The Developing Person Through the **Life Span**

Christian Pierre. *The Swing,* **2010 (front cover)** "Fro and to," my immigrant grandmother used to say as she rocked me to sleep, verbalizing a universal process (albeit not in the familiar English sequence). In *The Swing,* Christian Pierre captures the essence of our study of the life span: We move back and forth through space and time, eyes wide open.

The Developing Person Through the Life Span

EIGHTH EDITION

KATHLEEN STASSEN BERGER

Bronx Community College
City University of New York

WORTH PUBLISHERS

Publisher: Catherine Woods

Executive Editor: Jessica Bayne

Developmental Editors: Cecilia Gardner, Tom Churchill

Executive Marketing Manager: Katherine Nurre

Supplements and Media Editor: Sharon Prevost

Associate Managing Editor: Tracey Kuehn

Production Editor: Vivien Weiss

Art Director: Barbara Reingold

Interior Designer: Lissi Sigillo

Photo Treatments: Lyndall Culbertson

Layout Designer: Paul Lacy

Photo Editor: Christine Buese

Photo Researcher: Jacqui Wong

Senior Illustration Coordinator: Bill Page

Illustrations: Todd Buck Illustrations, MPS Limited, TSI Graphics, Inc.

Production Manager: Barbara Seixas

Composition: TSI Graphics, Inc.

Printing and Binding: RR Donnelley

Cover Art: Christian Pierre, *The Swing*

Library of Congress Control Number: 2010942672

ISBN-13: 978-1-4292-3203-6

ISBN-10: 1-4292-3203-X

ISBN-13: 978-1-4292-3205-0 (ppbk.)

ISBN-10: 1-4292-3205-6 (ppbk.)

Printed in the United States of America

Third printing

Worth Publishers

41 Madison Avenue

New York, NY 10010

www.worthpublishers.com

Credit is given to the following sources for permission to use the photos indicated:

Part Openers

Jose Luiz Pelaez Inc./Jupiter Images, p. xxxv

Jose Luiz Pelaez Inc./Jupiter Images, pp. vii, ix, 1

Alex Cao/Getty Images, p. 120

John Lund/Annabelle Breakey/Jupiter Images, pp. vi, x, 121, 205

BLOOM Images/Getty Images, p. 206

Digital Vision/Getty Images, pp. vi, xi, 207, 291

Ronnie Kaufman/Larry Hirshowitz/Getty Images, p. 292

George Doyle/Getty Images, pp. vi, xi, 293, 377

Tyler Edwards/Getty Images, p. 378

Mark Anderson/Getty Images, pp. vi, xii, 379, 461

Paul Burns/Getty Images, p. 462

Asia Images Group/Getty Images, pp. vii, xiii, 463, 545

WIN-Initiative/Getty Images, p. 546

Jeff Randall/Getty Images, pp. vii, xiv, 547, 635

Jimmy Cohrssen/Getty Images, p. 636

Rubberball/Getty Images, pp. vii, xiv, 637, 725

Chapter Openers

Tony Savino/The Image Works, pp. ix, 2

Fancy/Alamy, pp. ix, 32

David M. Phillips/Photo Researchers, Inc., pp. ix, 60

Rick Gomez/Corbis, pp. ix, 88

Nigel Pavitt/awl images, pp. x, 122, 205

Jacques Charlas/Stock Boston/PictureQuest, pp. x, 152, 205

Bruce Yuan-Yue Bi/Lonely Planet, pp. x, 178, 205

Elizabeth Crews, pp. xi, 208, 291

Alloy Photography/Veer, pp. xi, 236, 291

Little Blue Wolf Productions/Photolibrary, pp. xi, 264, 291

Osamu Koyata/Pacific Press Service, pp. xii, 294, 377

Ellen B. Senisi, pp. xii, 320, 377

Sean Sprague/The Image Works, pp. xii, 348, 377

Paul Miles/Axiom, pp. xii, 380, 461

Jutta Klee/Corbis, pp. xii, 406, 461

Digital Vision/Getty Images, pp. xiii, 432, 461

Junko Kimura/Getty Images, pp. xiii, 464, 545

Jon Arnold Images/DanitaDelimont.com, pp. xiii, 490, 545

Patrick Horton/Lonely Planet, pp. xiii, 518, 545

Lilly Doug/Botanica/Getty Images, pp. xiv, 548, 635

John Lund/Marc Romane/age fotostock, pp. xiv, 578, 635

Tony Anderson/Taxi/Getty Images, pp. xiv, 604, 635

Julie Larsen Maher, pp. xv, 638, 725

Russell Underwood/Uppercut Images/Photolibrary, pp. xv, 664, 725

INC Superstock/Photolibrary, pp. xv, 692, 725

Christophe Boisvieux/Corbis, pp. xv, Ep-0

About the Author

Kathleen Stassen Berger received her undergraduate education at Stanford University and Radcliffe College, earned an M.A.T. from Harvard University and an MS and PhD from Yeshiva University. Her broad experience as an educator includes directing a preschool, serving as chair of philosophy at the United Nations International School, teaching child and adolescent development to graduate students at Fordham University and undergraduates at Montclair State University in New Jersey and at Quinnipiac University in Connecticut, as well as teaching social psychology to inmates at Sing Sing Prison.

Throughout most of her professional career, Berger has worked at Bronx Community College of the City University of New York, first as an adjunct and for the past two decades as a full professor. She has taught introduction to psychology, child and adolescent development, adulthood and aging, social psychology, abnormal psychology, and human motivation. Her students—who come from many ethnic, economic, and educational backgrounds and who have a wide range of ages and interests—consistently honor her with the highest teaching evaluations.

Berger is also the author of *The Developing Person Through Childhood and Adolescence* and *Invitation to the Life Span.* Her developmental texts are currently being used at more than 700 colleges and universities worldwide and are available in Spanish, French, Italian, and Portuguese, as well as English. Her research interests include adolescent identity, immigration, and bullying, and she has published many articles on developmental topics in the *Wiley Encyclopedia of Psychology* and in publications of the American Association for Higher Education and the National Education Association for Higher Education. She continues teaching and learning every semester and in every edition of her books.

BRIEF CONTENTS

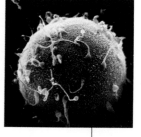

PART II

The First Two Years

Preface

"Another edition? Has anything really changed?" People often ask.

I suppress the impulse to tell them that if they understood human development, they would realize that change is pervasive. Scientists know more about the brain, about culture, about education, and about virtually everything else today than they did just a year ago. Humans themselves change, too, as each cohort experiences new events around the world—electronic media, chemicals in the food supply, globalization, HIV, longer lives, fewer babies . . . The list of sociocultural shifts that affect all our lives is long indeed.

Instead I talk about my own life, a small window on the larger changes around us. For example, in the past 18 months, my first grandchildren, Asa and Caleb, were born. As I watch them develop, I learn, again, about early childhood and motherhood. Among the dramatic changes since I first became a mother are recommendations to breast-feed longer, heightened worry about toxins, anticipated maternal employment, saving for college some day. And some of the accoutrements are new: bigger and better strollers and paper diapers, no-slip slippers, automatic rockers, books for babies, attractive mobiles.

Where does the science of human development fit into all this? Consider my experience.

When my daughter Bethany was pregnant, she knew of my extensive knowledge of development and asked me to be her birth partner, a great honor. We went to classes together, and I felt ready for the big day. She was told to also find a good midwife and doula—fortunate for me because, although I knew what was happening, understood the monitored vital signs, and had confidence in the professionals taking care of my daughter in labor, tears flowed down my cheeks as I watched.

I stayed in a corner, where Bethany could not see how emotional I was. At the birth, I helped her push, holding one leg as a nurse held the other—just as the midwife had told us. Caleb was born, small and perfect; Bethany cradled and fed him. A miracle.

And then I fainted.

I suddenly found myself on the floor, with six medical people clustered around me instead of attending to my daughter and new grandson.

"I'm fine," I assured them, telling them to focus on Bethany. They did not. They insisted that, per hospital policy, I'd have to be wheeled down to emergency intake. I protested until one nurse said, "You can refuse treatment when you're there."

So, to get them to focus on Bethany, I sat in the wheelchair—and soon told a triage nurse that a night of high emotion without food, water, or sleep made me faint. Thus, I said, "I refuse treatment." She checked with her supervisor and then allowed me to return to Bethany. The midwife was patiently waiting for the placenta to be expelled.

How does this relate to development? In three ways:

1. Emotions can overtake reason. As you will read, we are all dual-process thinkers. My knowledge led me to ignore my emotions—big mistake.
2. Knowledge helps. I have since learned that many family members faint at births. If I had been aware of this, I would have nourished my body rather

than deprived it in solidarity with Bethany (she could not eat). I would have noticed that I felt dizzy and lightheaded and thus would have sat down. Lack of knowledge is harmful in many ways—sharing vital information is why I write this book, and why you study human development.

3. Development brings change. Personal changes were evident: Giving birth to four wonderful daughters (without ever fainting) is quite different from witnessing one of those daughters give birth herself. Cohort changes are evident as well: Now that fathers, friends, and grandmothers are often allowed in delivery rooms, new education is needed—like how to avoid fainting. I did not know; now I do. That is why updating developmental textbooks is necessary.

All this makes me remember again why I study human development. We all need to know more; it will help us, our loved ones, and every person develop with more joy and fulfillment and less harm and despair.

Teaching and writing remain my life's work and passion. I strive to make this text both challenging and accessible to every student, remembering that my students were the inspiration for writing a developmental text in the first place. They deserve a book that respects their intellect and experiences, without making development seem dull or obscure.

Overall, I believe that a better world is possible because today's students will become tomorrow's wise leaders. My hope is that the knowledge they gain from reading this book will benefit all their family members from one generation to the next.

To learn more about the specifics of this text, including the material that is new to this edition, read on. Or simply turn to the beginning of Chapter 1 and start your study.

BIL BACHMANN / DANITADELIMONT.COM

Stranger Danger Some parents teach their children to be respectful of any adult; others teach them to fear any stranger. No matter what their culture or parents say, each of these two sisters in Nepal reacts according to her inborn temperament.

New Material

Every year, scientists discover and explain more concepts and research. The best of these are integrated into the text, including hundreds of new references on many topics—among them the genetics of delinquency, infant nutrition, bipolar and autistic spectrum disorders, attachment over the life span, high-stakes testing, drug use and drug addiction, brain changes throughout adulthood, and ways to die. Cognizant of the interdisciplinary nature of human development, I reflect research in biology, sociology, education, anthropology, political science, and more—as well as in my home discipline, psychology.

Genetics and social contexts are noted throughout. The variations and hazards of infant day care and preschool education are described; emerging adulthood is further explained in a trio of chapters; the blurry boundaries of adulthood are stressed; the various manifestations, treatment, and prevention of dementia (not just Alzheimer disease) are discussed; and much more.

Research on the Brain

Every page of this text reflects new research and theory. Brain development is the most obvious example: Every trio of chapters includes a section on the brain, often enhanced with charts and photos to help students understand its inner workings. The following list highlights some of this material:

Correlation between MAOA production and violent crime, pp. 6–7
A View from Science feature on mirror neurons, pp. 16–17
Plasticity of brain and balance, p. 17
Piaget's sensorimotor intelligence, pp. 45–48
Fronto-striatal deficits and ADHD, pp. 48, 311

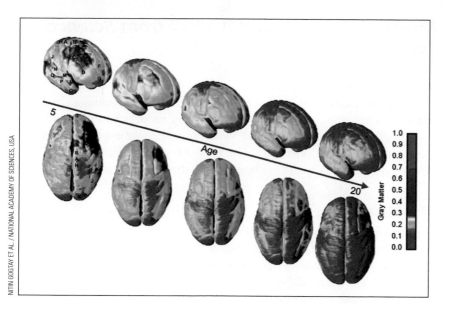

Same People, But Not the Same Brain
These brain scans are part of a longitudinal study that repeatedly compares the proportion of gray matter from childhood through adolescence. Gray matter is reduced as white matter increases, in part because pruning during the teen years (the fourth and fifth images here) allows intellectual connections to build. As the authors of one study that included this chart explain, teenagers may "look like an adult, but cognitively they are not there yet" (Powell, 2006, p. 865).

A Growing Trend The rate of first births to women in their 40s tripled from 1990 to 2008, although most newborns (96%) have mothers under age 40. Nonetheless, prenatal testing and medical advances have made late motherhood less risky than it was, with some happy results. This mother is 42.

New *Thinking Critically* and *A View from Science* Features

We all need to develop our critical thinking skills (if I had been better at this, I would not have fainted). Virtually every page of this book presents not only facts but also questions with divergent interpretations. In addition, a *Thinking Critically* boxed feature appears in many chapters, challenging readers to examine basic assumptions. Furthermore, boxes titled *A View From Science* explain surprising insight from recent scientific research. (The previous edition featured *Thinking Like a Scientist* boxes; now two distinct boxes cover that perspective.)

New Pedagogical Aids

This edition incorporates learning objectives at the beginning of each chapter: The "What Will You Know?" questions indicate important concepts for students to focus on. There is also a new element at the end of each chapter: The "What Have You Learned?" questions help students assess their learning in more detail. Some further explanation follows.

Peak Performance Because this is a soccer match, of course we see skilled feet and strong legs—but also notice the arms, torsos, and feats of balance. Deniz Naki (age 21) and Luis Gustavo (age 23) are German soccer team members in better shape than most emerging adults, but imagine these two a decade earlier (at age 11 and 13) or later (at age 31 and 33) and you will realize why, physiologically, one's early 20s are considered the prime of life.

Learning Objectives

Much of what students learn from this course is a matter of attitude, approach, and perspective—all hard to quantify. In addition, there are specific learning objectives, which supplement the key terms that should also be learned. For the first time in this edition, two sets of objectives are listed for each chapter. The first set ("What Will You Know?"), asked at the beginning of each chapter, lists the general ideas that students might remember and apply lifelong. At the end of each chapter are more specific learning objectives ("What Have You Learned?") that connect to each major heading within that chapter.

Ideally, students answer the learning objective questions in sentences, with specifics that demonstrate knowledge. Some items on the new lists are straightforward, requiring only close attention to the chapter content. Others require comparisons, implications, or evaluations.

Balancing the Range of Difficulty

To illustrate, the first question from Chapter 5 is straightforward: *What specific facts indicate that infants grow rapidly in the first year?* But the nineteenth question is more difficult: *What are the reasons for and against breast-feeding until the child is at least 1 year old?*

The first question might be answered simply as follows: *Birthweight doubles in four months and triples by one year, while infants grow about a foot*—or with several other specific details. However, students may, at first, be stumped by Question 19, since the chapter is overwhelmingly in favor of breast-feeding. A good answer might be:

> *There are dozens of strong reasons for breast-feeding, including protection against disease, early immunity, better digestion, easier bonding, and perhaps long-term intellectual ability. Breast-feeding has advantages for the mother and family as well. Disadvantages are more difficult to find. However, if the mother is taking drugs or is unable to breast-feed, formula may be best. And if a woman or culture insists that no other foods, supplements, or vitamins are needed for a year or more, an infant might become malnourished, as occurred with Kiana.*

As you can see from these examples, good answers may vary, but students should always use their own words and critical thinking skills, referring to specifics in the chapter.

Content Changes to the Eighth Edition

Life-span development, like all sciences, builds on past learning. Many facts and concepts are scaffolds that remain strong over time: stages and ages, norms and variations, dangers and diversities, classic theories and fascinating applications. However, the study of development is continually changed by discoveries and experiences, so no paragraph in this eighth edition is exactly what it was in the seventh edition, much less the first. Some major revisions have been made, and hundreds of new examples are cited. Highlights of this updating appear below.

Part I: The Beginnings

1. Introduction

- Scientific method explained at the outset of the book, with research on SIDS as example of a mystery that became hypotheses and then life-saving practices
- Nature–nurture interaction and critical versus sensitive periods explained in Chapter 1
- Cultural/ethnic differences made clear with example of Chinese and U.S. mothers reading books to toddlers
- Vygotsky now in Chapter 1, joining Bronfenbrenner and dynamic systems
- Juvenile delinquency as example of multidisciplinary perspective, including genetics, neuroscience, child rearing, and social context
- Clarification of correlation and causation via research on teenage marriages

And If I Die Not likely. To die of SIDS "before I wake" was not rare in many nations before 1990, but not in Mongolia (shown here) or other Asian countries. The reason, as scientists hypothesized and then confirmed, is that Asian parents put their infants "back to sleep."

SEAN SPRAGUE / THE IMAGE WORKS

2. Theories of Development

- Distinction between theories, facts, and norms
- Contemporary examples of the need for theories, e.g., love/hate of the Hummer
- Examples of behaviorism include white coat syndrome and toilet training
- Humanism highlighted as a major theory (also described in Chapter 22)
- Evolutionary theory explained, including sex differences in romantic jealousy

3. Heredity and Environment

- Epigenetics explained in more detail, including methylation and gene expression
- Sex selection in the United States (previously only China and India)
- Stem cells explained; possible applications
- Multiple births (including "Octomom")
- Controversy regarding genetic testing for psychological conditions
- Genetics of schizophrenia, with hypothesized impact of environment

Family Pride Grandpa Charilaos is proud of his tavern in northern Greece (central Macedonia), but he is even more proud of his talented grandchildren, including Maria Soni (shown here). Note her expert fingering. Her father and mother also play instruments—is that nature or nurture?

KUTTIG-RF-KIDS / ALAMY

4. Prenatal Development and Birth

- Home births and international rates of birth complications as examples of the need for critical thinking
- Research on the benefits of the doula, for high-risk infants and low-risk births
- Greater emphasis on father involvement (or absence) during pregnancy and birth, including couvade
- Various measures of newborn health—weight, age, Apgar score, Brazelton assessment scale, and reflexes
- Complications of risk analysis and advice (e.g., alcohol, fish, prenatal testing)

Part II: The First Two Years

5. The First Two Years: Biosocial Development
- Bed-sharing, co-sleeping, and infant sleep patterns as issues for critical thinking
- The fusiform face area of the brain, both nature and nurture, including specialized and differentiated recognition of human faces
- Current infant immunization, including California's 2010 whooping cough epidemic
- Infant survival worldwide; specifics include breast-feeding to combat malnutrition, vitamin D to prevent rickets, and bed nets to reduce malaria

6. The First Two Years: Cognitive Development
- Sharper yet more sympathetic coverage of limitations of Piaget's research
- Applications of information processing, especially for infant memory
- Stress on developing language before the first words, including in bilingual families
- Norms and theories of language learning explained with practical examples

7. The First Two Years: Psychosocial Development
- Extensive discussion of the influence of brain maturation on the emotional development of infants and toddlers
- Description of synesthesia and how it might differ in infancy and later on
- Variations in age of toilet training and how toilet-training approaches reflect theories of infant development
- Ethnotheories explained in more detail, with research examples comparing Germany and Cameroon
- Expanded discussion of infant day care, including national policies, international variations, possible negative effects

Part III: Early Childhood

8. Early Childhood: Biosocial Development
- New section on oral health, including what parents should do for their children's teeth
- Expanded discussion of brain development, including prefrontal cortex and limbic system, as well as the benefits and harm from stress
- Comparison of social understanding in humans and in chimpanzees
- Focus on environmental hazards, with lead as an example

9. Early Childhood: Cognitive Development
- Role of imitation in children's learning, comparing non-Western and Western children
- Emphasis on specific strategies to help children become bilingual without losing their original language
- Updated research on preschool programs, including new benefits found in Montessori schools, costs and advantages of Reggio Emilia schools, and federal evaluation of Head Start programs

10. Early Childhood: Psychosocial Development
- Expanded discussion of play, including cultural differences and learning from peers
- Moral development now a major section, with types and origins of prosocial and antisocial behavior and the moral lessons learned from methods of punishment
- The impact of electronic media, especially video games

Part IV: Middle Childhood

11. Middle Childhood: Biosocial Development
- Two case studies of children with asthma, illustrating the impact of SES
- Oral health now included

- International data on obesity and stress on macrocosm influences
- Variations of intelligence and IQ, including data from Sudan
- Bipolar disorder in childhood explained and contrasted with ADHD
- In psychopathology, examples of equifinality and multifinality

12. Middle Childhood: Cognitive Development

- Cultural differences in methods of learning (individual versus collaborative; discovery versus direct instruction)
- Advent of universal primary education (e.g., India)
- Updates on various measures of learning—TIMSS, PIRLS, NAEP, NCLB
- Who decides what is part of the curriculum (e.g., religion, charter schools, vouchers)

13. Middle Childhood: Psychosocial Development

- Self-esteem presented as complex; problems with high self-esteem and international variations explained
- Updated data on family structures—nuclear, step, extended, single parents, and others
- SES effects on children from both high- and low-income families
- Moral values, including peer influence, bullies, retribution, and restitution

Part V: Adolescence
14. Adolescence: Biosocial Development

- Specifics about the role that weight and stress play in the onset of puberty
- Problems with early teen sex as contrasted with later teen sex (pregnancy, STIs)
- Complications and benefits of brain development in adolescence
- Eating disorders now in this chapter; drug use now in Chapter 16

15. Adolescence: Cognitive Development

- Logical fallacies now include base rate neglect
- Contrast clarified between college-bound students and high school dropouts
- Methods of student engagement critically examined
- Technology and cognition discussed, with recent data on networking, cyberbullying, computers in instruction
- International contrasts include results from the PISA

16. Adolescence: Psychosocial Development

- Identity crisis refers to gender identity and identity politics
- Norms, expectations, and roles of parents and peers presented in cross-cultural contexts—variations by nation (e.g., Hong Kong), by SES, and by ethnicity
- Updated data on drug use, including brain changes, depression, anxiety

Part VI: Emerging Adulthood
17. Emerging Adulthood: Biosocial Development

- Debate among scholars as to whether contemporary emerging adults are more selfish or more transformative than those of earlier generations
- Psychopathology updated and moved to this section; includes discussion of mood disorders, anxiety, and schizophrenia
- Risk taking explained as a benefit to society as well as a problem

18. Emerging Adulthood: Cognitive Development

- Connection between social understanding and maturation of the prefrontal cortex
- New *A Case to Study* feature describes one professor's journey to postformal thought
- Updated data on college, including statistics on 25- to 34-year-olds who are college graduates, in many nations

19. Emerging Adulthood: Psychosocial Development
- Impact of recent cultural and economic changes on ethnic and vocational identity
- Hookups compared with cohabitation and marriage
- Choice overload as applied to mate selection
- Crucial role of parental support during emerging adulthood

Part VII: Adulthood
20. Adulthood: Biosocial Development
- Updated research on international tobacco and alcohol abuse, as well as obesity
- Strategies for breaking bad habits, from awareness to maintenance, including role of motivational interviewing
- Coping with stress and stressors, including the burden of allostatic load and weathering

21. Adulthood: Cognitive Development
- New examples of *selective optimization with compensation* throughout this chapter
- Research on unconscious processing related to intuition and expertise
- Exploration of the intellectual abilities and knowledge needed to be a good mother and recognition of "women's work"
- Expanded discussion of expertise, including London taxi drivers

22. Adulthood: Psychosocial Development
- Intimacy interactions and needs now include "consequential strangers"
- Midlife crisis, sandwich generation, and empty nest concepts thoroughly debunked
- Same-sex and other-sex partnerships compared
- Linked lives used to illuminate family interactions, including impact of employment schedules

Part VIII: Late Adulthood
23. Late Adulthood: Biosocial Development
- Clearer, data-based explanation of compression of morbidity
- More balanced discussion of nature and nurture regarding sleep, ageism, longevity
- Updated research on theories of aging, especially cellular and oxidative damage

24. Late Adulthood: Cognitive Development
- An expanded section on the aging brain, particularly neurological changes and variations
- Dementias described now include Lewy body and frontal lobe dementia

25. Late Adulthood: Psychosocial Development
- Positivity effect more extensively explained, including a new *Research Design*
- Intergenerational relationships discussed in more detail, including caregiving, filial obligations, and grandparent–grandchild interactions—sometimes not grand
- Social networking among the elderly—more social support versus less personal contact

Epilogue: Death and Dying
- Rational, irrational, and religious understanding of death, with trolley car dilemma explained as one example
- Meta-analysis of end-of-life brain functioning, including medical definitions of death
- Updated and culturally varied understanding of complicated grief, including enduring bonds, roadside memorials, cremation

Ongoing Features

Many characteristics of this book have been acclaimed since the first edition and have been retained in this revision.

Writing That Communicates the Excitement and Challenge of the Field

An overview of the science of human development should be lively, just as real people are. Each sentence conveys tone as well as content. Chapter-opening vignettes bring student readers into the immediacy of development. Examples and explanations abound, helping students make the connections among theory, research, and their own experiences.

Coverage of Diversity

Cross-cultural, international, multiethnic, sexual orientation, wealth, age, gender—all these words and ideas are vital to appreciating how people develop. Research uncovers surprising similarities and notable differences: We have much in common, yet each human is unique. From the discussion of social contexts in Chapter 1 to the coverage of cultural differences in mourning in the Epilogue, each chapter highlights possibilities and variations.

New research on family structures, immigrants, bilingualism, single adults, and ethnic differences in health are among the many topics that illustrate human diversity. Listed here is a smattering of the discussions of culture and diversity in this new edition. Respect for human differences is evident throughout. You will note that examples and research findings from many parts of the world are included, not as add-on highlights, but as integral parts of the description of each age.

Bright-Eyed and Nearsighted These are star students from Beijing, China, waiting in line for visas to the United States. If they had spent less time studying, would they be here?

Inclusion of all kinds of people in the study of development, pp. 7–8
Ethnicity, race, and culture defined, pp. 14–15
Male and female chromosomes, p. 65
Sex-selection policies in China, India, and other countries, p. 66
National differences in incidence of twin births, pp. 68–70
Nature–nurture interaction in nearsightedness among children in Britain, Africa, and Asia, pp. 76–78
Sex-chromosome abnormalities, pp. 78–82
Rates of cesarean births internationally, pp. 97–98
Birthing practices in various cultures, pp. 99–101
Low-birthweight rates in different nations, pp. 110–112
Co-sleeping and bed-sharing customs, pp. 125–126
Ethnic variations in development of motor skills, pp. 139–140
Cultural values and practices in infants' language learning, pp. 170–172
Cultural divergence in emotions encouraged in toddlers, p. 181
Toilet-training practices by place, income, and cohort, pp. 186–187
Erikson on autonomy versus shame, pp. 187–188
Ethnotheories in emotional development, pp. 189–190
Proximal and distal parenting, pp. 190–192
Latino fathers as toddlers' social references, p. 198
International variations in rates of infant day care, p. 199
Ethnic differences in young children's height and weight, pp. 207–208
Influence of culture on young children's theory of mind, pp. 243–245

STEPHEN SHAVER / POLARIS

Her Parents' Love Three-month-old Avery is blessed by having two adoring parents, Jared and Wendy Kennedy. It could even be said that she has a third parent—the woman who donated the ovum. Through ART, that egg was fertilized to help this couple realize their dream of parenthood.

Dedication Is Universal This young mother in the doorway of her Rajastan, India, home is typical of emerging adults worldwide: active, healthy, and working for the future.

JEAN MICHEL FOUJOLS/GETTY IMAGES

No Reason to Cry Over Spilt Milk Friendship and useful chores both correlate with happy children, as these boys seem to be.

PATRICK FRASER / CORBIS OUTLINE

A Trick Question How old is he? His leg muscles and the angle of his stretch make him comparable to a fit 30-year-old. However, the placement of this photo should give you a clue about his real age—he is 61.

Up-to-Date Coverage

My mentors welcomed curiosity, creativity, and skepticism; as a result, I am eager to read and analyze thousands of articles and books on everything from Alzheimer disease to zygosity. The recent explosion of research in neuroscience and genetics has challenged me, once again, first to understand and then to explain many complex findings and speculative leaps. My students continue to ask questions and share their experiences, always providing new perspectives and concerns.

Topical Organization within a Chronological Framework

The book's basic organization remains unchanged. Four chapters begin the book with coverage of definitions, theories, genetics, and prenatal development. These chapters function not only as a developmental foundation but also as the structure for explaining the life-span perspective, plasticity, nature and nurture, multicultural awareness, risk analysis, gains and losses, family bonding, and many other concepts that yield insights for all of human development.

The other seven parts correspond to the major periods of development. Each part contains three chapters, one for each of the three domains: biosocial, cognitive, and psychosocial. The topical organization within a chronological framework is a useful scaffold for students' understanding of the interplay between age and domain. The chapters are color-coded with tabs on the right-hand margins. The pages of the biosocial chapters have blue tabs, the cognitive chapters have purple tabs, and the psychosocial chapters have green tabs.

Three Series of Integrated Features

Three series of deeper discussions appear as integral parts of the text, and only where they are relevant. Readers of earlier editions will remember the *A Case to Study* feature; new to this edition are *Thinking Critically* and *A View from Science*.

End-of-Chapter Summary

Each chapter ends with a summary, a list of key terms (with page numbers indicating where the word is introduced and defined), key questions, and three or four application exercises designed to let students apply concepts to everyday life. Key terms appear in boldface type in the text and are defined in the margins and again in a glossary at the back of the book. The outline on the first page of each chapter, the new learning objectives, and the system of major and minor subheads facilitate the survey-question-read-write-review (SQ3R) approach.

A "Summing Up" feature at the end of each section provides an opportunity for students to pause and reflect on what they've just read. Observation quizzes inspire readers to look more closely at certain photographs, tables, and graphs. The "Especially for . . . " questions in the margins, many of which are new to this edition, apply concepts to real-life careers and social roles.

TIM GRAHAM / GETTY IMAGES

Keep Smiling Good humor seems to be a cause of longevity, and vice versa. This is as true among the elderly in nations where few reach old age as it is in countries where the aged outnumber the young.

Photographs, Tables, and Graphs That Are Integral to the Text

Students learn a great deal from this book's illustrations because Worth Publishers encourages authors to choose the photographs, tables, and graphs and to write captions that extend the content. Appendix A furthers this process by presenting numerous charts and tables that contain detailed data for further study.

Supplements

As an instructor myself, I know that supplements can make or break a class. I personally have rejected textbook adoptions because I knew that that publisher historically had provided inaccurate test banks, dull ancillaries, and slow service. That is not the case with Worth Publishers, which has a well-deserved reputation for providing supplements that are extensive and of high quality, for both professors and students. With this edition you will find the following.

Human Development: A Video Tool Kit

This edition of *The Developing Person Through the Life Span* is supplemented with the vast library of human development video and student activities on the Human Development Tool Kit. There are **17 new student activities** added especially for this edition. The tool kit was prepared by a talented team of instructors, including: Victoria Cross, University of California, Davis; Sheridan Dewolf, Grossmont College; Pamela B. Hill, San Antonio College; Lisa Huffman, Ball State University; Thomas Ludwig, Hope College; Cathleen McGreal, Michigan State University; Amy Obegi, Grossmont College; Michelle L. Pilati, Rio Hondo College; Tanya Renner, Kapiolani Community College; Catherine Robertson, Grossmont College; Stavros Valenti, Hofstra University; and Pauline Zeece, University of Nebraska, Lincoln.

The collection of 100 student activities offer a full range of material, from investigations of classic experiments (like the visual cliff and the Strange Situation) to observations on children's play and adolescent risk taking. For instructors, the tool kit includes more than 400 video clips and animations, along with discussion starters and PowerPoint slides available to download for free. We also offer a selection of videos taken from the online library (215, to be exact) on a DVD called "The Human Development Video Collection," as well as a DVD with 40 of our best Student Activities packageable for students.

PsychPortal

This is the complete online gateway to all the student and instructor resources available with the textbook. PsychPortal brings together all the resources of the video tool kits, integrated with an eBook and powerful assessment tools to complement your course.

The ready-to-use course template is fully customizable and includes all the teaching and learning resources that go along with the book, preloaded into a ready-to-use course; sophisticated quizzing, personalized study plans for students, and powerful assessment analyses that provide timely and useful feedback on class and individual student performance; and seamless integration of student resources, eBook text, assessment tools, and lecture resources. The quiz bank features more than 100 questions per chapter.

eBook

The beautiful and interactive eBook fully integrates the complete text and its electronic study tools in a format that instructors and students can easily customize—at a significant savings on the price of the printed text. It offers easy access from any Internet-connected computer; quick, intuitive navigation to any section or subsection, as well as any printed book page number; a powerful notes feature that allows you to customize any page; a full-text search; text highlighting; and a full, searchable glossary.

Companion Web Site

The companion Web site (at www.worthpublishers.com/berger) is an online educational setting for students and instructors. It is free, and tools on the site include interactive flashcards in both English and Spanish, a Spanish language glossary, quizzes, learning objectives, and Frequently Asked Questions About Development. A password-protected Instructor Site offers a full array of teaching resources, including PowerPoint slides, an online quiz gradebook, and links to additional tools.

"Journey Through the Life Span" Observational Videos

Bringing observational learning to the classroom, this video series allows students to watch and listen to real children as a way of amplifying their reading of the text. "Journey Through the Life Span" offers vivid footage of people of all ages from around the world (North America, Europe, Africa, Asia, and South America), as seen in everyday environments (homes, hospitals, schools, and offices) and at major life transitions (birth, marriage, divorce, being grandparents).

Interviews with prominent developmentalists—including Charles Nelson, Barbara Rogoff, Ann Peterson, and Steven Pinker—are integrated throughout to help students link research and theory to the real world. Interviews with a number of social workers, teachers, and nurses who work with children, adults, and the aged give students direct insight into the practical challenges and rewards of their vocations. One hour of unedited footage helps students sharpen their observation skills. Available on VHS and DVD.

Life-Span Development Telecourse

Transitions Through the Life Span, developed by Coast Learning Systems and Worth Publishers, teaches fundamentals of human development. The course also explores the variety of individual and developmental contexts that influence development, such as socioeconomic status, culture, genetics, family, school, and society. Each video lesson includes specific real-life examples interwoven with commentary by subject matter experts. The course includes 26 half-hour video lessons, a telecourse study guide, and a faculty manual with test bank. The test bank is also available electronically.

Instructor's Resources

This collection of resources written by Richard O. Straub (University of Michigan, Dearborn) has been hailed as the richest collection of instructor's resources in developmental psychology. The Lecture Guides preview learning objectives, springboard topics for discussion and debate, handouts for student projects, and supplementary readings from journal articles. Course planning suggestions, ideas for term projects, and a guide to audiovisual and software materials are also included.

Study Guide

The *Study Guide* by Richard O. Straub helps students evaluate their understanding and retain their learning longer. Each chapter includes a review of key concepts, guided study questions, and section reviews that encourage students' active participation in the learning process. Two practice tests and a challenge test help them assess their mastery of the material.

PowerPoint Slides

A number of different presentation slides are available. There are two prebuilt PowerPoint slide sets for each text chapter—one featuring chapter outlines, the other featuring all chapter art and illustrations. These slides can be used as is or can be customized to fit individual needs. Video presentation slides provide an easy way to connect chapter content to the selected video clip and follow each clip with discussion questions designed to promote critical thinking. In addition, a set of interactive, enhanced lecture slides focus on key themes from the text and feature tables, graphs, and figures.

Test Bank and Computerized Test Bank

The test bank, prepared by Susan Higgins (Penn Valley Community College and University of Kansas) and myself, includes at least 100 multiple-choice and 70 fill-in, true-false, and essay questions for each chapter. Each question is keyed to the textbook by topic, learning objective, and level of difficulty.

The Diploma computerized test bank, available on a dual-platform CD-ROM for Windows and Macintosh, guides instructors step by step through the process of creating a test. It also allows them to quickly add an unlimited number of questions; edit, scramble, or resequence items; format a test; and include pictures, equations, and media links. The accompanying gradebook enables instructors to record students' grades throughout the course and includes the capacity to sort student records, view detailed analyses of test items, curve tests, generate reports, and add weights to grades.

The CD-ROM is also the access point for Diploma Online Testing, which allows instructors to create and administer secure exams over a network or over the Internet. In addition, Diploma has the ability to restrict tests to specific computers or time blocks. Blackboard- and WebCT-formatted versions of each item in the Test Bank are available on the CD-ROM.

Thanks

I'd like to thank the academic reviewers who have read this book in every edition and who have provided suggestions, criticisms, references, and encouragement. They have all made this a better book. I want to mention especially those who have reviewed this edition:

Sindy Armstrong, *Ozarks Technical College*
Melanie Arpaio, *Sussex County Community College*
Lisa Brown, *Frederick Community College*
Randi Burton, *Brevard Community College*
Deborah Caldwell, *Indiana University*
Toni Campbell, *San Jose State University*
Kathryn Canter, *Pennsylvania State University*
Juanita Cole, *Azusa Pacific University*
Robin Deak, *McHenry County College*
Linda Emerson, *College of the Desert*
Lisa End-Berg, *Kennesaw State University*
Pamela Fergus, *Inver Hills College*
Rita Fike, *Troy University*
Krista Forrest, *University of Nebraska at Kearney*
Ellen Firestone, *Wilkes Community College*
Winona Fleenor, *Virginia Highlands Community College*
Albert Gardner, *University of Maryland*
Jan Garske, *Hocking College*
Robert Gates, *Cisco College*
Margie Goulden, *Pierce College*
Troianne Grayson, *Florida State College, Jacksonville*
Jerry Green, *Tarrant County College*
Corinne Greenberg, *Santa Fe College*
Donna Hardy, *California State University, Northridge*
Lora Harpster, *Salt Lake Community College*
Alvin Heard, *Salt Lake Community College*
Jennifer Hedrick, *Southern Utah University*
Dani Hodge, *California State University, San Bernardino*
Alycia Hund, *Illinois State University*

Kimberly Kinsey, *Agnes Scott College*
Kristina Klassen, *North Idaho College*
Harold Kotch, *Metropolitan Community College– Penn Valley*
Karen Kwan, *Salt Lake Community College*
Jennifer Lee, *Cabrillo College*
Amy Lindsey, *Utica College*
Geri Lotze, *Virginia Commonwealth University*
Pam MacDonald, *Emporia State University*
James Markusic, *Ozarks Technical Community College*
Alex McEntire, *Metropolitan Community College– Penn Valley*
Antoinette Miller, *Clayton State University*
Marcie Miller, *South Plains College, Levelland Campus*
Lonna Murphy, *Passaic County Community College*
Nancy Ogden, *Mount Royal University*
Ian Payton, *Bethune-Cookman University*
Debbie Phythian, *Assiniboine Community College*
Michelle Pilati, *Rio Hondo College*
Ron Ponsford, *Northwest Nazarene University*
Amy Ressing, *Arizona State University*
Armida Rosiles, *South Plains College, Levelland Campus*
Rachel Schmale, *North Park University*
David Schwalb, *Southern Utah University*
Robert Schwartz, *Bergen Community College*
Sean Seepersad, *California State University, Fresno*
Kaveri Subrahmanyam, *California State University, Los Angeles*
Stephen Tracy, *Southern Nevada College*

Anne Unterkoefler, *Delaware County Community College*
Bethany Van Vleet, *Arizona State University*
Sheree Watson, *University of Southern Mississippi*
Kyle Weir, *California State University, Fresno*

Shelly Wooldridge, *University of Arkansas Community College at Batesville*
Sheri Young, *John Carroll University*
Julie Zink, *University of Southern Maine*

In addition, I wish to thank the instructors who participated in our online survey. We've tried to apply the insights gained from their experiences with the last edition to make this new edition better.

Farah Alam, *De Anza College*
Sindy Armstrong, *Ozarks Technical Community College*
Deborah Barton, *York College of Pennsylvania*
Sherry Black, *Western Nevada College*
Don Bower, *University of Georgia*
Cornelia Brentano, *California State Dominguez Hills*
Diane Brown, *Everett Community College*
Dr. Sandra Broz, *Northeast Community College*
Stephen Burgess, *Southwestern Oklahoma State University*
Lanthan Camblin, *University of Cincinnati*
Catherine Camilletti, *University of Texas at El Paso*
Toni Campbell, *San Jose State University*
Donna Carey, *Keystone College*
Maria Casey, *Immaculata University*
Carolyn Cohen, *Northern Essex Community College*
Lauren Coodley, *Napa Valley College*
Catherine Currell, *Central Michigan University*
Jennifer DeCicco, *Hunter College*
Gretchen DeHart, *Community College of Vermont*
Sorah Dubitsky, *Florida International University*
Natalie Ebner, *Yale University*
Robert C. Gates, *Cisco College*
Amy Gerney, *Misericordia University*
Zebbedia Gibb, *University of Northern Iowa*
Margie Goulden, *Pierce College*
Troianne Grayson, *Florida State College at Jacksonville*
Jerry Green, *Tarrant County College–NW Campus*
Christine Grela, *McHenry County College*
Robert Hagstrom, *Northern Arizona University*
Danelle Hodge, *California State University, San Bernardino*
Kristin Homan, *Grove City College*
Alishia Huntoon, *Oregon Institute of Technology*
Matthew Isaak, *University of Louisiana at Lafayette*
Mehraban Khodavandi, *Lakeland College*
Jennifer King-Cooper, *Sinclair Community College*
Timothy L. Kitzman, *Blackhawk Technical College*
Kristina T. Klassen, *North Idaho College*
Charles P. Kraemer, *LaGrange College*

Alison Kulak, *Concordia University of Alberta*
Karen Kwan, *Salt Lake Community College*
Kathy Lein, *Community College of Denver*
Pei-Wen Ma, *William Paterson University*
Alisha Marciano, *Lynchburg College*
Dorothy Marsil, *Kennesaw State University*
Kris McAleavey, *Longwood University*
Alex McEntire, *Penn Valley Community College*
Kittie Myatt, *Argosy University*
Nancy Neveau, *Northeast Wisconsin Technical College East Region*
Alan Oda, *Azusa Pacific University*
Liz Odell, *Northwest State Community College*
Nancy Ogden, *Mount Royal University*
Bonnie Ortega, *Trinidad State Junior College*
Andrea Phronebarger, *York Technical College*
Cynthia Putman, *Charleston Southern University*
Cyd Quarterman, *Toccoa Falls College*
Jennifer Reid Reichert, *Marquette University*
Michael Rhoads, *University of Northern Colorado*
Nancy E. Rizzo, *Valencia Community College*
George Sayre, *Seattle University*
David J. Schieffer, *Minnesota West Community & Technical College*
Sheryl R. Schindler, *University of Utah*
Pamela Schuetze-Pizarro, *Buffalo State College*
Robert Schwartz, *Bergen Community College*
Deborah Sedik, *Bucks County Community College*
Sean Seepersad, *California State University*
Jane Tiedt, *Gonzaga University*
Tonya Toutge, *Bethel University*
Anne Unterkoefler, *Delaware County Community College*
Michael Vallante, *Quinsigamond Community College*
Ruth A. Wallace, *Butler Community College*
Steve Wisecarver, *Lord Fairfax Community College*
Susan Wolle, *Kirkwood Community College*
Rebecca Wood, *Central Connecticut State University*

The editorial, production, and marketing people at Worth Publishers are dedicated to meeting the highest standards of excellence. Their devotion of time, effort, and talent to every aspect of publishing is a model for the industry. I particularly would like to thank Stacey Alexander, Jessica Bayne, Christine Buese, Anthony Calcara, Tom Churchill, Adam Frese, Tracey Kuehn, Paul Lacy, Sharon Prevost, Katherine Nurre, Babs Reingold, Barbara Seixas, Ted Szczepanski, Vivien Weiss, Catherine Woods, and Jacquelyn Wong.

Dedication

Every edition of this book is dedicated to people who made this textbook better than I could have alone. I dedicate this to Cele Gardner, my editor for more than ten years, who died in April 2010. We all miss her.

Kathleen Stassen Berger

New York, December 2010

I

the beginnings

The science of human development has many beginnings. Chapter 1 introduces what we study, why, and how, explaining some research strategies and methods used to understand how people grow and change.

Chapter 2 introduces theories of development to focus our study. It describes major theories that lay the foundation for hundreds of other theories and thousands of observations.

Chapter 3 traces the interaction of nature (heredity) and nurture (environment). Chemical instructions on the genes and chromosomes influence everything from the thickness of toenails to the swiftness of brain waves, from quick temper to memory for faces. Genes never act alone; Chapter 3 also examines some effects of education, child rearing, and culture on a person's development.

Chapter 4 details the biological start of each developing person, from one dividing cell to a newborn's birth. Together these four chapters begin our study of human development.

Introduction

WHAT WILL YOU KNOW?

1. Why do developmentalists consider themselves scientists?
2. Does life get better or worse as people grow older?
3. At what age do people stop changing?
4. Why is it important for scientists of many disciplines to combine their conclusions about human development?
5. What makes an experiment ethical or not?

"We had our baby," my brother phoned me one November day in 1967.

"Wonderful. Boy or girl?" I said.

"Boy. David. [*Long sigh*] He has some problems. He is scheduled for heart surgery tomorrow. Both eyes have thick cataracts. And more."

"Oh, no. I am so sorry."

"Don't worry. It's not genetic. Dot had rubella when he was an embryo. We didn't tell you because the doctor wasn't sure and we didn't want to worry you. They found rubella virus in him. It's not in my genes; it doesn't affect you."

I was heartsick for my brother and his wife. But he was concerned about me, six months pregnant with our first child. The hormones of pregnancy increase fear and anxiety, but at that moment I was far more concerned about his baby than mine.

My concerns were justified. Over the next four years, our child, Bethany, was fine, but David was not. I watched him slowly learn to chew, to walk, to hum, and finally, at age 4, to talk. Hundreds of special doctors, nurses, teachers, and neighbors helped him. Thousands of developmental scientists contributed indirectly by describing how children like David can learn.

Four decades have passed since that first phone call. David—at right in the photograph, with his brothers Mike and Bill—is in his 40s. He told me:

> I am generally quite happy, but secretly a little happier lately, especially since November, because I have been consistently getting a pretty good vibrato when I am singing, not only by myself but also in congregational hymns in church. [*He explained vibrato:*] When a note bounces up and down within a quartertone either way of concert pitch, optimally between 5.5 and 8.2 times per second.

As you see, David is knowledgeable as well as happy.

He also has a wry sense of humor. When I complained that my writing wasn't progressing as fast as I wished, David replied, "That sounds just like a certain father I know." This was an acute observation: David's dad and I live three thousand miles apart, but we share half our genes and most of childhood; we are similar in many ways.

This chapter begins to describe the myriad influences on human life, including genes and experience. It introduces the science of development over the life span,

Family Bonds Note the friendly smiles of these three brothers; from left to right, Mike, Bill, and David. No wonder I am proud of my nephews.

GLEN STASSEN

3

defining domains, perspectives, methods, and ethics—all crucial for mastery of this subject. But always remember the goal: to enable David, Bethany, and all the other 6.9 billion people on Earth to fulfill their potential throughout their lives.

David's life continues to be amazing, filled with joys and sorrows. So is yours. This chapter, and those that follow, trace that reality.

>> Defining Development

The **science of human development** *seeks to understand how and why people— all kinds of people, everywhere, of every age—change over time.* Growth is *multidirectional, multicontextual, multicultural, multidisciplinary,* and *plastic.* These five terms will be explained soon, but first we delve deeper into the definition: how and why, all kinds of people, and change over time.

Understanding How and Why

Developmental study is a *science* that seeks to understand the changes that occur as people age (Bornstein & Lamb, 2005). It depends on theories, data, analysis, critical thinking, and sound methodology—like every other science. And like all scientists, developmentalists ask questions and seek answers, trying to ascertain "how and why"—that is, trying to discover the processes of development and the reasons for those processes.

Science is needed because our lives depend on the answers. People disagree vehemently about how children should be raised; whether emerging adults should marry; when adults should divorce, or retire, or die. Such subjective opinions arise from emotions and upbringing, not necessarily from evidence. Scientists seek to progress from opinion to truth, from subjective to objective, from wishes to outcomes. "The empirical sciences will show us the way, the means, and the obstacles" in making life what we want it to be (Koops, 2003, p. 18).

To say that something is **empirical** means it is based on data, on demonstrations, on facts. Empirical sciences enable people to live full lives. Without scientific conclusions and then applications, human life would be "solitary, poor, nasty, brutish, and short," as Hobbes (1651/1997) wrote before the scientific revolution.

The Scientific Method

To avoid unexamined opinions and to rein in personal biases, scientists follow the five basic steps of the **scientific method:**

1. *Begin with curiosity.* On the basis of theory, prior research, or a personal observation, pose a question.
2. *Develop a hypothesis.* Shape the question into a hypothesis, a specific prediction that can be tested.
3. *Test the hypothesis.* Design and conduct research to gather empirical evidence (data).
4. *Draw conclusions.* Use the evidence to support or refute the hypothesis.
5. *Report the results.* Share the data, conclusions, and alternative explanations.

Developmentalists begin with curiosity and then seek facts, drawing conclusions only after careful research and analysis of data. **Replication**—the repetition of a study, using different participants—often becomes a sixth step, needed before the scientific community accepts conclusions. Although reliance on evidence is

---

science of human development The science that seeks to understand how and why people of all ages and circumstances change or remain the same over time.

empirical Based on observations, repeated experiences, verifiable experiments; not theoretical.

scientific method A way to answer questions using empirical research and data-based conclusions.

replication The repetition of a study, using different participants.

intended to eliminate bias, scientists realize that any single study may include unknown distortions; therefore replication, elaboration, and analysis by other scientists are needed.

Thousands of studies reported in this book are examples of the scientific method. Here we present just one, to illustrate the method clearly. Every year until the mid-1990s, thousands of 2- to 4-month-olds died of sudden infant death syndrome (SIDS, called "crib death" in North America and "cot death" in England), including 5,000 annually in the United States. They seemed healthy, went to sleep, and never woke up. As their parents mourned, scientists asked why (*step 1*) and developed numerous hypotheses (the cat? the quilt? natural honey? brain damage? spoiled milk?).

For years, a scientist named Susan Beal chronicled every SIDS death in South Australia, seeking factors that increased the risk. She found several (maternal smoking, lambskin blankets) and noted ethnic variations: Australian babies of Chinese descent died of SIDS less often than did other Australian babies. Genetic? Most experts thought so. But Beal also noticed that Chinese babies usually slept on their backs, contrary to the European custom. She hypothesized (*step 2*) that sleeping position might matter.

Beal convinced a large group of Australian parents to put their infants to sleep on their backs (*step 3*). Very few of the babies died of SIDS. After several years, she had enough data to draw conclusions (*step 4*): Back-sleeping infants survived more often. Her published reports (*step 5*) (Beal, 1988) caught the attention of scientists in the Netherlands, where pediatricians had told parents that babies should sleep on their stomachs. Two Dutch scientists (Engelberts & de Jong, 1990) recommended back-sleeping; thousands of parents took heed. As a result, SIDS was reduced in Holland by 40 percent in one year, a stunning replication (*step 6*).

Replication then occurred elsewhere. By 1994, a "Back to Sleep" campaign cut the SIDS rate dramatically, saving tens of thousands of young lives (Kinney & Thach, 2009; Mitchell, 2009). In the United States, 5,245 babies died of SIDS in 1984—but only 2,034 in 2005. In nation after nation, back-sleeping cut SIDS in half. Scientists are now working on that other half (Kinney & Thach, 2009; Mitchell, 2009).

The Nature–Nurture Debate

This example highlights a historic puzzle, often called the *nature–nurture debate*. **Nature** refers to the influence of the genes that people inherit. **Nurture** refers to environmental influences, beginning with the health and diet of the embryo's mother and continuing lifelong, including family, school, culture, and society.

The nature–nurture debate has many other names, among them *heredity–environment, maturation–learning, nativist–empiricist*. Under whatever name, the basic question is: How much of any characteristic, behavior, or emotion results from genes and how much from experience? Note that the question is "how much," not "which," because both genes and the environment affect every characteristic. Nature always affects nurture, and then nurture affects nature.

Indeed, some scientists think that the ongoing interaction between genes and experiences is so varied, explosive, and profound that even "how much" is an outdated concept (Gottlieb, 2007; Meaney, 2010; Spencer et al., 2009). "How much" implies proportions, but many developmentalists believe that the dynamic interaction makes "how much" a misleading question.

SEAN SPRAGUE / THE IMAGE WORKS

And If I Die Not likely. To die "before I wake" was not rare in many nations before 1990, but not in Mongolia (shown here) or other Asian countries. The reason, as scientists hypothesized and then confirmed, is that Asian parents put their infants "back to sleep."

Observation Quiz Back-sleeping babies sometimes squirm so that the blankets covering them come loose—another risk factor for SIDS. What detail makes that unlikely here? (see answer, page 7)

nature A general term for the traits, capacities, and limitations that each individual inherits genetically from his or her parents at the moment of conception.

nurture A general term for all the environmental influences that affect development after an individual is conceived.

Critical and Sensitive Periods

The fact that nature and nurture interact helps clarify another question: whether or not timing is crucial. Thanks to scientific inquiry, we have learned that there are both *critical periods* and *sensitive periods* in development.

A **critical period** is a time when something *must* occur to ensure normal development. For example, genes normally program the human fetus to develop arms and legs, hands and feet, fingers and toes, each over a specific period between 28 and 54 days after conception. Tragically, between 1957 and 1961, thousands of newly pregnant women in 30 nations took thalidomide, an antinausea drug. This disrupted prenatal development: If a woman ingested thalidomide between day 28 and day 54, the limbs of her newborn were malformed or absent (Moore & Persaud, 2007). Specifics depended on the precise day she swallowed the drug; before or after the critical period, no harm occurred.

For most of development, no critical period is evident, but a **sensitive period,** when a particular development occurs most easily, is common. One example is language, best learned early in life. If children do not master their first language between ages 1 and 3, they may do so later (hence this is not a critical period), but their grasp of grammar may be impaired. Similarly, childhood is a sensitive period for fluent pronunciation in a second or third language. As often occurs with development, a sweeping generalization (as in the preceding sentence) does not apply in every case. Accent-free speech *usually* must be learned in the sensitive period before adolescence, but some adults with exceptional nature and nurture (naturally adept at speech and then immersed in a new language) learn to speak a second language flawlessly (Birdsong, 2006; Herschensohn, 2007). Now consider a more complex example of nature and nurture.

Genetic Vulnerability

Some young people become violent, hurting others as well as themselves. Indeed, if a person is ever going to kill someone, he (or less often, she) is most likely to do so between ages 15 and 25. Sociologists, psychologists, and economists have found many factors that contribute to youth violence, including past child abuse and current circumstances. The violent delinquent is often a boy who was beaten in childhood and who lives in a drug-filled, crowded neighborhood (Maas et al., 2008).

Yet some such boys never become violent. A fourth discipline—biology—suggests why. One genetic variant occurs in the code for an enzyme (monoamine oxidase A, abbreviated MAOA) that affects *neurotransmitters* (chemicals in the brain). This gene comes in two versions, producing people with lower or higher levels of that enzyme. Both versions are normal; about one-third have low MAOA.

A famous developmental study began with virtually every child born in Dunedin, New Zealand, between April 1, 1972, and March 31, 1973. The children and their families were examined on dozens of measures from early childhood on, providing literally hundreds of published studies based on a wealth of data, including parental practices and variants of the MAOA gene. Researchers found that boys who were mistreated by their parents were about twice as likely to be overly aggressive (to develop a conduct disorder, to be violent, to be antisocial, and eventually to be convicted of a violent crime) if, *and only if,* they had the low-MAOA gene instead of the high-MAOA one (Caspi et al., 2002; see Figure 1.1).

critical period A time when a particular type of developmental growth (in body or behavior) must happen if it is ever going to happen.

sensitive period A time when a certain type of development is most likely, although it may still happen later. For example, early childhood is considered a sensitive period for language learning.

Doing Good Someone threw that garbage onto this beach in south Miami, but these two teen volunteers are cleaning it up. It is easy to trace such good behavior to culture, family, and community, but genes may also play a role. Some people are naturally much less selfish than others.

JEFF GREENBERG / ALAMY

Does this mean that becoming violent is inevitable for those with less of that enzyme? No. As Figure 1.1 shows, *if* they were not maltreated, boys with the low-MAOA gene were more likely than those with the high-MAOA gene to become law-abiding, peaceable adults. Such results were surprising at the time, but recently many other scientists have found genes, or circumstances, that predispose people to be either unusually successful or unusually pathological (Belsky et al., 2007; Keri, 2009). Such vulnerability is now accepted, although many still debate the specifics.

Replication of this exact study has been problematic. Many other studies also show that inherited risk influences later behavior, but the impact varies from one place and group of participants to another. People are particularly vulnerable to some risks in certain developmental periods (e.g,, in infancy to malnutrition, in adolescence to drug abuse, and so on).

Now consider a study of a very different population: African American 11-year-olds in rural Georgia, the United States (Brody et al., 2009). Parents and children in some families were taught to develop racial pride, family encouragement, honest communication, and house rules. Teenagers from this study who had a genetic risk (in this case, the short version of the 5-HTTLPR gene) benefited from the special learning, engaging in relatively few risky behaviors. But those with the short gene and without family training often broke the law. (This study is further explained in Chapter 16.)

Note that these examples involve nature *and* nurture. No period is either critical or sensitive unless a combination of maturation and experience makes it so. Most of the time growth proceeds smoothly, and people develop hands, language, morals, and everything else that characterize our species. When things go awry, developmentalists look to both nature and nurture to understand the cause and the cure.

Searching for cause and cure raises the issue of what science can and cannot do. Science cannot decide the purpose of life; we need philosophy or religion for that (National Academy of Sciences, 2008). Literature, film, and the other arts provide insights as well. As you will learn throughout this chapter, statistics, research methods, and ethics have both scientific validity and notable limitations. Don't idealize science, and don't trash it—use it well.

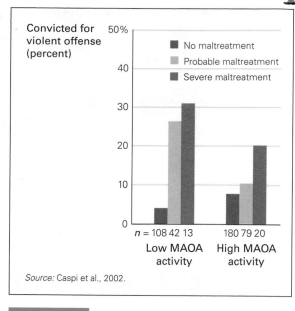

Source: Caspi et al., 2002.

FIGURE 1.1

Genetic Origins for Violent Crime Two variables—parental treatment and a variant of the gene that produces the enzyme MAOA—interact to affect the likelihood that a child will commit a violent crime. Of the boys in the "probable maltreatment" category, 10 percent were convicted of a violent crime if their MAOA level was high, but 26 percent were convicted if their MAOA was low.

Including All Kinds of People

As the second element of our definition indicates, developmental science studies *all kinds of people*—young and old; rich and poor; of every ethnicity, background, sexual orientation, culture, and nation. The challenge is to identify both universalities and differences and then to describe them in ways that simultaneously unify humanity and distinguish each individual. The danger is in drawing conclusions based on a limited group.

Both the universal and the unique are evident in everyone. For example, your father's father was once a boy who never sent a text message, was not vaccinated against chicken pox, and did not fear nuclear war. That much is universal, useful for understanding almost every grandfather. Also universal is the fact that his values and actions affect all of his descendents by his nature (you have one-eighth of his genes, and if you are male, his Y chromosome) and his nurture (his absence or presence affected your parents' lives as well as your own).

>> Answer to Observation Quiz (from page 5) The swaddling blanket is not only folded under the baby but also tied in place.

Family Pride Grandpa Charilaos is proud of his tavern in northern Greece (central Macedonia), but he is even more proud of his talented grandchildren, including Maria Soni (shown here). Note her expert fingering. Her father and mother also play instruments—is that nature or nurture?

Yet he is (or was) unique. No one exactly like him will ever live again. His effect on you depends on dozens of other factors, involving both genes and culture. For example, some people, genetically, are inclined to rebel against tradition while others cling to it; some people, culturally, revere their ancestors and others, as one Italian immigrant quipped, become "American by learning how to be ashamed of our parents" (Leonard Covello, quoted in Kasinitz et al., 2008, p. 10). As you learn more about the life span, you will recognize the influence of hundreds of people and circumstances on your personality, thoughts, and decisions.

Not every difference between one developing person and the norm is a deficit, as people once thought. By studying all kinds of people, of every age and background, developmentalists have come to appreciate the diversity of humankind, instead of assuming that someone unusual is to be pitied or changed. Some differences are welcome diversities, not deficits.

For instance, by age 75, 96 percent of all U.S. residents have married at least once in their lives (U.S. Bureau of the Census, 2009). Some of them thought being single was deficient, as the term *old maid* implied.

However, research now finds that difference (in this case, not marrying) is not necessarily a deficit. When "all kinds of people" include some who avoid marriage and some in same-sex partnerships, we find that some of those people are happy, successful, and accomplished just as they are. This does *not* mean that everyone unmarried is happy or that all variations are benign, but it does mean that judgments about deviations should be made carefully, based on evidence, not opinion.

Observing Changes over Time

The third crucial element in the definition of developmental science is that individuals *change over time*. Continuity and discontinuity, consistencies and transformations, from conception until death—these are our focus. Age is significant. Is it normal for a boy to throw himself down, kicking and screaming, when he is frustrated? Yes, if he is 2 years old; no, if he is 12. Is it normal for adults to plan their funeral? Yes at 90, no at 19.

dynamic-systems theory A view of human development as an ongoing, ever-changing interaction between the physical and emotional being and between the person and every aspect of his or her environment, including the family and society.

Every aspect of development interacts with every other; every person interacts with other people; all conditions and experiences interact continuously over time, each affecting the other. Consequently, scientists now envision development as the result of **dynamic systems.** The word *systems* captures the idea that a change in one aspect of a person, or family, or society affects all the other aspects because each part is connected to all the other parts (Thelen & Smith, 2006). The body is a system, or actually many systems (cardiovascular, respiratory, reproductive, and so on); a family is a system; so are neighborhoods, cities, nations, the world. Each part of development in each person is connected to many other parts of the system, and thus each part is affected by changes in other parts as time goes on. To pick a simple example, a birth turns a woman into a mother and a man into a father, a dramatic transformation of the individuals and the family system, and then other changes—in habits, goals, sleep, and so on—occur.

This approach to development is "relatively new" for social scientists, but all of nature is dynamic.

AP PHOTO / JIM MONE

Dynamic Interaction A dynamic-systems approach highlights the ever-changing impact that each part of a system has on all the other parts. This classroom scene reflects the eagerness for education felt by many immigrants, the reticence of some boys in an academic context, and a global perspective (as demonstrated by the world map). These facets emerge from various systems—family, gender, and culture—and they have interacted to produce this moment.

Observation Quiz What country is this? (see answer, page 11)

Especially for Future Teachers Does the classroom furniture shown in the photograph above affect instruction? (see response, page 11)

. . . seasons change in ordered measure, clouds assemble and disperse, trees grow to certain shape and size, snowflakes form and melt, minute plants and animals pass through elaborate life cycles that are invisible to us, and social groups come together and disband.

[Thelen & Smith, 2006, p. 271]

Since change is the nature of things, it is not surprising that the study of human development itself has changed. Fifty years ago, scholars concentrated on children, who were thought to grow until age 18 or so, when change stopped. A few researchers focused on the "sad ending" of life and none on the "empty middle" (Bronfenbrenner, 1974).

Then an insightful book around thirty years ago recognized that children affect adults just as adults affect children (Bell & Harper, 1977). And now with the dynamic-systems perspective, it is apparent that adults as well as children are continually affected by one another and by life circumstances. No one is the same at age 35 and age 45, or even 35 and 36. Every day is new; every age is open to change. Consequently, the science of development must encompass the entire life span. With that insight, the life-span perspective has emerged; it is described in the next section.

SUMMING UP

Developmental study is a science, which makes it useful in discovering and validating facts. All sciences follow the scientific method, beginning with questions to answer and drawing conclusions after empirical research. Developing persons of every age, culture, and background teach us what is universal as well as what is unique. Some periods of life are critical or sensitive periods for certain developmental changes, yet the interaction between nature and nurture is always evident. Differences among people are not necessarily deficits, although some people mistakenly assume that their own path is best for everyone. Change is systematic, ongoing, and dynamic throughout the entire life span.

life-span perspective An approach to the study of human development that takes into account all phases of life, not just childhood or adulthood.

>> The Life-Span Perspective

The **life-span perspective**, as set forth by Paul and Margret Baltes and their associates (Baltes et al., 2006; Staudinger & Lindenberger, 2003), views human development as (1) multidirectional, (2) multicontextual, (3) multicultural, (4) multidisciplinary, and (5) plastic. Each of these characteristics includes implications that need to be described.

Development Is Multidirectional

Change is apparent in each aspect of life and in every direction. Over time, human characteristics change in multiple ways—increasing, decreasing, or holding steady; in a line (linear), a curve (curvilinear), or up and down (zigzag). The curvilinear trajectory is the most difficult to capture statistically, but many things (from visual acuity to knowledge of calculus) advance and then decline over the life span. The dynamic variability of change is contrary to the traditional idea that development advanced bit by bit until about age 18, was stable until about age 50, and then declined.

Sometimes *discontinuity* is evident when a rapid shift occurs, as happens at puberty when a child's body becomes that of a woman or a man. Sometimes *continuity* is found: From age 2 to age 10, children ordinarily gain a few pounds each year. Some things do not change: Each person is born and dies with about 20,000 genes, present in his or her body cells lifelong. Thus, many directions are possible; specifics vary.

Many people believe that development occurs in stages, like a set of steps on a stairway (up, stable, up, stable, up, stable . . .). As you will read in Chapter 2, several major theorists—including Freud, Erikson, and Piaget—describe age-related stages. Others—including Skinner and Maslow—do not. Research shows that some shifts seem stagelike (when one development triggers several others) and other shifts are gradual. From a life-span perspective, a multidirectional view allows us to understand when, how, and whether stages occur.

A multidirectional perspective enables researchers to recognize that gains and losses often occur simultaneously: Losses can lead to gains and vice versa (Baltes et al., 2006). Every change—going to college, getting married or divorced, moving to another neighborhood, the death of a parent—produces unexpected advances and retreats.

Consider an example. When a man's wife dies, his physical, intellectual, and social well-being often decline (van den Brink et al., 2004). One study found that, in the month after the death of a spouse, widowers entered nursing homes three times more often than did other men of similar age, education, and health (Nihtilä & Martikainen, 2008). That is one pattern, when the direction of every aspect of life seems downward.

SPENCER GRANT / PHOTOEDIT INC.

What Will He Do Without Her? With the death of his wife, life has suddenly changed for this man. The direction that change will take is difficult to predict. Compared with other men their age, widowers are more likely to die *or* to remarry.

But the life-span perspective examines variations as well as averages, avoiding simple generalizations. Decline is common among widowers, but not inevitable. Some men expand their social worlds after mourning, and that triggers movement in other directions. A widower may develop new friendships, while income, intellectual stimulation, and nutrition may zigzag. Trends and trajectories sometimes follow unexpected paths.

Development Is Multicontextual

The second insight from the life-span perspective is that development is multi-contextual, occurring in many contexts, including physical surroundings (climate, noise, population density, etc.) and family constellations. The impact of various physical and social environments is explained throughout this book.

The need to consider many contexts was first emphasized by Urie Bronfenbrenner, who recommended an **ecological-systems approach** to developmental study (1977). He argued that developmentalists need to examine the systems that surround each person just as a naturalist examines the ecology, or the interrelationship, of each organism and its environment. Toward the end of his life, Bronfenbrenner renamed his theory *bioecological* (Bronfenbrenner & Morris, 2006) to ensure that its name reflected the natural settings and biological processes that the theory includes.

Bronfenbrenner described three nested levels that affect each person (diagrammed in Figure 1.2): *microsystems* (elements of the immediate surroundings, such as family and friends, school and religious classes), *exosystems* (local institutions such as school system, religious organization, and workplace), and *macrosystems* (the larger contexts, including cultural values, economic policies, and political processes). Appreciating the dynamic interaction among the microsystem, the exosystem, and the macrosystem, Bronfenbrenner named a fourth system, the *mesosystem*, which connects the other systems. One example of a mesosystem is the interface between employment and family. Some mesosystems between work and home are obvious, such as family-leave policies and overtime schedules. Some are indirect, originating in the macrosystem, such as unemployment rates, minimum-wage standards, and male–female hiring practices. Finally, recognizing the

ecological-systems approach The view that in the study of human development, the person should be considered in all the contexts and interactions that constitute a life. (Later renamed *bioecological theory.*)

>> **Answer to Observation Quiz** (from page 9) The three Somali girls wearing headscarves may have thrown you off, but these first-graders attend school in Minneapolis, Minnesota, in the United States. Clues include the children's diversity (this school has students from 17 nations), clothing (obviously Western), and—for the sharp-eyed—the flag near the door.

>> **Response for Future Teachers** (from page 9) Yes. Every aspect of the ecological context affects what happens. In this classroom, tables and movable chairs foster group collaboration and conversation—potent learning methods that are difficult to achieve when desks and seats are bolted to the floor and the teacher sits behind a large desk.

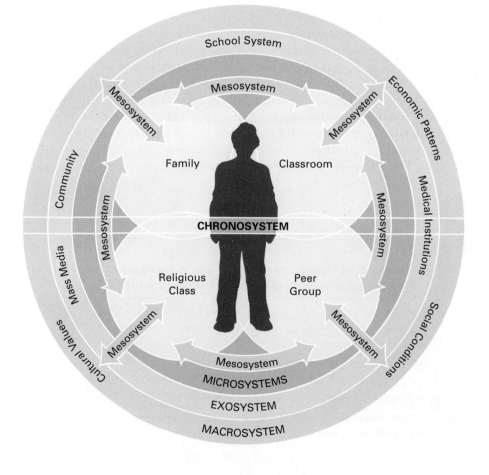

FIGURE 1.2

The Ecological Model According to developmental researcher Urie Bronfenbrenner, each person is significantly affected by interactions among a number of overlapping systems, which provide the context of development. *Microsystems*—family, peer groups, classroom, neighborhood, house of worship—intimately and immediately shape human development. Surrounding and supporting the microsystems are the *exosystems*, which include all the external networks, such as community structures and local educational, medical, employment, and communications systems, that influence the microsystems. Influencing all three of these systems is the *macrosystem*, which includes cultural values, political philosophies, economic patterns, and social conditions. *Mesosystems* refer to interactions among systems, as when parents and teachers coordinate to educate a child. Bronfenbrenner added a fifth system, the *chronosystem*, to emphasize the importance of historical time.

importance of historical conditions, Bronfenbrenner described the *chronosystem* (literally, "time system"), which affects the other systems.

Following through on Bronfenbrenner's pioneering work, developmentalists take many contexts into account. Two of them are highlighted here because they are pervasive yet sometimes ignored: the historical and the socioeconomic contexts.

The Historical Context

All persons born within a few years of one another are said to be a **cohort,** a group who travel through life together, experiencing similar circumstances. Members of each cohort are affected by the values, events, technologies, and culture of their era. For example, political opinions lifelong are particularly influenced by events in emerging adulthood. Consequently, attitudes about war differ for the U.S. cohorts who came of age during World War II, the Cold War, or the conflicts in Vietnam, the Persian Gulf, Iraq, and Afghanistan.

Sometimes demographic characteristics rather than headline-making events shape the historical context. For example, the cohort born between 1946 and 1964 is called the baby-boom generation because of a marked spike in the birth rate. The older members of that cohort are now beginning late adulthood, and their experiences are unlike those of their parents. One reason is the size of their cohort, making them a large voting bloc that shapes policies regarding retirement and health care.

If you doubt that national trends and events touch individuals, consider your first name—a word chosen especially for you. Look at Table 1.1, which lists the most popular names for boys and girls born into cohorts 20 years apart, beginning in 1928. Your name and your reaction to it are influenced by the era.

The Socioeconomic Context

Another context of development is the socioeconomic one, reflected in a person's **socioeconomic status,** abbreviated **SES,** sometimes called *social class* (as in *middle class* or *working class*). SES reflects more than income: Education is often crucial.

SES brings advantages and disadvantages, opportunities and limitations—all affecting housing, nutrition, knowledge, and habits. Although low income obviously limits a person, other SES factors can make poverty better or worse. Even income is not a straightforward indication of poverty: Financial assets over a long period affect children's learning more than their parents' current income does (Yeung & Conley, 2008).

Not the Typical Path This woman's lifelong ambition is to walk the 2,160-mile Appalachian Trail from Maine to Georgia. She is considerably more active than the average member of her cohort.

cohort A group defined by the shared age of its members. Each cohort was born at about the same time and moves through life together, experiencing the same historical events and cultural shifts.

socioeconomic status (SES) A person's position in society as determined by income, wealth, occupation, education, and place of residence. (Sometimes called *social class*.)

Guess First If your answers, in order from top to bottom, were 1928, 1968, 2008, 1948, and 1988, you are excellent at detecting cohort influences. If you made a mistake, perhaps that's because the data are compiled from applications for Social Security numbers, so the names of those who did not get a Social Security number are omitted.

TABLE 1.1		
Which First Names for U.S. Girls and Boys Were Most Popular in 1928, 1948, 1968, 1988 and 2008?		
Year	Top Five Girls' Names	Top Five Boys' Names
_____	Mary, Betty, Dorothy, Helen, Margaret	Robert, John, James, William, Charles
_____	Lisa, Michelle, Kimberly, Jennifer, Mary	Michael, David, John, James, Robert
_____	Emma, Isabella, Emily, Madison, Ava	Jacob, Michael, Ethan, Joshua, Daniel
_____	Linda, Mary, Barbara, Patricia, Susan	James, Robert, John, William, David
_____	Jessica, Ashley, Amanda, Sarah, Jennifer	Michael, Christopher, Matthew, Joshua, Andrew

Source: Social Security Administration Web site (http://www.ssa.gov/OACT/babynames), retrieved September 11, 2010.

Gambling on the Help of Others? Since 2008 in Atlantic City, more than 3,000 adults have lost their jobs because casinos and hotels have fewer patrons. Kristin and her son Thomas do not go hungry, thanks to the Atlantic City Mission.

Observation Quiz Can you see signs that malnutrition might nevertheless be a problem? (see answer, page 15)

A question for developmentalists: When does low SES do most damage? In infancy, poverty may mean inferior medical care and malnutrition, stunting the brain; in adulthood, job and marriage prospects are reduced as SES falls; in late adulthood, the accumulation of past stresses (including low SES) can overwhelm the body's reserves, causing disease and death. Which is worse? The answer is not clear; SES is powerful at every age.

Development Is Multicultural

When social scientists use the term *culture*, they refer to a "meaning and information system, shared by a group and transmitted across generations, that allows the group to meet basic needs of survival . . . pursue happiness and well-being, and derive meaning from life" (Matsumoto, 2009, p. 5). Citizens of a nation, residents of a region within a nation, members of an ethnic group, people living in one neighborhood, or even students in a college class can have their own culture, in that they have their own method of gathering information and ascribing meaning, or value, to life. Culture affects every action—indeed, every thought.

What's for Dinner? Markets are universal, but each culture has a unique mix of products, stores, and salespeople. Compare this floating food market in Bangkok, Thailand, with a North American supermarket.

Learning Within a Culture

Russian developmentalist Lev Vygotsky (1896–1934) was a leader in describing the interaction between culture and education. He noted that each community in his native Russia (which included Asians and Europeans, of many faiths and languages) taught their children whatever beliefs and habits their culture valued.

As discussed in more detail in Chapters 2 and 9, Vygotsky developed the concept of *guided participation,* in which entire societies teach novices the skills and habits expected within the particular culture. Guided participation often happens informally through "mutual involvement in several widespread cultural practices with great importance for learning: narratives, routines, and play" (Rogoff, 2003, p. 285).

That we are unaware of the culture we transmit is evident from a study of Chinese and U.S. parents of 20-month-olds. Parents in both cultures have small families and devote time and effort to their

▶ **Research Design**

Scientists: Cheri C. Y. Chan, Amanda C. Brandone, and Twila Tardif.

Publication: *Journal of Cross-Cultural Psychology* (2009).

Participants: A total of 49 mother/toddler pairs, 25 of them from middle America and 24 of them from Beijing, China, participated. The two groups were comparable in age and education.

Design: The mothers and toddlers were brought into a playroom and recorded in three 10-minute play sessions (1) with mechanical toys, (2) with regular toys, and (3) reading a picture book. To equalize both groups, the book was created for this study by laminating an equal number of pages from picture books used in the United States and China.

Major conclusions: Some universals were evident. For example, all the mothers were influenced by context—using more verbs when the toys were mechanical, for instance. Differences also emerged. The U.S. mothers gave fewer commands, such as "sit down" and "listen," and allowed children to add irrelevant comments about their own memories. Regarding joint book reading, the Chinese mothers used somewhat more verbs than nouns (about 20 percent more), but the opposite was true for the U.S. mothers.

Comments: This study shows cultural similarities as well as differences. Many studies suggest that Chinese culture encourages people to see themselves in relation to others rather than as isolated individuals and to see objects in context rather than detached from their uses and surroundings. This study suggests that even in joint book reading with 20-month-olds, differences appear. Note that the researchers tried to find parents of equivalent education: Without that similarity, a difference that seems to be cultural might be due to SES.

Not the Same At first glance, this seems a standard scene; educated mothers the world over often read books to their toddlers. A closer look reveals differences—in the billboard, in hairstyles, in the mother's ring. However, the pivotal cultural variation cannot be seen: her words and his focus (see text).

IMAGINE CHINA

children's language development. Book reading is common. In all of this, cultural similarities are apparent.

However, researchers designed a picture book (no words)—with half the pictures from U.S. picture books and half from Chinese ones—and asked the parents to look at the book with their toddlers. Everything said was recorded and analyzed. The U.S. mothers used more nouns than verbs, and the opposite was true for the Chinese mothers. For example, at a picture of a dandelion, the U.S. mothers pointed out the petals, leaves, and stem, while the Chinese mothers noted that a dandelion could be picked or smelled (Brody et al., 2009). That difference reflects the cultures of the United States and China.

Ethnicity, Race, and Culture

Confusion arises whenever people—scientists or nonscientists—refer to *ethnic groups, races,* and *cultures.* Each of these terms has a distinct meaning: The following definitions may help.

People of an **ethnic group** share certain attributes, almost always including ancestral heritage and usually national origin, religion, and language (Whitfield & McClearn, 2005). Ethnic group is not the same as cultural group: some people of a particular ethnicity may not share a culture, and some cultures are followed by people of several ethnic groups.

The term **race** has been used to categorize people on the basis of biology, particularly as it affects outward appearance. However, appearance is not a reliable indicator of biology, genetics, or development (Race, Ethnicity, and Genetics Working Group, 2005). Skin color (often used as a racial marker) is particularly misleading, since dark-skinned people whose ancestors were African are even more genetically diverse than light-skinned people whose

ethnic group People whose ancestors were born in the same region and who often share a language, culture, and religion.

race A group of people who are regarded by themselves or by others as distinct from other groups on the basis of physical appearance. Social scientists think race is a misleading concept.

ancestors were European (Tishkoff & Kidd, 2004). As one team of psychologists expressed it, "Race is a social construction wherein individuals [who are] labeled as being of different races on the basis of physical characteristics are often treated as though they belong to biologically defined groups" (Goldston et al., 2008, p. 14). Unlike genetic differences, social constructions (ideas created by a society) can change (Rothenberg, 2007). Most social scientists agree that "the idea of race distorts, exaggerates, and maximizes human differences" (Smedley & Smedley, 2005, p. 22).

Social constructions have power, given by people, not biology. Perceived racial differences can lead to discrimination, which can cause physical and psychological illness. Indeed, even when discrimination is not evident, each person's racial self-concept affects his or her cognition (see the discussion of *stereotype threat* in Chapter 18).

Some data in official documents (such as the U.S. Census), in research reports, and therefore in this book differentiate people by African, European, Hispanic, and Asian ancestry, sometimes thought to be races. When you encounter such data, remember that race may be misleading and that, although ethnicity, culture, and SES may overlap, "membership in an ethnic minority group is not equivalent to a common cultural experience," as developmentalist Vonnie McLoyd explains (2006, p. 1145).

Development Is Multidisciplinary

Scientists often specialize, studying one phenomenon in one species within one domain at one age, using the methods and strategies of their particular discipline. For example, laboratory experiments with genetically altered mice are more likely reported by biologists than by sociologists; psychologists are intrigued by the development of various types of memory, and they experiment with nonsense words in order to understand it; anthropologists are fascinated by various forms of family life and rely on scientific observation "in the field" to learn more.

All recognize, however, that human development over the life span is such a vast subject that insight and information from diverse disciplines are required to understand it. As a team of psychologists explain: "An integrative life-span developmental framework [involves] interdisciplinary collaborations and multiple methodological approaches for understanding how and why individuals change" (Hofer & Piccinin, 2010, p. 269).

To make it easier to study, development is usually segmented into three domains—biological, cognitive, and social—each one the specialty of scientists in a particular discipline. Development is also segmented into discrete age divisions, such as childhood, adolescence, and adulthood, each with approximate ages (see Table 1.2).

Domains and age periods may be further divided. For example, some scholars study hormonal, moral, or emotional development, each of which is primarily (but not exclusively) within one of the domains (respectively, biological, cognitive, and social). Similarly, the life span can be divided into three periods, or seven (as in this text), or many more. For example, there is intriguing research on vision in the first weeks of life (newborns have particular trouble seeing contrasts, as well as the color pink) (Brown & Lindsey, 2009; Franklin et al., 2008); on the relationship between intellectual ability and grip strength in the "oldest old"—one of three age stages within late adulthood (Takata et al., 2008); and on the sequence of self-assessed appearance, self-esteem, and dieting (all three domains) during the first few years of adolescence. Weaving together all these multidisciplinary and multiage strands reveals the pattern of human life.

>> **Answer to Observation Quiz** (from page 13) Eating enough does not always mean eating well—a reality ignored by many low-SES parents and by many charity groups who help them. Note the lack of green or deep yellow vegetables, the french fry dipped in ketchup, the glasses that are too large for milk or orange juice, and the baby bottle for a child who is old enough to have real food at mealtime. All of these are ominous signs, as is this statistic: In the United States, as income falls, obesity rises. Low SES is not just about tangible stuff.

TABLE 1.2	
Age Ranges for Different Stages of Development	
Infancy	0 to 2 years
Early childhood	2 to 6 years
Middle childhood	6 to 11 years
Adolescence	11 to 18 years
Emerging adulthood	18 to 25 years
Adulthood	25 to 65 years
Late adulthood	65 years and older

Of course, words and pages follow in linear succession and the brain thinks one idea at a time: It is impossible to consider all ages and domains simultaneously. All developmental scholars use discrete ages and topics to organize and focus their work, but here is the underlying truth: Although life is studied by domain and age, each domain and each stage affect the others. For example, your ability to learn from the paragraph you just read depends on your current maturity (a child wouldn't grasp it) and all three domains: your physical state (hunger, sleep, temperature, and so on), mental ability (familiar words), and social influences (cultural values, people around you). Furthermore, your past education and anticipated future affect your current motivation. Only a multidisciplinary approach can begin to encompass all that.

Two relatively new disciplines, genetics and neuroscience, have already affected our understanding of every age and aspect of development, as you will see now and in every chapter of this book.

mirror neurons Cells in an observer's brain that respond to an action performed by someone else in the same way they would if the observer had actually performed that action.

A VIEW FROM SCIENCE

Mirror Neurons

The multidisciplinary approach means that hundreds of factors, noted by many disciplines, combine to protect or undermine development. Often scientists in one discipline discover something that intrigues those in other disciplines, who hypothesize, experiment, conclude, and replicate.

About two decades ago, scientists were surprised to discover that a particular region of a macaque monkey's brain responded to actions the monkey had merely observed as if it had actually performed those actions itself (Gallese et al., 1996). For example, when one macaque saw another reach for a banana, the same brain areas were activated (lit up in brain scans) in both monkeys. Certain neurons, dubbed **mirror neurons,** in the F5 area of the premotor cortex, responded to what was observed. Using increasingly advanced technology, neuroscientists now find mirror neurons in several parts of the human brain (Keysers & Gazzola, 2010).

Human brains mirror much more than reaching for bananas. Indeed, "[The] human mirror neuron system may allow us to go beyond imitating the observed motor acts of others to infer their intentions and perhaps even their states of mind" (Coward,

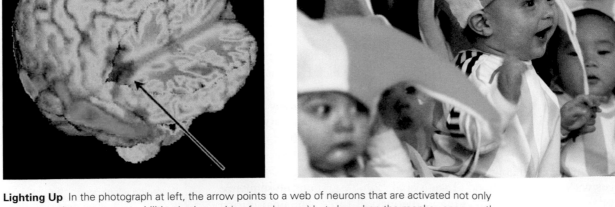

Lighting Up In the photograph at left, the arrow points to a web of neurons that are activated not only when a monkey uses motor abilities (as in reaching for a banana) but also when the monkey sees another monkey perform that action. At right, these toddlers in Buenos Aires may be exhibiting mirror neurons at work as they get ready to join other fans in cheering on Argentina's soccer team in a match against Peru.

2008, p. 1494). Scientists in many disciplines continue to explore the implications of this discovery (Rizzolatti & Sinigaglia, 2008; Soekadar et al., 2008):

- Anthropologists think that mirror neurons might explain cultural transmission and social organization (Losin et al., 2009).

- Psychopathologists connect autism with lost mirror neurons (Di Martino et al., 2009; Williams et al., 2006).

- Psychiatrists believe that abnormalities of the mirror neurons may be involved in symptoms of schizophrenia (Buccino & Amore, 2008).

- Linguists wonder whether mirror neurons aid language learning (Buccino et al., 2004; Corballis, 2010).

- Social psychologists think mirror neurons help people empathize with one another (Decety & Meyer, 2008; Iacoboni, 2009).

- Cognitive psychologists suggest that mirror neurons explain newborns' ability to imitate what they see (Diamond & Amso, 2008).

Although scientists are excited by these multidisciplinary possibilities, they are cautious as well. Research on human brains is notoriously difficult (Hunt & Thomas, 2008). Neural networks are complex; mirror neurons certainly do not explain all of human learning or social responsiveness (Wheatley et al., 2007). Yet because developmental research is multidisciplinary, thousands of scientists in multiple fields are pursuing implications suggested by a discovery in a monkey's brain.

Development Is Plastic

The term *plasticity* denotes two complementary aspects of development: Human traits can be molded (as plastic can be), yet people maintain a certain durability of identity (as plastic does). The concept of plasticity in development provides both hope and realism—hope because change is possible and realism because development builds on what has come before.

Even the brain is plastic (Stiles, 2008). Part of the normal brain is dedicated to balance; we don't fall down when we stand up, run, or even hop on one foot. However, this part of the brain was destroyed (by an overdose of a prescription drug) in a woman named Cheryl. An observer wrote:

> First her head wobbles and tilts to one side, and her arms reach out to try to stabilize her stand. Soon her whole body is moving chaotically back and forth, and she looks like a person walking a tightrope in the frantic seesaw moment before losing his balance—except that both her feet are firmly planted on the ground.
>
> *[Doidge, 2007, p. 1]*

A few neuroscientists, hoping that plasticity would allow recovery, tried to reprogram Cheryl's brain. They succeeded. Although the balance area in her brain remains dead, another part of her brain took over, and Cheryl now stands steady. This has implications for learning disabilities, for depression, for prejudice, for stroke victims, and for much more, as "[we] are all born with a far more adaptable, all-purpose, opportunistic brain than we have understood" (p. 26). Yet caution is stressed again here; plasticity does not mean that anything is possible, just that change may occur—for better or worse.

Plasticity and David's Future

In some ways, plasticity underlies the other four characteristics of development. My nephew David, whose story opened this chapter, required heart surgery two days after he was born and again at age 5. His first eye surgery, at 6 months, destroyed one eye. As he grew older, malformations of his thumbs, ankles, feet, teeth, spine, and brain became evident. Predictions were dire: Some people wondered why his parents did not place him in an institution. As a young child, David was severely retarded.

Time and time again, experts from many disciplines nurtured David's abilities. For example, at 9 months he did not crawl because his parents kept him safe in

Especially for Parents Who Want Their Children to Enjoy Sports While your baby is still too young and uncoordinated to play any sports, what does the research on mirror neurons suggest you might do? (see response, page 18)

>> Response to for Parents Who Want Their Children to Enjoy Sports
(from page 17) The results of mirror-neuron research imply that people of all ages learn by observing body movements in others. This suggests that parents should make sure their baby gets many chances to watch them (or someone else) throwing balls, running, and playing sports.

their arms. Fortunately, a consultant from the Kentucky School for the Blind put him on a large rug, so he learned to feel the boundaries and crawl safely. Later he attended three specialized preschools, then a mainstreamed public school, then a special high school, then the University of Louisville—each with educators guided by research on learning. Surgical advances kept his heart beating, allowed his remaining eye to see, caused his jaw to realign, and improved his life in many other ways that would not have been tried by doctors a few decades earlier.

As I have watched David's development, plasticity is evident. Remember, plasticity cannot erase genetic endowment, childhood experiences, or permanent damage. David's disabilities are always with him (he still lives at home). But by age 10, David had skipped a year of school and was a fifth-grader, reading at the eleventh-grade level. He learned languages (German and Russian, with some Spanish and Korean). In young adulthood, after one failing semester, he earned several As and graduated from college.

David now works as a translator of German texts, which he enjoys because "I like providing a service to scholars, giving them access to something they would otherwise not have." As his aunt, I have seen him repeatedly defy pessimistic predictions. All five of the characteristics of the life-span perspective are evident, summarized in Table 1.3.

TABLE 1.3

Five Characteristics of Development

Characteristic	Application in David's Story
Multidirectional. Change occurs in every direction, not always in a straight line. Gains and losses, predictable growth, and unexpected transformations are evident.	David's development seemed static (or even regressive, as when early surgery destroyed one eye) but then accelerated each time he entered a new school or college.
Multidisciplinary. Numerous academic fields—especially psychology, biology, education, and sociology, but also neuroscience, economics, religion, anthropology, history, medicine, genetics, and many more—contribute insights.	Two disciplines were particularly critical: medicine (David would have died without advances in surgery on newborns) and education (special educators guided him and his parents many times).
Multicontextual. Human lives are embedded in many contexts, including historical conditions, economic constraints, and family patterns.	The high SES of David's family made it possible for him to receive daily medical and educational care. His two older brothers protected him.
Multicultural. Many cultures—not just between nations but also within them—affect how people develop.	Appalachia, where David and his family lived, has a particular culture, including acceptance of people with disabilities and willingness to help families in need. Those aspects of that culture benefited David and his family.
Plasticity. Every individual, and every trait within each individual, can be altered at any point in the life span. Change is ongoing, although neither random nor easy.	David's measured IQ changed from about 40 (severely mentally retarded) to about 130 (far above average), and his physical disabilities became less crippling as he matured.

SUMMING UP

Development is multidirectional, with gains and losses evident at every stage and in every domain. All the dimensions of development are affected, sometimes in opposite ways, by human experience. Among the many contexts of development are historical circumstances and economic conditions. A person's life is affected partly by income and education, which encourage or restrict opportunity. Culture always shapes development, and it should not be confused with ethnicity or race. Each discipline uses particular methodology to focus on one aspect of life; consequently, a multidisciplinary approach is needed to study the entire life span. Development is plastic: Both the brain and experience are connected to prior events and open to change.

>> Using the Scientific Method

Now we focus on the crux of the scientific method: designing research and analyzing evidence. Statistical measures often help scientists discover relationships between various aspects of the data. (Some statistical perspectives are presented in Table 1.4) Every research design, method, and statistical measure has strengths as well as weaknesses. You will notice that every chapter in this text includes a Research Design in which the design of a particular study is explained and critiqued, to help you see the variations that, together, provide evidence for what is known about development. Now we consider three major types of research and then discuss three ways in which research focuses on change over time.

ALAMY

Can They See Her? No, and they cannot hear one another. This scientist is observing three deaf boys through a window that is a mirror on the other side. Her observations will help them learn to communicate.

Observation

We are all observers: As a scientific method, observation includes many techniques in order to be less subjective. **Scientific observation** requires the researcher to record behavior systematically and objectively. Observations often occur in a naturalistic setting (such as a home, school, or public place), where people are likely

scientific observation A method of testing a hypothesis by unobtrusively watching and recording participants' behavior in a systematic and objective manner—in a natural setting, in a laboratory, or in searches of archival data.

TABLE 1.4	
Statistical Measures Often Used to Analyze Research Results	
Measure	**Use**
Effect size	Indicates how much one variable affects another. Effect size ranges from 0 to 1: An effect size of 0.2 is called small, 0.5 moderate, and 0.8 large.
Significance	Indicates whether the results might have occurred by chance. A finding that chance would produce the results fewer than 5 times in 100 is significant at the 0.05 level. A finding that chance would produce the results once in 100 times is significant at 0.01; once in 1,000 times is significant at 0.001.
Cost-benefit analysis	Calculates how much a particular independent variable costs versus how much it saves. This is particularly useful to analyze public spending. For instance, one cost-benefit analysis showed that an expensive preschool program cost $15,166 per child but saved $215,000 by age 40, in reduced costs of special education, unemployment, prison, and so on (Belfield et al., 2006).
Odds ratio	Indicates how a particular variable compares to a standard, set at 1. For example, one study found that, although less than 1 percent of all child homicides occurred at school, the odds were similar for public and private schools. The odds of such deaths occurring in high schools, however, were 18.47 times that of elementary or middle schools (set at 1.0) (MMWR, January 18, 2008).
Factor analysis	Hundreds of variables could affect any given behavior. In addition, many variables (such as family income and parental education) may overlap. To take this into account, analysis reveals variables that can be clustered together to form a factor, which is a composite of many variables. For example, SES might become one factor, child personality another.
Meta-analysis	A "study of studies." Researchers use statistical tools to synthesize the results of previous, separate studies. Then they analyze the accumulated results, using criteria that weight each study fairly. This approach improves data analysis by combining the results of studies that used so few participants that the conclusions did not reach significance.

Who Participates? For all these measures, the characteristics of the people who participate in the study (formerly called the *subjects*, now called the *participants*) are important, as is the number of people who are studied. Even a tiny effect size that could be applied to a large population may indicate a useful benefit. For example, the effect size of exercise on heart health is small, but millions of lives would be saved if everyone walked at least an hour a day.

experiment A research method in which the researcher tries to determine the cause-and-effect relationship between two variables by manipulating one (called the *independent variable*) and then observing and recording the ensuing changes in the other (called the *dependent variable*).

independent variable In an experiment, the variable that is introduced to see what effect it has on the dependent variable. (Also called *experimental variable*.)

dependent variable In an experiment, the variable that may change as a result of whatever new condition or situation the experimenter adds. In other words, the dependent variable *depends* on the independent variable.

Especially for Nurses In the field of medicine, why are experiments conducted to test new drugs and treatments? (see response, page 22)

to behave as they usually do. Scientific observation can also occur in a laboratory, where scientists record how people react in various situations.

Observation is the mainstay of anthropologists, who try to be unobtrusive when they observe a culture. Historians use observation when they pore over old records to gain insight. Even with meticulous practice so as to achieve objectivity, observation is limited: It cannot prove what causes people to do what they do.

The Experiment

The **experiment** is designed to establish what causes what. In the social sciences, experimenters typically impose a particular treatment on a group of volunteer participants or expose them to a specific condition. Then they record whether their behavior changes.

In technical terms, the experimenters manipulate an **independent variable,** which is the imposed treatment or special condition (also called the *experimental variable*; a *variable* is anything that can vary). This independent variable may affect whatever they are studying, called the **dependent variable** (which *depends* on the independent variable). Thus, the independent variable is the new, special treatment; any change in the dependent variable is the result.

The purpose of an experiment is to find out whether an independent variable affects the dependent variable. In a typical experiment (as diagrammed in Figure 1.3), at least two groups of participants are studied. One group is called the *experimental group*, which gets the particular treatment (the independent variable). The other group is the *comparison group* (also called a *control group*), which does not.

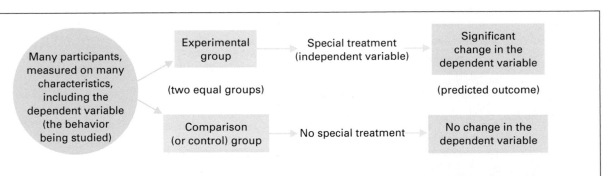

Procedure:

1. Divide participants into two groups that are matched on important characteristics, especially the behavior that is the dependent variable on which this study is focused.

2. Give special treatment, or intervention (the independent variable), to one group (the experimental group).

3. Compare the groups on the dependent variable. If they now differ, the cause of the difference was probably the independent variable.

4. Publish the results.

FIGURE 1.3

How to Conduct an Experiment The basic sequence diagrammed here applies to all experiments. Many additional features, especially the statistical measures listed in Table 1.4 and various ways of reducing experimenter bias, affect whether publication occurs. (Scientific journals reject reports of experiments that were not rigorous in method and analysis.)

The Survey

A third research method is the **survey.** Information is collected from a large number of people by interview, questionnaire, or some other means. The survey is a quick and direct way to obtain data.

However, acquiring valid survey data is far more difficult than it appears. For example, elections would be easy to predict (never "too close to call") if people voted as they said they would, if the undecided followed the trends, and if those who refused to tell or who were not asked were similar to those surveyed. But none of that is true: People lie or change their minds; those who never talk to strangers are unlike those who talk freely; those who are not surveyed are more likely to be at college, or in prison, or available only on cell phone—all of which makes them younger and less predictable than those surveyed. Good scientists correct for all this, but total accuracy is unattainable.

Furthermore, survey answers are influenced by the wording and the sequence of the questions, as well as by selective memory. For example, every year since 1991, thousands of high school students throughout the United States have been asked if they had sexual intercourse before age 13. Every year, about twice as many ninth-graders (14 percent in 2007) as twelfth-graders (7 percent) say yes. How could that be? Do twelfth-graders forget, do ninth-graders lie, or do sexually active ninth-graders drop out of school? Surveys, involving more than 200,000 students over the years, cannot tell.

Studying Development over the Life Span

Social scientists from every discipline use these three methods (observations, experiments, and surveys) to explore human behavior. In addition, for developmentalists time is pivotal. To study change over time, researchers use one of three basic research designs: cross-sectional, longitudinal, or cross-sequential (see Figure 1.4 on page 24).

Cross-Sectional Research

The most convenient (quickest and least expensive) way to study developmental change over time is with **cross-sectional research.** Groups of people of one age are compared with a similar group of people of another age. For instance, in

survey A research method in which information is collected from a large number of people by interviews, written questionnaires, or some other means.

cross-sectional research A research design that compares groups of people who differ in age but are similar in other important characteristics.

Compare These with Those The apparent similarity of these three groups in gender and ethnic composition makes them candidates for cross-sectional research. Before we could be sure that any difference among the three groups is the result of age, we would have to be sure the groups are alike in other ways, such as socioeconomic status and religious affiliation. Even if three groups seem identical in everything but age, there may be unknown differences.

>> Response for Nurses (from page 20)
Experiments are the only way to determine cause-and-effect relationships. If we want to be sure that a new drug or treatment is safe and effective, an experiment must be conducted to establish that the drug or treatment improves health.

longitudinal research A research design in which the same individuals are followed over time and their development is repeatedly assessed.

the United States in 2008, 92 percent of men aged 35 to 44 but only 70 percent of those aged 55 to 64 were in the labor force (U.S. Bureau of the Census, 2010). Does this mean one out of every four men retires between age 40 and 60?

Cross-sectional design might lead to that conclusion. However, might the groups differ in ways besides age? In this example, the younger U.S. men, on average, had more education than the older ones. Perhaps education, not age, accounted for their higher official employment, while some less educated, older men worked off the books—the study cannot determine this.

A related problem is that the number of people in a cohort affects the experience of that cohort. Perhaps the 60-year-old men, who were baby boomers, had more trouble finding work because there are so many of them. If so, a cohort effect might appear to be an age effect.

Longitudinal Research

To help discover whether age itself, not historical context, causes a developmental change, scientists undertake **longitudinal research.** This research design involves collecting data repeatedly on the same individuals as they age. Longitudinal research is particularly useful in studying development over many years (Elder & Shanahan, 2006; Hofer & Piccinin, 2010).

You have already read about the links among the MAOA gene, child maltreatment, and adult criminality. That was among hundreds of findings from a longitudinal study of an entire cohort in New Zealand. Some other surprising findings of longitudinal research are given in Table 1.5. Developmentalists agree that longitudinal research is more accurate than cross-sectional research. However, because so much effort and time are required, many longitudinal studies include far fewer participants than would be ideal, especially when developmentalists seek to study the interaction between several variables. The famous New Zealand study began with 1,037 participants, and only 13 boys were in the severely maltreated, low-MAOA group. Four of them were convicted of violent crimes as adults, as were 11 of the 42 "probably maltreated" low-MAOA boys. These are high proportions, but, as you see, low numbers.

Six Stages of Life These photos show Sarah-Maria, born in 1980 in Switzerland, at six stages of her life: infancy (age 1), early childhood (age 3), middle childhood (age 8), adolescence (age 15), emerging adulthood (age 19), and adulthood (age 30).

TABLE 1.5
Some Findings from Longitudinal Research

- *The effect of poverty in early childhood.* Young children whose parents were poor tend to become young adults who have lower incomes and who work fewer hours per week. This was found even when many other variables were considered, which suggests cause, not merely correlation (Duncan et al., 2010).

- *Parenting difficult babies.* Although some babies are difficult (crying, irregular), responsive and encouraging parenting results in better than average development for them by first grade (Belsky et al., 2007; Stright et al., 2008).

- *Preventing arrest and violence.* Dozens of factors, measured in infancy, make it more likely that a baby will become a violent, antisocial young adult. Among the most powerful are that the mother was severely depressed in the months after the birth (Hay et al., 2010).

- *Loneliness and high blood pressure.* Adults aged 50 to 68 who are unusually lonely are more likely to develop high blood pressure than adults who have many social contacts. This was found for both sexes and many ethnic groups (Hawkley et al., 2010).

- *The stability of personality.* Early temperament and childhood personality predict later personality in adolescence and beyond, although some change is always possible (Kagan, 2007; McCrae & Costa, 2003; Roberts et al., 2007).

The New Zealand study was successful in following the arrest rate of most participants (since most stayed in New Zealand and the court records are excellent), but in most decades-long studies, some participants withdraw, move to an unknown address, or die. This skews the final results because those who disappear are unlike those who remain in the study. Another problem is that participants become aware of the questions or the goals of the study and therefore may change in ways that most other people do not.

Probably the biggest problem in longitudinal research comes from the changing historical context. Science, popular culture, and politics alter life experiences, and those changes limit the current relevance of data collected on people born

Multidirectional and Plastic Longitudinal research that follows the same individuals as they age reveals the course of the life span in ways not possible in cross-sectional research. Sarah-Maria's hair color changed in ways that might not be predicted, but her engaging smile was evident at every stage.

ALL: MARILYN GENTNER / THE IMAGE WORKS

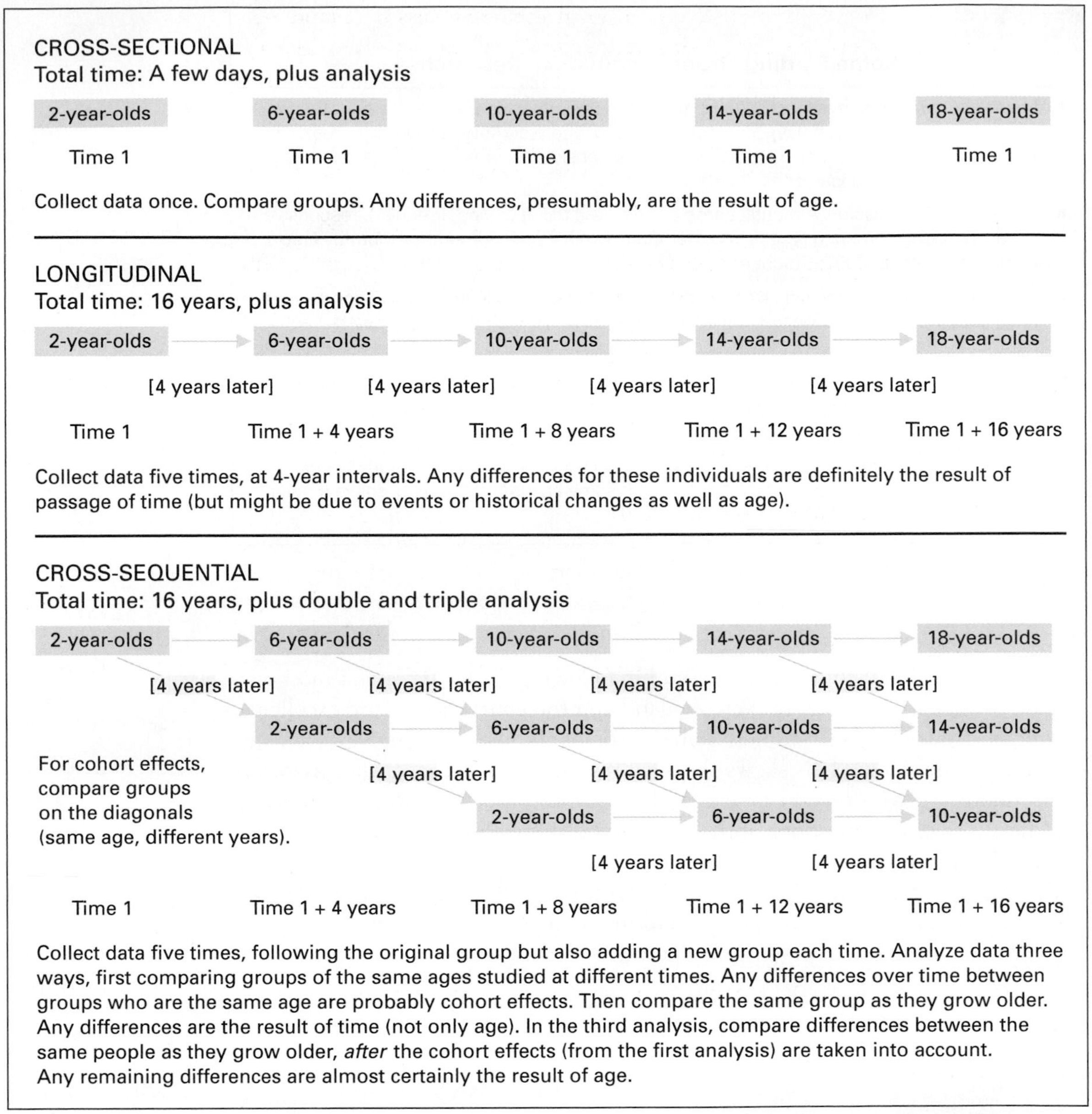

CROSS-SECTIONAL
Total time: A few days, plus analysis

2-year-olds	6-year-olds	10-year-olds	14-year-olds	18-year-olds
Time 1	Time 1	Time 1	Time 1	Time 1

Collect data once. Compare groups. Any differences, presumably, are the result of age.

LONGITUDINAL
Total time: 16 years, plus analysis

2-year-olds → 6-year-olds → 10-year-olds → 14-year-olds → 18-year-olds

[4 years later]   [4 years later]   [4 years later]   [4 years later]

Time 1	Time 1 + 4 years	Time 1 + 8 years	Time 1 + 12 years	Time 1 + 16 years

Collect data five times, at 4-year intervals. Any differences for these individuals are definitely the result of passage of time (but might be due to events or historical changes as well as age).

CROSS-SEQUENTIAL
Total time: 16 years, plus double and triple analysis

2-year-olds → 6-year-olds → 10-year-olds → 14-year-olds → 18-year-olds

[4 years later]   [4 years later]   [4 years later]   [4 years later]

    2-year-olds → 6-year-olds → 10-year-olds → 14-year-olds

For cohort effects, compare groups on the diagonals (same age, different years).

    [4 years later]   [4 years later]   [4 years later]

    2-year-olds → 6-year-olds → 10-year-olds

    [4 years later]   [4 years later]

Time 1	Time 1 + 4 years	Time 1 + 8 years	Time 1 + 12 years	Time 1 + 16 years

Collect data five times, following the original group but also adding a new group each time. Analyze data three ways, first comparing groups of the same ages studied at different times. Any differences over time between groups who are the same age are probably cohort effects. Then compare the same group as they grow older. Any differences are the result of time (not only age). In the third analysis, compare differences between the same people as they grow older, *after* the cohort effects (from the first analysis) are taken into account. Any remaining differences are almost certainly the result of age.

FIGURE 1.4

Which Approach Is Best? Cross-sequential research is the most time-consuming and complex, but it yields the best information. One reason that hundreds of scientists conduct research on the same topics, replicating one another's work, is to gain some advantages of cross-sequential research without waiting for decades.

decades ago. Results from longitudinal studies of people born in 1900, as they made their way through childhood, adulthood, and old age, may not be relevant to people born in 2000.

Finally, the need to wait decades for conclusions from longitudinal research makes it difficult to apply findings to current problems. The connection between smoking in adolescence and lung cancer in late adulthood took decades to prove. Currently, because of alarm about the possible harm caused by ingesting industrial compounds, called *phthalates,* from the plastic of baby bottles, many parents now use glass baby bottles. Might the risk of occasional shattered glass hurt more people than chemicals in plastic? Longitudnal research will tell us—in a few decades.

Cross-Sequential Research

As you see, cross-sectional and longitudinal research each has advantages that compensate for the other's disadvantages. Scientists have discovered a third strategy that involves using these two together, often with complex statistical analysis (Hartmann & Pelzel, 2005). This combination is called **cross-sequential research** (also referred to as *cohort-sequential* or *time-sequential research*). With this design, researchers study several groups of people who are of different ages (a cross-sectional approach) and follow them over the years (a longitudinal approach).

A cross-sequential design lets researchers compare findings for a group of, say, 18-year-olds, with findings for the same individuals at age 8, as well as with findings for groups who were 18 a decade or two earlier (see Figure 1.4). Cross-sequential research thus allows scientists to disentangle differences related to chronological age from those related to historical period.

One well-known cross-sequential study (the Seattle Longitudinal Study) found that some intellectual abilities—including the ability to build one's vocabulary—increase throughout adulthood, whereas others—such as speed of thinking—start to decline at about age 30 (Schaie, 2005). This study also discovered that declines in math ability are related more closely to changes in school curricula than to age, a finding that neither cross-sectional nor longitudinal research alone could reveal.

cross-sequential research A hybrid research design in which researchers first study several groups of people of different ages (a cross-sectional approach) and then follow those groups over the years (a longitudinal approach). (Also called *cohort-sequential research* or *time-sequential research*.)

Especially for Future Researchers What is the best method for collecting data? (see response, page 27)

SUMMING UP

Developmentalists use many research methods, each with advantages and disadvantages. Observational research requires careful and systematic recording of whatever actually occurs. Experiments seek to establish cause and effect, as revealed by change in the dependent variable. A true experiment compares at least two groups, similar in many ways except that one receives a particular treatment (the independent variable) that the other does not. Surveys are useful for large groups, but accuracy depends on factors not always evident. To study change over time, cross-sectional and longitudinal research are both useful, but a combination of the two, often called cross-sequential, is best.

>> Cautions from Science

The scientific method illuminates and illustrates human development as nothing else does. Facts, hypotheses, and possibilities have emerged that would not be known without science—and people of all ages are healthier and more capable because of it. For example, infectious diseases in children, illiteracy in adults, depression in late adulthood, and racism and sexism at every age are much less prevalent today than a century ago. The average life span in developed nations is about 80, not 50 as it was a century ago. Science contributed to all these changes; many of us would be dead without it.

Developmental scientists have also discovered unexpected sources of harm. As detailed in later chapters, cigarettes, television, shift work, lead paint, video games, and even automobiles are less benign than people first thought. Although the benefits of science are many, so are the pitfalls. We now discuss three of them: misinterpreting correlation, relying exclusively on numbers, and ignoring ethics.

Correlation and Causation

Probably the most common mistake in interpreting data is to think that correlation means causation. It does not. A **correlation** exists between two variables if one variable is more (or less) likely to occur when the other does. A correlation is *positive* if both variables tend to increase together or decrease together, *negative* if one variable tends to increase while the other decreases, and *zero* if no connection is evident. To illustrate: From birth to age 9, there is a positive correlation between age and height (children grow taller as they grow older), a negative correlation between age and hours of sleep (children sleep less as they grow older), and zero correlation between age and number of toes (barring a rare accident or late-life diabetes, after the eighth prenatal week, humans have ten toes lifelong). (Now take the quiz on correlation in Table 1.6.)

correlation A number between +1.0 and −1.0 that indicates the degree of relationship between two variables, expressed in terms of the likelihood that one variable will (or will not) occur when the other variable does (or does not). A correlation indicates only that two variables are related, not that one variable causes the other to occur.

For each of these three pairs of variables, indicate whether the correlation between them is positive, negative, or nonexistent. Then try to think of a third variable that might determine the direction of the correlation. The correct answers are printed upside down below.

TABLE 1.6

Quiz on Correlation

Two Variables	Positive, Negative, or Zero Correlation?	Why? (Third Variable)
1. Ice cream sales and murder rate	_____	_____
2. Learning to read and number of baby teeth	_____	_____
3. Sex of adult and their average number of offspring	_____	_____

Expressed in statistics, correlations vary from +1 (the most positive) to −1 (the most negative). Totally positive or totally negative correlations are virtually never found: There are always exceptions that reduce the strength of the correlation. Indeed, a correlation of +0.3 or −0.3 is noteworthy; a correlation of +0.8 or −0.8 is amazingly high.

Many correlations are unexpected. For instance, first-born children develop asthma more often than later-born children, teenage boys commit suicide more often than teenage girls, and immigrants have fewer low-birthweight babies than the native born within the same ethnic group.

Now consider another example. In the United States, there is a positive correlation between a couple's age at marriage and the length of the marriage: The older a newlywed couple, the more likely their marriage will last. Teenage brides are particularly divorce-prone. As one would expect from this correlation, if a place has many young marriages, that place will also have many divorces. Oklahoma and Massachusetts are examples. To be specific, the median age at first marriage in Oklahoma is 25, two years lower than the national average, and 10 percent of Oklahoma adults have divorced three (or more) times. The median marriage age in Massachusetts is 29; only 2 percent of adults have been divorced three times (American Community Survey, 2008).

Does this mean that marrying young *causes* divorce? No. Remember the mantra: Correlation is not causation. Perhaps a third variable, education, underlies the correlation between the other two. People who are college graduates marry later and divorce less, and Massachusetts has more such people than Oklahoma. Cohort and culture may be pivotal. In nineteenth-century America, the correlation was negative: Younger (not older) marriages tended be long-lasting. A negative

Answers:
1. Positive; third variable: heat
2. Negative; third variable: age
3. Zero; each child must have a parent of each sex; no third variable

correlation between age and length of marriage is also reported in some developing nations. As this example shows, correlations are intriguing—but conclusions about causes may be wrong.

Quantity and Quality

A second caution concerns how heavily scientists rely on data produced by **quantitative research** (from the word *quantity,* such as more or less, higher or lower, in rank order, in percents, or in numerical scores). Because quantitative research data fit neatly into categories and statistics, they can be easily translated across cultures and for diverse populations. One example of quantitative research is school test scores, used to measure the effectiveness of education, or to allow promotion, or to admit a high school student to college.

Since quantities can be easily summarized, compared, charted, and replicated, many scientists prefer quantitative research. Statistics require numbers. Quantitative data are said to provide "rigorous, empirically testable representations" (Nesselroade & Molenaar, 2003, p. 635). Without the test scores to measure achievement, students might be rejected by colleges because of their ethnicity, or religion, or income.

However, when data are reduced to numbers, some nuances and individual distinctions are lost. Many developmental researchers thus turn to **qualitative research** (from *quality*)—asking open-ended questions, reporting answers in narrative (not numerical) form, and generating "a rich description of the phenomena of interest" (Hartmann & Pelzel, 2005, p. 163). Qualitative research reflects diversity and complexity, but it is vulnerable to personal bias and hard to replicate. Particularly if one person, *a single case study,* is used, conclusions may be idiosyncratic. (In this chapter, I refer to one case, my nephew David. Is he an example of proven generalities, or is he atypical and thus misleading?)

Quantitative research has serious drawbacks as well, especially for a dynamic-systems approach to the life span. Since each person is unique, and change is multidirectional and multicontextual, numbers may obscure individuality. The solution: a combination of quantitative and qualitative methods. Sometimes scientists translate qualitative research into quantifiable data; sometimes they use qualitative studies to suggest hypotheses for quantitative research.

Ethics

The most important caution for all scientists, especially for those studying humans, is to uphold ethical standards. Each academic discipline and professional society involved in the study of human development has a **code of ethics** (a set of moral principles). Most educational and medical institutions have an **Institutional Review Board (IRB),** a group that permits only research that follows certain guidelines. Although IRBs often slow down scientific study, some research conducted before they were established was clearly unethical, especially when the participants were children, members of minority groups, prisoners, or animals (Blum, 2002; Washington, 2006).

Protection of Research Participants

Central to every IRB is the attempt to ensure that participation in research is voluntary, confidential, and harmless. In Western nations, this entails the *informed consent* of the participants—that is, their understanding of the research procedures and of any risks involved. If children are involved, consent must be obtained from the parents as well as the children, and the children must be allowed to stop

>> Response for Future Researchers (from page 25) There is no best method for collecting data. The method used depends on many factors, such as the age of participants (infants can't complete questionnaires), the question being researched, and the time frame.

quantitative research Research that provides data that can be expressed with numbers, such as ranks or scales.

qualitative research Research that considers qualities instead of quantities. Descriptions of particular conditions and participants' expressed ideas are often part of qualitative studies.

Especially for People Who Have Applied to College or Graduate School Is the admissions process based on quality or quantity? (see response, page 29)

code of ethics A set of moral principles that members of a profession or group are expected to follow.

Institutional Review Board (IRB) A group that exists within most educational and medical institutions whose purpose is to ensure that research follows established guidelines and remains ethical.

Especially for Future Researchers and Science Writers Do any ethical guidelines apply when an author writes about the experiences of family members, friends, or research participants? (see response, page 29)

TABLE 1.7
Code of Ethics: Canadian Psychological Association
The four principles have been ordered according to the weight each generally should be given when they conflict, namely: **Principle I: Respect for the Dignity of Persons.** This principle, with its emphasis on moral rights, generally should be given the highest weight, except in circumstances in which there is a clear and imminent danger to the physical safety of any person. **Principle II: Responsible Caring.** This principle generally should be given the second highest weight. Responsible caring requires competence and should be carried out only in ways that respect the dignity of persons. **Principle III: Integrity in Relationships.** This principle generally should be given the third highest weight. Psychologists are expected to demonstrate the highest integrity in all of their relationships. However, in rare circumstances, values such as openness and straightforwardness might need to be subordinated to the values contained in the Principles of Respect for the Dignity of Persons and Responsible Caring. **Principle IV: Responsibility to Society.** This principle generally should be given the lowest weight of the four principles when it conflicts with one or more of them. Although it is necessary and important to consider responsibility to society in every ethical decision, adherence to this principle must be subject to and guided by Respect for the Dignity of Persons, Responsible Caring, and Integrity in Relationships.
Source: Canadian Psychological Association, 2000.

at any time. In some other nations, ethical standards also require consent of the family and village elders (Doumbo, 2005).

Protection of participants may conflict with the goals of science. The Canadian Psychological Association (2000) is quite explicit about such conflicts (see Table 1.7).

Implications of Research Results

Once a study has been completed, additional ethical issues arise. Scientists are obligated to "promote accuracy, honesty, and truthfulness" (American Psychological Association, 2002); that obligation precludes distorting results to support any political, economic, personal, or cultural position.

Deliberate falsification is rare, but insidious dangers include unintentionally slanting the conclusions or withholding publication, especially when there is "ferocious . . . pressure from commercial funders to ignore good scientific practice" (Bateson, 2005, p. 645). Even nonprofit research groups and academic institutions may put undue pressure on scientists to produce publishable results.

For this reason, scientific training, collaboration, and replication are essential. Numerous safeguards are built into scientific methodology, including the fact that reports in professional journals are typically "peer reviewed," meaning that each article is evaluated by scientists not connected with the author(s) before it can be published. Reports also include (1) the researchers' affiliations and sources of funding, (2) details for replication, (3) the limitations of the research, and (4) alternative interpretations.

What Should We Study?

Long before designing and publishing research, the first ethical question for every scientist is what research is needed to enable more humans to live satisfying and productive lives. Consider these questions, for instance:

off the mark.com   by Mark Parisi

...AND I FIGURE BY GENETICALLY COMBINING TREES AND PITBULLS, THE RAIN FORESTS MIGHT HAVE A FIGHTING CHANCE...

A crucial question for all scientists is whether their research is ethical and will help solve human problems.

- Do we know enough about prenatal drug abuse to protect every fetus?
- Do we know enough about poverty to enable everyone to be healthy?
- Do we know enough about sex to eliminate AIDS, unwanted pregnancy, and sexual abuse?
- Do we know enough about dying to enable everyone to die with dignity?

The answer to all these questions is a resounding *NO*. The reasons are many, but a major one is that these topics are controversial. Some researchers avoid them, fearing unwelcome and uninformed publicity (Kempner et al., 2005). Few funders eagerly support scientific studies of drug abuse, poverty, sex, or death, partly because opinions on these subjects may conflict with the facts. Yet developmentalists have an obligation to study whatever helps the human family. Many people suffer because questions go unanswered—or even unasked.

The next cohort of developmental scientists will build on what is known, mindful of what needs to be understood. Remember the goal: to help the Earth's 6.9 billion people. Much more needs to be learned. The next 25 chapters are only the beginning.

SUMMING UP

Science has helped people in many ways over the past century. However, there are several potential pitfalls in scientific research. For instance, correlations are useful, but they may be mistakenly used to "prove" cause rather than simply indicate connection. Quantitative research is easier to analyze and compare, but qualitative research reveals more nuances. Scientists follow codes of ethics that require them to be respectful of research participants by getting their informed consent and protecting their confidentiality. Scientists must not let their opinions influence their research results as they study issues that are crucial for human development.

■

>> **Response for People Who Have Applied to College or Graduate School** (from page 27) Most institutions of higher education emphasize quantitative data—the SAT, the GRE, GPA, class rank, and so on. Decide for yourself whether this is fairer than a more qualitative approach.

>> **Response for Future Researchers and Science Writers** (from page 27) Yes. Anyone you write about must give consent and be fully informed about your intentions. They can be identified by name only if they give permission. For example, family members gave permission before anecdotes about them were included in this text. My nephew David read the first draft of his story (see pages 3–4) and is proud to have his experiences used to teach others.

SUMMARY

Defining Development

1. The study of human development is a science that seeks to understand how people change or remain the same over time. As a science, it begins with questions and hypotheses, gathers empirical data, and reports results.

2. All kinds of people, of every age, culture, and background, are studied by developmental scientists. The goal is to help all people develop well, by finding the universal patterns of human growth and by recognizing that each person is unique.

3. A dynamic-systems approach emphasizes that change is ongoing, with each aspect of development affecting every other part. Children influence adults just as surely as adults guide children. Continuity and discontinuity, consistency and transformation are evident throughout the life span.

The Life-Span Perspective

4. The life-span approach recognizes that development is multi-directional, multicontextual, multicultural, multidisciplinary, and plastic.

5. Change is *multidirectional*: Both continuity (sameness) and discontinuity (sudden shifts) are evident, as are many other trajectories.

6. A *multicontextual* approach to development recognizes the power of ecological circumstances that surround each person. Historical contexts—events or innovations—shape people of each cohort, and socioeconomic status (SES) affects development lifelong.

7. The *multicultural* approach recognizes that culture promotes customs, values, and perceptions that guide human life. Culture is not the same as ethnicity; race is a social construction, not a biological one.

8. Understanding development over the life span requires research and insights from many academic disciplines. This *mul-* *tidisciplinary* approach uses methods and investigates questions from each field, with discoveries from neuroscience recently reverberating in many other disciplines.

9. Human development is *plastic*, which means that individuals can be molded as time goes on by their circumstances, efforts, and unexpected events. Although change is always possible, earlier experiences and genetic tendencies influence people lifelong.

Using the Scientific Method

10. Research methods include observation (to record what normally occurs), the experiment (to learn what causes what), and the survey (to assess many people quickly). Each method has strengths and weaknesses.

11. To study how people change as the days and years go by, scientists use three research designs: cross-sectional research (comparing people of different ages), longitudinal research (studying the same people repeatedly over time), and cross-sequential research (combining longitudinal and cross-sectional methods).

Cautions from Science

12. A correlation shows that two variables are related in some way. However, correlation is not causation: A connection between two variables can arise in many ways for many reasons.

13. Research can be quantitative (reported with numbers or quanitities) or qualitative (reported with words or narratives). Qualitative research captures the nuances of individual lives, but quantitative research is easier to replicate, interpret, and verify. Each complements the other.

14. Ethical behavior is crucial in all the sciences. Not only must participants be protected and their identities kept confidential, but results must be reported clearly and interpreted carefully. The most important ethical question is whether scientists conduct and analyze the research that is most critically needed to improve human development in all cultures, generations, and conditions.

KEY TERMS

science of human development (p. 4)
empirical (p. 4)
scientific method (p. 4)
replication (p. 4)
nature (p. 5)
nurture (p. 5)
critical period (p. 6)
sensitive period (p. 6)

dynamic-systems theory (p. 8)
life-span perspective (p. 10)
ecological-systems approach (p. 11)
cohort (p. 12)
socioeconomic status (SES) (p. 12)
ethnic group (p. 14)
race (p. 14)

mirror neurons (p. 16)
scientific observation (p. 19)
experiment (p. 20)
independent variable (p. 20)
dependent variable (p. 20)
survey (p. 21)
cross-sectional research (p. 21)
longitudinal research (p. 22)
cross-sequential research (p. 25)

correlation (p. 26)
quantitative research (p. 27)
qualitative research (p. 27)
code of ethics (p. 27)
Institutional Review Board (IRB) (p. 27)

WHAT HAVE YOU LEARNED?

Defining Development

1. What makes the study of human development a science?

2. What are the five steps of the scientific method?

3. Why have recommendations regarding the sleeping circumstances of infants changed?

4. Why is it a mistake to ask whether a specific characteristic is the result of nature or nurture?

5. What are examples of a critical period and a sensitive period of development?

6. What factors make it more or less likely that a person will be a juvenile delinquent?

7. Why do developmentalists insist that differences among people not be assumed to be deficits?

8. How does the dynamic-systems concept interpret family relationships?

The Life-Span Perspective

9. Does the multidirectional concept support continuity or discontinuity? Why?

10. How does the ecological systems concept affect the way individual growth is perceived?

11. What are the differences among Bronfenbrenner's five systems of development?

12. How does cohort affect attitudes?

13. What impact does family SES have? Explain for one particular stage; include three domains.

14. What are examples of the impact of culture on adolescents?

15. Why do the three domains overlap?

16. What are the implications of the research on mirror neurons?

17. What is the evidence that development is plastic?

Using the Scientific Method

18. How do scientific observation and experimentation differ?

19. What are the advantages and disadvantages of cross-sectional research?

20. What are the advantages and disadvantages of longitudinal research?

21. Why do experiments need a control (or comparison) group?

22. How do independent and dependent variables make it easier to learn what causes what?

Cautions from Science

23. Why does correlation not prove causation?

24. Why do some researchers prefer quantitative research and others, qualitative research?

25. Why do most colleges have an Institutional Review Board (IRB)?

26. What are the ethical priorities when scientists use human subjects in research?

27. Why are some questions about human development not yet answered with scientific research?

APPLICATIONS

1. It is said that culture is pervasive but that people are unaware of it. List 30 things you did *today* that you might have done differently in another culture.

2. How would your life be different if your parents were much higher or lower in SES than they are? What if you had been born in another cohort?

3. Design an experiment to answer a question you have about human development. Specify the question and the hypothesis and then describe the experiment, including the sample size and the variables. (Look first at Appendix B.)

>>ONLINE CONNECTIONS

To accompany your textbook, you have access to a number of online resources, including quizzes for every chapter of the book, flashcards (in English and Spanish), critical thinking questions, and case studies. For access to any of these links, go to www.worthpublishers.com/bergerls8e. In addition to these free resources, you'll also find links to the podcasts, video clips, diagnostic quizzing with personalized study advice, and an ebook. Some of the videos and activities available online include:

- *Ethics in Human Research: Violating One's Privacy?* This video introduces the controversies around a research project in Iceland that collects the genetic and health information about private citizens.

- *What's Wrong with this Study?* This activity allows you to review some of the pitfalls in various research designs.

2

Theories of Development

WHAT WILL YOU KNOW?

1. Why are theories neither true nor false?
2. How are theories useful?
3. What are the basic assumptions of the psychoanalytic, behaviorist, and cognitive theories?
4. How do sociocultural and universal theories reflect recent perspectives of social scientists?
5. Why do many people object to humanism and evolutionary theory?

When I was little, on special occasions we drove to my grandparents' farm, where my father grew up with his three brothers and one sister, all married with children. My mother sang, "Over the river and through the woods, to grandmother's house we go." When we arrived, my brother and I played with our twelve cousins, including three other girls my age. I remember turkey, mashed potatoes, and lemon meringue pie; horses and hay in the barn; grandma wearing an apron; grandpa resting his big hands over a huge coffee mug; and enormous wooden rocking chairs in the sitting room. But my strongest single memory is a bitter one: One time, Grandma gave us girls presents, precursors of Barbie dolls. Mine had a peach-colored gown; my cousin's had a white bride's dress and veil.

Why did I feel rejected? Now I can think of many good reasons that particular cousin got the bride doll. But as a girl, my simple theory about presents and brides led to resentment.

This chapter outlines five theories of human development, or actually ten, since each theory has several versions. There are hundreds more theories about the human life span, some explained later. Before beginning, however, you should know that theorizing is part of human nature. In fact, according to "theory theory," young children spontaneously develop theories to explain whatever they observe, because that is what humans do (Gopnik & Schulz, 2007). My theory led me to believe that Grandma loved my cousin more than me.

>> What Theories Do

A **developmental theory** is a systematic statement of general principles that provides a coherent framework for understanding how and why people change as they grow older. "Developmental theorists try to make sense out of observations . . . [and] construct a story of the human journey from infancy through childhood or adulthood" (Miller, 2011, p. 2). Such a story, or theory, connects facts and observations with patterns and explanations, weaving the details of life into a meaningful whole. A developmental theory is more than a hunch or a hypothesis and is far more comprehensive than my simple theorizing about beautiful brides. The

developmental theory A group of ideas, assumptions, and generalizations that interpret and illuminate the thousands of observations that have been made about human growth. A developmental theory provides a framework for explaining the patterns and problems of development.

crucial aspect is that theories provide frameworks of understanding and thus are broader than the many observations from which they arise.

As an analogy, imagine building a house. A person could have a heap of lumber, nails, and other materials, but without a plan and labor, the heap cannot become a building. Furthermore, not all houses are alike: People have theories about houses that lead to preferences for the number of stories, bedrooms, entrances, and so on. Likewise, the observations and empirical studies of human development are essential raw materials, but theories put them together.

As Kurt Lewin (1943) once quipped, "Nothing is as practical as a good theory." Theories differ; some are less comprehensive or adequate than others (why did we forget a back door?), and each is constructing a somewhat different home, but without theory, we have only a heap.

Questions and Answers

As we saw in Chapter 1, the science of human development begins with questions. Among the thousands of important questions are the following, each central to one of the five theories described in this chapter:

1. Do early experiences—of breast-feeding or attachment or neglect—linger into adulthood, even if they seem to be forgotten?
2. Does learning depend on specific instruction, punishment, and examples?
3. Do children develop moral principles, even if they are not taught right from wrong?
4. Does culture guide behavior? Is that why Okinawa has more voters than Ohio?
5. Is survival a human instinct, the bedrock value for all of us?

Each of the five questions above is answered "yes" by one of the five major theories—in order: question 1 by psychoanalytic theory, question 2 by behaviorism, question 3 by cognitive theory, question 4 by sociocultural theory, and question 5 by universalism. Each question is answered "no" or "not necessarily," however, by several others. For every answer, more questions arise: Why or why not? When and how? And so what? This last question is crucial for the science of human development, because the implications and applications of the answers affect everyone's daily life.

To be more specific about what theories do:

- Theories produce *hypotheses*.
- Theories generate *discoveries*.
- Theories offer practical *guidance*.

If a 5-year-old shouts "I hate you!" at his father, the man's reaction (smiling, ignoring, spanking, or asking "Why?") depends on his theory of development, whether or not he knows it. Then his wife's reaction to him (perhaps approval or dismay, delivered with a kiss or a slap) depends on her theory of child rearing and marriage, again whether she knows it or not.

Facts and Norms

Do not confuse theories with facts. Theories raise questions, suggesting hypotheses that lead to research that gathers empirical data, which are facts that may lead to conclusions. Each of the theories soon to be explained has led to research, which has verified and refuted aspects of the theory and thereby moved the science of development forward.

Thus, a theory is neither true nor false; it is provocative and useful, leading to insight and exploration. For example, some people dismiss Darwin's theory of evolution as "just a theory," while others believe it explains all of nature since the beginning of time. No to both. Good theories should neither be dismissed nor equated with facts. Instead, theories deepen thought; they are useful (like a house plan), leading to new interpretations, hypotheses, and perspectives.

As already explained, developmental theories are comprehensive, detailed, and useful, unlike the simple theories of children or the implicit theories of customs. But those simpler theories make the distinction between theory and fact quite clear, so we return to the bride doll. My bitterness grew from a dominant theory when I was a child—that it was best for everyone to marry one person lifelong, have at least two children, and visit their parents, who should stay in their own house. That is what my grandparents' children all did. They pitied my mother's two unmarried sisters, Aunt Ida and Aunt Marie.

Consequently, I fantasized about my wedding; I named my seven imagined children; I was happy when my Aunt Marie, about age 40, finally married. My theory was held by many in my culture, in which having more than one spouse was illegal ("bigamists" went to jail), divorce meant a "failed" marriage, "only" children had psychological problems, and if elders were "put away" in nursing homes, their relatives felt ashamed. As you see, emotions, assumptions, and laws followed from this commonly held theory.

That theory of adulthood is no longer potent, as the "difference is not deficit" maxim in Chapter 1 explains. Research finds that many adults avoid marriage or parenthood but nonetheless seem happy. Indeed, some say that the pro-family theory I knew as a child has been replaced, at least in Western middle-class culture, by another untested theory—that personal happiness is the goal of life. That leads to another set of ideas—that unhappy spouses should divorce, childless marriages are fine, and older adults should not burden their offspring.

Obviously, people agree or disagree with these theories. Scientists design studies to investigate them because the theories themselves are not facts, and "each theory of developmental psychology always has a view of humans that reflects philosophical, economic, and political beliefs" (Miller, 2011, p. 17). Awareness of the possible bias within each theory helps in research, as the facts may make a scientist switch to another theory. You will see this as we explain various changes in developmental theories, but first let's look at another common example that shows how quickly humans develop theories.

The Same Situation, Many Miles Apart: Reality and Theory Both the German and Thai weddings are official ceremonies, complete with religious words and/or rituals that will unite these partners as a recognized married couple. But developmental theories are also implicit in every such occasion. For instance, note the following cultural differences: The German pair is seated a few feet apart, whereas the Thai couple lies prone with arms touching; the German bride wears a formal white dress and veil, whereas the Thai celebrants are barefoot and less formally adorned; the Germans are in their mid-20s to early 30s, whereas the Thai mates are closer to age 20. Even the difference in the color of flowers implies varying developmental theories. Every wedding expresses beliefs and theories about human development.

People buy many makes and models of cars. They are influenced by facts, such as fuel efficiency and popularity. But they are also affected by their theories of life, quite apart from facts. Consider the Hummer, a vehicle "widely loathed" by some, who judge owners as "callous Earthkillers," and loved by others, including one person who told the critics to "grow up and join us Americans that believe in our freedom. . . . Stop trying to oppress others that don't share your beliefs, color, and religion" (quoted in Walker, 2009, p. 22). Callous? Oppression? Perhaps. But before you agree with either side, some research is needed. That's why we need theories, to show us what studies might verify or dispute common assumptions about life.

Theories give insight and guidance—especially when developmental problems occur: the misbehaving child, the drug-using adolescent, the risk-taking young adult, the angry parent, the disoriented older adult. Without theories, we would be merely reactive and bewildered, adrift and increasingly befuddled, blindly following our culture and our prejudices. Unless we recognize that theories are useful, but in need of verification and exploration, we might be stuck with a limiting, inaccurate, or childish theory—as I was with the bride doll.

SUMMING UP

Theories provide a framework for organizing and understanding the thousands of observations and daily behaviors that occur in every aspect of development. Theories are not facts, but they powerfully affect thought and behavior, suggesting hypotheses and providing guidance. Thus, theories are practical—they frame and organize our millions of experiences, influencing the entire life span.

>> Grand Theories

In the first half of the twentieth century, two opposing theories—psychoanalytic theory and behaviorism (also called *learning theory*)—began as general theories of psychology. By mid-century, cognitive theory had emerged, becoming the dominant seedbed of research hypotheses. All three theories are "grand" in that they are comprehensive, enduring, and widely applied (McAdams & Pals, 2006).

Psychoanalytic Theory

Inner drives, deep motives, and unconscious needs rooted in childhood are the foundation of **psychoanalytic theory.** These basic underlying forces are thought to influence every aspect of thinking and behavior, from the smallest details of daily life to the crucial choices of a lifetime.

psychoanalytic theory A grand theory of human development that holds that irrational, unconscious drives and motives, often originating in childhood, underlie human behavior.

Freud's Ideas

Psychoanalytic theory originated with Sigmund Freud (1856–1939), an Austrian physician who treated patients suffering from mental illness. He listened to their accounts of dreams and fantasies and to their uncensored streams of thought, and he constructed an elaborate, multifaceted theory.

According to Freud, development in the first six years occurs in three stages, each characterized by sexual interest and pleasure centered on a particular part of the body. In infancy, the erotic body part is the mouth (the *oral stage*); in early childhood, it is the anus (the *anal stage*); in the preschool years, it is the penis (the *phallic stage*), a source of pride and fear among boys and a reason for sadness and envy among girls. Two more developmental periods then follow early childhood. After the phallic stage, *latency* occurs and then, at puberty, the *genital stage* arrives, lasting throughout adulthood (Table 2.1 on the next page describes the stages in Freud's theory).

Freud maintained that at each stage, sensual satisfaction (from stimulation of the mouth, anus, or penis) is linked to major developmental needs and challenges. During the oral stage, for example, sucking provides not only nourishment but also pleasure for the baby and attachment to the mother. Next, during the anal stage, pleasures that arise from control and self-control—initially with defecation and toilet training—are paramount. Freud called each stage *psychosexual* because children derive erotic pleasure from whatever body part is central at each stage. This idea (infantile sexuality) was one reason psychoanalytic theory was rejected at first.

Among Freud's most influential ideas was that each stage includes its own potential conflicts. Conflict occurs, for instance, when parents try to wean their babies (oral stage) or teachers expect 6-year-olds to become independent of their parents (phallic stage). According to Freud, how people experience and resolve these conflicts—especially those related to weaning, toilet training, and sexual pleasure—determine personality patterns, because "the early stages provide the foundation for adult behavior" (Salkind, 2004, p. 125.)

Freud did not believe that new stages occurred in the adult years; rather, he believed that adult personalities and habits were influenced by earlier stages. Unconscious conflicts rooted in a childhood stage may be evident in behavior—for instance, smoking cigarettes (oral) or keeping careful track of money (anal) or becoming romantically attracted to a much older partner (phallic). For all of us, psychoanalytic theory contends, childhood fantasies and memories remain powerful lifelong, particularly as they affect the sex drive (which Freud called the *libido*). If you have ever wondered why lovers call each other "baby" or why many people refer to their spouse as their "old lady" or "sugar daddy," then Freud's theory provides an explanation: The parent–child relationship is the model for all forms of intimacy.

Many other aspects of psychoanalytic theory may explain adult behavior. According to Freud, the personality has three parts: the *id* (unconscious drives, inborn and animal-like, mostly sexual and aggressive), the *superego* (the moral ideal, the conscience, learned from parents and society), and the *ego* (the conscious self). The id is dominant in infancy, the superego develops in the phallic stage, and by adulthood, a strong ego is able to defend itself against attacks from the id and superego. That defense occurs with *defense mechanisms* that keep the id and superego under control.

Freud identified many defense mechanisms, some more effective than others. Two that are often used in adulthood are rationalization (finding a logical reason to justify something that actually springs from the irrational id or superego) and sublimation (transforming energy from the libido to create something acclaimed by others, such as a musical masterpiece).

Erikson's Ideas

Many of Freud's followers became famous theorists themselves. They acknowledged the importance of the unconscious and of early childhood experience, but each of them expanded and modified Freud's ideas. Anna Freud (Sigmund's

Freud at Work In addition to being the world's first psychoanalyst, Sigmund Freud was a prolific writer. His many papers and case histories, primarily descriptions of his patients' bizarre symptoms and unconscious sexual urges, helped make the psychoanalytic perspective a dominant force for much of the twentieth century.

AKG / PHOTO RESEARCHERS, INC.

SUSAN LAPIDES / DESIGN CONCEPTIONS

Childhood Sexuality The girl's interest in the statue's anatomy may just reflect simple curiosity, but Freudian theory would maintain that it is a clear manifestation of the phallic stage of psychosexual development, when girls are said to feel deprived because they lack a penis.

daughter) and Carl Jung are mentioned later in this text. We turn now, though, to the most notable developmental theorist, Erik Erikson (1902–1994).

Erikson never knew his Danish father. He spent his childhood in Germany, his adolescence wandering through Italy, and his young adulthood in Austria, working with Freud. He married an American, fleeing to the United States just before World War II began. His experiences in many nations, as well as his studies of Harvard students, Boston children at play, and Sioux and Yurok Indians, led Erikson to stress cultural diversity, social change, and psychological crises throughout the life span. These elements are all present in Erikson's massive psychoanalytic study of Mahatma Gandhi, who was born in India, educated in Britain, and practiced law in South Africa. According to Erikson, those experiences forged Gandhi's psychosocial identity, enabling him to lead the fight for Indian independence (Erikson, 1969).

Erikson described eight developmental stages, each characterized by a particular challenge, or *developmental crisis* (summarized in Table 2.1). Although Erikson named two polarities at each crisis, he recognized a wide range of outcomes between these opposites. For most people, development at each stage leads to neither extreme but to something in between. The resolution of each crisis depends on the interaction between the individual and the social environment. In the stage of *initiative versus guilt,* for example, children between ages 3 and 6 often want to undertake activities that exceed the limits set by their parents and culture. They jump into swimming pools, put their pants on backwards, mix cakes according to their own recipes, wander off alone. Such efforts to act independently leave them open to feelings of pride or of failure, producing guilt if adults are too critical.

As you can see from Table 2.1, Erikson's first five stages are closely related to Freud's stages. Erikson, like Freud, believed that problems of adult life echo unresolved conflicts of childhood. For example, an adult who has difficulty establishing a secure, mutual relationship with a life partner may never have resolved the first crisis of early infancy, *trust versus mistrust.* Even in late adulthood, one older person may be outspoken while another fears saying the wrong thing, because they resolved their initiative-versus-guilt stage in opposite ways. In one crucial way, Erikson's stages differ significantly from Freud's: They emphasize each person's relationships to family and culture, not sexual urges.

TED STRESHINSKY / TIME LIFE PICTURES / GETTY IMAGES

A Legendary Couple In his first 30 years, Erikson never fit into a particular local community, considering he so frequently changed nations, schools, and professions. Then he met Joan. In their five decades of marriage, they raised a family and wrote several books. If he had published his theory at age 73 (when this photograph was taken) instead of in his 40s, would he still have described life as a series of crises?

Especially for Teachers Your kindergartners are talkative and always moving. They almost never sit quietly and listen to you. What would Erik Erikson recommend? (see response, page 42)

SAMANTHA SCOTT / ALAMY

Who Are We? The most famous of Erikson's eight crises is the identity crisis, during adolescence, when young people find their own answer to the question "Who am I?" Erikson did this for himself by choosing a last name that, with his first name, implies "son of myself" (Erik, Erik's son). These *hara juko* girls in Japan are among the millions of teenagers worldwide who display an identity unlike that of their parents.

TABLE 2.1

Comparison of Freud's Psychosexual and Erikson's Psychosocial Stages

Approximate Age	Freud (Psychosexual)	Erikson (Psychosocial)
Birth to 1 year	*Oral Stage* The lips, tongue, and gums are the focus of pleasurable sensations in the baby's body, and sucking and feeding are the most stimulating activities.	*Trust vs. Mistrust* Babies either trust that others will care for their basic needs, including nourishment, warmth, cleanliness, and physical contact, *or* develop mistrust about the care of others.
1–3 years	*Anal Stage* The anus is the focus of pleasurable sensations in the baby's body, and toilet training is the most important activity.	*Autonomy vs. Shame and Doubt* Children either become self-sufficient in many activities, including toileting, feeding, walking, exploring, and talking, *or* doubt their own abilities.
3–6 years	*Phallic Stage* The phallus, or penis, is the most important body part, and pleasure is derived from genital stimulation. Boys are proud of their penises; girls wonder why they don't have one.	*Initiative vs. Guilt* Children either want to undertake many adultlike activities *or* internalize the limits and prohibitions set by parents. They feel either adventurous *or* guilty.
6–11 years	*Latency* Not really a stage, latency is an interlude during which sexual needs are quiet and children put psychic energy into conventional activities like schoolwork and sports.	*Industry vs. Inferiority* Children busily learn to be competent and productive in mastering new skills *or* feel inferior, unable to do anything as well as they wish they could.
Adolescence	*Genital Stage* The genitals are the focus of pleasurable sensations, and the young person seeks sexual stimulation and sexual satisfaction in heterosexual relationships.	*Identity vs. Role Confusion* Adolescents try to figure out "Who am I?" They establish sexual, political, religious, and vocational identities *or* are confused about what roles to play.
Adulthood	Freud believed that the genital stage lasts throughout adulthood. He also said that the goal of a healthy life is "to love and to work."	*Intimacy vs. Isolation* Young adults seek companionship and love *or* become isolated from others because they fear rejection and disappointment. *Generativity vs. Stagnation* Middle-aged adults contribute to the next generation through meaningful work, creative activities, and/or raising a family, *or* they stagnate. *Integrity vs. Despair* Older adults try to make sense out of their lives, either seeing life as a meaningful whole *or* despairing at goals never reached.

Behaviorism

The second grand theory arose in opposition to the psychoanalytic notion of the unconscious. John B. Watson (1878–1958) argued that, if psychology was to be a true science, psychologists should examine only what they could see and measure: behavior, not irrational thoughts and hidden urges. In Watson's words:

> Why don't we make what we can *observe* the real field of psychology? Let us limit ourselves to things that can be observed, and formulate laws concerned only with those things. . . . We can observe behavior—what the organism does or says.
>
> [*Watson, 1924/1998, p. 6*]

According to Watson, if psychologists focus on behavior, they will realize that everything can be learned. He wrote:

> Give me a dozen healthy infants, well-formed, and my own specified world to bring them up in and I'll guarantee to take any one at random and train him to become any type of specialist I might select—doctor, lawyer, artist, merchant chief, and yes, even beggar-man and thief, regardless of his talents, penchants, tendencies, abilities, vocations, and race of his ancestors.
>
> [*Watson, 1924/1998, p. 82*]

An Early Behaviorist John Watson was an early proponent of learning theory. His ideas are still influential and controversial today.

behaviorism A grand theory of human development that studies observable behavior. Behaviorism is also called *learning theory* because it describes the laws and processes by which behavior is learned.

conditioning According to behaviorism, the processes by which responses become linked to particular stimuli and learning takes place. The word *conditioning* is used to emphasize the importance of repeated practice, as when an athlete *conditions* his or her body to perform well by training for a long time.

classical conditioning The learning process in which a meaningful stimulus (such as the smell of food to a hungry animal) is connected with a neutral stimulus (such as the sound of a tone) that had no special meaning before conditioning. (Also called *respondent conditioning.*)

SOVFOTO

A Contemporary of Freud Ivan Pavlov was a physiologist who received the Nobel Prize in 1904 for his research on digestive processes. It was this line of study that led to his discovery of classical conditioning.

Observation Quiz In appearance, how is Pavlov similar to Freud, and how do both look different from the other theorists pictured? (see answer, page 42)

Other psychologists, especially in the United States, agreed. They developed **behaviorism** to study actual behavior, objectively and scientifically. Behaviorism is also called *learning theory* because it describes how people learn and develop habits, step by step. For every individual at every age, from newborn to centenarian, behaviorists describe laws detailing how simple actions and environmental responses shape complex competencies, such as reading a book or making a family dinner.

Learning theorists believe that development occurs in small increments: A person learns to read, or cook, or anything else bit by bit over a long time. Because change is cumulative, behaviorists, unlike Freud and Erikson, describe no specific stages (Bijou & Baer, 1978). The laws of learning apply to **conditioning,** the processes by which responses become linked to particular stimuli, sometimes called *S–R (stimulus–response) conditioning.* There are two main types of conditioning: classical and operant.

Classical Conditioning

A century ago, Russian scientist Ivan Pavlov (1849–1936), after winning the Nobel Prize for his work on animal digestion, began to examine the link between stimulus and response. While studying salivation, Pavlov noted that his experimental dogs drooled not only at the smell of food but also, eventually, at the footsteps of the attendants who brought the food. This observation led Pavlov to perform his famous experiment in which he conditioned dogs to salivate when they heard a particular noise.

Pavlov began by sounding a tone just before presenting food. After a number of repetitions of the tone-then-food sequence, dogs began salivating at the sound even when there was no food. This simple experiment demonstrated **classical conditioning** (also called *respondent conditioning*).

In classical conditioning, a person or animal is conditioned to associate a neutral stimulus with a meaningful stimulus, gradually responding to the neutral stimulus in the same way as to the meaningful one. In Pavlov's original experiment, the dog associated the tone (the neutral stimulus) with food (the meaningful stimulus) and responded to the tone as though it were the food itself. The conditioned response to the tone, which is no longer neutral but has now become a conditioned stimulus, is evidence that learning had occurred.

Behaviorists see dozens of examples of classical conditioning in human development. One is called *white coat syndrome,* in which patients' blood pressure rises when they see a doctor. (This used to occur for nurses as well, in their white uniforms. To avoid this, most nurses now wear colorful blouses.) Another example of classical conditioning is very practical for parents of young children: After a period of conditioning, a child's bladder automatically releases urine when the child sits on the toilet.

Operant Conditioning

The most influential North American proponent of behaviorism was B. F. Skinner (1904–1990). Skinner agreed that psychology should focus on the scientific study of behavior and that classical conditioning explains some behavior. However, he recognized another type of conditioning— **operant conditioning** (also called *instrumental conditioning*)—in which animals do something and experience a consequence. If the consequence is useful or pleasurable, the animal may repeat the behavior. If the consequence is unpleasant, the animal is unlikely to do so.

Pleasant consequences are sometimes called "rewards," and unpleasant consequences are sometimes called "punishments." Behaviorists hesitate to use those words, however, because what some people think is punishment can actually be a reward, and vice versa. For example, parents punish their children by withholding dessert, by spanking them, by not letting them play, by speaking harshly to them, and so on. But a particular child might, for instance, dislike the dessert, so that being deprived of it is no punishment. Another child might not mind a spanking, especially if that is the only time the parent pays attention to the child. For that child, the intended punishment is actually a reward.

Similarly, teachers sometimes punish misbehaving children by sending them out of the classroom or even suspending them from school, but if a child dislikes the teacher and school, being sent out is actually a reward for misbehaving. In fact, recent research on school discipline finds that some measures, including school suspension, actually increase the frequency of later misbehavior (Osher et al., 2010). The true test is the *effect* a consequence has on the individual's future behavior, not whether it is intended to be a reward or a punishment. A child, or an adult, who commits the same offense a second time may have been reinforced, not punished, for the first infraction. Consequences that increase the likelihood that a particular action will be repeated are called reinforcers, in a process called **reinforcement** (Skinner, 1953).

Once a behavior has been conditioned (learned), animals (including humans) continue to perform it even if pleasurable consequences occur only occasionally, or they continue to avoid it even if punishment is rare. Almost all of our daily behavior, from socializing with others to earning a paycheck, can be understood as a result of past operant conditioning. More than half of all adult behavior is habitual, not a result of conscious thought (Neal et al., 2006). Conditioning, as described by behaviorists, led developmentalists to ask whether behavior that psychoanalytic theory attributed to deeply rooted psychological problems was learned instead.

Social Learning

At first behaviorists interpreted all behavior as arising from a chain of learned responses, the result of conditioning. Behavior depended on associations between one stimulus and another or on what consequences an individual experienced. That was valid, but humans are active and social, not just reactive. Instead of responding merely to their own experiences, "people act on the environment. They create it, preserve it, transform it, and even destroy it . . . in a socially embedded interplay" (Bandura, 2006, p. 167).

This insight led Albert Bandura to develop **social learning theory** (see Figure 2.1), which holds that humans sometimes learn without personal reinforcement. This may occur through **modeling,** when people copy what they see others do

© SAM FALK / PHOTO RESEARCHERS, INC.

Rats, Pigeons, and People B. F. Skinner is best known for his experiments with rats and pigeons, but he also applied his knowledge to human problems. For his daughter, he designed a glass-enclosed crib in which temperature, humidity, and perceptual stimulation could be controlled to make her time in the crib enjoyable and educational. He wrote about an ideal society based on principles of operant conditioning, where, for example, workers in less desirable jobs would earn greater rewards.

operant conditioning The learning process by which a particular action is followed by something desired (which makes the person or animal more likely to repeat the action) or by something unwanted (which makes the action less likely to be repeated). (Also called *instrumental conditioning*.)

reinforcement A technique for conditioning behavior in which that behavior is followed by something desired, such as food for a hungry animal or a welcoming smile for a lonely person.

social learning theory An extension of behaviorism that emphasizes the influence that other people have over a person's behavior. Even without specific reinforcement, every individual learns many things through observation and imitation of other people.

modeling The central process of social learning, by which a person observes the actions of others and then copies them. (Also called *observational learning*.)

Learning occurs through:

- **Classical conditioning** Through association, neutral stimulus becomes conditioned stimulus.
- **Operant conditioning** Through reinforcement, weak or rare response becomes strong, frequent response.
- **Social learning** Through modeling, observed behaviors become copied behaviors.

FIGURE 2.1

Three Types of Learning Behaviorism is also called *learning theory* because it emphasizes the learning process, as shown here.

PHOTOGRAPHER'S CHOICE/GETTY

Social Learning in Action Social learning validates the old maxim, "Actions speak louder than words." If the moment here is typical for this child, she is likely to grow up with a ready sense of the importance of this particular chore of infant care.

Observation Quiz What shows that this child imitates her mother? (see answer, page 44)

self-efficacy In social learning theory, the belief of some people that they are able to change themselves and effectively alter the social context.

>> Response for Teachers (from page 38) Erikson would note that the behavior of 5-year-olds is affected by their developmental stage and by their culture. Therefore, you might design your curriculum to accommodate active, noisy children.

Especially for Teachers Same problem as previously (talkative kindergartners), but what would a behaviorist recommend? (see response, page 44)

>> Answer to Observation Quiz (from page 40) Both are balding, with white beards. Note also that none of the other theorists in this chapter have beards—a cohort difference, not an ideological one.

(also called *observational learning*). Modeling is not simple imitation; people model only some actions, of some individuals, in some contexts. As an example, you may know adults who, as children, saw their parents hit each other. Some such adults abuse their own partners, while others scrupulously avoid marital conflict. These two responses seem opposite, but both are social learning produced by childhood observation.

Generally, modeling is most likely to occur when the observer is uncertain or inexperienced (which explains why modeling is especially powerful in childhood) and when the model is admired, powerful, nurturing, or similar to the observer (Bandura, 1986, 1997). If your speech, hairstyle, or choice of shoes is similar to those of a celebrity, ask yourself what made you model that person's behavior. Admiration? Similarity?

Social learning is connected to perceptions and interpretations of experience. One crucial interpretation involves a sense of **self-efficacy,** the belief that a personal achievement depends on personal actions. People develop a sense of efficacy when they see other people solve problems successfully, which teaches them to have high aspirations and to strive for notable accomplishments (Bandura et al., 2001).

Social learning is evident in groups of people perhaps even more than in individuals. For example, humans have innate aggressive impulses that, Freud thought, arose from the id. Controlling those impulses is a notable example of self-efficacy. In Sweden, where "for ages the Vikings plundered," the people collectively "transformed a warring society into a peaceful one. Sweden is now a mediator for peace among warring nations" (Bandura, 2006, p. 172). Currently Swedes are proud of their collective efficacy at international cooperation and of their laws against physical punishment of children.

Self-efficacy explains a paradox: One might think that strict parents would believe they are powerful, but the opposite seems true. Parents who feel powerless and who think their babies are strong-willed are stricter and less responsive than other parents (Guzell & Vernon-Feagans, 2004). Social learning theory provides an explanation: Their own parents may not have let them become proud of themselves; thus, they learned to be helpless, still feeling ineffective as adults. Their lack of self-efficacy makes them overly controlling with their children.

Psychoanalytic Versus Behaviorist Theories

These first two theories have endured because they are provocative; they were innovative, comprehensive, and surprising. Until these theories were developed, few imagined that the unconscious or childhood experiences exert such power (psychoanalytic) or that adult behavior arises from reinforcement (behaviorist) or observation (social learning). Both theories have also been soundly criticized, with many psychologists rejecting psychoanalytic theory as unscientific (Mills, 2004) and rejecting behaviorism as demeaning of human potential (Chein, 1972/2008). Another theory, humanism (described later in this chapter), arose in direct opposition to these theories. Nonetheless, like all good theories, both behaviorism and psychoanalytic theory have led to hypotheses that were examined in thousands of experiments. Here is one example.

What's a Mother For?

Why do children love their mothers? Both behaviorism and psychoanalytic theory originally hypothesized that mothers are loved because they satisfy the newborn's hunger and sucking needs. In other words, "The infant's attachment to the mother stemmed from internal drives which triggered activities connected with the libations of the mother's breast. This belief was the only one these two theoretical groups ever had in common" (H. Harlow, 1986). During infancy, mothers were for feeding, and not much else.

Even earlier than Freud and Pavlov, Louis Pasteur developed the germ theory of disease, proposing that invisible bacteria could make a person sick. This idea was first rejected by the medical establishment, even as thousands of new mothers and babies died (including three of Pasteur's children). Once the germ theory was accepted, medical personnel sterilized equipment and washed their hands, saving millions of lives in an impressive example of the application of concepts first proposed as theory.

However, some physicians took the theory too far. They concluded that people who kissed and hugged babies would give them germs and make them sick. Caregivers were thus kept away from hospitalized or orphaned children because "human contact was the ultimate enemy of health" (Blum, 2002, p. 35).

In the 1950s, Harry Harlow (1905–1981), a psychologist who studied learning in monkeys, observed something surprising.

> We had separated more than 60 of these animals from their mothers 6 to 12 hours after birth and suckled them on tiny bottles. . . . During the course of our studies, we noticed that the laboratory-raised babies showed strong attachment to the folded gauze diapers which were used to cover the . . . floor of their cages.
>
> *[H. Harlow, 1958, p. 673]*

In fact, the infant monkeys seemed more attached to the cloth diapers than to their bottles. This was contrary to the two prevailing theories, since psychoanalytic theory predicted that infants would love whatever satisfied their oral needs and behaviorism predicted that infants would cherish whatever provided reinforcing food. Motherless monkeys should have loved their bottles, not their floor cloths.

Harlow set out to make a "direct experimental analysis" of human love via his monkeys because he believed that "the basic processes relating to affection, including nursing, contact, clinging, and even visual and auditory exploration, exhibit no fundamental differences in the two species" (H. Harlow, 1958). He raised eight infant monkeys, each caged alone with two "surrogate" (artificial) mothers, both mother-monkey size. One surrogate was made of bare wire and the other was covered by soft terrycloth, with a face designed to be ugly—two red bicycle reflectors for eyes and a strip of green tape for a mouth—but "soft,

TIME & LIFE PICTURES / GETTY IMAGES

Clinging to "Mother" Even though it gave no milk, this "mother" was soft and warm enough that infant monkeys spent almost all their time holding on to it. Many infants, some children, and even some adults cling to a familiar stuffed animal when life becomes frightening. According to Harlow, the reasons are the same: All primates are comforted by something soft, warm, and familiar.

warm, and tender, a mother with infinite patience." Four of the baby monkeys were fed by a bottle stuck through the chest of the ugly cloth "mother," the other four by a bottle on the wire "mother" (see the Research Design on the next page).

Harlow measured how much time the infant monkeys spent clinging to each of the two surrogates. The four monkeys who had a cloth mother clung to it and ignored the wire mother; this was to be expected, since feeding is connected with mothering. However, even the four babies that fed from the wire mother clung to the cloth mother, going to the wire mother only when hunger compelled them (see Figure 2.2). In short, no attachment to, or love for, the nourishing wire mother could be observed, but the cloth mother had the infants' affection whether or not it provided food. The answer to the question, "Does feeding produce mother love?" was a resounding "No!"

Would the cloth mothers reassure infants when frightening events occurred, just as a live mother does? Harlow devised another experiment. He put a clanking mechanical toy into each cage. The monkeys immediately sought comfort from their cloth mother, clinging to the soft belly with one hand and then

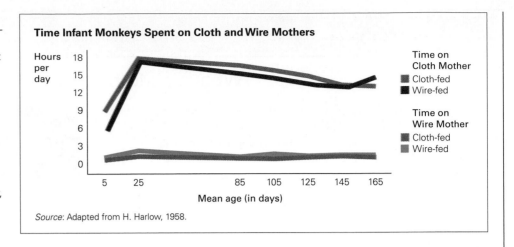

FIGURE 2.2

Softer Is Better During the first three weeks of Harlow's experiment, the infant monkeys developed a strong preference for the cloth-covered "mothers." That preference lasted throughout the experiment, even among the monkeys who were fed by a wire-covered mother.

Observation Quiz At five days, how much time did the wire-fed monkeys (compared with the cloth-fed monkeys) spend on the cloth mothers? (see answer, page 47)

Time Infant Monkeys Spent on Cloth and Wire Mothers

Hours per day

Time on Cloth Mother
Cloth-fed
Wire-fed

Time on Wire Mother
Cloth-fed
Wire-fed

Mean age (in days)

Source: Adapted from H. Harlow, 1958.

timidly exploring the new object with the other. Monkeys confronted by the same toy with only their wire mother present were terrified—freezing, screaming, shivering, hiding, urinating. Harlow concluded that mothering is not primarily about feeding but about what he called "contact comfort" or "love." Harlow and his students extended their research with dozens of other monkey studies. They discovered that mother love involves more than contact. To become psychologically healthy adults, infant monkeys (and humans as well) need interaction with another living, responsive creature (who could be of either sex) (Blum, 2002).

These experiments are a classic example of how theory is used in good science. Although aspects of both behaviorism and psychoanalytic theory were disproved, that is not the most significant point. Because Harlow was a good scientist, he knew what the classic theories predicted about love and comfort,

which made him notice the baby monkeys' attraction to the gauze diapers covering the floors of their cages (Suomi et al., 2008). That led to a hypothesis, a clever series of experiments, and some amazing results.

Harlow's work revolutionized the treatment of sick or motherless children. Even very tiny, preterm infants now have contact with their parents, typically including very gentle touch—and their chances of survival are better because of it. Both full-term and premature newborns may experience "kangaroo care," spending most of their time snuggled on their mother's naked body, and they thrive (see Chapter 4). Infants are no longer housed in orphanages but are sent home with adoptive or foster parents. Throughout infancy, parents hold their infants more and babies cry less than was true a few generations ago—all because one creative scientist compared theory and observations, and then designed ingenious experiments (Suomi et al., 2008).

>> Answer to Observation Quiz (from page 42) The obvious part is that she is feeding her doll, but modeling goes far beyond that. Notice that she is holding her spoon at exactly the same angle as her mother is holding hers.

>> Response for Teachers (from page 42) Behaviorists believe that anyone can learn anything. If your goal is quiet, attentive children, begin by reinforcing a moment's quiet or a quiet child, and soon all the children will be trying to remain attentive for several minutes at a time.

▶ **Research Design**

Scientists: Harry Harlow and many others.

Publication: Reprinted in *From Learning to Love: The Selected Papers of H. F. Harlow* (1986), edited by Clara Mears Harlow.

Subjects: Eight infant rhesus monkeys born in Harlow's laboratory.

Design: The monkeys were raised from birth in separate cages, each with two "surrogate mothers": one made of bare wire and the other of wire covered with terrycloth. Half the monkeys were fed by a bottle stuck onto the wire mother, the other half by a bottle stuck onto the cloth mother. Harlow recorded how much time the monkeys spent feeding from and clinging to each mother.

Major conclusion: Monkeys, and presumably all primate infants, need "contact comfort," the warm and soft reassurance of a mother's touch.

Comments: Many design problems are apparent: too few subjects, ethical questions about the treatment of animals, and uncertainty about whether data on lab-reared, socially isolated rhesus monkeys applies to humans or even to other primates in nature. However, the results of this experiment were so dramatic that it has been replicated and revised by dozens of other researchers. Harlow's research revolutionized child care.

Cognitive Theory

According to **cognitive theory,** thoughts and expectations profoundly affect attitudes, beliefs, values, assumptions, and actions. This theory has dominated psychology since about 1980 and has branched into many versions.

Thinking According to Piaget

The first major cognitive theorist was the Swiss scientist Jean Piaget (1896–1980), whose academic training was in biology. He became interested in human thought when he was hired to validate a standardized test of intelligence. His job was to note the age at which children answered each question correctly, setting the norms for the IQ test. However, the wrong answers caught his attention. *How* children think is much more revealing, Piaget concluded, than *what* they know.

In those days, most scientists believed that babies did not think until they could talk, but Piaget used the methods of scientific observation with his own three infants, finding them curious and thoughtful. Later he studied hundreds of schoolchildren. From this work Piaget formed the central thesis of cognitive theory: How children think changes with time and experience, and their thought processes always affect their behavior. According to cognitive theory, to understand human behavior, one must understand how a person thinks.

Piaget maintained that cognitive development occurs in four age-related periods, or stages: *sensorimotor, preoperational, concrete operational,* and *formal operational* (see Table 2.2). Each period fosters certain thinking processes, with

cognitive theory A grand theory of human development that focuses on changes in how people think over time. According to this theory, our thoughts shape our attitudes, beliefs, and behaviors.

YVES DEBRAINE / BLACK STAR

Would You Talk to This Man? Children loved talking to Jean Piaget, and he learned by listening carefully—especially to their incorrect explanations, which no one had paid much attention to before. All his life, Piaget was absorbed with studying the way children think. He called himself a "genetic epistemologist"—one who studies how children gain knowledge about the world as they grow up.

TABLE 2.2			
Piaget's Periods of Cognitive Development			
Age Range	Name of Period	Characteristics of the Period	Major Gains During the Period
Birth to 2 years	Sensorimotor	Infants use senses and motor abilities to understand the world. Learning is active; there is no conceptual or reflective thought.	Infants learn that an object still exists when it is out of sight (*object permanence*) and begin to think through mental actions.
2–6 years	Preoperational	Children think magically and poetically, using language to understand the world. Thinking is *egocentric,* causing children to perceive the world from their own perspective.	The imagination flourishes, and language becomes a significant means of self-expression and of influence from others.
6–11 years	Concrete operational	Children understand and apply logical operations, or principles, to interpret experiences objectively and rationally. Their thinking is limited to what they can personally see, hear, touch, and experience.	By applying logical abilities, children learn to understand concepts of conservation, number, classification, and many other scientific ideas.
12 years through adulthood	Formal operational	Adolescents and adults think about abstractions and hypothetical concepts and reason analytically, not just emotionally. They can be logical about things they have never experienced.	Ethics, politics, and social and moral issues become fascinating as adolescents and adults take a broader and more theoretical approach to experience.

(a) © IGAL JUSIDMAN

(b) DAVINA GRAHAM / ISTOCKPHOTO.COM

(c) RANDY DUCHAINE, BROOKLYN, NY

(d) PHOTODISC / PUNCHSTOCK

How to Think About Flowers A person's stage of cognitive growth influences how he or she thinks about everything, including flowers. (*a*) To 7-month-old Maya, in the sensorimotor stage, flowers are "known" through pulling, smelling, and even biting. (*b*) A slightly older child does not yet realize that dandelions are not fragrant, but like many children her age, her egocentric, two-handed curiosity will teach her. (*c, d*) At the adult's formal operational stage, flowers can be part of a larger, logical scheme—either to earn money or to cultivate beauty. Thinking is an active process from the beginning of life until the end.

cognitive equilibrium In cognitive theory, a state of mental balance in which people are not confused because they can use their existing thought processes to understand current experiences and ideas.

assimilation The reinterpretation of new experiences to fit into old ideas.

accommodation The restructuring of old ideas to include new experiences.

abstract logic absent in children but possible for adolescents and adults (Inhelder & Piaget, 1958; Piaget, 1952b).

Some aspects of Piaget's cognitive theory apply throughout the life span. Intellectual advancement occurs because humans at every age and developmental period seek **cognitive equilibrium**—a state of mental balance. The easiest way to achieve this balance is to interpret new experiences through the lens of preexisting ideas. For example, infants discover that new objects can be grabbed in the same way as familiar objects, and adults explain the day's headlines as evidence for their existing worldviews. Even a word can evoke a framework that short-circuits analysis, allowing quick equilibrium. For instance, people respond differently to the identical proposal depending on whether it is called a carbon *offset* or a carbon *tax* (Hardisty et al., 2010).

However, easy equilibrium is not always possible. Sometimes a new experience or question is jarring or incomprehensible. Then the individual experiences *cognitive disequilibrium,* an imbalance that creates confusion. As Figure 2.3 illustrates, disequilibrium can cause cognitive growth, because people adapt. Piaget describes two types of cognitive adaptation:

- **Assimilation:** New experiences are reinterpreted to fit into, or *assimilate* with, old ideas.
- **Accommodation:** Old ideas are restructured to include, or *accommodate,* new experiences.

Accommodation is harder than assimilation, but it is necessary when new ideas and experiences do not make sense using existing cognitive structures. Accommodation produces intellectual growth, including advancement to the next stage of cognition. For example, if a friend's ideas reveal cognitive inconsistencies in your own opinions, or if your favorite chess strategy puts you in checkmate, or if your mother says something completely unexpected, disequilibrium occurs. In the last example, you might *assimilate* by deciding your mother didn't mean what she said. You might tell yourself that she was repeating something she had read or that you misheard her. However, intellectual growth would occur if, instead, you changed your view of your mother to *accommodate* a new, expanded understanding.

Ideally, when two people disagree, or when they surprise each other by things they say, adaptation is mutual. For example, parents are often startled by their grown children's opinions. If the parents are able to grow intellectually, they revise their concepts of their children, accommodating their new perceptions. If an honest discussion occurs, the children, too, might accommodate. Cognitive growth is an active process, dependent on clashing and challenging concepts.

Information Processing

Piaget is justly credited with discovering that thoughts, not just experiences, affect development, an idea that is accepted by most social scientists today. However, many think Piaget's theorizing was too limited. Contemporary cognitive theory has benefited from brain research, cross-cultural studies, and step-by-step understanding of how people develop concepts. In later chapters, you will read details about Piaget's ideas and specifics regarding the limitations of his theory. Here we will describe one newer version of cognitive theory, called *information processing*.

Information processing "is not a single theory but, rather, a framework characterizing a large number of research programs" (Miller, 2011, p. 266). Inspired by computer functioning, instead of merely interpreting the answers given by children and adults, information processing explores the process, not just the outcome—that is, how people think before they respond. This information-processing approach has led researchers to use many modern techniques, among them brain scans and specific tests to investigate the details of attention and thought. The underlying theoretical base of all information processing is that those details reveal how the mind functions.

Scientists using an information-processing approach believe that a step-by-step description of the mechanisms of human thought aids our understanding of cognitive development at every age. Cognition begins with input picked up by the five senses; proceeds to brain reactions, connections, and stored memories; and concludes with some form of output. For infants, the output might consist of moving a hand, making a sound, or staring a split second longer at one stimulus than at another. With the aid of sensitive technology, information-processing research has overturned some of Piaget's findings.

Information processing also describes the relationship between one person's thinking and another's. For instance, under some conditions, people think better when they are part of a group, but under other conditions, groups slow down thought. Information processing helps us understand the difference (De Dreu et al., 2008). Similarly, some people say that watching television is destructive for young children; others disagree. Information-processing studies help researchers weigh in on this debate: Such studies can pinpoint exactly which cognitive processes are impaired by which images on the screen and at what age (Roseberry et al., 2009).

This approach to understanding cognition has many other applications. For example, it has long been recognized that children with ADHD (attention-deficit/

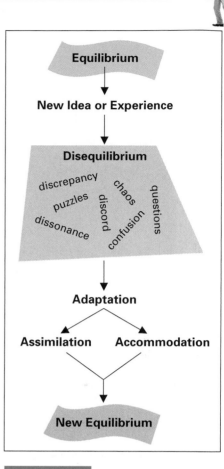

FIGURE 2.3

Challenge Me Most of us, most of the time, prefer the comfort of our conventional conclusions. According to Piaget, however, when new ideas disturb our thinking, we have an opportunity to expand our cognition with a broader and deeper understanding.

information processing A perspective that compares human thinking processes, by analogy, to computer analysis of data, including sensory input, connections, stored memories, and output.

>> **Answer to Observation Quiz** (from page 44) Six hours, or one-third less time. Note that later on, the wire-fed monkeys (compared with the cloth-fed monkeys) spent equal, or even more, time on the cloth mothers.

hyperactivity disorder) are not simply excessively active but also tend to have difficulties learning in school, obeying their parents, and making friends. Information processing has led to the discovery that a particular part of the brain (called fronto-striatal) does not function normally in children with ADHD. That makes it hard for them to interpret emotions from facial expressions and tone of voice (Uekermann et al., 2010). They may not realize when their father's "Come here" is an angry command and when it is a friendly suggestion. Knowing this helps in remediation: If that part of the brain can be strengthened, children may learn more, obey more, and gain friends.

SUMMING UP

The three grand theories of development originated almost a century ago. Each was pioneered by men who are still admired for their ability to set forth psychological theories so comprehensive and creative that they deserve to be called "grand." Each grand theory has a different focus: emotions (psychoanalytic theory), actions (behaviorism), or thoughts (cognitive theory) (see Figure 2.4).

The theories' methods and conclusions also differ. Freud and Erikson thought unconscious drives and early experiences formed the basis for later personality and behavior, so they listened to people's dreams and memories. Behaviorists instead stress experiences in the more recent past and focus on learning by association, by reinforcement, and by observation, so they experimented with dogs, rats, and humans. Cognitive theory holds that, to understand a person, one must learn how that person thinks—an ability that, according to Piaget, develops in four distinct stages, as measured by the response to various objects and questions. Information-processing theory agrees that cognition is crucial, but it breaks down cognition into thousands of components rather than into four stages and attends to details of thinking. ▪

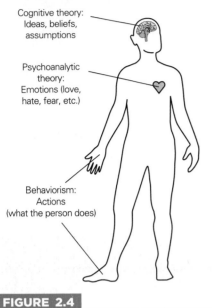

FIGURE 2.4

Major Focuses of the Three Grand Theories This simplified figure emphasizes that, while all three of the grand theories recognize that thoughts, emotions, and actions interact within each person, each theory focuses on a different aspect of the person.

(Figure labels)
Cognitive theory:
Ideas, beliefs,
assumptions

Psychoanalytic
theory:
Emotions (love,
hate, fear, etc.)

Behaviorism:
Actions
(what the person does)

>> Newer Theories

You have surely noticed that the seminal grand theorists (Freud, Erikson, Pavlov, Skinner, Piaget) were all men, scientists from western Europe or North America, born more than a hundred years ago. These background variables are limiting. (Of course, women, non-Western, and contemporary theorists are limited by their backgrounds as well.) Despite their impressive insights, the three grand theories no longer seem as comprehensive as they once did.

New theories have emerged that, unlike the grand theories, are multicultural and multidisciplinary. The first theory described here, sociocultural theory, draws on research in education, anthropology, and history; the second one, universal theory, arises from theology, political science, and history (humanism), or archeology, ethology, and biology (evolution). This multidisciplinary approach makes these theories particularly pertinent to current developmental science.

Sociocultural Theory

Chapter 1 emphasized that humans develop within social contexts. Barbara Rogoff (2003), a leading proponent of this idea, insists that "individual development must be understood in, and cannot be separated from, its social and cultural-historical context" (p. 50). The central thesis of **sociocultural theory** is that human development results from the dynamic interaction between developing persons and their surrounding society. Culture is viewed not as an external variable that impinges on developing persons but as integral to each person's development.

sociocultural theory An emergent theory that holds that development results from the dynamic interaction of each person with the surrounding social and cultural forces.

Social Interaction

The pioneer of the sociocultural perspective was Lev Vygotsky (1896–1934), a psychologist from the former Soviet Union. As you remember from Chapter 1, Vygotsky was particularly interested in the cognitive competencies that developed among the culturally and ethnically diverse people of his huge nation, as well as among children who were considered mentally retarded. He studied how farmers used tools, how illiterate people used abstract ideas, and how children of all abilities learned in school. In his view, each person, schooled or not, develops competencies taught by more skilled members of the society, who are tutors or mentors in an **apprenticeship in thinking** (Vygotsky, 1934/1986).

The implicit goal of this apprenticeship is to provide the instruction and support that novices need to acquire whatever knowledge and capabilities their culture values. Tutors engage learners in joint activities, offering not only instruction but also "mutual involvement in several widespread cultural practices with great importance for learning: narratives, routines, and play" (Rogoff, 2003, p. 285). Active apprenticeship is a central concept of sociocultural theory because each person depends on others to learn. This process is informal, pervasive, and social.

For example, one of my students recently came to my office with her young son, who eyed my candy dish but did not take any.

"He can have one if it's all right with you," I whispered to his mother.

She nodded and told him, "Dr. Berger will let you have one piece of candy."

He smiled shyly and quickly took one.

"What do you say?" she prompted.

"Thank you," he replied, glancing at me out of the corner of his eye.

"You're welcome," I said.

In that brief moment, all three of us were engaged in cultural transmission. We were surrounded by cultural traditions and practices, including my authority as professor, the fact that I have an office and a candy dish (a custom that I learned from one of my teachers), and the direct authority of the mother over her son. This mother had taught her son that *thank you* is the "magic word," as many North Americans call it. Specifics differ, but all adults teach children skills they may need in the society in which they live.

At the beginning of this chapter, you read about the concept that everyone should love and then marry once and only once. That is not true in some eras and cultures: Sometimes having several wives was (and is) a sign of prosperity, sometimes widowhood was quickly followed by marrying the brother of one's dead husband, sometimes (as among the nineteenth-century Shakers) marriage was forbidden, sometimes love was not sought in marriage (Coontz, 2005).

That cultural patterns and beliefs are *social constructions,* not natural laws, is obvious to sociocultural theorists. They find customs to be powerful, shaping the development of every person. Vygotsky stressed this point, arguing that mentally and physically disabled children should be educated (Vygotsky, 1925/1994), a cultural belief that has emerged in the United States in the past few decades but is not accepted in many other nations (Rogoff, 2003).

The Zone of Proximal Development

According to sociocultural theory, people always learn in the same way, whether they are learning a manual skill, a social custom, or a language. As part of the apprenticeship of learning, a mentor (parent, peer, or professional) must locate the learner's **zone of proximal development,** which consists of the skills, knowledge, and concepts that the learner is close to acquiring but cannot yet master without help.

apprenticeship in thinking Vygotsky's term for how cognition is stimulated and developed in people by older and more skilled members of society.

COURTESY OF DR. MICHAEL COLE, LABORATORY OF COMPARATIVE HUMAN COGNITION, UC, SAN DIEGO

The Founder of Sociocultural Theory Lev Vygotsky, now recognized as a seminal thinker whose ideas are revolutionizing education and the study of development, was a contemporary of Freud, Skinner, Pavlov, and Piaget. Vygotsky did not attain their eminence in his lifetime, partly because his work, conducted in Stalinist Russia, was largely inaccessible to the Western world and partly because he died young, at age 38.

zone of proximal development In sociocultural theory, a metaphorical area, or "zone," surrounding a learner that includes all the skills, knowledge, and concepts that the person is close ("proximal") to acquiring but cannot yet master without help.

DAVE KING / GETTY IMAGES

Gourmet Cook in the Making Some children have skilled mentors who engage them in learning. It would be much easier for this cook to cut, dip, and fry without help, but the child is an apprentice and will soon learn to use a knife himself.

Through sensitive assessment of the learner, the mentor engages the mentee and together, in a "process of joint construction," new knowledge is attained (Valsiner, 2006). The mentor must avoid two opposite dangers: boredom and failure. Some frustration is permitted, but the learner must be actively engaged, never passive or overwhelmed (see Figure 2.5).

To make this seemingly abstract process more concrete, consider an example: a father teaching his daughter to ride a bicycle. He begins by rolling her along, supporting her weight while telling her to keep her hands on the handlebars, to push the right and left pedals in rhythm, and to look straight ahead. As she becomes more comfortable and confident, he begins to roll her along more quickly, praising her for steadily pumping. Within a few lessons, he is jogging beside her, holding only the handlebars. When he senses that she could maintain her balance by herself, he urges her to pedal faster and slowly loosens his grip. Perhaps without even realizing it, she is riding on her own.

Note that this is not instruction by preset rules. Sociocultural learning is active: No one learns to ride a bike by reading and memorizing written instructions, and no good teacher merely repeats a prepared lesson. Because each learner has personal traits, experiences, and aspirations, education must be individualized. Learning styles vary: Some people need more assurance than others; some learn best by looking, others by hearing. A mentor needs to sense when support or freedom is needed and how peers can help (they are sometimes the

FIGURE 2.5

The Magic Middle Somewhere between the boring and the impossible is the zone of proximal development, where interaction between teacher and learner results in knowledge never before grasped or skills not already mastered. The intellectual excitement of that zone is the origin of the joy that both instruction and study can bring.

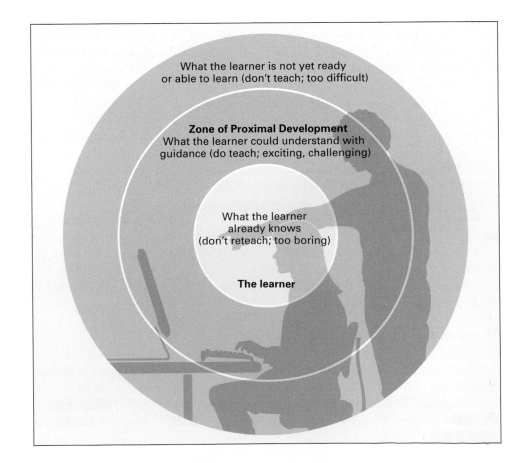

What the learner is not yet ready or able to learn (don't teach; too difficult)

Zone of Proximal Development
What the learner could understand with guidance (do teach; exciting, challenging)

What the learner already knows (don't reteach; too boring)

The learner

best mentors). Teachers know how the zone of proximal development expands and shifts.

Excursions into and through the zone of proximal development, as illustrated by the boy prompted to say "thank you" and the girl learning to balance on a bike, are commonplace for all of us. Examples are everywhere: a new mother learning to breast-feed a baby may meet with other breast-feeding mothers as well as a consultant who adjusts the latch, an adult trying a new food looks to other diners to know what utensils to use, and so on. Mentors, attuned to ever-shifting abilities and motivation, continually urge a new level of competence; learners ask questions, show interest, and demonstrate progress, thus guiding and inspiring the mentors. When education goes well, both are fully engaged and productive. Particular skills and processes vary enormously from culture to culture, but the overall social interaction is the same.

The Universal Perspective: Humanism and Evolutionary Theory

No developmentalist doubts that each person is unique. Yet many social scientists contend that focusing on cultural (or ethnic, or sexual, or economic) differences results in an unbalanced vision of humanity. We are one species, sharing universal impulses and needs. This universal perspective has been articulated several times in developmental theory, each time expressed in particular ways, but all contending that humans are, at the basic level, alike. Here we describe two of the most prominent of these: humanism and evolutionary theory.

Humanism

Many scientists are convinced that there is something hopeful, unifying, and noble in the human spirit, something ignored by psychoanalytic theory (which stresses the animalistic, selfish id) and by behaviorism (which seems to ignore free will). The limits of those two major theories were especially apparent to two Americans: Abraham Maslow, a deeply religious man who was the eldest son of uneducated Jewish immigrants, and Carl Rogers, who was preparing to become a Christian minister until he switched to psychology. Although they did not know each other as young men, both had studied at the University of Wisconsin in the 1920s when Harry Harlow set up his laboratory there and both witnessed the effects of the Great Depression and World War II, concluding that traditional psychological theories underrated the potential of all humans for good. They founded a theory called **humanism** that became prominent after World War II, as millions read Maslow's book *Toward a Psychology of Being* (1962/1999) and Rogers's book *On Becoming a Person* (1961/2004).

As he expressed it first in 1943, Maslow believed that all people—no matter what their culture, gender, or background—have the same basic needs and drives. He arranged these needs in a hierarchy:

1. Physiological: needing food, water, warmth, and air
2. Safety and security: feeling protected from injury and death
3. Love and belonging: having loving friends, family, and a community (often religious)
4. Respect and esteem: being respected by the wider community as well as by oneself
5. Self-actualization: becoming truly oneself, fulfilling one's unique potential while appreciating all of humanity

BETTMANN / CORBIS

Hope and Laughter Maslow studied law before psychology, and he enjoyed deep discussions with many psychoanalytic theorists who escaped Nazi Europe. Nonetheless, he believed in the human spirit and that it could overcome oppression and reach self-actualization where faith, hope, and humor abound.

humanism A theory that stresses the potential of all humans for good and the belief that all people have the same basic needs, regardless of culture, gender, or background.

Especially for Nurses Maslow's hierarchy is often taught in health sciences because it alerts medical staff to the needs of patients. What specific hospital procedures might help? (see response, page 52)

Rogers also stressed the need to accept and respect one's own personhood as well as that of everyone else. He thought that people should give each other *unconditional positive regard,* which meant that they should see (regard) each other with appreciation (positive) without conditions (unconditional). He did not think that everything people do is good, but he believed that people themselves are good, as in "Hate the sin but love the sinner." Rogers spent the last years of his life trying to reconcile the factions in Northern Ireland, South Africa, and Russia; he thought that all sides needed to learn to listen to each other.

As you can see, humanists emphasize what all people have in common, not their national, ethnic, or cultural differences. Maslow contended that everyone must satisfy each lower level of his hierarchy of needs before moving higher. A hungry man, for instance, might jeopardize his own safety to get food (level 1 precedes level 2), or an unloved woman might sacrifice her self-respect for the comfort of love (level 3 precedes level 4). He explained the destructive and inhumane actions of some people as the consequence of unmet lower needs, which meant they could not reach self-actualization. At the end of his life, he explained that the highest level transcended selfishness and became selflessness, when a person is able to appreciate all of humanity (Maslow, 1971).

Although humanism does not postulate stages, a developmental application of this theory is that the satisfaction of childhood needs is crucial for later self-acceptance. Thus, babies cry in hunger, and that basic need should subsequently be satisfied. Similarly, children cling to abusive parents, and people become thieves or even killers if they were unsafe or unloved as children, or disrespected as adults, unable to reach their potential, to self-actualize. Rogers agreed that people who were deprived in childhood, not given unconditional positive regard, might become selfish and antisocial adults.

This theory is still prominent in hospitals and hospices because caregivers realize that pain can be physical (the first two levels) and social (the next two) (Majercsik, 2005; Zalenski & Raspa, 2006). Even the very old and sick need love (family should be allowed to stay with them) and dignity (the dying need respect). Echoes of humanism are also evident in education and sports, in which the basic idea is that people are more effectively motivated when they try to master a body of knowledge or a skill to achieve a "personal best," that is, to reach the peak of their own potential, than when they strive to be the best in their class or on their team (Ravizza, 2007).

At the highest level, when basic needs have been met, people can be fully themselves—creative, spiritual, appreciative of nature, able to respect everyone else. Peak experiences occur when the intense joy of life makes time stop, makes self-seeking disappear, and makes the music of the heavens echo in daily life. Given the stresses and deprivations of modern life, humanists believe that relatively few people reach the self-actualization of level 5. But everyone *can*—that is the universality of humanism.

Humanism flourished in the 1960s and accrued a backlash of criticism. It was blamed for the abuse of psychedelic drugs, for sexual liberation, and for New Age philosophy (Cooke et al., 2005; Dye et al., 2005). Another major theorist of the time, Rollo May, said that humanists were led astray because they had "no theory of evil" (Hoffman, 2009). Perhaps ironically, humanism is also criticized for not appreciating the diverse cultures of people (e.g., Heslop, 2008). Maslow himself was suspected of being too enamored of personal freedom and thus too pro-American and anti-Communist. On the other hand, the values enshrined in self-actualization are credited with enabling some Rwandans to reject participation in the genocide that gripped their nation in 1994 (Baum, 2008). They realized that ethnic hatred was beneath them, that all human life has value.

>> Response for Nurses (from page 51) Reassurance from nurses (explaining procedures, including specifics and reasons) helps with the first two, and visitors, cards, and calls might help with the next two. Obviously, specifics depend on the patient, but everyone needs respect as well as physical care.

Evolutionary Theory

You are familiar with Darwin and his ideas, which were first published 150 years ago—essentially that plants, insects, birds, and animals developed over billions of years as life evolved from primitive cells to humans (Darwin, 1859). But you may not realize that serious research on human development (not on the biology of lower organisms) inspired by this theory is quite recent. As two leaders in this field write:

> During the last two decades, the study of the evolutionary foundations of human nature has grown at an exponential rate. In fact, it is now a booming interdisciplinary scientific enterprise, one that sits at the cutting edge of the social and behavioral sciences.
>
> *[Gangestad & Simpson, 2007, p. 2]*

Evolutionary theory has intriguing explanations for many issues in human development, including women's nausea in early pregnancy, 1-year-olds' attachment to their parents, onset of puberty in young adolescents, emerging adults' sexual preferences, adults' investment in their children, and even dementia in late adulthood. According to this theory, many human impulses, needs, and behaviors evolved to help humans survive and thrive over the millions of years since the human species began. To understand the life span today, we may need to recognize our past, including such puzzling things as why humans still fear snakes (which cause about 1 death in a billion) but not automobiles (which caused about 1 death in 5,000 in the United States in 2009—rates are higher in some other nations). This does not mean that we are stuck with our evolutionary past; for example, although we do not have an instinctive fear of cars, the motor-vehicle death rate has been cut in half by better-designed roads, laws, and cars. But it does mean that to understand human development, we need to recognize our impulses, some of which are useful and some not.

According to evolutionary theory, two long-standing, biologically based drives for every species are survival and reproduction. Understanding these two provides insight into lust, romance, protective parenthood, onset of disease, fear of death, as well as many other life-span topics. Current humans react in ways that helped survival and reproduction millions of years ago because of **selective adaptation,** a process essential to evolutionary theory.

Essentially, over time, selective adaptation means that genes for traits that made it more likely that people would live and bear children are selected to allow the species to thrive. The process worked like this: If one person happened to have a gene that made survival more likely, that gene was likely to be more common in later generations. Having such a beneficial gene could happen through mutation or simply through someone's having a gene that specified expression at one end of the natural variation in height, body type, anxiety, or any other characteristic that varies slightly from one person to another.

For example, originally humans were probably all lactose-intolerant, getting sick if they drank cow's milk. This was irrelevant in most regions because there were no cows, but in some places cattle were domesticated and raised for their meat. Of course, malnutrition was a common cause of death, and "killing the fatted calf" provided a rare feast for the entire community when a major celebration occurred. In cattle-raising locations, if a starving person chanced to have an aberrant gene for the enzyme that allowed digestion of cow's milk, and that person drank some milk produced for a calf, he or she might survive to procreate. Indeed, a woman with that gene might be fat enough to have early puberty, to sustain many pregnancies, and to breast-feed more thriving babies than her lactose-intolerant sisters. In that way, the next generation would include more people who inherited that gene.

Especially for Teachers and Counselors of Teenagers Teen pregnancy is destructive of adolescent education, family life, and sometimes even health. According to evolutionary theory, what can be done about this? (see response, page 55)

selective adaptation The process by which living creatures (including people) adjust to their environment. Genes that enhance survival and reproductive ability are selected, over generations, to become more frequent.

Got Milk! Many people in Sweden (like this pair) and the other Scandinavian countries regularly drink cow's milk and digest it easily. That may be because their ancient occupation of cattle herding coincided with a genetic tendency toward lactose tolerance.

This process of selective adaptation would continue over many generations. That odd gene would become widespread in cold climates where plant proteins were less abundant and cow's milk meant survival. That might explain why few Scandinavians are lactose-intolerant but many Africans are—a useful fact to know should Wisconsin dairy farmers want to ship milk to feed starving children in Ethiopia. In fact, although world hunger remains a global problem, fewer people are starving anywhere partly because nutritionists now know which foods are more digestible and nourishing for which people.

For groups as well as individuals, the interaction of genes and environment affects survival and reproduction, the basic evolutionary drives. Genetic variations are particularly beneficial when the environment changes, which is one reason the diversity of humans throughout the world benefits humanity. If a species' gene pool does not include variants that allow survival in difficult circumstances (such as a new disease or an environmental toxin), the entire species may become extinct. About 90 percent of nonhuman species that ever existed have disappeared because, as conditions changed, every member of that species died without progeny (Buss et al., 1998).

Genetic variation among humans and inherited flexibility (the plasticity explained in Chapter 1) enable humans to survive and multiply. This is true not only for biological traits (such as digestion) but also for traits that originate in the brain (Tomasello, 2009). For example, genes foster socialization, communication, and language, which helped our ancestors a million years ago and allowed societies a few thousand years ago to develop writing, then books, and then universities, allowing humans to learn from one another. Because of those same genes, people know the importance of clean water, good nutrition, and immunization, and the average life expectancy has increased from about 20 years a thousand years ago, to 35 years a century ago, to about 75 today (with marked regional variation). The very fact that you are reading this book, accepting some ideas and rejecting others, is part of the heritage that will allow future generations to survive, according to evolutionary theory.

To show how evolution works, consider a physical example. Humans and chimpanzees share 99 percent of their genes, a fact that means chimps can be used to test new drugs, study social organizations, investigate nutrition, and so on, with results applicable to humans. Within the study of human development, ethology (the study of nonhuman species) has provided many insights, such as the one you read about in Harlow's research on motherless monkeys. Obviously, however, there are some crucial genetic differences between species of primates. Evolution helps us recognize and appreciate them.

One such difference is the fact that humans walk on two legs, not four. Our bodies are designed for that, with longer legs, shorter arms, and different hip/pelvic structures than those of chimpanzees. This is not always helpful (many adults develop back trouble), but it enabled humans (but not chimps) to journey from Africa to distant fertile regions, carrying tools, seeds, and babies. Because of the genetic adaptability of our species, humans are the only mammals to have traveled, reproduced, and thrived on every landmass of the world (except Antarctica). In each place, particular characteristics evolved that made survival possible thousands of miles from our ancestral home. This explains why traits that are sometimes harmful (such as pale skin, high blood pressure, fear of spiders) continue: They were once adaptive. In medicine, this means that some drugs benefit some people but harm others; in education, it means that some children learn by doing and others by listening; in family organization, it means that some adults thrive in larger groups and others do not; and so on. The idea from Chapter 1 that difference is not deficit is central to evolutionary theory, as is the reality that we are all one human race, with many traits (those longer legs) that unify us.

Within developmental science, evolutionary theory is now considered insightful and intriguing, but some interpretations are hotly disputed. For instance, an evolutionary account of mental illness suggests that disorders are extremes of adaptive traits, such as anxiety about new situations or vivid imagination. The implications of this interpretation might include less diagnosis and treatment for mental illness.

An even more controversial idea arises from the evolutionary explanation for male–female differences. According to some, since human biology requires that the females, not the males, become pregnant and breast-feed, for species survival (especially during childbearing years) women benefit if they have a man to protect them and their children from predators. By contrast, men spread their genes more widely if they have many sexual partners and dozens of offspring.

This may explain male and female behavior even today, with women seeking one steady mate, kept near the campfire (or suburban home) by feeding him and satisfying his sexual drive. Males, however, may stray, being less faithful. Because of these ancient biological and genetic differences between males and females, evolutionary theory explains, men are likely to have more sex partners than women have. Current research on adolescent boys and adult men in many nations confirms this male–female difference, but many adults of both sexes believe that this difference is sociocultural, not evolutionary.

Evolutionary psychologists have done some intriguing research to support their interpretations, first with mostly White North Americans and later in many nations throughout the world (Buss, 2007). One of the most recent studies involved 212 college students, all U.S. citizens whose parents were born in Mexico (Cramer et al., 2009). The participants were asked to imagine their romantic partner either "forming a deep emotional attachment" or "enjoying passionate sexual intercourse" with someone else, and then they were asked which of those two possibilities would distress them more. As with every other population that has been surveyed with a similar query, most women (60 percent) were more distressed at the emotional infidelity and most men (66 percent) at the sexual infidelity. Evolutionary theory explains this oft-replicated result by noting that women need men to be soul mates who stick by them throughout life, whereas men need women to be sexually faithful, in part because that was the only way they could be sure their children were really theirs (Buss, 2003), that is, until recent advances in paternity testing.

As already mentioned, this is hotly disputed. The data find that worldwide, men are more likely to go into a jealous rage if they suspect infidelity, sometimes beating their sex partners to death, which women almost never do (Mize et al., 2009). However, the evolutionary interpretation may be in error (Harris, 2004). Some believe that sexist upbringing, not genes that evolved over millions of years, leads to mating and sexual patterns.

Similar problems occur for many other applications of evolutionary theory. The belief that some behaviors are universal, deeply rooted in human genes, may undermine efforts to change human actions. The interplay of nature and nurture, mentioned in the previous chapter and further discussed in the next chapter, suggests that genes alone never determine behavior. Note than even in the survey of Mexican American college students, more than one-third did not follow the

>> **Response for Teachers and Counselors of Teenagers** (from page 53) Evolutionary theory stresses the basic human drive for reproduction, which gives teenagers a powerful sex drive. Thus, merely informing teenagers of the difficulty of caring for a newborn (some high school sex education programs simply give teenagers a chicken egg to nurture) is not likely to work. A better method would be to structure teenagers' lives so that pregnancy is impossible—for instance, with careful supervision or readily available contraception.

typical pattern for their sex. Other surveys also find that many people act in ways counter to evolutionary predictions. Evolutionary theorists do not deny that, but they say that ignoring the human tendencies for sexism, aggression, and hostility to strangers makes it harder to understand, and then change, what people do. Furthermore, some of the best aspects of human behavior, including cooperation, spirituality, and self-sacrifice, may also originate from selective adaptation (Ackerman & Kenrick, 2009; Bulbulia, 2007; Gintis et al., 2007).

Many hypotheses from evolutionary theory have not been carefully tested, much less accepted, partly because this is the newest theory to be applied to life-span development. Some critics contend that evolutionary theory about human development is an unscientific leap from current human behavior to conditions that existed before written history. Nonetheless, evolutionary theory offers intriguing explanations for universal human tendencies that are difficult to explain.

SUMMING UP

Newer theories of development are more multicultural, expansive, and multidisciplinary than the earlier grand theories. Sociocultural theory emphasizes the varied cultural contexts of development, that even such basic behaviors as infant care and childhood education are guided by the community. Learning occurs within the zone of proximal development, as the result of sensitive collaboration between a teacher (who could be a parent or a child) and a learner who is ready for the next step.

Universal theories include humanism and evolution, both of which stress that, beneath all our diversities, humans have the same underlying needs. Humanism holds that each unique person merits respect and positive regard in order to become a fully self-actualized human being. Evolutionary theory contends that thousands of years of selective adaptation has led humans to experience strong emotions and impulses to satisfy two universal needs of every species: to survive and to reproduce. ▪

>> What Theories Contribute

Each major theory discussed in this chapter has contributed a great deal to our understanding of human development (see Table 2.3):

- *Psychoanalytic theories* have made us aware of the impact of early-childhood experiences, remembered or not, on subsequent development.
- *Behaviorism* has shown the effect that immediate responses, associations, and examples have on learning, moment by moment and over time.
- *Cognitive theories* have brought an understanding of intellectual processes and how our thoughts and beliefs affect every aspect of our development.
- *Sociocultural theories* have reminded us that development is embedded in a rich and multifaceted cultural context, which is evident in every social interaction.
- *Universal theories* stress that human differences are less significant than what all humans, in every place and era, share.

No comprehensive view of development can ignore any of these theories, yet each has encountered severe criticism. Psychoanalytic theory has been faulted for being too subjective; behaviorism, for being too mechanistic; cognitive theory, for undervaluing emotions; sociocultural theory, for neglecting individuals; and uni-

TABLE 2.3

Five Perspectives on Human Development

Theory	Area of Focus	Fundamental Depiction of What People Do	Relative Emphasis on Nature or Nurture?
Psychoanalytic theory	Psychosexual (Freud) or psychosocial (Erikson) stages	Battle unconscious impulses and overcome major crises	More nature (biological, sexual impulses, and parent–child bonds)
Behaviorism	Conditioning through stimulus and response	Respond to stimuli, reinforcement, and models	More nurture (direct environment produces various behaviors)
Cognitive theory	Thinking, remembering, analyzing	Seek to understand experiences while forming concepts and cognitive strategies	More nature (person's own mental activity and motivation are key)
Sociocultural theory	Social context, expressed through people, language, customs	Learn the tools, skills, and values of society through apprenticeships	More nurture (interaction of mentor and learner, within cultural context)
Universal perspective	Needs and impulses that all humans share as a species	Develop impulses, interests, and patterns to satisfy needs and survive as a species	More nature (needs that apply to all humans; genetic evolution)

versal theory, for slighting cultural, gender, and economic variations. Most developmentalists prefer an **eclectic perspective.** That is, rather than adopt any one of these theories exclusively, they make selective use of all of them. The state of research in human development has been accurately characterized as "theoretical pluralism" because no single theory fully explains the behavior of humans as they go through life (Dixon & Lerner, 1999).

Being eclectic, not tied to any one theory, is beneficial because everyone, scientists as well as laypeople, tends to be biased. It is easy to dismiss alternative points of view, but using all five theories opens our eyes and minds to aspects of development that we might otherwise ignore. As one overview of seven developmental theories, including those explained here, concludes, "Because no one theory satisfactorily explains development, it is critical that developmentalists be able to draw on the content, methods, and theoretical concepts of many theories" (Miller, 2011, p. 437).

As you will see in many later chapters, theories provide a fresh look at behavior. Imagine a parent and a teacher discussing a child's actions. Each suggests a possible explanation that makes the other say, "I never thought of that," and together they understand the child better. Having five theories is like having five perceptive observers. All five are not always on target, but it is better to use a theory to expand perception than to stay stuck in one narrow groove. A hand functions best with five fingers, although each finger is different, some more useful than others.

eclectic perspective The approach taken by most developmentalists, in which they apply aspects of each of the various theories of development rather than adhering exclusively to one theory.

SUMMING UP

Theories are needed to suggest hypotheses, investigation, and, finally, answers so that objective research and empirical evidence can replace untested and personal assumptions. All five of the major theories have met with valid criticism, but they have all helped to move the scientific process forward. Most developmentalists are eclectic, making selective use of all these theories and more. This helps guard against bias and keeps scientists, parents, students, and everyone else open to alternative explanations for the complexity of human life.

SUMMARY

What Theories Do

1. A theory provides a framework of general principles to guide research and to explain observations. Each of the five major developmental theories—psychoanalytic, behaviorist, cognitive, sociocultural, and universal—interprets human development from a distinct perspective, and each provides guidance for understanding how human experiences and behaviors change over time.

2. Theories are neither true nor false. They are not facts; they suggest hypotheses to be tested. Good theories are practical: They aid inquiry, interpretation, and daily life.

Grand Theories

3. Psychoanalytic theory emphasizes that human actions and thoughts originate from unconscious impulses and childhood conflicts. Freud theorized that sexual urges arise during three stages of childhood development—oral, anal, and phallic—and continue in latency and the genital stage.

4. Erikson described psychosocial, not psychosexual, stages. He described eight successive stages of development, each involving a crisis as people mature within their context. Societies, cultures, and family members respond to each person's development, affecting the resolution of each crisis.

5. All psychoanalytic theories stress the legacy of childhood. Conflicts associated with children's erotic impulses have a lasting impact on adult personality, according to Freud. Erikson thought that the resolution of each crisis impinges on adult development.

6. Behaviorists, or learning theorists, believe that scientists should study observable and measurable behavior. Behaviorism emphasizes conditioning—a lifelong learning process as reinforcement and punishment continue to guide behavior.

7. Social learning theory recognizes that people learn by observing others. Children are particularly susceptible to social learning, but everyone learns to be more or less effective. Ideally, individuals and communities recognize problems and then work to solve them, without the defeatism of those who have learned to be helpless.

8. Cognitive theorists believe that thoughts and beliefs powerfully affect attitudes, actions, and perceptions. Piaget proposed four age-related periods of cognition, propelled by an active search for cognitive equilibrium. Information processing focuses on each aspect of cognitive input, processing, and output.

Newer Theories

9. Sociocultural theory explains human development in terms of the guidance, support, and structure provided by knowledgeable members of the society, via culture and personal mentoring. Vygotsky described how learning occurs through social interactions, when mentors guide learners through their zone of proximal development.

10. The universal perspective focuses on the shared impulses and common needs of all humanity. One universal theory is humanism. Maslow believed that all humans have five basic needs, which he arranged in sequence, beginning with survival and ending with self-actualization. Rogers believed that each person merits respect and appreciation, with unconditional positive regard.

11. Evolutionary theory has recently been applied to life-span development. It contends that contemporary humans have inherited genetic tendencies that fostered survival and reproduction of the human species a million years ago. Some hypotheses from this theory are particularly provocative, such as the explanation for male–female differences in romantic liaisons.

What Theories Contribute

12. Psychoanalytic, behavioral, cognitive, sociocultural, and universal theories have each aided our understanding of human development, yet no one theory is broad enough to describe the full complexity and diversity of human experience. Most developmentalists are eclectic, drawing upon many theories.

KEY TERMS

developmental theory (p. 33)
psychoanalytic theory (p. 36)
behaviorism (p. 40)
conditioning (p. 40)
classical conditioning (p. 40)
operant conditioning (p. 40)

reinforcement (p. 41)
social learning theory (p. 41)
modeling (p. 41)
self-efficacy (p. 42)
cognitive theory (p. 45)
cognitive equilibrium (p. 46)

assimilation (p. 46)
accommodation (p. 46)
information processing (p. 47)
sociocultural theory (p. 48)
apprenticeship in thinking (p. 49)

zone of proximal development (p. 49)
humanism (p. 51)
selective adaptation (p. 53)
eclectic perspective (p. 56)

WHAT HAVE YOU LEARNED?

What Theories Do

1. How can a theory be practical?

2. How do theories differ from facts?

Grand Theories

3. What is the basic idea of psychoanalytic theory?

4. What is Freud's theory of infantile sexuality?

5. What body parts are connected to the oral, anal, and phallic stages?

6. In what ways does Erikson's theory differ from Freud's?

7. What is the basic idea of behaviorism?

8. Why is behaviorism considered "in opposition" to psycho-analytic theory?

9. How do classical and operant conditioning differ?

10. What reinforcers are emphasized by social learning theory?

11. What is the basic idea of cognitive theory?

12. How are Piaget's stages similar to, and different from, Freud's stages?

13. In what ways are assimilation and accommodation similar?

14. How does the information-processing approach differ from Piaget's approach to cognition?

15. What might information-processing theorists study to understand how babies learn to talk?

Newer Theories

16. What are the underlying differences between the newer theories and the grand theories?

17. How is "apprenticeship in thinking" an example of socio-cultural theory?

18. What do mentors do when mentees are in their zone of proximal development?

19. Is there a contradiction between humanism and the ideas of major religions? Explain.

20. How does Maslow's hierarchy of needs differ from Erikson's stages?

21. How does evolutionary psychology explain human instincts?

22. Why is the evolutionary theory of sexual infidelity controversial?

23. What does the idea of selective adaptation imply about the nature–nurture controversy?

What Theories Contribute

24. What is the key criticism and key contribution of psychoanalytic theory?

25. What is the key criticism and key contribution of behaviorism?

26. What is the key criticism and key contribution of cognitive theory?

27. What is the key criticism and key contribution of sociocultural theory?

28. What is the key criticism and key contribution of universal theories?

29. What are the advantages and disadvantages of an eclectic perspective?

APPLICATIONS

1. Developmentalists sometimes talk about "folk theories," which are theories developed by ordinary people who may not know that they are theorizing. Choose three sayings commonly used in your culture, such as (from the dominant U.S. culture) "A penny saved is a penny earned" or "As the twig is bent, so grows the tree." Explain the underlying assumptions, or theory, that each saying reflects.

2. Behaviorism has been used to change personal habits. Think of a habit you'd like to change (e.g., stop smoking, exercise more,

watch less TV). Count the frequency of that behavior for a week, noting the reinforcers for each instance. Then, and only then, develop a substitute behavior, reinforcing yourself for it. Keep careful records; chart data over several days. What did you learn?

3. Ask three people to give you their explanation of male–female differences in mating and sexual behaviors. Which theory in this text is closest to each person's explanation, and which theory (or theories) is not mentioned?

>>ONLINE CONNECTIONS

To accompany your textbook, you have access to a number of online resources, including quizzes for every chapter of the book, flashcards (in English and Spanish), critical thinking questions, and case studies. For access to any of these links, go to www.worthpublishers.com/bergerls8e. In addition to these free resources, you'll also find links to the podcasts, video clips, diagnostic quizzing with personalized study advice, and an ebook. Some of the videos and activities available online include:

■ *Modeling: Learning from Observation.* This activity includes clips from Albert Bandura's classic Bobo doll experiment on observational learning.

■ *Harlow's Studies of Infant Monkeys.* Original footage from Harry Harlow's lab of his studies.

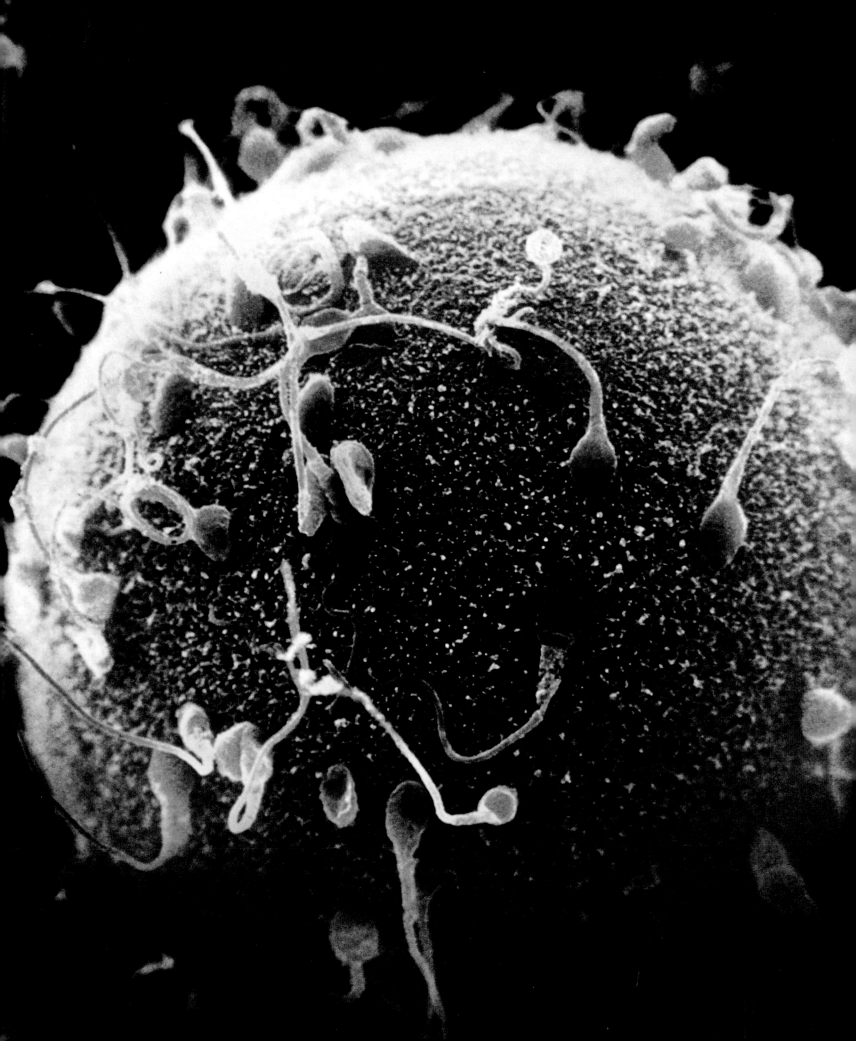

Heredity and Environment

WHAT WILL YOU KNOW?

1. To what extent does a baby take after the mother or father?
2. What does it mean to say that all human characteristics are epigenetic, not just genetic?
3. What is the relationship between genotype and phenotype?
4. What happens when someone has more or fewer than 46 chromosomes?
5. What do genetic counselors do?

As I came to pick up my daughter Rachel after school, Stephanie (another mother) pulled me aside. She whispered that she had seen my daughter fall and that her little finger was probably broken. A month ago, her son had fallen and broken his finger; it looked just like Rachel's.

Rachel was playing happily, but I examined her finger. It was crooked. Hoping to avoid both needless panic and medical neglect, I walked her home to consult with my husband. He smiled and spread out his hands, revealing the same bent finger. Aha! An inherited anomaly, not an injury.

That bent finger is one small example of millions of genetic surprises in human development, usually unnoticed unless a problem appears. This chapter anticipates and explains some of these mysteries, going behind the scenes to reveal not only what genes are but also how they work. Many ethical issues are raised by genetics; we will explore those, too. First, the basics.

>> The Genetic Code

You already know that genes affect every aspect of development and that they come from parents and are passed on to children. The specifics of that genetic transmission are intricate and miraculous, as you will soon read. Always remember, however, that the development of every person is dynamic, ongoing, and interactional; individuals are much more than the product of genes.

For example, conception, birth, growth, puberty, and death are all powerfully affected by genes. Genes dictate the maximum life span for each species: For mice it is 4 years; for humans, 122; for the tortoise, 150 (Crews, 2003). If you were a mouse, you couldn't live past age 4.

But whether one person outlives another depends much more on where the person lives than on his or her genes. The life-span range by nation is 43 years (averaging 83 in Japan, 40 in Swaziland) (United Nations, 2007). As you remember from Chapter 1, nature and nurture always interact: Many people inherit genes for a long life but die years before their organs reach programmed death. Similarly, genes for language fluency, for diabetes, for strong teeth, and even for bent fingers are expressed (or not) depending on nurture. To understand development, we begin with genes. But never forget that genetics describes possibilities (you could live to 122), not outcomes (you probably won't).

What Genes Are

First, we review some biology. All living things are made up of tiny cells. The work of these cells is done by *proteins*. Each cell manufactures certain proteins according to instructions stored by molecules of **deoxyribonucleic acid (DNA)** at the heart of each cell. These DNA molecules are on a **chromosome.**

Humans have 23 pairs of chromosomes (46 in all), which contain the instructions to make all the proteins that a person needs (see Figure 3.1). The instructions in the 46 chromosomes are organized into units called genes, with each **gene** usually located at a specific spot on a particular chromosome. Humans have between 18,000 and 23,000 genes, and each gene contains the chemical recipe for making a specific protein (Brooker, 2009).

What exactly is a protein? A protein is composed of a sequence of chemicals, a long string of building blocks called *amino acids*. The recipe for manufacturing a protein consists of instructions for stringing together the right amino acids in the right order.

These instructions are transmitted to the cell via pairs of four chemicals called *bases* (adenine, thiamine, cytosine, and guanine, abbreviated A, T, C, and G). The bases pair up in only four possible ways (A-T, T-A, C-G, and G-C). Humans have more than 3 billion base pairs, which are arranged in triplets (three base pairs) on those 20,000 or so genes.

Most genes have thousands of precise base pairs arranged in precise triplets, making the 20 types of amino acids needed for development into a human being. The codes for each particular gene can vary, although usually they do not. Some genes have alternate versions of base pairs, with transpositions, deletions, or repetitions of base pairs not found in other versions of the same gene. Each of these variations is called an **allele** of that gene. Most alleles cause only minor differences (such as the shape of an eyebrow); some seem inconsequential; some are notable (such as the amount of the MAOA enzyme, as you read in Chapter 1).

Although all mammals have most of the same genes, and although each person has almost all the same genes as every other person, everyone also has some significant alleles. This is precisely what makes each of us genetically unique. Variations in base pairs (called *SNPs*, single nucleotide polymorphisms) are not rare, nor are extra repeats of a piece of a gene or sometimes a whole gene. One expert said: "What's cool is that we are a mosaic of pieces of genomes. None of us is truly normal" (Eichler, quoted in Cohen, 2007, p. 1315). Everyone also has additional DNA and RNA (another molecule) that are not genes but that enhance, transcribe, connect, empower, and alter genes (Shapiro, 2009). This material used to be called "junk DNA"—no longer. Thousands of scientists seek to discover what those molecules do (more on that later), but no one thinks they are junk anymore.

The entire packet of instructions to make a living organism is called the **genome.** There is a genome for every species and variety of plant and animal— even for every bacteria and virus. Knowing the genome of the human species is a start (it was fully decoded in 2001), but each person (except monozygotic twins) has a slightly different code. One international group of scientists seeks to sequence the genome of a thousand people; another group hopes to sequence the genome of 10,000 other vertebrates (Kaiser, 2008; Pennisi, 2009). Everyone agrees, however, that each person is distinct, even though the human genome is

---

deoxyribonucleic acid (DNA) The chemical composition of the molecules that contain the genes, which are the chemical instructions for cells to manufacture various proteins.

chromosome One of the 46 molecules of DNA (in 23 pairs) that virtually each cell of the human body contains and that, together, contain all the genes. Other species have more or fewer chromosomes.

gene A small section of a chromosome; the basic unit for the transmission of heredity. A gene consists of a string of chemicals that provide instructions for the cell to manufacture certain proteins.

allele A variation that makes a gene different in some way from other genes for the same characteristics. Many genes never vary; others have several possible alleles.

genome The full set of genes that are the instructions to make an individual member of a certain species.

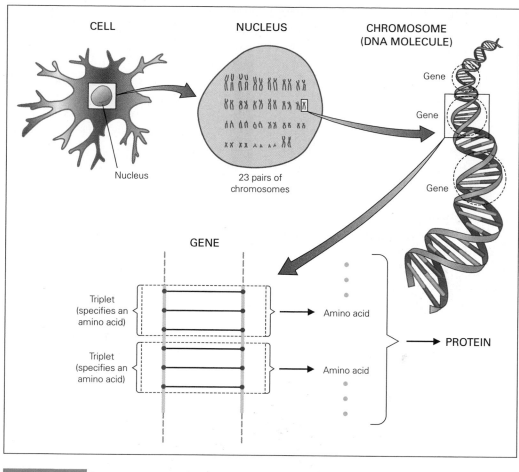

CELL   NUCLEUS   CHROMOSOME (DNA MOLECULE)

Nucleus

23 pairs of chromosomes

Gene

Gene

Gene

GENE

Triplet (specifies an amino acid)

Triplet (specifies an amino acid)

Amino acid

Amino acid

PROTEIN

FIGURE 3.1

How Proteins Are Made The genes on the chromosomes in the nucleus of each cell instruct the cell to manufacture the proteins needed to sustain life and development.

99.9 percent identical for any two persons. It is natural to focus on differences, but similarities far outweigh them.

Thus, the human genome contains hundreds of thousands of molecules, forming about 20,000 genes on 46 chromosomes, using 3 million base pairs of 4 chemicals to instruct production of 20 amino acids to create proteins that make each person unique, yet similar to all other humans. This entire instruction code is contained in one cell, smaller than the head of a pin. That is just one amazing fact of human genetics. More to come.

The Beginnings of Life

Development begins at conception, when a male reproductive cell (*sperm*; plural: *sperm*) penetrates the membrane of a female reproductive cell (*ovum*; plural: *ova*), creating a new cell called a **zygote.** Each human reproductive cell, or **gamete,** contains 23 chromosomes, half of the 46 of the zygote.

That one-celled zygote copies itself again and again, creating an embryo, a fetus, a baby, and eventually an adult with trillions of cells that contain the same 46 chromosomes (and thousands of genes) of the original zygote. Most human cells have all 46 chromosomes of the zygote that began that particular person; however,

Especially for Scientists A hundred years ago, it was believed that humans had 48 chromosomes, not 46; 10 years ago, it was thought that humans had 100,000 genes, not 20,000 or so. Why? (see response, page 64)

zygote The single cell formed from the union of two gametes, a sperm and an ovum.

gamete A reproductive cell; that is, a sperm or ovum that can produce a new individual if it combines with a gamete from the other sex to make a zygote.

>> **Response for Scientists** (from page 63) There was some scientific evidence for the wrong numbers (e.g., chimpanzees have 48 chromosomes), but the reality is that humans tend to overestimate many things, from the number of genes to their grades on the next test. Scientists are very human: They are inclined to overestimate until the data prove them wrong.

each gamete has only 23 chromosomes. Obviously, in the creation of sperm or ova, a cell splits in half, each half with only one of the two chromosomes at each location. Thus, a gamete has only one chromosome number 10, for instance, although the man or woman who formed it has two chromosomes at the 10th site. The zygote will have a pair of number 10 chromosomes as well—one from the father and one from the mother.

The particular member of each chromosome pair on a given gamete is randomly selected. That means each person can produce 2^{23} different gametes—more than 8 million versions of his or her own 46 chromosomes. If a given man and woman conceived a billion children, each would be genetically unlike the others because of the chromosomes of the particular sperm and ovum that created them.

Matching Genes

At the moment of conception, the father's chromosomes match up with the mother's chromosomes (his number 10 with her number 10, for instance) so that the zygote's 23 pairs of chromosomes are arranged in father/mother pairs. (A few zygotes have more or fewer than 46 chromosomes, discussed later.) The genes on the chromosomes constitute the organism's genetic inheritance, or **genotype,** which endures throughout life, repeated in almost every cell. Growth requires duplication again and again of the code of that original cell, so almost every cell of a person contains the entire genetic code.

genotype An organism's entire genetic inheritance, or genetic potential.

In 22 of the 23 pairs of chromosomes, both members of the pair are closely matched. Each of these 44 chromosomes is called an *autosome,* which means that it is independent (*auto* means "self") of the sex chromosomes (the 23rd pair). Each autosome, from number 1 to number 22, contains hundreds of genes in the same positions and sequence. At conception, each gene on each autosome matches with its counterpart from the other parent. If the code of the gene from one parent is exactly like the code on that gene from the other parent, the gene pair is **homozygous** (literally, "same-zygote").

homozygous Referring to two genes of one pair that are exactly the same in every letter of their code. Most gene pairs are homozygous.

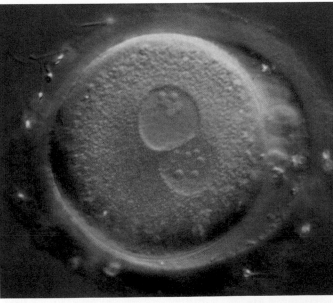

COURTESY OF LENNART NILSSON / BONNIER FAKTA / STOCKHOLM

The Moment of Conception This ovum is about to become a zygote. It has been penetrated by a single sperm, whose nucleus now lies next to the nucleus of the ovum. Soon, the two nuclei will fuse, bringing together about 20,000 genes to guide development.

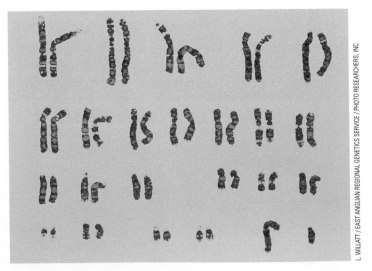

L. WILLATT / EAST ANGLIAN REGIONAL GENETICS SERVICE / PHOTO RESEARCHERS, INC

Mapping the Karyotype A *karyotype* portrays a person's chromosomes. To create a karyotype, a cell is grown in a laboratory, magnified, and then usually photographed. The photo is cut into pieces and rearranged so that the matched pairs of chromosomes are lined up from largest (*top left*) to smallest (*bottom row, fourth pair from the left*). Shown at the bottom right is the 23rd chromosome pair: These two do not match, meaning that this karyotype shows a male (XY).

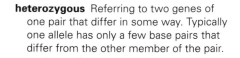

However, the match is not always letter perfect because some genes are alleles, and the mother might have a different allele than the father. If the code of one gene differs from that of its counterpart, the two genes still pair up, but the zygote (and later, the person) is **heterozygous** ("different-zygote") for the trait that specific gene influences.

Male or Female?

The **23rd pair** of chromosomes is a special case. These two are the sex chromosomes. In females, the 23rd pair is composed of two X-shaped chromosomes. Accordingly, it is designated **XX.** In males, the 23rd pair has one X-shaped chromosome and one Y-shaped chromosome. It is called **XY.**

Because a female's 23rd pair is XX, every ovum contains either one X or the other—but always an X. And because a male's 23rd pair is XY, half of his sperm carry an X chromosome and half a Y. The X chromosome is bigger and has more genes, but the Y chromosome has a crucial gene, called SRY, that directs the fetus to make male organs and hormones. Thus, sex depends on which sperm penetrated the ovum—a Y sperm with the SRY gene, creating a boy (XY), or an X sperm, creating a girl (XX) (see Figure 3.2).

The natural sex ratio at birth is close to 50:50. This ratio is affected by serious adversity (such as famine), when males are more likely to be spontaneously aborted (also called *miscarried*). For some species, environmental conditions dramatically tilt the sex ratio. In certain reptiles, for instance, the temperature during incubation can produce almost all males or almost all females (Quinn et al., 2007). For a New Zealand parrot (the kakapo), females are infertile when malnourished, produce more males than females (2:1) when overfed, but reach equity (1:1) when fed just right (Robertson et al., 2006). For humans, ovulation stops with severe malnutrition, but once conception occurs, the zygote is either XX or XY and nothing changes that. However, survival depends partly on prenatal conditions: Ordinarily, slightly more boys are conceived, but the sex ratio is close to even at birth.

heterozygous Referring to two genes of one pair that differ in some way. Typically one allele has only a few base pairs that differ from the other member of the pair.

23rd pair The chromosome pair that, in humans, determines sex. The other 22 pairs are autosomes; inherited equally by males and females.

XX A 23rd chromosome pair that consists of two X-shaped chromosomes, one each from the mother and the father. XX zygotes become females.

XY A 23rd chromosome pair that consists of an X-shaped chromosome from the mother and a Y-shaped chromosome from the father. XY zygotes become males.

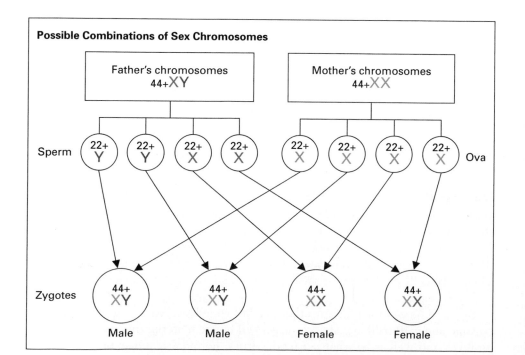

FIGURE 3.2

Determining a Zygote's Sex Any given couple can produce four possible combinations of sex chromosomes; two lead to female children and two, to male. In terms of the future person's sex, it does not matter which of the mother's Xs the zygote inherited. All that matters is whether the father's Y sperm or X sperm fertilized the ovum. However, for X-linked conditions it matters a great deal, because typically one, but not both, of the mother's Xs carries the trait.

Observation Quiz In the chapter-opening photograph (page 60), can you distinguish the Y sperm from the X sperm? (see answer, page 66)

THINKING CRITICALLY

Too Many Boys?

Prenatal sex selection is possible; millions of couples have done it, usually to have a boy. Is this a problem?

Historically, some newborns were killed in every culture. One of the moral advances of Islam, in the sixth century, was to forbid female infanticide. Currently, killing a newborn girl is rare; there are three other ways used to prevent female births— (1) inactivating X sperm before conception, (2) in vitro fertilization (IVF; to be described soon), or (3) aborting XX fetuses.

In China, a "one-child" policy initiated in 1990 cut the birth rate in half. This policy (sometimes enforced with sterilization and abortion) alleviated poverty, but many Chinese couples wanted their only child to be a boy (Greenhalgh, 2008). Since 1993, the Chinese government has forbidden prenatal testing to reveal sex, but records show that in 1999, only 83 girls were born for every 100 boys. Recently, the one-child policy has become a two-child policy, and the sex ratio is more balanced (Greenhalgh, 2008).

My Strength, My Daughter That's the slogan these girls in New Delhi are shouting at a demonstration against abortion of female fetuses in India. The current sex ratio of children in India suggests that this campaign has not convinced every couple.

Parents elsewhere also prefer boys. The Indian government forbids abortion to prevent female births, but India nonetheless has 92 girls for every 100 boys. One elderly Indian man said, "We should have at least four children per family, three of them boys" (quoted in Khanna, 2010, p. 66). Worldwide, one estimate is that 100 million fetuses have been aborted since 1990 because they were female (Sharma, 2008), perhaps 20,000 of them in the United States (Abrevaya, 2009).

Many nations recognize that society's needs clash with parental wishes and forbid abortion of the "wrong" sex. Some also forbid sorting sperm to change the proportion of X and Y sperm before insemination, a technique that works for humans about 85 percent of the time (Karabinus, 2009).

In the United States, individuals make their own choices before and after conception. Most fertility doctors and some parents believe that sex selection is a reproductive right and that couples who can afford it should be able to decide to have either a boy or a girl (Puri & Nachtigall, 2009). Some people who personally would not abort a fetus just because it is male or female do not want the government to forbid personal freedom—in this case, freedom to "balance" the family.

Chinese doctors worry that AIDS will spread if there are too many men with no available brides (J. Cohen, 2004). Other concerns are that male-heavy societies might have too many learning disabilities, drug abusers, violent crimes, wars, heart attacks, and suicides but fewer nurses, day-care centers, or close family bonds. Do you object because culture, not biology, affects these gender proportions? That is a valid objection. Chromosomes and genes do not determine behavior. Every male–female difference is context specific: Even traits that originate with biology, such as heart attacks and suicide rates, now higher among males, are affected more by environment (in this case, diet and culture) than by sex. As in every Thinking Critically feature, the answers here are not obvious. What do you think about sex selection?

>> **Answer to Observation Quiz** (from page 65) Probably not. The Y sperm are slightly smaller, which can be detected via scientific analysis (some cattle breeders raise only steers using such analysis), but visual inspection, even magnified as in the photo, may be inaccurate.

New Cells, New Functions

Within hours after conception, the zygote begins *duplication* and *division*. First, the 23 pairs of chromosomes duplicate, forming two complete sets of the genome. These two sets move toward opposite sides of the zygote, and the single cell splits neatly down the middle into two cells, each containing the original genetic code. These two cells duplicate and divide, becoming four, which duplicate and divide, becoming eight, and so on.

By the time you (or I, or any other person) were born, your original zygote had become about 10 trillion cells, all influenced by the material that was once called junk DNA as well as by whatever foods, drugs, hormones, and so on came to the

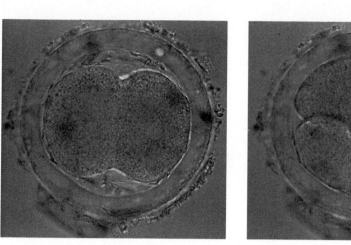

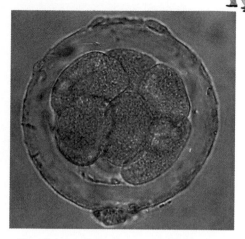

First Stages of the Germinal Period The original zygote as it divides into (*a*) two cells, (*b*) four cells, and (*c*) eight cells. Occasionally at this early stage, the cells separate completely, forming the beginning of monozygotic twins, quadruplets, or octuplets.

embryo from the mother. By adulthood, those cells become more than 100 trillion—again, all affected by the environment. But no matter how old a person, how large the total number of cells, or how much division and duplication occur, almost every cell carries a copy of the complete genetic instructions inherited by the one-celled zygote. This explains why DNA testing of any body cell, even from a drop of blood or a snip of hair, can identify "the real father," "the guilty criminal," or "the long-lost brother." DNA lingers long after death, as evident in living African Americans who have claimed Thomas Jefferson as an ancestor: DNA testing proved one of them right and one of them wrong (Foster et al., 1998).

The fact that every cell in the embryo contains the developing person's complete genetic code does not mean that any cell could become a person—far from it. If the two-celled organism was artificially split apart (illegal for humans, successful with mice), it might create monozygotic twins, but that is impossible after the first few hours. At about the eight-cell stage, a third process, *differentiation,* is added to duplication and division. Cells begin to specialize, taking different forms and reproducing at various rates, depending on where they are located. As one expert explains, "We are sitting with parts of our body that could have been used for thinking" (Gottlieb, 1992/2002, p. 172).

Stem Cells

As a result of this specialization and differentiation, cells change soon after conception from being **stem cells,** which are cells that are able to produce any other cell, to being only one kind of cell. For instance, specialization causes some cells to be part of an eye, others part of a finger.

Thousands of scientists are trying to make differentiated cells switch back to being stem cells, and success has been reported with mice. Although stem cells are present in the first stages of human development, ethical considerations have limited research on them, especially in the United States. Some of the legal U.S. restrictions were lifted in 2009, but others remain. Apparently human cells, like mice cells, can become stem cells after the first days of development (Armstrong et al., 2010), but application of stem cell research to remedy human genetic diseases is not

stem cells Cells from which any other specialized type of cell can form.

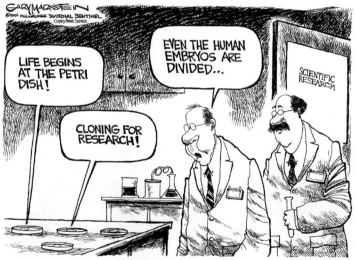

Politics and Genetics If life is the ability to grow, then life begins at conception. The question, of course, is at what point developing cells become human. Most zygotes, created inside a woman, do not implant—but this is largely irrelevant because the fact that they did not implant means no one knew they existed in the first place. Laboratory researchers, however, do notice when zygotes do not implant. This is of significance to many because zygotes have the potential to produce stem cells that could be used to cure fatal diseases—the ethics of which is a subject of considerable ongoing debate.

imminent. As the head of the Michael J. Fox Foundation for Parkinson's Research said, "All my exposure was pop media. I thought it was all about stem cells. I have not totally lost hope on cell replacement, I just don't think it's a near-term hope" (Hood, quoted in Holden, 2009).

Twins

Thousands of twins who would never have been born two decades ago are increasing the demand for twin strollers, rhyming names, and newborn intensive care. Why?

Monozygotic Twins

Although every zygote is genetically unique, about once in 250 human conceptions, the zygote not only duplicates but splits apart completely, creating two, or four, or even eight separate zygotes, each identical to that first single cell. (An incomplete split creates *conjoined twins,* formerly called Siamese twins.)

If each of those separated cells implants and grows, multiple births occur. One separation results in **monozygotic (MZ)** twins, from one (*mono*) zygote (also called *identical twins*). Two or three separations create monozygotic quadruplets or octuplets. Because monozygotic multiples originate from the same zygote, they have the same genotype, with identical genetic instructions for physical appearance, psychological traits, vulnerability to diseases, and everything else. One monozygotic twin can donate a kidney for surgical implantation in the other twin with no organ rejection, thus avoiding a major problem for the twin whose organs are failing.

Dizygotic Twins

Most twins (about two-thirds when naturally conceived) are **dizygotic (DZ),** also called *fraternal twins.* They began life as two separate zygotes created by the fertilization of two ova by two sperm at roughly the same time. (Usually, women release only one ovum per month, but sometimes double or triple ovulation occurs.) The incidence of dizygotic twins varies by ethnicity and age. For example, DZ twins occur about once in every 11 births among Yoruba women from Nigeria, once in 100 births among British women, and once in 700 births among Japanese women (Gall, 1996; Piontelli, 2002). Women in their late 30s are three times as likely to have DZ twins as are women in their early 20s.

---

monozygotic (MZ) twins Twins who originate from one zygote that splits apart very early in development. (Also called *identical twins*.) Other monozygotic multiple births (such as triplets and quadruplets) can occur as well.

dizygotic (DZ) twins Twins who are formed when two separate ova are fertilized by two separate sperm at roughly the same time. (Also called *fraternal twins*.)

Same Birthday, Same (or Different?) Genes Twins who are of different sexes or who have obvious differences in personality are dizygotic, sharing only half of their genes. Many same-sex twins with similar looks and temperaments are dizygotic as well. One of these twin pairs is dizygotic; the other is monozygotic.

Observation Quiz Can you tell which pair is monozygotic? (see answer, page 70)

DAVID YOUNG-WOLFF / PHOTOEDIT

JOHNER IMAGES / GETTY IMAGES

Like all siblings from the same two parents, DZ twins have about half of their genes in common. And like any other siblings, they can differ markedly or they can appear quite similar. Most differ in obvious ways—hair color, height, and so on. Half the time, one is a boy and the other a girl. But some dizygotic twins are the same sex and look so much alike that only genetic tests can determine whether they are monozygotic or dizygotic.

Assisted Reproduction

The preceding discussion describes multiple births through natural conception, but many twins and almost all triplets and quadruplets currently born in the United States and several other nations are conceived by choice, not by chance (see Figure 3.3). Let us explain.

When a couple are not fertile, they may turn to **assisted reproductive technology (ART).** A woman can take drugs to cause ovulation, usually of several ova at once. If they all are fertilized, multiple births occur. Or ova can be surgically removed from an ovary, fertilized in a glass lab dish, and then inserted into the uterus, where they might implant. This is **in vitro fertilization (IVF)**—*in vitro* literally means "in glass." Technicians can insert only one zygote, or only zygotes of one sex, or several zygotes. Often IVF fertilization occurs via *intra-cytoplasmic sperm injection (ICSI)*, in which a sperm is inserted directly into an ovum. Since the first "test-tube" baby in 1973, IVF has produced 2 million babies worldwide, including more than 1 percent of all U.S. newborns since 2000 (MMWR, June 12, 2009).

Assisted reproduction allows people to have children who are not biologically theirs if others provide the sperm, the ova, and/or the uterus. Donated sperm have been used for decades, resulting in millions of babies born after intrauterine insemination (formerly called artificial insemination). Donor ova and donor wombs (when an IVF embryo is implanted in a woman who did not provide the ovum) have become more common in the past decade. The word *donor* may be misleading, since people are paid for their sperm (up to $1,100), ova (up to $10,000), or

PACIFIC PHOTOS / NEWSCOM

Perfectly Legal Nadya Suleman takes 10 of her 14 children to the park, with the help of a nanny and two strollers designed for four. She was a medical miracle when her eight newborns all survived, thanks to expert care in a Los Angeles hospital. Soon thereafter, however, considerable controversy began: She was dubbed "Octomom" because—as a single mother of six children, including twins, already—she still opted to undergo in vitro fertilization, which resulted in implantation of her octuplets. Many believe implanting more than two zygotes is unethical and should be illegal. The debate continues.

assisted reproductive technology (ART) A general term for the techniques designed to help infertile couples conceive and then sustain a pregnancy.

in vitro fertilization (IVF) Fertilization that takes place outside a woman's body (as in a glass laboratory dish). The procedure involves mixing sperm with ova that have been surgically removed from the woman's ovary. If a zygote is produced, it is inserted into the woman's uterus, where it may implant and develop into a baby.

FIGURE 3.3

Why More Multiple Births? Historically in the United States, the natural rate of multiple births, particularly triplets and higher orders, tended to increase as mothers aged. Women in their mid- to late 30s were more likely to have twins than those who were younger. The advent of assisted reproductive technology (ART) led to a dramatic increase in multiple births overall starting in the early 1990s; it is now women aged 40 and over who are most likely to experience this phenomenon. Curiously, however, after peaking in the late 1990s, rates of triplet and higher-order births appear to be on the decline.

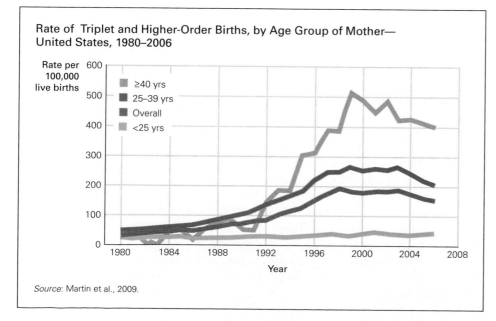

Rate of Triplet and Higher-Order Births, by Age Group of Mother— United States, 1980–2006

Rate per 100,000 live births

- ≥40 yrs
- 25–39 yrs
- Overall
- <25 yrs

Source: Martin et al., 2009.

>> **Answer to Observation Quiz** (from page 68) The Japanese American girls are the monozygotic twins. If you were not sure, look at their teeth, their eyebrows, and the shape of their faces, compared with the ears and chins of the boys.

pregnancies ($22,000) in addition to medical expenses. Some children who have three biological progenitors are raised by parents who have no biological connection to them at all.

Birth defects increase with IVF: Compared with spontaneously conceived infants, the odds ratio for birth defects in IVF newborns is about 1.5 (El-Chaar et al., 2009). Nonetheless, the risk is small: About 97 percent of all IVF newborns have no apparent defects. Not small, however, is the risk of prematurity and low birthweight, because often several zygotes are inserted and more than one implants. In the United States, almost half of all IVF babies are low-birthweight twins or triplets (MMWR, June 12, 2009). Many couples who feared they could never have children suddenly have two tiny ones. Is this a problem? Consider the following.

THINKING CRITICALLY

Two Babies for the Price of One?

If you were infertile, would you welcome twins? Most scientists and doctors wish the answer was no. Most couples say yes. They want to avoid a second IVF cycle (IVF costs a couple about $45,000 per cycle, with marked variations from clinic to clinic). It succeeds less than half the time; twins seem a bonus. In the United States, fewer minority women undergo IVF, but when military insurance covered it, the rate increased markedly for African Americans (but not for Latinos) (McCarthy-Keith et al., in press).

Why do doctors hope for single births? Multiple births increase medical complications for the mother and children and are costly for fathers, other siblings, and society as well because multiples have higher rates of death, disease, and disabilities lifelong. Multiples usually weigh less at birth, and even when compared with equally small singletons, they develop more slowly and form weaker social bonds (Feldman & Eidelman, 2004).

Finland allows insertion of only one IVF embryo per cycle, a move that increased the rate of full-term single births but did not reduce the rate of successful pregnancies (Yli-Kuha et al., 2009). Similar results were found in the United States with an experiment that subsidized single-embryo transfer (Stillman et al., 2009). Most European nations limit numbers per IVF cycle when government health care pays for the procedure.

In the United States, any limitation might be considered rationing. If more than two embryos implant, doctors may recommend selective reduction (abortion) of some embryos to protect the others. Not every woman agrees, as dramatically illustrated by the eight fragile infants born in California in 2009—a miracle or a disaster. Which was it? (See photo on page 69.)

SUMMING UP

The fusion of two gametes (sperm and ovum) creates a zygote, a tiny one-celled creature that has the potential to become a baby. One way to describe that process is chemically: DNA is composed of four chemicals that pair up in twos, three of those pairs (a triplet) direct the formation of an amino acid, amino acids make up proteins, and proteins make a person. Another way to describe it is with numbers: The genetic code for a human being consists of about 3 billion base pairs on about 20,000 genes on 46 chromosomes, half from the mother and half from the father. The father's 23rd chromosome pair is XY, which means that half his sperm are X and half are Y, determining the future baby's sex. Twins are monozygotic (one zygote) or dizygotic (two zygotes), with assisted reproduction increasing the rate of multiple births. ART has led to millions of much-wanted, healthy infants but also to new dilemmas, including whether people should be able to choose the sex, the genetic and biological parentage, and the number of newborns they have. ■

>> From One Cell to Many

As already explained, when sperm and ovum combine into a zygote, they establish the *genotype*: all the genes that the developing person has. Creation of an actual person from one cell involves several complex processes to form the **phenotype,** which is the actual appearance and manifest behavior of the person. Nothing is totally genetic, and nothing is untouched by genes, which means that the genotype and phenotype are intimately connected.

Keep in mind that "genes merely produce proteins, not mature traits" (Gottlieb, 1992/2002, p. 164). In other words, the genotype instigates body and brain formation, but the phenotype (the visible traits and behaviors) depends on many genes and on the environment. Most traits are **polygenic** (affected by many genes) and **multifactorial** (influenced by many factors, including biological and psychological ones). A zygote might have the genes for becoming, say, a musical genius, but that potential is not usually realized. Some crucial factors in development of the zygote are in the genome itself, because

> genes occupy only about 1.5 percent of the genome. The other 98.5 percent, dubbed "junk DNA" now appear to produce transcription of its genetic code, boosting the raw information output of the genome to about 62 times what the gene alone would produce.
>
> *[Barry, 2007, p. 154]*

Almost daily, researchers describe additional complexities in polygenic and multifactorial interaction. To understand this, we begin with epigenetics.

Epigenetics

Research over the past two decades has found that every trait—psychological as well as physical—is influenced by genes. At first, some scientists thought that genes *determined* everything, that humans became whatever their genes destined them to be—heroes, killers, or ordinary people. Research quickly revealed the limitations of this hypothesis. Even monozygotic twins are not totally identical—biologically, psychologically, or socially: Genes affect everything but determine nothing (Poulsen et al., 2007).

Instead, all important human characteristics are **epigenetic.** The prefix *epi-* means "with," "around," "before," "after," "beyond," or "near." The word *epigenetic,* therefore, refers to the environmental factors that surround the genes, affecting genetic expression. Some "epi" influences occur in the first hours of life, as biochemical elements silence certain genes in a process called *methylation*. These elements have been the subject of extensive research involving what used to be called junk DNA. Thousands of biologists are trying to understand exactly how methylation develops, in what ways it is passed down from parents to children, how it alters genetic expression, and so on (Margueron & Reinberg, 2010).

For developmentalists, one fascinating finding is that methylation changes over the life span (Mazin, 2009). Why do people get old, develop cancer, die? The cause is epigenetic: The elderly have the same genes they had as newborns, but methylation changes the expression of those genes as time goes on. Another important finding is that all the diseases known to be genetic (including cancer, schizophrenia, and autism) are actually epigenetic (Saey, 2008).

Certain environmental influences (such as injury, temperature extremes, drug abuse, and crowding) can impede genetic development, whereas others (nourishing food, loving care, play) can facilitate it. No trait—even one with strong, proven, genetic origins, such as blood pressure or social anxiety—is determined by genes alone because via "epigenetic programming . . . , health and behavior are mediated

phenotype The observable characteristics of a person, including appearance, personality, intelligence, and all other traits.

polygenic Referring to a trait that is influenced by many genes.

multifactorial Referring to a trait that is affected by many factors, both genetic and environmental expression; enhancing, halting, shaping, or altering the expression of genes, resulting in a phenotype that may differ markedly from the genotype..

epigenetic Referring to environmental factors that affect genes and genetic expression; enhancing, halting, shaping, or altering the expression of genes, resulting in a phenotype that may differ markedly from the genotype.

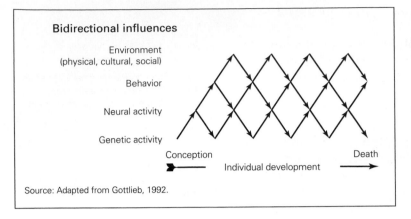

Source: Adapted from Gottlieb, 1992.

FIGURE 3.4

An Epigenetic Model of Development
Notice that there are as many arrows going down as going up, at all levels. Although development begins with genes at conception, it requires that all four factors interact.

Human Genome Project An international effort to map the complete human genetic code. This effort was essentially completed in 2001, though analysis is ongoing.

Twelve of Three Billion Pairs This is a computer illustration of a small segment of one gene, with several triplets. Even a small difference in one gene, such as a few extra triplets, can cause major changes in the phenotype of a person.

through altered gene expression" (Moffit et al., 2006, p. 6). Indeed, "development is an epigenetic process that entails cascades of interactions across multiple levels of causation, from genes to environments" (Spencer et al., 2009, p. 80).

The inevitable epigenetic interaction between genes and the environment (nature and nurture) is illustrated in Figure 3.4. That simple diagram, with arrows going up and down over time, has been redrawn and reprinted dozens of times since it was first published in 1992, reiterating that genes interact with environmental conditions again and again in each person's life (Gottlieb, 2007). The following explanation of genetic interaction is helpful for understanding genes, but remember that genes are only the beginning.

Gene–Gene Interactions

Many discoveries have followed the completion of the **Human Genome Project** in 2001. One of the first surprises was that humans have far fewer than 100,000 genes, the number everyone believed throughout the twentieth century. The total number of genes in a person is between 18,000 and 23,000; the precise number is elusive because—another surprise—it is not always easy to figure out where one gene starts and another stops, or even if a particular stretch of DNA is actually a gene (Rouchka & Cha, 2009).

Another unexpected finding is that all living creatures share many genes. For example, the eyes of flies, mice, and people all originate from the *Pax6 gene*; another gene produces legs in many species, including the butterfly, the cat, the centipede, and the person. Although chimpanzees have 48 chromosomes, humans and chimpanzees nonetheless have 99 percent of their genes in common. All this might make you wonder what makes humans unlike other animals. The answer lies partly in that "junk" around the genes (lower creatures have far less of it) and partly in 100 or so regulator genes, all of which influence thousands of other genes (Shapiro, 2009), directing formation of a creature who talks, walks, and thinks as people do.

Probably the crucial difference is in the brain. Adult brain size (about 1,400 cubic centimeters) is highly heritable and is quite similar among humans worldwide, especially when compared with the small brains (about 370 cubic centimeters) of chimpanzees (Holden, 2006). Of course, bigger animals (elephants) have bigger brains, but the proportion of brain to body is significantly greater for humans than for other creatures.

Additive Heredity

Some alleles are *additive* because their effects *add up* to influence the phenotype. When genes interact additively, the phenotype reflects the contributions of every gene that is involved. Height, hair curliness, and skin color, for instance, are usually the result of additive genes. Indeed, height is affected by an estimated 100 genes, each contributing a small amount—some to make a person a little taller; some, a little shorter (Little, 2002).

Most people have ancestors of various heights, hair curliness, skin color, and so on, so their children's phenotype does not mirror the parents' phenotypes (although it does always reflect their genotypes). I see this example in my family: Rachel is of average height, shorter than my husband or I but taller than our mothers. She apparently inherited some of her grandmothers' height genes from us.

How any additive trait turns out depends partly on all the genes a child happens to inherit (half from each parent, which means one-fourth from each grandparent). Some genes amplify or dampen the effects of other genes, aided by all the other DNA and RNA (not junk!) in the zygote.

Dominant–Recessive Heredity

Some genes are not additive. In one nonadditive form, alleles interact in a **dominant–recessive pattern,** which occurs when one allele, the *dominant gene,* is more influential than the other, the *recessive gene.*

The dominant gene controls the characteristic even when a recessive gene is the other half of a pair. When someone has a recessive gene on the genotype that is not apparent in the phenotype, that person is said to be a **carrier** of that gene. The recessive gene is *carried* on the genotype.

Most recessive genes are harmless. For example, blue eyes are determined by a recessive allele and brown eyes by a dominant one, which means that a child conceived by a blue-eyed person and a brown-eyed one will have brown eyes unless the brown-eyed parent is a carrier of the blue-eye gene. In that case, every child will have at least one blue-eye gene (from the blue-eyed parent) and half will have the blue-eye recessive gene from the other parent, and thus have blue eyes. The other half will have a brown-eye dominant gene and thus have brown eyes. If two brown-eyed parents both have the blue-eye recessive gene, they could have a blue-eyed child (one chance in four).

A special case of the dominant–recessive pattern occurs with genes that are **X-linked** (located on the X chromosome). If an X-linked gene is recessive—as are the genes for most forms of color blindness, many allergies, several diseases, and some learning disabilities—the fact that it is on the X chromosome is critical (see Table 3.1).

Especially for Future Parents Suppose you wanted your daughters to be short and your sons to be tall. Could you achieve that? (see response, page 74)

dominant–recessive pattern The interaction of a heterozygous pair of alleles in such a way that the phenotype reveals the influence of one allele (the dominant gene) more than that of the other (the recessive gene).

carrier A person whose genotype includes a gene that is not expressed in the phenotype. Such an unexpressed gene occurs in half of the carrier's gametes and thus is passed on to half of the carrier's children, who will most likely be carriers, too. Generally, only when such a gene is inherited from both parents does the characteristic appear in the phenotype.

X-linked Referring to a gene carried on the X chromosome. If a male inherits an X-linked recessive trait from his mother, he expresses that trait because the Y from his father has no counteracting gene. Females are more likely to be carriers of X-linked traits but are less likely to express them.

TABLE 3.1			
The 23rd Pair and X-Linked Color Blindness			

X indicates an X chromosome with the X-linked gene for color blindness.

23rd Pair	Phenotype	Genotype	Next Generation
1. XX	Normal woman	Not a carrier	No color blindness from mother
2. XY	Normal man	Normal X from mother	No color blindness from father
3. XX	Normal woman	Carrier from father	Half her children will inherit her X. The girls with her X will be carriers; the boys with her X will be color-blind.
4. XX	Normal woman	Carrier from mother	Half her children will inherit her X. The girls with her X will be carriers; the boys with her X will be color-blind.
5. XY	Color-blind man	Inherited from mother	All his daughters will have his X. None of his sons will have his X. All his children will have normal vision, unless their mother also had an X for color blindness.
6. XX	Color-blind woman (rare)	Inherited from both parents	Every child will have one X from her. Therefore, every son will be color-blind. Daughters will be only carriers, unless they also inherit an X from the father, as their mother did.

>> Response for Future Parents (from page 73) Yes, but you wouldn't want to. You would have to choose one mate for your sons and another for your daughters, and you would have to use sex-selection methods. Even so, it might not work, given all the genes on your genotype. More important, the effort would be unethical, unnatural, and possibly illegal.

Since the Y chromosome is much smaller than the X, an X-linked recessive gene almost never has a counterpart on the Y chromosome. Therefore, recessive traits carried on the X affect the phenotypes of sons more often than those of daughters because the daughters have another X chromosome, which usually has a dominant gene. This explains, for instance, why males with an X-linked disorder got it from their mothers, not their fathers. Because of their mothers, 20 times more boys than girls are color-blind (McIntyre, 2002).

More Complications

As complex as the preceding explanation may seem, it simplifies genetic interaction by making genes appear to be separately functioning entities. But remember that genes merely direct the creation of 20 types of amino acids, which combine to produce thousands of proteins, which then form the body's structures and direct biochemical functions, influenced by genetic molecules at conception and by other epigenetic factors. The proteins of each cell interact with other proteins, nutrients, and toxins, beginning at conception and continuing throughout life (Allis et al., 2007).

For any living creature, the outcome of all the interactions involved in heredity is difficult to predict. A small deletion, repetition, or transposition in base pairs, or several extra repetitions of a triplet, may be inconsequential or may cause a major problem. Furthermore, many early genetic interactions seem to be random.

For instance, sometimes one half of a gene pair switches off during prenatal development, allowing the other free rein. When and why this happens is unpredictable—the very fact that it happens is a new discovery (Gimelbrant et al., 2007). Not quite so new is the realization that one of a female's X chromosomes becomes inactive about 10 days after conception. It seems a matter of chance whether the inactive X is from the mother or the father.

Another complication is *imprinting*, which means that some genes function differently depending on which parent they came from. The best-known examples of imprinting are two syndromes, Prader-Willi and Angelman. Both result in cognitive impairment, and both are caused by a deletion of the same small part of chromosome 15. However, if that deletion occurs on the father's chromosome 15, the child will develop Prader-Willi syndrome and become obese and slow-moving. But if that deletion is from the mother's chromosome 15, the child will have Angelman syndrome and be thin and hyperactive.

MARIA PLATT-EVANS / SCIENCE PHOTO LIBRARY

She Laughs Too Much No, not the smiling sister, but the 10-year-old on the right, who has Angelman syndrome. She inherited it from her mother's chromosome 15. Fortunately, her two siblings inherited the mother's other chromosome 15 and are normal. If she had inherited the identical deletion on her *father's* chromosome 15, she would have developed Prader-Willi syndrome, which would cause her to be overweight as well as always hungry and often angry. With Angelman syndrome, however, laughing, even at someone's pain, is a symptom.

SUMMING UP

The genes of the original zygote duplicate themselves, and then the zygote becomes two cells, four, eight, and so on. Although those first cells are stem cells, and each could become a whole person (as with monozygotic twins), soon the cells begin to differentiate as they multiply. Each cell becomes a particular type, traveling to the location on the body where it will perform whatever is needed, becoming skin, blood, bone, part of the brain, and so on. The distinction between genotype (heredity) and phenotype (manifest appearance and observed behavior) is only one of the many complexities involved in trying to understand the influence of genes on development. Genes interact with one another in many ways—some additively, some in a dominant–recessive pattern—and all are influenced by other genes. All important traits are polygenic, multifactorial, and epigenetic. ■

>> Genotype and Phenotype

The main goal of this chapter is to help every reader grasp the complex interaction between genotype and phenotype. For the past 100 years in virtually every nation, almost a million scientists have struggled to understand this complexity, with each new decade bringing advances in statistics and molecular analysis, as well as more longitudinal data that uncover various patterns.

Current Consensus

Developmentalists today accept four generalities that were surprising when first reported (Fowler & Schreiber, 2008; Plomin et al., 2008; Rutter, 2006; Worthman et al., 2010):

1. Genes affect every aspect of behavior, including social interactions, intellectual abilities, even political values and reactions.
2. Most environmental influences on children raised in the same home are *not* shared.
3. A person's genes elicit responses that shape development. Thus, personality may not be the result of childhood experience but instead may have caused those experiences.
4. Lifelong, people choose friends and environments that accept and encourage their genetic predispositions (called *niche-picking*). Thus, genetic effects *increase* with age.

Every trait, action, and attitude has a genetic component: Without genes, no development could occur; without context, genes have no power. An easy example is height, which is powerfully influenced by genes, yet in Korea, those in the North are 3 inches shorter than those in the South (Johnson, 2010; Schwekendiek, 2009). Now we examine two complex traits: addiction and visual acuity. As you read about two specific expressions of those traits (alcoholism and nearsightedness), you will see that understanding the progression from genotype to phenotype has many practical uses.

Alcoholism

At various times, people have thought of alcoholism as a moral weakness, a social scourge, or a personality defect. Alcoholics were locked up, doused with cold water, or burned at the stake. Some nations made alcohol illegal (as in the United States from 1919 to 1933). Every nation has passed laws forbidding certain drugs, restricting others, and accepting still others—including those forbidden elsewhere. Now we know that inherited biochemistry makes some people vulnerable to alcoholism and drug use, so various proposed cures do not apply equally to everyone.

Of course, anyone can abuse drugs, but genes create an addictive pull that can be overpowering, extremely weak, or somewhere in between. Each person's biochemistry reacts to alcohol, causing sleep, nausea, aggression, joy, relaxation, forgetfulness, sexiness, or tears. How their bodies metabolize alcohol allows some

Shyness Is Universal Inhibition is a psychological trait that is influenced by genetics. It is more common at some ages (late infancy and early adolescence) and in some gene pools (natives of northern Europe and East Asia) than others. But every community includes some individuals who are unmistakably shy, such as this toddler in Woleai, more than 3,000 miles west of Hawaii.

Especially for Future Drug Counselors Is the wish for excitement likely to lead to addiction? (see response, page 76)

AP PHOTO / PELLE RINK / POLFOTO

Is He Drunk? This worker at Carlsberg Breweries in Copenhagen was one of many who benefited from company policy—beer available all day long from coolers placed throughout the work floor. In 2010, the policy changed: No more coolers, and beer could be consumed only at lunch. Many employees walked off their jobs in protest. Social attitudes about alcohol added intensity to this labor–management conflict.

heritability A statistic that indicates what percentage of the variation in a particular trait within a particular population, in a particular context and era, can be traced to genes.

>> Response for Future Drug Counselors (from page 75) Maybe. Some people who love risk become addicts; others develop a healthy lifestyle that includes adventure, new people, and exotic places. Any trait can lead in various directions. You need to be aware of the connection so that you can steer your clients toward healthy adventures.

people to "hold their liquor" and therefore abuse alcohol, while others (including many East Asians) sweat and become red-faced after just a few sips, an embarrassing response that may lead to abstinence.

Alcoholism is inherited via psychological as well as biochemical tendencies (Macgregor et al., 2009). Some inherited personality traits (a quick temper, sensation seeking, high anxiety) encourage drinking and drugging. Furthermore, certain contexts, such as fraternity parties, make it hard to avoid alcohol; other contexts, such as a church social in a "dry" county, make it hard to swallow anything stronger than lemonade.

Biological sex (XX or XY) and gender (cultural) also affect the risk of alcoholism. For biological reasons (body size, fat composition, metabolism), women become drunk after consuming less alcohol than would make men drunk, but how much they drink is cultural. For example, in Japan, both sexes have the same genes for metabolizing alcohol, yet women drink only about one-tenth as much as men. When Japanese women live in the United States, their alcohol consumption increases about fivefold, on average (Higuchi et al., 1996). It seems as if some genes on chromosome 11 increase the risk of alcoholism, but no scientist thinks the cause of this disease is solely genetic (Edenberg et al., 2010).

Nearsightedness

Age, genes, and culture affect vision as well. First consider age. Newborns cannot focus on anything more than 2 feet away; children see better each year until about age 8; at adolescence, the eyeball shape changes, increasing nearsightedness (myopia); in middle age, shape changes again, decreasing myopia.

Now consider genes. A study of British twins found that the Pax6 gene, which governs eye formation, has many alleles that make people somewhat nearsighted (Hammond et al., 2004). This research found heritability of almost 90 percent, which means that if one monozygotic twin is nearsighted, the other twin is almost always nearsighted, too.

However, **heritability** is a statistic that indicates only how much of the variation in a particular trait *within a particular population* in a particular context and era can be traced to genes. For example, the heritability of height is very high (about 95 percent) when children receive good medical care and ample nourishment but low (about 20 percent) when children are malnourished. Thus, the 90 percent heritability of nearsightedness among the British children may not apply elsewhere.

Indeed it does not. In some places, visual problems are caused by the environment. In many African nations, heritability of visual acuity is close to zero because a dietary lack of vitamin A is the main reason some children see less well than others. Scientists are working to develop a strain of maize (the local staple) high in vitamin A. If they succeed, heritability will increase as both nearsightedness and farsightedness decrease (Harjes et al., 2008). But what about children who are well nourished? Is their vision entirely inherited? Cross-cultural research suggests that it is not.

One report claims "myopia is increasing at an 'epidemic' rate, particularly in East Asia" (Park & Congdon, 2004, p. 21), and another cites "very strong environmental impacts" on Asian children's vision (Morgan, 2003, p. 276). The first published research on this phenomenon appeared in 1992, when scholars noticed that, in army-mandated medical exams of all 17-year-old males in Singapore, 43 percent were nearsighted in 1990 compared with only 26 percent a decade earlier (Tay et al., 1992). Further studies found nearsightedness increasing from 12 to 84 percent between ages 6 and 17 in Taiwan, with increases in myopia during middle childhood also in Singapore and Hong Kong (cited in Grosvenor, 2003).

One possible culprit is homework. In Chapter 12, you will learn that, unlike their parents, contemporary East Asian children are amazingly proficient in math and science, partly because they spend far more time studying than did their parents or than do their peers in other nations. As their developing eyes focus on the pages in front of them, those with a genetic vulnerability to myopia may lose acuity for objects far away—which is exactly what nearsightedness means.

A study of Singaporean 10- to 12-year-olds found a correlation between nearsightedness (measured by optometric exams) and high achievement, especially in language (presumably reflecting more reading). Correlation is not causation, but statistics (odds ratio of 2.5 and significance of 0.001) suggest a link (Saw et al., 2007).

Ophthalmologists believe that the underlying problem is not time studying but inadequate time spent in daylight. Perhaps if Asian children spent more time outside playing, walking, or relaxing, fewer might need glasses (Goss, 2002; Grosvenor, 2003). This recommendation is supported by an editorial in a leading U.S. journal for opthalmologists:

Bright-Eyed and Nearsighted These are star students from Beijing, China, waiting in line for visas to the United States. If they had spent less time studying, would they be here?

> The probability of becoming myopic by the eighth grade is about 60% if a child has two myopic parents and does less than 5 hours per week of sports/outdoor activity. . . . [It is] about 20% if a two-myopic-parent child does 14 hours or more per week of sports/outdoor activity.
>
> [Mutti & Zadnik, 2009, p. 77]

Between the early 1970s and the early 2000s, nearsightedness in the United States increased from 25 to 42 percent (Vitale et al., 2009). Other research finds that urbanization, television, and fear of strangers has kept many U.S. children indoors most of the time. The correlation between these two sets of statistics does not prove cause. A longitudinal experiment, with some children kept indoors while others from the same families play outside, is obviously impossible. Nonetheless, the accumulated evidence on the relationship among genotype, environment, and phenotype has many applications.

Practical Applications

Since genes affect every disorder, no one should be blamed or punished for inherited problems. However, knowing the importance of the environment leads to action whenever a genetic vulnerability is apparent. For instance, if alcoholism is in the genes, parents can keep alcohol away from their home and children, which might let the potential alcoholic become cognitively and socially mature before drinking. If nearsightedness runs in the family, parents can make sure that children spend time each day playing outdoors.

Of course, abstention from alcohol and ample outdoor play are recommended for every child, as are dozens of other behaviors, such as flossing the teeth, saying "thank you," getting enough sleep, eating vegetables, and writing thank-you notes. However, no parent can enforce every recommendation. Awareness of genetic risks helps parents set priorities and act on them.

Ignoring the nature–nurture interaction can be lethal. Consider baseball superstar Mickey Mantle, who hit more home runs in World Series baseball than any other player. Most of his male relatives were alcoholics and died before middle age, including his father, who died of Hodgkin disease (a form of cancer) at age 39. Mantle became "a notorious alcoholic [because he] believed a family history of early mortality meant he would die young" (Jaffe, 2004, p. 37). He ignored his genetic predisposition to alcohol.

At age 46 Mantle said, "If I knew I was going to live this long I would have taken better care of myself." He never developed Hodgkin disease, and if he had, chemotherapy developed since his father's death would have saved him, an example of environment prevailing over genes. However, drinking destroyed his liver. He understood only too late what he had done: When he was dying, he told his fans at Yankee Stadium: "Please don't do drugs and alcohol. God gave us only one body, keep it healthy. If you want to do something great, be an organ donor" (quoted in Begos, 2010). Despite a last-minute liver transplant, he died at age 63—15 years sooner than most men of his time.

SUMMING UP

Genes affect every trait—whether it is something wonderful, such as a wacky sense of humor; something fearful, such as a violent temper; or something quite ordinary, such as a tendency to be bored. The environment affects every trait as well, in ways that change as maturational, cultural, and historical processes unfold. Genes themselves can be modified through epigenetic factors, including drugs and nutrition. Furthermore, genetic expression can be directed or deflected, depending on the culture and the society as well as on the individual and the family. This is apparent in alcoholism, nearsightedness, and almost every other physical and psychological condition. All have genetic roots, developmental patterns, and environmental triggers. ■

>> Chromosomal and Genetic Problems

We now focus on conditions caused by an extra chromosome or a single gene. These are abnormalities in that they are not the usual, the typical, the norm (hence abnormal). Three reasons make these conditions relevant to our study:

1. They provide insight into the complexities of nature and nurture.
2. Knowing their origins helps limit their effects.
3. Information combats prejudice: Difference is not deficit.

Not Exactly 46

Usually, each sperm and each ovum has 23 chromosomes, and the zygote they create has 46. However, some gametes have more or fewer than 23 chromosomes. One variable that correlates with chromosomal abnormalities is the parents' age, particularly the age of the mother. A suggested explanation is that, since ova begin to form before a girl is born, older mothers have older ova, which are more likely to split 22–24 instead of 23–23.

These miscounts are not rare—about 5 to 10 percent of all zygotes have more or fewer than 46 chromosomes (Brooker, 2009). Far fewer are born, less than 1 percent, primarily because most such zygotes never duplicate, divide, and differentiate. Many of the rest are aborted spontaneously or by choice. Birth itself is hazardous; About 5 percent of stillborn (dead-at-birth) babies have 47 chromosomes (O. J. Miller & Therman, 2001).

Once in about every 200 births, a newborn survives with 45, 47, or, rarely, 48 or 49 chromosomes. Each abnormality leads to a recognizable *syndrome*, a cluster of distinct characteristics that tend to occur together. Usually the cause is three chromosomes (a condition called a *trisomy*) at a particular location instead of the usual two.

Down Syndrome

The most common extra-chromosome condition that results in a surviving child is **Down syndrome,** also called *trisomy-21* because the person has three copies of chromosome 21. According to one estimate, a 20-year-old woman has about 1 chance in 800 of carrying a fetus with Down syndrome; a 39-year-old woman, 1 in 67; and a 44-year-old woman, 1 in 16.

Some 300 distinct characteristics can result from the presence of that third chromosome 21. No individual with Down syndrome is identical to another, but most have specific facial characteristics—a thick tongue, round face, slanted eyes—as well as distinctive hands, feet, and fingerprints. Many also have hearing problems, heart abnormalities, muscle weakness, and short stature. They are usually slower to develop intellectually, especially in language (W. I. Cohen, 2005). Their eventual intellect varies: Some are severely retarded; others are of average or even above-average intelligence, partly because of epigenetics and partly because of family support.

Problems of the 23rd Pair

Every human has at least 44 autosomes and one X chromosome; an embryo cannot develop without those 45. However, about 1 in every 500 infants is born with only one sex chromosome (no Y) or with three or more (not just two) (Hamerton & Evans, 2005). Having an odd number of sex chromosomes impairs cognitive and psychosocial development as well as sexual maturation. The specifics depend on the particular configuration as well as on other genetic factors (Mazzocco & Ross, 2007).

Gene Disorders

Everyone carries alleles that *could* produce serious diseases or handicaps in the next generation (see Table 3.2). Most such genes have no serious consequences because they are recessive. The phenotype is affected only when the inherited condition is dominant or when a zygote is homozygous for a particular recessive condition.

Dominant-Gene Disorders

Most of the 7,000 *known* single-gene disorders are dominant (always expressed). They are usually easy to notice: Their effects are evident in the phenotype. Severe dominant disorders are rare because children with such disorders rarely live to pass the gene on.

One exception is *Huntington disease,* a fatal central nervous system disorder caused by a genetic miscode—more than 35 repetitions of a particular triplet. Unlike most dominant traits, the effects do not begin until middle adulthood. By then a person could have several children, and odds are that half would inherit the same dominant gene. This was true for the original Mr. Huntington (Bates et al., 2002). Another exception is a rare but severe form of Alzheimer disease that causes dementia before age 60.

Universal Happiness All young children delight in painting brightly colored pictures on a big canvas, but this scene is unusual for two reasons: Daniel has trisomy-21, and this photograph was taken at the only school in Chile where normal and special-needs children share classrooms.

REUTERS / CLAUDIA DAUT

Down syndrome A condition in which a person has 47 chromosomes instead of the usual 46, with 3 rather than 2 chromosomes at the 21st site. People with Down syndrome typically have distinctive characteristics, including unusual facial features, heart abnormalities, and language difficulties. (Also called *trisomy-21*.)

Especially for Future Doctors Might a patient who is worried about his or her sexuality have an undiagnosed abnormality of the sex chromosome? (see response, page 82)

Especially for Teachers Suppose you know that one of your students has a sibling who has Down syndrome. What special actions should you take? (see response, page 83)

TABLE 3.2

Common Genetic Diseases and Conditions

Name	Description	Prognosis	Probable Inheritance	Incidence*	Carrier Detection?[†]	Prenatal Detection?
Albinism	No melanin; person is very blond and pale	Normal, but must avoid sun damage	Recessive	Rare overall; 1 in 8 Hopi Indians is a carrier	No	No
Alzheimer disease	Loss of memory and increasing mental impairment	Eventual death, often after years of dependency	Early onset—dominant; after age 60—multifactorial	Fewer than 1 in 100 middle-aged adults; perhaps 25 percent of adults over age 85	Yes, for some genes; ApoE4 allele increases incidence	No
Cancer	Tumors that can spread	With early diagnosis and treatment, most are cured; without them, death usually within 3 years	Multifactorial; almost all cancers have a genetic component	More than half of all people develop some form of cancer; about one-fourth die of it	No	No
Cleft palate, cleft lip	The two sides of the upper lip or palate are not joined	Correctable by surgery	Multifactorial	1 in every 700 births; more common in Asian Americans and American Indians	No	Yes
Club foot	The foot and ankle are twisted	Correctable by surgery	Multifactorial	1 in every 200 births; more common in boys	No	Yes
Cystic fibrosis	Mucous obstructions, especially in lungs and digestive organs	Most live to middle adulthood	Recessive gene; also spontaneous mutations	1 in 3,200; 1 in 25 European Americans is a carrier	Sometimes	Yes, in most cases
Deafness (congenital)	Inability to hear	Deaf children can learn sign language; early cochlear implants allow normal language	Multifactorial; some forms are recessive	1 in 1,000 births; more common in people from Middle East	No	No
Diabetes	Abnormal sugar metabolism because of insufficient insulin	Early onset (type 1) fatal without insulin; for later onset (type 2), variable risks	Multifactorial; for later onset, body weight is significant	Type 1: 1 in 500 births; more common in American Indians and African Americans Type 2: 1 adult in 6 by age 60	No	No
Hemophilia	Absence of clotting factor in blood	Death from internal bleeding; blood transfusions prevent damage	X-linked recessive; also spontaneous mutations	1 in 10,000 males; royal families of England, Russia, and Germany had it	Yes	Yes
Hydrocephalus	Obstruction causes excess fluid in the brain	Brain damage and death; surgery can make normal life possible	Multifactorial	1 in every 100 births	No	Yes

*Incidence statistics vary from country to country; those given here are for the United States. All these diseases can occur in any ethnic group. Many affected groups limit transmission through genetic counseling; for example, the incidence of Tay-Sachs disease is declining because many Jewish young adults obtain testing and counseling before marriage.
[†]"Yes" refers to carrier detection. Family history can also reveal genetic risk.

Name	Description	Prognosis	Probable Inheritance	Incidence*	Carrier Detection?[†]	Prenatal Detection?
Muscular dystrophy (30 diseases)	Weakening of muscles	Inability to walk, move; wasting away and sometimes death	Recessive or multifactorial	1 in every 3,500 males develops Duchenne's	Yes, for some forms	Yes, for some forms
Neural-tube defects (open spine)	Anencephaly (parts of the brain missing) or spina bifida (lower spine not closed)	Anencephalic—severe retardation; spina bifida—poor lower body control	Multifactorial; folic acid deficit and genes	Anencephaly—1 in 1,000 births; spina bifida—3 in 1,000; more common in Welsh and Scots	No	Yes
Phenylketo-nuria (PKU)	Abnormal digestion of protein	Mental retardation, preventable by diet begun soon after birth	Recessive	1 in 100 European Americans is a carrier, especially those of Norwegian or Irish descent	Yes	Yes
Pyloric stenosis	Overgrowth of muscle in intestine	Vomiting, loss of weight, eventual death; correctable by surgery	Multifactorial	1 male in 200, 1 female in 1,000; less common in African Americans	No	No
Rett syndrome	Neurological developmental disorder	Boys die at birth. At 6–18 months, girls lose communication and motor abilities	X-linked	1 in 10,000 female births	No	Sometimes
Schizo-phrenia	Severely distorted thought processes	No cure; drugs, hospitalization, psychotherapy ease symptoms	Multifactorial	1 in 100 people develop it by early adulthood	No	No
Sickle-cell anemia	Abnormal blood cells	Possible painful "crisis"; heart and kidney failure; treatable with drugs	Recessive	1 in 11 African Americans and 1 in 20 Latinos are carriers	Yes	Yes
Tay-Sachs disease	Enzyme disease	Healthy infant becomes weaker, usually dying by age 5	Recessive	1 in 30 U.S. Jews and 1 in 20 French Canadians are carriers	Yes	Yes
Thalassemia	Abnormal blood cells	Paleness and listlessness, low resistance to infections, slow growth	Usually recessive, occasionally dominant	1 in 10 Americans from southern Europe, northern Africa, or south Asia is a carrier	Yes	Yes
Tourette syndrome	Uncontrollable tics, body jerking, verbal outbursts	Appears at about age 5; worsens then improves with age	Dominant, but variable penetrance	1 in 250 children	Sometimes	No

Sources: Benacerraf, 2007; Briley & Sulser, 2001; Butler & Meaney, 2005; Haydon, 2007; Hemminki et al., 2008; Klug et al., 2008; Mange & Mange, 1999; McKusick, 2007; K. L. Moore & Persaud, 2007; Shahin et al., 2002.

>> Response for Future Doctors
(from page 79) That is highly unlikely. Chromosomal abnormalities are evident long before adulthood. It is quite normal for adults to be worried about sexuality for social, not biological, reasons. If necessary, you could test the karyotype, but that may be needlessly alarmist.

fragile X syndrome A genetic disorder in which part of the X chromosome seems to be attached to the rest of it by a very thin string of molecules. The cause is a single gene that has more than 200 repetitions of one triplet.

Especially for Historians Some genetic diseases may have changed the course of history. For instance, the last czar of Russia had four healthy daughters and one son with hemophilia. Once called the *royal disease*, hemophilia is X-linked. How could this rare condition have affected the monarchies of Russia, England, Austria, Germany, and Spain? (see response, page 85)

genetic counseling Consultation and testing by trained experts that enable individuals to learn about their genetic heritage, including harmful conditions that they might pass along to any children they may conceive.

Recessive Disorders

Several genetic disorders are sex-linked. The most famous of these is hemophilia, a blood disorder carried by Queen Victoria of England. She passed it on to her descendants, including Empress Alexandra, who bore the only male heir to the Russian throne, Crown Prince Alexi (Rogaev et al., 2009). Historians suggest that X-linked hemophilia was a pivotal cause of antimonarchy revolutions, including the one that led to Communism in Russia in 1917. Alexi's parents were distracted from leading the nation and were vulnerable to irrational advice from Rasputin, a psychopathic "healer."

Another X-linked condition, **fragile X syndrome,** is caused by more than 200 repetitions of one triplet on one gene (Plomin et al., 2003). (Some repetitions are normal, but not this many.) The cognitive deficits caused by fragile X syndrome are the most common form of *inherited* mental retardation (many other forms, such as trisomy-21, are not inherited) (Sherman, 2002).

Since this is an X-linked, single-gene disorder, fragile X syndrome may be recessive; however, the exact inheritance pattern of fragile X is more complex than that of other X-linked conditions. Repetitions of the damaging triplet increase when the affected X chromosome passes from one generation to the next; more repetitions correlate with lower IQ, especially in boys.

Most recessive disorders are on the autosomes and thus are not X-linked. For example, cystic fibrosis, thalassemia, and sickle-cell anemia are all equally common and devastating in both sexes (see Table 3.2). About 1 in 12 North Americans is a carrier for one of these three. That high incidence occurs because carriers benefit from the gene (Brooker, 2009).

The most studied example is sickle-cell anemia. Carriers of sickle cell die less often from malaria, still prevalent in parts of Africa. Indeed, there are four distinct alleles that cause it, each originating in a malaria-prone region. Selective adaptation allowed the gene to become widespread because it protected more people (the carriers) than it killed. About 11 percent of Americans whose ancestors were African carry the gene. Similarly, cystic fibrosis is more common among Americans with ancestors from northern Europe; carriers may once have been protected from cholera.

Genetic Counseling and Testing

Until recently, after the birth of a child with a disorder, couples blamed witches or fate, not genes or chromosomes. Today, many young adults worry about their genes long before they marry. Virtually everyone has a relative with a serious condition, and everyone wonders what their children will inherit.

Genetic counseling relieves some worries by providing facts and helping prospective parents discuss sensitive issues. Counselors must be carefully trained to communicate clearly, because many people, especially when considering personal and emotional information, misinterpret words such as *risks* and *probability* (O'Doherty, 2006). Even doctors do not always understand. Consider the experience of one of my students. A month before she became pregnant, Jeannette was required to have a rubella vaccination for her job. Hearing this, her prenatal care doctor gave her the following prognosis:

> My baby would be born with many defects, his ears would not be normal, he would be mentally retarded. . . . I went home and cried for hours and hours. . . . I finally went to see a genetic counselor. Everything was fine, thank the Lord, thank you, my beautiful baby is okay.

[Jeannette, personal communication, 2008]

Preconception, prenatal, or even prenuptial (before marriage) genetic testing and counseling are recommended for everyone, especially for these groups:

- Individuals who have a parent, sibling, or child with a serious genetic condition
- Couples who have had several spontaneous abortions or stillbirths
- Couples who are infertile
- Couples from the same ethnic group, particularly if they are relatives
- Women over age 35 and men over age 40

Genetic counselors follow two ethical guidelines. First, tests are confidential, beyond the reach of insurance companies and public records. Second, decisions are made by the clients, not by the counselors. However, these guidelines are not always easy to follow.

A quandary arises when genetic tests on a child with a severe recessive disease reveal that the husband does not carry the gene. Should the counselor tell the couple that they have zero chance of having another baby with this problem without revealing that the man is not the biological father? Counselors vary in how they handle this (Lucast, 2007). Sometimes couples make a decision (such as to continue or to abort a pregnancy) that is not what the counselor would do. The professional must explain facts and risks, probabilities and projections, and then let the clients' decide.

Genetic counselors, scientists, and the general public usually favor testing, reasoning that knowledge is better than ignorance. However, high-risk individuals (who might hear bad news) do not always agree: They fear the truth might jeopardize their marriage, their insurance coverage, or their willingness to become parents.

Sometimes people have no choice because testing is legally required. This is the case for **phenylketonuria (PKU).** Newborns with the double recessive gene for PKU become severely retarded if they consume phenylalanine, an amino acid found in many foods. But if they maintain a diet free of phenylalanine, they develop almost normally (Hillman, 2005). Parents need to start newborns on the special diet immediately (which is why testing is required), but knowing that a child has PKU itself might change the parenting (which is why the information needs to be sensitively transmitted).

Tests for dozens of other conditions are routinely administered to newborns (specifics vary by U.S. state and by nation). Although many developmentalists advocate testing, since early diagnosis can reduce many problems, counseling is also needed. In one study of newborn testing, some parents wanted facts and others wanted emotional support. They were often distressed if they wanted one of these but received the other (Tluczek et al., 2006).

Many factors require individualized counseling. Decisions affect the adults' relationship, other children, and relatives, as well as the larger community (McConkie-Rosell & O'Daniel, 2007). Some people want tests that counselors would not recommend (see the following feature); counseling is especially needed when risks and benefits are not understood. Unfortunately, misunderstanding is common. For example, half of a large group of women misinterpreted an explanation (written for the general public) about tests for genes that make breast cancer more likely (Hanoch et al., 2010).

>> **Response for Teachers** (from page 79) As the text says, "information combats prejudice." Your first step would be to make sure you know about Down syndrome, reading material about it. You would learn, among other things, that it is not usually inherited (your student need not worry about his or her progeny) and that some children with Down syndrome need extra medical and educational attention. This might mean you need to pay special attention to your student.

ROBERT SPENCER / THE NEW YORK TIMES

"The Hardest Decision I Ever Had to Make" That's how this woman described her decision to terminate her third pregnancy when genetic testing revealed that the fetus had Down syndrome. She soon became pregnant again with a male fetus that had the normal 46 chromosomes, as did her two daughters and as will her fourth child, not yet born. Many personal factors influence such decisions. Do you think she and her husband would have made the same choice if they had had no other children?

phenylketonuria (PKU) A genetic disorder in which a child's body is unable to metabolize an amino acid called phenylalanine. Unless the infant immediately begins a special diet, the resulting buildup of phenylalanine in body fluids causes brain damage, progressive mental retardation, and other symptoms.

A VIEW FROM SCIENCE

Genetic Testing for Psychological Disorders

Might your genes increase your chances of developing a psychological disorder—say schizophrenia, or dementia, or bipolar disorder, or autism, or addiction? If so, should you seek genetic testing to learn more? The answer to these two questions from science is yes, and then no.

Psychological disorders are multifactorial, and everyone is vulnerable to some inherited conditions. Genes increase vulnerability, but the environment has a crucial influence. You have already seen this in the discussion of the MAOA gene and development of an antisocial personality in Chapter 1. The same is true for almost every psychological condition.

Consider, for example, schizophrenia, a devastating condition that distorts thought and gives rise to hallucinations, delusions, garbled talk, and irrational emotions. When one monozygotic twin becomes schizophrenic, often—but not always—the other identical twin develops a psychological disorder. For dyzygotic twins and other siblings, the risk is much lower—about 12 percent for schizophrenia—but higher than the 1 percent incidence of schizophrenia for people who have no relatives with the disease. This leaves no doubt that genes are one factor (Castle & Morgan, 2008).

Yet dozens of environmental conditions correlate with schizophrenia. Of course, twins are no more vulnerable to any genetic condition than nontwins, but if one MZ twin develops schizophrenia, about half of the time the other one does, too. That means that about half the time the other twin escapes, even though having the same genes puts the co-twin at risk. Similar

evidence for both nature and nurture comes from children born to schizophrenic parents: If both parents have the disease, 27 percent of their children develop it; if one parent is affected, 7 percent of the children will be as well. The other way to present these statistics is to say that 73 percent of the children with two schizophrenic parents escape the disease, and half of them have no serious psychiatric conditions at all (Gottesman et al., 2010) (see the Research Design).

These numbers make it obvious that schizophrenia is not simply genetic. Among the environmental causes are undernutrition of the mother during pregnancy, birth in the summer, use of psychoactive drugs in adolescence, emigration to another nation as a young adult, and family emotionality during adulthood. Because environment is crucial and many genes that increase vulnerability to schizophrenia remain to be found, few scientists think anyone would benefit from genetic testing for schizophrenia. Some worry that a positive test would lead to depression, lack of therapy, and more stigma against those who have mental illness than already exists (Mitchell et al., 2010).

Another example is testing for the ApoE4 allele. Compared to people without that allele, a person with one ApoE4 allele has 8 times the risk of developing Alzheimer-type dementia in old age and a person with two such alleles has 20 times the risk. Many researchers test adults for ApoE4, but almost none tell them the results. Why? Some people with the double allele never become demented and some people without it do. The results create worry for carriers and perhaps bring false assurance to those who are not.

Despite the reluctance of researchers to tell people their ApoE status, many people seek out laboratories that will perform the tests. If they learn that their risk is higher than average, many buy long-term-care insurance—which may be a good investment for them but is a bad one for insurance companies (D. H. Taylor et al., 2010). The goal of good health care for everyone is another reason genetic testing may be harmful: If insurance is bought only by those at high risk, then costs will skyrocket, and if people get sick but did not buy insurance because they thought they wouldn't need it, either they will get inferior care or their fellow citizens will pay.

Genes have been discovered that add a small bit of risk regarding virtually every condition, not only diseases but also personality and intellectual traits. Many people are curious, and many companies want to sell diagnostic tests. In several U.S. states (California and New York among them), selling genetic tests is illegal without a physician's request. Some people break the law to get the information they want. Should those lawbreakers be punished, or are laws and scientists interfering with personal freedom?

COURTESY OF EDNA MORLOK

Too Cute? This portrait of the Genain sisters was taken 20 years before they all developed schizophrenia. However, from their identical hair ribbons to the identical position of their feet, it is apparent that their unusual status as quadruplets set them apart as curiosities. Could their life in the spotlight have nurtured their potential for schizophrenia? There is no way to know for sure.

> ### Research Design
>
> **Scientists:** Irving I. Gottesman, Thomas Munk Laursen, Aksel Bertelsen, and Preben Bo Mortensen.
>
> **Publication:** *Archives of General Psychiatry* (2010).
>
> **Participants:** Everyone born in Denmark between 1968 and 1997 whose parents were listed in the Denmark population archives.
>
> **Design:** The researchers traced the hospital admissions of the children's parents, noting admission for psychiatric disorders. They found 196 couples (with 270 children) in which both the mother and father were hospitalized for schizophrenia and 83 couples (with 146 children) who were both admitted for bipolar disorder. The psychiatric records of all the children (more than 2 million of them), aged 10 to 52 at the time of the study, were examined.
>
> **Results:** Children born to parents with psychological disorders had much higher rates than average of developing a disorder. When both parents were schizophrenic, 27 percent of the children were hospitalized for schizophrenia and 12 percent had other severe disorders. With only one schizophrenic parent, 7 percent developed the disorder, and when no parent was hospitalized for schizophrenia, less than 1 percent (0.86 percent) of the children were. Disorders (including depression) were also common among children of bipolar parents, although the rate was lower than for children whose parents were schizophrenic.
>
> **Major conclusions:** Genes confer vulnerability for serious mental disorders, especially schizophrenia. However, more than half of the children born to a schizophrenic mother and father escaped serious disorders themselves, and about 20,000 Danes who were hospitalized for schizophrenia had neither parent with the disorder.
>
> **Comments:** This is an impressive study, since it included both parents of more than 2 million children. Such powerful research on a large population group with verified records (not just a selected sample with the researchers' assessment) is possible only in relatively small developed nations with accurate records. Note, however, that the data are correlational. Even in Denmark, where every child gets good medical care, social services, and education, some of the burden of family schizophrenia may result from nurture, not nature.

For every condition, including unusual talents, learning abilities, and diseases, the interaction of genes and the environment makes development over the life span unpredictable, even if the genes are known. Some leaders in genetic research stress that changes in the environment, not in the genes, are the most promising direction for "disease prevention and more effective health maintenance" (Schwartz & Collins, 2007, p. 696). Much depends on the family and society. Genes are part of the human story, influencing every page, but they do not determine the plot or the final paragraph.

SUMMING UP

Every person is a carrier for some serious genetic conditions. Most of them are rare, which makes it unlikely that the combination of sperm and ovum will produce severe disabilities. A few exceptional recessive-gene diseases are common because carriers were protected against some lethal conditions in their communities. They survived to reproduce, and the gene spread throughout the population. Most serious dominant diseases disappear because the person dies before they have children, but a few dominant conditions continue because their effects are not evident until after the childbearing years are over.

Often a zygote does not have 46 chromosomes. Such zygotes rarely develop to birth, with two primary exceptions: Down syndrome (trisomy-21) and abnormalities of the sex chromosomes. Genetic counseling helps couples clarify their values and understand the risks before they conceive, but every decision raises ethical questions. Counselors try to explain facts and probabilities. The final decision is made by those directly involved. ∎

>> **Response for Historians** (from page 82) Hemophilia is a painful chronic disease that (before blood transfusions became feasible) killed a boy before he could reach adulthood. Though rare, it ran in European royal families, whose members often intermarried, which meant that many queens (including England's Queen Victoria) were carriers of hemophilia and thus were destined to watch half their sons die of it. All families, even rulers of nations, are distracted from their work when they have a child with a mysterious and lethal illness. Some historians believe that hemophilia among European royalty was an underlying cause of the Russian Revolution of 1917 as well as of the spread of democracy in the nineteenth and twentieth centuries.

SUMMARY

The Genetic Code

1. Genes are the foundation for all development, first instructing the living creature to form the body and brain and then influencing thought and behavior. Human conception occurs when two gametes (an ovum and a sperm, each with 23 chromosomes) combine to form a zygote, 46 chromosomes in a single cell.

2. Genes and chromosomes from each parent match up to make the zygote. The match is not always perfect because of genetic variations called alleles.

3. The sex of an embryo depends on the sperm: A Y sperm creates an XY (male) embryo; an X sperm creates an XX (female) embryo. Virtually every cell of every living creature has the unique genetic code of the zygote that began that life. The human genome contains about 20,000 genes in all.

4. Twins occur if a zygote splits into two separate beings (monozygotic, or identical, twins) or if two ova are fertilized by two sperm (dizygotic, or fraternal, twins). Monozygotic multiples are genetically the same. Dizygotic multiples have only half of their genes in common, as do all other siblings who have the same parents.

5. Assisted reproductive technology (ART), including drugs and in vitro fertilization, have led not only to the birth of millions of much-wanted babies but also to an increase in multiple births, which have a higher rate of medical problems. Several aspects of ART raise ethical and medical questions.

From One Cell to Many

6. Genes interact in various ways, sometimes additively, with each gene contributing to development, and sometimes in a dominant–recessive pattern. Environmental factors influence the phenotype as well. Epigenetics is the study of all the environmental factors that affect the expression of genes, including the DNA that surrounds the genes at conception.

7. The environment interacts with the genetic instructions for every trait, even for physical appearance. Every aspect of a person is almost always multifactorial and polygenic.

8. The first few divisions of a zygote are stem cells, capable of becoming any part of a person. Then cells differentiate, specializing in a particular function.

9. Combinations of chromosomes, interactions among genes, and myriad influences from the environment all ensure both similarity and diversity within and between species. This aids health and survival.

Genotype and Phenotype

10. Environmental influences are crucial for almost every complex trait, with each person experiencing different environments. Customs and contexts differ markedly.

11. Genetic makeup can make a person susceptible to a variety of conditions; nongenetic factors also affect susceptibility. Examples include alcoholism and nearsightedness. Cultural and familial differences in both of these problems are dramatic evidence for the role of nurture.

12. Knowing the impact of genes and the environment can be helpful. People are less likely to blame someone for a characteristic that is inherited, and realizing that someone is at risk of a serious condition helps with prevention.

Chromosomal and Genetic Problems

13. Often a gamete has fewer or more than 23 chromosomes. The result is a zygote with an odd number of chromosomes.

14. Usually zygotes with other than 46 chromosomes do not develop. The main exceptions involve three chromosomes at the 21st location (Down syndrome, or trisomy-21) or an odd number of sex chromosomes. In such cases, the affected child has physical and cognitive problems but can live a nearly normal life.

15. Everyone is a carrier for genetic abnormalities. Usually genetic disorders are recessive (not affecting the phenotype); if they are dominant, the trait is usually mild, varied, or inconsequential until late adulthood. When carrier status is protective, then selective adaptation results in that gene becoming widespread, as with malaria and the sickle-cell trait.

16. Genetic testing and counseling can help many couples. Testing usually provides information about possibilities, not actualities. Couples, counselors, and cultures differ in the decisions they make when risks are known.

KEY TERMS

deoxyribonucleic acid (DNA) (p. 62)
chromosome (p. 62)
gene (p. 62)
allele (p. 62)
genome (p. 62)
zygote (p. 63)
gamete (p. 63)
genotype (p. 64)

homozygous (p. 64)
heterozygous (p. 65)
23rd pair (p. 65)
XX (p. 65)
XY (p. 65)
stem cells (p. 67)
monozygotic (MZ) twins (p. 68)
dizygotic (DZ) twins (p. 68)

assisted reproductive technology (ART) (p. 69)
in vitro fertilization (IVF) (p. 69)
phenotype (p. 71)
polygenic (p. 71)
multifactorial (p. 71)
epigenetic (p. 71)
Human Genome Project (p. 72)

dominant–recessive pattern (p. 73)
carrier (p. 73)
X-linked (p. 73)
heritability (p. 76)
Down syndrome (p. 79)
fragile X syndrome (p. 82)
genetic counseling (p. 82)
phenylketonuria (PKU) (p. 83)

WHAT HAVE YOU LEARNED?

The Genetic Code

1. How many pairs of chromosomes and pairs of genes does a person usually have?

2. What is the relationship between genes, base pairs, and alleles?

3. Why is a person's genotype not usually apparent in the phenotype?

4. In nature, what determines a person's sex and how can nurture affect that?

5. What are the advantages and disadvantages of being a monozygotic twin?

6. Why does in vitro fertilization increase the incidence of dizygotic twins?

From One Cell to Many

7. What is the difference between an epigenetic characteristic and a multifactorial one?

8. Why do polygenetic traits suggest that additive genes are more common than dominant–recessive ones?

9. What surprises came from the Human Genome Project?

Genotype and Phenotype

10. Regarding heritability, why is it important to know which group provided the data?

11. What nature and nurture reasons make one person an alcoholic and another not?

12. What nature and nurture reasons make one person nearsighted and another not?

13. What can be learned from Micky Mantle's life?

Chromosomal and Genetic Problems

14. Why does this textbook on normal development include abnormal development?

15. What usually happens when a zygote has fewer or more than 46 chromosomes?

16. What are the consequences if a newborn is born with trisomy-21?

17. Why are relatively few genetic conditions dominant?

18. Why are a few recessive traits (such as sickle cell) quite common?

19. What are the advantages and disadvantages of genetic testing?

20. Why do people need genetic counselors, not merely fact sheets about genetic conditions?

APPLICATIONS

1. Pick one of your traits, and explain the influences that both nature *and* nurture have on it. For example, if you have a short temper, explain its origins in your genetics, your culture, and your childhood experiences.

2. Many adults have a preference for having a son or a daughter. Interview adults of several ages and backgrounds about their preferences. If they give the socially preferable answer ("It does not matter"), ask how they think the two sexes differ. Listen and take notes—don't debate. Analyze the implications of the responses you get.

3. Draw a genetic chart of your biological relatives, going back as many generations as you can, listing all serious illnesses and causes of death. Include ancestors who died in infancy. Do you see any genetic susceptibility? If so, how can you overcome it?

4. List a dozen people you know who need glasses (or other corrective lenses) and a dozen who do not. Are there any patterns? Is this correlation or causation?

>>ONLINE CONNECTIONS

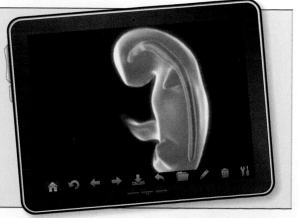

To accompany your textbook, you have access to a number of online resources, including quizzes for every chapter of the book, flashcards (in English and Spanish), critical thinking questions, and case studies. For access to any of these links, go to www.worthpublishers.com/bergerls8e. In addition to these free resources, you'll also find links to the podcasts, video clips, diagnostic quizzing with personalized study advice, and an ebook. Some of the videos and activities available online include:

- *Genetic Code.* This activity includes animations of basic genetic processes in our earliest development.

- *Identical Twins.* This video features footage of two identical twins, separated at birth and unknown to each other until adulthood.

Prenatal Development and Birth

WHAT WILL YOU KNOW?

1. What are several astonishing or amazing prenatal developments?
2. Why would any woman in a developed nation try to avoid a hospital birth?
3. What are the consequences of most severe teratogens?
4. What are the causes and consequences of low birthweight?
5. How do fathers help or harm prenatal development and newborn health?

My friend Judy taught history at the United Nations International School. Since her students came from many parts of the world, Judy often contrasted the broad generalities of human history and the current local particulars. When she was pregnant, she rubbed her bulging belly and told her students, "According to international statistics, this is probably a Chinese boy."

Judy was right: Most fetuses are male (about 52 percent) and Chinese. However, given Judy's particulars (genes, age, sonogram), I was not surprised when she gave birth to her new European American daughter. Judy herself seemed awestruck, repeatedly recounting tiny details, as if no baby like hers had ever appeared before. She was right about that, too.

This example illustrates the dual themes of this chapter, which describes human development from conception through birth. Every topic—embryonic growth, teratogens, sonograms, low birthweight, medical assistance, bonding, reflexes, and so on—relates to the almost 200 million births in the world every year. Yet each pregnancy, birth, and newborn is unique. This chapter includes both generalities and particulars. Learn all you can and then, if you become a parent, expect to be awed by your personal miracle.

>> Prenatal Growth

The most dramatic and extensive transformation of the entire life span occurs before birth. To make it easier to study, prenatal development is often divided into three main periods. The first two weeks are called the **germinal period;** the third through the eighth week is the **embryonic period;** the ninth week until birth is the **fetal period.** (Alternative terms are explained in Table 4.1.)

Germinal: The First 14 Days

You learned in Chapter 3 that the one-celled zygote, traveling slowly down the fallopian tube toward the uterus, begins to duplicate and multiply (see Figure 4.1). At about the eight-cell stage, differentiation begins. The early cells take on distinct characteristics and gravitate toward particular locations, foreshadowing the types of cells they will become.

germinal period The first two weeks of prenatal development after conception, characterized by rapid cell division and the beginning of cell differentiation.

embryonic period The stage of prenatal development from approximately the third through the eighth week after conception, during which the basic forms of all body structures, including internal organs, develop.

fetal period The stage of prenatal development from the ninth week after conception until birth, during which the fetus gains about 7 pounds (more than 3,000 grams) and organs become more mature, gradually able to function on their own.

TABLE 4.1

Timing and Terminology

Popular and professional books use various phrases to segment pregnancy. The following comments may help to clarify the phrases used.

- *Beginning of pregnancy:* Pregnancy begins at conception, which is also the starting point of *gestational age.* However, the organism does not become an *embryo* until about two weeks later, and pregnancy does not affect the woman (and cannot be confirmed by blood or urine testing) until implantation. Paradoxically, many obstetricians date the onset of pregnancy from the date of the woman's last menstrual period (LMP), about 14 days *before* conception.

- *Length of pregnancy:* Full-term pregnancies last 266 days, or 38 weeks, or 9 months. If the LMP is used as the starting time, pregnancy lasts 40 weeks, sometimes expressed as 10 lunar months. (A lunar month is 28 days long.)

- *Trimesters:* Instead of *germinal period, embryonic period,* and *fetal period,* some writers divide pregnancy into three-month periods called *trimesters.* Months 1, 2, and 3 are called the *first trimester;* months 4, 5, and 6, the *second trimester;* and months 7, 8, and 9, the *third trimester.*

- *Due date:* Although doctors assign a specific due date (based on the woman's LMP), only 5 percent of babies are born on that exact date. Babies born between three weeks before and two weeks after that date are considered "full term" or "on time." Babies born earlier are called *preterm;* babies born later are called *post-term.* The words *preterm* and *post-term* are more accurate than *premature* and *postmature.*

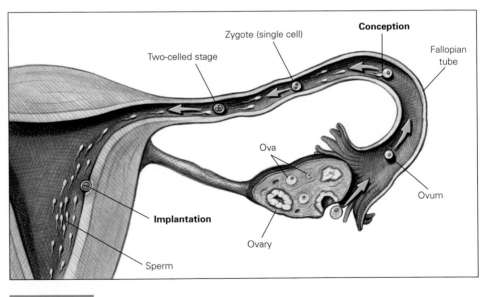

FIGURE 4.1

The Most Dangerous Journey In the first 10 days after conception, the organism does not increase in size because it is not yet nourished by the mother. However, the number of cells increases rapidly as the organism prepares for implantation, which occurs successfully about one-third of the time.

implantation The process, beginning about 10 days after conception, in which the developing organism burrows into the placenta that lines the uterus, where it can be nourished and protected as it continues to develop.

About a week after conception, the multiplying cells (now numbering more than 100) separate into two distinct masses. The outer cells form a shell that will become the *placenta* (the organ that surrounds and protects the developing creature), and the inner cells form a nucleus that will become the embryo.

The first task of the outer cells is to achieve **implantation**—that is, to embed themselves in the nurturing lining of the uterus. This is far from automatic; about

TABLE 4.2

Vulnerability During Prenatal Development

The Germinal Period

At least 60 percent of all developing organisms fail to grow or implant properly and thus do not survive the germinal period. Most of these organisms are grossly abnormal.

The Embryonic Period

About 20 percent of all embryos are aborted spontaneously,* most often because of chromosomal abnormalities.

The Fetal Period

About 5 percent of all fetuses are aborted spontaneously before viability at 22 weeks or are stillborn, defined as born dead after 22 weeks.

Birth

About 31 percent of all zygotes grow and survive to become living newborn babies.

*Spontaneous abortions are also called miscarriages. This table does not include *induced* abortions.
Sources: Bentley & Mascie-Taylor, 2000; K. L. Moore & Persaud, 2003.

60 percent of natural conceptions and 70 percent of in vitro conceptions do not implant (see Table 4.2). Thus, most new life ends before an embryo begins.

Embryo: From the Third Through the Eighth Week

The start of the third week after conception initiates the *embryonic period,* during which the formless mass of cells becomes a distinct being—not yet recognizably human but worthy of a new name, **embryo.** (The word *embryo* is often used loosely, but each stage of development has a particular name; embryo refers to the developing human from day 14 to day 56).

First, a thin line (called the *primitive streak*) appears down the middle of the embryo, becoming the neural tube 22 days after conception and eventually developing into the central nervous system, the brain and spinal column (Moore & Persaud, 2003). The head begins to take shape in the fourth week, as eyes, ears, nose, and mouth start to form. Also in the fourth week, a minuscule blood vessel that will become the heart begins to pulsate. By the fifth week, buds that will become arms and legs emerge. The upper arms and then forearms, palms, and webbed fingers appear. Legs, feet, and webbed toes, in that order, are apparent a few days later, each having the beginning of a skeletal structure. Then, 52 and 54 days after conception, respectively, the fingers and toes separate.

embryo The name for a developing human organism from about the third through the eighth week after conception.

The Embryonic Period (*a*) At 4 weeks past conception, the embryo is only about ⅛ inch (3 millimeters) long, but already the head (*top right*) has taken shape. (*b*) At 5 weeks past conception, the embryo has grown to twice the size it was at 4 weeks. Its primitive heart, which has been pulsing for a week now, is visible, as is what appears to be a primitive tail, which will soon be enclosed by skin and protective tissue at the tip of the backbone (the coccyx). (*c*) By 7 weeks, the organism is somewhat less than an inch (2½ centimeters) long. Eyes, nose, the digestive system, and even the first stage of toe formation can be seen. (*d*) At 8 weeks, the 1-inch-long organism is clearly recognizable as a human fetus.

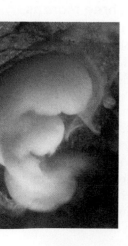
(a)

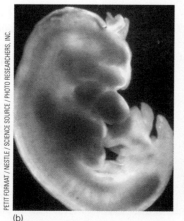
(b)

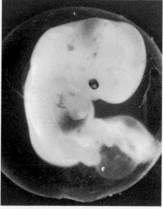
(c)

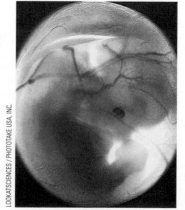
(d)

At the end of the eighth week after conception (56 days), the embryo weighs just one-thirtieth of an ounce (1 gram) and is about 1 inch (2½ centimeters) long. It has all the basic organs and body parts (except sex organs) of a human being, including elbows and knees. It moves frequently, about 150 times per hour, but such movement is random and imperceptible (Piontelli, 2002).

Fetus: From the Ninth Week Until Birth

The organism is called a **fetus** from the ninth week after conception until birth. The fetal period involves dramatic change, from a tiny, sexless creature smaller than the final joint of your thumb to a boy or girl about 20 inches (51 centimeters) long.

fetus The name for a developing human organism from the start of the ninth week after conception until birth.

Especially for Biologists Many people believe that the differences between the sexes are sociocultural, not biological. Is there any prenatal support for that view? (see response, page 94)

There's Your Baby For many parents, their first glimpse of their future child is an ultrasound image. This is Alice Morgan, 63 days before birth.

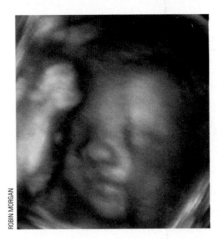
ROBIN MORGAN

The Third Month

In the ninth week, if an embryo is male (XY), the SRY gene triggers the development of male sexual organs. Otherwise, female organs develop. The male fetus experiences a rush of testosterone, shaping the brain (Morris et al., 2004; Neave, 2008). Of course, the range of brain and behavioral variations *among* males and *among* females is greater than those *between* the average man and woman. Nonetheless, some neurological sex differences begin in the third month.

Prenatally, the head develops first, in a *cephalocaudal* (literally, "head to tail") pattern, and the extremities form last, in a *proximodistal* (literally, "near to far") pattern. The head comprises about half of the total body weight of the early fetus. By the end of the third month, the sex organs are visible via **ultrasound** (similar to an X-ray, but using sound waves instead of radiation; also called *sonogram*).

ultrasound An image of a fetus (or an internal organ) produced by using high-frequency sound waves. (Also called *sonogram*.)

The 3-month-old fetus weighs approximately 3 ounces (87 grams) and is about 3 inches (7.5 centimeters) long. Early prenatal growth is very rapid, with considerable variation from fetus to fetus, especially in body weight (Moore & Persaud, 2003). The numbers just given—3 months, 3 ounces, 3 inches,—are rounded off for easy recollection. (For those on the metric system, "100 days, 100 grams, 100 millimeters" is similarly imprecise but useful.)

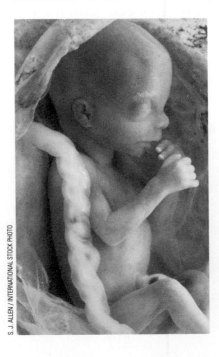
S. J. ALLEN / INTERNATIONAL STOCK PHOTO

The Fetus At the end of 4 months, the fetus, now 6 inches long, looks fully formed but out of proportion—the distance from the top of the skull to the neck is almost as long as that from the neck to the rump. For many more weeks, the fetus must depend on the translucent membranes of the placenta and umbilical cord (the long white object in the foreground) for survival.

Observation Quiz Can you see eyebrows, fingernails, and genitals? (see answer, page 94)

The Middle Three Months

In the fourth, fifth, and sixth months, the heartbeat becomes stronger. Digestive and excretory systems develop. Fingernails, toenails, and buds for teeth form, and hair grows (including eyelashes). The brain increases about six times in size and develops many new neurons (*neurogenesis*) and synapses (*synaptogenesis*). Indeed, up to half a million brain cells per minute are created at peak growth during mid-pregnancy (Dowling, 2004). Some neurons extend long axons to distant neurons, and brain parts (first the brain stem above the back of the

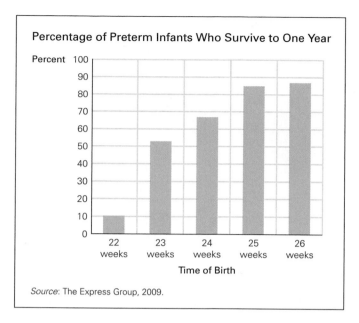

Percentage of Preterm Infants Who Survive to One Year

Percent

Time of Birth

Source: The Express Group, 2009.

FIGURE 4.2

Each Critical Day Even with advanced medical care, survival of extremely preterm newborns is in doubt. These data come from a thousand births in Sweden, where prenatal care is free and easily obtained. As you see, the age of viability (22 weeks) means only that an infant *might* survive, not that it will. By full term (not shown), the survival rate is almost 100 percent.

neck, then the midbrain, and finally the cortex) develop and connect within the central nervous system (Kolb & Whishaw, 2008).

The entire central nervous system becomes responsive during mid-pregnancy. As you will see in later chapters, in which neurons, synapses, and axons are discussed and illustrated, brain growth and neurological organization continue for years.

Because the brain regulates basic body functions such as breathing and sucking, advances in neurological functioning are essential for a newborn to reach the **age of viability,** when a preterm newborn can survive. With intensive medical care, some babies survive at 22 weeks past conception (The Express Group, 2009). If born before that, death is almost inevitable, because even the most advanced technology cannot maintain life without some brain response. Reports of survivors born at fewer than 22 weeks are suspect because the date of conception is unknown. Figure 4.2 indicates known survival rates for extremely preterm newborns who receive advanced medical care.

With brain maturation, the organs of the body begin to work in harmony, so the heart beats faster during activity, and fetal movement as well as heart rate quiet down during rest (which may not be when the mother wants to sleep).

age of viability The age (about 22 weeks after conception) at which a fetus may survive outside the mother's uterus if specialized medical care is available.

The Final Three Months

Attaining viability simply means that life outside the womb is *possible*. Each day of the final three months of prenatal growth improves the odds. A viable preterm infant born in the seventh month is a tiny creature requiring intensive care for each gram of nourishment and every shallow breath. By contrast, after nine months or so, the typical full-term infant is a vigorous person, ready to thrive at home on mother's milk—no expert help, oxygenated air, or special feeding required.

The critical difference between life and death, or between a fragile preterm baby and a robust newborn, is maturation of the neurological, respiratory, and cardiovascular systems. In the last three months of prenatal life, the lungs begin to expand and contract, exercising muscles involved in breathing by using the amniotic fluid as a substitute for air. The valves of the heart go through a final

Can He Hear? A fetus, just about at the age of viability, is shown fingering his ear. Such gestures are probably random; but, yes, he can hear.

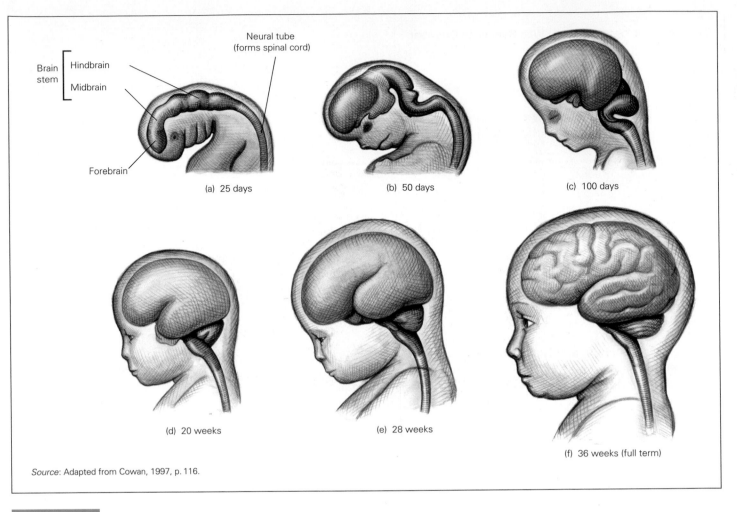

(a) 25 days

(b) 50 days

(c) 100 days

(d) 20 weeks

(e) 28 weeks

(f) 36 weeks (full term)

Source: Adapted from Cowan, 1997, p. 116.

FIGURE 4.3

Prenatal Growth of the Brain Just 25 days after conception (*a*), the central nervous system is already evident. The brain looks distinctly human by day 100 (*c*). By the 28th week of gestation (*e*), at the very time brain activity begins, the various sections of the brain are recognizable. When the fetus is full term (*f*), all the parts of the brain, including the cortex (the outer layers), are formed, folding over one another and becoming more convoluted, or wrinkled, as the number of brain cells increases.

>> Response for Biologists (from page 92) Only one of the 46 human chromosomes determines sex, and the genitals develop last in the prenatal sequence. On the other hand, several sex differences develop before birth.

>> Answer to Observation Quiz (from page 92) Yes, yes, and no. Genitals are formed, but they are not visible in this photo. The object growing from the lower belly is the umbilical cord.

maturation, as do the arteries and veins throughout the body. Among other things, this helps to prevent "brain bleeds," one of the hazards of preterm birth in which paper thin blood vessels in the skull collapse.

The fetus usually gains at least 4½ pounds (2.1 kilograms) in the third trimester, increasing to almost 7½ pounds (about 3.4 kilograms) at birth (see At About This Time). By full term, human brain growth is so extensive that the *cortex* (the brain's advanced outer layers) form several folds in order to fit into the skull (see Figure 4.3).

The relationship between mother and child intensifies during the final three months, for a fetus's size and movement make the pregnant woman very aware of it. In turn, her sounds, diet (via amniotic fluid), and behavior become part of fetal consciousness. Auditory communication from mother to child begins at the 28th week and improves each week as fetal hearing (or newborn hearing if the baby is born early) becomes more acute (Bisiacchi et al., 2009). The fetus startles and kicks at loud noise, becomes used to the mother's heartbeat and voice, and is

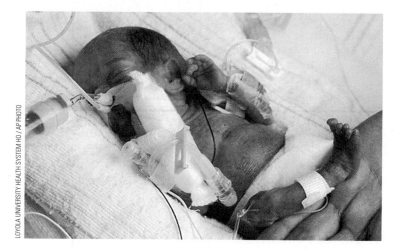

LOYOLA UNIVERSITY HEALTH SYSTEM HO / AP PHOTO

One of the Tiniest Rumaisa Rahman was born after 26 weeks and 6 days weighing only 8.6 ounces (244 grams). Nevertheless, she has a good chance of living a full, normal life. Rumaisa gained 5 pounds (2,270 grams) in the hospital and then, 6 months after her birth, went home. Her twin sister, Hiba, who weighed 1.3 pounds (590 grams) at birth, had gone home two months earlier. At their one-year birthday, the twins seemed normal, with Rumaisa weighing 15 pounds (6,800 grams) and Hiba 17 pounds (7,711 grams) (CBS News, 2005).

AT ABOUT THIS TIME

Average Prenatal Weights*

Period of Development	Weeks After Conception	Weight (nonmetric)	Weight (metric)	Notes
End of embryonic period	8	1/30 oz.	1 g	This is the most common time for spontaneous abortion (miscarriage).
End of first trimester	13	3 oz.	85 g	
At viability (50/50 chance of survival)	22	20 oz.	570 g	A birthweight less than 2 lb., 3 oz. (1,000 g) is considered extremely low birthweight (ELBW).
End of second trimester	26–28	2–3 lb.	900–1,400 g	Less than 3 lb., 5 oz. (2,500 g) is very low birthweight (VLBW).
End of preterm period	35	5½ lb.	2,500 g	Less than 5½ lb. (2,500 g) is low birthweight (LBW).
Full-term	38	7½ lb.	3,400 g	Between 5½ lb. and 9 lb. (2,500–4,000 g) is considered normal weight.

*To make them easier to remember, the weights are rounded off (which accounts for the inexact correspondence between metric and nonmetric measures). Actual weights vary. For instance, a normal full-term infant can weigh between 5½ and 9 pounds (2,500 and 4,000 grams or more); a viable infant, especially one of several born at 26 or more weeks, can weigh less than shown here.

comforted by rhythmic music, especially if the mother walks or rocks as she sings. When the mother is highly fearful or anxious, the fetal heart beats faster and body movements increase (DiPietro et al., 2002).

SUMMING UP

In two weeks of rapid cell duplication, differentiation, and finally implantation, the newly conceived organism is transformed from a one-celled zygote to a many-celled embryo. The embryo soon develops the beginning of the central nervous system (3 weeks), a heart and a face (4 weeks), arms and legs (5 weeks), hands and feet (6 weeks), and fingers and toes (7 weeks), while the inner organs take shape. By 8 weeks, all the body structures, except male and female sex organs, are in place. Fetal growth then proceeds rapidly, including mid-trimester weight gain (about 2 pounds, or 1 kilogram) and brain maturation, which make viability possible. By full term, the 35- to 40-week-old newborn is a survivor, with organs functioning well, ready for life. ∎

>> Birth

About 38 weeks (266 days) after conception, the fetal brain signals the release of hormones, specifically *oxytocin,* which prepares the fetal brain for delivery and starts labor (Tyzio et al., 2006). Contractions are weak and irregular at first (some occur weeks before birth and then fade), but eventually they become strong and regular. The average baby is born after 12 hours of active labor for first births and 7 hours for subsequent births (Moore & Persaud, 2003), although labor often takes twice or half as long. Women's birthing positions also vary—sitting, squatting, lying down, or even immersed in warm water (although many physicians believe the latter is hazardous [Tracy, 2009]). Figure 4.4 shows the sequence of stages in the birth process.

The Newborn's First Minutes

Newborns usually breathe and cry on their own. Between spontaneous cries, the first breaths of air bring oxygen to the lungs, as the infant's color changes from bluish to pinkish. (This refers to the color of the blood, visible beneath the skin, and applies to newborns of all hues.) The eyes open wide; the tiny fingers grab; even tinier toes stretch and retract. The newborn is instantly, zestfully, ready for life.

Nevertheless, there is much for birth attendants to do. Mucus in the baby's throat is removed, especially if the first breaths seem shallow or strained. The umbilical cord is cut to detach the placenta, leaving the "belly button." The infant is examined, weighed, and given to the mother to preserve body heat.

FIGURE 4.4

A Normal, Uncomplicated Birth
(*a*) The baby's position as the birth process begins. (*b*) The first stage of labor: The cervix dilates to allow passage of the baby's head. (*c*) Transition: The baby's head moves into the "birth canal," the vagina. (*d*) The second stage of labor: The baby's head moves through the opening of the vagina ("crowns") and (*e*) emerges completely.

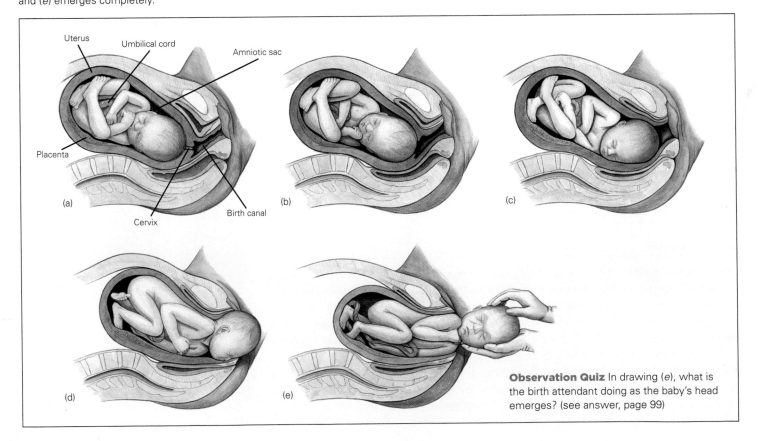

Observation Quiz In drawing (*e*), what is the birth attendant doing as the baby's head emerges? (see answer, page 99)

TABLE 4.3

Criteria and Scoring of the Apgar Scale

			Five Vital Signs		
Score	Color	Heartbeat	Reflex Irritability	Muscle Tone	Respiratory Effort
0	Blue, pale	Absent	No response	Flaccid, limp	Absent
1	Body pink, extremities blue	Slow (below 100)	Grimace	Weak, inactive	Irregular, slow
2	Entirely pink	Rapid (over 100)	Coughing, sneezing, crying	Strong, active	Good; baby is crying

Source: Apgar, 1953.

One widely used assessment of infant health is the **Apgar scale** (see Table 4.3), first developed by Dr. Virginia Apgar, who became an anesthesiologist because in 1933, when she earned her MD, she was told that only men did surgery. She saw that "delivery room doctors focused on mothers and paid little attention to babies. Those who were small and struggling were often left to die" (M. Beck, 2009, p. D-1). In 1949, Apgar developed a simple rating scale of five vital signs—color, heart rate, cry, muscle tone, and breathing—to alert doctors to the health of the newborn. Now birth attendants worldwide use the Apgar (often using it as an acronym to denote appearance, pulse, grimace, activity, and respiration) at one minute and again at five minutes after birth, assigning each vital sign a score of 0, 1, or 2 (Moster et al., 2001).

If the five-minute Apgar is at least 7, all is well. If the five-minute total is below 7, the infant needs help. If the score is below 4, a neonatal pediatrician rushes to the delivery room to provide emergency care. Most newborns score 8 or 9, which comforts the new parents, who cradle their infant and congratulate each other. Typically, fathers praise the mothers for giving birth, while mothers point out the resemblance between the father and his child ("She has your ears!"), perhaps to reassure him that the baby is his.

Medical Assistance

How closely any particular birth matches the foregoing depends on the parents' preparation, the skill of the birth attendants, the position and size of the fetus, and the customs of the culture. In developed nations, births usually include drugs to dull pain or speed contractions, sterile procedures, and electronic monitoring.

Surgery

More than one-third of U.S. births occur via **cesarean section** (**c-section,** or simply *section*), whereby the fetus is removed through incisions in the mother's abdomen and uterus (Hamilton et al., 2004). This surgery is controversial: Critics contend that about half of all c-sections are unwarranted. Culture and cohort affect the rates: Most nations have fewer cesareans than the United States but some have more (see Figure 4.5). In every nation, cesareans have increased as risks have decreased. For example, in China, rates were 5 percent in the early 1990s and 20 percent by 2001 (Guo et al., 2007). Usually, cesareans

Apgar scale A quick assessment of a newborn's health. The baby's color, heart rate, reflexes, muscle tone, and respiratory effort are given a score of 0, 1, or 2 twice—at one minute and five minutes after birth—and each time the total of all five scores is compared with the maximum score of 10 (rarely attained).

cesarean section (c-section) A surgical birth, in which incisions through the mother's abdomen and uterus allow the fetus to be removed quickly, instead of being delivered through the vagina. (Also called simply *section*.)

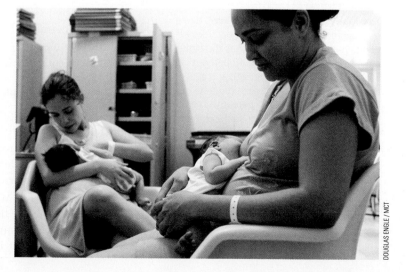

From Day One For various reasons, some countries have much higher rates of cesarean deliveries than others. These new mothers in Brazil, which has a high cesarean rate, have safely delivered their babies and, with the encouragement of the hospital, are breastfeeding them from the very beginning.

DOUGLAS ENGLE / MCT

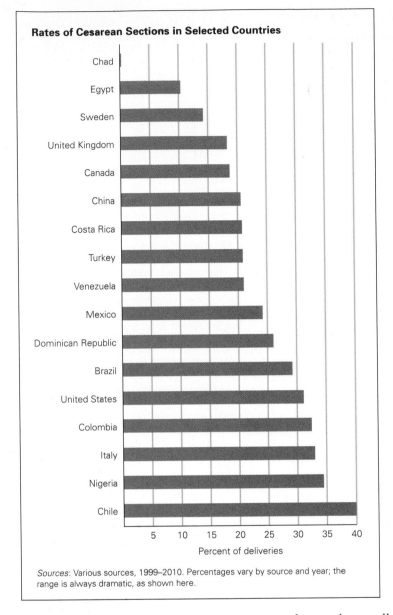

Rates of Cesarean Sections in Selected Countries

Percent of deliveries

Sources: Various sources, 1999–2010. Percentages vary by source and year; the range is always dramatic, as shown here.

FIGURE 4.5

Too Many Cesareans or Too Few? Rates of cesarean deliveries vary widely from nation to nation. Latin America has the highest rates in the world (note that 40 percent of all births in Chile are by cesarean), and sub-Saharan Africa has the lowest (the rate in Chad is less than half of 1 percent). The underlying issue is whether some women who should have cesareans do not get them, while other women have unnecessary cesareans.

are completely safe for mother and baby and have many advantages for hospitals (easier to schedule, quicker, and more expensive than vaginal births), but if they occur before labor begins, the rate of complications rises (Malloy, 2009).

Newborn Survival

A century ago, at least 5 of every 100 newborns in the United States died (De Lee, 1938). Currently in the United States, safe surgery, the Apgar, and intensive care have reduced newborn mortality to less than 1 in 100—a statistic that includes very high-risk newborns such as those weighing only 1 pound. In many nations, newborns are screened immediately for serious diseases, including phenylketonuria, sickle-cell anemia, and more (some U.S. states test for 40 diseases). Initial results might indicate that more testing and special treatment are needed to reduce the potential harm.

Every year worldwide, obstetricians, midwives, and nurses save millions of lives—of mothers as well as of infants. Indeed, the major reason motherhood is still hazardous in the least developed nations is the lack of medical attention during abortion (spontaneous or induced) and childbirth. In sub-Saharan Africa, where only one-third of all births are attended by a doctor or trained midwife, about 1 in 16 women dies of complications of pregnancy and birth (Kruk et al., 2008), and almost 2 million newborns die each year (Rajaratnam et al., 2010). The main reason for maternal death is bleeding after birth, and the main reason for newborn death is inadequate oxygen. Both of these are routinely prevented in modern hospitals.

Nonetheless, several aspects of hospital birth have been criticized as arising from custom or politics, not from necessity. A particular issue concerns the attention lavished on "miracle babies" who require intensive care, microsurgery, and weeks in the hospital. Those who survive often need special care all their lives. Critics note the public expense of keeping them alive and then the lifelong burden borne privately by the parents. As one author says, "Any country that is rich enough to afford neonatal intensive care also has the moral obligation to accept responsibility for the care of impaired children throughout their lives, but . . . none of them does" (Guyer, 2006).

Alternatives to Hospital Technology

Questions of cost and benefits, both financial and emotional, abound. For instance, c-section rates vary more by the particular doctor, hospital, day of the week, or region than by the specifics of the birth. Fear of lawsuits dictates that women who have had one cesarean section need cesareans for all subsequent births to avoid a rupture of the uterus, even though that complication is unusual. Juries blame doctors who do not operate.

Most U.S. births now take place in hospital labor rooms (which are smaller and more private than operating rooms) with high-tech operating rooms nearby. Another 5 percent of U.S. births occur in freestanding birthing centers, and less than 1 percent occur at home (illegal in some jurisdictions). About one-half of these home births occur by plan, attended by a doctor or midwife going against protocol, and half occur because of unexpectedly rapid births. The latter are hazardous because there is likely no one available who is trained to rescue a newborn in distress (Tracy, 2009). A careful comparison of an excellent hospital and an excellent birthing center found that medical procedures were less common in birthing centers (e.g., fewer intravenous fluids, fewer c-sections, more eating, more walking during labor) but that birth outcomes were similar (Jackson et al., 2003). Outcomes are not as good for U.S. home births, but valid comparisons are elusive, as the following explains.

>> **Answer to Observation Quiz** (from page 96) The birth attendant is turning the baby's head after it has emerged; doing this helps the shoulders come out more easily.

THINKING CRITICALLY

Home Births

Compared with the United States, planned home births are much more common in many European nations (2 percent in England, 30 percent in the Netherlands), with midwives licensed and paid by the government. In the Netherlands, special ambulances called *flying storks* speed mother and infant to a hospital if needed. In European nations, outcomes for home births are better than for hospital births.

In the poorest nations, most babies are born at home: Doctors are called only for emergencies, often arriving too late, and women never go to the hospital unless they think they are dying. The following describes a home birth in Ghana:

> Huddled in a corner of the hut, she was lying on the floor. . . . She lay curled into a small ball on her left side, her pregnant and contracting uterus protruding from her thin frame. No sound came from her. No sound came from the midwife either. She

was seated in the corner of the dark, hot hut, waiting. Suddenly, Emefa gave a low whimper and hauled herself into a sitting and then squatting position. The midwife crept over to her and gently supported Emefa's back as she bore down. No words, no commands, no yelling. . . . The baby's head appeared gradually, slowly making its progress into the world. How did the midwife know that it was time? . . . A soft whoosh and the baby's body was born into the steady and confident hands of the midwife. And still there was no sound. The baby did not cry, not because there was any problem, but because it was a gentle birth. The baby was breathing as he was handed to his mother.

[Hillier, 2003, p. 3]

The idea of a "gentle birth" is appealing, but this newborn may have been lucky. The infant mortality rate in Ghana is 10 times that in the United States. Some people wish gentle home births would become more common in the United States; others shudder at the thought of home births. Two opposite risks are apparent: Home births might suddenly become emergencies and then transport to the hospital would delay care; on the other hand, hospital births might cause needless intervention, harming the new family. Comparing the Netherlands and Ghana makes it obvious that one crucial question is how supportive the medical professionals are. Critical thinking is needed to analyze the costs and benefits of home birth.

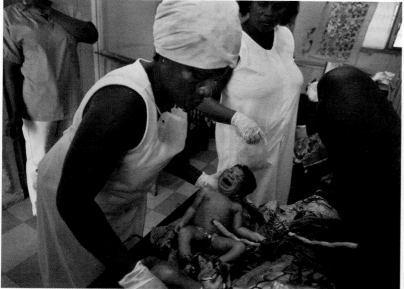

RANDY OLSON / NGS IMAGE COLLECTION

Celebration? The lusty cry of this infant is a good sign, as is his color (not bluish) and muscle tone. Moreover, this birth occurred in a clinic, which bodes well for the mother's recovery—unlike many other births in Ghana. So why does no one seem very happy?

Observation Quiz Is this infant minutes, hours, or days old? (see answer, page 101)

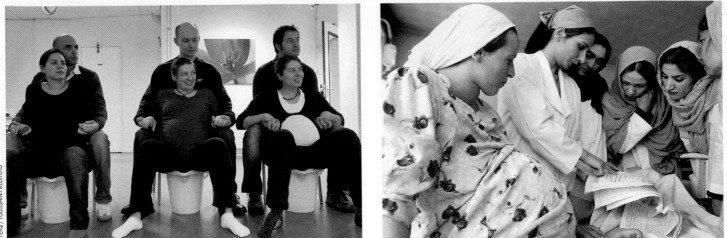

REUTERS / TOUSSAINT KLUITERS

AP PHOTO / LYNNE SLADKY

The Same Situation, Many Miles Apart: Getting Ready There are many similarities here: Six adults and three fetuses on the left and six adults and two fetuses (twins) on the right. But the differences are tragic, evident in the faces of the expectant mothers. The husbands in the Netherlands are learning how to help their wives give birth at home, as most Dutch couples do. The Afghan doctor on the right, however, is explaining why this woman's labor will be induced, with neither baby expected to survive—a devastating blow this woman has already faced, having twice lost a baby less than a week old.

Learning from Tradition

Traditional and modern practices can be combined. An example is reported regarding the Inuit people of northern Canada:]

> Until thirty or forty years ago every woman, and most men, learned midwifery skills and knew what to do to help at a birth if they were needed. . . . They helped the woman kneel or squat on caribou skins, and tied the cord with caribou sinews. . . . Since the 1950s, as the medical system took control in the belief that hospital birth was safer, more and more pregnant women were evacuated by air to deliver in large hospitals in Winnipeg and other cities. . . . Around three weeks before her due date, a woman is flown south to wait in bed and breakfast accommodation for labor to start, and to have it induced if the baby does not arrive when expected. Anxious about their children left at home, mothers became bored and depressed. . . . Women . . . deliver in a supine position [on their back] instead of an upright one, which was part of their tradition, and also describe being tied up while giving birth. Many women say that children who have been born in a hospital are different and no longer fit into the Inuit lifestyle. . . . Several new birth centres have now been created [in the Inuit homeland] and nurse-midwives are bringing in traditional midwives as assistants during childbirth, training some Inuit midwives to work alongside them, and at the same time learning some of the old Inuit ways themselves.

> [Kitzinger, 2001, pp. 160–161]

doula A woman who helps with the birth process. Traditionally in Latin America, a doula was the only professional who attended childbirth. Now doulas are likely to arrive at the woman's home during early labor and later work alongside a hospital's staff.

Pressure Point Many U.S. couples, like this one, benefit from a doula's gentle touch, strong pressure, and sensitive understanding—all of which make doula births less likely to include medical intervention.

JADA SHAPIRO / BIRTH DAY PRESENCE

Another example of a traditional custom incorporated into a modern birth is the presence of a **doula.** Long a fixture in many Latin American countries, a doula is a woman who helps other women with labor, delivery, breast-feeding, and newborn care. Doulas have been shown to benefit low-income women with no partner. Moreover, in one study, 420 middle-class married women

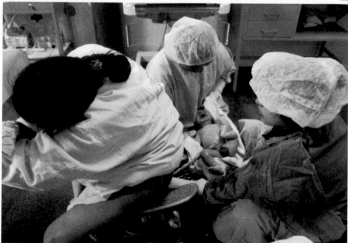

The Same Situation, Many Miles Apart: A Better Position The most obvious difference between these births in Chicago, Illinois *(left)*, and Cuzco, Peru, is the mother's body position. In the United States, the horizontal position was designed to give doctors a better view when the head emerges *(left)*. In Peru, women prefer "vertical births," and this maternity center has had more patients as a result of their willingness to perform them. Note other differences—the father present in Chicago, the protective head coverings in Cuzco. It is not so clear-cut which practices make better medical sense and which are simply social customs.

▶ Research Design

Scientists: Susan McGrath and John Kennell.

Publication: *Birth* (2008).

Participants: A total of 420 pregnant women, all healthy, middle class, and accompanied by their male partner when they arrived in labor at a major hospital in Cleveland, Ohio. They all gave birth to their first baby, attended by their obstetrician.

Design: All received the usual care from medical professionals as well as the support of their partners. At arrival at the hospital, half were randomly assigned a doula, who provided physical care (e.g., massage), expertise, and reassurance until the baby was born. Mothers and their partners were questioned 24 hours and 6 weeks later.

Major conclusion: The births with a doula had lower rates of cesareans (13 versus 25 percent) and epidural anesthesia (65 versus 76 percent). More than 99 percent of the women and their partners rated the doula's help positively or very positively. The authors conclude: "Continuous labor support by a doula is a risk-free obstetric technique that could benefit all laboring women" (p. 97).

Comment: Three factors in this study design made the conclusions especially valid: (1) There was random assignment (to avoid the selection factors that occur because women who choose doulas tend to be healthy, educated women); (2) the fathers were present, which showed that the results were not simply the result of having a support person; (3) the doula did not join the couple until their arrival at the hospital (which avoided the confounding benefits that occur when doulas come to the woman's home during early labor).

were randomly given a doula or not. Those who had the doula needed much less medical intervention, including surgery: Their cesarean rate was 13 percent, compared with 25 percent for the women who chanced to have no doula (McGrath & Kennell, 2008). (See the Research Design.)

SUMMING UP

Most newborns weigh about 7½ pounds (3.4 kilograms), score at least 7 out of 10 on the Apgar scale, and thrive without medical assistance. If necessary, neonatal surgery and intensive care save lives. Although modern medicine has reduced maternal and infant deaths, many critics deplore treating birth as a medical crisis instead of a natural event. Responses to this critique include births in hospital labor rooms rather than operating rooms, in birthing centers instead of hospitals, or even in homes. The assistance of a doula is another recent practice that reduces the need for medical intervention. ∎

>> Answer to Observation Quiz (from page 99) Probably ten minutes or less. His umbilical cord is still attached to the placenta, which is still inside the woman. Usually, placentas are expelled with contractions a few minutes after birth.

>> Problems and Solutions

The early days of life place the developing person on the path toward health and success—or not. Fortunately, resilience is apparent from the beginning; healthy newborns are the norm, not the exception. Sadly, if something is amiss, it is often part of a cascade that may become overwhelming.

Harmful Substances

teratogens Agents and conditions, including viruses, drugs, and chemicals, that can impair prenatal development and result in birth defects or even death.

Many toxins, illnesses, and experiences can harm a fetus. Every day scientists learn more about **teratogens,** which are substances (such as drugs and pollutants) and conditions (such as severe malnutrition and extreme stress) that increase the risk of prenatal abnormalities. Many abnormalities can be avoided, and others (such as cleft palate) can be remedied. Thus, prenatal development is not a dangerous period to be feared as much as a natural process to be protected.

Some teratogens do not cause obvious physical defects but harm the brain, making a child hyperactive, antisocial, or learning-disabled. These are **behavioral teratogens.** About 20 percent of all children have difficulties that could be connected to behavioral teratogens, although the link is not straightforward. One of my students described her little brother as follows:

behavioral teratogens Agents and conditions that can harm the prenatal brain, impairing the future child's intellectual and emotional functioning.

> I was nine years old when my mother announced she was pregnant. I was the one who was most excited. . . . My mother was a heavy smoker, Colt 45 beer drinker. . . . I asked, "Why are you doing it?" She said, "I don't know."
>
> During this time I was in the fifth grade and we saw a film about birth defects. My biggest fear was that my mother was going to give birth to a fetal alcohol syndrome (FAS) infant. . . . My baby brother was born right on schedule. The doctors claimed a healthy newborn. . . . Once I heard healthy, I thought everything was going to be fine. I was wrong, then again I was just a child. . . . My baby brother never showed any interest in toys . . . he just cannot get the right words out of his mouth . . . he has no common sense . . .
>
> *[J, personal communication]*

My student blames her mother, adding, "Why hurt those who cannot defend themselves?" But she may be wrong: Genes, postnatal experiences, and even J's own perceptions could be the explanation. As you remember from Chapter 1, one example is not proof. Nonetheless, J is right to wonder why her mother took a chance.

Risk Analysis

One of the crucial insights that applies to all of human development is that life entails risks (National Research Council, 2009). Risk analysis involves knowing which risks are worth taking and how to minimize the chance of harm. To pick an easy example: Crossing the street is a risk, yet it would be harmful to avoid all street-crossing. Knowing this, we cross carefully, looking both ways.

Sixty years ago, no one applied risk analysis to prenatal development. It was believed that the placenta screened out all harmful substances. Then two tragic episodes showed otherwise: (1) On an Australian military base, an increase in babies born blind was linked to a rubella (German measles) epidemic on the same base seven months earlier (Gregg, 1941, reprinted in Persaud et al., 1985), and (2) a sudden rise in British newborns with deformed limbs was traced to maternal use of thalidomide, a new drug widely prescribed in Europe in the late 1950s (Schardein, 1976). Thus began teratology, a science of risk analysis. Although all teratogens increase the *risk* of harm, none *always* cause damage. The impact of teratogens depends on the interplay of many factors, both destructive and protective, an example of the dynamic-systems perspective described in Chapter 1.

One crucial factor is *timing*—the age of the developing organism when it is exposed to the teratogen. Some teratogens cause damage only during a critical period, when a particular part of the body is forming (see Figure 4.6). Because the early days are critical, most obstetricians today recommend that *before* pregnancy women need to avoid drugs (especially alcohol); supplement a balanced diet with extra folic acid, iron, and other crucial vitamins; and update their immunizations. Indeed, preconception health is at least as important as health during pregnancy. Unfortunately, almost half the births in the United States are unplanned, and most of those women are not in the best of health before conception (D'Angelo et al., 2007) (see Figure 4.7). Of course, plans should include care of the child for years to come. Data on fertility rate and economic status (see Figure 4.8) indicate that many parents are well aware of the cost of child rearing.

The first days and weeks after conception are critical for body formation during the germinal and embryonic periods, but health during the entire fetal period is crucial for the brain. Some teratogens that cause preterm birth or low birthweight are particularly harmful in the second half of pregnancy. Indeed, one study found that, although smoking cigarettes throughout pregnancy can be lethal for

FIGURE 4.6

Critical Periods in Human Development
The most serious damage from teratogens (*orange bars*) is likely to occur early in prenatal development. However, significant damage (*purple bars*) to many vital parts of the body, including the brain, eyes, and genitals, can occur during the last months of pregnancy as well.

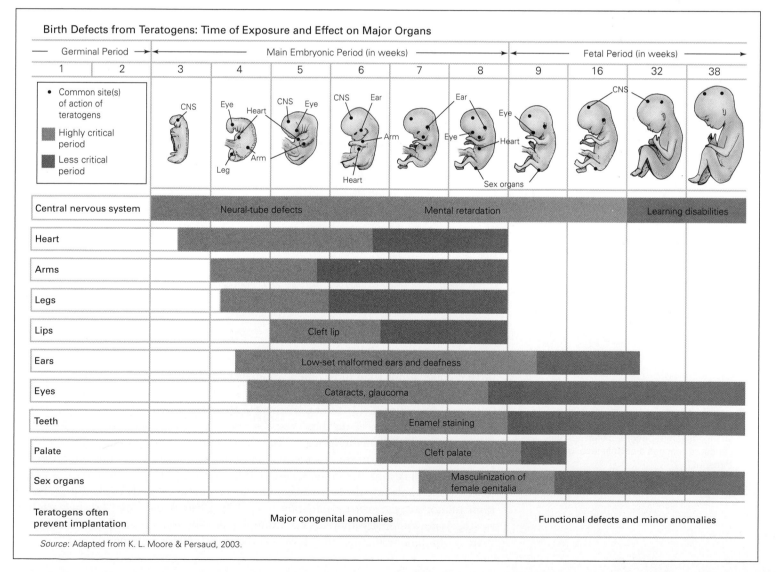

Birth Defects from Teratogens: Time of Exposure and Effect on Major Organs

Source: Adapted from K. L. Moore & Persaud, 2003.

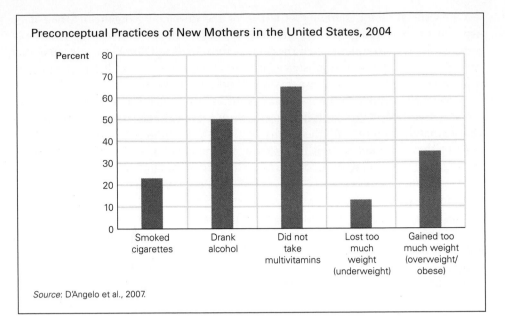

Preconceptual Practices of New Mothers in the United States, 2004

Source: D'Angelo et al., 2007.

FIGURE 4.7

No One Is Perfect Blaming pregnant women is easy, but almost no one avoids all drugs and stresses, sleeps and eats well, weighs just the right amount, exercises at least an hour each day, and completely avoids fried or salty foods. If you are the exception, could you keep it up for a year, while gaining 35 pounds; sometimes feeling nauseous; coping with stares and the questions of friends, relatives, and strangers; and going to the doctor every few weeks?

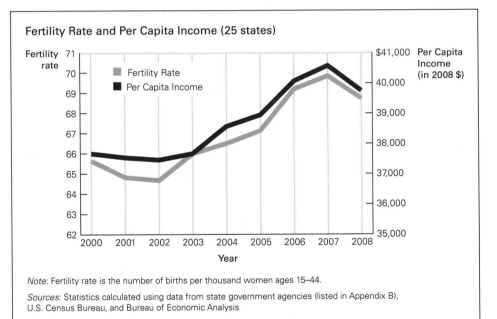

Fertility Rate and Per Capita Income (25 states)

Note: Fertility rate is the number of births per thousand women ages 15–44.

Sources: Statistics calculated using data from state government agencies (listed in Appendix B), U.S. Census Bureau, and Bureau of Economic Analysis

FIGURE 4.8

Can We Afford College? Fertility rates in the United States seem to reflect the economic recession that began in 2007. States with higher unemployment experienced a greater decline. The problem continues. The 2009 fertility rate was the lowest in U.S. history.

threshold effect A situation in which a certain teratogen is relatively harmless in small doses but becomes harmful once exposure reaches a certain level (the threshold).

the fetus, smokers who quit in the first weeks of pregnancy had no higher risks of birth complications than did women who never smoked (McCowan et al., 2009).

A second factor affecting the harm from any teratogen is the dose and/or frequency of exposure. Some teratogens have a **threshold effect;** they are virtually harmless until exposure reaches a certain level, at which point they "cross the threshold" and become damaging (O'Rahilly & Müller, 2001). Indeed, a few substances are beneficial in small amounts but fiercely teratogenic in large quantities. One is vitamin A, which is essential for healthy development, but 50,000 units per day (obtained only in pills) can cause many abnormalities (Naudé et al., 2007). For most teratogens, experts are reluctant to specify a threshold, partly because each teratogen may intensify another. For example, alcohol, tobacco, and marijuana do more harm in combination, thus lowering the threshold for each on its own.

Genes of the developing organism are a third factor. When a woman carrying dizygotic twins drinks alcohol, for example, the twins' blood alcohol levels are equal, yet one twin may be more severely affected than the other. The probable reason: Only one twin has an allele that affects the enzyme that metabolizes alcohol. Genetic vulnerability is suspected for many birth defects.

Data are definitive on a maternal allele that results in low levels of folic acid, which can produce *neural-tube defects*—either *spina bifida,* when the tail of the spine is not enclosed properly (in healthy embryos, enclosure occurs at about week 7) or *anencephaly,* when part of the brain is missing. Neural-tube defects are more common in certain ethnic groups (Irish, English, and Egyptian) than in others (most Asian and African groups), which led researchers to discover the allele that prevents the normal utilization of folic acid (Mills et al., 1995). There is not yet a preconception test for this allele, and Americans of all ethnicities sometimes have it. Consequently, folic acid is now added to all U.S. packaged bread and breakfast cereal by law; the result has been a 26 percent reduction in the rate of neural-tube defects since 1990 (MMWR, September 13, 2002).

Risk analysis cannot precisely predict the results of teratogenic exposure in individual cases. However, much is known about destructive and damaging teratogens and about what individuals and society can do to reduce the risks. Table 4.4 on pages 106–107 lists some teratogens and their possible effects, as well as preventive measures.

Especially for Nutritionists Is it beneficial that most breakfast cereals are fortified with vitamins and minerals? (see response, page 107)

Applying the Research

Remember that the effects of teratogens vary. Many fetuses are exposed with no evident harm, and about 20 percent of all serious defects occur for reasons unknown. Women are advised to eat healthy foods and to avoid all possible teratogens, especially chemicals in pesticides, cleaning fluids, and cosmetics (bug spray, hair dye, and some plastics are among the substances recently discovered to be teratogenic). Some medications are essential, but caution should begin even *before* pregnancy is confirmed.

Unfortunately, sometimes research results leave room for doubt. In addition, conclusions do not always reach those who need to know. Even doctors are not always as careful as they could or should be. According to a massive study of 152,000 new mothers in eight health maintenance organizations (HMOs) in the United States, doctors wrote an average of three prescriptions per pregnant woman, including drugs that had not been declared safe during pregnancy (prescribed for 40 percent) and drugs with proven risks to fetuses (prescribed for 2 percent) (Andrade et al., 2004). We hope that these doctors did not know their patients were pregnant and that the women did not take the medications.

Sadly, women who are most vulnerable are most likely to be exposed and least likely to be aware of thresholds and interactions. Examples include: those who smoke cigarettes are likely to be highly stressed and to drink alcohol; those who are exposed to chemicals and pesticides are likely to be malnourished; those who have low incomes are also likely to receive substandard medical care and to have jobs (such as in factories, not offices) that increase exposure to teratogens (Ahmed & Jaakkola, 2007; Hougaard & Hansen, 2007).

Even scientists apply the research in contradictory ways. For instance, pregnant women in the United States have been warned not to eat much fish, but pregnant women in the United Kingdom have been advised that fish consumption is beneficial to the fetus. The reason for these opposite messages is that fish contains both mercury (a teratogen) and DHA (needed for brain development) (Oken & Bellinger, 2008; Ramón et al., 2009), and scientists weigh the benefits and risks of

TABLE 4.4		
Teratogens: Effects of Exposure and Prevention of Damage		
Teratogens **Diseases**	Effects on Child of Exposure	Measures for Preventing Damage
Rubella (German measles)	In embryonic period, causes blindness and deafness; in first and second trimesters, causes brain damage	Get immunized before pregnancy
Toxoplasmosis	Brain damage, loss of vision, mental retardation	Avoid eating undercooked meat and handling cat feces, garden dirt
Measles, chicken pox, influenza	May impair brain functioning	Get immunized before pregnancy; avoid infected people during pregnancy
Syphilis	Baby is born with syphilis, which, untreated, leads to brain and bone damage and eventual death	Early prenatal diagnosis and treatment with antibiotics
AIDS	Baby may catch the virus. If so, illness and death are likely during childhood.	Prenatal drugs and cesarean birth make AIDS transmission rare
Other sexually transmitted infections, including gonorrhea and chlamydia	Not usually harmful during pregnancy but may cause blindness and infections if transmitted during birth	Early diagnosis and treatment; if necessary, cesarean section, treatment of newborn
Infections, including infections of urinary tract, gums, and teeth	May cause premature labor, which increases vulnerability to brain damage	Get infection treated, preferably before pregnancy
Pollutants		
Lead, mercury, PCBs (polychlorinated biphenyls), dioxin, and some pesticides, herbicides, and cleaning compounds	May cause spontaneous abortion, preterm labor, and brain damage	Most common substances are harmless in small doses, but pregnant women should still avoid regular and direct exposure, such as drinking well water, eating unwashed fruits or vegetables, using chemical compounds, eating fish from polluted waters
Radiation		
Massive or repeated exposure to radiation, as in medical X-rays	In the embryonic period, may cause abnormally small head (microcephaly) and mental retardation; in the fetal period, suspected but not proven to cause brain damage. Exposure to background radiation, as from power plants, is usually too low to have an effect.	Get ultrasounds, not X-rays, during pregnancy; pregnant women who work directly with radiation need special protection or temporary assignment to another job
Social and Behavioral Factors		
Very high stress	Early in pregnancy, may cause cleft lip or cleft palate, spontaneous abortion, or preterm labor	Get adequate relaxation, rest, and sleep; reduce hours of employment; get help with housework and child care
Malnutrition	When severe, may interfere with conception, implantation, normal fetal development, and full-term birth	Consume adequate vitamins and minerals, especially folic acid, iron, and vitamin A; achieve normal weight before getting pregnant, then gain 25–35 lbs (10–15 kg)
Excessive, exhausting exercise	Can affect fetal development when it interferes with pregnant woman's sleep or digestion	Get regular, moderate exercise

Teratogens	Effects on Child of Exposure	Measures for Preventing Damage
Medicinal Drugs		
Lithium	Can cause heart abnormalities	Avoid all medicines, whether prescription or over-the-counter, during pregnancy unless they are approved by a medical professional who knows about the pregnancy and is aware of the most recent research
Tetracycline	Can harm the teeth	
Retinoic acid	Can cause limb deformities	
Streptomycin	Can cause deafness	
ACE inhibitors	Can harm digestive organs	
Phenobarbital	Can affect brain development	
Thalidomide	Can stop ear and limb formation	
Psychoactive Drugs		
Caffeine	Normal use poses no problem	Avoid excessive use: Drink no more than three cups a day of beverages containing caffeine (coffee, tea, cola drinks, hot chocolate)
Alcohol	May cause fetal alcohol syndrome (FAS) or fetal alcohol effects (FAE)	Stop or severely limit alcohol consumption during pregnancy; especially dangerous are three or more drinks a day or five or more drinks on one occasion
Tobacco	Increases risk of malformations of limbs and urinary tract, and may affect the baby's lungs	Stop smoking before and during pregnancy
Marijuana	Heavy exposure may affect the central nervous system; when smoked, may hinder fetal growth	Avoid or strictly limit marijuana consumption
Heroin	Slows fetal growth and may cause premature labor; newborns with heroin in their bloodstream require medical treatment to prevent the pain and convulsions of withdrawal	Get treated for heroin addiction before becoming pregnant; if already pregnant, gradual withdrawal on methadone is better than continued use of heroin
Cocaine	May cause slow fetal growth, premature labor, and learning problems in the first years of life	Stop using cocaine before pregnancy; babies of cocaine-using mothers may need special medical and educational attention in their first years of life
Inhaled solvents (glue or aerosol)	May cause abnormally small head, crossed eyes, and other indications of brain damage	Stop sniffing inhalants before becoming pregnant; be aware that serious damage can occur before a woman knows she is pregnant

Note: This table summarizes some relatively common teratogenic effects. As the text makes clear, many individual factors in each pregnancy affect whether a given teratogen will actually cause damage and what that damage might be. This is a general summary of what is known; new evidence is reported almost daily, so some of these generalities will change. Pregnant women or women who want to become pregnant should consult with their physicians.

Sources: Briggs et al., 2008; R. D. Mann & Andrews, 2007; O'Rahilly & Müller, 2001; Reece & Hobbins, 2007; Shepard & Lemire, 2004.

>> **Response for Nutritionists** (from page 105) Useful, yes; optimal, no. Some essential vitamins are missing (too expensive), and individual needs differ, depending on age, sex, health, genes, and eating habits. The reduction in neural-tube defects is good, but many women don't eat cereal or take vitamin supplements before becoming pregnant.

fish differently. Another dispute involves bisphenol A (commonly used in plastics), banned in Canada but allowed in the United States. The effect of bisphenol A is disputed because

> epidemiological research on fetal exposure would be logistically difficult and costly because exposures must be measured at several different time points, including gestation, whereas the outcome may not be manifest in some cases until 50 or more years after the initial fetal exposure.

[*Diamanti-Kandarakis et. al. 2009, p. 320*]

Prenatal teratogens can cause behavioral problems, reproductive impairment, and several diseases many years after birth. Almost every common disease, almost every food additive, most prescription and nonprescription drugs (even caffeine and aspirin), trace minerals in the air and water, emotional stress, exhaustion, and poor nutrition *might* impair prenatal development—but only at some times, in some amounts, in some mammals. Most research has been done with mice; harm to humans is rarely proven to everyone's satisfaction, and even when it is, the proper response can be controversial.

fetal alcohol syndrome (FAS) A cluster of birth defects, including abnormal facial characteristics, slow physical growth, and retarded mental development, that may occur in the child of a woman who drinks alcohol while pregnant.

Consider a proven teratogen, alcohol, which can cause **fetal alcohol syndrome** (FAS), distorting the facial features (especially the eyes, ears, and upper lip) in the first weeks of prenatal development. It later causes *fetal alcohol effects (FAE)*, leading to hyperactivity, poor concentration, impaired spatial reasoning, and slow learning (Niccols, 2007; Streissguth & Connor, 2001).

That much is known. But it is not known whether timing, high doses, other teratogens, or particular genetics are necessary for alcohol to be teratogenic. Many American experts advise women to abstain completely and to avoid any other drug that could interact with alcohol, including marijuana, heroin, and cocaine. However, FAS is rare: If occasional drinking during pregnancy caused it, most people born in Europe before 1980 would be affected. Total abstinence requires pregnant and potentially pregnant women to avoid a legal substance that most adults use routinely. Wise? Probably. Necessary? Maybe not.

© DAVID H. WELLS / CORBIS

Yes, But . . . An adopted boy points out something to his father—a positive interaction between the two. The shapes of the boy's eyes, ears, and upper lip indicate that he was born with fetal alcohol syndrome (FAS). Scientists disagree about the strength of the correlation between FAS and drinking alcohol during pregnancy.

Since 1998, five states (Minnesota, North Dakota, Oklahoma, South Dakota, and Wisconsin) have authorized "involuntary commitment" (jail or forced residential treatment) for pregnant women who drink. The legal basis is that the fetus is a future child and that therefore drinking during pregnancy is child abuse. Advocates for women consider such laws discriminatory, especially since women who are poor or American Indian are most likely to be imprisoned (Schroedel & Fiber, 2001). The threat of jail may cause women who most need prenatal care to instead avoid it.

Prenatal Care

The benefits of early prenatal care are many: Women are told which substances to avoid, they learn what to eat and what to do, and they are treated for some conditions (syphilis and HIV/AIDS among them) that may not harm the fetus if treated early in pregnancy. Prenatal tests (of blood, urine, and fetal heart rate as well as ultrasound) reassure the parents long before fetal movement is apparent.

In general, early care protects fetal growth, makes birth easier, and renders parents better able to cope. For example, nutritional and exercise needs are met, and, if complications (twins, gestational diabetes, infections) are recognized early, that increases the chance of a healthy, happy birth. Unfortunately, about 20 percent of early pregnancy tests *raise* anxiety instead of reducing it. For instance, the level of alpha-fetoprotein (AFP) may be too high or too low, or ultrasound may indicate multiple fetuses, abnormal growth, Down syndrome, or a too-narrow pelvis. Many such warnings are "false positives," which means they suggest a problem that does not actually exist. Any warning, whether false or accurate, requires further testing but also leads to worry and soul-searching. Some choose to abort, some to give birth, and in both cases the decision may not be what the parents assumed before prenatal testing, as the following illustrates.

Especially for Social Workers When is it most important to convince women to be tested for HIV: before pregnancy, after conception, or immediately after birth? (see response, page 111)

A CASE TO STUDY

"What Did That Say About Me?"

When Tom Horan and his wife learned in April 2004 that their fetus's legs were bowed and shortened, they were told that the condition could be healed through braces, growth hormones, and surgical procedures in childhood.

Closer examination by a specialist with a 3-D ultrasound machine revealed other deformities: The left arm was missing below the elbow and the right hand was only partially developed. Moreover, sometimes such features are a sign of a neurological impairment, the doctors told them, but in this case it was impossible to tell.

"Our main concern was the quality of life that the child would have growing up with such extensive limb deformities, even in the absence of cognitive problems," Mr. Horan said. He and his wife, who have three other children, were reared Roman Catholic and had never considered terminating a pregnancy. Yet even

his father, Mr. Horan said, who had long been opposed to abortion, supported their decision to end the pregnancy.

"Confronted with this question and knowing what we knew, it changed his mind," Mr. Horan said. "It's not just a question of right and wrong; it introduces all sorts of other questions that one has to consider, whether it is the survivability of the child, quality of life of parents, quality of life of siblings, social needs. And it becomes much more real when you're confronted with an actual situation."

After the termination, an examination showed . . . an extremely rare condition, Cornelia de Lange syndrome would have been severely mentally and physically disabled.

The news was a relief to Mr. Horan, who said he felt sadness and grief, but no regrets. . . . Before the diagnosis, he felt guilt and uncertainty. . . . "I wondered about the ethical implications. . . . What did that say about me?"

[Harmon, 2004, p. A19]

A CASE TO STUDY

"What Do People Live to Do?"

John and Martha, graduate students at Harvard, were expecting their second child. Martha was four months pregnant, and her initial prenatal screening revealed an abnormally low level of alpha-fetoprotein, which could indicate that the fetus had Down syndrome. Another blood test was scheduled.

After a nurse had drawn the second blood sample, before the laboratory reported the result, Martha wrote that John asked:

"What exactly is the problem?" . . .

"We've got a one in eight hundred and ninety-five shot at a retarded baby."

John smiled, "I can live with those odds."

"I'm still a little scared."

He reached across the table for my hand. "Sure," he said, "That's understandable. But even if there is a problem, we've

caught it in time. . . . The worst case scenario is that you might have to have an abortion, and that's a long shot. Everything's going to be fine."

. . . "I might *have to have* an abortion?" The chill inside me was gone. Instead I could feel my face flushing hot with anger. "Since when do you decide what I *have* to do with my body?"

John looked surprised. "I never said I was going to decide anything," he protested. "It's just that if the tests show something wrong with the baby, of course we'll abort. We've talked about this."

"What we've talked about," I told John in a low, dangerous voice, "is that I am pro-choice. That means I decide whether or not I'd abort a baby with a birth defect. . . . I'm not so sure of this."

"You used to be," said John.

"I know I used to be." I rubbed my eyes. I felt terribly confused. "But now . . . look, John, it's not as though we're deciding whether or not to have a baby. We're deciding what *kind* of baby we're willing to accept. If it's perfect in every way, we keep it. If it doesn't fit the right specifications, whoosh! Out it goes.". . .

John was looking more and more confused. "Martha, why are you on this soapbox? What's your point?"

"My point is," I said, "that I'm trying to get you to tell me what you think constitutes a 'defective' baby. What about . . . oh, I don't know, a hyperactive baby? Or an ugly one?"

"They can't test for those things and—"

"Well, what if they could?" I said. "Medicine can do all kinds of magical tricks these days. Pretty soon we're going to be aborting babies because they have the gene for alcoholism, or homosexuality, or manic depression. . . . Did you know that in China they abort a lot of fetuses just because they're female?" I growled. "Is being a girl 'defective' enough for you?"

"Look," he said, "I know I can't always see things from your perspective. And I'm sorry about that. But the way I see it, if a baby is going to be deformed or something, abortion is a way to keep everyone from suffering—*especially* the baby. It's like shooting a horse that's broken its leg. . . . A lame horse dies slowly, you know? . . . It dies in terrible pain. And it can't run anymore. So it can't enjoy life even if it doesn't die. Horses live to run; that's what they do. If a baby is born not being able to do what other people do, I think it's better not to prolong its suffering."

". . . And what is it," I said softly, more to myself than to John, "what is it that people do? What do we live to do, the way a horse lives to run?"

[M. N. Beck, 1999, pp. 132–133, 135]

The second AFP test came back low but in the normal range, "meaning there was no reason to fear that [the fetus] had Down syndrome" (p. 137).

Note that John thought they had already discussed and decided to abort a fetus if a serious problem was evident. However, an unexpected test result distresses many prospective parents. As you read in Chapter 3, a genetic counselor not only explains the odds but also helps a couple discuss their choices *before* becoming pregnant. John and Martha had no counseling before conceiving because the pregnancy was unplanned and their risk for any problems, especially chromosomal ones, was low.

The opposite of a false positive is a false negative, a mistaken assurance that all is well. Even though the second AFP test suggested "no reason to fear," amniocentesis later revealed that the second AFP was a false negative. Their fetus had Down syndrome. Martha decided against abortion.

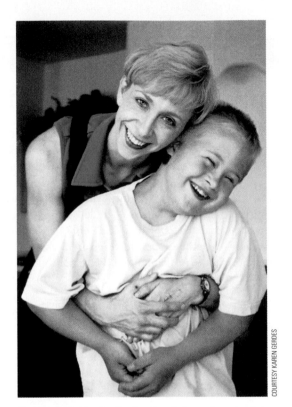

Happy Boy Martha Beck not only loves her son Adam (shown here), but she also writes about the special experiences he has brought to the whole family's life—hers, John's, and their other children's. She is "pro-choice"; he was a chosen child.

Low Birthweight

Some newborns are small and immature, a problem that originates months or even years before birth because women who are undernourished are likely to have undernourished babies. With modern hospital care, tiny infants usually survive, but it would be better for everyone—mother, father, baby, and society—if all newborns were in the womb for at least 35 weeks and weighed more than 2,500 grams (5½ pounds). (Usually, pounds are given before grams in this text, but hospitals worldwide measure birthweight using the metric system, so grams precede pounds and ounces here.)

Low birthweight (LBW) is defined by the World Health Organization as under 2,500 grams. LBW babies are further grouped into **very low birthweight (VLBW),** under 1,500 grams (3 pounds, 5 ounces), and **extremely low birthweight (ELBW),** under 1,000 grams (2 pounds, 3 ounces).

low birthweight (LBW) A body weight at birth of less than 5½ pounds (2,500 grams).

very low birthweight (VLBW) A body weight at birth of less than 3 pounds, 5 ounces (1,500 grams).

extremely low birthweight (ELBW) A body weight at birth of less than 2 pounds, 3 ounces (1,000 grams).

Causes of Low Birthweight

Remember that fetal weight normally doubles in the last trimester of pregnancy, with 900 grams (about 2 pounds) of that gain occurring in the final three weeks. Thus, a baby born **preterm** (three or more weeks early; no longer called *premature*) is probably LBW.

Early birth is only one cause of low birthweight. Some fetuses gain weight slowly throughout pregnancy and are *small-for-dates,* or **small for gestational age (SGA).** A full-term baby weighing only 2,500 grams and a 30-week-old fetus weighing only 1,000 grams are both SGA, even though the first is not quite low birthweight. Maternal or fetal illness might cause SGA, but maternal drug use is a more common cause. Every psychoactive drug slows fetal growth, with tobacco implicated in 25 percent of all low-birthweight births worldwide. Smoking among young women is declining in the United States but rising in other nations; the worldwide rate of SGA may rise as well.

Another common reason for slow fetal growth is maternal malnutrition. Women who begin pregnancy underweight, who eat poorly during pregnancy, or who gain less than 3 pounds (1.3 kilograms) per month in the last six months are more likely to have an underweight infant. Malnutrition (not age) is the primary reason teenagers often have small babies. Unfortunately, many of the risk factors just mentioned—underweight, undereating, underage, and smoking—tend to occur together.

Consequences of Low Birthweight

You already read that life itself is uncertain for the smallest newborns. Ranking worse than most developed nations—and tied with Poland and Slovakia in infant deaths (MacDorman & Mathews, 2008)—the United States has a distressing incidence of infant mortality, primarily because of low birthweight. When LBW infants survive, their problems are not over. Even when compared with newborns conceived at the same time but born later, very-low-birthweight infants are later to smile, to hold a bottle, to walk, and to communicate. As the months go by, cognitive difficulties as well as visual and hearing impairments may emerge. Survivors who were high-risk newborns tend to become infants and children who cry more, pay attention less, disobey, and experience language delays (Aarnoudse-Moens et al., 2009; Spinillo et al., 2009).

Even in adulthood, some risks persist. Ironically, low-birthweight infants have higher rates of obesity, heart disease, and diabetes. The data provide hope as well as caution: Some LBW infants develop normally, overcoming their early problems if they receive excellent early care in the hospital and then at home (Spittle et al., 2009).

International Low Birthweight

In some northern European nations, only 3 percent of newborns weigh under 2,500 grams; in several South Asian nations, 30 percent do. Worldwide, fewer low-birthweight babies are born than 20 years ago, and neonatal deaths have been reduced by one-third as a result (Rajaratnam et al., 2010). Some nations, China and Chile among them, show dramatic improvement. In 1970, about 50 percent of Chinese newborns were LBW; recent estimates are that about 15 percent are, with continued improvement every year.

In other nations, notably some in sub-Saharan Africa, LBW births have been steady or even rising, as global warming, AIDS, food shortages, wars, and other problems affect pregnancy. Another nation with increases is the United States, where the LBW rate fell steadily throughout most of the twentieth century,

preterm A birth that occurs 3 or more weeks before the full 38 weeks of the typical pregnancy—that is, at 35 or fewer weeks after conception.

small for gestational age (SGA) A term for a baby whose birthweight is significantly lower than expected, given the time since conception. For example, a 5-pound (2,265-gram) newborn is considered SGA if born on time but not SGA if born two months early. (Also called *small-for-dates.*)

>> Response for Social Workers (from page 109) Testing and then treatment are useful at any time, because women who know they are HIV-positive are more likely to get treatment, reduce the risk of transmission, or avoid pregnancy. If pregnancy does occur, early diagnosis is best. Getting tested after birth is too late for the baby.

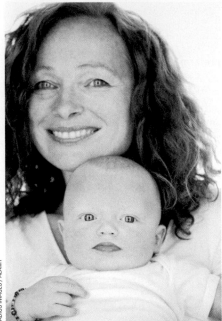

A Growing Trend The rate of first births to women in their 40s tripled from 1990 to 2008, although most newborns (96%) have mothers under age 40. Nonetheless, prenatal testing and medical advances have made late motherhood less risky than it was, with some happy results. This mother is 42.

reaching a low of 7.0 percent in 1990. Then the rate rose again, with the 2008 rate at 8.2 percent—higher than that of almost every other developed nation.

Many scientists have explored various hypotheses for the rise in U.S. rates. One logical idea is that the increase in assisted reproduction is the problem, since the result is often twins and triplets, and multiples are usually LBW. However, rates are rising even for naturally conceived babies (Pinborg et al., 2004). Add to the puzzle the fact that several changes in maternal ethnicity, age, and health since 1990 would be expected to decrease the LBW rate, not increase it. For example, African Americans have LBW newborns twice as often as the national average (almost 14 percent compared with 7 percent), and younger teenagers have smaller babies than do women in their 20s; but the birth rate among both African Americans and teenagers was significantly lower in 2010 than in 1990. Furthermore, two increasingly common health problems, obesity and diabetes, tend to result in heavier babies, not lighter ones.

Something systemic must be amiss. One possibility is nutrition. Those African nations with high rates of LBW are also nations where hunger is prevalent, and Chile and China have both reduced malnutrition. Could this be relevant to the United States? A study sponsored by the United States Department of Agriculture found that *food insecurity* (a term that includes skipping meals, using food stamps, and outright hunger) increased between 2000 and 2007. About 15 percent of households are food insecure, with rates higher among young mothers than among the middle-aged (Nord et al., 2009).

Another possibility is drug use. As you will see in Chapters 14 and 17, the rate of smoking, drinking, and other drug use among high school girls reached a low in 1992, then increased, and is now decreasing again. Most U.S. women now giving birth were in the cohort that exhibited rising drug use; they may still be affected by it. If that is the reason, the current decrease in drug use will mean that LBW should fall again in the United States. In developing nations, more young women are smoking and drinking than a decade ago: Will their newborns be underweight as a result?

Complications During Birth

cerebral palsy A disorder that results from damage to the brain's motor centers. People with cerebral palsy have difficulty with muscle control, so their speech and/or body movements are impaired.

anoxia A lack of oxygen that, if prolonged, can cause brain damage or death.

When a fetus is already at risk because of low birthweight, preterm birth, genetic abnormality, or exposure to a teratogen, or when a mother is unusually young, old, small, or ill, birth complications become likely. As an example, **cerebral palsy** (difficulties with movement control resulting from brain damage) was once thought to be caused solely by birth procedures: excessive pain medication, slow breech birth, or delivery by forceps (an instrument sometimes used to pull the fetus's head through the birth canal). In fact, however, cerebral palsy often results from genetic vulnerability and may be worsened by teratogens, maternal infection (J. R. Mann et al., 2009), and then a preterm birth involving insufficient oxygen to the brain.

The term for a temporary lack of oxygen is **anoxia,** which often occurs for a second or two during birth. When anoxia lasts longer than that, or when the fetus is immature, the heart beats more slowly and brain damage can occur. To avoid the damage of anoxia, the fetal heart rate is monitored during labor and the newborn's color, breathing, and heart rate are measured (they are three of the five criteria on the Apgar scale). How long anoxia can continue without harming the brain depends on genes, birthweight, gestational age, drugs in the bloodstream (either taken by the mother before birth or given to the mother during birth), and a host of other factors.

SUMMING UP

Risk analysis is a complex but necessary aspect of prenatal development because the placenta does not protect the fetus from all teratogens, including diseases, drugs, and pollutants. Many factors reduce risk, including the mother's health and nourishment before pregnancy and early prenatal care (to diagnose and treat problems and to teach the woman how to protect her fetus). The timing of exposure to teratogens and their dose, as well as the genes of the mother and fetus, may be crucial. Low birthweight, slow growth, and early birth increase vulnerability: Maternal illness, drug use, and malnutrition are among the most common causes of these complications. The birth process can add to the problems of the vulnerable infant, especially if anoxia lasts more than a moment or two.

>> The New Family

Humans are social creatures, seeking interaction with their families and their societies. Each person is affected by every other person, particularly within each family.

The Newborn

Even before birth, developing humans contribute to their families, not only indirectly by making some people mothers, fathers, sisters, or brothers, but directly via fetal movements and hormones (causing protective impulses in the mother early in pregnancy and nurturant impulses at the end). The appearance of the newborn (big hairless head, tiny feet, and so on) stirs the human heart, evident in brain activity and heart rate. Fathers are often enraptured by their scraggly infant and protective of the exhausted mother.

Newborns are responsive social creatures, even in the first hours of life. They listen, stare, cry, stop crying, and cuddle. In the first day or two, a professional might administer the **Brazelton Neonatal Behavioral Assessment Scale (NBAS),** which records 46 behaviors, including 20 reflexes. Parents who watch their infant perform on the NBAS are amazed at the newborn's responses—and this fosters early parent–child connection (Hawthorne, 2009).

Technically, a **reflex** is an involuntary response to a particular stimulus, a definition that makes reflexes seem automatic, with the new person having no role. Actually, the strength of reflexes varies from one newborn to the next, an early indication that each person is unique. Humans of every age instinctively seek to protect themselves (the eyeblink is one example). Newborns do this, too, with three sets of reflexes that aid survival:

- *Reflexes that maintain oxygen supply.* The *breathing reflex* begins even before the umbilical cord, with its supply of oxygen, is cut. Additional reflexes that maintain oxygen are reflexive *hiccups* and *sneezes,* as well as *thrashing* (moving the arms and legs about) to escape something that covers the face.
- *Reflexes that maintain constant body temperature.* When infants are cold, they *cry, shiver,* and *tuck in their legs* close to their bodies, thereby helping to keep themselves warm. When they are hot, they try to *push away* blankets and then stay still.
- *Reflexes that manage feeding.* The *sucking reflex* causes newborns to suck anything that touches their lips—fingers, toes, blankets, and rattles, as well as natural and artificial nipples of various textures and shapes. The *rooting*

Brazelton Neonatal Behavioral Assessment Scale (NBAS) A test often administered to newborns that measures responsiveness and records 46 behaviors, including 20 reflexes.

reflex An unlearned, involuntary action or movement that responds to a stimulus. A reflex occurs without conscious thought.

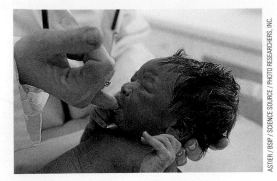

Never Underestimate the Power of a Reflex For developmentalists, newborn reflexes are mechanisms for survival, indicators of brain maturation, and vestiges of evolutionary history. For parents, they are mostly delightful and sometimes amazing. Both of these viewpoints are demonstrated by three star performers: a newborn boy sucking peacefully on the doctor's finger, a newborn grasping so tightly that his legs dangle in space, and a 1-day-old girl stepping eagerly forward on legs too tiny to support her body.

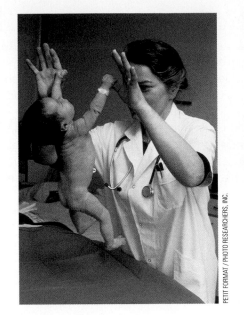

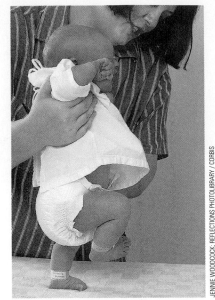

reflex causes babies to turn their mouths toward anything that brushes against their cheeks—a reflexive search for a nipple—and start to suck. *Swallowing* is another important reflex that aids feeding, as are *crying* when the stomach is empty and *spitting up* when too much has been swallowed too quickly.

Other reflexes are not necessary for survival but signify the state of brain and body functions. Among them:

- *Babinski reflex.* When a newborn's feet are stroked, the toes fan upward.
- *Stepping reflex.* When newborns are held upright, feet touching a flat surface, they move their legs as if to walk.
- *Swimming reflex.* When held horizontally on their stomachs, newborns stretch out their arms and legs.
- *Palmar grasping reflex.* When something touches newborns' palms, they grip it tightly.
- *Moro reflex.* When someone bangs on the table they are lying on, newborns fling their arms outward and then bring them together on their chests, crying with wide-open eyes.

It is a mistake to dismiss such behaviors as merely reflexive; they are responses to experiences, not unlike an adult's quick fear, or lust, or anger. The senses are also responsive: New babies listen more to voices than to traffic sounds, for instance. Thus, in many ways newborns connect with the people of their world, who usually respond. If the baby performing all these actions were your own, you would be proud and amazed; that is part of being human.

The Father's Role

Fathers can be crucial to a newborn's development. During pregnancy, supportive fathers-to-be help mothers-to-be stay healthy, well nourished, and drug-free.

Father Presence

At birth, the father's presence reduces complications, in part because his presence helps his wife. I observed this with my own daughter, whose anxiety rose when the

Especially for Scientists Research with animals can benefit people, but it is sometimes wrongly used to support conclusions about people. When does that happen? (see response, page 116)

doctor and midwife discussed a possible cesarean without asking her opinion. Her husband said, "All you need to do is relax between contractions and push when a contraction comes. I will do the rest." She listened. No cesarean.

A study of all live single births in Milwaukee from 1993 to 2006 (151,869 babies!) found that medical complications correlated with several expected variables (such as African American ethnicity, maternal cigarette smoking) and one unexpected one—no father listed on the birth record. This was especially apparent for European American births: Father absence correlated with long labor, cesarean sections, and other complications (Ngui et al., 2009).

Fathers may be the explanation for what is called the *immigration paradox,* which finds that although immigrants to the United States are poorer, with less adequate prenatal care, they have healthier newborns than native-born mothers of the same ethnic background (Cunningham et al., 2008). The reason may be related to another fact: Immigrant women are almost always married when they give birth, unlike the circumstances in about 40 percent of births in the United States since 2005 (U.S. Bureau of the Census, 2009). Perhaps immigrant husbands make sure their expectant wives eat well, avoid alcohol and cigarettes, and get enough rest.

Paternal Pride Twins mean trouble—less sleep, less money, more worry. Yet, like most parents of newborns, no matter what special complications they entail, this father is enraptured with his 1-day-old sons.

Couvade

Pregnancy and birth may be biologically (not just psychologically) experienced by fathers. For example, levels of the stress hormone cortisol correlate between expectant fathers and mothers, probably because they make each other anxious or relaxed (Berg & Wynne-Edwards, 2002). Beyond that, many fathers experience symptoms of pregnancy and birth, including weight gain and indigestion during pregnancy and pain during labor. Indeed, among some Latin American Indians, fathers are expected to go through the motions of labor when their wives do, to help ensure an easy birth.

Paternal experiences of pregnancy and birth are called **couvade,** expected in some cultures, a normal variation in many, and considered pathological in still others (M. Sloan, 2009). In developed nations, couvade is unnoticed and unstudied, but researchers find that fathers are often intensely involved with pregnancy and birth (Brennan et al., 2007).

Remember John and Martha, the young couple whose amniocentesis revealed that their fetus had trisomy-21 (Down syndrome)? One night at 3:00 A.M., after about seven months of pregnancy, Martha was crying uncontrollably. She told John she was scared.

> "Scared of what?" he said. "Of a little baby who's not as perfect as you think he ought to be?"
>
> "I didn't say I wanted him to be perfect," I said. "I just want him to be normal. That's all I want. Just normal."
>
> "That is total bullshit. . . . You don't want this baby to be normal. You'd throw him in a dumpster if he just turned out to be normal. What you really want is for him to be superhuman."
>
> "For your information," I said in my most acid tone, "I was the one who decided to keep this baby, even though he's got Down's. You were the one who wanted to throw him in a dumpster."
>
> "How would you know?" John's voice was still gaining volume. "You never asked me what I wanted, did you? No. You never even asked me. . . ."
>
> [M. N. Beck, 1999, p. 255]

couvade Symptoms of pregnancy and birth experienced by fathers.

parental alliance Cooperation between a mother and a father based on their mutual commitment to their children. In a parental alliance, the parents support each other in their shared parental roles.

A Good Beginning The apparent joy and bonding between this expectant couple and their unborn child is a wonderful sign. Although this couple in Germany may experience discrimination from society—one reason the divorce rate is higher among multiracial couples than monoracial ones—their own parental alliance is crucial for their child. Many multiracial children become adults with higher achievement, greater self-understanding, and more tolerance than others.

postpartum depression A new mother's feelings of inadequacy and sadness in the days and weeks after giving birth.

parent–infant bond The strong, loving connection that forms as parents hold, examine, and feed their newborn.

>> Response for Scientists (from page 114) Animal research should not, by itself, confirm an assertion that has popular appeal but no scientific evidence. This occurred in the social construction that physical contact was crucial for parent–infant bonding.

This episode ended well, with a long, warm, and honest conversation between the two prospective parents. Both parents learned what their fetus meant to the other, a taboo topic until that night. Adam, their future son, became an important part of their relationship. Their lack of communication up to this point, and the sudden eruption of unexpressed emotions, is not unusual, because pregnancy itself raises memories from childhood and fears about the future. Yet honest and intimate communication is crucial throughout pregnancy, birth, and child rearing, to create the foundation for a **parental alliance,** a commitment by both parents to cooperate in raising the child.

A parental alliance is especially beneficial when the infant is physically vulnerable, such as having a low birthweight. The converse is also true: Family conflict when a newborn needs extra care makes child maladjustment and parental divorce more likely (Whiteside-Mansell et al., 2009).

Postpartum Depression

About half of all women experience physical problems after birth, such as healing from a c-section, or painfully sore nipples, or problems with urination (Danel et al., 2003). However, worse than any physical problems are psychological ones. When the birth hormones decrease, between 8 and 15 percent of women experience **postpartum depression,** a sense of inadequacy and sadness (called *baby blues* in the mild version and *postpartum psychosis* in the most severe form) (Perfetti et al., 2004). Normal baby care (feeding, diapering, bathing) feels very burdensome, babies are not always comforted, and the mother may have thoughts of neglecting or abusing the infant.

Since maternal depression can have a long-term impact on the child, postpartum depression should be recognized and treated. Fathers are the first responders to this complication; they are often instrumental in getting the help the mother and baby need (Cuijpers et al., 2010; Goodman & Gotlib, 2002).

From a developmental perspective, some causes of postpartum depression (such as financial stress or marital problems) predate the pregnancy; others occur during pregnancy (especially if the women is worried about the fetus or the birth process); others correlate with birth (especially if the mother is unprepared, alone, or surrounded with unsupportive medical professionals); and still others are specific to the particular infant (health, feeding, or sleeping problems). In every case, support from the father may be pivotal. Of course, this is easier said than done: Fathers may also become depressed, and other people need to help.

Bonding

To what extent are the first hours crucial for the **parent–infant bond,** the strong, loving connection that forms as parents hold, examine, and feed their newborn? It has been claimed that this bond develops in the first hours after birth when a mother touches her naked baby, just as sheep and goats must immediately smell and nuzzle their newborns if they are to nurture them (Klaus & Kennell, 1976).

Although the concept of bonding has been used to argue against the impersonal medicalization of birth, research does not find that early skin-to-skin contact is essential for humans (Eyer, 1992; Lamb, 1982). Unlike sheep and goats, most mammals do not need immediate contact for parents to nurture their offspring.

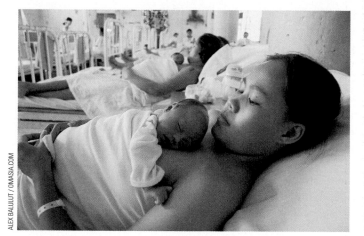

A Beneficial Beginning These new mothers in a maternity ward in Manila are providing their babies with kangaroo care.

In fact, substantial research on monkeys begins with *cross-fostering*, a strategy in which newborns are removed from their biological mothers in the first days of life and raised by another female or even a male. A strong and beneficial relationship sometimes develops (Suomi, 2002).

However, the fact that mother–infant contact is not essential for bonding does not contradict the fact that the prospective mother's and father's active involvement in pregnancy, birth, and newborn care benefits all three. This has recently become apparent with **kangaroo care,** when the newborn lies between the mother's breasts, skin-to-skin, listening to her heartbeat and feeling her body heat. Many studies find that kangaroo-care newborns sleep more deeply, gain weight more quickly, and spend more time alert than do infants who receive standard care (Feldman et al., 2002; Ferber & Makhoul, 2004; Gathwala et al., 2008).

Kangaroo care has been used particularly with low-birthweight newborns and their mothers, with good results. Recently, it has also been successful with healthy newborns and their fathers—evidence that the entire new family benefits from early contact (Thomas, 2008). All the research finds that kangaroo care benefits babies, not only in the hospital but months later, either because of improved infant adjustment to life outside the womb or because of increased parental sensitivity and effectiveness. It probably is both.

Implementation of many strategies, especially for fragile infants and their parents, is especially needed in developing nations, where kangaroo care and other measures could reduce deaths by 20 to 40 percent (Bhutta et al., 2008). From a developmental perspective, the most difficult time for high-risk infants occurs when they leave the hospital, typically weeks after birth. At this juncture, measures to involve parents in early care are shown to be most beneficial. As we will see in later chapters, the bond between parent and child is mutual, developing over months, not merely hours. Birth is one step of a lifelong journey.

SUMMING UP

Every member of the new family contributes to their shared connection, enabling them all to thrive. The new baby has responsive senses and many reflexes. Close observation and reflection reveal how much the new baby can do. Father support of the new family is crucial, sometimes being the reason for a healthy, happy newborn and mother. Postpartum depression is not rare; factors before and after birth affect how serious and long-lasting it is. Family relationships begin before conception, may be strengthened throughout pregnancy and birth, and continue throughout the life span.

Especially for Nurses in Obstetrics Can fathers be of any practical help in the birth process? (see response, page 118)

kangaroo care A form of newborn care in which mothers (and sometimes fathers) rest the baby between their breasts, like a kangaroo that carries her immature newborn in a pouch on her abdomen.

A Teenage Mother This week-old baby, born in a poor village in Myanmar (Burma), has a better chance of survival than he might otherwise have had, because his 18-year-old mother has bonded with him.

SUMMARY

Prenatal Growth

1. The first two weeks of prenatal growth are called the germinal period. During this period, the single-celled zygote multiplies into more than 100 cells that will eventually form both the placenta and the embryo, travels down the fallopian tube, and implants. Most zygotes do not develop.

2. The period from the third through the eighth week after conception is called the embryonic period. The heart begins to beat, and the eyes, ears, nose, and mouth form. By the eighth week, the embryo has the basic organs and features of a human, with the exception of the sex organs.

3. The fetal period extends from the ninth week until birth. In the ninth week, the sexual organs develop. By the end of the third month, all the organs and body structures have formed. The fetus attains viability at 22 weeks, when the brain is sufficiently mature to regulate basic body functions. Babies born before the 26th week are at high risk of death or disability.

4. The average fetus gains approximately 4½ pounds (2,000 grams) during the last three months of pregnancy and weighs 7½ pounds (3,400 grams) at birth. Maturation of brain, lungs, and heart ensures survival of more than 99 percent of all full-term babies born in developed nations.

Birth

5. Birth typically begins with contractions that push the fetus out of the uterus and then through the vagina. The Apgar scale, which rates the neonate's vital signs at one minute and again at five minutes after birth, provides a quick evaluation of the infant's health.

6. Medical assistance can speed contractions, dull pain, and save lives. However, many aspects of medicalized birth have been criticized as impersonal and unnecessary. Contemporary birthing practices are aimed at finding a balance, protecting the baby but also allowing more parental involvement and control. In some cultures, traditional birthing practices are being revisited and implemented.

Problems and Solutions

7. Some teratogens (diseases, drugs, and pollutants) cause physical impairment. Others, called behavioral teratogens, harm the brain and therefore impair cognitive abilities and affect personality traits.

8. Whether a teratogen harms an embryo or fetus depends on timing, amount of exposure, and genetic vulnerability. To protect against prenatal complications, good public and personal health practices are strongly recommended.

9. Low birthweight (under 5½ pounds, or 2,500 grams) may arise from multiple births, placental problems, maternal illness, malnutrition, smoking, drinking, drug use, and age. Compared with full-term newborns, preterm and underweight babies experience more medical difficulties. Fetuses that grow slowly (and thus are small for gestational age, or SGA) are especially vulnerable.

10. Birth complications, such as unusually long and stressful labor that includes anoxia (a lack of oxygen to the fetus), have many causes. Long-term handicaps, such as cerebral palsy, are not inevitable for such children, but careful nurturing from their parents may be needed.

The New Family

11. Humans are social animals. Newborns respond to others in many ways. The Brazelton Neonatal Behavioral Assessment Scale measures 46 newborn behaviors, 20 of which are reflexes.

12. Fathers can be supportive during pregnancy as well as helpful in birth; such support correlates with shorter labor and fewer complications. Some fathers become so involved with the pregnancy and birth that they experience couvade.

13. Many women feel unhappy, incompetent, or unwell after giving birth. Postpartum depression gradually disappears with appropriate help; fathers are crucial to the well-being of mother and child.

14. Kangaroo care is beneficial when the newborn is of low birthweight. Mother–newborn interaction should be encouraged, although the parent–infant bond depends on many factors in addition to birth practices.

KEY TERMS

germinal period (p. 89)
embryonic period (p. 89)
fetal period (p. 89)
implantation (p. 90)
embryo (p. 91)
fetus (p. 92)
ultrasound (p. 92)
age of viability (p. 93)
Apgar scale (p. 97)

cesarean section (c-section) (p. 97)
doula (p. 100)
teratogens (p. 102)
behavioral teratogens (p. 102)
threshold effect (p. 103)
fetal alcohol syndrome (FAS) (p. 108)
low birthweight (LBW) (p. 110)

very low birthweight (VLBW) (p. 110)
extremely low birthweight (ELBW) (p. 110)
preterm (p. 111)
small for gestational age (SGA) (p. 111)
cerebral palsy (p. 112)
anoxia (p. 112)

Brazelton Neonatal Behavioral Assessment Scale (NBAS) (p. 113)
reflex (p. 113)
couvade (p. 115)
parental alliance (p. 116)
postpartum depression (p. 116)
parent–infant bond (p. 116)
kangaroo care (p. 117)

>> **Response for Nurses in Obstetrics** (from page 117) Usually not, unless he is experienced, well-taught, or has expert guidance. But his presence provides emotional support for the woman, which makes the birth process easier and healthier for mother and baby.

WHAT HAVE YOU LEARNED?

Prenatal Growth

1. What are three critical developments in the germinal period?

2. What events begin and end the embryonic period?

3. What occurs about halfway through the fetal period?

4. Why does pregnancy continue months after the fetus could live outside the uterus?

Birth

5. Why has the Apgar scale increased newborns' survival rate?

6. Why has the rate of cesarean sections increased?

7. Why are developmentalists concerned that surgery is often part of birth?

8. Why is the newborn mortality rate much higher in some countries than in others?

9. What are the differences between the role of the doula and that of the doctor?

Problems and Solutions

10. What teratogens harm the developing body structure?

11. What teratogens harm the brain of the developing person?

12. How does timing affect the risk of harm to the fetus?

13. Why does risk analysis not predict precise damage to a fetus?

14. What factors increase or decrease the risk of spina bifida?

15. What are the differences between LBW, VLBW, and ELBW?

16. What are the reasons a baby might be born a month or more before the due date?

17. How have U.S. LBW rates changed in the past decade?

18. What are the long-term consequences if a very tiny or vulnerable newborn survives?

19. What causes cerebral palsy?

The New Family

20. What do newborns do to aid their survival?

21. What role do fathers have during and after birth?

22. How do fathers affect pregnancy?

23. What are the causes of postpartum depression?

24. What affects the parent–infant bond?

25. What happens if a mother does not see her newborn until several days after birth?

APPLICATIONS

1. Go to a nearby greeting-card store and analyze the cards about pregnancy and birth. Do you see any cultural attitudes (e.g., variations depending on the sex of the newborn or of the parent)? If possible, compare those cards with cards from a store that caters to another economic or cultural group.

2. Interview three mothers of varied backgrounds about their birth experiences. Make your interviews open-ended—let them choose what to tell you, as long as they give at least a 10-minute description. Then compare and contrast the three accounts, noting especially any influences of culture, personality, circumstances, or cohort.

3. People sometimes wonder how any pregnant woman could jeopardize the health of her fetus. Consider your own health-related behavior in the past month—exercise, sleep, nutrition, drug use, medical and dental care, disease avoidance, and so on. Would you change your behavior if you were pregnant? Would it make a difference if you, your family, and your partner did not want a baby?

>>ONLINE CONNECTIONS

To accompany your textbook, you have access to a number of online resources, including quizzes for every chapter of the book, flashcards (in English and Spanish), critical thinking questions, and case studies. For access to any of these links, go to www.worthpublishers.com/bergerls8e. In addition to these free resources, you'll also find links to the podcasts, video clips, diagnostic quizzing with personalized study advice, and an ebook. Some of the videos and activities available online include:

- *Brain Development: In the Beginning.* Three-dimensional animation follows brain development from the formation of the neural tube until birth. Animations of microscopic changes in the brain including synaptic pruning.

- *Periods of Prenatal Development.* A series of detailed animations shows the stages of prenatal development from fertilization to birth.

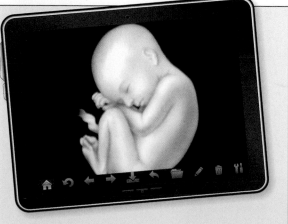

II

the first two years

Adults don't change much in a year or two. Their hair might grow longer, grayer, or thinner; they might be a little fatter; or they might learn something new. But if you saw friends you hadn't seen for two years, you'd recognize them immediately.

By contrast, if you cared for a newborn 24 hours a day for a month, went away for two years, and then came back, you might not recognize him or her, because the baby would have quadrupled in weight, grown taller by more than a foot, and sprouted a new head of hair. Behavior would have changed, too. Not much crying, but some laughter and fear—including of you.

A year or two is not much compared with the 80 or so years of the average life span. However, in two years newborns reach half their adult height, talk in sentences, and express almost every emotion— not just joy and fear but also love, jealousy, and shame. The next three chapters describe these radical and awesome changes.

The First Two Years: Biosocial Development

WHAT WILL YOU KNOW?

1. What are the usual weight and motor skills of a 6-month-old?
2. What are the usual weight and motor skills of a 1-year-old?
3. How do both genes and experience influence brain growth?
4. How do vision and hearing change in the first two years?
5. What major health practices have saved millions of young lives?

Our first child, Bethany, was born when I was in graduate school, a time when I dutifully memorized the timetable of developmental norms, including "sitting at 6 months, walking and talking at 12." Bethany, at 14 months, spoke a dozen words but had not yet taken any steps on her own. Instead of worrying, I decided genes were more influential than parenting. My hypothesis was confirmed when our next two children, Rachel and Elissa, were also slow to walk.

When Sarah was born, I could afford a full-time caregiver, Mrs. Todd, from Jamaica. I cautioned her that Berger children walk late.

"Sarah will be walking by one year," Mrs. Todd told me. "My daughter walked at 10 months."

"We'll see" I replied, confident of my genetic explanation.

I underestimated Sarah and Mrs. Todd, who bounced my baby on her lap, day after day, and spent hours giving her "walking practice"—to Sarah's great delight. My fourth child took her first step at 12 months, late for a Todd baby, early for a Berger, and a humbling lesson for me.

This chapter describes physical development in the first two years of life, emphasizing changes in the body and brain, including cortex maturation, perceptions, and muscle control. All these changes make toddlers much different people than newborns. Individual variations in development abound, some genetic and some contextual, including, as I now believe, some changes due to cultures and caregivers.

HAZEL HANKIN

My Youngest at 8 Months When I look at this photo of Sarah, I see evidence of Mrs. Todd's devotion. Sarah's hair is washed and carefully brushed, her jumper and blouse are clean and pressed, and the carpet and stepstool are perfect equipment for standing practice. Sarah's legs—chubby and far apart—indicate that she is not about to walk early; but, given all these signs of Mrs. Todd's attention to caregiving, it is not surprising, in hindsight, that my fourth daughter was my earliest walker.

>> Body Changes

In infancy, growth is so rapid and the consequences of neglect are so severe that gains are closely monitored. Medical checkups, including measurement of height, weight, and head circumference, should occur every few weeks at first to determine whether an infant is progressing as expected.

Body Size

Exactly how rapidly does growth usually occur? Infants typically double their birthweight by the fourth month and triple it by age 1. For example, a 7-pound newborn might be 14 pounds at 4 months and 21 pounds at 1 year (from 3,250 to 6,500 to 9,750 grams). Physical growth then slows but is still rapid. By 24 months, most children weigh almost 28 pounds (13 kilograms) and have grown from about 20 inches at birth to about 34 inches tall (51 to 86 centimeters). This means that 2-year-olds are half their adult height and about a fifth of their adult weight, four times heavier than they were at birth. (See Appendix A, pp. A-6, A-7.)

Much of the weight increase in the early months is fat, with small babies experiencing extra gain to catch up to the norm. Baby fat is stored to keep the brain nourished if teething or the sniffles interfere with eating. If nutrition is temporarily inadequate, the body stops growing but not the brain—a phenomenon called **head-sparing** (Georgieff & Rao, 2001; Yeung, 2006). (Chronic malnutrition is discussed later in this chapter.)

Remember that these norms are simply averages and that individual variation is common. To interpret such variations, it helps to know an infant's **percentile** score, a number that indicates the rank of the person compared with that of other similar people. Percentiles range from zero to 100 for any variable in a population.

A child of average weight would be close to the 50th percentile. Some children would be heavy (above the 75th percentile) and some quite light (below the 25th). Half the children would be outside the 25th to 75th percentile norms, but most of them would be fine. The advantage of percentiles is that children can be compared not only to others the same age but also to themselves. Thus, a baby whose weight *and* height are at the 90th percentile at birth and again at 6 months is normal for that child; so is a child who is consistently at the 20th percentile.

Percentiles may alert professionals and parents that something is amiss. If a newborn is at the 50th percentile in height and weight but later is at the 40th percentile in height but the 80th percentile in weight, that infant may be getting too heavy. Neither the 40th nor the 80th percentiles are worrisome alone, but the combination and the change are warning signs.

head-sparing A biological mechanism that protects the brain when malnutrition affects body growth. The brain is the last part of the body to be damaged by malnutrition.

percentile A point on a ranking scale of 0 to 100. The 50th percentile is the midpoint; half the people in the population being studied rank higher and half rank lower.

Same Boy, Much Changed All three photos show Riley, first at 3 months, then at 12 months, and finally at 24 months. Note the rapid growth within the first two years, especially apparent in proportions of the head and use of the legs—sprawling while propped against a pillow, steadying while sitting upright, or racing across an autumn lawn.

Sleep

Newborns spend most of their time sleeping, about 15 to 17 hours a day. Hours of sleep decrease rapidly with maturity; the norm for the first 2 months is 14¼ hours; the norm for the next 3 months is 13¼ hours; the norm from 6 to 17 months is 12¾ hours. Variation is particularly apparent in the early months, when 5 percent of new babies sleep 9 hours or fewer a day and another 5 percent sleep 19 hours or more (Sadeh et al., 2009) (see Figure 5.1).

The specifics vary not only because of the age and characteristics of the particular baby but also because of the social environment. With responsive parents, children who are well fed and full term usually sleep more than the low-birthweight ones, who need to eat every two hours. Babies who are fed cow's milk and cereal sleep more soundly, which is not necessarily good. If parents respond to predawn cries with food and play, babies learn to wake up night after night; again, not necessarily good (Sadeh et al., 2009).

Throughout childhood, regular and ample sleep correlates with normal brain maturation, learning, emotional regulation, academic success, and psychological adjustment (Mindell & Owens, 2010). Children who wake up frequently and sleep too little often have other physical or psychological problems. Lifelong, sleep deprivation can cause health problems—and vice versa (Murphy & Delanty, 2007).

Over the first months, the relative amount of time spent in each type or stage of sleep changes. Babies born preterm may always seem to be dozing. Full-term newborns dream a lot; about half their sleep is **REM sleep** (rapid eye movement sleep), characterized by flickering eyes and rapid brain waves. Dreaming declines over the early weeks, as does "transitional sleep," the dozing, half-awake stage. At 3 or 4 months, quiet sleep (also called *slow-wave sleep*) increases markedly.

By about 3 months, all the various states of waking and sleeping become more evident. Thus, although newborns often seem half asleep, neither in deep sleep nor wide awake, by 3 months most babies have periods of alertness (when they are not hungry or sleepy) and periods of deep sleep (when noises do not rouse them).

First-born infants typically "receive more attention" (Bornstein, 2002, p. 28), which may be why they have more sleep problems than do later-borns. Overall, a study of more than 5,000 North American 0- to 3-year-olds found that, according

PETER SOLNESS / LONELY PLANET IMAGES

Protective Sleeping It matters little what infants sleep in—bassinet, cradle, crib, or Billum bag made from local plants in Papua, New Guinea, as shown here. In fact, this kind of bag is very useful since babies can easily be carried in it. It can also be used for carrying food, tools, and much else. What does matter is the infant's sleeping position—always on the back, as this healthy infant does.

REM sleep Rapid eye movement sleep, a stage of sleep characterized by flickering eyes behind closed lids, dreaming, and rapid brain waves.

Especially for New Parents You are aware of cultural differences in sleeping practices, and this raises a very practical issue: Should your newborn sleep in bed with you? (see response, page 127)

(see response, page 127)

FIGURE 5.1

Good Night, Moon Average sleep per 24-hour period is given in percentiles because there is much variation in how many hours a young child normally sleeps. Other charts from this study show nighttime sleep and daytime napping. Most 1-year-olds sleep about 10 hours a night, with about 2 hours of napping, but some sleep much less; by age 3, about 10 percent have given up naps altogether. Note that these data are drawn from reports by U.S. parents, based on an Internet questionnaire. Actual sleep monitors, or reports by a more diverse group of parents, would probably show even more variation.

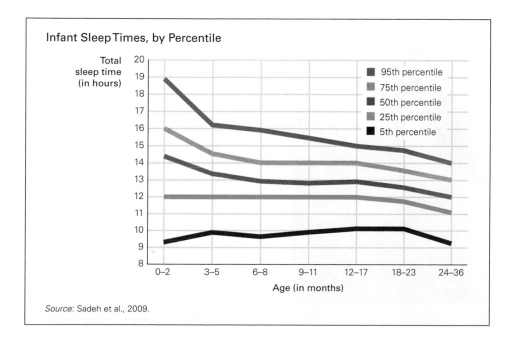

Infant Sleep Times, by Percentile

Total sleep time (in hours)

- 95th percentile
- 75th percentile
- 50th percentile
- 25th percentile
- 5th percentile

Age (in months)

Source: Sadeh et al., 2009.

to their parents, sleep was a problem for 25 percent, with 2 percent saying the problem was serious (Sadeh et al., 2009). Such problems are more troubling for parents than for infants. This does not render them insignificant; sleep-deprived parents may be less patient and responsive (Bayer et al., 2007).

Developmentalists agree that insisting an infant conform to the parents' sleep–wake schedule can be frustrating and, in some cases, harmful to the infant, whose brain patterns and digestion are not ready for a long night's sleep. However, when children frequently interrupt the adults' sleep, parents suffer. Parent reactions to infant sleep shape the baby's sleep patterns, which in turn affect the parents (Sadeh et al., 2010), as explained in the following. Ideally, families interact and adapt until everyone's needs are met.

co-sleeping A custom in which parents and their children (usually infants) sleep together in the same room.

THINKING CRITICALLY

Where Should Babies Sleep?

Traditionally, most Western infants slept in a crib in a separate bedroom; it was thought that they might be traumatized by the parents' sexual interactions. By contrast, parents in Asia, Africa, and Latin America slept in the same room with their infants, a practice called **co-sleeping.** It was thought that parent–child separation at night was heartless.

Co-sleeping is increasingly common among Western parents, although reports differ as to exactly how common. About half of a group of British parents slept with their infants some of the time (Blair & Ball, 2004), and about one-third of a group of California families practiced co-sleeping from the infant's birth (Keller & Goldberg, 2004). A North American Internet survey found that 20 percent of the youngest babies were put to sleep in the parents' bed and 19 percent were put in a crib alone in another room (many of the rest were in their own room with the parents present until the baby fell asleep). By age 2, 18 percent were put to sleep in the parents' bed and 63 percent were put to sleep alone in a crib in their own room (Sadeh et al., 2009). Unlike the British study, this study asked parents where sleep began. When the parents were asked what they did if infants of any age wakened during the night, another 21 percent replied "bring child to parents' bed."

Cultural customs affect sleep patterns (in many cultures, husbands and wives do not share a bed). Developmentalists hesitate to declare that any particular pattern is best (Tamis-Lemonda et al., 2008). Sleeping alone may encourage a child's independence and individuality—traits appreciated in some cultures, abhorred in others.

Both those who advocate co-sleeping and those who oppose it cite evidence (Hormann,

2007). With co-sleeping, breast-feeding is easier and more common. So is sudden infant death (Ruys et al., 2007). Everyone agrees that co-sleeping is harmful if the adult is drugged or drunk—and thus in danger of "overlying" the baby. Some say that co-sleeping is beneficial but *bed-sharing* is not, partly because adult beds, unlike cribs, are often soft, with comforters and pillows that can increase a baby's risk of suffocation (Alm, 2007).

A crucial issue is sleep deprivation. A videotape analysis found that, although co-sleeping infants wake up twice as often as solo-sleeping infants (six times a night versus three times), co-sleepers get just as much sleep as solo sleepers because they go back to sleep more quickly (Mao et al., 2004). One of the main reasons parents opt for co-sleeping—and a powerful argument for it—is that they are less tired if they do not need to get out of bed to feed the baby during the night. On the other hand, if a child is used to co-sleeping, parents may find their 10-year-old still crawling into their bed at night, thus causing the parents to be sleep-deprived

Logical arguments on both sides are many, but they are usually overwhelmed by cultural practices. Whatever you think best, do your conclusions reflect values and emotions that are disconnected from practical considerations?

STEPHEN CHANG / JUPITERIMAGES

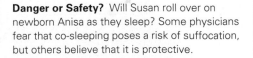

Danger or Safety? Will Susan roll over on newborn Anisa as they sleep? Some physicians fear that co-sleeping poses a risk of suffocation, but others believe that it is protective.

Birthweight doubles, triples, and quadruples by 4 months, 12 months, and 24 months, respectively. Height increases by about a foot (about 30 centimeters) in the first two years. Such norms are useful as general guidelines, but personal percentile rankings over time indicate whether a particular infant is growing appropriately. With maturation, sleep becomes regular, dreaming becomes less common, and distinct sleep–wake patterns develop. The youngest infants sleep more hours in total but for less time at a stretch; by age 1, most babies sleep longer at night, with a nap or two during the day. Cultural and caregiving practices influence norms, schedules, and expectations for sleep.

>> **Response for New Parents** (from page 125) From the psychological and cultural perspectives, babies can sleep anywhere as long as the parents can hear them if they cry. The main consideration is safety: Infants should not sleep on a mattress that is too soft, nor should a baby sleep beside an adult who is drunk or drugged or sleeps very soundly. Otherwise, the family should decide for itself where its members would sleep best.

>> Brain Development

Recall that the newborn's skull is disproportionately large. That's because it must be big enough to hold the brain, which at birth is already 25 percent of its adult weight. The neonate's body, by comparison, is typically only 5 percent of its adult weight. By age 2, the brain is almost 75 percent of adult brain weight; the child's total body weight is about 20 percent of adult weight (see Figure 5.2).

Connections in the Brain

Head circumference provides a rough idea of how the brain is growing, which is why medical checkups include measurement of skull circumference. The distance around the head typically increases about 35 percent (from 13 to 18 inches, or from 33 to 46 centimeters) in the first year. Much more significant (although harder to measure) are changes in the brain's communication system. To understand this, we review the basics of neurological development (see Figure 5.3).

Basic Brain Structures

The brain's communication system begins with nerve cells, called **neurons.** Most neurons are created before birth, at a peak production rate of 250,000 new brain cells per minute in mid-pregnancy (Purves et al., 2004). In infancy, the human brain has billions of neurons. Some are deep inside the brain in a region called the

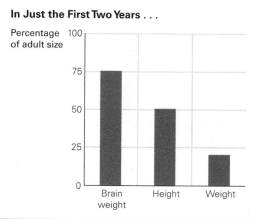

In Just the First Two Years . . .

Percentage of adult size

FIGURE 5.2

Growing Up Two-year-olds are barely talking and are totally dependent on adults, but they have already reached half their adult height and three-fourths of their adult brain size. This is dramatic evidence that biosocial growth is the foundation for cognitive and social maturity.

neurons The billions of nerve cells in the central nervous system, especially the brain.

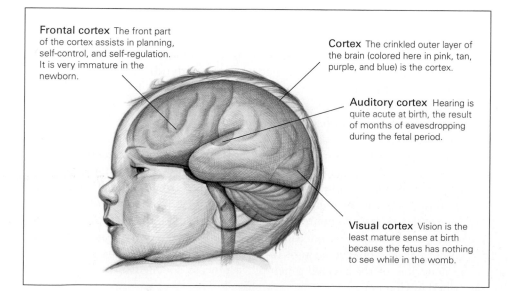

Frontal cortex The front part of the cortex assists in planning, self-control, and self-regulation. It is very immature in the newborn.

Cortex The crinkled outer layer of the brain (colored here in pink, tan, purple, and blue) is the cortex.

Auditory cortex Hearing is quite acute at birth, the result of months of eavesdropping during the fetal period.

Visual cortex Vision is the least mature sense at birth because the fetus has nothing to see while in the womb.

FIGURE 5.3

The Developing Cortex The infant's cortex consists of four to six thin layers of tissue that cover the brain. It contains virtually all the neurons that make conscious thought possible. Some areas of the cortex, such as those devoted to the basic senses, mature relatively early. Others, such as the frontal cortex, mature quite late, after age 20.

cortex The outer layers of the brain in humans and other mammals. Most thinking, feeling, and sensing involve the cortex. (Sometimes called the *neocortex*.)

brain stem, which controls automatic responses such as heartbeat, breathing, temperature, and arousal. Others are in the midbrain, in areas that affect emotions and memory. About 70 percent of neurons are in the **cortex,** the brain's six outer layers (sometimes called the *neocortex*). The cortex is crucial for humans: Most thinking, feeling, and sensing occur in the cortex, although parts of the midbrain join in (Kolb & Whishaw, 2008).

Various areas of the cortex specialize in particular functions. For instance, there is a visual cortex, an auditory cortex, and an area dedicated to the sense of touch for each body part—including for each finger of a person or each whisker of a rat (Barnett et al., 2006). Regional specialization within the cortex occurs not only for motor skills and senses but also for particular aspects of cognition.

One of the fascinating details of brain specialization is that a particular part of the brain (called the *fusiform face area*) seems dedicated to perception of faces. Other parts of the brain are also involved, including the prefrontal cortex, which is not fully mature until emerging adulthood (which may explain why children are less adept than adults at recognizing individuals or reading facial expressions of emotion). However, the fusiform face area is active in infants. It responds to monkey faces as well as human ones and to visual stimuli (e.g., pictures) as well as live faces.

Experiences refine perception, so 2-month-olds recognize their mothers and fathers, 3-month-olds examine faces of strangers, 6-month-olds no longer pay careful attention to monkey faces (M. H. Johnson, 2005), and people as young as 1 year recognize faces of people from their ethnic group (called *own-race effect*) more readily than the faces of others (Meissner & Brigham, 2001). The own-race effect persists throughout life, making it hard for adults who have always known people of one background to distinguish individuals from another group or to read facial expressions of emotion in someone from an unfamiliar race. This is the result of limited multiethnic experience, not innate prejudice against those who look different from oneself, as shown by Korean adults who were adopted between ages 3 and 9 by European Americans. They were better at distinguishing White faces than Korean ones (Sangrigoli et al., 2005).

Surprisingly, infants who are repeatedly exposed to pictures of the faces of six monkeys, each with a name, recognize monkey faces at 9 months, unlike infants without named pictures of monkeys—a clear indication that experience is crucial (Scott & Monesson, 2009). Many aspects of early experience shape face recognition (Moulson et al., 2009).

Within and between brain areas, neurons are connected to other neurons by intricate networks of nerve fibers called **axons** and **dendrites** (see Figure 5.4). Each neuron has a single axon and numerous dendrites, which spread out like the branches of a tree. The axon of one neuron meets the dendrites of other neurons at intersections called **synapses,** which are critical communication links within the brain.

To be more specific, neurons communicate by sending electrochemical impulses through their axons to synapses, to be picked up by the dendrites of other neurons. The dendrites bring the message to the cell bodies of their neurons, which, in turn, convey the message via their axons to still other neurons.

Axons and dendrites do not touch at synapses. Instead, the electrical impulses in axons typically cause the release of chemicals called *neurotransmitters,* which carry information from the axon of the sending neuron, across the *synaptic gap,* to the dendrites of the receiving neuron, a process speeded up by myelination (described in Chapter 8).

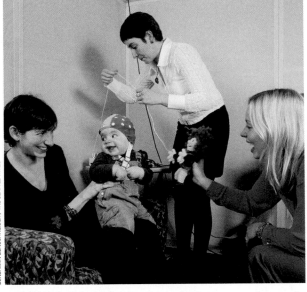

BENJAMIN BENSCHNEIDER / THE SEATTLE TIMES

Electric Excitement Milo's delight at his mother's facial expressions is visible, not just in his eyes and mouth but also in the neurons of the outer layer of his cortex. Electrodes map his brain activation region by region and moment by moment. Every month of life up to age 2 shows increased electrical excitement.

axon A fiber that extends from a neuron and transmits electrochemical impulses from that neuron to the dendrites of other neurons.

dendrite A fiber that extends from a neuron and receives electrochemical impulses transmitted from other neurons via their axons.

synapse The intersection between the axon of one neuron and the dendrites of other neurons.

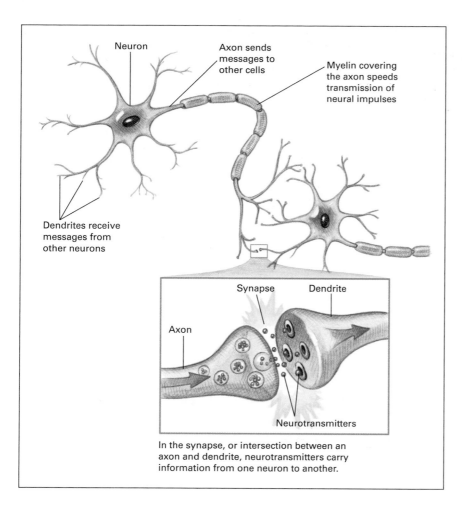

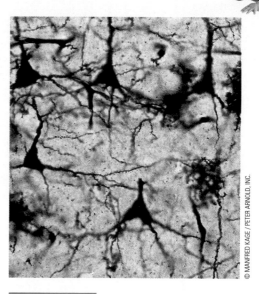

In the synapse, or intersection between an axon and dendrite, neurotransmitters carry information from one neuron to another.

FIGURE 5.4

How Two Neurons Communicate The link between one neuron and another is shown in the simplified diagram at left. The infant brain actually contains billions of neurons, each with one axon and many dendrites. Every electrochemical message to or from the brain causes thousands of neurons to fire simultaneously, each transmitting the message across the synapse to neighboring neurons. The electron micrograph directly above shows several neurons, greatly magnified, with their tangled but highly organized and well-coordinated sets of dendrites and axons.

Transient Exuberance and Pruning

At birth, the brain contains more than 100 billion neurons, more than any person will ever use (de Haan & Johnson, 2003). By contrast, the newborn brain has far fewer dendrites and synapses than the person will eventually possess. During the first months and years, rapid growth and refinement in axons, dendrites, and synapses occur, especially in the cortex. Dendrite growth is the major reason that brain weight increases 300 percent from birth to age 2 (M. H. Johnson, 2005).

An estimated fivefold increase in dendrites in the cortex occurs in the 24 months after birth, with about 100 trillion synapses being present at age 2 (Schwartz & Begley, 2002). This early growth is called **transient exuberance,** *exuberant* because it is so rapid and *transient* because some of it is temporary. The expansive growth of dendrites is followed by *pruning* (see Figure 5.5), in which unused neurons and misconnected dendrites atrophy and die (Barinaga, 2003), just as a gardener might prune a rose bush by cutting away parts to enable more, or more beautiful, roses to bloom.

Transient exuberance enables neurons to connect to, and communicate with, a greatly expanding number of other neurons within the brain. Synapses, dendrites, and even neurons continue to form and die throughout life, though more rapidly in infancy than at any other time (Nelson, Thomas et al., 2006).

Thinking and learning require connections among many parts of the brain. For example, to understand any sentence in this text, you need to understand the letters and word, the surrounding text, the ideas they convey, and how they relate to

transient exuberance The great but temporary increase in the number of dendrites that occurs in an infant's brain during the first two years of life.

Brain Growth in Response to Experience
These curves show the rapid rate of experience-dependent synapse formation for three functions of the brain (senses, language, and analysis). After the initial increase, the underused neurons are gradually pruned, or inactivated, as no functioning dendrites are formed from them.

Observation Quiz Why do both "12 months" and "1 year" appear on the "Age" line? (see answer, page 132)

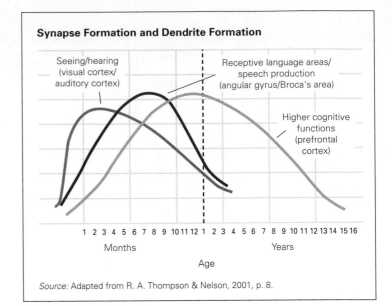

Synapse Formation and Dendrite Formation

Seeing/hearing (visual cortex/auditory cortex)

Receptive language areas/speech production (angular gyrus/Broca's area)

Higher cognitive functions (prefrontal cortex)

1 2 3 4 5 6 7 8 9 10 11 12   1 2 3 4 5 6 7 8 9 10 11 12 13 14 15 16
Months   Years
Age

Source: Adapted from R. A. Thompson & Nelson, 2001, p. 8.

your other thoughts and experiences. Baby brains have the same requirement, although at first they have few experiences to build on, and the various parts of the brain have not yet developed to the adult level or even to the level of a 2-year-old.

Experience Shapes the Brain

The specifics of brain structure and growth depend on genes and also on experience, which produces the "postnatal rise and fall" of synapses (de Haan & Johnson, 2003, p. 5). As you have just read, soon after exuberant expansion, some dendrites wither away because they are underused—that is, no experiences have caused them to send a message to the axons of other neurons. This expansion and pruning of dendrites occurs for almost every aspect of early experience, from noticing musical rhythms to understanding emotions (Scott et al., 2007).

Strangely enough, this loss of dendrites increases brainpower by promoting a more intricate organization of existing connections. The "increasing cognitive complexity of childhood is related to a loss rather than a gain of synapses" (de Haan & Johnson, 2003, p. 8). Further evidence of the benefit of cell death comes from one of the sad symptoms of fragile X syndrome (described in Chapter 3), "a persistent failure of normal synapse pruning" (Irwin et al., 2002, p. 194). Affected children become mentally retarded without this pruning; their dendrites are too dense and long, making thinking difficult.

Pruning is necessary. Normally, as brains mature, the process of extending and eliminating neurons is exquisitely attuned to experience, as the appropriate links in the brain need to be established, protected, and strengthened. One group of scientists speculates that "lack of normative experiences may lead to overpruning of neurons and synapse, both of which may lead to reduction of brain activity" (Moulson et al., 2009, p. 1051).

Stress and the Brain

An unfortunate example of the effect of experience in brain development begins when the brain produces cortisol and other hormones in response to stress. Cortisol production is evident in infants and continues throughout life (Adam et al., 2007).

If the brain produces an overabundance of stress hormones early in life (as when an infant is frequently terrified), then the brain becomes incapable of normal stress responses. Later, that person's brain may either overproduce stress hormones, making the person hypervigilant (always on the alert), or underproduce them, making the person emotionally flat (never happy, sad, or angry).

A kindergarten teacher might notice that one child becomes furious or terrified at a mild provocation and another child seems indifferent to everything. Why? In both cases, the underlying cause could be excessive stress-hormone production in infancy, which changed the way that child's brain responds to stress.

Necessary and Possible Experiences

A scientist named William Greenough has identified two experience-related aspects of brain development (Greenough et al., 1987):

- **Experience-expectant brain function.** Certain functions of the brain require basic experiences in order to develop, just as a tree requires water. Those experiences are part of almost every infant's life, and thus almost every human brain develops as it should. Brains need and expect such experiences; development is impaired without them.

- **Experience-dependent brain function.** Some brain functions are not required but rather depend on particular experiences, the way a bonsai tree might be shaped. These specific experiences happen to infants in some families and cultures but not in others.

experience-expectant brain functions Brain functions that require certain basic common experiences (which an infant can be expected to have) in order to develop normally.

experience-dependent brain functions Brain functions that depend on particular, variable experiences and that therefore may or may not develop in a particular infant.

The basic, expected experiences *must* happen for normal brain maturation to occur, and they almost always do. The human brain is designed to expect them and needs them for growth. For example, in deserts and in the Arctic, on isolated farms and in crowded cities, almost all babies have things to see, objects to manipulate, and people to love them. As a result, their brains develop normally.

In contrast, dependent experiences *might* happen; because of them, one brain differs from another. Particular experiences vary, such as which language babies hear, what faces they see, or how their mother reacts to frustration. *Depending* on those particulars, infants' brains are structured and connected one way or another, as some dendrites grow and some neurons thrive while others die. Consequently, all people are similar, but each person is unique, because each has particular early experiences.

This distinction can be made for all mammals. Some of the most persuasive research has been done with songbirds. All male songbirds have a brain region dedicated to listening and reproducing sounds (experience-expectant), but birds of the same species who happen to live in different locations learn to produce slightly different songs (experience-dependent). This is not unlike regional accents, as with English-speaking adults who grew up in Kingston or Kansas, or, for that matter, one neighborhood of Brooklyn or another.

Birds are genetically designed to develop the neurons that they need, which might be neurons dedicated to learning new songs (canaries) or to finding hidden seeds (chickadees). Both of these functions require experiences that circumstances offer to some birds but not to others (Barinaga, 2003).

An intriguing example of this is the ability to recognize newborns—specifically, to see a photo of one infant and then distinguish that face from a photo of another infant. Most children and adults are less adept at distinguishing between baby photos than they are at distinguishing between photos of adults. Some even believe that "all newborns look alike." However, 3-year-olds with younger siblings are much better at this than 3-year-olds without younger siblings, presumably because of experience (Cassia et al., 2009).

>> **Answer to Observation Quiz** (from page 130) "One year" signifies the entire year, from day 365 to day 729, and that is indicated by its location between "12 months" and "2 years."

prefrontal cortex The area of cortex at the front of the brain that specializes in anticipation, planning, and impulse control.

shaken baby syndrome A life-threatening injury that occurs when an infant is forcefully shaken back and forth, a motion that ruptures blood vessels in the brain and breaks neural connections.

self-righting The inborn drive to remedy a developmental deficit; literally, to return to sitting or standing upright, after being tipped over. People of all ages have self-righting impulses, for emotional as well as physical imbalance.

Knowledge of which developmental events are experience-expectant is helpful. For example, proliferation and pruning occur at about 4 months in the visual and auditory cortexes (which explains why young infants are eager to see and listen). Consequently, remedies for blind or deaf infants (such as surgery, glasses, or hearing aids) should occur early in life to prevent atrophy of those brain regions that expect sights and sounds (Leonard, 2003). Deaf infants whose difficulties are recognized and remediated in the early months (such as with a cochlear implant) become more proficient at understanding and expressing language than those with the same deficits whose remedy occurred later. Brain expectancy is the critical difference (Kennedy et al., 2006).

The language areas of the brain develop most rapidly between the ages of 6 and 24 months, so infants need to hear speech during that period in order to talk fluently. In fact, speech heard between 6 and 12 months helps infants recognize the characteristics of their local language long before they utter a word (Saffran et al., 2006).

The last part of the brain to mature is the **prefrontal cortex,** the area for anticipation, planning, and impulse control. It is virtually inactive in early infancy but gradually becomes more efficient over the years of childhood and adolescence (Wahlstrom et al., 2010). Thus, telling an infant to stop crying is pointless because the infant cannot decide to stop crying. Such decisions require brain functions that are not yet present.

Much worse is for adults to shake a baby to stop the crying. This can cause **shaken baby syndrome,** a life-threatening condition that occurs when infants are shaken back and forth sharply and quickly. Shaking stops the crying because blood vessels in the brain rupture and neural connections break, which is why shaken baby syndrome is recognized by pediatricians as an example of *abusive head trauma* (Christian et al., 2009). In the United States, brain scans show that more than one in five of all children hospitalized for maltreatment (broken bones, burns, and so on) also suffer from shaken baby syndrome (Rovi et al., 2004).

Implications for Caregivers

What does early brain development mean for caregivers? First, early brain growth is rapid and dependent on experience. This means that caressing a newborn, talking to a preverbal infant, and showing affection toward a toddler may be essential to develop the child's full potential. If such experiences are missing from the child's early weeks and months, lifelong damage may result.

Second, each brain region follows a sequence of growing, connecting, and pruning. Some stimulation is meaningless before the brain is ready. Adults should follow the baby's curiosity. Infants respond most strongly and positively to whatever their brains need; that is why very young babies like to look at and listen to musical mobiles, strangers on the street, and, best of all, their animated caregivers.

This preference reflects **self-righting,** the inborn drive to remedy deficits. Infants with few toys develop their brains by using whatever is available. They do not need the latest educational playthings—their brains will develop with normal human interaction. One-year-olds do not appreciate blocks with letters and numbers on them. Just don't keep them in a dark, quiet place all day long. Human brains are designed to grow and adapt; some plasticity is retained throughout life, but plasticity is especially apparent in the beginning (Baltes et al., 2006; Tomalski & Johnson, 2010).

Neuroscientists once thought that brains were influenced *solely* by genes and prenatal influences, with infants seeking stimulation when they needed it and shielding themselves from too much excitement (usually by crying or sleeping) when they became overwhelmed. The opposite assumption was held by many social scientists, who thought that environment was all that mattered: Cultures (according to anthropologists) or societies (according to sociologists) or parents (according to psychologists) could be credited or blamed for a child's every emotion and action.

Now most scientists, especially developmentalists, are multidisciplinary. They incorporate both neuroscience and social science, noting the specific influence of genes and environment (Tomalski & Johnson, 2010). They believe that plasticity is an "inherent property of development" (M. H. Johnson, 2005, p. 189), but they also know there are biological limitations to growth.

As you remember from Chapter 1, humans have sensitive periods, when particular kinds of development are primed to occur (Baltes et al., 2006). The first two years of life are a sensitive period, an experience-expectant time, when brains need some experiences to develop normally. The following explains this in detail.

Especially for Social Workers An infertile couple in their late 30s asks for your help in adopting a child from eastern Europe. They particularly want an older child. How do you respond? (see response, page 134)

A VIEW FROM SCIENCE

Plasticity and Orphans

The developmental community was stunned and saddened by a girl named Genie, who spent most of her childhood tied to a chair, never hearing human speech (her father barked and growled at her) or feeling love, because her parents were severely disturbed. After being rescued, she eventually responded to affection and learned to speak, but she never developed normally. Most developmentalists concluded that her normal experiences came too late; her brain had already passed the sensitive period for development of many abilities.

But Genie was just one person, and you remember from Chapter 1 that one case proves nothing. Perhaps she had been born brain-damaged and therefore never learned what most people take for granted. Or perhaps her early care after rescue was itself traumatic (Rymer, 1945/1994).

More research, with more participants, was needed but would be unethical and thus impossible to perform with humans. Consequently, Marion Diamond, William Greenough, and their colleagues studied some "deprived" rats (raised alone in small, barren cages) and compared them with "enriched" rats (raised in large cages with other rats as well as toys). At autopsy, the brains of the enriched rats were larger and heavier, with more dendrites (M. Diamond, 1988; Greenough & Volkmar, 1973). Much research with other mammals confirms that isolation and sensory deprivation harm the developing brain but that a complex social environment enhances neurological growth.

Such experiments are unthinkable with humans, but history provided a laboratory: When Romanian dictator Nicolae Ceausescu forbade birth control and abortions in the 1980s, illegal abortions became the leading cause of death for Romanian women aged 15 to 45 (Verona, 2003), and more than 100,000 children were abandoned to crowded, impersonal, state-run orphanages (D. E. Johnson, 2000). The children experienced severe deprivation, including virtually no normal interaction, play, or conversation (Rutter et al., 2007).

In the two years after Ceausescu was ousted in 1989, thousands of these children were adopted by American and western European families. Those who were adopted before 6 months of age fared best; most of them, by age 11, were quite normal. However, for many, but not all, of those who had been adopted *after* they were 6 months old, deprivation was evident, particularly in abilities controlled by the cortex: At age 11, they scored an average of only 85 on the WISC IQ test, 15 points below normal.

Neither dire nor sunny predictions about maltreated children are completely accurate. A team of scientists who have devoted

A Fortunate Pair Elaine Himelfarb (shown in the background), of San Diego, California, is shown here in Bucharest to adopt 22-month-old Maria. This joyous moment may be repeated through Maria's childhood—or maybe not.

AP / WIDE WORLD PHOTOS

their lives to studying impaired children advise: "Be skeptical about 'miracle' cures of severely affected individuals which appear in the media, or even in scientific journals, while recognizing that partial amelioration can occur in individual cases" (Clarke & Clarke, 2003, p. 131).

Further research in Romania has found that early experience, not genetics, is the main problem with these abandoned children. Romanian infants develop best in their own families, second best in foster families, and much worse in institutions (Nelson et al., 2007). Research on institutionalized infants from many nations of eastern Europe, adopted by western European or North American families, again finds that they have a higher rate of emotional problems, especially evident at puberty, but also finds that more recent adoptees develop better than those severely deprived Romanian orphans adopted in the early 1990s (Merz & McCall, 2010). All infants need basic love and stimulation. Head-sparing, plasticity, self-righting, catch-up growth, and experience-expectant events compensate for the many imperfections and lapses of human parenting, but they cannot overcome extreme early deprivation.

>> Response for Social Workers (from page 133) Tell them that such a child would require extra time and commitment, more than a younger adoptee would. Ask whether both are prepared to cut down on their working hours in order to meet with other parents of international adoptees; to obtain professional help (for speech, nutrition, physical development, and/or family therapy); and to help the child with schoolwork, play dates, and so on. You might encourage them instead to adopt a special-needs child from their own area, to become foster parents, or to volunteer at least 10 hours a week at a day-care center. Their response would indicate their willingness to help a real—not imagined—child. If they demonstrate their understanding of what is required, then you might help them adopt the child they want.

SUMMING UP

Brain growth is rapid during the first months of life, when dendrites and the synapses within the cortex increase exponentially. By age 2, the brain already weighs three-fourths of its adult weight. Pruning of underused and unconnected dendrites begins in the sensory and motor areas and then occurs in other areas. Although some brain development is maturational, experience is also essential—both the universal experiences that almost every infant has (experience-expectant brain development) and the particular experiences that reflect the child's family or culture (experience-dependent brain development). ▪

>> Sensation and Movement

You learned in Chapter 2 that Piaget called the first period of intelligence the *sensorimotor* stage, emphasizing that cognition develops from the senses and motor skills. The same concept—that infant brain development depends on sensory experiences and early activity—underlies the discussion you have just read.

The Five Senses

Every sense functions at birth. Newborns have open eyes; sensitive ears; and responsive noses, tongues, and skin. Throughout their first year, infants use those senses to sort and classify everything they experience. Indeed, "infants spend the better part of their first year merely looking around" (Rovee-Collier, 2001, p. 35). As they look, they also listen, smell, taste, and touch anything they can. Indeed, very young babies seem to attend to everything without much focus or discrimination. For instance, they smile at strangers and put almost anything in their mouths (Adolph & Berger, 2005).

Why are they not more selective? Because sensation precedes perception. **Sensation** occurs when a sensory system detects a stimulus, as when the inner ear reverberates with sound or the retina and pupil of the eye intercept light. Thus, sensations begin when an outer organ (eye, ear, nose, tongue, or skin) meets anything that can be seen, heard, smelled, tasted, or touched. But what appear to be simple responses to every stimulus actually show some selection: Even in the early months, infants are attracted to social stimuli, preferring sensations from people, not objects (Lloyd-Fox et al., 2009). They would rather suck your finger than a scrap of cloth, but they will settle for the cloth when no finger is available.

Perception occurs when the brain notices and processes a sensation. This happens in the cortex, usually as the result of a message from one of the sensing

sensation The response of a sensory system (eyes, ears, skin, tongue, nose) when it detects a stimulus.

perception The mental processing of sensory information when the brain interprets a sensation. Perception occurs in the cortex.

organs—a message based on past experience that suggests that a particular sensation might be worth interpreting (M. E. Diamond, 2007).

Some sensations are beyond comprehension at first. A newborn has no idea that the letters on a page might have significance, that Mother's face should be distinguished from Father's, or that the smells of roses and garlic have different connotations. Perceptions require experience, either direct experience or messages from other people.

Infants' brains are especially attuned to their own repeated social experiences. Thus, a newborn named Emily has no concept that *Emily* is her name, but she has the brain and auditory capacity to hear sounds in the usual speech range (not the high sounds that only dogs can hear) and an inborn preference for repeated patterns, so she attends to people saying her name.

At about 4 months, when her auditory cortex is rapidly creating and pruning dendrites, the repeated word *Emily* is perceived as well as sensed, especially because that sound emanates from the people Emily has learned to love (Saffran et al., 2006). Before 6 months, Emily may open her eyes and turn her head when her name is called. It will take many more months before she tries to say "Emmy" and still longer before she knows that *Emily* is indeed her name.

Thus, cognition follows perception, when people think about what they have perceived. (Later, cognition no longer requires sensation: People imagine, fantasize, hypothesize!) The sequence from sensation to perception to cognition requires that an infant's sense organs function. No wonder the parts of the cortex dedicated to the senses develop rapidly: That is the prerequisite for human intellect. Now the specifics.

Hearing

The sense of hearing develops during the last trimester of pregnancy and is already quite acute at birth (Saffran et al., 2006). At birth, certain sounds trigger reflexes, even without conscious perception. Sudden noises startle newborns, making them cry; rhythmic sounds, such as a lullaby or a heartbeat, soothe them and put them to sleep.

A newborn's hearing can be checked with advanced equipment, routine at most hospitals in North America and Europe, since early remediation benefits deaf infants. Screening is needed later as well, because some infants acquire hearing losses in the early months (Harlor & Bower, 2009). Normally, even in the first days of life, infants turn their heads at a sound. Soon they can pinpoint the actual source of the noise.

Infants particularly attend to voices, developing expectations of the rhythm, segmentation, and cadence of spoken words long before comprehension. As time goes on, sensitive hearing combines with the developing brain to distinguish patterns of sounds and syllables. Infants become accustomed to the rules of their language, such as which syllable is usually stressed (various English dialects have different rules), whether changing inflection is significant (as in Chinese), whether certain sound combinations are repeated, and so on. All this is based on very careful listening to human speech, even speech not directed toward them with words they do not yet understand.

Especially for Parents of Grown Children Suppose you realize that you seldom talked to your children until they talked to you and that you never used a stroller or a walker but put them in cribs and playpens. Did you limit their brain growth and their sensory capacity? (see response, page 136)

Before Leaving the Hospital As mandated by a 2004 Ohio law, 1-day-old Henry has his hearing tested via vibrations of the inner ear in response to various tones. The computer interprets the data and signals any need for more tests—as is the case for about 1 baby in 100. Normal newborns hear quite well; Henry's hearing was fine.

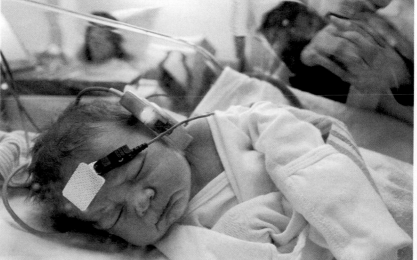

AP PHOTO / THE PLAIN DEALER, DAVID I. ANDERSEN

>> **Response for Parents of Grown Children** (from page 135) Probably not. Experience-expectant brain development is programmed to occur for all infants, requiring only the stimulation that virtually all families provide—warmth, reassuring touch, overheard conversation, facial expressions, movement. Extras such as baby talk, music, exercise, mobiles, and massage may be beneficial but are not essential.

binocular vision The ability to focus the two eyes in a coordinated manner in order to see one image. This ability is absent at birth.

Learning About a Lime As with every other normal infant, Jacqueline's curiosity leads to taste and then to a slow reaction, from puzzlement to tongue-out disgust. Jacqueline's responses demonstrate that the sense of taste is acute in infancy and that quick brain reactions are still to come.

Seeing

Vision is the least mature sense at birth. Although the eyes open in mid-pregnancy and are sensitive to bright light (if the pregnant woman is sunbathing in a bikini, for instance), the fetus has nothing much to see. Newborns are legally blind; they see only objects between 4 and 30 inches (10 and 75 centimeters) away (Bornstein et al., 2005).

Soon experience combines with maturation of the visual cortex to improve the ability to see shapes and then notice details. By 2 months, infants look more intently at a human face and, tentatively and fleetingly, smile. Soon visual scanning becomes organized and more efficient, centered on important points. Thus, 3-month-olds look closely at the eyes and mouth, the parts of a face that contain the most information, and they prefer photos of faces with features over photos of faces with the features blanked out. They pay attention to patterns, colors, and motion (Kellman & Arterberry, 2006).

Binocular vision is the ability to coordinate the two eyes to see one image. Because using both eyes together is impossible in the womb (nothing is far enough away to need two eyes), many newborns seem to focus with one eye or the other, or to use their two eyes independently, so that they momentarily look wall-eyed or cross-eyed. At about 14 weeks, binocular vision appears quite suddenly, probably because the underlying brain mechanisms are activated, allowing both eyes to focus on one thing (Atkinson & Braddick, 2003).

Smelling, Tasting, and Touching

As with vision and hearing, the senses of smell, taste, and touch function at birth and rapidly adapt to the social world. Infants learn to appreciate whatever their mothers eat, first through the breast milk and then through spoonfuls of whatever the family has for dinner. Some herbs and plants contain natural substances that are medicinal. Thus, the foods of a particular culture may aid survival: Bitter foods seem to provide some defense against malaria, spicy ones preserve food and thus work against food poisoning, and so on (Krebs, 2009).

Similar adaptation occurs for the senses of smell and touch. As babies learn to recognize each person's smell and handling, they relax only when cradled by their familiar caregiver, even when their eyes are closed. The ability to be comforted by touch is one of the important skills tested in the Neonatal Behavioral Assessment Scale (NBAS, described in Chapter 4). Although almost all newborns respond to swaddling, massage, and cuddling, over time they perceive what each touch communicates. For instance, 12-month-olds respond differently to their mother's tense or relaxed holding (Hertenstein & Campos, 2001). Tickling, too, produces a social

ALL CINDY CHARLES / PHOTOEDIT, INC.

reaction, which is why you can't tickle yourself but 6-month-olds laugh at being kissed on the stomach.

The entire package of the five senses furthers two goals: social interaction (to respond to familiar caregivers) and comfort (to be soothed amid the disturbances of infant life). Infants even adapt the senses of pain and motion (not among the five senses because no body part is dedicated to them) for socialization and comfort. The most important experiences are perceived with all the senses. Breast milk, for instance, is a mild sedative, so the newborn literally feels happier at the mother's breast, connecting pleasure with taste, touch, smell, and sight.

Infants respond to motion as well as to sights and sounds. Knowing this, many new parents soothe their baby's distress by rocking, carrying, or even driving (with the baby in a safety seat) while humming a lullaby; here again, infant comfort is connected with social interaction. Similarly, massage is calming for infants, especially because they soon realize that the touch comes from someone: Massage is a social touch, not a random one. Surprisingly, even vacuuming the carpet with the baby in a sling may quiet a fussy baby because steady noise, movement, and carrying combine to soothe distress. By 6 months, infants have learned to coordinate the senses, expecting lip movements to synchronize with speech, for instance (Lewkowicz, 2010). In sum, infant senses are immature, but they function and coordinate to help babies join the human family.

Basic Infant Care In many cultures, infant massage is considered an essential part of daily care, no less important than diapering or feeding. In other cultures, mothers attend classes to learn how best to touch their infants—firmly on the stomach, as shown here, or rhythmically moving the arms and legs, as these mothers will soon practice.

Motor Skills

We now come to the most visible and dramatic advances of infancy, those that ultimately allow the child to "stand tall and walk proud." Thanks to ongoing changes in size and proportion and to increasing brain maturation, infants markedly improve their **motor skills,** which are the abilities needed to move and control the body.

Gross Motor Skills

Deliberate actions that coordinate many parts of the body, producing large movements, are called **gross motor skills.** These emerge directly from reflexes (discussed in Chapter 4). Crawling is one example. As you remember from that chapter, newborns, when placed on their stomachs, reflexively move their arms and legs as if they were swimming. As young infants gain muscle strength, they start to wiggle, attempting to move forward by pushing their arms, shoulders, and upper bodies against whatever surface they are lying on. Usually by 5 months or so, they become able to use their arms, and then legs, to inch forward on their bellies. That is a gross motor skill.

Between 8 and 10 months after birth, most infants can lift their midsections and crawl (or *creep,* as the British call it) on "all fours," coordinating the movements of their hands and knees in a smooth, balanced manner. Crawling is experience-dependent. Some normal babies never do it, especially if the floor is cold, hot, or rough, or if they have always slept on their backs (Pin et al., 2007). It is not true that babies *must* crawl to develop normally. All babies figure out some way to move before they can walk (inching, bear-walking, scooting, creeping, or crawling), but many resist "tummy time" by rolling over and fussing (Adolph & Berger, 2005).

Sitting also develops gradually, a matter of developing the muscles to steady the heavy top half of the body. By 3 months, babies have sufficient muscle control

motor skills The learned abilities to move some part of the body, in actions ranging from a large leap to a flicker of the eyelid. (The word *motor* here refers to movement of muscles.)

gross motor skills Physical abilities involving large body movements, such as walking and jumping. (The word *gross* here means "big.")

Young Expert This infant is an adept crawler. Note the coordination between hands and knees as well as the arm and leg strength needed to support the body in this early version of push-ups. This boy probably will become an expert walker and runner, as do many babies who bypass the crawling phase altogether.

Bossa Nova Baby? This boy in Brazil demonstrates his joy at acquiring the gross motor skill of walking, which quickly becomes dancing whenever music plays.

fine motor skills Physical abilities involving small body movements, especially of the hands and fingers, such as drawing and picking up a coin. (The word *fine* here means "small.")

Fingers and Toes When infants first catch sight of their own feet, they are fascinated—wiggling, stretching, kicking as they learn they have some connection to that distant part of themselves. At about 4 months, they grab successfully—a major achievement.

Observation Quiz How is this infant's grab still immature? (see answer, page 140)

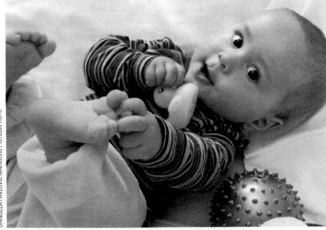

to be lap-sitters if the lap's owner provides supportive arms. By 6 months, they can usually sit unsupported. Walking progresses from reflexive, hesitant, adult-supported stepping to a smooth, coordinated gait. Some children step while holding on at 9 months, stand alone momentarily at 10 months, and walk well, unassisted, at 12 months. Three factors combine to allow toddlers to walk (Adolph et al., 2003):

1. *Muscle strength*. Newborns with skinny legs and infants buoyed by water make stepping movements, but 6-month-olds on dry land do not; their legs are too chubby for their underdeveloped muscles.
2. *Brain maturation within the motor cortex*. The first leg movements—kicking (alternating legs at birth and then kicking both legs together or one leg repeatedly at about 3 months)—occur without much thought or aim. As the brain matures, deliberate leg action becomes possible.
3. *Practice*. Unbalanced, wide-legged, short strides become a steady, smooth gait after hours of practice.

Once the first two developments have made walking possible, infants become passionate walkers, logging those needed hours of practice. They take steps on many surfaces, barefoot or wearing socks, slippers, or shoes. They hate to be pushed in their strollers when they can walk.

> Walking infants practice keeping balance in upright stance and locomotion for more than 6 accumulated hours per day. They average between 500 and 1,500 walking steps per hour so that by the end of each day, they have taken 9,000 walking steps and traveled the length of 29 football fields.
>
> [Adolph et al., 2003, p. 494]

Fine Motor Skills

Small body movements are called **fine motor skills.** Hand and finger movements are fine motor skills, enabling humans to write, draw, type, tie, and so on. Movements of the tongue, jaw, lips, and toes are fine movements, too.

Actually, mouth skills precede finger skills by many months, and skillful grabbing with the feet sometimes precedes grabbing with the hands (Adolph & Berger, 2005). However, hand skills are more valued by society. Every culture encourages hand skills, so every child practices them. By contrast, skilled spitting or chewing is not praised; even a child's mastery of blowing bubbles with gum is admired only by other children.

Regarding finger skills, newborns have a strong reflexive grasp but seem to lack hand and finger control. During their first 2 months, babies excitedly stare and wave their arms at objects dangling within reach. By 3 months of age, they can usually touch such objects, but they cannot yet grab and hold on unless an object is placed in their hands, partly because their eye–hand coordination is limited.

By 4 months, infants sometimes grab, but their timing is off: They close their hands too early or too late. Finally, by 6 months, with a concentrated, deliberate stare, most babies can reach for, grab at, and hold onto almost any object that is of the right size. Some can even transfer it from one hand to the other. Almost all can hold a bottle, shake a rattle, and yank a sister's braids. Once grabbing is possible, babies practice it enthusiastically; in fact, "from 6 to 9 months, reaching appears as a quite compulsive behaviour for small objects presented within arm's reach" (Atkinson & Braddick, 2003, p. 58).

Toward the end of the first year and throughout the second, finger skills improve, as babies master the pincer movement (using thumb and forefinger to pick up tiny objects) and self-feeding (first with hands, then fingers, then utensils). In the second year, grabbing becomes more selective. Toddlers learn when not to pull at a sister's braids, or Mommy's earrings, or Daddy's glasses. However, as you will learn in the next chapter, the curiosity of the "little scientist" may overwhelm inhibition.

Ethnic Variations

All healthy infants develop skills in the same sequence, but they vary in the age of acquisition. The At About This Time shows age norms for gross motor skills, based on a large, representative, multiethnic sample of U.S. infants. When infants are grouped by ethnicity, generally African Americans are ahead of Latinos, who are ahead of babies of European descent. Internationally, the earliest walkers are in Uganda, where well-nourished and healthy babies walk at 10 months, on average. Some of the latest walkers are in France.

What accounts for this variation? The power of genes is suggested not only by ethnic differences but also by identical twins, who begin to walk on the same day more often than fraternal twins do. Striking individual differences are apparent in infants' strategies, effort, and concentration in mastering motor skills, again suggesting something inborn (Thelen & Corbetta, 2002).

But genes are only part of ethnic differences, as the example that opened this chapter shows. Cultural patterns of child rearing affect sensation, perception, and motor skills. For instance, early reflexes may not fade if culture and conditions allow extensive practice. This has been demonstrated with legs (the stepping reflex), hands (the grasping reflex), and crawling (the swimming reflex). Senses and motor skills are part of a complex and dynamic system in which practice counts (Thelen & Corbetta, 2002).

AT ABOUT THIS TIME

Age Norms (in Months) for Gross Motor Skills

Skill	When 50% of All Babies Master the Skill (months)	When 95% of All Babies Master the Skill (months)
Sit, head steady	3	4
Sit, unsupported	6	7
Pull to stand (holding on)	9	10
Stand alone	12	14
Walk well	13	15
Walk backward	15	17
Run	18	20
Jump up	26	29

Note: As the text explains, age norms are approximate and are affected by culture and cohort. These are U.S. norms, mostly for European American children. Mastering skills a few weeks earlier or later is not an indication of health or intelligence. Mastering them very late, however, is a cause for concern.

Source: Coovadia & Wittenberg, 2004; based primarily on Denver II (Frankenburg et al., 1992).

Observation Quiz Which of these skills has the greatest variation in age of acquisition? Why? (see answer, page 140)

MIKE GREENLAR / THE IMAGE WORKS

Safe and Secure Like this Algonquin baby in Quebec, many American Indian infants spend hours each day on a cradle board, to the distress of some non-Native adults until they see that most of the babies are quite happy that way. The discovery in the 1950s that Native American children walked at about the same age as European American children suggested that maturation, not practice, led to motor skills. Later research found that most Native American infants also received special exercise sessions each day, implying that practice plays a larger role than most psychologists once thought.

>> Answer to Observation Quiz (from page 138) In several more months, he will be able to do a full hand grab, not the less secure two-finger grab shown here.

>> Answer to Observation Quiz (from page 139) Jumping up, with a three-month age range for acquisition. The reason is that the older an infant is, the more impact culture has.

For example, Jamaican caregivers provide rhythmic stretching exercises for their infants as part of daily care; their infants are among the world's youngest walkers (Adolph & Berger, 2005). Other cultures discourage or even prevent infants from crawling or walking. The people of Bali, Indonesia, never let their infants crawl, because babies are considered divine and crawling is for animals (Diener, 2000). Similar reasoning appeared in colonial America, where "standing stools" were designed for children so they could strengthen their legs without sitting or crawling (Calvert, 2003).

By contrast, the Beng people of the Ivory Coast are proud when their babies start to crawl but do not let them walk until at least 1 year. Although the Beng do not recognize the connection, one reason for this prohibition may be birth control: Beng mothers do not resume sexual relations until their baby begins walking (Gottlieb, 2000).

Although variation in the timing of the development of motor skills is normal, slow development relative to the norm within an infant's ethnic group suggests that the infant needs careful examination.

SUMMING UP

The five senses (seeing, hearing, smelling, tasting, touching) function at birth, although hearing is far superior to vision, probably because of experience: The fetus has much more to hear than to see. After birth, vision develops rapidly, leading to binocular vision at about the 14th week. By one year, infants heed stimuli from all the sense organs; sensitive perception and preferences for the familiar are evident. The senses work together and are particularly attuned to human interaction.

Motor skills begin with reflexes but quickly expand to include various body movements. Infants lift their heads, then sit, then stand, then walk and run. Sensory and motor skills follow a genetic and maturational timetable, but they are also powerfully influenced by experiences, guided by caregivers and culture, and by practice, which infants do as much as their immature and top-heavy bodies allow. Fine motor skills, especially hand skills, mature over the first two years, although many more years of practice and maturation are needed.

>> Surviving in Good Health

Although precise worldwide statistics are unavailable, at least 10 billion children were born between 1950 and 2010. More than 2 billion of them died before age 5. Although 2 billion is far too many, twice as many would have died without public health measures. As best we know, in earlier centuries more than half of all newborns died in infancy.

In the twenty-first century, most people live to adulthood. In the healthiest nations, 99.9 percent who survive the first month (when the sickest and smallest newborns may die) live to age 15, and most live for decades more (although accidents, suicide, and homicide kill some, far more than die of disease).

Even in the poorest nations, where a few decades ago half the children died, now about three-fourths live (see Table 5.1). Improvement in public health measures (clean water, nourishing food, immunization) is the main reason childhood mortality has declined; more medical professionals (rare in some rural areas) would result in a 15 percent decline in infant deaths in the short term and an almost 50 percent decline in the long term (Farahani et al., 2009). One particular medical treatment, oral rehydration therapy (giving restorative liquids to sick children who have diarrhea), is now widely used, saving 3 million young children *per year.* Most such children are in developing nations, but oral rehydration saves lives in developed nations as well (Spandorfer et al., 2005).

Every year in Africa, 1 million people die of malaria, most of them children. Although immediate drug treatment can save lives, health workers may not be available, children are brought to clinics too late, and undernourished children (a category that includes many young Africans) are especially vulnerable. Furthermore, resistance to many drugs is developing (Kun et al., 2010). A simple and inexpensive measure to prevent malaria is to have children sleep under bed nets treated with insect repellant; children who do so are much less likely to develop the disease. Many foundations in developed nations now provide bed nets in Africa and Asia, saving young lives (Roberts, 2007).

Immunization

Immunization—not yet possible with malaria but successful with measles, whooping cough, small pox, pneumonia, and many other illnesses that once killed thousands of babies each year—has prevented many diseases. Also called *vaccination,* immunization primes the body's immune system to resist a specific contagious disease. Immunization is said to have had "a greater impact on human mortality reduction and population growth than any other public health intervention besides clean water" (J. P. Baker, 2000, p. 199).

When people catch a contagious disease, their immune system produces antibodies to prevent a recurrence. In a healthy person who has not had the disease, a vaccine—a small dose of inactive virus (often via a "shot" in the arm)—stimulates the same antibodies. (Immunization schedules, with recommendations for the United States, appear in Appendix A, p. A-4.)

Dramatic Successes

Stunning successes in immunization include the following:

- Smallpox, the most lethal disease for children in the past, was eradicated worldwide as of 1971. Vaccination against smallpox is no longer needed.
- Polio, a crippling and sometimes fatal disease, is rare. Widespread vaccination, begun in 1955, has eliminated polio in most nations (including the United States). Just 784 cases worldwide were reported in 2003. In the same year, however, rumors about the safety of the polio vaccine halted immunization in northern Nigeria; consequently, polio reappeared. There were 1,948 cases, almost all in West Africa, in 2005 (Arita et al., 2006).
- Measles (rubeola, not rubella) is disappearing, thanks to a vaccine developed in 1963. Prior to that time, 3 to 4 million cases occurred each year in the United States alone (Centers for Disease Control and Prevention, 2007). In 2007, in the United States, only 43 people had measles, most of them born in nations without widespread immunization (MMWR, July 24, 2009).
- A recent success is a newly developed vaccine against rotavirus, which causes severe diarrhea and killed half a million children in 2005. Far fewer children caught rotavirus in 2009, although the vaccine is not yet widespread in developing nations, where most deaths occur (Glass & Parashar, 2006; MMWR, October 23, 2009).

Immunization protects children not only from temporary sickness but also from serious complications, including deafness, blindness, sterility, and meningitis. Sometimes the damage from illness is not apparent until decades later. Childhood mumps, for instance, can cause sterility and doubles the risk of schizophrenia in adults (Dalman et al., 2008).

TABLE 5.1

Deaths of Children Under Age 5 in Selected Countries

Country	Number of Deaths per 1,000
Singapore	3[†]
Iceland	3[†]
Sweden	3[†]
Japan	4[*]
Italy	4[†]
Spain	4[†]
Australia	6[*]
United Kingdom	6[*]
Canada	6[*]
New Zealand	6[*]
United States	8[†]
Russia	13[†]
Vietnam	14[†]
Mexico	17[†]
China	21[†]
Brazil	22[†]
Philippines	32[*]
India	69[*]
Nigeria	186
Sierra Leone	194
Afghanistan	257

[*] Reduced by at least one-third since 1990.
[†] Reduced by half or more since 1990.
Source: UNICEF, 2009.

This table shows the number of deaths per 1,000 children under age 5 for 20 of the 192 members of the United Nations. Most nations have improved markedly on this measure since 1990. Only when war destroys families and interferes with public health measures (as it has in Afghanistan and Sierra Leone) are nations not improving.

STEVEN RUBIN / THE IMAGE WORKS

Look Away! The benefits of immunization justify the baby's brief discomfort, but many parents still do not appreciate the importance of following the recommended schedule of immunizations.

Furthermore, each vaccinated child stops the spread of the disease and thus protects others, including those who cannot be safely immunized. Newborns may die if they catch a disease; the fetus of a pregnant woman who contracts rubella (German measles) may be born blind, deaf, and brain-damaged; adults who contract mumps or rubeola (measles) may become very ill; and those with impaired immune systems (HIV-positive, very old, or undergoing chemotherapy) sometimes die from "childhood" diseases.

Problems with Immunization

Parents do not notice if their child does *not* get seriously ill. One doctor, who wants people to attend to disease prevention, laments, "No one notices when things go right" (Bortz, 2005, p. 389). Before the varicella (chicken pox) vaccine, more than 100 people in the United States died each year from that disease and 1 million were itchy and feverish for a week. Now almost no one dies, and far fewer get chicken pox.

Many parents are concerned about potential side effects of vaccinations. However, the risks of the diseases are far greater than the risks from immunization (as Table 5.2 indicates). Doctors agree that vaccines "are one of the most cost-effective, successful interventions in the history of public health" and fear only that that success has made parents, physicians, and governments less vigilant than they should be (Hannan et al., 2009, p. S571). A hypothesis that the MMR (measles-mumps-rubella) vaccine causes autism has been repeatedly disproved (Mrozek-Budzyn et al., 2010; Shattuck, 2006).

More than 1 million children in developing nations die each year because effective vaccines against AIDS, malaria, cholera, typhoid, and shigellosis are not yet available. Another 2 to 3 million die each year from diphtheria, tetanus, and measles because they have not been immunized (Mahmoud, 2004); 100,000 children in India died in 2005 from measles alone (Dugger, 2006). Although most U.S. children eventually are fully immunized, only one-third get all their vaccinations on time (Mell et al., 2005). Late and inadequate immunization is blamed for a spike in infant whooping cough deaths in California in 2010, causing that state to declare an epidemic (McKinley, 2010). Failure to immunize infants may constitute medical neglect.

TABLE 5.2

Details About Vaccinations: United States

Vaccine	Year of Introduction*	Peak Annual Disease Total*	2007 Total[†]	Worst Consequences of Natural Disease*[†]	Percent of Children Vaccinated (U.S.)[†]	Known Vaccine Side Effects[†]
Chicken pox (varicella)	1995	4 million (est.)	34,507	Encephalitis (2 in 10,000 cases), bacterial skin infections, shingles (300,000 per year)	90.0	Fever (1 in 10 doses); mild rash (1 in 20 doses)
DTaP (diphtheria, tetanus, and pertussis)					84.5	Seizures (1 in 14,000), crying for 3 hours or more (1 in 1,000), fever of 105°F or higher (1 in 16,000)
Diphtheria	1923	206,939	0	Death (5 to 10 in 100 cases), muscle paralysis, heart failure		Adult Td (tetanus and diphtheria) vaccine may cause deep, aching pain and muscle wasting in upper arms
Tetanus	1927	1,560 (est.)	20	Death (1 in 10 cases), fractured bones, pneumonia		
Pertussis	1926 (whole cell) 1991 (acellular)	265,269	8,739	Death (2 in 1,000 cases), pneumonia (10 in 100 cases), seizures (1 to 2 in 100 cases)		Brain disease (0 to 10 in 1 million doses—whole-cell vaccine only)
H. influenzae (Type B) (childhood) (all serotypes)	1985	20,000 (est.)	2,231	Death (2 to 3 in 100 cases), meningitis, pneumonia, blood poisoning, inflammation of epiglottis, skin or bone infections	92.6	Redness, warmth, or swelling at injection site (1 in 4); fever of 101°F or higher (1 in 20)
IPV (inactivated polio vaccine)	1955; improved version used in U.S. since 1987	21,269	0	Death (2 to 5 in 100 cases in children), respiratory failure, paralysis, postpolio syndrome	92.6	Soreness and redness at injection site
MMR (measles, mumps, and rubella)					92.3	Seizure caused by fever (1 in 3,000 doses); low platelet count (1 in 30,000 doses)
Measles	1963	894,134	30	Encephalitis (1 in 1,000 cases), pneumonia (6 in 100 cases), death (1 to 2 in 1,000 cases), seizure (6 to 7 in 1,000 cases)		Temporary joint pain and stiffness (1 in 4 teenaged girls and women)
Mumps	1967	152,209	715	Deafness (1 in 20,000 cases), inflamed testicles (20 to 50 in 100 postpubertal males)		
Rubella	1969	56,686	11	Blindness, deafness, heart defects, and/or mental retardation in 85 percent of children born to mothers infected in early pregnancy		
PCV7 (pneumococcal conjugate vaccine)[†] (childhood)	2000	93,000 (est.)	20,000 (2005 est.)	Death or serious illness caused by meningitis, pneumonia, blood poisoning, ear infections		Fever over 100.4°F (1 in 3); redness, tenderness, or swelling at injection site (1 in 4)

Sources: *Lieu et al., 2000; [†]Centers for Disease Control and Prevention, 2009.

Nutrition

Infant mortality worldwide has plummeted in recent years. Several reasons have already been mentioned: fewer sudden infant deaths (explained in Chapter 1), advances in prenatal and newborn care (explained in Chapter 4), and, as you just read in this chapter, immunization. Better nutrition would further reduce infant deaths and disease.

Breast Is Best

Ideally, nutrition starts with *colostrum*, a thick, high-calorie fluid secreted by the mother's breasts at birth. After about three days, the breasts begin to produce milk. Compared with formula based on cow's milk, human milk is sterile; always at body temperature; and rich in iron, vitamins, and other newly discovered nutrients for brain and body (Drover et al., 2009).

Babies who are exclusively breast-fed are less often sick. This is true in infancy because breast milk provides antibodies against any disease to which the mother is immune, as well as decreases the risk of allergies and asthma. It is also true later on because breast-feeding decreases the risk of obesity and heart disease in adulthood.

The specific fats and sugars in breast milk make it more digestible, and better for an infant's brain, than any prepared formula (Drover et al., 2009; Riordan, 2005). The composition of breast milk adjusts to the age of the baby, with breast milk for premature babies distinct from breast milk for older infants. Quantity increases to meet the demand: Twins and even triplets can grow strong while being exclusively breast-fed for months.

In fact, breast milk appears to have so many advantages over formula (see Table 5.3) that critics question the validity of the research: Although scientists control for education and income, these critics wonder whether women who breast-feed might be better caregivers in ways not indexed by socioeconomic status (SES). In the United States, a survey found that parents of breast-fed babies were more likely to be married, college graduates, and/or immigrants (Gibson-Davis & Brooks-Gunn, 2006; see the Research Design). Could one of those variables account for the advantages of breast-feeding? Perhaps somewhat, but almost every developmentalist agrees that breast is best.

▶ **Research Design**

Scientists: Christina Gibson-Davis and Jeanne Brooks-Gunn.

Publication: *American Journal of Public Health* (2006).

Participants: A study called Fragile Families surveyed about 5,000 new mothers from 75 U.S. hospitals. The focus was on low-income families.

Design: Mothers and fathers were asked about their social status (e.g., education, marital status, immigration, income, employment) and breast-feeding, with assurance of confidentiality. Questions were asked of both parents soon after birth and again of the mothers a year later.

Major conclusions: A mother's decision to start and continue breast-feeding is affected by many aspects of her social context, including her education and relationship with the baby's father. U.S.-born mothers are less likely to breast-feed than immigrant mothers.

Comment: This research includes a population often omitted from other surveys and thus is particularly useful. For instance, other research has found that college graduation increases breast-feeding; this study finds that parents with more education at any level are more likely to breast-feed, even when the comparison is between those who did, or did not, graduate from high school.

© JENNIE HART / ALAMY

ALAIN EVRARD / PHOTOLIBRARY

The Same Situation, Many Miles Apart: Breast-Feeding Breast-feeding is universal. None of us would exist if our foremothers had not successfully breast-fed their babies for millennia. Currently breast-feeding is practiced worldwide, but it is no longer the only way to feed infants, and each culture has particular practices.

Observation Quiz (see answer, page 146) What three differences do you see between these two breast-feeding women—one in the United States and one in Laos?

TABLE 5.3
The Benefits of Breast-Feeding

For the Baby

Balance of nutrition (fat, protein, etc.) adjusts to age of baby

Breast milk has micronutrients not found in formula

Less infant illness, including allergies, ear infections, stomach upsets

Less childhood asthma

Better childhood vision

Less adult illness, including diabetes, cancer, heart disease

Protection against measles and all other childhood diseases, since breast milk contains antibodies

Stronger jaws, fewer cavities, advanced breathing reflexes (less SIDS)

Higher IQ, less likely to drop out of school, more likely to attend college

Later puberty, less teenage pregnancy

Less likely to become obese or hypertensive by age 12

For the Mother

Easier bonding with baby

Reduced risk of breast cancer and osteoporosis

Natural contraception (with exclusive breast-feeding, for several months)

Pleasure of breast stimulation

Satisfaction of meeting infant's basic need

No formula to prepare; no sterilization

Easier travel with the baby

For the Family

Increased survival of other children (because of spacing of births)

Increased family income (because formula and medical care are expensive)

Less stress on father, especially at night (he cannot be expected to feed the baby)

Sources: Beilin & Huang, 2008; DiGirolamo et al., 2005; Oddy, 2004; Riordan & Wambach, 2009.

>> Answer to Observation Quiz (from page 145): The babies' ages, the settings, and the mothers' apparent attitudes. The U.S. mother (*left*) is indoors in a hospital and seems attentive to whether she is feeding her infant the right way. The mother in Laos (*right*) seems confident and content as she feeds her older baby in a public place, enjoying the social scene.

Bottle-feeding is preferable only in unusual cases, such as when the mother is HIV-positive or uses toxic or addictive drugs. Even then, however, breast milk without supplementation may be better than alternative nutrition. In some African nations, HIV-positive women are encouraged to breast-feed because their infants' risk of catching HIV from their mothers is lower than the risk of dying from infections, diarrhea, or malnutrition as a result of bottle-feeding (Cohen, 2007; Kuhn et al., 2009). Pediatricians agree that it "is clear and incontrovertible that human milk is the best nutritive substance for infants during the first year" (Wagner et al., 2008. p. 1148).

For all these reasons, virtually all doctors worldwide recommend exclusive breast-feeding for the first six months. Some hospitals encourage breast-feeding by putting the infant to the breast soon after birth, avoiding bottle-feeding, and allowing the baby to room with the mother (Murray et al., 2007). Hospitals could do more because successful breast-feeding involves some learning (how to latch on and off, for instance) and often some pain (cracked nipples) in the early weeks. Encouragement from family members, especially new fathers, is crucial. My son-in-law did well by my first grandson: When I noted that he did most of the diapering, he said, "That's because Elissa does most of the breast-feeding."

After six months, other foods can be added—especially cereals and bananas, which are easily digested and provide needed nutrients. Breast milk should remain in the diet for a year or more, however. Of course, none of this means that a diet of only breast milk is adequate throughout infancy, as the following explains.

A CASE TO STUDY

Breast-Fed Kiana, Close To Death

Thinking his 10-month old daughter, Kiana, had a bad case of flu, Ian Barrow took her to the emergency room earlier this year. Doctors immediately noticed something more serious: soft bones, an enlarged heart, and organs close to shutting down. The diagnosis was a shock: rickets. Barrow, a technician at the National Cancer Institute, says, "Rickets is something that has supposedly disappeared."

[Stokstad, 2003, p. 1886]

Rickets is caused by severe deficiency of vitamin D, a vitamin naturally produced by the body in response to sunshine. For light-skinned adults, even a few minutes of direct sun exposure three days a week is enough to make adequate vitamin D. Rickets was once common in children who did not often play outside; that is why vitamin D is added to milk. Although few older children now get rickets, the disease has not disappeared: Now exclusively breast-fed babies, aged 6 to 18 months, are at highest risk. Rickets is the worst consequence, but people of all ages may suffer from inadequate vitamin D, resulting in reduced immunity and less energy (Wagner et al., 2008).

Many modern mothers prevent the exposure of even an inch of infant skin to direct sunlight in order to avoid later cancer. Many also believe that breast milk provides complete nutrition. But if this latter belief prevents infants from getting vitamin D (88 percent of U.S. mothers do not give vitamin D to their babies), serious deficiencies may occur (J. A. Taylor et al., 2010).

Beach Baby Infants need to be protected from sunburn, as this child is with hat and coverup designed especially to keep out ultraviolet rays. Infants also need vitamin D, which the body produces naturally in response to sunlight on the skin. It can also be obtained with vitamin supplements.

SCIENCE FACTION / SUPERSTOCK

Some researchers "blame public health experts who have urged women to breast feed without emphasizing the need for supplements. And they're even more angry at those who recommend that infants under 6 months avoid all sunlight to reduce cancer risks" (Stokstad, 2003, p. 1887). Many pediatricians do not prescribe vitamin D for breast-fed babies, and, even if they do, about half of their breast-feeding mothers do not follow that advice. Actually, only a blood test reveals how much vitamin D an infant has; many babies need no extra dose, but others do—rickets should never occur.

Remember how shocked Ian Barrow was. He knew that his child should be breast-fed, and he was proud of his wife for doing so. However, he did not know that rickets was still pos-

sible or that Kiana's dark skin meant that more sunlight was needed. Fortunately, this case ended well, because an alert father noticed that something was wrong and took his daughter to doctors who diagnosed her quickly and provided immediate vitamin D. Kiana not only survived; she thrived.

Experts are still debating how much vitamin D a person needs. In 2008, the American Academy of Pediatrics doubled its recommendation (from 200 to 400 IU a day) (Wagner et al., 2008). Not every doctor or parent agrees (J. A. Taylor et al., 2010), but "Ian Barrow, for one, says that he's making sure that Kiana and her brothers spend more time outside" (Stokstad, 2003, p. 1888). No expert doubts that breast is best, but that does not mean that breast-fed babies always have every nutrient they need.

Breast-feeding dramatically reduces infant disease and death. In the United States and worldwide, more than 90 percent of infants are breast-fed at birth, but only 36 percent are exclusively breast-fed for the first six months. By their second birthday, half of the world's infants (especially in poor nations, rarely in rich ones) are still being nursed, usually at night (UNICEF, 2007).

How long a mother continues to breast-feed is strongly affected by her experiences in the first week, when encouragement and practical help are most needed (DiGirolamo et al., 2005). Ideally, nurses visit new parents at home for several weeks; such visits (routine in some nations, rare in others) increase the likelihood that breast-feeding will continue.

Malnutrition

Protein-calorie malnutrition occurs when a person does not consume sufficient food of any kind. Roughly a third of the world's children in developing nations suffer from **stunting,** being very short for their age because severe and chronic malnutrition kept them from growing. Stunting is most common in the poorest nations (see Figure 5.6).

protein-calorie malnutrition A condition in which a person does not consume sufficient food of any kind. This deprivation can result in several illnesses, severe weight loss, and even death.

stunting The failure of children to grow to a normal height for their age due to severe and chronic malnutrition.

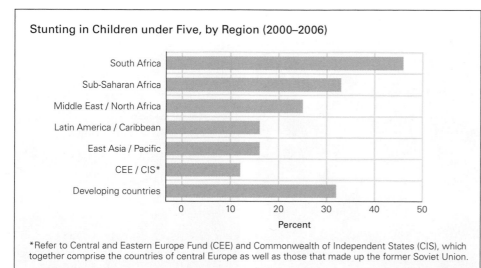

Stunting in Children under Five, by Region (2000–2006)

*Refer to Central and Eastern Europe Fund (CEE) and Commonwealth of Independent States (CIS), which together comprise the countries of central Europe as well as those that made up the former Soviet Union.

Source: UNICEF, 2007.

FIGURE 5.6

Genetic? The data show that basic nutrition is still unavailable to many children in the developing world. Some critics contend that Asian children are genetically small and therefore that Western norms make it appear as if India and Africa have more stunted children than they really do. However, children of Asian and African descent born and nurtured in North America are as tall as those of European descent. Thus, malnutrition, not genes, accounts for most stunting worldwide. (Western Europe and North America are not shown here; stunting in these areas is low—much less than 5 percent.)

wasting The tendency for children to be severely underweight for their age as a result of malnutrition.

Another measure of malnutrition is **wasting,** when children are severely underweight for their age (2 or more standard deviations below average). About 25 percent of the world's children are wasted (UNICEF, 2007). Many nations, especially in East Asia, Latin America, and central Europe, have seen improvement in child nutrition in the past decades; but in some other nations, primarily in Africa, child malnutrition has increased since 2000. Most stunted children are also wasted. However, it is possible to be wasted without being stunted (such as when malnutrition has not gone on for years) or stunted without being wasted (such as when a short child has started to overeat; adult obesity correlates with childhood thinness).

To measure a particular child's nutritional status, compare weight and height with the detailed norms presented in Appendix A, pages A-6 and A-7, and consider percentiles from birth on. A child may simply be genetically short or thin, but a decline in percentile ranking during the first two years is an ominous sign—and being in the bottom 3 percent is almost always a sign of malnutrition.

Chronically malnourished infants and children suffer in three ways, as indicated by the United Nations World Food Program (2008) and many other sources:

1. Their brains may not develop normally. If malnutrition has continued long enough to affect the baby's height, it may also have affected the brain.
2. Malnourished children have no body reserves to protect them against common diseases. About half of all childhood deaths occur because malnutrition makes a childhood disease lethal.
3. Some diseases result directly from malnutrition.

marasmus A disease of severe protein-calorie malnutrition during early infancy, in which growth stops, body tissues waste away, and the infant eventually dies.

The worst disease directly caused by malnutrition is **marasmus.** Growth stops, body tissues waste away, and the infant victim eventually dies. Prevention of marasmus begins long before birth, with good nutrition for the pregnant woman. Then breast-feeding on demand (eight or more times a day) and frequent checkups to monitor the baby's weight can stop marasmus before it begins. Infants who

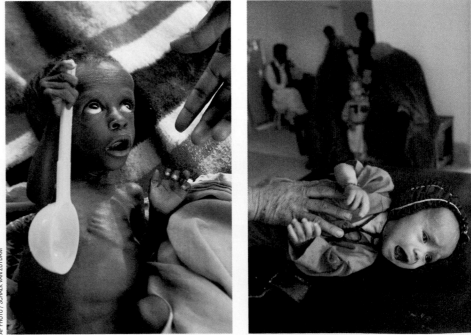

The Same Situation, Many Miles Apart: Children Still Malnourished Infant malnutrition is common in nations at war (like Afghanistan, *at right*) or with crop failure (like Niger, *at left*). UNICEF relief programs reach only half the children in either nation. The children in these photographs are among the lucky ones who are being fed.

show signs of "failure to thrive" (they do not gain weight) can be hospitalized and treated before brain damage occurs.

Malnutrition after age 1 may cause **kwashiorkor.** Ironically, *kwashiorkor* means "a disease of the older child when a new baby arrives"—signifying cessation of breast-feeding and less maternal attention. In kwashiorkor, growth is retarded; the liver is damaged; the immune system is weakened; the face, legs, and abdomen swell with fluid (edema); energy is reduced (malnourished children play less); and hair becomes thin, brittle, and colorless. Treatment includes providing protein that the body has long lacked. However, partly because the bodies of children with kwashiorkor may have become less efficient at digesting good food, the survival rate of hospitalized children with kwashiorkor is lower than that of those hospitalized with marasmus (Badaloo et al., 2006).

Prevention, more than treatment, stops childhood malnutrition. Maternal prenatal nutrition defends against marasmus after birth; breast-feeding throughout toddlerhood defends against kwashiorkor in childhood. A study of two poor African nations (Niger and Gambia) found several specific factors that reduced wasting and stunting: mother's secondary education, breast-feeding, both parents at home, water piped to the house, a tile (not dirt) floor, a toilet, electricity, a radio, and immunization (for measles, polio, and several other diseases) (Oyekale & Oyekale, 2009).

Several items on this list are taken for granted by readers of this book. However, two themes apply to everyone at any age: (1) Prevention is better than treatment, and (2) people with some knowledge are more likely to protect their health and that of their loved ones. The next chapters continue these themes.

> **kwashiorkor** A disease of chronic malnutrition during childhood, in which a protein deficiency makes the child more vulnerable to other diseases, such as measles, diarrhea, and influenza.

SUMMING UP

Many public health practices save millions of infants each year. Immunizing children and breast-feeding are simple yet life-saving steps. These are called public health measures rather than parental practices because they are affected by culture and national policies.

An underlying theme of this chapter is that healthy biological growth is the result not simply of genes and nutrition but also of a social environment that provides opportunities for growth: lullabies and mobiles for stimulating the infant's senses, encouragement for developing the first motor skills, and protection against disease. Each aspect of development is linked to every other aspect, and each developing person is linked to family, community, and world.

SUMMARY

Body Changes

1. In the first two years of life, infants grow taller, gain weight, and increase in head circumference—all indicative of development. The norm at birth is 7½ pounds in weight, 20 inches in length (about 3,400 grams, 51 centimeters). Birthweight doubles by 4 months, triples by 1 year, and quadruples by 2 years, when toddlers weigh about 30 pounds (13½ kilograms).

2. Sleep gradually decreases over the first two years. As with all areas of development, variations in sleep patterns are normal, caused by both nature and nurture. In developed nations, co-sleeping is increasingly common for very young infants, and many (but not all) developmentalists consider it a harmless, or even beneficial, practice.

Brain Development

3. The brain increases dramatically in size, from about 25 to 75 percent of adult weight, in the first two years. Complexity increases as well, with cell growth, development of dendrites, and formation of synapses. Both growth and pruning aid cognition.

4. Experience is vital for dendrites and synapses to link neurons. In the first year, the parts of the cortex dedicated to the senses and motor skills mature. If neurons are unused, they atrophy, and the brain regions are rededicated to processing other sensations. Normal stimulation, which almost all infants obtain, fosters experience-expectant maturation.

5. Most experience-dependent brain growth reflects the varied, culture-specific experiences of the infant. Therefore, one person's brain differs from another's. However, in the basic capacities that humans share—emotional, linguistic, and sensory—all normal infants are equally capable.

Sensation and Movement

6. At birth, the senses already respond to stimuli. Prenatal experience makes hearing the most mature sense. Vision is the least mature sense at birth, but it improves quickly. Infants use all their senses to strengthen their early social interactions.

7. Infants gradually improve their motor skills as they begin to grow and brain maturation increases. Gross motor skills are soon evident, from rolling over to sitting up (at about 6 months), from standing to walking (at about 1 year), from climbing to running (before age 2).

8. Fine motor skills are difficult for infants, but babies gradually develop the hand and finger control needed to grab, aim, and manipulate almost anything within reach. Experience, time, and motivation allow infants to advance in all their motor skills.

Surviving in Good Health

9. About 2 billion infant deaths have been prevented in the past half-century because of improved health care. More medical professionals are needed to prevent, diagnose, and treat the diseases that still cause many infant deaths.

10. One major innovation is immunization, which has eradicated smallpox and virtually eliminated polio and measles in developed nations. In recent years, there has been much debate over potential side effects of immunization, but the benefits have consistently been shown to greatly outweigh any risks.

11. Breast-feeding is best for infants, partly because breast milk helps them resist disease and promotes growth of every kind. Most babies are breast-fed at birth, but in North America less than half are exclusively breast-fed for six months, as most doctors worldwide recommend.

12. Severe malnutrition stunts growth and can cause death, both directly through marasmus or kwashiorkor and indirectly through vulnerability if a child catches measles, an intestinal disorder, or some other illness.

KEY TERMS

head-sparing (p. 124)
percentile (p. 124)
REM sleep (p. 125)
co-sleeping (p. 126)
neurons (p. 127)
cortex (p. 128)
axon (p. 128)
dendrite (p. 128)

synapse (p. 128)
transient exuberance (p. 129)
experience-expectant brain
  functions (p. 131)
experience-dependent brain
  functions (p. 131)
prefrontal cortex (p. 132)
shaken baby syndrome (p. 132)

self-righting (p. 132)
sensation (p. 134)
perception (p. 134)
binocular vision (p. 136)
motor skills (p. 137)
gross motor skills (p. 137)
fine motor skills (p. 138)

protein-calorie malnutrition
  (p. 147)
stunting (p. 147)
wasting (p. 148)
marasmus (p. 148)
kwashiorkor (p. 149)

WHAT HAVE YOU LEARNED?

Body Changes

1. What specific facts indicate that infants grow rapidly in the first year?

2. Why is it fine for an infant to be consistently at the 20th percentile in height and weight?

3. How much do newborns usually sleep and dream?

4. How much and where do 1-year-olds usually sleep?

Brain Development

5. What is the difference between the cortex and the rest of the brain?

6. How does the brain change in weight from birth to age 2?

7. What factors increase the accuracy of perception via the fusiform face area?

8. How can loss of dendrites increase brain potential?

9. What is the difference between experience-expectant and experience-dependent brain function?

10. How does the concept of plasticity apply to early brain development?

11. What should caregivers remember about brain development when an infant cries?

Sensation and Movement

12. What is the relationship between perception and the five senses?

13. What particular sounds and patterns do infants pay attention to?

14. How does an infant's vision change over the first year?

15. What changes occur in the infant's senses of smell, taste, and touch over the first two years?

16. What is universal and what is cultural in the development of gross motor skills in infancy?

17. Which fine motor skills are developed in infancy and which not until later in childhood?

Surviving in Good Health

18. Why do public health doctors hope that all infants worldwide have been immunized?

19. What are the reasons for and against breast-feeding until a child is at least 1 year old?

20. What is the relationship between malnutrition and disease?

21. As an indication of malnutrition, which is better, stunting or wasting? Why?

APPLICATIONS

1. Immunization regulations and practices vary, partly for social and political reasons. Ask at least two faculty or administrative staff members what immunizations students at your college must have and why. If you hear, "It's a law," ask why that law is in place.

2. Observe three infants (whom you do not know) in public places such as a store, playground, or bus. Look closely at body size and motor skills, especially how much control each baby has over legs and hands. From that, estimate the age in months and then ask the caregiver how old the infant is. (Most caregivers know the infant's exact age and are happy to tell you.)

3. *This project can be done alone, but it is more informative if several students pool responses.* Ask 3 to 10 adults whether they were bottle-fed or breast-fed and, if breast-fed, for how long. If anyone does not know, or if anyone expresses embarrassment about how long they were breast-fed, that itself is worth noting. Is there any correlation between adult body size and mode of infant feeding?

>>ONLINE CONNECTIONS

To accompany your textbook, you have access to a number of online resources, including quizzes for every chapter of the book, flashcards (in English and Spanish), critical thinking questions, and case studies. For access to any of these links, go to www.worthpublishers.com/bergerls8e. In addition to these free resources, you'll also find links to the podcasts, video clips, diagnostic quizzing with personalized study advice, and an ebook. Some of the videos and activities available online include:

- *Infant Reflexes.* Watch video clips of some of the most common infant reflexes, from the Babinski to the Moro.

- *Nutritional Needs of Infants and Children.* Including video footage from UNICEF of children around the world, this activity provides an overview of the nutritional needs challenges children face in both developed and developing countries.

The First Two Years: Cognitive Development

WHAT WILL YOU KNOW?

1. What is the evidence that infants are learning in the first year of life?
2. Why are curiosity and exploration signs of intelligence in toddlers?
3. How are physiological maturation and information processing connected?
4. When do infant comprehension, gestures, words, and sentences normally begin?
5. How do the implications of each major theory of early language learning differ?

My aunt's husband, Uncle Henry, boasted that he did nothing with his three children—all boys—until they were smart enough to talk. He may have found an excuse to avoid diapering, burping, and bathing, but his beliefs about cognition were wrong. Babies are smart from the first days of life; they communicate long before they say their first words.

Uncle Henry missed his children's most impressive cognitive accomplishments. His sons grew up to be devoted to their mother and much more involved with their own infants than Uncle Henry had been with them. The research and conclusions presented in this chapter help explain all this.

We begin with Piaget's framework for observing intellectual progression over the first two years. Newborns know almost nothing; two years later they make a wish, say it out loud, and blow out their birthday candles. Piaget traced this progression in six stages. We then describe some research on early cognition, including a theoretical approach (information processing) and specific methods that reveal preverbal infants to be avid learners (habituation, brain scans). Then we outline the progress of language learning, from reactionary cries to deliberate two-word sentences—like that 2-year-old's wish might have been. We end by exploring how early cognitive accomplishments, particularly acquisition of language, occur.

>> Sensorimotor Intelligence

As you remember from Chapter 2, Jean Piaget was a Swiss scientist, born in 1896. He was "arguably the most influential researcher of all times within the area of cognitive developmental psychology" (Birney et al., 2005, p. 328). Contrary to most people of his day (including my Uncle Henry), Piaget realized that infants are smart and active learners, adapting to experience. Adaptation, according to Piaget, is the core of intelligence.

Piaget described four distinct periods of cognitive development. The first begins at birth and ends at about 24 months. Piaget called it **sensorimotor intelligence** because infants learn through their senses and motor skills. This two-year-long period is subdivided into six stages (see Table 6.1).

sensorimotor intelligence Piaget's term for the way infants think—by using their senses and motor skills—during the first period of cognitive development.

Stages One and Two: Primary Circular Reactions

In every aspect of sensorimotor intelligence, the brain and the senses interact with experiences, each shaping the other (Ambady & Bharucha, 2009). Sensation, perception, and cognition cycle back and forth in what Piaget called *circular reactions*. The first two stages of sensorimotor intelligence involve **primary circular reactions,** which involve the infant's own body.

Stage one, called the *stage of reflexes*, lasts only for a month. It includes senses as well as motor reflexes, the foundations of infant thought. Reflexes become deliberate; sensation leads to perception and then to cognition. Sensorimotor intelligence begins.

As reflexes adjust, the 1-month-old enters stage two, *first acquired adaptations* (also called the *stage of first habits*). Adaptation is cognitive; it includes both assimilation and accommodation (see page 46), which people use to understand their experience. Infants adapt their reflexes as repeated responses provide information about what the body does and how that action feels.

Here is one example. In a powerful reflex, newborns suck anything that touches their lips. By about 1 month, infants adapt this reflex, to bottles or breasts, pacifiers or fingers, each requiring specific types of tongue pushing. This adaptation is

primary circular reactions The first of three types of feedback loops in sensorimotor intelligence, this one involving the infant's own body. The infant senses motion, sucking, noise, and other stimuli, and tries to understand them.

Time for Adaptation Sucking is a reflex at first, but adaptation begins as soon as an infant differentiates a pacifier from her mother's breast or realizes that her hand has grown too big to fit into her mouth. This infant's expression of concentration suggests that she is about to make that adaptation and suck just her thumb from now on.

Especially for Parents When should parents decide whether to feed their baby only by breast, only by bottle, or using some combination? When should they decide whether or not to let their baby use a pacifier? (see response, page 158)

TABLE 6.1	
The Six Stages of Sensorimotor Intelligence	

For an overview of the stages of sensorimotor thought, it helps to group the six stages into pairs. The first two stages involve the infant's responses to its own body.

Primary Circular Reactions

Stage One (birth to 1 month)	*Reflexes:* sucking, grasping, staring, listening
Stage Two (1–4 months)	*The first acquired adaptations:* accommodation and coordination of reflexes. *Examples:* sucking a pacifier differently from a nipple; grabbing a bottle to suck it

The next two stages involve the infant's responses to objects and people.

Secondary Circular Reactions

Stage Three (4–8 months)	*Making interesting sights last:* responding to people and objects. *Example:* clapping hands when mother says "patty-cake"
Stage Four (8–12 months)	*New adaptation and anticipation:* becoming more deliberate and purposeful in responding to people and objects. *Example:* putting mother's hands together in order to make her start playing patty-cake

The last two stages are the most creative, first with action and then with ideas.

Tertiary Circular Reactions

Stage Five (12–18 months)	*New means through active experimentation:* experimentation and creativity in the actions of the "little scientist." *Example:* putting a teddy bear in the toilet and flushing it
Stage Six (18–24 months)	*New means through mental combinations:* considering before doing provides the child with new ways of achieving a goal without resorting to trial-and-error experiments. *Example:* before flushing, remembering that the toilet overflowed the last time, and hesitating

a sign that infants have begun to interpret their perceptions; as they accommodate to pacifiers, they are "thinking."

After several months, additional adaptation of the sucking reflex is evident. Infant cognition may lead babies to suck in some ways for hunger, in other ways for comfort—and never to suck fuzzy blankets or large balls. Once adaptation is successful, it sticks. For instance, breast-fed babies may reject milk from a bottle, and if parents of a 3-month-old thumb-sucker decide that a pacifier would be better, the infant may refuse to adapt. Piaget believed that people of all ages tend to be stuck in their ways for cognitive reasons; this is one early example.

Stages Three and Four: Secondary Circular Reactions

In stages three and four, development advances from primary to **secondary circular reactions.** Those reactions are an *interaction* between the baby and something else.

During stage three (4 to 8 months), infants attempt to produce exciting experiences, *making interesting events last*. Realizing that rattles make noise, for example, they wave their arms and laugh whenever someone puts a rattle in their hand. The sight of something delightful—a favorite book, a smiling parent—can trigger active efforts for interaction.

Next comes stage four (8 months to 1 year), *new adaptation and anticipation*, also called the *means to the end* because babies have goals that they try to reach. Often they ask for help (fussing, pointing, gesturing) to accomplish what they want. Thinking is more innovative in stage four than in stage three because adaptation is more complex. For instance, instead of always smiling at Daddy, an infant might first assess Daddy's mood, and then try to engage. Stage-three babies know how to continue an experience; stage-four babies initiate and anticipate.

New Directions

A 10-month-old girl might crawl over to her mother, bringing a bar of soap as a signal to start her bath, and then remove her clothes to make her wishes crystal clear—finally squealing with delight when the bath water is turned on. Similarly, if a 10-month-old boy sees his mother putting on her coat to leave, he might drag over his own jacket to signal that he wants to go along.

These examples reveal *goal-directed behavior*—that is, purposeful action. The baby's obvious goal-directedness stems from (1) an enhanced awareness of cause and effect, (2) memory for actions already completed, and (3) understanding of other people's intentions (Behne et al., 2005; Brandone & Wellman, 2009; Willatts, 1999). These cognitive advances coincide with new motor skills (e.g., crawling, grabbing), both the result of brain maturation.

Object Permanence

Piaget thought that, at about 8 months, babies first understand the concept of **object permanence,** the realization that objects or people continue to exist when they are no longer in sight. As Piaget predicted, not until about 8 months do infants search for toys that have fallen from the crib, rolled under a couch, or disappeared under a blanket. As they grow older, toddlers become better at seeking hidden objects, which Piaget again considered symptomatic of their sensorimotor intelligence. However, many scientists now question Piaget's interpretations, as the following explains.

secondary circular reactions The second of three types of feedback loops in sensorimotor intelligence, this one involving people and objects. Infants respond to other people, to toys, and to any other object they can touch or move.

Intelligence in Action At four months, he already has learned that every sense and motor skill connects with daddy—or is it the other way around?

object permanence The realization that objects (including people) still exist when they can no longer be seen, touched, or heard.

A VIEW FROM SCIENCE

Object Permanence Revisited

Before Piaget, it was assumed that infants understood objects just as adults do. Piaget demonstrated otherwise in a basic experiment in which an adult shows an infant an interesting toy, covers it with a lightweight cloth, and observes the response. The results:

- Infants younger than 8 months do not search for the object (by removing the cloth).

- At about 8 months, infants search immediately after the object is covered but not if they have to wait a few seconds.

- By 2 years, children fully understand object permanence, progressing through several stages of ever-advanced cognition (Piaget, 1954).

As you learned in Chapter 1, the scientific method includes (1) replication (thousands of scientists in dozens of nations have replicated Piaget's original research design) and (2) seeking alternative interpretations of the results. In recent years, alternative explanations have proliferated. Piaget claimed that failure to search meant the child had no concept of object permanence. Might other immaturities, such as imperfect motor skills or fragile memory, mask an infant's understanding that objects still exist when they are no longer visible (Charles & Rivera, 2009)?

As one researcher points out, "Amid his acute observation and brilliant theorizing, Piaget . . . mistook infants' motor incompetence for conceptual incompetence" (Mandler, 2004, p. 17). A series of clever experiments, in which objects seemed to disappear behind a screen while researchers traced eye movements and brain activity, revealed some inkling of object permanence in infants as young as 4½ months (Baillargeon & DeVos, 1991; Spelke, 1993).

The specific finding that contradicted Piaget's conclusions is that long before infants were 8 months old, they showed surprise at an experimental event by such reactions as staring longer, for instance. In one experiment, a screen at first momentarily obscured an object that the infants saw; when the screen was removed, the object had vanished or had become two objects or had moved in an unexpected way. The infants' surprise (evident in longer stares) suggests they understood object permanence; it indicated that they seemed to think the object still existed in its original form behind the screen (Baillargeon, 1994).

The idea that such surprise indicates object permanence is accepted by some scientists, who believe that "infants as young as 2 and 3 months of age can represent fully hidden objects" (Cohen & Cashon, 2006, p. 224), but not by everyone (Kagan, 2008). Some psychologists may be too eager to interpret shifts in infant eye gaze as evidence of infant thought. Further research on object permanence continues to raise questions and produce surprises. For instance, many other creatures (cats, monkeys, dogs, birds) develop object permanence at younger ages than humans do. Slow development in humans indicates slower cognition—which may or may not reflect brain activity or language facility (Bruce & Muhammad, 2009).

No matter which side of this debate an adult is on, this research provides many practical suggestions. If very young infants fuss because they want something they see but cannot have (your keys, a cigarette, a piece of candy), all an adult needs to do is to put it out of sight. Fussing stops. By contrast, for toddlers, merely hiding the forbidden object is not enough. It must be securely locked or thrown away, or else a young child might remember where it is hidden and later retrieve it.

The fact that object permanence develops gradually also lets caregivers know that games such as peek-a-boo and hide-and-seek are too advanced at early ages—although they are great fun for infants who understand object permanence but are not yet bored by another demonstration of it. Peek-a-boo brings gales of laughter from 8- to 12-month-olds. Try it.

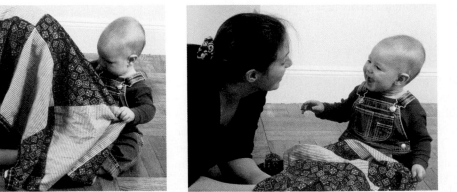

BOTH: LAURA DWIGHT

Peek-a-Boo The best hidden object is Mom under an easily moved blanket, as 7-month-old Elias has discovered. Peek-a-boo is fun from about 7 to 12 months. In another month, Elias will search for more conventionally hidden objects. In a year or two, his surprise and delight at finding Mom will fade.

Stages Five and Six: Tertiary Circular Reactions

In their second year, infants start experimenting in thought and deed, in the opposite sequence—acting first and thinking later. **Tertiary circular reactions** begin when 1-year-olds take independent actions to discover the properties of other people, animals, and things. Infants no longer respond simply to their own bodies (primary reactions) or to other people or objects (secondary reactions). They explore in a cognitive pattern more like a spiral than a closed circle.

The first stage of tertiary circular reactions, Piaget's stage five (age 12 to 18 months), is called *new means through active experimentation.* This builds on the accomplishments of stage four. Now goal-directed and purposeful activities become more expansive and creative. Toddlers delight in squeezing all the toothpaste out of the tube, taking apart your iPod, uncovering the anthill. Piaget referred to the stage-five toddler as a **"little scientist"** who "experiments in order to see." Their scientific method is trial and error. Their devotion to discovery is familiar to every adult scientist—and to every parent.

Finally, in the sixth stage (age 18 to 24 months), toddlers begin to anticipate and solve simple problems by using *mental combinations,* an intellectual experimentation that sometimes supersedes the active experimentation of stage five. Thankfully, the sequence may begin with thought (especially if an adult previously said something was forbidden) and then move on to action.

Also in the sixth stage, children are able to combine ideas. For instance, they know that a doll is not a real baby but can instead be a pretend baby, belted into a stroller and taken for a walk. Two words can be combined by this point as well, an impressive intellectual accomplishment discussed later in this chapter.

Because they combine ideas, stage-six toddlers think about consequences, hesitating a moment before yanking the cat's tail or dropping a raw egg on the floor. Of course, their strong impulse to discover may overwhelm reflection; they do not always choose wisely. Piaget describes another stage-six intellectual accomplishment, involving both thinking and memory. **Deferred imitation** occurs when infants copy behavior they noticed hours or even days earlier (Piaget, 1945/1962). A classic example is Piaget's daughter, Jacqueline, who observed another child

> who got into a terrible temper. He screamed as he tried to get out of a playpen and pushed it backward, stamping his feet. Jacqueline stood watching him in amazement, never having witnessed such a scene before. The next day, she herself screamed in her playpen and tried to move it, stamping her foot lightly several times in succession.

[Piaget, 1945/1962, p. 63]

Piaget and Modern Research

Infants reach the various stages of sensorimotor intelligence earlier than Piaget predicted. Not only do many 5-month-olds show surprise when object permanence seems compromised, but many babies pretend and defer imitation (both stage-six

tertiary circular reactions The third of three types of feedback loops in sensorimotor intelligence, this one involving active exploration and experimentation. Infants explore a range of new activities, varying their responses as a way of learning about the world.

"little scientist" The stage-five toddler (age 12 to 18 months) who experiments without anticipating the results, using trial and error in active and creative exploration.

deferred imitation A sequence in which an infant first perceives something that someone else does and then performs the same action a few hours or even days later.

Especially for Parents One parent wants to put all the breakable or dangerous objects away because a toddler is now able to move around independently. The other parent says that the baby should learn not to touch certain things. Who is right? (see response, page 159)

Exploration at 15 Months One of the best ways to investigate food is to squish it in your hands, observing any changes in color and texture and listening for any sounds. Taste and smell are primary senses for adults when eating, but it looks as if Jonathan has already had his fill of those.

I'm Listening This 14-month-old is a master at deferred imitation. He knows how to hold a cell phone and what gestures to use as the "conversation" goes on.

>> Response for Parents (from page 154)
Both decisions should be made within the first month, during the stage of reflexes. If parents wait until the infant is 4 months or older, they may discover that they are too late. It is difficult to introduce a bottle to a 4-month-old who has been exclusively breast-fed or a pacifier to a baby who has already adapted the sucking reflex to a thumb.

habituation The process of getting used to an object or event through repeated exposure to it.

capabilities, according to Piaget) before 1 year (Bauer, 2006; Fagard & Lockman, 2010; Hayne & Simcock, 2009; Meltzoff & Moore, 1999).

Piaget underestimated infant cognition because his basic insights were based on his own infants. Direct observation of three children is a start, and Piaget's observations were extraordinarily meticulous and creative, but no contemporary researcher would stop there. Given the immaturity and variability of babies, dozens of infants must be studied in creative yet logical ways. For instance, to prove that object permanence occurred before 6 months, Baillargeon (2000) listed 30 studies involving more than a thousand infants.

When studying infants, there are always problems with "fidelity and credibility" (Bornstein et al., 2005, p. 287). To overcome these problems, modern researchers use innovative statistics, research designs, sample sizes, and strategies that were not available to Piaget—often finding that object permanence, deferred imitation, and other sensorimotor accomplishments occur earlier, and with more variation, than Piaget had assumed (Hartmann & Pelzel, 2005; Kolling et al., 2009).

Boredom as a Research Method

For the past several decades, hundreds of studies have depended on a research method called **habituation** (from the word *habit*). Habituation refers to getting used to an experience after repeated exposure, as when the school cafeteria serves macaroni day after day or when infants repeatedly encounter the same sound, sight, toy, or so on. Evidence of habituation is loss of interest (or, for macaroni, loss of appetite).

Using habituation as a research strategy involves repeating one stimulus until babies lose interest and then presenting another, slightly different stimulus (a new sound, sight, or other sensation). Babies can indicate in many ways that they detect a difference between the two stimuli—a longer or more focused gaze; a faster or slower heart rate; more or less muscle tension around the lips; a change in the rate, rhythm, or pressure of suction on a nipple. Subtle indicators are recorded by technology that was unavailable to Piaget (such as eye-gaze cameras, heart monitors, and brain scans).

By inducing habituation and then presenting a new stimulus, scientists have learned that even 1-month-olds can detect the difference between a *pah* sound and a *bah* sound, between a circle with two dots inside it and a circle without any dots, and much more. Babies younger than 6 months perceive far more than Piaget imagined. Indeed, habituation has spawned so much research that developmentalists are concerned that it may be relied on too much. As Jerome Kagan (2008) says:

> The next cohort of developmental psychologists . . . should gather additional
> sources of evidence besides fixation time: these include ERPs, skin conductance,
> muscle tension, blood flow, changes in heart rate, smiling, and vocalizing.
>
> *[p. 1620]*

Measuring the Brain

fMRI Functional magnetic resonance imaging, a measuring technique in which the brain's electrical excitement indicates activation anywhere in the brain; fMRI helps researchers locate neurological responses to stimuli.

Included in Kagan's list are several techniques that measure brain activity (see Table 6.2) (M. H. Johnson, 2005). Brain research suggests that babies are thinking long before they talk. In functional magnetic resonance imaging, or **fMRI,** a burst of electrical activity measured by blood flow within the brain is recorded, indicating that neurons are firing. This leads researchers to conclude that a particular stimulus has been noticed and processed. Based on such advanced methods, scientists are convinced that infants have memories, goals, deferred imitation, and even mental combinations in advance of Piaget's stages (Bauer et al., 2010; Morasch & Bell, 2009).

TABLE 6.2

Some Techniques Used by Neuroscientists to Understand Brain Function

SPL / PHOTO RESEARCHERS

Technique
EEG (electroencephalogram)

Use
Measures electrical activity in the top layers of the brain, where the cortex is.

Limitations
Especially in infancy, much brain activity of interest occurs below the cortex.

EEG, normal brain

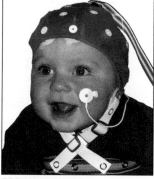

©2001 UNIVERSITY OF WASHINGTON, INSTITUTE FOR LEARNING AND BRAIN SCIENCES

Technique
ERP (event-related potential)

Use
Notes the amplitude and frequency of electrical activity (as shown by brain waves) in specific parts of the cortex in reaction to various stimuli.

Limitations
Reaction within the cortex signifies perception, but interpretation of the amplitude and timing of brain waves is not straightforward.

ERP when listening

VOLKER STEGER / PETER ARNOLD

Technique
fMRI (functional magnetic resonance imaging)

Use
Measures changes in blood flow anywhere in the brain (not just the outer layers).

Limitations
Signifies brain activity, but infants are notoriously active, which can make fMRIs useless.

fMRI when talking

HANK MORGAN / PHOTO RESEARCHERS

Technique
PET (positron emission tomography)

Use
Also (like fMRI) reveals activity in various parts of the brain. Locations can be pinpointed with precision, but PET requires injection of radioactive dye to light up the active parts of the brain.

Limitations
Many parents and researchers hesitate to inject radioactive dye into an infant's brain unless a serious abnormality is suspected.

PET scan of sleep

For both practical and ethical reasons, these techniques have not been used with large, representative samples of normal infants. One of the challenges of neuroscience is to develop methods that are harmless, easy to use, and comprehensive for the study of normal children. A more immediate challenge is to depict the data in ways that are easy to interpret.

As detailed in Chapter 5, early brain development is wide-ranging: Dendrites proliferate, and pruning is extensive. The first years of life are filled with mental activity and may be prime time for cognitive development (M. H. Johnson, 2005), although, of course, brain development and cognitive advances continue long past infancy. Significant advances in brain networks and functioning are apparent at ages 2, 4, 6, and throughout puberty (Kagan, 2008). Overall, there is "ample data to suggest that learning and memory are correlated with changes in the brain at multiple levels" (Nelson, de Haan et al., 2006, p. 17). Brain scans with normal infants are difficult and costly, but all the evidence so far indicates that babies are avid learners.

SUMMING UP

Piaget discovered, described, and then celebrated active infant learning, which he described in six stages of sensorimotor intelligence. Babies use their senses and motor skills to gain an understanding of their world, first with reflexes and then by adapting through assimilation and accommodation. Piaget's description of active learning during the first months of life rings true and was a welcome contrast to the earlier

>> **Response for Parents** (from page 157)
It is easier and safer to babyproof the house, because toddlers, being "little scientists," want to explore. However, it is important for both parents to encourage and guide the baby, so it is preferable to leave out a few untouchable items if that will help prevent a major conflict between husband and wife.

assumption that babies did not think until they could talk. Yet we now know that object permanence, pursuit of goals, and deferred imitation all develop before the time Piaget assigned to his stages. The infant is a "little scientist" not only at 1 year, as Piaget described, but long before that. Thinking develops before infants have the motor skills through which they can execute thoughts. ■

>> Information Processing

information-processing theory A perspective that compares human thinking processes, by analogy, to computer analysis of data, including sensory input, connections, stored memories, and output.

As explained in Chapter 2, Piaget's sweeping overview of four periods of cognition contrasts with **information-processing theory,** a perspective modeled on computer functioning, including input, memory, programs, calculation, and output. For infants, the output might be moving a hand to uncover a toy (object permanence), saying a word to signify recognition (e.g., *mama*), or simply glancing briefly at a photo (habituation).

Especially for Computer Experts In what way is the human mind not like a computer? (see response, page 162)

Instead of the newborn's reflexive cry of hunger, a slightly older hungry infant might perceive a bottle, reach, and then suck. Each step of this process requires information to be processed; older infants are much more thoughtful and effective than newborns because of more advanced information processing. Researchers have demonstrated that these advances occur week by week in the first year, contrary to Piaget's notion that they occurred in much longer, separate stages (Cohen & Cashon, 2006). Furthermore, knowing the incremental details of cognitive development has many practical implications, as information-processing research reveals. For example, information processing is especially helpful in suggesting ways to avoid the later intellectual deficits many preterm children experience (Rose et al., 2008).

With the aid of the sensitive technology just described, information-processing research has found impressive intellectual capacities: Concepts and categories seem to develop in infants' brains by about 6 months (Mandler, 2007; Quinn, 2004). Research inspired by information processing finds detailed sequences in number sense. For instance, habituation and brain scans reveal that 6-month-olds can detect the difference between a display of 8 dots and one of 16 dots but not the difference between 8 and 12 dots. By 9 months old, they can (Lipton & Spelke, 2003). Overall number sense may appear as early as 3 months but is not fully mature until adulthood (Libertus & Brannon, 2009).

The information-processing perspective helps tie together many aspects of infant cognition. We review two of these now: affordances and memory. Affordances concern perception or, by analogy, input. Memory concerns brain organization and output—that is, information storage and retrieval.

Affordances

Perception, remember, is mental processing of information that arrives at the brain from the sensory organs. It is the first step of information processing. One puzzle of development is that two people can have discrepant perceptions of the same situation, not only interpreting it differently but actually observing it differently.

Decades of thought and research led Eleanor and James Gibson to conclude that perception is far from automatic (E. J. Gibson, 1969; J. J. Gibson, 1979). Perception—for infants, as for the rest of us—is a cognitive accomplishment that requires selectivity: "Perceiving is active, a process of obtaining information about the world. . . . We don't simply see, we look" (E. J. Gibson, 1988, p. 5); or, as a neuroscientist said, "You see what you expect or are trained to see, not what is there" (Freeman, quoted in Bower, 2007, p. 106).

The Gibsons contend that the environment (people, places, and objects) *affords,* or offers, many opportunities for interaction with what is perceived (E. J. Gibson, 1997). Each of these opportunities is called an **affordance.** Which particular affordance is perceived and acted on depends on four factors: sensory awareness, immediate motivation, current development, and past experience.

As an example, imagine that you are lost in an unfamiliar city. Who will you ask for directions? Not necessarily the first person you see: You will look for someone who seems both knowledgeable and approachable. Approach-ability is an affordance, connected to people's expressions, body language, gender, and more (Miles, 2009).

An important concept for developmentalists is that age affects affor-dances. A toddler's idea of what affords running might be any unobstructed surface—a meadow, a long hallway in an apartment building, or a road. To an adult eye, the degree to which these places afford running may be re-stricted by such factors as a bull grazing in the meadow, neighbors along the hallway, or traffic on the road. Moreover, young children love to run, so they notice affordances for running. By contrast, many adults prefer to stay put—so they do not perceive whether running is afforded or not.

Selective perception is characteristic of every age and culture, as psy-chologists have realized and as a visitor to another nation may be shocked to discover. Just as an American in, say, Afghanistan, might miss an important sign of the social network, a baby might be oblivious to something adults consider crucial—or vice versa.

Research on Early Affordances

As information-processing abilities improve over the first year, infants become quicker to recognize affordances. A detailed study traced the responses of infants to eight different displays on a TV screen (Courage et al., 2006). The scientists who conducted the study measured, among other things, how many times the in-fants glanced away from the displays, how long their most extensive look lasted, and whether their heart rate changed as they saw one set of images or another.

The older infants were quicker to process the display and decide whether it was interesting to them. This is a sign of more advanced information processing. For example, the 14-week-olds looked at static dots for 10 seconds at a time, the 20-week-olds for 6 seconds, and infants aged 6 to 12 months for only 5 seconds.

Sudden Drops

The fact that experience affects which affordances are perceived is quite apparent in studies of depth perception. Research that demonstrates this fact began with an apparatus called the **visual cliff,** designed to provide the illusion of a sudden drop-off between one horizontal surface and another. Mothers were able to urge their 6-month-olds to wiggle toward them over the supposed edge of the cliff, but even with their mothers urging them on, 10-month-olds fearfully refused to budge (E. J. Gibson & Walk, 1960).

Researchers once thought that a visual deficit—specifically, inadequate depth perception—prevented young babies from seeing the drop. According to this hypothesis, as the visual cortex matured, 8-month-olds could see that crawling into the gap afforded falling. Later research (using more advanced technology) disproved that interpretation. Even 3-month-olds notice a drop: Their heart rate slows and their eyes open wide when they are placed over the cliff. But until they can crawl, they do not realize that crawling over an edge affords falling, perhaps with a frightening and painful consequence.

affordance An opportunity for perception and interaction that is offered by a person, place, or object in the environment.

visual cliff An experimental apparatus that gives an illusion of a sudden drop-off between one horizontal surface and another.

Chewable? Motivation is crucial for af-fordances. This baby's toy was designed to afford pulling, but he is teething, so he is motivated to recognize that it also affords chewing.

Depth Perception This toddler in a labora-tory in Berkeley, California, is crawling on the experimental apparatus called a visual cliff. She stops at the edge of what she perceives as a drop-off.

The infant's awareness of the affordance of the visual cliff depends on past experience. The difference is in processing, not input; in affordance, not mere stimulus. Further research on affordances of the visual cliff included the social context, with the tone of the mother's encouragement being a significant indicator of whether the cliff affords crawling or not (Kim et al., 2010). The same sequence happens with walking: Novice walkers are fearless and reckless; experienced walkers are more cautious and deliberate (Adolph & Berger, 2005).

Movement and People

Despite all the variations from one infant to another in the particular affordances they perceive, all seek to understand two kinds of affordances. Babies pay close attention to things that move and to people. This was demonstrated by the study of the eight TV-screen displays mentioned above: Motion was more interesting than static displays, and people were more interesting than dots (Courage et al., 2006).

Dynamic perception is perception that focuses on movement and change. Infants love motion. As soon as they can, they move their bodies—grabbing, scooting, crawling, walking. To their delight, such motion changes what the world affords them. As a result, infants work hard to master the next motor accomplishment (Adolph & Berger, 2005).

Other creatures that move, especially an infant's own caregivers, are among the main sources of pleasure, again because of dynamic perception. It's almost impossible to teach a baby not to chase and grab any moving creature, including a dog, a cat, or even a cockroach.

Infants' interest in motion was the beginning of another experiment that sought to learn what affordances were perceived by babies too young to talk or walk (van Hof et al., 2008). A ball was moved at various speeds in front of infants aged 3 to 9 months. Most tried to touch or catch the ball as it passed within reach. However, marked differences appeared in their perception of the affordance of "catchableness."

Sometimes younger infants did not reach for slow-moving balls yet tried (unsuccessfully) to grasp the faster balls. They tried but failed, touching the ball only about 20 percent of the time. By contrast, the 9-month-olds knew when a ball afforded catching. They grabbed the slower balls and refused to try for the very fast ones, and their success rate was almost 100 percent. This result "follows directly from one of the key concepts of ecological psychology, that animals perceive the environment in terms of action possibilities or affordances" (van Hof et al., 2008, p. 193).

The other universal principle of infant perception is **people preference.** This is in accord with a key principal of evolutionary psychology: that over the centuries, humans of all ages survived by learning to attend to, and rely on, one another. You just read that the affordance of the visual cliff depends partly on the mother's voice (Kim et al., 2010). Infants soon recognize their regular caregivers and expect certain affordances (comfort, food, entertainment) from them.

Very young babies are particularly interested in the emotional affordances of their caregivers, using their limited perceptual abilities and intellectual understanding to respond to smiles, shouts, and so on. Infants connect facial expressions with tone of voice long before they understand language. This ability has led to an interesting hypothesis:

> Given that infants are frequently exposed to their caregivers' emotional displays and further presented with opportunities to view the affordances (Gibson, 1959, 1979) of those emotional expressions, we propose that the expressions of familiar persons are meaningful to infants very early in life.
>
> [Kahana-Kalman & Walker-Andrews, 2001, p. 366]

Especially for Parents of Infants When should you be particularly worried that your baby will fall off the bed or down the stairs? (see response, page 164)

dynamic perception Perception that is primed to focus on movement and change.

MARINA RAITH / PHOTOLIBRARY

The Next Move These infants are intrigued by things and people, as would be expected. However, they have much to learn about how to grab a ball or play with a friend. It would not be surprising if, a minute later, the ball rolled away, one child cried, and the wide-eyed redhead hit her playmate.

people preference A universal principle of infant perception, consisting of an innate attraction to other humans, which is evident in visual, auditory, tactile, and other preferences.

>> Response for Computer Experts (from page 160) In dozens of ways, including speed of calculation, ability to network across the world, and vulnerability to viruses. In one crucial way, the human mind is better: Computers wear out within a few years, while human minds keep working until death.

Building on earlier studies, researchers presented infants with two moving images on one video screen (Kahana-Kalman & Walker-Andrews, 2001). Both images were of a woman, either two views of the infant's own mother or of a stranger. In one image, the woman was joyful; in the other, sad. Each presentation was accompanied by an audiotape of that woman's happy *or* sad talk. Previous studies had found that 7-month-olds could reliably match emotional words with facial expressions. At that age, but not earlier, they looked longer at a stranger whose voice and face expressed the same emotion and less at a person whose facial expression did not match the tone they heard.

Some infants in this experiment were only 3½ months old. When they did not know the woman, they failed to match the verbal emotion with the facial expression. In other words, when the face was that of a stranger, these young infants did not look longer at the happy face when they heard happy talk or the sad face when they heard the sad voice. That result was expected from previous research.

However, when the 3½-month-olds saw two images of their own mother and heard her happy or her sad voice, they correctly matched visual and vocal emotions. They looked longest at their happy mothers talking in a happy way, but they also looked at their sad mothers when they heard their mother's sad voice—thus connecting sound and sight. The researchers noticed something else. When infants saw and heard their happy mothers, they smiled twice as fast, seven times as long, and much more brightly (cheeks raised and lips upturned) than for the happy strangers. Experience had taught them that a smiling mother affords joy. The affordances of a smiling stranger are more difficult to judge.

Memory

Both a certain amount of experience and a certain amount of brain maturation are required in order to process and remember anything (Bauer et al., 2010). Infants have great difficulty storing new memories in their first year, and older children are often unable to describe events that occurred when they were younger. Many adults have what Freud called "childhood amnesia"—they forget experiences, people, and even languages they knew when they were young. One reason is linguistic: People use words to store (and sometimes distort) memories, so preverbal children have difficulty with recall (Richardson & Hayne, 2007), and adults cannot access early memories.

Especially for Parents This research on early affordances suggests a crucial lesson about how many babysitters an infant should have. What is it? (see response, page 165)

Calvin & Hobbes

Selective Amnesia As we grow older, we forget about spitting up, nursing, crying, and almost everything else from our early years. However, strong emotions (love, fear, mistrust) may leave lifelong traces.

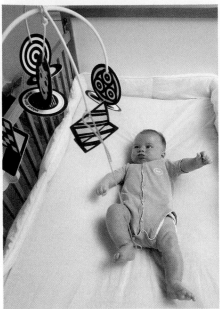

MICHAEL NEWMAN / PHOTOEDIT

He Remembers! In this demonstration of Rovee-Collier's experiment, a young infant immediately remembers how to make the familiar mobile move. (Unfamiliar mobiles do not provoke the same reaction.) He kicks his right leg and flails both arms, just as he learned to do several weeks ago.

Observation Quiz How and why is this mobile unlike those usually sold for babies? (see answer, page 166)

reminder session A perceptual experience that is intended to help a person recollect an idea, a thing, or an experience, without testing whether the person remembers it at the moment.

>> Response for Parents of Infants (from page 162) Constant vigilance is necessary for the first few years of a child's life, but the most dangerous age is from about 4 to 8 months, when infants can move but do not yet fear falling over an edge.

However, a series of experiments reveals that very young infants *can* remember, even if they cannot later put memories into words. Memories are particularly evident in these circumstances:

- Experimental conditions are similar to those of real life.
- Motivation is high.
- Retrieval is strengthened by reminders and repetition.

The most dramatic evidence for infant memory comes from innovative experiments in which 3-month-olds were taught to make a mobile move by kicking their legs (Rovee-Collier, 1987, 1990). The infants lay on their backs, in their own cribs, connected to a mobile by means of a ribbon tied to one foot (see photograph).

Virtually all the infants began making some occasional kicks (as well as random arm movements and noises) and realized, after a while, that kicking made the mobile move. They then kicked more vigorously and frequently, sometimes laughing at their accomplishment. So far, this is no surprise—self-activated movement is highly reinforcing to infants, part of dynamic perception.

When some infants had the mobile-and-ribbon apparatus reinstalled in their cribs *one week later,* most started to kick immediately; this reaction indicated that they remembered their previous experience. But when other 3-month-old infants were retested *two weeks later,* they began with only random kicks. Apparently they had forgotten what they had learned—evidence that memory is fragile early in life.

Reminders and Repetition

The lead researcher, Carolyn Rovee-Collier, developed another experiment that demonstrated that 3-month-old infants *could* remember after two weeks *if* they had a brief reminder session before being retested (Rovee-Collier & Hayne, 1987). A **reminder session** is any experience that helps people recollect an idea, a thing, or an event.

In this particular reminder session, two weeks after the initial training, the infants watched the mobile move but were *not* tied to it and were positioned so that they could *not* kick. The next day, when they were again connected to the mobile and positioned so that they *could* move their legs, they kicked as they had learned to do two weeks earlier.

Watching the mobile move on the previous day had revived their faded memory. The information about making the mobile move was stored in their brains, but they needed processing time to retrieve it. The reminder session provided that time.

Other research finds that repeated reminders are more powerful than single reminders and that context is crucial, especially for infants younger than 9 months old: Being tested in the same room as the initial experience aids memory (Rovee-Collier & Cuevas, 2009a). Many other studies have found that infant memory is fragile but that reminders and repetition may help even 4-month-olds to remember (S. P. Johnson & Shuwairi, 2009).

A Little Older, a Little More Memory

After about 6 months of age, infants retain information for a longer time than younger babies do, with less training or reminding. Toward the end of the first year, many kinds of memory are apparent. For example, suppose a 9-month-old watches someone playing with a toy he or she has never seen. The next day, if given the toy, the 9-month-old will play with it in the same way as he or she had observed. Younger infants will not.

Many experiments show that toddlers can transfer learning from one object or experience to another and that they learn from various people and events—from parents and strangers, from other babies and older siblings, from picture books and family photographs (Hayne & Simcock, 2009). The dendrites and neurons of the brain change to reflect their experiences and memories even in the first years of life.

Aspects of Memory

Brain activity patterns shown on fMRI and PET scans indicate that one region of the brain is devoted to memory for faces and others to memory for sounds, events, sights, phrases, and much more. Several additional brain regions also participate in these various memories, although memory is not necessarily localized to discrete regions in early life (Rovee-Collier & Cuevas, 2009b). An infant could lose one part of the brain and still remember things that supposedly were stored there. Gradual brain maturation and growth constitute one reason some kinds of memories are better consolidated in infancy than others.

An important developmental distinction can be made between **implicit memory,** which is memory that remains hidden until a particular stimulus brings it to mind (like the mobile reminder session), and **explicit memory,** which is memory that can be recalled on demand. Explicit memories are usually verbal, and thus "although explicit memory *emerges* sometime between 6 and 12 months, it is far from fully developed" (Nelson, de Haan et al., 2006, p. 23).

The particular part of the brain on which explicit memory depends is the hippocampus (explained in Chapter 8), present at birth but very immature until about age 5 or 6. It is no surprise that this timing coincides with the beginning of formal education, because children are much better at memorizing at that age.

Implicit memories begin much earlier. For instance, adults who knew a language in childhood retain an implicit memory of it, even though they have no explicit memories for that language (Bowers et al., 2009). Interestingly, when first tested, such adults are no better at understanding the language than those who never knew that language, but repeated exposure reveals their earlier, implicit memories. Apparently, reminders are significant for adults as well as infants. This may explain why some people, places, and smells seem familiar or emotionally evocative to you, but you don't know why.

Infants probably store in their brains many emotions and sensations that they cannot readily retrieve, but memories of motion (dynamic perception) are more readily remembered once a particular action is cued by the context (as when the infants remembered how to kick to make the mobile move). The information-processing approach to infants' cognition finds that memory is crucial for later development—far more so than are other components of early thought, such as attention and processing speed (Rose et al., 2009). Extensive research finds that early memories help infants and toddlers learn words, and then language helps encode memories (Richardson & Hayne, 2007).

Memory Aid Personal motivation and action are crucial to early memory, which is why Noel has no trouble remembering which shape covers the photograph of herself as a baby.

implicit memory Unconscious or automatic memory that is usually stored via habits, emotional responses, routine procedures, and various sensations.

explicit memory Memory that is easy to retrieve on demand (as in a specific test), usually with words. Most explicit memory involves consciously learned words, data and concepts.

SUMMING UP

Infant cognition can be studied using the information-processing perspective, which analyzes each component of how thoughts begin; how they are organized, remembered, and expressed; and how cognition builds, day by day. Infants' perception is powerfully influenced by particular experiences and motivation, so the affordances perceived by one infant differ from those perceived by another. Memory depends on both brain maturation and experience. That is why memory is fragile in the first year (although it can be triggered by dynamic perception and reminders) and becomes more evident, although still fragile, in the second year, especially before language develops.

>> Response for Parents (from page 163) It is important that infants have time for repeated exposure to each caregiver, because infants adjust their behavior to maximize whatever each particular caregiver affords in the way of play, emotions, and vocalization. Parents should find one steady babysitter rather than several.

>> **Answer to Observation Quiz** (from page 164) It is black and white, with larger objects—designed to be particularly attractive to infants, not to adult shoppers.

>> Language: What Develops in the First Two Years?

No other species has anything approaching the neurons and networks that support the 6,000 or so human languages. The human ability to communicate, even at age 2, far surpasses that of full-grown adults from every other species, including dolphins and chimpanzees, which have much better communication mechanisms than was formerly believed. Here we describe the specific steps in early language learning and then raise the crucial question: How do babies do it?

The Universal Sequence

The timing of language acquisition varies; the most advanced 10 percent of 2-year-olds speak more than 550 words, and the least advanced 10 percent speak fewer than 100 words—a fivefold difference (Merriman, 1999). But, although timing varies, the sequence is the same worldwide (see At About This Time). Even deaf children who become able to hear before age 3 (thanks to cochlear implants) follow the sequence. Although they got a late start, they often catch up to their age-mates within a year or so (Ertmer et al., 2007).

AT ABOUT THIS TIME

The Development of Spoken Language in the First Two Years

Age*	Means of Communication
Newborn	Reflexive communication—cries, movements, facial expressions
2 months	A range of meaningful noises—cooing, fussing, crying, laughing
3–6 months	New sounds, including squeals, growls, croons, trills, vowel sounds
6–10 months	Babbling, including both consonant and vowel sounds repeated in syllables
10–12 months	Comprehension of simple words; speechlike intonations; specific vocalizations that have meaning to those who know the infant well. Deaf babies express their first signs; hearing babies also use specific gestures (e.g., pointing) to communicate.
12 months	First spoken words that are recognizably part of the native language
13–18 months	Slow growth of vocabulary, up to about 50 words
18 months	Naming explosion—three or more words learned per day. Much variation: Some toddlers do not yet speak.
21 months	First two-word sentence
24 months	Multiword sentences. Half the toddler's utterances are two or more words long.

*The ages of accomplishment in this table reflect norms. Many healthy children with normal intelligence attain these steps in language development earlier or later than indicated here.
Sources: Bloom, 1993, 1998; Fenson et al., 2000; Lenneberg, 1967.

Listening and Responding

Infants begin learning language before birth, via brain organization and hearing. Habituation to noises has been demonstrated in fetuses several weeks before birth, which suggests that listening and remembering are inborn, basic to being human (Dirix et al., 2009). They even learn to prefer the language their mother speaks over an unheard language, with newborns of bilingual mothers preferring both languages and differentiating between them (Byers-Heinlein et al., 2010). (See the Research Design.)

▶ Research Design

Scientists: Krista Byers-Heinlein, Tracey C. Burns, & Janet Werker.

Publication: *Psychological Science* (2010).

Participants: In three experiments, data were collected from 94 newborns (0–5 days old) in a large hospital in Vancouver, Canada. Half were born to mothers who spoke both English and Tagalog (the native language of Filipinos), one-third to mothers who spoke only English, and one-sixth to mothers who spoke English and Chinese.

Design: The infants sucked as they listened to 10 minutes of sentences matched for pitch, duration, and number of syllables, alternating each minute in English or Tagalog. When they sucked at "high amplitude" (predetermined for each infant), the recording played, so that more frequent sucking was taken as a preference for one language or the other. The total number of intense sucks for English was subtracted from the Tagalog sucks.

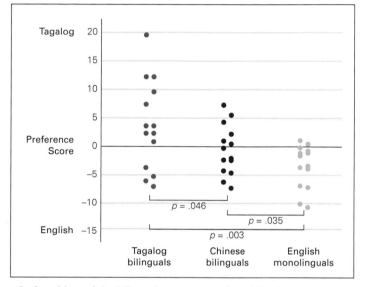

Major conclusion: Most of the bilingual newborns preferred Tagalog, whereas the monolinguals preferred English. The Chinese bilinguals (who had not heard Tagalog in utero) were tested to rule out alternate explanations. As you see in the figure, newborn preferences were affected by language heard before birth. The researchers believe that it is the rhythm of the language that becomes familiar, and they note that the rhythm of Chinese is somewhat similar to Tagalog, leading to the results of the Chinese bilinguals.

Comments: Other research had already shown that the fetus responds to the language spoken by the mother; this study suggests that some children begin to become bilingual before they are born. One advantage of this study is that all the participants were born in a large Canadian hospital, and thus all probably had adequate prenatal nutrition, health care, and birth experiences. More details, controls, and replication would help confirm the results. For example, although the bilingual mothers said they spoke at least 30 percent of each language, direct observation may have found otherwise. Replication with other bilingual infants would rule out the possibility that these results are related to something specific in Tagalog or English, or to when and how much the mothers spoke each language. Nonetheless, this study confirms and extends a conclusion from thousands of studies: Humans have an amazing ability to learn languages, evident long before the first spoken word.

Newborns look closely at facial expressions and prefer to hear speech over other sounds. Infants have an early preference for the sights and sounds that humans use to communicate. By 6 months of age, infants can distinguish, just by looking at someone's mouth movements (no sound), whether that person is speaking their native language or not (Weikum et al., 2007).

Careful analysis has found that adult communication with babies is distinct in many ways from adult–adult interaction (Falk, 2004). For instance, adults talk to

Lip-Reading Communication begins in early infancy. Infants closely watch speakers' mouth movements and facial expressions. By this baby's age, 5 months, bilingual infants can tell by looking who is speaking French and who is speaking English.

STOCK CONNECTION DISTRIBUTION / ALAMY

CORBIS / ANTHONY BANNISTER

Too Young for Language? No. The early stages of language are communication through noises, gestures, and facial expressions, very evident here between this !Kung grandmother and granddaughter.

child-directed speech The high-pitched, simplified, and repetitive way adults speak to infants. (Also called *baby talk* or *motherese*.)

babbling The extended repetition of certain syllables, such as *ba-ba-ba,* that begins when babies are between 6 and 9 months old.

Especially for Nurses and Pediatricians
The parents of a 6-month-old have just been told that their child is deaf. They don't believe it, because, as they tell you, the baby babbles as much as their other children did. What do you tell them? (see response, page 170)

babies with higher pitch, simpler words, repetition, varied speeds, and exaggerated and emotional tones (Bryant & Barrett, 2007). This special language form is sometimes called *baby talk,* since it is talk directed to babies, and sometimes called *motherese,* since mothers universally speak it. Both these terms have misleading implications, so scientists prefer the more formal term **child-directed speech.**

No matter what term is used, child-directed speech fosters early language learning. Even at 7 months of age, infants begin to recognize words that are highly distinctive (Singh, 2008): *Bottle, dog,* and *mama,* for instance, might be distinguished from one another before words that sound alike (such as *baby, Bobbie,* and *Barbie*). Infants respond vocally to adult noises and expressions (as well as to their own internal pleasures and pain) in many ways—crying, cooing, and a variety of other sounds. Their responses gradually become more varied. By 4 months, most babies squeal, growl, gurgle, grunt, croon, and yell, telling everyone what is on their minds.

Also within the first months, infants' listening becomes more selective. Not only do infants prefer child-directed speech, they like alliteration, rhymes, repetition, rhythm, and varied pitch (Hayes & Slater, 2008; Schön et al., 2008). Think of your favorite lullaby (itself an alliterative word); obviously babies prefer sounds over content.

Babbling

Between 6 and 9 months of age, babies begin to repeat certain syllables (*ma-ma-ma, da-da-da, ba-ba-ba*), a phenomenon referred to as **babbling** because of the way it sounds. Babbling is experience-expectant; all babies do it, even deaf ones. Responses from other people encourage babbling (remember, this is the age of "making interesting events last"). Deaf babies stop babbling because they cannot hear responses; hearing babies continue.

All babies make rhythmic gestures, again in response to the actions of others (Iverson & Fagan, 2004). Toward the end of the first year, babbling begins to sound like the infant's native language; infants imitate what they hear in accents, consonants, and so on.

Videotapes of deaf infants whose parents sign to them show that 10-month-olds use about a dozen distinct hand gestures in a repetitive manner similar to babbling. All babies express concepts with gestures sooner than with speech (Goldin-Meadow, 2006). Many caregivers, recognizing the power of gestures,

Happy Talk Ty's mother and the teacher demonstrate the sign for "more" in a sign-language class at the public library in Hudson, Florida. Ty takes the lesson very seriously: Learning language in any form is crucial for 1-year-olds.

NEWSCOM

teach "baby signs" to their 6- to 12-month-olds, allowing them to have conversations months before the infants talk (Pizer et al., 2007).

Pointing is an advanced social gesture that requires understanding another person's perspective. Most animals cannot interpret pointing; most humans can do so at 10 months, even pointing at the place where an object should be but no longer is (Liszkowski et al., 2009). This is one of the intriguing aspects of human development, since pointing indicates a strong preference for social interaction and an ability to understand another's viewpoint (Tomasello et al., 2007).

First Words

Finally, at about 1 year of age, the average hearing baby speaks a few words. Caregivers usually understand the first words before strangers do, which makes it hard for researchers to pinpoint exactly what a 12-month-old can say. For example, at 13 months, Kyle knew standard words such as *mama,* but he also knew *da, ba, tam, opma,* and *daes,* which his parents knew to be, respectively, "downstairs," "bottle," "tummy," "oatmeal," and "starfish" (yes, that's what *daes* meant) (Lewis et al., 1999).

Show Me Where Pointing is one of the earliest forms of communication, emerging at about 10 months.

Gradual Beginnings

In the first months of the second year, spoken vocabulary increases very gradually (perhaps one new word a week). However, 6- to 15-month-olds learn meanings rapidly; they understand about 10 times more words than they can say (Schafer, 2005; Snow, 2006). The first words soon take on nuances of tone, loudness, and cadence that are precursors of the first appearance of grammar. A single word can convey many messages by the way it is spoken. Imagine meaningful sentences encapsulated in "Dada!" "Dada?" and "Dada." Each is a **holophrase,** a single word that expresses an entire thought.

Intonation (variations of tone and pitch) is extensive in early babbling and again in holophrases at about 18 months, with a dip in between (at about 12 months). At that one-year point, infants seem to reorganize their vocalization from universal to language-specific (Snow, 2006). They are no longer just singing and talking to themselves (babbling) but communicating in language.

holophrase A single word that is used to express a complete, meaningful thought.

The Naming Explosion

Once vocabulary reaches about 50 *expressed* words (understood words are far more extensive), it builds rapidly, at a rate of 50 to 100 words per month, with 21-month-olds saying twice as many words as 18-month-olds (Adamson & Bakeman, 2006). This language spurt is called the **naming explosion** because many early words are nouns, although the word *noun* is a linguist category, not an infant's preference (Waxman & Lidz, 2006).

In almost every language, the name of each significant caregiver (often *dada, mama, nana, papa, baba, tata*) and sibling (and sometimes each pet) is learned between 12 and 18 months (Bloom, 1998). (See Appendix A, p. A-4.) Other frequently uttered words refer to the child's favorite foods (*nana* can mean "banana" as well as "grandma") and to elimination (*pee-pee, wee-wee, poo-poo, ka-ka, doo-doo*). No doubt you notice that all these words have two identical syllables, each a consonant followed by a vowel sound. Many more words follow that pattern—not just *baba* but also *bobo, bebe, bubu, bibi.* Other early words are only slightly more complicated—*ma-me, ama,* and so on.

naming explosion A sudden increase in an infant's vocabulary, especially in the number of nouns, that begins at about 18 months of age.

Especially for Caregivers A toddler calls two people "Mama." Is this a sign of confusion? (see response, page 171)

WOLFGANG KAEHLER / CORBIS

Cultural Values If they are typical of most families in the relatively taciturn Otavalo culture of Ecuador, these three children hear significantly less conversation than children elsewhere. In most Western cultures, that might be called maltreatment. However, each culture encourages the qualities it values, and verbal fluency is not a priority in this community. In fact, people who talk too much are ostracized and those who keep secrets are valued, so encouragement of talking may constitute maltreatment in the Otavalo culture.

Cultural Differences

Cultures and families vary a great deal in how much child-directed speech children hear. Some parents read to their infants, teach them signs that communicate, and respond to every noise, including a burp or a fart, as if it is an attempt to talk. Others are much less verbal, using gestures, touch, and tone, saying "hush" and "no" instead of words that the toddler might say.

The idea that children should be "seen but not heard" is contrary to the emphasis on communication within many American families. The emphasis on listening, not talking, is common among other families, including Latino families (Cabrera et al., 2006), and many fathers, especially of low socioeconomic status (SES). Nonetheless, all infants quickly appreciate the sounds of their culture—even musical tempo is culture-specific; 4- to 8-month-olds seem to like their own native music best (Soley & Hannon, 2010).

Like everyone else, I am guided by my SES and cultural background. Thus, I often spoke, sang, and read to my infants. But as a developmental scientist, I know that my assumptions about child care may be social constructions, not adaptive in every culture and cohort. Not every family appreciates talkative children, and some cultures consider children who interrupt adult conversation (as my children did) to be rude and uncultured.

Parts of Speech

Although all new talkers say names, use similar sounds, and say more nouns than any other part of speech, the ratio of nouns to verbs and adjectives varies from place to place. For example, by 18 months, English-speaking infants use relatively more nouns but fewer verbs than Chinese or Korean infants do. Why?

One explanation goes back to the language itself. Chinese and Korean are "verb-friendly" in that verbs are placed at the beginning or end of sentences, which makes them easier to learn. In English, verbs occur in various positions within sentences, and their forms change in illogical ways (e.g., *go, gone, will go, went*). This irregularity makes English verbs harder to learn than nouns (Gentner & Boroditsky, 2001).

>> **Response for Nurses and Pediatricians** (from page 168) Urge the parents to begin learning sign language immediately and investigate the possibility of cochlear implants. Babbling has a biological basis and begins at a specified time, in deaf as well as hearing babies. However, deaf babies eventually begin to use gestures more and to vocalize less than hearing babies. If their infant can hear, sign language does no harm. If the child is deaf, however, noncommunication may be devastating.

An alternative explanation for cultural differences in the proportion of nouns and verbs considers the entire social context: Playing with a variety of toys and learning about dozens of objects are crucial in North American culture, whereas East Asian cultures emphasize human interactions—specifically, how one person responds to another. Accordingly, North American infants are expected to name many objects, whereas Asian infants are expected to encode social interactions into language, as explained in Chapter 1.

Thus, the Chinese toddler might learn the equivalent of *come, play, love, carry, run,* and so on before the Canadian one. (This is the result of experience, not genes. A toddler of Chinese ancestry, growing up in an English-speaking Canadian home, has the learning patterns of other English toddlers.)

Every language has some concepts that are easy and some that are hard for infants. English-speaking infants confuse *before* and *after;* Dutch-speaking infants misuse *out* when it refers to taking off clothes; Korean infants need to learn two meanings of *in* (Mandler, 2004). Learning adjectives is easier in Italian and Spanish than in English or French because of patterns in those languages (Waxman & Lidz, 2006). Specifically, adjectives can stand by themselves without the nouns. If I want a blue cup from a group of multicolored cups, I would ask for "a blue cup" or "a blue one" in English but simply "uno azul" (a blue) in Spanish. Despite such variations, in every language, infants demonstrate impressive speed and efficiency in acquiring both vocabulary and grammar

Putting Words Together

Grammar includes all the methods that languages use to communicate meaning. Word order, prefixes, suffixes, intonation, verb forms, pronouns and negations, prepositions and articles—all of these are aspects of grammar. Grammar is obvious when two-word combinations begin, at about 21 months. The sentences "Baby cry" or "More juice" follow the proper English word order rather than the reverse. No child says "juice more," and already by age 2 children know that "cry baby" has an entirely different meaning. Soon the child combines three words, usually in subject–verb–object order in English (for example, "Mommy read book"), rather than any of the five other possible sequences of those words.

A child's grammar correlates with the size of his or her vocabulary (Snow, 2006). The child who says "Baby is crying" is advanced in language development compared with the child who says "Baby crying" or simply the holophrase "Baby." Comprehension advances as well. Their expanding knowledge of both vocabulary and grammar helps toddlers understand what others are saying (Kedar et al., 2006).

Listening to two languages does not necessarily slow down the acquisition of grammar, but "development in each language proceeds separately and in a language specific manner" (Conboy & Thal, 2006, p. 727).

Most studies suggest that a young child can master two languages, not just one, but that the crucial variable is how much speech in both languages the child hears. If children know that a particular person speaks only one language, they will answer accordingly. Most bilingual children have parents who also are bilingual, and these children may mix vocabulary because they expect the parents to understand.

>> Response for Caregivers (from page 169) Not at all. Toddlers hear several people called "Mama" (their own mother, their grandmothers, their cousins' and friends' mothers) and experience mothering from several people, so it is not surprising if they use "Mama" too broadly. They will eventually narrow the label down to one person.

grammar All the methods—word order, verb forms, and so on—that languages use to communicate meaning, apart from the words themselves.

Look Who's Talking Men have a reputation for being strong and silent, but these three are more typical of today's men—sharing the joys and tribulations of fatherhood. Such conversations are distinctly human; other animals communicate, but only people use language so extensively.

Observation Quiz Which of these three strollers is best for encouraging infant language? (see answer, page 172)

Theories of Language Learning

Worldwide, people who are not yet 2 years old already speak in their native tongue. By adolescence, some teenagers compose lyrics or deliver orations that move thousands of their co-linguists. How is language learned so easily and so well?

Answers come from three schools of thought, each connected to a theory (behaviorism, sociocultural theory, and universalism). The first says that infants are directly taught, the second that social impulses propel infants to communicate, and the third that infants naturally understand language because of a brain advance thousands of years ago that allowed survival of our species.

Theory One: Infants Need to Be Taught

The seeds of the first perspective were planted more than 50 years ago, when the dominant theory in North American psychology was behaviorism, or learning theory. The essential idea was that all learning is acquired, step by step, through association and reinforcement. Just as Pavlov's dogs learned to associate the sound of a tone with the presentation of food (see Chapter 2), behaviorists believe that infants associate objects with words they have heard often, especially if reinforcement occurs.

B. F. Skinner (1957) noticed that spontaneous babbling is usually reinforced. Typically, every time the baby says "ma-ma-ma-ma," a grinning mother appears, repeating the sound as well as showering the baby with attention, praise, and perhaps food. These affordances of mothers are exactly what infants want, so babies repeat those sounds, and, via operant conditioning, talking begins.

Most parents worldwide are excellent instructors, responding to their infants' gestures and sounds (Gros-Louis et al., 2006). Even in preliterate societies, parents use child-directed speech, responding quickly with high pitch, short sentences, stressed nouns, and simple grammar—exactly the techniques that behaviorists would recommend.

The core ideas of this theory are the following:

- Parents are expert teachers, although other caregivers help.
- Frequent repetition is instructive, especially when linked to daily life.
- Well-taught infants become well-spoken children.

Behaviorists note that some 3-year-olds converse in elaborate sentences; others just barely put one simple word with another. Such variations correlate with the amount of language that child has heard. Parents of the most verbal children teach language throughout infancy—singing, explaining, listening, responding, and reading to them every day, even before age 1 (Forget-Dubois et al., 2009).

In a detailed U.S. study, researchers analyzed the language that mothers used with their 9-month-old infants (Tamis-LeMonda et al., 2001). Although all the mothers in that study were from the same nation and all were middle-class, in 10 minutes one mother never imitated her infant's babbling; another mother imitated 21 times, babbling back in conversation. Mothers often described things or actions (e.g., "That is a spoon you are holding—spoon"), but one mother provided only 4 descriptions while another provided 33.

The frequency of maternal responsiveness at 9 months predicted language acquisition at 17 months (see Figure 6.1). It was not that noisy infants, whose genes would soon make them start talking, elicited more talk. Some quiet infants had mothers who frequently suggested play activities, described things, and asked questions. Quiet infants with talkative mothers usually became talkative later on. Those results are confirmed by research from many nations. For example, in one

Especially for Nurses and Pediatricians
Bob and Joan have been reading about language development in children. They are convinced that because language is "hardwired" they need not talk to their 6-month-old son. How do you respond? (see response, page 174)

>> Answer to Observation Quiz (from page 171) The one on the left, which allows the baby to listen, watch, and talk to the father. One-on-one interaction is pivotal for learning language no matter which theory is right—reinforcement, brain stimulation, or social interaction.

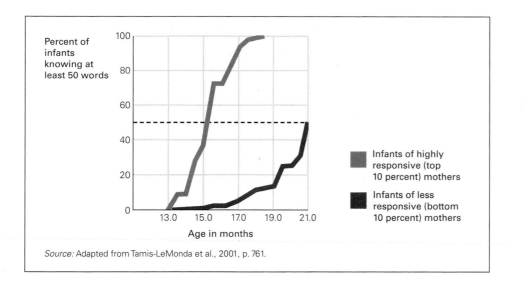

Source: Adapted from Tamis-LeMonda et al., 2001, p. 761.

FIGURE 6.1

Maternal Responsiveness and Infants' Language Acquisition Learning the first 50 words is a milestone in early language acquisition, as it predicts the arrival of the naming explosion and the multiword sentence a few weeks later. Researchers found that the 9-month-old infants of highly responsive mothers (top 10 percent) reached this milestone as early as 15 months. The infants of nonresponsive mothers (bottom 10 percent) lagged significantly behind.

large study in Australia, parents who provided extensive language to their preverbal infants had children who spoke early and well (Reilly et al., 2006).

Thus, many studies confirm the behaviorist theory that adults teach language and infants learn it. According to this perspective, if adults want children who speak, understand, and (later) read well, they must talk to their babies.

Theory Two: Social Impulses Foster Infant Language

The second theory is called *social-pragmatic*. It arises from the sociocultural reason for language: communication. According to this perspective, infants communicate because humans are social beings, dependent on one another for survival and joy. Each culture has practices that further social interaction; talking is one of those practices.

It is the emotional messages of speech, not the words, that are the focus of early communication, according to this perspective. In one study, people who had never heard English (Shuar hunter-gatherers living isolated near the Andes mountains) listened to tapes of North American mothers talking to their babies. The Shuar successfully distinguished speech conveying comfort, approval, attention, and prohibition, without knowing any of the words (Bryant & Barrett, 2007). Thus, the social content of speech is universal, which is why babies learn whatever specifics their culture provides.

Suppose an 18-month-old is playing with an unnamed toy and an adult utters a word. Does the child connect that word to the toy? A behaviorist, learning-by-association prediction would be yes, but the answer is no. In an experiment, when toddlers played with a fascinating toy and adults said a word, the toddlers looked up, figured out what the adult was looking at, and assigned the new word to that, not to the fascinating toy (Baldwin, 1993). This supports theory two: The toddlers wanted to know what the adults intended.

Another study also suggests social learning. Many 1-year-olds enjoy watching television (e.g., *Teletubbies*), but they probably do not learn much from it. In a controlled experiment, 1-year-olds learned vocabulary much better when someone directly taught them than when the same person taught the same lesson in the same way on a video (Roseberry et al., 2009). This suggests personal, social language acquisition, not impersonal learning.

Especially for Educators An infant day-care center has a new child whose parents speak a language other than the one the teachers speak. Should the teachers learn basic words in the new language, or should they expect the baby to learn the majority language? (see response, page 175)

College Grad, Class of '33? Reading to an infant correlates with talking at age 1, reading at age 5, and college graduation at age 21. Of course, correlation is not causation, but in any case, this shared joy bodes well for the future.

OCEAN PHOTOGRAPHY / VEER

>> **Response for Nurses and Pediatricians** (from page 172) While much of language development is indeed hardwired, many experts assert that exposure to language is required. You don't need to convince Bob and Joan of this point, though—just convince them that their baby will be happier if they talk to him.

language acquisition device (LAD)
Chomsky's term for a hypothesized mental structure that enables humans to learn language, including the basic aspects of grammar, vocabulary, and intonation.

According to theory two, then, social impulses, not explicit teaching, lead infants to learn language "as part of the package of being a human social animal" (Hollich et al., 2000). They seek to understand what others want and intend; "children acquire linguistic symbols as a kind of by-product of social action with adults" (Tomasello, 2001).

Theory Three: Infants Teach Themselves

A third theory holds that language learning is innate; adults need not teach it, nor is it simply a by-product of social interaction. The seeds of this perspective were planted soon after Skinner proposed his theory of verbal learning. Noam Chomsky (1968, 1980) and his followers felt that language is too complex to be mastered merely through step-by-step conditioning. Although behaviorists focus on variations among children in vocabulary size, Chomsky focused on similarities in language acquisition—the universals (see Chapter 2), not the differences.

Noting that all young children master basic grammar at about the same age, Chomsky cited this *universal grammar* as evidence that humans are born with a mental structure that prepares them to seek some elements of human language—for example, the use of a raised tone at the end of an utterance to indicate a question. Chomsky labeled this hypothesized mental structure the **language acquisition device (LAD).** The LAD enables children to derive the rules of grammar quickly and effectively from the speech they hear every day, regardless of whether their native language is English, Thai, or Urdu.

Other scholars agree with Chomsky that infants are innately ready to use their minds to understand and speak whatever language is offered. This idea does not strip languages and cultures of their differences in sounds, grammar, and almost everything else, but the basic idea is that "language is a window on human nature, exposing deep and universal features of our thoughts and feelings" (Pinker, 2007, p. 148).

The various languages of the world are all logical, coherent, and systematic. Infants are primed to grasp the particular language they are exposed to, making caregiver speech "not a 'trigger' but a 'nutrient'" (Slobin, 2001, p. 438). There is no need for a trigger, according to theory three, because words are expected by the developing brain, which quickly and efficiently connects neurons to support whichever language the infant hears. Thus, language itself is experience-expectant, although obviously the specific language is experience-dependent.

Research supports this perspective as well. As you remember, newborns are primed to listen to speech (Vouloumanos & Werker, 2007) and all infants babble *ma-ma* and *da-da* sounds (not yet referring to mother or father). No reinforcement or teaching is needed; all infants need is for dendrites to grow, mouth muscles to strengthen, neurons to connect, and speech to be heard.

Nature even provides for deaf infants. All 6-month-olds, hearing or not, prefer to look at sign language over nonlinguistic pantomime. For hearing infants, this preference disappears by 10 months because their affinity for gestural language is not helpful (Krentz & Corina, 2008). Deaf infants are signing by then.

A Hybrid Theory

Which of these three perspectives is correct? Perhaps all of them. In one monograph with 12 experiments, the authors presented a hybrid (which literally means "a new creature, formed by combining other living things") of previous theories (Hollich et al., 2000). Since infants learn language to do numerous things—indicate intention, call objects by name, put words together, talk to family members, sing to themselves, express their wishes, remember the past, and much more—some aspects of language learning may be best explained by one theory at one age and other aspects by another theory at another age.

One study supporting the hybrid theory began, as did the study previously mentioned, with infants looking at pairs of objects that they had never seen and never heard named. One of each pair was fascinating to babies and the other was boring, specifically "a blue sparkle wand . . . [paired with] a white cabinet latch . . . a red, green, and pink party clacker . . . [paired with] a beige bottle opener" (Pruden et al., 2006, p. 267).

The experimenter said a made-up name (not an actual word), and then the infants were tested to see if they assigned the word to the object that had the experimenter's attention (the dull one) or the one that was interesting to the child. Unlike the previous study that involved 18-month-olds, this one studied 10-month-olds and found different results: The young infants seemed to assign the word to the fascinating object, not the dull one.

These researchers' interpretation was that *how* language is learned depends on the age of the child as well as on the particular circumstances. Behaviorism may work for young children, social learning for slightly older ones: "The perceptually driven 10-month-old becomes the socially aware 19-month-old" (Pruden et al., 2006, p. 278). After intensive study, another group of scientists also endorsed a hybrid theory, concluding that "multiple attentional, social and linguistic cues" contribute to early language (Tsao et al., 2004, p. 1081). It makes logical and practical sense for nature to provide several paths toward language learning and for various theorists to emphasize one or another (Sebastián-Gallés, 2007).

As one expert concludes:

> In the current view, our best hope for unraveling some of the mysteries of language acquisition rests with approaches that incorporate multiple factors, that is, with approaches that incorporate not only some explicit linguistic model, but also the full range of biological, cultural, and psycholinguistic processes involved.
>
> *[Tomasello, 2006, pp. 292–293]*

What conclusion can we draw from all this? That infants are active learners, not only of language, concepts, objects, and goals as explained in this chapter but also of the motor skills detailed in Chapter 5 and the social understanding described in Chapter 7.

Back to Uncle Henry: My cousins loved their mother because she knew instinctively that her infant boys were ready to learn. When they grew up they realized, with Piaget, that even in the first weeks of life, fathers can join mothers as the first, and perhaps best, teachers.

SUMMING UP

From the first days of life, babies attend to words and expressions, responding as well as their limited abilities allow—crying, cooing, and soon babbling. Before age 1, they understand simple words and communicate with gestures. At 1 year, most infants speak. Vocabulary accumulates slowly at first, but then more rapidly with the naming explosion and with the emergence of the holophrase and the two-word sentence.

The impressive language learning of the first two years can be explained in many ways: that caregivers must teach language, that infants learn because they are social beings, that inborn cognitive capacity propels infants to acquire language as soon as maturation makes that possible. Because infants vary in culture, learning style, and social context, a hybrid theory contends that each theory may be valid for some aspects and ages of language learning.

>> **Response for Educators** (from page 173) Probably both. Infants love to communicate, and they seek every possible way to do so. Therefore, the teachers should try to understand the baby, and the baby's parents, but should also start teaching the baby the majority language of the school.

SUMMARY

Sensorimotor Intelligence

1. Piaget realized that very young infants are active learners, seeking to understand their complex observations and experiences. Sensorimotor intelligence, the first of Piaget's four periods of cognitive development, involves early adaption to experience.

2. Sensorimotor intelligence develops in six stages, beginning with reflexes and ending with mental combinations. The six stages occur in pairs, with each pair characterized by a circular reaction, or feedback loop, as infants first react to their own bodies, then respond to other people and things. Finally, in the tertiary circular reaction, infants become more goal-oriented, creative, and experimental as "little scientists."

3. Infants gradually develop an understanding of objects. As shown in Piaget's classic experiment, infants understand object permanence and begin to search for hidden objects at about 8 months. Other research finds that Piaget underestimated infant cognition, in object permanence and many other ways.

Information Processing

4. Another approach to understanding infant cognition is information-processing theory, which looks at each step of the thinking process, from input to output. The perceptions of a young infant are attuned to the particular affordances, or opportunities for action, that are present in the infant's world.

5. Objects that move are particularly interesting to infants, as are other humans. Objects as well as people afford many possibilities for interaction and perception, and therefore these affordances enhance early cognition.

6. Infant memory is fragile but not completely absent. Reminder sessions help trigger memories, and young brains learn motor sequences long before they can remember with words. Memory is multifaceted; explicit memories are rare in infancy.

Language: What Develops in the First Two Years?

7. Language learning may be the most impressive cognitive accomplishment of infants, distinguishing the human species from the other animals. The universal sequence of early language development is well known; the reasons for it are in dispute.

8. Eager attempts to communicate are apparent in the first weeks and months. Infants babble at about 6 to 9 months, understand words and gestures by 10 months, and speak their first words at about 1 year.

9. Vocabulary begins to build very slowly until the infant knows approximately 50 words. Then the naming explosion begins. Toward the end of the second year, toddlers put words together, showing that they understand the rudiments of grammar.

10. Various theories explain how infants learn language as quickly as they do. The three main theories emphasize different aspects of early language learning: that infants must be taught, that their social impulses foster language learning, and that their brains are genetically attuned to language.

11. Each theory of language learning is confirmed by some research. The challenge for developmental scientists has been to formulate a hybrid theory that uses all the insights and research on early language learning. The challenge for caregivers is to respond to the infant's early attempts to communicate, expecting neither too much nor too little.

KEY TERMS

sensorimotor intelligence (p. 153)

primary circular reactions (p. 154)

secondary circular reactions (p. 155)

object permanence (p. 155)

tertiary circular reactions (p. 157)

"little scientist" (p. 157)

deferred imitation (p. 157)

habituation (p. 158)

fMRI (p. 158)

information-processing theory (p. 160)

affordance (p. 161)

visual cliff (p. 161)

dynamic perception (p. 162)

people preference (p. 162)

reminder session (p. 164)

implicit memory (p. 165)

explicit memory (p. 165)

child-directed speech (p. 168)

babbling (p. 168)

holophrase (p. 169)

naming explosion (p. 169)

grammar (p. 171)

language acquisition device (LAD) (p. 174)

WHAT HAVE YOU LEARNED?

Sensorimotor Intelligence

1. Why did Piaget call his first stage of cognition *sensorimotor* intelligence?

2. How do the first two sensorimotor stages illustrate primary circular reactions?

3. If a parent speaks and a baby babbles in response, how does that illustrate stage three?

4. How is object permanence an example of stage four of sensorimotor intelligence?

5. In sensorimotor intelligence, what is the difference between stages five and six?

6. What steps of the scientific method does the "little scientist" follow?

7. Why is becoming bored a sign of infant cognitive development?

Information Processing

8. How do the affordances of this book differ at age 1 month, 12 months, and 20 years?

9. What are several hypotheses to explain why infants refuse to crawl over visual cliffs?

10. What two preferences show that infants are selective in early perception?

11. What conditions help 3-month-olds remember something?

12. What is the crucial difference between implicit and explicit memory?

13. Why is explicit memory difficult for babies under age 2?

Language: What Develops in the First Two Years?

14. What linguistic abilities do infants have at 6 months?

15. What is typical of the rate and nature of the first words that infants speak?

16. What have developmentalists discovered about the way adults talk to babies?

17. What are the early signs of grammar in infant speech?

18. According to behaviorism, how do adults teach infants to talk?

19. According to sociocultural theory, why do infants try to communicate?

20. What does the idea that child speech results from brain maturation imply for caregivers?

21. How does the hybrid theory compare to the eclectic approach described in Chapter 2.

APPLICATIONS

1. Elicit vocalizations from an infant—babbling if the baby is under age 1, using words if older. Write down all the baby says for 10 minutes. Then ask the primary caregiver to elicit vocalizations for 10 minutes, and write these down. What differences are apparent between the baby's two attempts at communication? Compare your findings with the norms described in the chapter.

2. Piaget's definition of intelligence is adaptation. Others consider a good memory or an extensive vocabulary to be a sign of intelligence. How would you define intelligence? Give examples.

3. Many educators recommend that parents read to babies even before the babies begin talking. What theory of language development does this reflect?

4. Test an infant's ability to search for a hidden object. Ideally, the infant should be about 7 or 8 months old, and you should retest over a period of weeks. If the infant can immediately find the object, make the task harder by pausing between the hiding and the searching or by secretly moving the object from one hiding place to another.

>>ONLINE CONNECTIONS

To accompany your textbook, you have access to a number of online resources, including quizzes for every chapter of the book, flashcards (in English and Spanish), critical thinking questions, and case studies. For access to any of these links, go to www.worthpublishers.com/bergerls8e. In addition to these free resources, you'll also find links to the podcasts, video clips, diagnostic quizzing with personalized study advice, and an ebook. Some of the videos and activities available online include:

- *The Visual Cliff.* Includes footage from Joseph Campos's lab at the University of California, Berkeley.

- *Language Development in Infancy.* How easy is it to understand a newborn's coos? Or a 6-month old's babbling? But we can almost all make out the voice of a toddler singing "Twinkle, Twinkle." Video clips from a variety of real-life contexts bring to life the development of children's language.

The First Two Years: Psychosocial Development

WHAT WILL YOU KNOW?

1. How do emotions change from birth to age 1 and from age 1 to age 2?

2. What differences in temperament are apparent in the first two years?

3. How do the major theories of development differ in their emphasis on mothers and cultures?

4. What are the forms of attachment, and how might each affect humans lifelong?

5. How are fathers similar to, and different from, mothers in infant care?

As I sat on a crowded subway car, a young woman boarded with a heavy shopping bag in one arm and an infant, about 8 months old, in the other. She stood in front of me, trying to steady herself as the train started to move. "Can I help?" I asked. Wordlessly, she handed me . . . the baby. I began softly singing a children's song. The baby was quiet, neither crying nor smiling, keeping her eyes intently on her mother. We traveled for about 10 minutes; I wondered why I was holding a living human being, not a shopping bag.

Adults express cultural and personal values as they provide various experiences for infants, and each individual reacts with his or her particular emotions. That is the basis of psychosocial development. This mother chose to let a stranger hold her infant, and I was happy the baby did not cry. All three of us were part of a psychosocial interaction; our reactions were affected by our ages, past experiences, and circumstances.

This chapter opens by tracing infants' emotions as their brains mature and their experiences accumulate over the first two years, noting temperamental and cultural differences. Then we describe how each of the five theories introduced in Chapter 2 explains psychosocial development during infancy. Toilet training and ethnotheories are included in that section. This leads to an exploration of caregiver–infant interaction, particularly *synchrony, attachment,* and *social referencing.* For every aspect of caregiving, we consider fathers as well as mothers.

We then consider infant day care (a common experience for babies worldwide), paying special attention to its impact on psychosocial development. The chapter ends with practical suggestions. That subway mother may have made a wise choice in handing me her baby—just not the choice I expected.

AT ABOUT THIS TIME

Ages When Emotions Emerge

Birth	Crying; contentment
6 weeks	Social smile
3 months	Laughter; curiosity
4 months	Full, responsive smiles
4–8 months	Anger
9–14 months	Fear of social events (strangers, separation from caregiver)
12 months	Fear of unexpected sights and sounds
18 months	Self-awareness; pride; shame; embarrassment

As always, culture and experience influence the norms of development. This is especially true for emotional development after the first 8 months.

social smile A smile evoked by a human face, normally evident in infants about 6 weeks after birth.

Kazakhstan Kid Joy is universal when an infant smiles at her beaming grandparents—a smile made even better when the tongue joins in. This particular scene takes place in Kazakhstan in central Asia, an independent nation only since 1991. So it may take some time for them to get used to a slang term like *kid*.

stranger wariness An infant's expression of concern—a quiet stare, clinging to a familiar person, or sadness—when a stranger appears.

>> Emotional Development

Within the first two years, infants progress from reactive pain and pleasure to complex patterns of social awareness (see At About This Time). This is the period of "high emotional responsiveness" (Izard et al., 2002, p. 767), expressed in speedy, uncensored reactions—crying, startling, laughing, raging—and, by toddlerhood, complex responses, from self-satisfied grins to mournful pouts.

Infants' Emotions

At first, there is pleasure and pain. Newborns look happy and relaxed when fed and drifting off to sleep. They cry when they are hurt or hungry, are tired or frightened (as by a loud noise or a sudden loss of support), and about one-third of infants have bouts of uncontrollable crying, called *colic*—probably the result of immature digestion.

Smiling and Laughing

Soon, additional emotions become recognizable (Lavelli & Fogel, 2005). Curiosity is evident as infants (and people of all ages) respond to objects and experiences that are new but not too novel. Happiness is expressed by the **social smile,** evoked by a human face at about 6 weeks. Preterm babies are later to smile at people, because the social smile is affected by age since conception. Infants worldwide express social joy, even laughter, between 2 and 4 months (Konner, 2007).

Among the Navajo, whoever brings forth that first laugh gives a feast to celebrate that the baby is becoming a person (Rogoff, 2003). Laughter builds as curiosity does; a typical 6-month-old laughs loudly upon discovering new things, particularly social experiences that have the right balance between familiarity and surprise, such as Daddy making a funny face.

Anger and Sadness

The basic positive emotions of joy and contentment are soon joined by basic negative emotions, more common in infancy than later on (Izard, 2009). Anger is evident at 6 months, usually triggered by frustration. It is obvious when infants are prevented from grabbing an object they want or from moving as they wish (Plutchik, 2003). Infants hate to be strapped in, caged in, closed in, or even just held tightly when they want to explore.

Anger in infancy is a healthy response to frustration, unlike sadness, which also appears in the first months. Sadness indicates withdrawal and is accompanied by an increase in the body's production of *cortisol,* a stress hormone (Lewis & Ramsay, 2005). Since sadness is accompanied by signs of stress, sorrow is probably not a superficial emotion for infants. Many researchers believe that the infant brain is shaped by the early social emotions, particularly sadness and fear (Fries & Pollak, 2007; M. H. Johnson, 2007).

Fear

Fully formed fear in response to some person, thing, or situation (not just distress at a surprise) emerges at about 9 months and then rapidly becomes more frequent as well as more apparent (Witherington et al., 2004). Two kinds of social fear are obvious:

- **Stranger wariness,** evident when an infant no longer smiles at any friendly face but cries if an unfamiliar person moves too close, too quickly

- **Separation anxiety,** expressed in tears, dismay, or anger when a familiar caregiver leaves

Separation anxiety is normal at age 1, intensifies by age 2, and usually subsides after that. If it remains strong after age 3, it is considered an emotional disorder (Silverman & Dick-Niederhauser, 2004). Many 1-year-olds fear not just strangers but also anything unexpected, from the flush of a toilet to the pop of a jack-in-the-box, from the closing of elevator doors to the tail-wagging approach of a dog. With repeated experiences and caregiver reassurance, older infants might themselves enjoy flushing the toilet (again and again) or calling the dog (crying if the dog does *not* come).

Toddlers' Emotions

Emotions take on new strength during toddlerhood (Izard, 2009). For example, throughout the second year and beyond, anger and fear become less frequent but more focused, targeted toward infuriating or terrifying experiences. Similarly, laughing and crying become louder and more discriminating.

New emotions appear: pride, shame, embarrassment, disgust, and guilt (Stevenson et al., 2010; Thompson, 2006). These emotions require social awareness, emerging from family interactions, influenced by the culture (Mesquita & Leu, 2007). For example, parents encourage pride in North American toddlers (saying, "You did it yourself"—even when that is untrue), but Asian families discourage pride and cultivate modesty and shame (Rogoff, 2003). Disgust is strongly influenced by other people: Many 18-month-olds (but not younger infants) express disgust at touching a dead animal, but none have learned to be disgusted when a teenager curses at an elderly person, something that parents and older children may find disgusting (Stevenson et al., 2010).

By age 2, children can display the entire spectrum of emotional reactions. They have been taught what is acceptable in their family and culture—sometimes fear, sometimes boldness (Saarni et al., 2006). For example, if a toddler hides his face in his mother's skirt when a friendly dog approaches, the mother could hastily pick the child up or enthusiastically pet the dog, teaching fear or welcome the next time a dog appears.

Self-Awareness

In addition to social awareness, another foundation for emotional growth is **self-awareness,** the realization that one's body, mind, and actions are separate from those of other people (R. A. Thompson, 2006). At about age 1, an emerging sense of "me" and "mine" leads to a new consciousness of others.

Very young infants have no sense of self—at least of *self* as most people define it (Harter, 2006). In fact, a prominent psychoanalyst, Margaret Mahler, theorized that for the first 4 months of life infants see themselves as part of their mothers. They "hatch" at about 5 months and spend the next several months developing a sense of self (Mahler et al., 1975).

Actually, some aspects of selfhood emerge even before age 1, but

> more complex self-representations are reflected [in] . . . self-referential emotions. . . . By the end of the second year and increasingly in the third [ages 1 and 2] the simple joy of success becomes accompanied by looking and smiling to an adult and calling attention to the feat; the simple sadness of failure becomes accompanied either by avoidance of eye contact with the adult and turning away or by reparative activity and confession . . .
>
> *[Thompson, 2006, p. 79]*

separation anxiety An infant's distress when a familiar caregiver leaves, most obvious between 9 and 14 months.

JOURNAL-COURIER / TIFFANY HERMON / THE IMAGE WORKS

Stranger Wariness Becomes Santa Terror For toddlers, even a friendly stranger is cause for alarm, especially if Mom's protective arms are withdrawn. The most frightening strangers are men who are unusually dressed and who act as if they might take the child away. Ironically, therefore, Santa Claus remains terrifying until children are about 3 years old.

Especially for Nurses and Pediatricians Parents come to you concerned that their 1-year-old hides her face and holds onto them tightly whenever a stranger appears. What do you tell them? (see response, page 182)

self-awareness One's realization that he or she is a distinct individual, whose body, mind, and actions are separate from those of other people.

Mirror, Mirror This toddler clearly recognizes herself in the reflection in the mirror, and her careful combing indicates that she also knows that her culture admires long hair in females.

Observation Quiz This little girl may end up tangling her hair instead of smoothing it. Besides the comb, what else do you see that she might misuse? (see answer, page 184)

In a classic experiment (M. Lewis & Brooks, 1978), babies aged 9 to 24 months looked into a mirror after a dot of rouge had been surreptitiously put on their noses. If the babies reacted by touching their noses, that meant they knew the mirror showed their own faces. None of the babies younger than 12 months old reacted as if they recognized themselves (they sometimes smiled and touched the dot on the "other" baby in the mirror). However, between 15 and 24 months, babies usually showed self-awareness, touching their own noses with curiosity and puzzlement.

Self-recognition in the mirror/rouge test (as well as in photographs) usually emerges at about 18 months, along with two other advances: pretending and using first-person pronouns (*I, me, mine, myself, my*). Therefore, some developmentalists connect self-recognition with self-understanding (e.g., Gallup et al., 2002), although "the interpretation of this seemingly simple task is plagued by controversy" (Nielsen et al., 2006, p. 176).

For example, one study found that self-recognition in the mirror/rouge test *negatively* correlated with embarrassment when a doll's leg fell off (it had been rigged to do so) as each toddler played with it (Barrett, 2005). Many 17-month-olds who recognized themselves, particularly boys, were *less* embarrassed at this mishap and more likely to tell the examiner about it. Does a sense of self diminish shame as it increases pride? Perhaps. Pride may be linked to the maturing self-concept, not necessarily to other people's opinions (Barrett, 2005).

Brain Maturation and the Emotions

Brain maturation is involved in all the emotional developments just described. There is no doubt that varied experiences, as well as good nutrition, promote both brain maturation and emotional development. Nor is there any doubt that emotional reactions begin in the brain (M. H. Johnson, 2007).

Social Impulses

Many aspects of brain maturation support social emotions (Lloyd-Fox et al., 2009). For instance, most developmentalists agree that the social smile and the first laughter appear as the cortex matures (Konner, 2007). The same is probably true for nonreflexive fear, self-awareness, and anger. The maturation of a particular part of the cortex (the anterior cingulate gyrus) is directly connected to emotional self-regulation, which allows a child to moderate these emotions (Posner et al., 2007).

One important aspect of the infant's emotional development is that particular people (typically those the infant sees most often) begin to arouse specific emotions. This is almost certainly the result of brain development, as a sequence of neurons that fire together become more closely and quickly connected in the brain.

All emotional reactions, particularly those connected to self-awareness, depend partly on memory (Harter, 2006). As already explained in Chapter 6, memory is fragile at first and gradually improves as dendrites and axons connect. No wonder children over age 1 are more quickly angered than those under 8 months when teased by an older sibling or are easily frightened when entering the doctor's office. The toddlers now remember the last time that sibling frustrated them or the doctor gave them a shot. (Anger appears earlier when an infant is restricted or frustrated, no memory needed for that.)

Stress

Chapter 5 suggested that excessive stress impairs the brain, particularly in areas associated with emotions (Adam et al., 2007). Brain imagery and cortisol measure-

>> Response for Nurses and Pediatricians (from page 181) Stranger wariness is normal up to about 14 months. This baby's behavior actually sounds like secure attachment!

ments suggest that the hypothalamus (part of the brain that regulates bodily functions and hormone production) grows more slowly if an infant is often stressed. (The hypothalamus is discussed further in Chapter 8.)

The brain damage from abuse in infancy is difficult to prove experimentally, for obvious ethical reasons. However, brain scans of maltreated children reveal abnormal activation not only to stress and other emotions but even to photographs of frightened people (Gordis et al., 2008; Masten et al., 2008). Such abnormal neurological responses are likely caused by early abuse.

This research has important applications. Everything should be done to prevent excessive stress in infants. One obvious way is to support new mothers, but support for new fathers may be crucial as well. For example, when the father of a baby delivered via cesarean section provides *kangaroo care,* holding the newborn against his naked chest (see Chapter 4), that baby tends to cry less and to be more relaxed (Erlandsson et al., 2007). Throughout early development, the father's behavior toward the mother affects her stress level, and her stress is then transmitted to the baby (Talge et al., 2007).

Synesthesia

Brain maturation may affect an infant's ability to differentiate emotions—for instance, distinguishing between fear and joy. Some infants seem to cry at everything. Early emotional confusion seems similar to *synesthesia,* when one sense triggers another in the brain. For older children and adults, the most common form of synesthesia is when a number or letter evokes a vivid color. Among adults, synesthesia is unusual; often it is partly genetic and indicates artistic creativity (K. J. Barnett et al., 2008).

Synesthesia seems more common in infants because the boundaries between the sensory parts of the cortex are still forming (Walker et al., 2010). Textures seem associated with vision, sounds with smells, and the infant's own body seems connected to the bodies of others. The sensory connections are called *cross-model perception;* the interpersonal connections may become the basis for early social understanding (Meltzoff, 2007).

The tendency of one part of the brain to activate another may occur for emotions. An infant's cry can be triggered by pain, fear, tiredness, surprise, or excitement; laughter can turn to tears. Discrete emotions in the early months are less easy to recognize, differentiate, or predict than are an adult's emotions; infants emotions seem to erupt, increase, or disappear for unknown reasons (Camras & Shutter, 2010). One likely explanation is immaturity of brain structures.

Temperament

Every human emotion is influenced by a person's genotype. Thus, an infant might be happy or fearful not only because of maturation but also because of genes. Among each person's genetic predispositions are the traits of **temperament,** defined as "constitutionally based individual differences" in emotions, activity, and self-regulation (Rothbart & Bates, 2006, p. 100). "Constitutionally based" means that these traits originate with nature (genes). Confirmation that temperament is constitutionally, not experientially, based comes from an analysis of newborn cries after the hepatitis B inoculation: Cry variations correlated with later temperament (Jong et al., 2010).

Temperament may overlap with personality (Caspi & Shiner, 2006). Generally, however, personality traits (e.g., honesty and humility) are thought to be primarily learned, whereas temperamental traits (e.g., shyness and aggression) are considered primarily genetic. Of course, even though temperamental traits originate

On Top of His World This boy's blissful expression is evidence that fathers can prevent or relieve stress in infants, protecting a baby's brain and promoting the mother's peace of mind.

temperament Inborn differences between one person and another in emotions, activity, and self-regulation. Temperament originates in genes and prenatal development and is affected by early experiences.

>> Answer to Observation Quiz (from page 182) Perfume. She might splash too much of her mother's perfume on herself, ending up reeking instead of wafting.

FIGURE 7.1

Do Babies' Temperaments Change? The data suggest that fearful babies are not necessarily fated to remain that way. Adults who are reassuring and do not act frightened themselves can help children overcome an innate fearfulness. Some fearful children do not change, however, and it is not known whether that's because their parents are not sufficiently reassuring (nurture) or because they are temperamentally more fearful (nature).

Observation Quiz Out of 100 4-month-olds who react positively to noises and other experiences, how many are fearful at later times in early childhood? (see answer, page 186)

with the genes, the actual expression of the traits over the life span is modified by experience—the result of child-rearing methods, culture, and learning (Rothbart & Bates, 2006).

The New York Longitudinal Study

In laboratory studies of temperament, infants are exposed to events that are frightening. Four-month-olds might see spinning mobiles or hear unusual sounds. Older babies might confront a noisy, moving robot or a clown who quickly moves close. At such experiences, some children laugh (and are classified as "easy"), some cry ("difficult"), and some are quiet ("slow to warm up"). These three categories come from the *New York Longitudinal Study* (NYLS). Begun in the 1960s, the NYLS was the first among many large studies to recognize that each newborn has distinct inborn traits (Thomas & Chess, 1977).

According to the NYLS, by 3 months, infants manifested nine temperamental traits that could be clustered into four categories (the three described above and a fourth category of infants who are "hard to classify"). The proportion of infants in each category was as follows:

- Easy (40 percent)
- Difficult (10 percent)
- Slow to warm up (15 percent)
- Hard to classify (35 percent)

Later research has confirmed that newborns differ in temperament and that some babies are unusually difficult. However, although the NYLS began a rich research endeavor, the nine dimensions of the NYLS have not held up to later research (Caspi & Shiner, 2006; Zentner & Bates, 2008). Generally, only three (not nine) dimensions of temperament are clearly present in early childhood (Else-Quest et al., 2006):

- Effortful control (ability to regulate attention)
- Negative mood (fearful, angry, unhappy)
- Surgency (active, social, not shy)

Each study of infant temperament uses somewhat different terms. One longitudinal study (Fox et al., 2001) identified three distinct types among 4-month-olds—exuberant, negative, and inhibited (fearful). These researchers used laboratory measures, gathered mothers' reports, and scanned brains of the same children at 4, 9, 14, 24, and 48 months.

Half of the participants did not change much, reacting the same way and having similar brainwave patterns when confronted with frightening experiences every time they were tested. The other half altered their responses as they grew older. Inhibited, fearful infants were most likely to change and exuberant infants, least likely (see Figure 7.1). That speaks to the influence of child-rearing methods: Adults coax frightened children to be brave and encourage exuberant children to stay happy.

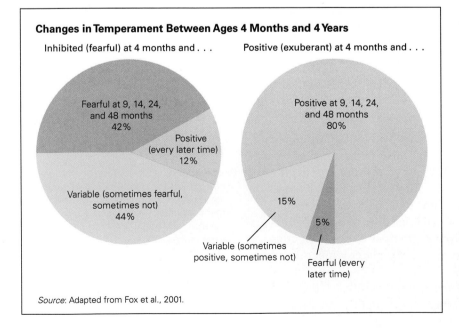

Changes in Temperament Between Ages 4 Months and 4 Years

Inhibited (fearful) at 4 months and . . .

Fearful at 9, 14, 24, and 48 months 42%

Positive (every later time) 12%

Variable (sometimes fearful, sometimes not) 44%

Positive (exuberant) at 4 months and . . .

Positive at 9, 14, 24, and 48 months 80%

15%

5%

Variable (sometimes positive, sometimes not)

Fearful (every later time)

Source: Adapted from Fox et al., 2001.

Longitudinal studies of the relationship between infant temperament and adolescent personality (especially antisocial traits) find similar results: Continuity is evident, but so is the effect of family and culture, which sometimes diminishes difficult or negative traits (Kagan et al., 2007; Zentner & Bates, 2008).

Goodness of Fit

All the research finds that traces of childhood temperament endure and also that context shapes behavior. Ideally, parents find a **goodness of fit**—that is, an adjustment that allows smooth infant–caregiver interaction. With a good fit, parents of difficult babies build a close relationship; parents of exuberant infants learn to protect them from harm; parents of slow-to-warm-up toddlers give them time to adjust. Note that the parents do most of the accommodating, as is evident in this example of a man and his daughter:

> Kevin is a very active, outgoing person who loves to try new things. Today he takes his 11-month-old daughter, Tyra, to the park for the first time. Tyra is playing alone in the sandbox, when a group of toddlers joins her. At first, Tyra smiles and eagerly watches them play. But as the toddlers become more active and noisy, Tyra's smiles turn quickly to tears. She . . . reaches for Kevin, who picks her up and comforts her. But then Kevin goes a step further. After Tyra calms down, Kevin gently encourages her to play near the other children. He sits at her side, talking and playing with her. Soon Tyra is slowly creeping closer to the group of toddlers, curiously watching their moves.
>
> *[Lerner & Dombro, 2004, p. 42]*

Tyra needed Kevin. In general, anxious, difficult children are more affected by their parents' responsiveness than are easygoing children (Belsky & Pluess, 2009; Leerkes et al., 2009; Pauli-Pott et al., 2004). Ineffective or harsh parenting *combined with* a negative temperament creates antisocial, destructive children (Cicchetti et al., 2007). Some children naturally cope with life's challenges; others must make an effort. For example, "a shy child must control his or her fear and approach a stranger, and an impulsive child must constrain his or her desire and resist a temptation" (Derryberry et al., 2003, p. 1061).

Of course, childhood temperament is linked to adult personality in another way, via the adults who care for the children. Adult personality is discussed later in this text, but let us note here that adults who are high in extroversion (surgency), high in agreeableness (effortful control), and low in neuroticism (negative mood) tend to be warmer and more competent parents (de Haan et al., 2009).

Especially for Nurses Parents come to you with their fussy 3-month-old. They say that they have read that temperament is "fixed" before birth, and they are worried that their child will always be difficult. What do you tell them? (see response, page 186)

goodness of fit A similarity of temperament and values that produces a smooth interaction between an individual and his or her social context, including family, school, and community.

SUMMING UP

Newborns seem to have only two simple emotions, distress and contentment, expressed by crying or looking peaceful. Very soon curiosity and obvious joy, with social smiles and laughter, appear. By the second half of the first year, anger and fear are increasingly evident, especially in reaction to social experiences, such as encountering a stranger. In the second year, as infants become self-aware, they express emotions connected to themselves—including pride, shame, embarrassment, and guilt—and to other people. Maturation makes these emotions possible, but context and learning affect the timing, frequency, and intensity of their expression. Underlying all emotional development is brain maturation and the connections between neurons. From birth on, temperamental differences are apparent; some infants are easier than others.

>> Answer to Observation Quiz (from page 184) Out of 100 4-month-olds who react positively, 20 are fearful at least occasionally later in childhood, but only 5 are consistently fearful.

>> Response for Nurses (from page 185) It's too soon to tell. Temperament is not truly "fixed" but variable, especially in the first few months. Many "difficult" infants become happy, successful adolescents and adults.

Especially for Nursing Mothers You have heard that if you wean your child too early, he or she will overeat or become an alcoholic. Is it true? (see response, page 188)

>> Theories of Infant Psychosocial Development

We now consider the theories discussed in Chapter 2 and look at some possible applications of those theories to early emotional development. As you will see, theories lead to applications. Thumb sucking, toilet training, diapering, and bonding are all issues that concern theory and practice.

Psychoanalytic Theory

Psychoanalytic theory connects biosocial and psychosocial development. Both major psychoanalytic theorists, Sigmund Freud and Erik Erikson, described two distinct early stages of development. Freud (1935, 1940/1964) wrote about the *oral stage* and the *anal stage.* Erikson (1963) called his first stages *trust versus mistrust* and *autonomy versus shame and doubt.*

Freud: Oral and Anal Stages

According to Freud (1935), the first year of life is the *oral stage,* so named because the mouth is the young infant's primary source of gratification. In the second year, with the *anal stage,* the infant's main pleasure comes from the anus—particularly from the sensual pleasure of bowel movements and, eventually, the psychological pleasure of controlling them.

Freud believed that the oral and anal stages are fraught with potential conflicts that have long-term consequences. If a mother frustrates her infant's urge to suck—weaning the infant too early, for example, or preventing the child from sucking—the child may become distressed and anxious, eventually becoming an adult with an *oral fixation.* Such a person is stuck (fixated) at the oral stage and therefore eats, drinks, chews, bites, or talks excessively, in quest of the mouth-related pleasure denied in infancy.

Similarly, if toilet training is overly strict or if it begins before the infant is mature enough, parent–infant interaction may become locked into a conflict over the toddler's refusal, or inability, to comply. The child develops an anal personality—as an adult, seeking self-control with an unusually strong need for regularity in all aspects of life. Most developmentalists no longer agree with this part of Freud's theory, although diverse opinions flourish about the optimal timing and method of toilet training, as the following illustrates.

THINKING CRITICALLY

Toilet Training: How and When?

Remember that theories are practical. This is particularly apparent in infancy. One example is toilet training. A century ago, parents believed that body functions should be controlled as soon as possible; they began toilet training infants in the first months of life (Accardo, 2006). Then psychoanalytic theory pegged the first year as the oral stage (Freud) or the time when trust was crucial (Erikson), before the toddler's anal stage or autonomy needs. Thus, psychoanalytic theory influenced parents to postpone toilet training to avoid serious personality problems later on. This was reflected in the recommendation of a leading pe-

diatrician, Barry Brazelton (who designed the NBAS, mentioned in Chapter 4). Brazelton wrote that toilet training should not begin until the child is cognitively, emotionally, and biologically ready, around age 2 for daytime training and age 3 for nighttime dryness (Brazelton & Sparrow, 2006).

> As a society, we are far too concerned about pushing children to be toilet trained early. I don't even like the phrase "toilet training." It really should be toilet learning.
>
> [*Brazelton & Sparrow, 2006, p. 193*]

By the middle of the twentieth century, many U.S. researchers had rejected psychoanalytic theory and had become behaviorists. They proposed a toilet-training method that could occur whenever the parent and the child wished, not at a particular age (Azrin & Foxx, 1974). In this method, children drink quantities of their favorite juice, sit on the potty with a parent nearby to keep them entertained, and then, when the inevitable occurs, the parent praises and rewards them. They soon learn (within a day, according to some behaviorists) to head for the potty whenever the need arises.

Which method is best? One comparison study found that this behaviorist approach was often effective for older children with serious disabilities. However, this study also found that almost every method of toilet training succeeded with normal children, as long as the parents did not expect impossible bladder or bowel control. No method seemed to result in marked negative emotional consequences (Klassen et al., 2006).

Later training may be quickest. One study followed hundreds of toddlers whose parents began training between 18 months and 3 years. Early starters took about a year to be toilet-trained completely (doing everything without help), while later starters took only about three months (Blum et al., 2003). Other research in industrialized nations found that the age of success depends mostly on the child's bladder size and sleep habits (Jansson et al., 2005).

Neither psychoanalytic nor behaviorist theory reflects sociocultural influences, yet toilet training occurs "in very diverse ways . . . at different ages, with different degrees of attention and harshness" (Rozin, 2007, p. 405). In some cultures, parents expect their children to be trained by 6 months; in others, parents never train their children because toddlers watch slightly older children and imitate what they do. A survey in the United States found that some parents thought toilet training should begin as early as 6 months, others as late as 4 years. The preferred age was affected by the parents' socioeconomic

status (SES): More years of education correlated with later age of training (Horn et al., 2006). That suggests that cognition as well as culture is influential

Rejecting this relaxed, child-centered approach, some Western parents prefer to start potty training very early. One U.S. mother began training her baby just 33 days after birth. She noticed when her son was about to defecate, held him above the toilet, and had trained him by 6 months (Sun & Rugolotto, 2004). Similar disparities are evident in many aspects of infant care, such as thumb sucking or pacifier use. Some parents forbid any sucking, covering infants' hands so sucking is impossible, and others stick a pacifier into the mouths of their 1-day-old babies.

This diversity raises a question: What is the goal? What values are imbedded in each theory, each practice? There is no easy answer: Critical thinking is required.

All Together, Now Toddlers in an employees' day-care program at a flower farm in Colombia learn to use the potty on a schedule.

Erikson: Trust and Autonomy

According to Erikson, the first crisis of life is **trust versus mistrust,** when infants learn whether the world can be trusted to satisfy basic needs. Babies feel secure when food and comfort are provided with "consistency, continuity, and sameness of experience" (Erikson, 1963, p. 247). If social interaction inspires trust and security, the child (and later the adult) confidently explores the social world.

The second crisis is **autonomy versus shame and doubt,** beginning at about 18 months, when self-awareness emerges. Toddlers want autonomy (self-rule) over their own actions and bodies. Without it, they feel ashamed and doubtful. Like Freud, Erikson believed that problems in early infancy could last a lifetime, creating adults who are suspicious and pessimistic (mistrusting) or easily shamed (lacking autonomy).

Erikson was aware of cultural variations. He knew that mistrust or shame could be destructive or not, depending on norms and expectations. Some cultures

trust versus mistrust Erikson's first psychosocial crisis. Infants learn basic trust if their basic needs (for food, comfort, attention, and so on) are met.

autonomy versus shame and doubt Erikson's second crisis of psychosocial development. Toddlers either succeed or fail in gaining a sense of self-rule over their own actions and bodies.

A Mother's Dilemma Infants are wonderfully curious, as this little boy demonstrates. Parents, however, must guide as well as encourage the drive toward autonomy. Notice this mother's expression as she makes sure her son does not crush or eat the flower.

social learning Learning that is accomplished by observing others—both what they do and how other people react to that behavior.

>> **Response for Nursing Mothers** (from page 186) Freud thought so, but there is no experimental evidence that weaning, even when ill timed, has such dire long-term effects.

encourage independence and autonomy; in others (for example, in China), "shame is a normative emotion that develops as parents use explicit shaming techniques" to encourage children's loyalty and harmony within their families (Mascolo et al., 2003, p. 402). Westerners expect toddlers to go through the stubborn and defiant "terrible twos"; parents elsewhere expect toddlers to be docile and obedient. Autonomy may be prized among North Americans, but it is considered immature by many other peoples (Morelli & Rothbaum, 2007).

Behaviorism

From the perspective of behaviorism, emotions and personality are molded as parents reinforce or punish a child's spontaneous behaviors. Behaviorists believe that parents who smile and pick up their infant at every glimmer of a grin will have children with a sunny disposition. The opposite is also true, according to behaviorist John Watson:

> Failure to bring up a happy child, a well-adjusted child—assuming bodily health—falls squarely upon the parents' shoulders. [By the time the child is 3] parents have already determined . . . [whether the child] is to grow into a happy person, wholesome and good-natured, whether he is to be a whining, complaining neurotic, an anger-driven, vindictive, over-bearing slave driver, or one whose every move in life is definitely controlled by fear.
>
> *[Watson, 1928, pp. 7, 45]*

Later behaviorists recognized that infants also experience **social learning.** Albert Bandura conducted a classic experiment: Children watched an adult hitting a rubber Bobo clown with a mallet and then treated the doll the same way (Bandura, 1977). In this experiment, those children had good reason to follow the example; they were frustrated by being told they could not play with some attractive toys and were then left alone with a mallet and the Bobo doll. Both boys and girls pounded and kicked Bobo.

Since that experiment, developmentalists have demonstrated that social learning occurs throughout life (Morris et al., 2007; Nielsen, 2006). In many families, toddlers express emotions in various ways—from giggling to cursing—just as they have seen their parents or older siblings do. A boy might develop a hot temper, for instance, if his father's outbursts seem to win his mother's respect. Social learning

Hammering Bobo These images are stills from the film of Bandura's original study of social learning, in which frustrated 4-year-olds imitated the behavior they had observed an adult perform. The children used the same weapon as the adult, with the same intent—whether that involved hitting the doll with a hammer, shooting it with a toy gun, or throwing a large ball at it.

theory acknowledges inborn temperament but stresses parental example: Shyness may be inborn, for instance, but parents who model social interaction will help a withdrawn child become more outgoing (Rubin et al., 2009).

Cognitive Theory

Cognitive theory holds that thoughts and values determine a person's perspective. Early experiences are important because beliefs, perceptions, and memories make them so, not because they are buried in the unconscious (psychoanalytic theory) or burned into the brain's patterns (behaviorism). Early relationships help infants develop a **working model,** a set of assumptions that become a frame of reference for later life. It is a "model" because these early relationships are a prototype, or blueprint, for later relationships; it is "working" because, although it is used, it is not necessarily fixed or final.

Ideally, infants develop "a working model of the self as valued, loved, and competent" and "a working model of parents as emotionally available, loving, sensitive and supportive" (Harter, 2006, p. 519). However, reality does not always conform to this ideal. A 1-year-old girl might develop a model, based on her parents' inconsistent responses to her, that people are unpredictable. She will apply that model to everyone: Her childhood friendships will be insecure, and her adult relationships will be guarded.

To use Piaget's terminology, such a girl develops a cognitive *schema* to organize her perceptions. According to cognitive theory, it is not necessarily a child's early experiences themselves that are crucial but rather the child's *interpretation* of them (Schaffer, 2000). The hopeful message from cognitive theory is that people can rethink and reorganize their thoughts, developing new working models. Our mistrustful girl can change if her later experiences—such as marriage to a faithful and loving man—provide a new model.

Sociocultural Theory

No one doubts that "human development occurs in a cultural context" (Kagitcibasi, 2003, p. 166). The crucial question is *how much* influence culture has. Sociocultural theorists argue that the influence is substantial, that the entire social and cultural context shapes infant emotional development.

Ethnotheories

An **ethnotheory** is a theory that is embedded in a particular culture or ethnic group. Although people are rarely aware of it—as you have already seen with breast-feeding, co-sleeping, child-directed speech, and toilet training—many child-rearing practices arise from ethnotheories (H. Keller et al., 2006).

This is certainly true for emotional development. For example, if a culture's ethnotheory includes the idea that ancestors are reincarnated in the younger generation, then "children are not expected to show respect for adults, but adults [are expected to show respect] for their reborn ancestors." Consequently, children are allowed to express many emotions. Such cultures favor indulgent child-rearing with no harsh punishment, which "Western people perceive as extremely lenient" (Dasen, 2003, pp. 149–150).

Remember that cultures can change as circumstances do. This was found in a study of the values of grandmothers and mothers of 3-month-olds (Lamm et al., 2008). The grandmother–mother pairs were from four contexts: urban Germany, urban India, and urban and rural West Africa. Women in each place held ethnotheories unlike women living elsewhere. In all four cultures, generational

working model In cognitive theory, a set of assumptions that the individual uses to organize perceptions and experiences. For example, a person might assume that other people are trustworthy and be surprised by evidence that this working model of human behavior is erroneous.

Stranger Danger Some parents teach their children to be respectful of any adult; others teach them to fear any stranger. No matter what their culture or parents say, each of these two sisters in Nepal reacts according to her inborn temperament.

ethnotheory A theory that underlies the values and practices of a culture but is not usually apparent to the people within the culture.

Especially for Linguists and Writers
U.S. culture has given rise to the term *empty nest,* signifying an ethnotheory about mothers whose children have grown up and moved out of the family home. What cultural values are expressed by that term? (see response, page 192)

proximal parenting Caregiving practices that involve being physically close to a baby, with frequent holding and touching.

distal parenting Caregiving practices that involve remaining distant from a baby, providing toys, food, and face-to-face communication with minimal holding and touching.

Especially for Pediatricians A mother complains that her child refuses to stay in the car seat, spits out disliked foods, and almost never does what she says. How should you respond? (see response, page 192)

differences were apparent, with the mothers valuing children's autonomy more than the grandmothers did.

The generation gap was smallest, however, in the two cultures that were most different from each other. Among urban Germans, grandmothers tended to agree with mothers in valuing autonomy; among rural Africans, mothers tended to agree with grandmothers in valuing obedience. The greatest mother–grandmother gap was in urban Africa, probably because dramatic social change meant that the grandmothers' traditions were quite unlike those learned by their daughters (Lamm et al., 2008).

Since theories of development are open to change, parents tempted to be abusive—either because of their own stresses or expectations or because their infants are difficult—can reframe their perceptions. They can stop blaming the infant and instead become more responsive, as cognitive theory would hope (Bugental & Schwartz, 2009).

Proximal and Distal Parenting

Another example of ethnotheory involves a culture's ideas about how frequently parents should carry and cuddle their babies. **Proximal parenting** involves being physically close to a baby, often holding and touching. **Distal parenting** involves keeping some distance—providing toys, feeding by putting finger food within reach, and talking face-to-face instead of communicating by touch. Caregivers who believe that one of these is better are usually unaware that they are expressing an ethnotheory.

A longitudinal study comparing child-rearing methods of the Nso people of Cameroon with those of Greeks in Athens found marked differences in proximal and distal parenting (H. Keller et al., 2004). The researchers videotaped 78 mothers as they played with their 3-month-olds. Coders (who did not know the study's hypothesis) counted frequency of proximal play (e.g., carrying, swinging, caressing, exercising the child's body) and distal play (e.g., face-to-face talking) (see Table 7.1 and the Research Design). The Nso mothers were proximal, holding their babies all the time and almost never using toys or bottles. The Greek mothers were relatively distal, using objects almost half the time.

The researchers hypothesized that proximal parenting would result in toddlers who were less self-aware but more compliant—traits needed in an interdependent and cooperative society such as that of rural Cameroon. By contrast, distal parenting might produce children who were self-aware but less obedient, as needed when a culture values independence and self-reliance. The predictions were accurate. At 18 months, the same infants were tested on self-awareness (via the mirror/rouge test) and obedience to their parents. The African toddlers didn't recognize themselves in the mirror but were compliant; the opposite was true of the Greek toddlers.

Replicating their own work, these researchers studied a dozen mother–infant pairs in Costa Rica. In that Central American nation, caregiver–infant distance was midway between the Nso and the Greeks, as was later toddler behavior. The researchers reanalyzed all their data, child by child. They found that, even apart from culture, proximal or distal play at 3 months was highly predictive: Greek mothers who, unlike most of their peers, were proximal parents had more obedient toddlers (H. Keller et al., 2004). Research with German father–infant pairs replicated these results (Borke et al., 2007).

Every aspect of early emotional development interacts with cultural beliefs, expressed in parental actions. Other research has found more separation anxiety in Japan than in Germany, because Japanese infants "have very few experiences

TABLE 7.1

Infants in Rural Cameroon and Urban Greece

	Cameroon	Athens, Greece
I. Infant–mother play at 3 months		
Percent of time held by mother	100%	31%
Percent of time playing with objects	3%	40%
II. Toddler behavior at 18 months		
Self-recognition	3%	68%
Immediate compliance with request	72%	2%

Source: Adapted from Keller et al., 2004.

▶ **Research Design**

Scientists: A team of six from three nations (Germany, Greece, Costa Rica): Heidi Keller, Relindis Yovsi, Joern Borke, Joscha Kärtner, Henning Jensen, and Zaira Papaligoura.

Publication: *Child Development* (2004).

Participants: A total of 90 mothers participated when their babies were 3 months old and again when they were 18 months old (32 from Cameroon, 46 from Greece, 12 from Costa Rica). In Greece and Costa Rica, researchers recruited mothers in hospitals. In Cameroon, permission was first sought from the local leader, and then announcements were made among local people.

Design: First, mothers played with their 3-month-olds, and that play was videotaped and coded for particular behaviors by researchers who did not know the hypothesis. Fifteen months later, the toddlers' self-recognition was assessed with the mirror/rouge test, and compliance with preset maternal commands was measured. The mother's frequency of eye contact and body contact with the infant at 3 months was compared with the toddler's self-awareness and compliance at 18 months.

Major conclusion: Toddlers with proximal mothers were more obedient but less self-aware; toddlers with distal mothers tended to show the opposite pattern.

Comments: This is a good comparison study of child-rearing practices in various cultures in that it is longitudinal, using the same measures in each nation. However, with only three locations and relatively few mother–infant pairs (12 in Costa Rica), it is possible that factors unrelated to proximal/distal parenting affected the results. For example, the mothers in Athens were wealthier and more urbanized than the ones in Cameroon; these variables need to be explored in other research.

---

with separation from the mother," whereas in Germany "infants are frequently left alone outside of stores or supermarkets" while their mothers shop (Saarni et al., 2006, p. 237).

Such cultural differences may become encoded in the infant brain, called "a cultural sponge" by one group of scientists (Ambady & Bharucha, 2009, p. 342). It is difficult to measure whether infant brains are molded by their context, but one study of adults born either in the United States or in China found that in both places a particular area of the brain (the medial prefrontal cortex) was activated when the adults judged whether certain adjectives applied to them. However, only in the Chinese was that area activated when they were asked if those adjectives applied to their mothers. The researchers consider this to be "neuroimaging evidence that culture shapes the functional anatomy of self-representation" (Zhu et al., 2007, p. 1310) and speculate that the Chinese learned, as babies, that they are closely aligned with their mothers, whereas the Americans learned to be independent.

>> Response for Linguists and Writers
(from page 190) The implication is that human mothers are like sad birds, bereft of their fledglings, who have flown away.

From the beginning of life, some emotions are dampened and others are fueled by family, as influenced by culture. We noted earlier that infants become angry when they are restrained. Some Western parents rarely hold their infants except to restrain them (and the purpose of the restraint is often to enforce parent–infant separation). Parents force protesting toddlers to sit in strollers, ride in car seats, stay in cribs or behind gates—all examples of distal parenting. If toddlers do not passively allow diapers to be changed (and few do), some parents simply hold the protesting child down to get the task done. Compare this approach to that of Roberto's parents, who used nursing (very proximal) and the threat of separation to get their son diapered and dressed.

A CASE TO STUDY

"Let's Go to Grandma's"

Mayan parents from Mexico and Guatemala hold the ethnotheory that children should not be forced to obey their parents. Roberto, at 18 months, was playing with a ball and did not want to wear a diaper or put on his pants.

> "Let's put on your diaper . . . Let's go to Grandma's . . . We're going to do an errand." This did not work, and the mother invited Roberto to nurse, as she swiftly slipped the diaper on him with the father's assistance. The father announced, "It's over."

Roberto's mother felt

> increasing exasperation that the child was wiggling and not standing to facilitate putting on his pants. Her voice softened as Roberto became interested in the ball, and she increased the stakes: "Do you want another toy?" They [father and mother] continued to try to talk Roberto into cooperating, and handed him various objects, which Roberto enjoyed. But still he stubbornly refused to cooperate with dressing. They left him alone for a while. When his father asked if he was ready, Roberto pouted "nono!"
>
> After a bit, the mother told Roberto that she was leaving and waved goodbye. "Are you going with me?" Roberto sat quietly with a worried look. "Then put on your pants, put on your pants to go up the hill." Roberto stared into space, seeming to consider the alternatives. His mother started to walk away, "OK then, I'm going. Goodbye." Roberto started to cry, and his father persuaded, "Put on your pants then!" and his mother asked, "Are you going with me?"
>
> Roberto looked down worriedly, one arm outstretched in half a take-me gesture.
>
> "Come on, then," his mother offered the pants and Roberto let his father lift him to a stand and cooperated in putting his legs into the pants and in standing to have them fastened. His mother did not intend to leave; instead she suggested that Roberto dance for the audience. Roberto did a baby version of a traditional dance.
>
> *[Rogoff, 2003, p. 204]*

This is an example of an ethnotheory that "elders protect and guide rather than giving orders or dominating" (Rogoff, 2003, p. 205). A second ethnotheory is apparent as well: The parents readily used deception to get their child to do what they wanted.

>> Response for Pediatricians (from page 190) Remember the origins of the misbehavior—probably a combination of the child's inborn temperament and the mother's distal parenting. Blended with ethnotheory, all contribute to the child's being stubborn and independent. Acceptance is more warranted than anger. On the other hand, this mother may be expressing hostility toward the child—a sign that intervention may be needed. Find out.

SUMMING UP

Theories differ in their explanations of the origins of early emotions and personality. Psychoanalytic theory stresses a mother's responses to an infant's need for food and elimination (Freud) or for security and independence (Erikson). Behaviorism also stresses caregiving—especially as parents reinforce the behaviors they want their baby to learn or as they thoughtlessly teach unwanted behaviors.

Cognitive theory highlights the child's concept, or working model, of the world. Sociocultural theory emphasizes that the diversity of nurture explains much of the diversity of emotions. According to sociocultural theory, child-rearing practices arise from ethnotheories, implicit and unexpressed but very powerful. ■

>> The Development of Social Bonds

You surely have noticed that the fifth theory was omitted from the preceding discussion. It is evident, however, in the following discussion, as both humanism and evolutionary theory stress the social interaction of infant and parent. Both the "love and belonging" and "unconditional positive regard," essential to humanism, and the urgency of species survival and reproduction, central to evolutionary psychology, are best explained within the context of social bonds.

Synchrony

Synchrony is a coordinated interaction between caregiver and infant, an exchange in which they respond to each other with split-second timing, evident in the first three months and then more frequently and elaborately as the infant matures (Feldman, 2007). Parents and infants average about an hour a day in face-to-face play.

Detailed research reveals the mutuality of the interaction: Adults rarely smile at newborns until the infants smile at them, at which point adults grin broadly and talk animatedly (Lavelli & Fogel, 2005). Synchrony is evident not only through careful observation but also via computer calculation of the timing of smiles, arched eyebrows, and so on (Messinger et al., 2010). Via synchrony, infants learn to read others' emotions and to develop the skills of social interaction, such as taking turns and paying attention.

Although infants imitate adults, synchrony usually begins with parents imitating infants (Lavelli & Fogel, 2005). When parents detect an emotion from an infant's facial expressions and body motions and then respond, the infant learns to connect an internal state with an external expression (Rochat, 2001). Such responsive parenting is particularly apparent in Asian cultures, perhaps because interpersonal sensitivity is crucial, and thus very small infants begin to learn it (Morelli & Rothbaum, 2007).

synchrony A coordinated, rapid, and smooth exchange of responses between a caregiver and an infant.

(a)

(b)

The Same Situation, Many Miles Apart: Intimate Parenting Some parents are proximal, encouraging mutual touch, as shown by this pair in the Sudan *(left)*; other parents are distal, as shown by this father in Germany *(right)*. Each is part of a cultural pattern that teaches values essential to that society—in this case, intimate family interdependence or individual self-sufficiency.

Learning Emotions Infants respond to their parents' expressions and actions. If the moments shown here are typical, one young man will be happy and outgoing and the other will be sad and quiet.

Observation Quiz For the pair at the left, where are their feet? (see answer, page 196)

still-face technique An experimental practice in which an adult keeps his or her face unmoving and expressionless in face-to-face interaction with an infant.

In Western cultures, parents can become partners to their infants. This is especially important when the infant is at medical risk and the parent ignores psychosocial needs because of urgent and time-consuming biological needs (Newnham et al., 2009). Note that synchrony is exactly what Maslow and the other humanists would recommend. Once basic needs (safety, food) are satisfied, people need love and belonging—responsiveness without conditions, judgment, or rejection. That is synchrony.

When Synchrony Disappears

Is synchrony necessary? If no one plays with an infant, what will happen? Experiments using the **still-face technique** have addressed these questions (Tronick, 1989; Tronick & Weinberg, 1997). An infant is placed facing an adult, who responds normally while video cameras record each partner's reactions. Frame-by-frame analysis typically reveals that mothers instinctively synchronize their responses to the infants' movements, with exaggerated tone and expression. Babies reciprocate with smiles and moving limbs.

Then, on cue, the adult erases all facial expression and stares with a "still face" for a minute or two. Sometimes by 2 months, and clearly by 6 months, babies are very upset by the still face, especially from their parents (less so from strangers). Babies frown, fuss, drool, look away, kick, cry, or suck their fingers. By 5 months, they also increase their babbling, as if to say, "Pay attention to me" (Goldstein et al., 2009).

Many research studies such as those with the still face lead to the same conclusion: Responsiveness to an infant aids development, measured both psychosocially and biologically—by heart rate, weight gain, and brain maturation (Moore & Calkins, 2004; Newnham et al., 2009). Particularly in the first year of life (more than prenatally or after infancy), if a mother is depressed, her child suffers, and fathers, other relatives, and day-care providers need to help (Bagner et al., 2010). Young brains need social interaction—an essential, expected stimulant—to develop to their fullest.

Attachment

Toward the end of the first year, face-to-face play almost disappears. Once infants can move around, they are no longer content to respond to adult facial expressions and vocalizations. Another connection, called *attachment,* overtakes synchrony.

Attachment is a lasting emotional bond between people. It begins before birth, solidifies by age 1, and influences relationships throughout life (see At About This Time). Adults' attachment to their parents, formed decades earlier, affects their behavior with their own children as well as their relationship with their partners (Grossmann et al., 2005; Kline, 2008; Simpson & Rholes, 2010; Sroufe et al., 2005).

Infants show their attachment through *proximity-seeking* (such as approaching and following their caregivers) and through *contact-maintaining* (such as touching, snuggling, and holding). A securely attached toddler is curious and eager to explore but maintains contact by occasionally looking back at the caregiver. Caregivers show attachment as well. They keep a watchful eye on their baby and maintain contact by responding to vocalizations, expressions, and gestures. For example, many mothers or fathers, awakening in the middle of the night, tiptoe to the crib to gaze at their sleeping infant. During the day, many parents instinctively smooth their toddler's hair or caress a hand or cheek, evidence of proximity-seeking.

Attachment is a reflection of a universal trait, as expressed in evolutionary theory. Over humanity's history, proximity-seeking and contact-maintaining fostered the survival of the species by keeping toddlers near their caregivers and caregivers vigilant. All of us inherited these impulses from our great, great . . . grandparents, who would have died without them.

attachment According to Ainsworth, an affectional tie that an infant forms with a caregiver—a tie that binds them together in space and endures over time.

AT ABOUT THIS TIME	
Stages of Attachment	
Birth to 6 weeks	*Preattachment.* Newborns signal, via crying and body movements, that they need others. When people respond positively, the newborn is comforted and learns to seek more interaction. Newborns are also primed by brain patterns to recognize familiar voices and faces.
6 weeks to 8 months	*Attachment in the making.* Infants respond preferentially to familiar people by smiling, laughing, babbling. Their caregivers' voices, touch, expressions, and gestures are comforting, often overriding the infant's impulse to cry. Trust (Erikson) develops.
8 months to 2 years	*Classic secure attachment.* Infants greet the primary caregiver, show separation anxiety when the caregiver leaves, play happily when the caregiver is present. Both infant and caregiver seek to be close to each other (proximity) and frequently look at each other (contact). In many caregiver–infant pairs, physical touch (patting, holding, caressing) is frequent.
2 to 6 years	*Attachment as launching pad.* Young children seek their caregiver's praise and reassurance as their social world expands. Interactive conversations and games (hide-and-seek, object play, reading, pretending) are common. Children expect caregivers to comfort and entertain.
6 to 12 years	*Mutual attachment.* Children seek to make their caregivers proud by learning what adults want them to learn, and adults reciprocate. In concrete operational thought (Piaget), specific accomplishments are valued by adults and children.
12 to 18 years	*New attachment figures.* Teenagers explore and make friendships on their own, using their working models of earlier attachments as a base. With more advanced, formal operational thinking (Piaget), physical contact is less important; shared ideals and goals are more influential.
18 years on	*Attachment revisited.* Adults develop relationships with others, especially relationships with romantic partners and children, influenced by earlier attachment patterns. Past insecure attachments from childhood can be repaired rather than repeated, although this does not always happen.

Source: Adapted from Grobman, 2008.

>> **Answer to Observation Quiz** (from page 194) The father uses his legs and feet to support his son at just the right distance for a great fatherly game of foot-kissing.

secure attachment (type B) A relationship in which an infant obtains both comfort and confidence from the presence of his or her caregiver.

insecure-avoidant attachment (type A) A pattern of attachment in which an infant avoids connection with the caregiver, as when the infant seems not to care about the caregiver's presence, departure, or return.

insecure-resistant/ambivalent attachment (type C) A pattern of attachment in which anxiety and uncertainty are evident, as when an infant becomes very upset at separation from the caregiver and both resists and seeks contact on reunion.

disorganized attachment (type D) A type of attachment that is marked by an infant's inconsistent reactions to the caregiver's departure and return.

Secure and Insecure Attachment

The concept of attachment was originally developed by John Bowlby (1969, 1973, 1988), a British developmentalist influenced by both psychoanalytic theory and *ethology,* the study of animals, a precursor to evolutionary psychology. Inspired by Bowlby's work, Mary Ainsworth, then a young American graduate student, studied the relationship between parents and infants in Uganda (Ainsworth, 1973).

Ainsworth realized that most infants become attached to their caregivers despite sociocultural differences in expression and style (van IJzendoorn et al., 2006). (For example, Ugandan mothers almost never kiss their infants, but nonetheless they may be securely attached to them.) Attachment is classified into four types, labeled A, B, C, and D (see Table 7.2). Infants with **secure attachment** (type B) feel comfortable and confident. The caregiver becomes a *base for exploration,* providing assurance that enables exploration. A toddler might, for example, scramble down from the caregiver's lap to play with an intriguing toy but periodically look back, vocalize a few syllables, or return for a hug.

By contrast, insecure attachment (types A and C) is characterized by fear, anxiety, anger, or indifference. Some insecure children play independently without maintaining contact with the caregiver; this is **insecure-avoidant attachment** (type A). By contrast, another insecure child might be unwilling to leave the caregiver's lap; this is **insecure-resistant/ambivalent attachment** (type C). The fourth category (type D) is **disorganized attachment.** Type D infants may shift from hitting to kissing their mothers, from staring blankly to crying hysterically, from pinching themselves to freezing in place.

Almost two-thirds of all infants are secure (type B). Their mother's presence gives them courage to explore. A caregiver's departure may cause distress; the caregiver's return elicits positive social contact (such as smiling or hugging) and then more playing. A balanced reaction, being concerned but not overwhelmed by departure, is secure attachment.

About one-third of infants are insecure, either indifferent (type A) or unduly anxious (type C). About 5 to 10 percent of infants fit into none of these categories and are disorganized (type D). Disorganization prevents them from developing a strategy for social interaction (even an avoidant or resistant one, type A or C). Sometimes they become hostile and aggressive, difficult for anyone to relate to (Lyons-Ruth et al., 1999). (Many Romanian children adopted after age 2, described in Chapter 5, were type D.)

TABLE 7.2

Patterns of Infant Attachment

Type	Name of Pattern	In Play Room	Mother Leaves	Mother Returns	Toddlers in Category (%)
A	Insecure-avoidant	Child plays happily	Child continues playing	Child ignores her	10–20
B	Secure	Child plays happily	Child pauses, is not as happy	Child welcomes her, returns to play	50–70
C	Insecure-resistant/ ambivalent	Child clings, is preoccupied with mother	Child is unhappy, may stop playing	Child is angry; may cry, hit mother, cling	10–20
D	Disorganized	Child is cautious	Child may stare or yell; looks scared, confused	Child acts oddly— may scream, hit self, throw things	5–10

Measuring Attachment

Ainsworth (1973) developed a now-classic laboratory procedure called the **Strange Situation** to measure attachment. In a well-equipped playroom, an infant is closely observed for eight episodes, each lasting three minutes. First, the caregiver and child are together. Then, according to a set sequence, a stranger arrives, and the caregiver and the stranger come and go. Infants' responses indicate which type of attachment they have formed to their caregivers. (Reactions to the caregiver indicate attachment; reactions to the stranger are influenced more by temperament than by attachment.)

Strange Situation A laboratory procedure for measuring attachment by evoking infants' reactions to stress in eight episodes, lasting three minutes each.

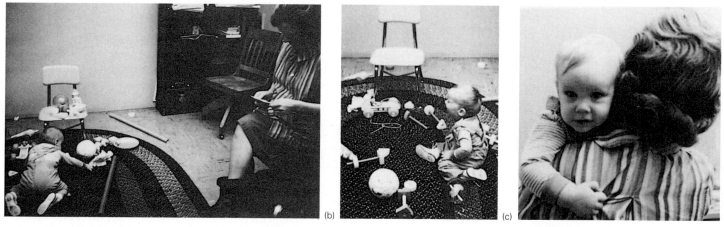

(a)　　　(b)　　　(c)

The Attachment Experiment In this episode of the Strange Situation, Brian shows every sign of secure attachment. (*a*) He explores the playroom happily when his mother is present; (*b*) he cries when she leaves; and (*c*) he is readily comforted when she returns.

ALL COURTESY OF MARY AINSWORTH

Researchers are trained and certified as able to distinguish types A, B, C, and D. They focus on the following:

- *Exploration of the toys.* A secure toddler plays happily.
- *Reaction to the caregiver's departure.* A secure toddler notices when the caregiver leaves and shows some sign of missing him or her.
- *Reaction to the caregiver's return.* A secure toddler welcomes the caregiver's reappearance and then plays again.

Attachment is not always measured via the Strange Situation, however, especially when researchers want to study a large number of people (Andreassen & West, 2007). Instead, researchers use surveys and interviews. Sometimes parents sort out 90 questions about their children's characteristics, and sometimes adults are interviewed extensively (according to a detailed protocol) about their relationships with their own parents, again with various specific measurements (Fortuna & Roisman, 2008).

Insecure Attachment and Social Setting

At first, developmentalists expected secure attachment to "predict all the outcomes reasonably expected from a well-functioning personality" (R. A. Thompson & Raikes, 2003, p. 708). But this expectation turned out not to be valid.

Securely attached infants *are* more likely to become secure toddlers, socially competent preschoolers, high-achieving schoolchildren, and capable parents (R. A. Thompson, 2006) (see Table 7.3). Some researchers find that secure attachment affects early brain development, one reason these later outcomes occur (Diamond & Fagundes, 2010). However, attachment status often shifts with family circumstances as children grow older and parents change. Harsh contexts, especially the stress of poverty, make secure attachment less likely (Seifer et al.,

TABLE 7.3	
Predictors of Attachment Type	

Secure attachment (type B) is more likely if:

- The parent is usually sensitive and responsive to the infant's needs.
- The infant–parent relationship is high in synchrony.
- The infant's temperament is "easy."
- The parents are not stressed about income, other children, or their marriage.
- The parents have a working model of secure attachment to their own parents.

Insecure attachment is more likely if:

- The parent mistreats the child. (Neglect increases type A; abuse increases types C and D.)
- The mother is mentally ill. (Paranoia increases type D; depression increases type C.)
- The parents are highly stressed about income, other children, or their marriage. (Parental stress increases types A and D.)
- The parents are intrusive and controlling. (Parental domination increases type A.)
- The parents are active alcoholics. (Alcoholic father increases type A; alcoholic mother increases type D.)
- The child's temperament is "difficult." (Difficult children tend to be type C.)
- The child's temperament is "slow to warm up." (This correlates with type A.)

2004; van IJzendoorn & Bakermans-Kranenburg, 2010). Thus, attachment is an important and useful measure, but it does not totally determine later development; plasticity is apparent with attachment as with other indicators.

Social Referencing

social referencing Seeking information about how to react to an unfamiliar or ambiguous object or event by observing someone else's expressions and reactions. That other person becomes a social reference.

At every age, people want to know what other people feel about the experiences they encounter. **Social referencing** refers to seeking emotions or information from other people, much as a student might consult a dictionary or other reference work. A glance of reassurance or words of caution; an expression of alarm, pleasure, or dismay—each becomes a social reference.

After age 1, when infants reach the stage of active exploration (Piaget) and the crisis of autonomy versus shame and doubt (Erikson), the need to consult others becomes urgent. Toddlers search for clues in gazes and facial expressions, paying close attention to emotions and intentions to understand what people do. Toddlers are selective in their social referencing: Even 16-month-olds notice which strangers are reliable references and which are not (Poulin-Dubois & Chow, 2009).

Social referencing has many practical applications. Consider mealtime. Caregivers the world over smack their lips, pretend to taste, and say "yum-yum," encouraging toddlers to eat and enjoy their first beets, liver, or spinach. For their part, toddlers become astute at reading expressions, insisting on the foods that the adults *really* like. Through this process, children in some cultures develop a taste for raw fish or curried goat or smelly cheese—foods that children in other cultures refuse. Similarly, toddlers are able to use their mother's cues to understand the difference between real and pretend eating (Nishida & Lillard, 2007).

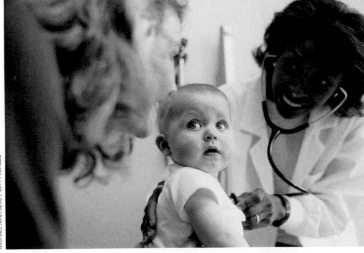

Whose Smile to Believe? Logically, the doctor is the one to watch: She has the stethoscope, and she is closer. But this baby references her mother, as any securely attached 1-year-old would.

MICHAEL MALYSZKO / GETTY IMAGES

Fathers as Social Partners

In most nations and ethnic groups, fathers spend much less time with infants than mothers do (Parke & Buriel, 2006; Tudge, 2008). Ethnotheories often limit father–child involvement, with some mothers believing that child care is the special domain of women (Gaertner et al., 2007) and some fathers thinking it unmanly to dote on an infant.

Some of these ethnotheories are changing. One obvious example is that of Latino fathers, who were said to be less involved with their infants than many other fathers. Research refutes this ethnotheory (Cabrera et al., 2006; Tamis-LaMonda et al., 2009). In the United States, many fathers of Mexican, Cuban, and Dominican heritage are active caregivers for their infants. Similar findings occur worldwide: Brazilian fathers seem to spend more time caring for their infants than do fathers in any other nation (Tudge, 2008). Among low-income families in the United States, the best predictor of a father's involvement with his infant is the father's relationship with the mother.

The normative involvement of Latino fathers has an unfortunate downside. If a biological Hispanic American father is absent, single Latinas seem to be more demanding of and less responsive to their infants than other single mothers (Cooper et al., 2009). Similar findings come from rural Mexico, where most infants are born to married parents, with fathers helping with infant care. However, when fathers are absent (usually because they have migrated to the United States to alleviate family poverty), infants are significantly more likely to become sick—a sign that the mothers find infant care more difficult (Schmeer, 2009).

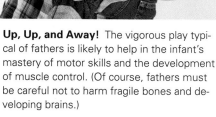

Up, Up, and Away! The vigorous play typical of fathers is likely to help in the infant's mastery of motor skills and the development of muscle control. (Of course, fathers must be careful not to harm fragile bones and developing brains.)

Comparing Fathers and Mothers

Fathers enhance their children's social and emotional development in many ways (Lamb, 2010). Synchrony, attachment, and social referencing are all apparent with fathers. Indeed, fathers are more likely to elicit smiles and laughter from their infants than mothers are. Close father–infant relationships can teach infants (especially boys) appropriate expressions of emotion (Boyce et al., 2006), particularly anger. The results may endure: Teenagers are less likely to lash out at friends and authorities if, as infants, they experienced a warm, responsive relationship with their fathers (Trautmann-Villalba et al., 2006). Close relationships with infants help the men, too, reducing the risk of depression (Borke et al., 2007; Bronte-Tinkew et al., 2007).

Contemporary fathers can and do feed, diaper, and bathe infants as well as mothers, but typically "mothers engage in more caregiving and comforting, and fathers in more high intensity play" (Kochanska et al., 2008, p. 41), such as moving their infant's limbs in imitation of walking, kicking, or climbing or swinging the baby through the air, sideways or even upside down. Fathers provide excitement; mothers caress, read, or sing.

Research on father–infant care has focused on three different questions over the past two decades (Bretherton, 2010; Lamb, 2010). The first and second questions were: Can fathers provide the same care as mothers? Is father–infant interaction different from mother–infant interaction? As you just read, many studies found that the answer to both questions was yes. The current question is: How do fathers and mothers interact to provide infant care? The answer seems to be that, in a well-functioning family, they cooperate and complement each other, each giving the infant what the other does not (Bretherton, 2010). Mothers are the usual caregivers and fathers the best playmates, but not always—each set of parents, given their circumstances (which might include being immigrant, gay, or low-income parents, or having a premature or disabled infant), finds their own way to make sure their infant thrives (Lamb, 2010).

Infant Day Care

Most infants are cared for exclusively by their mothers, with the rest usually cared for by relatives, usually fathers in the United States and grandmothers in most other nations (Leach, 2009). Worldwide, only about 15 percent of infants receive regular care from a nonrelative who is both paid and trained to provide it.

International Comparisons

The actual percentage of infants in nonrelative care varies markedly from nation to nation (Leach, 2009; Melhuish & Petrogiannis, 2006). Center-based care is common in France, Israel, China, and Sweden, where it is heavily subsidized by the government, and scarce in India, Ethiopia, and most Latin American nations, where it is not. North America is in between these extremes, but variation from place to place is apparent.

In the United States, only 20 percent of infants are cared for *exclusively* by their mothers (no other relatives or babysitters) in the first year, but in Canada 70 percent are (Côté et al., 2008). In England, only 9 percent of 4-month-olds are in regular nonmaternal care, but 48 percent of 1-year-olds are (Leach, 2009).

Both maternal employment and national policy have an impact. In Canada and England (as well as in most European nations), mothers have paid leave for a year after birth, and many wait even longer to return to work. In the United States, paid leave is shorter and less certain, and 58 percent of married mothers of babies younger than 12 months are in the labor force (rates are higher for mothers who are not married or who have slightly older infants) (U.S. Bureau of the Census, 2009). Obviously, these national differences are determined more by politics and culture than by the nature of babies.

Data from many European nations as well as Australia and New Zealand find that national policies regarding maternal leave (many nations pay mothers to stay home with their infants) as well as ethnotheories that include father caretaking markedly reduce the rate of out-of-home infant care. Divergent statistics on the incidence and consequences of such care in each nation are found because "informal in-family arrangements speak to the ingenuity of parents trying to cope but bedevil child care statistics" (Leach, 2009, p. 44).

Types of Nonmaternal Care

Most mothers who need someone else to provide some infant care prefer help from the baby's father. Many parents thus coordinate their work schedules so one or the other parent is always present. Grandmothers are also often caregivers in the first year, less so in the second as infants become more mobile and social (Leach, 2009).

When parents turn to paid nonrelatives, they may hire someone to come to the home, but usually they use **family day care,** in which the caregiver looks after a small group of young children in her (almost never his) home. The quality of family day care varies; sometimes, for example, infants and toddlers get less attention than older children, who resent them (Kryzer et al., 2007). As you know, providing physical care and ensuring safety are only the beginning of quality caretaking; ideally, the caregiver talks to and plays with the baby frequently.

family day care Child care that occurs in the home of someone to whom the child is not related and who usually cares for several children of various ages.

A better option may be **center day care,** in which licensed and educated adults care for several infants in a place designed for children. Most centers separate infants from older children. Ideally, the center (see Table 7.4) has ample safe space, appropriate equipment, trained providers, and two adults for a group of five or fewer infants (de Schipper et al., 2006). That setting advances cognitive and social skills: Toddlers are intrigued by other toddlers, and they have much to learn from interaction. No matter what form of day care is chosen, responsive, individualized continuity of care seems best (Morrissey, 2009)—changes in caregivers are difficult early in life, when each gesture or sound requires interpretation.

The Effects of Infant Day Care

The evidence is overwhelming that good preschool education (discussed in Chapter 9) benefits young children, especially in cognition. However, when it comes to infants, "disagreements about the wisdom (indeed, the morality) of nonmaternal child care for the very young remain" (NICHD Early Child Care Research Network, 2005, p. xiv). A major concern is that quality varies. Some caregivers with no training look after many infants—the result is inadequate care (Waldfogel, 2006).

The consequences of nonmaternal care are a subject of debate. The concern is that infants with extensive nonmaternal care tend to become more aggressive later on (Jacob, 2009), although some babies seem far more affected than others (Pluess & Belsky, 2009). In England, one study found that infants who were not exclusively in their mothers' care were less advanced emotionally (Fergusson et al., 2008). However, most of those infants were cared for by grandmothers, especially when the mothers were young and poor. Thus, nonmaternal care, grandmothers, maternal immaturity, or family SES could each be the reason for the emotional immaturity.

A large study in Canada found that when children were cared for by someone other than their mothers (usually relatives) in their first year, boys from high-income families fared less well than similar boys in exclusive maternal care: By age 4, they were slightly more assertive or aggressive and had more emotional problems (e.g., a teacher might note that a boy "seems unhappy"). The opposite was true for boys from low-income families: They seemed to benefit from nonmaternal care, again according to teacher reports. No effects were found for girls. The researchers insist that no policy implications can be derived from this study, partly because care varied so much in quality, location, and provider (Côté et al., 2008).

Research in the United States on low-income families also finds that center care is beneficial (Peng & Robins, 2010). For less impoverished children, an ongoing longitudinal study by the Early Child Care Network of the National Institute of Child Health and Human Development (NICHD) has followed the development of more than 1,300 children from birth to age 11. It has found many cognitive benefits of early day care, especially in language development. The social consequences are less clear (Loeb et al., 2005). Most analyses find that secure attachment to the mother was as common among infants in center care as among infants cared for at home. Like other, smaller studies, the NICHD research confirms that infant day care, even for 40 hours a week before age 1, has much less influence on child development than does the warmth of the mother–infant relationship.

The NICHD study has also found that infant day care seems detrimental when the mother is insensitive *and* the infant spends more than 20 hours a week in a poor-quality program with too many children per group (McCartney et al., 2010). Again, boys sometimes become more quarrelsome, having more conflicts with their teachers than did the girls or other boys with a different mix of maternal traits and day-care experiences.

center day care Child care that occurs in a place especially designed for the purpose, where several paid adults care for many children. Usually, the children are grouped by age, the day-care center is licensed, and providers are trained and certified in child development.

TABLE 7.4

High-Quality Day Care

High-quality day care during infancy has five essential characteristics:

1. *Adequate attention to each infant.* A small group of infants (no more than five) needs two reliable, familiar, loving caregivers. Continuity of care is crucial.

2. *Encouragement of language and sensorimotor development.* Infants need language—songs, conversations, and positive talk—and easily manipulated toys.

3. *Attention to health and safety.* Cleanliness routines (e.g., handwashing), accident prevention (e.g., no small objects), and safe areas to explore are essential.

4. *Professional caregivers.* Caregivers have experience and degrees/certificates in early-childhood education. Turnover is low, morale high, and enthusiasm evident.

5. *Warm and responsive caregivers.* Providers engage the children in active play and guide them in problem solving. Quiet, obedient children may indicate unresponsive care.

For a more detailed evaluation of day care, see the checklist in NICHD Early Child Care Research Network, 2005.

Especially for Day-Care Providers
A mother who brings her child to you for day care says that she knows she is harming her baby but must work out of economic necessity. What do you say? (see response, page 202)

The research is subject to many complications because of international variations, uncertainty about quality and extent of care (both at home and elsewhere), and the fact that choices are not random. It seems likely that family income and education affect choice of care, and those same variables affect child development. It also seems possible that mothers are less likely to stay home for two years with their active, difficult sons, which is why the average 5-year-old boy who was in family or center care at age 1 is slightly more aggressive than his classmate who had full-time maternal care in his early years. A careful summary of the longitudinal outcomes of nonmaternal infant care finds that "externalizing behavior is predicted from a constellation of variables in multiple contexts . . . and no study has found that children of employed mothers develop serious emotional or other problems *solely* because their mothers are working outside the home" (McCartney et al., 2010, pp. 1, 16).

Another complication is that children generally benefit if their mothers are employed (Goldberg et al., 2008), in part because maternal income reduces parental depression and increases family wealth, both of which correlate with happier and more successful children. It is certainly possible for employed mothers to make infant care their top priority, sometimes at the expense of their own self-care or marriage. A time-use study found that mothers who worked full time outside the home spent almost as much time playing with their babies (14½ hours a week) as did mothers with no outside jobs (16 hours a week) (Huston & Aronson, 2005). To make more time for their babies, the employed mothers spent half as much time on housework, less time with their husbands, and almost no time on leisure. The study concludes:

> There was no evidence that mothers' time at work interfered with the quality of their relationship with their infants, the quality of the home environment, or children's development. In fact, the results suggest the opposite. Mothers who spent more time at work provided slightly higher quality home environments.
>
> [Huston & Aronson, 2005, p. 479]

As you can see, researchers find mixed evidence on infant day care. Many factors are relevant: infant sex and temperament, family income and education, and especially the quality of care at home and elsewhere. As with many topics in this chapter, the numerical averages seem less revealing than the need for personal responsiveness to each infant.

SUMMING UP

Infants seek social bonds, which they develop with one or several people. Synchrony begins in the early months: Infants and caregivers interact face-to-face, making split-second adjustments in their emotional responses to each other. Synchrony evolves into attachment, an emotional connection. Secure attachment allows infants to learn; insecure infants are less confident and may develop emotional impairments. As infants become more curious and encounter new toys, people, and events, they use social referencing to learn whether such new things are fearsome or fun.

The emotional connections evident in synchrony, attachment, and social referencing may occur with mothers, fathers, other relatives, and day-care providers. Nations and families vary in how much nonmaternal infant care is provided and in the quality of that care; consequences also vary. Most employed mothers provide responsive care. Problems with later development may occur if an infant receives unresponsive care (as when one caregiver has too many infants or a depressed mother is the sole caregiver). Quality and continuity of care matter.

>> **Response for Day-Care Providers** (from page 201) Reassure the mother that you will keep her baby safe and will help to develop the baby's mind and social skills by fostering synchrony and attachment. Also tell her that the quality of mother–infant interaction at home is more important than anything else for psychosocial development; mothers who are employed full time usually have wonderful, secure relationships with their infants. If the mother wishes, you can discuss ways in which she can be a more responsive mother.

SUMMARY

Emotional Development

1. Two emotions, contentment and distress, appear as soon as an infant is born. Smiles and laughter are evident in the early months. Anger emerges after 4 months, when the infant is restricted, and becomes stronger and connected to experience by age 1.

2. Reflexive fear is apparent in very young infants. Fear of something specific, including fear of strangers and of separation, appears toward the end of the first year.

3. In the second year, social awareness produces more selective fear, anger, and joy. As infants become increasingly self-aware, emotions emerge that encourage an interface between the self and others—specifically, pride, shame, and affection.

4. Brain maturation has an obvious impact on emotional development, although specifics are not yet known. Synesthesia (connections between senses and emotions) is apparent early in life. Self-recognition (on the mirror/rouge test) emerges at about 18 months.

5. Stress impedes early brain and emotional development. Some infants are particularly vulnerable to the effects of early mistreatment.

6. Temperament is a set of genetic traits whose expression is influenced by the context. Inborn temperament is linked to later personality, although plasticity is also evident.

7. Parental practices inhibit and guide a child's emotions. Ideally, a good fit develops between the parents' actions and the child's personality.

Theories of Infant Psychosocial Development

8. According to all major theories, caregiver behavior is especially influential in the first two years. Freud stressed the mother's impact on oral and anal pleasure; Erikson emphasized trust and autonomy.

9. Behaviorists focus on learning; parents teach their babies many things, including when to be fearful or joyful. Cognitive theory holds that infants develop working models based on their experiences.

10. The sociocultural approach notes the impact of social and cultural factors on the parent–infant relationship. Ethnotheories shape infant emotions and traits so that they fit well within the culture. Some cultures encourage proximal parenting (more physical touch); others, distal parenting (more talk and object play).

The Development of Social Bonds

11. Sometimes by 2 months, and clearly by 6 months, infants become more responsive and social, and synchrony begins. Synchrony involves moment-by-moment interaction. Infants are disturbed by a still face because they expect and need social interaction.

12. Attachment, measured by the baby's reaction to the caregiver's presence, departure, and return in the Strange Situation, is crucial. Some infants seem indifferent (type A attachment—insecure-avoidant) or overly dependent (type C—insecure-resistant/ambivalent), instead of secure (type B). Disorganized attachment (type D) is the most worrisome.

13. Secure attachment provides encouragement for infant exploration. As they play, toddlers engage in social referencing, looking to other people's facial expressions to detect what is frightening and what is fun.

14. Fathers are wonderful playmates for infants, who frequently use them as social references, learning about emotions and exploration. Male ethnotheories sometimes inhibit father involvement; mothers sometimes discourage it, but many modern fathers complement the mother's infant care: Babies are happier because of it.

15. The impact of nonmaternal care depends on many factors; it varies from one nation to another and probably from one child to another. Quality of care (responsive, individualized) is crucial, no matter who provides that care.

KEY TERMS

social smile (p. 180)
stranger wariness (p. 180)
separation anxiety (p. 181)
self-awareness (p. 181)
temperament (p. 183)
goodness of fit (p. 185)
trust versus mistrust (p. 187)

autonomy versus shame and
  doubt (p. 187)
social learning (p. 188)
working model (p. 189)
ethnotheory (p. 189)
proximal parenting (p. 190)
distal parenting (p. 190)
synchrony (p. 193)

still-face technique (p. 194)
attachment (p. 195)
secure attachment (type B)
  (p. 196)
insecure-avoidant attachment
  (type A) (p. 196)
insecure-resistant/ambivalent
  attachment (type C) (p. 196)

disorganized attachment
  (type D) (p. 196)
Strange Situation (p. 197)
social referencing (p. 198)
family day care (p. 200)
center day care (p. 201)

WHAT HAVE YOU LEARNED?

Emotional Development

1. What are the first emotions to appear in very young infants?

2. What are 1-year-olds afraid of?

3. How do the emotions of the second year of life differ from those of the first year?

4. How does stress during infancy affect brain development?

5. Why does synesthesia seem to be more common in infants than in adults?

6. Why are temperamental traits more apparent in some people than others?

Theories of Infant Psychosocial Development

7. What are the similarities and differences between the oral stage and the trust-versus-mistrust stage?

8. What are the similarities and differences between the anal stage and the autonomy-versus-shame-and-doubt stage?

9. How would behaviorists explain family and cultural patterns of personality traits?

10. Why does the idea of a "working model" arise from cognitive theory instead of the other theories?

11. What would be the beliefs of an ethnotheory that supports proximal parenting?

12. What would be the beliefs of an ethnotheory that supports distal parenting?

The Development of Social Bonds

13. How does synchrony help infants learn about emotions?

14. Is it possible to overemphasize the importance of secure attachment? Why or why not?

15. In what circumstances would an infant develop type A attachment?

16. In what circumstances would an infant develop type C attachment?

17. In what circumstances would an infant develop type D attachment?

18. For infants, how is father care different from, and similar to, mother care?

19. Why are most infants, in most nations, cared for exclusively by their mothers?

20. What are the differences among grandmother care, family day care, and center day care?

21. For which infants does early day care correlate with aggression in kindergarten?

22. Why is it difficult to draw definite conclusions about infant day care?

APPLICATIONS

1. One cultural factor influencing infant development is how infants are carried from place to place. Ask four mothers whose infants were born in each of the past four decades how they transported them—front or back carriers, facing out or in, strollers or carriages, car seats or on mother's lap, and so on. Why did they choose the mode(s) they chose? What are their opinions and yours on how that cultural practice might affect infants' development?

2. Observe synchrony for three minutes. Ideally, ask the parent of an infant younger than 8 months of age to play with the infant.

If no infant is available, observe a pair of lovers as they converse. Note the sequence and timing of every facial expression, sound, and gesture of both partners.

3. Telephone several day-care centers to try to assess the quality of care they provide. Ask about such factors as adult–child ratio, group size, and training for caregivers of children of various ages. Is there a minimum age? If so, why was that age chosen? Analyze the answers, using Table 7.4 as a guide.

>>ONLINE CONNECTIONS

To accompany your textbook, you have access to a number of online resources, including quizzes for every chapter of the book, flashcards (in English and Spanish), critical thinking questions, and case studies. For access to any of these links, go to www.worthpublishers.com/bergerls8e. In addition to these free resources, you'll also find links to the podcasts, video clips, diagnostic quizzing with personalized study advice, and an ebook. Some of the videos and activities available online include:

- *Attachment Behaviors in the Strange Situation.* You'll get a chance to watch—and take your best guess about attachment states—as some infants are left in the company of strangers.

- *Child Care.* A variety of videos showcase different types of early child care and different strategies for best practices.

The First Two Years

BIOSOCIAL

Body Changes Over the first two years, body weight quadruples and brain weight triples. Connections between brain cells grow dense, with complex networks of dendrites and axons. Neurons become coated with myelin, sending messages more efficiently. Experiences that are universal (experience-expectant) and culture-bound (experience-dependent) aid brain growth, partly by pruning unused connections between neurons.

Senses and Motor Skills Brain maturation underlies the development of all the senses. Seeing, hearing, and mobility progress from reflexes to coordinated voluntary actions, including focusing, grasping, and walking. Culture is evident in sensory and motor development, as brain networks respond to the particulars of each infant's life.

Public Health Infant health depends on immunization, parental practices (including "back to sleep"), and nutrition. Breast milk protects health and has so many other benefits that the World Health Organization recommends exclusive breast-feeding for the first six months. Survival rates are much higher today than even a few decades ago, yet in some regions, infant growth is still stunted because of malnutrition.

COGNITIVE

Sensorimotor Intelligence and Information Processing As Piaget describes it, in the first two years, infants progress from knowing their world through immediate sensory experiences to "experimenting" on that world through actions and mental images. Information-processing theory stresses the links between sensory experiences and perception. Infants develop their own ideas regarding the possibilities offered by the objects and events of the world. Research over the past two decades finds traces of memory at 3 months, of object permanence at 4 months, and of deferred imitation at 9 months—all much younger ages than Piaget described.

Language Interaction with responsive adults exposes infants to the structure of communication and language. By age 1, infants usually speak a word or two; by age 2, language has exploded—toddlers talk in short sentences and add vocabulary each day. Language develops through reinforcement, neurological maturation, and social motivation; all three processes combine to create a very conversational toddler.

PSYCHOSOCIAL

Emotions and Theories Emotions develop from newborn reactions to complex, self-conscious responses. Infants' self-awareness and independence are shaped by parents, in a transition explained by Freud's oral and anal stages, by Erikson's crises of trust versus mistrust and autonomy versus shame and doubt, by behaviorism's focus on parental responses, and by cognitive theory's working models. Much of basic temperament is inborn and apparent throughout life. Sociocultural theory stresses cultural norms, evident in parents' ethnotheories in raising their infants; some parents are more proximal (encouraging touch), others more distal (encouraging cognition).

The Development of Social Bonds Parents and infants respond to each other by synchronizing their behavior. Toward the end of the first year, secure attachment to the parent sets the stage for the child's increasingly independent exploration of the world. Insecure attachment—avoidant, resistant, or disorganized—signifies a parent–child relationship that hinders learning. Infants actively participate socially, using social referencing to interpret their experiences. Mothers, fathers, and day-care providers encourage infants' social confidence.

early childhood

From age 2 to age 6, children spend most of their waking hours discovering, creating, laughing, and imagining, as they acquire the skills they need. They chase each other and attempt new challenges (developing their bodies); they play with sounds, words, and ideas (developing their minds); they invent games and dramatize fantasies (learning social skills and morals).

These years have been called *the preschool years,* but that has become a misnomer. School no longer means sitting at desks in rows. Many 2- to 6-year-olds are in "school," learning and playing. These years have also been called *the play years.* The young child's delight in life seems magical—whether quietly tracking a beetle through the grass or riotously turning a bedroom into a shambles. Young children's minds seem playful, too; they explain that "a bald man has a barefoot head" or that "the sun shines so children can go outside to play." But people of all ages play, so we should not imply these are the only play years.

Therefore, we now call this *early childhood*, the traditional term to refer to ages 2 to 6. Early childhood is a period of extraordinary growth, learning, and play, joyful not only for young children but also for anyone who knows them—and a time for impressive growth in every domain.

CHAPTER **8**

Early Childhood: Biosocial Development

WHAT WILL YOU KNOW?

1. How does the shape of the child's body change from age 2 to age 6?
2. What should parents remember about young children's eating and appetite?
3. What is the relationship among brain development, hand preference, and emotional control?
4. Why are young children vulnerable to serious injuries, abuse, and neglect?
5. What are the three levels of prevention that reduce injury and maltreatment?

I remember as a child leaping off the back of our couch again and again, trying to fly. My mother laughed but also wondered whether it had been a mistake to let me see *Peter Pan*. An older family friend warned that jumping would hurt my uterus. I didn't know what a uterus was, nor did I stop until I decided I could not fly because I had no pixie dust.

When you were 3 years old, I hope you also wanted to fly and I hope someone laughed while making sure to keep you safe. Protection and appreciation are needed, as well as fantasy. Do you remember trying to skip, tie your shoes, or write your name? Three-year-olds try, fail, try again until they are able to master various skills. Later they understand some of life's limitations: Humans have no wings. Advances in brain and body, and the need for adult protection, are the themes of this chapter.

>> Body Changes

In early childhood as in infancy, the body and brain develop according to powerful epigenetic forces, biologically driven and socially guided, experience-expectant and experience-dependent (as explained in Chapter 5). Bodies and brains mature in size and function.

Growth Patterns

Just comparing a toddling 1-year-old and a cartwheeling 6-year-old makes some differences obvious. During early childhood, children slim down as the lower body lengthens and fat turns to muscle. In fact, the body mass index (or BMI, the ratio of weight to height) is lower at age 5 than at any other age in the first five years (Guillaume & Lissau, 2002). Gone are the toddler's protruding belly, round face, short limbs, and large head. The center of gravity moves from the breast to the belly, enabling cartwheels, somersaults, and many other motor skills. The joys of dancing, gymnastics, and pumping a swing become possible; changing body proportions enable new achievements year by year.

Not Much Difference? The 6-year-old is only about a foot taller than her 2-year-old sister, and the width of their upper legs is almost the same. However, we perceive the older girl as much bigger than the younger one because we notice proportions: The older girl's legs are almost twice as long, and they account for half her height.

Victory! Well, maybe not quite yet, but he's certainly on his way. This boy is part of a British effort to combat childhood obesity; mother and son exercising in Liverpool Park is part of the solution. Harder to implement are dietary changes—many parents let children eat as much as they want.

Increases in weight and height accompany these new proportions. Each year of early childhood, well-nourished children gain about 4½ pounds (2 kilograms) and grow almost 3 inches (about 7 centimeters). By age 6, the average child in a developed nation:

- Weighs between 40 and 50 pounds (between 18 and 22 kilograms)
- Is at least 3½ feet tall (more than 100 centimeters)
- Looks lean, not chubby (ages 5–6 are lowest in body fat)
- Has adultlike body proportions (legs constitute about half the total height)

When many ethnic groups live together in a nation with abundant food and adequate medical care, children of African descent tend to be tallest, followed by those of European descent, then Asians, and then Latinos. However, height differences are greater *within* ethnic groups than *between* groups.

Nutrition

Over the centuries, low-income families encouraged their children to eat, protecting them against famine. This saved lives. Even today in the poorest nations, malnutrition contributes to one-third of all child deaths (UNICEF, 2008) and slows later growth. For instance, hungry young children in Ghana often became depressed or mentally impaired adolescents, although few are delinquents (Appoh, 2004; Appoh & Krekling, 2004).

Unfortunately, the well-intentioned practice of encouraging young children to eat can become destructive when food is abundant. This is true in many nations: In Brazil 30 years ago, the most common nutritional problem was undernutrition; now it is overnutrition (Monteiro et al., 2004), with low-income Brazilians particularly vulnerable (Monteiro et al., 2007). A detailed study of 2- to 4-year-olds in low-income families in New York City found many overweight children, with an increase in weight as family income fell (J. A. Nelson et al., 2004) and as children grew older (14 percent at age 2; 27 percent at age 4). This suggests that eating habits, not genes, were the cause. Overweight children were more often Latino (27 percent) or Asian American (22 percent) than Americans or African (14 percent) or European (11 percent) descent.

One explanation for these ethnic differences is that many of these children lived with grandparents who knew firsthand the dangers of malnutrition. This possibility is supported by generational data: Latino and Asian American grandparents are unlikely to be obese themselves but often have overweight grandchildren (Bates et al., 2008).

An epidemic of heart disease and diabetes is spreading worldwide as overfed children become overweight adults (Gluckman & Hanson, 2006). An article in *Lancet* (the leading medical journal in England) predicted that by 2020, 228 million adults worldwide will have diabetes (more in India than in any other nation) as a result of unhealthy eating habits acquired in childhood. This article suggests that measures to reduce childhood overeating in the United States have been inadequate and that "U.S. children could become the first generation in more than a century to have shorter life spans than their parents if current trends of excessive weight and obesity continue" (Devi, 2008, p. 105).

Appetite decreases between ages 2 and 6 because, compared with infants, young children need fewer calories per pound. This is especially true for the current generation, since children play outdoors less than their parents or grandparents did. However, instead of accepting this natural change, many parents fret, threaten, and cajole their children to overeat ("Eat all your dinner and you can have ice cream").

Nutritional Deficiencies

Although most children in developed nations consume more than enough calories, they do not always obtain adequate iron, zinc, and calcium. For example, children drink less milk, which means less calcium. Another problem is too much sugar. Many cultures encourage children to eat sweets—in birthday cake, holiday candy, desserts, and other treats.

Sweetened cereals and drinks (advertised as containing 100 percent of daily vitamins) are a poor substitute for a balanced, varied diet, partly because some nutrients have not yet been identified, much less listed on food labels. This means that eating a wide variety of foods may be essential. Preschoolers who eat more orange and dark green vegetables and less fried food than the average child their age benefit in many ways. They gain bone mass but not fat, according to a study that controlled for other factors that might correlate with body fat, such as gender (girls have more), ethnicity (people of some ethnic groups are genetically thinner), and income (poor children have worse diets) (Wosje et al., 2010).

Oral Health

Too much sugar and too little fiber cause tooth decay, the most common disease of young children in developed nations, affecting more than one-third of all U.S. children under age 6 (Brickhouse et al., 2008). Sugary fruit drinks and soda are prime culprits; even diet soda contains acid that makes decay more likely (Holtzman, 2009).

Fortunately, "baby" teeth are replaced at about ages 6 to 10. However, severe tooth decay in early childhood harms those permanent teeth (which form below the first teeth) and can cause jaw malformation, chewing difficulties, and speech problems. The teeth are affected by diet and illness, which means that the state of a young child's teeth can alert adults to other health problems.

Many preschoolers visit the dentist if they have U.S.-born, middle-class parents but not if their parents were born elsewhere. A study in San Francisco found that fear of the dentist was common among immigrants from China, who were unlikely to take their young children for an oral health checkup (Hilton et al., 2007). Many low-income parents of all ethnic groups are overwhelmed with work and child care and do not realize that tooth brushing is vital (Mofidi et al., 2009).

Hazards of "Just Right"

Many young children are compulsive about their daily routines, including meals. They insist on eating only certain foods, prepared and placed in a particular way. This rigidity, known as the "just right" or "just so" phenomenon, would be a sign of a pathological obsessive-compulsive disorder in adults but is normal and widespread among young children (Evans & Leckman, 2006). For example:

> Whereas parents may insist that the child eat his vegetables at dinner, the child may insist that the potatoes be placed only in a certain part of the plate and must not touch any other food; should the potatoes land outside of this area, the child may seem to experience a sense of near-contamination, setting off a tirade of fussiness for which many 2- and 3-year-olds are notorious.
>
> [Evans et al., 1997, p. 59]

Most children's food preferences and rituals are far from ideal. (One 3-year-old I know wanted to eat only cream cheese sandwiches on white bread; one 4-year-old,

"I'm not hungry. I ate with Rover."

Eat Your Veggies On their own, children do not always eat wisely.

Especially for Nutritionists A parent complains that she prepares a variety of vegetables and fruits, but her 4-year-old wants only French fries and cake. What should you advise? (see response, page 214)

only fast-food chicken nuggets.) When 1,500 parents of 1- to 6-year-olds were surveyed (Evans et al., 1997), they reported that the just-right phase peaked at about age 3, when children:

- Preferred to have things done in a particular order or in a certain way
- Had a strong preference to wear (or not wear) certain articles of clothing
- Prepared for bedtime by engaging in a special activity, routine, or ritual
- Had strong preferences for certain foods

By age 6, this rigidity fades somewhat (see Figure 8.1). Another team of experts puts it this way: "Most, if not all, children exhibit normal age-dependent obsessive compulsive behaviors [that are] usually gone by middle childhood" (March et al., 2004, p. 216). The best reaction may be patience: A young child's insistence on a particular routine, a preferred pair of shoes, or a favorite cup can be accommodated for a year or two. After all, adults also have preferred routines, keeping obsessions in check with some rational thinking (Evans & Leckman, 2006).

Overeating is another story. If the social context of early childhood (television commercials, store displays, other children's eating) encourages too much consumption, childhood obesity will lead to later illness. Unfortunately, most parents believe that a child who is consistently in the 20th weight percentile is less healthy than one in the 80th percentile, although the opposite is true (Laraway et al., 2010). Pediatricians need to provide parents of 2- to 5-year-olds with "anticipatory guidance" (Collins et al., 2004), since prevention is better than putting a 6-year-old on a diet (as some pediatricians do).

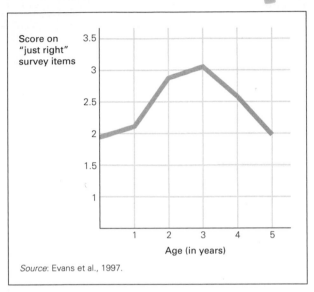

Source: Evans et al., 1997.

FIGURE 8.1

Young Children's Insistence on Routine
This chart shows the average scores of children (who are rated by their parents) on a survey indicating the child's desire to have certain things—including food selection and preparation—done "just right." Such strong preferences for rigid routines tend to fade by age 6.

SUMMING UP

Between ages 2 and 6, children grow taller and proportionately thinner, with variations depending on genes, nutrition, income, and ethnicity. Nutrition and oral health are serious concerns, as many children are overweight and have cavities. Young children usually have small appetites and picky eating habits. Unfortunately, many adults encourage overeating, particularly if malnutrition was a problem in their childhood culture, not realizing that too much fat, once protective, now leads to life-threatening illness. ■

>> Brain Development

Brains grow rapidly before birth and throughout infancy, as you saw in Chapter 5. By age 2, most neurons connect to other neurons and substantial pruning has occurred. The 2-year-old's brain weighs 75 percent of what it will weigh in adulthood. (The major structures of the brain are diagrammed in Figure 8.2.)

Since most of the brain is already present and functioning by age 2, what remains to develop? The most important parts! Those functions of the brain that make us most human are the ones that develop after infancy, enabling quicker, better coordinated, and more reflective thought (Kagan & Herschkowitz, 2005). Between ages 2 and 6, the brain grows from 75 percent to 90 percent of adult weight, with increases particularly in the areas that allow advanced language and social understanding. The size of the cortex is a crucial difference between humans and other animals. Elephants, crows, lower primates, and dolphins have all surprised researchers in recent decades with their intelligence, but none are close to *Homo sapiens* in their social understanding.

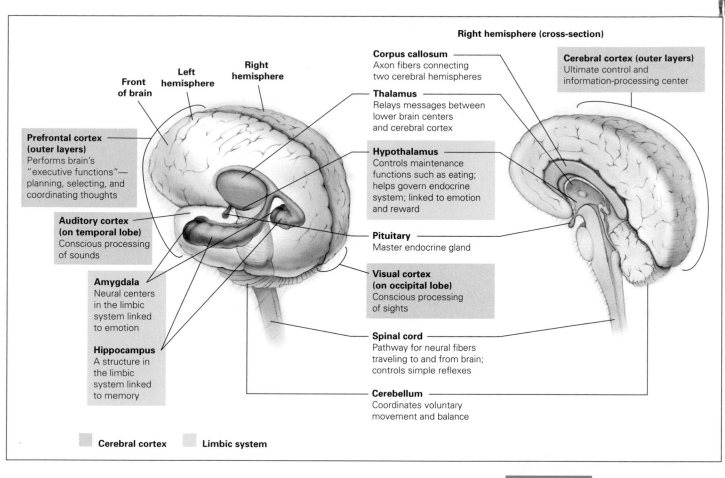

Corpus callosum
Axon fibers connecting
two cerebral hemispheres

Cerebral cortex (outer layers)
Ultimate control and
information-processing center

Left hemisphere

Right hemisphere

Front of brain

Thalamus
Relays messages between
lower brain centers
and cerebral cortex

Prefrontal cortex (outer layers)
Performs brain's
"executive functions"—
planning, selecting, and
coordinating thoughts

Hypothalamus
Controls maintenance
functions such as eating;
helps govern endocrine
system; linked to emotion
and reward

Auditory cortex (on temporal lobe)
Conscious processing
of sounds

Pituitary
Master endocrine gland

Amygdala
Neural centers
in the limbic
system linked
to emotion

Visual cortex (on occipital lobe)
Conscious processing
of sights

Hippocampus
A structure in
the limbic
system linked
to memory

Spinal cord
Pathway for neural fibers
traveling to and from brain;
controls simple reflexes

Cerebellum
Coordinates voluntary
movement and balance

Cerebral cortex   Limbic system

FIGURE 8.2

Connections A few of the dozens of named parts of the brain are shown here. Although each area has particular functions, the entire brain is interconnected. The processing of emotions, for example, occurs primarily in the limbic system, but many other brain areas are involved.

For example, a careful series of tests given to 106 chimpanzees, 32 orangutans, and 105 human 2½-year-olds found that young children were "equivalent . . . to chimpanzees [and better than orangutans] on tasks of physical cognition but far outstripped both chimpanzees and orangutans on tasks of social cognition" such as pointing or following someone's gaze (Herrmann et al., 2007, p. 1365).

Speed of Thought

After infancy, some brain growth is the result of proliferation of the communication pathways (dendrites and axons). However, most increased brain weight occurs because of **myelination.** *Myelin* is a fatty coating on the axons that speeds signals between neurons.

The effects of myelination are notable in early childhood (Nelson, Thomas et al., 2006), partly because the areas of the brain that show greatest early myelination are the motor and sensory areas (Kolb & Whishaw, 2008). Greater speed of thought becomes pivotal when several thoughts must occur in rapid succession. By age 6, most children can see an object and immediately name it, catch a ball and throw it, write their ABCs in proper sequence, and so on.

Parents must still be patient when listening to young children talk, helping them get dressed, or watching them write the first letter of their name. Everything is done more slowly by 6-year-olds than by 16-year-olds, because information processing is slower. However, thanks to myelination, preschoolers are much quicker than toddlers, who may forget what they were doing before they finish.

myelination The process by which axons become coated with myelin, a fatty substance that speeds the transmission of nerve impulses from neuron to neuron.

Especially for Early-Childhood Teachers You know you should be patient, but you feel your frustration rising when your young charges dawdle on the walk to the playground a block away. What should you do? (see response, page 215)

corpus callosum A long, thick band of nerve fibers that connects the left and right hemispheres of the brain and allows communication between them.

lateralization Literally, sidedness, referring to the specialization in certain functions by each side of the brain, with one side dominant for each activity. The left side of the brain controls the right side of the body, and vice versa.

Signing His Artwork A large sheet of paper and a marker are excellent equipment for brain exercise in early childhood.

Observation Quiz How is this boy different from more than 90 percent of other 3-year-olds? (see answer, page 216)

>> Response for Nutritionists (from page 212) The nutritionally wise advice would be to offer only fruits, vegetables, and other nourishing, low-fat foods, counting on the child's eventual hunger to drive him or her to eat them. However, centuries of cultural custom make it almost impossible for parents to be wise in such cases. A physical checkup, with a blood test, may be warranted to make sure the child is healthy.

Connecting the Brain's Hemispheres

One part of the brain that grows and myelinates rapidly during early childhood is the **corpus callosum,** a long, thick band of nerve fibers that connects the left and right sides of the brain. Growth of the corpus callosum makes communication between the hemispheres more efficient, allowing children to coordinate the two sides of the brain or body. Failure of the corpus callosum to develop results in serious disorders: This is one of several possible causes of autism (Frazier & Hardan, 2009).

To understand the significance of the corpus callosum, note that the two sides of the body and of the brain are not identical. Each side specializes, each being dominant for certain functions—the result of **lateralization,** literally "sidedness," which is apparent not only in right- or left-handedness but also in the feet, the eyes, the ears, and the brain itself. Genes, prenatal hormones, and early experiences all affect which side does what. Lateralization advances with development of the corpus callosum (Boles et al., 2008).

The Left-Handed Child

Infants and toddlers usually prefer one hand over the other for grabbing spoons and rattles. Handedness is partly genetic (Goymer, 2007), but many cultures have tried to make everyone right-handed. When parents forced their left-handed children to use their right hands, the result was a left-handed child who wrote right-handedly. However, neurological success was incomplete: Their brains were only partly reprogrammed (Klöppel et al., 2007).

Even today, many cultures endorse the belief that being right-handed is best, an example of the *difference-equals-deficit error,* explained in Chapter 1. Consider language. In English, a "left-handed compliment" is insincere, and no one wants to have "two left feet" or be "out in left field." In Latin, *dexter* (as in *dexterity*) means "right" and *sinister* means "left" (and also "evil"). *Gauche,* the French word for *left,* means "socially awkward" in English. Most languages are written from left to right.

Customs also favor the right hand. Doorknobs, scissors, baseball mitts, instrument panels, and other objects are designed for right-handed people. (Some manufacturers have special versions for lefties, but few young children know to ask for them.) In many Asian and African cultures, the left hand is used only for wiping after defecation; it is an insult to give someone anything with that "dirty" hand.

Developmentalists advise against switching a child's handedness, not only because this causes conflict but also because it interferes with lateralization. Left-handed adults tend to have a thicker corpus callosum, probably because growing up in a world that favors right-handedness means they had a greater need as children to coordinate the two sides of their bodies (Cherbuin & Brinkman, 2006). This may correlate with creativity and flexibility. A disproportionate number of artists, musicians, and sports stars were/are left-handed, including Michelangelo, Seal, Jimi Hendrix, Paul McCartney, Larry Bird, and Sandy Koufax. Four of the past six presidents of the United States were/are lefties: Ronald Reagan, Jimmy Carter, Bill Clinton, and Barack Obama.

The Whole Brain

Through studies of people with brain damage as well as through brain imaging of humans and many other vertebrates, scientists have discovered how the brain's hemispheres specialize (Rogers & Andrew, 2008). Generally, the left half controls the right side of the body and contains areas dedicated to logical reasoning, detailed analysis, and the basics of language; the right half controls the left side of the body and contains areas dedicated to generalized emotional and creative impulses, including appreciation of most music, art, and poetry. Thus, the left side notices details and the right side grasps the big picture—a distinction that should provide a clue in interpreting Figure 8.3.

This distinction has been exaggerated, especially when applied to people. No one is exclusively left-brained or right-brained (except severely brain-damaged individuals). Every cognitive skill requires both sides of the brain. Because older children have more myelinated fibers in the corpus callosum to speed signals between the two hemispheres, they are better at thinking as well as less clumsy.

Planning and Analyzing

You learned in Chapter 5 that the *prefrontal cortex* (sometimes called the *frontal cortex* or *frontal lobe*) is an area in the very front part of the brain's outer layers (the cortex), just behind the forehead. The prefrontal cortex is crucial for humans; it is said to be the executive of the brain because all the other areas of the cortex are ruled by the planning, prioritizing, and reflection in the prefrontal cortex. For example, someone might feel anxious on meeting a new person whose friendship might be valuable. The prefrontal cortex can calculate and plan, not letting the anxious feelings interfere. Young children are much less adept than adults at such social understanding and planning because the crucial functions of this part of the brain have not yet developed (Kolb & Whishaw, 2008).

Brain maturation is partly genetic, but early experience matters (Lenroot & Giedd, 2008). Control of anxiety, for instance, depends not only on the child's age and temperament but also on parental understanding and guidance. At age 18, brain scans of the prefrontal cortex and amygdala (soon described) still show inborn inhibition, but most people no longer act in extremely anxious ways (Schwartz et al., 2010).

Maturation of the Prefrontal Cortex

The frontal lobe "shows the most prolonged period of postnatal development of any region of the human brain" (M. H. Johnson, 2005, p. 210), with dendrite density and myelination increasing throughout childhood and adolescence. Although much remains to develop, over the years of early childhood maturation of the prefrontal cortex is already evident as:

- Sleep becomes more regular.
- Emotions become more nuanced and responsive to specific stimuli.
- Temper tantrums subside.
- Uncontrollable laughter and tears become less common.

In one series of experiments, 3-year-olds consistently made a stunning mistake (Zelazo et al., 2003). The children were given a set of cards with clear outlines of trucks or flowers, some red and some blue. They were asked to "play the shape game," putting trucks in one pile and flowers in another. Three-year-olds can do this correctly, as can some 2-year-olds and almost all older children.

Then the children were asked to "play the color game," sorting the cards by color. Most of them failed at this task, instead sorting by shape again. This study has been replicated in many nations; 3-year-olds usually get stuck in their initial sorting pattern (Diamond & Kirkham, 2005). Most older children, even 4-year-olds, can make the switch.

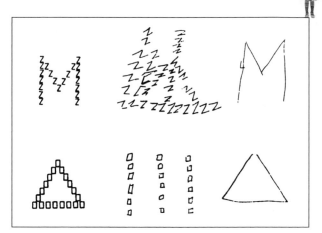

FIGURE 8.3

Copy What You See Brain-damaged adults were asked to copy the leftmost figure in each row. One person drew the middle set, another the set at the right.

Observation Quiz Which set was drawn by someone with left-side damage and which set by someone with right-side damage? (see answer, page 217)

>> Response for Early-Childhood Teachers (from page 213) One solution is to remind yourself that the children's brains are not yet myelinated enough to enable them to quickly walk, talk, or even button their jackets. Maturation has a major effect, as you will observe if you can schedule excursions in September and again in April. Progress, while still slow, will be a few seconds faster in April than it was in September.

>> **Answer to Observation Quiz** (from page 214) He is left-handed.

When this result was first obtained, experimenters wondered whether the problem was that the children didn't know their colors; so the scientists switched the order, first playing "the color game." Most 3-year-olds did that correctly. Then, when they were asked to play "the shape game," they sorted by color again. Even with a new set of cards, such as yellow or green rabbits or boats, they still tended to sort by the criterion that was used in their first trial (either color or shape).

Researchers are looking into many possible explanations for this surprising result (Müller et al., 2006; Yerys & Munakata, 2006). All agree, however, that something in the executive function of the brain must mature before children are able to switch from one way of sorting objects to another.

Prefrontal maturation is also demonstrated in the game Simon Says, in which children are supposed to follow the leader *only* when orders are preceded by the words "Simon says." Thus, when leaders touch their noses and say, "Simon says touch your nose," children are supposed to touch their noses; but when leaders touch their noses and merely say, "Touch your nose," no one is supposed to follow the example. Young children quickly lose at Simon Says because they impulsively do what they see and are told to do. Older children can think before acting. (Maturation of the prefrontal cortex is also discussed in Chapters 5, 11, and 14.)

Impulsiveness and Perseveration

Neurons have only two kinds of impulses: on or off, to activate or to inhibit. Each is signaled by biochemical messages from axon to dendrite. Both activation and inhibition are necessary for thoughtful adults, who neither leap too quickly nor hesitate too long. A balanced brain is most effective throughout life.

Many young children have not yet found the balance. Some 3-year-olds cannot stay on one task, even in church or any other place that requires quiet. Similarly, a young child may want a toy that another child has but then lose interest when the toy becomes available. Few 3-year-olds are capable of the kind of sustained attention that is pivotal for most learning in elementary school.

By contrast, some children play with a single toy for hours. **Perseveration** refers to the tendency to persevere in, or stick to, one thought or action—evident in the card-sorting study just described. It is also apparent to anyone who listens to a young child repeat one phrase or question again and again, or to anyone who witnesses a tantrum if a child's favorite TV show is interrupted. That tantrum itself may perseverate: The young child's crying may become uncontrollable and unstoppable, as if the child is stuck in the emotion that triggered the tantrum.

Impulsiveness and perseveration are opposite manifestations of the same underlying cause: immaturity of the prefrontal cortex. Remember from Chapter 7 that the ability to regulate attention is one trait that varies notably from child to child. Of course, no young child excels at regulating attention, and both impulsiveness and perseveration are evident (Else-Quest et al., 2006). However, over the years of childhood, with brain maturation (innate) and emotional regulation (learned), children gradually can pay attention as needed (de Haan & Johnson, 2003).

As with all biological maturation, some of this is related to culture—hence the reason this chapter is called *biosocial development,* not simply *physical development.* A study of Korean preschoolers found that the children had earlier attention control and less perseveration than a comparable group of English children (Oh & Lewis, 2008). This study included the shape/color task: Of the 3-year-olds, 40 percent

perseveration The tendency to persevere in, or stick to, one thought or action for a long time.

Ashes to Ashes, Dust to Dust Many religious rituals have sustained humans of all ages for centuries, including listening quietly in church on Ash Wednesday—as Nailah Pierre tries to do. This is developmentally difficult for young children, but for three reasons she probably will succeed: (1) gender (girls mature earlier than boys), (2) experience (she has been in church many times) and (3) social context (she is one of 750 students in her school attending a special service at Nativity Catholic Church).

ZUMA PRESS PHOTOS VIA NEWSCOM

of the Koreans but only 14 percent of the Britons successfully shifted from sorting by shape to sorting by color. The researchers explored many possible explanations, including genes, but they "feel that a cultural explanation is more likely" (Oh & Lewis, 2008, p. 96). They also called for replication of the study, particularly with Korean-born children who are adopted and raised in British homes.

Emotions and the Brain

Now that we have looked at the executive functions of the prefrontal cortex, we turn to another region of the brain, sometimes called the *limbic system.* Both the expression and the regulation of emotions advance during early childhood (more about that in Chapter 10). Three major areas of the limbic system—the amygdala, the hippocampus, and the hypothalamus—are part of this advance.

The Amygdala

The **amygdala** is a tiny structure deep in the brain, named after an almond because it is about the same shape and size. It registers emotions, both positive and negative, especially fear (Kolb & Whishaw, 2008). Increased amygdala activity is one reason some young children have terrifying nightmares or sudden terrors, which overwhelms the prefrontal cortex and disrupts reason. If a child is terrified of, say, a lion in the closet, an adult should not laugh but might open the closet door and command the lion to go home.

Children watch their parents' emotions closely. If a parent looks worried when entering an elevator, that child may fearfully cling to the parent when the elevator moves. If this sequence recurs often enough, the child's amygdala may become hypersensitive to elevators. If, instead, the parent seems calm and makes elevator riding fun (letting the child push the buttons, for instance), the child will overcome initial feelings of fear.

The Hippocampus

Another structure in the brain's limbic system, the **hippocampus,** is located right next to the amygdala. A central processor of memory, especially memory for locations, the hippocampus responds to the anxieties of the amygdala by summoning memory; a child can remember, for instance, whether elevator riding was scary or fun. Memories of location are fragile in early childhood because the hippocampus is still developing. Nonetheless, deep emotional memories from early childhood can interfere with expressed, rational thinking in adulthood: A person might have a panic attack in a certain situation but not know why.

The interaction of the amygdala and the hippocampus is sometimes helpful, sometimes not; fear can be constructive or destructive (LaBar, 2007). Studies performed on some animals show that when the amygdala is surgically removed, the animals are fearless in situations that should scare them; for instance, a cat will stroll nonchalantly past monkeys—something no normal cat would do (Kolb & Whishaw, 2008).

The Hypothalamus

A third part of the limbic system, the **hypothalamus,** responds to signals (arousing) from the amygdala and to signals (usually dampening) from the hippocampus by producing cortisol and other hormones that activate parts of the brain and body (see Figure 8.4). Ideally, this hormone production occurs in moderation (Tarullo & Gunnar, 2006). As you remember from previous chapters, excessive cortisol (the primary stress hormone) may flood the brain and destroy part of the hippocampus.

>> **Answer to Observation Quiz** (from page 215) The middle set, with its careful details, reflects damage to the right half of the brain, where overall impressions are formed. The person with left-brain damage produced the drawings that were just an M or a △, without the details of the tiny z's and rectangles. With a whole functioning brain, people can see both "the forest and the trees."

Especially for Neurologists Why do many experts think the limbic system is an oversimplification? (see response, page 219)

amygdala A tiny brain structure that registers emotions, particularly fear and anxiety.

hippocampus A brain structure that is a central processor of memory, especially memory for locations.

hypothalamus A brain area that responds to the amygdala and the hippocampus to produce hormones that activate other parts of the brain and body.

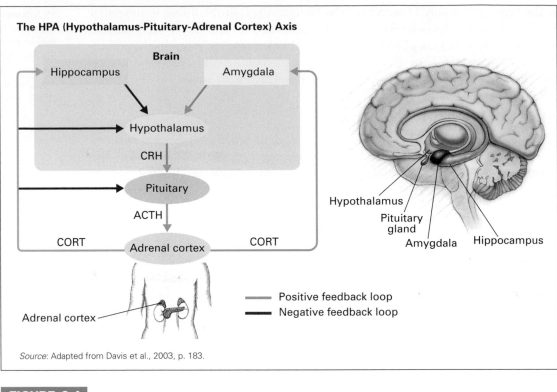

The HPA (Hypothalamus-Pituitary-Adrenal Cortex) Axis

Source: Adapted from Davis et al., 2003, p. 183.

FIGURE 8.4

A Hormonal Feedback Loop This diagram simplifies a hormonal linkage, the HPA (hypothalamus–pituitary–adrenal) axis. Both the hippocampus and the amygdala stimulate the hypothalamus to produce CRH (corticotropin-releasing hormone), which in turn signals the pituitary gland to produce ACTH (adrenocorticotropic hormone). ACTH then triggers the production of CORT (glucocorticoids) by the adrenal cortex (the outer layers of the adrenal glands, atop the kidneys). Fear may either build or disappear, depending on other factors, including how the various parts of the brain interpret that first alert from the amygdala.

Permanent deficits in learning and memory may result as "children exposed to traumatic or stressful events have an increased probability of developing major depression, post traumatic stress disorder, and attention deficit hyperactivity" because stress hormones affect the hippocampus (Garcia-Segura, 2009, p. 169), which therefore has less impact on the hypothalamus.

Stress may also be helpful, not harmful. Emotionally arousing experiences—meeting new friends, entering school, visiting a strange place—are beneficial if a young child has someone or something to moderate the stress. In an experiment, brain scans and hormone measurements were taken of 4- to 6-year-olds immediately after a fire alarm. Some children were upset; some not. Two weeks later, either a friendly or a stern adult questioned them about the event. Those with higher cortisol reactions to the alarm remembered more details than did those with less stress; in all the children, memory was better with a friendly interviewer (Quas et al., 2004).

Other research also finds that preschoolers remember a stressful experience better when an interviewer is warm and attentive (Bruck et al., 2006). Context is crucial: Stress can facilitate memory and cognitive growth if the inquiring adults are reassuring. However, because developing brains are fragile, "prolonged physiological responses to stress and challenge put children at risk for a variety of problems in childhood, including physical and mental disorders, poor emotional regulation, and cognitive impairments" (Quas et al., 2004, p. 797). Such problems originating in early development of the limbic system may impair health decades later (Shonkoff et al., 2009).

Sadly, this topic leads to an update on those adopted Romanian children first mentioned in Chapter 5. When they saw pictures of happy, sad, frightened, and angry faces, their limbic systems were less reactive than were those of Romanian children living with their parents. Their brains were also less lateralized, suggesting less specialized, less efficient thinking (Parker & Nelson, 2005).

Romania no longer permits wholesale international adoptions. Nonetheless, there are still many Romanian infants and young children in institutions. In one study, some were randomly assigned to foster homes at about age 2 while others stayed in their institutions. Two years later, those in foster homes were significantly smarter (by about 10 IQ points) than those who remained institutionalized (Nelson et al., 2007). As you remember from Chapter 7, age 6 to 24 months may be crucial for developing social bonds; this research suggests that ages 2 to 4 may be a sensitive time for intellectual growth.

SUMMING UP

The brain continues to mature during early childhood, with myelination occurring in several crucial areas. One is the corpus callosum, which connects the left and right sides of the brain and therefore the right and left sides of the body. Increased myelination speeds up actions and reactions. The prefrontal cortex enables a balance between action and inhibition, allowing children to think before they act as well as to stop one action in order to begin another. As impulsiveness and perseveration decrease, children become better able to learn.

Several key areas of the brain—including the amygdala, the hippocampus, and the hypothalamus—make up the limbic system, which matures from ages 2 to 6, aiding emotional expression and control. Children whose early experience was highly stressful and who lacked nurturing caregivers may have impaired limbic systems. ∎

>> Response for Neurologists (from page 217) The more we discover about the brain, the more complex we realize it is. Each part has specific functions and is connected to every other part.

"I would share, but I'm not there developmentally."

Good Excuse It is true that emotional control of selfish instincts is difficult for young children because the prefrontal cortex is not yet mature enough to regulate some emotions. However, family practices can advance social understanding.

>> Improved Motor Skills

Maturation of the prefrontal cortex improves impulse control, while myelination of the corpus callosum and lateralization of the brain permit better physical coordination. No wonder children move with greater speed and grace as they age from 2 to 6, becoming better able to direct and refine their actions. (At About This Time lists approximate ages for the acquisition of various motor skills in early childhood.)

According to a study in Brazil, Kenya, and the United States, young children spend most of their waking time playing, more than the combined time they spend on three other important activities: doing chores, learning lessons, or having conversations with adults (Tudge et al., 2006; see the Research Design and Figure 8.5). Mastery of gross and fine motor skills is one result of the extensive, active play of young children.

Gross Motor Skills

Gross motor skills improve dramatically during early childhood. When children play, clumsy 2-year-olds fall down and bump into each other, but some 5-year-olds are skilled and graceful, performing coordinated dance steps or sports moves.

Specific Skills

Most North American 5-year-olds can ride a tricycle, climb a ladder, pump a swing, as well as throw, catch, and kick a ball. Some can skate, ski, dive, and ride a bicycle—activities that demand balance as well as coordination of both brain hemispheres. In some nations, 5-year-olds swim in oceans or climb cliffs. Brain maturation, motivation, and guided practice make these skills possible.

AT ABOUT THIS TIME

Motor Skills at Ages 2–6*

Approximate Age	Skill or Achievement
2 years	Run for pleasure without falling (but bumping into things) Climb chairs, tables, beds, out of cribs Walk up stairs Feed self with spoon Draw lines, spirals
3 years	Kick and throw a ball Jump with both feet off the floor Pedal a tricycle Copy simple shapes (e.g., circle, rectangle) Walk down stairs Climb ladders
4 years	Catch a ball (not too small or thrown too fast) Use scissors to cut Hop on either foot Feed self with fork Dress self (no tiny buttons, no ties) Copy most letters Pour juice without spilling Brush teeth
5 years	Skip and gallop in rhythm Clap, bang, sing in rhythm Copy difficult shapes and letters (e.g., diamond shape, letter *S*) Climb trees, jump over things Use knife to cut Tie a bow Throw a ball Wash face, comb hair
6 years	Draw and paint with preferred hand Write simple words Scan a page of print, moving the eyes systematically in the appropriate direction Ride a bicycle Do a cartwheel Tie shoes Catch a ball

*Context and culture are crucial for acquisition of all these skills. For example, many 6-year-olds cannot tie shoelaces because they have no shoes with laces.

JEFFREY L. ROTMAN / CORBIS

Could Your Child Do This? Perhaps. If your family's profession and passion were acrobatics, you might encourage your toddler to practice headstands, and years later, your child could balance on your head. Everywhere, young children try to do whatever their parents do.

Observation Quiz Was this photo taken in the United States? (see answer, page 224)

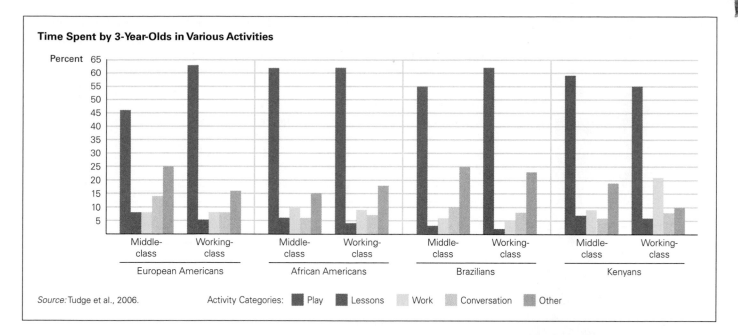

Time Spent by 3-Year-Olds in Various Activities

Source: Tudge et al., 2006.

Activity Categories: ■ Play ■ Lessons ■ Work ■ Conversation ■ Other

▶ **Research Design**

Scientists: Jonathan Tudge, Dolphine Odero, Cesar A. Piccinini, Fabienne Doucet, Tania M. Sperb, and Rita S. Lopes.

Publication: *Child Development* (2006).

Participants: About 20 3-year-olds from each of four ethnic groups: European American and African American in Greensboro, North Carolina; Luo in Kisumu, Kenya; and European descent in Porto Alegre, Brazil. On the basis of parents' education and occupation, half the children in each group were from middle-class families and half were from working-class families.

Design: Data were collected on each child for 20 hours in their usual daytime activities. Children wore wireless microphones; every 6 minutes, observers recorded the child's activity in five categories: lessons (deliberate attempts to impart information), work (household tasks), play (activities for enjoyment), conversation (sustained talk with adults not about the current activity), and other (eating, bathing, sleeping).

Major conclusions: All eight groups spent much more time playing than doing anything else. Some differences based on socioeconomic status (SES) and cultural group were apparent—for example, middle-class European Americans talked most with their children, and working-class Kenyan children did the most work.

Comments: Strengths of this study include contrasting cultures and SES and the frequent observation intervals (especially useful with young children, for whom questionnaires filled out by parents often produce inaccurate results). The weakness of this study is the small number of children in each group; larger samples might find other differences or fewer differences, or they might confirm these differences. The "other" category was also high; it would be interesting to break it down further. For instance, had some groups given up napping while others still napped?

FIGURE 8.5

Mostly Playing When researchers studied 3-year-olds in the United States, Brazil, and Kenya, they found that, on average, the children spent more than half their time playing. Note the low percentages of both middle- and working-class Brazilian children in the "Lessons" category, which included all intentional efforts to teach children something. There is a cultural explanation: Unlike parents in Kenya and the United States, most Brazilian parents believe that children of this age should not be in organized day care.

Adults need to make sure children have safe spaces, time, and playmates; skills will follow. According to sociocultural theory, children learn best from peers who demonstrate whatever skills the child is ready to try—from catching a ball to climbing a tree. Of course, the culture and the locale influence which skills children display—some small children learn to sled; others learn to sail.

Recent urbanization concerns many developmentalists. Compared with a century ago, when almost all children played together in empty lots or fields without adult supervision, half the world's children now live in cities. Many of these are

The Joy of Climbing Would you delight in climbing on an unsteady rope swing, like this 6-year-old in Japan (and almost all his contemporaries worldwide)? Each age has special sources of pleasure.

Exploring the Great Outdoors Two children climb over a rock outcrop in Shenandoah National Park in Virginia. Such outdoor play is important for the development of motor skills, even though many parents are tempted to try to keep their children safer by keeping them indoors.

"megacities . . . overwhelmed with burgeoning slums and environmental problems" (Ash et al., 2008, p. 739). Crowded, violent streets not only impede development of gross motor skills but also add to the natural fears of the immature limbic system.

The next generation of young children may have few older playmates and insufficient safe space to practice motor skills. Gone are the days when parents told their children to go out and play, expecting them safely back when hunger, weather, or nightfall brought them home. Now parents fear strangers, cars, trucks, and stray animals and therefore keep their 3- to 5-year-olds inside, perhaps watching television or playing video games, but not developing gross motor skills (Taylor et al., 2009).

Environmental Hazards

Pollutants do more harm to young, growing brains and bodies than to older, more developed ones; they are of particular concern for urban young children. Much depends on local regulations. For example, in India, one city of 14 million (Calcutta/Kolkata) has such extensive air pollution that childhood asthma rates are soaring and lung damage is prevalent. In another Indian city (Mumbai, formerly Bombay), air pollution has been reduced and children's health improved through several measures, including an extensive system of public buses that are required to use clean fuels (Bhattacharjee, 2008).

Research on lower animals raises concern about dozens of substances in the air, food, and water that can affect the brain and thus impede balance, finger dexterity, and motivation. The data are not clear-cut, leading one research team to implore that "developmental researchers direct basic and applied research about the effects of pollutant exposures and ways to reduce children's pollutant burdens" (Dilworth-Bart & Moore, 2006, p. 264).

Some substances—including lead in the water and air, pesticides in the soil or on clothing, bisphenol A (BPA) in plastic, and secondhand cigarette smoke—are already proven to be harmful. Lead, in particular, has been thoroughly researched: High exposure reduces intelligence and increases behavior problems in young children.

Over the past 20 years, U.S. regulations have reduced the amount of lead in paint, gasoline, and manufacturing, and children's blood lead levels have dropped sharply—in some states (e.g., Colorado and Wyoming), the average is close to zero. In other states (e.g., Michigan and Ohio), average lead levels are still too high, defined as above 10 micrograms per deciliter of blood among children under age 6 (MMWR, May 27, 2005). Some sources of lead remain unregulated, including lead in city water from old pipes, in manufacturing, and in jet fuel. It is not known precisely how high blood levels of lead must be before harm occurs, but some scientists are convinced that even 5 micrograms per deciliter is probably too much (Cole & Winsler, 2010).

Lead must be reduced by laws and policies, but parents can take action as well. Specifics include increasing consumption of calcium, wiping window ledges clean of dust, testing drinking water, and making sure the child never eats peeling chips of lead-based paint (still found in old buildings) (Dilworth-Bart & Moore, 2006).

Fine Motor Skills

Fine motor skills, especially small movements of the hands and fingers, are harder to master than gross motor skills. Pouring juice into a glass, cutting food with a knife and fork, and achieving anything more artful than a scribble with a pencil all require a level of muscular control, patience, and judgment that are beyond most 2-year-olds.

Many fine motor skills involve two hands and thus both sides of the brain: The fork stabs the meat while the knife cuts it; one hand steadies the paper while the other writes; tying shoes, buttoning shirts, pulling on socks, and zipping zippers require both hands. An immature corpus callosum and prefrontal cortex may be the underlying reason that shoelaces get knotted, paper gets ripped, and zippers get stuck. Short, stubby fingers add to the problem. As with gross motor skills, practice and maturation are key: By kindergarten, many of these skills are mastered if adults are patient and provide appropriate tools (no tiny buttons).

Traditional academic learning depends on fine motor skills and body control. Writing requires finger control, reading a line of print requires eye control, sitting for hours at a desk requires bladder control, and so on. These are beyond most young children, so even the brightest 3-year-old is not allowed in first grade, and some slower-developing 6-year-olds are frustrated if their teachers expect them to write neatly and cut straight.

Fine motor skills—like many other biological characteristics, such as bones, brains, and teeth—typically mature about 6 months earlier in girls than in boys. This may be one reason girls typically outperform boys on elementary school tests of school achievement and many young girls consider boys "stupid." Some educators suggest waiting until a child is "ready" for school; others suggest that school expectations should adjust to the immaturity of the child, a controversy explored in Chapter 9.

Artistic Expression

Young children are imaginative, creative, and not yet self-critical. They love to express themselves, especially if their parents applaud, display their artwork, and otherwise communicate approval. The fact that fine motor skills are immature, and thus their creations lack precision, is not yet important. Perhaps the immaturity of the prefrontal cortex allows the imagination to flourish without the social anxiety of the older child, who might say, "I can't draw" or "I am horrible at dancing."

All forms of artistic expression blossom during early childhood. Psychologists have diverse opinions about whether drawings reveal anything about children's emotions or needs (Burkitt, 2004). But there is no doubt that 2- to 6-year-olds love to dance around the room, build an elaborate tower of blocks, make music by pounding in rhythm, and put bright marks on shiny paper. In every artistic domain, skill gradually comes with practice.

Maturation is evident in the progression of skills development. When drawing the human figure, 2- to 3-year-olds usually draw a "tadpole"—a circle for a head with dots for eyes and sometimes a smiling mouth, and then a line or two beneath to indicate the rest of the body. Gradually, children's drawings of people evolve from tadpoles into more human forms as fine motor skills and perceptual abilities advance. Similarly, children seek places to climb, jump from, and crawl into—on rocky hillsides, playground structures, and the dining room table—imagining as they play. They like to sing, to beat rhythms, to mold clay or dirt, and so on. Creativity brings joy as well as the honing of skills in every culture.

No Spilled Milk This girl is demonstrating her mastery of the motor skills involved in pouring milk, to the evident admiration of her friend. The next skill will be drinking it—not a foregone conclusion, given the lactose intolerance of some children and the small appetites and notorious pickiness of children this age.

Especially for Immigrant Parents
You and your family eat with chopsticks at home, but you want your children to feel comfortable in Western culture. Should you change your family's eating customs? (see response, page 224)

Snip, Snip Cutting paper with scissors is a hard, slow task for a 3-year-old, who is just beginning to develop fine motor control. Imagine wielding blunt "safety" scissors and hoping that the paper will be sliced exactly where you want it to be.

LAURA DWIGHT

BLEND IMAGES / ALAMY

No Ears? (*left*) Elizabeth takes pride in drawing her family from memory. All have belly buttons and big smiles that reach their foreheads, but they have no arms or hair. (*right*) By age 6, this Virginia girl draws just one family member in detail—nostrils and mustache included.

>> Answer to Observation Quiz (from page 220) No, not because of ethnicity (many U.S. citizens are of Indian descent) but because of child labor laws. This duo is part of a circus (note the rigging), and no child in North America is allowed to perform such feats for pay.

>> Response for Immigrant Parents (from page 223): Children develop the motor skills that they see and practice. They will soon learn to use forks, spoons, and knives. Do not abandon chopsticks completely, because young children can learn several ways of doing things, and the ability to eat with chopsticks is a social asset.

SUMMING UP

Maturation of the brain leads to better hand and body control. Gross motor skills advance every year as long as young children have space to play, older children to emulate, and freedom from environmental toxins. Fine motor skills also develop, preparing children for the many requirements of formal education. Underlying all this is brain development, particularly of the prefrontal cortex and the corpus callosum, which gradually allows control of the limbic system, including the amygdala, the hippocampus, and the hypothalamus. ■

>> Injuries and Abuse

In almost all families of every income, ethnicity, or national group, parents want to protect their children while fostering their growth. Yet in developed nations, more children die of violence—either accidental or deliberate—than from any other cause. In the United States in 2006, out of every 100,000 1- to 4-year-olds, 9.9 died accidentally, 2.3 died of cancer (the leading fatal disease at this age), and 2.2 were murdered (U.S. Bureau of the Census, 2009).

Young children experience more injuries and abuse than slightly older children, partly because they are impulsive, immature, and dependent. But much harm can be prevented.

Avoidable Injury

Worldwide, injuries cause millions of premature deaths among young adults as well as children: Not until age 40 does any specific disease overtake accidents as a cause of mortality, and worldwide 14 percent of all life years lost are the result of injuries (WHO, 2010). Of course, in many nations, malaria and other infectious diseases combined cause more deaths than injuries do, but everywhere young children die of accidents that could have been prevented. In the United States, children are twice as likely to be seriously hurt in early childhood as in middle childhood (Safe Kids USA, 2008).

Immaturity of the prefrontal cortex makes young children impulsive, so they plunge into dangerous places and activities. Their motor skills allow them to run, leap, scramble, and grab in a flash. Their curiosity is boundless; their impulses are uninhibited; and, if they do something forbidden such as play with matches, their limbic system might make them hide rather than get help.

Age-related trends are apparent in particular injuries. Teenagers and young adults are most often killed in motor-vehicle crashes. Falls are more often fatal for the very young (under 24 months) and very old (over 80 years) than for preschoolers, for whom fatal accidents are more likely to involve poison, fire, or drowning (Safe Kids USA, 2008)

Injury Control

Instead of using the term *accident prevention,* public health experts prefer **injury control** (or **harm reduction**). Consider the implications of terminology. *Accident* implies that an injury is a random, unpredictable event; if anyone is at fault, it's a careless parent or an accident-prone child. This is called the "accident paradigm"; as if "injuries will occur despite our best efforts," allowing the public to feel blameless (Benjamin, 2004, p. 521).

A better phrase is *injury control,* which implies that harm can be minimized with appropriate controls. Minor mishaps are bound to occur, but serious injury is unlikely if a child falls on a safety surface instead of on concrete, if a car seat protects the body in a crash, if a bicycle helmet cracks instead of a skull, if swallowed pills come from a tiny bottle.

Only half as many 1- to 5-year-olds in the United States were fatally injured in 2005 as in 1985, thanks to laws that govern poisons, fires, and cars. But as more households in California, Florida, Texas, and Arizona install swimming pools, drowning has become a leading cause of unintentional death for young children (Safe Kids USA, 2008).

Three Levels of Prevention

Injury prevention begins long before any particular child, parent, or politician does something foolish. Three levels of prevention apply to every childhood health and safety issue (Tercyak, 2008; Towner & Mytton, 2009):

- In **primary prevention,** the overall situation is structured to make injuries less likely. Primary prevention fosters conditions that reduce everyone's chance of injury.
- **Secondary prevention** is more specific, averting harm in high-risk situations.
- **Tertiary prevention** begins after an injury, limiting the damage it causes.

In general, tertiary prevention is most visible, but primary prevention is most effective (Cohen et al., 2007). A good example of this comes from data on pedestrian deaths. Fewer people in the United States die after being hit by a motor vehicle than did 25 years ago (see Figure 8.6). How does each level of prevention contribute?

Primary prevention includes sidewalks, speed bumps, pedestrian overpasses, streetlights, and traffic circles (Retting et al., 2003; Tester et al., 2004). Cars have been redesigned (e.g., better headlights, bumpers, and brakes) and drivers' competence has improved (e.g., with stronger drunk-driving penalties and tougher licensing exams). If

injury control/harm reduction Practices that are aimed at anticipating, controlling, and preventing dangerous activities; these practices reflect the beliefs that accidents are not random and that injuries can be made less harmful if proper controls are in place.

primary prevention Actions that change overall background conditions to prevent some unwanted event or circumstance, such as injury, disease, or abuse.

secondary prevention Actions that avert harm in a high-risk situation, such as stopping a car before it hits a pedestrian.

tertiary prevention Actions, such as immediate and effective medical treatment, that are taken after an adverse event (such as illness or injury) occurs and that are aimed at reducing the harm or preventing disability.

FIGURE 8.6

While the Population Grew This chart shows dramatic evidence that prevention measures are succeeding in the United States. Over the same time period, the total population has increased by about one-third, making these results even more impressive.

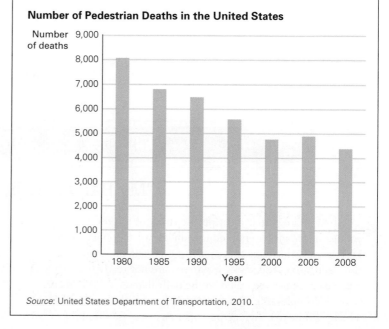

Number of Pedestrian Deaths in the United States

Source: United States Department of Transportation, 2010.

And If He Falls . . .   None of these children are injured, so no tertiary prevention is needed. Photos (*b*) and (*c*) both illustrate secondary prevention. In (*c*), crossing the street in a clearly marked crosswalk, under adult supervision, is safest for children. A five-point car seat (the safest kind) protects the Russian child in (*b*). In photo (*a*), the metal climbing equipment with large gaps and peeling paint is hazardous. Primary prevention suggests that this "attractive nuisance" be dismantled.

Especially for Urban Planners Describe a neighborhood park that would benefit 2- to 5-year-olds. (see response, page 228)

congestion is reduced via traffic regulations and improved mass transit, that is additional primary prevention.

Secondary prevention reduces danger in high-risk situations. For child pedestrians, this includes flashing lights on stopped school buses, school-crossing guards, and fences to keep children from running into streets. For teenagers, this includes later ages for permits and/or licenses. For everyone, salt on icy roads, warning signs before blind curves, and walk signals at busy intersections are examples of secondary prevention.

Finally, *tertiary prevention* reduces damage after crashes, such as laws against hit-and-runs, speedy ambulances, efficient emergency room procedures, and effective rehabilitation. Medical personnel are aware of the *golden hour*. Although there is nothing magical about 60 minutes in contrast to 59 or 61 minutes, the faster an injury victim reaches a trauma center, the better the chance of survival (Bansal et al., 2009).

Especially for Economists In the feature below, how did Kathleen Berger's SES protect Bethany from serious harm? (see response, page 228)

A CASE TO STUDY

"My Baby Swallowed Poison"

The first strategy that most people think of to prevent injury to young children is parental education. However, public health research finds that laws that apply to everyone are more effective than education, especially if parents are not ready to learn and change or are overwhelmed by the daily demands of child care.

For example, infant car seats have saved thousands of lives. The best time to convince parents to use one is before they take

their newborn home from the hospital. Use of car seats, though, is much less common when it is voluntary than when it is mandated. As one expert explains: "Too often, we design our physical environment for smart people who are highly motivated" (S. P. Baker, 2000). But in real life, everyone has moments of foolish indifference. At those moments, automatic safety measures save lives.

I know this firsthand; my own experience is "a case to study." Our daughter Bethany, at age 2, climbed onto the kitchen counter to find, open, and swallow most of a bottle of baby aspirin. Where was I? A few feet away, nursing our second child and watching television. I did not notice what Bethany was doing until I checked on her during a commercial.

Bethany is alive and well today. She was protected not by her foolish mother but by all three levels of prevention. Primary prevention included laws limiting the number of baby aspirin per container, secondary prevention included my pediatrician's written directions on my first well-baby checkup to buy syrup of ipecac, and tertiary prevention was my phone call to Poison Control.

I told the helpful stranger who answered the phone, "My baby swallowed poison." He calmly asked me a few questions and then advised me to give Bethany ipecac to make her throw up the pills she had swallowed. I did, and she did. I still blame myself, but I am grateful for all three levels of prevention that protected my child. I am also well aware that my background helped me avert a tragedy. I had chosen a wise pediatrician and followed his advice; I had a phone and knew whom to call. As I remember all the mistakes I made in parenting (only a few of them detailed in this book), I am grateful that I knew how to prevent serious harm.

Child Maltreatment

The next time you read headlines about some horribly neglected or abused child, think of these words from a leading researcher in child maltreatment:

> Make no mistake—those who abuse children are fully responsible for their actions. However, creating an information system that perpetuates the message that offenders are the only ones to blame may be misleading. . . . We all contribute to the conditions that allow perpetrators to succeed.
>
> [Daro, 2002, p. 1133]

"We all contribute" in the sense that the causes of child maltreatment are multifaceted, involving not only the parents but also the neighbors, the community, the culture, and even the maltreated children themselves. Difficult infants (fragile, needing frequent feeding, crying often) are at greatest risk of being maltreated, especially if their mothers are depressed and feel they have no control over their lives. Family financial stress adds to the risk (Bugental & Happaney, 2004). Each of these factors could be mitigated or prevented by the community, through laws, practices, or direct help.

Maltreatment Noticed and Defined

Noticing is the first step. Until about 1960, people thought child maltreatment was rare and consisted of a sudden attack by a disturbed stranger. Today we know better, thanks to a pioneering study based on careful observation in one Boston hospital (Kempe & Kempe, 1978): Maltreatment is neither rare nor sudden, and the perpetrators are usually one or both of the child's own parents. That makes the situation much worse: Ongoing maltreatment, with no protector, is much more damaging than a single incident, however injurious.

With this recognition came a broader definition: **Child maltreatment** now refers to all intentional harm to, or avoidable endangerment of, anyone under 18 years of age. Thus, child maltreatment includes both **child abuse,** which is deliberate action that is harmful to a child's physical, emotional, or sexual well-being, and **child neglect,** which is failure to meet a child's basic physical or emotional needs. The more that researchers study the long-term harm of child maltreatment, the worse neglect seems to be, especially in early childhood.

Nobody Watching? Madelyn Gorman Toogood looks around to make sure no one is watching before she slaps and shakes her 4-year-old daughter, Martha, who is in a car seat inside the vehicle. A security camera recorded this incident in an Indiana department store parking lot. A week later, after the videotape was repeatedly broadcast nationwide, Toogood was recognized and arrested. The haunting question is: How much child abuse takes place that is not witnessed?

child maltreatment Intentional harm to or avoidable endangerment of anyone under 18 years of age.

child abuse Deliberate action that is harmful to a child's physical, emotional, or sexual well-being.

child neglect Failure to meet a child's basic physical, educational, or emotional needs.

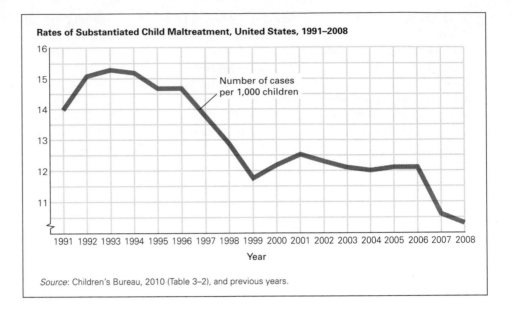

Rates of Substantiated Child Maltreatment, United States, 1991–2008

Number of cases per 1,000 children

Year

Source: Children's Bureau, 2010 (Table 3–2), and previous years.

FIGURE 8.7

Still Far Too Many The number of reported and substantiated cases of maltreatment of children under age 18 in the United States is too high, but there is some good news: The rate has declined significantly from its peak in 1993.

Observation Quiz The data point for 2008 is close to the bottom of the graph. Does that mean it is close to zero? (see answer, page 230)

reported maltreatment Harm or endangerment about which someone has notified the authorities.

substantiated maltreatment Harm or endangerment that has been reported, investigated, and verified.

>> Response for Urban Planners (from page 226): The adult idea of a park—a large, grassy open place—is not best for young children. For them, you would design an enclosed area, small enough and with adequate seating to allow caregivers to socialize while watching their children. The playground surface would have to be protective (since young children are clumsy), with equipment that encourages both gross motor skills (such as climbing) and fine motor skills (such as sandbox play). Swings are not beneficial, since they do not develop many motor skills. Teenagers and dogs should have their own designated area, far from the youngest children.

>> Response for Economists (from page 226) Children from families at all income levels have accidents, but Kathleen Berger's SES allowed her to have a private pediatrician as well as the income to buy ipecac "just in case." She also had a working phone and the education to know about Poison Control.

Reported maltreatment means that the authorities have been informed. Since 1993, the number of *reported* cases of maltreatment in the United States has ranged from about 2.7 million to 3.5 million a year (Children's Bureau, 2010). **Substantiated maltreatment** means that a reported case has been investigated and verified (see Figure 8.7). With the exception of sexual abuse (discussed in Chapter 14), most victims are under age 6. The substantiated maltreatment rate in early childhood is about 1 maltreated child in every 80; the reported rate is triple that (U.S. Bureau of the Census, 2009).

The overall ratio of 3-to-1 for reported versus substantiated cases can be attributed to three factors:

- Each child is counted once, even if repeated maltreatment is reported.
- Substantiation requires proof in the form of unmistakable injuries, severe malnutrition, or a witness willing to testify. Such evidence is not always available.
- A report may be false or deliberately misleading (though few are) (Kohl et al., 2009).

Frequency of Maltreatment

How often does maltreatment occur? No one knows. Not all cases are noticed, not all are reported, and not all that are reported are substantiated. According to official U.S. statistics, the rate of substantiated child maltreatment decreased by 18 percent between 2001 and 2008 (see Figure 8.8), even though cases of neglect increased. Other sources also report less maltreatment over the past two decades.

Although it seems that maltreatment has, in fact, declined, the data are not solid because official reports of substantiated data leave room for doubt. For example, Pennsylvania and Maine reported almost identical numbers of victims in 2007 (4,117 and 4,118), but the child population of Pennsylvania is ten times that of Maine (U.S. Bureau of the Census, 2009). It also seems that some communities are better at noticing and reporting maltreatment than others. The most marked variation occurs for educational professionals, who are mandated by law to

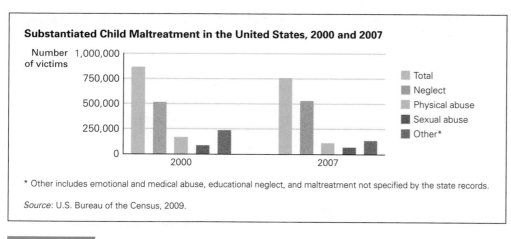

Substantiated Child Maltreatment in the United States, 2000 and 2007

* Other includes emotional and medical abuse, educational neglect, and maltreatment not specified by the state records.

Source: U.S. Bureau of the Census, 2009.

FIGURE 8.8

Getting Better? As you can see, the number of victims of child maltreatment in the United States has declined in the past decade. The legal and social-work response to serious maltreatment has improved over these years, which is a likely explanation for the decline. Other, less sanguine, explanations are possible, however.

report suspected maltreatment. However, the percent of the reports from educators is ten times higher in Minnesota than in North Carolina (24 percent versus 2.5 percent) (Children's Bureau, 2010).

Overall, only about one-fourth of investigated cases are substantiated, but some cases are not reported. According to a confidential nationwide survey of young adults in the United States, 1 in 4 had been physically abused ("slapped, hit, or kicked" by a parent or other adult caregiver) before sixth grade and 1 in 22 had been sexually abused ("touched or forced to touch someone else in a sexual way") (Hussey et al., 2006; see the Research Design). Almost never had their abuse been reported. The authors of this study think the rates they found are *underestimates* (Hussey et al., 2006)!

Especially for Criminal Justice Professionals Over the past decade, the rate of sexual abuse has gone down by almost 20 percent. What are three possible explanations? (see response, page 231)

▶ **Research Design**

Scientists: Jon Hussey and others at the University of North Carolina.

Publication: *Pediatrics* (2006).

Participants: A total of 15,197 young adults, interviewed at age 18–26 as part of the third wave of Add Health, a longitudinal study that began in 1995 with a representative sample of over 20,000 U.S. adolescents.

Design: Participants were asked to report, confidentially (via headphones and a computer, a method that yields more accurate answers than face-to-face or written questions do), whether their caregivers had ever maltreated them. Questions were specific (e.g., "slapped, hit, or kicked"), and participants indicated how often the behavior occurred (once, twice, or more).

Major conclusions: Maltreatment was common: One in four had been physically abused. Each type of maltreatment was associated with multiple health risks.

Comments: Although one would hope that these rates are overestimates, actual rates may be even higher, for three reasons: (1) Young adults tend to idealize their childhood; (2) the original participants were all in high school and had their parents' permission to respond to the survey; and (3) the participants in this third wave of interviews were, on average, more advantaged than those who dropped out or could not be found.

>> Answer to Observation Quiz (from page 228) No. The number is actually 11.8 per 1,000. Note the little squiggle on the graph's vertical axis below the number 11. This means that numbers between 0 and 11 are not shown.

Especially for Nurses While weighing a 4-year-old, you notice several bruises on the child's legs. When you ask about them, the child says nothing and the parent says the child bumps into things. What should you do? (see response, page 232)

post-traumatic stress disorder (PTSD) An anxiety disorder that develops as a delayed reaction to having experienced or witnessed a profoundly shocking or frightening event, such as rape, severe beating, war, or natural disaster. Its symptoms may include flashbacks to the event, hyperactivity and hypervigilance, displaced anger, sleeplessness, nightmares, sudden terror or anxiety, and confusion between fantasy and reality.

One reason for these high rates of unreported abuse may be that these young adults were asked if they had *ever* been mistreated by someone who was caring for them, while most other sources report annual rates. Another reason is that few children report their own abuse; many do not know that they are mistreated until later, when they compare their experiences with that of their friends. Indeed, some adults who were slapped, hit, or kicked in childhood do not think they were abused. Reinterpretation of childhood experiences is controversial: Some memories are false and others are accurate, finally recognized as abuse (McNally & Geraerts, 2009).

Warning Signs

Often the first sign of maltreatment is delayed development, such as slow growth, immature communication, lack of curiosity, or unusual social interactions. All these difficulties may be evident even at age 1 (Valentino et al., 2006).

During early childhood, maltreated children may seem fearful, startled by noise, defensive and quick to attack, and confused between fantasy and reality. These are symptoms of **post-traumatic stress disorder (PTSD),** first identified in combat veterans, then in adults who had experienced some emotional injury or shock (after a serious accident, natural disaster, or violent crime, for example), and more recently in some maltreated children, who suffer neurologically as well as behaviorally (Neigh et al., 2009; Yehuda, 2006).

Table 8.1 lists signs of child maltreatment, both neglect and abuse. None of these signs are proof that a child has been abused, but whenever any of them occurs, it signifies trouble. Many nations, including the United States, require all professionals who deal with children (teachers, nurses, social workers, doctors, police officers) to report suspected maltreatment.

Abuse or Athletics? Four-year-old Budhia Singh ran 40 miles in 7 hours with adult marathoners. He says he likes to run, but his mother (a widow who allowed his trainer to "adopt" him because she could not feed him) has charged the trainer with physical abuse. The government of India has declared that Singh cannot race again until he is fully grown. If a child, the parent, and the community approve of some activity, can it still be maltreatment?

TABLE 8.1
Signs of Maltreatment in Children Aged 2 to 10
Injuries that do not fit an "accidental" explanation: bruises on both sides of the face or body; burns with a clear line between burned and unburned skin; "falls" that result in cuts, not scrapes
Repeated injuries, especially broken bones not properly tended
Fantasy play, with dominant themes of violence or sexual knowledge
Slow physical growth, especially with unusual appetite or lack of appetite
Ongoing physical complaints, such as stomachaches, headaches, genital pain, sleepiness
Reluctance to talk, to play, or to move, especially if development is slow
No close friendships; hostility toward others; bullying of smaller children
Hypervigilance, with quick, impulsive reactions, such as cringing, startling, or hitting
Frequent absences from school, changes of address, or new caregivers
Expressions of fear rather than joy on seeing the caregiver
Source: Adapted from Scannapieco & Connell-Carrick, 2005.

Consequences of Maltreatment

The impact of any child-rearing practice is affected by the cultural context. Certain customs (such as circumcision, pierced ears, and spanking) are considered abusive in some cultures but not in others; their effects on children vary accordingly. Children suffer if their parents seem not to love them as much as other parents in their community love their children. However, although cultural standards are always relevant, the more scientists use a life-span approach, the more widespread and long-lasting the impact of maltreatment is found to be.

A VIEW FROM SCIENCE

The Neglect of Neglect

The biological and academic impairment from maltreatment are substantial but are thus relatively easy to notice—the teacher sees that a child is bruised, broken, or failing despite ability. However, when researchers follow maltreated children over the years, enduring deficits in social skills seem more crippling. Abused children typically regard other people as hostile and exploitative; hence, they are less friendly, more aggressive, and more isolated than other children. The earlier abuse starts and the longer it continues, the worse their peer relationships are (Scannapieco & Connell-Carrick, 2005). Neglected children may have even worse social deficits than abused ones, because they were unable to relate to their parents (Stevenson, 2007).

Deficits are lifelong. Maltreated children may become bullies or victims or both, not only in childhood and adolescence but also in adulthood (Dietrich, 2008). They tend to dissociate, that is, to disconnect their memories from their understanding of themselves (Valentino et al., 2008). Adults who were severely maltreated (physically, sexually, or emotionally) often abuse drugs or alcohol, enter unsupportive relationships, become victims or aggressors, sabotage their own careers, eat too much or too little,

and engage in other self-destructive behavior (M. G. Smith & Fong, 2004). They also have a much higher risk of emotional disorders and suicide attempts, even after other risk factors (e.g., poverty) are considered (Afifi et al., 2008).

In the current economic climate, finding and keeping a job is a critical aspect of well-being; adults who were maltreated suffer in this way as well. One study carefully matched 807 children who had experienced substantiated abuse with other children who were of the same sex, ethnicity, and family SES. About 35 years later, as adults, the employment rates of those who had been mistreated were 14 percent lower than the employment rates of those who had not been abused. The researchers concluded that "abused and neglected children experience large and enduring economic consequences" (Currie & Widom, 2010, p. 111). In this study, the women were more impaired than the men: It may be that self-esteem and social skills are even more important for female employment than for male.

This is just one of hundreds of longitudinal studies, all of which find that maltreatment affects children decades after the specifics of broken bones, or skinny bodies, or neglected care.

Three Levels of Prevention, Again

Just as with injury control, there are three levels of prevention of maltreatment. The ultimate goal is *primary prevention* that focuses on the macrosystem and exosystem (see Chapter 1). Examples of primary-prevention conditions include stable neighborhoods; family cohesion; financial support; and any measure that decreases financial instability, family isolation, and teenage parenthood.

Secondary prevention involves spotting the warning signs and intervening to keep a risky situation from getting worse. For example, insecure attachment, especially of the disorganized type (described in Chapter 7), is a sign of a disrupted parent–child relationship. Someone needs to help repair that interaction. Secondary prevention includes home visits by helpful nurses or social workers, high-quality day care, and preventive medical treatment—all designed to help high-risk families. Medical professionals are now trained to notice early warning signs, such as repeated accidents or illnesses, that suggest that additional, more devastating, maltreatment is likely (Giardino & Alexander, 2011).

>> **Response for Criminal Justice Professionals** (from page 229): Hopefully, more adults or children are aware of sexual abuse and stop it before it starts. A second possibility is that sexual abuse is less often reported and substantiated because the culture is more accepting of teenage sex (most victims of sexual abuse are between ages 10 and 18). A third possible explanation is that the increase in single mothers means that fathers have less access to children (fathers are the most frequent sexual abusers).

PHOTO JAPAN / ALAMY

JOACHIM LADEFOGED / VII

The Same Situation, Many Miles Apart: Fun with Grandpa Grandfathers, like those shown here in Japan and Sweden, often delight their grandchildren. Sometimes, however, they protect them—either in kinship care, when parents are designated as neglectful, or as secondary prevention before harm is evident. (The grandparents in Sweden are refugees from Iraq.)

permanency planning An effort by child-welfare authorities to find a long-term living situation that will provide stability and support for a maltreated child. A goal is to avoid repeated changes of caregiver or school, which can be particularly harmful to the child.

foster care A legal, publicly supported system in which a maltreated child is removed from the parents' custody and entrusted to another adult or family, which is reimbursed for expenses incurred in meeting the child's needs.

kinship care A form of foster care in which a relative of a maltreated child, usually a grandparent, becomes the approved caregiver.

>> Response for Nurses (from page 230) Any suspicion of child maltreatment must be reported, and these bruises are suspicious. Someone in authority must find out what is happening so that the parent as well as the child can be helped.

Tertiary prevention includes everything intended to reduce harm when maltreatment has already occurred. Reporting and substantiating abuse are the first steps. Then someone in authority must help the family or remove the child. If hospitalization is required, that is a sign of failure: Intervention should have begun much earlier. At that point, treatment is very expensive, harm has already been done, and hospitalization itself further strains the parent–child bond (Rovi et al., 2004).

Children need caregivers they trust, in safe and stable homes, whether they live with their biological parents, a foster family, or an adoptive family. Whenever a child is legally removed from an abusive or neglectful home and placed in foster care, federal law in the United States requires authorities to begin **permanency planning,** an effort to find a family that will nurture the child until adulthood. This is a complex task, requiring cooperation among social workers, judges, and psychologists as well as the caregivers themselves (Edwards, 2007).

In **foster care,** children are officially removed from their parents' custody and entrusted to another adult or family; foster parents are reimbursed for the expenses they incur in meeting the children's needs. In every year from 2000 to 2009, about half a million children in the United States were in foster care. More than half of them were in a special version of foster care called **kinship care,** in which a relative—usually a grandparent—becomes the foster caregiver. This estimate is for official kinship care; three times as many children are unofficially cared for by relatives who are not their parents.

In the United States, most foster children are from low-income families; half are African American and many of the others are Latino. Those officially in foster care often have a history of severe maltreatment and multiple physical, intellectual, and emotional problems (Pew Commission on Children in Foster Care, 2004). Despite these problems, children develop better in foster care (including kinship care) than with their original abusive families if a supervising agency screens foster families effectively and provides ongoing financial support and counseling (MacMillan et al., 2009; Oosterman et al., 2007).

Many agencies, however, do not provide adequate support. One obvious failing is that many move children from one foster home to another for reasons that are unrelated to the child's behavior or wishes. Foster children average three place-

STEPHANIE MAZE / CORBIS

Tertiary Prevention Adoption has been these children's salvation, particularly for 9-year-old Leah, clinging to her mother. The mother, Joan, has five adopted children. Adoption is generally better than foster care for maltreated children because it is a permanent, stable arrangement.

ments before permanent placement (Pew Commission on Children in Foster Care, 2004). Each move increases the risk of a poor outcome (Oosterman et al., 2007). Another problem is that kinship care is sometimes used as an easy, less expensive solution. Kinship care may be better than stranger care, but supportive services are needed (Edwards, 2010; Fechter-Leggett & O'Brien, 2010).

Adoption (when an adult or couple unrelated to the child is legally granted the obligations and joys of parenthood) is the preferred permanent option, but it is difficult for many reasons. For example, judges and biological parents are reluctant to release children for adoption; most adoptive parents prefer infants, yet most maltreated children available for adoption are older; and some agencies accept only families headed by a heterosexual married couple who are the same ethnicity and religion as the child.

As detailed many times in this chapter, caring for young children is not easy, from making sure they brush their teeth to helping them learn motor skills. Parents usually shoulder most of the burden, and their love and protection result in strong and happy young children. The benefit to the entire community of having well-nurtured children is obvious; the ways to achieve that seem not so clear. No child should be mistreated, yet millions are.

adoption A legal proceeding in which an adult or couple unrelated to a child is granted the joys and obligations of being that child's parent(s).

SUMMING UP

As they move with more speed and agility, young children encounter new dangers, becoming seriously injured more often than older children. They also are more often mistreated, either deliberately (abuse) or because essential care is not provided (neglect). Three levels of prevention are needed. Laws and customs can protect everyone (primary prevention); supervision, forethought, and protective care can prevent harm to those at risk (secondary prevention); and when injury or maltreatment occurs, quick and effective medical and psychosocial intervention, and prevention of further harm, are needed (tertiary prevention). Stopping maltreatment of all kinds is urgent but complex, because the sources are often the family, the culture, the community, and the laws. ■

SUMMARY

Body Changes

1. Children continue to gain weight and add height during early childhood. Many become quite picky eaters. One reason this occurs is that many adults overfeed children, not realizing that young children are naturally quite thin.

2. Culture, income, and family customs all affect children's growth. In contrast to past decades, children of low-income families are twice as likely to be overweight as their wealthier counterparts. Worldwide, an increasing number of children are eating too much, risking heart disease and diabetes.

3. Many young children consume too much sugar and too little calcium and other nutrients. One consequence is poor oral health. Children need to brush their teeth and visit the dentist years before the permanent teeth erupt.

Brain Development

4. The brain continues to grow in early childhood, reaching 75 percent of its adult weight at age 2 and 90 percent by age 5.

5. Myelination is substantial during early childhood, speeding messages from one part of the brain to another. The corpus callosum becomes thicker and functions much better. The prefrontal cortex, known as the executive of the brain, is strengthened as well.

6. Brain changes enable more reflective, coordinated thought and memory; better planning; and quicker responses. Left/right specialization is apparent in the brain as well as in the body, although the entire brain and the entire body work together for most skills.

7. The expression and regulation of emotions are fostered by several brain areas, including the amygdala, the hippocampus, and the hypothalamus. Childhood abuse may cause overactivity in the amygdala and hippocampus, creating a flood of stress hormones that interfere with learning. Some stress aids learning if reassurance is also present.

Improved Motor Skills

8. Gross motor skills continue to develop; clumsy 2-year-olds become 6-year-olds who move their bodies well, guided by their culture. Play is their main activity, and it helps them practice the skills needed for formal education.

9. Fine motor skills are difficult to master during early childhood. Young children enjoy expressing themselves artistically, developing their body and finger control as well as self-expression.

10. Urbanization and chemical pollutants hamper development. More research is needed, but it is already apparent that high lead levels in the blood can impair the brain and that opportunities to develop gross motor skills are restricted when play space is scarce.

Injuries and Abuse

11. Accidents are by far the leading cause of death for children in developed nations, and young children are more likely to suffer a serious injury or premature death than older children. Close supervision and public safeguards are needed to protect young children from their own eager, impulsive curiosity.

12. Injury control occurs on many levels, including long before and immediately after each harmful incident. Primary prevention protects everyone. Secondary and tertiary prevention also save lives.

13. Child maltreatment includes ongoing abuse and neglect, usually by a child's own parents. Each year, about 3 million cases of child maltreatment are reported in the United States, almost 1 million of which are substantiated.

14. Physical abuse is the most obvious form of maltreatment, but neglect is more common and may be more harmful. Health, learning, and social skills are all impeded by abuse and neglect, not only during childhood but also decades later.

15. Tertiary prevention may include placement of a child in foster care, including kinship care. Permanency planning is required because frequent changes are harmful to children. Primary and secondary prevention help parents care for their children and reduce the need for tertiary prevention.

KEY TERMS

myelination (p. 213)
corpus callosum (p. 214)
lateralization (p. 214)
perseveration (p. 216)
amygdala (p. 217)
hippocampus (p. 217)

hypothalamus (p. 217)
injury control/harm reduction (p. 225)
primary prevention (p. 225)
secondary prevention (p. 225)
tertiary prevention (p. 225)

child maltreatment (p. 227)
child abuse (p. 227)
child neglect (p. 227)
reported maltreatment (p. 228)
substantiated maltreatment (p. 228)

post-traumatic stress disorder (PTSD) (p. 230)
permanency planning (p. 232)
foster care (p. 232)
kinship care (p. 232)
adoption (p. 233)

WHAT HAVE YOU LEARNED?

Body Changes

1. About how much does a well-nourished child grow in height and weight from age 2 to 6?

2. Why do many parents overfeed their children?

3. The incidence of what adult diseases increases with childhood obesity?

4. What specific measures should be part of oral health in early childhood?

5. When is it normal for children to be picky about eating and other daily routines?

Brain Development

6. How much does the brain grow from ages 2 to 5?

7. Why is *myelination* important for thinking and motor skills?

8. What is the function of the corpus callosum?

9. What should parents do if their toddler seems left-handed?

10. How does the prefrontal cortex affect impulsivity and perseveration?

11. Is stress beneficial or harmful to young children? Explain why.

Improved Motor Skills

12. What factors help children develop their motor skills?

13. What is known and unknown about the effects on young children of chemicals in the food, air, and water?

14. How does brain and body maturation affect the artistic expression of children?

Injuries and Abuse

15. Why is the term *injury control* preferred instead of *accident prevention*?

16. What primary measures prevent childhood injury, abuse, and neglect?

17. What secondary measures prevent childhood injury, abuse, and neglect?

18. What tertiary measures prevent childhood injury, abuse, and neglect?

19. Why did most people not recognize childhood maltreatment 50 years ago?

20. Why is neglect in childhood considered as harmful as abuse?

21. Why is it difficult to know exactly how often childhood maltreatment occurs?

22. What are the signs that a child may be mistreated?

23. What are the long-term consequences of childhood maltreatment?

24. Why would a child be placed in foster care?

APPLICATIONS

1. Keep a food diary for 24 hours, writing down what you eat, how much, when, how, and why. Then think about nutrition and eating habits in early childhood. Do you see any evidence in yourself of imbalance (e.g., not enough fruits and vegetables, too much sugar or fat, eating when you are not really hungry)? Did your food habits originate in early childhood, in adolescence, or at some other time?

2. Go to a playground or other place where young children play. Note the motor skills that the children demonstrate, including abilities and inabilities, and keep track of age and sex. What differences do you see among the children?

3. Ask several parents to describe each accidental injury of each of their children, particularly how it happened and what the consequences were. What primary, secondary, or tertiary prevention measures would have made a difference?

4. Think back to your childhood and the friends you had at that time. Was there any maltreatment? Considering what you have learned in this chapter, why or why not?

>>ONLINE CONNECTIONS

To accompany your textbook, you have access to a number of online resources, including quizzes for every chapter of the book, flashcards (in English and Spanish), critical thinking questions, and case studies. For access to any of these links, go to www.worthpublishers.com/bergerls8e. In addition to these free resources, you'll also find links to the podcasts, video clips, diagnostic quizzing with personalized study advice, and an ebook. Some of the videos and activities available online include:

- *Brain Development in Early Childhood.* Animations illustrate the macroscopic and microscopic changes as children's brains grow.

- *Stolen Childhoods.* Some children, because of poverty or abuse, never have the opportunities for schooling and nurture that many of us take for granted. Children in a variety of difficult circumstances, from sex work to work in carpet factories, tell their stories in a variety of video clips.

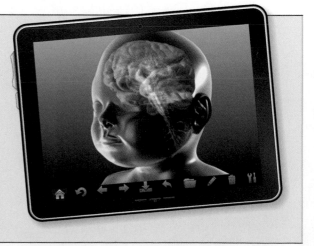

Early Childhood: Cognitive Development

WHAT WILL YOU KNOW?

1. What did Piaget discover about the thinking of young children?
2. What are the practical uses of Vygotsky's ideas about learning?
3. What does the research say about learning two languages in early childhood?
4. What are two opposite perspectives on the role of preschool education?

I was one of dozens of subway riders who were captivated by a little girl, about age 3, with sparkling eyes and many braids. She sat beside a large man, her legs straight out in front of her. Her mother was standing about 6 feet away. The little girl repeatedly ducked her head behind the man and said, "You can't see me, Mama," unaware that her legs (in colorful striped stockings) were constantly visible to her mother.

Like that little girl, every young child has much to learn. Young children are sometimes *egocentric,* understanding only their own perspective. Among their developing ideas is a *theory of mind,* an understanding of how minds work (as in knowing that your mother would not lose sight of you on a subway).

Early childhood is a time of prodigious new learning. Examples abound. Toddlers' simple block towers become elaborate cities, with tunnels, bridges, and houses designed and built by kindergartners. The youngest children are easy to fool; by age 5, they do the fooling. The halting, simple sentences of a typical 2-year-old become the nonstop, complex outpourings of a talkative 6-year-old.

How does such rapid cognitive development happen? How much is maturation and how much is deliberate education? Many young children are now taught, not merely babysat (as if adults merely sat) or cared for (as in day care or home care). This chapter describes thinking and learning from ages 2 to 6, including advances in thought, language, and education, and explores how all this develops.

>> Piaget and Vygotsky

Jean Piaget and Lev Vygotsky are justly famous for their descriptions of cognition. Their theories are "intertwined" (Fox & Riconscente, 2008, p. 373), especially when they describe young children. As you read, look for the commonalities.

Piaget: Preoperational Thinking

Early childhood is the second of Piaget's four stages of cognition. He called cognitive development between about 2 and 6 years of age **preoperational intelligence,** a time for symbolic thought, especially language and imagination. It is *pre*-operational, in that children do not yet use logical operations (reasoning processes), but intelligence is no longer limited to senses and motor skills (sensorimotor) (Inhelder & Piaget, 1964).

preoperational intelligence Piaget's term for cognitive development between the ages of about 2 and 6; it includes language and imagination (which involve symbolic thought), but logical, operational thinking is not yet possible.

centration A characteristic of preoperational thought in which a young child focuses (centers) on one idea, excluding all others.

egocentrism Piaget's term for children's tendency to think about the world entirely from their own personal perspective.

focus on appearance A characteristic of preoperational thought in which a young child ignores all attributes that are not apparent.

static reasoning A characteristic of preoperational thought in which a young child thinks that nothing changes. Whatever is now has always been and always will be.

irreversibility A characteristic of preoperational thought in which a young child thinks that nothing can be undone. A thing cannot be restored to the way it was before a change occurred.

conservation The principle that the amount of a substance remains the same (i.e., is conserved) even when its appearance changes.

Especially for Nutritionists How can Piaget's theory help you encourage children to eat healthy foods? (see response, page 240)

Demonstration of Conservation My youngest daughter, Sarah, here at age 5¾, demonstrates Piaget's conservation-of-volume experiment. First, she examines both short glasses to be sure they contain the same amount of milk. Then, after the contents of one are poured into the tall glass and she is asked which has more, she points to the tall glass, just as Piaget would have expected. Later she added, "It looks like it has more because it's taller," indicating that some direct instruction might change her mind.

Obstacles to Logical Operations

Piaget described four limitations of preoperational thought that make logic difficult: centration, focus on appearance, static reasoning, and irreversibility.

Centration is the tendency to focus on one aspect of a situation to the exclusion of all others. Young children may, for example, insist that lions and tigers seen at the zoo or in picture books cannot be cats, because the children "center" on the house-pet aspect of the cats they know. Or they may insist that Daddy is a father, not a brother, because they center on the role that each family member fills for them.

The daddy example illustrates a particular type of centration that Piaget called **egocentrism**—literally, "self-centeredness." Egocentric children contemplate the world exclusively from their personal perspective, as the little girl on the subway did. Egocentrism is not selfishness. Consider, for example, a 3-year-old who chose to buy a model car as a birthday present for his mother: His "behavior was not selfish or greedy; he carefully wrapped the present and gave it to his mother with an expression that clearly showed that he expected her to love it" (Crain, 2005, p. 108).

A second characteristic of preoperational thought is a **focus on appearance** to the exclusion of other attributes. A girl given a short haircut might worry that she has turned into a boy. In preoperational thought, a thing is whatever it appears to be.

Third, preoperational children use **static reasoning,** believing that the world is unchanging, always in the state in which they currently encounter it. A young boy might want the television turned off while he goes to the bathroom, assuming that when he returns, he can pick up the program exactly where he left off.

The fourth characteristic of preoperational thought is **irreversibility.** Preoperational thinkers fail to recognize that reversing a process sometimes restores whatever existed before. A young child might cry because her mother put lettuce on her hamburger. Overwhelmed by her desire to have things "just right" (as explained in Chapter 8), she might reject the hamburger even after the lettuce is removed because she believes that what is done cannot be undone.

Conservation and Logic

Piaget lauded the development of symbolic thought, allowing chidren to talk about what they think, but he also highlighted the many ways in which preoperational intelligence overlooked logic. A famous set of experiments involved **conservation,** the notion that the amount of something remains the same (is conserved) despite changes in its appearance.

Suppose two identical glasses contain the same amount of liquid, and the liquid from one of these glasses is poured into a taller, narrower glass. If young children are asked whether one glass contains more liquid or both glasses contain the same

COURTESY OF KATHLEEN BERGER

Tests of Various Types of Conservation

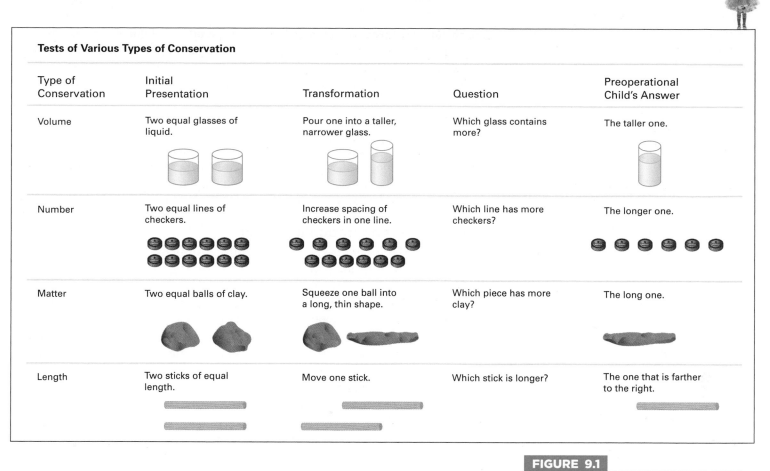

Type of Conservation	Initial Presentation	Transformation	Question	Preoperational Child's Answer
Volume	Two equal glasses of liquid.	Pour one into a taller, narrower glass.	Which glass contains more?	The taller one.
Number	Two equal lines of checkers.	Increase spacing of checkers in one line.	Which line has more checkers?	The longer one.
Matter	Two equal balls of clay.	Squeeze one ball into a long, thin shape.	Which piece has more clay?	The long one.
Length	Two sticks of equal length.	Move one stick.	Which stick is longer?	The one that is farther to the right.

FIGURE 9.1

Conservation, Please According to Piaget, until children grasp the concept of conservation at (he believed) about age 6 or 7, they cannot understand that the transformations shown here do not change the total amount of liquid, checkers, clay, and wood.

amount, they will insist that the narrower glass (in which the liquid level is higher) has more.

All four characteristics of preoperational thought are evident in this mistake. Young children fail to understand conservation of liquids because they focus (*center*) on what they see (*appearance*), noticing only the immediate (*static*) condition. It does not occur to them that they could reverse the process and re-create the liquid's level of a moment earlier (*irreversibility*). (See Figure 9.1 for other examples.)

Limitations of Piaget's Research

Notice that Piaget's tests of conservation require the child's words, not actions or brain scans. Later research has found that, when the tests of logic are simplified, young children often succeed. In many ways, children indicate that they know something via their gestures before they can say it in words (Goldin-Meadow, 2009).

Furthermore, even when words are the measure, some young children demonstrate conservation and other logical ideas in a gamelike setting, although not in Piaget's experiments (Donaldson, 1963/2003). For example, if a "naughty bear" lengthens a row of checkers, 4-year-olds say that the new row has the same number as before. That's conservation of number, a concept Piaget did not expect children to grasp until age 6.

Researchers now believe that Piaget underestimated cognition during early childhood, just as he had underestimated it during infancy (Halford & Andrews, 2006). He relied on the children's words in an experimental setting rather than on nonverbal signs in a play context. Other experiments to distinguish preoperational thought from Piaget's next stage (concrete operational thought) show the same results. For instance, he thought that preoperational children cannot classify objects properly, in that they do not firmly grasp that dogs, cats, and cows are all categories of animals.

To some extent, Piaget was right: Children are confused about the relationship between superordinate categories (such as animals), subcategories (such as dogs), and further subcategories (such as collies). (Classification is discussed further in Chapter 12.) However, even 3-year-olds can classify things if the categories are ones they themselves often use, such as that cereal and toast are part of break-fast or that ice cream and cake both belong to the dessert category (Nguyen & Murphy, 2003). Piaget was right that young children are not as logical as adults or older children, but he did not realize how much they actually do understand.

Animism in Preoperational Thought

animism The belief that natural objects and phenomena are alive.

A final aspect of preoperational thought is called **animism,** the belief that natural objects and phenomena are alive (Piaget, 1929). With egocentric reasoning, many children strongly believe that clouds, mountains, and trees have feelings and goals, and that they are capable of deliberate action in certain circumstances. Closely related to animism, an egocentric concept of nonhuman animals is common. For example, a dead bird discovered by a child might bring forth tears and require a burial ceremony. A dog might be told wishes and worries by a child who believes that the pet understands and sympathizes. Many children's stories include ani-mals or objects that talk and help people.

Attempts to measure children's animism find that many children simultane-ously hold rational and magical ideas (Meshcheryakov, 2005). Magical happenings and magical sayings are also common in the daily lives of young children. Wish-ing on a star or an eyelash, saying "Cross my heart and hope to die," holding one's breath when passing a cemetery, and many more such behaviors are frequent, even if the parents belittle them.

Regarding animism, not only Piaget but adults of all persuasions may have un-derestimated children. Adults who are bemused by children's superstitions need to remember that talking animals are found in every religion and that many adults encourage children's illogical, quasi-religious beliefs when they promote Santa Claus and the tooth fairy (Barrett, 2008).

Vygotsky: Social Learning

For decades, the magical, illogical, and self-centered aspects of early childhood cognition dominated research; scientists were understandably awed by Piaget. Vygotsky was the first leading developmentalist to emphasize another side of early cognition—that young children, instead of being egocentric, are affected by the wishes and emotions of others. He emphasized the sociocultural aspects of young children's cognition, in contrast to Piaget's emphasis on the individual.

Children and Mentors

>> **Response for Nutritionists** (from page 238) Take each of the four characteristics of preoperational thought into account. Because of egocentrism, having a special place and plate might assure the child that this food is exclusively his or hers. Since appearance is important, food should look tasty. Since static thinking dominates, if something healthy is added (e.g., grate carrots into the cake, add milk to the soup), do it before the food is given to the child. In the reversibility example in the text, the lettuce should be removed out of the child's sight and the "new" hamburger presented.

Vygotsky believed that every aspect of children's cognitive development is embed-ded in a social context (Vygotsky, 1934/1987). Children are curious and observant. They ask questions—about how machines work, why weather changes, where the sky ends—and seek answers from more knowledgeable mentors.

As you remember from Chapter 2, a child is an *apprentice in thinking,* someone whose intellectual growth is stimulated and directed by older and more skilled members of society. Parents are the first mentors (teachers) for young children, although many others are mentors as well. For example, the verbal proficiency of children in day-care centers is affected by the language of their playmates, who teach vocabulary without consciously doing so (Mashburn et al., 2009).

According to Vygotsky, children learn because their mentors:

- Present challenges
- Offer assistance (without taking over)
- Add crucial information
- Encourage motivation

Thinking occurs as the mentor and the child join in **guided participation,** sharing social experiences and explorations. For example, children learning to draw or write or dance copy one another, with the child who is copied not resenting it (as an adult might) but appreciating that someone else follows her lead. The ability to learn from mentors indicates intelligence, according to Vygotsky: "What children can do with the assistance of others might be in some sense even more indicative of their mental development than what they can do alone" (1934/1987, p. 5).

guided participation The process by which people learn from others who guide their experiences and explorations.

Scaffolding

Vygotsky believed that each individual has a **zone of proximal development (ZPD),** first described in Chapter 2 but emphasized again here because it is crucial to understanding cognition in early childhood. *Proximal* means "near," so the ZPD includes the ideas and skills that a child is close to learning but is not yet able to do independently. How and when children master various skills depends, in part, on the wisdom and willingness of mentors to provide **scaffolding,** or temporary sensitive support, to help them within their developmental zone.

Good caregivers provide plenty of scaffolding, encouraging children to look both ways before crossing the street (while holding the child's hand) or letting them stir the cake batter (perhaps the hands of both the adult and the child on the spoon handle, in guided participation). Scaffolding is particularly important for experiences that are directly cognitive—that is, ones that will produce better understanding of words and ideas. Fortunately, when an adult reads to a child, the adult usually scaffolds—explaining, pointing, listening—within the child's zone of development. A sensitive reader would never tell the child to be quiet but might instead prolong the session by expanding on the child's questions and the pictures in the book.

Scaffolding occurs everywhere. For instance, a program to introduce 2- and 3-year-olds to science occurred in the sandbox: Adults helped children experiment with sand and water, and later these children did more exploration on their own than children who had not undergone this apprenticeship in learning (van Schijndel et al., 2010). Even in conversation, scaffolding is possible and helpful. Parents often answer young children's questions, not with a simple answer, but with a response that builds vocabulary and understanding (Chouinard, 2007). If a child asks, "What is that?" the mother, instead of simply saying, "That is a truck," might say, "That is a kind of t-r-r . . ." (guiding the child to respond "truck") or "That is a garbage truck. What do you think it has inside?" Older siblings can be excellent mentors, too.

In Chiapas, Mexico, 8-year-old Tonik taught his 2-year-old sister, Katal, how to wash a doll. After several minutes of demonstrating and describing, Tonik continues:

zone of proximal development (ZPD) Vygotsky's term for the skills—cognitive as well as physical—that a person can exercise only with assistance, not yet independently.

scaffolding Temporary support that is tailored to a learner's needs and abilities and aimed at helping the learner master the next task in a given learning process.

Weaving Skills Baskets made in the Pacific island nation of Palau are known worldwide for their beauty and durability. The skills involved in weaving them are taught through scaffolding and apprenticeship.

TIM ROCK / LONELY PLANET

Tonik: Pour it like this. *[Demonstrates]*
Tonik: Sister, pour it. *[Hands glass]*
Tonik: Look! Pour it.
 Katal: *[Pours, with some difficulty]*
Tonik: Like that. *[Approval]*
 Katal: *[Looks away]*
Tonik: It's finished now.

[quoted in Maynard, 2002, p. 977]

Note that when Katal looks away, Tonik wisely declares the session finished. This response encourages the learner to participate in later apprenticeships. Motivation is crucial in early education—one reason why sensitive social interaction is so powerful. The social learning emphasized by Vygotsky is transmitted in every culture through scaffolding (Gauvain, 2005). Toys, clothes, playground equipment, eating routines, social interactions—everything scaffolds certain skills and behaviors that children learn.

The power of scaffolding is demonstrated when 2- to 6-year-olds imitate adult actions that are irrelevant, time-consuming, and inefficient. This is called *over-imitation*, evident in children from many cultures but not in other animals. Over-imitation is thought to be a way that children learn from older members of their community, allowing "rapid, high-fidelity intergenerational transmission of cultural forms" (Nielsen & Tomaselli, 2010, p. 735). (See the Research Design.)

Especially for Driving Instructors
Sometimes your students cry, curse, or quit. How would Vygotsky advise you to proceed? (see response, page 244)

▶ **Research Design**

Scientists: Mark Nielsen and Keyan Tomaselli.

Publication: *Psychological Science* (2010).

Participants: Sixty-one 2- to 6-year-olds from Bushman communities in South Africa and Botswana; 16 young children from Brisbane, Australia; and 17 older Bushman children. Over-imitation has been repeatedly demonstrated among Western children, but Bushman adults rarely explicitly teach children how to use objects. Thus, if apprenticeship in learning is the outcome of deliberate training, the children raised in the Bushman culture would not do it.

Design: Experimenters tested the children, one by one, on overimitation of irrelevant and inefficient ways to open three boxes. For example, a blue box could be easily opened by pulling a knob; but in the experimental condition, an adult (sometimes a Western scientist, sometimes a member of the local community) waved a red stick above the box three times and then used that stick to push down the knob to open the box. The children were given the stick and the box, and their actions were noted.

In the control condition, the children were simply given the stick and the box with no demonstration; again, their actions were noted. In an extension of this basic design, some of the control-group participants were shown the stick-waving demonstration after they had discovered on their own how to open the box the easy way.

Major conclusions: No matter who tested them, children of every age and culture performed the irrelevant and inefficient actions they saw, even if they had already opened the box the easy way. Apparently, children are universally predisposed to learn from mentors. Scaffolding occurs in many ways; children learn whatever routines and procedures they witness. These researchers believe that the cross-cultural "similarity of performance is profound" (p. 734). (Soon you will read applications to preschool education: Young children learn whatever adults encourage—imaginative play, artistic activities, social cooperation, or writing the alphabet.)

Comments: Originally, the researchers hypothesized that overimitation resulted from the practice in Western cultures, in which parents explicitly teach their young children, explaining as they demonstrate. The scientists were surprised that the Bushman children imitated as often as Western children do. Such cross-cultural research is needed to discover which aspects of cognitive development are part of Western culture and which are universal. Other developmentalists have found that children's imitation is sometimes selective (they don't imitate untrustworthy adults or accidental acts). More research will "determine when children will do precisely as others have done and when they instead choose their own actions" (p. 735).

Language as a Tool

Although all the objects of a culture guide children, Vygotsky believed that words are especially pivotal. Empirical research finds this to be the case, in every culture and with children of every ability (e.g., Baker et al., 2007; Philips & Tolmie, 2007; Schick & Melzi, 2010). Just as a builder needs tools to construct a house, the mind needs language. Talking, listening, reading, and writing are tools to advance thought, and informal scaffolding leads to advances in language and cognition.

Language advances thinking in two ways, according to Vygotsky (Fernyhough, 2010). The first way is with internal dialogue, or **private speech,** in which people talk to themselves (Vygotsky, 1934/1987). Young children use private speech often, although they do not realize it (Manfra & Winsler, 2006). They talk aloud to review, decide, and explain events to themselves (and, incidentally, to anyone else within earshot).

Older preschoolers are more selective, effective, and circumspect, sometimes whispering. Audible or not, private speech aids cognition and self-reflection; adults should encourage it (Perels et al., 2009; Winsler et al., 2007). Many people of all ages talk to themselves when alone or write down ideas to help them think. That is private speech as well. Preschool curricula based on Vygotsky's ideas use games, play, social interaction, and private speech to develop executive functioning (Diamond et al., 2007).

The second way in which language advances thinking, according to Vygotsky, is by mediating the social interaction that is vital to learning. This **social mediation** function of speech occurs during both formal instruction (when teachers explain things) and casual conversation. Words entice people into their zone of proximal development, as mentors guide children to learn numbers, recall memories, and follow routines. Words are tools that enable children, between ages 2 and 6, to do the following:

- Count objects, with one number per item (called *one-to-one correspondence*)
- Remember accurately (although false memories can confuse anyone)
- Verbalize standard experiences (called *scripts,* such as the normal sequence of a birthday party or a restaurant meal)

Each of these cognitive accomplishments has been the subject of extensive research; mentoring and language are crucial for all of them. By age 3 or 4, children's brains are mature enough to comprehend numbers, store memories, and recognize routines. Whether or not a child actually demonstrates such understanding depends on mentoring within family, school, and culture. Words are the mediator between brain potential and what children understand, and they become crucial for the social interaction that leads to brain maturation (Fernyhough, 2010; Gelman & Kalish, 2006).

One application in particular makes the point. Some children are the only witnesses to crimes, especially of sexual abuse or domestic violence. Adult mentors can plant false ideas in young children, whose shaky grasp of reality makes them vulnerable to guided participation. One result is that children recount memories of events that never happened (Bruck et al., 2006). How can adults know when a verbal report is accurate? Language can be the crucial mediator. Children who have already learned to tell coherent narratives provide more accurate accounts (Kulkofsky & Klemfuss, 2008).

private speech The internal dialogue that occurs when people talk to themselves (either silently or out loud).

social mediation Human interaction that expands and advances understanding, often through words that one person uses to explain something to another.

SUMMING UP

Cognition develops rapidly from age 2 to 6. Children's active search for understanding was first recognized by Piaget, who believed that young children are generally incapable of performing logical operations (hence *preoperational intelligence*). Piaget thought that

>> **Response for Driving Instructors**
(from page 242) Use guided participation and
scaffold the instruction so your students are
not overwhelmed. Be sure to provide lots of
praise and days of practice. If emotion erupts,
do not take it as an attack on you.

egocentrism limits understanding, as young childen center on only one thing at a time, focusing on appearance. Their thinking is magical and animistic.

Vygotsky emphasized the social and cultural aspects of children's cognition. He believed that children are guided as apprentices, within their zones of proximal development. Other people are mentors, providing the scaffolding that helps children master various skills and concepts. Language is a crucial learning tool, in private speech and social mediation.

theory-theory The idea that children attempt to explain everything they see and hear by constructing theories.

>> Children's Theories

Piaget and Vygotsky realized that children actively work to understand their world. Many other developmentalists have attempted to show exactly how children's knowledge develops. One discovery is that children do not simply learn words and ideas—they develop theories.

Theory-Theory

Humans of all ages try to explain whatever happens. The term **theory-theory** refers to the idea that children naturally construct theories to explain whatever they see and hear:

> More than any animal, we search for causal regularities in the world around us. We are perpetually driven to look for deeper explanations of our experience, and broader and more reliable predictions about it. . . . Children seem, quite literally, to be born with . . . the desire to understand the world and the desire to discover how to behave in it.
>
> *[Gopnik, 2001, p. 66]*

FIGURE 9.2

Unfold the Turkey This recipe (from *Smashed Potatoes*, edited by Jane Martel) shows many characteristics of preschool thought, among them literal interpretation of words ("Sometimes you can call it a bird, but it's not") and an uncertain idea of time ("Push in the stuffin' for a couple of hours") and quantity ("A giant lump of stuffin'").

A whole turkey

1 big bag full of a whole turkey
   (Get the kind with no feathers on,
   not the kind the Pilgrims ate.)
A giant lump of stuffin'
1 squash pie
1 mint pie
1 little fancy dish of sour berries
1 big fancy dish of a vegetable mix
20 dishes of all different candies;
   chocolate balls, cherry balls,
   good'n plenties and peanuts

Get up when the alarm says to and get busy fast. Unfold the turkey and open up the holes. Push in the stuffin' for a couple of hours. I think you get stuffin' from that Farm that makes it.

I know you have to pin the stuffin' to the turkey or I suppose it would get out. And get special pins or use big long nails.

Get the kitchen real hot, and from there on you just cook turkey. Sometimes you can call it a bird, but it's not.

Then you put the vegetables in the cooker—and first put one on top, and next put one on the bottom, and then one in the middle. That makes a vegetable mix. Put 2 red things of salt all in it and 2 red things of water also. Cook them to just ½ of warm.

Put candies all around the place and Linda will bring over the pies.

When the company comes put on your red apron.

Thus, according to theory-theory, the best explanation for cognition in young children is that humans always seek reasons, causes, and underlying principles to make sense of their experience. Figure 9.2, with its narrative-style "recipe" for cooking a turkey, captures the essential idea of theory-theory: that children don't want logical definitions but rather explanations of various things, especially things that involve them.

Exactly how are explanations sought in early childhood? In one study, Mexican American mothers kept detailed diaries of every question their 3- to 5-year-olds asked and how they themselves had responded (Kelemen et al., 2005). Most of the questions were about human behavior and characteristics (see Figure 9.3); for example, "Why do you give my mother a kiss?" "Why is my brother bad?" "Why do women have breasts?" and "Why are there Black kids?" Fewer questions were about nonliving things ("Why does it rain?") or objects ("Why is my daddy's car white?").

Questions were often about the underlying purpose of whatever the child observed, although parents usually responded as if children were asking about science instead. An adult might interpret a child's one-word question "Why?" to mean "What causes X to happen?" when the child intended "Why?" to mean "I want to know more about *X*" (Leach, 1997). For example, if a child asks why women have breasts, a parent's first thought would be about hormones and maturation, but a child-centered explanation would be that breasts are for feeding babies. From a child's egocentric perspective, any query includes "How does this relate to me?" Accordingly, the parent might add that the child got his or her first nourishment from mother's breast.

A series of experiments that explored when and how 3-year-olds imitate others provides some support for theory-theory (Williamson et al., 2008). Children seem to figure out *why* adults act as they do before deciding to copy those actions. If an adult intended to accomplish something and succeeded, a child is likely to follow the example, but if the same action and result seemed inadvertent or accidental, the child is less likely to copy. Indeed, even when asked to repeat something un-grammatical that an adult says, children are likely to correct the grammar based on their theory of the adult's intentions (Over & Gattis, 2010). This is another example of a general principle: Children develop theories before they employ their impressive ability to imitate.

Theory of Mind

Human mental processes—thoughts, emotions, beliefs, motives, and intentions—are among the most complicated and puzzling phenomena that we encounter every day. Adults seek to understand why people fall in love, or vote as they do, or make foolish choices. Children are puzzled about a playmate's unexpected anger, a sibling's generosity, or an aunt's too-wet kiss.

To know what goes on in another's mind, people develop a *folk psychology,* an understanding of others' thinking called **theory of mind.** Theory of mind is an emergent ability, slow to develop in autistic children and animals, but typically beginning in most human children at about age 4 (Sterck & Begeer, 2010).

Belief and Reality: Understanding the Difference

The idea that thoughts may not reflect reality is beyond very young children, but then it occurs to each child rather suddenly sometime after age 3. This idea leads to the theory-of-mind concept that people can be deliberately deceived or fooled—which younger children do not realize.

In one of several false-belief tests that researchers developed, a child watches as a doll named Max puts a puppy in a red box. Then Max leaves and the child sees the puppy taken out of the red box and put in a blue box. When Max returns, the child is asked, "Where will Max look for the puppy?" Most 3-year-olds confidently say, "In the blue box"; most 6 year-olds correctly say, "In the red box," a pattern found in a dozen nations (Wellman et al., 2001).

Indeed, 3-year-olds almost always confuse what they know now with what they once thought and what someone else might think. Another way of describing this is to say that they are "cursed" by their own knowledge (Birch & Bloom, 2003), too egocentric to grasp others' perspectives.

This can been seen in everyday life: Young children are notoriously bad at deception. They play hide-and-seek by hiding in the same place time after time, or their facial expression betrays them when they tell a fib. Parents sometimes say, "I know when you are lying" and, to the consternation of most 3-year-olds, parents are usually right. (This is not true at older ages because children become better at fooling their parents; knowing this, parents thus become suspicious of the truth as well as of the lie.)

Closely related to young children's trouble with lying are their belief in fantasy (the magical thinking noted earlier) and their static reasoning (characteristic of

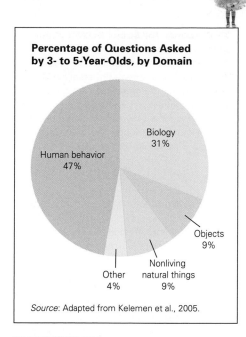

Percentage of Questions Asked by 3- to 5-Year-Olds, by Domain

Human behavior 47%
Biology 31%
Objects 9%
Nonliving natural things 9%
Other 4%

Source: Adapted from Kelemen et al., 2005.

FIGURE 9.3

Questions, Questions Parents found that most of their children's questions were about human behavior—especially the parents' behavior toward the child. Children seek to develop a theory to explain things, so the question "Why can't I have some candy?" is not satisfactorily answered by "It's almost dinnertime."

theory of mind A person's theory of what other people might be thinking. In order to have a theory of mind, children must realize that other people are not necessarily thinking the same thoughts that they themselves are. That realization is seldom possible before age 4.

Especially for Social Scientists Can you think of any connection between Piaget's theory of preoperational thought and 3-year-olds' errors in this theory-of-mind task? (see response, page 246)

>> **Response for Social Scientists** (from page 245) According to Piaget, preschool children focus on appearance and on static conditions (so they cannot mentally reverse a process). Furthermore, they are egocentric, believing that everyone shares their point of view. No wonder they believe that they had always known the puppy was in the blue box and that Max would know that, too.

Brains at Work Neuroscience confirms the critical role of the prefrontal cortex for development of theory of mind. Adults and 4- to 6-year-olds were questioned on 40 theory of mind examples. The adults answered correctly, as did some 4- to 6-year-olds (passers), though not all (failers). The leftmost images are brain wave patterns, the middle ones represent brain activity (fMRI), and the far right trio contrasts mental activity when distinguishing reality and belief. Adult brain waves show quick answers, and the contrast (*right*) shows that they answered quickly with little effort; but the child passers needed to think longer before they answered. The authors concluded that "social cognition and the brain develop together" (Liu et al., 2009, pp. 318, 325).

preoperational thought), which makes it difficult for them to change their minds (remember perseveration from Chapter 8).

Brain and Context

Developmentalists wonder what, precisely, strengthens theory of mind at about age 4. Is this change more nature or nurture, brain maturation or experience? Age-related maturation of the prefrontal cortex seems crucial, according to brain scans of 4-, 5-, and 6-year-olds and adults as they figured out theory-of-mind puzzles (Liu et al., 2009) (see photo).

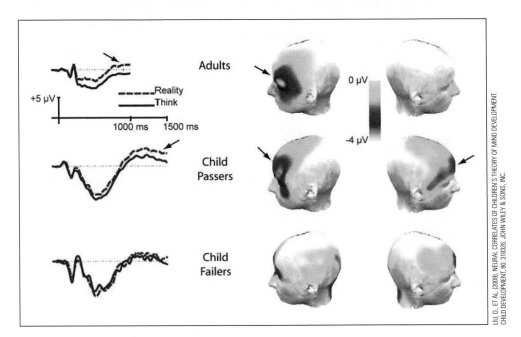

Does the significance of brain maturation mean that context is irrelevant? Not at all (Sterck & Begeer, 2010). Language, siblings, and culture have an effect. At any age, children with greater verbal fluency are more likely to demonstrate theory of mind. This is partly the result of experience, especially experiencing mother–child conversations that involve thoughts and wishes (Ontai & Thompson, 2008). Furthermore, in the development of theory of mind, "Two older siblings are worth about a year of chronological age" (Perner, 2000, p. 383). As siblings argue, agree, compete, and cooperate, and as older siblings try to fool them, it dawns on 3-year-olds that not everyone thinks as they do. By age 5, their theory of mind is well established: They know how to gain parental sympathy to protect themselves against their older siblings.

Culture also matters. A study comparing theory of mind among young children in preschools in Canada, India, Peru, Samoa, and Thailand found that the Canadian 5-year-olds were slightly more advanced and the Samoan 5-year-olds were slightly slower in their understanding of theory of mind; but across cultures, most 5-year-old children passed the false-belief tests (see Figure 9.4). The researchers concluded that brain maturation was critical for theory of mind and that language, social interaction, and culture were also influential (Callaghan et al., 2005). Similar conclusions were reached by a meta-analysis of 254 studies in China and North America (in which about 5,000 children were tested) (Liu et al., 2008, p. 527).

Cultural effects were also evident in a series of studies comparing children in Korea and in England. Some Korean 3-year-olds passed tests that almost no

Ready to Learn When 2-year-olds quarrel, they grab toys and, if expedient, push and kick. Such fights between siblings seem to advance theory of mind: By age 4, these two may use deception to get what they want.

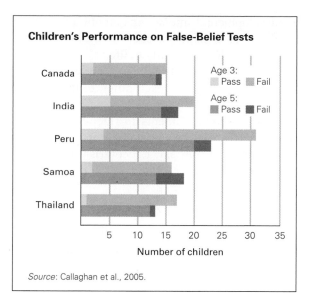

Children's Performance on False-Belief Tests

Age 3:
Pass ■ Fail

Age 5:
■ Pass ■ Fail

Number of children

Source: Callaghan et al., 2005.

FIGURE 9.4

Few at Age 3, Most by Age 5 The advantage of cross-cultural research is that it can reveal universal patterns. Although the number of children in each group is small (from 31 3-year-olds in Peru to 13 5-year-olds in Thailand), the pattern is obvious. Something changes at about age 4 that enables most children to acquire theory of mind by age 5.

English child did. However, in both cultures, notable progress occurred from ages 3 to 5 (U.S. Department of Health and Human Services, 2010), indicating the influence of maturation (Oh & Lewis, 2008).

SUMMING UP

Scholars have recently noted that children develop theories to explain whatever they observe and that those theories do not necessarily spring from explanations given to them by adults. Children are interested in the underlying purpose of events; adults are more focused on immediate scientific causes. Many researchers have explored the development of theory of mind, the realization that other people's thoughts and ideas might differ from one's own. Neurological maturation, linguistic competence, family context, and culture all affect the attainment of theory of mind, which appears at about age 4.

A Shared Pleasure As they read stories to young children, many adults express exaggerated surprise, excitement, worry, and relief. They realize that words are better understood and remembered when they are connected to emotions.

>> Language

Language is not only a tool for learning, it is the premier accomplishment of early childhood: 2-year-olds use short, telegraphic sentences, but 6-year-olds seem able to understand and discuss almost anything (see At About This Time on the next page).

Brain maturation, myelination, scaffolding, and social interaction make early childhood ideal for learning language. As you remember from Chapter 1, scientists once thought that early childhood was a critical period for language learning—the only time when a first language could be mastered and the best time for learning a second or third language. However, millions of people have learned languages after age 6; the critical-period hypothesis is false (Birdsong, 2006; Herschensohn, 2007).

Instead, early childhood is a sensitive period for language learning—for rapidly and easily mastering vocabulary, grammar, and pronunciation. Young children are "language sponges" because they soak up every drop of language they encounter. There are "multiple sensitive periods . . . auditory, phonological, semantic, syntactic, and motor systems, along

AT ABOUT THIS TIME	
Language in Early Childhood	
Approximate Age	**Characteristic or Achievement in First Language**
2 years	*Vocabulary:* 100–2,000 words *Sentence length:* 2–6 words *Grammar:* Plurals, pronouns, many nouns, verbs, adjectives *Questions:* Many "What's that?" questions
3 years	*Vocabulary:* 1,000–5,000 words *Sentence length:* 3–8 words *Grammar:* Conjunctions, adverbs, articles *Questions:* Many "Why?" questions
4 years	*Vocabulary:* 3,000–10,000 words *Sentence length:* 5–20 words *Grammar:* Dependent clauses, tags at sentence end ("... didn't I?" "... won't you?") *Questions:* Peak of "Why?"; many "How?" and "When?" questions
5 years	*Vocabulary:* 5,000–20,000 words *Sentence length:* Some seem unending ("... and ... who ... and ... that ... and ...") *Grammar:* Complex, sometimes using passive voice ("Man bitten by dog"); subjunctive ("If I were ...") —if a child has heard these forms used correctly *Questions:* Some about differences (male/female, old/young, rich/poor) and many other issues

fast-mapping The speedy and sometimes imprecise way in which children learn new words by tentatively placing them in mental categories according to their perceived meaning.

with the developmental interactions among these components" (Thomas & Johnson, 2008, p. 2), all of which facilitate language learning early in life.

One of the valuable traits of young children is that they talk a lot—to adults, to each other, to themselves, to their toys—unfazed by mispronunciation, misuse, stuttering, or other impediments to fluency. Language comes easily partly because young children are less self-conscious about what they say. Egocentrism has advantages; this is one of them.

The Vocabulary Explosion

Children add new words to their vocabulary rapidly. The average child knows about 500 words at age 2 and usually more than 10,000 at age 6 (Herschensohn, 2007). Precise estimates of vocabulary size vary because contexts are diverse; some children learn four times as many words as others. For every young child, however, vocabulary builds quickly and language potential is greater than is demonstrated by spoken vocabulary. Every child could become fluently bilingual given the proper circumstances.

Fast-Mapping

How does the vocabulary explosion occur? After painstakingly learning one word at a time at age 1, children develop an interconnected set of categories for words, a kind of grid or mental map, which makes speedy vocabulary acquisition possible. The process is called **fast-mapping** (Woodward & Markman, 1998) because, rather than figuring out an exact definition after hearing a word used in several contexts, children hear a word once and quickly stick it into one of the categories in their mental language map.

Like more conventional mental mapping, language mapping is not always precise. Thus, when asked where Cameroon is, most people can locate it approximately ("It's in Africa"), but few can name the six countries that border it (Nigeria, Chad, Central African Republic, Equitorial Guinea, Gabon, Congo). Similarly, children quickly map new animal names close to already-known animal names, without knowing all the precise details. Thus, *tiger* is easy to map if you know *lion*. A trip to the zoo facilitates fast-mapping of dozens of animal words, especially since zoos scaffold learning by placing similar animals nearby.

Egocentrism is an asset here—children say "tiger" for any animal that is fast-mapped in that category, from cheetah to jaguar. They do not worry that they might be wrong; they center on their own concept. Adults, however, might be silent if they cannot distinguish a lynx from an ocelot; that slows down their learning.

Fast-mapping is evident even before age 2, accelerating as new words are learned because each word makes it easier to map other words (Gershkoff-Stowe & Hahn, 2007). Generally, the more linguistic clues children already have, the better their fast-mapping is (Mintz, 2005). One set of experiments in vocabulary learning began in cultures whose languages had only a few counting words: the equivalents of *one, two,* and *many*. People in such cultures were much worse at estimating quantity because they did not have the words to guide them (Gordon, 2004). Mapping and understanding a new number word, such as *nineteen*, is easier if one already knows a related word, such as *nine*.

An experiment in teaching the names of parts of objects (e.g., the spigot of a faucet) found that children learned much better if the adults named the object that had the part and then spoke of the object in the possessive (e.g., "See this butterfly? Look, this is the butterfly's thorax") (Saylor & Sabbagh, 2004). This finding shows that it is easier to map a new word when it is connected to a familiar one.

Words and the Limits of Logic

Closely related to fast-mapping is a phenomenon called logical extension: After learning a word, children use it to describe other objects in the same category. One child told her father she had seen some "Dalmatian cows" on a school trip to a farm. He understood because he remembered that she had petted a Dalmatian dog the weekend before. Bilingual children might insert a word from another language if they don't know the word in the language they are speaking, although soon they separate one language from the other and know who speaks which—and talk in only one language when speaking to a monolingual person.

Young children have difficulty with words that express comparisons (such as *tall* and *short*, *near* and *far*, *high* and *low*, *deep* and *shallow*) because they do not understand that the meaning of these words depends on the context (Ryalls, 2000). If they have been taught that one end of the swimming pool is the deep end, children might obey parental instructions to stay out of deep puddles by splashing through every puddle they see, insisting that none of them are deep.

Words expressing relationships of place and time—such as *here*, *there*, *yesterday*, and *tomorrow*—are difficult as well. More than one child has awakened on Christmas morning and asked, "Is it tomorrow yet?" A child told to "stay there" or "come here" may not follow instructions because the terms are confusing.

Acquiring Basic Grammar

We noted in Chapter 6 that the *grammar* of language includes the structures, techniques, and rules that are used to communicate meaning. Word order and word repetition, prefixes and suffixes, intonation and emphasis—all are part of grammar.

By age 3, children understand basic aspects of grammar. English-speaking children know word order (subject/verb/object), saying, "I eat the apple," not any of the 23 other possible sequences of those four words. They use plurals; tenses (past, present, and future); and nominative, objective, and possessive pronouns (*I*/ *me*/*mine* or *my*). Some even use articles (*the, a, an*) correctly, even though proper article use in English is bewilderingly complex, as those who learn English as adults know all too well.

Learning each aspect of each language (grammar, vocabulary, pronunciation, etc.) follows a particular developmental path, partly because parts of the brain myelinate at specific rates and every language has both easy and difficult constructions. In general, genes affect *expressive* (spoken or written) language more than *receptive* (heard or read) language. Thus, some children are relatively talkative or quiet because they inherit that tendency, but experience determines which words and grammatical constructions they understand (Kovas et al., 2005).

Young children sometimes apply the rules of grammar when they should not, an error called **overregularization.** For example, English-speaking children learn the rule to add an *-s* to form the plural: Toddlers ask for two *cookies* or more *blocks.* They apply this to nonsense words as well: If they are shown a drawing of an abstract shape, are told it is called a *wug,* and are then shown two of these

Horse or Dromedary? These children might fast-map and call it a horse since it is horse-sized, horse-colored, and has a horse-like head and legs. Fast-mapping is misleading. However, if you think this is a dromedary, you made a similar mistake. All dromedaries are camels, but not all camels are dromedaries. This one is not.

Observation Quiz Is this scene set in the United States or some other country? (see answer, page 250)

overregularization The application of rules of grammar even when exceptions occur, making the language seem more "regular" than it actually is.

shapes, they say there are two *wugs*. However, many young children overregularize that final -*s*, talking about *foots, tooths,* and *mouses*. This is evidence for increasing knowledge: Many children first say words correctly because they repeat what they have heard, yet later, when they grasp the grammar and try to apply it, they overregularize.

Learning Two Languages

Language-minority children (those who speak a language that is not the dominant language of their nation) suffer if they do not speak the majority language well. In the United States, those who are not proficient in English tend to have lower school achievement, diminished self-esteem, and inadequate employment, as well as many other problems. Fluency in English can erase these liabilities, and fluency in another language is an asset. In the United States in 2010, 20 percent of schoolchildren spoke one language at home and English at school, with most of that 20 pecent (75 percent) also speaking English well. But how and when should a second language be learned?

What Is the Goal?

Is a nation better off if all its citizens speak one language or if there is more than one official language (Switzerland has three, Canada has two)?

Some say that young children need to become proficient in one, and only one, language. "English only" advocates in the United States believe that children should speak only English. They believe that national identity requires everyone to speak English well, that children taught two languages might become confused and end up being semilingual, not bilingual, "at risk for delayed, incomplete, and possibly even impaired language development" (Genesee, 2008, p. 17).

Others say that everyone should speak at least two languages and that "there is absolutely no evidence that children get confused if they learn two languages" (Genesee, 2008, p. 18). This second position has more research support: Soon after the vocabulary explosion, children who have heard two languages since birth usually master two distinct sets of words and grammar, along with each language's characteristic pauses, pronunciations, intonations, and even gestures (Genesee & Nicoladis, 2007).

No doubt early childhood is the best time to learn language, whether it is one, two, or three languages. Neuroscience finds that young bilingual children site both languages in the same areas of their brains yet manage to keep them separate. This separation allows them to activate one language and temporarily inhibit the other, experiencing no confusion when they speak to a monolingual person (Crinion et al., 2006). By contrast, the brains of those who learn a second language in adulthood usually show different activation sites for each language. Sometimes they silently translate as they listen and speak, which slows them down. A few fortunate adults who learn a second language after puberty activate the same brain area for both; these people tend to be unusually skilled bilingualists (Thomas & Johnson, 2008).

Pronunciation is hard to master after childhood. Indeed, young children have pronunciation difficulties in their first language, but they are blithely unaware of their mistakes. English-only children transpose sounds (*magazine* becomes *mazagine*), drop consonants (*truck* becomes *ruck*), and convert difficult sounds to easier ones (*father* becomes *fadder*). Mispronunciation does not impair fluency primarily because young children are more receptive than expressive—they hear better than they talk. When 4-year-old Rachel asked for a "yeyo yayipop," her father repeated, "You want a yeyo yayipop?" She replied, "Daddy, sometimes you talk funny."

Student and Teachers Children at the Lawrence, Massachusetts, YWCA show Rashon McCloud of the Boston Celtics how they use a computer to learn reading. They are participating in an NBA-sponsored program called Read to Achieve. Children are often faster than adults to catch on to technological innovations.

RAY AMATI / NBAE / GETTY IMAGES

>> **Answer to Observation Quiz** (from page 249) It is not set in the United States. One clue is the boys' haircuts, the girl's headscarf, and the clothes on all three—each possible in the United States, but unlikely on three U.S. children together. Another clue is that camels with two humps are rare in U.S. zoos. But one thing is definitive: the fence. By law and custom, no U.S. zoos have fences children can crawl through. Is this cultural scaffolding, leading U.S. preschoolers to fear camels more than these Italians do?

To speak well, young children need to be "bathed in language," as some early-childhood educators express it. The emphasis is on hearing and speaking in every situation, just as a person taking a bath is surrounded by water. Television is a poor teacher because children need personalized, responsive instruction in the zone of proximal development.

Language Loss

Schools in all nations stress the dominant language, but language-minority parents fear that their children will make a *language shift,* becoming more fluent in the school language than in their home language (Min, 2000). Language shift occurs everywhere: Some language-minority children in Mexico shift to Spanish (Messing, 2007), some children from the First Nations in Canada shift to English (Allen, 2007), and so on—often to the consternation of their elders.

Some children shift in talking but not in comprehending. It is not unusual for 5-year-olds to understand their parents' language but refuse to speak it. Nor is it unusual for immigrant adults to depend on a child as spokesperson and interpreter when they deal with monolingual bureaucrats. This dependency may be a practical necessity, but it represents a role reversal that widens the generational gap between child and parent.

Language shift and role reversal are unfortunate, not only for the child but also for the society. Having many fluently bilingual citizens is a national strength, especially in this era of globalization, and respect for family traditions is a bulwark against adolescent rebellion. Yet young children are preoperational: They center on the immediate status of the "foreign" language, not on its global usefulness; on appearances more than on past history; on parental dress and customs, not on traditions and wisdom. No wonder many shift toward the dominant culture. Since language is integral to culture, if a child is to become fluently bilingual, everyone who speaks with the child should appreciate both cultures (Pearson, 2008; Snow & Kang, 2006).

Becoming a **balanced bilingual,** speaking two languages so well that no audible hint suggests the other language, is accomplished by millions of young children in many nations. However, many millions of other children abandon their first language or do not learn the second as well as they might. There are many cognitive and linguistic advantages to bilingual proficiency (Bialystok & Viswanathan, 2009; Pearson, 2008). However, although skills in one language can be transferred to benefit another, "transfer is neither automatic nor inevitable" (Snow & Kang, 2006, p. 97). Scaffolding is needed. The basics of language learning—the naming and vocabulary explosions, fast-mapping, overregularization, extensive practice—apply to every language a young child learns.

MARY KNOX MERRILL / THE CHRISTIAN SCIENCE MONITOR / GETTY IMAGES

Smiling Faces Sometimes Everyone in this group is an immigrant, born far from their current home in Burlington, Vermont. Jean Luc Dushime escaped the 1994 genocide in Rwanda, central Africa, when he was 14. He eventually adapted to his new language, climate, surroundings, and culture. Today he helps immigrant children make the same transition.

balanced bilingual A person who is fluent in two languages, not favoring one over the other.

Especially for Immigrant Parents You want your children to be fluent in the language of your family's new country, even though you do not speak that language well. Should you speak to your children in your native tongue or in the new language? (see response, page 252)

SUMMING UP

Children aged 2 to 6 have impressive linguistic talents. They explode into speech, from about a hundred words to many thousands, from halting baby talk to fluency. Fast-mapping and grammar are among the sophisticated devices they use, although both can backfire: Many young children misuse words or assume grammar regularities that do not exist. No other time in the entire life span is as sensitive for language learning, especially for mastering pronunciation. Extensive exposure to two languages, with strong encouragement and repeated practice, can result in children being balanced bilinguals, which confers not only fluency but also cognitive and social benefits.

>> Early-Childhood Education

A hundred years ago, children had no formal education until first grade, which is why it was called "first" and why young children were "preschoolers." Today many 3- to 6-year-olds are in school (see Figure 9.5 for U.S. trends) not only because of changing family patterns but also because research now "documents the rapid development and great learning potential of the early years" (Hyson et al., 2006, p. 6). Especially by age 3 or 4, children learn best if they have extensive practice in hearing and speaking, in fine and gross motor skills, and in literacy and numeracy, which most preschools provide.

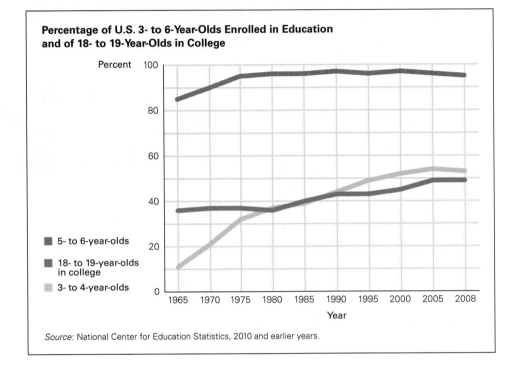

FIGURE 9.5

Changing Times As research increasingly finds that preschool education provides a foundation for later learning, most young children are enrolled in educational programs. Note the contrast with 18- to 19-year-olds in college (not shown are the 18- to 19-year-olds still in high school—about 15 percent).

Observation Quiz At what point did the percentage of 3- to 4-year-olds in school exceed that of 18- to 19-year-olds in college? (see answer, page 254)

Source: National Center for Education Statistics, 2010 and earlier years.

A key research conclusion is that the quality of both the home and the school matter. If the home educational environment is poor, a quality preschool program is especially beneficial (Hindman et al., 2010). When early education programs are compared, the most important variable are teachers who know how to respond to the needs of young children and have time to do so.

Some characteristics of quality day care were described in Chapter 7: safety, adequate space and equipment, a low child/adult ratio, positive social interactions among children and adults, and trained staff who are likely to stay in the program. One of the best questions that parents comparing options can ask is, "How long has each staff member worked at this center?"

Educational institutions for young children are referred to by various names—preschool, nursery school, day care, pre-primary—but a program's label is not a reliable indicator of its nature. Each early-childhood educational program (and sometimes each teacher) emphasizes somewhat different skills, goals, and methods (Chambers et al., 2010; Walsh & Petty, 2007). We will now consider three general categories of early-childhood education: child-centered, teacher-directed, and intervention programs. Remember, however, that home quality and warm, experienced teachers are more important for young children than the particular philosophy of the program.

>> Response for Immigrant Parents (from page 251) Children learn by listening, so it is important to speak with them often. Depending on how comfortable you are with the new language, you might prefer to read to your children, sing to them, and converse with them primarily in your native language and find a good preschool where they will learn the new language. The worst thing you could do would be to restrict speech in either tongue.

"We teach them that the world can be an unpredictable, dangerous, and sometimes frightening place, while being careful not to spoil their lovely innocence. It's tricky."

Tricky Indeed Young children are omnivorous learners, picking up habits, curses, and attitudes that adults would rather not transmit. Deciding what to teach—by actions more than words—is essential.

Child-Centered Programs

Many programs are called *developmental,* or *child-centered,* because they stress children's development and growth. They emphasize children's need to follow their own interests rather than adult directions (Weikart, 1999). Many child-centered programs allow children to discover ideas at their own pace. The physical space and the materials (such as dress-up clothing, art supplies, puzzles, blocks of many sizes, and other toys) are arranged to allow self-paced exploration.

Most child-centered programs encourage artistic expression (Lim, 2004). Some educators argue that young children "are all poets" in that they are gifted in seeing the world more imaginatively than older people do. According to advocates of child-centered programs, this peak of creative vision should be encouraged; children are given many opportunities to tell stories, draw pictures, dance, and make music for their own delight (Egan & Ling, 2002).

Child-centered programs are often influenced by Piaget, who emphasized that each child will discover new ideas, and by Vygotsky, who thought that children learn much from other children, with adult guidance (Bodrova & Leong, 2005). In order to learn number skills, for example, children in child-centered programs play games that include math (counting objects, keeping score), follow routines that use measurements (daily calendars, schedules), and use number rules (only three children in the block corner at one time, two volunteers to get the juice).

Montessori Schools

One type of child-centered school began a hundred years ago, when Maria Montessori opened nursery schools for poor children in Rome. She believed that children needed structured, individualized projects to give them a sense of accomplishment. They completed puzzles, used sponges and water to clean tables, traced shapes, and so on.

Like Piaget (her contemporary), Montessori (1870–1952) realized that children's thoughts and needs are different from those of adults. In her schools, children learned from activities that some adults might call play. Teachers gave each child tasks that dovetailed with his or her cognitive eagerness. For example, because

Especially for Unemployed Early-Childhood Teachers You are offered a job in a program that has 10 children for every one adult. You know that is too many, but you want a job. What should you do? (see response, page 255)

Tibet, China, India, and . . . Italy? Over the past half-century, as China increased its control of Tibet, thousands of refugees fled to northern India. Tibet traditionally had no preschools, but young children adapt quickly, as here in Ladakh, India. This Tibetan boy is working a classic Montessori board.

Montessori schools Schools that offer early-childhood education based on the philosophy of Maria Montessori, which emphasizes careful work and tasks that each young child can do.

Reggio Emilia A famous program of early-childhood education that originated in the town of Reggio Emilia, Italy, and that encourages each child's creativity in a carefully designed setting.

>> Answer to Observation Quiz (from page 252) Between 1985 and 1990. The exact year (not shown) was 1988.

they have a need for order, for language learning, and for using all their senses, children learned from systematic exercises that allowed them to augment their language skills as they touched and smelled various objects. The child's own wish to explore and to practice various fine motor skills was used to aid learning.

Today's **Montessori schools** still emphasize individual pride and achievement, presenting many literacy-related tasks (such as outlining letters and looking at books) to young children (Lillard, 2005). Many of the specifics differ from those that Montessori developed, but the underlying philosophy is the same. Children seek out learning tasks and are not made to sit quietly while a teacher instructs them. That is what makes Montessori programs child-centered, although traditional Montessori schools exclude some activities that children enjoy (pretend play, for example).

The goal is for the children to feel proud of themselves and engaged in learning. Many aspects of Montessori's philosophy are in accord with current developmental research. That is one reason this kind of school remains popular. A study of 5-year-olds in inner-city Milwaukee who were chosen by lottery to attend Montessori programs found that they were better at prereading and early math tasks, as well as at developing a theory of mind, than were their peers in other schools (Lillard & Else-Quest, 2006).

Reggio Emilia

Another form of early-childhood education is called **Reggio Emilia** because it began in the Italian town of that name, where virtually every young child attends preschool. In Reggio Emilia, children are encouraged to master skills that are not usually seen in North American schools until age 7 or so, such as writing and using tools. There is no large-group instruction, with formal lessons in, say, forming letters or cutting paper. Instead, "Every child is a creative child, full of potential" (Gandini et al., 2005, p. 1), with personal learning needs and artistic drive. Measurement of learning, such as testing to see whether children have learned their letters, is not part of the core belief that each child should explore and learn in his or her own way (Lewin-Benham, 2008).

ATELIER—FROM "OPEN WINDOWS," © MUNICIPALITY OF REGGIO EMILIA INFANT-TODDLER CENTERS AND PRESCHOOLS, PUBLISHED BY REGGIO CHILDREN 1994.

Another Place for Children High ceilings, uncrowded play space, varied options for art and music, a glass wall revealing trees and flowers—all these features reflect the Reggio Emilia approach to individualized, creative learning for young children. Such places are rare in nations other than Italy.

>> **Observation Quiz** How many children appear in this photograph and how many are engaged in creative expression? (see answer, page 257)

Appreciation of the arts is evident. Every Reggio Emilia school has a studio and an artist who encourages the children to be creative. The space also fosters creativity. Reggio Emilia schools have a large central room where children gather, children's art is displayed on white walls and hung from high ceilings, and floor-to-ceiling windows open to a spacious, plant-filled playground. Big mirrors are part of the school's décor—again, with the idea of fostering individuality. Reggio Emilia programs have a low child/teacher ratio, ample space, and abundant materials for creative expression.

One distinctive feature of the curriculum is that a small group of children become engaged in long-term projects of their choosing. Such projects foster the children's pride in their accomplishments (which are displayed for all to admire) while teaching them to plan and work together. Teachers are also encouraged to plan and collaborate. For six hours each week, they work without the children: planning activities, having group discussions, and talking to parents. Parents collaborate as well, teaching special subjects and learning about their child, with reports that include photographs, detailed observations written by the teachers, and artwork.

Teacher-Directed Programs

Unlike child-centered schools, teacher-directed preschool programs stress academics, usually taught by one adult to the entire group. The curriculum includes learning the names of letters, numbers, shapes, and colors according to a set timetable; every child naps, snacks, and goes to the bathroom on schedule as well. Children are taught to sit quietly and listen to the teacher. Praise and other reinforcements are given for good behavior, and time-outs (brief separation from activities) are imposed to punish misbehavior.

>> **Response for Unemployed Early-Childhood Teachers** (from page 253) Best for you to wait for a job where children learn well, organized along the lines explained in this chapter. You would be happier, as well as learn more, if your workplace were good for children, but realistically, you might take the 10-children-to-1-adult job. If you do, change the child/adult ratio—choose a helper, perhaps a college intern or a volunteer grandmother. But choose carefully—some adults are not helpful at all. Before you take the job, remember that children need continuity: You can't leave simply because you find something better.

In teacher-directed programs, the serious work of schooling is distinguished from the unstructured play of home. As one young boy explained:

> So home is home and kindergarten is kindergarten. Here is my work and at home is off-time, understand? My mum says work is me learning something. Learning is when you drive your head, and off-time is when the head slows down.
>
> *[quoted in Griebel & Niesel, 2002, p. 67]*

The teachers' goal is to make all children "ready to learn" when they enter elementary school by teaching basic skills, including precursors to reading, writing, and arithmetic, perhaps via teachers asking questions that children answer together. Children practice forming letters, sounding out words, counting objects, and writing their names. If a 4-year-old learns to read, that is success. (In a child-centered program, early reading might arouse suspicion that the child had too little time to play or socialize.) Many teacher-directed programs were inspired by behaviorism, which emphasizes step-by-step learning and repetition.

The contrast between child-centered and teacher-directed philosophies is evident not only in lessons but also in attitudes and expectations. For instance, if one child bothers another child, should the second child tell the teacher, or should the two children work it out by themselves? If one child bites another, should the biter be isolated, counseled, admonished, punished, or—as sometimes happens—should the victim be allowed to bite back? Preschools need rules for such situations, and rules vary because of contrasting philosophies. In a child-centered program, the offender might be asked to think of the effect of his or her actions; in a teacher-directed program, punishment might be immediate.

It may seem easier for each teacher to do whatever he or she believes is best, but this may confuse the children and the parents. According to a detailed study of early childhood staff in the Netherlands, differences are notable among adults raised in diverse cultures. In this study, the native-born Dutch teachers emphasized individual achievement more than the adults from the Caribbean or Mediterranean, who stressed sharing and group learning (Huijbregts et al., 2009). New

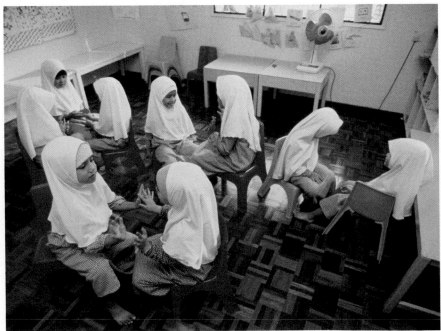

Learning from One Another Every nation creates its own version of early education. In this scene at a nursery school in Kuala Lumpur, Malaysia, note the head coverings, uniforms, bare feet, and absence of boys. None of these elements would be found in most early-childhood-education classrooms in North America or Europe.

Observation Quiz What seemingly universal aspects of childhood are visible in this photograph? (see answer, page 258)

PAUL CHESLEY / STONE / GETTY IMAGES

teachers were particularly likely to believe their way was best; teachers who had worked together for years were more similar in their beliefs and practices than those who had not, probably because they had discussed various concerns and learned from one another.

This study highlights the complexities that can result when parents, teachers, and aides are from different backgrounds, as is often the case in North American programs. As many studies have shown, children can learn whatever academic and social skills are taught to them, with those who attended preschool usually advanced in cognitive skills over those who did not (Camilli et al., 2010; Chambers et al., 2010). However, all young children need personal attention, consistency, and continuity.

Intervention Programs

Many nations try to narrow the learning gap evident between the most and least proficient kindergartner by offering early education to everyone (e.g., China, France, Italy, and Sweden) or at least to families who cannot afford private care. Public support for the early education of children from low-income families varies by cohort and culture. In the United States in the early 1960s, many people sought to improve learning among children who had been disadvantaged. The television program *Sesame Street* was one such effort; so were hundreds of new books published for early readers. In the area of early-childhood education, one large-scale national effort, called Head Start (and several intensive but small efforts) began.

Head Start

Since 1965, Head Start has served millions of young children who were thought to need a "head start" on their formal education. In 2007–2008, nearly a million children attended Head Start programs. Both health and cognition are Head Start goals. The first wave of research found dramatic improvement in participants' intelligence and language; the first follow-up found that the advances faded by second grade; then, just as the funding was about to vanish, a third wave of research found that former Head Start students were more likely to graduate from high school and have jobs than those who never had preschool education (Zigler & Styfco, 2004). That conclusion stands: In England as well as in the United States, numerous studies find that early education helps disadvantaged children (Camilli et al., 2010; Coghlan et al., 2009).

The federal government has funded Head Start since it began and has legislated several changes over the decades, including longer hours, stricter limits on the income level that determines eligibility, earlier entry age (in a program called Early Start), and special programs for children with disabilities. Evaluation has been difficult, in part because assessment of outcomes was not part of the original design. In addition, the goals and implementation methods of various Head Start centers differ so much that assessment of the outcomes at any one center will clash with the goals of many other centers.

Furthermore, the goals of the legislators, the parents, and the teachers often differ. The intent of Head Start has changed over the decades, from lifting families out of poverty to promoting literacy, from providing dental care and immunizations to teaching standard English, from teaching parents better discipline methods to teaching children to solve their own conflicts. As more children speak a language other than English, literacy has become increasingly stressed; as the United States seems to fall behind other nations in science, children are encouraged to enjoy math and discovery. Some teachers practice child-centered education and others

>> **Answer to Observation Quiz** (from page 255) Eight children, and all of them are engaged in creative projects—if the boy standing at right is making music, not just noise, with that cymbal.

Especially for Teachers In trying to find a preschool program, what should parents look for? (see response, page 259)

ELLEN B. SENISI / THE IMAGE WORKS

Disaster Recovery The success of Head Start led to Early Head Start, for children such as this 2-year-old in Biloxi, Mississippi. When Hurricane Katrina destroyed most of the community, it was the first program to reemerge there. Small children recover from disasters *if* their parents can reestablish a normal life—which is why this Head Start program is helping entire families.

All Together Now Socialization is part of every early education program, in ways almost impossible for children who stay at home to benefit from. In this intervention program in Washington, D.C., children learn Spanish and English culture, with the help of a Peruvian-American foster grandparent. All four are also learning computer skills—best mastered as one person shows another.

>> **Answer to Observation Quiz** (from page 256) Three aspects are readily apparent: These girls enjoy their friendships; they are playing a hand-clapping game, some version of which is found in every culture; and, most important, they have begun the formal education that their families want for them.

prefer a teacher-directed approach; some consider parents to be a problem and others regard parents as allies (D. R. Powell, 2006). Some programs enroll only children of citizens; others encourage all young children to participate.

Head Start increasingly enrolls children who are at highest risk, either because they are from very-low-income families or because they have disabilities that are already apparent by age 3. There is no doubt that specific educational experiences help such children. For example, the recent push for math fluency has made educators aware that many low-income 3- and 4-year-olds are not exposed to math at home; as a solution, one Head Start program engaged children in playing a board game with numbers, and their mathematical understanding advanced (Siegler, 2009).

A recent congressional authorization of funding for Head Start included a requirement for extensive evaluation to learn the answers to two sets of questions:

1. What difference does Head Start make to key outcomes of development and learning (in particular, the multiple domains of school readiness) for low-income children? What difference does Head Start make to parental practices that contribute to children's school readiness?
2. Under what circumstances does Head Start achieve the greatest impact? What works for which children? What Head Start services are most related to impact?

The answers that the evaluation found were not as dramatic, in either direction, as advocates or detractors had hoped (U.S. Department of Health and Human Services, 2010). Head Start did improve children's literacy and math skills while they were in the program; their oral health and their parents' responsiveness also improved. However, this study found that most benefits faded by first grade, when the Head Start participants were compared to other children with the same backgrounds. An important difference between the control group for this study and the control group from earlier research is that children who were not in Head Start were often enrolled in other programs, sometimes in excellent center-based care but more often in poor patchwork care.

This major evaluation found that certain Head Start initiatives benefited some children more than others, with benefits most apparent for children with the lowest family income, or those in rural areas, or those with disabilities (U.S. Department of Health and Human Services, 2010). These were the children least likely to find other sources of early education. The strongest overall benefits were advances in language and social skills during early childhood, but those advances did not endure past kindergarten, with one exception—vocabulary.

Long-Term Gains from Intensive Programs

As you see, evaluation is complex. Fortunately, good longitudinal evaluation exists for three intensive interventions that began when Head Start did. Unlike Head Start, these programs were research-based and enrolled children full time for years, sometimes beginning with home visits in infancy, sometimes continuing in after-school programs through first grade. One program, called Perry or High/Scope, was spearheaded in Michigan (Schweinhart & Weikart, 1997; Schweinhart et al., 2005); another, called Abecedarian, got its start in North Carolina (Campbell et al., 2001); and a third, called Child–Parent Centers, began in Chicago (Reynolds, 2000; Reynolds et al., 2007). All took place in a public-school environment.

All three programs enrolled children from low-income families, all compared experimental groups of children with matched control groups, and all reached the same conclusion: Early education can have substantial long-term benefits that become most apparent when the children are in the third grade or later. Children in these three programs scored higher on math and reading achievement tests at age 10 than did other children from the same backgrounds, schools, and neighborhoods. They were significantly less likely to be placed in special classes for slow or disruptive children or to repeat a year of school. In adolescence, they had higher aspirations and a greater sense of achievement and were less likely to have been abused. As young adults, they were more likely to attend college and less likely to go to jail, usually paying taxes rather than being on welfare.

For example, consider some details of longitudinal data from the High/Scope program (see Figure 9.6). From a developmental perspective, early education makes financial sense, saving public money on special education (four times more expensive per student per year); unemployment (no income-tax revenue); and prison. The immediate cost, the small numbers, and the intensity of research

>> **Response for Teachers** (from page 257) Tell parents to look at the people more than the program. Parents should see the children in action and note whether the teachers show warmth and respect for each child.

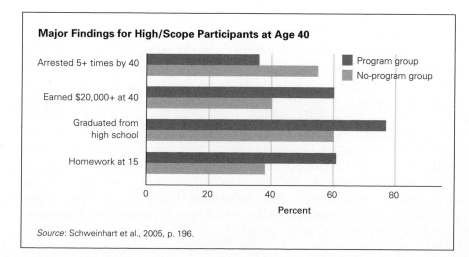

Major Findings for High/Scope Participants at Age 40

Legend: Program group / No-program group

Categories: Arrested 5+ times by 40; Earned $20,000+ at 40; Graduated from high school; Homework at 15

X-axis: Percent (0, 20, 40, 60, 80)

Source: Schweinhart et al., 2005, p. 196.

FIGURE 9.6

And in Middle Age Longitudinal research found that two years in the intensive High/Scope preschool program changed the lives of dozens of children from impoverished families. The program had a positive impact on many aspects of their education, early adulthood, and middle age. (This graph does not illustrate another intriguing finding: The girls who attended High/Scope fared much better than the boys.)

effort required for these early programs are among the reasons why comparable studies are not now underway.

All three research projects found that providing direct cognitive training (rather than simply letting children play), with specific instruction in various school-readiness skills, was useful as long as each child's needs and talents were considered. The curricular approach was a combination of child-centered and teacher-directed. Teachers were encouraged to involve parents in their child's education, and each program included measures to make sure this happened. These programs were expensive (perhaps as much as $17,000 annually per child in 2010 dollars). From a developmental perspective, the decreased need for special education and other social services later on eventually made such programs a wise investment, perhaps saving $4 for every dollar spent (Barnett, 2007).

Other Government Programs

Inspired by these intensive programs as well as by the research on young children, many developmentalists have advocated for widespread early education. Many state legislators and governors have agreed, and 38 states sponsor public education for young children—usually only for low-income 4-year-olds. In 2007–2008, more than a million children (1,134,687) attended state-sponsored preschools—double the number a decade earlier (W. S. Barnett et al., 2008).

From a developmental perspective, the leading state is Oklahoma, which provides full-day kindergarten and preschool education for all children. Attendance is voluntary, but most children are enrolled. The results surpassed those reported by Head Start and other state programs (Gormley et al., 2008). The curriculum emphasizes literacy and math; benefits are particularly strong for children whose home language is Spanish (Phillips et al., 2009). However, the major problem with most state programs, including Oklahoma's, is that they do not begin early enough: Few 3-year-olds are allowed to enroll (Illinois and Arkansas are notable exceptions) (W. S. Barnett et al., 2008). In the United States overall, only about half of 3- and 4-year-olds are enrolled in preschool, which reduces the "chance for success" in elementary school for the other half (*Education Week,* January 14, 2010).

Twelve states provide no state-sponsored preschools for children of any age: Alaska, Hawaii, Idaho, Indiana, Mississippi, Montana, New Hampshire, North Dakota, Rhode Island, South Dakota, Utah, and Wyoming. Some of these states have many church-sponsored day-care centers, occasionally excellent but usually not, with teachers who are underprepared and overworked. One bright spot is found in military day-care centers: With 200,000 children enrolled nationwide beginning at age 2 or 3, they have trained teachers and an academic curriculum (W. S. Barnett et al., 2008).

For the 38 states that sponsor schools for early education, the average funding is only $4,000 per year per student. The adult/child ratio and teacher training are crucial elements of a successful, high-quality program. Four thousand dollars per child per year is obviously inadequate to support a program that hires a head teacher with a BA in early-childhood education to teach a small group of children in a safe, well-equipped space. Priorities change with each new legislature, but the variation in one recent year will help you grasp the range. New Jersey allocated almost $11,000 per child in the same year that Maine and South Carolina allocated less than $2,000. Because of the cost of good preschool education, too many centers increase class size to more than 10 children per adult— a ratio that precludes the personal attention to language and learning that young children need (W. S. Barnett et al., 2008).

THINKING CRITICALLY

Costs and Benefits

The financial aspect of early-childhood education looms large, especially in the current economic climate. For many early-childhood educators, Reggio Emilia is the gold standard because the child/teacher ratio is low, the physical space is luxurious, and the children learn a prodigious amount while gaining self-confidence and social skills. However, the cost per child for such a program is more than double that of other types of preschool care; for example, the cost at one Reggio Emilia nursery school in Massachusetts is $15,000 per year for a three-hour school day. In Italy, the nation and town heavily subsidize the cost of Reggio Emilia preschools; that is not the case in most other cities or nations.

In the United States, parents pay almost all the cost of preschool education, and a Reggio Emilia school is beyond the means of most families. Good programs open to all children may be feasible only in places with high community support and a low birth rate (the Italian average is 1 child per couple, compared with 2.1 in the United States).

Especially when community support is low, when some of the children have backgrounds and cultures unlike those of most of the voters, the question of costs and benefits becomes urgent. For example, all the research on Head Start over the years has shown that participating children learn more than their peers who are not in school. Long-term cost benefits—due to less special education, more jobs, less crime, less teen pregnancy—accrue with intensive, research-based programs, but not everyone is convinced.

The programs with intensive intervention, showing that adults who attended them as children cost society less than do other adults, were characterized by careful, ongoing training of the teachers—an expense that few current public programs subsidize. From a life-span perspective, the problem is that immediate costs and benefits are the focus of most elections and thus of most legislators. Funding for programs that promise benefits decades down the line is scarce, especially considering that tax dollars could instead be immediately directed toward hospitals, colleges, or police officers. Certainly money would be saved if parents handled all the educating of their young children, but some parents might do a poor job; or, if the parents are employed, they might enroll their young children in a crowded place with poorly trained caregivers.

The quality of parenting, and the quality of early education, may be crucial to children's learning and ongoing success in life. Every cost-benefit analysis of early education has found that most efforts eventually paid off but that merely extending kindergarten from three to six hours, or providing inferior care to more 4-year-olds, was not worth the investment (Barnett, 2007; Reynolds & Temple, 2008). The fact that the most recent large-scale evaluation of Head Start found few benefits by first grade could be attributed to the nature of the evaluation: Remember that the quality of Head Start centers varied, that the comparison children also experienced extensive nonmaternal care, and that the evaluation stopped at age 7 (U.S. Department of Health and Human Services, 2010).

Do you think Head Start should be curtailed, expanded, or maintained? If you live in a state without state-sponsored early education, would you push your legislature to support it? And the final question for deeper reflection, crucial for every student of human development: What data, what research, would change your mind?

SUMMING UP

Research, particularly on preschool programs for children in low-income families, has proven that high-quality early education benefits children by improving language learning, social skills, and prospects for the future. Many different programs, including child-centered (Montessori and Reggio Emilia) and teacher-directed programs, are available—although sometimes good programs are very expensive. Massive intervention programs such as Head Start and state-sponsored pre-kindergarten and smaller ones such as High/Scope, Abecedarian, and Chicago's Child–Parent Centers seem to improve the life course of low-income children who attend them. Nations, states, and parents differ in what they seek from early education for their children, and programs vary in teacher preparation, curriculum, physical space, and child/adult ratios. Quality matters.

SUMMARY

Piaget and Vygotsky

1. Piaget stressed the egocentric and illogical aspects of thought during the play years. He called this stage preoperational thought because young children often cannot yet use logical operations to think about their observations and experiences.

2. Young children, according to Piaget, sometimes focus on only one thing (centration) and see things only from their own viewpoint (egocentrism), remaining stuck on appearances and current reality. They may believe that living spirits reside in inanimate objects, a belief called animism.

3. Vygotsky stressed the social aspects of childhood cognition, noting that children learn by participating in various experiences, guided by more knowledgeable adults or peers. That guidance assists learning within the zone of proximal development, which encompasses the knowledge and skills that the child has the potential to learn.

4. According to Vygotsky, the best teachers use various hints, guidelines, and other tools to provide the child with a scaffold for new learning. Language is a bridge that provides social mediation between the knowledge that the child already has and the learning that the society hopes to impart. For Vygotsky, words are a tool for learning.

Children's Theories

5. Children develop theories, especially to explain the purpose of life and their role in it. Among these is theory of mind—an understanding of what others may be thinking. Notable advances in theory of mind occur at around age 4. Theory of mind is partly the result of brain maturation, but culture and experiences also have an impact.

Language

6. Language develops rapidly during early childhood, a sensitive period but not a critical one for language learning. Vocabulary increases dramatically, with thousands of words added between ages 2 and 6. In addition, basic grammar is mastered.

7. Many children learn to speak more than one language, gaining cognitive as well as social advantages. Ideally, children become balanced bilinguals, equally proficient in two languages, by age 6.

Early-Childhood Education

8. Organized educational programs during early childhood advance cognitive and social skills, although specifics vary a great deal. Montessori and Reggio Emilia are two child-centered programs that began in Italy and are now offered in many nations. Behaviorist principles led to many specific practices of teacher-directed programs.

9. Head Start is a U.S. federal government program primarily for low-income children. Longitudinal research finds that early-childhood education reduces the risk of later problems, such as needing special education. High-quality programs increase the likelihood that a child will become a law-abiding, gainfully employed adult.

10. Many types of preschool programs are successful. It is the quality of early education that matters. Children learn best if teachers follow a defined curriculum and if the child/adult ratio is low. The training, warmth, and continuity of early-childhood teachers benefits the children in many ways.

KEY TERMS

preoperational intelligence (p. 237)	irreversibility (p. 238)	scaffolding (p. 241)	overregularization (p. 249)
centration (p. 238)	conservation (p. 238)	private speech (p. 243)	balanced bilingual (p. 251)
egocentrism (p. 238)	animism (p. 240)	social mediation (p. 243)	Montessori schools (p. 254)
focus on appearance (p. 238)	guided participation (p. 241)	theory-theory (p. 244)	Reggio Emilia (p. 254)
static reasoning (p. 238)	zone of proximal development (ZPD) (p. 241)	theory of mind (p. 245)	
		fast-mapping (p. 248)	

WHAT HAVE YOU LEARNED?

Piaget and Vygotsky

1. What are the strengths and weaknesses of preoperational thought?

2. How does children's understanding of categories show the limitations of Piaget's theory?

3. How does the animism of young children differ from the animism of adults?

4. How do the toys given to young children scaffold particular behaviors and values?

5. How does guided participation increase a child's zone of proximal development?

6. Why did Vygotsky think talking to yourself was not a sign of illness but an aid to cognition?

Children's Theories

7. Is theory-theory as valid for adults as for children?

8. Why does development of theory of mind make it more difficult to fool a child?

9. What factors spur the development of theory of mind?

Language

10. What is the evidence that early childhood is a sensitive time for learning language?

11. How does fast-mapping aid the language explosion?

12. How does overregularization signify a cognitive advance?

13. What evidence in language learning shows the limitations of logic in early childhood?

14. What are the advantages of teaching a child two languages?

15. How can language loss be avoided?

Early-Childhood Education

16. What do most preschools provide for children that most homes do not?

17. In child-centered programs, what do the teachers do?

18. What makes Reggio Emilia different from most other preschool programs?

19. Why are Montessori schools still functioning, 100 years after the first such schools opened?

20. What are the advantages and disadvantages of teacher-directed preschools?

21. What are the goals of Head Start?

22. Why have various evaluations of Head Start reached different conclusions?

23. What are the long-term results of intervention preschools?

APPLICATIONS

The best way to understand thinking in early childhood is to listen to a child, as applications 1 and 2 require. If some students have no access to children, they should do application 3 or 4.

1. Replicate one of Piaget's conservation experiments. The easiest one is conservation of liquids (Figure 9.1). Work with a child under age 5 who tells you that two identically shaped glasses contain the same amount of liquid. Then carefully pour one glass of liquid into a narrower, taller glass. Ask the child if one glass now contains more or if the glasses contain the same amount.

2. To demonstrate how rapidly language is learned, show a preschool child several objects and label one with a nonsense word the child has never heard. (*Toma* is often used; so is *wug*.) Or choose a word the child does not know, such as *wrench, spatula,* or the name of a coin from another nation. Test the child's fast-mapping.

3. Theory of mind emerges at about age 4, but many adults still have trouble understanding other people's thoughts and motives. Ask several people why someone in the news did whatever they did (e.g., a scandal, a crime, a heroic act). Then ask your informants how sure they are of their explanation. Compare and analyze the reasons as well as the degrees of certainty. (One person may be sure of an explanation that someone else thinks is impossible.)

4. Think about an experience in which you learned something that was initially difficult. To what extent do Vygotsky's concepts (guided participation, language mediation, apprenticeship, zone of proximal development) explain the experience? Write a detailed, step-by-step account of your learning process as Vygotsky would have described it.

>>ONLINE CONNECTIONS

To accompany your textbook, you have access to a number of online resources, including quizzes for every chapter of the book, flashcards (in English and Spanish), critical thinking questions, and case studies. For access to any of these links, go to www.worthpublishers.com/bergerls8e. In addition to these free resources, you'll also find links to the podcasts, video clips, diagnostic quizzing with personalized study advice, and an ebook. Some of the videos and activities available online include:

- *Theory of Mind.* Watch a variety of children challenged by false-belief tasks.

- *Early Childhood Language Development.* Six-year-olds can tell jokes and 3-year-olds engage in private speech. A variety of video clips showcases the development of children's speech through early childhood.

Early Childhood: Psychosocial Development

WHAT WILL YOU KNOW?

1. How do young children learn when and how to be afraid?
2. What skills do children develop when they are playing?
3. What would happen if children never watched television?
4. Is it normal for young children to hit each other?
5. When do children realize that they are male or female?

My daughter Bethany, at about age 5, challenged one of my students to a fight.

"Girls don't fight," he said, laughing.

"Nobody fights," I corrected him.

We were both teaching Bethany how to express emotions. She learned well; by age 6, she no longer challenged young men to fight.

I remember this incident because I am troubled by what I said. "Nobody" refers to both sexes, but could my response have originated from my gender? Was I teaching Bethany to be passive? Should I have asked my student to play-fight with her, as men do with young boys? Or should I have allowed him to express gender norms?

Emotional control, rough play, parenting, morality, and sex differences are all discussed in this chapter. On some aspects experts agree. For instance, no developmentalist doubts that play teaches social understanding, that parents should guide and discipline their children, that bullies should be stopped. However, other aspects are controversial. My "Nobody fights" reaction may have been wrong . . . or right.

>> Emotional Development

Children gradually learn when and how to express emotions, becoming more capable in every aspect of their lives (Buckley & Saarni, 2009; Denham et al., 2003; Morrison et al., 2010). This **emotional regulation** becomes possible as the emotional hot spots of the limbic system connect to the prefrontal cortex; regulating the expression of emotions is the preeminent psychosocial accomplishment between ages 2 and 6 (N. Eisenberg et al., 2004). With emotional regulation, children learn how to be angry but not explosive, frightened but not terrified, sad but not unconsolable, anxious but not withdrawn, proud but not boastful, and so on.

emotional regulation The ability to control when and how emotions are expressed.

Initiative Versus Guilt

During Erikson's third developmental stage, **initiative versus guilt,** pride naturally emerges from the acquisition of the skills and competencies described in

initiative versus guilt Erikson's third psychosocial crisis, in which children undertake new skills and activities and feel guilty when they do not succeed at them.

Close Connection Unfamiliar events often bring developmental tendencies to the surface, as with the curious boy and his worried brother, who are attending Colorado's Pikes Peak or Bust Rodeo breakfast. Their attentive mother keeps the livelier boy calm and reassures the shy one.

Observation Quiz Mother is obviously a secure base for both boys, who share the same family and half the same genes but are different ages: One is 2 and the other is 4. Can you tell which boy is younger? (see answer, page 268)

self-concept A person's understanding of who he or she is, in relation to self-esteem, appearance, personality, and various traits.

A Poet and We Know It She is the proud winner of a national poetry contest. Is she as surprised, humbled, and thankful as an adult winner would be?

intrinsic motivation A drive, or reason to pursue a goal, that comes from inside a person, such as the need to feel smart or competent.

the previous two chapters. Initiative is saying something new, extending a skill, beginning a project. Depending on the outcome (including the parents' response), children can feel either proud or guilty. Usually, parents encourage the natural enthusiasm, effort, and pride of their 3- to 6-year-olds. If, instead, parents dismiss a child's emotions—fear, anger, or any other emotion—that child may not learn emotional regulation (Morris et al., 2007).

Children's beliefs about their worth are connected to parental confirmation, especially when parents remind their children of their positive accomplishments (Reese et al., 2007). ("Remember when you helped Daddy sweep the sidewalk? You made it very clean.") The autonomy of 2-year-olds, often expressed as stubbornness, becomes initiative, and children enter kindergarten ready to learn new skills (Rubin et al., 2009). In the process, children form their **self-concept,** or understanding of themselves, including their gender and size. Girls are usually happy to be girls, boys to be boys, and both are glad they aren't babies. "Crybaby" is a major insult.

Erikson recognized that young children often lack modesty. They believe that they are strong, smart, and good-looking—and thus that any goal is achievable. Whatever they are (self-concept) is thought to be good. For instance, they believe that their nation and religion are best; they feel sorry for children who do not belong to their country or church. Young children are confident that their good qualities will endure but that bad qualities (even biological traits such as poor eyesight) will disappear (Lockhart et al., 2002).

The new initiative that Erikson describes is aided by increased attention span, made possible by neurological maturity. Concentrated attention aids social competence (Murphy et al., 2007), as children proudly practice and then master various skills. They learn to pour juice, zip pants, or climb trees, undeterred by overflowing juice, stuck zippers, or a perch too high to climb down from. Faith in themselves, sometimes called "protective optimism," helps them try new things (Lockhart et al., 2002).

Erikson believed that as children develop self-awareness, they feel guilt when they realize their own mistakes. Many people believe that guilt is a more mature emotion than shame because guilt comes from within the person (Kochanska et al., 2002; Tangney et al., 2007), whereas shame comes from outside and depends on other people. Unlike guilt, shame can be based on gender, ethnicity, or background. To counter such feelings, many parents of minority children (Mexican, African, or Indian American, among others) encourage ethnic pride in their children (Brown et al., 2007; Parke & Buriel, 2006). Guilt and pride help children develop moral values, a topic discussed later in this chapter.

Motivation

The idea that guilt comes from within the child highlights the distinction between *intrinsic motivation* and *extrinsic motivation*. **Intrinsic motivation** occurs when people do something for the joy of doing it: A musician might enjoy making music, even when all alone. **Extrinsic motivation** comes from outside, when people do something to gain praise (or some other reinforcement): A musician who plays for the reward of applause is an example.

For the most part, preschool children are intrinsically motivated. They enjoy learning, playing, and practicing whether or not someone else wants them to. For instance, when they play a game, young children might not keep score; the fun is in playing, not winning. Intrinsic motivation is seen when children invent dialogues for their toys, concentrate on a work of art or architecture, and converse with *imaginary friends* who exist only in the child's imagination. Imaginary friends are increasingly common from ages 3 through 7, as initiative builds. They combat loneliness and aid emotional regulation. For example, one girl had an imaginary friend named Elephant, "7 inches tall, grey color, black eyes, wears tank top and shorts . . . plays with the child [but] sometimes is mean" (Taylor et al., 2004, p. 1178). By having an imaginary friend who is sometimes mean, this girl developed strategies to deal with mean people.

An Experiment in Motivation

In a classic experiment, preschool children were given markers and paper and assigned to one of three groups who received, respectively: (1) no award, (2) an expected award (they were told *before* they had drawn anything that they would get a certificate), and (3) an unexpected award (*after* they had drawn something, they heard, "You were a big help" and got a certificate) (Lepper et al., 1973). Later, observers noted how often children in each group chose to draw on their own. Those who received the expected award were less likely to draw later than those who were unexpectedly rewarded. The interpretation was that extrinsic motivation (condition 2) undercut intrinsic motivation.

This research triggered a flood of studies seeking to understand whether, when, and how positive reinforcement should be given. The consensus is that praising or paying a person after an accomplishment sometimes encourages that behavior. However, if payment is promised in advance, that extrinsic reinforcement may backfire (Cameron & Pierce, 2002; Deci et al., 1999; Gottfried et al., 2009).

Culture and Emotional Control

Cultures differ in what emotions they expect children to regulate, and children try to follow the norms of their culture. Some research finds that specific cultures emphasize control of particular emotions (Hong et al., 2000; J. G. Miller, 2004; Stubben, 2001):

- Fear (United States)
- Anger (Puerto Rico)
- Pride (China)
- Aggression (Japan)
- Impatience (many Native American communities)

Cultures differ in control strategies as well (Matsumoto, 2004). Shame is used when a family's reputation is a priority. Indeed, in some cultures, "pride goeth before a fall" and people who "have no shame" are considered mentally ill (Stein, 2006). Of course, cultures change, and parents do not always follow their cultural norms. No matter what the culture, children of depressed parents are less able to regulate their emotions (Kovacs et al., 2008). Neglectful or inconsistent caregivers make an impulsive child's emotional problems worse, whereas nurturing caregivers guide impulsive children to be *more* competent than other children (Belsky et al., 2007; Hane & Fox, 2006; Quas et al., 2004).

extrinsic motivation A drive, or reason to pursue a goal, that arises from the need to have one's achievements rewarded from outside, perhaps by receiving material possessions or another person's esteem.

Especially for Teachers One of your students tells you about playing, sleeping, and talking with an imaginary friend. Does this mean that that child is emotionally disturbed? (see response, page 269)

Especially for College Students Is extrinsic or intrinsic motivation more influential in your study efforts? (see response, page 269)

Especially for Teachers of Young Children Should you put gold stars on children's work? (see response, page 269)

Glad to be Navajo These sisters are about to join the procession for the annual Intertribal Indian Ceremonial in Gallup, New Mexico. More important, they are gaining pride in their ancestry, a key aspect of childhood emotional development.

psychopathology An illness or disorder of the mind.

externalizing problems Difficulty with emotional regulation that involves expressing powerful feelings through uncontrolled physical or verbal outbursts, as by lashing out at other people or breaking things.

internalizing problems Difficulty with emotional regulation that involves turning one's emotional distress inward, as by feeling excessively guilty, ashamed, or worthless.

Who's Chicken? Genes and good parenting have made this boy neither too fearful nor too bold. Appropriate caution is probably the best approach to meeting a chicken.

>> Answer to Observation Quiz (from page 266) Size is not much help, since children grow slowly during these years and the heads of these two boys appear about the same size. However, emotional development is apparent. Most 2-year-olds, like the one at the right, still cling to their mothers; most 4-year-olds are sufficiently mature, secure, and curious to watch the excitement as they drink their juice.

Seeking Emotional Balance

In every culture and at every age, developmentalists seek to prevent **psychopathology,** an illness or disorder (*-pathology*) of the mind (*psycho-*). Although specific symptoms and diagnoses are influenced by culture, a lack of emotional regulation is universally accepted as a sign of psychopathology.

Externalizing and Internalizing Problems

Without adequate regulation, emotions may be overpowering. Intense emotional reactions occur in two seemingly opposite ways. Some people have **externalizing problems:** Their powerful feelings burst out uncontrollably. They may externalize a feeling of rage, for example, by lashing out at other people or breaking things. Without emotional regulation, an angry child might flail at another person or lie down screaming and kicking. That might be acceptable in a typical 2-year-old's temper tantrum, but 5-year-olds usually have more self-control, perhaps pouting and cursing, but not hitting and screaming.

Other people have **internalizing problems:** They are fearful and withdrawn, turning distress inward. Again, with maturity, the extreme fears of some 2-year-olds (e.g., of the bathtub drain, of an imagined tidal wave, of a stranger with a hat) diminish. Neither externalizing nor internalizing children regulate their emotions very well—or, more precisely, they do not regulate the *expression* of emotions. Either they have too little self-control or they control themselves too much (Caspi & Shiner, 2006; Hart et al., 2003).

Sex Differences in Emotional Regulation

Girls usually develop emotional regulation ahead of boys, especially evident when comparing boys' and girls' externalizing emotions. In adolescence, girls are more often depressed; this may be the result of too much internalizing.

In one study, researchers gave 5-year-olds toy figures and told them the start of a story (Zahn-Waxler et al., 2008). Two children (named Mark and Scott for the boys, Mary and Sarah for the girls) were said to start yelling at each other, and the 5-year-olds were asked to show what happened next.

Many boys had Mark and Scott hitting and kicking each other. Boys whose behavior problems got worse between ages 5 and 9 (as rated by their teachers and parents) were the most likely to show such externalizing at age 5. By contrast, 5-year-old girls were more likely to have Mary and Sarah talk about their conflict or change the subject. Curiously, those girls whose behavior problems got worse from age 5 to 9 were more likely than either the boys or the other girls to engage in "reparative behavior," such as Mary hugging Sarah and saying, "I'm sorry." This response may indicate internalized guilt or shame. The authors explain:

> Gender-role stereotypes or exaggerations of masculine qualities (e.g., impulsive, aggressive, uncaring) and feminine qualities (submissive, unassertive, socially sensitive) are reflected not only in the types of problems males and females tend to develop but also in different forms of expression.
>
> [Zahn-Waxler et al., 2008, p. 114]

These researchers suggest that, for both sexes, extreme externalization or extreme internalization predicts future psychopathology.

The Brains of Boys and Girls

For both sexes, emotional regulation requires thinking before acting (deciding whether and how to display joy, anger, fear, or any other emotion). Such thinking occurs in the prefrontal cortex, the executive area of the brain. As you remember from Chapter 8, the prefrontal cortex regulates the limbic system (especially the amygdala), where powerful emotions form.

Normally, neurological advances in the prefrontal cortex at about age 4 or 5 make children less likely to throw a temper tantrum, provoke a physical attack, or burst into giggles during prayer (Kagan & Herschkowitz, 2005). Throughout early childhood, violent outbursts, uncontrolled crying, and terrifying phobias (irrational, crippling fears) diminish. The capacity for self-control—such as not opening a present immediately if asked to wait and not expressing disappointment at an undesirable gift—becomes more evident (Carlson, 2003; Grolnick et al., 2006).

Children of both sexes learn emotional regulation and avoid either extreme of emotional imbalance, but neurological vulnerability and parents who maltreat them combine to lead to dysregulated emotions. Neurological and hormonal effects may make boys more likely to externalize and girls to internalize, a difference found in every culture and thus probably genetic—the result of the XX or XY chromosomes, although social expectation and guidelines also have an impact. By age 5, boys with immature emotional regulation are likely to throw things and vulnerable girls are likely to sob uncontrollably.

SUMMING UP

Erikson and many others find that pride, purpose, and initiative are integral components of the self-concept of young children, who want to try new activities. Children who have difficulty with emotional regulation may develop internalizing or externalizing problems, which may be early signs of psychopathology. Many factors—including genes, gender, brain development, culture, and hormones—influence emotional regulation. ■

Learning Emotional Regulation Like this girl in Hong Kong, all 2-year-olds burst into tears when something upsets them—a toy breaks, a pet refuses to play, or it's time to go home. A mother who comforts them and helps them calm down is teaching them to regulate their emotions.

>> Play

Play is timeless and universal—apparent in every part of the world for thousands of years. Many developmentalists believe that play is the most productive as well as enjoyable activity that children undertake (Elkind, 2007; Frost, 2009), although whether play is critical or merely fun is controversial. As you learned in Chapter 8, some educators want to reduce playtime so children will focus on reading and math skills; others predict dire consequences for children who do not play enough (Pellegrini, 2009).

Playmates

Young children play best with *peers,* that is, people of about the same age and social status. Two-year-olds are intrigued by peers but are not yet good playmates: They might throw a ball and expect a playmate to throw it back rather than keep it. By contrast, most 6-year-olds are quite skilled: They can gain entry to a peer group, manage conflict, take turns, find friends, and keep playmates. Over those years, peers provide practice in emotional regulation, empathy, and social understanding (Cohen, 2006).

Not surprisingly, children usually prefer to play with peers rather than alone or with parents. They prefer playmates of the same sex, who encourage boy or girl play (Berenbaum et al., 2008). Young children who never play may later have emotional and academic problems (Rubin et al., 2009). There is an obvious application for parents: Find a playmate. Even the most playful parent is outmatched by another child at negotiating the rules of tag, at wrestling on the grass, at pretending to be sick, at killing a dragon.

>> **Response for Teachers** (from page 267) No. In fact, imaginary friends are quite common, especially among creative children. The child may be somewhat lonely, though; you could help him or her find a friend.

>> **Response for College Students** (from page 267) Both are important. Extrinsic motivation includes parental pressure and the need to get a good job after graduation. Intrinsic motivation includes the joy of learning. Have you ever taken a course that was not required and was said to be difficult? That was intrinsic motivation.

>> **Response for Teachers of Young Children** (from page 267) Perhaps, but only after the work is completed and the child put genuine effort into it. You do not want to undercut intrinsic motivation, as happens with older students who know a particular course will be an "easy A."

Play Ball! In every nation, young children play with balls, but the specific games they play vary with the culture. Soccer is the favorite game in many countries, including Brazil, where these children are practicing their dribbling on Copacabana Beach in Rio de Janeiro.

Cultural Differences in Play

All young children play, whether they are on Arctic ice or desert sand. Children create dramas that reflect their culture and play games that have been passed down from older generations (Kalliala, 2006; Roopnarine et al., 1994). Because play varies by culture, gender, and age, it teaches children values and skills required in their particular context (Sutton-Smith, 1997). Chinese children fly kites, Alaskan natives tell dreams and stories, Lapp children pretend to be reindeer, and so on.

As children grow older, play becomes more social and more affected by their physical setting (a small playroom, a large park, a wild hillside) and culture. Recent studies of young children's play show plots and characters that originated on television, including plots that indicate sexual awareness by age 6 (Kalliala, 2006). Once such knowledge was a sign of child abuse; now young children become sexually aware (albeit confused) simply by watching television.

The development of social play was first noted by American researcher Mildred Parten (1932). She distinguished five kinds of play, each more interactive than the previous one:

1. *Solitary play:* A child plays alone, unaware of any other children playing nearby.
2. *Onlooker play:* A child watches other children play.
3. *Parallel play:* Children play with similar toys in similar ways, but not together.
4. *Associative play:* Children interact, observing one another and sharing material, but their play is not yet mutual and reciprocal.
5. *Cooperative play:* Children play together, creating dramas or taking turns.

Ages and patterns are affected by culture. Some normal U.S. 4-year-olds prefer to play alone (Henderson et al., 2004), but many families in China expect 3-year-olds to take turns, share, and otherwise cooperate in social play. They do.

Active Play

Children need physical activity to develop muscle strength and control. Peers provide an audience, role models, and sometimes competition. For instance, running skills develop best when children chase or race each other, not when a child runs alone. Gross motor play is favored among young children, who enjoy climbing, kicking, and tumbling (Case-Smith & Kuhaneck, 2008). Active play—not solitary play—correlates with peer acceptance and a healthy self-concept (Nelson et al., 2008), something adults might remember when they prefer young children to be quiet. One 5-year-old boy came to his parents' bedroom every night to entertain them with an "action show," which involved elaborate jumps and acrobatics. As soon as his 1-year-old brother could, he joined in (Cohen, 2006).

Rough-and-Tumble Play

rough-and-tumble play Play that mimics aggression through wrestling, chasing, or hitting, but in which there is no intent to harm.

The most common form of active play is called **rough-and-tumble** because it looks quite rough and because the children seem to tumble over one another. The term was coined by British scientists who studied primates in East Africa (Blurton-Jones, 1976). They noticed that monkeys often chased, attacked, rolled over in the dirt, and wrestled, quite roughly, but without hurting one another. If a young monkey wanted to play, all it had to do was come close, catch the eye of a peer, and then run a few feet, looking back. This invitation was almost always accepted, with the other monkey responding with a *play face* rather than an angry one. Puppies, kittens, and young chimpanzees similarly invite rough-and-tumble play.

When the scientists returned to their own children, they saw that human youngsters, like baby monkeys, enjoy rough-and-tumble play (Pellegrini & Smith, 2005). They chase, wrestle, and grab each other, developing games like tag and cops-and-robbers, with play faces, lots of chasing, and various conventions, expressions, and gestures that children use to signify "just pretend."

Rough-and-tumble play appears everywhere (although cops-and-robbers can be robots-and-humans or many other iterations), particularly among young males (human and otherwise) when they are allowed to play freely with ample space and minimal supervision (Berenbaum et al., 2008; Hassett et al., 2008). Many scientists think that rough-and-tumble play helps the prefrontal cortex to develop, as children learn to regulate emotions, practice social skills, and strengthen their bodies (Pellegrini et al., 2007). Indeed, some believe that play in childhood, especially rough-and-tumble play between boys and their fathers, not only teaches regulation of aggression but may prevent antisocial behavior (even murder) later on (Wenner, 2009).

Rough-and-tumble play advances planning and self-control. Two-year-olds just chase and catch one another, but older children keep the play fair, long-lasting, and fun. In tag, for instance, older players set rules (which vary, depending on availability of base, safety, and terrain) and then each child decides when and how far to venture. If one child is "It" for too long, another child (often a friend) makes it easy to be caught.

Male Bonding Sometimes the only way to distinguish aggression from rough-and-tumble play is to look at the faces. The hitter is not scowling, the hittee is laughing, and the hugger is just joining in the fun. Another clue that this is rough-and-tumble play comes from gender and context. These boys are in a Head Start program, where they are learning social skills, such as how to avoid fighting.

Drama and Pretending

Another major type of active play is **sociodramatic play,** in which children act out various roles and plots, taking on "any identity, role, or activity that they choose. They can be mothers, babies, Cinderella, or Captain Hook. They can make tea or fly to the moon. Or they can fight, hurt others, or kill or imprison someone" (Dunn & Hughes, 2001, p. 491).

Sociodramatic play allows children to:

- Explore and rehearse social roles
- Learn how to explain their ideas and convince playmates to agree
- Practice emotional regulation by pretending to be afraid, angry, brave, and so on
- Develop self-concept in a nonthreatening context

sociodramatic play Pretend play in which children act out various roles and themes in stories that they create.

Sociodramatic play builds on pretending and social interest, both of which emerge in toddlerhood. But preschool children do more than pretend; they combine their own imagination with that of others. The beginnings of sociodramatic play are illustrated by this pair, a 3-year-old girl and a 2-year-old boy. The girl wanted to act out the role of a baby, and she persuaded the boy to play a parent.

> **Boy:** Not good. You bad.
> **Girl:** Why?
> **Boy:** 'Cause you spill your milk.
> **Girl:** No. 'Cause I bit somebody.
> **Boy:** Yes, you did.
> **Girl:** Say, "Go to sleep. Put your head down."
> **Boy:** Put your head down.
> **Girl:** No.
> **Boy:** Yes.

Girl: No.

Boy: Yes. Okay, I will spank you. Bad boy. *[Spanks her, not hard]*

Girl: No. My head is up. *[Giggles]* I want my teddy bear.

Boy: No. Your teddy bear go away.

> *[At this point she asked if he was really going to take the teddy bear away.]*

> *[from Garvey, reported in Cohen, 2006, p. 72]*

Note that the girl not only directed the play but also played her part, sometimes accepting what the boy said and sometimes not. The boy took direction yet also made up his own dialogue and actions ("Bad boy!").

Compare their simple plot to the play of four boys, about age 5, in a day-care center in Finland. Joni plays the role of the evil one who menaces the other boys; Tuomas directs the drama and acts in it as well.

Tuomas: And now he *[Joni]* would take me and would hang me. . . . This would be the end of all of me.

Joni: Hands behind.

Tuomas: I can't help it. I have to. *[The two other boys follow his example.]*

Joni: I would put fire all around them.

> *[All three brave boys lie on the floor with hands tied behind their backs. Joni piles mattresses on them, and pretends to light a fire, which crackles closer and closer.]*

Tuomas: Everything is lost.

> *[One boy starts to laugh.]*

Petterl: Better not to laugh, soon we will all be dead. . . . I am saying my last words.

Tuomas: Now you can say your last wish. . . . And now I say I wish we can be terribly strong.

> *[At that point, the three boys suddenly gain extraordinary strength, pushing off the mattresses and extinguishing the fire. Good triumphs over evil, but not until the last moment, because, as one boy explains, "Otherwise this playing is not exciting at all."]*

> *[adapted from Kalliala, 2006, p. 83]*

Good versus evil is a favorite theme of boys' sociodramatic play. In contrast, girls often act out domestic scenes. Such gender differences are found in many cultures. In the same day-care center where Joni piles mattresses on his play-mates, the girls say their play is "more beautiful and peaceful . . . [but] boys play all kinds of violent games" (Kalliala, 2006, p. 110).

Ladies and Babies A developmental difference is visible here between the 14-month-old's evident curiosity and the 4-year-old friends' pleasure in sociodramatic play. The mother's reaction—joy at the children's imaginative play or irritation at the mess they've made—is less predictable.

FELICIA MARTINEZ / PHOTOEDIT, INC.

Playing with other children is a boon for children's emotional regulation, as they learn how to get along with one another. Although play is universal, the particular form it takes varies not only by age but also by gender and culture. Many forms of play, including rough-and-tumble and sociodramatic, require social understanding and compromise. Younger children chase each other and act out simple dramas; older children have more nuanced and elaborate rules and scripts.

>> Challenges for Parents

We have seen that young children's emotions and actions are affected by many factors, including brain maturation, culture, and peers. Now we focus on another primary influence on young children: their parents.

Parenting Styles

Although thousands of researchers have traced the effects of parenting on child development, the work of one person, 40 years ago, continues to be influential. Diana Baumrind (1967, 1971) studied 100 preschool children, all from California, almost all middle-class European Americans. (The cohort and cultural limitations of this sample were not obvious at the time.)

Baumrind found that parents differed on four important dimensions:

1. *Expressions of warmth.* Some parents are warm and affectionate; others, cold and critical.
2. *Strategies for discipline.* Parents vary in whether and how they explain, criticize, persuade, ignore, and punish.
3. *Communication.* Some parents listen patiently; others demand silence.
4. *Expectations for maturity.* Parents vary in the degree of responsibility and self-control they expect from their children.

Baumrind's Three Styles of Parenting

On the basis of the dimensions listed above, Baumrind identified three parenting styles (summarized in Table 10.1).

- **Authoritarian parenting.** The authoritarian parent's word is law, not to be questioned. Misconduct brings strict punishment, usually physical (but not so harsh as to be considered abusive). Authoritarian parents set down clear rules and hold high standards. They do not expect children to offer opinions; discussion about emotions is especially rare. (One adult from such a family said that "How do you feel?" had only two possible answers: "Fine" and "Tired.") Authoritarian parents love their children, but they seem aloof, rarely showing affection.
- **Permissive parenting.** Permissive parents (also called *indulgent*) make few demands, hiding any impatience they feel. Discipline is lax, partly because permissive parents have low expectations for maturity. Instead, permissive parents are nurturing and accepting, listening to whatever their offspring say. They try to be helpful; they do not feel responsible for shaping their children.
- **Authoritative parenting.** Authoritative parents set limits and enforce rules, yet they also listen to their children. They encourage maturity, but they usually forgive (not punish) if the child falls short. They consider themselves guides, not authorities (unlike authoritarian parents) and not friends (unlike permissive parents).

Especially for Political Scientists Many observers contend that children learn their political attitudes at home, from the way their parents treat them. Is this true? (see response, page 275)

authoritarian parenting An approach to child rearing that is characterized by high behavioral standards, strict punishment of misconduct, and little communication.

permissive parenting An approach to child rearing that is characterized by high nurturance and communication but little discipline, guidance, or control.

authoritative parenting An approach to child rearing in which the parents set limits but listen to the child and are flexible.

TABLE 10.1					
Characteristics of Parenting Styles Identified by Baumrind					
Style				**Communication**	
	Warmth	Discipline	Expectations of Maturity	Parent to Child	Child to Parent
Authoritarian	Low	Strict, often physical	High	High	Low
Permissive	High	Rare	Low	Low	High
Authoritative	High	Moderate, with much discussion	Moderate	High	High

neglectful/uninvolved parenting An approach to child rearing in which the parents are indifferent toward their children and unaware of what is going on in their children's lives.

A fourth style, called **neglectful/uninvolved parenting,** is sometimes mistaken for the permissive style but is actually quite different (Steinberg, 2001). The similarity is that neither permissive nor neglectful parents use physical punishment; the difference is that neglectful parents are strikingly unaware of what their children are doing—they seem not to care. By contrast, permissive parents are very involved in their children's lives: defending them from criticism, arranging play dates, and sacrificing to buy them coveted toys.

The following long-term effects of parenting styles have been reported, not only in the United States but in many other nations as well (Baumrind, 2005; Chan & Koo, 2010; Huver et al., 2010; Rothrauff et al., 2009; Steinberg et al., 1994):

- *Authoritarian* parents raise children who are likely to become conscientious, obedient, and quiet but not especially happy. Such children tend to feel guilty or depressed, internalizing their frustrations and blaming themselves when things don't go well. As adolescents, they sometimes rebel, leaving home before age 20.
- *Permissive* parents raise unhappy children who lack self-control, especially in the give-and-take of peer relationships. Inadequate emotional regulation makes them immature and impedes friendships, which is the main reason for their unhappiness. They tend to continue to live at home, still dependent, in early adulthood. In middle and late adulthood, they fare quite well.
- *Authoritative* parents raise children who are successful, articulate, happy with themselves, and generous with others. These children are usually liked by teachers and peers, especially in the United States and other societies in which individual initiative is valued.
- *Uninvolved* parents raise children who are immature, sad, lonely, and at risk of abuse. All children need parents who care about them because, no matter what their practices regarding punishment and expectations, "parental involvement plays an important role in the development of both social and cognitive competence" (Parke & Buriel, 2006, p. 437).

Problems with Baumrind's Parenting Styles

Baumrind's classification of parenting styles is often criticized as too simplistic. Among the problems of her original research are the following:

- Her participants were very similar in socioeconomic status (SES), ethnicity, and culture.
- She focused more on parental attitudes than on behavior.
- She overlooked the child's contribution to parent–child relationships.
- She did not realize that some authoritarian parents are very affectionate.
- She did not realize that some permissive parents provide extensive verbal guidance (Bornstein, 2006; Lamb & Lewis, 2005; Parke & Buriel, 2006).

The child's temperament and the prevailing cultural standards powerfully affect parenting style, and this is as it should be. Fearful or impulsive children require particular styles (reassurance for the fearful ones and restraint for the impulsive ones). Parents need to provide guidance and protection, but not too much—overprotection seems to be both a cause and a consequence of childhood anxiety (McShane & Hastings, 2009).

Cultural Variations

The significance of the context is particularly obvious when children of various ethnic groups are compared. American parents of Chinese, Caribbean, or African heritage are often stricter than those of European backgrounds, yet their children may develop better than if the parents were more easygoing (Chao, 2001; Parke & Buriel, 2006). Latino parents are sometimes thought to be too intrusive, other times too permissive—but their children seem to be happier than the children of North American parents who behave the same way (García & Gracia, 2009; Ispa et al., 2004). Sometimes minority and non-Western parents are categorized as authoritarian because of their punishment styles, but that label may be misapplied since many are also warm and affectionate.

In a detailed study of 1,477 instances when Mexican American mothers of 4-year-olds tried to get their children to do something they were not doing, most of the time the mothers simply uttered a command and the children complied (Livas-Dlott et al., 2010). This simple strategy, with the mother asserting authority and the children obeying without question, might be considered authoritarian. However, almost never did the mothers use physical punishment or even harsh threats, even when the children did not immediately do as they were told—which happened 14 percent of the time. For example,

> Hailey decided to look for another doll and started digging through her toys, throwing them behind her as she dug. Maricruz [the mother] told Hailey she should not throw her toys. Hailey continued to throw toys, and Maricruz said her name to remind her to stop. Hailey continued her misbehavior, and her mother repeated "Hailey" once more. When Hailey continued, Maricruz raised her voice but calmly directed, "Hailey, look at me." Hailey continued but then looked at Maricruz as she explained, "You don't throw toys; you could hurt someone." Finally, Hailey complied and stopped.
>
> [Livas-Dlott et al., 2010, p. 572]

Note that the mother's first three efforts failed, and then there was a look accompanied by a calmly expressed but inaccurate explanation (actually, in that setting, no one could be hurt). The researchers explain that these families do not fit any of Baumrind's categories; respect for adult authority is rarely accompanied by a hostile mother–child relationship. Instead, the relationship shows evident "cariono" (caring) (Livas-Dlott et al., 2010).

Similarly, a study of parents in Hong Kong found that almost all believed that young children need strong parental guidance, including punishment; but most classified themselves as authoritative, not authoritarian, because they listened to their children and adjusted their expectations when needed (S. M. Chan et al., 2009).

In general, multicultural and international research has found that specific discipline methods and family rules are less important than parental warmth, support, and concern. Children from every ethnic group and every country benefit if they believe that their parents appreciate them; children everywhere suffer if they feel rejected and unwanted (Khaleque & Rohner, 2002; Maccoby, 2000).

>> **Response for Political Scientists** (from page 273) There are many parenting styles, and it is difficult to determine each one's impact on children's personalities. At this point, attempts to connect early child rearing with later political outlook are speculative.

"He's just doing that to get attention."

Socioeconomic factors may be even more crucial than ethnic ones. Authoritarian parenting increases as income falls, perhaps because low-income families tend to be larger or because parents want to raise obedient children who will not challenge police or employers later on. Parents everywhere try to raise their children to adjust to the culture they know, which may differ from that of the families Baumrind studied.

In addition, culture and family patterns change with time and place. A multicultural study of Canadian parents found that, contrary to past U.S. research, East Asian and Caribbean immigrants were *less* harsh with their children than the average Canadian parent, and teachers rated their children as less aggressive than the norm (Ho et al., 2008). Studies of Latinos find that parents who have been in the United States longer are less authoritarian than are new immigrants (Hill et al., 2003: Parke et al., 2004).

Given a multicultural perspective, developmentalists hesitate to recommend any particular style of parenting (Dishion & Bullock, 2002; J. G. Miller, 2004). That does not mean that all parents function equally well—far from it. Signs of trouble are obvious in children's behavior, including overcontrol, undercontrol, and inability to play with others. Ineffective or uninvolved parenting is one cause of these problems, but it is not the only one.

"Why don't you get off the computer and watch some TV?"

Children, Parents, and the New Media

New challenges confront each generation of parents. One of today's great challenges is the influence of electronic media on children. All media—television, the Internet, electronic games, and so on—*can* be harmful, especially when the content is violent (Anderson et al., 2007, 2008; Bailey et al., 2010; Gentile et al., 2007; Smyth, 2007).

Media for young children have become a multimillion-dollar industry, seeking profit, education, and entertainment for billions of young viewers (Steemers, 2010). Yet six major organizations (the American Psychological Association, the American Academy of Pediatrics, the American Medical Association, the American Academy of Child and Adolescent Psychiatry, the American Academy of Family Physicians, and the American Psychiatric Association) recommend that parents limit their children's television watching, with no electronic media at all allowed for children under age 2.

Few parents follow that recommendation. Most young children in the United States spend more than three hours each day using one electronic medium or another (see Table 10.2). Almost every North American family owns at least two televisions, and most preschoolers watch apart from their parents, often in their own rooms.

The new media are not always harmful, a topic discussed further in later chapters. During early childhood, some children may learn basic literacy from educational programs, especially if their parents watch with them and reinforce the lessons. However, children rarely select educational programs over fast-paced cartoons, in which everyone hits, shoots, and kicks, and parents are often more concerned about eating and health habits than about viewing preferences.

Good choices are particularly hard for parents to enforce because many parents themselves, as well as older siblings, are more engaged with electronic media (television, texting, e-mail, social networking) than with each other. Young children learn from that example. Even when they are too young to understand television dialogue, and television is merely background noise, children play less and parent–child interaction is markedly reduced when the TV is on (Kirkorian et al., 2009;

TABLE 10.2	
Average Daily Exposure to Electronic Media	
Age 2 to 4 Years	**Hours per Day**
White	3:18
Black	4:30
Hispanic	3:37
Age 5 to 7 Years	**Hours per Day**
White	3:17
Black	4:16
Hispanic	3:38
Source: Adapted from Roberts & Foehr, 2004.	

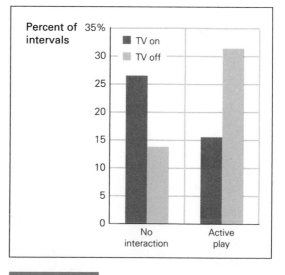

Video: Good, Bad, or Indifferent? A modest amount of time spent watching television and videos does not seem to be harmful for young children, especially when parents watch with them and the content is educational. However, the effects are not yet known for certain because adequate longitudinal research has not yet been conducted.

Schmidt et al., 2008). Yet language development depends on conversation that is individualized to each child, and emotional regulation depends on parental guidance. (See the Research Design.)

Thus, the problem is not only that violent media teach destructive behavior but also that all media take time from constructive interactions. According to the *displacement hypothesis*, whatever time children devote to electronic media reduces time spent in social and educational activities, a hypothesis proven in school-age children and likely true in younger children as well (Weis & Cerankosky, 2010).

▶ Research Design

Scientists: Heather L. Kirkorian, Tiffany A. Pempek, Lauren A. Murphy, Marie E. Schmidt, and Daniel R. Anderson, all at the University of Massachusetts.

Publication: *Child Development* (2009).

Participants: Fifty-one parents and their 1- to 3-year olds, mostly middle-class European Americans.

Design: Children and parents were videotaped in a well-equipped playroom for an hour, with a television in the corner showing an adult program (chosen by the parent) for half of the time. Magazines were also available for the adults to read. Parents were asked to relax, interacting with their child as they would at home. Observations of interaction were noted every 10 seconds (360 segments per parent–child dyad) and tallied for language and parental involvement by coders blind to the hypothesis of the study.

Major conclusions: Most (not all) parents interacted and spoke less when the television was on. This was true for adults of both sexes (two fathers were included), all ethnicities, and children of all ages, especially for the 2-year-olds, as shown in Figure 10.1.

Comment: This study has many strengths: detailed observation (every 10 seconds) by blind coders, each dyad exposed to both conditions (thus controlling for individual differences in interaction patterns), and inclusion of very young children (most earlier research assumed 1-year-olds were not affected by television). However, only 51 parent–child dyads were studied, all from one region of the United States and almost all middle class, even though background television is more prevalent in low-income families. Furthermore, the researchers were all from one university. Do any of these factors limit this study?

FIGURE 10.1

Don't Bother Me For dyads with 2-year-olds and their parents, having a TV on in the background reduced play by half. The effect was not as dramatic (although still evident) for 1-year-olds. Have 2-year-olds learned to be quiet when the television is on?

SUMMING UP

Over the past 40 years, Diana Baumrind and most other developmentalists have found that authoritative parenting (warm, with guidance) is more effective than either authoritarian (very strict) or permissive (very lenient) parenting. Other researchers have found that uninvolved parents are the least effective of all. In any culture, children thrive when their parents appreciate them and care about their accomplishments. The children of parents who are uninvolved, uncaring, or abusive seldom become happy, well-adjusted, and high-achieving adults.

Good parenting is not achieved by following any one simple rule; children's temperaments vary, and so do cultural patterns. The media pose a particular challenge worldwide because children are attracted to colorful, fast-paced images; yet violent TV programs, in particular, lead to more aggressive behavior. Educational television may be instructive, but all television reduces parent–child interaction.

>> Moral Development

Children develop increasingly complex moral values, judgments, and behaviors as they mature. The social bonds described in Chapter 7, the theory of mind described in Chapter 9, and the emotional development and social awareness described in this chapter are the foundation for morality. Piaget thought that moral development began when children learned games with rules, which he connected with concrete operational thought at about age 7 (Piaget, 1932/1997). We now know that Piaget underestimated young children: Games with rules and moral development are both evident during early childhood. Indeed, some researchers see moral judgement beginning in infancy (Narvaez & Lapsley, 2009).

Many parents and teachers consider morality more important than any of the other developments already described (physical strength, motor skills, intelligence, and so on). Perhaps for this reason, debate rages over how children internalize standards, develop virtues, and avoid vices. Conflicting perspectives are taken by theories and scholars of psychology, philosophy, theology, and sociology. This conflict reflects the primal debate over development: nature versus nurture:

- The "nature" perspective suggests that morality is genetic, an outgrowth of natural bonding, attachment, and cognitive maturation. That would explain why young children help and defend their parents, no matter what the parents do, and punish other children who violate moral rules.

- The "nurture" perspective contends that culture is crucial, as children learn the values of their community. That would explain why young children in diverse cultures reject or emulate people who follow the moral rules of their community, even if the actual behavior is not innately good or bad. Some children believe that people who eat raw fish, or hamburgers, or bacon, or crickets are immoral.

Both nature and nurture are always important, but developmentalists disagree about which is more important for morality (Killen & Smetana, 2007; Krebs, 2008; Narvaez & Lapsley, 2009; Turiel, 2006). That debate is not to be settled here. Our discussion centers on two moral issues that arise from age 2 to age 6: prosocial and antisocial behavior (especially aggression), as well as the moral lessons inherent in parental discipline.

Empathy and Antipathy

Two moral emotions are evident as children play with one another. With increasing social experiences and decreasing egocentrism, they develop **empathy,** an understanding of other people's feelings and concerns, and **antipathy,** dislike or even hatred.

Empathy is not the same as sympathy, which means feeling sorry *for* someone. Rather, empathy means feeling sorry *with* someone, experiencing the other person's pain or sadness as if it were one's own. This recalls the research with mirror neurons (see Chapter 1), which suggests that observing someone else's behavior activates the same areas in the brain of the observer as in the person performing the action. Scientists studying young humans and other primates report spontaneous efforts to help others who are hurt, crying, or in need of help: That is evidence of empathy (Warneken & Tomasello, 2009). Empathy leads to **prosocial behavior,** extending helpfulness and kindness without any obvious benefit to oneself. Expressing concern, offering to share food or a toy, and including a shy child in a game or conversation are examples of prosocial behavior among young children. Jack, age 3, showed empathy when he

> refused to bring snacks with peanuts to school because another boy had to sit alone during snack because he was allergic to nuts. Jack wanted to sit with him.
>
> *[Lovecky, 2009, p. 161]*

Antipathy can lead to **antisocial behavior,** deliberate hurtfulness or destructiveness aimed at another person, including people who have not actually harmed the antisocial person. Antisocial actions include verbal insults, social exclusion, and physical assaults (Calkins & Keane, 2009). An antisocial 4-year-old might look another child in the eye, scowl, and then kick him hard without provocation. Brain scans show that adults who want to punish others for violating social norms do so with pleasure, even if it means some loss (of money, time, or effort) to themselves (Takahashi et al., 2009). By age 4 or 5—as a result of brain maturation, theory of mind, emotional regulation, and interactions with caregivers—most children can be deliberately prosocial or antisocial.

Emotional regulation, moral development, and the emergence of antipathy are nowhere more apparent than in the way children learn to deal with their aggressive impulses. The gradual control of aggression is evident on close observation of rough-and-tumble play, or in the fantasies of domination and submission acted out in sociodramatic play, or in the sharing of art supplies, construction materials, and toys (J. B. Peterson & Flanders, 2005).

Researchers recognize four general types of aggression, described in Table 10.3. Not surprisingly, given the moral sensibilities of children, already by age 5 children judge when aggression is justified (Etchu, 2007). As with adults, self-defense is easier to justify than is a deliberate, unprovoked attack—although most aggressors feel they had a reason to do what they did, and children are more egocentric than adults.

Instrumental aggression is common among young children, who often want something they do not have and who try, without thinking, to get it. **Reactive aggression** is common as well; this type becomes better controlled as emotional regulation increases. **Relational aggression** (usually verbal) destroys another child's self-esteem and disrupts the victim's social networks, becoming more hurtful as children mature. The fourth and most ominous type is **bullying aggression,** done to dominate someone else. It is fairly common in young children but should be stopped before school age, when it can become particularly destructive for both victims and bullies (see Chapter 13).

empathy The ability to understand the emotions and concerns of another person, especially when they differ from one's own.

antipathy Feelings of dislike or even hatred for another person.

prosocial behavior Feelings and actions that are helpful and kind but are of no obvious benefit to oneself.

antisocial behavior Feelings and actions that are deliberately hurtful or destructive to another person.

instrumental aggression Behavior that hurts someone else because the aggressor wants to get or keep a possession or a privilege.

reactive aggression An impulsive retaliation for another person's intentional or accidental action, verbal or physical.

relational aggression Nonphysical acts, such as insults or social rejection, aimed at harming the social connection between the victim and other people.

bullying aggression Unprovoked, repeated physical or verbal attack, especially on victims who are unlikely to defend themselves.

TABLE 10.3		
The Four Forms of Aggression		
Type of Aggression	Definition	Comments
Instrumental aggression	Hurtful behavior that is aimed at gaining something (such as a toy, a place in line, or a turn on the swing) that someone else has	Often increases from age 2 to 6; involves objects more than people; quite normal; more egocentric than antisocial.
Reactive aggression	An impulsive retaliation for a hurt (intentional or accidental) that can be verbal or physical	Indicates a lack of emotional regulation, characteristic of 2-year-olds. A 5-year-old can usually stop and think before reacting.
Relational aggression	Nonphysical acts, such as insults or social rejection, aimed at harming the social connections between the victim and others	Involves a personal attack and thus is directly antisocial; can be very hurtful; more common as children become socially aware.
Bullying aggression	Unprovoked, repeated physical or verbal attack, especially on victims who are unlikely to defend themselves	In both bullies and victims, a sign of poor emotional regulation; adults should intervene before the school years. (Bullying is discussed in Chapter 13.)

Parental Discipline

Many developmentalists believe that children's attachment to their parents, and then to others, is the beginning of morality. According to evolutionary theory, humans protect, cooperate, and even sacrifice for each other precisely because social groups evolved to encourage such prosocial behavior (Krebs, 2008). A particular issue for many developmentalists is discipline, when a child violates a standard of behavior held by his or her family and culture.

Ideally, parents anticipate misbehavior and guide their children toward patterns of behavior and internalized standards of morality that will help them lifelong. Parents need to take developmental immaturity into account, as shown in Table 10.4—but parents cannot always prevent problems. A study of mothers and 3-year-olds during late afternoon (a stressful time) found that conflicts (including verbal disagreements) arose about every two minutes (Laible et al., 2008). Here is one example:

> **Child:** I want my other shoes.
> **Mother:** You don't need your other shoes. You wear your Pooh sandals when we go for a walk.
> **Child:** Noooooo.
> **Mother:** *[Child's name]*! You don't need your other shoes.
> **Child:** *[Cries loudly]*
> **Mother:** No, you don't need your other shoes. You wear your Pooh sandals when we go for a walk.
> **Child:** Ahhhh. Want pretty dress. *[Crying]*
> **Mother:** Your pretty dress.
> **Child:** Yeah.
> **Mother:** You can wear them some other day.
> **Child:** Noooooo. *[Crying]*
>
> *[Laible et al., 2008, pp. 442–443]*

In this study, securely attached children had as many conflicts as the insecurely attached ones. However, unlike the exchange in the dialogue above, their mothers often compromised and explained (Laible et al., 2008).

In every nation and family, adults vary in their expectations for proper words, actions, and appearance and in their response to transgressions. What is "rude" or "nasty" behavior in one community is accepted, even encouraged, in another.

TABLE 10.4

Discipline and Children's Thinking

1. *Remember theory of mind.* Young children gradually come to understand things from other viewpoints. Encouraging empathy ("How would you feel if someone did that to you?") increases prosocial behavior and decreases antisocial behavior by age 5.

2. *Remember egocentrism.* Young children are developing a sense of who they are. Adults might protect that emerging self by, for example, not insisting on sharing.

3. *Remember fast-mapping.* Young children are eager to talk and think, but they say more than they understand. A child who "doesn't listen" may have not understood.

4. *Remember that young children are not logical.* Children confuse a lie and a wish because their minds are not yet logical, and they may disconnect a misdeed from the punishment. If you were spanked as a child, do you remember why?

Many developmentalists have studied how children's thinking affects behavior. Here are four reminders from Chapter 9 that apply to disciplining of young children. None of this means that children should never be punished. However, parents need to consider the child's perspective. Often children attribute punishment to parental anger and rejection, not to their own misbehavior.

Parents are often unaware of their ethnotheories—no wonder they do not explain them and no wonder their children disagree, disobey, and disappoint (Bornstein, 2006; Bugental & Grusec, 2006). When adult authorities were raised differently, as when parents have different backgrounds or the culture of the school differs from the culture of the home, the children are more likely to be confused and considered disobedient.

Physical Punishment

In the United States, young children are slapped, spanked, or beaten more often than are children over age 6. Many parents remember such punishment and think it works. Some researchers agree; others do not (Gershoff, 2002; Larzelere & Kuhn, 2005). Physical punishment (called *corporal punishment* because it hurts the body) succeeds at the moment—spanking stops misbehavior—but longitudinal research finds that children who are physically punished are more likely to become bullies, delinquents, and then abusive adults. They are less likely to advance cognitively (Straus & Paschall, 2009). The moral value they learn is "might makes right."

Of course, children who are spanked do not always become violent adults. Spanking increases the risk, but other factors (poverty and temperament, among others) are stronger influences. Nonetheless, many developmentalists wonder why parents would increase any risk. Physical punishment seems to increase the possibility of long-term aggression while it increases obedience only temporarily.

Psychological Control

Spanking is not the only punishment with unintended consequences. Another method is **psychological control,** in which children's guilt and gratitude are used to control their behavior (Barber, 2002). Psychological control may reduce academic achievement.

Consider the results of a study of an entire cohort (the best way to obtain an unbiased sample) of children born in Finland (Aunola & Nurmi, 2004). Their parents were asked 20 questions about their approach to child rearing. The following four items, which the parents rated from 1 ("Not at all like me") to 5 ("Very much like me") measured psychological control:

DAVID STRICKLER / MONKMEYER

Angela at Play Research suggests that being spanked is a salient and memorable experience for young children, not because of the pain but because of the emotions. Children seek to do what they have learned; they know not only how to place their hands but also that an angry person does the hitting. The only part of the lesson they usually forget is what particular misdeed precipitated the punishment. Asked why she is spanking her doll, Angela will likely explain, "She was bad."

psychological control A disciplinary technique that involves threatening to withdraw love and support and that relies on a child's feelings of guilt and gratitude to the parents.

1. "My child should be aware of how much I have done for him/her."
2. "I let my child see how disappointed and shamed I am if he/she misbehaves."
3. "My child should be aware of how much I sacrifice for him/her."
4. "I expect my child to be grateful and appreciate all the advantages he/she has."

The higher the parents scored on psychological control, the lower the children's math scores—and this connection grew stronger over time. Surprisingly, math achievement suffered most if parents were high in both affection (e.g., they frequently hugged their children) and psychological control (Aunola & Nurmi, 2004). Other research finds that psychological control can depress children's achievement, creativity, and social acceptance (Soenens & Vansteenkiste, 2010). Psychological control seems less likely to produce bullies, but it may increase relational aggression (Kuppens et al., 2009).

time-out A disciplinary technique in which a child is separated from other people for a specified time.

Bad Boy or Bad Parent?
For some children and cultures, sitting alone is an effective punishment; for others, it produces an angry child.

SW PRODUCTIONS/AGE FOTOSTOCK

Exclusion and Conversation

The disciplinary technique most often used in North America is the **time-out,** in which an adult requires the misbehaving child to sit quietly, without toys or playmates, for a short time (Barkin et al., 2007). The time-out must be brief; one minute for each year of the child's age is suggested. Time-out is favored by experts: In the large, longitudinal evaluation of Head Start highlighted in Chapter 9, an increase in use of time-out and a decrease in use of spanking were considered signs of improved parental discipline (U.S. Department of Health and Human Services, 2010).

Another alternative to physical punishment and psychological control is *induction,* in which the parents talk extensively with the offending child, getting the child to understand why his or her behavior was wrong. Conversation helps children internalize standards, but induction takes time and patience. Since 3-year-olds confuse causes with consequences, they cannot answer an angry "Why did you do that?" or appreciate a lengthy explanation. Simple induction ("You made him sad") may be appropriate for 3-year-olds. In general, induction is recommended if the goal is an internalized standard of right and wrong (Turiel, 2006).

Methods of discipline vary in consequences and effectiveness, depending on temperament, culture, and the adult–child relationship. For example, time-out is effective *if* the child prefers to be with other people. As explained in Chapter 2, one version of time-out for older children is suspension from school. However, if a child hates school, suspension amounts to reinforcement, not punishment. In fact, if a teacher finds teaching easier when a particular child is absent, the teacher may unconsciously provoke the child to misbehave and thus be suspended. Both the child and the teacher are thereby reinforced, not punished. Similarly, induction might be rewarding if the child wants a parent to pay attention to him or her.

Children vary in their personalities, and parents have powerful emotions, memories, and stresses. No wonder punishment is not a simple issue. One young child who was disciplined for fighting protested, "Sometimes the fight just crawls out of me." Ideally, punishment won't "just crawl out" of the parent.

SHE USED TO HAVE 'TIME OUT' IN HER BEDROOM BUT WE FIND MAKING HER WATCH RERUNS OF THE 'ANTIQUES ROADSHOW' IS **FAR** MORE EFFECTIVE!

©FRAN

CARTOONSTOCK.COM

Cruel and Unusual? The PBS series *Antiques Roadshow* is popular among adults, but for a child whose sense of the finer things in life is still developing, it might be an apt punishment.

A VIEW FROM SCIENCE

Culture and Punishment

Worldwide, cultural differences in child discipline are apparent. For example, only half as many Canadian parents slap, pinch, or smack their children as parents in the United States (Oldershaw, 2002). The U.S. Supreme Court decided in 2004 that teachers and parents could use "reasonable force" to punish children (Bugental & Grusec, 2006), but physical punishment is illegal in many other developed nations—among them Austria, Croatia, Cyprus, Denmark, Finland, Germany, Israel, Italy, Norway, and Sweden—because it is considered a violation of human rights (Bitensky, 2006).

Perhaps the United States has more authoritarian parents than other nations do. However, cultural differences are evident by region and income even within the United States (Giles-Sims & Lockhart, 2005). Parents in the southern states and parents in low-income families do more spanking than do parents in New England and in wealthier families.

Cultural differences may lie behind a controversy that recently arose in the United States over a recommendation by some evangelical Christians that parents put a drop of hot sauce (which burns) on a child's tongue as punishment for forbidden speech. This method is included in a book on "creative correction" (Whelchel, 2000). Most evangelical parents as well as developmentalists consider this method abusive. Yet opinions are strongly divided. For example, most comments (posted on Amazon.com in 2008) regarding this book were either highly favorable or highly unfavorable. One man wrote:

> This lady is crazy. A sadistic monster. I wouldn't treat my dog like this, much less my kid. Tell me, how many kids did Jesus Hotsauce?

A woman who highly recommended the book wrote:

> Like most moms, I want to have obedient, fun children. I was, however, struggling to find effective means to discipline the children when they strayed.

Remember the study of Latino mothers and their 4-year-olds (Livas-Dlott et al., 2010)? Induction was rare and time-out was almost never used: The implicit belief was that the connection between the child and the mother was so important that it should not be broken, even in discipline. In those Mexican American families, disobedient children needed to listen to their mothers; if they didn't comply, the child might be moved from the scene of the forbidden action or told the social reason to obey (one mother got her son to help tidy the living room by saying that she should not be the only one cleaning up). In only 3 percent of the instances was corporal punishment used.

As for international comparisons, Americans consider Japanese mothers too permissive. They almost never punish children younger than 6. Instead, they use reason, empathy, and expres-

sions of disappointment. However, although U.S. children in permissive families tend to be immature and unhappy, Japanese children usually develop well. The reason may be summed up in the word: *amae,* which refers to the strong and affectionate bond that is typical of Japanese mother–child relationships (Rothbaum et al., 2000). For many Japanese children, their mother's approval is so important that no punishment is needed. Six-year-olds who, to a Western eye, might appear overly dependent and affectionate toward their indulgent mothers seem quite normal in Japan.

The parents' underlying attitude may be crucial. One study of African American mothers found that if they disapproved of spanking but did it nonetheless, their children were likely to be depressed; however, their children were okay if the spanking mothers were convinced that spanking was what they should do (McLoyd et al., 2007). Similarly, Chinese American parents who used physical punishment and shame raised children who were relatively happy and well adjusted *if* the parents used those methods because they agreed with the Chinese ideology that led to them (Fung & Lau, 2009).

Do all these observations lead to any general conclusions? Perhaps only that a multicultural understanding of discipline makes it difficult to judge any one tactic as best. All children need parental love and guidance; there are many ways to provide it.

Laughing? Pulling an ear is physical punishment—and this would be considered abuse in some cultures. Here, however, no one seems upset.

Especially for Parents Suppose you agree that spanking is destructive, but you sometimes get so angry at your child's behavior that you hit him or her. Is your reaction appropriate? (see response, page 284)

>> Response for Parents (from page 283) No. The worst time to spank a child is when you are angry. You might seriously hurt the child, and the child will associate anger with violence. You would do better to learn to control your anger and develop other strategies for discipline and for prevention of misbehavior.

SUMMING UP

Moral development occurs throughout childhood and adolescence. During early childhood, the most powerful moral lessons are learned from other children, particularly the need to be appropriately prosocial and antisocial, with aggression controlled. Ideally, children learn to be good friends to each other, particularly avoiding unprovoked aggression. Parents discipline their children in many ways, with each method teaching lessons about right and wrong. Induction seems most likely to lead to internalized standards of morality.

>> Becoming Boys and Girls

Biology determines whether a person is male or female. As you know from Chapters 3 and 4, the SRY gene on the Y chromosomes directs the reproductive organs to develop outside the body, and then it starts the production of hormones that exert subtle control over the brain and later behavior. The female organs produce other hormones, again beginning in prenatal development and affecting the brain.

However, sexual identity is more than biology, and it is during early childhood that patterns and preferences become apparent. Children become more gender conscious with every year of childhood (Ruble et al., 2006). Even 2-year-olds apply gender labels (*Mrs., Mr., lady, man*) consistently. By age 4, children are convinced that certain toys (such as dolls or trucks) are appropriate for one sex but not the other and that certain roles (not just Daddy or Mommy, but also nurse, teacher, police officer, soldier) are best for one sex or the other.

Sex and Gender

sex differences Biological differences between males and females, in organs, hormones, and body type.

gender differences Differences in the roles and behavior of males and females that are prescribed by the culture.

Scientists distinguish **sex differences,** which are biological differences between males and females, from **gender differences,** which are culturally prescribed roles and behaviors. In theory, this seems like a straightforward separation, but, as with every nature–nurture distinction, the interaction between sex and gender makes it hard to separate the two (Hines, 2004).

Young children are particularly confused about gender and sex, partly because culture emphasizes gender. One little girl said she would grow a penis when she got older, and one little boy offered to buy his mother one. Uncertainty about the biological determination of sex was demonstrated by a 3-year-old who went with his father to see a neighbor's newborn kittens. Returning home, the child told his mother that there were three girl kittens and two boy kittens. "How do you know?" she asked. "Daddy picked them up and read what was written on their tummies," he replied.

In recent years, sex and gender issues have become increasingly complex as cultural acceptance of varied sexual orientations has increased—to the outrage of some and the joy of others. Adults may be bisexual, homosexual, "mostly straight," or heterosexual (Thompson & Morgan, 2008, p. 15). Despite the increasing acceptance of sexual diversity, at least in North America, at around age 5 many children become quite rigid in their ideas of sex and gender. If a 5-year-old boy needs new shoes, but the only ones that fit him are pink, he would rather go barefoot.

Theories of Sex Role Development

There are many theories to explain the reasons why boys and girls, and men and women, see the two sexes so differently. Biologically, the differences may seem minor: a matter of one of the 46 chromosomes that affect almost everything (rough-and-tumble play, emotional regulation, parental reactions to misbehavior, to name just a few in this chapter alone) but nothing very much. For instance, the fact that boys are more likely to chase and catch each other does not keep millions of little girls from chasing and catching. Most neighborhood play groups are of both sexes and several ages.

Nonetheless, if given many playmates to choose from, as when a child is in preschool with a dozen peers, girls prefer to play with the girls and boys with the boys. Despite their parents' and teachers' wishes, children of either sex might say, "No girls [or boys] allowed." How can this be explained?

Psychoanalytic Theory

Freud (1938) called the period from about ages 3 to 6 the **phallic stage** because he believed its central focus is the *phallus,* or penis. At about 3 or 4 years of age, said Freud, the process of maturation makes a boy aware of his male sexual organ. He begins to masturbate, to fear castration, and to develop sexual feelings toward his mother.

These feelings make every young boy jealous of his father—so jealous, according to Freud, that every son wants to replace his dad. Freud called this the **Oedipus complex,** after Oedipus, son of a king in Greek mythology. Abandoned as an infant and raised in a distant kingdom, Oedipus later returned to his birthplace and, not realizing who they were, killed his father and married his mother. When he discovered what he had done, he blinded himself in a spasm of guilt.

Freud believed that this ancient story has been replayed for over two millennia because it dramatizes emotions that all boys feel about their parents—both love and hate. Every male feels guilty about the incestuous and murderous impulses that are buried in his unconscious. In self-defense, boys develop a powerful conscience called the **superego,** which is quick to judge and punish. That marks the beginning of morality, according to psychoanalytic theory, which contends that a young boy's fascination with superheroes, guns, kung fu, and the like arises from his unconscious impulse to kill his father. An adult man's homosexuality, homophobia, or obsession with punishment might be explained by an imperfectly resolved phallic stage. Later psychoanalytic theorists agree that morality originates from the clash between unconscious wishes and parental prohibitions in childhood (Hughes, 2007).

Freud offered several descriptions of the phallic stage in girls. One centers on the **Electra complex** (also named after a figure in classical mythology). The Electra complex is similar to the Oedipus complex in that the little girl wants to eliminate the same-sex parent (her mother) and become intimate with the opposite-sex parent (her father). Girls may also develop a superego, although Freud thought it weaker than in boys.

According to psychoanalytic theory, children of both sexes cope with their guilt and fear through **identification;** that is, they try to become like the same-sex parent. Consequently, young boys copy their father's mannerisms, opinions, actions, and so on, and girls copy their mother's. Both sexes exaggerate the male or female role. Since the superego arises from the phallic stage, and since Freud believed that sexual identity and expression were crucial for mental health, this theory encourages parents to teach sexual identity to children during early childhood.

Many social scientists from the mid-twentieth century on believe that Freud's explanation of sexual and moral development "flies in the face of sociological and historical evidence" (David et al., 2004, p. 139). In graduate school, I learned that

Two Trios at Play Sex differences are apparent by age 3, not only in haircuts and clothing but also in physical closeness (girls hold hands) and preferred activities (boys more readily take risks).

phallic stage Freud's third stage of development, when the penis becomes the focus of concern and pleasure.

Oedipus complex The unconscious desire of young boys to replace their father and win their mother's romantic love.

superego In psychoanalytic theory, the judgmental part of the personality that internalizes the moral standards of the parents.

Electra complex The unconscious desire of girls to replace their mother and win their father's romantic love.

identification An attempt to defend one's self-concept by taking on the behaviors and attitudes of someone else.

Freud was unscientific. However, as explained in Chapter 1, developmental scientists seek to connect research, theory, and experience. I have softened my criticism of Freud, as the following explains.

Berger and Freud

My family's first "Electra episode" occurred in a conversation with my eldest daughter, Bethany, when she was about 4 years old:

> **Bethany:** When I grow up, I'm going to marry Daddy.
> **Mother:** But Daddy's married to me.
> **Bethany:** That's all right. When I grow up, you'll probably be dead.
> **Mother:** [*Determined to stick up for myself*] Daddy's older than me, so when I'm dead, he'll probably be dead, too.
> **Bethany:** That's OK. I'll marry him when he gets born again.

At this point, I couldn't think of a good reply, especially since I had no idea where she had gotten the concept of reincarnation. Bethany saw my face fall, and she took pity on me:

> **Bethany:** Don't worry, Mommy. After you get born again, you can be our baby.

The second episode was a conversation I had with my daughter Rachel when she was about 5:

> **Rachel:** When I get married, I'm going to marry Daddy.
> **Mother:** Daddy's already married to me.
> **Rachel:** [*With the joy of having discovered a wonderful solution*] Then we can have a double wedding!

The third episode was considerably more graphic. It took the form of a "valentine" left on my husband's pillow by my daughter Elissa, who was about 8 years old at the time. It is reproduced here.

Finally, when my youngest daughter, Sarah, turned 5, she also expressed the desire to marry my husband. When I told her she couldn't, because he was married to me, her response revealed one more hazard of watching TV: "Oh, yes, a man can have two wives. I saw it on television."

I am not the only feminist developmentalist to be taken aback by her own children's words. Nancy Datan (1986) wrote about the Oedipal conflict: "I have a son who was once five years old. From that day to this, I have never thought Freud mistaken." As you remember from Chapter 1, however, a single example, or four children from one family, does not prove that Freud was correct. A behaviorist explanation would be that my daughters wanted to model themselves after me and thus naively thought that marrying my husband was the way to do it. Cohort changes, which my two infant grandsons remind me of daily, may mean that my children's children may not expect to marry—or that my grandsons (no granddaughters yet) may seek someone quite unlike their mothers.

Or they may change my mind again. You have your own theories and experiences, and I still think Freud was wrong on many counts. But his description of the phallic stage seems less bizarre than I once thought.

Pillow Talk Elissa placed this artwork on my husband's pillow. My pillow, beside it, had a less colorful, less elaborate note—an afterthought. It read "Dear Mom, I love you too."

Behaviorism

In contrast to psychoanalytic theorists, behaviorists believe that virtually all roles, values, and morals are learned. To behaviorists, gender distinctions are the product of ongoing reinforcement and punishment, as well as social learning.

Some evidence supports this aspect of learning theory. Parents, peers, and teachers all reward behavior that is "gender appropriate" more than behavior that is "gender inappropriate" (Berenbaum et al., 2008). For example, "adults compliment a girl when she wears a dress but not when she wears pants" (Ruble et al., 2006, p. 897). According to social learning theory, children notice the ways men and women behave, and they experience punishment when they act inappropriately ("boys don't cry" or "be a good girl"). They internalize the standards they observe, becoming proud of themselves when they act like a man or a lady (Bandura & Bussey, 2004; Bussey & Bandura, 1999).

Interestingly, sex roles seem more significant for males than for females (Banerjee & Lintern, 2000; David et al., 2004). Boys are criticized for being "sissies" more than girls are for being "tomboys." Fathers, particularly, expect their daughters to be sweet and their sons to be tough.

Behaviorists believe children learn about proper behavior not only directly (as by receiving a gender-appropriate toy or an adult's praise) but also indirectly, through *social learning*. Children model their behavior after people they perceive to be nurturing, powerful, and yet similar to themselves. For young children, those people are usually their parents, and men and women are usually most sextyped when they are raising young children. For instance, if ever an adult woman quits work to become a housewife, she does so when she has young children; the children do not realize that their family's arrangement, with their mother doing domestic work and their father working outside the home, is not how men and women always behave.

Cognitive Theory

Cognitive theory offers an alternative explanation for the strong gender identity that becomes apparent at about age 5. Remember that cognitive theorists focus on how children understand various ideas. Children develop concepts about their experiences. In this case, a **gender schema** is the child's understanding of sex differences (Kohlberg et al., 1983; Martin et al., 2002; Renk et al., 2006).

Young children have many gender-related experiences but not much cognitive depth. They tend to see the world in simple terms. For this reason, they categorize male and female as opposites, even when evidence contradicts such a sexist view. Nuances, complexities, exceptions, and gradations about gender (as well as about everything else) are beyond the preoperational child. Furthermore, as they try to make sense of their culture, they see numerous customs, taboos, and terminology that enforce the gender norms. Remember that for preoperational children, appearance is crucial and static thinking makes them believe that whatever is has always been and is irreversible.

gender schema A cognitive concept or general belief based on one's experiences— in this case, a child's understanding of sex differences.

Toy Guns for Boys, Cinderella for Girls
Young boys throughout the world are the ones who aim toy guns, while young girls imagine themselves as a Disney Cinderella, waiting for her handsome prince. The question is why: Are these young monks in Laos and this girl in Mexico responding to biology or to culture?

JEFF GREENBERG / ALAMY

Imagine Halloween is a time for fantasy. Can you imagine these two boys dressed like the girl while she wore a pirate's outfit? If you can, you are not stuck in cultural norms, but you probably also realize that none of these children would be smiling if their costumes violated gender norms. In fact, they would probably refuse to leave their homes.

In addition, the need to develop a self-concept leads young children to a cognitive need to categorize themselves as male or female and then to behave in a way that fits their concept. For that reason, cognitive theorists see "Jill's claim that she is a girl because she is wearing her new frilly socks as a genuine expression of her gender identity" (David et al., 2004, p. 147). Similarly, a 3½-year-old boy whose aunt called him *cute* insisted that he should be called *handsome* instead (Powlishta, 2004). Obviously, he had developed gender-based categories, and he wanted others to see him as he conceptualized himself.

Gender and Universal Social Order

As you can see, the three grand theories differ in how they explain the young child's understanding of male and female. The newer theories have other explanations. Evolutionary theory holds that sexual attraction is crucial for humankind's most basic urge, to reproduce; thus, males and females try to look attractive to the other sex, taking on many behaviors to do so. Sociocultural theory holds that sexual behavior depends on the culture (men holding hands with men is taboo or expected, depending on local customs) and that some of the distinctions are tied to general patterns of social organization. Therefore, evolutionary theory would encourage male–female differences and sociocultural theory would conclude that sex differences are changeable if they interfere with other values.

The theories all raise a question: What gender patterns *should* children learn? Should everyone combine the best of both sexes (called *androgyny*), and should gender stereotypes disappear with age (like Santa Claus and the tooth fairy)? Or should male–female distinctions be encouraged as essential for the human family? Answers vary among developmentalists as well as among mothers, fathers, and cultures. Was I right or wrong to stop my student who told Bethany, "Girls don't fight"?

SUMMING UP

Gender stereotypes are held most forcefully at about age 6. Each theory, each discipline, and probably each parent has an explanation for this phenomenon: Freud described unconscious incestuous urges; behaviorists highlight social reinforcement; cognitive theorists describe immature categorization. Moreover, people differ as to the moral response: from considering gender identification as the bedrock of morality to seeing gender stereotypes as childish and destructive. ▪

SUMMARY

Emotional Development

1. Learning to regulate and control emotions is crucial during early childhood. Emotional regulation is made possible by maturation of the brain, particularly of the prefrontal cortex, as well as by experiences with parents and peers.

2. In Erikson's psychosocial theory, the crisis of initiative versus guilt occurs during early childhood. Children normally feel pride, sometimes mixed with feelings of guilt. Shame is also evident, particularly in some cultures.

3. Both externalizing and internalizing problems indicate impaired self-control. Some emotional problems that indicate psychopathology are first evident during these years.

4. Boys more often manifest externalizing behaviors and girls, internalizing behaviors. For both sexes, brain maturation and the quality of early caregiving affect emotional control.

Play

5. All young children enjoy playing—with other children of the same sex (preferably), alone, or with parents.

6. Rough-and-tumble play teaches many social skills and occurs everywhere, especially among boys who have space to run and chase.

7. Sociodramatic play allows development of emotions and roles within a safe setting. Both sexes engage in dramatic play, with girls preferring more domestic, less violent themes.

Challenges for Parents

8. Three classic styles of parenting have been identified: authoritarian, permissive, and authoritative. Generally, children are more successful and happy when their parents express warmth and set guidelines.

9. A fourth style of parenting, uninvolved, is always harmful. The particulars of parenting reflect the culture as well as the temperament of the child.

10. Children are prime consumers of many kinds of media, usually for several hours a day and often without their parents' involvement. Content is crucial. The problems that arise from the media include increased aggression and less creative play.

Moral Development

11. The sense of self and the social awareness of the young child become the foundation for morality. This is evident in both prosocial and antisocial behavior.

12. There are four types of aggression: instrumental, reactive, relational, and bullying. Instrumental aggression is used by all children but becomes less common with age. Unprovoked injury (bullying) is considered wrong by children as well as by adults.

13. Parents' choice of punishment can have long-term consequences. Physical punishment may teach lessons that parents do not want their children to learn. Other forms of punishment have long-term consequences as well.

Becoming Boys and Girls

14. Even 2-year-olds correctly use sex-specific labels. Young children become aware of gender differences in clothes, toys, future careers, and playmates.

15. Freud emphasized that children are attracted to the opposite-sex parent and eventually seek to identify, or align themselves, with the same-sex parent. Behaviorists hold that gender-related behaviors are learned through reinforcement and punishment (especially for males) and social modeling.

16. Cognitive theorists note that simplistic preoperational thinking leads to gender schema and therefore stereotypes. Sociocultural theorists point to the many male–female distinctions that are apparent in every society and are taught to children.

17. Evolutionary theory contends that sex and gender differences are crucial for the survival and reproduction of the species.

KEY TERMS

emotional regulation (p. 265)	sociodramatic play (p. 271)	antisocial behavior (p. 279)	phallic stage (p. 285)
initiative versus guilt (p. 265)	authoritarian parenting (p. 273)	instrumental aggression (p. 279)	Oedipus complex (p. 285)
self-concept (p. 266)	permissive parenting (p. 273)	reactive aggression (p. 279)	superego (p. 285)
intrinsic motivation (p. 266)	authoritative parenting (p. 273)	relational aggression (p. 279)	Electra complex (p. 285)
extrinsic motivation (p. 267)	neglectful/uninvolved parenting	bullying aggression (p. 279)	identification (p. 285)
psychopathology (p. 268)	(p. 274)	psychological control (p. 281)	gender schema (p. 287)
externalizing problems (p. 268)	empathy (p. 279)	time-out (p. 282)	
internalizing problems (p. 268)	antipathy (p. 279)	sex differences (p. 284)	
rough-and-tumble play (p. 270)	prosocial behavior (p. 279)	gender differences (p. 284)	

WHAT HAVE YOU LEARNED?

Emotional Development

1. What aspects of brain development aid emotional regulation?

2. What are the differences between shame and guilt?

3. How is initiative different from autonomy (Erikson's third and second stages)?

4. What is the connection between psychopathology and emotional regulation?

5. What emotions are hard for people to regulate and why?

6. How do children learn emotional regulation?

7. What would be an example of intrinsic and extrinsic motivation in reading a book?

Play

8. What do children learn from rough-and-tumble play?

9. Why do children prefer to play with peers rather than adults?

10. How is the development of social play affected by culture?

11. What does sociodramatic play help children learn?

12. What are the differences in the typical play of young boys and young girls?

Challenges for Parents

13. In Baumrind's three parenting styles, how do parents differ in expectations?

14. Why are children of permissive parents often unhappy?

15. Why do many non–European American parents seem stricter than other parents?

16. What do most American professionals advise about television and young children?

17. What is likely to be displaced when young children are using electronic media?

Moral Development

18. What did Piaget believe about the moral development of children?

19. What is the nature perspective on how people develop morals?

20. What are the differences among sympathy, empathy, and antipathy?

21. What are the advantages and disadvantages of prosocial behavior?

22. What are the similarities and differences of the four kinds of agression?

23. Why do developmentalists hope that parents will discuss discipline with each other before their child needs it?

24. What are the advantages and disadvantages of physical punishment?

25. Why have many nations made corporal punishment illegal?

26. When is time-out an effective punishment and when is it not?

27. What are the advantages and disadvantages of using induction as punishment?

Becoming Boys and Girls

28. How and when do children learn about sex differences between males and females?

29. How and when do children learn about gender differences between boys and girls?

30. Why do many social scientists dispute Freud's theory of sex-role development?

31. What would be easy and what difficult for society if sex roles changed?

APPLICATIONS

1. Observe the interactions of two or more young children. Sort your observations into four categories: emotions, reasons, results, and emotional regulation. Note every observable emotion (expressed by laughter, tears, etc.), the reason for it, the consequences, and whether or not emotional regulation was likely. For example: "Anger: Friend grabbed toy; child suggested sharing; emotional regulation probable."

2. Ask three parents about punishment, including their preferred type, at what age, for what misdeeds, and by whom. Ask your three informants how they were punished as children and how that affected them. If your sources agree, find a parent (or a classmate) who has a different view.

3. Children's television programming has been accused of stereotyping ethnicity, gender, and morality. Watch an hour of children's TV, especially on a Saturday morning, and describe the content of both the programs and the commercials. Draw conclusions about stereotyping, citing specific evidence (rather than merely reporting your impressions).

4. Gender indicators often go unnoticed. Go to a public place (park, restaurant, busy street) and spend at least 10 minutes recording examples of gender differentiation, such as articles of clothing, mannerisms, interaction patterns, and activities. Quantify what you see, such as baseball hats on eight males and two females or (better but more difficult) four male–female conversations, with gender differences in length and frequency of talking, interruptions, vocabulary, and so on.

>>ONLINE CONNECTIONS

To accompany your textbook, you have access to a number of online resources, including quizzes for every chapter of the book, flashcards (in English and Spanish), critical thinking questions, and case studies. For access to any of these links, go to www.worthpublishers.com/bergerls8e. In addition to these free resources, you'll also find links to the podcasts, video clips, diagnostic quizzing with personalized study advice, and an ebook. Some of the videos and activities available online include:

- *Children at Play.* Watch video clips of children at play, identify the types of play you see, and review how each type contributes to children's development.

- *Bullying.* With video clips of bullying, this covers physical and relational aggression, gender differences in bullying, and the impact on victims. Presents causes and preventive measures.

Early Childhood

BIOSOCIAL

Body Changes Children continue to grow from ages 2 to 6, but at a slower rate. Normally the BMI (body mass index) is lower at about age 5 than at any other time of life. Children often eat too much unhealthy food and refuse to eat certain other foods altogether, insisting that food and other routines be "just right."

Brain Development The proliferation of neural pathways and myelination continue. Parts of the brain (e.g., the corpus callosum, prefrontal cortex, amygdala, hippocampus, and hypothalamus) connect, allowing lateralization and coordination of left and right as well as less impulsivity and perseveration. Gross motor skills slowly develop.

Injuries and Maltreatment Injury control is particularly necessary in these years, since far more children worldwide die of avoidable accidents than of diseases. Child abuse and neglect can occur in any family but are especially likely in homes with many children and few resources. Prevention requires that abused children be protected from further harm (tertiary prevention), that risk factors be reduced (secondary prevention), and that social changes make maltreatment less likely (primary prevention).

COGNITIVE

Piaget and Vygotsky Piaget stressed the young child's egocentric, illogical perspective, which prevents the child from grasping concepts such as conservation. Vygotsky stressed the cultural context, noting that children learn from mentors, which include parents, teachers, peers, and the social context. Children develop their own theories, including a theory of mind, as they realize that not everyone thinks as they do.

Language Language abilities develop rapidly. By age 6, the average child knows 10,000 words and demonstrates extensive grammatical knowledge. Young children can become balanced bilinguals during these years if their social context is encouraging.

Early Childhood Education Young children are avid learners. Child-centered, teacher-directed, and intervention programs can all nurture learning; the outcome depends on the skill and attention from teachers, as well as on the specifics of the curriculum.

PSYCHOSOCIAL

Emotional Development Self-esteem is usually high during early childhood. Self-concept emerges in Erikson's stage of initiative versus guilt, as does the ability to regulate emotions. Externalizing problems may be the result of too little emotional regulation; internalizing problems may result from too much control. Empathy produces prosocial behavior; antipathy leads to antisocial actions. Aggression takes many forms: Instrumental aggression is quite normal; bullying aggression is ominous.

Parents Parenting styles that are warm and encouraging, with good communication as well as high expectations (called authoritative), are most effective in promoting the child's self-esteem, autonomy, and self-control. The authoritarian and permissive styles are less beneficial, especially if spanking or psychological control is used as discipline. Extensive use of television and other media by children can disrupt family life.

Becoming Boys and Girls Children develop stereotypic concepts of sex differences (biological) and gender differences (cultural). Current theories give contradictory explanations of nature and nurture, but all agree that sex and gender identities become increasingly salient to young children.

P A R T

IV

CHAPTERS 11 • 12 • 13

middle childhood

If someone asked you to pick the best years of the entire life span, you might say that every age has joys and sorrows, gains and losses. But if you were pushed to choose one, you could select ages 6 to 11, a time when many children experience good health and steady growth as they master new athletic skills, learn thousands of words, become less dependent on families. Almost all children throughout the world attend school during these years, learning to read and write, which expands their worldview. Usually, schoolchildren appreciate their parents; make new friends; and are proud of their nationality, gender, and ethnicity. Life is safe and happy; the dangers of adolescence (drugs, sex, and so on) are not yet on the horizon.

Yet some readers of this book remember these years as the worst, not the best. Some school-age children struggle with school; some live in dysfunctional families; some have no permanent home; some contend with obesity, asthma, learning disabilities, or bullies. The next three chapters celebrate the joys and acknowledge the difficulties of ages 6 to 11.

Middle Childhood: Biosocial Development

WHAT WILL YOU KNOW?

1. Why do many parents think child rearing is easiest during middle childhood?
2. Why are many children overweight?
3. How does society favor children who are right-handed?
4. Why do many professionals recommend medication for children with ADHD?
5. Why are more children considered autistic today than 50 years ago?

In the middle of the second grade, my family and I moved a thousand miles. Entering a new school where my accent was unusual, I was self-conscious and lonely. Cynthia had a friendly smile, a quick wit, and red hair. More important, she talked to me; I asked her to be my friend.

"We cannot be friends," she said, "because I am a Democrat."

"So am I," I answered. (I knew my family believed in democracy.)

"No, you're not. You are a Republican," she said.

I was stunned and sad. We never became friends.

Neither Cynthia nor I realized that each child is unusual in some way (perhaps because of culture, family type, or, in this case, political background) and yet capable of friendship with children unlike themselves. Cynthia and I could have been good friends, but neither of us knew it. Her parents told her something about my parents' politics that I did not understand. Cynthia left the school after that year, friendless.

This chapter describes not only the similarities among all school-age children but also the differences that suddenly become significant—in size, in health, in learning ability, and in almost everything else. At the end of this chapter, we focus on children with special needs—who often need friends but have trouble finding them.

>> A Healthy Time

Genetic and environmental factors safeguard **middle childhood** (about age 6 to 11), the period after early childhood and before adolescence. Genes that protect species survival mean that most fatal diseases and accidents occur before age 6 or after age 11. Contemporary schoolchildren have two added protections: education about risks and several doses of vaccine. All in all, these factors mean that middle childhood is the healthiest period of the entire life span (see Figure 11.1).

Slower Growth, Greater Strength

Unlike infants or adolescents, school-age children's growth is slow and steady. Self-care is easy—from brushing their new adult teeth to dressing themselves,

middle childhood The period between early childhood and early adolescence, approximately from ages 6 to 11.

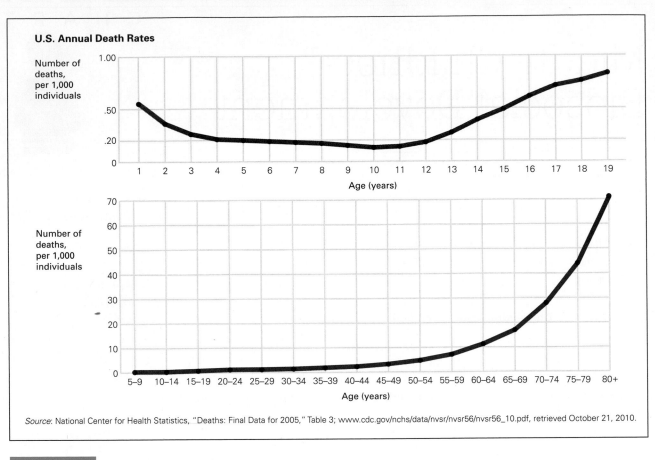

U.S. Annual Death Rates

Source: National Center for Health Statistics, "Deaths: Final Data for 2005," Table 3; www.cdc.gov/nchs/data/nvsr/nvsr56/nvsr56_10.pdf, retrieved October 21, 2010.

FIGURE 11.1

Death at an Early Age? Almost Never! Schoolchildren are remarkably hardy, as measured in many ways. These charts show that death rates for 6- to 11-year-olds are lower than those for children under 6 or over 11 and about 100 times lower than for adults.

Observation Quiz From the bottom graph, it looks as if ages 9 and 19 are equally healthy, but they are dramatically different in the top graph. What is the explanation for this? (see answer, page 298)

from making their own lunch to walking to school. In these middle years, children depend less on their families and do not yet need to cope with the body changes and impulses of adolescence.

Muscles become steadily stronger. For example, the average 10-year-old can throw a ball twice as far as a 6-year-old. Hearts and lungs are muscles, too, increasing in strength as well as capacity. Consequently, with each passing year, children can run faster and exercise longer (Malina et al., 2004). Many sports most valued by adults (such as basketball and football) require taller, bigger bodies, but school-age children are far superior to younger children in every athletic skill.

Most children eat enough: Parents need to ensure they eat healthy foods and not too much junk. However, as long as their entire community is not starving, school-age children are able to find enough food. As the "just right" obsession fades, children try new foods, especially if they are having dinner at a friend's house. As discussed in Chapter 8, in most nations overweight is more likely than underweight. Earlier malnutrition is evident in height, not weight: Children from the poorest nations are several inches shorter than those from richer ones (Worthman et al., 2010).

Improved Medical Care

Immunization has reduced deaths dramatically, and serious accidents, fatal illnesses, and even minor diseases are less common than they were a few decades ago. In the United States, the 1950 death rate for 5- to 14-year-olds was 70 per 100,000; in 2008, it was 15 per 100,000. Compared with 60 years ago, chronic illnesses are less prevalent, exposure to environmental toxins is reduced, and childhood surgery is unusual. Hearing impairments and anemia are half as frequent as they were even two decades ago, partly because both conditions are usually diagnosed and treated earlier. In just one decade (1994 to 2004), exposure to secondhand smoke between ages 4 and 11 was reduced by 28 percent, according to measures of cotine in the blood (not just parents' reports) (MMWR, July 11, 2008).

Expert Eye–Hand Coordination The specifics of motor-skill development in middle childhood depend on the culture. These flute players are carrying on the European Baroque musical tradition that thrives among the poor, remote Guarayo people of Bolivia.

Oral Care

Oral health is a good example of improvements. Sixty years ago, many children neither brushed their teeth nor saw a dentist, and fluoride was almost never added to water. That's why many elderly people have lost their teeth. This is still true among younger adults in developing nations, where one sign of poverty is missing teeth and one sign of wealth is a gold front tooth.

Now, in developed nations, most school-age children brush their teeth; most communities add fluoride to drinking water; and 75 percent of U.S. 6- to 11-year-olds have no untreated cavities (MMWR, August 26, 2005). North American children with poor oral health tend to have parents from nations where dentists are scarce (Chattopadhyay, 2008). Since school-age children respect most authorities, this is the time for dentists to teach good habits. For instance, dentists could explain that tobacco is the leading cause of gum disease, yellowed teeth, and bad breath among adults—but few dentists do so (Kast et al., 2008).

Back Teeth, Too Under age 5, children brush their teeth quickly and superficially, unlike this thorough, conscientious 8-year-old.

Children's Health Habits

School-age children are influenced by peers and many adults. Thus, if people they know have good health habits, children develop them as well. For this reason, camps for children with asthma, cancer, diabetes, and other chronic illnesses are particularly helpful during these years. When children are with peers, guided by knowledgeable adults, they become better at self-care.

Childhood habits protect adult health. For example, the more regular exercise children get, the less likely they are to suffer a stroke or a heart attack decades later (Branca et al., 2007). The good health that most school-age children naturally enjoy may either continue or be disrupted, depending on basic practices—such as eating a balanced diet, getting enough exercise and sleep, and breathing clean air. Unfortunately, the data also show that children who have poor health for economic or social reasons (such as those with no regular medical care) are vulnerable lifelong, even if their circumstances improve in adulthood (Buckhalt et al., 2007; Dilworth-Bart & Moore, 2006).

Especially for School Nurses For the past month, a 10-year-old fifth-grade girl has been eating very little at lunch and has visibly lost weight. She has also lost interest in daily school activities. What should you do? (see response, page 299)

>> Answer to Observation Quiz (from page 296) Look at the vertical axis. From age 1 to 20, the annual death rate is less than 1 in 1,000.

Physical Activity

Children often play joyfully, "fully and totally immersed" (Loland, 2002, p. 139). Beyond the sheer fun of playing, the benefits of physical activity—especially playing games with rules, which school-age children are now able to follow—can last a lifetime. These benefits include:

- Better overall health
- Less obesity
- Appreciation of cooperation and fair play
- Improved problem-solving abilities
- Respect for teammates and opponents of many ethnicities and nationalities

However, there are hazards as well:

- Loss of self-esteem as a result of criticism from teammates or coaches
- Injuries (the infamous "Little League elbow" is one example)
- Reinforcement of prejudices (especially against the other sex)
- Increased stress (evidenced by altered hormone levels, insomnia)

Where can children reap the benefits and avoid the hazards of active play? Three possibilities are neighborhoods, schools, and sports leagues.

Neighborhood Games

Neighborhood play is flexible. Rules and boundaries (out of bounds is "past the tree" or "behind the parked truck") are adapted to the context. Stickball, touch football, tag, hide-and-seek, and dozens of other running and catching games go on forever—or at least until dark. The play is active, interactive, and inclusive—ideal for children. It also teaches ethics. As one scholar notes:

> Children play tag, hide and seek, or pickup basketball. They compete with one another but always according to rules, and rules that they enforce themselves without recourse to an impartial judge. The penalty for not playing by the rules is not playing, that is, social exclusion . . .
>
> [Gillespie, 2010, p. 398]

Tree Hugging? Some adults disparage other adults who seek to preserve nature, but for children worldwide, climbing trees is a joy. Not every child has this opportunity. These fortunate boys are playing on a South African estate.

IMAGE100 / ALAMY

For school-age children, social exclusion is a steep price for insisting on their own way. Instead, they learn to cooperate. Unfortunately, modern life undercuts informal neighborhood games, as there are fewer open spaces today. A century ago, 90 percent of the world's children lived in rural areas; now more than half live in cities. The cities that have exploded most rapidly are in developing nations, where playgrounds and parks are particularly rare; but even in the slower-growing developed nations, population increases are notable. For instance, in 1990 slightly fewer than 4 million people lived in metropolitan Dallas, Texas; in 2010, nearly 7 million did so.

An added problem, especially for city children, is that their parents keep them at home because of "stranger danger"—although one expert writes that "there is a much greater chance that your child is going to be dangerously overweight from staying inside than that he is going to be abducted" (quoted in Layden, 2004, p. 86). Indoor activities like homework, television, and video games compete with outdoor play in every nation, perhaps especially in the United States. According to another scholar:

> Australian children are lucky. Here the dominant view is that children's after school time is leisure time. In the United States, it seems that leisure time is available to fewer and fewer children. If a child performs poorly in school, recreation time rapidly becomes remediation time. For high achievers, after school time is often spent in academic enrichment.
>
> [Vered, 2008, p. 170]

Exercise in School

When opportunities for neighborhood play are scarce, physical education in school is a logical alternative. Dedicated and trained gym teachers know developmentally appropriate, cooperative games and exercises for children (Belka, 2004). However, given the way gym class is conducted in many schools, children may love sports but hate physical education. One author cites an example of two children who enjoy team games every weekend but whose participation at school is quite different:

> Their current softball unit in physical education hardly provokes any excitement. There are 18 students on each side, sides that are formed in an ad hoc manner each lesson. . . . Few students get turns to pitch, and many are satisfied playing the deepest of outfield positions in order to have minimal involvement in the game.
>
> *[Hastie, 2004, p. 63]*

As U.S. schools are pressured to increase reading and math knowledge (see Chapter 12), time for physical education and recess has declined. Many children share a confined exercise space, spending more time waiting their turn than moving. Paradoxically, school exercise may improve academic achievement (Carlson et al., 2008). The Centers for Disease Control recommends that schools require physical education classes in which children are active at least 50 percent of the time (Khan et al., 2009). These are minimal goals; many schools do not meet them.

Athletic Clubs and Leagues

Private or nonprofit clubs and organizations offer additional opportunities for children to play. Culture and family affect the specifics: Some children learn golf, others tennis, others boxing. Cricket and rugby are common in England and in former British colonies such as India, Australia, and Jamaica; baseball is common in Japan, the United States, Cuba, Panama, and the Dominican Republic; soccer is central in many European, African, and Latin American nations.

The best-known organized recreation program for children is Little League. When it began in 1939, Little League had only three teams of boys aged 9–12. Now it includes girls, younger and older children, and 22,000 children with disabilities, with an annual total of 2.7 million children playing baseball or softball on more than 180,000 teams in 100 nations. Coaches are usually parent volunteers, not necessarily adept at encouraging every child. Nonetheless, most children enjoy it. One adult confesses:

> I was a lousy Little League player. Uncoordinated, small, and clueless are the accurate adjectives I'd use if someone asked politely. . . . What I did possess, though, was enthusiasm. Wearing the uniform—cheesy mesh cap, scratchy polyester shirt, old-school beltless pants, uncomfortable cleats and stirrups that never stayed up—gave me a sort of pride. It felt special and made me think that I was part of something important.
>
> *[Ryan, 2005]*

Being "part of something important" raises a problem: Many children are left out (Collins, 2003). Not all parents can pay for after-school sports or can afford the time to transport children to practices and games; many do not have the energy to cheer on the teams. Children from poor families, or those who are not well coordinated, or those who have disabilities are less likely to belong to sports teams—yet those are the very children who could benefit most from the strength, activity, and teamwork that organized play provides.

Indeed, especially for low-income children, participation in structured sports activities correlates with academic achievement, less delinquency, and development

>> **Response for School Nurses** (from page 297) Something is wrong, and you (or the school psychologist, or both) should talk to the girl's parents. Ask whether they, too, have noticed any changes. Recommend that the child see her pediatrician for a thorough physical examination. If the girl's self-image turns out to be part of the problem, stress the importance of social support.

Why Helmets? Sports organized by adults, such as this football team of 7- to 8-year-old boys sponsored by the Lyons and Police Athletic League of Detroit, may be harmful to children. The best games are those that require lots of running and teamwork—but no pushing or shoving.

Especially for Physical Education Teachers A group of parents of fourth- and fifth-graders has asked for your help in persuading the school administration to sponsor a competitive sports team. How should you advise the group to proceed? (see response, page 301)

"Just remember, son, it doesn't matter whether you win or lose—unless you want Daddy's love."

of friendships. Ironically, in difficult economic times, public sports programs are often cut. The problem is personal choice as well as political agenda. Although participation in extracurricular activities, especially sports, benefits low-income children more than others, such children are less likely to join even when after-school activities are free and available. The reasons are many; the consequences, sad (Dearing et al., 2009).

SUMMING UP

School-age children are usually healthy, strong, and capable. Genes as well as immunization protect them against contagious diseases; medical care has improved over the past 60 years; and their own developmental advances give them the strength, understanding, and coordination to undertake self-care, providing a foundation for adult health. Exercise is crucial for joy and learning. Although neighborhood play, school physical education, and community sports leagues all provide the activity that children need, not every child has access to these.

>> Health Problems in Middle Childhood

Chronic conditions may become more troubling if they interfere with school and friendship. Some worsen during the school years, including Tourette syndrome, stuttering, and allergies. Even minor problems—wearing glasses, repeatedly coughing or blowing one's nose, or having a visible birthmark—make children self-conscious. Learning good health habits is vital before adolescence: Teenagers might dye their hair green or get a tattoo, but hopefully they still take their medication and see the doctor. If adolescent rebellion includes medical noncompliance, those with serious, chronic conditions (including diabetes, phenylketonuria [PKU], epilepsy, cancer, asthma, sickle-cell anemia) ignore special diets, pills, and so on and get sicker (Dean et al., 2010; Suris et al., 2008).

Researchers increasingly recognize that every physical and psychological problem is affected by the social context and, in turn, affects that context (Jackson & Tester, 2008). Parents and children are not merely reactive: In a dynamic-systems manner (see Chapter 1), individuals and contexts influence each other. We now focus on two examples: obesity and asthma.

Childhood Obesity

BMI (body mass index) A person's weight in kilograms divided by the square of height in meters.

overweight In a child, having a BMI above the 85th percentile, according to the U.S. Centers for Disease Control's 1980 standards for children of a given age.

obesity In a child, having a BMI above the 95th percentile, according to the U.S. Centers for Disease Control's 1980 standards for children of a given age.

Of any age group, 6-year-olds have the least body fat and lowest **BMI (body mass index),** a number expressing the relationship of height to weight. Childhood **overweight** is defined as having a BMI above the 85th percentile for age; childhood **obesity** is defined as having a BMI above the 95th percentile. Both percentiles are measured against growth charts for a reference group of children that were published by the U.S. Centers for Disease Control in 1980.

Childhood obesity has increased since then, although it may have stopped increasing in the United States in 2005, with one-third (32 percent) of those under 18 overweight, half of them (16 percent) obese, and 11 percent extremely obese (Ogden et al., 2008).

An International Problem

As already made clear in Chapter 8, historically, undernourished children were common worldwide. Now the opposite is true, with obesity "increasing at especially alarming rates in children" (Branca et al., 2007, p. 9). Overweight children are more likely to have asthma, high blood pressure, and elevated levels of cholesterol (especially LDL, the "bad" form of cholesterol). Furthermore, on average, school achievement decreases, self-esteem falls, and loneliness rises as excessive weight builds (Dietz & Robinson, 2005). If they stay heavy (and most do), they risk diabetes, heart disease, and strokes. Because of obesity, today's children may be the first generation to die at younger ages than their parents did (Devi, 2008; Yajnik, 2004).

Why Childhood Obesity?

To halt the epidemic of childhood obesity, we need to understand what causes it. Researchers have focused on three major areas: heredity, parenting practices, and social influences.

Some people are genetically predisposed to having a high proportion of body fat. More than 200 genes affect weight by influencing activity level, food preference, body type, and metabolism (Gluckman & Hanson, 2006). Having two copies of an allele called FTO (inherited by 16 percent of all European Americans) increases the likelihood of both obesity and diabetes (Frayling et al, 2007).

However, genes change little from one generation to the next and thus cannot have caused the marked increase in obesity. Parenting practices, on the other hand, *have* changed dramatically. Obesity is more common in infants who are not breast-fed, in preschoolers who watch TV and drink soda, and in school-age children who ride to school and rarely exercise (Institute of Medicine, 2006; Patrick et al., 2004; Rhee, 2008). All these factors are typical for many children today.

Especially for children, family eating habits are crucial. One critic of parents who says weight is genetic writes, "Fat runs in families but so do frying pans" (S. Jones, 2006, p. 1879). Many American families eat meat daily and snack regularly on chips, cakes, and ice cream, once rare treats.

A third source of childhood obesity is "embedded in social policies" (Branca et al., 2007). It is governments, not parents, that determine the quality of school lunches; the presence of snack vending machines; the prevalence of parks, bike paths, and sidewalks; and the subsidies for corn oil but not fresh vegetables. One report lists 24 specific strategies that local governments could employ to reduce overweight (Khan et al., 2009).

Particularly potent for children is food advertising. In the United States, billions of dollars are spent on ads that entice children to eat unhealthy foods. Parents rarely realize how many such ads their children see (Linn & Novosat, 2008). Such advertising is illegal in some nations, limited in others, and unrestricted in still others—and a country's rate of childhood obesity correlates with the frequency of children's exposure to food commercials on television (Lobstein & Dibb, 2005; see Figure 11.2 on the next page).

Nature and Nurture

Since all three factors—genes, parents, and policies—are relevant, it is not surprising that parents blame genes or policies while others (medical professionals, political leaders) blame parents. Everyone may be right: It is unclear which particular measures would markedly reduce obesity. For instance, childhood weight correlates with hours of TV watched per day (Philipsen & Brooks-Gunn, 2008)—but remember that correlation does not prove cause. If families that allow unlimited television also allow unlimited snacking, then the snacking, not the TV, might be the problem. Or maybe content is crucial: One study found that neither educational television nor commercial-free videos correlated with childhood obesity but that commercials for calorie-dense foods did (Zimmerman & Bell, 2010).

GAETAN BALLY / KEYSTONE / CORBIS

A Happy Meal A close look at this photograph reveals that this scene is a McDonald's in Switzerland—one of hundreds of fast-food chain branches in Europe, where many normal-weight 6-year-olds become overweight 12-year-olds.

Especially for Teachers A child in your class is overweight, but you are hesitant to say anything to the parents, who are also overweight, because you do not want to insult them. What should you do? (see response, page 302)

Especially for Parents Suppose that you always serve dinner with the television on, tuned to a news broadcast. Your hope is that your children will learn about the world as they eat. Can this practice be harmful? (see response, page 303)

>> **Response for Physical Education Teachers** (from page 299) Discuss with the parents their reasons for wanting the team. Children need physical activity, but some aspects of competitive sports are better suited to adults than to children.

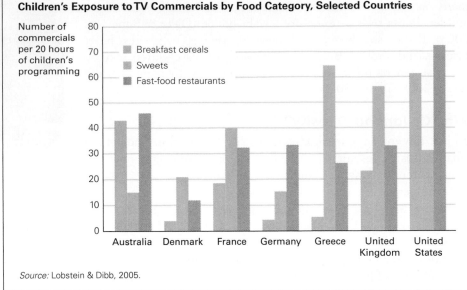

Children's Exposure to TV Commercials by Food Category, Selected Countries

Source: Lobstein & Dibb, 2005.

FIGURE 11.2

A Greek Sweet Tooth? Regulations restricting the number of commercials in children's television programming are one reason for the national differences in exposure shown here. Equally important are cultural differences. Breakfast cereal, for instance, is heavily advertised in the United States because it is much more common in that country than elsewhere.

asthma A chronic disease of the respiratory system in which inflammation narrows the airways from the nose and mouth to the lungs, causing difficulty in breathing. Signs and symptoms include wheezing, shortness of breath, chest tightness, and coughing.

>> **Response for Teachers** (from page 301) Speak to the parents, not accusingly (because you know that genes and culture have a major influence on body weight) but helpfully. Alert them to the potential social and health problems their child's weight poses. Most parents are very concerned about their child's well-being and will work with you to improve the child's snacks and exercise level.

Asthma

Asthma is a chronic inflammatory disorder of the airways that makes breathing difficult. Although asthma affects people of every age, rates are highest among school-age children, with marked increases in that age group worldwide (Cruz et al., 2010). In the United States, asthma rates among every group of children have tripled since 1980. Of all U.S. children under age 18, 14 percent have been diagnosed at least once with asthma, with ethnic variations (Puerto Rican, 26 percent; African American, 21 percent; Mexican American 10 percent) (Bloom et al., 2009).

Curiously, compared with Mexican American children born in the United States, Mexican Americans who were born in Mexico have half the rate of asthma; yet compared with children of Puerto Rican heritage born in New York, children born in Puerto Rico more often have asthma (Lara et al., 2006). It is not known why.

Causes of Asthma

Many researchers seek the causes of asthma. A few alleles have been identified, but asthma has many genetic roots, none of which act in isolation (Bossé & Hudson, 2007). Environment combined with genes is crucial (Akinbami et al., 2010). Air pollution, especially that caused by traffic congestion, increases the prevalence of asthma among vulnerable children (Gilliland, 2009).

Some experts suggest a *hygiene hypothesis:* that contemporary children are overprotected (too hygienic) from viruses and bacteria, which means they do not get infections and diseases that would strengthen their immune systems (Busse & Lemanske, 2005; Tedeschi & Airaghi, 2006). Several aspects of modern life—carpets, pets inside the home, airtight windows, less outdoor play—contribute to the increased rates of asthma (Tamay et al., 2007). Many allergens (pet dander, cigarette smoke, dust mites, cockroaches, and mold among them) that trigger attacks are concentrated in today's well-insulated homes.

The hygiene hypothesis might explain why dramatic increases in asthma occur when nations improve in national wealth (such as Brazil and China) and why first-born children (more protected) are at greater risk than later-born ones. However, increasing urbanization—which correlates with national income, automobile use, more pollution, and smaller families—may be the environmental trigger correlated with prosperity, not hygiene (Cruz et al., 2010).

Prevention of Asthma

The three levels of prevention (in Chapter 8) apply to asthma and every other health problem.

Primary prevention requires changes in the entire society. Better ventilation of schools and homes, less pollution, fewer cockroaches, and more outdoor play areas would benefit everyone while reducing asthma.

Secondary prevention decreases asthma attacks among high-risk children. If asthma runs in the family, then breast-feeding, family exercise, less dust and smoke, and no cats or cockroaches cut the onset of asthma in half (Elliott et al., 2007; Gdalevich et al., 2001).

Finally, *tertiary prevention* includes the prompt use of injections and inhalers. The use of hypoallergenic materials (e.g., for mattress covers) also reduces asthma attacks—but not by much, probably because it occurs too late (MMWR, January 14, 2005). Without tertiary prevention, childhood asthma is devastating, as the following illustrates.

>> **Response for Parents** (from page 301) Habitual TV watching correlates with obesity, so you may be damaging your children's health rather than improving their intellect. Your children would probably profit more if you were to make dinner a time for family conversation about world events.

A CASE TO STUDY

Asthma in Two Active 8-Year-Olds

A team of social scientists analyzed statistics and interviewed individuals to produce *The Measure of America,* a book comparing development in the United States and elsewhere (Burd-Sharps et al., 2008). Among their case studies were those of Sophie and Alexa, two 8-year-olds with asthma.

Sophie is a vibrant eight-year-old who was diagnosed with severe asthma when she was two. She lives in a house in a New York City suburb with a park down the street and fresh air outside—an environment with few asthma triggers.

Her family has private health insurance, a benefit of her father's job, with extensive provisions for preventative care and patient education. Her parents' jobs have personal and sick days that give them time off from work to take her to the doctor. After some early difficulty finding a suitable medication regime, she has settled into a routine of daily inhaled medication (at a cost of $500 per month, fully covered by insurance), annual flu shots, and a special medication she takes only when she is sick with a cold. Sophie sees her pediatrician regularly and a top-flight asthma specialist yearly, to monitor her progress; has a nebulizer for quick relief in case of a serious attack; and can rely on nebulizers in her school and after-school program as well.

Sophie has never had to go to the emergency room for an attack, almost always participates in gym, and misses about two or three days of school a year due to asthma related problems.

Alexa is also an active eight-year-old, first diagnosed with severe asthma at age three. She lives with her mother in a Brooklyn apartment three blocks from a waste transfer station that receives, sorts, and dispatches thirteen thousand tons of garbage each weekday. In addition to the acrid smell of garbage, the cockroaches that frequent her apartment also trigger Alexa's asthma attacks through allergens in their droppings. Her mother works at a minimum-wage job; she loses income when she takes Alexa to the doctor, fills emergency prescriptions, or stays home with Alexa when she is sick.

Alexa's mother could qualify for SCHIP, which would provide health insurance for Alexa, but she has never heard of it. Instead, Alexa is officially listed as living with her grandmother, whose Medicaid coverage extends to Alexa. Alexa sees a doctor annually, though her grandmother fears Alexa is not benefitting from the latest advances in asthma care.

Alexa misses twelve to fifteen days of school each year, does not participate in gym, and spends up to eight fearful nights each year in a hospital emergency room. When she misses consecutive days of school, she struggles with schoolwork. She wishes she could run around like her classmates.

[Burd-Sharps et al., 2008, p. 67]

These cases were presented to illustrate economic disparities in health. Few families can afford the excellent care Sophie receives, and programs such as SCHIP do not reach every low-income child like Alexa. However, as with obesity, severe asthma in childhood can be blamed on genes, parents, schools, medical professionals, neighborhoods, and public policies. Whom to blame is a hotly disputed political question, but Alexa should not spend "eight fearful nights" in the hospital each year. Someone, or perhaps everyone, should help her.

Pride and Prejudice In some city schools, asthma is so common that using an inhaler is a sign of prestige, as suggested by the facial expressions of these two boys. The "prejudice" is more apparent beyond the walls of this school nurse's room, in a society that allows high rates of childhood asthma to occur.

The increase in childhood asthma is disheartening. But improvement may be possible. One hundred and thirty-three Latino (primarily Puerto Rican) caregivers—all adult smokers not necessarily willing to quit—who look after children with asthma agreed to allow a Spanish-speaking counselor to visit them repeatedly at home (Borrelli et al., 2010). The counselor placed a smoke monitor in each child's room and a week later told the caregiver how much smoke exposure the child had experienced. Then, in three sessions, she provided specific counseling on quitting, based on the best research on addiction, with particular sensitivity to Latino values.

Three months later, one-fourth of the caregivers had quit smoking completely, many of the rest had cut down, and the children's exposure to smoke was cut in half. Asthma problems diminished (Borrelli et al., 2010). Other research confirms that most parents want to provide good care (many wonder how) and that many adults, parents or not, consider protecting all children a priority.

SUMMING UP

Some children have chronic health problems that interfere with school and friendship. Among these are obesity and asthma, both increasing in every nation and both having genetic and environmental causes. Childhood obesity may seem harmless, but it leads to severe health problems later on. Asthma's harm is more obvious: Asthmatic children often miss school and are rushed to emergency rooms, gasping for air. Family practices and lifestyle are part of the reason for increases in obesity and asthma, and many society-wide policies and cultural customs make the problems worse. ■

>> Brain Development

Recall that emotional regulation, theory of mind, and left–right coordination emerge in early childhood. The maturing corpus callosum connects the hemispheres of the brain, enabling balance and two-handed coordination, while myelination speeds up thoughts and behavior. The prefrontal cortex—the executive part of the brain—begins to plan, monitor, and evaluate. All of these neurological developments continue in middle childhood and beyond. We now look at additional advances in middle childhood.

Coordinating Connections

Increasing maturation results "by 7 or 8 years of age, in a massively interconnected brain" (Kagan & Herschkowitz, 2005, p. 220). Such connections are crucial for the complex tasks that children must master (M. H. Johnson et al., 2009). One example is learning to read, perhaps the most important intellectual accomplishment of the school-age child. Reading is not instinctual: Our ancestors never did it, and until recent centuries only a few scribes and scholars were expected to make sense of those marks on paper. Consequently, the brain has no areas dedicated to reading as it does for talking or gesturing (Gabrieli, 2009).

How do humans read without brain-specific structures? The answer is "massive interconnections": We use several parts of our brains—one for sounds, another for recognizing letters, another for sequencing, another for comprehension, and so on (Booth, 2007). That is true for many social skills as well—deciding whom to trust, figuring out what is fair, interpreting ambiguous gestures and expressions.

Children are not proficient at reading social cues (that's why they are told, "Don't talk to strangers"). During childhood, various parts of the brain connect to allow social decision making (Crone & Westenberg, 2009). Indeed, for many activities, children use more parts of their brains than adults do, thus requiring more connections (M. H. Johnson et al., 2009).

A crucial measure of better brain coordination is the ability of the prefrontal cortex to control various impulses, as already described in the discussion of early childhood. Advances in the "mental control processes that enable self-control" (Verté et al., 2005, p. 415) allow planning for the future, beyond the ability of the impatient younger child. School-age children can analyze possible consequences before they lash out in anger or dissolve in tears, and they can figure out when a curse word seems advisable (on the playground to a bully, perhaps) and when it does not (in the classroom or at home). Planning for the future means they can count the days until summer vacation.

The prefrontal cortex takes decades to mature. For children who want to be rocket scientists, billionaire stock analysts, or brain surgeons, connecting those distant goals with current behavior is not yet possible.

Think Quick; Too Slow

Advance planning and impulse control are aided by fast **reaction time,** which is how long it takes to respond to a stimulus. Thus, reaction time indicates speed of thought as an impulse travels from one neuron to another, and increasing myelination reduces reaction time every year from birth until about age 16.

A simple example is being able to kick a speeding soccer ball toward a teammate; a more complex example is being able to calculate when to utter a witty remark and when to stay quiet. Young children find both impossible; fast-thinking older children sometimes succeed; few adults can beat a teenager at a quick-paced video game.

Pay Attention

Neurological advances allow children not only to quickly process information but also to pay special heed to the most important elements of their environment. **Selective attention,** the ability to concentrate on some stimuli while ignoring others, improves noticeably at about age 7. School-age children not only notice various stimuli (which is one form of attention) but also select appropriate responses when several possibilities conflict (Rueda et al., 2007).

In the classroom, selective attention allows children to listen, take concise notes, and ignore distractions (all difficult at age 6, easier by age 10). In the din of the cafeteria, children can understand one another's gestures and expressions and react. On the baseball diamond, older batters ignore the other team's attempts to distract them, and older fielders start moving into position as soon as a ball is hit their way. Indeed, selective attention underlies all the abilities that gradually mature during the school years. "Networks of collaborating cortical regions" (M. H. Johnson et al., 2009, p. 151) are required because attention is not just one brain function but three: alerting, orienting, and executive control (Posner et al., 2007).

Automatization

One final advance in brain function in middle childhood is **automatization,** the process by which a sequence of thoughts and actions is repeated until it becomes automatic, or routine. At first, almost all behaviors under conscious control require careful and slow thought. After many repetitions, as neurons fire in

reaction time The time it takes to respond to a stimulus, either physically (with a reflexive movement such as an eyeblink) or cognitively (with a thought).

Finger Math Few schools teach children to count with their fingers, and some teachers forbid it. Yet concrete operational children learn best when they begin with visible examples, as this wise 8-year-old and millions of others know.

selective attention The ability to concentrate on some stimuli while ignoring others.

automatization A process in which repetition of a sequence of thoughts and actions makes the sequence routine, so that it no longer requires conscious thought.

sequence, actions become automatic and patterned. Less thinking is needed because firing one neuron sets off a chain reaction: That is automatization.

Consider again learning to read. At first, eyes (sometimes aided by a finger) focus intensely, painstakingly making out letters and sounding out each one. This leads to perception of syllables and then words. Eventually, the process becomes so automatic that, for instance, as you read this text, automatization allows you to concentrate on concepts without thinking about the letters. Automatization aids every skill. Learning to speak a second language, to recite the multiplication tables, and to write one's name are all slow at first but gradually become automatic.

One study used brain scans to trace how children and adults understood irony. Although the context made irony obvious, children exerted considerable mental effort (using the prefrontal cortex and left inferior frontal gyrus) to understand the intent of the words. For the adults, because automatization had occurred, conscious mental effort was not evident; irony was recognized, but the prefrontal cortex was relatively inactive (Wang et al., 2006). In many other ways as well, widespread activity of the prefrontal cortex is typical in childhood but less so in adulthood because automatization has occurred (M. H. Johnson et al., 2009).

Brains at Work Like all 10-year-olds, Luna and Carlotta love games. Frequently playing games makes some brain connections automatic, allowing players to concentrate on the most challenging aspects. Unlike 10-year-olds in previous generations, however, today's games usually involve small gadgets rather than big balls.

BEN WELSH

Measuring the Mind

In ancient times, if an adult was strong and fertile, that was enough, worthy of admiration. By the twentieth century, however, cognitive abilities had become important; therefore, many ways to measure intellect were developed.

Aptitude, Achievement, and IQ

In theory, **aptitude** is the potential to master a specific skill or to learn a certain body of knowledge. Intellectual aptitude is often measured by **IQ tests.** Originally, an IQ score was literally an intelligence quotient: Mental age (the age of a typical child who had reached a particular intellectual level) was divided by a child's chronological age, and the result of that division (the quotient) was multiplied by 100. Obviously, if mental age was the same as chronological age, the quotient would be 1, and the child's IQ would be 100, exactly average. The current method of calculating IQ is more complicated, but an IQ of 100 is still considered average (see Figure 11.3).

aptitude The potential to master a specific skill or to learn a certain body of knowledge.

IQ test A test designed to measure intellectual aptitude, or ability to learn in school. Originally, intelligence was defined as mental age divided by chronological age, times 100—hence the term *intelligence quotient,* or *IQ.*

FIGURE 11.3

In Theory, Most People Are Average Almost 70 percent of IQ scores fall within the normal range. Note, however, that this is a norm-referenced test. In fact, actual IQ scores have risen in many nations; 100 is no longer exactly the midpoint. Furthermore, in practice, scores below 50 are slightly more frequent than indicated by the normal curve shown here, because severe retardation is the result not of the normal distribution but of genetic and prenatal factors.

Observation Quiz If a person's IQ is 110, what category is he or she in? (see answer, page 309)

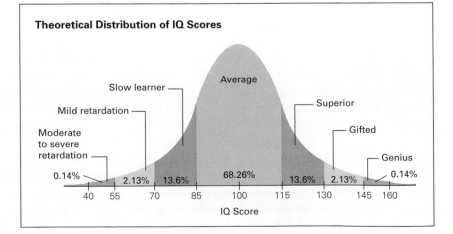

Theoretical Distribution of IQ Scores

Moderate to severe retardation — 0.14%
Mild retardation — 2.13%
Slow learner — 13.6%
Average — 68.26%
Superior — 13.6%
Gifted — 2.13%
Genius — 0.14%

IQ Score: 40 55 70 85 100 115 130 145 160

In theory, achievement is actual learning, not learning potential (aptitude). **Achievement tests** in school (see Chapter 12) compare scores to norms established for each grade. The words *in theory* precede the definitions of aptitude and achievement because, although potential and accomplishment are supposed to be distinct, IQ and achievement scores are strongly correlated for individuals, for groups of children, and for nations (Lynn & Mikk, 2007).

It was once assumed that aptitude was a fixed characteristic, present at birth. Longitudinal data show that this is not the case. Children with a low IQ could become above average, or even gifted, like my nephew David (in Chapter 1). Indeed, the average IQs of the populations of entire nations have risen substantially—a phenomenon called the **Flynn effect,** after the researcher who first described it (Flynn, 1999; 2007). An IQ score is only a snapshot, a static view of the dynamic, developing brain.

Criticisms of Testing

Beyond the fact that scores change, a more fundamental criticism is that no test can measure the complexities of the human brain. This criticism has been targeted particularly at IQ tests that assume that there is one general thing called *intelligence* (often referred to as *g*, for general intelligence). Many studies suggest instead that people inherit a set of abilities, some high and some low, rather than a general intellectual ability (e.g., Zhu et al., 2010). Two leading developmentalists (Sternberg and Gardner) are among the many who believe that humans have **multiple intelligences,** not just one.

Robert Sternberg (1996) describes three distinct types of intelligence:

1. *Academic,* measured by IQ and achievement tests
2. *Creative,* evidenced by imaginative endeavors
3. *Practical,* seen in everyday problem solving

These three intelligences are particularly significant in adulthood, when academic intelligence is less relevant but practical intelligence is crucial (explained further in Chapter 21).

Howard Gardner originally described seven intelligences: linguistic, logical-mathematical, musical, spatial, bodily-kinesthetic (movement), interpersonal (social understanding), and intrapersonal (self-understanding), each associated with a particular brain region (Gardner, 1983). He subsequently added an eighth intelligence (naturalistic: understanding nature, as in biology, zoology, or farming) and a ninth (existential: asking questions about life and death) (Gardner, 1999, 2006; Gardner & Moran, 2006). Although every normal person has at least a little of all nine intelligences, each individual excels in some more than others. For example, a person might be gifted spatially but not linguistically (a visual artist who cannot describe her work) or might have interpersonal but not naturalistic intelligence (a gifted clinical psychologist whose houseplants die).

Gardner's theory has been influential in education, especially the education of children (e.g., Rettig, 2005), as teachers allow children to demonstrate knowledge in their own ways, illustrating history with a drawing rather than an essay, for instance. Gardner's theory has been used to suggest that some children learn by listening, others by looking, others by doing—an idea that led to research on learning styles. Similarly, Sternberg believes that matching instruction to a person's analytic, creative, or practical ability advances his or her comprehension. However, these applications do not seem to be supported by scientific research (Pashler et al., 2008). Debate continues about whether intelligence is general or multiple, as well as what the educational implications of IQ and achievement scores might be.

achievement test A measure of mastery or proficiency in reading, mathematics, writing, science, or some other subject.

Flynn effect The rise in average IQ scores that has occurred over the decades in many nations.

multiple intelligences The idea that human intelligence is comprised of a varied set of abilities rather than a single, all-encompassing one.

Trial and Understanding This youngster completes one of the five performance tests of the Wechsler Intelligence Scale for Children (WISC). If her score is high, is that because of superior innate intelligence? ["Wechsler Intelligence Scale for Children" and "WISC" are trademarks, in the U.S. and/or other countries, of Pearson Education, Inc. or its affiliate(s).]

Especially for Teachers What are the advantages and disadvantages of using Gardner's nine intelligences to guide your classroom curriculum? (see response, page 309)

One final criticism arises from the multicultural understanding that is part of the life-span perspective. Every test reflects the culture of the people who create, administer, and take it. This is obviously true for achievement tests: A child may score low because of the school, the teacher, the family, or the culture, not because of his or her ability. Indeed, one reason IQ tests are still used is that achievement tests do not necessarily reflect ability.

Some experts have tried to develop aptitude tests that are culture-free, by asking children to draw shapes, repeat stories, identify letters, hop on one foot, name their classmates, sort objects, and much more. However, even with such tests, culture is relevant. One group reports that Sudanese children averaged 40 points lower (from average to notably retarded) when IQ tests required using a pencil because they had no experience with pencils (Wicherts et al., 2010).

Beyond such specifics, though, most tests assume that ability and achievement are characteristic of an individual. Consequently, accurate IQ tests (the WISC [Wechsler Intelligence Scale for Children] and the Stanford-Binet) and educational evaluations used in North America entail one professional testing one child. Yet in some cultures, individuals are taught to consider themselves part of a group, and a child's intellect is evident in social interaction, not in isolation. In Africa, for instance, testing a single child's IQ might not indicate potential (Nsamenang, 2004).

Brain Scans

One way to measure the mind might be to measure the brain directly, avoiding the pitfalls of written exams. Yet even with such measures, interpretations of brain scans, especially those of normal children, are controversial. Although it seems logical to interpret less activation as less thinking, that would be a mistake; many areas of a child's brain are activated simultaneously and, with practice, automatization reduces the need for brain activity. Similarly, some research finds that a thick cortex correlates with higher ability and also that thickness develops slower in gifted children (Karama et al., 2009; Miller, March 2006). This gifted pattern is puzzling—but so is much brain research.

Genius at Work Ten-year-old Kishan Shrikanth is a Bollywood director, shown here shooting his first full-length feature film (about street children in India). He excels at some intelligences (spatial, interpersonal) but not others (kinesthetic, naturalistic). Such variations may be much more common than traditional IQ tests measure.

AMI VITALE / GETTY IMAGES

Brain Fitness Aerobic fitness was measured (by VO_2—volume of oxygen expelled after exercise) in 59 children (average age 10, none of whom had ADHD or were pubescent); then the children's brains were scanned. Overall brain size did not correlate with fitness—genes and early nutrition are more important for that. However, volume of crucial areas for cognitive control (attention, contextualizing, planning) were significantly greater in the children who were in better shape. This is one more reason to go biking, running, or swimming with your child.

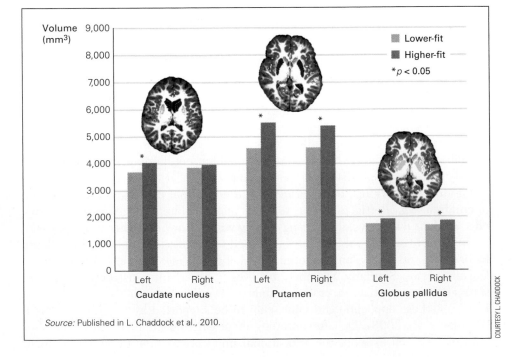

Volume (mm^3)

Legend: ▨ Lower-fit ▦ Higher-fit $*p < 0.05$

Source: Published in L. Chaddock et al., 2010.

COURTESY L. CHADDOCK

Neuroscientists agree, however, on three conclusions:

- Brain development depends on a person's specific experiences because "brain, body, and environment are . . . dynamically coupled" (Marshall, 2009, p. 119) and thus any brain scan is accurate only for that moment.
- Brain development continues throughout life. Middle childhood is crucial, but so are developments before and after these years.
- Children with disorders often have unusual brain patterns, and training their brains may help. However, brain complexity means that no neuroscience remediation always succeeds.

This leads to the final topic of this chapter, children with special needs.

SUMMING UP

During middle childhood, neurological maturation allows faster, more automatic reactions. Selective attention enables focused concentration in school and in play. Aptitude tests, including IQ tests, compare mental age to chronological age, while actual learning is measured by achievement tests. IQ scores change much more than was originally imagined, as children and cultures adapt to changing contexts. The concept that an IQ score measures one underlying aptitude is challenged by Robert Sternberg, Howard Gardner, and others, who believe that people have not just one type of intelligence but many.

>> Children with Special Needs

Developmental psychopathology links the study of typical development with the study of disorders (Cicchetti & Toth, 2009). Every topic already described including "genetics, neuroscience, developmental psychology . . . must be combined to understand how psychopathology develops and can be prevented" (Dodge, 2009, p. 413).

At the outset, four general principles of developmental psychopathology should be emphasized.

1. *Abnormality is normal.* Most children sometimes act oddly. At the same time, children with serious disorders are, in many respects, like everyone else.
2. *Disability changes year by year.* Most disorders are **comorbid,** which means that more than one problem is evident in the same person. Which particular disorder is most disabling changes with development, as does the degree of impairment for each disorder.
3. *Life may be better or worse in adulthood.* Prognosis is difficult. Many children with severe disabilities (e.g., blindness) become productive adults. Conversely, some conditions (e.g., bipolar disorder) become more disabling as a person matures.
4. *Diagnosis and treatment reflect the social context.* In a dynamic system, each individual interacts with the surrounding setting—including family, school, community, and culture—to modify, worsen, or even create psychopathology.

Developmental psychopathology is especially relevant in middle childhood, when children are grouped by age and expected to learn on schedule. Moreover, many disorders can be mitigated if diagnosed long before adolescence and if treatment begins early.

>> **Answer to Observation Quiz** (from page 306) He or she is average. Anyone with a score between 85 and 115 is of average IQ.

>> **Response for Teachers** (from page 307): The advantages are that all the children learn more aspects of human knowledge and that many children can develop their talents. Art, music, and sports should be an integral part of education, not just a break from academics. The disadvantage is that they take time and attention away from reading and math, which might lead to less proficiency in those subjects on standard tests and thus to criticism from parents and supervisors.

developmental psychopathology The field that uses insights into typical development to understand and remediate developmental disorders, and vice versa.

comorbid Refers to the presence of two or more unrelated disease conditions at the same time in the same person.

Therein lies a problem: Although treatment is more likely to succeed the earlier it begins, accurate diagnosis is more difficult the younger a child is, not only because many disorders are comorbid but also because symptoms differ by age. There is no simple link between cause and effect, which means that a specific behavior might be normal for children or might be an early sign of serious problems.

Two basic principles of developmental psychopathology are *multifinality* and *equifinality,* which lead to caution in diagnosis and treatment (Cicchetti & Toth, 2009). Multifinality means that one cause can have many (multiple) final manifestations (as when a child who has been flooded with stress hormones in infancy may be hypervigilant or unusually calm, easily angered or quick to cry). Equifinality (equal in final form) means that one manifestation can have many causes (for instance, a 2-year-old who does not talk may be autistic, hard of hearing, mentally retarded, or electively mute). We focus here on only three topics (attention-deficit and bipolar disorders, learning disabilities, and autism spectrum disorder) to illustrate these general principles of childhood psychopathology. (Readers interested in any specific condition are urged to read some of the extensive relevant research).

Attention-Deficit and Bipolar Disorders

These are two distinct disorders, but they are discussed together here because they are often comorbid. Especially in children, one is often mistaken for the other, partly because of equifinality—both can result in explosive rage and deep regret.

Attention-Deficit Disorder

Perhaps 10 percent of all young children have an *attention-deficit disorder* (ADD), which means they have difficulty paying attention. Often ADD is accompanied by an impulse to be unusually active, in which case it is called **attention-deficit/ hyperactivity disorder (ADHD).** Children with ADHD are inattentive, impulsive, and overactive and are thus disruptive when adults want them to be still (Barkley, 2006).

A typical child with ADHD, when sitting down to do homework, might look up, ask questions, think about playing, get a drink, fidget, squirm, tap the table, jiggle his or her legs, and go to the bathroom—and then start the whole sequence again. Not surprisingly, such children tend to have academic difficulties; they are less likely to graduate from high school and college (Loe & Feldman, 2007).

Adults with ADHD often have the same characteristics, but they are not as disruptive because usually they find work that allows them to be active (they hate desk jobs), a family who understands them (they are allowed to "blow off steam"), and ways to manage their impulses (running instead of attacking, writing down things to remember).

The number of children diagnosed with ADHD has increased in the United States from about 5 percent in 1980 to almost 10 percent in the early twenty-first century. Rates are affected by gender and ethnicity, with about three times as many boys as girls considered to have ADHD, and more European American children than Latino ones—at least as measured by medication use. The rate has doubled in Europe as well (e.g., Hsia & Maclennan, 2009; van den Ban et al., 2010). Worldwide, marked variations in ADHD rates are reported: Rates in some nations are higher than in the United States; in most, they are lower (Faraone et al., 2003).

attention-deficit/hyperactivity disorder (ADHD) A condition in which a person not only has great difficulty concentrating for more than a few moments but also is inattentive, impulsive, and overactive.

Almost Impossible The concentration needed to do homework is almost beyond Clint, age 11, who takes medication for ADHD. Note his furrowed brow, resting head, and sad face.

Observation Quiz Will he complete his homework on his own? (see answer, page 313)

SACRAMENTO BEE / LEZLIE STERLING / ZUMA PRESS

Bipolar Disorder

Bipolar disorder is characterized by extreme mood swings, from euphoria to deep depression, not caused by outside circumstances such as a good grade in school or a move to another neighborhood. A child with bipolar disorder experiences at least one episode of grandiosity, believing, for instance, that he (or less often she) is the smartest person in the school, a genius destined to save the entire world. At other periods, that child is severely depressed and unwilling to do usual things, such as playing with friends and going to school (Miklowitz & Cicchetti, 2010).

In adults who have bipolar disorder, grandiosity usually lasts at least several days; this is less true for children. In adolescents and adults, bipolar depression often leads to suicidal thoughts and even suicide itself. This is one reason bipolar disorder should be diagnosed in childhood—to prevent suicide attempts later on.

One U.S. study reports that medical visits for youth under age 18 with a primary diagnosis of bipolar disorder (one-third of them comorbid with attention-deficit disorder) increased 40-fold between 1995 and 2003, a period when adult diagnosis of bipolar disorder merely doubled (Moreno et al., 2007). Such a rapid increase could not have occurred in the actual behavior of children, which led some critics to suggest that childhood bipolar disorder was a diagnosis more in the mind of the observer than in the moods of the child. However, careful analysis suggests that the problem is real and often becomes worse with age (Geller et al., 2008). The probable reason for the rapid increase in diagnosis is earlier misdiagnosis, not current overdiagnosis (Miklowitz & Cicchetti, 2010; Santosh & Canagaratnam, 2008).

Distinguishing Between Disorders

Bipolar disorder "remains notoriously difficult to differentiate from other psychiatric illnesses in youth" (Phillips, 2010, p. 4). Many children diagnosed with either ADHD or bipolar disorder may be more accurately diagnosed with the other. Some symptoms are the same: Children with either disorder tend to be irritable, even rageful, when adults demand that they behave normally. Most who have either condition have trouble sleeping, are sometimes notably active, and other times are depressed.

Both are more common in children whose parents have a disorder, which strongly suggests a genetic link. However, the specifics of parent disability differ. In some cases, the parent has the same disorder as the child. If not, parents of children with ADHD often have learning disabilities, whereas parents of children with bipolar disorder are likely to have mood disturbances, including depression and eating disorders.

Both disorders in children are linked to unusual brain patterns, either in structures or activity, although, again, some differences may be apparent (Riccio et al., 2010; Santosh & Canagaratnam, 2008). In one study, children observed pictures of faces while their brain activity was measured. Children with either disorder were less able to differentiate emotions than were the control-group children, but different parts of the amygdala were aroused in children with ADHD and in those with bipolar disorder (Brotman et al., 2008; Brotman et al., 2010). There is not yet any definitive biological or neurological sign of either disorder, however.

Treatment involves psychological counseling and training for the family and the child, showing teachers how to help the children learn, and medication to stabilize

bipolar disorder A condition characterized by extreme mood swings, from euphoria to deep depression, not caused by outside experiences.

Go Team Remember that abnormality is normal. Which of these boys has been diagnosed with a serious disability? Michael, second from the right, has bipolar disorder.

MARC ASNIN / REDUX

Especially for Health Workers Parents ask that some medication be prescribed for their kindergarten child, who they say is much too active for them to handle. How do you respond? (see response, page 315)

moods for the bipolar child and quiet down the ADHD child. With medication, ongoing monitoring is crucial because stimulants usually help children with ADHD but harm bipolar ones. Furthermore, even if diagnosis is accurate, each child responds differently to each drug. Medication use in childhood raises many issues, as the following explains.

A VIEW FROM SCIENCE

Drugs for Children

In the United States, more than 2 million children and adolescents under age 18 take prescription drugs to regulate their emotions and behavior. The rate has leveled off in recent years but remains high, with about 1 in 20 children aged 6 to 12 taking psychoactive drugs, usually for ADHD (Scheffler et al., 2009; Vitiello et al., 2006; Zuvekas et al., 2006). In many other nations, drug use in middle childhood has recently increased (e.g., Hsia & Maclennan, 2009; van den Ban et al., 2010).

The most common drug is Ritalin for ADHD, but at least 20 other psychoactive drugs treat depression, anxiety, developmental delay, autism, bipolar disorder, and many other conditions in middle childhood. Younger children (age 2–5) are taking these drugs at increasing rates, although the rates (about 1 child in 600) are still far lower than for older children (Olfson et al., 2010). Because testing is inadequate for children, many drugs are prescribed "off label"—they have not been approved for patients of that age or condition. The incidence, ages, rates, and off-label uses all raise questions; much of the American public is suspicious of any childhood psychiatric medicine (dosReis & Myers, 2008; McLeod et al., 2004; Rose, 2008).

Many child psychologists raise additional issues (Mayes et al., 2009). They find that some parents punish their children instead of seeking help, and they know that, for every child, finding the best drug at the right strength is difficult. Furthermore, since children's weight and metabolism change, the right dose at one point will be wrong at another. Underdosing and overdosing are especially destructive when brains and habits are developing, yet only about half of all 2- to 5-year-olds who take psychoactive drugs are evaluated and monitored by a mental health professional (Olfson et al., 2010).

Many of these concerns are valid. Most professionals are convinced by many studies that medication helps schoolchildren with emotional problems, particularly ADHD (Epstein et al., 2010; King et al., 2009; Scheffler et al., 2009). Some professionals also believe that contextual interventions (teaching strategies to parents and teachers, for instance) should be tried first (Daley et al., 2009; Pelham & Fabiano, 2008).

By contrast, parents are less sure. One study of parents whose children were diagnosed with ADHD found that about 20 percent believed drugs should *never* be used for children, and about 29 percent believed that drugs were *necessary* to treat illnesses; the other 51 percent were in neither camp (dosReis

et al., 2009). That was a small study (48 families), but large-scale research finds that only about half (56 percent) of the parents of U.S. children who are diagnosed with ADHD give them medication every day (Scheffler et al., 2009). African American children have more ADHD symptoms but are less often medicated, for reasons that include fragmented medical care and distrust of doctors (Miller et al., 2009).

The result of the discrepancy between public attitude and research data is that some children who would benefit are never given medication, other children are given medication without the necessary monitoring, and still other children are given medication only until their symptoms subside. Eight years after a group of children from many cities in the United States and Canada were given appropriate medication and improved in symptoms of ADHD, many had stopped taking medication, and both those who were on and off medication were likely to have learning difficulties and lower grades in school (Molina et al., 2009).

What about other long-term effects? Much remains to be learned, and opinions are divided. However, two concerns—that children who take drugs in childhood will become adolescent addicts and that their growth will be stunted—seem invalid. In fact, longitudinal research comparing nonmedicated and medicated children with ADHD finds the opposite: Childhood medication reduces the risk of illegal drug use in adolescence and does not seem to adversely affect growth (Biederman et al., 2010; Faraone & Wilens, 2003). One caution, however: As more drugs are prescribed, more abuse of those specific drugs occurs (Setlik et al., 2009). Government regulators have raised other concerns, specifically that psychoactive drugs might cause hallucinations, suicide attempts, or overactive hearts. These results do occur, but rarely: Professionals need to monitor their patients (Elia & Vetter, 2010; Mosholder et al., 2009; Riccio et al., 2010).

When appropriately used, drugs help children make friends, learn in school, feel happier, and behave better. However, problems do not disappear: Adolescents who had childhood emotional problems are less successful academically and personally (Geller et al., 2008; Loe & Feldman, 2007; Molina et al., 2009). When children have special needs, parents and teachers need training, and professionals need to monitor treatment. Drugs do not cure, but they may make childhood better.

Learning Disabilities

Many people have some specific **learning disability** that leads to difficulty in mastering a particular skill that most other people acquire easily. Indeed, according to Gardner's view of multiple intelligences, almost everyone has a specific inadequacy or two. Perhaps one person is clumsy (low in kinesthetic intelligence), while another sings off key (low in musical intelligence).

Most such learning disabilities are minor, but every schoolchild is expected to learn reading and math, and learning disabilities in either of these two subjects often undercut academic achievement and make a child feel inadequate, ashamed, and stupid. Hopefully, such children find (or are taught) ways to compensate: They learn strategies, and in adulthood their other abilities shine. Winston Churchill, Albert Einstein, and Hans Christian Andersen all are said to have had learning disabilities as children.

The most commonly diagnosed learning disability is **dyslexia,** unusual difficulty with reading. No single test accurately diagnoses dyslexia (or any learning disability) because every academic achievement involves many specifics (Riccio & Rodriguez, 2007). A child with a reading disability might have trouble sounding out words but might excel in comprehension and memory of printed text, for example. Dozens of types and causes of dyslexia have been identified.

Early theories hypothesized that visual difficulties—for example, reversals of letters (reading *was* instead of *saw*) and mirror writing (*b* instead of *d*)—were the cause of dyslexia, but we now know that dyslexia often originates with speech and hearing difficulties (Gabrieli, 2009). An early warning occurs if a 3-year-old does not talk clearly or have a naming explosion (see Chapter 6). Not only might early speech therapy improve talking, but it might also reduce or prevent later dyslexia (Gabrieli, 2009).

Similar conditions apply to learning disabilities in math, called *dyscalculia.* Early help with numbers and concepts (long before first grade), thus avoiding the emotional anxiety that occurs if a child is made to feel stupid, can help. Remember that in early childhood, maybe even in infancy, most children can look at a series of dots and estimate how many there are. This basic number sense is deficient in children with dyscalculia, which provides a clue for early remediation (Piazza et al., 2010). It is helpful to remember that although every child has different strengths and interests, all children can learn basic academic skills if given extensive and specific help, encouragement, and practice.

Autistic Spectrum Disorders

Of all the special-needs children, those with autism are probably the most troubling, not only because their problems are severe but also because many causes and treatments are hotly disputed. Most children with autism can be spotted in the early weeks, but some seem quite normal at first and then deteriorate later on. Parent responses vary, from irrational hope to deep despair, from blaming doctors to wondering what they did wrong.

Symptoms

Autism is characterized by woefully inadequate social skills. Half a century ago, it was considered a single, rare disorder affecting fewer than 1 in 1,000 children with "an extreme aloneness that, whenever possible, disregards, ignores, shuts out

learning disability A marked delay in a particular area of learning that is not caused by an apparent physical disability, by mental retardation, or by an unusually stressful home environment.

dyslexia Unusual difficulty with reading; thought to be the result of some neurological underdevelopment.

She Knows the Answer Physical disabilities often mushroom into additional emotional and cognitive problems. However, a disability can be reduced to a minor complication if it is recognized and if appropriate compensation or remediation is made part of the child's education. As she signs her answer, this deaf girl shows by her expression that she is ready to learn.

>> **Answer to Obseration Quiz** (from page 310) No. His mother is writing the answers for him.

autism A developmental disorder marked by an inability to relate to other people normally, extreme self-absorption, and an inability to acquire normal speech.

autistic spectrum disorder Any of several disorders characterized by inadequate social skills, impaired communication, and unusual play.

PHANIE / PHOTO RESEARCHERS INC.

Precious Gifts Many children with autism are gifted artists. This boy attends a school in Montmoreau, France, that features workshops in which children with autism develop social, play, and learning skills.

anything . . . from the outside" (Kanner, 1943). Children who developed slowly but were not so withdrawn were diagnosed as being mentally retarded or as having a "pervasive developmental disorder." Now such children are usually said to have an **autistic spectrum disorder,** which characterizes about 1 in every 150 8-year-olds (three times as many boys as girls and more European Americans than Latino, Asian, or African Americans), according to official U.S.statistics (MMWR, February 9, 2007), and 1 in 100 according to parent reports (Kogan et al., 2009).

There are three signs of an autistic spectrum disorder: delayed language; impaired social responses; and unusual, repetitive play. Underlying all three is a kind of emotional blindness (Scambler et al., 2007). Children with any form of autism find it difficult to understand the emotions of others, which makes them feel alien, like "an anthropologist on Mars," as Temple Grandin, an educator and writer with autism, expressed it (quoted in Sacks, 1995). Consequently, they do not want to talk, play, or otherwise interact with anyone, and they are especially delayed in developing a theory of mind (Senju et al., 2010).

Autistic spectrum disorders include many symptoms of varied severity. Some children never speak, rarely smile, and often play for hours with one object (such as a spinning top or a toy train). Others are called "high-functioning" (or are said to have *Asperger syndrome*)—they are extremely talented in some specialized area, such as drawing or geometry, and their speech is close to normal. Many are brilliant in unusual ways (Dawson et al., 2007), including Grandin, a well-respected expert on animal care (Grandin & Johnson, 2009). However, social interaction is always impaired. Grandin was bewildered by romantic love.

Most children with autistic spectrum disorder show signs in early infancy (no social smile, for example) and resist social contact as they grow. Some improve by age 3 (Chawarska et al., 2007) whereas others deteriorate (MMWR, February 9, 2007). Amazingly, 40 percent of parents who were told their child was autistic say that is no longer the case (Kogan et al., 2009). On the other hand, late onset of autism occurs with *Rett syndrome,* in which a newborn girl (never a boy, since they do not survive if they have the Rett gene) seems fine, but then her brain develops much more slowly than normal (Bienvenu, 2005).

Many children with autism have an opposite problem—too much neurological activity, not too little. Their heads are slightly larger than average, and parts of their brain (especially the limbic system) are unusually sensitive to noise, light, and other sensations (Schumann et al., 2004). Temple Grandin described the effect:

> Every time you take the kid into Wal-Mart, he's screaming. Well, the reason for that is that the fluorescent lights are flickering and driving him crazy, the noise in there hurts his ears, the smells overpower his nose. Wal-Mart is like being inside the speaker at a rock and roll concert.
>
> *[Medscape Psychiatry & Mental Health, 2005]*

Far more children have autistic spectrum disorders now than in 1990, either because the incidence of this disorder has increased or because more children receive that diagnosis. The hypothesis that the diagnosis, not the disorder, is more common is supported by a detailed study in Texas showing that in the wealthiest school districts the number of children diagnosed with autism tripled over six years, but the number did not change in the poorest districts (Palmer et al., 2005; see the Research Design).

▶ **Research Design**

Scientists: Raymond Palmer, Stephen Blanchard, and David Mandall designed the study, and C. R. Jean provided critical interpretation.

Publication: *American Journal of Public Health* (2005).

Participants: All 1,040 school districts in Texas over six school years, 1994 to 2001.

Design: The school districts were sorted into tenths according to wealth—a composite of average income, salaries, proportion of disadvantaged students, and so on. Within each tenth, the number of students designated as autistic was tallied each year.

Major conclusion: Increases in diagnosis of students with autistic spectrum disorders correlated with wealth, from an increase of 300 percent in districts in the top two-tenths to no change in the bottom tenth. For every 10,000 children, 21 in the top districts and 3 in the bottom districts were designated as having autism.

Comment: These findings, covering an entire state, suggest that increases in the incidence of autism are caused by better diagnosis, more available physicians, advanced special education, and perhaps parental insistence on diagnosis and treatment.

Treatment

Equifinality certainly applies to autism: A child can have autistic symptoms for many reasons, which makes treatment difficult, as an intervention that seems to help one child proves worthless for another. It is known, however, that biology is crucial (genes, birth complications, prenatal injury, or perhaps chemicals) and that brain patterns are unusual; autism is not caused by family nurture (G. Dawson, 2010).

A vast number of treatments have been used to help autistic children, none of them completely successful; some parents are convinced that a particular treatment helped their child, whereas other parents say the treatment was a failure. Scientists disagree as well. For instance, one popular new regime is putting the child in a hyperbaric chamber to breathe more oxygen than in everyday air. Two studies of hyperbaric treatments—both randomized in participant selection and both with control groups—reported contradictory results, either benefits (Rossignol et al., 2009) or no effect (Granpeesheh et al., 2010). Part of the problem may be multifinality and equifinality: Children with autism spectrum disorders have core symptoms in common, but they also differ in cause and consequence.

An added problem is the gap between parents of autistic children and medical professionals. This has been dramatically illustrated with the controversy about thimerosal, an antiseptic containing mercury that was once used in childhood immunizations. Many parents of autistic children first noticed their infants' impairments after their MMR (measles-mumps-rubella) vaccinations and believe thimerosal was the cause. No scientist who examines the evidence agrees: Extensive research has disproven the immunization hypothesis many times (Offit, 2008). Thimerosal was removed from vaccines a decade ago, but the rates of autism are still rising. Many doctors fear that parents who cling to this hypothesis are not only wrong but are harming millions of children who suffer needless illnesses because their parents refuse to immunize them.

Many children with autism are on special diets, take vitamin supplements, or are on medication. One drug in particular, rispridone, relieves some symptoms (although research finds side effects), but no treatment has proven successful at relieving the basic condition. As you already know, all medication use is controversial: Whether or not a child takes rispridone depends on many factors other than symptoms (Arnold et al., 2010; Rosenberg et al., 2010).

Many behavior methods to improve talking and socialization have been tried, again with mixed results (Granpeesheh et al., 2009; Hayward et al., 2009; Howlin et al., 2009). Early and individualized education, of both the child and the parents, has had some success, although the connection between disorder and special education is an uncertain one, as you will now see.

Special Education

The overlap of the biosocial, cognitive, and psychosocial domains is evident to developmentalists, who envision each child's growth in every area as affected by the other areas. However, whether or not a child is designated as needing special education is not straightforward, nor is it closely related to specific special needs. We discussed education because it pertains to developmental psychopathology, but, as you will see, the link between disorder and education is problematic.

Changing Laws and Practices

Recognition that the distinction between normal and abnormal development is not clear-cut (the first principle of developmental psychopathology) led to a series of reforms in the treatment and education of children with special needs. According

>> Response for Health Workers (from page 312): Medication helps some hyperactive children, but not all. It might be useful for this child, but other forms of intervention should be tried first. Compliment the parents on their concern about their child, but refer them to an expert in early childhood for an evaluation and recommendations. Behavior-management techniques geared to the particular situation, not medication, will be the first strategy.

least restrictive environment (LRE) A legal requirement that children with special needs be assigned to the most general educational context in which they can be expected to learn.

response to intervention An educational strategy intended to help children in early grades who demonstrate below-average achievement by means of special intervention.

individual education plan (IEP) A document that specifies educational goals and plans for a child with special needs.

to a 1975 U.S. law called the *Education of All Handicapped Children Act,* children with special needs must learn in the **least restrictive environment (LRE).**

Most of the time, that has meant educating them with children in a regular class, with added help (sometimes called *mainstreaming*), rather than in a special classroom or school. Sometimes a child is sent to a *resource room,* with a teacher who provides targeted tutoring. Sometimes a class is an *inclusion class,* which means that children with special needs are "included" in the general classroom, with "appropriate aids and services" (usually from a trained teacher who works with the regular teacher) (Kalambouka et al., 2007).

The latest educational strategy for children in the United States is called **response to intervention** (Fletcher & Vaughn, 2009). All children in the early grades who are below average in achievement (which may be half the class) are given some special intervention. Most of them respond by improving their achievement, but for those who do not, more intervention occurs. If the problem persists, the child is then referred for testing and observation to diagnose the problem. Professionals use a battery of tests (not just IQ or achievement tests) to reach their diagnosis and develop recommendations. If they find that a child has special needs, they discuss an **individual education plan (IEP)** with the parents, to specify educational goals for the child.

Cohort and Culture

Developmentalists tend to see the biological and brain development of children as the starting point for whatever special assistance will allow each child to reach full potential. However, as Table 11.1 shows, of all the children in the United States who are recognized as having special needs, cohort changes are notable, and some basic categories (e.g., attention-deficit disorder) are missing. In the United States, only 8 percent of all 3- to 21-year-olds were officially designated as having special needs in 1980, compared with 13 percent in 2007.

From looking at Table 11.1, you can also see cohort effects. Twice as many of the 8 percent in 1977 were called "mentally retarded," a category much less used today, but about 4.5 percent of children with special needs are currently desig-

TABLE 11.1						
Proportion of Children with Special Education Needs by Specific Designation* (percent of children)						
	1977		1997		2007	
Learning disabilities	21.5	(1.8**)	46	(5.9)	39	(5.2)
Speech impairment	35.2	(2.9)	17	(2.3)	22	(3.0)
Mentally retarded	28	(2.2)	10.0	(1.3)	7.6	(1.0)
Emotionally disturbed	7.7	(0.6)	7.7	(1.0)	6.7	(0.9)
Deafness and hearing loss	2.4	(0.2)	1.2	(0.2)	1.2	(0.2)
Blindness and low vision	1	(0.1)	0.4	(0.1)	0.4	(0.1)
Developmental delay	—		—		5.4	(0.7)
Autism spectrum	—		0.7	(0.1)	4.5	(0.6)
Orthopedic handicap	2.4	(0.2)	1.2	(0.1)	1.0	(0.1)
Other health problems***	2.8	(0.3)	3.2	(0.5)	9.7	(1.3)

*Based on evaluation by U.S. public school professionals.
**Numbers in parentheses are percentages of all public school children.
***Limited strength, vitality, or alertness due to chronic health problems, such as asthma, sickle-cell anemia, and diabetes.
Source: Snyder & Dillow (2010).

nated as autistic and 5.4 percent as developmentally delayed. Neither category existed in 1977 (some of those children earlier considered mentally retarded would fall under one of these newer categories if diagnosed today). As you have read, many schoolchildren are considered to have ADHD, which has no separate category. To receive special services, they usually need to prove they are learning disabled. See Table 11.2 for examples of legislation relating to special education.

TABLE 11.2

Laws Regarding Special Education in the United States*

PL (Public Law) 91-230: Children with Specific Learning Disabilities Act, 1969

Recognized learning disabilities as a category within special education. Before 1969, learning-disabled children received no special education or services.

PL 94-142: Education of All Handicapped Children Act, 1975

Mandated education of all school-age children, no matter what disability they might have, in the *least restrictive environment (LRE)*—which meant with other children in a regular classroom, if possible. Fewer children were placed in special, self-contained classes and even fewer in special schools. This law required an *individual education plan (IEP)* for each child with special needs, specifying educational goals and periodic reassessment.

PL 105-17: Individuals with Disabilities Education Act (IDEA), 1990; updated 1997 and 2004

Refers to "individuals," not children (to include education of infants, toddlers, adults), and to "disabilities," not handicaps. Emphasizes parents' rights in placement and IEP.

*Other nations have quite different laws and practices, and states and school districts within the United States vary in interpretation and practice. Consult local support groups, authorities, and legal experts, if necessary.

Looking internationally, it seems that the connection between special needs and education varies even more for cultural reasons, not child-related reasons. In many African and Latin American nations, no children are designated as having special needs; in many Asian nations, the diagnosis of special needs refers primarily to the physically disabled. As a result, in Taiwan, for example, less than 1 percent of the students receive special education of any kind (Tzeng, 2007).

In another oddity, children who are unusually gifted are generally thought to have special needs, but they are so designated by the state, not the federal government. Some states have 15 percent or more children in gifted-and-talented classes (e.g., Maryland); others, less than 1 percent (Massachusetts).

Children with any of these special needs are given more individualized help, a boon for any child. Many strategies to teach them are effective with all children, as you might expect from knowing that "abnormality is normal." The next chapter, on cognitive development in middle childhood, makes that point again: As the Education of All Handicapped Children law states, all children can learn; we need all schools to teach them.

SUMMING UP

Many children have special learning needs that originate with problems in the development of their brains. Developmental psychopathologists emphasize that no one is typical in every way; the passage of time sometimes brings improvement to children with special needs and sometimes not. Children with attention-deficit disorders, learning disabilities, and autistic spectrum disorders may function adequately or may have lifelong problems, depending on many variables—the severity of the problem; family, school, and cultural environments; and the presence of comorbid conditions. Specifics of diagnosis, prognosis, medication, and education are debatable; no child learns or behaves exactly like another, and no educational strategy is entirely successful with every child. ∎

SUMMARY

A Healthy Time

1. Middle childhood is a time of steady growth and few serious illnesses. Increasing independence and self-care allow most school-age children to be relatively happy and competent.

2. Advances in medical care have reduced childhood sickness and death. Immunization is effective, fewer children are exposed to toxins, and early diagnosis and treatment have mitigated many conditions.

3. Physical activity aids health and joy in many ways. However, current social and environmental conditions make informal neighborhood play scarce, school physical education less prevalent, and sports leagues less welcoming for some school-age children.

Health Problems in Middle Childhood

4. Childhood obesity is a worldwide epidemic. Although genes are part of the problem, less exercise and the greater availability of unhealthy foods are the main reasons today's youth are heavier than youth were 50 years ago. Parents and policies share the blame.

5. The incidence of asthma is increasing overall, with notable ethnic differences. The origins of asthma are genetic; the triggers are specific environmental allergens. Preventive measures include longer breast-feeding, increased outdoor play, and less air pollution, particularly from cars.

Brain Development

6. Brain development continues during middle childhood, enhancing every aspect of development. Notable are advances in reaction time and automatization, allowing faster and better coordination of many parts of the brain.

7. IQ tests quantify intellectual aptitude. Most such tests emphasize language and logical ability and predict school achievement. IQ scores sometimes change over time.

8. Achievement tests measure accomplishment, often in specific academic areas. Aptitude and achievement are correlated, both for individuals and for nations.

9. Critics contend that intelligence is manifested in multiple ways that conventional IQ tests are too limited to measure. Multiple intelligences include creative and practical abilities and many skills not usually valued in typical North American schools.

Children with Special Needs

10. Developmental psychopathology uses an understanding of normal development to inform the study of unusual development. Four general lessons have emerged: Abnormality is normal; disability changes over time; adolescence and adulthood may make a condition better or worse; and diagnosis depends on context.

11. Children with attention-deficit/hyperactivity disorder (ADHD) have potential problems in three areas: inattention, impulsiveness, and overactivity. Stimulant medication often helps children with ADHD to learn, but any drug use by children must be carefully monitored.

12. Children with bipolar disorder have marked mood swings, from grandiosity to depression. This disorder is often mistaken for attention-deficit/hyperactivity disorder.

13. People with learning disabilities have unusual difficulty in mastering a specific skill that other people learn easily. The most common learning disability that manifests itself during the school years is dyslexia, unusual difficulty with reading.

14. Children with autistic spectrum disorders typically show odd and delayed language ability, impaired interpersonal skills, and unusual play. Many causes are hypothesized. Autism is partly genetic; no one now views autism as primarily the result of inadequate parenting. Treatments are diverse: All are controversial and none are certain to help.

15. About 13 percent of all school-age children in the United States receive special education services. These services begin with an IEP (individual education plan) and assignment to the least restrictive environment (LRE), usually the regular classroom.

KEY TERMS

middle childhood (p. 295)
BMI (body mass index) (p. 300)
overweight (p. 300)
obesity (p. 300)
asthma (p. 302)
reaction time (p. 305)
selective attention (p. 305)
automatization (p. 305)

aptitude (p. 306)
IQ test (p. 306)
achievement test (p. 307)
Flynn effect (p. 307)
multiple intelligences (p. 307)
developmental psychopathology (p. 309)
comorbid (p. 309)

attention-deficit/hyperactivity disorder (ADHD) (p. 310)
bipolar disorder (p. 311)
learning disability (p. 313)
dyslexia (p. 313)
autism (p. 313)
autistic spectrum disorder (p. 314)

least restrictive environment (LRE) (p. 316)
response to intervention (p. 316)
individual education plan (IEP) (p. 316)

WHAT HAVE YOU LEARNED?

A Healthy Time

1. What physical abilities emerge from age 6 to age 11?

2. How do childhood health habits affect adult health?

3. What are the main advantages and disadvantages of physical play during middle childhood?

4. How do children benefit from physical education in school?

5. How are after-school activities affected by socioeconomic status (SES), gender, and culture?

Health Problems in Middle Childhood

6. What are the national and cohort differences in childhood obesity?

7. Why does a thin 6-year-old not need to fatten up?

8. What roles do nature and nurture play in childhood asthma?

9. What would be primary prevention for childhood obesity?

10. Why does good tertiary prevention for childhood asthma not reach every child who needs it?

Brain Development

11. Why does quicker reaction time improve the ability to learn?

12. How do changes in brain functioning make it easier for a child to sit in a classroom?

13. When would a teacher give an aptitude test instead of an achievement test?

14. If the theory of multiple intelligences is correct, should IQ tests be discarded? Why or why not?

15. Why are some intellectual abilities valued more than others? Give examples.

16. Should brain scans replace traditional intelligence tests? Why or why not?

Children with Special Needs

17. What would be normal child behavior in one culture but not in another?

18. What examples illustrate the difference between multifinality and equifinality?

19. Why is medication recommended for children with ADHD?

20. Why might parents ask a doctor to prescribe Ritalin for their child?

21. Why is bipolar disorder hard to diagnose in children?

22. What is the difference between bipolar disorder in children and in adults?

23. What specific learning disabilities do not matter much in the United States currently?

24. How could an adult have a learning disability that has never been diagnosed?

25. If a successful adult has high-functioning autism, what professions and sorts of family life would you expect him or her to have?

26. Why does the frequency of some kinds of developmental psychopathology increase while that of others decreases?

27. What are the signs of autistic spectrum disorders?

APPLICATIONS

1. Compare play spaces for children in different neighborhoods—ideally, urban, suburban, and rural areas. Note size, safety, and use. How might children's weight and motor skills be affected?

2. Developmental psychologists believe that every teacher should be skilled at teaching children with a wide variety of needs. Does the teacher-training curriculum at your college or university reflect this goal? Should all teachers take the same courses, or should some teachers be specialized? Give reasons for your opinions.

3. Internet sources vary in quality on any topic, but this may be particularly true of Web sites designed for parents of children with special needs. Pick one childhood disability or disease and find several Web sources devoted to that condition. How might parents evaluate the information provided?

4. Special education teachers are in great demand. In your local public school, what is the ratio of regular to special education teachers? How many are in self-contained classrooms, resource rooms, and inclusion classrooms? What do your data reveal about the education of children with special needs in your community?

>>ONLINE CONNECTIONS

To accompany your textbook, you have access to a number of online resources, including quizzes for every chapter of the book, flashcards (in English and Spanish), critical thinking questions, and case studies. For access to any of these links, go to www.worthpublishers.com/bergerls8e. In addition to these free resources, you'll also find links to the podcasts, video clips, diagnostic quizzing with personalized study advice, and an ebook. Some of the videos and activities available online include:

- *Autism.* This activity explores the symptoms of autism and the importance of early diagnosis. Video clips give a glimpse into the world of parents and autistic children.

- *Educating the Girls of the World.* Girls around the world talk about the challenges that hinder their enrolment in all levels of education. Highlights initiatives for change.

Middle Childhood: Cognitive Development

C H A P T E R

12

WHAT WILL YOU KNOW?

1. What can school-age children learn, and what is beyond them?
2. How do memory abilities change in middle childhood?
3. Why do many children talk one way at school and another way with their friends?
4. What are the differences in schools from place to place?
5. Why is education a controversial issue in the United States?

■ **Building on Theory**
Piaget and School-Age Children
Vygotsky and School-Age Children
Information Processing
THINKING CRITICALLY: Balls Rolling Down

■ **Language**
Vocabulary
Differences in Language Learning
A CASE TO STUDY: Two Immigrants

■ **Teaching and Learning**
International Schooling
In the United States

At age 9, I wanted a puppy. My parents said no—we already had Dusty, our family dog. I dashed off a poem, promising "to brush his hair as smooth as silk" and "to feed him milk." Wrong, of course: Puppies should not have cow's milk. My father praised my poem; I got Taffy, a blonde cocker spaniel.

At age 10, Sarah wanted her ears pierced. I said no—it wouldn't be fair to her three older sisters, who had had to wait until they were teenagers before ear-piercing. Sarah wrote an affidavit and persuaded her sisters to sign it, saying that they had no objection. She got gold posts.

Sarah and I were typical, although our wishes differed by cohort and our strategies by family. Sarah knew I wouldn't budge for doggerel but that I respect signed documents. All school-age children master whatever their context presents: dividing fractions, surfing the Web, memorizing rap songs, loading rifles, or persuading parents.

This chapter describes that impressive cognitive development. We begin by examining how Piaget, Vygotsky, and information-processing theory describe cognition in middle childhood. Then we discuss applications of those theories to language, as well as the many disputes about how and what children should learn in school.

concrete operational thought Piaget's term for the ability to reason logically about direct experiences and perceptions.

His Science Project Concrete operational 10-year-olds like Daniel, shown here with some of his family's dairy cows, can be logical about anything they see, hear, or touch. Daniel's science experiment, on the effect of music on milk production, won first place in a Georgia regional science fair.

>> Building on Theory

Learning is rapid in childhood. Some children, by age 11, beat their elders at chess, play music that adults pay to hear, publish poems, win trophies. Others live on the streets or fight in civil wars, learning lessons that no child should know.

Piaget and School-Age Children

Piaget called the cognition of middle childhood **concrete operational thought,** characterized by concepts that enable children to use logic. *Operational* comes from the Latin word *operare*, "to work; to produce"; Piaget emphasizes productive thinking. The school-age child, no longer limited by egocentrism, performs logical operations.

AP PHOTO / THE AUGUSTA CHRONICLE, CHRIS THELEN

321

Children apply their new reasoning skills to *concrete* situations—that is, situations with visible, tangible, real things (not abstractions). Children become more systematic, objective, scientific—and educable.

A Hierarchy of Categories

classification The logical principle that things can be organized into groups (or categories or classes) according to some characteristic they have in common.

One logical concept is **classification,** the organization of things into groups (or *categories* or *classes*) according to some characteristic that they share. For example, *family* includes parents, siblings, and cousins. Other common classes are people, animals, toys, and food. Each class includes some elements and excludes others, and each is part of a hierarchy. Food, for instance, is a category, with the next-lower level of that hierarchy being meat, grains, fruits, and so on. Most subclasses can be further divided: Meat includes poultry, beef, and pork, each of which can be divided again. Adults realize that items at the bottom of a classification hierarchy belong to every higher level: Bacon is always pork, meat, and food. This hierarchical understanding eludes some children.

Piaget devised many experiments to reveal children's understanding of classification. For example, an examiner shows a child a bunch of nine flowers—seven yellow daisies and two white roses (revised and published in Piaget et al., 2001). The examiner makes sure the child knows the words *flowers, daisies,* and *roses.* Then comes the crucial question: "Are there more daisies or more flowers?" Until about age 7, most children say, "More daisies." Younger children can offer no justification for their answers, but some 6- or 7-year-olds explain that "there are more yellow ones than white ones" or that "because daisies are daisies, they aren't flowers" (Piaget et al., 2001). By age 8, most children can classify: "More flowers than daisies," they say.

After "Gee Whiz!" After he sees the magnified image that his classmate expects will amaze him, will he analyze his observations? Ideally, concrete operational thought enables children to use their new logic to interpret their experiences.

Other Logical Concepts

transitive inference The ability to figure out the unspoken link between one fact and another.

Another example of logic is the ability to grasp connections that are implied, not stated. Piaget studied **transitive inference,** the ability to figure out (infer) the unspoken link (transfer) between one fact and another. For example, "John is taller than Jim. Jim is taller than David. Who is taller, John or David?" Preoperational children are stumped. They cannot do this simple transitive inference because they know only what they have been told directly, not implications. By contrast, school-age children infer relationships.

Later research connects transitive inference to the maturation of the hippocampus, which reaches a critical point at about age 7, making inferences and other kinds of mental logic possible (DeVito et al., 2010; Zalesak & Heckers, 2009). This may seem to confirm Piaget's findings, but neurological and comparative research finds that transitive inference is both more complex and simpler than Piaget imagined (Goodwin & Johnson-Laird, 2008), with some nonhuman animals succeeding at simple versions of it.

Nonetheless, transitive inference is related to another logical concept that Piaget called *seriation,* the knowledge that things can be arranged in a logical series. Seriation is crucial for using (not merely memorizing) the alphabet or for understanding the number sequence. By age 5, most children can count up to 100, but they cannot correctly estimate where any particular two-digit number would be placed on a line that starts at 0 and ends at 100. Generally, this is possible by age 8 (Meadows, 2006).

The logical abilities of school-age children may allow them to understand arithmetic. For example, children need to understand that 12 plus 3 equals 3 plus 12, and that 15 is always 15 no matter how it was reached (conservation). Reversibility eventually allows the realization that if 5 times 7 equals 35, then 35 divided by 5 must be 7. Seriation and classification abilities correlate with math skills in primary school, although many other factors contribute to math achievement (Desoete et al., 2009).

The Significance of Piaget's Findings

Although logic connects to math concepts, researchers have found more continuity than discontinuity in number skills. Thus, Piaget was mistaken: There is no sudden shift between preoperational and concrete operational logic. In fact, some children learn logic via math, not vice versa. As explained in Chapter 9, the ability to classify appears long before middle childhood (Halford & Andrews, 2006), and you have just read that transitive inference is not unique to humans.

Nonetheless, Piaget's experiments revealed something important. School-age children can use mental categories and subcategories more flexibly, inductively, and simultaneously than younger children can (Meadows, 2006). They are more advanced thinkers, intellectually capable in ways that younger children are not.

Vygotsky and School-Age Children

Like Piaget, Vygotsky felt that educators should consider children's thought processes. He recognized that younger children are confused by some concepts that older children understand. Children are curious, creative, learned. For that reason, Vygotsky believed that an educational system based on rote memorization rendered the child "helpless in the face of any sensible attempt to apply any of this acquired knowledge" (Vygotsky, 1934/1994, pp. 356–357).

The Role of Instruction

Unlike Piaget, Vygotsky regarded instruction as crucial. He thought that peers and teachers provide the bridge between developmental potential and needed skills and knowledge, via guided participation, scaffolding, and the zone of proximal development (see Chapters 2 and 9).

Confirmation of the role of social interaction and instruction comes from children who, because of their school's entry-date cutoff, are either relatively old kindergartners or quite young first-graders. Spring achievement scores of 6-year-old first-graders far exceed those of kindergarten 6-year-olds who are only one month younger (Lincove & Painter, 2006; NICHD, 2007).

Remember that Vygotsky believed education occurs everywhere, not only in school. Children mentor one another as they play together. They learn from television, dinner with their families, people they see on the street, and every other daily experience. This education accumulates from infancy on.

For instance, a study of the reading and math achievement of more than a thousand third- and fifth-grade children from ten U.S. cities found that high-scoring primary school children were likely to have had extensive cognitive stimulation. There were three main sources of intellectual activity: their families (e.g., parents read to them daily when they were toddlers), preschool programs (e.g., a variety of learning activities), and the first grade (e.g., literacy emphasis with individual evaluation). Although children from families of low socioeconomic status (SES) were least likely to have been highly stimulated in all three contexts, achievement scores of low-income children who had these crucial three influences showed even more advances than did scores of the high-SES children (Crosnoe et al., 2010).

Especially for Teachers How might Piaget's and Vygotsky's ideas help in teaching geography to a class of third-graders? (see response, page 324)

DAVID R. FRAZIER PHOTOLIBRARY, INC. / ALAMY

He Knows His Stuff Many child vendors, like this boy selling combs and other grooming aids on the streets of Manaus, Brazil, understand basic math and the give-and-take of social interaction. But, deprived of formal education, they know little or nothing about history and literature.

>> **Response for Teachers** (from page 323) Here are two of the most obvious ways. (1) Use logic. Once children can grasp classification and class inclusion, they can understand cities within states, states within nations, and nations within continents. Organize your instruction to make logical categorization easier. (2) Make use of children's need for concrete and personal involvement. You might have the children learn first about their own location, then about the places where relatives and friends live, and finally about places beyond their personal experience (via books, photographs, videos, and guest speakers).

International Contexts

In general, Vygotsky's emphasis on sociocultural contexts contrasts with Piaget's maturational, self-discovery approach. Vygotsky believed that cultures (tools, customs, and mentors) teach. For example, if a child is surrounded by adults reading for pleasure, by full bookcases, by daily newspapers, and by street signs, that child will read better than a child who has had little exposure to print, even if both are in the same classroom.

The most detailed international example of the influence of context on learning comes from Brazil, where street children sell fruit, candy, and other products. Many never attend school and consequently score poorly on standard math achievement tests. This is no surprise to developmentalists, who have data from numerous nations showing that unschooled children score lower in every academic area (Rogoff et al., 2005).

However, some young Brazilian peddlers are skilled at pricing their wares and making change. Some cannot read, but they use colors and pictures to identify how many *reals* each bill is worth (Saxe, 2004). They may recalibrate selling prices daily in response to inflation, wholesale costs, and customer demand, calculating "complex markup computations . . . by using procedures that were widespread in their practice but not known to children in school" (Saxe, 1999, p. 255). Ratios and fractions, not usually taught until the end of middle childhood, are understood by young street sellers. They learn math from:

- The social context
- Other sellers (especially older children)
- Daily experience

None of this would surprise Vygotsky, who believed that peers are good mentors. Much other research shows that children's understanding of arithmetic depends on context: If they learn math in school, they are proficient at school math; if they learn math out of school, they are adept at problems encountered in similar situations (Abreu, 2008). The transfer of knowledge from one context to another is not automatic: In a series of experiments, when schoolchildren were given real coins and bills to help them calculate problems, they did worse than when they worked as usual, with pencils and paper (McNeil et al., 2009). Thus, real money (and practical necessity) distracts some children as it helps others. Piaget's stress on concrete operations, using blocks and marks to teach math, is not always helpful (McNeil & Uttal, 2009).

Culture affects the methods of learning, not just the content. This was evident in a study of 80 Mexican American children in California (Silva et al., 2010). Half were from families where indigenous Indian learning was the norm: Children were expected to learn by watching others and to help each other if need be. The other half were from families more acculturated to U.S. norms; the children were used to direct instruction, not observational learning, and expected to work on their own.

In the first session of this study, each child was shown how to make a toy while his or her sibling sat nearby. First, the younger sibling waited while the older sibling made a toy mouse and then the older sibling waited while the younger sibling made a toy frog. Each waiting child's behavior was videotaped and coded every 5 seconds as *sustained attention* (alert and focused on the sibling's activity), *glancing* (sporadic interest, but primary focus on something else), or *not attending* (looking elsewhere). (See Figure 12.1 and the Research Design.) Unexpectedly, a week later, each child was individually given the materials to make the toy his or her sibling had made but was not told how unless necessary.

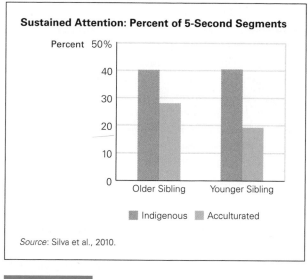

Sustained Attention: Percent of 5-Second Segments

Source: Silva et al., 2010.

FIGURE 12.1

Watch Your Brother! When a brother (or sister) is learning how to make a toy, do you focus your attention on that, or do you look elsewhere? Apparently, it depends partly on what your mother has taught you, not directly but in the way she expects you to learn.

Observation Quiz Among those children accustomed to U.S. styles of learning, were older or younger siblings more likely to pay attention to their siblings? Why? (see answer, page 326)

► **Research Design**

Scientists: Katie G. Silva, Maricela Correa-Chávez, and Barbara Rogoff.

Publication: *Child Development* (2010).

Participants: Forty 5- to 11-year-old pairs of siblings, living in southern California and attending public school. All were Mexican American, most born in the United States to families originally from rural areas in the state of Michoacán. The groups differed in maternal education: Some mothers were high school graduates, an accomplishment that signified more acculturation to U.S. ways of learning, while other mothers averaged six years of schooling (range 0–9) and were more indigenous (Indian) in their ways. Other indicators also showed that the two groups were different: family size (2.4 versus 3.3 children), fathers' birthplace (half in the United States versus almost all in Mexico).

Design: A Spanish-speaking "toy lady" showed each child how to make a toy, with the younger sibling waiting while the older child made a mouse, and then the older child waiting while the younger child made a frog. A week later, each child individually was given the materials to make the toy that his or her sibling had made. The toy lady ostensibly was involved in paperwork, giving hints about making the toy only when needed. Coders noted the waiting children's attention during the first session and the number of hints needed during the second. The coders and the toy ladies did not know the hypothesis, nor did they know the background of the children.

Results: The children from the indigenous backgrounds were more likely to pay close attention to the instructions and actions of their siblings; they did so in 40.4 percent of the 5-second segments versus 23.6 percent for the acculturated group. Virtually none of the children in either group were disruptive, and most simply waited their turn. Some of the indigenous siblings tried to help, but virtually none of the acculturated children did so. Moreover, the indigenous children better remembered what they saw: A week later, they needed an average of 37 percent of the possible hints versus 47 percent for the other pairs.

Major conclusion: Even when children currently live in the same settings and attend the same schools, they follow family cultural traditions in how they learn. This is reflected in their achievement.

Comment: That cultural ways of learning differ is useful for teachers as well as testers to know. Note that several parts of the design helped the children feel comfortable (sibling nearby, Spanish-speaking toy lady), and several measures made the data detailed and objective (videotapes, "blind" coders, 5-second segments). These features suggest that the conclusion—that children from rural, lower-SES backgrounds learn better under some conditions than similar children who ordinarily are better students—is probably valid.

Children from indigenous backgrounds were more attentive in the first session and needed less help a week later (Silva et al., 2010).

Information Processing

Today's educators and psychologists regard both Piaget and Vygotsky as insightful; international research confirms the merits of their theories. Piaget described universal changes; Vygotsky noted cultural impact.

A third, and more recent, approach to understanding cognition adds crucial details. As you learned earlier, the information-processing perspective benefits from technology that allows much more detailed understanding than 50 years ago.

Like computers, people sense and perceive large amounts of information. They then: (1) seek specific units of information (as a search engine does), (2) analyze (as software programs do), and (3) express their conclusions so another person can understand (as a networked computer might do). By tracing the paths and links of each of these functions, scientists better understand the process of learning. This has become particularly useful in educating children with learning disabilities, whose processing of information is often impaired. Dyslexia or dyscalculia may be symptoms, not causes (Waber, 2010).

The brain's gradual growth confirms the information-processing perspective. Ongoing brain connections and pathways allow advances in mental processing.

Memory

Information processing requires memory. Various types of input, and many methods of storage and retrieval, affect the increasing cognitive ability of the schoolchild. Each of the three major steps in the memory process—sensory memory, working memory, and long-term memory—is affected by development.

Sensory memory (also called the *sensory register*) is the first component of the human information-processing system. It stores incoming stimuli for a split second after they are received, with sounds retained slightly longer than sights. To use terms explained in Chapter 5, *sensations* are retained for a moment, and then some become *perceptions*. This first step of sensory awareness is already quite good in early childhood, improves slightly until about age 10, and remains adequate until late adulthood.

Once some sensations become perceptions, the brain selects meaningful perceptions to transfer to working memory for further analysis. It is in **working memory** (formerly called *short-term memory*) that current, conscious mental activity occurs. Working memory improves steadily and significantly every year from about age 4 to age 15 (Gathercole et al., 2004) as the brain matures and experiences build (Baddelely, 2007). Especially significant is increased myelination and dendrite formation in the prefrontal cortex—increases that allow the massive interconnections described in Chapter 11.

Processing, not mere exposure, is essential to getting information into working memory, which is why working memory improves markedly in middle childhood (Cowan & Alloway, 2009). Improvement in working memory during the school years includes advances in two crucial areas—one called the *phonological loop*, which stores sounds, and one called the *visual–spatial sketchpad*, which stores sights (Meadows, 2006). As the brain matures, schoolchildren are able to use memory strategies that are inaccessible to young children (see Table 12.1). These strategies do not appear suddenly; gradual improvement is evident from early childhood through adolescence (Schneider & Lockl, 2008).

The relationship among strategy, classification, and working memory was demonstrated by an experiment in which 7- and 9-year-olds memorized two

sensory memory The component of the information-processing system in which incoming stimulus information is stored for a split second to allow it to be processed. (Also called the *sensory register*.)

working memory The component of the information-processing system in which current conscious mental activity occurs. (Formerly called *short-term memory*.)

>> **Answer to Observation Quiz** (from page 325) Older siblings were more attentive. The reasons are speculative—whatever reason you thought of, does it reflect your own sibling experience or your cultural values?

TABLE 12.1	
Advances in Memory from Infancy to Age 11	
Child's Age	**Memory Capabilities**
Under 2 years	Infants remember actions and routines that involve them. Memory is implicit, triggered by sights and sounds (an interactive toy, a caregiver's voice).
2–5 years	Words are now used to encode and retrieve memories. Explicit memory begins, although children do not yet use memory strategies. Children remember things by rote (their phone number, nursery rhymes) without truly understanding them.
5–7 years	Children realize that some things should be remembered, and they begin to use simple strategies, primarily rehearsal (repeating an item again and again). This is not a very efficient strategy, but with enough repetition, automatization occurs.
7–9 years	Children use new strategies if they are taught them. Children use visual clues (remembering how a particular spelling word looks) and auditory hints (rhymes, letters), evidence of advances in the visual–spatial sketchpad and phonological loop. They become able to take advantage of the organization of things to be remembered.
9–11 years	Memory becomes more adaptive and strategic as children become able to learn various memory techniques from teachers and other children. They can organize material themselves, developing their own memory aids.

Source: Based on information in Meadows, 2006.

lists of 10 items each (M. L. Howe, 2004). Some children had one list of toys and another of vehicles; others had two mixed lists, with toys and vehicles in both. A day later, each child was asked to remember one of the two lists. Having had separate lists of toys and vehicles helped the 7-year-olds somewhat but benefited the 9-year-olds more. Those older children used the organized topical lists well: Not only did they surpass all the 7-year-olds, they also remembered much more than the 9-year-olds with mixed lists.

Older children's ability to use memory strategies is evident in other research as well. For instance, when asked to remember lists that were not grouped together, 10-year-olds did much better than 8-year-olds because fewer of them relied on rote item-by-item memory and more of them used active memory, repeating a string of items as they memorized them (Lehmann & Hasselhorn, 2010). Stringing, or chunking, items is crucial: The size of each chunk seems far less important than the number of chunks, with about five the usual maximum (Cowan, 2010).

Finally, information from working memory may be transferred to **long-term memory,** which stores it for minutes, hours, days, months, or years. The capacity of long-term memory—how much information can be crammed into one brain—is very large by the end of middle childhood. Together with sensory memory and working memory, long-term memory assists in organizing ideas and reactions. Crucial to long-term memory is not merely *storage* (how much material has been deposited) but also *retrieval* (how readily past learning can be brought into working memory). Retrieval is easier for some memories (especially memories of vivid, highly emotional experiences) than for others. Children's long-term memory is imperfect, but this is true at every age: Everyone forgets or distorts items that should be remembered (Meadows, 2006).

AP PHOTO / THE HERALD, DAVID E. DALE

Verbs and Adverbs Erin, Ally, Paige, and Sabrina perform rap lyrics they wrote to review key concepts for an upcoming assessment test. Such mnemonic devices are beyond younger children but may be very helpful in middle childhood.

Especially for Teachers How might your understanding of memory help you teach a 2,000-word vocabulary list to a class of fourth-graders? (see response, page 328)

Knowledge

Information processing finds that the more people know, the more they learn. Having an extensive **knowledge base,** or a broad body of knowledge in a particular subject, makes it easier to master related new information.

Three factors facilitate increases in the knowledge base: past experience, current opportunity, and personal motivation. That explains why children's knowledge base is not what their parents or teachers would like. Some schoolchildren memorize words and rhythms of hit songs, know plots and characters of television programs, and can recite the names and histories of football players but do not know the century of World War I or whether Pakistan is in Asia or Africa. The importance of motivation provides a clue for teachers: New concepts are learned best if they are connected to personal and cultural experiences (Schneider & Lockl, 2008; Wittrock, 1974/2010).

Control Processes

The mechanisms that put memory, processing speed, and the knowledge base together are **control processes;** they regulate the analysis and flow of information within the system. Control processes include *emotional regulation* and *selective attention,* explained in Chapters 10 and 11. Equally important is **metacognition,** sometimes defined as "thinking about thinking." Metacognition is the ultimate control process because it allows a person to evaluate a cognitive task, determine how to accomplish it, and then monitor performance and make adjustments.

long-term memory The component of the information-processing system in which virtually limitless amounts of information can be stored indefinitely.

knowledge base A body of knowledge in a particular area that makes it easier to master new information in that area.

control processes Mechanisms (including selective attention, metacognition, and emotional regulation) that combine memory, processing speed, and knowledge to regulate the analysis and flow of information within the information-processing system. (Also called *executive processes.*)

metacognition "Thinking about thinking," or the ability to evaluate a cognitive task in order to determine how best to accomplish it, and then to monitor and adjust one's performance on that task.

>> **Response for Teachers** (from page 327) Children this age can be taught strategies for remembering by making links between working memory and long-term memory. You might break down the vocabulary list into word clusters, grouped according to root words, connections to the children's existing knowledge, applications, or (as a last resort) first letters or rhymes. Active, social learning is useful; perhaps in groups the students could write a story each day that incorporates 15 new words. Each group could read its story aloud to the class.

Control processes require an executive in the information-processing system to organize, prioritize, and direct mental operations, as the CEO (chief executive officer) of a business does. For that reason, control processes are also called *executive processes*, evident whenever someone concentrates only on the relevant parts of a task and uses his or her knowledge base to connect new information or applies memory strategies. Such controlling is more evident among 10-year-olds than among 4- or 6-year-olds (Bjorklund et al., 2009). A fourth-grade student listens to what the teacher is saying about the river Nile, ignoring the classmate who is chewing gum or tying his shoe.

Both metacognition and control processes continue to improve with age and school experience. For instance, in one study, children took a fill-in-the-blanks test, indicated how confident they were of each answer, and then were allowed to delete some questions (with the remaining ones counting more). Already by age 9, they were able to estimate correctness; by age 11, they were skilled at knowing what to delete (Roebers et al., 2009).

Control processes develop spontaneously, but they can also be taught. Sometimes such teaching is explicit, more so in some nations (e.g., Germany) than in others (e.g., the United States) (Bjorklund et al., 2009). For instance, teachers may provide spelling rules ("*i* before *e* except after *c*") and sentences to help pupils remember the notes of the treble clef ("Every Good Boy Does Fine"—E, G, B, D, F). Children can use simple rules by about age 7 and can combine rules by age 9; younger children ignore them or use them only on command (Meadows, 2006). Often children with special needs require explicit teaching of control processes (Riccio et al., 2010). The issue of what needs to be taught and what discovered is one that requires critical thinking, as the following explains.

THINKING CRITICALLY

Balls Rolling Down

Should metacognition be taught, or should children develop it spontaneously when they are old enough? This question has been the focus of decades of research (Orlich et al., 2009; Pressley & Hilden, 2006). Such research has looked at both discovery learning (inspired by Piaget) and explicit teaching (from an information-processing perspective), always with awareness of differences (as Vygotsky stressed).

The answer depends partly on cultures and goals. Some cultures value single-minded concentration, others multitasking; some stress explicit instruction, others implicit learning. The latter is not necessarily inefficient: One commentator explained, "Simultaneous attention may be important when learning relies on observation of ongoing events" (Correa-Chavez et al., 2005, p. 665), a point made by the research cited earlier on toy-making (Silva et al., 2010).

To illustrate the impact of instruction, one study sought to help children realize that, in order to be valid, scientific experiments need to control the relevant variables and to measure each, one by one (Klahr & Nigam, 2004). The researchers showed 112 third- and fourth-graders an apparatus consisting of a downhill ramp connected to an uphill ramp (see Figure 12.2). There were four variables: golf ball or rubber ball, steep or shallow slope, smooth or rough ramp surface, and long or short downhill run.

First, the children were asked to design four experiments on their own: two to determine the effect of distance and two to determine the effect of steepness. Only 8 of the 112 children designed experiments that controlled the variables. Unless the variables were controlled, the results would be confounded (inappropriately combined). Thus, for example, a child might confound the conclusions by comparing one trial with a steep ramp and a golf ball to a second trial with a shallow ramp and a rubber ball.

The 104 children who did not already know the importance of controlling variables were then divided into two groups. Half were allowed to create their own experiments; the other half received explicit instruction by watching an experimenter create pairs of demonstrations. The experimenter asked the children whether a demonstrated pair allowed them to "tell for sure" how a particular variable affected the distance traveled by the ball. After each response, the experimenter explained the correct answer and emphasized the importance of testing a single variable at a time.

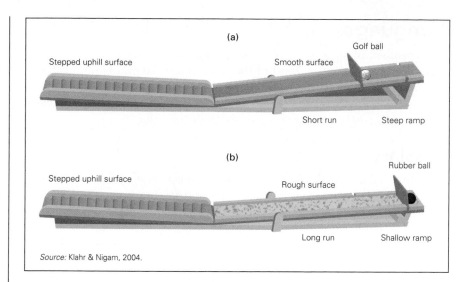

(a)

Stepped uphill surface   Smooth surface   Golf ball

Short run   Steep ramp

(b)

Stepped uphill surface   Rough surface   Rubber ball

Long run   Shallow ramp

Source: Klahr & Nigam, 2004.

FIGURE 12.2

Design for a Confounded Experiment On each of these two ramps, children could vary the steepness, surface, and length of the ramp, as well as the type of ball. The confounded experiment depicted here contrasts (*a*) a golf ball on a steep, smooth, short ramp with (*b*) a rubber ball on a shallow, rough, long ramp.

Then all 104 children were asked to design four experiments, as before. Far more children who received direct instruction (40 of 52) correctly isolated the variables than did children who explored on their own (12 of 52). A week later, to assess whether the children had really learned the importance of controlling variables, those children who seemed to understand (the 40 and the 12) were asked to examine two science posters created by 11-year-olds. The researcher requested suggestions to make the posters "good enough to enter in a state science fair." The 40 children who had been instructed were virtually as perceptive in their critiques of the posters as the 12 who had learned through discovery. This study suggests that strategy can be taught—if the teacher actively engages the students. That is exactly what information-processing theory would predict.

Of course, scientific understanding is about more than understanding variables: It is about questioning conclusions and realizing that answers can and do change. How children develop this ability—whether by discovery and experience as Piaget might expect, whether by explicit instruction as information-processing theory suggests—is a matter of intense concern to educators. Furthermore, a logical and skeptical approach to life is pivotal for scientists, but that itself may be culturally determined: questions, critiques, and doubts may be handicapping in some communities. An understanding of human development can be helpful here. As one expert explains:

> The developmentalist can contribute knowledge of what needs to develop, sketch its course, and hopefully even gain insight into the mechanisms involved. Developmentalists and educators in collaboration can seek to identify the kinds of experiences that make it more likely to happen.
>
> *[Kuhn, 2009, p. 115]*

Whatever you think about teaching metacognitive skills, Vygotsky would ask, "How does your personal experience and cultural heritage affect your answer?"

SUMMING UP

Every theory of cognitive development recognizes that school-age children are avid learners who actively build on the knowledge they already have. Piaget emphasized children's own logical thinking, as they come to understand classification and develop transitive inference during concrete operational thought. Research inspired by Vygotsky and the sociocultural perspective reveals that cultural differences can be powerful; specific instruction and practical experience vary from one context to another, and therefore each child learns different skills.

An information-processing analysis highlights the many components of thinking that advance during middle childhood. Although sensory and long-term memory do not change much during these years, the speed and efficiency of working memory improve dramatically, making school-age children better thinkers as well as more strategic learners than previously. Another advantage for older children is that they develop a greater knowledge base. As control processes and metacognition advance, children are able to direct their minds toward whatever they want to learn.

>> Language

As you remember, many aspects of language advance during early childhood. By age 6, children have mastered most of the basic vocabulary and grammar of their first language, and many speak a second language fluently. Those linguistic abilities form a strong knowledge base, enabling some school-age children to learn up to 20 new words a day and to apply complex grammar rules.

Vocabulary

By age 5, children already know the names of thousands of objects, and they understand many parts of speech. After that point, they become more flexible and logical; they can understand prefixes, suffixes, compound words, phrases, and figures of speech. For example, 2-year-olds know *egg*, but 10-year-olds also know *egg salad, egg-drop soup, last one in is a rotten egg*. They understand that each of these expressions is connected to *egg* but is also distinct from the dozen uncooked eggs in the refrigerator.

Understanding Metaphors

Metaphors, jokes, and puns are finally comprehended. Some jokes ("What is black and white and red all over?" "Why did the chicken cross the road?") are funny only during middle childhood. They are not understood by younger children and are no longer funny for teenagers, but in middle childhood they are evidence of normally developing cognitive flexibility and social awareness. Indeed, a lack of metaphorical understanding, even when a child has a large vocabulary, signifies cognitive problems (Thomas et al., 2010).

Many adults do not realize how difficult it is for young children or adults who are learning a new language to grasp figures of speech. The humorist James Thurber remembered:

> the enchanted private world of my early boyhood. . . . In this world, businessmen who phoned their wives to say they were tied up at the office sat roped to their swivel chairs, and probably gagged, unable to move or speak except somehow, miraculously, to telephone. . . . Then there was the man who left town under a cloud. Sometimes I saw him all wrapped up in the cloud and invisible. . . . At other times it floated, about the size of a sofa, above him wherever he went. . . . [I remember] the old lady who was always up in the air, the husband who did not seem able to put his foot down, the man who lost his head during a fire but was still able to run out of the house yelling.
>
> [*Thurber, 1999, p. 40*]

Adjusting Vocabulary to the Context

One aspect of language that advances markedly in middle childhood is **pragmatics,** the practical use of language, which includes the ability to adjust one's language to communicate with varied audiences in different contexts. This ability is obvious to linguists when they listen to children talk informally with their friends and formally with their teachers or parents (never calling the latter a *rotten egg*). It is also very helpful to children: Shy 6-year-olds who are adept at pragmatics cope far better with the social pressures of elementary school than do those who are not as adept (Coplan & Weeks, 2009).

Children are able to switch back and forth, depending on the audience, using different styles of speech, or "codes." Each code includes many aspects of language—tone, pronunciation, gestures, sentence length, idioms, vocabulary, and grammar. Sometimes the switch is between *formal code* (used in academic contexts) and *informal code* (used with friends); sometimes it is between standard (or proper)

RADIUS IMAGES / PHOTOLIBRARY

Homework Despite first appearances, this is not teacher and student but father and daughter, as Dad becomes excited about his 7-year-old's science project. Actually, if she is as intrigued as she appears to be, he is teacher as well as father. Children learn most of their vocabulary with friends and family, not in class.

pragmatics The practical use of language that includes the ability to adjust language communication according to audience and context.

Especially for Parents You've had an exhausting day but are setting out to buy groceries. Your 7-year-old son wants to go with you. Should you explain that you are so tired that you want to make a quick solo trip to the supermarket this time? (see response, page 333)

speech and dialect or vernacular (used on the street). Many children use a code in text messaging, with numbers (411), abbreviations (LOL), and emoticons (:-D).

Children need instruction from teachers to become fluent in the formal code because the logic of grammar—whether *who* or *whom* is correct or when a sentence is incomplete—is almost impossible to deduce. The peer group teaches the informal code, and each local community transmits dialect and pronunciation. Teachers sometimes consider such talk ungrammatical, but they are mistaken: Grammar is embedded in the informal code. Pragmatics is evident when curses, slang, and alternate grammar are employed with some friends but not others.

Pragmatic code use becomes most obvious when children speak one language at home and another at school. Every nation includes many such children; most of the world's 6,000 languages are not school languages. For instance, English is the language of instruction in Australia, but 17 percent of the children speak one of 246 other languages at home (Centre for Community Child Health, 2009). In the United States, 20 percent of all students speak a language other than English at home; half of them are fluent with their parents in one language and fluent in English at school.

Can You Text Me? Few adults over 40 know how to "text" anyone, but many schoolchildren quickly become masters of text messaging. Their universal use of the informal texting code—terse, ungrammatical, symbol-laden—is evidence of their ability to learn rapidly from one another.

Differences in Language Learning

Learning to speak, read, and write the language of the school is pivotal for achievement, the foundation of all primary school education. Yet children differ in how well they do. Some of these differences may be genetic, but many educators describe the importance of the social context.

Family Poverty

Decades of research throughout the world have found a strong correlation between academic achievement and socioeconomic status (Hauser-Cram et al., 2006; Plank & MacIver, 2003). Language is a major reason. Not only do children from low-SES families usually have smaller vocabularies, but their grammar is simpler (fewer compound sentences, dependent clauses, and conditional verbs) and their sentences are shorter (Hart & Risley, 1995; E. Hoff, 2003). They fall behind their peers in talking, in reading, and then in other subjects, and even their brains signal linguistic weaknesses (Hackman & Farah, 2009).

The information-processing perspective focuses on specifics that might affect the brain and thus the ability to learn. Possibilities abound—inadequate prenatal care, exposure to lead, no breakfast, overcrowded households, few books at home, teenage parents, authoritarian child rearing, inexperienced teachers . . . the list could go on and on. All of these correlate with low SES and less learning, but none have been proven to be a major cause (not merely a correlate) of low achievement during primary school.

Three factors, however, *do* appear causal. One is limited early exposure to words. Unlike parents who attended college, many less educated parents do not speak extensively or elaborately with their children. Daily book-reading to 2-year-olds, for instance, occurs for 24 percent of the children of mothers with less than a high school education as opposed to 70 percent of the children of mothers with at least a BA (National Center for Education Statistics, 2009) (see Figure 12.3).

The reasons correlate with low income (financial stress, not enough time for each child, neighborhood noise) but are not directly caused by it. Indeed, children from high-SES families who rarely hear language also do poorly in school, and deaf children with cochlear implants (allowing them to hear) whose parents

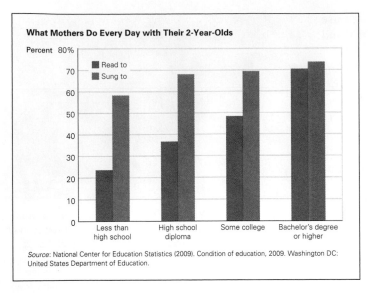

What Mothers Do Every Day with Their 2-Year-Olds

Source: National Center for Education Statistics (2009). Condition of education, 2009. Washington DC: United States Department of Education.

FIGURE 12.3

Red Fish, Blue Fish As you can see, most mothers sing to their little children, but the college-educated mothers are much more likely to know that book-reading is important. Simply knowing how to turn a page or hearing new word combinations (fish with a little car?) correlates with reading ability later on.

do not encourage talking have language difficulties later on (DesJardin et al., 2009). Remember that dendrites grow to reflect children's experiences, including how much language they hear.

A second cause of low achievement is teachers' and parents' expectations, a finding supported by research in many nations (Melhuish et al., 2008; Phillipson & Phillipson, 2007; Rosenthal, 1991; Rubie-Davies, 2007). Expectations are closely connected to the third causal factor, the macrosystem, which affects whether or not a child is taught advanced words and concepts, especially the vocabulary words that are the foundation for later learning, such as *negotiate, evolve, respire, allegation, deficit* (Snow et al., 2007). International achievement test scores indicate that the income gap, and consequent variation in school resources and student achievement, is much greater in some nations than in others. One of the largest spreads is in the United States, where the fourth-grade reading scores among the schools with the most low-income children are 35 points below the national average; in 40 nations studied, the average gap is 23 points, with much smaller gaps in most European nations (e.g., 11 points in France).

We should note that, although these three factors (language exposure, adult expectations, and macrosystem resources) correlate with low SES, the connection between SES and learning is not inevitable. A detailed study of children's literacy recognizes the income differences in achievement, but "we reject social class as an explanation for our findings" (Snow et al., 2007, p. 22). One of many exceptions to the general SES trends is E. P. Jones, who won the 2004 Pulitzer Prize for his novel *The Known World* (2003). He grew up in a very poor family, headed by a single mother who was illiterate but who had high expectations for her son. Jones writes:

> For as many Sundays as I can remember, perhaps even Sundays when I was in the womb, my mother has pointed across "I" street to Seaton [school] as we come and go to Mt. Carmel [church].
> "You gonna go there and learn about the whole world."
>
> *[E. P. Jones, 1992/2003, p. 29]*

The process works in reverse as well. Low expectations lead to low achievement. The importance of the teacher's attitude is demonstrated by Yolanda and Paul in the following.

A CASE TO STUDY

Two Immigrants

Two children, both Mexican American, describe their experiences in their local public school in California.

Yolanda:
When I got here [from Mexico at age 7], I didn't want to stay here, 'cause I didn't like the school. And after a little while, in third grade, I started getting the hint of it and everything and I tried real hard in it. I really got along with the teachers. . . . They would start talking to me, or they kinda like pulled me up some grades, or moved me to other classes, or took me somewhere. And they were always congratulating me.

Paul:
I grew up . . . ditching school, just getting in trouble, trying to make a dollar, that's it, you know? Just go to school, steal from the store, and go sell candies at school. And that's what I was doing in the third or fourth grade. . . . I was always getting in the principal's office, suspended, kicked out, everything, starting from the third grade.

My fifth grade teacher, Ms. Nelson . . . she put me in a play and that like tripped me out. Like, why do you want me in a play? Me, I'm just a mess-up. Still, you know, she put me in a play. And in the fifth grade, I think that was the best year out of the whole six years. I learned a lot about the Revolutionary War. . . . Had good friends. . . . We had a project we were involved in. Ms. Nelson . . . just involved everyone. We made books, this and that. And I used to write, and wrote two, three books. Was in a book fair. . . . She got real deep into you. Just, you know, "Come on now, you can do it." That was a good year for me, fifth grade.

[quoted in Nieto, 2000, pp. 220, 249]

Note that initially Yolanda didn't like the United States because of school, but her teachers "kind of pulled me up." By third grade, she was beginning to get "the hint of it." For Paul, school was where he sold stolen candy and where his third-grade teacher sent him to the principal, who suspended him. Ms. Nelson's fifth grade was "a good year," but it was too late—he had already learned he was "just a mess-up." Paul was sent to a special school, and the text implies (but does not confirm) that he was arrested and jailed by age 18. Yolanda became a successful young woman, fluently bilingual.

It would be easy to conclude that the difference was gender, since girls generally do better in school than boys. But that is too simple: Some Mexican-born boys do well in California schools—which raises the question of how teachers impact children: Was there anything else the third-grade teacher could have done for Paul?

Culture Clash: Question and Response

Since languages spring from cultures, not from dictionaries, children learn best if teaching reflects their culture. This was evident in a Canadian school where Inuit children were taught in their native language by Inuit teachers for their first two years and then in French or English by non-Inuit teachers from the third grade up. Few Inuit children became fluent in their second language, and most dropped out before graduation. Why?

There were marked differences in teaching methods from grades 2 to 3 (Eriks-Brophy & Crago, 2003). The non-Inuit teachers discouraged talk that the Inuit teachers had encouraged, including cooperation (which the non-Inuit teachers called "talking out of turn"), helping each other ("cheating"), and attempts to answer ("mistakes").

A specific example illustrates this pattern. A common routine in North American schools is initiation/response/evaluation: The teacher asks a question, a child responds, and the teacher judges the response. Initiation/response/evaluation was used by the non-Inuit teachers 60 percent of the time, compared with 18 percent of the time by the Inuit teachers (Eriks-Brophy & Crago, 2003). For example, an Inuit teacher showed a picture and asked:

Teacher: This one. What is it?
Student: Tutuva *[an insect]*.
Teacher: What is it?
Student: Tutuva.
Teacher: All of us, look carefully.
Student: Kituquianluti *[another insect, this time correct. The teacher nodded and breathed in.]*

In contrast, a non-Inuit teacher asked:

Teacher: Richard, what is this?
Richard: It is an ear.
Teacher: Good.
Teacher: Rhoda, what is this?
Rhoda: Hair.
Teacher: No. What is this?
Rhoda: Face.
Teacher: It is a face.
Rhoda: It is a face.
Teacher: Very good, Rhoda.

[quoted in Eriks-Brophy & Crago, 2003, pp. 406–407]

ALASKA STOCK IMAGES

The Best of Both Worlds An Inupiat boy works at a computer keyboard in his classroom. His teachers want him and his classmates to benefit from both cultures—traditional and modern.

>> Response for Parents (from page 330) Your son would understand your explanation, but you should take him along if you can do so without losing patience. You wouldn't ignore his need for food or medicine; don't ignore his need for learning. While shopping, you can teach vocabulary (does he know *pimientos, pepperoni, polenta*?), categories ("root vegetables," "freshwater fish"), and math (which size box of cereal is cheaper?). Explain in advance that you need him to help you find items and carry them and that he can choose only one item that you wouldn't normally buy. Seven-year-olds can understand rules, and they enjoy being helpful.

Note that the Inuit teacher never verbally evaluated the child (nodding and breathing to signal correctness), but the second teacher did three times ("good," "no," "very good"). Teaching methods are the outcome of cultural beliefs, a "social system that evolves over time" (Eriks-Brophy & Crago, 2003, p. 397), often hidden from the teachers themselves. Children feel the effects, becoming talkative or quiet.

SUMMING UP

Children continue to learn language rapidly during the school years. They become more flexible, logical, and knowledgeable, figuring out the meanings of new words and grasping metaphors, jokes, and compound words. Many converse with friends using informal speech and master a more formal code to use in school. They learn whatever grammar and vocabulary they are taught, and they succeed at pragmatics, the practical task of adjusting their language to friends, teachers, or family. Millions become proficient in a second language, a process facilitated by teachers and peers. ■

>> Teaching and Learning

As we have just described, school-age children are great learners, developing strategies, accumulating knowledge, expanding language, and using logic. Throughout history and worldwide, children are given new responsibility and instruction in middle childhood because that is when the human body and brain are ready. Traditionally, this occurred at home, but now 90 percent of the world's 7-year-olds are in school; that is where their parents and political leaders want them to be (Cohen & Malin, 2010). In 2010, for instance, India passed a law providing free education to all 6- to 14-year olds, regardless of caste or income (no more school fees).

Parents rate their children's schools more favorably than do nonparents in the same community, and a U.S. survey found that nationwide, everyone grades schools lower (C−) than their local schools (C+) and that parents of public school children rate their local schools higher still (B−) (Snyder & Dillow, 2010). (About 10 percent of children attend private or parochial schools; their parents were not separately tallied.) Other research finds that most parents, no matter what schooling they choose for their children, are satisfied with their choice. However, many educators and developmentalists are less satisfied, as you will now see.

International Schooling

Everywhere in the world, children are taught to read, write, and do arithmetic. There are some generally accepted goals: Because of brain maturation and the necessity of learning in sequence, no nation teaches 6-year-olds to multiply three-digit numbers or read paragraphs fluently out loud, but every nation expects 10-year-olds to do so. Some of the sequences for reading and math that are recognized universally are listed in Tables 12.2 and 12.3. Nations also want their children to be good citizens, although there is no consensus as to exactly what that means or what developmental paths (a specific class? at what age?) it should follow (Cohen & Malin, 2010).

Differences by Nation

Although literacy and math are valued everywhere, many specifics of the educational curriculum vary by nation, by community, and by school subject. These variations are evident in the results of international tests; in the mix of school subjects; and in the relative power of parents, educators, and political leaders.

TABLE 12.2	
Sequence of Norms and Expectations for Reading	
Age	Norms and Expectations
4–5 years	Understand basic book concepts, including that English books are written from front to back, with print from left to right, and that words describe pictures.
	Recognize letters—name the letters on sight. Recognize own name.
6–7 years	Know the sounds of the consonants and vowels, including those that have two sounds (e.g., *c, g, o*). Use sounds to figure out words.
	Read simple words, such as *cat, sit, ball, jump*.
8 years	Read simple sentences out loud, 50 words per minute, including words of two syllables.
	Understand basic punctuation, consonant/vowel blends.
	Comprehend what is read.
9–10 years	Read paragraphs and chapters.
	Understand more advanced punctuation (e.g., the colon).
	Answer comprehension questions about concepts as well as facts.
	Read polysyllabic words (e.g., *vegetarian, population, multiplication*).
11–12 years	Demonstrate rapid and fluent oral reading (more than 100 words per minute).
	Comprehend paragraphs about unfamiliar topics.
	Sound out new words, figuring out meaning using cognates and context.
	Read for pleasure.
13+ years	Continue to build vocabulary, with emphasis more on comprehension than on speech.

Reading is a complex mix of skills, and children's skill at reading depends on brain maturation, education, and culture. The sequence given here is approximate; it should not be taken as a standard to measure any particular child.

TABLE 12.3	
Sequence of Norms and Expectations for Math	
Age	Norms and Expectations
4–5 years	Count to 20.
	Understand one-to-one correspondence of objects and numbers.
	Understand *more* and *less*.
	Recognize and name shapes.
6 years	Count to 100.
	Understand *bigger* and *smaller*.
	Add and subtract one-digit numbers.
8 years	Add and subtract two-digit numbers.
	Understand simple multiplication and division.
10 years	Add, subtract, multiply, and divide multidigit numbers.
	Understand simple fractions, percents, area, and perimeter of shapes.
	Understand word problems.
12 years	Begin to use abstract concepts, such as formulas, algebra.

Math learning depends heavily on direct instruction and repeated practice, which means that some children advance more quickly than others. This list is only a rough guide, to illustrate the importance of sequence.

Daily physical activity is mandated in some schools, absent in others. For instance, many schools in Japan have swimming pools; virtually no school in Africa or Latin America does. Geography, music, and art are an essential part of the curriculum in some places, not in others. In France, for example, every week children take physical education for three hours and arts education for more than two hours (Marlow-Ferguson, 2002).

Reasoned speaking and logical argument are taught in Russia and France but not in India (where children are expected to be quiet) or the United States (where children are expected to have opinions, not necessarily logical ones) (R. Alexander, 2000). Memorization is important in India but is less so in England. Educational practices may differ between nations that are geographically and culturally close. For example, the average child in a primary school in Germany spends three times as much school time studying science as does the average child in the Netherlands (Snyder & Dillow, 2010).

Variation from nation to nation is even greater in the **hidden curriculum,** the implicit values and assumptions evident in course selection, tracking, teacher characteristics, discipline, teaching methods, sports competition, student government, extracurricular activities, and so on. For example, if most teachers differ from most students in gender, ethnicity, or economic background, the hidden message may be that education is not relevant for the children's daily lives. If some students are

hidden curriculum The unofficial, unstated, or implicit rules and priorities that influence the academic curriculum and every other aspect of learning in a school.

in gifted classes, the message is that they are more capable of learning and, by implication, that less is expected of the other students. A message regarding the importance of education is expressed in the physical setting, which might be spacious classrooms, wide hallways, and large, grassy playgrounds; or small, poorly equipped rooms and cement play yards or play streets; or outdoor spaces with no chairs, desks, or books.

Learning a Second Language

The questions of when, how, to whom, and whether second-language instruction should be provided are answered with marked variations from nation to nation, with some nations teaching two or more languages throughout elementary school and others not teaching any language except the majority one. For children who do not speak the majority language, instruction again varies. Teaching approaches range from **immersion,** in which instruction occurs entirely in the new language, to the opposite, in which children learn in their first language until the second language can be taught as a "foreign" tongue. Between these extremes lies **bilingual schooling,** with instruction in two languages and, in North America, **ESL (English as a second language),** in which non-English speakers are taught intensively and exclusively in English to prepare them for regular classes.

Methods for teaching a second language sometimes succeed and sometimes fail, with the research not yet clear as to which approach is best (Gandara & Rumberger, 2009). The success of any method seems to depend on the literacy of the home environment (frequent reading, writing, and listening in any language helps); the national culture; and the warmth, training, and skill of the teacher. In some schools, every teacher is bilingual; in other schools, none are—and children quickly understand the hidden curriculum of such discrepancies. Almost every European child speaks two languages by age 10, as does almost every Canadian child. Those African children who are talented and fortunate enough to graduate from high school often speak three languages.

Although cognitive research leaves no doubt that school-age children *can* learn a second language if taught logically, step by step, and that they *can* maintain

immersion A strategy in which instruction in all school subjects occurs in the second (usually the majority) language that a child is learning.

bilingual schooling A strategy in which school subjects are taught in both the learner's original language and the second (majority) language.

ESL (English as a second language) An approach to teaching English in which all children who do not speak English are placed together in an intensive course to learn basic English so that they can be educated in the same classroom as native English speakers.

Especially for Parents Suppose you and your school-age children move to a new community that is 50 miles from the nearest location that offers instruction in your faith or value system. Your neighbor says, "Don't worry, they don't have to make any moral decisions until they are teenagers." Is your neighbor correct? (see response, page 338)

Together They Learn Thousands of children worldwide do not understand the language used in their schools because their families are refugees, asylum seekers, or immigrants. Ideally, teachers, like this one in London, use guided participation to individualize instruction as they help these children learn the new language. Note that both the teacher and the student point, listen, and speak.

their original language, whether they do so is affected by factors beyond cognitive research: SES, family ethnotheories, and national policies. Indeed, "Language teaching has always been susceptible to political and social influences" (Byram & Feng, 2005, p. 926). This is obvious currently for the 20 percent of the 5- to 13-year-olds in the United States who are of Hispanic heritage, many entering school knowing Spanish better than English. It was equally true a century ago, when German was the language of instruction in many U.S. public schools. Then, in 1914, World War I patriotism converted German-language schools to English-only ones (Geitz et al., 2006).

Religious Education

Another aspect of education that varies markedly by nation is religious instruction. In some nations, every public school teaches religion, either the national religion, if there is one, or one of several. For instance, Finnish public schools provide parents three choices: Lutheran, Christian Orthodox, or nonsectarian (Marlow-Ferguson, 2002). Education in Islam is assumed in many Muslim nations, just as Christian education is assumed elsewhere. In some nations, including the United States, the constitutional separation of church and state precludes religious instruction in public schools.

Every nation has some private schools sponsored by religious groups. Again, international variation is large. Sixteen percent of French children attend church-related schools; only 1 percent of Japanese children do (Marlow-Ferguson, 2002). In the United States, 87 percent of children attend public schools, but for the 3 percent who are home-schooled, most parents (72 percent) cite religious/moral education as one of the reasons (Snyder et al., 2006); for the remaining 10 percent who attend private schools, most receive religious instruction (Snyder & Dillow, 2010).

International Testing

Over the past two decades, about 50 nations have participated in at least one massive international testing program. We focus here on the results for fourth-graders, the youngest children usually tested.

The primary test of reading is the **Progress in International Reading Literacy Study (PIRLS),** given every five years. The next scheduled time is 2011, with results to be published a year or two later. In the 2006 study, Canadian children from the western provinces were close to the top, and the United States ranked 15th out of 45 groups (most groups are nations, but some, as with the provinces of Canada, are not). Russia scored first in the PIRLS, up from 16th only five years earlier, probably because of extensive changes in education in the early grades. Only two East Asian groups took the PIRLS, Hong Kong and Singapore, where instruction is in English; they scored second and fourth among the groups. Africa and Middle Eastern groups scored low.

Science and math achievement are tested in the **Trends in Math and Science Study (TIMSS).** In every assessment, East Asian nations are advanced. Indeed, the average 10-year-old in Singapore scored higher than the top 5 percent of U.S. students. Despite national attention to the relatively low scores in the United States, U.S. children have not improved much on the TIMSS over the past several years. Furthermore, the gap between European American children and their Latino and African American peers remains what it was 15 years ago (see Table 12.4).

The lowest-ranking nations in the TIMSS have only recently required universal fourth-grade education and do not yet have a network of preschools. Many nations

Progress in International Reading Literacy Study (PIRLS) Inaugurated in 2001, a planned five-year cycle of international trend studies in the reading ability of fourth-graders.

Trends in Math and Science Study (TIMSS) An international assessment of the math and science skills of fourth- and eighth-graders. Although the TIMSS is very useful, different countries' scores are not always comparable because sample selection, test administration, and content validity are hard to keep uniform.

TABLE 12.4

TIMSS Ranking and Average Scores of Math Achievement for Fourth-Graders, 2007

Rank*	Country	Score
1.	Hong Kong	667
2.	Singapore	599
3.	China/Taipei	576
4.	Japan	568
5.	Kazakhstan	549
6.	Russian Federation	544
7.	England	541
8.	Latvia	537
9.	Netherlands	535
10.	United States	531
11.	Lithuania	530
12.	Germany	525
	Denmark	523
	Canada/Quebec	519
	Australia	516
	Hungary	516
	Canada/Ontario	512
	Italy	507
	New Zealand	492
	Iran	402
	Columbia	355
	Yemen	224

*The top 12 groups are listed in order, but after that not all the jurisdictions that took the test are listed. Some nations have improved over the past 15 years (notably, Hong Kong, England) and some have declined (Austria, Netherlands), but most continue about where they have always been.

Source: TIMSS 2007 International Mathematics Report (Mullis et al., 2008).

"Big deal, an A in math. That would be a D in any other country."

(especially developing ones) participate in neither the PIRLS nor the TIMSS, finding them too expensive, too discouraging, or too difficult. This may be a mistake, since test results focus a nation's efforts on educational achievement, and when school learning advances, the national economy advances as well. This link seems causal, not merely correlational (Hanushek & Woessmann, 2009), probably because better-educated adults become more productive workers. Since four of the top twelve are in eastern Europe, we will see if their economies improve.

Problems with International Benchmarks

Elaborate and extensive steps have been taken to ensure that the test items on both the PIRLS and the TIMSS are fair and culture-free, that the children who take the tests are representative (of both sexes, many incomes, many regions, and so on), and that they have had four (or eight) years of education. Most researchers have great respect for the science and the data. However, national differences mean that absolute comparability of results is impossible. For example, children in Scotland begin school at age 4 and thus had a three-year advantage over Russian children, who used to begin at age 7 (Mullis et al., 2004). The age for school entry in Russia recently dropped to age 5, and that may be one reason the scores of Russian fourth-graders have improved.

Furthermore, agreement on test items is difficult. For example, should fourth-graders be expected to understand fractions, graphs, and simple geometry, or should the emphasis be on basic operations with whole numbers? Even specific items may inadvertently be culturally biased. One item testing fourth-grade math on the most recent TIMSS was as follows:

> Al wanted to find out how much his cat weighed. He weighed himself and noted that the scale read 57 kg. He then stepped on the scale holding his cat and found that it read 62 kg. What was the weight of the cat in kilograms?
>
> Answer: _____ kilograms

This is simple subtraction. However, 40 percent of U.S. fourth-graders got it wrong. Were they unable to subtract 57 from 62, or did they not understand the example, or did the abbreviation for kilograms confuse them because—unlike children in most nations—they are more familiar with pounds? On this item, children from Yemen were at the bottom, with 95 percent of them failing. Is that because few of them have cats for pets or weigh themselves on a scale?

Gender Differences in School Performance

In addition to ethnic and economic differences in the achievement scores, many critics note gender differences. Some argue that these differences are biological and thus that schools should not be blamed for them. For instance, the 2006 PIRLS finds girls ahead of boys in verbal skills in every nation. A possible reason is that processing speed develops more slowly in boys, a finding that implies the existence of differences in male and female brains (Camarata & Woodcock, 2006). In math and science, boys traditionally were ahead of girls, but the recent TIMSS finds this no longer to be true. In the 2007 TIMSS, boys overall were 10 points higher than girls, but national and economic differences were far greater. For example, the district of Hong Kong, with a score of 667, was 443 points ahead of the lowest-scoring nation (Yemen, 224); within the United States, the high- and low-SES difference was 103 points. Such results lead to a *gender-similarities hypothesis* that males and females are similar on most test measures, with "trivial" exceptions (Hyde et al., 2008, p. 494).

>> **Response for Parents** (from page 337) No. In fact, these are prime years for moral education. You might travel those 50 miles once or twice a week or recruit other parents to organize a local program. Whatever you do, don't skip moral instruction. Discuss and demonstrate your moral and religious values, and help your children meet other children who share those values.

Catching Up with the West These Iranian girls are acting out a poem they have memorized from their third-grade textbook. They attend school in a UNICEF-supported Global Education pilot project. Their child-centered classes encourage maximum participation.

The gender gap is narrow on tests, but school performance still shows gender differences. In middle childhood, girls typically get higher grades than boys do. Then at puberty, girls' achievement dips. Many reasons for these differences have been suggested (Williams & Ceci, 2007): Young girls may have an easier time sitting at their desks and concentrating (because of brain maturation); girls at puberty may fear appearing smarter than boys; since most elementary school teachers are women, girls in the early grades may feel (or be) more encouraged. Or perhaps when children begin to prepare for adult roles, they seek the skills and jobs that characterize people of their sex (Weisgram et al., 2010).

Research on fifth-graders with high IQs found an intriguing gender difference: When academic material became confusing, girls were less likely to persevere but boys enjoyed the challenge (Dweck, 2007). Such discrepancies could be explained by nature, nurture, or a combination of the two. However, remember that whenever comparing scores of males and females, either person by person or nation by nation, only a small bit of the difference seems to be due to biological sex.

In the United States

The relatively low performance of U.S. children on international tests has led to many ideas for improving education. As you will see, developmental theories have been used to support some ideas—though not always well.

National Standards

In the United States, the reality that U.S. children were below those in many other nations led to the **No Child Left Behind Act** of 2001 (NCLB), a federal law that promotes high national standards for public schools. One controversial aspect of the law is the requirement for frequent testing to measure whether standards are being met. One unfortunate result is that children of middling achievement are pushed to make sure they meet the benchmark, but children far above it are ignored because they will do well enough without help. Children far below are ignored as well, because they will never be average. If schools do not meet certain benchmarks, parents can transfer their children out. Low-scoring schools lose funding and may close.

No Child Left Behind Act A U.S. law enacted in 2001 that was intended to increase accountability in education by requiring states to qualify for federal educational funding by administering standardized tests to measure school achievement.

How Many Fingers? It looks as if teacher Alvin Yardley and fourth-grader Matthew are fully engaged in figuring out a math problem. However, a curriculum that includes solving math problems by counting fingers is one of the reasons U.S. fourth-graders score far below those in East Asia. Some critics blame the teachers, some the students, others the schools, and still others the culture.

Some states (e.g., Utah) have opted out of No Child Left Behind, preferring their own tests and standards, even though they lose federal funds by doing so. Many states developed their own standards and then created achievement tests that allow most schools to progress (and thus get federal funds). Many political leaders agree with the goals of NCLB (accountability and higher achievement) but not with the strategies, and strong opinions for and against No Child Left Behind are common—such as two opposite opinions expressed in the same issue of *Science* (Hanushek, 2009; Koretz, 2009). NCLB troubles those who value the arts, social studies, or physical education because those subjects are often squeezed out when reading and math achievement is the priority (Rentner, 2006).

National Assessment of Educational Progress (NAEP) An ongoing and nationally representative measure of U.S. children's achievement in reading, mathematics, and other subjects over time; nicknamed "the Nation's Report Card."

In the United States, a series of federally sponsored tests called the **National Assessment of Educational Progress (NAEP)** measure achievement in reading, mathematics, and other subjects. Many critics believe that state tests are inadequate measures of learning and that the NAEP is better (Applegate et al., 2009). One reason is that fewer children achieve proficiency levels in various subjects on the NAEP than on state tests (see Figures 12.4 and 12.5), and the TIMSS shows that even the NAEP itself may overestimate achievement (Cavanagh, 2007).

Disagreement about state tests has led to another effort, the Common Core Standards Initiative, developed by the National Governors Association. The gover-

FIGURE 12.4

Better or Worse? Should a country's education policy emphasize helping more students become "proficient" or better in mathematics or trying to make sure that fewer students score "below basic"? The United States seems to be choosing the former policy, with more resources allocated to the schools where students score high in math achievement.

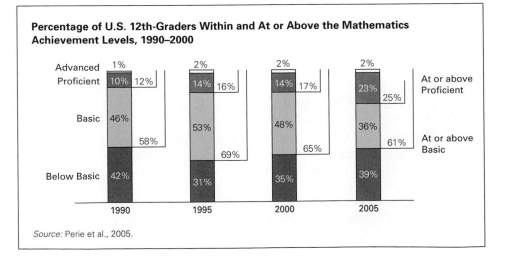

Percentage of U.S. 12th-Graders Within and At or Above the Mathematics Achievement Levels, 1990–2000

Source: Perie et al., 2005.

nors of all 50 states designated a group of experts to consider all the state, federal, and international standards for education and develop a Common Core, finalized in 2010, for use nationwide. The standards are quite specific, with half a dozen or more specifics in each subject for each grade. Table 12.5 provides a sample of the specific standards.

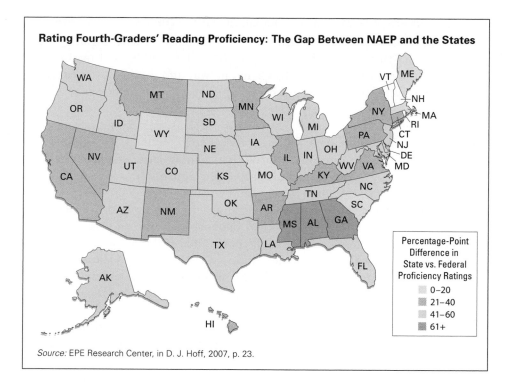

Rating Fourth-Graders' Reading Proficiency: The Gap Between NAEP and the States

Percentage-Point Difference in State vs. Federal Proficiency Ratings
- 0–20
- 21–40
- 41–60
- 61+

Source: EPE Research Center, in D. J. Hoff, 2007, p. 23.

FIGURE 12.5

Local Standards Each state sets its own level of proficiency, which helps states in which children score low on the NAEP to obtain more federal money for education. That practice may undercut high standards for student learning.

TABLE 12.5

The Common Core: Sample Items for Each Grade

Grade	Reading and Writing	Math
Kindergarten	Pronounce the primary sound for each consonant	Know number names and the count sequence
First	Decode regularly spelled one-syllable words	Relate counting to addition and subtraction (e.g., by counting 2 more to add 2)
Second	Decode words with common prefixes and suffixes	Measure the length of an object twice, using different units of length for the two measurements; describe how the two measurements relate to the size of the unit chosen
Third	Decode multisyllabic words	Understand division as an unknown-factor problem; for example, find $32 \div 8$ by finding the number that makes 32 when multiplied by 8
Fourth	Use combined knowledge of all letter–sound correspondences, syllable patterns, and morphology (e.g., roots and affixes) to read accurately unfamiliar multisyllabic words in context and out of context	Apply and extend previous understandings of multiplication to multiply a fraction by a whole number
Fifth	With guidance and support from peers and adults, develop and strengthen writing as needed by planning, revising, editing, rewriting, or trying a new approach	Graph points on the coordinate plane to solve real-world and mathematical problems

Source: National Governor's Association, 2010

All This and More This is a small sample of the elements in the Common Core, but it is enough for you to see that the grade-by-grade standards are explicit and not easy. Teachers are encouraged to make sure all the children in each grade achieve the skills and knowledge listed for that grade.

Most states have adopted this Common Core, a few states have rejected it, and several are undecided. These national standards are higher than most state standards, and thus adopting them adds pressure to many educators. One of the few states where standards were higher than the Common Core (Massachusetts) nonetheless adopted the national standards in order to allow students and teachers to move from one place to another without being confused.

Reading Wars, Math Wars, and Cognitive Theory

To help you understand why children have been confused by teaching in the past, we now explain the disputes in teaching methods for reading and math. Many children were taught these core subjects in one way and were confronted by another method when they changed schools (or even changed grades or teachers), losing ground as a result.

Clashes over teaching reading have led to "serious, sometimes acrimonious debate, fueling the well-named 'reading wars'" (Keogh, 2004, p. 93). The dispute pitted advocates of the **phonics approach** (teaching letter–sound correspondence) versus advocates of the **whole-language approach** (which encourages all language—talking, listening, reading, and writing).

The phonics proponents believe that decoding letters and sounds is essential to reading and that, without it, children will flounder and become frustrated. This is particularly likely if families have not prepared their children for reading. Without phonics, many of them fail. One critic said such failures occurred because a "child-centered anti-academic" approach does not teach the basics of reading, rendering children helpless without explicit standards and foundations (Hirsch, 2008, p. 9).

The whole-language proponents counter that phonics drills destroy motivation, reduce comprehension, and lead to the "fourth-grade slump," when 10-year-olds no longer want to learn. Offering children a choice of books on various subjects, encouraging children to read what they have written to each other, and guiding learners within their particular zone of proximal development are all part of the whole-language approach. As you can see, this approach can be seen as an application of the ideas of Vygotsky.

The other battle involves math. According to one report, "U.S. mathematics instruction has been scorched in the pedagogical blaze known as the 'math wars'—a divide between those who see a need for a greater emphasis on basic skills in math and others who say students lack a broader, conceptual understanding of the subject" (Cavanagh, 2005, p. 1).

Historically, children in the United States memorized number facts, such as the multiplication tables, filling page after page of workbooks. In reaction to this approach, many educators, inspired again by Piaget and Vygotsky, sought to make math instruction more active and engaging—less a matter of memorization than of discovery. Children used blocks or marks to add and subtract; algebra was introduced in middle childhood because the idea of an unknown added mystery to math. Curiosity, discovery, peer discussion of problems were all considered more important than memorizing formulas or facts.

As you remember, the newest cognitive approach is information processing, which stresses a step-by-step sequence in learning. That might seem to support explicit, sequenced standards such as phonics and number facts, and you can see evidence of this in the move toward national and international tests and in the Common Core standards. However, before deciding that current cognitive theory supports one side of these wars, you need to remember that all children are great learners and that they learn in various ways. That means that phonics may be

phonics approach Teaching reading by first teaching the sounds of each letter and of various letter combinations.

whole-language approach Teaching reading by encouraging early use of all language skills—talking and listening, reading and writing.

"You Wud Be Sad Like Me" Although Karla uses invented spelling, her arguments show that she is reasoning quite logically; her school-age mind is working quite well. (If you have trouble deciphering Karla's note, turn the book upside down for a translation.)

"From Karla to my mom. It's no fair that you made me let my lady bug go. What if I was your mom and I made you take your lady bug. I am sure you would be sad like me. That lady bug might have been an orphan. So you should have let me have it anyway."

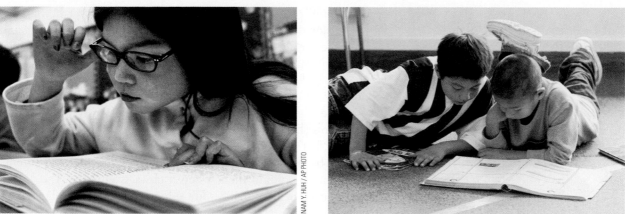

Reading with Comprehension (*left*) Reading and math scores in third-grader Monica's Illinois elementary school showed improvement under the standards set by the No Child Left Behind Act. However, the principal noted a cost for this success in less time spent on social studies and other subjects. (*right*) Some experts believe that children should have their own books and be able to read them wherever and however they want. This strategy seems to be working with Josue and Cristo, two 8-year-olds who were given books through their after-school program in Rochester, Washington.

essential for children who need help learning how to sound out new words; the whole-language approach may be needed to help children expand their knowledge base.

Similar resolution is available in math. TIMSS experts videotaped 231 math classes in three nations—Japan, Germany, and the United States (Stigler & Hiebert, 2009). The U.S. teachers presented math at a lower level than did their German and Japanese counterparts, with more definitions but less connection to what the students had already learned. Math was a dull subject because their "teachers seem to believe that learning terms and practicing skills is not very exciting" (p. 89).

In contrast, the Japanese teachers were excited about math instruction, working collaboratively and structuring lessons so that the children developed proofs and alternative solutions, alone and in groups. Teachers used social interaction and followed an orderly sequence (lessons built on previous knowledge). Such teaching reflected all three theories of cognition: problem solving from Piaget, learning collaboratively from Vygotsky, and sequencing from information processing. Remember that Japanese students excelled at math on the TIMSS, which suggests that all three theories might be relevant.

Who Determines Educational Practice?

In most nations, matters regarding public education—including curriculum, funding, teacher training, and so on—are set by the central government. In the United States, by contrast, local jurisdictions provide most of the funds and guidelines. Parents determine education as well, not only by the mesosystem of parent–teacher conferences and parent–teacher associations (PTAs), but by choosing residences based on zoning for public schools, by paying for private schools, or by home schooling (illegal in some nations). Charter schools and vouchers are two recent phenomena in the United States that signify the role of parents and local communities in education.

Charter schools are funded and licensed by states or local districts and also have private money and sponsors. They are exempt from some regulations that

"The path to becoming an astronaut is rougher than I thought."

Especially for School Administrators
Children who wear uniforms in school tend to score higher on reading tests. Why? (see response, page 345)

charter school A public school with its own set of standards that is funded and licensed by the state or local district in which it is located.

Collaborative Learning Japanese children are learning mathematics in a more structured and socially interactive way than are their North American counterparts.

voucher Permission for a parent to choose the school for the child, with some or all of the cost of that's chld's education borne by the local government. Parents who have vouchers for their children often can choose a public or private school, although the specifics vary a great deal from one jurisdiction to another.

apply to public schools. Most have some control over admissions and expulsions, and for that reason they are more racially segregated and have fewer children with special needs. Compared with public schools, standards are higher, teachers work longer, and school size is smaller—all factors known to enhance learning. Some charter schools are remarkably successful; others are not—and overall, children and teachers leave charter schools more often than they leave other schools (Education Sector, 2009).

In an effort to increase competition between schools, some jurisdictions have issued pay **vouchers** for students, allowing parents to choose a school and then, when a child is enrolled, the school collects the money for that child's education. One complication is that some families choose private, church-sponsored schools, thus violating the separation of church and state because funding comes from the public purse. Another complication is that parents may not choose well. For example, many good primary schools have small class sizes and nightly homework, but several nations whose children score high on international tests also have large class sizes (Korea's average is 26; that of the United States is 15). Furthermore, data find that fourth-graders with no homework have higher achievement scores than do those with homework (Snyder & Dillow, 2010). This is not definitive—perhaps weaker students are assigned to smaller classes with more homework—but it does raise doubts.

Should developmental experts decide what children should learn and how? Probably not. It is apparent from this chapter that children are great learners. However, what and how they learn is determined by their culture. Every developmental theory can lead to suggestions for teaching and learning (Farrar & Al-Qatawneh, 2010), but none endorse one curriculum or method to the exclusion of all others.

There is, however, one solid conclusion that almost all social scientists would endorse: More quantitative and qualitative research is needed. A 19-member panel of experts seeking the best math curricula for the United States examined 16,000 studies but "found a serious lack of studies with adequate scale and design for us

Chance or Design These third-graders are using dice to play a game that may teach them multiplication.

Observation Quiz This is a charter school in New Jersey. What three signs are visible here that few typical public schools share? (see answer, page 347)

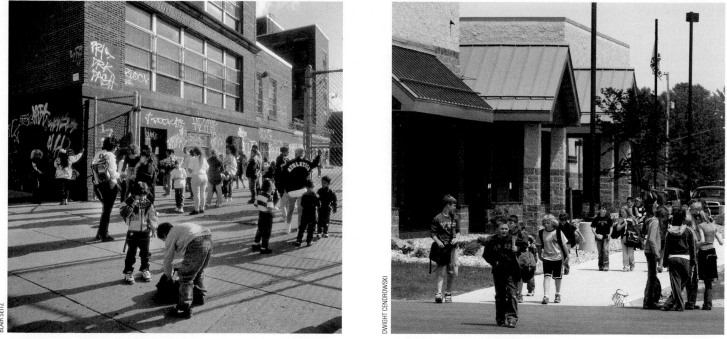

Coming and Going These photos are of students arriving *(left)* and leaving *(right)* their local public schools. Because each jurisdiction pays for the education of the children, class size, teacher quality, and—as evidenced by the contrast between Philadelphia and Ann Arbor—buildings vary markedly from one town or city to another.

to reach conclusions" (Faulkner, quoted in Mervis, 2008, p. 1605). Similarly, a review of home schooling, charter schools, and vouchers complains of "the difficulty of interpreting the research literature on this topic, most of which is biased and far from approaching balanced social science" (Boyd, 2007, p. 7). The same complaint could apply to research on the reading and math wars, controversies about testing and standards, and mixed results on class size and homework: All would benefit from large-scale, controlled studies.

Fortunately, some such research is under way, and compared to even a decade ago, much more national and international interest in education is evident. School-age children are great learners; soon we will know how best to teach them.

SUMMING UP

Societies throughout the world recognize that school-age children are avid learners and that educated citizens are essential to economic development, which has led to increased enrollment: More than 90 percent of the world's 6- to 11-year-olds are in school. Schools differ in what and how children are taught, and international tests find some nations are far more successful than others in educating their young. Test scores, as well as the nature and content of education, raise ideological and political passions: Examples are found in the reading wars, the math wars, and many other aspects of the overt and the hidden curricula. Research finds that direct instruction (in phonics; in mathematical symbols and procedures; in the vocabulary, grammar, and syntax of second languages) is useful. Also crucial are motivation, pride, and social interaction. School-age children are great learners, but they cannot learn everything. Adults must decide the specifics.

>> **Response for School Administrators**
(from page 343) The relationship reflects correlation, not causation. Wearing uniforms is more common when the culture of the school emphasizes achievement and study, with strict discipline in class and a policy of expelling disruptive students.

SUMMARY

Building on Theory

1. According to Piaget, middle childhood is the time of concrete operational thought, when egocentrism diminishes and logical thinking begins. School-age children can understand classification and conservation, and they develop transitive inference.

2. Vygotsky stressed the social context of learning, including the specific lessons of school and learning from peers and adults. Culture affects not only what children learn but also how they learn.

3. An information-processing approach examines each step of the thinking process, from input to output, using the computer as a model. This approach is useful for understanding memory, perception, and expression.

4. Memory begins with information that reaches the brain from the sense organs. Then selection processes allow some information to reach working memory. Finally, long-term memory stores images and ideas indefinitely, retrieving parts when needed.

5. Selective attention, a broader knowledge base, logical strategies for retrieval, and faster processing advance every aspect of cognition. Children become better at controlling and directing their thinking as the prefrontal cortex matures. Metacognition advances.

Language

6. Language learning improves in many practical ways, including expanded vocabulary, as words are logically linked together and the understanding of metaphors begins.

7. Children of low SES are usually lower in linguistic skills, primarily because they hear less language and because adult expectations for their learning are low.

8. Children excel at pragmatics during middle childhood, often using one code with their friends and another in school. Many children learn a second language, succeeding if they are well taught, while speaking their first language at home.

Teaching and Learning

9. Nations and experts agree that education is critical during middle childhood. The vast majority of the world's children now attend primary school. Schools differ in what and how they teach.

10. International assessments are useful as comparisons, partly because few objective measures of learning are available. Reading is assessed with the PIRLS, math and science with the TIMSS. On both measures, children in East Asia excel and children in the United States are middling.

11. In the United States, the No Child Left Behind Act and the National Assessment of Educational Progress (NAEP) attempt to raise the standard of education, with mixed success. A Common Core of standards developed with the sponsorship of the governors of the 50 states is an effort to raise national standards and improve accountability.

12. The reading wars pitted advocates of phonics against advocates of the whole-language approach. Math learned by rote and math learned via social interaction are the two sides of the math wars. A truce has been reached, however. Research finds that both methods may be needed, as children require both basic skills and more advanced thinking.

13. Cultural differences in assumptions about education are frequent, but scientific research on the best way for children to learn is scarce. For example, many people believe that children learn better in small classes, but the research is inconclusive.

KEY TERMS

concrete operational thought (p. 321)
classification (p. 322)
transitive inference (p. 322)
sensory memory (p. 326)
working memory (p. 326)
long-term memory (p. 327)
knowledge base (p. 327)

control processes (p. 327)
metacognition (p. 327)
pragmatics (p. 330)
hidden curriculum (p. 335)
immersion (p. 336)
bilingual schooling (p. 336)
ESL (English as a second language) (p. 336)

Progress in International Reading Literacy Study (PIRLS) (p. 337)
Trends in Math and Science Study (TIMSS) (p. 337)
No Child Left Behind Act (p. 339)

National Assessment of Educational Progress (NAEP) (p. 340)
phonics approach (p. 342)
whole-language approach (p. 342)
charter school (p. 343)
voucher (p. 344)

WHAT HAVE YOU LEARNED?

Building on Theory

1. Why did Piaget call cognition in middle childhood *concrete operational* thought?

2. How would you express classification in categories of transportation or plants?

3. How might you use transitive inference when trying to talk with someone you have not met before?

4. How do Vygotsky and Piaget differ in their understanding of middle childhood?

5. If children never went to school, how would cognitive development occur?

6. What have developmentalists learned from child vendors in Brazil?

7. How does information processing differ from traditional theories of cognition?

8. What aspects of memory do not change much during middle childhood?

9. What aspects of memory change markedly during middle childhood?

10. How might metacognitive skills help a college student?

Language

11. How does the process of learning language differ between age 3 and age 10?

12. What metaphors are better understood by adolescents and what by senior citizens?

13. Why are prefixes and suffixes useful in expanding vocabulary?

14. Why would a child's code be criticized by teachers but admired by friends?

15. How does metacognition affect the ability to learn something new?

16. Which factors affect a child's ability to learn grammar and advanced vocabulary?

17. What was the hidden curriculum of your primary school?

Teaching and Learning

18. What is the best way to teach a second language in middle childhood?

19. What are the benefits and liabilities of teaching all children in English-only classes?

20. Why do nations vary in the religious education they provide in school?

21. Why do some nations set an educational goal of all children becoming bilingual?

22. Why are international tests of learning taken in some nations but not all?

23. What national, SES, and gender differences are found on educational tests?

24. Why are some disagreements about education called "wars," not merely differences?

25. What problems does the Common Core attempt to solve?

APPLICATIONS

1. Visit a local elementary school and look for the hidden curriculum. For example, do the children line up? Why or why not, when and how? Does gender, age, ability, or talent affect the grouping of children or the selection of staff? What is on the walls? Are parents involved? If so, how? For everything you observe, speculate about the underlying assumptions.

2. Interview a 7- to 11-year-old child to find out what he or she knows *and understands* about mathematics. Relate both correct and incorrect responses to the logic of concrete operational thought.

3. What do you remember about how you learned to read? Compare your memories with those of two other people, one at least 10 years older and the other at least 5 years younger than you are. Can you draw any conclusions about effective reading instruction? If so, what are they? If not, why not?

4. Talk to two parents of primary school children. What do they think are the best and worst parts of their children's education? Ask specific questions and analyze the results.

>> Answer to Observation Quiz (from page 344) Carpets and rugs, students lying down to do schoolwork, clipboards and dice—all are highly unusual for traditional schools.

>>ONLINE CONNECTIONS

To accompany your textbook, you have access to a number of online resources, including quizzes for every chapter of the book, flashcards (in English and Spanish), critical thinking questions, and case studies. For access to any of these links, go to www.worthpublishers.com/bergerls8e. In addition to these free resources, you'll also find links to the podcasts, video clips, diagnostic quizzing with personalized study advice, and an ebook. Some of the videos and activities available online include:

- *Conservation.* Half empty or half full? Watch as children of different ages perform the Piagetian conservation of liquid task, and note the differences as they explain their reasoning.

- *Motivation and Learning.* Are children really "little scientists," as Piaget believed? Explores intrinsic motivation and classroom strategies that inspire it.

CHAPTER

Middle Childhood: Psychosocial Development

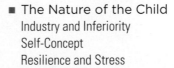

WHAT WILL YOU KNOW?

1. Is it best for children to have high self-esteem?
2. What makes a child resilient, bouncing back after stress?
3. Ideally, should all children live with their married biological parents?
4. What can be done to stop a school bully?
5. Why do the morals of children sometimes clash with the morals of adults?

A student of mine drove to a garage to get a flat tire fixed. She wrote:

> As I pulled up, I saw a very short boy sitting at the garage door. I imagined him to be about 8 or 9 years old and wondered why he was sitting there by himself. He directed me to park, and summoned a man who looked at my tire and spoke to the boy in a language I did not understand. This little boy then lifted my car with a jack, removed all the bolts, and fixed the flat. I was in shock. When I paid the man (who was his father), I asked how long his son had been doing this. He said about three years.
>
> [adapted from Tiffany, personal communication, March 15, 2008]

Adults like Tiffany are shocked to learn that many of the world's children are forced to work, in defiance of the United Nations' declaration that children have the right

> to be protected from economic exploitation and from performing any work that is likely to be hazardous or to interfere with the child's education, or to be harmful to the child's health or physical, mental, spiritual, moral, or social development.
>
> [Convention on the Rights of the Child]

Caught in a Net Forced child labor, in which young bodies are exploited and young minds are neglected, is never beneficial. These boys are among the thousands who work in the fishing industry on Ghana's Lake Volta. Their impoverished parents gave them to fishermen, hoping that they would get some education and an apprenticeship in fishing. They are receiving neither; instead, they, like the fish they catch, are tangled in a net.

In 2008, the International Labour Organization (ILO) of the United Nations estimated that this right was violated for 165 million child laborers worldwide.

Did the tire-changer's work harm him? The answer is not obvious. With almost every aspect of middle childhood, specific details are crucial to understanding. As this chapter explains, all children need friends, families, and skills, but some peers are destructive, some families are harmful, and some skills should not be mastered. This chapter describes circumstances that affect a child's "physical, mental, spiritual, moral, or social development." You will learn when influences such as child labor, peer culture, bullying, single-parent families, poverty, divorce, and so on are harmful and when they are not. We begin with the children themselves and then discuss families, peers, and morality.

>> The Nature of the Child

As explained in the previous two chapters, steady growth, brain maturation, and intellectual advances make middle childhood a time when children gain independence and autonomy (see At About This Time). They acquire an "increasing ability to regulate themselves, to take responsibility, and to exercise self-control"—all strengths that make this a period of positive growth (Huston & Ripke, 2006, p. 9).

One simple result is that school-age children can finally care for themselves. They not only feed themselves but make their own dinner, not only dress themselves but pack their own suitcases, not only walk to school but organize games with friends at the playground. They venture outdoors alone, with boys in particular putting some distance between themselves and home, as they engage in activities without their parents' awareness or approval (Munroe & Romney, 2006). This budding independence fosters growth.

AT ABOUT THIS TIME
Signs of Psychosocial Maturation Between Ages 6 and 11
Children are likely to have specific chores to perform at home.
Children are likely to have a weekly allowance.
Children are expected to tell time, and they have set times for various activities.
Children have more homework, some assignments over several days.
Children are less often punished physically, more often verbally or with loss of privileges.
Children try to conform to peers in clothes, language, and so on.
Children voice preferences about their after-school care, lessons, and activities.
Children use media (TV, computers, video games) without adult supervision.
Children are responsible for younger children, pets, and, in some places, work.
Children strive for independence from parents.

Industry and Inferiority

One particular characteristic of school-age children, throughout the centuries and in every culture, is that they are industrious, busily and actively mastering whatever skills their culture values.

Erikson's Insights

industry versus inferiority The fourth of Erikson's eight psychosocial crises, during which children attempt to master many skills, developing a sense of themselves as either industrious or inferior, competent or incompetent.

The tension between feeling productive and feeling useless is the fourth psychosocial crisis highlighted by Erik Erikson: **industry versus inferiority.** Erikson noted that middle childhood is a time when the child "must forget past hopes and wishes, while his exuberant imagination is tamed and harnessed to the laws of impersonal things," becoming "ready to apply himself to given skills and tasks" (Erikson, 1963, pp. 258, 259).

Think of learning to read and add—painstaking and boring tasks. For instance, how exciting can it be to slowly sound out "Jane has a dog" or to write "3 + 4 = 7" for the hundredth time? Yet school-age children busily practice reading and math: They are intrinsically motivated to read a page, finish a worksheet, memorize a spelling word, color in a map, and so on. Similarly, they enjoy collecting, categorizing, and counting whatever they accumulate—perhaps stamps, stickers, stones, or seashells.

Overall, children judge themselves as either *industrious* or *inferior*—that is, competent or incompetent, productive or failing, winners or losers. Being productive is intrinsically joyous, and it fosters the self-control that is a crucial defense against emotional problems (Bradley & Corwyn, 2005).

Freud on Latency

Sigmund Freud described this period as **latency,** a time when emotional drives are quiet and unconscious sexual conflicts are submerged. Some experts complain that "middle childhood has been neglected at least since Freud relegated these years to the status of an uninteresting 'latency period'" (Huston & Ripke, 2006, p. 7).

But in one sense, at least, Freud was correct: Sexual impulses are quiet. Even when children were betrothed before age 12 (rare today, but not uncommon in earlier centuries), the young husband and wife had little interaction. Everywhere, boys and girls typically choose to be with others of their sex (Munroe & Romney, 2006). Indeed, boys who write "Girls stay out!" and girls who complain that "boys smell bad" are quite typical. Parents sometimes worry about sexual predators. However, school-age children are not sexual beings; strangers rarely attempt to seduce children who have yet to reach puberty (Wolak et al., 2008).

Self-Concept

The following self-description could have been written by many 10-year-olds:

> I'm nice to people and can keep secrets. Mostly I am nice to my friends, although if I get in a bad mood I sometimes say something that can be a little mean. I try to control my temper. . . . I also like myself because I know my parents like me and so do other kids. That helps you like yourself.

> *[quoted in Harter, 1999, p. 48]*

This excerpt (written by a scholar who studies the developing self-concept) captures the nature of school-age children. It includes *effortful control* ("I try to control my temper"), loyalty ("can keep secrets"), and appreciation from peers and parents ("I know my parents like me and so do other kids"), all of which are explained soon. Most children, like the one described above, are happy with themselves and have friends who appreciate them.

The Me-Self

The schoolchild's self-concept no longer mirrors the parents' perspective. Every theory and every perceptive observer notes that school-age children are much more concerned with the opinions of their peers than those of their parents because during preadolescence, "the peer group exerts an increasingly salient socializing function" (Thomaes et al., 2010, p. 812).

In describing school-age children's self-concept, it is useful to distinguish between "two distinct but intimately intertwined aspects of self" (Harter, 2006, p. 508): the "I-self" and the "me-self." The I-self is the self as subject—a person who thinks, acts, and feels independently. The me-self is the self as object—a person reflected, validated, and critiqued by others (Harter, 2006).

The I-self predominates in early childhood, but the me-self ascends in middle childhood. This is evident in **social comparison,** which is comparing one's attributes to those of other people (Carpendale & Lewis, 2004; Davis-Kean et al.,

Celebrating Spring No matter where they live, 7- to 11-year-olds seek to understand and develop whatever skills are valued by their culture. They do so in active, industrious ways, as described in every theory. This is illustrated here, as four friends in Assam, northeastern India, usher in spring with a Bihu celebration. Soon they will be given sweets and tea, which is the sociocultural validation of their energy, independence, and skill.

latency Freud's term for middle childhood, during which children's emotional drives and psychosexual needs are quiet (latent). Freud thought that sexual conflicts from earlier stages are only temporarily submerged, bursting forth again at puberty.

social comparison The tendency to assess one's abilities, achievements, social status, and other attributes by measuring them against those of other people, especially one's peers.

No Reason to Cry Over Spilt Milk Friendship and useful chores both correlate with happy children, as these boys seem to be.

effortful control The ability to regulate one's emotions and actions through effort, not simply through natural inclination.

2009). Ideally, social comparison with peers helps school-age children value themselves and abandon the imaginary, rosy self-evaluation of preschoolers. However, some children—especially those from minority ethnic or religious groups—become aware of social prejudices they need to overcome (Kiang & Harter, 2008; McKown & Strambler, 2009).

For all children, their increasing self-understanding and social awareness come at a price. Self-criticism and self-consciousness rise from ages 6 to 11, and "by middle childhood this [earlier] overestimate of their ability or judgments decreases" (Davis-Kean et al., 2009, p. 184) while self-esteem falls. Children's self-concept becomes increasingly vulnerable to the opinions of others, even other children whom they do not know (Thomaes et al., 2010). In addition, partly because children think concretely during middle childhood, materialism increases, and attributes adults might find superficial become important, which makes self-esteem more fragile (Chaplin & John, 2007). Insecure 10-year-olds might especially want the latest shoes, cell phones, and so on.

Complications of Unrealistic Self-Esteem

Academic and social competence are aided by this more realistic self-perception (Baumeister et al., 2003). Unrealistically high self-esteem reduces **effortful control** (deliberately modifying one's impulses and emotions), which lowers a child's achievement and increases aggression. The same consequences occur if self-esteem is unrealistically low.

Ideally, "children develop feelings of self-esteem, competence, and individuality during middle childhood as they begin comparing themselves with peers" (Ripke et al., 2006, p. 261). A program that teaches anxious children to confide in friends as well as to understand their own emotions helps them develop a better self-concept; such programs have been successful not only in the United States but also in many other cultures (Siu, 2007). After-school activities, particularly sports, can provide a foundation for friendship and realistic self-esteem. Team sports benefit not only self-concept but also academic achievement (Morris & Kalil, 2006), perhaps because the effortful control needed to practice skills and to cooperate with teammates also can be applied to academics.

Culture and Self-Esteem

High self-esteem is not universally valued nor universally criticized, as many examples make clear (Yamaguchi et al., 2007). Many cultures expect children to be modest, not prideful. For example, Australians say that "tall poppies" are cut down, and the Japanese discourage social comparison aimed at making oneself feel superior (Toyama, 2001).

Although Japanese children often excel at mathematics on international tests, only 17 percent have a high opinion of their math ability. In the United States, 53 percent of the students taking the TIMSS (Trends in Math and Science Study) are very confident of their math ability, yet they score significantly lower than the Japanese (Snyder & Dillow, 2010). In Estonia, low self-esteem correlates with high academic achievement (Pullmann & Allik, 2008).

Currently in the United States, children's successes are praised and teachers are wary of being too critical, especially in middle childhood. For example, many schools issue report cards with grades ranging from "Excellent" to "Needs improvement" instead of from A to F. An opposite trend is found in the national reforms of education explained in Chapter 12, which rate some schools as failing. Obviously culture, cohort, and age all influence self-concept, with the long-term effects debatable (Heine, 2007).

Resilience and Stress

In infancy and early childhood, children depend on their immediate families for food, learning, and life itself. Then "experiences in middle childhood can sustain, magnify, or reverse the advantages or disadvantages that children acquire in the preschool years" (Huston & Ripke, 2006, p. 2). Children may escape destructive family influences by finding their own niche in the larger world.

Surprisingly, some children seem unscathed by early experiences. They have been called "resilient" or even "invincible." Current thinking about resilience (see Table 13.1), with insights from dynamic-systems theory, makes it clear that, although some children cope better than others, none are impervious to their past history or current context (Jenson & Fraser, 2006; Luthar et al., 2003). Some children are hardy, more like dandelions than orchids, but all are influenced by their situation (Ellis & Boyce, 2008).

Resilience has been defined as "a dynamic process encompassing positive adaptation within the context of significant adversity" (Luthar et al., 2000, p. 543). Note the three parts of this definition:

resilience The capacity to adapt well to significant adversity and to overcome serious stress.

- Resilience is *dynamic,* not a stable trait. That means a given person may be resilient at some periods but not others.
- Resilience is a *positive adaptation* to stress. For example, if rejection by a parent leads a child to establish a closer relationship with another adult, perhaps a grandparent or the parent of a neighbor child, that is positive adaptation, not mere passive endurance. Thus, the child may be resilient.
- Adversity must be *significant.* Some adversities are comparatively minor (large class size, poor vision), and some are major (victimization, neglect).

TABLE 13.1	
Dominant Ideas About Challenges and Coping in Children, 1965–Present	
1965	All children have the same needs for healthy development.
1970	Some conditions or circumstances—such as "absent father," "teenage mother," "working mom," and "day care"—are harmful for every child.
1975	All children are *not* the same. Some children are resilient, coping easily with stressors that cause harm in other children.
1980	Nothing inevitably causes harm. Indeed, both maternal employment and preschool education, once thought to be risk factors, usually benefit children.
1985	Factors beyond the family, both in the child (low birthweight, prenatal alcohol exposure, aggressive temperament) and in the community (poverty, violence), can be very risky for the child.
1990	Risk–benefit analysis finds that some children seem to be "invulnerable" to, or even to benefit from, circumstances that destroy others. (Some do well in school despite extreme poverty, for example.)
1995	No child is invincibly resilient. Risks are always harmful—if not in educational achievement, then in emotions.
2000	Risk–benefit analysis involves the interplay among all three domains (biosocial, cognitive, and psychosocial), including factors within the child (genes, intelligence, temperament), the family (function as well as structure), and the community (including neighborhood, school, church, and culture). Over the long term, most people overcome problems, but the problems are real.
2008	The focus is on strengths, not risks. Assets in the child (intelligence, personality), the family (secure attachment, warmth), the community (good schools, after-school programs), and the nation (income support, health care) must be nurtured.
2010	Strengths vary by culture and national values. Both universal ethics and local variations must be recognized and respected.

Healing Time Children who survived Hurricane Katrina participate in a fire drill at their new charter school, Lafayette Academy in New Orleans. The resumption of school routines helps them overcome the stress they experienced in the chaos of the deadly storm.

Cumulative Stress

One important discovery is that accumulated stresses over time, including minor ones (called "daily hassles"), are more devastating than an isolated major stress. Almost every child can withstand one stressful event, but repeated stresses make resilience difficult (Jaffee et al., 2007). One example comes from research on children in New Orleans who survived Hurricane Katrina (see Figure 13.1). Years after the hurricane, about half were resilient but the other half (especially those in middle childhood) were still traumatized. Their risk of developing serious psychological problems was affected not so much by the hurricane itself as by ongoing problems—frequent moves, changes in caregivers, disruption of schooling, and so on (Kronenberg et al., 2010; Viadero, 2007). Similarly, children who witness their father beating their mother are obviously stressed, but one study found that 20 percent of them were resilient, especially if their mother left the abuser, found a better life, and was not herself depressed (Graham-Bermann et al., 2009).

An international example comes from Sri Lanka, where many children were exposed to war, the 2004 tsunami, poverty, death of relatives, and relocation. The accumulated stresses, more than any single problem, increased the rate of pathology and decreased achievement. The authors point to "the importance of multiple contextual, past, and current factors in influencing children's adaptation" (Catani et al., 2010, p. 1188).

Coping measures also reduce the impact of repeated stress. One factor is the child's own interpretation. Cortisol (the stress hormone) increased in low-income children *if* they interpreted events connected to their family's poverty as a personal threat and *if* the family lacked order and routines (thus increasing daily hassles) (E. Chen et al., 2010). When low-income children did not take things personally and their family was not chaotic, they were more resilient.

FIGURE 13.1

Enough Stress for a Lifetime Many children experienced more than one kind of severe stress during Hurricane Katrina and its aftermath. That disaster inflicted more stress on the children of New Orleans than most adults ever experience in their lifetime, and its long-term impact will likely be dramatic.

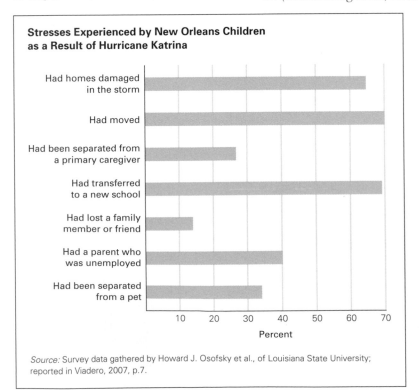

Stresses Experienced by New Orleans Children as a Result of Hurricane Katrina

Source: Survey data gathered by Howard J. Osofsky et al., of Louisiana State University; reported in Viadero, 2007, p.7.

Many adults who by objective standards were poor in childhood did not consider themselves poor; thus, they were not much affected by it.

In general, a child's interpretation of a family situation (poverty, divorce, and so on) determines how that situation affects him or her (Olson & Dweck, 2008). Some children consider the family they were born into a temporary hardship; they look forward to the day when they can leave childhood behind. Other children experience *parentification*: They act as parents, trying to take care of everyone, including their actual parents (Byng-Hall, 2008). Children who endured Katrina were affected by their thoughts, both positive and negative, even more than by factors one might expect, such as the distress of their caregivers (Kilmer & Gil-Rivas, 2010).

An intriguing study of 8- to 11-year-olds assessed the impact of two related factors on children's stress: (1) conflict between parents and (2) the child's emotional reactions to the conflict. The strongest correlate with children's psychic and academic problems was not how severe the conflict was but how vulnerable or at fault they felt. When children "do not perceive that marital conflict is threatening to them and do not blame themselves" (El-Sheikh & Harger, 2001, p. 883), they are much less troubled (see Figure 13.2).

Some children develop their own friends, activities, and skills, blossoming once they are old enough, becoming "increasingly autonomous and industrious" (Pagani et al., 2006, p. 132). Many activities, from 4-H to midnight basketball, from choir to Little League, help children develop a view of themselves as industrious, not inferior.

A 40-year study in Hawaii began with children born into poverty, often to parents who were alcoholic or mentally ill. In infancy, many of these children had symptoms of deprivation. Experts at the time predicted a troubled future for them. One was Michael, born preterm, weighing under 5 pounds. His parents were low-income teenagers, and his father was absent for the first two years of his life, returning later only to impregnate Michael's mother again and again and again. When Michael was 8 years old, both parents left him and three younger siblings with his grandparents. Yet Michael became a successful, happy, loving adult (E. Werner, 1979).

Michael was not the only resilient one. Amazingly, about one-third of the high-risk Hawaiian babies coped well. By middle childhood, they had discovered ways

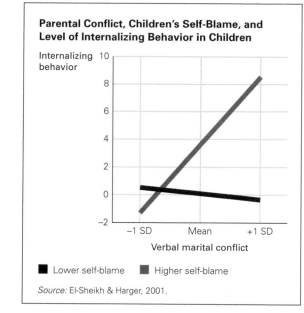

Parental Conflict, Children's Self-Blame, and Level of Internalizing Behavior in Children

Source: El-Sheikh & Harger, 2001.

FIGURE 13.2

When Parents Fight and Children Blame Themselves Husbands and wives who almost never disagree are below the first standard deviation (–1 SD) in verbal marital conflict. Couples who frequently have loud, screaming, cursing arguments are in the highest 15 percent (+1 SD). In such high-conflict households, children are not much affected—if they do not blame themselves for the situation. However, if children do blame themselves, they are likely to have internalizing problems, such as nightmares, stomachaches, panic attacks, and feelings of loneliness.

Grandmother Knows Best About 20,000 grandmothers in Connecticut are caregivers for their grandchildren. This 15-year-old boy and his 17-year-old sister came to live with their grandmother in New Haven after their mother died several years ago. This type of family can help children cope with stress, especially when the grandmother is relatively young and has her own house, as is the case here.

to avoid family stresses, to achieve in school, to make good friends, and to find adult mentors. As adults, they left family problems behind (many moved far away) and established their own healthy relationships (E. Werner & Smith, 1992, 2001).

As was true for many of these children, school and then college can be an escape. An easygoing temperament and a high IQ help (Curtis & Cicchetti, 2003), but that is not essential. In the Hawaiian study, "a realistic goal orientation, persistence, and 'learned creativity' enabled . . . a remarkable degree of personal, social, and occupational success," even for children with evident learning disabilities (E. Werner & Smith, 2001, p. 140).

Social Support and Religious Faith

Social support is a major factor that strengthens the ability to deal with stress. Compared with the homebound lives of younger children, the expanding social world of school-age children allows new possibilities (Morris & Kalil, 2006). Relatives, teachers, peers, pets, community programs (even free libraries and concerts)—all help children cope with stress (Bryant & Donnellan, 2007). One study concludes:

> When children attempt to seek out experiences that will help them overcome adversity, it is critical that resources, in the form of supportive adults or learning opportunities, be made available to them so that their own self-righting potential can be fulfilled.
>
> [Kim-Cohen et al., 2004, p. 664]

A specific example is children's use of religion, which often provides support via adults from the same faith group (P. E. King & Furrow, 2004, p. 709). Church involvement particularly helps African American children in communities rife

Become Like a Child Although the particulars vary a great deal, school-age children's impulses toward industriousness, stability, and dedication place them among the most devout members of every religious faith.

BILL ARON / PHOTOEDIT, INC.

with social stress and racial prejudice (Akiba & García Coll, 2004). Faith is psychologically protective when it helps children reinterpret their experiences (Crawford et al., 2006).

Prayer may also foster resilience. In one study, adults were required to pray for a specific person for several weeks. Their attitude about that person changed (Lambert et al., 2010). Ethics precludes such an experiment with children, but it is known that children often pray in middle childhood, expecting that prayer will make them feel better, especially when they are sad or angry (Bamford & Lagattuta, 2010). As already explained, expectations and interpretations can be powerful.

SUMMING UP

Children gain in maturity and responsibility during the school years. According to Erikson, the crisis of industry versus inferiority generates feelings of confidence or self-doubt. Freud thought latency enables children to master new skills. Often children develop more realistic self-concepts. Children cope with family stresses by becoming more independent, using school achievement, after-school activities, supportive adults, and religious beliefs to help them overcome whatever problems they face. ■

>> Families and Children

No one doubts that genes affect personality as well as ability, that peers are vital, and that schools and cultures influence what, and how much, children learn. Many people believe that parental practices also affect how children develop, an idea that led to extensive research on authoritarian, authoritative, and permissive parenting (see Chapter 10). However, some researchers suggest that genes, peers, and communities are so influential that parenting has little impact (Harris, 1998, 2002; McLeod et al., 2007).

Shared and Nonshared Environments

Many studies find that children are much less affected by *shared environment* (influences that are the same for people, such as for children raised by the same parents in the same home) than by *nonshared environment* (e.g., the different experiences two people have). Most characteristics of siblings can be traced to genes and nonshared environments, with little left over for the shared influence of having the same parents. Nonshared environment is far more influential than shared environment for personality traits (Ganiban et al., 2008), child psychopathology (Burt, 2009), and sexual orientation (Långström et al., 2010). Since shared environment has little impact on so many characteristics, perhaps being raised by the same parents has little effect.

More recent findings, however, reassert parent power. The analysis of shared and nonshared influences was correct, but the conclusion about parents was based on the false assumption that children raised together share the same home environment. If the family moves, if parents divorce, or if one or both lose a job, for example, every child is affected—but the impact depends on age, genes, resilience, and gender.

In addition, some nonshared influences—school, neighborhood, after-school activity—are not shared because family income and neighborhood contexts change (Simpkins et al., 2006). Indeed, even children who share the same genes, age, sex, and home may not have a shared environment, as the following makes clear.

MASTERFILE / RADIUS IMAGES

Family Unity Thinking about any family—even a happy, wealthy family like this one—makes it apparent that each child's family experiences differ. For instance, would you expect the 5-year-old boy to be treated the same way as his two older sisters? And how about each child's feelings toward the parents? Even though the 12-year-olds are twins, one may favor her mother while the other favors her father.

Especially for Scientists How would you determine whether or not parents treat all their children the same? (see response, page 359)

A VIEW FROM SCIENCE

"I Always Dressed One in Blue Stuff . . ."

An expert team of scientists compared 1,000 sets of monozygotic twins reared by their biological parents (Caspi et al., 2004). Obviously, the pairs were identical in genes, sex, and age. They assessed each child's temperament by asking the mothers and teachers to fill out a detailed, standardized checklist. They also asked every mother to describe each twin. Maternal attitudes ranged from very positive ("my ray of sunshine") to very negative ("I wish I never had her. . . . She's a cow, I hate her") (quoted in Caspi et al., 2004, p. 153). Many mothers described personality differences between their

twins. For example, one mother spoke of her identical-twin daughters:

> Susan can be very sweet. She loves babies . . . she can be insecure . . . she flutters and dances around. . . . There's not much between her ears. . . . She's exceptionally vain, more so than Ann. Ann loves any game involving a ball, very sporty, climbs trees, very much a tomboy. One is a serious tomboy and one's a serious girlie girl. Even when they were babies I always dressed one in blue stuff and one in pink stuff.
>
> *[quoted in Caspi et al., 2004, p. 156]*

Some mothers were much more cold and rejecting toward one twin than toward the other:

> He was in the hospital and everyone was all "poor Jeff, poor Jeff" and I started thinking, "Well, what about me? I'm the one's just had twins. I'm the one's going through this, he's a seven-week-old baby and doesn't know a thing about it" . . . I sort of detached and plowed my emotions into Mike.
>
> *[quoted in Caspi et al., 2004, p. 156]*

After she was divorced, this mother blamed Jeff for favoring his father: "Jeff would do anything for Don but he wouldn't for me, and no matter what I did for either of them [Don or Jeff] it wouldn't be right" (p. 157). She said Mike was much more lovable.

In this longitudinal study, the researchers measured personality at age 5 (by calculating, among other things, antisocial behavior as reported by kindergarten teachers) and then assessed each twin's personality two years later. They found that if the mothers were more negative toward one of their twins, that twin *became* more antisocial than the co-twin. The rejected twins were more likely to fight, steal, and hurt others at age 7 than at age 5, after all background factors were taken into account.

These researchers acknowledge that many other nonshared factors—peers, teachers, and so on—are significant. But this difference in monozygotic twins confirms that parents matter. As every sibling knows, each child's family experiences are unique.

---

family structure The legal and genetic relationships among relatives living in the same home; includes nuclear family, extended family, stepfamily, and so on.

family function The way a family works to meet the needs of its members. Children need families to provide basic material necessities, to encourage learning, to help them develop self-respect, to nurture friendships, and to foster harmony and stability.

What Must She Leave Behind? In every nation, children are uprooted from familiar places as a result of adult struggles and/or aspirations for a better life. This girl is leaving a settlement in the Gaza Strip, due to the Israeli–Palestinian conflict that has disrupted millions of lives. Worldwide, it's the children who suffer most.

Family Function and Family Structure

The data reaffirm that parents are important, which raises another question: What family structures make it likely (or unlikely) that families will function well? **Family structure** refers to the legal and genetic connections among related people living in the same household. **Family function** refers to how a family cares for its members.

Function is more important than structure in every developmental period. No matter what the structure, people need family love and encouragement. Specifics vary by age. Infants need responsive caregiving and social interaction; teenagers need freedom and guidance; young adults need peace and privacy; the aged need respect and appreciation.

What do school-age children need?

1. *Material necessities.* Although children at this stage eat, dress, and sleep without help, families can furnish food, clothing, and shelter.
2. *Learning.* Families can support, encourage, and guide education.
3. *Self-respect.* Because children become self-critical and socially aware, families can provide opportunities for success.
4. *Peer relationships.* Families can welcome friendships.
5. *Harmony and stability.* Families can provide protective, predictable routines.

No family always functions perfectly, but children worldwide fare better in families than in other structures (such as group living). The final item on the list above is especially crucial in middle childhood, when children resist change.

Ironically, many parents move from one neighborhood or school to another during these years, thinking they are securing a better life for their children. To be specific, in one year (2008) 17 percent of U.S. 5- to 9-year-olds moved from one home to another, a rate four times that of adults over age 50 (U.S. Bureau of the Census, 2010).

A surprising study of children who moved with their fathers revealed the value of continuity (Tanaka & Nakazawa, 2005). Many Japanese companies transfer junior employees from one place to another, and if the employee is a father, about half the time his family moves with him. Usually children do better, emotionally as well as academically, if they live with their fathers, so the researchers expected that children who moved would benefit. They found the opposite to be the case (Tanaka & Nakazawa, 2005). School-age children did better if they stayed put, probably because they kept their friends.

Lack of stability also seems to harm U.S. children in military families. Such children have an advantage because enlisted parents average more income and education than civilians from the same backgrounds. However, parents repeatedly depart and return, and the entire family relocates every few years (Titus, 2007). Military children (dubbed "military brats") have more emotional problems and lower school achievement than do other children of the same age and background. As one author explains:

> Military parents are continually leaving, returning, leaving again. School work suffers, more for boys than for girls, and . . . reports of depression and behavioral problems go up when a parent is deployed.

[Hall, 2008, p. 52]

Diversity of Structures

About two-thirds of all U.S. school-age children live in two-parent homes (see Table 13.2 on the next page), most often with their biological parents—an arrangement called a **nuclear family.** In U.S. nuclear families, the parents are usually married, although many European nuclear families are headed by couples who are not legally wed. Other two-adult families include adoptive parents, foster parents, grandparents without parents, a biological parent with a stepparent, and same-sex couples.

In the United States, about 28 percent of all school-age children currently live in a **single-parent family,** with one parent and no other adults. Many more children live in a single-parent family at some time before adulthood (they were born into single-parent families, or their parents divorced), but in any given year of middle childhood, about twice as many children live with two parents rather than just one.

Two-parent and single-parent structures are often contrasted with the **extended family,** which includes other relatives, usually grandparents, and often aunts, uncles, and cousins as well. In 2009, about one in six U.S. families was an extended family, an increase from 1980 (one in eight) and a decrease from 1940 (one in five) (Pew Social Trends Staff, 2010). The primary reason is financial: Extended families are more common among low-income households.

>> **Response for Scientists** (from page 357) Proof is very difficult when human interaction is the subject of investigation, since random assignment is impossible. Ideally, researchers would find identical twins being raised together and would then observe the parents' behavior over the years.

nuclear family A family that consists of a father, a mother, and their biological children under age 18.

single-parent family A family that consists of only one parent and his or her biological children under age 18.

extended family A family of three or more generations living in one household.

AP PHOTO / CHARLES REX ARBOGAST

GREG ELMS / LONELY PLANET IMAGES

The Same Situation, Many Miles Apart: Happy Families The boys in both photos are about 4 years old. Roberto *(left)* lives with his single mother in Chicago. She pays $360 a month for her two children to attend a day-care center. The youngest child in the Balmedina family *(right)* lives with his nuclear family—no day care needed—in the Philippines. Which boy has the better life? The answer is not known; family function is more crucial than family structure.

TABLE 13.2

Family Structures (with percent of U.S. 6- to 11-year-olds in each type)

Two-Parent Families (67%)

1. **Nuclear family** (54%). Named after the nucleus (the tightly connected core particles of an atom), the nuclear family consists of a husband and wife and their biological offspring under 18 years of age. About half of all school-age children live in nuclear families.

2. **Stepparent family** (9%). Divorced fathers usually remarry; divorced mothers remarry about half the time. When children from a former relationship live with the new couple in their home, that makes a stepparent family. If the stepparent family includes children born to two or more couples (such as children from the spouses' previous marriages and/or children of the new couple), that is called a *blended family*.

3. **Adoptive family** (2%). Although as many as one-third of infertile married couples adopt children, few adoptable children are available and so most adoptive couples have only one or two children. Thus, the number of school-age children who are adopted is only 2 percent, although the overall percentage of adoptive families is higher than that.

4. **Grandparents alone** (2%). Grandparents take on parenting for some school-age children because the children's biological parents are absent (dead, imprisoned, sick, addicted, and so on). This is increasing, especially in communities where many parents have died of AIDS.

5. **Two same-sex parents** (0%). Less than 1 percent of two-parent families are headed by a same-sex couple, whose legal status (married, step-, adoptive) varies.

Single-Parent Families (28%)

One-parent families are increasing, but they average fewer children than two-parent families, so the number of school-age children in such families is only 28%.

1. **Single mother, never married** (10%). Almost 40 percent of all U.S. births are to unmarried mothers, but many such mothers marry by the time the child is in school.

2. **Single mother—divorced, separated, or widowed** (13%). Although many marriages end in divorce (almost half in the United States, fewer in other nations), many divorcing couples have no children. Others remarry. Thus, only 13 percent of school-age children currently live with single, formerly married mothers.

3. **Single father** (4%). About one in five divorced, separated, or widowed fathers has physical custody of his children and raises them without a new wife.

4. **Grandparent alone** (1%). Sometimes a single grandparent (usually the grandmother) becomes the sole caregiving adult for a child.

More Than Two Adults (5%)

1. **Extended family** (5%). Some children live with a grandparent or other relatives as well as with one or both of their parents.

2. **Polygamous family** (0%). In some nations (not the United States), men can legally have several wives. This family structure is more favored by adults than children. Everywhere, polyandry (one woman, several husbands) is rare.

Source: Estimated from data in U.S. Bureau of the Census, 2010, *Statistical Abstract* and Current Population Reports: *America's Families and Living Arrangements*, 2009.

---

polygamous family A family consisting of one man, several wives, and the biological children of the man and his wives.

None of these distinctions are as simple in practice as on paper. Many parents live near relatives who share meals, offer emotional support, provide money and child care, and otherwise function as an extended family. The opposite is true as well, especially in developing nations, where many extended families create separate quarters for each set of parents, making these units somewhat like two-parent families (Georgas et al., 2006).

In some nations, the **polygamous family** (one husband with two or more wives) is not unusual. Generally, in polygamous families, income per child is reduced and education, especially for the girls, may be curtailed (Omariba & Boyle, 2007).

Connecting Structure and Function

Family structure and family function affect each other. The crucial question for schoolchildren is whether the structure makes it more or less likely that the five family functions mentioned earlier will be fulfilled. In general, nuclear families function best; their children tend to achieve in school with fewer psychological problems.

Some advantages of nuclear families begin before the wedding because education, earning potential, and emotional maturity all make it more likely that people will marry and have children, bringing personal assets to their new family. Ideally, both partners encourage each other, becoming wealthier and healthier than either would be alone. Shared parenting decreases the risk of maltreatment and makes it more likely that children will have someone to read to them, check their homework, invite their friends over, buy them new clothes, and save for their education.

Considerable controversy has focused on how well same-sex couples provide for their children. Research is particularly spotty on male–male couples, since only recently have they been able to marry and raise children, and thus longitudinal research on a large sample has not been possible. Some research on female–female couples has been published, and it seems that their children develop at least as well as children from other two-parent families (Biblarz & Stacey, 2010).

Overall, the single-parent structure functions less well for children because income and stability tend to be reduced. Most single parents fill many roles—including wage earner, daughter or son (single parents often depend on their own parents), and lover (many seek a new partner)—which makes it harder for single parents to provide steady emotional and academic support for their schoolchildren.

The stepparent structure has advantages and disadvantages for children. The primary advantage is financial, especially when compared with most single-parent families, but the primary disadvantage is instability: Compared to other nuclear families, in stepfamilies it is more likely that older children leave, new babies arrive, and the marriages themselves dissolve (Teachman, 2008a). An added complication is that many children are loyal to both biological parents, who may disagree with each other as well as with the stepparent.

Finally, ethnicity and nationality affect family structure and function. For example, many French parents do not marry, but they generally live together and

A Texas Family Two-year-old Jackson's adoptive parents have been in a committed relationship for 13 years. Their home is in Dallas, where gay couples can adopt but cannot marry.

Especially for Single Parents You have heard that children raised in one-parent families will have difficulty in establishing intimate relationships as adolescents and adults. What can you do about this possibility? (see response, page 363)

A Comfortable Combination The blended family—husband, wife, and children from both spouses' previous marriages—often breeds resentment, depression, and rebellion in the children. That is apparently not the case for the family shown here, which provides cheerful evidence that any family structure is capable of functioning well.

share child rearing, separating less often than do married couples in the United States. Since divorce is disruptive for children, this means that cohabitation functions better in France than does marriage in the United States. However, in the United States, cohabiting parents separate more often than do married parents, making the cohabiting structure worse for children. Thus, the functioning of a cohabiting family is affected by national mores (S. L. Brown, 2004).

Ethnic culture matters as well. Single parenthood is more common among African Americans (54 percent of African American 6- to 11-year-olds live with only one parent) and more accepted. As a result, relatives and friends routinely help African American single parents, who would likely be more isolated and dysfunctional if they were of another ethnicity (Cain & Combs-Orme, 2005; Taylor et al., 2008). By contrast, only 10 percent of Asian American mothers are single parents, which makes it harder for them to raise their children alone (U.S. Census Bureau, 2009).

All these are generalities: Contrary to the averages, thousands of nuclear families are destructive, thousands of single-parent families are wonderful, and thousands of stepparents provide good care. Structure and ethnicity tend to protect or undercut healthy function, but many parents overcome structural problems to support their children.

Family Trouble

Two factors interfere with family function in every structure, ethnic group, and nation: low income and high conflict. Many families experience both, because financial stress increases conflict and vice versa (McLanahan, 2009). Suppose a 6-year-old spills his milk, as every 6-year-old sometimes does. In a well-functioning, financially stable family, one parent then guides him to mop up the spill, while the other parent pours more milk, perhaps encouraging family harmony by saying, "Everyone has an accident sometimes."

What if the 6-year-old lives with a single parent struggling with overdue rent, unemployment, and an older child who wants money for a school trip? What if the last of the food stamps bought that milk? Shouting, crying, and accusations are almost inevitable (perhaps the sibling claims, "He did it on purpose," to which the 6-year-old responds, "You pushed me," and a visitor adds, "You should teach him to be careful"). As in this example, poverty makes anger spill over when the milk does.

Family income correlates with both function and structure. The effects of poverty are cumulative; low-SES (socioeconomic status) may be especially damaging for children from ages 6 to 10 (Duncan et al., 2010). Many researchers want to know exactly why income affects development. Several have developed the *family-stress model,* which holds that the crucial question about any risk factor (such as low income, divorce, single parenthood, unemployment) is whether it increases stress. Poverty is less stressful *if* low income is temporary and the family's net worth (home ownership, investments, and so on) buffers the strain (Yeung & Conley, 2008). However, if economic hardship is ongoing and parents have little education, that increases stress, making adults tense and hostile toward their partners and children (Conger et al., 2002; Parke et al., 2004). Thus, the *reaction* to poverty is crucial.

Reaction to wealth may cause problems, too. Children in high-income families develop more than their share of developmental problems. One reason may be parental pressure on the children to excel, causing stress in middle childhood and creating externalizing and internalizing problems that lead to drug use, delinquency, and poor academic performance in high school (Ansary & Luthar, 2009).

> **Research Design**
>
> **Scientists:** Greg J. Duncan, Kathleen M. Ziol-Guest, and Ariel Kalil.
>
> **Publication:** *Child Development* (2010).
>
> **Participants:** Individuals born between 1968 and 1975 to parents who were part of the Panel Study of Income Dynamics, a longitudinal study in the United States that traces the effect of income on families. Only people with repeated measures throughout childhood and adulthood (1,589 of them) were included. The goal of this study was to seek developmental outcomes, not merely correlates, of income.
>
> **Design:** Data were collected at many stages of each person's life, including detailed and repeated family economic indicators and adult body mass index (BMI), health, education, arrests, income, employment, and psychological distress.
>
> **Major conclusions:** Childhood poverty had a decided effect on adult functioning, 20 and even 30 years later, particularly on work hours and earnings. This study controlled for many factors that vary with income, such as parents' education and family structure. Childhood poverty itself, especially during middle childhood, impaired well-being in adulthood.
>
> **Comment:** Since low income correlates with large family size, single parenthood, low education, and so on, studies that simply link poverty to outcomes may reflect third variables. Because this study has longitudinal data on many individuals and variables, the conclusion—that childhood poverty itself impairs development—is probably valid.

Some intervention programs aim to teach parents to be more encouraging and patient (McLoyd et al., 2006). In low-income families, however, this focus on child-rearing methods may be misplaced. Poverty itself—with attendant problems such as inadequate schools, poor health, and the threat of homelessness—may cause stress (see the Research Design).

If that is so, more income means better family functioning. Some support for that possibility is that children in single-mother households do much better if their father pays child support even if he is not actively involved in the child's daily life (Huang, 2009). Nations that subsidize single parents (e.g., Austria and Iceland) also have smaller achievement gaps between low- and middle-SES children on the TIMSS. This is suggestive, but controversial and value-laden. Some developmentalists report that raising income does *not*, by itself, improve parenting (L. M. Berger et al., 2009).

There is no controversy about conflict: It is harmful for children, especially when adults fight about child rearing (more common in stepfamilies, divorced families, and extended families). Of course, nuclear families are not immune: Children suffer if their parents abuse each other or if one parent walks out, leaving the other distraught.

>> **Response for Single Parents** (from page 361) Do not get married mainly to provide a second parent for your child. If you were to do so, things would probably get worse rather than better. Do make an effort to have friends of both sexes with whom your child can interact.

SUMMING UP

Parents influence child development. For school-age children, families serve five crucial functions: to supply basic necessities, to encourage learning, to develop self-respect, to nurture friendships, and to provide harmony and stability. Low income and family conflict interfere with these functions, no matter what the family structure.

The nuclear, two-parent family is the most common, but many families are headed by a single parent (including more than one-fourth of all families of school-age children in the United States). Families headed by two biological parents tend to provide more income, stability, and adult attention, all of which benefit children. Families that are extended, grandparent, one-parent, stepparent, same-sex parents, or adoptive sometimes raise successful children, although each type has vulnerabilities. No structure inevitably harms children, and none (even two married biological parents) guarantee optimal function.

>> The Peer Group

Peers are increasingly important in middle childhood. Younger children learn from their friends, but their egocentrism buffers them from peer acceptance or rejection. School-age children, in contrast, are well aware of their classmates' opinions, judgments, and accomplishments.

The Culture of Children

Peer relationships, unlike adult–child relationships, involve partners who negotiate, compromise, share, and defend themselves as equals. Children learn social lessons from one another that grown-ups cannot teach. Adults sometimes command obedience, sometimes allow dominance, but always they are much older and bigger, with the values and experiences of their own cohort, not the child's.

Remember from Chapter 1 that culture includes customs and values as well as more obvious manifestations such as clothing and food. Each age group can have a culture. Adults have mixed emotions about child culture: Modern society isolates children from adults yet often restricts unsupervised play with other children, which may make it more difficult for children to form their culture (Gillis, 2008).

The **culture of children** includes the particular rules and behaviors that are passed down to younger children from slightly older ones without adult approval; it includes not only fashions and gestures but also values and rituals. Jump-rope rhymes, insults, and superstitions are often part of the peer culture. Even nursery games echo the culture of children. For instance, "Ring around the rosy/Pocketful of posy/Ashes, ashes/We all fall down," originated with children coping with death (Kastenbaum, 2006). (*Rosy* is short for *rosary*.)

culture of children The particular habits, styles, and values that reflect the set of rules and rituals that characterize children as distinct from adult society.

Throughout the world, the culture of children encourages independence from adults. Classmates pity those (especially boys) whose parents kiss them ("mama's boy"), tease children who please the teachers ("teacher's pet," "suckup"), and despise those who betray children to adults ("tattletale," "grasser," "snitch," "rat"). Keeping secrets is part of the culture of children, even as parents want to know the details of their children's lives (Gillis, 2008). A clash may develop. For instance, many children reject clothes that parents buy as too loose, too tight, too long, too short, or wrong in color, style, brand, or some other aspect that adults do not notice.

The culture of children is not always benign. For example, because communication with peers is a priority, parents are often proud because their children quickly master a second language, but parents may be upset when the children spout their peers' curses, accents, and slang. As they seek autonomy, children find friends who defy authority (J. Snyder et al., 2005), sometimes harmlessly (a child might pass a note during class), sometimes not (shoplifting, spray-painting graffiti, cigarette smoking).

Attitudes are affected by friends. Remember Yolanda and Paul (Chapter 12)?

Yolanda:
There's one friend . . . she's always been with me, in bad or good things. . . .
She's always telling me, "Keep on going and your dreams are gonna come true."

Paul:
I think right now about going Christian, right? Just going Christian, trying to do good, you know? Stay away from drugs, everything. And every time it seems like I think about that, I think about the homeboys. And it's a trip because a lot of the homeboys are my family, too, you know?

[*quoted in Nieto, 2000, pp. 220, 149*]

How to Play Boys teach each other the rituals and rules of engagement. The bigger boy shown here could hurt the smaller one, but he won't; their culture forbids it in such situations.

BOB DAEMMRICH / THE IMAGE WORKS

The Rules of the Game These young monks in Myanmar (formerly Burma) are playing a board game that adults also play, but the children have some of their own refinements of the general rules. Children's peer groups often modify the norms of the dominant culture, as is evident in everything from superstitions to stickball.

Friendship and Social Acceptance

Children want to be liked; they learn faster as well as feel happier when they have friends. Indeed, if they had to choose between being friendless but popular (widely accepted by peers) or having close friends but being unpopular, most would choose friends.

Friendships become more intense and intimate as social cognition and effortful control advance. Compared with 6-year-olds, 10-year-olds demand more of their friends, change friends less often, become more upset when a friendship breaks up, and find it harder to make new friends. Gender differences persist in activities (girls converse more, whereas boys play more active games), but both boys and girls want best friends, and not having a close friend at age 11 is likely to lead to depression at age 13 (Brendgen et al., 2010).

Most children learn during middle childhood how to be a good friend. For example, when fifth-graders were asked how they would react if other children teased their friend, almost all said they would ask their friend to do something fun with them and would reassure the friend that "things like that happen to everyone" (Rose & Asher, 2004).

Older children tend to choose best friends whose interests, values, and backgrounds are similar to their own. By the end of middle childhood, close friendships are almost always between children of the same sex, age, ethnicity, and socioeconomic status. This occurs not because children become more prejudiced over the course of middle childhood (they do not) but because they seek friends who understand and agree with them (Aboud & Amato, 2001; Aboud & Mendelson, 1998; Powlishta, 2004).

Friends and Culture Like children everywhere, these children—two 7-year-olds and one 10-year-old, of the Surma people in southern Ethiopia—model their appearance after that of slightly older children, in this case adolescents who apply elaborate body paint for courtship and stick-fighting rituals.

Observation Quiz Are they boys or girls? (see answer, page 367)

Popular and Unpopular Children

Culture and cohort affect what makes a child well liked or not. For example, in North American culture, shy children are not popular. In contrast, a study conducted in 1990 in Shanghai found that shy children were respected and often popular (X. Chen et al., 1992). Over the next 12 years, however, in Chinese culture assertiveness became more valued, especially in cities. A new survey from the same Shanghai schools found that shy children were less popular than their shy predecessors had been, and fewer children identified themselves as shy (X. Chen et al., 2005). In rural China, however, shyness was still valued and predicted adult adjustment (X. Chen et al., 2009). Obviously, cohort and context matter.

Over the years of middle childhood, two types of popular children and three types of unpopular children become apparent in the United States. In the early grades, the most popular children are "kind, trustworthy, cooperative." Around fifth grade, a new popular group appears: Children who are "athletic, cool, dominant, arrogant, and . . . aggressive" (Cillessen & Mayeux, 2004a, p. 147; Rodkin & Roisman, 2010).

Some unpopular children are *neglected,* not rejected; ignored, but not shunned. The neglected child does not enjoy school but is psychologically unharmed, especially if the child has a supportive family and outstanding talent (in music or the arts, say) (Sandstrom & Zakriski, 2004). Harm (usually depression and anger) becomes greater over the years of middle childhood for other unpopular children, both **aggressive-rejected** (disliked because they are antagonistic and confrontational) and **withdrawn-rejected** (disliked because they are timid and anxious). Children of these two types have much in common, often misinterpreting social situations, lacking emotional regulation, and experiencing mistreatment at home (Pollak et al., 2000).

aggressive-rejected Rejected by peers because of antagonistic, confrontational behavior.

withdrawn-rejected Rejected by peers because of timid, withdrawn, and anxious behavior.

social cognition The ability to understand social interactions, including the causes and consequences of human behavior.

Social Awareness

Understanding social situations, called **social cognition,** may be crucial for peer acceptance (Ladd, 2005). Social cognition begins in infancy (with *social referencing;* see Chapter 7), continues to develop in early childhood (*theory of mind;* see Chapter 9), and advances in middle childhood. For example, when siblings fight in middle childhood, those who are older tend to have a better understanding of how to resolve the conflict (discussion, compromise) (Recchia & Howe, 2009). Similarly, a two-year study began with 4½- to 8-year-olds. School-age children improved not only in social cognition but also in effortful control (their ability to control their emotions depending on the social situation). As a result, the older children had fewer externalizing or internalizing problems, according to parents' reports (N. Eisenberg et al., 2004).

Well-liked children tend to like themselves and generally assume that social slights, from a push to an unkind remark, are accidental (Clark & Symons, 2009; Dodge et al., 2006). Therefore, a social slight does not provoke fear, self-doubt, or anger, as it often does in rejected children. When a direct conflict occurs between themselves and another child, well-liked children think about the future of that relationship, compromising to maintain the friendship (Rose & Asher, 1999). These prosocial impulses and attitudes are a sign of social maturity, and they are rare in rejected children (Gifford-Smith & Rabiner, 2004).

CARTOONSTOCK.COM

WELCOME BACK CLASS!

IT'S AN ESPRESSO LATTE, I THOUGHT YOU MIGHT NEED IT.

Pity the Teacher The culture of children encourages pranks, jokes, and defiance of authorities at school. At the same time, as social cognition develops, many children secretly feel empathy for their teachers.

Bullies and Victims

From a developmental perspective, childhood bullying is connected to many other aspects of aggression, including maltreatment (Chapter 8), special needs (Chapter 11), and delinquency (Chapter 16). Here we consider bullies and victims in school during middle childhood.

Bullying is defined as repeated, systematic attacks intended to harm those who are unable or unlikely to defend themselves. It occurs in every nation, in every community, and in every kind of school (religious or secular, public or private, progressive or traditional, large or small). Bullying may be *physical* (hitting, pinching, or kicking), *verbal* (teasing, taunting, or name-calling), or *relational* (designed to destroy peer acceptance). *Cyberbullying* (using electronic means to harm

bullying Repeated, systematic efforts to inflict harm through physical, verbal, or social attack on a weaker person.

another) is a particularly devastating form of relational bullying, more common in high school than in primary school, and thus discussed in Chapter 15.

A key word in the definition of bullying is *repeated*. Almost everyone experiences isolated attacks or social slights in middle childhood, but victims of bullying endure shameful experiences again and again—being forced to hand over lunch money, laugh at insults, drink milk mixed with detergent, and so on, with no one defending them. Victims tend to be "cautious, sensitive, quiet . . . lonely and abandoned at school. As a rule, they do not have a single good friend in their class" (Olweus et al., 1999, p. 15). Although it is often thought that victims are particularly ugly or odd, this is not usually true. Victims are chosen because of their emotional vulnerability and social isolation, not their appearances.

Most victims are withdrawn-rejected, but some are aggressive-rejected. The latter are **bully-victims** (or *provocative victims*) (Unnever, 2005), "the most strongly disliked members of the peer group," with neither friends nor sympathizers (Sandstrom & Zakriski, 2004, p. 110). One study found that teachers tend to mistreat bully-victims, making their problems worse (Khoury-Kassabri, 2009).

Most bullies are *not* rejected. They have a few admiring friends (henchmen). Unless they are bully-victims, they are socially perceptive—but they lack the empathy of prosocial children. Especially over the years of middle childhood, they become skilled at avoiding adult awareness, attacking victims who can be counted on not to resist effectively. This seems to be as true for relational bullying as for physical and verbal bullying, with bully-victims suffering most, no matter what form the bullying takes (Dukes et al., 2009).

Boys bully more than girls, and during childhood most bullies pick on their own sex. Boy bullies are often big; they target smaller, weaker boys. Girl bullies are often sharp-tongued; they harass shyer, more soft-spoken girls. Boys tend to use force (physical aggression), while girls tend to mock, ridicule, or spread rumors (verbal aggression). Both sexes may also use relational aggression, especially cyberbullying, which becomes more common with age.

>> **Answer to Observation Quiz** (from page 365) They are all girls. Boys would not be likely to stand so close together. Also, the two 7-year-olds have decorated their soon-to-be budding breasts.

bully-victim Someone who attacks others and who is attacked as well. (Also called *provocative victims* because they do things that elicit bullying, such as stealing a bully's pencil.)

Picking on Someone Your Own Sex Bullies usually target victims of the same sex. Boy victims tend to be physically weaker than their tormentors, whereas girl victims tend to be socially out of step—unusually shy or self-conscious, or unfashionably dressed. In the photograph at right, notice that the bystanders seem very interested in the bullying episode, but no one is about to intervene.

MICHELLE D. BRIDEWELL / PHOTOEDIT, INC.

JONATHAN NOUROK / PHOTOEDIT, INC.

Causes and Consequences of Bullying

Bullying may originate with a genetic predisposition or a brain abnormality, but parents, teachers, and peers usually teach young children to rein in aggressive impulses, part of developing effortful control. However, the opposite may occur (Granic & Patterson, 2006). Families that create insecure attachment, provide a stressful home life, are ineffective at discipline, or include hostile siblings tend to intensify children's aggression. Peers are influential as well. Some peer groups approve of relational bullying, and children in those groups are influenced more by their peers than by their own beliefs, increasing relational bullying (N. E. Werner & Hill, 2010). On the other hand, when students themselves disapprove of bullying, its incidence is reduced (Guerra & Williams, 2010).

The consequences of bullying can echo for years. Many victims develop depression; many bullies become increasingly cruel. However, this is not inevitable. Both bullies and victims can be identified in first grade and "need active guidance and remediation" before their behavior patterns become destructive (Leadbeater & Hoglund, 2009, p. 857). Unless they are deterred, bullies and victims risk impaired social understanding, lower school achievement, and relationship difficulties (Ma et al., 2009; Pepler et al., 2004). Bystanders suffer, too (Nishina & Juvonen, 2005; Rivers et al., 2009).

Can Bullying Be Stopped?

Most victimized children find ways to halt ongoing bullying—by ignoring, retaliating, defusing, or avoiding. A study of older children who were bullied in one year but not in the next indicated that finding new friends was crucial (P. K. Smith et al., 2004). Friendships help victims, but what can be done to halt bullying altogether?

We know what does *not* work: increasing students' awareness, instituting zero tolerance for fighting, or putting troubled students together in a therapy group or a classroom. This last measure tends to make daily life easier for some teachers, but it increases aggression (Kupersmidt et al., 2004).

The whole school needs to change—teachers and bystanders, parents and aides, bullies and victims. Peers are crucial: If they empathize with victims and refuse to admire bullies, that reduces classroom aggression (Salmivalli, 2010). Dan Olweus, a pioneer in antibullying efforts, advocates this *whole-school strategy* (Olweus, 1993), which is credited with recent successful efforts to decrease bullying (Hahn et al., 2007). A review of all research on successful ways to halt bullying (Berger, 2007) finds the following:

- Everyone in the school must change, not just the identified bullies.
- Intervention is more effective in the earlier grades.
- Evaluation is critical. Programs that appear to be good might actually be harmful.

This final point merits special emphasis. Some programs make a difference, some do not; only objective follow-up can tell. The best recent success was reported from a multifaceted effort that involved an entire town for eight years. Bit by bit, victimization declined in the schools, from 9 to 3 percent (Koivisto, 2004). Sustained, comprehensive efforts seem needed.

ELLEN B. SENISI / THE IMAGE WORKS

Only an Act? Fifth-grade boys play passengers on a bus as they act out a scene in which three of them reject a fourth (at right). They are participating in a curriculum designed to increase empathy and reduce bullying.

Especially for Parents of an Accused Bully Another parent has told you that your child is a bully. Your child denies it and explains that the other child doesn't mind being teased. (see response, page 370)

School-age children develop their own culture, with customs that encourage them to be loyal to one another. All 6- to 11-year-olds want and need social acceptance and close, mutual friendships to protect against loneliness and depression. Friendship is more valued than popularity; being rejected is painful.

Most children experience occasional peer rejection. However, some children are victims, repeatedly rejected and friendless, experiencing physical, verbal, or relational bullying. Some efforts to reduce bullying are not successful; a whole-school approach seems best.

>> Children's Moral Values

Although the origins of morality are debatable (see Chapter 10), there is no doubt that middle childhood is prime time for moral development. Ages 7 to 11 are:

> years of eager, lively searching on the part of children . . . as they try to understand things, to figure them out, but also to weigh the rights and wrongs. . . .
> This is the time for growth of the moral imagination, fueled constantly by the willingness, the eagerness of children to put themselves in the shoes of others.
>
> *[Coles, 1997, p. 99]*

That optimistic assessment seems validated by detailed research. In middle childhood, children are quite capable of making moral judgments, differentiating universal principles from mere conventional norms (Turiel, 2008). Empirical studies show that throughout middle childhood, children readily suggest moral arguments to distinguish right from wrong (Killen, 2007).

Many forces drive children's growing interest in moral issues. These include (1) peer culture, which judges some behaviors as fair and others not, and (2) personal experience. Both of these typically give schoolchildren greater exposure to more diverse people and ideas than the preschoolers have, which makes a difference. For example, children in multiethnic schools are better able to argue against prejudice than are children who attend racially and ethnically homogeneous schools (Killen et al., 2006). A final factor is (3) empathy, stronger in middle childhood because children are more aware of one another.

However, moral advances are not automatic. Children who are slow to develop theory of mind—which, as you remember from Chapter 9, is affected by family and culture—are also slow to develop empathy (Caravita et al., 2010). The authors of a study of 7-year-olds "conclude that moral *competence* may be a universal human characteristic, but that it takes a situation with specific demand characteristics to translate this competence into actual prosocial performance" (van IJzendoorn et al., 2010, p. 1). In other words, school-age children can think and act morally, but they do not always do so.

JOHN ANTHONY RIZZO / UPPERCUT IMAGES / PHOTOLIBRARY

Empathy Building Look at their facial expressions, not just their matching hats and gloves. For this 9-year-old sister and 7-year-old brother, moral development is apparent. This is not necessarily the case for all siblings, however; imagine the same behavior but with angry expressions.

Moral Reasoning

Much of the developmental research on children's moral thinking began with Piaget's descriptions of the rules used by children as they play (Piaget, 1932/1997). This led to Lawrence Kohlberg's description of cognitive stages of morality (Kohlberg, 1963).

Kohlberg's Levels of Moral Thought

Kohlberg described three levels of moral reasoning and two stages at each level (see Table 13.3) with parallels to Piaget's stages of cognition. **Preconventional moral reasoning** is similar to preoperational thought in that it is egocentric, with children seeking their personal pleasure or pain more than social concerns. **Conventional moral reasoning** parallels concrete operational thought in that it relates to current, observable practices: Children see what their parents, their teachers, and their friends do and try to follow suit. **Postconventional moral reasoning** is similar to formal operational thought because it uses logic and abstractions, going beyond what is concretely observed in a particular society, willing to question "what is" in order to decide "what should be."

According to Kohlberg, intellectual maturation advances moral thinking. During middle childhood, children's answers shift from being primarily preconventional to being more conventional: Concrete thought and peer experiences help children move past the first two stages (level I) to the next two (level II). Postconventional reasoning is not usually present until adolescence or adulthood.

Kohlberg posed moral dilemmas to school-age boys (and eventually girls, teenagers, and adults). The story of a poor man named Heinz, whose wife was dying,

preconventional moral reasoning
Kohlberg's first level of moral reasoning, emphasizing rewards and punishments.

conventional moral reasoning Kohlberg's second level of moral reasoning, emphasizing social rules.

postconventional moral reasoning Kohlberg's third level of moral reasoning, emphasizing moral principles.

>> Response for Parents of an Accused Bully (from page 368) The future is ominous if the charges are true. Your child's denial is a sign that there is a problem. (An innocent child would be worried about the misperception instead of categorically denying that any problem exists.) You might ask the teacher what the school is doing about bullying. Family counseling might help. Because bullies often have friends who egg them on, you may need to monitor your child's friendships and perhaps befriend the victim. Talk matters over with your child. Ignoring the situation might lead to heartache later on.

TABLE 13.3

Kohlberg's Three Levels and Six Stages of Moral Reasoning

Level I: Preconventional Moral Reasoning
The goal is to get rewards and avoid punishments; this is a self-centered level.

- *Stage One: Might makes right* (a punishment and obedience orientation). The most important value is to maintain the appearance of obedience to authority, avoiding punishment while still advancing self-interest. Don't get caught!

- *Stage Two: Look out for number one* (an instrumental and relativist orientation). Each person tries to take care of his or her own needs. The reason to be nice to other people is so that they will be nice to you.

Level II: Conventional Moral Reasoning
Emphasis is placed on social rules; this is a community-centered level.

- *Stage Three: "Good girl" and "nice boy."* Proper behavior is behavior that pleases other people. Social approval is more important than any specific reward.

- *Stage Four: "Law and order."* Proper behavior means being a dutiful citizen and obeying the laws set down by society, even when no police are nearby.

Level III: Postconventional Moral Reasoning
Emphasis is placed on moral principles; this level is centered on ideals.

- *Stage Five: Social contract.* Obey social rules because they benefit everyone and are established by mutual agreement. If the rules become destructive or if one party doesn't live up to the agreement, the contract is no longer binding. Under some circumstances, disobeying the law is moral.

- *Stage Six: Universal ethical principles.* General, universally valid principles, not individual situations (level I) or community practices (level II), determine right and wrong. Ethical values (such as "life is sacred") are established by individual reflection and may contradict egocentric (level I) or social and community (level II) values.

serves as an example. A local druggist had the only cure for the wife's illness, a drug that Heinz could not pay for and that sold for 10 times what it cost to make.

> Heinz went to everyone he knew to borrow the money, but he could only get together about half of what it cost. He told the druggist that his wife was dying and asked him to sell it cheaper or let him pay later. But the druggist said "no." The husband got desperate and broke into the man's store to steal the drug for his wife. Should the husband have done that? Why?
>
> *[Kohlberg, 1963, p. 19]*

The crucial element in Kohlberg's scheme is not the answer given but the *reasons* for it. For instance, someone might say that the husband should steal the drug because he needs his wife to care for him (preconventional), or because people will blame him if he lets his wife die (conventional), or because trying to save her life is more important than obeying the law (postconventional).

Criticisms of Kohlberg

Kohlberg has been criticized for not taking cultural or gender differences into account. For example, caring for family members is much more important to people in some cultures than in others, which might make them avoid postconventional actions even as they are acting according to the highest morals of their society. Similarly, Kohlberg's original participants were all boys, which may have led him to downgrade female values of nurturance and relationships (Gilligan, 1982). Kohlberg's highest stages of moral reasoning require standards of justice that supersede individual needs, but caring for people may be no less moral than impartial justice (Sherblom, 2008).

Furthermore, Kohlberg did not seem to recognize that although children's moral values differ from those of adults, they may be equally valid and strong. School-age children are quite capable of questioning or ignoring adult rules that seem unfair (Turiel, 2006, 2008), and in that way they are postconventional.

In one respect, however, Kohlberg was undeniably correct. Children use their intellectual abilities to justify their moral actions. This was shown in an experiment in which trios of children aged 8 to 18 had to decide how to divide a sum of money with another trio of children. Some groups chose to share equally; other groups were more selfish. There were no age differences in the actual decisions, but there were age differences in the arguments voiced. Older children suggested more complex rationalizations for their choices, both selfish and altruistic (Gummerum et al., 2008).

What Children Value

Many lines of research have shown that children develop their own morality, guided by peers, parents, and culture (Turiel, 2006). Some prosocial values are evident in early childhood. Among these are caring for close family members, cooperating with other children, and not hurting anyone directly (Eisenberg et al., 2006). Even very young children think stealing is wrong.

As children become more aware of themselves and others in middle childhood, they realize that values sometimes conflict. Concrete operational cognition, which gives them the ability to observe and to use logic, propels them to think about morality and to try to behave ethically (Turiel, 2006). As part of growing up, children become conscious of immorality in their peers (Abrams et al., 2008) and, later, in their parents, themselves, and their culture. That is considered a developmental advance, but inherent in that judgment are values that some might question, as the following explores.

THINKING CRITICALLY

Evidence for Morality

Kohlberg's hierarchy may reflect his Western, masculine, elitist values—he was a European American professor, first at the University of Chicago and then at Harvard. For some, those background factors are enough to call his entire scheme into question, but others suggest that the moral message of any leader, from the Pope to the Dalai Lama, from Jesus to Mohammed, from Buddha to Confucius, should not be judged by personal background but by the integrity of their message.

The emphasis in life-span development on multicultural understanding adds complexity to this issue. As one social scientists notes:

> On the basis of the historical and ethnographic record, we know that different people in different times and places have found it quite natural to be spontaneously appalled, outraged, indignant, proud, disgusted, guilty and ashamed by all sorts of things [such as] Islam, Christianity, Judaism, capitalism, democracy, flag burning, miniskirts, long hair, no hair, alcohol consumption, meat eating, medical inoculation . . . .
>
> *[Shweder, 1994, p. 26]*

Most everyone tends to endorse the morals of their own culture, especially if their religious leaders guide them in that direction. Parents quite rightly hope that their children will follow their moral principles, and developmentalists, including Kohlberg, believe that as children become more educated and mature, they will become less selfish and more honest—that is, morally more advanced.

Indeed, the underlying message of this discussion, this chapter, this textbook, and the entire field of human development is that critical thinking and empirical evidence are better than unquestioned acceptance of current conditions and emotional impulses. Most instructors would agree with the sentiments behind the bumper sticker "If you think education is expensive, try ignorance." Do you agree as well? Is that a moral position?

As already noted, school-age children are intensely interested in moral issues, but when child culture conflicts with adult morality, children often align themselves with peers. A child might lie to protect a friend, for instance. On a broader level, one study found that 98 percent of a group of children believed that no child should be excluded from a sports team because of gender or race, even when adult society was less tolerant. Some of the same children, however, justified excluding another child from a friendship circle (Killen et al., 2002).

The conflict between the culture of children and that of adults is evident in the value that children place on education. Adults usually prize school, but children may encourage one another to play hooky, cheat on tests, or drop out. The morality of peers sometimes outweighs the morality endorsed by adults.

Consider another comment from Paul:

> I try not to get influenced too much, pulled into what I don't want to be into. But mostly, it's hard. You don't want people to be saying you're stupid. "Why do you want to go to school and get a job? . . . Drop out."
>
> *[quoted in Nieto, 2000, p. 252]*

Not surprisingly, Paul later left school.

It is apparent that three common values among 6- to 11-year-olds are:

- Protect your friends
- Don't tell adults what is happening
- Don't be too different from your peers

These three values can explain both apparent boredom and overt defiance, as well as standards of dress that mystify adults (such as jeans so loose that they fall off or so tight that they impede digestion). Given what we know about middle childhood, it is no surprise that children do not echo adult morality.

In many ways, peers help one another develop morals. You have already seen this in the discussion of bullies. The best way to stop a bully is for the bystanders to take action, defending the victim and isolating the bully. This is exactly what occurs when the whole-school approach is effective: The adults do not lecture (that can backfire), but everyone—children, parents, and school staff alike—works together to stop bullying. Since bullies tend to be low on empathy, they need peers to teach them that their actions are not admired (which many bullies believe). During middle childhood, morality can be scaffolded just as cognitive skills are, with mentors—peers or adults—structuring moral dilemmas to advance moral understanding (Turner & Berkowitz, 2005).

A detailed examination of this process began with an update on one of Piaget's moral issues: whether punishment should seek *retribution* (hurting the transgressor) or *restitution* (restoring what was lost). Piaget found the latter to be more advanced: he also found that between ages 8 and 10 children do indeed move from retribution to restitution.

To learn how this occurs, researchers arranged for 133 9-year-olds to ponder the following:

> Late one afternoon there was a boy who was playing with a ball on his own in the garden. His dad saw him playing with it and asked him not to play with it so near the house because it might break a window. The boy didn't really listen to his dad, and carried on playing near the house. Then suddenly, the ball bounced up high and broke the window in the boy's room. His dad heard the noise and came to to see what had happened. The father wonders what would be the fairest way to punish the boy. He thinks of two punishments. The first is to say: "Now, you didn't do as I asked. You will have to pay for the window to be mended, and I am going to take the money from your pocket money." The second is to say: "Now, you didn't do as I asked. As a punishment you have to go to your room and stay there for the rest of the evening." Which of these punishments do you think is the fairest?
>
> *[Leman & Björnberg, 2010, p. 962]*

The children were split equally in their answers. Then 48 of them were paired with a child who answered the other way, and each pair was asked to discuss the broken window event and try to reach agreement on the fairest punishment. As a control, the rest of the children were not paired and did not discuss the dilemma. Six pairs were boy–boy; six, boy–girl with the boy favoring restitution; six, boy–girl with the girl favoring restitution; and six, girl–girl. The conversations typically took only five minutes, and the retribution side was more often chosen—which Piaget would consider a moral backslide. However, all the children were queried again, two weeks and eight weeks later, and their responses changed toward the more advanced, restitution thinking (see Figure 13.3). This was particularly true for the children who engaged in conversation.

The authors of this study noted that the boy–boy pairs included many more hostile interruptions (is that rude or immoral?), but hostile interruptions did not impede advancement of thought. Instead, such hostility seemed to be the middle school boys' conventional way of interacting. The main conclusion, however, was that children's "conversation on a topic may stimulate a process of individual reflection that triggers developmental advances" (Leman & Björnberg, 2010, p. 969). Parents and teachers take note: Raising moral issues, and letting children talk about them, may advance morality—not immediately, but eventually.

Now we are ready to reexamine the tire-changing boy from the opening vignette of this chapter. Child labor is deemed immoral by the United Nations, but that international body has had difficulty educating children about their rights and

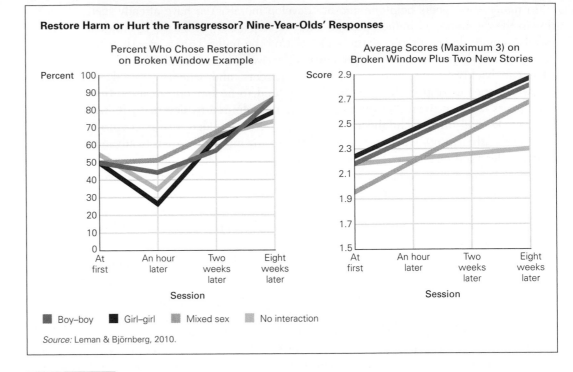

Restore Harm or Hurt the Transgressor? Nine-Year-Olds' Responses

Source: Leman & Björnberg, 2010.

FIGURE 13.3

Benefits of Time and Talking The chart on the left shows that most children, immediately after their initial punitive response, became even more likely to seek punishment rather than to repair damage. However, after some time and reflection, they affirmed the response Piaget would consider more mature. The chart on the right indicates that children who had talked about the broken window example moved toward restorative justice even in examples they had not heard before, which was not true for those who had not talked about the first story. Gender differences were apparent in how children discussed the story, but reflection about moral dilemmas yielded similar results for both sexes, no matter how they got there.

convincing nations to enforce child labor standards (Print et al., 2008). Morality is quite variable, not only among children but also among cultures. Thus, to decide whether that young boy should be helping his father would require finding out whether his life situation allows him to satisfy the five needs that are thought to be universal during middle childhood. Are his material needs met, is he learning in school, does he have friends, is he proud of himself, is his work keeping his family supportive and stable? If the answer to all these questions is yes, then Tiffany's understandable shock, or the father's acceptance of child labor, may be more reflective of their respective cultures than of the boy's condition.

SUMMING UP

Moral issues are of great interest to school-age children, who are affected by their cultures, by their parents, and particularly by their peers. Kohlberg's stages of moral thought parallel Piaget's stages of development, suggesting that the highest level of morality goes beyond the norms of any particular nation. Children develop moral standards that they try to follow, although these may differ from adult morals. Maturation, reflection, and discussion all foster moral development.

▪

SUMMARY

The Nature of the Child

1. All theories of development acknowledge that school-age children become more independent and capable in many ways. Erikson emphasized industry, when children are busy mastering various tasks; in psychoanalytic theory, Freud described latency, when psychosexual needs are quiet.

2. Children develop their self-concept during these years, basing it on a more realistic assessment of their competence than they had in earlier years. High self-esteem may reduce effort and is not valued in every culture.

3. Both daily hassles and major stresses take a toll on children, with accumulated stresses more likely to impair development than any single event. The child's interpretation of the situation, and the availability of supportive adults and peers, aid resilience.

Families and Children

4. Families influence children in many ways, as do genes and peers. Each child in a family experiences different (nonshared) circumstances.

5. The five functions of a supportive family are to satisfy children's physical needs; to encourage them to learn; to help them develop friends; to protect their self-respect; and to provide them with a safe, stable, and harmonious home.

6. The most common family structure worldwide is the nuclear family, usually with other relatives nearby and supportive. Other two-parent families include adoptive, same-sex, grandparent, and stepfamilies, each of which sometimes functions well for children. However, each has vulnerabilities as well.

7. Generally, it seems better for children to have two parents rather than one because a parental alliance can support their development. Single-parent families have higher rates of change in residence and family composition, and change adds stress in middle childhood.

8. Income affects family function. Poor children are at greater risk for emotional and behavioral problems because the stress of poverty hinders effective parenting. Instability and conflict are harmful.

The Peer Group

9. Peers are crucial for social development during middle childhood. Each cohort of children has a culture of childhood, passed down from slightly older children. Close friends are particularly helpful during these years.

10. Popular children may be cooperative and easy to get along with or may be competitive and aggressive. Much depends on the age and culture of the children.

11. Rejected children may be neglected, aggressive, or withdrawn. Aggressive and withdrawn children have difficulty with social cognition; their interpretation of the normal give-and-take of childhood is impaired.

12. Bullying is common among school-age children and has long-term consequences for both bullies and victims. Bullying is hard to stop without a multifaceted, long-term, whole-school approach.

Children's Moral Values

13. School-age children are very interested in differentiating right from wrong. Kohlberg described three levels of moral reasoning, each related to cognitive maturity. When values conflict, children often choose loyalty to peers over adult morality.

KEY TERMS

industry versus inferiority (p. 350)
latency (p. 351)
social comparison (p. 351)
effortful control (p. 352)
resilience (p. 353)

family structure (p. 358)
family function (p. 358)
nuclear family (p. 359)
single-parent family (p. 359)
extended family (p. 359)
polygamous family (p. 360)

culture of children (p. 364)
aggressive-rejected (p. 366)
withdrawn-rejected (p. 366)
social cognition (p. 366)
bullying (p. 366)
bully-victim (p. 367)

preconventional moral reasoning (p. 370)
conventional moral reasoning (p. 370)
postconventional moral reasoning (p. 370)

WHAT HAVE YOU LEARNED?

The Nature of the Child

1. How do Erikson's stages for school-age children and for preschool children differ?

2. Why is social comparison particularly powerful during middle childhood?

3. Why do cultures differ in how they value pride or modesty?

4. How does the accumulation of minor stresses compare to the impact of a major stress?

5. What factors help a child become resilient despite severe early stresses?

Families and Children

6. Why does research on nonshared environments *not* prove that parents are irrelevant?

7. Which of the five family functions is most difficult for divorcing parents?

8. What is the difference between family function and family structure?

9. Why might poverty be harder for school-age children than for children of other ages?

10. What are the advantages and disadvantages of a stepparent family?

11. Why is a safe, harmonious home particularly important during middle childhood?

12. Which of the five family functions is particularly difficult for single parents?

13. Does the increase in single parents mean that more children will have a difficult childhood? Why or why not?

14. What is the evidence that school-age children benefit from continuity?

15. What are the advantages and disadvantages for children in an extended family?

The Peer Group

16. How does the disapproval of tattletales affect bullies and victims?

17. How do children's games reflect the culture of children?

18. Did children's clothing in your primary school reflect the culture of children? Explain.

19. How is a child's popularity affected by culture?

20. What is the difference between being a bully and being a bully-victim?

21. Who is best able to stop a bully and why—victim, teacher, another child?

Children's Moral Values

22. What are the the main criticisms of Kohlberg's theory of moral development?

23. How does children's conversation impact their moral reasoning?

24. Why don't children always accept the moral standards of their parents?

APPLICATIONS

1. Go someplace where school-age children congregate (such as a schoolyard, a park, or a community center) and use naturalistic observation for at least half an hour. Describe what popular, average, withdrawn, and rejected children do. Note at least one potential conflict (bullying, rough-and-tumble play, etc.). Describe the sequence and the outcome.

2. Focusing on verbal bullying, describe at least two times when someone said a hurtful thing to you and two times when you said something that might have been hurtful to someone else. What are the differences between the two types of situations?

3. How would your childhood have been different if your family structure had been different, such as if you had (or had not) lived with your grandparents, if your parents had (or had not) gotten divorced, if you had (or had not) lived in a foster family?

>>ONLINE CONNECTIONS

To accompany your textbook, you have access to a number of online resources, including quizzes for every chapter of the book, flashcards (in English and Spanish), critical thinking questions, and case studies. For access to any of these links, go to www.worthpublishers.com/bergerls8e. In addition to these free resources, you'll also find links to the podcasts, video clips, diagnostic quizzing with personalized study advice, and an ebook. Some of the videos and activities available online include:

- *Moral Reasoning.* This activity reviews Kohlberg's theory of age-related changes in moral reasoning. Was he right? You can decide as you watch footage of people solving the famous Heinz dilemma.

- *Effects of Divorce and Remarriage on Children.* Learn three factors that affect a child's adjustment, and what parents can do to avoid potential problems.

Middle Childhood

BIOSOCIAL

A Healthy Time During middle childhood, children grow more slowly than they did earlier or than they will during adolescence. Physical play is crucial for health and happiness. Prevalent physical problems, including obesity and asthma, have genetic roots and psychosocial consequences.

Brain Development Brain maturation continues, leading to faster reactions and better self-control. Which specific skills are mastered depends largely on culture, gender, and inherited ability, all of which are reflected in intelligence tests. Children have multiple intellectual abilities, most of which are not reflected in standard IQ tests.

Special Needs Many children have special learning needs. Early recognition, targeted education, and psychological support can help them, including those with bipolar and attention-deficit disorders, specific learning disabilities, and the many disorders of the autism spectrum.

COGNITIVE

Building on Theory Beginning at about age 7, Piaget noted, children attain concrete operational thought, including the ability to understand the logical principles of classification and transitive inference. Vygotsky emphasized that children become more open to learning from mentors, both teachers and peers. Information-processing abilities increase, including greater memory, knowledge, control, and metacognition.

Language Children's increasing ability to understand the structures and possibilities of language enables them to extend the range of their cognitive powers and to become more analytical in vocabulary. Children have the cognitive capacity to become bilingual and bicultural, although much depends on the teacher's awareness.

Education International comparisons reveal marked variations in overt and hidden curriculum, as well as in learning, between one nation and another. The reading and math wars pit traditional education against a more holistic approach to learning. Alternate school structures, including vouchers and charter schools, are an attempt to increase learning among U.S. schoolchildren.

PSYCHOSOCIAL

The Nature of the Child Theorists agree that many school-age children develop competencies, emotional control, and attitudes to defend against stress. Some children are resilient, coping well with problems and finding support in friends, family, school, religion, and community.

Families Parents continue to influence children, especially as they exacerbate or buffer problems in school and the community. During these years, families need to meet basic needs, encourage learning, foster self-respect, nurture friendship, and—most important—provide harmony and stability. Nuclear families often provide this, but one-parent, foster, same-sex, or grandparent families can also function well for children. No family structure guarantees optimal functioning, however. Household income, little conflict, and family stability benefit children of all ages, particularly in middle childhood.

Peers and Morals The peer group becomes increasingly important as children become less dependent on their parents and more dependent on friends for help, loyalty, and sharing of mutual interests. Rejection and bullying become serious problems. Moral development, influenced by peers, advances during these years.

Adolescence

Would you ride in a car with an unskilled driver? When my daughter Bethany had her learner's permit, I tried to convey confidence. Not until a terrified, "Mom! Help!" did I grab the wheel to avoid hitting a subway kiosk. I should have intervened sooner, but it is hard to know when, and in what specific contexts, children become adults who no longer need their mother's assistance. Bethany was an adolescent, neither child nor adult.

A century ago, puberty began at age 15 or so. Soon after that, most girls married and most boys found work. It is said that *adolescence begins with biology and ends with culture*. If so, then a hundred years ago adolescence lasted a few months; now it lasts a decade or more. Puberty starts before the teen years, and adult responsibilities may not begin until the end of the next stage, emerging adulthood. One observer said adolescence is like "starting turbo-charged engines with an unskilled driver" (Dahl, 2004, p. 17).

In the next three chapters (covering ages 11 to 18), we begin with biology and move toward culture. Understanding adolescence is more than an intellectual challenge: Those turbo-charged engines need skilled guidance. Get ready to grab the wheel.

Adolescence: Biosocial Development

WHAT WILL YOU KNOW?

1. What parts of a teenager's body grow first during puberty?

2. How can you tell whether a child will begin puberty early (age 8) or late (age 14)?

3. What is the difference between normal dieting and an eating disorder?

4. Do hormones, brains, or cultures cause the problems parents have with teenagers?

I overheard a conversation among three teenagers, including my daughter Rachel, all past their awkward years, now becoming beautiful. They were discussing the imperfections of their bodies. One spoke of her fat stomach (what stomach? I could not see it), another of her long neck (hidden by her silky, shoulder-length hair). Rachel complained not only about her bent finger but also about her feet!

The reality that children grow into men and women is no shock to any adult. But for teenagers, heightened self-awareness often triggers surprise or even horror, joy or despair. Like these three, adolescents pay attention to details of their growth. This chapter describes some of those biosocial details of growing bodies and emerging sexuality. It all begins with hormones, but other invisible changes may be even more potent—such as the timing of neurological maturation that does not yet allow adolescents to realize that their minor imperfections are insignificant.

>> Puberty Begins

Puberty refers to the years of rapid physical growth and sexual maturation that end childhood, producing a person of adult size, shape, and sexuality. The forces of puberty are unleashed by a cascade of hormones that produce external growth and internal changes, including heightened emotions and sexual desires. The process normally starts between ages 8 and 14, and follows the sequence outlined in At About This Time on page 382. Most physical growth and maturation ends about four years after the first signs appear, although some individuals add height, weight, and muscle until age 20 or so.

For girls, the observable changes of puberty usually begin with nipple growth. Soon a few pubic hairs are visible, then peak growth spurt, widening of the hips, the first menstrual period (**menarche**), full pubic-hair pattern, and breast maturation (Susman et al., 2010). The average age of menarche among normal weight girls is about 12 years, 8 months (Rosenfield et al., 2009), although variation in timing is quite normal.

For boys, the usual sequence is growth of the testes, initial pubic-hair growth, growth of the penis, first ejaculation of seminal fluid (**spermarche**), appearance of facial hair, peak growth spurt, deepening of the voice, and final pubic-hair growth (Biro et al., 2001; Herman-Giddens et al., 2001; Susman et al., 2010). The typical age of spermarche is just under 13 years, close to the age for menarche.

puberty The time between the first onrush of hormones and full adult physical development. Puberty usually lasts three to five years. Many more years are required to achieve psychosocial maturity.

menarche A girl's first menstrual period, signaling that she has begun ovulation. Pregnancy is biologically possible, but ovulation and menstruation are often irregular for years after menarche.

spermarche A boy's first ejaculation of sperm. Erections can occur as early as infancy, but ejaculation signals sperm production. Spermarche may occur during sleep (in a "wet dream") or via direct stimulation.

AT ABOUT THIS TIME		
The Sequence of Puberty		
Girls	Approximate Average Age*	Boys
Ovaries increase production of estrogen and progesterone[†]	9	
Uterus and vagina begin to grow larger	9½	Testes increase production of testosterone[†]
Breast "bud" stage	10	Testes and scrotum grow larger
Pubic hair begins to appear; weight spurt begins	11	
Peak height spurt	11½	Pubic hair begins to appear
Peak muscle and organ growth (also, hips become noticeably wider)	12	Penis growth begins
Menarche (first menstrual period)	12½	Spermarche (first ejaculation); weight spurt begins
First ovulation	13	Peak height spurt
Voice lowers	14	Peak muscle and organ growth (also, shoulders become noticeably broader)
Final pubic-hair pattern	15	Voice lowers; visible facial hair
Full breast growth	16	
	18	Final pubic-hair pattern

*Average ages are rough approximations, with many perfectly normal, healthy adolescents as much as three years ahead of or behind these ages.
[†]Estrogens and testosterone influence sexual characteristics, including reproduction. Charted here are the increases produced by the gonads (sex glands). The ovaries produce estrogens and the testes produce androgens, especially testosterone. Adrenal glands produce some of both kinds of hormones (not shown).

Unseen Beginnings

Just described are the visible changes of puberty, but the entire process begins with an invisible event, a marked hormonal increase. **Hormones** are body chemicals that regulate hunger, sleep, moods, stress, sexual desire, immunity, reproduction, and many other bodily reactions, including puberty. Hormones start the process: Spermarche and menarche are "a very late event," long after hormonal beginnings (J. L. Cameron, 2004, p. 116). Throughout adolescence hormone levels correlate with physiological changes and self-reported developments (Shirtcliff et al., 2009).

You learned in Chapter 8 that the production of many hormones is regulated deep within the brain, where biochemical signals from the hypothalamus signal another brain structure, the **pituitary,** to go into action. The pituitary produces hormones that stimulate the **adrenal glands,** located above the kidneys at either side of the lower back. The adrenal glands produce more hormones.

Many hormones that regulate puberty follow this route, known as the **HPA (hypothalamus–pituitary–adrenal) axis** (see Figure 14.1). Abnormalities of the HPA axis in adolescence are associated with eating disorders, anxiety, and depression; all of these conditions and many other types of psychopathology are connected to hormones and appear for the first time or worsen at puberty (Dahl & Gunnar, 2009).

Sex Hormones

At adolescence, the pituitary activates not only the adrenal glands but also the **gonads,** or sex glands (ovaries in females; testes, or testicles, in males), follow-

hormone An organic chemical substance that is produced by one body tissue and conveyed via the bloodstream to another to affect some physiological function.

pituitary A gland in the brain that responds to a signal from the hypothalamus by producing many hormones, including those that regulate growth and control other glands, among them the adrenal and sex glands.

adrenal glands Two glands, located above the kidneys, that produce hormones (including the "stress hormones" epinephrine [adrenaline] and norepinephrine).

HPA (hypothalamus–pituitary–adrenal) axis A sequence of hormone production originating in the hypothalamus and moving to the pituitary and then to the adrenal glands.

gonads The paired sex glands (ovaries in females, testicles in males). The gonads produce hormones and gametes.

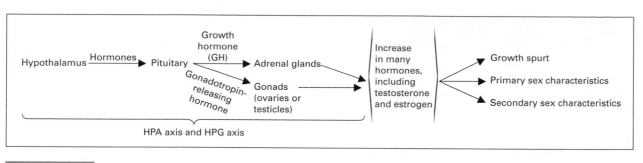

FIGURE 14.1

Biological Sequence of Puberty Puberty begins with a hormonal signal from the hypothalamus to the pituitary gland. The pituitary, in turn, signals the adrenal glands and the ovaries or testes to produce more of their hormones.

Especially for Parents of Teenagers Why would parents blame adolescent moods on hormones? (see response, page 387)

HPG (hypothalamus–pituitary–gonad) axis A sequence of hormone production originating in the hypothalamus and moving to the pituitary and then to the gonads.

estradiol A sex hormone, considered the chief estrogen. Females produce much more estradiol than males do.

testosterone A sex hormone, the best known of the androgens (male hormones); secreted in far greater amounts by males than by females.

ing another sequence called the **HPG (hypothalamus–pituitary–gonad) axis.** One hormone in particular, GnRH (gonadotropin-releasing hormone), causes the gonads to enlarge and dramatically increase their production of sex hormones, chiefly **estradiol** in girls and **testosterone** in boys. These hormones affect the body's entire shape and functioning, including production of additional hormones that regulate stress and immunity (E. A. Young et al., 2008).

Estrogens (including estradiol) are female hormones and *androgens* (including testosterone) are male hormones, although the adrenal glands produce estrogens and androgens in everyone. The gonads, however, produce sex-specific hormones: The ovaries produce much more estrogens than androgens; the reverse is true of the testes. Testosterone skyrockets in boys—up to 20 times the prepubescent level (Roche & Sun, 2003). Estradiol increases to about 8 times a girl's childhood level (Malina et al., 2004).

The activated gonads eventually produce mature sperm or ova, released in spermarche or menarche. That signifies the potential for parenthood, although peak fertility occurs four to six years later. Hormonal increases and differences may underlie sex differences in psychopathology (Steiner & Young, 2008), with males twice as likely to become schizophrenic and females twice as likely to become depressed. For both sexes, interest in sexual experiences awakens and strengthens as hormones increase. The first sexual objects are usually unattainable—a film star, a teacher, someone's older sibling—but by mid-adolescence, fantasies may settle on another teenager.

Not only are brain and body affected by hormones, but behavior is as well. Surges of emotions and sudden lustful impulses are partly hormonal, but thoughts *cause* physiological and neurological processes as well as result from them (Damasio, 2003). For example, when other people react to an adolescent's emerging breasts, beard, or body shape, these reactions evoke thoughts and frustrations in the young person, which then raise hormone levels and produce emotional outbursts, each increasing the other.

Body Rhythms

The brain of every living creature responds to the environment with natural rhythms. One of these *biorhythms* is a day–night cycle of biological activity that occurs approximately every 24 hours, called the *circadian rhythm.* (*Circadian* means "about a day.") Puberty alters these biorhythms.

PHOTOALTO / ALAMY

Primping, Bonding, or Both? Lip gloss and eyelash-curling have the full concentration of these three, as the two "older" girls (the one on the left is 13) work on the youngest one. Critics lament society's focus on superficial appearance, but this scene may be more biological than cultural, since similar moments have occurred throughout history and in every nation.

Observation Quiz This moment was captured fairly recently, in 2007. Are these girls North American? For a clue—look at their hair. (see answer, page 387)

Too Early It is 8:00 A.M. on their first day of high school, and these freshmen are having trouble staying awake for orientation in their homeroom.

As just described, the hypothalamus and the pituitary gland regulate hormones that affect stress, appetite, sleep, and so on. Hormones cause a "phase delay" in sleep–wake patterns, making many teens wide awake at midnight but half asleep all morning. By contrast, many adult brains are naturally alert in the morning and sleepy at night.

Added to the adolescent day–night pattern, some people (especially males) are naturally more alert in the evening than in the morning, a genetic trait called *eveningness*. Exacerbated by the pubescent phase delay, eveningness puts adolescents at high risk for antisocial activities (Susman et al., 2007) because they are awake when adults are sound asleep. One result: "Teenagers are notoriously sleep deprived" (Ruder, 2008, p. 10). Uneven sleep schedules (more sleep on weekends, erratic bedtimes) decrease well-being, as does sleep deprivation (Fuligni & Hardway, 2006; Holm et al., 2009).

Sleep deprivation and irregular sleep schedules lead to several specific dangers, including falling asleep while driving, insomnia, nightmares, and mood disorders (depression, conduct disorder, anxiety). Individuals who are sleep deprived do not think or learn as well as they might when rested. The implications of that may be ignored by adults, as the following explains.

A VIEW FROM SCIENCE

Get Real

Some parents fight biology. They command their wide-awake teen to "go to sleep," they hang up on classmates who phone after 10:00 P.M., they set curfews and stay awake until their teenagers come home, and they drag their offspring out of bed for school. (An opposite developmental clash occurs when parents tell their toddlers to stay in their cribs after dawn.) But this fight goes against natural design, so teenagers sometimes fall asleep in school (see Figure 14.2).

Data on the adolescent phase delay convinced social scientists at the University of Minnesota to ask 17 school districts to start high school at 8:30 A.M. or later. Few parents agreed. Many (42 percent) thought high school should begin before 8:00 A.M., and some (20 percent) wanted their teenagers out of the house by 7:15 A.M., as did only 1 percent of parents with younger children.

Members of various occupations had their own reasons for believing school should begin by 8 A.M. Teachers generally thought that learning was more efficient early in the morning; bus drivers hated rush hour; cafeteria workers wanted to leave by mid-afternoon; police said teenagers should be home by 4:00 P.M.; coaches needed after-school sports events to end before dark; employers wanted teens to staff the afternoon shift; community program directors liked to use school gyms for nonschool events in the late afternoon (Wahlstrom, 2002).

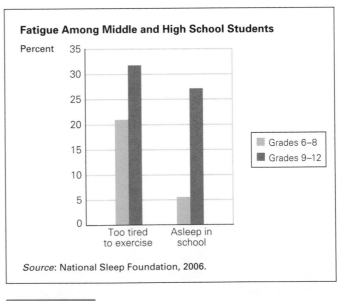

Fatigue Among Middle and High School Students

Source: National Sleep Foundation, 2006.

FIGURE 14.2

Dreaming and Learning? This graph shows the percentage of U.S. students who, once a week or more, fall asleep in class or are too tired to exercise. Not shown are those who are too tired overall (59 percent for high school students) or who doze in class "almost every day" (8 percent).

Only one school district experimented. In Edina, Minnesota, high school schedules changed to 8:30 A.M. to 3:10 P.M. instead of 7:25 A.M. to 2:05 P.M. After a trial year, most parents (93 percent) and virtually all students liked the new schedule. One student said, "I have only fallen asleep in school once this whole year, and last year I fell asleep about three times a week" (quoted in Wahlstrom, 2002, p. 190). The data showed fewer absent, late, disruptive, or sick students (the school nurse became an advocate) as well as higher grades.

Other school districts reconsidered. Minneapolis, which had started high school at 7:15 A.M., changed the starting time to 8:40 A.M. Again, attendance improved, as did the graduation rate. School boards in South Burlington (Vermont), West Des Moines (Iowa), Tulsa (Oklahoma), Arlington (Virginia), and Milwaukee (Wisconsin) voted in favor of later starting times, switching on average from 7:45 A.M. to 8:30 A.M. (Tonn, 2006). Unexpected advantages appeared: financial savings (more efficient energy use) and, at least in Tulsa, unprecedented athletic championships.

But change is hard. Many school districts stick to their old schedules. From 2006 to 2009, the community of Fairfax (Virginia) argued, forming two opposing groups: SLEEP (Start Later for Excellence in Education Proposal) versus WAKE (Worried About Keeping Extra-Curriculars). One high school sports reporter argued:

> The later start would hinder teams without lighted practice fields. Hinder kids who work after-school jobs to save for college or to help support their families. Hinder teachers who work second jobs or take late-afternoon college classes. Hinder commuters who would get stopped behind more buses during peak traffic times. Hinder kids who might otherwise seek after-school academic help, or club or team affiliation. Hinder families that depend on high school children to watch younger siblings after school. Hinder community groups that use school and park facilities in the late afternoons and evenings.
>
> *[Williams, 2009]*

This writer also wrote that science was on the side of change but reality was not. Of course, to developmentalists, science *is* reality. However, the Fairfax school board worried about the cost of school buses in rush hour. It voted to keep high school start times at 7:20 A.M.

Age and Puberty

A practical question is: "When will adolescence begin?" Some fear *precocious puberty* (sexual development before age 8) or very late puberty (after age 16), but both are rare (Cesario & Hughes, 2007). Quite normal is hormonal activity beginning any time from age 8 to age 13, with visible signs a year later. Many parents, teachers, and children want to be prepared, but not years before the events. Fortunately, genes, gender, body fat, and stress all aid in prediction.

Genes and Gender

About two-thirds of the variation in age of puberty is genetic, evident not only in families but also in ethnic groups (Ge et al., 2007; Susman et al., 2010; van den Berg & Boomsma, 2007). African Americans reach puberty about 7 months earlier than European or Hispanic Americans, while Chinese Americans average several months later. Ethnic differences are apparent on other continents as well. For instance, northern European girls reach menarche at 13 years, 4 months, on average; southern European girls do so at 12 years, 5 months (Alsaker & Flammer, 2006).

Genes of the sex chromosomes have a marked effect. The average girl is about two years ahead of the average boy in height. However, a girl's height spurt occurs before menarche, whereas for boys, the increase in height is a late event, occurring after spermarche. Thus, when it comes to hormonal and sexual changes, girls are only a few months ahead of boys (Hughes & Gore, 2007). Therefore, the sixth-grade boy with sexual fantasies about the taller girls in his class is neither perverted nor precocious; his hormones are simply ahead of his height.

Body Fat

Body fat affects the onset of puberty, at least in girls. Heavy girls reach menarche years earlier than do those who are malnourished. Most girls must reach at least

Both 12 The ancestors of these two Minnesota 12-year-olds came from northern Europe and West Africa, respectively. Their genes have dictated some differences between them, including the timing of puberty, but these differences are irrelevant to their friendship.

100 pounds (45 kilograms) before they can experience their first period (Berkey et al., 2000).

Worldwide, urban children are more often overfed and underexercised compared with rural children. That is probably why puberty starts earlier in the cities of India and China than it does in more remote villages, a year earlier in Warsaw than in rural Poland, and earlier in Athens than in other parts of Greece (Malina et al., 2004).

Body fat explains why, in some parts of Africa, youth reach puberty at age 15 or later, although their genetic relatives in North America mature much earlier. Malnutrition may also be the reason why puberty began at about age 17 in sixteenth-century Europe. Puberty has occurred at younger ages every century since then (an example of what is called the **secular trend**) as nutrition and medicine have improved, allowing not only earlier puberty but also taller average height.

One curious bit of evidence of the secular trend is that U.S. presidents are taller in recent decades than they were earlier (James Madison, the fourth president, was shortest at 5 feet, 4 inches; Barack Obama is 6 feet, 1 inch tall). Over most of the twentieth century, each generation experienced puberty a few weeks earlier and grew a centimeter or so taller than did the preceding one (Alsaker & Flammer, 2006). The secular trend has stopped in developed nations, perhaps because nutrition is now sufficient for everyone's developmental potential to be attained (Roche & Sun, 2003). Unlike their grandparents, today's young men are unlikely to look down at their short fathers, or girls at their little mothers.

Beyond nutrition, many scientists suspect that hormones in the food supply affect the age of puberty. As evidence, they point to the steroids fed to cattle to increase their bulk and their milk supply, as well as to many other substances in meat and other foods consumed by children that may affect appetite, body fat, and sex hormones (Wang et al., 2005).

One hormone in particular has been implicated in the onset of puberty: **leptin,** which stimulates the appetite and naturally increases over childhood, peaking at puberty (Rutters et al., 2008). Curiously, leptin affects appetite in females more than it does in males (Geary & Lovejoy, 2008), and body fat is more closely connected to the onset of puberty in girls than in boys. In fact, the well-established finding that body fat precipitates puberty may not be true for boys in nations where malnutrition is rare: One study found that U.S. boys who are heavy in childhood reach puberty later, not earlier, than others (J. M. Lee et al., 2010).

It is not yet known for certain exactly what the effects of leptin are; what factors increase or decrease leptin in the bloodstream; and how various chemicals in the air, water, or diet affect the human sexual-reproductive system. We know more about female than male puberty, partly because menarche is easier to date than spermarche, but that makes it harder to know whether the same substances and factors affect both sexes. It is certain that malnutrition slows down growth and reproduction for everyone; beyond that, there remains some uncertainty.

Stress

A bit of ambiguity remains regarding stress as well. What *is* known is that stress affects fertility and puberty by making reproduction more difficult when either partner is stressed and, paradoxically, by *increasing* (not decreasing) the hormones of puberty. It is also established that puberty arrives earlier if a child's parents are sick, addicted, or divorced or if the neighborhood is violent and impoverished. Corroborating evidence comes from other animals. Opossums experience earlier puberty and earlier death if their environment is stressful (Warshofsky, 1999), and

secular trend The long-term upward or downward direction of a certain set of statistical measurements, as opposed to a smaller, shorter cyclical variation. As an example, over the last two centuries, because of improved nutrition and medical care, children have tended to reach their adult height earlier and their adult height has increased.

leptin A hormone that affects appetite and is believed to affect the onset of puberty. Leptin levels increase during childhood and peak at around age 12.

Especially for Parents Worried About Early Puberty Suppose your cousin's 9-year-old daughter has just had her first period, and your cousin blames hormones in the food supply for this "precocious" puberty. Should you change your young daughter's diet? (see response, page 389)

mice mature later if their mother is highly nurturant, as measured by frequent licking and grooming during infancy (which protects young mice against stress later on) (N. M. Cameron et al., 2008).

However, although the link between stress and puberty is known, not every scientist agrees that stress *causes* early puberty (Ellis, 2004). Since puberty is largely genetic, it could be that adults who reached puberty early were more likely to become teenage parents, passing the genes that triggered early puberty on to their offspring. Since teenage parenthood correlates with low education, high anger, and divorce, many children of teenage parents may live in conflicted, divorce-prone homes. Their early puberty appears to result from that home life, but genes may be the real cause.

The same caveats apply to early sexual intercourse. No doubt, early puberty correlates with early sex and with absence of the biological father—and those three characteristics correlate not only with teen pregnancy and disease but also with depression and delinquency. However, the underlying cause may be genes, not stress (Mendle et al., 2009).

That genetic link is plausible, but several longitudinal studies suggest that stress hormones are a direct cause of early puberty. For example, one study followed 756 children from infancy to adolescence and found that earlier puberty correlated with harsh parenting in early childhood. This included behaviors such as demanding quiet and respect, spanking often, and rarely hugging or kissing. Although parents punish sons more than daughters, the effects on puberty were evident only for daughters, especially for girls who cried a lot as infants, which suggests that they were particularly vulnerable (Belsky et al., 2007).

A further study of the same girls at age 15, taking genetic differences into account, considered genes and still found that harsh treatment in childhood led not only to earlier menarche, but also to increased sexual risk taking (e.g., more partners, pregnancies, diseases) and not to other overall risks (e.g., drugs, crime) (Belsky et al., 2010). This suggests that the effects of the stress were targeted to sexual hormones.

Why would stress trigger puberty? Developmentally, delayed puberty would seem better. Those in their early teens who look and act childlike might evoke adult protection, not lust or anger, which would be especially beneficial in conflicted or single-parent homes. But in such homes, the reverse occurs. One explanation comes from evolutionary theory:

> Maturing quickly and breeding promiscuously would enhance reproductive fitness more than would delaying development, mating cautiously, and investing heavily in parenting. The latter strategy, in contrast, would make biological sense, for virtually the same reproductive-fitness-enhancing reasons, under conditions of contextual support and nurturance.
>
> [Belsky et al., 2010, p. 121]

In other words, in past stressful times, for the species to continue, adolescents needed to replace themselves before they died. Of course, natural selection would favor genes that postponed puberty during extreme famine (so that pregnant girls or newborns would not die of malnutrition) and that hastened puberty when girls were well fed but the society was in turmoil and there was a risk of the parents dying. By contrast, in more peaceful times and families, puberty could occur later because each child would have benefited from years of parental attention.

Of course, this evolutionary rationale no longer applies. Today, early sexuality and reproduction are more likely to destroy societies than protect them. However, the genome has been shaped over millennia; timing takes centuries to change.

>> Response for Parents of Teenagers (from page 383) If something causes adolescents to shout "I hate you," to slam doors, or to cry inconsolably, parents may decide that hormones are the problem. This makes it easy to disclaim personal responsibility for the teenager's anger. However, research on stress and hormones suggests that this comforting attribution is too simplistic.

>> Answer to Observation Quiz (from page 383) This girlish behavior is universal, but the hairstyles are not. All three have braids; these girls are Argentinean.

Not Yet a Woman She may look like an attractive woman, but she is really an early-maturing girl. Notice her long and sandy feet, her relatively short torso, her thin upper arms. Her body is changing—in a photo taken two years earlier or two years later, her shape would be different.

Too Early, Too Late

For most adolescents, only one aspect of pubertal timing is important: their friends' schedules. Puberty can enhance or diminish a person's status with peers. No one wants to be too early or too late.

Girls

Think about the early-maturing girl. If she has visible breasts at age 10, the boys in her class tease her; they are distressed by the sexual creature in their midst. She must fit her developing body into a school chair designed for smaller children, she might hide her breasts in large T-shirts and bulky sweaters, she might refuse to undress for gym. Early-maturing girls tend to have lower self-esteem, more depression, and poorer body image than do other girls (Compian et al., 2009). They also exercise less than their classmates, which often contributes to their difficulties as well (Davison et al., 2007).

Sometimes early-maturing girls have boyfriends a few years their senior, which garners them status—but this also increases their risk of using drugs and alcohol (Weichold et al., 2003) and of facing relational bullying and physical violence (Schreck et al., 2007). Early-maturing girls enter abusive relationships more often than other girls do, perhaps because they are lonely or because their social judgment is immature.

Boys

Cohort is crucial for boys. Early-maturing boys who were born around 1930 often became leaders in high school and more successful as adults (M. C. Jones, 1965; Taga et al., 2006). Since about 1960, however, the problems with early male maturation have outweighed the benefits. Currently, early-maturing boys are more aggressive, law-breaking, and alcohol-abusing than later-maturing boys (Biehl et al., 2007; Lynne et al., 2007). For boys as well as girls, early puberty correlates with sexual activity and teenage parenthood, which in turn correlate with depression and other psychosocial problems (B. Brown, 2004; Siebenbruner et al., 2007).

Late puberty may also be difficult, especially for boys. Slow-developing boys tend to be more anxious, depressed, and afraid of sex, at least according to research in Finland (Lindfors et al., 2007). In fact, every adolescent wants to hit puberty "on time." They are likely to overestimate or underestimate their maturation, or become depressed, if they are not average (Conley & Rudolph, 2009; Shirtcliff et al., 2009).

Ethnic Differences

Puberty that is late by world norms, at age 14 or so, is not troubling if one's friends are late as well. Well-nourished Africans tend to experience puberty a few months earlier and Asians a few months later than Europeans, but they all develop well if their classmates are on the same schedule. However, variable timing may add to intergroup tensions in multiethnic schools, since peer approval is more important in adolescence than is approval from adults (see the Research Design).

For instance, in one New England high school, the shorter and thinner "quiet Asian boys" were teased, much to their dismay. When one larger Asian American boy fought back at an ethnic insult, he was a hero to his Asian peers, even though school authorities punished him for his actions (Lei, 2003).

▶ Research Design

Scientists: Melissa L. Greene, Niobe Way, and Kerstin Pahl.

Publication: *Developmental Psychology* (2006).

Participants: A total of 136 high school students at a multiethnic high school in New York City.

Design: Six times over the four years of high school, students answered questionnaires about discrimination, ethnic identity, depression, and self-esteem.

Major conclusions: For all four ethnic groups (Black, Asian American, Puerto Rican, and other Latino), perceived peer discrimination had a greater impact on self-esteem than did perceived adult discrimination or teacher or parent encouragement. The Asian Americans averaged higher levels of perceived discrimination than any other group; the African Americans were second. Other research also finds that, in multiethnic contexts, students of Asian heritage experience more bullying.

Comment: This study is a welcome step toward multifaceted, multiethnic, longitudinal research on adolescents. More is needed to provide, as the researchers write, "a thorough examination of the impact of experiences of discrimination on well-being."

In a California high school, Samoan students were a small minority of the school population but advanced in puberty, which earned them respect from their classmates of all backgrounds. They were accepted as peacemakers between the two more numerous groups, African and Mexican Americans (Staiger, 2006).

Size and maturation are important for many adolescents in every nation. For example, a study of more than 3,000 Australian students, primarily of English heritage, found that late developers had four times the rate of self-harm (cutting or poisoning themselves) as did other students. This is a marked indication of serious depression (Patton et al., 2007).

>> **Response for Parents Worried About Early Puberty** (from page 386) Probably not. If she is overweight, her diet should change, but the hormone hypothesis is speculative. Genes are the main factor; she shares only one-eighth of her genes with her cousin.

SUMMING UP

Puberty usually begins between ages 8 and 14 (typically around age 11) in response to a chain reaction of hormone production from the hypothalamus to the pituitary to the adrenal and sex glands. Hormones affect emotions as well as the body: Adolescent outbursts of sudden anger, sadness, and lust are caused by hormones combined with reactions from other people to the young person's changing body. Many factors, including genes, body fat, and stress, affect the onset of puberty, especially among girls. Early or late puberty is less desirable than puberty at the same age as one's peers, and such off-time maturation may lead to depression, drug abuse, and other problems. ■

>> Nutrition

All the changes of puberty depend on adequate nourishment, yet many adolescents do not consume enough vitamins or minerals. Teenagers often skip breakfast, eat at midnight, guzzle down soda, and munch on salty, processed snacks. One reason is that their hormones affect their diurnal rhythms, including their appetites; another reason is that they seek independence, which may mean refusing to sit down to a family dinner.

Cohort and age are crucial. In the United States, each new generation eats less well than the previous one, and each 18-year-old tends to eat a less balanced diet than he or she did at age 10 (N. I. Larson et al., 2007). Most adolescents consume enough calories, but in 2007 only 19 percent of high school seniors ate the recommended five or more servings of fruits and vegetables a day (MMWR, June 6, 2008)—down from 27 percent just a decade earlier (MMWR, August 14, 1998).

Diet Deficiencies

Deficiencies of iron, calcium, zinc, and other minerals are especially noteworthy during adolescence. For instance, because menstruation depletes iron, anemia is more common among adolescent girls than among any other age group (Belamarich & Ayoob, 2001). Boys are also at risk because many push their bodies in physical labor or sports: Muscles need iron for growth as well as strength (Blum & Nelson-Mmari, 2004). The recommended daily dose of iron is 15 milligrams; less than half of all U.S. teenagers consume that much. Many adolescents spurn iron-rich foods (green vegetables, eggs, and meat) in favor of iron-poor chips, sweets, and fries.

Similarly, although the daily recommended intake of calcium for teenagers is 1,300 milligrams, most consume less than 500 milligrams a day. About half of adult bone mass is acquired from

Come Here Often? Teenagers worldwide (like this group in Yangshuo, China) are attracted by fast-food restaurants because the cheap food and public setting of such places make them ideal for snacking and socializing. However, the food—usually high in fat and low in nutrition—contributes to overweight and undernourishment in many young customers.

LEE SNIDER / THE IMAGE WORKS

ages 10 to 20, which means many contemporary teenagers will develop osteoporosis (fragile bones), a major cause of disability, injury, and death in late adulthood among people of European descent.

One reason for calcium deficiency is that milk drinking has declined. In 1957, most North American children drank at least 24 ounces (about 3/4 liter) of milk each day, providing most (about 900 milligrams) of their daily calcium requirement. Fifty years later (2007), only 15 percent of U.S. ninth-graders drank that much. Among twelfth-graders, rates were only 9 percent for girls and 19 percent for boys (MMWR, June 6, 2008).

Choices Made

Economists advocate a "nudge" to encourage people to make better choices, not only in nutrition but in all aspects of their lives (Thaler & Sunstein, 2008). In many ways, however, teenagers are nudged in the wrong direction. Nutritional deficiencies result from the food choices that young adolescents are allowed, even enticed, to make.

Fast-food establishments cluster around high schools, often with additional seating on another floor, to encourage teenagers to socialize. Price influences food choices, especially for adolescents (Epstein et al., 2006), and unfortunately, milk and fruit juice are more expensive than fruit punch or soda. In New York City in 2010, a McDonald's salad cost five times more than a hamburger ($5.59 versus $1.09).

Furthermore, nutritional deficiencies increase when schools have vending machines that offer soda and snacks (Cullen & Zakeri, 2004). A nudge such as higher prices, less attractive placement, or healthier selections in school vending machines might improve nutrition.

A more drastic strategy would be to ban the purchase of unhealthy foods in schools altogether—a strategy used by 29 percent of U.S. high schools in 2002 and 69 percent in 2008. During the same years, obesity leveled off in the United States, although school policies are only one of several possible explanations. Experts call for "increased efforts" at schools and new awareness among adolescents (MMWR, October 9, 2009).

body image A person's idea of how his or her body looks.

Body Image

Another reason for poor nutrition among teenagers is anxiety about **body image**—that is, a person's idea of how his or her body looks. Few teenagers welcome every change in their bodies. Unfortunately, they tend to focus on, and exaggerate, imperfections (as did the three girls in the anecdote that opens this chapter).

Girls go on diets because they want to be thinner, partly because boys tend to prefer dating thin girls (Halpern et al., 2005). Boys want to look taller and stronger, a concern that increases from ages 12 to 17, partly because girls value well-developed muscles in males (D. Jones & Crawford, 2005). Thus, both sexes become less happy with their own bodies and more superficial in their evaluation of the other sex as sexual interest increases. This is true worldwide. A longitudinal study in Korea found that, as in the West, body image dissatisfaction began in early adolescence and increased until age 15 or so. For 10-year-old girls and 15-year-old boys, body dissatisfaction increased depression and thoughts of suicide (Kim & Kim, 2009).

In North America, the ideal body type and facial appearance is Anglo-Saxon: Many teenagers are bombarded by media images that differ markedly from those their mirrors reflect. Of course, few Anglo-

Does He Like What He Sees? During adolescence, all the facial features do not develop at the same rate, and the hair often becomes less manageable. If B. T. here is typical, he is not pleased with the appearance of his nose, lips, ears, or hair.

LAURA DWIGHT

Saxon youth achieve the media ideal, either. Again, the problems are worldwide. A longitudinal study in China found that adolescents in that region had similar anxieties about weight gain as do U.S. teenagers (Chen & Jackson, 2009). Everywhere, young adolescents wish their bodies looked different.

Eating Disorders

One result of dissatisfaction with body image is that many teenagers—mostly girls—eat erratically or ingest drugs (especially diet pills) to lose weight; others—mostly boys—take steroids to increase muscle mass. Eating disorders are rare in childhood but increase dramatically at puberty, with distorted body image, food obsession, and depression (Bulik et al., 2008; Hrabosky & Thomas, 2008).

Individual adolescents sometimes switch from obsessive dieting to overeating to overexercising and back again, without yet having any diagnosable disorder (Henig, 2004). Obesity is a problem at every age, discussed in Chapters 8, 11, and 20. Here we describe two eating disorders that are common in adolescence.

Anorexia Nervosa

Some individuals suffer from **anorexia nervosa,** a disorder characterized by voluntary starvation that, for between 5 and 20 percent of sufferers, leads to death by organ failure or suicide. If someone's body mass index (BMI) is 18 or lower, or if she (or, less often, he) loses more than 10 percent of body weight within a month or two, anorexia is suspected. The disorder is officially diagnosed when four symptoms are evident (American Psychiatric Association, 2000):

- Refusal to maintain a weight that is at least 85 percent of normal BMI
- Intense fear of weight gain
- Disturbed body perception and denial of the problem
- Absence of menstruation (in adolescent and adult females)

Although anorexia existed in earlier centuries (think of the saints who refused all food), the disease was undiagnosed until about 1950, when some high-achieving, upper-class young women became so emaciated that they died. Soon anorexia became evident among younger women (the rate spikes at puberty and again in emerging adulthood), among men, and in every nation and ethnic group (Chao et al., 2008). Certain alleles increase the risk of anorexia (J. K. Young, 2010), as is evident from the higher rates among people who have a close relative, especially a monozygotic twin, with anorexia or severe depression. However, not everyone with genetic vulnerability becomes anorexic: Context is pivotal.

Bulimia Nervosa

About three times as common as anorexia is **bulimia nervosa,** a disorder clinically present in 1 to 3 percent of young adult women in the United States. The person (again, usually female) with bulimia overeats compulsively, wolfing down thousands of calories within an hour or two, and then purges via vomiting or laxatives. Most people with bulimia are close to normal in weight and therefore unlikely to starve. However, they risk serious health problems, including damage to their gastrointestinal systems and cardiac arrest from electrolyte imbalance (Shannon, 2007).

Three things combine to warrant a clinical diagnosis of bulimia:

- Bingeing and purging at least once a week for three months
- Uncontrollable urges to overeat
- A distorted perception of body size

Guess Her Age Jennifer has gained some weight since she was first admitted to an eating-disorders clinic, but she still looks younger than her years. One hypothesis about anorexia is that it stems from an unconscious desire to avoid growing up. (Jennifer is 18 years old.)

anorexia nervosa An eating disorder characterized by self-starvation. Affected individuals voluntarily undereat and often overexercise, depriving their vital organs of nutrition. Anorexia can be fatal.

bulimia nervosa An eating disorder characterized by binge eating and subsequent purging, usually by induced vomiting and/or use of laxatives.

These symptoms and those for anorexia are from DSM-IV, the fourth edition of the *Diagnostic and Statistical Manual of Mental Disorders*, published by the American Psychiatric Association. Many experts think that eating disorders are much more widespread among adolescents than these official statistics and listed symptoms portray. For all eating problems, treatment that begins in early adolescence has a better chance of halting the problem than treatment begun later on (Keel & Brown, 2010).

Origins of Disordered Eating

Many adolescents have unhealthy eating habits: They try new diets, go without food for 24 hours (as did 12 percent of U.S. high school students in 2007), or take diet drugs (6 percent) (MMWR, June 6, 2008). Some become so hungry that they binge; some dieters become anorexic; others eat oddly (only rice, or only once a day) for awhile.

Each episode of bingeing, purging, or fasting makes the next one easier. A combination of causes leads to obesity, anorexia, or bulimia, with at least five general elements—cultural images, stress, puberty, hormones, and childhood patterns—all making disordered eating more likely (Shannon, 2007).

One family practice reduces the risk of adolescent eating disorders: eating together during childhood (Franko et al., 2008). It is not known whether family cohesion is the protective factor or whether family meals directly encourage good nutrition. Nonetheless, developmentalists agree that nutrition begins with childhood habits and family routines. Some infants who are overweight or underweight do not develop nutritional problems, but the older an overweight or underweight child is, the more likely an eating disorder will occur.

SUMMING UP

All adolescents are vulnerable to poor nutrition; few are well nourished. Insufficient consumption of iron and calcium is particularly common, as fast food and nutrient-poor snacks often replace family meals. Both boys and girls often choose junk food instead of a balanced diet, in part because they are concerned about peer opinions regarding their appearance. The combination of nutritional deficiencies, peer culture, and anxiety about body image sometimes causes obesity, anorexia, and bulimia, influenced by heredity and childhood patterns. All adolescent nutrition problems have lifelong, potentially life-threatening, consequences. ■

>> The Transformations of Puberty

Every body part changes during puberty. For simplicity, the study of this transformation from a child into an adult is traditionally divided into two parts: growth and sexuality. We will use that division here. We will also describe a third transformation—changes in the adolescent brain. All three relate to adolescent cognitive and psychosocial development, described in Chapters 15 and 16, making this chapter division somewhat artificial. However, it is useful to consider each major transformation separately.

Growing Bigger and Stronger

growth spurt The relatively sudden and rapid physical growth that occurs during puberty. Each body part increases in size on a schedule: Weight usually precedes height, and growth of the limbs precedes growth of the torso.

The first set of changes is called the **growth spurt**—a sudden, uneven jump in the size of almost every body part, turning children into adults. Growth proceeds from the extremities to the core (the opposite of the earlier proximodistal growth). Thus, fingers and toes lengthen before hands and feet, hands and feet before arms and legs, arms and legs before the torso. This growth is not always symmetrical: One foot, one breast, or even one ear may grow later than the other.

Because the torso is the last body part to grow, many pubescent children are temporarily big-footed, long-legged, and short-waisted. If young teenagers complain that their jeans don't fit, they are probably correct, even if those same jeans fit when their parents bought them a month earlier. (At least the parents had advance warning when they had to buy their children's shoes in the adult section.)

Sequence: Weight, Height, Muscles

As the bones lengthen and harden (visible on X-rays) and the growth spurt begins, children eat more and gain weight. Exactly when, where, and how much weight they gain depends on heredity, hormones, diet, exercise, and gender. For instance, at age 17, the average girl has twice the percentage of body fat as her male classmate, whose increased weight is mostly muscle (Roche & Sun, 2003).

A height spurt follows the weight spurt, then a year or two later a muscle spurt occurs. Thus, the pudginess and clumsiness of early puberty are usually gone by late adolescence. (The young teenager who took nutritional supplements or lifted weights could have simply waited a year or two.)

Arm muscles develop more in boys. On average, a boy's arm muscles are twice as strong at age 18 as at age 8, enabling him to throw a ball four times as far (Malina et al., 2004) (see Figure 14.3). Other muscles are gender-neutral. For instance, both sexes run faster, with boys not much faster than girls (unless the girls choose to slow down) (see Figure 14.4).

Organ Growth

In both sexes, organs mature. Lungs triple in weight; consequently, adolescents breathe more deeply and slowly. The heart doubles in size and beats more slowly, decreasing the pulse rate while increasing blood pressure (Malina et al., 2004). Consequently, endurance improves: Some teenagers can run for miles or dance for hours.

Both weight and height increase *before* muscles and internal organs: Athletic training and weight lifting should be tailored to an adolescent's size the previous year, to protect immature muscles and organs. Sports injuries are the most common school accidents, and they increase at puberty, partly because the height spurt precedes increases in bone mass, making young adolescents vulnerable to fractures (Roche & Sun, 2003).

Only one organ system, the lymphoid system (which includes the tonsils and adenoids), *decreases* in size, making teenagers less susceptible to respiratory ailments. Mild asthma, for example, often switches off at puberty (Busse & Lemanske, 2005), and teenagers have fewer colds than younger children do. This is aided by growth in the larynx, which gives deeper voices to both sexes, dramatically noticeable in boys.

Another organ system, the skin, becomes oilier, sweatier, and more prone to acne. Hair also changes. During puberty, hair on the head and limbs becomes coarser and darker. New hair grows under arms, on faces, and over sex organs (pubic hair, from the same Latin root as *puberty*). Visible facial and chest hair is sometimes

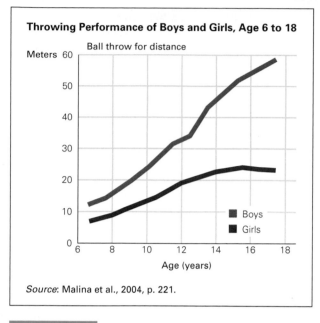

Throwing Performance of Boys and Girls, Age 6 to 18

Source: Malina et al., 2004, p. 221.

FIGURE 14.3

Big Difference All children experience an increase in muscles during puberty, but gender differences are much more apparent in some gross motor skills than in others. For instance, upper-arm strength increases dramatically only in boys.

Observation Quiz At what age does the rate of increase in the average boy's muscle strength accelerate? (see answer, page 394)

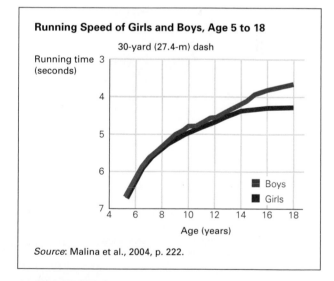

Running Speed of Girls and Boys, Age 5 to 18

Source: Malina et al., 2004, p. 222.

FIGURE 14.4

Little Difference Both sexes develop longer and stronger legs during puberty.

>> **Answer to Observation Quiz** (from page 393) About age 13. This is most obvious in ball throwing (Figure 14.3), but it is also apparent in the 30-yard dash (Figure 14.4).

primary sex characteristics The parts of the body that are directly involved in reproduction, including the vagina, uterus, ovaries, testicles, and penis.

secondary sex characteristics Physical traits that are not directly involved in reproduction but that indicate sexual maturity, such as a man's beard and a woman's breasts.

CLEVE BRYANT / PHOTOEDIT

Male Pride Teenage boys typically feel serious pride when they first need to shave. Although facial hair is taken as a sign of masculinity, a person's hairiness is actually genetic as well as hormonal. Further evidence that the Western world's traditional racial categories are not aligned with genetic variations comes from East Asia: Many Chinese men cannot grow beards or mustaches, but most Japanese men can.

considered a sign of manliness, although hairiness in either sex depends on genes as well as on hormones. Girls pluck or dye any facial hair they see; boys proudly shave or grow "soul patches." In these ways, both sexes display sexual/cultural reactions.

Sexual Maturation

Now we turn to the changes that transform boys into men and girls into women.

Sexual Characteristics

The body characteristics that are directly involved in conception and pregnancy are called **primary sex characteristics.** During puberty, every primary sex organ (the ovaries, the uterus, the penis, and the testes) increases dramatically in size and matures in function. By the end of the process, reproduction is possible.

At the same time as maturation of the primary sex characteristics, secondary sex characteristics develop. **Secondary sex characteristics** are bodily features that do not directly affect fertility (hence they are secondary) but that signify masculinity or femininity. One such characteristic is shape. Young boys and girls have similar shapes, but at puberty, males widen at the shoulders and grow about 5 inches taller than females, while girls develop breasts and a wider pelvis. Breasts and broad hips are often considered signs of womanhood, but neither is required for conception; thus, they are secondary, not primary, sex characteristics.

Secondary sex characteristics are important psychologically, if not biologically. Consider breasts. Many adolescent girls buy "minimizer," "maximizer," "training," or "shaping" bras, hoping that their breasts will conform to an idealized body image. During the same years, many boys are horrified to notice a swelling around their nipples—a normal and temporary result of the erratic hormones of early puberty. If a boy's breast growth is very disturbing, drugs can reduce the swelling, although many doctors prefer to let time, rather than tamoxifen, deal with the problem (Derman et al., 2003).

The pattern of growth at the scalp line differs for the two sexes as well, a secondary sex characteristic that few people notice. Instead, they notice gender markers in hair length and style, which can attain the status of a secondary sex characteristic. To become more attractive, many adolescents spend considerable time, money, and thought on their visible hair—growing, gelling, shaving, curling, straightening, highlighting, brushing, combing, styling, dyeing, wetting, drying . . .

Sexual Activity

The primary and secondary sex characteristics just described are not the only manifestations of the sex hormones. Fantasizing, flirting, hand-holding, staring, standing, sitting, walking, displaying, and touching are all done in particular ways to reflect gender, availability, and culture. As already explained, hormones trigger thoughts and emotions, but the social context shapes thoughts into enjoyable fantasies, shameful preoccupations, frightening impulses, or actual contact.

A recent study on sexual behaviors such as hand-holding and cuddling among young adolescents found that biological maturation was only one factor in whether or not such activities occurred: Especially among European Americans, those girls with lower self-esteem were more likely to engage in sexual intimacy (Hipwell et al., 2010).

Regarding sex-related impulses, some experts believe that boys are more influenced by hormones and girls by culture (Baumeister & Blackhart, 2007). Perhaps. If a relationship includes sexual intimacy, girls seem more concerned than boys do about the depth of the romance (Zani & Cicognani, 2006). Girls hope their partners say "I'll love you forever"; boys like to hear "I want you now."

However, everyone is influenced by both hormones and society. All adolescents have sexual interests they did not previously have (biology), which produce behaviors that teenagers in other nations would not do (culture) (Moore & Rosenthal, 2006). Since only girls can become pregnant, their wish for long-term commitment may be a consequence of biology, not culture. If this is so, the gender difference—girls' need for love versus boys' lust for sex—may disappear as advances in contraception make pregnancy unlikely. Already the gender gap in sexual experience is narrowing.

It may seem that choosing sexual partners is a private and personal matter. Yet culture rules. For example, most North Americans find partners who are about the same age as they are (Zani & Cicognani, 2006), but in Finland and Norway, girls are sexually active later than boys. So boys find older partners for their first encounter, and women might begin sexual intimacy with a younger man. In Greece and Portugal, the opposite occurs: Girls' first partners tend to be older (Teitler, 2002).

These generalities do not apply to everyone within any given nation. Subgroups as well as cohorts always differ. One specific was found in a survey of 704 adolescents in Ghana: More 16-year-old girls than boys were sexually experienced, but those experienced girls had usually had only one partner, whereas the experienced boys had had several. Muslim youth in Ghana were more likely to be virgins than were Christian youth, who themselves were more likely to be virgins than those of neither faith (Glover et al., 2003).

As in Ghana, religious teachings affect sexual behavior worldwide. In a study of Jewish and Muslim adolescents in Israel and the United States, the romances of Muslim youth seldom included sexual intimacy, even in thought (Magen, 1998). One Muslim boy in Israel reported "the most wonderful and happiest day of my life":

> A girl passed our house. And she looked at me. She looked at me as though I were an angel in paradise. I looked at her, and stopped still, and wondered and marveled. . . . [Later] she passed near us, stopped, and called my friend, and asked my name and who I am. I trembled all over and could hardly stand on my feet. I used my brain, since otherwise I would have fallen to the floor. I couldn't stand it any longer and went home.

[quoted in Magen, 1998, pp. 97–98]

A Daughter's Promise At a "purity ball" in Colorado, a father reads the pledge signed by his 14-year-old daughter, in which she promises that she will abstain from sex until she marries. Young adolescents who take a virginity pledge are more likely than their peers to be celibate in high school. However, they are also more likely to become parents before they graduate from college.

A 15-Year-Old A religious ceremony is part of the Quinceañera, a coming-of-age celebration for girls in Latino communities.

Cohort affects sexual activity as well. For most of the twentieth century, surveys in North America reported increasing sexual activity among adolescents. This trend reversed in the 1990s. In 1991, 62.4 percent of U.S. eleventh-graders said they had had intercourse, but in 2009 only 53 percent said so (MMWR, June 4, 2010).

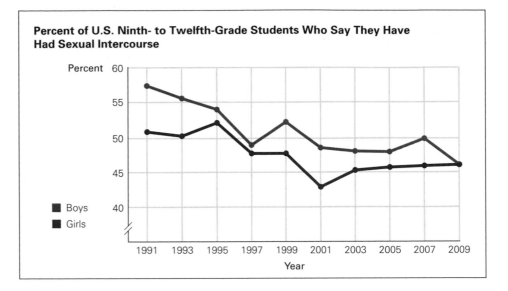

Percent of U.S. Ninth- to Twelfth-Grade Students Who Say They Have Had Sexual Intercourse

FIGURE 14.5

Boys and Girls Together Boys tend to be somewhat more sexually experienced than girls during the high school years, but since the Youth Risk Behavior Survey began in 1991, the overall trend has been toward equality in rates of sexual activity.

During the same time period, the double standard (with boys expected to be more sexually active than girls) decreased, and today boys and girls are quite similar in reported sexual activity (see Figure 14.5). These trends are apparent in every ethnic group, but some ethnic differences are apparent between 1991 and 2009. For ninth- through twelfth-graders, among African Americans, rates of sexual experience were down 15.8 percentage points (from 81 to 65.2 percent); among European Americans, down 8 percentage points (from 50 to 42 percent); among Latinos, down 3.7 percentage points (from 53 to 49.3 percent) (MMWR, June 4, 2010).

All these examples demonstrate that a universal experience (rising hormones) that produces another universal experience (growth of primary and secondary sex characteristics) is powerfully influenced by cohort, gender, and culture.

Problems with Sexual Activity

Before focusing specifically on the problems with sexual activity, we should acknowledge that sex has become less problematic worldwide in the past decades. Here are three specifics:

Pin It on Him Boutonniere, corsage, formal shirt with matching tie, bare arms—all are common at U.S. high school proms, including here, at Notre Dame in Harper Woods, Michigan. Yet these sights are unknown to most 17-year-olds in other nations. Despite such cultural oddities and this once-in-a-lifetime moment, Mariel West and John Felczak are evidence of a worldwide phenomenon: sexual attraction in late adolescence.

- *Teen births overall have decreased.* For example, between 1960 and 2005, the adolescent birth rate in China was cut in half (reducing the United Nations' projections of the world's population by about a billion). This decline is continuing in every ethnic group within every nation. For instance, in 1991, the birth rate overall for U.S. teenagers aged 15 to 17 was 39 per 1,000; in 2007, the ratio was 22 per 1,000 (U.S. Bureau of the Census, 2009).
- *The use of "protection" has risen.* Contraception, particularly condom use among adolescent boys, has increased markedly in most nations since 1990 (Santelli & Melnikas, 2010). The U.S. Youth Risk Behavior Survey found that 70 percent of sexually active ninth-grade boys had used a condom during their most recent intercourse (MMWR, June 4, 2010).

- *The teen abortion rate is down.* In the United States, the teen abortion rate in 2005 was less than the rate 15 years earlier (for all girls aged 14 to 19, the rate was 22.3 per 1,000 in 2006 and 48.5 per 1,000 in 1990) (U.S. Bureau of the Census, 2009).

Now we focus on biological consequences of sexual activity—pregnancy and infections—and on sexual abuse.

Sex Too Soon

Sex can, of course, be thrilling and affirming, a bonding experience for a couple. However, compared to 100 years ago, adolescent sexual activity—especially if it results in birth—is more hazardous because five circumstances have changed:

- Earlier puberty and weaker social taboos mean teens have sexual experiences at younger ages. Early sex correlates with depression and drug abuse.
- Most teenage mothers have no husbands to help them. A century ago, teenage mothers were married; now, in the United States, 85 percent are unwed.
- Raising a child has become more complex and expensive.
- Mothers of teenagers are usually employed and therefore are less available to help their young daughters and new grandchildren.
- Sexually transmitted infections are more common and dangerous.

As you just read, the overall rate of teen birth is declining, as is the teen abortion rate. However, the U.S. rate is the highest of any developed nation (true among every ethnic group), and since 2005 teen pregnancy has increased slightly—an alarming statistic (Santelli & Melnikas, 2010). If a pregnant girl is under 16 (most are not, but the rate of young pregnancies has also been rising over the past year or two), she is more likely to experience complications—including spontaneous and induced abortion, high blood pressure, stillbirth, preterm birth, and low-birthweight newborns—than are teenagers who are age 16 or more. Babies born to young parents (even as "old" as 17 or 18) have higher rates of medical, educational, and social problems lifelong.

There are many reasons in addition to maternal age for these hazards. Poverty and lack of education correlate with teenage pregnancy and with every problem just listed (Santelli & Melnikas, 2010). Beyond that, younger teenagers often postpone prenatal care (Borkowski et al., 2007), and after birth, adolescents are less likely to provide the responsive mothering that newborns need. Consequently, insecure attachment (see Chapter 7) is more common. However, some problems are a direct consequence of age: Immature bodies are less ready for pregnancy and birth, and nutritional needs for two growing people are harder to meet than for one.

Sexual Abuse

Teenage pregnancy is risky, as just described, but sexual abuse is much worse, as it harms a person's development lifelong. **Child sexual abuse** is any sexual activity between a juvenile and an adult, with age 18 a common demarcation (although legal age varies by state). The most common time for sexual abuse is in early puberty, with girls particularly vulnerable. Puberty is not only a risk factor for sexual abuse; it also makes the emotional consequences worse (Graber et al., 2010). Virtually every adolescent problem, including early pregnancy, drug abuse,

Rosie Will Be Fine Monica, here with her dog Rosie, is a mom-to-be—as are 13 percent of her female classmates at Timkin High School in Canton, Ohio. She is one of the fortunate ones; already a senior, she will probably earn her diploma. Plus, she is six months past conception, so the fetus is likely to be healthy. Teenagers typically welcome their unplanned babies but tend to have trouble raising them. This child will reach puberty before Monica is 30; their mutual immaturity will increase the child's risk of depression, delinquency, and another teen pregnancy.

child sexual abuse Any erotic activity that arouses an adult and excites, shames, or confuses a child, whether or not the victim protests and whether or not genital contact is involved.

TABLE 14.1

Age and Sex Abuse: United States, 2007

Age	Number of Sex-Abuse Victims	Percent of Maltreatment That Is Sex Abuse
Less than 1 year	315	0.3%
1–3	3,249	2.2
4–7	13,137	7.4
8–11	13,459	9.5
12–15	19,848	14.5
16–17	6,084	13.5

Source: U.S. Department of Health and Human Services, 2010.

sexually transmitted infection (STI) A disease spread by sexual contact, including syphilis, gonorrhea, genital herpes, chlamydia, and HIV.

Especially for Health Practitioners How might you encourage adolescents to seek treatment for STIs? (see response, page 400)

eating disorders, suicide, and so on, is more common in adolescents who are sexually abused.

The problem is worldwide. The United Nations reports that millions of girls in their early teens are forced into marriage, genital surgery, or prostitution (often across national borders) each year (Pinheiro, 2006). Exact numbers are elusive. Almost every nation has laws against child sexual abuse, but these laws are rarely enforced, and sensationalism about a single horrific case often crowds out systemic efforts to prevent, monitor, and eliminate the problem (Davidson, 2005).

In the United States, overall rates of abuse are declining (see Table 14.1), perhaps because adolescents are becoming better informed about sexual activity (Finkelhor & Jones, 2004). Evidence of this is condom use, more common among the young (see Figure 14.6). However, many adolescents remain ignorant. Some schools teach only the biology of sex and disease, peers brag and lie about their sexual exploits, and the teen media virtually never discuss healthy sexuality (Hust et al., 2008). That leaves youth to depend on their families—the worst possible source of information and protection for sexually abused adolescents, since the abusers are often family members, and relatives (including the abuser) sometimes blame the child. Many children trust their abusers. That makes them doubly distressed later on, when they realize what happened (Clancy, 2010).

As with other types of child maltreatment, the consequences extend far beyond the event. Young people who are sexually exploited tend to fear sexual relationships and to devalue themselves lifelong. Abusers often isolate adolescents from their peers, depriving them of the friendships and romances that aid a healthy and satisfying life.

Sexually Transmitted Infections

Unlike teen pregnancy and sexual abuse, the other major problem of teenage sex shows no signs of abating. A **sexually transmitted infection (STI)** (sometimes referred to as sexually transmitted disease [STD] or venereal disease [VD]) is any infection transmitted through sexual contact. Worldwide, sexually active teenagers have higher rates of the most common STIs—gonorrhea, genital herpes, and chlamydia—than sexually active people of any other age group (World Health Organization, 2005). In the United States, 15- to 24-year-olds constitute only one-fourth of the sexually active population but account for half of all sexually transmitted infections. On average for urban U.S. teenagers, an STI is diagnosed only two years after intercourse begins (Tu et al., 2009).

Those who have sexual intercourse before age 16 are twice as likely to catch an infection as are those who begin sexual activity at age 20 (Ryan et al., 2008). One reason is biological. Fully developed women have some natural biological defenses against STIs; this is less true for pubescent girls, who are more likely to catch any STI they are exposed to, including HIV-AIDS (World Health Organization, 2005). In addition, if symptoms appear, sexually active teens are slow to seek treatment or to alert their partners. In cultures or families where teenagers are forbidden to have sex, adolescents are particularly likely to avoid treatment for STIs because that would be evidence of sexual activity. In this regard, adolescents whose partners are of the same sex experience added hesitancy if their community considers such relationships shameful.

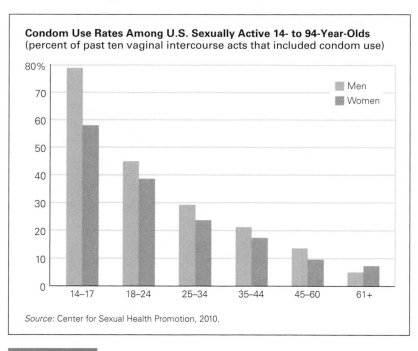

Condom Use Rates Among U.S. Sexually Active 14- to 94-Year-Olds
(percent of past ten vaginal intercourse acts that included condom use)

Source: Center for Sexual Health Promotion, 2010.

FIGURE 14.6

Pleasure and Protection Teenagers are much more likely to use condoms than are older adults, who probably never used them when they were young. This study found that sexual pleasure did not correlate with condom use. However, a negative correlation was found between condom use and having a steady partner—another reason for the age differences.

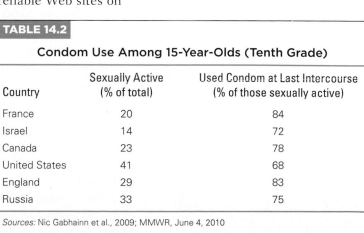

No Safer? Educational posters and even intense educational programs have little proven effect on the incidence of AIDS among adolescents. This poster was displayed outside an HIV testing center in Windhoek, Namibia, a country that has one of the highest HIV infection rates in the world.

There are hundreds of STIs (James, 2007). *Chlamydia* is the most frequently reported one; it often begins without symptoms, yet it can cause permanent infertility. A laboratory test can detect chlamydia, and it can be treated and cured, but many young people avoid doctors. Worse is *human papillomavirus (HPV),* which has no immediate consequences but, later in life, increases a female's risk of uterine cancer and death. Immunization before the first intercourse makes contracting HPV much less likely, but many parents hesitate to immunize their 11- and 12-year-olds. The interested reader is encouraged to consult other publications, doctors, and reliable Web sites on the topic.

National differences in laws and rates of STIs are notable, with rates among U.S. teenagers the highest in medically advanced nations. Internationally, a comparison of 30 nations found that French teenagers were among the most likely to use condoms and those in the United States, the least (Nic Gabhainn et al., 2009; MMWR, June 4, 2010) (see Table 14.2). One reason may be that, by law, every French high school (including Catholic ones) is required to provide students with free, confidential medical care as well as condoms; by contrast, providing either medical care or condoms was illegal at many U.S. schools when the data on the chart were collected.

TABLE 14.2

Condom Use Among 15-Year-Olds (Tenth Grade)

Country	Sexually Active (% of total)	Used Condom at Last Intercourse (% of those sexually active)
France	20	84
Israel	14	72
Canada	23	78
United States	41	68
England	29	83
Russia	33	75

Sources: Nic Gabhainn et al., 2009; MMWR, June 4, 2010

>> **Response for Health Practitioners** (from page 398): Many adolescents are intensely concerned about privacy and fearful of adult interference. This means your first task is to convince the teenagers that you are nonjudgmental and that everything is confidential.

Neurological Development

Like the other parts of the body, different parts of the brain grow at different rates (Blakemore, 2008). The limbic system, responsible for the intense fear and excitement from the amygdala, matures before the prefrontal cortex, where planning ahead, emotional regulation, and impulse control occur. Myelination and maturation continue, proceeding from the inner brain to the cortex and from back to front (Sowell et al., 2007). That means the adolescent instinctual and emotional areas develop before the reflective, analytic ones do. Furthermore, the hormones of puberty target the amygdala directly, whereas the cortex responds more to age and experience. As a consequence, early puberty means emotional rushes, unchecked by caution.

In addition, emotional control, as evidenced by fMRI studies of the brain, is not fully developed until adulthood (Luna et al., 2010). When compared with 18- to 23-year-olds, 14- to 15-year-olds show more fully aroused reward centers of the brain, making them seek more excitement and pleasure (Van Leijenhorst et al., 2010).

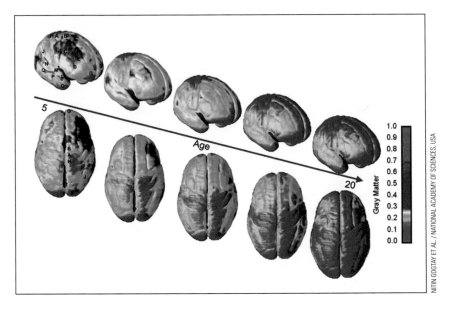

Same People, But Not the Same Brain
These brain scans are part of a longitudinal study that repeatedly compares the proportion of gray matter from childhood through adolescence. Gray matter is reduced as white matter increases, in part because pruning during the teen years (the fourth and fifth images here) allows intellectual connections to build. As the authors of one study that included this chart explain, teenagers may "look like an adult, but cognitively they are not there yet" (K. Powell, 2006, p. 865).

NITIN GOGTAY ET AL. / NATIONAL ACADEMY OF SCIENCES, USA

Caution Needed

Not only are adolescents likely to forget caution when excitement rises, but scientists are vulnerable to the same problem when studying the adolescent brain. As explained in Chapter 6, the fMRI, the PET scan, and other measures of neurological activity are expensive and complex. Furthermore, "the images generated by such methods may have a power to captivate that reaches beyond their power to explain" (Miller, 2008, p. 1413). Reliable, longitudinal, multidisciplinary, replicated research on the brains of typical 10- to 17-year-olds is scarce.

Although neuroscientists seek more detailed data, many scientists are understandably excited by recent discoveries about the adolescent brain. The fact that the frontal lobes (prefrontal cortex) are the last part of the brain to mature may explain something that has bewildered adults: Many adolescents are driven by the excitement of new experiences, sensations, and peers—forgetting the caution that their parents have tried to instill (Steinberg, 2008). The following case is one example.

A CASE TO STUDY

"What Were You Thinking?"

Laurence Steinberg is a noted expert on adolescent thinking. He is also a father.

> When my son, Benjamin, was 14, he and three of his friends decided to sneak out of the house where they were spending the night and visit one of their girlfriends at around two in the morning. When they arrived at the girl's house, they positioned themselves under her bedroom window, threw pebbles against her windowpanes, and tried to scale the side of the house. Modern technology, unfortunately, has made it harder to play Romeo these days. The boys set off the house's burglar alarm, which activated a siren and simultaneously sent a direct notification to the local police station, which dispatched a patrol car. When the siren went off, the boys ran down the street and right smack into the police car, which was heading to the girl's home. Instead of stopping and explaining their activity, Ben and his friends scattered and ran off in different directions through the neighborhood. One of the boys was caught by the police and taken back to his home, where his parents were awakened and the boy questioned.
>
> I found out about this affair the following morning, when the girl's mother called our home to tell us what Ben had done. . . . After his near brush with the local police, Ben had returned to the house out of which he had snuck, where he slept soundly until I awakened him with an angry telephone call, telling him to gather his clothes and wait for me in front of his friend's house. On our drive home, after delivering a long lecture about what he had done and about the dangers of running from armed police in the dark when they believe they may have interrupted a burglary, I paused.
>
> "What were you thinking?" I asked.
> "That's the problem, Dad," Ben replied, "I wasn't."

[Steinberg, 2004, pp. 51, 52]

Steinberg agrees with this last insight by his son. As he expresses it, "The problem is not that Ben's decision-making was deficient. The problem is that it was nonexistent" (Steinberg, 2004, p. 52). In his analysis, Steinberg points out a characteristic of adolescent thought: When emotions are intense, especially when one is with peers, the logical part of the brain shuts down. This shutdown is not reflected in questionnaires that require teenagers to respond to paper-and-pencil questions regarding hypothetical dilemmas. On those tests, most teenagers think carefully and answer correctly. They have been taught the risks of sex and drugs in biology or health classes in school. However,

> the prospect of visiting a hypothetical girl from class cannot possibly carry the excitement about the possibility of surprising someone you have a crush on with a visit in the middle of the night. It is easier to put on a hypothetical condom during an act of hypothetical sex than it is to put on a real one when one is in the throes of passion. It is easier to just say no to a hypothetical beer than it is to a cold frosty one on a summer night.

[Steinberg, 2004, p. 53]

Ben reached adulthood safely. Some other teenagers, with less cautious police or less diligent parents, do not. Ideally, research on adolescent brains will help protect teens from their dangerous impulses (Monastersky, 2007). Brain immaturity is not the origin of every "troublesome adolescent behavior," but it is true that teenage brains have underdeveloped "response inhibition, emotional regulation, and organization" (Sowell et al., 2007, p. 59) because their prefrontal cortexes are immature.

The combination of the normal sequence of brain maturation (limbic system, then cortex by the earlier 20s) and the early onset of puberty means that, for many contemporary teenagers, emotions rule behavior (Blakemore, 2008; Compas, 2004). The limbic system, unchecked by the slower-maturing prefrontal cortex, makes strong, immediate sensations attractive to teens. For this reason,

> adolescents *like* intensity, excitement, and arousal. They are drawn to music videos that shock and bombard the senses. Teenagers flock to horror and slasher movies. They dominate queues waiting to ride the high-adrenaline rides at amusement parks. Adolescence is a time when sex, drugs, *very* loud music, and other high-stimulation experiences take on great appeal. It is a developmental period when an appetite for adventure, a predilection for risks, and a desire for novelty and thrills seem to reach naturally high levels.

[Dahl, 2004, pp. 7–8]

When stress, arousal, passion, sensory bombardment, drug intoxication, or deprivation is extreme, the adolescent brain is flooded with impulses that might

Not Me! A young woman jumps into the Pacific Ocean near Santa Cruz, California, while at a friend's birthday party. The jump is illegal, yet since 1975, 52 people have died taking that leap off these cliffs. Hundreds of young people each year decide that the thrill is worth the risk, aided by what they think are sensible precautions. (Note that she is wearing shoes. Also note that the dog has apparently decided against risking a jump.) As Chapter 17 explains, slightly older adolescents now jump into the Pacific off the California coast via parachute—even riskier since sharks also live there.

NORBERT SCHWERIN / THE IMAGE WORKS

shame adults. As further explained regarding drug abuse in Chapter 16, teenagers brag about being so drunk they were "wasted," "bombed," "smashed"—a state most adults try to avoid. Also, unlike adults, some teenagers choose to spend a night without sleep, go through a day without eating, exercise for hours in pain, play football after a mild concussion. The parts of the brain dedicated to analysis may be immature until years after the young person has hormonal rushes; overwhelming sexual urges; and access to fast cars, lethal weapons, or dangerous drugs.

One dangerous example of the cautious part of the brain being overwhelmed by the emotions of the moment comes from teens sending text messages while they are driving. In a recent survey, 64 percent of U.S. 16- to 17-year-olds say they have been in a car when the driver was texting—a practice that occurs in every state even though it is illegal in many of them (Madden & Lenhart, 2009). More generally, by far the most common cause of teenage death is motor-vehicle accidents; poor decisions (despite quick reflexes and better vision than at later ages) are almost always the reason.

Every decision people make, from whether or not to eat a peach to whether or not to enroll in college, requires balancing risk and reward, caution and attraction. For all of us, experiences, memories, emotions, and the prefrontal cortex help us decide to avoid some actions and participate in others. Neurological research finds that the reward parts of adolescents' brains (the parts that respond to excitement and pleasure) are far stronger than the inhibition parts (the parts that urge caution) (Van Leijenhorst et al., 2010). That fact is used to explain many adolescent actions that seem foolhardy to adults.

Benefits of Adolescent Brain Development

It is easy to be critical of adolescent behavior and then to blame it on hormones, or brains, or the media. Evidence of this attitude abounds. Yet remember from Chapter 1 that difference is not always deficit, and gains as well as losses are part of every life development. Thus, the fact that the limbic system develops faster than the prefrontal cortex has benefits as well as hazards.

With increased myelination and slower inhibition, reactions become lightning fast; such speed is valuable in many aspects of life. For instance, adolescent ath-

letes are potential superstars, not only quick but fearless as they steal a base, tackle a fullback, or race when their lungs feel as if they will burst. Ideally, coaches have the wisdom to channel such bravery. Furthermore, as the reward areas of the brain activate and the production of positive neurotransmitters increases, teenagers become happier. Reaction to a new love, or a first job, or even an A on a term paper can be ecstasy, a joy to be cherished in memory lifelong.

Adolescence is a good time to question tradition and learn new things. Before the brain becomes fully mature (at about age 25) and before another wave of pruning (at about age 18), "young brains have both fast-growing synapses and sections that remain unconnected" (Ruder, 2008, p. 8). This allows new connections to facilitate acquisition of new ideas, words, memories, personality patterns, and dance steps (Keating, 2004).

Synaptic growth enhances moral development as well. Adolescents question their elders and seek to forge their own standards. Values acquired during adolescence are more likely to endure than those learned later, after brain connections are firmly established. This is an asset if values developed during adolescence are less self-centered than those of children or are more culturally attuned than those of older generations.

In short, several aspects of adolescent brain development can be positive. The fact that the prefrontal cortex is still developing "confers benefits as well as risks. It helps explain the creativity of adolescence and early adulthood, before the brain becomes set in its ways" (Monastersky, 2007, p. A17). The emotional intensity of adolescents "intertwines with the highest levels of human endeavor: passion for ideas and ideals, passion for beauty, passion to create music and art" (Dahl, 2004, p. 21). As a practical application, those who care about the next generation must attend to the life lessons that adolescents are learning. Adults should provide "scaffolding and monitoring" until adolescents' brains can function well on their own (Dahl, quoted in Monastersky, 2007, p. A18).

By age 18, not only brains but also bodies can be strong and healthy, as described in this chapter. Most 18-year-olds are capable of hard physical work, problem-free reproduction, and peak athletic performance. Growth and sexual awakening, strength and speed, emotional intensity and hormonal rushes—all of these can be wonderful. Of course, adolescent minds and contexts are not always benign, as the following chapters describe. But before learning about alienation from school, or addiction to drugs, or juvenile delinquency, pause to appreciate the transformations just described.

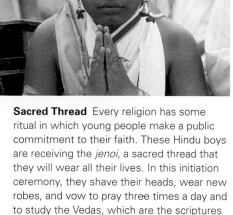

Sacred Thread Every religion has some ritual in which young people make a public commitment to their faith. These Hindu boys are receiving the *jenoi*, a sacred thread that they will wear all their lives. In this initiation ceremony, they shave their heads, wear new robes, and vow to pray three times a day and to study the Vedas, which are the scriptures of Hinduism.

SUMMING UP

Three transformations of puberty—the growth spurt, sexual differentiation, and brain maturation—are dramatic. Children become men or women, first in physical and sexual growth and then in brain maturation. Growth proceeds from the extremities to the center, so the limbs grow before the internal organs. Increase in weight precedes that in height, which precedes growth of the muscles and of the internal organs. Primary sex characteristics, which are connected to reproduction, and secondary sex characteristics, which signify masculinity or femininity, develop. Both boys and girls experience an increase in sexual interest as their bodies mature and their hormone levels rise. Adolescents' sexual behavior and thoughts are powerfully affected by culture.

The brain develops unevenly, with the limbic system ahead of the prefrontal cortex and the reward centers more active than the cautionary areas. As a result, adolescents are fast and fearless, qualities that may cause trouble or may benefit society. ∎

SUMMARY

Puberty Begins

1. Puberty refers to the various changes that transform a child's body into an adult one. Even before the teenage years, biochemical signals from the hypothalamus to the pituitary gland to the adrenal glands (the HPA axis) increase production of testosterone, estrogen, and various other hormones, which cause the body to develop.

2. Some emotional reactions, such as quick mood shifts and thoughts about sex, are directly caused by hormones. Others are caused by reactions (of others and then of the young person) to the physical changes of adolescence.

3. The body rhythms of life, both by the day and by the season, are regulated by hormones. In adolescence, these changes often result in sleep deprivation, partly because teenagers are often wide awake at night.

4. Puberty normally begins anytime from about age 8 to about age 14, most often between ages 10 and 13. The young person's sex, genetic background, body fat, and level of family stress all contribute to this variation in timing.

5. Girls generally begin and end the process of puberty before boys do, although the time gap in sexual maturity is much shorter than the two-year gender gap in reaching peak height.

6. Adolescents who do not reach puberty at about the same age as their friends experience additional stresses. Generally (depending on culture, community, and cohort), early-maturing girls and late-maturing boys have a particularly difficult time.

Nutrition

7. To sustain body growth, many adolescents consume large quantities of food, although they do not always make healthy choices. One reason for poor nutrition is the desire to lose (or, less often, gain) weight because of anxiety about body image.

8. Although eating disorders—overeating, anorexia, and bulimia—are not usually diagnosed until early adulthood, their precursors are evident during puberty. Many adolescents eat too much of the wrong foods or too little food overall.

The Transformations of Puberty

9. The growth spurt is an acceleration of growth in every part of the body. Peak weight usually precedes peak height, which is then followed by peak muscle growth. The lungs and the heart also increase in size and capacity.

10. Male–female differences become apparent at puberty. The maturation of primary sex characteristics means that by age 13 or so, after experiencing menarche or spermarche, teenagers are capable of reproducing.

11. Secondary sex characteristics are not directly involved in reproduction but do signify that the person is becoming a man or a woman. Body shape, breasts, voice, body hair, and numerous other features differentiate males from females. Sexual activity is influenced more by culture than by physiology.

12. Among the problems that adolescents face is the tendency to become sexually active before their bodies and minds are truly ready. Pregnancy before age 16 takes a physical toll on a growing girl, and STIs at any age can lead to infertility and even death.

13. Sexual abuse, which includes any sexually provocative activity that involves a juvenile and an adult, is more likely to occur in early adolescence than at other ages. Girls are most often victims; the perpetrators are most often family members.

14. Various parts of the brain mature during puberty, each at its own rate. The neurological areas dedicated to emotional arousal (including the amygdala) mature ahead of the areas that regulate and rationalize emotional expression (the prefrontal cortex).

15. Because of the sequence of brain development, many adolescents seek intense emotional experiences, untempered by rational thought. On the other hand, adolescents are quick to react and eager to learn. As a result, adolescents take risks, bravely or foolishly, with potential for harm as well as for social benefits.

KEY TERMS

puberty (p. 381)
menarche (p. 381)
spermarche (p. 381)
hormone (p. 382)
pituitary (p. 382)
adrenal glands (p. 382)

HPA (hypothalamus–pituitary–adrenal) axis (p. 382)
gonads (p. 382)
HPG (hypothalamus–pituitary–gonad) axis (p. 383)
estradiol (p. 383)

testosterone (p. 383)
secular trend (p. 386)
leptin (p. 386)
body image (p. 390)
anorexia nervosa (p. 391)
bulimia nervosa (p. 391)
growth spurt (p. 392)

primary sex characteristics (p. 394)
secondary sex characteristics (p. 394)
child sexual abuse (p. 397)
sexually transmitted infection (STI) (p. 398)

WHAT HAVE YOU LEARNED?

Puberty Begins

1. What are the first visible signs of puberty?

2. What parts of a teenager's body are the last to reach full growth?

3. What do hormones do?

4. Why do adolescents have sudden, intense emotions, such as anger, ecstasy, or despair?

5. Why is the genetic trait of eveningness a particular problem during adolescence?

6. Why do parents and adolescents fight about bedtime?

7. What are the gender differences in the growth spurt?

8. What are the ethnic and cultural differences in the changes of puberty?

9. How would society be affected if puberty occurred for everyone a few years later?

10. Why is early puberty more difficult for girls than for boys?

11. Why is late puberty more difficult for boys than for girls?

Nutrition

12. Why would anyone voluntarily starve herself to death?

13. Why would anyone make himself throw up?

14. What problems might occur if adolescents do not get enough iron or calcium?

The Transformations of Puberty

15. Why are most adolescents dissatisfied with their appearance?

16. Why is body image likely to be distorted in adolescence?

17. What are examples of the uneven growth patterns in adolescent bodies?

18. What problems result from the growth spurt sequence (weight/height/muscles)?

19. How do religion and culture affect adolescent sexual activity?

20. Among sexually active people, why do adolescents have more STIs than adults?

21. What are positive changes in adolescent sexuality over the past five decades?

22. Why is adolescent sexuality more hazardous now than it was five decades ago?

23. Why is it harmful for a young adolescent and an adult to have sex?

24. How might the timing of maturation of parts of the adolescent brain create problems?

25. In what ways is adolescent brain functioning better than adult brain functioning?

APPLICATIONS

1. Visit a fifth-, sixth-, or seventh-grade class. Note variations in the size and maturity of the students. Do you see any patterns related to gender, ethnicity, body fat, or self-confidence?

2. Interview two to four of your friends who are in their late teens or early 20s about their memories of menarche or spermarche, including their memories of others' reactions. Do their comments indicate that these events are, or are not, emotionally troubling for young people?

3. Talk with someone who became a parent before the age of 20. Were there any problems with the pregnancy, the birth, or the first years of parenthood? Would the person recommend teen parenthood? What would have been different had the baby been born three years earlier or three years later?

4. Find two or three adults who, as adolescents, acted impulsively and did something that could have potentially caused great harm to themselves and/or other people. What do they recall about their thinking at the time of the incident? How would their actions differ now? What do their answers reveal about the adolescent mind?

>>ONLINE CONNECTIONS

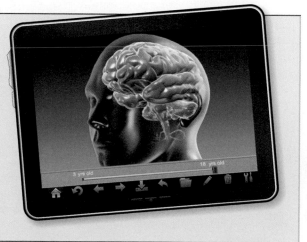

To accompany your textbook, you have access to a number of online resources, including quizzes for every chapter of the book, flashcards (in English and Spanish), critical thinking questions, and case studies. For access to any of these links, go to www.worthpublishers.com/bergerls8e. In addition to these free resources, you'll also find links to the podcasts, video clips, diagnostic quizzing with personalized study advice, and an ebook. Some of the videos and activities available online include:

- *Brain Development: Adolescence.* There's a lot going on in a teenager's brain! Animations and illustrations highlight that development and its effect on behavior.

- *The Timing of Puberty.* Too early? Too late? Teens tell their own stories about the impact of pubertal timing. Also reviews physical changes and gender differences in maturation.

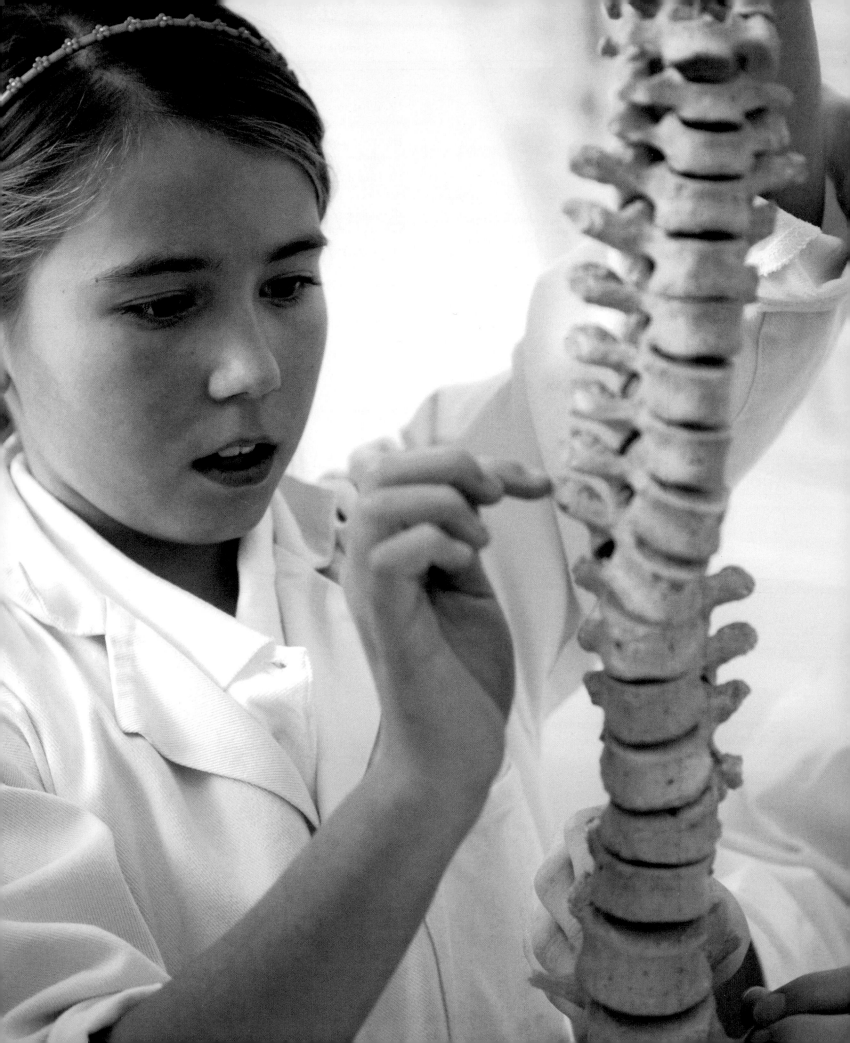

C H A P T E R

Adolescence: Cognitive Development

WHAT WILL YOU KNOW?

1. Why are young adolescents so concerned about how they look and what they say and do?

2. Is it typical for teenagers to lose their religious faith and become atheists?

3. Why do teenagers prefer to think with their emotions instead of logic?

4. Would it help learning if schools got tougher—banned cyberbullying, installed metal detectors, increased suspensions, and so on?

5. How is student learning in secondary school connected to the national economy?

Our eldest daughters, Bethany and Rachel, took public transportation to middle school with no problem. I expected the same of Elissa, our third child, who was almost always cooperative, outgoing, and happy. I rode the bus with her a few times, teaching her where to board, when to get off, and how to transfer. The first time she did it without me, I drove behind the bus—and saw her *not* get off at her stop. I zoomed ahead, yelling at her to exit. After many more trials, she finally succeeded on her own, still happy. I, however, was puzzled.

Other problems appeared. Elissa lost her books, her homework, her schedule. Her teachers praised her intelligence and personality, but tests diagnosed her as "severely spatially disorganized." The principal concluded that she belonged in a special school. Only then did Lissa analyze her current situation and study conscientiously; only then did we help by checking her homework and watching her pack her bookbag. Fortunately, she did brilliantly on her finals. Her school allowed her to continue. In the next two decades, she graduated from high school, college, and law school—as valedictorian.

Elissa made me realize that we all have vulnerabilities that might emerge when new stresses appear, especially during adolescence. As explained in detail in this chapter, adolescent cognition and secondary school challenges may be disorienting. This chapter also describes the positive aspects of adolescent thought. Adolescents become able to reason logically and rationally, with newfound abstract thought required for advanced academic courses. Yet often they prefer to think egocentrically and intuitively, using emotions instead of analysis. Lissa did not take her difficulties seriously until she realized that she might need to find new friends in the special school we visited. People of all ages have at least two ways to think: My husband and I did not notice the problem and figure out how to support our daughter until we had to.

>> Adolescent Thinking

Brain maturation, intense conversations, additional years of schooling, moral challenges, and increased independence all occur between ages 11 and 18. The combination propels impressive cognitive growth, from egocentrism to abstract logic.

Egocentrism

During puberty, young people center many of their thoughts on themselves, in part because maturation of the brain heightens self-consciousness (Sebastian et al., 2008). It is typical for young adolescents to try to make sense of their conflicting feelings about their parents, school, and classmates and to think deeply (but not always realistically) about their future. One reason adolescents spend so much time talking on the phone, e-mailing, and texting is that they want to ruminate about each nuance of everything they have done, are doing, and might do.

Young adolescents think intensely about themselves and about what others think about them. Together these two aspects of thought are called **adolescent egocentrism,** first described by David Elkind (1967). Egocentrism is common in early adolescence among youth of both sexes and every ethnic group (Beaudoin & Schonert-Reichl, 2006). It continues throughout adolescence, especially in teenagers who have problems such as delinquency, aggression, and eating disorders, and it may increase again at the start of college (Schwartz et al., 2008).

In egocentrism, adolescents regard themselves as unique, special, and much more socially significant (that is, noticed by everyone) than they actually are. Accurately imagining someone else's perspective is difficult when egocentrism rules (Lapsley, 1993). For example, it seems unlikely that adolescent girls are especially attracted to boys with pimples and braces, but Edgar did not realize this, according to his older sister:

> Now in the 8th grade, Edgar has this idea that all the girls are looking at him in school. He got his first pimple about three months ago. I told him to wash it with my face soap but he refused, saying, "Not until I go to school to show it off." He called the dentist, begging him to approve his braces now instead of waiting for a year. The perfect gifts for him have changed from action figures to a bottle of cologne, a chain, and a fitted baseball hat like the rappers wear.
>
> *[adapted from Eva, personal communication, 2007]*

Egocentrism leads adolescents to interpret everyone else's behavior as if it were a judgment on them. A stranger's frown or a teacher's critique could make a teenager conclude that "No one likes me" and then to deduce that "I am unlovable" or even to claim that "I can't leave the house." More positive casual reactions—a smile from a sales clerk or an extra-big hug from a younger brother—could lead to "I am great" or "Everyone loves me," with similarly distorted self-perception. Given the rapid mood changes described in the previous chapter, such conclusions are usually short-lived, susceptible to reversal with another offhand remark.

As an aspect of egocentrism, acute self-consciousness about one's physical appearance is probably more prevalent between ages 10 and 14 than earlier or later (Rankin et al., 2004). Young adolescents would rather not stand out from their peers, hoping instead to blend in. They also believe that everyone is as egocentric as they are.

As one girl said:

> I am a real worrier when it comes to other people's opinions. I care deeply about what they say, think and do. If people are very complimentary, it can give you a big confidence boost, but if people are always putting you down you feel less

adolescent egocentrism A characteristic of adolescent thinking that leads young people (ages 10 to 13) to focus on themselves to the exclusion of others.

ELLEN SENISI / THE IMAGE WORKS

Mirror, Mirror At 13, she is at the peak of adolescent egocentrism, carefully combining the appearance of rebellion (backward cap, overalls) with femininity (earrings, necklace, ring).

Observation Quiz In addition to her expression and the handheld mirror, what sign do you see of emotional stress? (see answer, page 410)

confident and people can tell. A lot of advice that is given is "Do what you want and don't listen to anyone else," but I don't know one person who can do that.

[quoted in J. H. Bell & Bromnick, 2003, p. 213]

Fables

Elkind named several aspects of adolescent egocentrism, among them the **personal fable** and the **invincibility fable,** which often appear together. The *personal fable* is the belief that one is unique, destined to have a heroic, fabled, even legendary, life. Some 12-year-olds plan to star in the NBA, or become billionaires, or cure cancer. Another example is the belief that one is destined to die a young and tragic death; thus, habits that could lead to midlife lung cancer or heart disease are considered no problem. In some adolescent minds, there is no contradiction between the personal fable and *invincibility,* the idea that, unless fate wills it, they will not be hurt by fast driving, unprotected sex, or addictive drugs. If they take risks and survive without harm, they feel invincible, not grateful.

In every nation, those who volunteer for military service—knowing or even hoping that they will be sent into combat—are more likely to be under age 20 than over it. Young recruits take risks more often than older, more experienced soldiers (Killgore et al., 2006). In this example, as in many others further detailed in Chapter 17, more boys than girls believe that they are invincible (Alberts et al., 2007).

The Imaginary Audience

Egocentrism creates an **imaginary audience** in the minds of many adolescents. They believe they are at center stage, with all eyes on them, and they imagine how others might react to their appearance and behavior.

I witnessed this with my daughter Bethany at age 16. She was already a gifted artist. Perhaps that is why I agreed to go with her to the Metropolitan Museum of Art on a humid midsummer afternoon. When we emerged from the subway, we encountered a sudden downpour. Bethany stopped and became angry—at me!

> **She:** You didn't bring an umbrella? You should have known.
> **Me:** It's OK—we'll walk quickly. It's a warm rain.
> **She:** But we'll get all wet.
> **Me:** No problem. We'll dry.
> **She:** But people will see us with our hair all wet.
> **Me:** Honey, no one cares how we look. And we won't see anyone we know.
> **She:** That's OK for you to say. You're already married.
> **Me:** (incredulous) Do you think you'll meet your future husband here?
> **She:** (exasperated) No, of course not. But people will look at me and think, "She'll never find a husband looking like that!"

The imaginary audience can cause teenagers to enter a crowded room as if they are the most attractive human beings alive. They might put studs in their lips or blast music for all to hear, calling attention to themselves. The reverse is also possible: Unlike Edgar, they might avoid scrutiny lest someone notice a blemish on their chin or make fun of their braces. Many a 12-year-old balks at going to school with a bad haircut or the wrong shoes.

Egocentrism Reassessed

After Elkind first described adolescent egocentrism, some psychologists blamed it for every teenage problem, from drug use to pregnancy (Eckstein et al., 1999). It still is a common explanation for the risk taking evident in adolescence (Leather, 2009). However, other research has found that some adolescents do not feel invincible; in fact, some have exaggerated perceptions of risks (Mills et al., 2008).

---

personal fable An aspect of adolescent egocentrism characterized by an adolescent's belief that his or her thoughts, feelings, and experiences are unique, more wonderful or awful than anyone else's.

invincibility fable An adolescent's egocentric conviction that he or she cannot be overcome or even harmed by anything that might defeat a normal mortal, such as unprotected sex, drug abuse, or high-speed driving.

imaginary audience The other people who, in an adolescent's egocentric belief, are watching and taking note of his or her appearance, ideas, and behavior. This belief makes many teenagers very self-conscious.

Ready for Battle? As uniformed Russian draftees, Yevgeny and Alexei might imagine that an audience sees them as tough men, but they would be mortified to know how boyishly naïve they appear.

AP PHOTO

>> **Answer to Observation Quiz** (from page 408) Look at her bitten fingernails.

Some developmentalists now believe that egocentrism "may signal growth toward cognitive maturity" (Vartanian, 2001, p. 378), that egocentrism may be protective "each time an individual enters into a new environmental context or dramatically new life situation" (Schwartz et al., 2008, p. 447) as the adolescent responds to culture and cohort. For example, a 13-year-old who moved to Los Angeles from a small town recalled:

> When I got to school the first day, everyone looked at me like I was from outer space or something. It was like, "Who's that? Look at her hair. Look at what she's wearing." That's all anybody cares about around here; what you look like and what you wear. I felt like a total outcast. As soon as I got home, I locked myself in my room and cried for about an hour. I was so lonely.
>
> *[Tina, quoted in R. Bell, 1998, p. 78]*

The phrase "all anybody cares about around here" applies not only to Los Angeles. The same words could have been written by a young adolescent who moved from Los Angeles to a small town or by almost any adolescent new to a school. This girl's reaction was egocentric if she imagined more scrutiny than actually occurred, but young adolescents do sometimes reject peers who dress or act in unusual ways. Self-awareness and cultural sensitivity may be helpful.

Every year, thousands of new students in middle and high schools are harassed, especially if they differ from the norm in sexual behavior, accent, or clothing. In 2010, 15-year-old Phoebe Prince killed herself three months after she moved from a small town in Ireland to Massachusetts. Other students had been taunting her—culminating in her suicide, which led to the indictment of nine of them. The bullies were wrong, of course. But this tragedy could have been anticipated and even halted by adults if they had understood adolescent egocentrism.

Formal Operational Thought

Adolescents move past concrete operational thinking and consider abstractions. Jean Piaget described a shift to what he called **formal operational thought,** including "assumptions that have no necessary relation to reality" (Piaget, 1972, p. 148).

One way to distinguish formal from concrete thinking is to compare curricula in primary school and high school. Here are three examples:

1. *Math.* Younger children multiply real numbers, such as $4 \times 3 \times 8$; adolescents can multiply unreal numbers, such as $(2x)(3y)$ or even $(25xy^2)(3zy^3)$.
2. *Social studies.* Younger children study other cultures by considering daily life— drinking goat's milk or building an igloo, for instance; adolescents can consider "gross national product" and "fertility rate" and how these affect global politics.
3. *Science.* Younger students water plants; adolescents test H_2O in the lab.

Piaget's Experiments

Piaget and his colleagues devised a number of tasks to assess formal operational thought (Inhelder & Piaget, 1958), when "in contrast to concrete operational children, formal operational adolescents imagine all possible determinants . . . [and] systematically vary the factors one by one, observe the results correctly, keep track of the results, and draw the appropriate conclusions" (P. H. Miller, 2011, p. 57).

In one experiment (diagrammed in Figure 15.1), children balance a scale by hooking weights onto the scale's arms. To master this task, a person must realize that the heaviness of the weights and their distance from the center interact reciprocally to affect balance. Therefore, a heavier weight close to the center can be counterbalanced with a lighter weight far from the center. For example, a 12-gram

formal operational thought In Piaget's theory, the fourth and final stage of cognitive development, characterized by more systematic logical thinking and by the ability to understand and systematically manipulate abstract concepts.

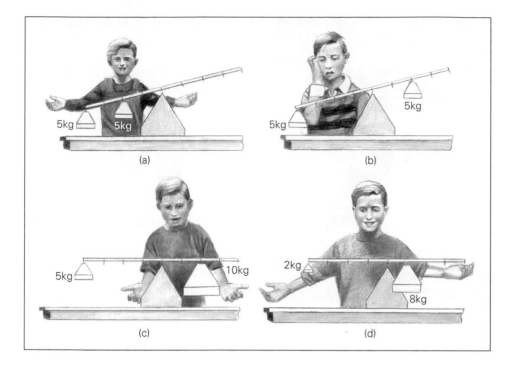

FIGURE 15.1

How to Balance a Scale Piaget's balance-scale test of formal reasoning, as it is attempted by *(a)* a 4-year-old, *(b)* a 7-year-old, *(c)* a 10-year-old, and *(d)* a 14-year-old. The key to balancing the scale is to make weight times distance from the center equal on both sides of the center; the realization of that principle requires formal operational thought.

weight placed 2 centimeters to the left of the center might balance a 6-gram weight placed 4 centimeters to the right.

This concept was completely beyond the 3- to 5-year-olds. By age 7, children balanced the scale by putting the same amount of weight on each arm, but they didn't realize that the distance from the center mattered. By age 10, children thought about location, but used trial and error, not logic. Finally, by about age 13 or 14, some children hypothesized and tested the reciprocal relationship between weight and distance and developed the formula (Piaget & Inhelder, 1969).

Hypothetical-Deductive Reasoning

One hallmark of formal operational thought is the capacity to think of possibility, not just reality. "Here and now" is only one of many alternatives, including "there and then," "long, long ago," "nowhere," "not yet," and "never." As Piaget said:

> The adolescent . . . thinks beyond the present and forms theories about everything, delighting especially in considerations of that which is not . . .
>
> *[Piaget, 1972, p. 148]*

Adolescents are therefore primed to engage in **hypothetical thought,** reasoning about *if–then* propositions that do not reflect reality. For example, consider this question:

> If all mammals can walk,
> And whales are mammals,
> Can whales walk?
>
> *[adapted from De Neys & Van Gelder, 2009]*

Younger adolescents often answer "No!" They know that whales swim, not walk, so the logic escapes them. Some adolescents answer "Yes." They understand *if.*

> *Possibility* no longer appears merely as an extension of an empirical situation or of action actually performed. Instead, it is *reality* that is now secondary to *possibility.*
>
> *[Inhelder & Piaget, 1958, p. 251; emphasis in original]*

hypothetical thought Reasoning that includes propositions and possibilities that may not reflect reality.

A Proud Teacher "Is it possible to train a cockroach?" This hypothetical question, an example of formal operational thought, was posed by 15-year-old Tristan Williams of New Mexico. In his award-winning science project, he succeeded in conditioning Madagascar cockroaches to hiss at the sight of a permanent marker. (His parents' logical reasoning about having 600 cockroaches living in their home is not known.)

deductive reasoning Reasoning from a general statement, premise, or principle, through logical steps, to figure out (deduce) specifics. (Also called *top-down reasoning*.)

inductive reasoning Reasoning from one or more specific experiences or facts to reach (induce) a general conclusion. (Also called *bottom-up reasoning*.)

Impressive Thinking "Correlating Genetic Signature with Surface Sugar Expression in *Vibrio Vulnificus*" is the title of Shilpa Argade's winning science project about a sometimes deadly bacteria. Like many of her peers in southern California, she is capable of deductive reasoning, but she does not always think that way.

Hypothetical thought transforms perceptions, not necessarily for the better. Adults sometimes become exasperated at the adolescent penchant for criticizing everything from the way their mother cooks spaghetti to why the Gregorian calendar, not the Chinese or Jewish one, is standard. They criticize what *is* precisely because of their hypothetical thinking about what might be. Adolescents' reflection about serious issues becomes complicated because they consider many possibilities, avoiding conclusions about the immediate issues (Moshman, 2005). They "naively underestimate the practical problems involved in achieving an ideal future for themselves or for society" (Miller, 2011, p. 59).

For example, a survey of U.S. teenagers' religious ideas found that most 13- to 17-year-olds considered themselves religious and thought that practicing their particular faith would help them avoid hell. However, they did not take the next logical step by trying to convince their friends to believe as they did and avoid hellfire. As one explained, "I can't speak for everybody, it's up to them. I know what's best for me, and I can't, I don't, preach" (C. Smith, 2005, p. 147).

Another said:

> I think every religion is important in its own respect. You know, if you're Muslim, then Islam is the way for you. If you are Jewish, well, that's great too. If you're Christian, well, good for you. It's just whatever makes you feel good about you.
>
> [quoted in C. Smith, 2005, p. 163]

In developing the capacity to think hypothetically, by age 14 or so adolescents become capable of **deductive reasoning,** or *top-down reasoning,* which begins with an abstract idea or premise and then uses logic to draw specific conclusions (Galotti, 2002; Keating, 2004). By contrast, **inductive reasoning,** or *bottom-up reasoning,* predominates during the school years, as children accumulate facts and personal experiences (the knowledge base) to aid their thought.

In essence, a child's reasoning goes like this: "This creature waddles and quacks. Ducks waddle and quack. Therefore, this must be a duck." This reasoning is inductive: It progresses from particulars ("waddles" and "quacks") to a general conclusion ("A duck"). By contrast, deduction progresses from the general to the specific: "If it's a duck, it will waddle and quack" (see Figure 15.2).

Research since Piaget finds marked variability: Some adolescents and adults still reason like concrete operational children, and "no contemporary scholarly reviewer of research evidence endorses the emergence of a discrete new cognitive structure at adolescence that closely resembles . . . formal operations" (Kuhn & Franklin, 2006, p. 954). Piaget may have "launched the systematic study of adolescent cognitive development" (Keating, 2004, p. 45), but his description is not the final word.

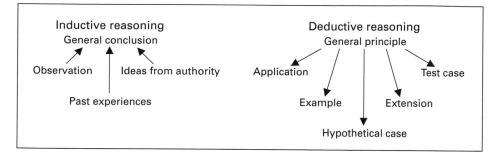

FIGURE 15.2

Bottom Up or Top Down? Children, as concrete operational thinkers, are likely to draw conclusions on the basis of their own experiences and what they have been told. This is called inductive, or bottom-up, reasoning. Adolescents can think deductively, from the top down.

SUMMING UP

Thinking reaches heightened self-consciousness at puberty, when adolescent egocentrism may be apparent. Some young adolescents have unrealistic notions about their place in the social world, including the personal fable and the imaginary audience. They often imagine themselves as invincible, unique, and the center of attention. Adults often criticize this self-awareness, but it shows a cognitive advance and may be shaped by the social context.

Piaget thought the fourth and final stage of intelligence, called *formal operational thought,* begins in adolescence. He found that adolescents improve in deductive logic and hypothetical reasoning. Other scholars note much more variability in adolescent thought than Piaget's description implies.

■

Especially for Natural Scientists Some ideas that were once universally accepted, such as the belief that the sun moved around the Earth, have been disproved. Is it a failure of inductive or deductive reasoning that leads to false conclusions? (see response, page 415)

>> Intuitive, Emotional Thought

The fact that adolescents *can* use hypothetical-deductive reasoning does not necessarily mean that they *do* use it (Kuhn & Franklin, 2006). Adolescents find it much easier and quicker to forget about logic and follow their impulses.

Two Modes of Thinking

Advanced logic is counterbalanced by the increasing power of intuitive thinking. A **dual-process model** of adolescent cognition has been formulated (Evans, 2008). Researchers are increasingly convinced that at least two modes characterize thought. Although various scholars choose different terms and somewhat distinct

dual-process model The notion that two networks exist within the human brain, one for emotional and one for analytical processing of stimuli.

Dual Processing Signs of both analysis and emotion are evident in these two girls at a school in south Texas. They are using wireless computers to study, perhaps analyzing information, formatting questions, and drawing logical conclusions. At the same time, intuitive thinking is also on display: The girls are sitting side by side for companionship and are dressed similarly, wearing shoes designed more for fashion than for walking.

BOB DAEMMRICH / THE IMAGE WORKS

definitions, broadly speaking these two modes are intuitive/analytic, implicit/explicit, creative/factual, contextualized/decontextualized, unconscious/conscious, gist/quantitative, emotional/intellectual, experiential/rational.

The thinking described by the first half of each pair is preferred in everyday life. Sometimes, however, circumstances compel the second mode, when deeper thought is demanded. Neuroscience confirms that the brain has multiple pathways, not all used at once. Research focuses on the intuitive/analytic pair in adolescence (Gerrard et al., 2008).

> **intuitive thought** Thought that arises from an emotion or a hunch, beyond rational explanation, and is influenced by past experiences and cultural assumptions.

> **analytic thought** Thought that results from analysis, such as a systematic ranking of pros and cons, risks and consequences, possibilities and facts. Analytic thought depends on logic and rationality.

- **Intuitive thought** begins with a belief, assumption, or general rule (called a *heuristic*) rather than logic. Intuition is quick and powerful; it feels "right."
- **Analytic thought** is the formal, logical, hypothetical-deductive thinking described by Piaget. It involves rational analysis of many factors whose interactions must be calculated, as in the scale-balancing problem.

When the two modes of thinking conflict, adults sometimes use one and sometimes the other (De Neys, 2006), but they try to coordinate them because there are "two systems but one reasoner" (De Neys, 2006, p. 428).

Comparing Intuition and Analysis

Paul Klaczynski has conducted many studies comparing the thinking of children, young adolescents, and older adolescents (usually 9-, 12-, and 15-year-olds) (Holland & Klaczynski, 2009; Klaczynski, 2001; Klaczynski et al., 2009). In one, he presented 19 logical problems to children and adolescents. For example:

> Timothy is very good-looking, strong, and does not smoke. He likes hanging around with his male friends, watching sports on TV, and driving his Ford Mustang convertible. He's very concerned with how he looks and with being in good shape. He is a high school senior now and is trying to get a college scholarship.

> *Based on this [description], rank each statement in terms of how likely it is to be true. . . The most likely statement should get a 1. The least likely statement should get a 6.*

> _____ Timothy has a girlfriend.
> _____ Timothy is an athlete.
> _____ Timothy is popular and an athlete.
> _____ Timothy is a teacher's pet and has a girlfriend.
> _____ Timothy is a teacher's pet.
> _____ Timothy is popular.

In ranking these statements, one study reported that most adolescents (73 percent) made at least one analytic error, ranking a double statement (e.g., popular *and* an athlete) as more likely than a single statement included in it (popular *or* an athlete). They intuitively jumped to the more inclusive statement, rather than sticking to logic. Almost all adolescents were analytical and logical on some of the 19 problems but not on others. Logical thinking improved with age and education, although not with IQ. In other words, being smarter as measured by an intelligence test did not advance logic as much as having more experience, in school and in life. Klaczynski (2001) concluded that, even though teenagers *can* use logic, "most adolescents do not demonstrate a level of performance commensurate with their abilities" (p. 854).

Her Whole Brain Chess players like this girl, who is competing in a Connecticut championship match, must be analytic, thinking several moves ahead. But sometimes an unexpected intuitive move unnerves the opponent and leads to victory.

What would motivate adolescents to use—or fail to use—their formal operational thinking? The students in Klaczynski's study had learned the scientific method in school, and they knew that scientists use empirical evidence and deductive reasoning. But they did not always think like scientists. Why not?

Dozens of experiments and extensive theorizing have found some answers (Klaczynski, 2005; Kuhn & Franklin, 2006; Sunstein, 2008). Essentially, logic is more difficult than intuition, and it requires examination of comforting, familiar prejudices. Once people of any age reach an emotional conclusion (sometimes called a "gut feeling"), they resist changing their minds. As people gain experience in making decisions and thinking things through, they become better at knowing when analysis is needed (Milkman et al., 2009).

Egocentrism makes rational analysis even more difficult, as one psychologist discovered when her teenage son called late one night to be picked up from a party that had "gotten out of hand." The boy heard

> his frustrated father lament "drinking and trouble—haven't you figured out the connection?" Despite the late hour and his shaky state, the teenager advanced a lengthy argument to the effect that his father had the causality all wrong and the trouble should be attributed to other covariates, among them bad luck.
>
> [*Kuhn & Franklin, 2006, p. 966*]

Common Fallacies

Many cognitive scientists study how people think, especially the ways in which logic eludes them. This is often more apparent during adolescence than during other years.

One example is the **sunk cost fallacy,** which is the conviction that when a person has already spent money, time, or effort that cannot be recovered (a cost already "sunk"), he or she should continue to try to achieve the desired goal because otherwise that previous effort is wasted. People of all ages make this error, investing money and time to repair a "lemon" of a car, remaining in a class they are failing, continuing a destructive marriage, and so on.

Another common fallacy is called **base rate neglect** (Barbey & Sloman, 2007), in which a person ignores statistical information about the frequency of a phenomenon and instead makes a decision on a personal basis, influenced perhaps by a vivid experience. For instance, a person might not wear a bicycle helmet, despite statistics, until a friend is brain-damaged in a biking accident. "When adolescents take unjustified risks, it is often because of the weakness of their analytic systems, which provide an inadequate check on impulsive or ill-considered decisions" (Sunstein, 2008, p. 145).

Better Thinking

Sometimes adults conclude that more mature thought processes are wiser, since they lead to a more cautious approach (as in the father's connection between "trouble" and alcohol in the excerpt above). Adults are particularly critical of the egocentrism that leads an impulsive teenager to risk future addiction by experimenting with drugs or to risk pregnancy and AIDS by avoiding the awkwardness of using a condom.

But adults may themselves be egocentric in making such judgments if they assume that adolescents share their values. Parents want healthy, long-living children, and they conclude that adolescents use faulty reasoning when they risk their lives. Adolescents, however, value social warmth and friendship. A 15-year-old who is offered a cigarette might rationally choose social acceptance over the distant risk of cancer (Engels et al., 2006).

Research on adults making complex decisions, such as whom to marry or which investment to make, finds that sometimes intuitive decisions are best and

>> **Response for Natural Scientists** (from page 413) Probably both. Our false assumptions are not logically tested because we do not realize that they might need testing.

sunk cost fallacy The mistaken belief that if money, time, or effort that cannot be recovered (a "sunk cost," in economic terms) has already been invested in some endeavor, then more should be invested in an effort to reach the goal. Because of this fallacy, people spend money trying to fix a "lemon" of a car or send more troops to fight a losing battle.

base rate neglect A common fallacy in which a person ignores the overall frequency of some behavior or characteristic (called the *base rate*) in making a decision. For example, a person might bet on a "lucky" lottery number without considering the odds that that number will be selected.

sometimes not (Dijksterhuis & Aarts, 2010). At every age, the best thinking may be "fast and frugal" (Gigerenzer, 2008). Weighing alternatives, and thinking of possibilities, could be paralyzing. The systematic, analytic thought that Piaget described is slow and costly, not fast and frugal, wasting precious time when a young person wants to act.

As the knowledge base increases and the brain matures, both modes of thought become more forceful. With maturity, adolescents are less likely to be paralyzed by too much analysis or to plummet into costly intuition. Logic increases from adolescence to adulthood (and then decreases somewhat in old age) (De Neys & Van Gelder, 2009). Ideally, people use whatever combination of dual-processing leads to a good decision (Gigerenzer, 2008). Adolescents may use formal, analytic thinking in science class and emotional, experiential thinking (which is quicker and more satisfying) for personal issues (Kuhn & Franklin, 2006).

Thinking About Religion

As you remember from Chapter 1, scientists build on previous research or theories, replicating, extending, or disputing the work of others. Scientists question assumptions, seeking empirical evidence to verify or refute both new theories and old cultural myths. This is a formal operational approach.

Some impressionistic descriptions of teenagers and religion (e.g., Flory & Miller, 2000) emphasize cults and sects. Young congregants gather, "dressed as they are, piercings and all, and express their commitment by means of hip-hop and rap music, multimedia presentations, body modification, and anything else that can be infused with religious meaning" (Ream & Savin-Williams, 2003, p. 51).

This description evokes emotions—the quick, intuitive responses that judge piercings and rap to be the antithesis of religion. When a team of researchers began by "reading many published overview reports on adolescence . . . [they found] the distinct impression that American youth simply do not have religious or spiritual lives" (C. Smith, 2005, p. 4). They decided to seek evidence, not impressions, and surveyed 3,360 13- to 17-year-olds and their parents, including confidential follow-up interviews with 287 of them.

They found that most adolescents (71 percent) felt close to God; believed in heaven, hell, and angels; and affirmed the same religion as their parents (78 percent Christian, 3 percent Jewish or Muslim, almost none Buddhist or Hindu). Some were agnostic (2 percent), and 16 percent said they were not religious—although many of those attended church and prayed. Less than 1 percent were "unconventional" (e.g., Wiccan).

Adolescents' religious beliefs tended to be egocentric, with faith considered a personal tool to be used in times of difficulty (e.g., while taking an exam). Many (82 percent) said their beliefs were important in daily life. One boy explained that religion kept him from doing "bad things, like murder or something," and one girl said:

> [Religion] influences me a lot with the people I choose not to be around. I would not hang with people that are, you know, devil worshipers because that's just not my thing. I could not deal with that negativity.
>
> *[quoted in C. Smith, 2005, p. 139]*

The researchers doubt that "socializing with Satanists is a real issue in this girl's life" or that this boy "struggles with murderous tendencies" (C. Smith, 2005, p. 139). They also noted that few

Living Their Faith? Theologians may separate faith from personal or political concerns, but few adolescents do. In a protest aimed at keeping their Catholic school open, one student leader carries a white cross with a quote from Thomas Jefferson (a deist who opposed clergy and religious doctrine); her classmate carries a bullhorn and a Bible. Secular concerns also affect adult religious thought: Despite community and student protests such as this one, the Detroit Archdiocese closed Holy Redeemer for financial reasons.

adolescents (less than 1 percent) used theology to guide them in the actual issues of daily life, such as seeking justice or loving one's neighbor. For most, religious beliefs were intuitive, not analytic.

What does this imply for adults who hope to instill values in the next generation? In many ways, these data are encouraging: Most children and adolescents adhere to the faith and values of their parents. However, the authors wish that adults would encourage teenagers to discuss complex spiritual issues (e.g., stewardship of the environment, economic disparity, the implications of scriptures). This would require parents and church leaders to engage in the more difficult mode of thinking.

As good scientists, the researchers surveyed the same individuals three years later. They found a "shifting away from conventional religious beliefs" (Denton et al., 2008, p. 3). But, despite less certainty about God, angels, or an afterlife, these older adolescents tended to feel they had become more rather than less religious over the three-year period. One possible reason is that "as adolescents develop and mature, they take more ownership over their own beliefs and practices so that their religiosity feels stronger and more authentic" (Denton et al., 2008, p. 32). In other words, maturation, independence, and deeper thought may advance cognition.

SUMMING UP

Current research recognizes that there are at least two modes of cognition: People sometimes use analytical thinking and other times prefer quick, intuitive reasoning. This second kind of thinking is experiential, quicker, and more intense than formal operational thought. Both forms develop during adolescence, although sometimes intuitive processes seem more powerful than logical ones. Each form of thinking is appropriate in some contexts, although with maturation, the logical, reflective thinking becomes more possible, as is evident in thoughts about religion.

>> Teaching and Learning

What does this understanding of adolescent thought imply about school? Educators, developmentalists, political leaders, and parents wonder exactly which curricula and school structures are best for 11- to 18-year-olds. There are dozens of options: academic knowledge or practical skills, single sex or co-ed, competitive or cooperative, large or small, public or private—and many more.

The research does not support any single answer. Various scientists, nations, and schools are trying many strategies, some based on opposite, but logical, hypotheses. To analyze these, we present some definitions, facts, issues, and possibilities.

Definitions and Facts

Every year of school advances human potential, as recognized by leaders and scholars in every nation and discipline. Adolescents are open to deep and wide-ranging thought, no longer limited by personal experience. Of course, the quality of education matters: A year can propel thinking forward or can have little impact (Hanushek & Woessmann, 2010).

Secondary education—traditionally grades 7 through 12—designates the school years after elementary or grade school (known as *primary education*) and before college or university (known as *tertiary education*). Adults are healthier and wealthier if they complete primary education, learning to read and write, and then continue on through secondary and tertiary education.

secondary education Literally, the period after primary education (elementary or grade school) and before tertiary education (college). It usually occurs from about age 12 to 18, although there is some variation by school and by nation.

Especially for Teachers You are stumped by a question your student asks. What do you do? (see response, page 420)

middle school A school for children in the grades between elementary and high school. Middle school usually begins with grade 6 and ends with grade 8.

Even such a seemingly unrelated condition as serious hearing loss in late adulthood is twice as common among those who never graduated from high school than among high school graduates (National Center for Health Statistics, 2010). This statistic comes from the United States, but data on almost every ailment, from every nation and every ethnic group, confirm that high school graduation correlates with health. Reasons include income and residence, but even when inadequate health resources and crowded, polluted neighborhoods are taken into account, health improves with education.

Partly because political leaders recognize that educated adults advance national wealth and health, every nation is increasing the number of students in secondary schools. Education is compulsory until at least age 12 almost everywhere (UNESCO, 2008).

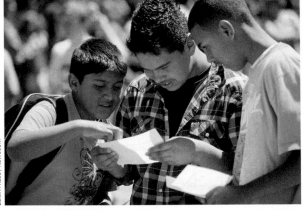

Lunch at Different Times Alex, Malik, and Luis examine their schedules for their upcoming seventh grade year. Most students prefer to be in the same classes together, but most schools try to separate friends as much as possible.

Middle School

Often, two levels of secondary education are provided, with schools traditionally divided into junior high (usually grades 7 and 8) and senior high (usually grades 9 through 12). As the average age of puberty has declined over the past century (see Chapter 14) and young adolescents are ready for intellectual challenge, **middle schools** have been created to educate 10- to 13-year-olds (grades 6, 7, and 8), and some nations add a year before college.

Less Learning

Often during middle school, academic achievement decreases and behavioral problems arise. The first year of middle school has been called the "low ebb" of learning (Covington & Dray, 2002), when many teachers feel ineffective (Eccles, 2004).

Puberty itself may be part of the problem. For rats and other animals, especially under stress, learning slows down at that point in their growth (McCormick et al., 2010).

A School Connection Middle schools are more likely to succeed when they combine high academic standards with consistent discipline and high motivation among both students and teachers. This public school in New York City's South Bronx is affiliated with the Knowledge Is Power Program, offering college preparation to students from low-income families.

However, most developmentalists think that learning suffers more because of the organizational structure of middle schools than because of the biological stresses of puberty. Unlike primary school teachers, middle and high school teachers specialize in a particular academic area, which they teach to hundreds of students each year. This reduces the personal connection between teacher and student, leading to less learning and more risk taking among adolescents (Crosnoe et al., 2004). Parents are influential as well: When they encourage academics, middle school children achieve more (unless the parents directly help with homework instead of merely guide) (Hill & Tyson, 2009). Consider James and his parents.

Especially for Middle School Teachers You think your lectures are interesting and you know you care about your students, yet many of them cut class, come late, or seem to sleep through it. What do you do? (see response, page 421)

A CASE TO STUDY

James, the High-Achieving Dropout

A longitudinal study in Massachusetts followed children from preschool through high school. James was one of the most promising. In his early school years, he was an excellent reader whose mother took great pride in him, her only child.

Once James entered middle school, however, something changed:

> Although still performing well academically, James began acting out. At first his actions could be described as merely mischievous, but later he engaged in much more serious acts, such as drinking and fighting, which resulted in his being suspended from school.
>
> *[Snow et al., 2007, p. 59]*

For James and many others, family problems increase at puberty (Shanahan et al., 2007). He and his father blamed each other for their poor relationship, and his mother was uninvolved in his schooling. She bragged "about how independent James was for being able to be left alone to fend for himself," whereas James "described himself as isolated and closed off" (Snow et al., 2007, p. 59).

James said, "The kids were definitely afraid of me but that didn't stop them" from associating with him (Snow et al., 2007, p. 59). James's experiences with other classmates are not unusual. Generally, aggressive and drug-using students are admired more than those who are conscientious and studious—a marked difference from elementary school (Allen et al., 2005; Mayeux & Cillessen, 2007). Students dislike those who are unlike them, which may mean general antipathy toward those who excel (Laursen et al., 2010). As a consequence, some adolescents sacrifice academics rather than risk social exclusion. This was verified in three nations (Germany, Canada, and Israel); mathematically gifted girls were particularly likely to underachieve (Boehnke, 2008).

Furthermore, puberty awakens sexual concerns, with each sex wanting to appear masculine or feminine, as the case may be. Boys particularly fear becoming a "nerd" or teacher's pet. Perhaps that is why boys are a majority (60 percent) of U.S. 18- to 19-year-olds who completed less than four years of high school (Snyder & Dillow, 2010). James may have been one of many "boys who choose to emphasize their masculine identities [and] may thus actively avoid literacy activities and academic success" (Snow et al., 2007, p. 64). At the end of primary school, James planned to go to college; in middle school, he said he had "a complete lack of motivation"; in tenth grade, he left school.

To pinpoint the developmental mismatch between students' needs and the middle school context, note that just when egocentrism leads young people to feelings of shame or fantasies of stardom (the imaginary audience), schools typically require them to change rooms, teachers, and classmates every 40 minutes or so. That makes public acclaim and personal recognition difficult. In retrospect, that added stress was enough to disorient our daughter Elissa (as explained at the start of this chapter); it affects millions more.

In middle school, grades usually fall because teachers mark more harshly and students become less conscientious. After-school activities that welcome all 11- to 13-year-olds, neither treating them like children nor expecting them to act like adults, are scarce. Sports become competitive; fragile egos avoid coaches, teammates, or observers.

>> **Response for Teachers** (from page 418) Praise the student by saying, "What a great question!" Egos are fragile, so it's best to always validate the question's relevance. Seek student engagement, perhaps asking whether any classmates know the answer, or telling students to discover the answer online. Whatever you do, don't fake it—if students lose faith in your credibility, you may lose them completely.

The Same Situation, Many Miles Apart: Where Is the Teacher? Free laptops are provided for every middle school student in Maine *(top)* and at some public schools in Uruguay *(bottom)*. Benefits include more active learning, collaboration, and independence—or are these liabilities instead?

HERB SWANSON / THE NEW YORK TIMES

AP PHOTO / MARCELO HERNANDEZ

Blaming Other People

One way to cope with stress is to blame trouble on others—classmates, teachers, parents, governments. This may explain the surprising results of a study in Los Angeles: Students in schools that were *more* ethnically mixed felt safer and *less* lonely. It was not that they had many friends from other groups, but students who felt rejected could "attribute their plight to the prejudice of other people" rather than blame themselves (Juvonen et al., 2006, p. 398). Another way to avoid feeling like a failure is to avoid effort—then the student can blame lack of trying ("I didn't study"), not stupidity. Some deliberately avoid earning As; they fear success as well as failure.

Meanwhile, teachers may blame students or their parents for problems they encounter, rather than reassessing their own classroom behavior. For example, one study found that, from the last year of primary school to the first year of middle school, student suspensions increased markedly for behavior that reflected the teachers' perceptions, such as "class disturbance" and "failure to follow the rules," but not for objective infractions such as carrying a weapon or engaging in a physical fight (Theriot & Dupper, 2010).

Many developmentalists find middle schools to be "developmentally regressive" (Eccles, 2004, p. 141)—they force children to step backward. Does this matter for later achievement? One team believes so: "Long-term academic trajectories—the choice to stay in school or to drop out and the selection in high school of academic college-prep courses versus basic-level courses—are strongly influenced by experience in grades 6–8" (Snow et al., 2007, p. 72).

Technology and Cognition

Adults debate the impact of technology on cognition. Two decades ago, no one knew about the World Wide Web, instant messaging, Twitter, blogs, cell phones, iPods, iPads, BlackBerries, or digital cameras. Yet today's teenagers (born during those decades) are "digital natives," creating texting languages and clicking to check facts. Cell phones, iPods, and other mobile devices are beside them day and night (Shuler, 2009).

The Digital Divide

The gap between those who did and did not have computers was bemoaned in the 1990s; it divided boys from girls and rich from poor (Dijk, 2005; Norris, 2001). However, in developed nations, that digital divide has virtually disappeared. Low-income children are somewhat less likely to have high-speed Internet at home, and Hispanic households lag behind others in technology, but virtually every secondary school in the United States is connected to the Internet, wired or wireless. Students take the Internet for granted. Most teenagers own computers; many others get them free from their schools (Ash, 2009).

Among older adolescents, African and Latino Americans are almost as likely to be online as are European Americans. The remaining digital divide is age: Of those over age 65, less than half (42 percent) are online, and only 31 percent have high speed (broadband) access at home (see Figure 15.3).

Learning via the Internet

Computers and cell phones are used as tools for learning. Internet use and video games improve visual-spatial skills and vocabulary (Greenfield, 2009). Recall that research conducted before the technology explosion found that, with education, conversation, and experience, adolescents move past egocentric thought. Social networking may speed up this process, as most teens communicate daily

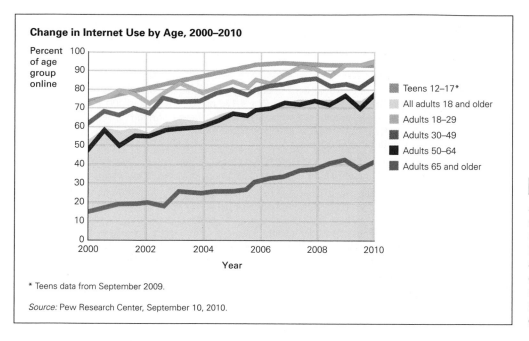

Change in Internet Use by Age, 2000–2010

Percent of age group online

- Teens 12–17*
- All adults 18 and older
- Adults 18–29
- Adults 30–49
- Adults 50–64
- Adults 65 and older

Year

* Teens data from September 2009.

Source: Pew Research Center, September 10, 2010.

FIGURE 15.3

Almost Every Teenager Most teenagers go online every day, more often for social reasons than academic ones. The challenge for American educators is no longer access (virtually every school has Internet capability) but guidance: Adolescents need to learn appropriate Web use, including how to identify and evaluate propaganda and how to avoid plagiarism.

with dozens—perhaps even hundreds or thousands—of friends via e-mail, texting, and cell phones.

Online connections bring friends closer together and reduce social isolation (Valkenburg & Peter, 2009). Although most social networking is between friends who know each other well, the Internet may be a lifeline for teenagers who are isolated because of their sexual orientation, culture, religion, or native language. For everyone, the Internet allows contact with like-minded people thousands of miles away in addition to expanding knowledge. Most secondary students (and teachers) check facts, read explanations, view videos, and thus grasp concepts they would not have understood just a few years earlier.

The Dangers of Technology

Adults worry about sexual abuse via the Internet. There is comforting research here: Although sexual predators lurk online, most teens avoid them, just as most adults avoid distasteful ads and pornography. Sexual abuse is a serious problem, but social networking does not increase the risk (Wolak et al., 2008).

There are some dangers, however. Technology encourages rapid shifts of attention, multitasking without reflection, visual learning instead of invisible analysis (Greenfield, 2009). For some, chat rooms, video games, or Internet gambling become addictive, taking time from the normal play, social outreach, schoolwork, and friendships that children and adolescents need (Shuler, 2009; Yen et al., 2008).

This is not mere speculation. A study using a representative sample of 8- to 18-year-olds in the United States found that one-third of the boys and one-eighth of the girls played video games every day (see the Research Design). Most of the rest played often: Only 3 percent of the boys and 21 percent of the girls said they never played. The average respondent played two hours a day. Those with symptoms of addiction (12 percent of the boys and 3 percent of the girls) played, on average, more than three hours a day, with some of them (about 10 percent) playing more than six hours a day (Gentile, 2009). (See Figure 15.4 for time spent playing video games, by age group.)

In this study, many adolescents admitted that video game playing took time away from household chores and homework. Worse, one-fourth used video games to escape from problems, and one-fifth had "done poorly on a school assignment

>> Response for Middle School Teachers (from page 419) Students need both challenge and involvement; avoid lessons that are too easy or too passive. Create small groups; assign oral reports, debates, and role-plays; and so on. Remember that adolescents like to hear one another's thoughts and their own voices.

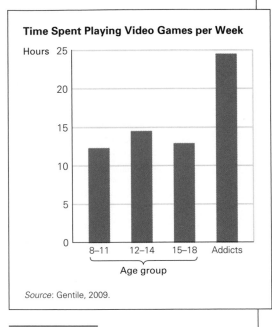

Time Spent Playing Video Games per Week

Source: Gentile, 2009.

FIGURE 15.4

Less Than Sleeping The average adolescent boy spends more time playing video games than reading, eating, doing homework, talking with friends, playing sports, or almost anything else except sleeping or sitting in class. Indeed, some skip school or postpone sleep to finish a game.

cyberbullying Bullying that occurs when one person spreads insults or rumors about another by means of e-mails, text messages, or cell phone videos.

> **▶ Research Design**
>
> **Scientist:** Douglas Gentile.
>
> **Publication:** *Psychological Science* (2009).
>
> **Participants:** All were part of a Harris interactive sample, selected to be representative of youth, aged 8 to 18, in the United States. The 1,178 participants (about 100 at each age) were equally divided by gender and ethnically diverse (about half non-Hispanic White; about one-sixth each African American and Latino; and the remaining mixed, Asian or Native American, or declining to specify).
>
> **Design:** The young people were asked questions, via computer, about their video game use, including frequency, parental policies, and signs of possible addiction.
>
> **Results:** Almost all played video games many hours a week, with boys doing so about twice as often as girls. Video game frequency peaked at ages 12 to 14. Younger students played slightly less often, and older students played for a longer time at a stretch. More than half of the boys had M games (rated mature, with explicit violence or sex), almost always with their parents' permission. Video game playing correlated with lower achievement and more behavior problems, especially attention-deficit disorder.
>
> **Major conclusions:** Many parents, teachers, and psychologists have worried that some teenagers are addicted to video games, curtailing important aspects of their lives and using games to avoid problems. Using criteria for addiction developed by psychiatrists for other addictions (gambling, drugs, and so on), this study found an answer: 12 percent of the boys and 3 percent of girls were addicted to playing video games. That addiction decreased their family and school involvement.
>
> **Comments:** These numbers are chillingly high. One hopes those in the sample are more likely than the average teenager to be game-addicted (they were all contacted via computer, for instance) or, since this study is correlational, that low school achievement leads to video game playing, rather than vice versa. However, a later controlled study began with children whose parents wanted to buy them a video game system. Those 6- to 9-year-old boys who were given a video game system had lower reading and writing achievement than did other boys from the same population with the same characteristics who had to wait four months (while their reading and writing scores rose) before the researchers gave them the promised gaming systems (Weis & Cerankosky, 2010). (A similar study with adolescents would be enlightening but is probably impossible, since almost every teenage boy whose parents allow a video game system already has it.)

or test" because of spending too much time on video games. The heaviest users got lower school grades and had more physical fights than did the average users. Sadly, the data from this study may underestimate the problem, since adolescents reported on themselves.

Addiction of any kind limits life experience, with the harm especially severe when the brain is still growing. Thus, adolescent video game addiction is a serious problem. This survey found that most game playing occured at home, often in the child's own bedroom, and that only half of the parents had rules about their adolescents' play (Gentile, 2009). One conclusion is that if parents allow video games, then more rule setting and monitoring are needed. As the next chapter will stress again, this needs to be carefully done: Especially with adolescents, overly restrictive parenting can backfire. A simple solution is to ban technology from schools and bedrooms, but, as one critic writes, "Cell phones have the potential to be negative in schools. But we don't ban pencils and paper because students pass notes" (Shuler, 2009, p. 35).

Now consider two other problems that are sometimes blamed on technology but that require much deeper understanding on the part of adults in order to protect children: cyberbullying and cutting.

Cyberbullying occurs when one person bullies another by spreading insults and rumors using electronic devices, usually via e-mail, text messages, or cell phone videos (Tokunaga, 2010). The adolescents most likely to be involved are already bullies or victims or both, with bully-victims the most likely to engage in and suffer from cyberbullying. Technology gives bullies another means and wider access. One study found that 23 percent of secondary school students had experienced cyberbullying and 16 percent of them had engaged in it (Dehue et al., 2008).

A scholar who has studied bullying in all its forms finds that cyberbullying is similar to other bullying (P. K. Smith et al., 2008), a conclusion reached by numerous other social scientists. For example, a study of 1,169 15-year-olds in New Zealand found that cyberbullying correlated with physical and relational bullying (Marsh et al., 2010). Relational bullying in particular accelerates with cyberbullying, since rumors can spread widely and insults can be transmitted day and night. The imaginary audience magnifies the shame (Englander et al., 2009). The solution is stressed in Chapters 10 and 13: Children need to learn prosocial rather than antisocial behaviors.

The second problem is less common but more devastating. Some teenagers use the Internet to pursue a secret action, such as extreme dieting, abusive prejudice, or self-mutilation, known as **cutting.** Over 400 Web sites are dedicated to cutting, an addictive activity (particularly among adolescent girls) that correlates with depression and drug abuse.

cutting An addictive form of self-mutilation that is most prevalent among adolescent girls and that correlates with depression and drug abuse.

Analysis of a representative sample of 3,219 posts on cutting sites found that most were positive and helpful, allowing self-injuring adolescents to "establish interpersonal intimacy . . . , [which is] especially difficult for young people struggling with intense shame, isolation, and distress" (Whitlock et al., 2006, p. 415). The most common theme of the messages was informal support (28 percent). Other posts described treatment (7 percent, usually positively) and emotional triggers (20 percent). Some posts, however, told how to conceal marks (9 percent) or described techniques of cutting (6 percent). One exchange:

> Poster 1: Does anyone know how to cut deep without having it sting and bleed too much?
>
> Poster 2: I use box cutter blades. You have to pull the skin really tight and press the blade down really hard. You can also use a tourniquet to make it bleed more.
>
> Poster 3: I've found that if you press your blade against the skin at the depth you want the cut to be and draw the blade really fast it doesn't hurt and there is blood galore. Be careful, though, 'cause you can go very deep without meaning to.
>
> *[quoted in Whitlock et al., 2006, p. 413]*

Note that with both cyberbullying and cutting, the danger lies not in the computer but in the antisocial attitudes and the depression of the person at the keyboard. Technology must be used with care. As with many aspects of adolescence (puberty, brain development, egocentric thought, and so on), context, adults, peers, and the adolescent's own personality and temperament "shape, mediate, and/or modify effects" of technology (Oakes, 2009, p. 1142).

The Transition to a New School

Changing schools during the growth spurt or when new sexual impulses arise is stressful. Remember from Chapter 13 that ongoing minor stresses can become overwhelming, causing pathology if they accumulate. One expert explains:

> A number of disorders and symptoms of psychopathology, including depression, self-injury behavior, substance abuse, eating disorders, bipolar disorder, and schizophrenia have striking developmental patterns corresponding to transitions in early and late adolescence.
>
> *[Masten, 2004, p. 310]*

REN YONG / XINHUA / PHOTOSHOT / NEWSCOM

International Communication The Russian girl on the left was one of 300 middle schoolers who crossed the border to visit a school in China, where students learn Russian and English, as well as Chinese. Adolescents learn from one another, either constructively when adults structure and plan the interaction (as shown here) or destructively when adults do not engage with them.

Of course, transitions are not the only cause of stress; hormones, body changes, sexual experiences, family conflict, and cultural expectations also contribute. In addition, the biology of puberty may activate genes that predispose a person to pathology (Erath et al., 2009). Nonetheless, many schools wisely have special grouping or programs for entering classes. When students enter a new school with classmates and customs unlike those in their old school, minority students in particular may feel alienated and fear failure (Benner & Graham, 2007). It is not diversity per se that is difficult; it is suddenly finding oneself in the minority, in a context that is unfamiliar.

Signs of stress—absenteeism, externalizing behavior, leaving school—are not inevitable, of course. For example, a middle school program that helped parents and other students support entering Mexican Americans (a particularly vulnerable minority, since few teachers share their background) had a significant impact: Fewer students left school than similar Mexican Americans without support (Gonzales et al., 2004).

High School

As we have seen, adolescents can think abstractly, analytically, hypothetically, and logically—as well as personally, emotionally, intuitively, and experientially. The curriculum and teaching style in high school often require the former mode. Students who need more individualized, personal attention may feel left out.

The College-Bound

From a developmental perspective, the fact that high schools emphasize formal thinking makes sense, since many older high schoolers are capable of attaining that level. High school teachers typically assume that their pupils have mastered formal thinking instead of teaching them how to do it (Kuhn & Franklin, 2006).

Some nations are trying to raise standards so that more students will be ready for college. International variations are vast, so we focus here on one example, the United States. Every year from 2006 to 2010, more than 1 million U.S. high school students enrolled in classes that led to externally scored exams, either the IB (International Baccalaureate) or the AP (Advanced Placement). The hope is that such classes will lead to better thinking—or at least satisfy some college requirements. Unfortunately, merely taking the class does not necessarily lead to either result: Many students in AP courses avoid or fail exams bestowing college credit (Sadler et al., 2010).

Another manifestation of the academic push is an increase in requirements that all students must fulfill to receive an academic diploma. In many U.S. schools, no one is allowed to earn a vocational or general diploma unless parents request it. Otherwise, graduation requirements include two years of math beyond algebra, two years of laboratory science, three years of history, and four years of English. Study of a language other than English is often required as well.

high-stakes test An evaluation that is critical in determining success or failure. If a single test determines whether a student will graduate or be promoted, it is a high-stakes test.

In 2009, in addition to these courses, 26 U.S. states required students to pass a **high-stakes test** in order to graduate (Zhang, 2009). (Any exam for which the consequences of failing are severe is called a high-stakes test.) As explained in Chapter 12, the National Association of Governors developed a Common Core of high standards for every year of school. Many people believe that high-stakes tests, raised standards, and rigorous course requirements will improve education; others fear these will destroy learning, especially if teachers "teach to the test," concentrating on rote memorization and ignoring analysis and intuition (Nichols &

The Same Situation, Many Miles Apart: Top Students The New York girls just won a classroom history contest, and the Kenyan boys are studying physics, a subject available only to the brightest African students.

Observation Quiz Although the two groups of winners are thousands of miles apart, there are three evident similarities between them. What are they? (see answer, page 427)

Especially for High School Teachers You are much more interested in the nuances and controversies than in the basic facts of your subject, but you know that your students will take high-stakes tests on the basics and that their scores will have a major impact on their futures. What should you do? (see response, page 427)

Berliner, 2007). Over the past eight years, some states with high-stakes tests have seen an increase in the percentage of students who pass, while others have seen a decrease (Zhang, 2009).

For the United States, there is no evidence yet that the push for high standards has led to more learning, at least according to international tests. As reviewed in Chapter 12, two such tests, the TIMSS and the PIRLS, show many nations ahead of the United States. That chapter highlighted the results at grade 4; the results at grade 8 are similar.

Ironically, just when more U.S. schools are instituting high-stakes tests and requiring more courses, many East Asian nations are moving in the opposite direction. According to a report on Chinese education,

> some prominent government officials have grown concerned that too many students have become the sort of stressed-out, test-acing drone who fails to acquire the skills—creativity, flexibility, initiative, leadership—said to be necessary in the global marketplace.

[Hulbert, 2007, p. 36]

The same concerns have led to changes in the Korean and Japanese educational systems. The trend in Japan is toward fewer academic requirements for high school, classes five days a week instead of six, and less "examination hell," as their high-stakes tests have been called. The science adviser to the prime minister of Japan recommends more flexibility in education in order to promote more innovation. He wants students to "study whatever they are interested in" rather than to narrow their learning so as to score high on one final test (Normile, 2007).

Those Who Do Not Go to College

In the United States, one result of pushing almost all high school students to pursue an academic curriculum is that most enroll in college. (College completion rates provide a different story, detailed in Chapter 18). However, about one-third of high school students in the United States and at least two-thirds worldwide do not aim for college.

Not every student who begins secondary school intends to finish it. Graduation rates vary from less than 10 percent in the poorest nations (such as Niger and Cambodia) to 99 percent in the richest (such as Japan and Sweden). The United States is neither the best nor the worst (see Figure 15.5). Whenever high-stakes tests are a requisite for graduation, there is a "potential unintended consequence" that more high school students will drop out (Christenson & Thurlow, 2004, p. 36). In the 26 U.S. states that now require exit exams to graduate, fewer

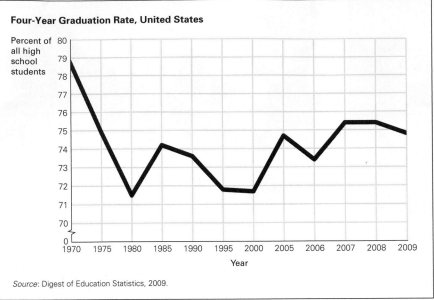

Four-Year Graduation Rate, United States

Source: Digest of Education Statistics, 2009.

FIGURE 15.5

Interpreting the Data These dropout rates measure how many ninth-graders graduate from high school four years later. Some say the decrease from 1970 to 1980 occurred because more adolescents dropped out before ninth grade; others say high school was easier.

TABLE 15.1

Measuring Dropout Rates

There are three commonly used ways to measure high school dropout rates.

1. Compare the number of students in the ninth grade with the number who graduate four years later. Students who transfer out, stop out, or take more than four years to graduate are counted as dropouts.

2. Count the percent of 16- to 24-year-olds who are not in school and have no high school diploma. (These are called *status dropouts*.) One problem with this mode is that newly arrived young adult immigrants who have not completed high school are considered dropouts.

3. Count only those students who formally register as school leavers, not those who simply stop coming to school. This method finds the lowest rates of dropouts but may be the least realistic.

PISA (Programme for International Student Assessment) An international test taken by 15-year-olds in 50 nations that is designed to measure problem solving and cognition in daily life.

students earn diplomas, not only because some who have completed four years of requirements fail the tests but also because some quit before their senior year. How many such students there are is uncertain, in part because school districts measure dropouts in various ways (see Table 15.1).

Unfortunately, even if they graduate from high school, young people may be ill prepared for the next step in their lives. According to a report by the United Nations Economic and Social Council (UNESCO),

> In many parts of the world, learning contents at the secondary level are still following a pattern tailored for the 19th or early 20th century contexts, which often emphasized the acquisition of academic knowledge over skills development. . . .
> [T]here is a challenging task to diversify and adapt the curriculum to all learners of various styles and interests . . .
>
> One effort to help such students is to provide job training in schools, with courses ranging from airplane repair to secretarial skills. However, the job market is changing rapidly, so few in-school programs provide vocational skills that are needed in the workplace.
>
> [UNESCO, 2005]

As you see, this report was published in 2005, but the same lament has echoed for decades and continues to this day. Meeting the needs of all secondary students is the universal goal, but people disagree as to the particulars as the world economy shifts. One solution is to arrange job-training apprenticeships, whereby students earn credits toward graduation while working in local businesses. Germany placed tens of thousands of high school students in apprenticeships during the 1980s, all guaranteed jobs if they did well.

That strategy succeeded when businesses needed workers. However, when unemployment increased, most employers left the program (Grollmann & Rauner, 2007). Furthermore, students were enrolled in apprenticeship programs because their parents had less education than the parents of more academically enrolled students, which was not what the creators intended (Lehmann, 2004).

Currently, employers in every nation provide on-the-job training (usually much more specific and current than any high school can provide) and want their newly trained employees to know how to think, explain, write, concentrate, and get along with other workers. Those skills are hard to measure on a high-stakes test or on the international tests explained in Chapter 12, the PIRLS and the TIMSS.

Another international test, the **PISA (Programme for International Student Assessment),** is designed to measure cognition needed in adult life. The PISA is taken by 15-year-olds in 50 nations, with that age picked deliberately because many students are close to the end of their formal school career. On this test, the questions are written to be practical, measuring the use of knowledge that might apply at home or on the job. As a PISA report described it:

> The tests are designed to generate measures of the extent to which students can make effective use of what they have learned in school to deal with various problems and challenges they are likely to experience in everyday life.
>
> [PISA, 2009, p. 12]

For example, among the questions to test math is this one:

Robert's mother lets him pick one candy from a bag. He can't see the candies. The number of candies of each color in the bag is shown in the following graph.

What is the probability that Robert will pick a red candy?
A. 10%   B. 20%   C. 25%   D. 50%

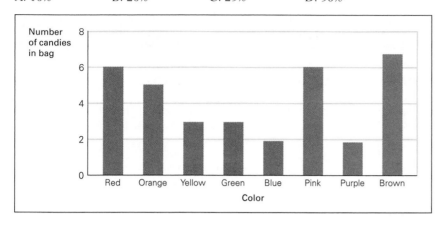

>> **Answer to Observation Quiz** (from page 425) The similarities have to do with gender, uniforms, and cooperation. Sex segregation and similar garb are evident in both photographs, although they are voluntary in U.S. public schools and compulsory in many African secondary schools. Adolescents everywhere enjoy working collaboratively.

For that and the other questions on the PISA, the calculations are quite simple—most 10-year-olds can do it; no calculus or complex formulas are needed. However, the mathematical reasoning may be challenging. On this question, only one-half of the students worldwide got it right (answer B), as did fewer than one-half of the students from the United States. Overall, the U.S. students did even worse on the PISA than on the PIRLS or TIMSS. On the PISA science questions, Finland was on top and Canada was second; the United States ranked 23rd. In math, the United States ranked a bit lower, with 25 nations scoring higher (see Table 15.2). (U.S. reading scores from the most recent PISA were invalid because of a printing error; it is possible that American 15-year-olds are better at reading literacy than they are at math.)

>> **Response for High School Teachers** (from page 425) It would be nice to follow your instincts, but the appropriate response depends partly on pressures within the school and on the expectations of the parents and administration. A comforting fact is that adolescents can think about and learn almost anything if they feel a personal connection to it. Look for ways to teach the facts your students need for the tests as the foundation for the exciting and innovative topics you want to teach. Everyone will learn more, and the tests will be less intimidating for your students.

TABLE 15.2

Math Scores on the PISA

Nation	Score	Nation	Score	Nation	Score
Chinese Taipei	549	Austria	505	Greece	459
Finland	548	Germany	504	Israel	442
Hong Kong	547	Sweden	502	Uruguay	427
South Korea	547	Ireland	501	Turkey	424
Netherlands	531	France	496	Thailand	417
Switzerland	530	United Kingdom	495	Romania	415
Canada	527	Poland	495	Chile	411
Japan	523	Hungary	491	Mexico	406
New Zealand	522	Norway	490	Indonesia	391
Belgium	520	Spain	480	Jordan	384
Australia	520	Russia	476	Argentina	381
Denmark	513	United States	474	Colombia	370
Czech Republic	510	Portugal	466	Brazil	370
Iceland	506	Italy	462	Tunisia	365

Source: PISA, test taken in 2006, scores published in 2009.

Not Geography The PISA is taken by 15-year-olds in many nations. Questions are designed to measure practical applications of school knowledge in science, reading, and math. Educators and political leaders for countries below average (including the United States) search for explanations for low achievement in geography, genes, or immigration, not schools and teachers, but the data do not support them. Although most East Asian nations do very well, note that Thailand is low, and nations with a higher proportion of immigrants than the United States (e.g., Canada) or very few immigrants (e.g., Japan) seem to do equally well. Scholars who study international variations in academic achievement agree that school practices are far more directly responsible for differences than any broader cultural differences—although controversy remains regarding exactly what those significant practices are.

Indications from the PISA and from international comparisons of high school dropout rates suggest that much more can be done to improve secondary education for those who do not go to college. Of course, nothing can be done if a student leaves school early, as many U.S. students do if they are disengaged from school. Efforts to increase engagement require critical thinking, as the following explains.

THINKING CRITICALLY

Increasing Adolescent Engagement in School

What can be done to encourage adolescents to be engaged with school? There is no single, definitive answer. However, developmental research provides three suggestions:

- *Keep high schools small.* Schools educate best if 200 to 400 students are enrolled because many teachers and staff will know every student and almost every student will be involved in some sort of team or club. That fosters a sense of belonging to the school as well as more engagement with education. Unfortunately, in 2009 the *average* secondary school in eight states (Florida, California, Georgia, Hawaii, Maryland, Nevada, New Jersey, and Virginia) enrolled over a thousand.

- *Encourage extracurricular activities.* There are "developmental benefits of participation in extracurricular activities for many high school adolescents" (Fredricks & Eccles, 2006, p. 712). Athletic teams elicit positive emotions and school bonding, for the athletes and everyone else. Even activities sponsored by nonschool groups help (Glanville et al., 2008). When extracurricular activities are cut, so is school attachment (Fredricks & Eccles, 2006). A North Carolina study found that high schools with more varied activities, and more students in them, had fewer dropouts and higher achievement, even after the socioeconomic statuses of students and schools were equalized (Stearns & Glennie, 2010).

- *Reduce harassment.* School violence is decreasing in the United States, but fear of violence is increasing. Clear rules for student behavior, rewards for attendance, and more sporting events within (not just between) schools all reduce in-school crime, according to a survey of Texas middle and high schools (Cheurprakobkit & Bartsch, 2005). The same study shows that both fear and violence increase when metal detectors are installed and strict punishments are handed out. For healthy development,

cooperation among the adults and friendly relationships among the students, with everyone feeling protected, is critical (Stewart, 2008).

Not everyone would agree with this list; each item increases cost. Ironically, every high school dropout saves money for the overall education budget. When taxpayers and political leaders set priorities, the education of secondary school students may not be among them. Furthermore, no measure always succeeds. A review of high school education worldwide finds that "no culture or nation has worked out a surefire educational psychology to guarantee that every one of the youth is motivated in school" (Larson & Wilson, 2004, p. 318). A positive school climate "requires explicit, targeted, and aligned change efforts at the leverage points" (McGuigan, 2008, p. 112). To agree on those levers, and pull them, requires effort from everyone.

Bored or Attentive? This girl explains an aspect of history to her classmates at the small Manhattan International School. This public school's size (300 students) might increase student engagement, but the four-year graduation rate is only 60 percent, suggesting that factors beyond class size are important.

Surprisingly, students who are capable of passing their classes drop out as often as those less capable. Persistence, engagement, and motivation seem more crucial than intellectual ability (Archambault et al., 2009; Fredricks et al., 2004). For many reasons, engagement in school and assessment of self-competence typically fall in each consecutive year of high school, particularly among boys (Fredricks & Eccles, 2006; Porche et al., 2004; Wigfield et al., 1997). One study that measured engagement and motivation reported that students achieved the highest scores in primary school, middling scores in college, and lowest scores in secondary school (Martin, 2009).

Secondary school teachers are hired for their academic expertise, not for their ability to engage adolescents. They model formal operational thinking—answering questions about the intricacies of theoretical physics, advanced calculus, and iambic pentameter—but they may not connect with students. Furthermore, the most qualified teachers tend to gravitate to schools with more able students (where salaries are higher and class sizes, smaller); even within schools, the best teachers are often assigned classes of the elite college-bound. This creates problems for the other students, who learn best when a master teacher guides active discussion, debate, and exposition but are less likely to have such teachers (Slavin et al., 2009).

Some nations provide equally qualified teachers for every school, but most do not. The disparity between teacher qualifications for students from low- and high-income families is twice as high in the United States as in Canada and Finland, two nations that do very well on the PISA (Cavanagh, 2007).

A final question arises for all three of the school groups discussed here: the college-bound, the students who quit after they earn their diploma, and those who drop out as soon as they can (legally age 16 in most U.S. states). That question is: Does learning during adolescence matter when considering the entire life span? For individuals, the answer is a resounding yes. Not only health but also almost every other indicator of a good life—high income, stable marriage, successful children, satisfying work—correlates with education. (There are a few exceptions, noted in later chapters.)

Beyond the benefits to the individual, entire nations gain from the quality of secondary education. A detailed calculation found that if the United States average PISA score increased by a mere 25 points (up to the scores for France, Ireland, or Sweden; still far below Finland or South Korea), that would result in an increase of $40 *trillion* in the U.S. GDP (gross domestic product, a number used by economists to measure national economic production) between 2010 and 2090 (Hanushek & Woessmann, 2010). How could this be?

The cognitive skills that boost economic development are creativity, flexibility, and analytic ability; they allow innovation and mastery of new technology. When nations raise their human capital by having more adults with those skills, their economies prosper (Cohen & Soto, 2007). Scores of various nations on the PISA and other tests predict later economic development (Hanushek & Woessmann, 2010).

Those cognitive abilities that nations need in the twenty-first century are exactly what adolescents can develop—with proper education and guidance. As you have read, every scientist who studies adolescent cognition notes that the logical and creative potential of the adolescent mind is not always realized, but it can be. Does this chapter end on a hopeful note?

Especially for High School Guidance Counselors Given what you know about adolescent thinking, should you spend more time helping students with college applications, with summer jobs, with family problems, or with course selection? (see response, page 431)

SUMMING UP

Middle schools tend to be less personal, less flexible, and more tightly regulated than elementary schools, which may contribute to a general finding: declining student achievement. In fostering adolescent cognition, technology seems to have many positive aspects but also allows cyberbullying and addiction to video games. School transitions are difficult but can be made less stressful. Ideally, secondary education advances thinking, although some measures that help students connect with their schools (such as sports) are too often undervalued. High school students who do not expect to attend college may be particularly unprepared for adult life. ∎

SUMMARY

Adolescent Thinking

1. Cognition in early adolescence may be egocentric, a kind of self-centered thinking. Adolescent egocentrism gives rise to the personal fable, the invincibility fable, and the imaginary audience.

2. *Formal operational thought* is Piaget's term for the last of his four periods of cognitive development. He tested and demonstrated formal operational thought with various problems that students in a high school science or math class might encounter.

3. Piaget realized that adolescents are no longer earthbound and concrete in their thinking; they prefer to imagine the possible, the probable, and even the impossible, instead of focusing on what is real. They develop hypotheses and explore, using deductive reasoning. However, most developmentalists believe that this is only part of the picture and that there is no sudden movement from concrete to formal thinking.

Intuitive, Emotional Thought

4. Intuitive thinking becomes more forceful during adolescence. Few teenagers always use logic, although they are capable of doing so. Emotional, intuitive thinking is quicker and more satisfying, and sometimes better, than analytic thought.

5. Contrary to popular belief, research has found that a large majority of adolescents consider themselves to be religious, with most following the faith of their parents. With time, they move away from traditional practices, but they believe their deeper cognition results in stronger rather than weaker faith.

Teaching and Learning

6. Secondary education—after primary (grade school) and before tertiary (college) education—correlates with the health and wealth of individuals and nations. Almost all of the world's children now receive some secondary schooling.

7. In middle school, many students tend to be bored, difficult to teach, and hurtful to one another. One reason may be that middle schools are not structured to accommodate egocentrism or intuitive thinking.

8. Many forms of psychopathology increase at the transitions to middle school, to high school, and to college. School changes may be particularly difficult in adolescence, when young people must also adjust to biological and family changes.

9. Adolescents use technology, particularly the Internet, more than people of any other age group. They reap many educational benefits from doing so, but there are hazards as well, in video game addiction, cyberbullying, and support for pathological activities.

10. Education in high school emphasizes formal operational thinking. In the United States, the demand for more accountability has led to more AP classes and high-stakes testing. This may have unintended consequences, including a higher dropout rate.

11. A sizable number of high school students do not graduate or go on to college. Current high school education does not seem to meet their needs.

12. A test (PISA) taken by many 15-year-olds in 50 nations measures how well they can apply the knowledge they have been taught. Students in the United States seem to have particular difficulty with such tests.

KEY TERMS

adolescent egocentrism (p. 408)
personal fable (p. 409)
invincibility fable (p. 409)
imaginary audience (p. 409)
formal operational thought (p. 410)

hypothetical thought (p. 411)
deductive reasoning (p. 412)
inductive reasoning (p. 412)
dual-process model (p. 413)
intuitive thought (p. 414)
analytic thought (p. 414)

sunk cost fallacy (p. 415)
base rate neglect (p. 415)
secondary education (p. 417)
middle school (p. 418)
cyberbullying (p. 422)
cutting (p. 423)

high-stakes test (p. 424)
PISA (Programme for International Student Assessment) (p. 426)

WHAT HAVE YOU LEARNED?

Adolescent Thinking

1. How does adolescent egocentrism differ from early childhood egocentrism?

2. What are the two extreme perceptions that arise from the imaginary audience?

3. Why are the personal fable and the invincibility fable called "fables"?

4. How does formal operational thinking differ from concrete operational thinking?

5. What are the advantages and disadvantages of using induction rather than deduction?

6. How certain are contemporary developmentalists that Piaget accurately described adolescent cognition?

Intuitive, Emotional Thought

7. When might intuition and analysis lead to contrasting conclusions?

8. What mode of thinking do most people prefer, intuitive or analytic, and why?

9. How does personal experience increase the probability of base rate neglect?

10. How does egocentrism account for the clashing priorities of parents and adolescents?

11. When is intuitive thinking better than analytic thinking?

Teaching and Learning

12. Why have most junior high schools disappeared?

13. What characteristics of middle schools make them more difficult for students than elementary schools?

14. How does being a young adolescent affect a person's ability to learn?

15. Why are transitions a particular concern for educators?

16. What benefits come from the adolescent use of technology?

17. How do video games affect student learning?

18. Who is most and least likely to be involved in cyberbullying?

19. If an adolescent consults Internet sites regarding cutting, what should adults do and why?

20. Why is the first year of attending a new school more stressful than the second year?

21. What is the United States doing to raise the education standards in secondary schools?

22. What are the advantages and disadvantages of high-stakes testing?

23. Why is Germany's apprentice/vocational education system no longer prevalent?

24. How does PISA differ from other international tests?

25. Why is high school achievement likely to advance the national economy?

APPLICATIONS

1. Describe a time when you overestimated how much other people were thinking about you. How was your mistake similar to and different from adolescent egocentrism?

2. Talk to a teenager about politics, families, school, religion, or any other topic that might reveal the way that young person thinks. Do you hear any adolescent egocentrism? Intuitive thinking? Systematic thought? Flexibility? Cite examples.

3. Think of a life-changing decision you have made. How did logic and emotion interact? What would have changed if you had given the matter more thought—or less?

4. Describe what happened and what you thought in the first year you attended a middle school or high school. What made it better or worse than later years in that school?

>> **Response for High School Guidance Counselors** (from page 429) It depends on what your particular students need; schools vary a great deal. However, all students need to talk and think about their choices and options so that they will not act impulsively. Therefore, providing information and a listening ear might be the most important thing you can spend time doing.

>>ONLINE CONNECTIONS

To accompany your textbook, you have access to a number of online resources, including quizzes for every chapter of the book, flashcards (in English and Spanish), critical thinking questions, and case studies. For access to any of these links, go to www.worthpublishers.com/bergerls8e. In addition to these free resources, you'll also find links to the podcasts, video clips, diagnostic quizzing with personalized study advice, and an ebook. Some of the videos and activities available online include:

- *Child Soldiers and Child Peacemakers.* More than 150 wars since World War II! See the effects of armed conflict on children's development and hear how some young people take a stand for peace.

- *HIV/AIDS.* A brief history of the global spread of HIV and successful promotion of educational intervention in Sri Lanka. Videos let affected people tell their stories.

Adolescence: Psychosocial Development

WHAT WILL YOU KNOW?

1. Why do adolescents need to establish their own identity rather than accepting what their parents want for them?

2. What special difficulties are encountered by adolescents who are gay or lesbian?

3. How can a person tell if an adolescent might attempt suicide?

4. Why are more young men in prison than young women?

5. Is it really harmful for adolescents to smoke cigarettes or drink alcohol?

"What does your mother do?" Emil, the head of Town Security, asked my daughter, who had a summer job as a security deputy.

"She writes books."

"How does she do that?"

"She spends a lot of time in the library, reading and writing."

"Oh, your poor mother!"

No need for pity. I love teaching and writing. Emil's pity made me realize that each of us has our own preferences, habits, and interests, with differences that become clearer as people begin to find their identity in adolescence. From ages 11 to 18, humans experiment to discover what they like. Emil liked riding around town, responding to emergencies, searching for "perps." I would hate that. Already in high school, I loved reading and writing and resented interruptions. I chose classes that rewarded me for figuring things out with paper and pencil: I was the only girl in advanced math, for instance.

In many ways, I was a rebel: I told my friends that I would never be a teacher (too conventional, especially for a girl), and I refused the colleges my parents suggested (more of that in the next chapter). But in some ways, I was a typical teenager. For example, I was thrilled when Bill invited me to his fraternity weekend, and I took it as a compliment when his roommate said of me, "That's not the kind of girl you date, that's the kind of girl you marry." That was my plan for myself.

This chapter describes the search for identity, how parents and peers influence each young person, and how each person refuses part of his or her familial heritage while accepting other parts. One important topic is romance; many adolescents try to discern and express their gender identity, via partners, aspirations, and sexuality. We also consider ethnic identity, parental influences, and friendships. A few adolescents plunge into despair and contemplate suicide; most experiment with drugs, alcohol, or minor lawbreaking—perhaps to be stopped by someone like Emil, who likes his job and would hate mine. All this is covered in this chapter, describing how 11- to 18-year-olds move through the psychosocial maze from childhood to adulthood.

>> Identity

Psychosocial development during adolescence is often understood as a search for a consistent understanding of oneself. Self-expression and self-concept become increasingly important, as the egocentrism described in Chapter 15 illustrates. Each young person wants to know "Who am I?"

According to Erik Erikson, life's fifth psychosocial crisis is **identity versus role confusion,** with the complexities of finding one's own identity being the primary task of adolescence (Erikson, 1968). He said this crisis is resolved with **identity achievement;** after adolescents reconsider the goals and values of their parents and culture, they accept some and discard others, discerning their own unique self.

The result is neither wholesale rejection nor unquestioning acceptance of society (Côté, 2009). With their new autonomy, teenagers maintain continuity with the past so they can move to the future, achieving their own identity—necessary since their context is not identical to that of their parents, and each person has a unique combination of genes and alleles.

Not Yet Achieved

Erikson's insights inspired many researchers. Notable among them was James Marcia, who described and measured four specific ways young people cope with this stage of life: (1) achievement, (2) role confusion, (3) foreclosure, (3) moratorium (Marcia, 1966). Over the past half-century, major psychosocial shifts have lengthened the duration of adolescence and made identity achievement more complex (Côté, 2006; Kroger et al., 2010; Nurmi, 2004). However, these four possible paths still seem evident.

Role confusion is the opposite of identity achievement. It is characterized by lack of commitment to any goals or values. Identity confusion is sometimes called *identity diffusion,* to emphasize that some adolescents seem diffuse, unfocused, unconcerned about their future (Phillips & Pittman, 2007). Even the usual social demands—such as putting away clothes, making friends, completing school assignments, and thinking about college or career—are beyond the ability of confused adolescents. Instead, they might sleep too much, immerse themselves in video games or mind-numbing television, and turn from one romance to another. Their thinking is disorganized, they procrastinate, they avoid issues and actions (Côté, 2009).

Identity **foreclosure** occurs when, in order to halt the confusion, young people accept traditional values without question (Marcia, 1966; Marcia et al., 1993). They might follow roles and customs transmitted from their parents or culture, never exploring alternatives. Or they might foreclose completely on an oppositional, negative identity, again without any thoughtful questioning. Foreclosure is a comfortable shelter.

A more mature shelter is **moratorium,** a kind of time-out. Societies provide many moratoria (such as college) that allow adolescents to postpone identity achievement. Adolescents can be in moratorium throughout their teen years, but since this status peaks at age 19 (Kroger et al., 2010), the specific modes of moratorium are described in the chapters on emerging adulthood.

Many aspects of the search for identity have become more arduous than when Erikson first described them. Fifty years ago, the drive to become independent and autonomous was thought to be the "key normative psychosocial task of adolescence" (Zimmer-Gembeck & Collins, 2003, p. 177). Developmentalists still believe that adolescents struggle through the identity crisis, but it now seems that attaining autonomy and achieving identity before age 18 are unlikely (Kroger et al., 2010).

---

identity versus role confusion Erikson's term for the fifth stage of development, in which the person tries to figure out "Who am I?" but is confused as to which of many possible roles to adopt.

identity achievement Erikson's term for the attainment of identity, or the point at which a person understands who he or she is as a unique individual, in accord with past experiences and future plans.

role confusion A situation in which an adolescent does not seem to know or care what his or her identity is. (Sometimes called *identity diffusion.*)

foreclosure Erikson's term for premature identity formation, which occurs when an adolescent adopts parents' or society's roles and values wholesale, without questioning or analysis.

moratorium An adolescent's choice of a socially acceptable way to postpone making identity-achievement decisions. Going to college is a common example.

Four Arenas of Identity Formation

Erikson (1968) highlighted four aspects of identity: religious, political, vocational, and sexual. Terminology and emphasis have changed for all four, as has timing. In none of these is identity usually achieved during adolescence. In fact, if an 18-year-old is no longer open to new possibilities in any of these areas, that may be foreclosure, not achievement—and might even shift again. (I did not marry Bill, or anyone, until relatively late for my cohort.) Nonetheless, each of these four arenas for identity is integral to understanding life-span development. For that reason, each is discussed in this text: religious identity in Chapter 15, political identity (now referred to as *ethnic identity*) later in this chapter, vocational identity in Chapter 19, and sexual identity (now referred to as *gender identity*) also later in this chapter. Now, we briefly summarize all four.

Religious identity, for most adolescents, is similar to that of their parents and community. Few adolescents totally reject religion if they grew up following a particular faith, partly because religion provides meaning as well as coping skills that are particularly useful during the stresses of the teen years (King & Roeser, 2009). Past parental practices influence adolescent religious identity, although some adolescents express that identity in ways that their parents did not anticipate: A Muslim girl might wear a headscarf, or a Catholic boy might study for the priesthood, or a Baptist teenager might join a Pentecostal youth group. Such new practices are relatively minor: Almost no young Muslim converts to Judaism, and almost no teenage Baptist becomes Hindu. Most adolescents accept the religious identity of their parents and culture, questioning specific beliefs as their cognitive processes allow more reflective, less concrete assumptions, but they do not have a crisis of faith unless unusual circumstances propel it (King & Roeser, 2009).

Political identity is similar, with most adolescents following the political traditions of their parents. In the twenty-first century in the United States, party identification is weakening among adults, with more adults saying they are independent rather than Republican or Democratic (Pew Research Center, 2009). Their teenagers reflect this; some proudly say they are not interested in politics, in which case an apolitical identity is likely to continue in adulthood (Côté, 2009).

A word here about political terrorism and religious extremism, however. It is true that people who are relatively young (under age 30) are often on the front lines of terrorism or are converts to groups that their elders consider cults. Political and religious fanatics have much in common: Age of new adherents is one of them (L. L. Dawson, 2010). However, adolescents are rarely drawn to these groups unless personal loneliness or a difficult family background (such as a parent's death caused by the opposing political group) compels them. The idea that every teenager might become a suicide bomber or willing martyr is an adult myth.

The topic of political identity also brings up "identity politics," the tendency to identify politically with others of one's group, such as those of the same race, religion, ethnicity, or national origin (Bernstein, 2005; McClain et al., 2009; Monroe et al., 2000). Identity politics is more limited than Erikson proposed, and in some ways the young are less devoted to group identity than are their elders (e.g., they are more likely to approve of interracial dating, accept neighbors of other groups, and oppose discrimination).

Not Just a Uniform Adolescents in moratorium adopt temporary roles to postpone achieving their final identity. High school students like these may sign up for an ROTC (Reserve Officers Training Corps) class, but few of them go on to enlist in the U.S. Marine Corps.

A Religious Life These young adolescents in Ethiopia are studying to be monks. Their monastery is a haven in the midst of civil strife. Will the rituals and beliefs also provide them with a way to achieve identity?

The Same Situation, Many Miles Apart: Learning in School For these two groups of Muslim girls, the distance between their schools in Dearborn, Michigan (*left*), and Jammu, Kashmir (*right*), is more than geographical. The schools' hidden curricula teach different lessons about the roles of women.

Observation Quiz What three differences are evident? (see answer, page 438)

Vocational identity originally meant envisioning oneself as a worker in a particular occupation. This made sense a century ago, when most women were wives and mothers, most men were farmers or factory workers, and those few others in particular professions were generalists (doctors were general practitioners, lawyers handled all kinds of cases, and so on). Vocational identity needed to be established when adolescent choices led to one career lifelong.

Obviously, such vocational identity is no longer relevant. Nor is anyone ready for a lifetime career at age 18. As detailed in Chapter 19, there are thousands of careers, and many adults change vocations (not just employers) several times. One popular book discussing more than a thousand careers is 3,376 pages long (Ferguson Publishing, 2007).

Friendship, Romance, or Passion? Sexual identity is much more complex for today's adolescents than it once was. Behavior, clothing, and hairstyles are often ambiguous. Girls with shorn hair, boys with pierced ears, or same-sex couples embracing are not necessarily homosexual for life—and may not be oriented toward the same sex.

gender identity A person's acceptance of the roles and behaviors that society associates with the biological categories of male and female.

Achieving *sexual identity* is also a lifelong task, in part because standards keep changing, especially for young adults. A half-century ago, Erikson and other theorists thought of the two sexes as opposites (P. Y. Miller & Simon, 1980). They assumed that adolescents who were confused about their sexual identity would soon adopt proper male or female roles (Erikson, 1968; A. Freud, 1958/2000). Adolescence was a time for "gender intensification," when people identified as male or female—but no longer (Priess et al., 2009).

As you remember from Chapter 10, for social scientists *sex* and *sexual* refer to biological male and female characteristics, whereas *gender* refers to cultural and social characteristics that differentiate males and females. Erikson's term *sexual identity* has been replaced by **gender identity** (Denny & Pittman, 2007), which refers primarily to a person's self-definition as male or female. Gender identity usually begins with the person's biological sex and leads to assumption of a gender role, behavior that society considers appropriate for that gender: nurse/doctor, secretary/businessman, housewife/breadwinner.

Adolescents still experience strong sexual drives as their hormone levels increase. They are often confused regarding when, how, and with whom to express those drives. That makes achieving gender identity complicated for many (Baumeister & Blackhart, 2007; Gilchrist & Sullivan, 2006). Some adolescents foreclose (exaggerating male or female roles), others seek a moratorium (avoiding all sexual contact), and still others move toward achievement. Changes and controversies regarding gender identity are discussed later in this chapter as well as throughout the adulthood chapters.

SUMMING UP

Erikson's fifth psychosocial crisis, identity versus role confusion, was first described more than 50 years ago. Adolescence was thought to be the time to search for a personal identity, with identity achievement representing the mark of adulthood. This crisis still occurs; role confusion, foreclosure, and moratorium are still apparent. However, timing has changed. The identity crisis lasts much longer, and fewer young people develop a firm sense of who they are and what path they will follow by age 18.

Specific aspects of identity—religious, political, vocational, and sexual—have new forms and timetables. All are still relevant to life-span development, but each has complexities that were not anticipated by Erikson.

>> Relationships with Adults

Adolescence is often characterized as a period of waning adult influence, when children distance themselves from the values of their elders. There is validity in this generalization, but it is not always accurate. In fact, when young people feel appreciated by their communities, trusted by teachers, and connected to parents or other adults, they are far less likely to abuse drugs, quit school, break the law, or hurt themselves or others.

bickering Petty, peevish arguing, usually repeated and ongoing.

Parents

The fact that parent–adolescent relationships are pivotal does not mean that they are peaceful (Eisenberg et al., 2008; Laursen & Collins, 2009). Disputes are common because the adolescent's drive for independence clashes with the parents' desire to maintain control. Normally, parent–adolescent conflict peaks in early adolescence, especially between mothers and daughters. It usually manifests as **bickering**—repeated, petty arguments (more nagging than fighting) about routine, day-to-day concerns such as cleanliness, clothes, chores, and schedules (Eisenberg et al., 2008).

Some bickering may indicate a healthy family, since close relationships almost always include some conflict (Smetana et al., 2004). Generally, parents adjust by granting more autonomy, and "friendship and positive affect [emotional state] typically rebound to preadolescent levels" (Collins & Laursen, 2004, p. 337). Teenagers adjust as well. By age 18, their emotional maturity and reduced egocentrism allow them to appreciate parents. Generally, over the years of adolescence, both parents and teenagers try to balance the need for independence and closeness, with less disclosure but improved communication as the young person matures (Masche, 2010).

You Don't Listen Adolescent girls are particularly likely to accuse their mothers of not understanding them. For their part, mothers' responses vary, from anger to support and guidance.

AP PHOTO / THE PLAIN DEALER, DALE OMORI

"So I blame you for everything—whose fault is that?"

In Chapter 10, you learned that authoritative parenting is usually the best parenting style for school-age children and that uninvolved parenting is the worst. The same holds true for adolescents. Although teenagers may act as if they no longer need their parents, neglect is always destructive—as you saw with James in Chapter 15. Another example is Joy. When she was 16, her stepfather said: "Teens all around here [are] doing booze and doing drugs. . . . But my Joy here ain't into that stuff" (quoted in C. Smith, 2005, p. 10). In fact, however, Joy was smoking pot, drinking alcohol, and having sex with her boyfriend. She later reported that she

> overdosed on a bunch of stuff once, pills or some prescription of my mom's—I took the whole bottle. It didn't work. I just went to sleep for a long time. . . . They never found out . . . pretty pitiful.
>
> [quoted in C. Smith, 2005, p. 12]

That suicide attempt was a clear indication that she was in far worse trouble than most "teens all around here."

Cultural Differences

Regarding parent–adolescent relationships, some cultures value harmony above all else. Some scholars wonder whether adolescent rebellion is a *social construction*, assumed by middle-class Westerners but not by others, or whether it is a consequence of the competitive global economy, not a developmental universal (Larson & Wilson, 2004). Or it could be that bickering and then autonomy are essential for healthy adulthood.

Certainly culture affects the topics and methods of conflict. Because of globalization, even adolescents who have never traveled far from home are aware of other ways of life (Arnett, 2002). The variations are many: Japanese youth expect autonomy in their musical choices but want parents to help them with romance (Hasebe et al., 2004); U.S. teenagers resist parental interference in romance or friendship (Kakihara & Tilton-Weaver, 2009). In Chile, adolescents usually obey their parents, even when they disagree (Darling et al., 2008); but if they do something their parents might not like, they keep it secret—unlike U.S. adolescents, who might instead provoke an argument (Cumsille et al., 2010).

Several researchers have focused specifically on the parent–child differences between young people in Hong Kong and those in the United States or Australia. In every culture, adolescents seem to benefit from increasing autonomy, but parents in the United States allow more independence than do parents in Hong Kong (Qin et al., 2009). Similarities outweigh differences. In the United States, Hong Kong, and Australia alike, parent–adolescent communication and encouragement benefit the youths, protecting them somewhat from depression, suicide, and low self-esteem and helping them have high aspirations and achievements (e.g., Kwok & Shek, 2010; Leung et al., 2010).

Filial devotion (the reciprocal obligations of parents and children) is particularly strong in Chinese culture and curbs adolescent rebellion somewhat. Some of the autonomy and rebellion expected for Western adolescents is not as apparent among Asian adolescents. The pervasive cultural influence is evident in a study that focused on language: Chinese adolescents expressed more self-assertion when they spoke English than when they spoke Chinese (Wang et al., 2010). (See Figure 16.1 and the Research Design.) It was not the words themselves, of course, but rather the context evoked (e.g., Hong Kong's British heritage or millennia of mainland Chinese culture) when a researcher spoke English or Chinese.

>> Answer to Observation Quiz (from page 436) Facial expressions, degree of adult supervision, and head covering. (Did you notice that the Kashmiri girls wear a tight-fitting cap under their one-piece white robes?)

Research Design

Scientists: Qi Wang, Yi Shao, and Yexin Jessica Li.

Publication: *Child Development* (2010).

Participants: A total of 125 children (aged 8, 10, 12, and 14) in Hong Kong, all proficient in both Chinese and English. (They spoke Chinese with their parents, but their education was in English.) All the children were exposed to both cultures because, in the words of these researchers, "Hong Kong is a culturally dynamic place where Western and Chinese values intertwine and where modernity and tradition coexist" (p. 557).

Design: Trained bilingual researchers asked the children to speak about memories, self-descriptions, and values. Children were randomly assigned to be interviewed in Chinese or English. Among the data were self-descriptions, judged by coders who did not know the hypothesis, about the individual alone (such as "I enjoy books," "My eyes are dark") or related to others or a group (e.g., "I am a student," "My family loves me"). The ratio of self- to social descriptions was calculated.

Results: Those interviewed in Chinese became more social at adolescence, while those interviewed in English were more likely to refer to themselves—a distinction especially apparent at age 10, an age characterized by accelerating hormones and the distortions of egocentrism.

Major conclusions: The researchers interpreted these results to mean that, at adolescence, autonomy becomes less prominent in Chinese but not in English, presumably because of cultural differences between China and Britain, and that adolescents' self-concepts are powerfully influenced by the context—signaled by the language.

Comment: Thousands of social scientists study culture, but it is difficult to determine that the differences or similarities they find are objective, not influenced by translation or the perceptions of the scientist. These researchers cleverly assigned bilingual participants randomly to an interview language. This study was small (about 30 adolescents at each age, 125 in total, and only two cultures), however, so replication is needed.

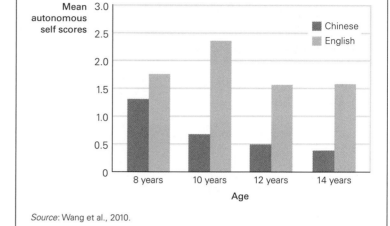

Effect of Age and Language on Autonomy

Source: Wang et al., 2010.

FIGURE 16.1

Words and Perceptions As they grew older, fluently bilingual students in Hong Kong who were interviewed in Chinese became less likely to refer to themselves as individuals distinct from their family and friends. By contrast, their classmates, who, by chance, were interviewed in English, were more self-focused—especially at age 10. Is that a shame? It depends on the culture (and maybe the language) of the observer.

Closeness Within the Family

More important than family conflict may be family closeness, which has four aspects:

1. Communication (Do family members talk openly with one another?)
2. Support (Do they rely on one another?)
3. Connectedness (How emotionally close are they?)
4. Control (Do parents encourage or limit adolescent autonomy?)

No developmentalist doubts that the first two, communication and support, are helpful, perhaps essential. Patterns set in place during childhood continue, ideally buffering some of the turbulence of adolescence (Cleveland et al., 2005; Laursen & Collins, 2009). Regarding connectedness and control, consequences vary and observers differ in what they see. Consider this example, written by one of my students:

> I got pregnant when I was sixteen years old, and if it weren't for the support of my parents, I would probably not have my son. And if they hadn't taken care of him, I wouldn't have been able to finish high school or attend college. My parents also helped me overcome the shame that I felt when . . . my aunts, uncles, and especially my grandparents found out that I was pregnant.

[I., personal communication]

parental monitoring Parents' ongoing awareness of what their children are doing, where, and with whom.

My student is grateful to her parents, but other observers might wonder whether her early motherhood allowed her parents too much control and required her to remain dependent when she should have been seeking her own identity. An added complexity is that my student's parents had emigrated from South America: Cultural expectations affected her family's response. A study of nonimmigrant pregnant adolescents found that most (not all) young mothers and their children fared best if the teen's parents were supportive but did not take over the care of the child (Borkowski et al., 2007).

An important issue is **parental monitoring**—that is, parental knowledge about each child's whereabouts, activities, and companions. When monitoring is part of a warm, supportive relationship, children are likely to become confident, well-educated adults, avoiding drugs and risky sex (G. M. Barnes et al., 2006; Fletcher et al., 2004).

Adolescents play an active role in their own monitoring: Some are eager to tell parents about their activities, whereas others are secretive (Vieno et al., 2009). Thus, monitoring is a good sign if it indicates mutual, close interaction. However, monitoring may be harmful when it derives from suspicion and secrecy instead of from a warm connection (Smetana, 2008; Stattin & Kerr, 2000).

Control is another aspect of parenting that can backfire. Adolescents expect parents to exert some control, especially over moral issues. However, overly restrictive and controlling parenting correlates with depression. Decreasing control is best, as documented in a longitudinal study of 12- to 14-year-olds in the suburbs of Chicago and Hong Kong. In both cultures, adolescents were given more autonomy over personal choices as they grew older, and in both cultures increased autonomy was associated with better emotional functioning (Qin et al., 2009). Overall, parental reaction to adolescent communication is crucial: Too much criticism and control are more likely to stop the dialogue than to improve the behavior (Tilton-Weaver et al., 2010).

A VIEW FROM SCIENCE

Parents, Genes, and Risks

Research on human development has practical applications. This was evident in a longitudinal study of African American families in rural Georgia that began with 611 parents and their 11-year-olds (Brody et al., 2009). Half of the families were randomly assigned to the control group, and the other half were invited to seven two-hour training sessions. Groups were small, and leaders were well prepared. Parents and their 11-year-olds were taught separately for an hour and then brought together.

The parents learned:

- To be nurturant and involved
- To convey pride in being African American (called *racial socialization*)
- Why monitoring and control benefit adolescents
- The need for clear norms and expectations concerning substance use
- Strategies for communication about sex

The 11-year-olds learned:

- The importance of having household rules
- Adaptive behaviors when encountering racism
- The need for making plans for the future
- The differences between them and peers who use alcohol

In their joint hour, games, structured interactions, and modeling improved family communication and cohesion. Three years later, both groups were reassessed regarding sex and alcohol/drug activity. Four years after the study began, the researchers read the new genetic research regarding the heightened risks for people with the short allele of the 5-HTTLPR gene. To see if this applied to their African American teenagers, they collected and analyzed the DNA of 16-year-olds who had been, at age 11, in either the control or experimental groups. As Figure 16.2 shows, the training had no decided impact on those with the long allele, but it did have a major impact on those with the short one.

That 14 hours of training had such an impact seems incredible, given all the other influences in these teenagers' lives. However, since the parent–child relationship begins at birth (even before) and continues throughout adolescence, those seven sessions might have provided some insights and connections that affected each dyad from then on.

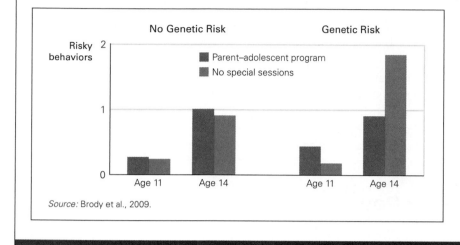

Source: Brody et al., 2009.

FIGURE 16.2

Not Yet The risk score was a simple 0 to 3, with one point for each of the following: had drunk alcohol, had smoked marijuana, had had sex. As shown, most of the 11-year-olds had done none of these; by age 14, most had done one (usually had drunk beer or wine)—except for those at genetic risk who did not have the seven-session training. Some at-risk 14-year-olds had done all three; and many had done at least two. As you see, for those youth without genetic risk, the usual parental advice limited risky behaviors such that the average 14-year-old had tried only one risky behavior. But for those at genetic risk, the special program made a decided difference. Extensive research has found that postponing these three behaviors is beneficial to adolescent development in many ways, which makes these results particularly noteworthy.

Other Adults

Parents are important, but so are many others—even those with no biological relationship to the young person (Scales et al., 2006). For the four arenas of identity development, there is no doubt that a church or temple youth minister can affect a young person's faith and morality; that a charismatic political leader can attract devotion (especially if the adolescents' own father is absent); that a school counselor or adult friend can influence vocational direction; and that, especially for sexual-minority youth, knowing an adult with a happy life and satisfying opposite- or same-sex relationship allows acceptance of sexuality (Lerner & Steinberg, 2009).

However, for many youth, other relatives are more influential than nonrelatives. An older sibling, cousin, aunt, or uncle can become a valued confidant, encouraging destructive or constructive behavior. For many adolescents, a close relationship with a grandparent is pivotal, whether or not their parents are single, married, or remarried (Attar-Schwartz et al., 2009). Details of all the adult–adolescent relationships are beyond the scope of this book, but one anecdote may make the point. Jim, age 21, was asked about mentors:

> My Mom's father—my grandfather. A very independent guy, but a very caring guy. They (grandparents) go down to Florida every winter. And our family often goes down to spend some time with them. My grandpa really loves swimming in the ocean. So he would go out floating on his back for hours at a time. . . . When I was younger, I used to stand on the shore and watch him float out. He would disappear and come back and ask me if I wanted to go out. I did once and people were worried because I was only ten. My parents and my grandma were concerned, "Oh, he's too small," even though I was with my grandpa. But what he said to me stuck. What he said was I need to know my own limits, my abilities. Other people are going to have their opinions and worries and concerns, but being independent is taking that stuff into consideration, but then also doing what you can.

[*cited in Pratt et al., 2010, p. 93*]

As with many adults whom adolescents admire, this grandfather helped his grandson affirm his own abilities, even when his parents wanted to hold him back. Of course, if young Jim needed rescuing, his grandfather would have done it, but that is not what "stuck." For many teenagers struggling to know "my own limits, my abilities," adult mentors can be crucial.

SUMMING UP

Relationships with adults are essential during adolescence. Parents and adolescents often bicker over small things, but parental guidance and ongoing communication promote adolescent psychosocial health. Among the signs of a healthy parent–adolescent relationship are that parents know what their child is doing (parental monitoring) and that adolescents talk with their parents about their concerns; both are affected by culture, by past relationships, and by the adolescent's maturity. Parental neglect or excessive parental control can foster adolescent rebellion; authoritative parenting continues to be effective. Other relatives and even strangers have an impact. ■

>> Peer Power

It is hard to overestimate the importance of peer approval for adolescents, although adults are not always aware of it. I did not recognize it at the time with my own children:

- Our oldest daughter wore the same pair of jeans to tenth grade, day after day. She washed them each night by hand and asked me to put them in the dryer early each morning. My husband was bewildered. "Is this some weird female ritual?" he asked. Years later, she explained that she was afraid that if she wore different pants each day, her classmates would think she cared about her clothes.
- Our second daughter, at 16, pierced her ears for the third time. When I asked if this meant she would do drugs, she laughed at my ignorance.
- At age 15, our third daughter was diagnosed with cancer. My husband and I weighed opinions from four physicians, each explaining how to minimize the risk of death. She had her own priorities: "I don't care what you choose, as long as I keep my hair." (Her hair fell out, but now her health is good.)
- Our youngest, in sixth grade, refused to wear her jacket (it was new; she had chosen it) even in midwinter. Not until high school did she tell me she wanted her middle school classmates to think she was tough.

For every adolescent, the judgment of peers is important, and having friends is vital. One high school boy said:

> A lot of times I wake up in the morning and I don't want to go to school, and then I'm like, you know, I have got this class and these friends are in it, and I am going to have fun. That is a big part of my day—my friends.
>
> [quoted in Hamm & Faircloth, 2005, p. 72]

Peer Pressure

peer pressure Encouragement to conform to one's friends or contemporaries in behavior, dress, and attitude; usually considered a negative force, as when adolescent peers encourage one another to defy adult authority.

Adults sometimes fear **peer pressure,** that an adolescent's peers will push him or her to try drugs, break the law, or do other things that child would never do alone. This fear ignores the fact that "friends generally encourage socially desirable behaviors" (Berndt & Murphy, 2002, p. 281), such as joining sports teams, studying for exams, rejecting cigarettes, and applying to college. Peers are more helpful than harmful (Audrey et al., 2006; Nelson & DeBacker, 2008), especially in early and middle adolescence, when biological and social stresses can be overwhelming. In later adolescence, teenagers are more likely to make their own decisions (Monahan et al., 2009).

To understand the role of peers, it is useful to realize how adolescents organize themselves. A cluster of close friends who are loyal to one another and who exclude outsiders is called a **clique.** A larger group of adolescents who share common interests is a **crowd.** Cliques and crowds provide social control and social support, via comments, exclusion, and admiration (B. Brown & Larson, 2009).

A crowd may exhibit small signs of identity (a certain brand of backpack, a particular greeting) that adults do not notice but that members of other crowds do (Strouse, 1999). Crowds may be based on ethnicity or on some personal characteristic or activity, such as the "brains," "jocks," "skaters," or "goths." They also provide encouragement for certain values. For instance, one study in the Midwest of the United States found that "tough" and "alternative" crowds felt that teenagers should behave as they choose, whereas the "prep" crowds thought that parental authority was usually legitimate (Daddis, 2010).

A major task for adolescents of minority and immigrant groups is to achieve ethnic identity, their own firm (not confused or foreclosed) understanding of what it means to be Asian, African, Latino, and so on. The larger society provides stereotypes and discrimination, and parents counter that with racial socialization (Umana-Taylor et al., 2010), but each young person needs to find his or her own ethnic identity, different from that of society or parents (Fuligni et al., 2009). For this, peers may be pivotal (Whitehead et al., 2009). In large schools with many ethnic groups, crowds based on ethnicity attract those in the minority who seek to avoid isolation while establishing their identity—not an easy or smooth process (Kiang et al., 2009).

Selecting Friends

The fact that peers are beneficial does not mean that they always are constructive. Young people *can* lead one another into trouble. Collectively, peers sometimes provide **deviancy training,** in which one person shows another how to rebel against social norms (Dishion et al., 2001). Especially if adolescents believe that the most popular, most admired peers are having sex, doing drugs, or ignoring homework, they become more likely to take up the destructive behavior themselves (Rodgers, 2003).

However, it is not accurate to imagine that an upstanding, innocent teen is somehow corrupted by deviant friends. Adolescents choose their friends and models—not always wisely, but never randomly. There is a developmental progression here, from "problem behavior, school marginalization, and low academic performance" at age 11, leading to gang involvement two years later, deviancy training two years after that, and violent behavior at age 18 or 19 (Dishion et al., 2010, p. 603). This cascade is far from inevitable; parents and teachers need to help the disengaged middle school child instead of waiting to blame his or her friends several years later.

To further understand the impact of peers, two concepts are helpful: *selection* and *facilitation*. Teenagers join a clique whose values and interests they share, abandoning former friends who follow other paths. Peers then facilitate destructive and constructive behaviors. It is easier to do the wrong thing ("Let's all skip school on Friday") or even the right thing ("Let's study together for that chemistry exam") if one's friends are doing it, too. Peer facilitation helps adolescents act in ways they are unlikely to act on their own.

clique A group of adolescents made up of close friends who are loyal to one another while excluding outsiders.

crowd A larger group of adolescents who have something in common but who are not necessarily friends.

Especially for Parents of a Teenager Your 13-year-old comes home after a sleepover at a friend's house with a new, weird hairstyle—perhaps cut or colored in a bizarre manner. What do you say and do? (see response, page 445)

deviancy training Destructive peer support in which one person shows another how to rebel against authority or social norms.

SERGE J. MICHAUT / VIEWFINDER EXIS, LLC

Beach Party These laughing barefoot girls, with the boys in the background displaying manly indifference, could be partying alongside any ocean and sandy shoreline—in California, Florida, New Jersey, or several other states and nations.

Observation Quiz This photo was taken in 2007. Is it set in the United States? (see answer, page 447)

Both selection and facilitation can work in any direction. One teenager joins a clique whose members smoke cigarettes and drink beer, and together they take the next step, perhaps sharing a joint at a party. Another teenager might choose friends who enjoy math puzzles, and, as demonstrated in this quote from Lindsay, they might all enroll in AP calculus together:

> [Companionship] makes me excited about calculus. That is a hard class, but when you need help with calculus, you go to your friends. You may think no one could be excited about calculus, but I am. Having friends in class with you definitely makes school more enjoyable.
>
> *[quoted in Hamm & Faircloth, 2005, p. 72]*

Thus, adolescents select and facilitate, choose and are chosen. Happy, energetic, and successful teens have close friends who themselves are high-achieving, with no major emotional problems. The opposite also holds: Those who are drug users, sexually active, and alienated from school choose compatible friends and support one another in continuing on that path (Crosnoe & Needham, 2004). A study of identical twins from ages 14 to 17 found that selection typically preceded facilitation, rather than the other way around. Young teenagers who were likely to rebel chose more lawbreaking friends than did their less externalizing twin (Burt et al., 2009).

Approval for Risk Taking

An experiment in peer facilitation involved adolescents (ages 13 to 16), emerging adults (ages 18 to 22), and adults (over age 24) in a video driving game (Gardner & Steinberg, 2005). As each player drove, every so often the screen would flash a yellow light, indicating that soon (in one to several seconds) a wall would appear. The goal was to drive as long as possible but brake before crashing into the wall. Points were gained for travel time; a crash erased the points from that round.

The participants were randomly assigned to one of two conditions: playing alone or with two strangers of the same sex and age as themselves. When they played alone, adolescents, emerging adults, and adults all averaged one crash per 15-round session. That single crash was enough to make them wary. Adults were equally cautious when playing with other adults. But when the adolescents were with peers, they became bolder, crashing three times, on average (see Figure 16.3)

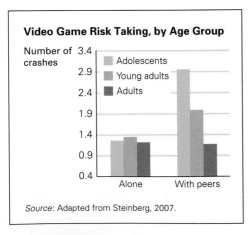

Video Game Risk Taking, by Age Group

Number of crashes

- Adolescents
- Young adults
- Adults

Source: Adapted from Steinberg, 2007.

FIGURE 16.3

Admire Me Everyone wants to accumulate points in a game, earn high grades, and save money—unless one is a teenager and other teens are watching. Then a desire to obtain peer admiration by taking risks may overtake caution. At least in this game, teenage participants chose to lose points and increase crashes when other teens were present.

(Gardner & Steinberg, 2005; Steinberg, 2007). They chose to lose points rather than to appear overly cautious.

Best Friends

For many teenagers, friends become "like family," "brothers and sisters" (Way et al., 2005). In violent neighborhoods, friends not only defend against attacks but also help each other avoid physical fights. One 16-year-old boy said about his friend:

> Well, with him when I'm in an argument with somebody that disrespected me and he just comes out and backs me up and says, "Yo, Chris, don't deal with that. Yo, let's just go on," you know, 'cause I could snap.
>
> *[quoted in Way et al., 2005, p. 48]*

"Snapping" is a potential danger for all adolescents, given their quick, intuitive reactions. Having a friend who says "Don't deal with that" can help them stay calm and protect them from self-destruction. Often teenagers rely on friends for reassurance, encouragement, and advice day and night—which explains why friends typically see each other at school, after school, and on weekends, as well as why they communicate by phone, e-mail, text, and on Facebook. Social networking is used primarily by close friends who see each other often (Mikami et al., 2010).

Contemporary adolescents often have friends of the other sex who are not their lovers. Adults sometimes worry, assuming that teenagers will have sex if adults are not watching. However, many teenagers do have close, even passionate, friendships with peers of both sexes, without romantic undertones. Disruptions of friendships (either same-sex or other-sex) can cause jealousy (e.g., if the friend befriends another person) or depression (e.g., if the friend moves away).

Romance

Decades ago, Dexter Dunphy (1963) described the sequence of male–female relationships during childhood and adolescence:

1. Groups of friends, exclusively one sex or the other
2. A loose association of girls and boys, with public interactions within a crowd
3. Small mixed-sex groups of the advanced members of the crowd
4. Formation of couples, with private intimacies

Culture affects the timing and manifestation of each step on Dunphy's list, but subsequent research in many nations validates the sequence. Youth in many countries (and even the young of many species) avoid members of the other sex in childhood and are attracted to them by adulthood. This suggests that biology underlies these changes.

First Love

In modern developed nations, where puberty begins at about age 10 and marriage occurs much later, each of these four stages typically lasts several years. Early, exclusive romances are more often a sign of social trouble than maturity, especially for girls (Eklund et al., 2010). Unlike the norm in earlier centuries, in North America and Europe a long-lasting commitment to one partner does not usually occur until adulthood.

The first romances usually appear in high school, rarely lasting more than a year, with girls having a steady partner more often than boys do. Breakups are common; so are unreciprocated crushes. Both can be devastating, in part because often entire high school crowds are witnesses (Schwartz, 2006). Adolescents are

FRANCES ROBERTS / ALAMY

Instant Connections Ignoring the rides at Coney Island, these two girls lean on each other; both have blue bracelets, green sleeveless shirts, and, most important, texts to read and send. As with their use of the automobile and the telephone, teens have taken an adult invention (the Internet was originally developed for military use) and turned it into a tool for increasing peer support.

>> Response for Parents of a Teenager (from page 443) Remember: Communicate, do not control. Let your child talk about the meaning of the hairstyle. Remind yourself that a hairstyle in itself is harmless. Don't say "What will people think?" or "Are you on drugs?" or anything that might give your child reason to stop communicating.

The Same Situation, Many Miles Apart: Teenagers in Love No matter where in the world they are, teenage couples broadcast their love in universally recognized facial expressions and body positions. Samantha and Ryan (*left*), visiting New York City from suburban Philadelphia, are similar in many ways to the teen couple (*right*) in Chicute, Mozambique, even though their social contexts are dramatically different.

crushed by rejection, often contemplating revenge or suicide (Fisher, 2006). In such cases, peer support can be a lifesaver. Indeed, adolescents as well as adults rely on same-sex friends, who help them cope with romantic ups and downs (Mehta & Strough, 2009).

Contrary to adult fears, many teenage romances do not include sexual intercourse. Rates and ages of sexual activity vary widely from nation to nation. In the United States in 2009, even though one-half of all high school students were sexually experienced by the eleventh grade, one-third were still virgins by their senior year (see Figure 16.4). However, every survey finds that norms vary markedly from crowd to crowd, school to school, city to city, and nation to nation. For instance, twice as many ninth- through twelfth-graders in Milwaukee as in Seattle say they have had intercourse (63 percent versus 29 percent) (MMWR, June 4, 2010).

Same-Sex Romances

sexual orientation A term that refers to whether a person is sexually and romantically attracted to others of the same sex, the opposite sex, or both sexes.

Some adolescents are sexually attracted to peers of the same sex. **Sexual orientation** refers to the direction of a person's erotic desires. One meaning of *orient* is to "turn toward"; thus, sexual orientation refers to whether a person is romantically

FIGURE 16.4

Many Virgins For 30 years, the Youth Risk Behavior Survey has asked high school students from all over the United States dozens of confidential questions about their behavior. As you can see, about one-third of all students have already had sex by the ninth grade, and about one-third have not yet had sex by their senior year, a group whose ranks have been increasing in recent years. Other research finds that sexual behaviors are influenced by peers, with some groups all sexually experienced by age 14 and others not until age 18 or later.

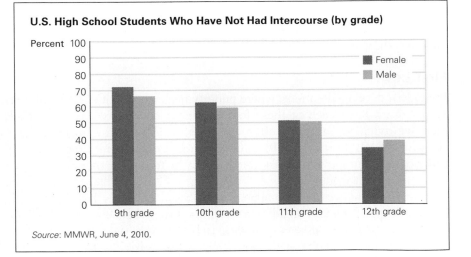

U.S. High School Students Who Have Not Had Intercourse (by grade)

Source: MMWR, June 4, 2010.

attracted to (turned on by) people of the other sex, the same sex, or both sexes. It is not known how many adolescents are romantically oriented toward people of the same sex because sexual orientation can be strong, weak, acted upon, secretive, or unconscious. Thus, asking teenagers to indicate their sexual orientation is bound to underestimate prevalence.

Currently in North America and western Europe, not just two (homosexual and heterosexual) but many gender roles and sexual orientations are evident (Denny & Pittman, 2007). Gender identity itself has become controversial; an increasing number of early adolescents do not identify with their biological sex and may be diagnosed with what the DSM-IV calls *gender-identity disorder,* the focus of an international conference in London (Asscheman, 2009). Some psychologists and psychiatrists believe that gender-identity problems originate in society, not individuals; thus, gender-identity disorder should be omitted from the DSM-V (to be published in 2013) (Ross, 2009).

Obviously, culture and cohort are powerful, not only in social acceptance but also in self-acceptance. For example, in many Latino cultures, "adolescents who pursue same-sex sexuality are viewed . . . as having fundamentally failed as men or women" (Diamond & Savin-Williams, 2003, p. 399). Many gay youth date members of the other sex to hide their orientation (B. Brown, 2006), and past cohorts had higher rates of clinical depression, drug abuse, and suicide than did their peers. This may be changing in nations where same-sex partnerships are accepted.

How many adolescents are gay, lesbian, bisexual, or asexual is unknown. Many youth refuse to commit to any orientation (Savin-Williams, 2005). In the mid-1990s, one large study of high school students in Massachusetts found that 1 in 200 identified as gay or lesbian (Garofalo et al., 1999). More recently, a large Dutch study of high school students found that 1 in 12 said they were attracted to people of the same sex as themselves (Bos et al., 2008). Research on adults conducted 15 years ago in the United States found that about 1 in 10 had same-sex encounters or desires as adolescents, yet most identified as heterosexual in adulthood (Laumann et al., 1994).

These variations may reflect culture, cohort, or simply the wording of the questions. When and with whom a person becomes sexually active depends on a cascade of factors, including age of puberty, parenting practices, and dating relationships (Longmore et al., 2009).

Learning About Sex

Adults and peers both provide sex education, either explicit or implicit (through examples, expressions, silences). Many adolescents have strong sexual urges but minimal logic about pregnancy and disease. They worry that they are oversexed, undersexed, or deviant, unaware that there are thousands, maybe millions, of people like themselves.

Obviously, there is much they need to learn. Explicit parental communication is influential but often absent (Longmore et al., 2009). Many parents wait too long to discuss sex. In one study, 12-year-old girls and their parents were asked if the girl had hugged or kissed a boy "for a long time" or hung out with older boys (signs that sex information is urgently needed). Only 5 percent of the parents said yes—compared with 38 percent of the girls (O'Donnell et al., 2008).

Adolescent sexual behavior is strongly influenced by peers. Many teens discuss details of romance and sex with other members of their clique, seeking advice and approval (Laursen & Mooney, 2007). Often, the boys brag and the girls worry about gaining a "reputation." Specifics depend on the group: All members of a clique may be virgins or all may be sexually active. Partners teach each other, but

>> **Answer to Observation Quiz** (from page 444) No. They are in Halong Bay, Vietnam. Beachgoing U.S. girls would be dressed differently.

Especially for Sex Educators Suppose adults in your community never talk to their children about sex or puberty. Is that a mistake? (see response, page 448)

"Smirking or Non-Smirking?"

only about half of U.S. adolescent couples discuss the risks of pregnancy and disease before they become sexually active (Ryan et al., 2007).

Almost all parents want other adults to provide their adolescents with up-to-date sex education, including information on safe sex and contraception (Landry et al., 2003; Yarber et al., 2005). Developmentalists agree that sex education belongs in the schools as well as in parent–child conversations, since adolescents need to learn from trusted and knowledgeable adults rather than misinform each other.

Sex-education policies vary dramatically by nation. Most European schools begin sex education in elementary school, and by middle school they teach about sexual responsibility, masturbation, same-sex romance, and oral and anal sex—subjects that are rarely covered in U.S. classes. Rates of teenage pregnancy in most European nations are less than half those in the United States, curriculum being one of many reasons why.

In the United States, the timing and content of sex education vary by state and community. Some schools provide comprehensive programs, free condoms, and medical treatment; others provide nothing at all. The research finds that most such programs succeed in delaying the age at which adolescents become sexually active and increase the use of condoms; but specific information and attitudes influence the the effectiveness of the curriculum—with some programs not effective at all (Kirby & Laris, 2009).

One controversy is whether abstinence should be taught as the best, or only, sexual strategy for adolescents. It is true, of course, that abstaining from sex (including oral sex) is an effective way to avoid sexually transmitted infections (STIs) and pregnancy, but that choice does not seem to result from abstinence-only classes. Longitudinal evaluations conducted four to six years after people had participated in several abstinence-only programs revealed that the programs made little difference. About half of students in both experimental (abstinence-only) and control groups had had sex by age 16. The number of partners and use of contraceptives were the same with and without the special curriculum (Trenholm et al., 2007). Students in the control groups knew slightly more about preventing disease and pregnancy, but this knowledge neither slowed down nor sped up their sexual initiation.

Overall, according to a nationwide, controlled study of sex education in the United Kingdom, whether or not an adolescent becomes sexually active depends more on family, peers, and culture than on information from classes (Allen et al., 2007). The crucial test of sex education is not whether adolescents can learn facts (most pass multiple-choice tests) but whether their knowledge affects their behavior (Kirby & Laris, 2009).

SUMMING UP

Crowds, cliques, and friends are all part of adolescence. Contrary to what some adults may think, peer pressure can be positive, and many adolescents rely on friends of both sexes to help them with the concerns and troubles of the teen years. Romances are typical in high school, but early, exclusive romances are more often a sign of emotional trouble than of maturity. Some adolescents are romantically attracted to others of their sex; it is not known how often this occurs.

Given the earlier onset of puberty and the later marriages today, adolescents spend a decade or more with intense sexual drives but no committed partner. They need accurate information regarding sex. Although parents are influential role models, many are slow to talk with their children about sex. Most adolescents learn from personal experience with peers. School instruction can delay sexual intercourse and increase condom use, but not every curriculum is equally effective.

>> Response for Sex Educators (from page 447) Yes, but forgive them. Ideally, parents should talk to their children about sex, presenting honest information and listening to the child's concerns. However, many parents find it very difficult to do this because they feel embarrassed and ignorant. You might schedule separate sessions for adults over 30, for emerging adults, and for adolescents.

>> Sadness and Anger

Adolescence is usually a wonderful time, perhaps better for current generations than for any generation before. Nonetheless, troubles plague about 20 percent of youth, who often have several problems at once. Distinguishing between normal moodiness and pathology is complex; many adolescents are more depressed and angry than they were as children. For a few, however, such emotions become intense and even deadly.

Depression

The general emotional trend from late childhood through adolescence is toward less confidence. A dip in self-esteem at puberty is found for children of every ethnicity and gender (Fredricks & Eccles, 2002; Greene & Way, 2005; Kutob et al., 2009). Some studies report rising self-esteem thereafter (especially for African American girls and European American boys), but variations are many, as are individual differences.

All studies find that parents and peers affect self-esteem (Hall-Lande et al., 2007) and that some communities are more conducive to strong relationships between teenagers and adults than others. For example, a study of Latino American youth found that self-esteem rose after puberty. Especially if familism was strong, Latino adolescents felt comfortable in the United States and proud of their culture. However, serious parental conflicts reduced Latino self-esteem even more than for other adolescents (Smokowski et al., 2010). Often young adolescents with very low self-esteem turn to drug use, early sex, and disordered eating—all of which further reduce esteem (Biro et al., 2006; Trzesniewski et al., 2006).

Clinical Depression

Some adolescents sink down into **clinical depression,** a deep sadness and hopelessness that disrupts all normal, regular activities. The causes predate puberty, including genes and early care. Then the onset of puberty—with its myriad physical and emotional ups and downs—pushes some vulnerable children, especially girls, into despair. The rate of clinical depression more than doubles during this time, to an estimated 15 percent, affecting about 1 in 5 girls and 1 in 10 boys (Graber, 2004).

It is not known whether the reasons for these gender differences are primarily biological, psychological, or social (Alloy & Abramson, 2007). Obviously, hormones differ, but girls also experience gender-specific pressures from their families, peers, and cultures. Perhaps the combination of biological and psychosocial development causes some to slide into depression.

Recently, a cognitive explanation has been offered. **Rumination**—talking about, remembering, and mentally replaying past experiences—is more common among girls than boys. If unpleasant incidents are replayed, rumination often leads to depression (Ayduk & Kross, 2008). Close mother–daughter relationships may contribute: When mothers and daughters ruminate about the mother's problems, daughters often become depressed (Waller & Rose, 2010).

Suicide

Stress can lead to depression and thoughts of suicide. Serious, distressing thoughts about killing oneself (called **suicidal ideation**) are most common at about age 15 (Rueter & Kwon, 2005). The 2009 Youth Risk Behavior Survey revealed that one-third (33.9 percent) of U.S. high school girls felt so hopeless that they stopped doing some usual activities for two weeks or more and one-sixth (17.4 percent)

Especially for Journalists You just heard that a teenage cheerleader jumped off a tall building and died. How should you report the story? (see response, page 450)

clinical depression Feelings of hopelessness, lethargy, and worthlessness that last two weeks or more.

rumination Repeatedly thinking and talking about past experiences; can contribute to depression.

suicidal ideation Thinking about suicide, usually with some serious emotional and intellectual or cognitive overtones.

>> Response for Journalists (from page 449) Since teenagers seek admiration from their peers, be careful not to glorify the victim's life or death. Facts are needed, as is, perhaps, including warning signs that were missed or cautions about alcohol abuse. Avoid prominent headlines or anything that might encourage another teenager to do the same thing.

TABLE 16.1

Suicidal Ideation and Parasuicide Among U.S. High School Students, 2009

		Seriously Considered Attempting Suicide (%)	Parasuicide (attempted suicide, %)	Parasuicide Requiring Medical Attention (%)	Actual Suicide (ages 15–19)*
Overall		**13.8%**	**6.3%**	**1.9%**	Less than 0.01% (about 7.5 per 100,000)
Girls:	9th grade	20.3	10.3	2.8	
	10th grade	17.2	8.8	2.3	Girls: About 3.5
	11th grade	17.8	7.8	2.6	per 100,000
	12th grade	13.6	4.6	1.0	
Boys:	9th grade	10.0	4.5	1.4	
	10th grade	10.0	5.2	2.0	Boys: About 11.5
	11th grade	11.4	4.7	1.7	per 100,000
	12th grade	10.5	3.8	1.4	

*Actual suicide numbers are based on data for 2007.
Source: MMWR, June 4, 2010; U.S. National Center for Health Statistics, 2010.

parasuicide Any potentially lethal action against the self that does not result in death.

FIGURE 16.5

Much Depends on Age A historical look at U.S. suicide statistics reveals two trends, both of which were still apparent in 2005. First, older teenagers today are twice as likely to take their own lives as in 1960 but less likely to do so than in 1980. Second, suicide rates overall are down, but they continue to be highest among elderly people age 80 and older.

seriously thought about suicide. The corresponding rates for boys were 19.1 percent and 10.5 percent (MMWR, June 4, 2010).

Suicidal ideation can lead to **parasuicide,** also called *attempted suicide* or *failed suicide.* Parasuicide includes any deliberate self-harm that could have been lethal; it is a preferred term because seriousness of intent is difficult to discern amidst the emotions typical in adolescence. Internationally, rates of teenage parasuicide range between 6 and 20 percent. Among U.S. high school students in 2009, 8.1 percent of the girls and 4.6 percent of the boys said they had tried to kill themselves in the past year (MMWR, June 4, 2010; see Table 16.1).

While suicidal ideation during adolescence is common, completed suicides are not. The U.S. annual rate of completed suicide for people aged 15 to 19 (in school or not) is about 8 per 100,000, or 0.008 percent. Adolescents are *less* likely to kill themselves than adults are. Many people mistakenly think suicide is more frequent in adolescence for four reasons:

1. The rate, low as it is, is much higher than it appeared to be 50 years ago (see Figure 16.5).

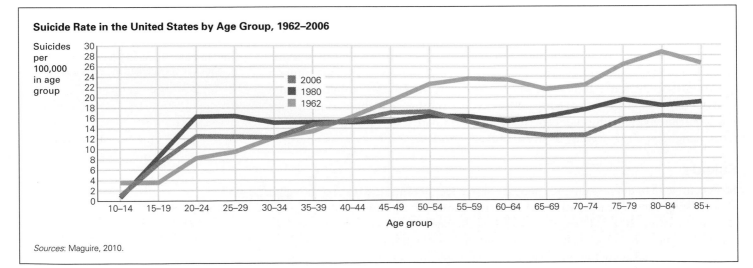

Suicide Rate in the United States by Age Group, 1962–2006

Suicides per 100,000 in age group

Legend: 2006, 1980, 1962

Age group: 10–14, 15–19, 20–24, 25–29, 30–34, 35–39, 40–44, 45–49, 50–54, 55–59, 60–64, 65–69, 70–74, 75–79, 80–84, 85+

Sources: Maguire, 2010.

2. Statistics on "youth" often include emerging adults aged 18 to 25, whose suicide rates are higher than those of adolescents aged 12 to 17.
3. Adolescent suicides capture media attention.
4. Parasuicides may be more common in adolescence than later.

Gender has a marked influence on the incidence of suicide. Although depression and parasuicide are far more common among females, completed suicide is higher for males in every nation except China. For instance, boys aged 15 to 19 in the United States kill themselves four times as often as girls that age do (National Center for Health Statistics, 2010). A major reason is that males typically shoot themselves (an immediately lethal method), whereas females typically swallow pills or hang themselves (methods that allow time for intervention).

Another hypothesis for the gender difference is that girls ruminate; thus, their friends and families can often tell that they are depressed before they reach the despair of contemplating suicide. Boys are more likely to withdraw; their warning signs are not as obvious. Furthermore, young men somehow think it unmanly to attempt suicide and survive, so they choose more deadly methods (Aseltine & DeMartino, 2004). Consider the following.

Nothing to Do Compared with most other Americans, these three adolescents are at higher risk of diabetes, alcoholism, unemployment, and suicide. They live on the Rosebud Sioux Reservation in South Dakota. The suicide rate among Native American teenagers is more than three times as high as the rate for U.S. adolescents overall.

A CASE TO STUDY

He Kept His Worries to Himself

A psychologist described an adolescent boy in these words:

> Bill is 17, a senior in high school. A good student, hard working, some would say "driven," Bill has achieved well and is hoping to go to either Harvard or Stanford next year. He is also hopeful that his college career will lead him to medical school and a career as a surgeon like his father. Bill is a tall, handsome boy, attractive to girls but surprisingly shy among them. When he socializes, he prefers to hang out in groups rather than date; in these groups, he is likely to be seen deep in introspective discussion with one girl or another. Introspection has no place on the school football team, where this past season Bill led all receivers in pass catches. Nor does he appear at all the quiet type in his new sports car, a gift from his parents on his 17th birthday. The elder of two sons, Bill has always been close to his parents, and a "good son." Perhaps for these reasons, he has been increasingly preoccupied as verbalized threats of separation and divorce become common in his parents' increasingly frequent conflicts. These worries he has kept largely to himself.
>
> [Berman et al., 2006, pp. 43–44]

If you were Bill's friend, would you make sure he obtained professional help? Unfortunately, Bill had no friends who were close enough to heed the warning signs. Even his parents did not realize he was troubled until

> Bill's body was brought to the local medical examiner's office; he put his father's .22-caliber handgun to his head and ended his life in an instant.
>
> [Berman et al., 2006, p. 44]

In retrospect, Bill had some risk factors and had shown danger signs—no close friends, male or female; his parents' conflicts; his foreclosure on his father's profession; his drive for perfection (Harvard or Stanford, football star); no older siblings to advise and comfort him. Did the gift of a sports car signify a problem—perhaps that Bill's parents provided material possessions instead of emotional closeness? Did his shyness around girls mean that he may have been worried about his sexuality? Why did his father own a handgun, and why was it loaded and accessible?

The report does not mention whether Bill's body was tested for alcohol or other drugs. Overall, about one-third of all U.S. suicides occur when a person has been drinking or taking drugs; rates of drug and alcohol use are higher for people under 25.

cluster suicides Several suicides committed by members of a group within a brief period of time.

Adolescents are particularly affected when they hear about a suicide, either via media reports or from peers (Insel & Gould, 2008). That makes them susceptible to **cluster suicides,** a term for the occurrence of several suicides within a group over a brief span of time—a few weeks or months. If a high school student's "tragic end" is sentimentalized, that elicits suicidal ideation among his or her peers, and then further media attention increases the risk.

Wealth and education decrease the incidence of many disorders, but *not* of suicide—quite the opposite. The reason may be news reports that typically highlight the lost potential of a suicidal adolescent (e.g., "Honor Student Kills Self"). This may encourage suicidal ideation in, say, other honor students. Or adolescents from families of high socioeconomic status (SES) may be particularly hard-hit by a failing grade or a broken relationship.

Since 1990, however, rates of adolescent suicide have fallen, especially among those with more family income and education. One reason may be that more adolescents are using antidepressants, and therefore fewer of them are desperately sad (Gould, 2003). A British study raised the possibility that such drugs might *increase* suicidal ideation (not suicide). However, a meta-analysis of 27 controlled clinical trials (similar to experiments, only with participants who have a particular illness or disorder) found that antidepressants, especially when combined with cognitive-behavioral therapy, helped depressed or anxious young people far more often than they increased their suicidal ideation (Bridge et al., 2007).

Delinquency and Disobedience

Like low self-esteem and suicidal ideation, bouts of anger are common in adolescence. Many adolescents slam doors, defy parents, and tell friends exactly how badly other teenagers (or siblings or teachers) have behaved. Some teenagers—particularly boys—"act out" by breaking laws. They steal, damage property, or injure others.

Is such behavior normal? Some developmentalists answer yes. One was Anna Freud (Sigmund's daughter, herself a prominent psychoanalyst), who wrote that adolescent resistance to parental authority was "welcome . . . beneficial . . . inevitable." She explained:

> We all know individual children who, as late as the ages of fourteen, fifteen or sixteen, show no such outer evidence of inner unrest. They remain, as they have been during the latency period, "good" children, wrapped up in their family relationships, considerate sons of their mothers, submissive to their fathers, in accord with the atmosphere, idea and ideal of their childhood background. Convenient as this may be, it signifies a delay of their normal development and is, as such, a sign to be taken seriously.

> *[A. Freud, 1958/2000, p. 263]*

Contrary to Freud, many psychologists, most teachers, and almost all parents are quite happy with well-behaved, considerate teenagers. Which view is valid? Actually, both. Adolescents vary, and understanding that helps all of them.

Most teenagers usually obey the law, and their lawfulness does not predict a later explosion or breakdown. In fact, according to the 30-year New Zealand study first mentioned in Chapter 1, by age 26, men who had never been arrested usually earned degrees, "held high-status jobs, and expressed optimism about their own futures" (Moffitt, 2003, p. 61). Dozens of other longitudinal studies confirm that increased anger during puberty is normal but that most adolescents express their anger in acceptable ways. They yell at their parents, curse at their peers, complain about school. For a minority, anger explodes, and they break something or

The Same Situation, Many Miles Apart: Following Tradition Adolescents worldwide flout adult conventions. Here, for instance, note the necklace on one of these boys in a Los Angeles high school *(top)* and the dyed red hair (or is it a wig?) on one of the girls in a Tokyo park *(bottom)*. As distinctive as each of these eight rebels is, all are following a tradition for their age group—just as their parents probably did when they were adolescents.

hurt someone. And a minority of that minority have been aggressive throughout childhood. They are the ones to be worried about.

Breaking the Law

Both the prevalence (how widespread) and the incidence (how frequent) of criminal actions are more common during adolescence. Arrest statistics in every nation reflect this, and confidential self-reports reveal that virtually every adolescent breaks the law at least once before age 20. Only about one-fourth of young lawbreakers are caught, and most of those are warned and released (Dodge et al., 2006).

In one study of 1,559 urban seventh-graders (both sexes, all races, from parochial as well as public schools), more than three-fourths had committed at least one offense (stolen something, damaged property, or hurt someone physically). Usually, however, adolescents are not chronic offenders: In the same study, less than one-third had committed five or more such acts (Nichols et al., 2006).

Gender and ethnic differences in arrest rates are dramatic. Adolescent males are arrested three times as often as females; African Americans are arrested three times as often as European Americans, who are arrested three times as often as Asian Americans (Pastore & Maguire, 2005). The Hispanic rate usually falls between that of African and European Americans (although this varies from state to state), unless they are immigrants or children of immigrants, in which case their arrest rates are very low. Self-reports of lawbreaking show much smaller gender and ethnic differences than official statistics (Dodge et al., 2006).

Causes of Delinquency

Two clusters of factors, one from childhood (primarily brain-based) and one from adolescence (primarily contextual), predict delinquency. The first of these clusters includes a short attention span, hyperactivity, inadequate emotional regulation, slow language development, low intelligence, early and severe malnutrition, autistic tendencies, maternal cigarette smoking, and being the victim of severe child abuse. Most of these factors are more common among boys than girls, which may be one reason for the gender difference in delinquency. Neurological impairment (either inborn or caused by early experiences) increases the risk that a child will become a **life-course-persistent offender** (Moffitt et al., 2001), someone who breaks the law before and after adolescence as well as during it.

The second cluster of factors that predict delinquency includes risk factors that are primarily psychosocial. They include having deviant friends; having few connections to school; living in a crowded, violent, unstable neighborhood; not having a job; using drugs and alcohol; and having close relatives (especially older siblings) in jail. These are more prevalent among low-income, urban adolescents, but adolescents at all income levels who experience them risk becoming an **adolescence-limited offender,** someone whose criminal activity stops by age 21 (Moffitt, 2003). They break the law with their friends, facilitated by their chosen antisocial clique. More boys than girls are in this group, but some lawbreaking cliques include both sexes (the gender gap in lawbreaking is narrower in late adolescence than earlier) (Moffitt et al., 2001).

The criminal records of both types of teenagers may be similar. However, if adolescence-limited delinquents can be protected from various snares (such as

Some Want Her Dead But Florida law did not allow 15-year-old Morgan Leppert to be executed for murdering a 63-year-old man when she and her 22-year-old boyfriend, Toby, stole the man's car. Instead, she was sentenced to life in prison without parole. Developmentalists agree that teenage criminals are not like adult ones, but they also wonder why Morgan's mother let Toby sleep in Morgan's bedroom when she was just 14.

life-course-persistent offender A person whose criminal activity typically begins in early adolescence and continues throughout life; a career criminal.

adolescence-limited offender A person whose criminal activity stops by age 21.

Especially for Police Officers You see some 15-year-olds drinking beer in a local park when they belong in school. What do you do? (see response, page 455)

quitting school, entering prison, drug addiction, early parenthood), they may out-grow their criminal behavior. This is confirmed by other research: Few delinquent youth who are not imprisoned continue lawbreaking in early adulthood (Monahan et al., 2009).

Of course, adolescence-limited lawbreaking is neither inevitable nor insignifi-cant. Antisocial behavior is dangerous, especially to other adolescents, who are victimized three times as often as adults (Baum, 2005). But maturation puts an end to adolescence-limited lawbreaking. By contrast, life-course-persistent offend-ing begins in childhood and correlates in adulthood with more crime, less educa-tion, lower income, unhappy marriages and disobedient children, and continued violence (Huesmann et al., 2009).

SUMMING UP

Compared with people of other ages, many adolescents experience sudden and ex-treme emotions that lead to powerful sadness and explosive anger. Supportive families, friendships, neighborhoods, and cultures usually contain and channel such feelings. For some teenagers, however, emotions are unchecked or intensified by their social con-texts. This situation can lead to parasuicide (especially for girls), to minor lawbreaking (for both sexes), and, less often, to completed suicide and arrests (especially for boys). Delinquents can be adolescent-limited or life-course-persistent, a distinction that may help the justice system target the best response. ▪

>> Drug Use and Abuse

Adolescents enjoy doing something forbidden, and their hormonal surges and cog-nitive immaturity may cause them to be particularly attracted to the sensations produced by drugs (Witt, 2007). But their immature bodies and brains make drug use particularly hazardous.

Variations in Drug Use

Most adolescents try *psychoactive drugs*. To a developmentalist (but not to a police officer), cigarettes, alcohol, and many prescription medicines are as addictive and damaging as illegal drugs like marijuana, cocaine, and heroin. Both prevalence and incidence of drug use increase from about age 10 to 25 and then decrease, with use before age 18 being the best predictor of later abuse.

The one exception is inhalants (fumes from aerosol containers, cleaning fluid, and so on), which are used more by younger adolescents, partly because they can be easily purchased. Sadly, the youngest adolescents are least able, cognitively, to analyze risks, and their parents rarely suspect a drug problem unless their child dies from breathing toxic vapors.

Variations by Place

Especially for Parents Who Drink Socially You have heard that parents should allow their children to drink at home, to teach them to drink responsibly and not get drunk elsewhere. Is that wise? (see response, page 456)

Nations vary markedly in drug use. Consider the most common drugs: alcohol and tobacco. In most European nations, alcohol is widely used, even by children. In much of the Middle East, alcohol use is illegal, and teenagers almost never drink. In many Asian nations, anyone may smoke anywhere; in the United States, smok-ing is often forbidden; in Canada, cigarette advertising is outlawed, and fewer Ca-nadian than U.S. teenagers smoke.

Variations within nations are marked as well. In the United States, most high school students have tried alcohol, and almost half have smoked cigarettes and marijuana—but a significant minority (about 20 percent) never use any drugs. Regional differences are apparent. For instance, 26.1 percent of high school students in Kentucky have smoked at least one cigarette in the past month, but only 14.8 New York students have (MMWR, June 4, 2010).

Variations by Generation and Gender

Cohorts vary. Use of most drugs, among adolescents as well as adults, has decreased in the United States since 1976 (as Figure 16.6 shows), but adolescent abuse of synthetic narcotics and prescription drugs has increased. During 2009, 10 percent of U.S. high school seniors used Vicodin and 6 percent used OxyContin (Johnston et al., 2010).

With some exceptions, adolescent boys use more drugs, and use them more often, than girls do. An international survey of 13- to 15-year-olds in 131 nations found that more boys are smokers (except in a few European nations), including three times as many boys as girls in Southeast Asia (Warren et al., 2006). According to another international survey of 31 nations, almost twice as many boys as girls have tried marijuana (26 versus 15 percent) (ter Bogt et al., 2006).

Gender differences are reinforced by social constructions about proper male and female behavior. In Indonesia, for instance, 38 percent of the boys smoke cigarettes, but only 5 percent of the girls do. One Indonesian boy explains, "If I don't smoke, I'm not a real man" (quoted in Ng et al., 2007). These worldwide gender differences are not evident in the United States, where more girls than boys smoked in the 1990s. Recent statistics show that girls smoke less than boys but are younger when they start drinking alcohol, with eighth-grade girls having notably higher rates than boys (Johnston et al., 2010).

>> **Response for Police Officers** (from page 453) Avoid both extremes: Don't let them think this situation is either harmless or serious. You might take them to the police station and call their parents. These adolescents are probably not life-course-persistent offenders; jailing them or grouping them with other lawbreakers might encourage more crime.

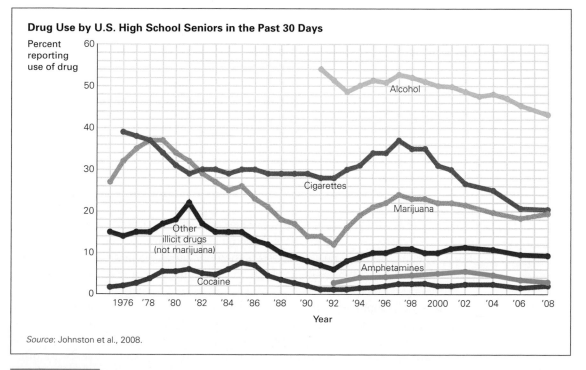

FIGURE 16.6

Rise and Fall By asking the same questions year after year, the Monitoring the Future study shows notable historical effects. It is encouraging that something in society, not in the adolescent, makes drug use increase and decrease and that the most recent data show a decline. However, as Chapter 1 emphasized, survey research cannot prove what causes change.

Harm from Drugs

Many teenagers believe that adults exaggerate the evils of drug use. That may be, but developmentalists see both immediate and long-term harm when adolescents take drugs. Addiction and brain damage are among "the deleterious consequences of drug use [that] appear to be more pronounced in adolescents than in adults, a difference that has been linked to brain maturation" (Moffit et al., 2006, p. 12). Few adolescents notice when they move past *use* (experimenting) to *abuse* (experiencing harm) and then to *addiction* (needing the drug to avoid feeling ill).

An obvious negative effect of *tobacco* is that it impairs digestion and nutrition, slowing down growth. This is true for bidis, cigars, pipes, and chewing tobacco as well as for cigarettes. In India, widespread tobacco use is one reason for chronic undernutrition (Warren et al., 2006). Since internal organs continue to mature after the height spurt, drug-using teenagers who appear full-grown may damage their developing hearts, lungs, brains, and reproductive systems.

Alcohol is the most frequently abused drug among North Americans. Heavy drinking impairs memory and self-control by damaging the hippocampus and the prefrontal cortex, perhaps distorting the reward circuits of the brain lifelong (Guerri & Pascual, 2010). Although some specifics of the impact of alcohol on the adolescent brain are still to be discovered, there is no doubt that alcohol affects adolescents more than adults because of their brain immaturity (Chin et al., 2009).

Like many other drugs, alcohol allows momentary denial of problems; worries seem to disappear when a person is under the influence. When problems get worse because they have been ignored, more alcohol is needed—a vicious cycle that often leads to addiction. Denial is a problem for all alcoholics, but particularly for teenagers who have not yet learned that they cannot drive, write, or even think after several drinks.

Similarly, *marijuana* seems harmless to many people (especially teenagers), partly because users seem more relaxed than inebriated. A girl named Johanna said:

> I started off using about every other weekend, and pretty soon it increased to three to four times a week. . . . I started skipping classes to get high. I quit soccer because my coach was a jerk. My grades dropped, but I blamed that on my not being into school. . . . Finally, some of my friends cornered me and told me how much I had changed, and they said it started when I started smoking marijuana. They came with me to see the substance-abuse counselor at school.
>
> *[quoted in Bell, 1998, p. 199]*

Johanna's future was in jeopardy. Adolescents who regularly smoke marijuana are more likely to drop out of school, become teenage parents, and be unemployed (Chassin et al., 2004). Marijuana affects memory, language proficiency, and motivation (Lane et al., 2005)—all of which are especially crucial during adolescence.

Those are correlations, which, as you know, do not reveal causation. Is it possible that adolescents who are not particularly clever or ambitious choose to smoke marijuana, rather than vice versa? Is some third variable (such as hostile parents) the cause of both the academic problems and the drug use, rendering the correlation deceptive? This seemed plausible because drug-using adolescents often distrust their parents, injure themselves, hate their schools, and break many laws.

These questions led to the hypothesis that the psychic strains of adolescence can lead to drug use. In fact, however, longitudinal research suggests that drug use *causes* more problems than it solves, often *preceding* anxiety disorders, depression, and rebellion (Chassin et al., 2009; Meririnne et al., 2010). Marijuana use is par-

>> **Response for Parents Who Drink Socially** (from page 454) No. Alcohol is particularly harmful for young brains. It is best to drink only when your children are not around. Children who are encouraged to drink with their parents are more likely to drink when no adults are present. It is true that adolescents are rebellious, and they may drink even if you forbid it. But if you allow alcohol, they might rebel with other drugs.

ticularly common among wealthier adolescents, who then become less motivated to achieve in school and more likely to develop other problems (Ansary & Luthar, 2009). Rather than lack of ambition leading to marijuana use, marijuana itself destroys ambition.

Preventing Drug Abuse: What Works?

Drug use is a progression, beginning with a social occasion and ending alone. The first use usually occurs with friends, which leads adolescents to believe that occasional use is an expression of friendship or generational solidarity. Few adolescent drug users are addicts, and, for those who are, usually they and their friends are unaware of it.

However, the Monitoring the Future study found the following: 25 percent of high school seniors report having had five drinks in a row in the past two weeks, 11 percent are daily cigarette smokers, and 5 percent are daily marijuana users (Johnston et al., 2010). These figures are ominous, suggesting that addiction is the next step. The younger a beginning drug user is, the more likely addiction will occur.

That may not persuade adolescents, who, as you remember, think they are exceptions to the general rule. However, every psychoactive drug excites the limbic system and interferes with the prefrontal cortex. Drug users are thus more emotional (specifics vary, from ecstasy to terror, paranoia to rage) than they otherwise would be, as well as less reflective. Every hazard of adolescence—including car crashes, unsafe sex, and parasuicide—is more common among teens who have taken a psychoactive drug.

With harmful drugs, as with many other aspects of life, each generation prefers to learn things for themselves. A common phenomenon is **generational forgetting,** the idea that each new generation forgets what the previous generation learned (Chassin et al., 2009; Johnston et al., 2010). Mistrust of the older generation, added to loyalty to one's peers, leads not only to generational forgetting but also to a backlash. If adults say something is forbidden, that may be an incentive to try it!

Some antidrug curricula and advertisements using scare tactics (such as the one that showed eggs being broken into a hot frying pan while an announcer intoned, "This is your brain on drugs") have the opposite effect from that intended, increasing rather than decreasing drug use. One reason may be that such advertisements make drugs seem exciting; another may be that adolescents recognize the exaggeration. Antismoking announcements produced by cigarette companies (such as one that showed a clean-cut young person advising viewers to think before they started smoking) actually increase use (Strasburger et al., 2008).

An added problem is that many parents do not know about their children's drug use, so their educational efforts may be too late, too general, or too ignorant. For instance, in one U.S. study, less than 1 percent of parents of sixth-graders thought their children had ever had alcohol, but 22 percent of the children said they had (O'Donnell et al., 2008). In general, adolescents follow their parents' example more than their advice.

This does not mean that trying to halt early drug use is hopeless. Massive ad campaigns in Florida and California have cut adolescent smoking almost in half,

generational forgetting The idea that each new generation forgets what the previous generation learned. As used here, the term refers to knowledge about the harm drugs can do.

Friendship As with these three in the Netherlands, the first lights, swallows, snorts, and even injections are social occasions for adolescents. Only later do the lonely and costly consequences become apparent.

HILLEN / HOLLANDSE HOOGTE / REDUX

in part because the publicity appealed to the young (Wakefield et al., 2003). A particularly effective ad depicted young people dumping 1,200 body bags in front of the corporate headquarters of a tobacco company to highlight the number of smoking-related deaths that occur in the United States each day (Farrelly et al., 2005). The anti-corporation message, with dramatic black-and-white footage (as if a teen had shot it), had an impact.

Changing the social context is also helpful. Throughout the United States, higher prices, targeted warnings, and better law enforcement have led to a marked decline in cigarette smoking among younger adolescents. In 2009, only 6.5 percent of eighth-graders had smoked cigarettes in the past month, compared with 21 percent 10 years earlier (Johnston et al., 2010).

All the research confirms that parents continue to be influential in adolescence. When parents forbid smoking in their homes, fewer adolescents smoke (Messer et al., 2008); when parents are careful with their own drinking, fewer teenagers abuse alcohol (Van Zundert et al., 2006). When parents provide guidance about drinking, teenagers not only drink less but use fewer other substances (Miller & Plant, 2010).

Looking broadly at the past three chapters and past 40 years in the United States, it is apparent that the universal biological processes do not lead to universal psychosocial problems. Sharply declining rates of teenage births and abortions (Chapter 14), increasing numbers graduating from high school, and less use of legal and illegal drugs are apparent in many nations. Looking forward to adulthood, you will see the same basic phenomenon: Human growth starts with biology, but the outcome depends on many social forces.

SUMMING UP

Most adolescents worldwide experiment with drugs, usually cigarettes and alcohol. Variations in adolescent drug use and abuse related to age, culture, cohort, and gender are evident. Drug use in adolescence is especially risky, since many drugs reduce learning and growth as well as smooth the path to addiction and abuse. Generational forgetting is one reason each cohort has distinctive drug-use patterns, and many efforts to stop drug use have failed, but the overall trend is positive: Drug use is lower in the United States and in many other places than it was a few decades ago. ▪

SUMMARY

Identity

1. Adolescence is a time for self-discovery. According to Erikson, adolescents seek their own identity, sorting through the traditions of their families and cultures.

2. Many young adolescents foreclose on their options without exploring possibilities, experience role confusion, or reach moratorium. Identity achievement takes longer for contemporary adolescents than it did half a century ago, when Erikson first described it.

3. Identity achievement occurs in many domains, including religion, politics, vocation, and sex. Each of these remains important over the life span, but timing, contexts, and often terminology have changed since Erikson and Marcia first described them.

Relationships with Adults

4. Parents continue to influence their growing children, despite bickering over minor issues. Ideally, communication and warmth remain high within the family, while parental control decreases and adolescents develop autonomy.

5. There are cultural differences in the timing of conflicts and particulars of parental monitoring. Too much parental control, with psychological intrusiveness, is harmful, as is neglect. Parents need to find a balance between granting freedom and providing guidance.

6. Adults who are not parents sometimes provide important mentoring and modeling for adolescents. Grandparents can be particularly influential.

Peer Power

7. Peers and peer pressure can be beneficial or harmful, depending on particular friends, cliques, and crowds. Adolescents select their friends, including friends of the other sex, who then facilitate constructive and/or destructive behavior.

8. Crowds and cliques are evident in high schools, necessary to help adolescents develop their values and life habits. Peers may be particularly crucial for ethnic-minority and immigrant adolescents, who need to establish their own ethnic identity, one not quite corresponding to the messages they have received from society or their parents.

9. Like adults, adolescents experience diverse sexual needs and may be involved in short-term or long-term romances, depending in part on their peer culture. This is a long process; early, exclusive sexual relationships are a sign of emotional immaturity.

10. The sexual orientation of some youth is toward same-sex romances. Depending on the culture and cohort, they may have a more difficult adolescence than others.

11. Most parents want schools to teach adolescents about sex, although such education often comes later than the personal experiences of the teen. No curriculum (including abstinence-only programs) markedly changes the age at which adolescents become sexually active, although some reduce pregnancy and STIs.

Sadness and Anger

12. Almost all adolescents become self-conscious and self-critical. A few become chronically sad and depressed. Many adolescents (especially girls) think about suicide, and some attempt it. Few adolescents actually kill themselves; most who do so are boys.

13. At least within Western societies, almost all adolescents become more independent and angry as part of growing up, although most still respect their parents. Lawbreaking as well as momentary rage are common; boys are more likely to be arrested for violent offenses than are girls.

14. Adolescence-limited delinquents should be prevented from hurting themselves or others; their criminal behavior will disappear with maturation. Life-course-persistent offenders are aggressive in childhood and may continue to be so in adulthood.

Drug Use and Abuse

15. Most adolescents experiment with drugs, especially alcohol and tobacco, although such substances impair growth of the body and the brain. National culture has a powerful influence on which specific drugs are used as well as on frequency of use. Age, gender, community, and parental factors are also influential

16. Prevention and moderation of adolescent drug use and abuse are possible. Antidrug programs and messages need to be carefully designed to avoid a backlash or generational forgetting.

KEY TERMS

identity versus role confusion (p. 434)	gender identity (p. 436)	deviancy training (p. 443)	cluster suicides (p. 452)
identity achievement (p. 434)	bickering (p. 437)	sexual orientation (p. 446)	life-course-persistent offender (p. 453)
role confusion (p. 434)	parental monitoring (p. 440)	clinical depression (p. 449)	adolescence-limited offender (p. 453)
foreclosure (p. 434)	peer pressure (p. 442)	rumination (p. 449)	generational forgetting (p. 457)
moratorium (p. 434)	clique (p. 443)	suicidal ideation (p. 449)	
	crowd (p. 443)	parasuicide (p. 450)	

WHAT HAVE YOU LEARNED?

Identity

1. What is the relationship between the identity crisis and the past and future?

2. How does identity confusion differ from identity moratorium?

3. Why is foreclosure considered less mature than identity achievement?

4. Why is it premature for adolescents today to achieve their vocational identity?

5. What role do parents play in religious and political identity?

6. What assumptions did most adults hold 50 years ago about sexual identity?

Relationships with Adults

7. Why do parents and adolescents often bicker?

8. When is parental monitoring a sign of a healthy parent–adolescent relationship and when is it not?

9. What are the differences between the influence of parents and that of nonparent adults on adolescents?

Peer Power

10. What are the differences between the influence of peers and the influence of parents?

11. Why do many adults misunderstand the role of peer pressure?

12. What are the similarities and differences in crowds and cliques?

13. What is the role of parents, peers, and society in helping an adolescent develop an ethnic identity?

14. What are the differences in friendship during adolescence and in adulthood?

15. When is an adolescent romance healthy and when is it not?

16. How does culture affect the development of sexual orientation?

17. Where and from whom do adolescents usually learn about sex?

18. What are the variations in sex education in schools, and how does this affect adolescent sexual behavior?

Sadness and Anger

19. What is the difference between adolescent sadness and clinical depression?

20. Why do many adults think adolescent suicide is more common than it is?

21. How can rumination contribute to gender differences in depression and suicide?

22. Why are cluster suicides more common in adolescence than later?

23. Why do arrest statistics show more gender and ethnic differences than self-reported lawbreaking?

24. What are the similarities between life-course-persistent and adolescence-limited delinquents?

25. What are the differences between life-course-persistent and adolescence-limited delinquents?

Drug Use and Abuse

26. Why are psychoactive drugs particularly attractive in adolescence?

27. Why are psychoactive drugs particularly destructive in adolescence?

28. What are the implications of national differences in drug use during adolescence?

29. What works and doesn't work in reducing adolescent drug use?

APPLICATIONS

1. Teenage cliques and crowds may be more important in large U.S. high schools than elsewhere. Interview people who spent their teenage years in U.S. schools of various sizes, or in another nation, about the peer relationships in their high schools. Describe and discuss any differences you find.

2. Locate a news article about a teenager who committed suicide. Can you find evidence in the article that there were warning signs that were ignored? Does the report inadvertently encourage cluster suicides?

3. Research suggests that most adolescents have broken the law but that few have been arrested or incarcerated. Ask 10 of your fellow students whether they broke the law when they were under 18 and, if so, how often, in what ways, with what consequences. (Assure them of confidentiality.) What hypothesis arises about lawbreaking in your cohort?

4. Cultures have different standards for drug use among children, adolescents, and adults. Interview three people from different cultures (not necessarily from different nations; each occupation, generation, or religion can be said to have a culture) about their culture's drug-use standards. Ask your respondents to explain the reasons for any differences.

>>ONLINE CONNECTIONS

To accompany your textbook, you have access to a number of online resources, including quizzes for every chapter of the book, flashcards (in English and Spanish), critical thinking questions, and case studies. For access to any of these links, go to www.worthpublishers.com/bergerls8e. In addition to these free resources, you'll also find links to the podcasts, video clips, diagnostic quizzing with personalized study advice, and an ebook. Some of the videos and activities available online include:

■ *Who Am I?* Reviews pathways to identity achievement and Marcia's dimensions of exploration and commitment. Teens talk about identity. The embedded questionnaire lets you gauge your progress in identity formation.

■ *Interview with Anne Petersen.* This expert talks about the role of parents in adolescence and the need for solid community services.

Adolescence

BIOSOCIAL

Puberty Puberty begins adolescence, as the child's body becomes much bigger (the growth spurt) and more sexual. Both sexes experience increased hormones, reproductive potential, and primary as well as secondary sexual characteristics. Brain growth, hormones, and social contexts combine to make every adolescent more interested in sexual activities, with possible hazards of early pregnancy and sexual abuse.

Nutrition The growth spurt requires adequate nutrition. Many teens do not get enough iron or calcium, since they often consume fast food and soda instead of family meals and milk. Some suffer from serious eating disorders like anorexia and bulimia.

Brain Neurological growth continues through adolescence; the limbic system typically matures faster than the prefrontal cortex. As a result, adolescents act impulsively.

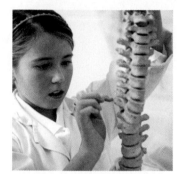

COGNITIVE

Adolescent Thinking Adolescents think differently than younger children do. Piaget stressed the new ability to use abstract logic (part of formal operational thought). Adolescents think hypothetically and deductively, as they are taught to do in school. Elkind recognized adolescent egocentrism; younger teens think they are invincible or that everyone notices what they do. Intuitive thought also increases during adolescence, with emotional and experiential thinking overcoming logic at times.

Teaching and Learning Secondary education promotes individual and national success. Nations vary in how many adolescents graduate from high school. Particularly in the United States, middle schools have been considered the "low ebb" of education: Grades and achievement fall, bullying increases, and teachers and students become disenchanted with learning. International tests find marked differences in achievement. In the United States, high-stakes tests and more rigorous course requirements before high school graduation are intended to improve standards of learning.

PSYCHOSOCIAL

Identity Adolescent development includes a search for identity, as Erikson described. Adolescents combine childhood experiences, cultural values, and their unique aspirations. The contexts of identity are religion, politics/ethnicity, vocation, and sex/gender. Few adolescents achieve identity; role confusion and foreclosure are more likely.

Relationships Families continue to be influential, despite rebellion and bickering. Adolescents seek autonomy but also rely on parental support. Friends and peers of both sexes are increasingly important. Romances often begin in adolescence. About half of all U.S. teens become sexually active. Among developed nations, the United States has higher rates of teen pregnancy and less comprehensive sex education.

Sadness and Anger Depression and rebellion become serious problems for a minority of adolescents. This troubled group is at some risk of suicide (rates are lower than for adults) and violent criminality (rates are higher than for adults). Many adolescents break the law, but their delinquency is adolescence-limited; they eventually become law-abiding adults. Some, however, are life-course-persistent delinquents.

Drugs Adolescents are attracted to psychoactive drugs. Specifics of use and legality vary by nation and culture. In North America, drug use is illegal for teenagers, but most adolescents drink alcohol, and many try cigarettes and marijuana.

emerging adulthood

Social scientists traditionally cite three roles as signifying adulthood: employee, spouse, and parent. Those roles were expected, even coveted, once puberty was over. Children looked forward to being "all grown up," anticipating privileges (like driving and drinking) that were previously denied them.

By contrast, many contemporary young adults avoid those three classic roles. Especially in developed nations, the ages 18 to 25 are characterized by more education, later marriage, fewer births, and postponed career choices. It is a time for exploration, not settling down. People in their early 20s try out various jobs, lifestyles, partners, ideas, and values.

Of course, not all young adults stretch the time between adolescence and adulthood. Particularly in developing nations, many begin work, marriage, and parenthood before age 20—just as their parents and grandparents did. But globalization has accelerated a trend first apparent among wealthier youth. Now adolescents and young adults everywhere put off adult roles as long as they can, seeking more education and independence than older generations in their community ever had. Emerging adulthood has become a new life stage and, here, a new trio of chapters.

CHAPTER 17

Emerging Adulthood: Biosocial Development

WHAT WILL YOU KNOW?

1. Why do emerging adults want sex but not marriage?
2. Why are emerging adults unlikely to go to doctors for checkups?
3. What do young-adult criminals, stockbrokers, and firefighters have in common?
4. Why would anyone voluntarily risk his or her life?
5. What can reduce drug abuse among college students?

"How does it feel to be your age?" Elissa asked me at my recent birthday dinner.

"I don't feel old," I told her, "but the number makes me think that I am."

"Twenty-five is old, too," Sarah said. (She had turned 25 two weeks earlier.)

We laughed, but understood. Although 18 or 21 was once considered the beginning of adulthood, age 25 has become a new turning point. By about age 18, the biology of the human body ends adolescence: A person is literally "grown-up." But biology is not the sole marker of adulthood. Many people do not consider themselves adults (which is what Sarah meant by *old*) until age 25 or later.

Accordingly, a shift has occurred worldwide. A new stage, called **emerging adulthood,** is evident, usually from ages 18 to 25. The specific ages vary: In some places, emerging adulthood ends sooner (perhaps 21 instead of 25) and in other places it ends later (some scholars suggest age 30 as the cutoff). Everywhere, however, marriage, parenthood, a chosen career path, and completed education (all traditional signs of adulthood) occur later than they used to (see At About This Time). The years between adolescence and adulthood have become a distinct new period.

As this chapter explains, emerging adults share particular biosocial characteristics. These traits have always been part of the human experience, but modern contexts are changing their meaning. This is the time when health habits lay the foundation for years to come, yet some specifics (eating disorders, lack of exercise) are more prevalent today than they once were. Sexual maturity is another case in point, described in detail: Men and women have always reached full reproductive ability between ages 18 and 25, but the significance of that maturation has changed. Overall, as bodies mature and health improves, new vulnerabilities appear. First, the strengths.

emerging adulthood The period of life between the ages of 18 and 25. Emerging adulthood is now widely thought of as a separate developmental stage.

AT ABOUT THIS TIME
Following Certain Patterns, by Age (U.S., 2008)
Age 18—Graduate from high school
Age 18–19—Enroll in college (65 percent of high school graduates go to college)
Age 22—Leave college (of those who entered college)
Age 25*—Steady employment
Age 26†—Women: Average age of first marriage (Asian American, 29; Native American, 22)
Age 26**—Women's first birth (of those who have children; about 20 percent do not)
Age 27†—Men: Average age of first marriage
*At age 20–24, many have jobs, but half this group has been with the current employer less than a year. †This is the age at which half the cohort has married. It is the median, but not the mean, because no one knows when, or if, the other half will marry. International variations are dramatic. In Sweden, Hong Kong, and Spain, first marriages usually occur after age 30. **Currently, 15 percent never marry. *Sources:* Dye, 2005; U.S. Bureau of the Census, 2009.

These are estimates, based primarily on data from the United States Bureau of the Census. Ages vary by source and nation, but all report older ages for the current cohort compared with prior generations.

>> Growth and Strength

Biologically, the years from ages 18 to 25 are prime time for hard physical work and safe reproduction. However, as you will see, the fact that an emerging adult could move stones, plow fields, or haul water better than older adults is no longer admired; and if a contemporary young couple had a baby every year, their neighbors would be more appalled than approving. Let's look at what is the same and what has changed over the centuries.

Peak Performance Because this is a soccer match, of course we see skilled feet and strong legs—but also notice the arms, torsos, and feats of balance. Deniz Naki (age 21) and Luis Gustavo (age 23) are German soccer team members in better shape than most emerging adults, but imagine these two a decade earlier (at age 11 and 13) or later (at age 31 and 33) and you will realize why, physiologically, one's early 20s are considered the prime of life.

Strong and Active Bodies

Maximum height is usually reached by age 16 for girls and 18 for boys, except for a few late-maturing boys who gain another inch or two by age 21. During emerging adulthood, muscles grow, bones strengthen, and shape changes, with males gaining more arm muscle and females more fat. By age 22, women have attained adult breast and hip shape and men have reached full shoulder width and upper-arm strength.

For both sexes, physical strength increases. Emerging adults are more able than people of any other age to race up a flight of stairs, lift a heavy load, or grip an object with maximum force. Strength gradually decreases over adulthood, with some muscles weakening more quickly than others: Back and leg muscles shrink faster than the arm muscles, for instance (McCarter, 2006). This is apparent in older baseball players who are still able to hit home runs long after they've ceased being able to steal bases.

Every body system—including the digestive, respiratory, circulatory, and sexual-reproductive systems—functions optimally at the beginning of adulthood (Aspinall, 2003). Serious diseases are not yet apparent, and some childhood ailments are outgrown. For example, childhood asthma disappears as often as it continues (Sears et al., 2003).

In a mammoth survey, 95.8 percent of young adults (aged 18 to 29) in the United States rated their health as good, very good, or excellent, whereas only 4.2 percent rated it as fair or poor (National Center for Health Statistics, 2010). Similarly, 95.3 percent of 18- to 24-year-olds reported no activity limitations due to chronic health conditions, a rate better than that of any other age group (see Figure 17.1). A Pew survey found that only 2 percent of emerging adults consid-

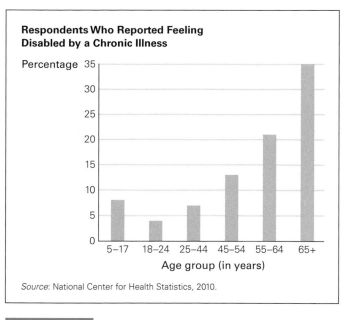

Respondents Who Reported Feeling Disabled by a Chronic Illness

Percentage

Source: National Center for Health Statistics, 2010.

FIGURE 17.1

Strong and Independent Looking at this graph, do you wonder why twice as many 5- to 17-year-olds as 18- to 24-year-olds are said to be limited in daily activities? The answer relates to who reports the limitations. Parents answer for children; adults answer for themselves. Parents tend to be more protective, reporting that chronic conditions (mostly ADHD and asthma) limit what their children can do.

▶ **Research Design**

Scientists: Andrew Kohut, Director of the Pew Research Center for the People and the Press, and hundreds of others.

Publication: *A Portrait of "Generation Next"* (2007).

Participants: A total of 1,501 adults from throughout the United States, with an "oversample" of emerging adults.

Design: People answered telephoned questions about habits, values, and opinions. Answers were compared by age group, with special care and methods to ensure validity.

Major conclusion: Emerging adults differ markedly from older generations in many ways (such as use of technology and attitudes about homosexuality) but not in others (such as views on abortion).

Comment: Although the Pew scientists designed their research to obtain valid results (e.g., contacting young adults via cell phone), surveys are always vulnerable to bias. The report notes two possible problems: wording and inadvertent selection bias (e.g., those who have no phones might have given different answers). A third possible problem is the human tendency to say one thing and do another. Good surveys, such as the Pew studies and several national and United Nations surveys cited in this chapter, are very useful for social scientists. However, no one method provides a complete picture: Replication via direct behavioral research is needed.

ered health their most important problem, compared with 15 percent of those over age 25 (Pew Research Center, 2007). (See the Research Design.)

However, there may be health problems that emerging adults ignore. In the same national survey in which only 4 percent of young adults rated their health as less than good, 15 percent said their doctor had told them they had a chronic disease—most often asthma, arthritis, or high blood pressure (National Center for Health Statistics, 2010). A comprehensive review of many studies finds that low birthweight, undernutrition in infancy, and rapid weight gain by early childhood tend to result in shorter height, reduced body functioning, and higher risk of disease by age 25 (Victora et al., 2008).

Lifelong, many serious conditions can be avoided or ameliorated with preventive medical care. If this were the only way to stay healthy, then many emerging adults would be sick, because most avoid doctors unless they are injured or pregnant. Each year in the United States, the average young adult sees a health professional once, compared with about 10 annual medical visits for the typical adult aged 75 or older. In one study, only about half (55 percent) of men aged 18 to 30 saw a doctor even once in a year. Most women in that age group (85 percent) had one or more doctor visit, often for birth control (National Center for Health Statistics, 2010).

Emblematic of the carelessness of emerging adults regarding health is handwashing among college students in Ontario, where a virus epidemic led the school's administration to advocate (with signs in bathrooms, public announcements, and so on) frequent, careful handwashing. Most students (85 percent) said they practiced proper hand hygiene, but observers discovered that only 17 percent actually did so (Surgeoner et al., 2009).

Especially for a Competitive Young Man Given the variations in aging muscle, how might a 20-year-old respond if he loses an arm-wrestling contest against his father? (see response, page 469)

TABLE 17.1	
U.S. Deaths from the Top Three Causes (Heart Disease, Stroke, Cancer)	
Age Group	Annual Rate per 100,000
15–24	7
25–34	18
35–44	65
45–54	219
55–64	561
65–74	1,313
75–84	2,971
85+	7,126

Source: National Center for Health Statistics, 2009.

Young and Healthy Young adults rarely die of diseases, including the top four: heart disease, cancer, stroke, and obstructive pulmonary disease. These are annual rates, which means that for each person, the chance of death in that decade is 10 times the yearly rate. Thus, a 15-year-old has less than 1 chance in 10,000 of dying of disease before age 25; a 75-year-old has more than 1 chance in 3 of dying of disease before age 85. (As reported later in this chapter, nondisease deaths show a different pattern.)

Observation Quiz How likely is a 90-year-old person to die in the next year? What about a 19-year-old? (see answer, page 472)

senescence The process of aging, whereby the body becomes less strong and efficient.

homeostasis The adjustment of all the body's systems to keep physiological functions in a state of equilibrium. As the body ages, it takes longer for these homeostatic adjustments to occur, so it becomes harder for older bodies to adapt to stress.

organ reserve The capacity of organs to allow the body to cope with stress, via extra, unused functioning ability.

Bodies Designed for Health

Fortunately, bodies are naturally healthy during emerging adulthood. The immune system is strong, fighting off everything from the sniffles to cancer and responding well to vaccines (Grubeck-Loebenstein, 2010). Usually, blood pressure is normal, teeth have no new cavities, heart rate is steady, the brain functions well, and lung capacity is sufficient. Many diagnostic tests, such as PSA (for prostate cancer), mammograms (for breast cancer), and colonoscopies (for colon cancer), are not recommended until age 40, or later, unless family history or warning signs suggest otherwise. Death from disease is rare worldwide during emerging adulthood, as Table 17.1 details for the United States.

This does not mean that emerging adults are unaffected by the passing years. The process of aging, called **senescence** (discussed in Chapter 20), begins in late adolescence. However, few emerging adults are aware of senescence because of two biological processes we now describe: homeostasis and organ reserve.

Bodies in Balance

Many body functions are designed for **homeostasis,** a state of equilibrium maintained by interactions of all the body's physiological systems. Homeostatic responses are regulated in the brain by the pituitary, sometimes called "the master gland," which defends the body via various hormonal shifts (see discussion of the *HPA axis*, page 382) to maintain homeostasis.

Examples of homeostasis are within us and all around us. If people exercise, they use more oxygen, so they automatically breathe faster and deeper while their hearts beat rapidly to deliver more oxygen to their cells. If the air temperature rises, people sweat, move slowly, and thirst for cold drinks—all to cool off. If it gets chilly, people shiver to increase body heat. If they are really cold, their teeth chatter, a more intense form of shivering. Homeostasis works most quickly and efficiently during emerging adulthood, which is one reason emerging adults are less likely to be sick, fatigued, or obese than older adults. When they catch a cold, they may be down for a day or two; older adults more often complain that they cannot "shake" a virus.

Each person's homeostatic systems are affected by age and past experiences, as well as by genes. For example, reaction to weather depends partly on childhood climate (an African may be cold when her roommate from northern Europe is warm), and younger people are generally warmer than older ones. If two people share a bed, one may want more blankets than the other. Your mother may tell *you* to put on a sweater because *she* is cold.

Unused Potential

The other major reason young adults rarely experience serious illness is **organ reserve,** an extra capacity of each organ that allows the body to cope with stress or physiological extremes. Senescence reduces the capacity of each organ and body system and slows down homeostasis; but because of organ reserve, the reduction is usually imperceptible (except in laboratory analysis) and rarely affects daily life until old age (Aspinall, 2003). For instance, hearing is most acute at about age 12: If a teenager and an adult are both listening for footsteps, the teenager usually hears those footsteps a few seconds earlier. Except in such special circumstances, adult hearing losses are unnoticed.

Thus, declines in organ reserve are usually ignored until old age. A 40-year-old pregnant woman might find more strain on her kidneys, blood pressure, and lung capacity than when she was pregnant at age 20, but she is unaware of any diminished organ reserve when she is not expecting.

Bodies have a muscle reserve as well, directly related to physical strength. Maximum strength *potential* typically begins to decline by age 25. However, few adults develop all their possible strength, and even if they did, 50-year-olds retain 90 percent of the muscle reserve they had at age 20 (Rice & Cunningham, 2002). If a 50-year-old begins lifting weights, he or she may become stronger than ever. The most important muscle of all, the heart, shows a similar pattern (Cameron & Bulpitt, 2003). The heart is amazingly strong during emerging adulthood: Only 1 in 50,000 North American young adults dies of heart disease each year. The average *maximum* heart rate—the number of times the heart can beat per minute under extreme stress—declines as the reserve is reduced, beginning at about age 25. But the *resting* heart rate remains very stable.

Even in the smaller changes of aging, such as the wearing down of the teeth or loss of cartilage in the knees, serious reductions are not normally evident until old age. As one expert explains, "A remarkable feature of aging is that various organs and structures have evolved to 'last a lifetime'" (Holliday, 1995, p. 144).

Appearance

Partly because of their overall health, strength, and activity, most emerging adults look vital and attractive. The oily hair, pimpled faces, and awkward limbs of adolescence are gone, and the wrinkles and hair loss of middle adulthood have not yet appeared. Obesity is less common during emerging adulthood than at other stages of life; skin is clear and taut (Whitbourne, 2008). Newly prominent fashion models, popular singers, and film stars tend to be in their early 20s, looking fresh and glamorous.

Vanity about personal appearance is discouraged, so it is not surprising that a cross-cultural study of 19- to 26-year-olds in the United States, New Zealand, India, and China found few who admitted that they were intensely concerned about their appearance (Durvasula et al., 2001). Yet emerging adults spend more money on clothes and shoes than adults of any other age. When they exercise, their main reason is fitness and weight control, unlike older adults, whose main motivation is organ strength. For example, a young person's primary motivation to run several miles a day may be to lose weight, not to reduce blood pressure.

Some of this concern about appearance is connected to sexual drives, since appearance attracts sexual interest. Young adults care about how they look because, quite naturally, they want attention from one another. Furthermore, these are the years when many people seek employment. Attractiveness (in clothing as well as body and face) correlates with better jobs and higher pay (Fletcher, 2009).

No wonder emerging adults try to look their best. Usually, they succeed. Remember the large-scale longitudinal study of U.S. teenagers called Add Health (see Chapter 8)? When the participants were interviewed for the third time as young adults, the interviewers rated only 7 percent as unattractive, a much smaller proportion of the very same people whose attractiveness had been rated a few years earlier (Blum et al., 2000). Other data also find that adults of all ages rate this age group as better looking than any other (Mocan & Tekin, 2006).

Sexual Activity

As already mentioned, the sexual-reproductive system is at its strongest during emerging adulthood. Fertility is greater; miscarriage is less common; serious birth complications are unusual; orgasms are more frequent; and testosterone (the hormone associated with sexual desire) is higher for both sexes at age 20 than at age 40 (Anis, 2007; Huang, 2007).

>> **Response for a Competitive Young Man** (from page 467) He might propose a stair-climbing race and win, since leg strength declines faster than arm strength. Of course, intergenerational competition has psychological ramifications; perhaps the son should simply say "congratulations" and leave it at that.

Love Without Pregnancy Not only government policy but also modern contraception have changed the nature of loving relationships for young Chinese couples. This Shanghai couple may marry, they may have sex, and they may be together for 50 years or more, but they will probably have only one child.

Especially for Marriage Counselors Sex is no longer the main reason for divorce—money is. If you are counseling a cohabiting couple who want to marry, do you still need to ask them about sex? (see response, page 472)

Historically, most babies were born to women under 25 years old, and peak newborn survival occurred when mothers were aged 18 to 25. With unprotected intercourse, pregnancy occurs during emerging adulthood within three months, on average. Both sexes become less fertile with age. (Infertility is discussed in Chapter 20.)

However, these physiological assets are liabilities for today's emerging adults because their hormones want sex but their minds know they are not ready for spouses or children (Lefkowitz & Gillen, 2006). In earlier times, women who did not want a baby had few options other than abstinence. Several unscientific "methods" were tried (such as walking in seven circles right after sex), but many unwanted babies were born. Today there is "a plethora of methods" (Bayer, 2007, p. 231) that usually work, including some for men who fear unexpectedly becoming a father. Almost every problem a child might have correlates with being unwanted (Hayatbakhsh et al., 2010), but fewer unwanted pregnancies occur for the current cohort of emerging adults. That increases the likelihood that every child will develop well.

The disconnect between sex and pregnancy is one reason for later marriage. Attitudes have changed along with practice. A national poll found that most 18- to 24-year-olds think premarital sex is "not wrong at all," while only 18 percent of those over age 65 agree (T. W. Smith, 2005). Is it bad for society that more people are living together without getting married? Few current young adults (27 percent) think so, but most of those over age 65 (64 percent) believe it is (Pew Research Center, 2010).

Most emerging adults believe that marriage is a serious and desirable commitment that they expect to make someday, but not yet. Although they accept *pre*marital sex, many emerging adults (80 percent) believe that *extra*marital sex is "always wrong" (T. W. Smith, 2005). Obviously, premarital sex postpones marriage without sexual deprivation; no wonder most emerging adults value it. However, premarital sex increases two complications: distress and disease, which we will discuss soon. But first consider the implication that the morals of young adults suit their own purposes.

THINKING CRITICALLY

Generation Me?

The cohort of emerging adults who became young adults in the years following the year 2000 are often called the Millennials, a name connected to chronology. Because they follow Generation X, they have also been called Generation Y or Generation Next. In the United States, one set of scholars calls them Generation Me, because they are more selfish, egotistical, and narcissistic than previous generations (Twenge, 2006; Twenge & Campbell, 2009).

Developmentalists have long recognized cohort differences (as explained in Chapter 1), and popular books have praised one generation over another (as with *The Greatest Generation*, which lauds Americans who fought in World War II) (Brokaw, 1998). Generational descriptions often assert that cohort influences transcend national boundaries: The 1960s countercultural generation may have begun in the United States, but it included thousands of youth in eastern and western Europe—together they changed politics, institutions, and the culture itself (Klimke & Scharloth, 2008).

However, the Generation Me nickname and several others (Trophy Generation, Me First Generation) (Lipkin & Perrymore, 2009; Tulgan, 2009) may be unfair. Some researchers find youth today similar to the youth a generation ago and suggest that age, not cohort, is the reason for any differences between them and their elders (Trzesniewski & Donnellan, 2010). By contrast, many contend that the selfishness of the current cohort is greater than that of earlier generations at the same age. They cite evidence, including social phenomena that signify a changed context (e.g., today, twice as many Americans are on antidepressants and twice as many undergo plastic surgery) (Twenge & Campbell, 2010).

Beyond these opposing views is a third perspective from Jeffrey Arnett, the scholar best known for recognizing, naming, and describing emerging adulthood. He agrees that this cohort is not the same as earlier ones, but he argues that the criticism is biased. Older adults call them selfish when they are merely self-focused, call them lazy when really they are dedicated workers if they believe the job is significant. Millennials simply avoid working slavishly at just any job, which may distress their adult supervisors but does not constitute laziness (Arnett, 2010). Finally, a fourth perspective is that age and history always interact; thus, "It is impossible to . . . distinguish cohort or generational effects from time-of-measurement or period effects" (Terracciano, 2010, p. 93).

All four perspectives are put forth by scientists who rely on empirical evidence and who debate the interpretation of the data, not the need for it. Here is a snippet of the dispute:

Trzesniewski & Donnellan do not perform standard significance testing and instead impose an arbitrary cutoff of $d = .20$. The result is a moving target of p values (because sample sizes differed across items) and a failure to discuss a large number of changes that were significant at, for example, $p < .0001$. They thus not only base their argument on null effects, but also expand the definition of "null" to include any effect they deem too small to matter. To say that there were no changes in a variable with statistically significant change at $p < .0001$—which they do numerous times—is highly questionable.

[Twenge & Campbell, 2010, p. 83]

Most readers of this text are not inclined to evaluate this controversy about statistics (although p and d were mentioned in Chapter 1), but it is useful to recognize that scientists argue about analysis in order to move past their personal biases. That propels critical thinking for all of us: Some may consider the emerging adults a disappointment; others see them as a bright hope. How can we move past our presuppositions?

Emotional Stress

One consequence of the current sexual patterns among emerging adults may be emotional stress as relationships begin and end. Contemporary emerging adults have more partners and sex than do somewhat older adults. Their physical relationships usually involve emotional connections because, at least in the United States, most sexually active adults have one steady partner at a time, a pattern called *serial monogamy*.

Emerging adults in France (reputedly a highly erotic culture) also follow this pattern of serial monogamy (Gagnon et al., 2001). Indeed, although solid research on sex among emerging adults in traditional cultures is largely unavailable, sex and commitment may be intertwined by nature. Human physiological responses affect neurological patterns as well as vice versa. As one scientist explains, those who engage in casual sex can trigger the brain system for attachment (as well as for romantic love), leading to "complex, unanticipated emotional entanglement with psychologically and socially unsuitable mating partners" (H. E. Fisher, 2006, p. 12).

"Unanticipated emotional entanglement" produces unanticipated stress because sexual interactions include unspoken assumptions. Generally speaking, attitudes about the purpose of sex fall into one of three categories (Laumann & Michael, 2001):

1. *Reproduction*. About one-fourth of all people in the United States (more women than men; more older adults than younger ones) believe that the primary purpose of sex is reproduction. For them, abstinence is the only acceptable contraception when a woman is fertile. Emerging adults with this perspective are likely to marry young, pressured not only by their parents but also by their values and sexual desires.
2. *Relationship*. Half of the people in the United States (more women than men) believe that the main purpose of sex is to strengthen pair bonding. This is the dominant belief among emerging adults. Their preferred sequence is dating, falling in love, deciding to be faithful, having sex, perhaps living together, and finally (if both are "ready"), marriage and parenthood. Emotional complexities

©ELLEN SINISI / THE IMAGE WORKS

Do They Talk? This couple in Schenectady, New York, are in a "long-term relationship," probably years from marriage. We hope they agree about what they would do if she got pregnant, or if he found someone else, or if either was offered a great job or university scholarship in another state. Few emerging adult couples discuss such matters until they happen.

arise if one partner is further along in this sequence—but at least both are on the same path.

3. *Recreation.* About one-fourth of all people in the United States (more men than women, especially young men) believe that sex is "a fundamental human drive and a highly pleasurable physical and mental experience" (Cockerham, 2006, p. 25), sought primarily for enjoyment. Ideally, both partners achieve orgasm, without commitment. As already explained, this attitude may be difficult to sustain.

These three labels and generalities come from the United States, but they are also evident elsewhere (although proportions differ). For example, a study of Canadian college students found that about 30 percent were celibate, waiting for their lifelong partner; about 60 percent were sexually active and faithful in their relationships; and about 10 percent were experimenters. The last group used condoms less frequently and were more accepting of sex with acquaintances (like the recreation group above) (Netting & Burnett, 2004).

Assumptions about the purpose of sex are usually mutual when partners were raised in the same religion and culture. In that case, attitudes about fidelity, pregnancy, love, and abortion are often understood by both partners, even when not discussed. Currently, however, many emerging adults leave their childhood community and "have a number of love partners in their late teens and early twenties before settling on someone to marry" (Arnett, 2004, p. 73). Without realizing it, each partner may hold a worldview that the other does not share—or even imagine. Each may feel misused and misled because "choices about sex are not the disassociated, disembodied, hedonistic and sensuous affairs of the fantasy world; they are linked, and rather tightly linked by their social embeddedness, to other domains of our lives" (Laumann & Michael, 2001, p. 22).

An added complication is gender identity (discussed in Chapter 16). Whereas former generations identified as either male or female, either heterosexual or homosexual, some emerging adults refuse to categorize themselves, saying they fall under all, or none, of these categories (Savin-Williams, 2005). Obviously, this complicates bonding.

If partners hold differing assumptions about the purpose of sex or the nature of gender, emotional pain and frustration are likely to follow. One might accuse the other of betrayal, an accusation the other considers patently unfair. Romantic breakups often result from such disagreements and may lead to depression, especially among adolescents and emerging adults (Davila, 2008). The more partners a person has from age 18 to 25, the more breakups occur—each stressful.

Sexually Transmitted Infections

Sexually transmitted infections (STIs) have been present since the beginning of time. However, the rate has suddenly reached epidemic proportions because of the sexual patterns of emerging adults. In the United States, most emerging adults have had at least one STI, and many have had several (Lefkowitz & Gillen, 2006). About half the time, STIs have no symptoms and require laboratory tests to diagnose; nonetheless, infertility and even death can result (James, 2007).

The best way to prevent STIs is lifelong monogamy. Even with AIDS, that strategy would work; if both partners had AIDS, then the virus would die with them. (Nonsexual transmission of AIDS is relatively rare since the current blood supply is tested and sterile needles are rigorously used in hospitals and available to IV drug users through needle exchange programs.) Lifelong monogamy is ideal for prevention, but serial monogamy would reduce STIs as well—provided sexually active people, after the end of a sexual relationship, are abstinent for six months

>> **Answer to Observation Quiz** (from page 468) Note that the rates are per 100,000 for the three leading diseases. This means that 1 out of every 14 90-year-olds and 1 out of every 14,000 19-year-olds will die of these diseases each year. However, people die from other causes as well. At age 90 in the United States, the rate of death doubles, meaning that a 90-year-old has about 1 chance in 7 of dying within a year. For emerging adults, the overall death rates are about 10 times higher, primarily because of violent deaths; 19-year-olds thus have an annual death rate of 1 per 1,400.

>> **Response for Marriage Counselors** (from page 470) Yes. The specifics of sex—frequency, positions, preferences—are no longer a taboo topic for most couples, but the couple still needs to discuss exactly what sex means to each of them. Issues of contraception, fidelity, and abortion can drive partners apart, each believing that he or she is right and the other is rigid, or loose, or immoral, or hidebound, or irresponsible, or unloving, and so on.

and then tested and treated for any STI before having sex with a new partner (Mah & Halperin, 2010). However, most emerging adults begin a new relationship almost immediately after one ends. Indeed, sometimes a new sexual liaison pushes them to stop the prior one (Foxman et al., 2006). Rapid transmission of STIs is one result.

Worldwide, globalization fuels every contagious disease (Herring & Swedlund, 2010). In earlier times, prostitution was localized. Now, with international travel, an STI caught from an infected sex worker in one place quickly spreads. HIV, for instance, has several variants, each prevalent in a specific part of the world—but all variants are found in every nation. This wildfire spread is particularly tragic with HIV/AIDS, first confined to gay men in major U.S. cities and then to injection drug users who shared needles. Within 20 years, primarily because of the sexual activities of young adults, HIV became a worldwide epidemic, with more heterosexual female than gay male victims (Davis & Squire, 2010). In nations where HIV is not yet prevalent, such as Croatia, the sexual risk taking of 18- to 25-year-olds means that many may soon become infected (Štulhofer et al., 2009).

Some countries (e.g., Thailand, Zimbabwe, and Uganda) have reduced the incidence of AIDS by persuading sex workers and their clients to use condoms and by encouraging young women to delay marriage. Ideally, if virginal brides are old enough to choose husbands, they will marry younger men who are HIV-negative. Rates of STIs are cut in half if men are circumcised or women take a new drug that is an antiretroviral microbicide (Tenofovir) (Abdool Karim et al., 2010; Sawires, 2007). Worldwide, however, young adults remain the prime STI vectors (those who spread disease) as well as the new victims.

Free Sample for Sex Rates of STIs and unplanned pregnancy are far lower in Europe than in the United States, and this photo shows one reason why. Young adults are often given free condoms and information in public places like this ferry terminal in Helsinki.

SUMMING UP

Emerging adulthood is a distinct period of life, often defined as between ages 18 and 25, when most people are strong, healthy, and attractive. They have well-functioning organ systems, protected by homeostasis and organ reserve. Typically, emerging adults satisfy their strong sexual appetites with a series of relationships that last for months or years—although they avoid marriage and parenthood. Two hazards from this new pattern, not always anticipated, are emotional distress and sexually transmitted infections. One result is that worldwide, STIs, including HIV/AIDS, have become epidemic. ∎

>> Psychopathology

Most emerging adults enjoy the freedom that modern life has given them. Not all do, however. Although physical health peaks during these years, the same is not true for psychological health. Average well-being increases in emerging adulthood, but so does the incidence of psychopathology (Mowbray et al., 2006; SAMHSA, 2009; Schulenberg & Zarrett, 2006).

Except for dementia, emerging adults experience more of every diagnosed disorder (sometimes called *mental illness*) than any older group. Their rate of serious mental illness is almost double that for adults over age 25 (SAMHSA, 2009). The first signs of such an illness may appear in childhood, and symptoms worsen in adolescence; but the full disorder often becomes evident during emerging adulthood. For society, the consequences of a mentally ill adult are severe, because although "mental disorders cause fewer deaths than infectious diseases, they cause as much or more disability because they strike early and can last a long time" (G. Miller, January 2006, p. 459).

Why an increase at this age? Part of it is that parents are less able to restrict and protect, so disturbed young adults are more likely to act in destructive ways. In addition, vocational, financial, educational, and interpersonal stresses may be greater in early adulthood than later on, because

> for the first time in their lives, young adults are faced with independence and its inherent rights and responsibilities. Given the novelty of these challenges, young adults may lack the requisite skills to effectively cope and subsequently experience negative mental health outcomes, including depression and anxiety.
>
> *[Cronce & Corbin, 2010, p. 92]*

diathesis–stress model The view that psychological disorders, such as schizophrenia, are produced by the interaction of a genetic vulnerability (the diathesis) and stressful environmental factors and life events.

Most psychologists and psychiatrists accept the **diathesis–stress model,** which "views psychopathology as the consequence of stress interacting with an underlying predisposition (biological, psychosocial, or sociocultural) to produce a specific disorder" (Hooley, 2004, p. 204). You will recognize this as related to the dynamic-systems model described in Chapter 1—that all the systems of the body, mind, and social context interact and influence one another as time goes on. Thus, the demands of emerging adulthood may cause psychopathology when added to preexisting vulnerability arising from genetic interactions, early childhood experiences, and social circumstances. As a result, many disorders appear; some (e.g., anorexia, bulimia) we have already discussed, and others (extreme sensation seeking, drug abuse) are topics later in this chapter. Here we focus on three others: mood disorders, anxiety disorders, and schizophrenia.

Mood Disorders

Before they reach age 30, 8 percent of U.S. residents suffer from a mood disorder: mania, bipolar disorder, or severe depression. Mood disorders can usually be treated with medication and therapy, but they often appear, disappear, and reappear—which means that the impairment for the individual, the family, and the society may be lifelong. Thus, the social cost of mood disorders is estimated to be higher than that of most physical illnesses, including cancer and heart disease, since mood disorders may begin in early adulthood (or before) and can prevent a person from fully functioning for decades (Kessler et al., 2009).

Bipolar Disorder

Bipolar disorder may begin in childhood, as described in Chapter 11, but it becomes more severe in adulthood, when the grandiosity of the mania and the despair of depression may be unchecked by the normal restraints on children (Geller et al., 2008; Merikangas & Pato, 2009). Once the problem is diagnosed, usually in early adulthood, it impacts the family lifelong, partly because many adults with bipolar disorder need to live with their parents or in a supervised setting.

Depression

The most common mood disorder is major depression, signaled by a loss of interest or pleasure in nearly all activities for two weeks or more. Other difficulties—in sleeping, concentrating, eating, carrying on friendships, and feeling hopeful—are also present (American Psychiatric Association, 2000, p. 249). About one-quarter of mood disorders begin in adolescence, and another one-quarter begin in young adulthood. About half of all depressed people have episodes of depression all their lives.

Major depression may be rooted in biochemistry, specifically imbalances in neurotransmitters and hormones, but, as the diathesis–stress model explains, problems that are more prevalent in late adolescence and emerging adulthood (e.g., romantic breakups, arrests) can set in motion a downward spiral. One reason is that young adults with psychological problems have fewer supportive friendships, which in itself can be depressing (King & Terrance, 2006). Women at all ages are more often depressed than men, but according to research on thousands of young adults in 15 nations, men are particularly vulnerable to the ups and downs of their love life: Marriage typically relieves their depression, but divorce may plummet them into despair (Scott et al., 2009; Seedat et al., 2009).

This disorder may be particularly debilitating in emerging adulthood because it undercuts achievements—higher education, vocational choices, romantic commitment—that normally occur between ages 18 and 25. Thus, depression at this stage makes the rest of adulthood more difficult (Howard et al., 2010; Zarate, 2010).

Failure to get treatment for depression is common among emerging adults (Zarate, 2010). They distance themselves from anyone who might know them well enough to realize that professional therapy is needed. Furthermore, depressed people of all ages characteristically believe that nothing will help; therefore, although effective treatment exists for most depressed individuals, they are unlikely to seek it on their own. This raises another issue: Why do scientists distinguish one period of adult life from another when many problems, such as depression, can appear at any age? The following suggests an answer.

A VIEW FROM SCIENCE

Ages and Stages

In most biological ways, a person aged 18 to 25 is no different from a person a few years younger or older, and thus the age parameters of emerging adulthood are somewhat arbitrary. This is not true earlier in life. For children, physical maturation is closely connected to chronological age and developmental stage. Infancy begins at birth; adolescence begins at puberty. Early and middle childhood also have biological markers.

Therefore, with children, age signifies norms and abilities. No one would mistake a 3-month-old for a 3-year-old or expect a 6-year-old to learn in the same way as an 11-year-old does. A controversial topic in education is "redshirting," starting a child in kindergarten a year later than the law allows, because that year adds physical, cognitive, and social maturity, making that late-starting child an advanced kindergartner. Obviously, each year of childhood matters (Weil, 2007).

For adults, however, chronological age is an imperfect guide. A 40-year-old, for instance, could have a body that functions like that of a typical person a decade older or younger. The same is true for intellect: College students are expected to learn the same material, whether they are 18, 28, or any other age. Social roles vary as well. Unlike in childhood, when virtually all 6- to 10-year-olds live with their parents and go to school, a group of 40-year-olds might include some never married, some divorced

several times, some expecting their first child, some grandparents, some employed, some not. Age is not determinative even within one group, much less when comparing cultures. Variation is apparent at every age of adulthood, including emerging adulthood and late adulthood, although the specifics of that variation differ.

Nonetheless, developmental scientists cluster adults into chronological age groups and report differences between one age group and another. For example, cited throughout the adulthood chapters are surveys conducted by the Pew Research Center comparing generations (see the Research Design on page 467). The authors acknowledge that "boundaries that separate generations are indistinct" but proceed to distinguish the following (Pew Research Center, 2007):

- Ages 18 to 25 (Generation Next, born 1981–1988)
- Ages 25 to 40 (Generation X, born 1965–1980)
- Ages 40 to 60 (baby boomers, born 1946–1964)
- Age 60 and older (seniors, born before 1946)

These birth-year designations were set several years ago, in 2006. And it's important to note that not only ages but also names will change as time goes on. For instance, baby boomers

THE FRESNO BEE / ZUMAPRESS.COM

PETE OXFORD / DANITADELIMONT.COM

The Same Situation, Many Miles Apart: Dedication Is Universal It may seem as if the activities and clothing of the Fresno college student in the bookstore *(left)* could not differ more from those of the young mother in the doorway of her Rajastan, India, home *(right)*. However, both are typical emerging adults: active, healthy, and working for their futures.

are fast becoming seniors: Should they still be considered boomers?

Given this fluidity, why do surveys and textbooks cluster adults into age groups? Because cohort and age influence behavior, particularly in adulthood, as people become more aware of each birthday, especially the ones ending in 5 or 0. Your maturation and experience (and those of others your age) make you not the same as you were five years ago or as you will be ten years hence. People born within a few years of one another share some biological and sociological characteristics.

The goal of developmental study remains to understand changes over time in order to allow optimal growth at each life period (Chapter 1). Since people follow patterns that vary by age, culture, and cohort, it helps to know what those patterns are. As you have read, later marriage creates problems as well as opportunities. Likewise, emerging adulthood may be stressful, and psychopathology may emerge. Knowing age-related characteristics helps us protect one another, increasing optimal health for everyone.

Don't Worry Isaiah Schaffer was wounded twice as a soldier in Iraq and now suffers from PTSD. Evident in the photo are two ways he is learning to readjust to civilian life. He is buying a book for his young daughter, and he has his trusty service dog, Meghan, by his side. Meghan calms him when being in public suddenly triggers a panic attack.

EVELYN HOCKSTEIN / POLARIS

Anxiety Disorders

Another major set of disorders, evident in one-fourth of all U.S. residents below the age of 25, is anxiety disorders. These include panic attacks, post-traumatic stress disorder (PTSD), and obsessive-compulsive disorder (OCD). Note that anxiety disorders are even more prevalent than depression; this is true worldwide, according to the World Mental Health surveys of the World Health Organization (Kessler et al., 2009). Incidence statistics vary from study to study, depending partly on definitions and cutoff scores, but all research finds that many emerging adults are anxious about themselves, their relationships, and their future.

Age and genetic vulnerability shape the symptoms of anxiety disorders. For instance, everyone with PTSD has had a frightening experience—such as a near-death encounter in battle or a rape at knifepoint. However, only about 15 percent of the people who undergo such trauma develop PTSD (Ozer & Weiss, 2004). Young adults, especially if they have no support from close friends or relatives, are more likely to develop the disorder than are people of other ages (Grant & Potenza, 2010). This is not surprising because young adults face a higher rate of trauma (military combat, rape, serious accidents) yet are less protected by parents or spouses (Odlaug et al., 2010).

Recovering A young Japanese man sits alone in his room, which until recently was his self-imposed prison. He is one of thousands of Japanese young people (80 percent of whom are male) who have the anxiety disorder known as *hikikomori*.

Anxiety disorders are affected by every aspect of the context. In the United States, social phobia—fear of talking to other people—is a common anxiety disorder, one that keeps young adults away from college, unable to make new friends, hesitant to apply for jobs. In Japan, a severe social phobia has appeared within the last 20 years that may affect more than 100,000 young adults. It is called **hikikomori,** or "pull away" (Teo, 2010).

The sufferer stays in his (or, less often, her) room almost all the time for six months or more. Typically, a person suffering with *hikikomori* is anxious about the social and academic pressures of high school and college. Parents bring food to their self-imprisoned children and "fear that their children won't survive without them" (M. Jones, 2005, p. 51). The close connection between parents and children (known as *amae,* mentioned in our discussion of childhood)—and the fact that Japanese parents usually have only one or two children—makes this particular social phobia more common in that culture.

It is easier to see how another culture or family enables a particular anxiety disorder than it is to recognize that aspects of one's own culture that raise anxiety in emerging adults. Japanese emerging adults are thought to experience more pressure, and parents are thought to be more indulgent. Yet everywhere, anxiety seems to be part of emerging adulthood. Manifestations vary, but the trait is universal.

Schizophrenia

About 1 percent of all adults experience schizophrenia, becoming overwhelmed by disorganized and bizarre thoughts, delusions, hallucinations, and emotions (American Psychiatric Association, 2000). Schizophrenia is found in every nation, but some cultures and contexts have much higher rates than others (Anjum et al., 2010).

No doubt, the cause of schizophrenia is partly genetic, although most people with this disorder have no immediate family members suffering from it. But beyond genetics, some other risk factors are known. One is malnutrition when the brain is developing: Women who are severely malnourished in the early months of pregnancy are twice as likely to have a child with schizophrenia as are other women (St Clair et al., 2005). Another factor is extensive social pressure. Among

hikikomori A Japanese word literally meaning "pull away," it is the name of an anxiety disorder common among young adults in Japan. Sufferers isolate themselves from the outside world by staying inside their homes for months or even years at a time.

Finally Almost 30 Beyoncé and Justin Timberlake are astonishingly talented and successful today, seen here in their opening performance for Spring Fashion Week 2009. Both shot to stardom in adolescence, but emerging adulthood was difficult for them. At age 19, after her singing group won a Grammy, Beyoncé experienced years of severe depression about how to handle the newfound fame, sometimes unable to leave her room or even eat. As for Justin, his two-year love affair with Britney Spears came "crashing down" at age 21, resulting in his writing the heartrending song "Cry Me a River."

Especially for Immigrants What can you do in your adopted country to avoid or relieve the psychological stresses of immigration? (see response, page 481)

immigrants, the rate of schizophrenia triples when young adults have no familial supports (Cantor-Graae & Selten, 2005; Morgan et al., 2007).

In every nation, symptoms of schizophrenia typically begin in adolescence. Diagnosis is most common from ages 18 to 24, with men particularly vulnerable (Anjum et al., 2010; Kirkbride et al., 2006). Men who have had no symptoms by age 35 almost never develop schizophrenia, although some older women do (Anjum et al., 2010). This raises the question: Does something in the bodies, minds, or social surroundings of young adult men trigger schizophrenia? The diathesis–stress model of mental illness, which (as you saw earlier) proposes that a combination of genetic vulnerability and environmental stresses produces mental disorders, suggests that the answer is yes for all three.

SUMMING UP

Most emerging adults enjoy their independence. However, those with inborn vulnerability whose childhood added emotional and cognitive burdens rather than emotional regulation and intellectual strengths may experience a serious disorder during emerging adulthood. Mood disorders, anxiety disorders, and schizophrenia are all diagnosed more often before age 25 than later, partly because the stresses of this period occur when family supports are less available. Mood disorders (especially depression) may appear at any age, but, anxiety disorders cluster during early adulthood, and schizophrenia almost never appears for the first time after age 35 in men (though it sometimes does in women). All of these disorders respond to therapy and medication, but all impose a substantial burden on individual development and the society overall. ■

≫ Good Health Habits

Emerging adults experiment and select from many options. Some begin good habits and sustain them lifelong; others make destructive choices. We focus first on two vital choices, exercise and nutrition.

Exercise

Exercise at every stage of life protects against serious illness, even if a person has other bad habits, such as smoking and overeating. Exercise reduces blood pressure; strengthens the heart and lungs; and makes depression, osteoporosis, heart disease, arthritis, and even some cancers less likely. Health benefits from exercise are substantial for men and women, old and young, former sports stars and those who never joined an athletic team.

By contrast, sitting for long hours correlates with almost every unhealthy condition, especially heart disease and diabetes, both of which pose additional health hazards (Hu et al., 2003). Even a little movement—gardening, light housework, walking up the stairs or to the bus—helps. Walking briskly for 30 minutes a day, five days a week, is better; more intense exercise (swimming, jogging, bicycling, and the like) is ideal.

The later health consequences of inactivity in early adulthood have been found in dozens of studies. One of the best, which showed cause not merely correlation, was a study called CARDIA (Coronary Artery Risk Development in Adulthood) that began with 18- to 30-year-olds who were followed into middle age. Those who were the least fit during emerging adulthood were four times more likely to have diabetes and high blood pressure 15 years later. Circulatory problems began, unnoticed, in early adulthood (Carnethon et al., 2003).

Especially for Emerging Adults Seeking a New Place to Live People move more often between the ages of 18 and 25 than at any later time. Currently, real estate agents describe sunlight, parking, and privacy as top priorities for their young clients. What else might emerging adults ask when selecting a new home? (see response, page 481)

SABINE LUBENOW / PHOTOLIBRARY

Coincidence or Cause? Many European cities boast far more cyclists than does the United States, largely thanks to exclusive bike paths (as here alongside an Amsterdam canal), public bike shares (as in Paris), or financial incentives (as in London's congestion pricing). Those cities also have lower rates of obesity, heart disease, and diabetes.

It is natural for most emerging adults to keep moving—to climb stairs, run to the store, join intramural college and company athletic teams, play neighborhood games, jog, sail, or bicycle. Especially in developing nations, they take jobs that require movement and strength. In the United States, emerging adults walk more and drive less than older adults, and more of them reach the standard of exercising 30 minutes a day, five days a week. However, although they exercise more than their elders (see Figure 17.2), many do not meet the minimal standard, and their rate of exercise has decreased in recent years.

Past generations quit exercising when marriage, parenthood, and career became more demanding. Young adults today, aware of this tendency, can choose friends and communities that support, rather than preclude, staying active. To be specific:

1. *Friendship.* People exercise more if their friends do so, too. Because social networks typically shrink with age, adults need to maintain, or begin, friendships that include movement, such as meeting a friend for a jog instead of a beer or playing tennis instead of going to a movie.

2. *Communities.* In some places, exercise is facilitated with easy access to walking and biking paths, ample fields and parks, and subsidized pools and gyms. Most colleges provide these amenities, but most neighborhoods and nations do not. Health experts cite extensive research showing that community design can have a positive effect on the levels of obesity, hypertension, and depression (Bors et al., 2009).

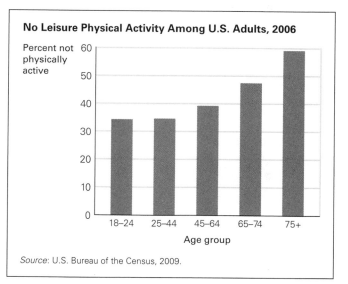

No Leisure Physical Activity Among U.S. Adults, 2006

Source: U.S. Bureau of the Census, 2009.

FIGURE 17.2

No Movement What did you expect? These data could be seen positively, since nearly two-thirds of all emerging adults get some exercise. However, minimal standards set by national health experts are that everyone should at least do one of the following: (1) Exercise moderately (e.g., walk fast) for half an hour, five times a week; (2) exercise strenuously (e.g., run) for 20 minutes three times a week; or (3) do muscle strengthening (e.g., lift weights) twice a week. One-third of emerging adults do far less.

Eating Well

Nutrition is another lifelong habit embedded in culture. "You are what you eat" is an oversimplification, but at every stage of life, diet affects future development. Indeed, a program in Guatemala that provided adequate nutrition to pregnant women and children under age 3 had benefits for emerging adults 20 years later—they had more education and better jobs than did other emerging adults who had

set point A particular body weight that an individual's homeostatic processes strive to maintain.

body mass index (BMI) The ratio of a person's weight in kilograms divided by his or her height in meters squared.

Calculating Adult BMI One objective assessment of appropriate weight is the amount of body fat as represented by the body mass index (BMI). A person's BMI is calculated by dividing his or her weight (in kilograms) by height (in meters) squared. Since most U.S. readers do not know their weight and height in the metric system, this table calculates BMI for them. A healthy BMI is between 19 and 25. A very muscular person may be healthy at a BMI of 26 or even 27 because muscle and bone weigh more than fat.

not been so fortunate when they were babies (Martorell et al., 2010). Fortunately, in most cultures, long before the invention of vitamin pills and bathroom scales, young adults ate enough but not too much.

For body weight, there is a homeostatic **set point,** or settling point, which makes people eat when they are hungry and stop eating when they are full. Of course, the set point may be altered by extreme dieting: The eating disorders explained in Chapter 14 (anorexia and bulimia nervosa) may get worse in early adulthood, and death from such disorders is more likely in the 20s than in the teens. For everyone, the set point is affected by age, genes, diet, hormones, and exercise; but for most people, nature works to keep every bodily system in balance.

Especially in emerging adulthood, the set point seems to function well. Weight is often measured via the **body mass index (BMI),** which is the ratio between weight and height (see Table 17.2). A BMI between 20 and 25 indicates a normal weight—above 25 is considered overweight, 30 or more is considered obese, below 18 is a symptom of anorexia. Emerging adulthood is the time when the greatest proportion of people are within the normal range. The BMI chart as a measure of overweight can be used for adults of all ages, although more precise measures are sometimes necessary for muscular individuals.

Once they are independent, emerging adults often change childhood eating patterns. As a generation, young adults consume more bottled water, organic foods,

TABLE 17.2

Body Mass Index (BMI)

To find your BMI, locate your height in the first column, then look across that row. Your BMI appears at the top of the column that contains your weight.

BMI	19	20	21	22	23	24	25	26	27	28	29	30	35	40
Height (in feet and inches)							**Weight** (in pounds)							
4'10"	91	96	100	105	110	115	119	124	129	134	138	143	167	191
4'11"	94	99	104	109	114	119	124	128	133	138	143	148	173	198
5'0"	97	102	107	112	118	123	128	133	138	143	148	153	179	204
5'1"	100	106	111	116	122	127	132	137	143	148	153	158	185	211
5'2"	104	109	115	120	126	131	136	142	147	153	158	164	191	218
5'3"	107	113	118	124	130	135	141	146	152	158	163	169	197	225
5'4"	110	116	122	128	134	140	145	151	157	163	169	174	204	232
5'5"	114	120	126	132	138	144	150	156	162	168	174	180	210	240
5'6"	118	124	130	136	142	148	155	161	167	173	179	186	216	247
5'7"	121	127	134	140	146	153	159	166	172	178	185	191	223	255
5'8"	125	131	138	144	151	158	164	171	177	183	190	197	230	262
5'9"	128	135	142	149	155	162	169	176	182	189	196	203	236	270
5'10"	132	139	146	153	160	167	174	181	188	195	202	207	243	278
5'11"	136	143	150	157	165	172	179	186	193	200	208	215	250	286
6'0"	140	147	154	162	169	177	184	191	199	206	213	221	258	294
6'1"	144	151	159	166	174	182	189	197	204	212	219	227	265	302
6'2"	148	155	163	171	179	186	194	202	210	218	225	233	272	311
6'3"	152	160	168	176	184	192	200	208	216	224	232	240	279	319
6'4"	156	164	172	180	189	197	205	213	221	230	238	246	287	328
			Normal					*Overweight*					*Obese*	

Source: National Heart, Lung, and Blood Institute, n.d.

and nonmeat diets than do older adults, and many become more fit than their parents were at the same age. A large British study found that about one-half of those who were obese as children become normal-weight young adults, with healthier eating and social patterns (Viner & Cole, 2005). A study in the United States found that emerging adults who lived on college campuses ate a more balanced, healthier diet than those living with their parents (Laska et al., 2010).

Of course, better eating is not automatic. Although some emerging adults lose excess weight, others gain. According to the British study cited above, 12 percent of normal-weight teenagers become obese by age 30 (Viner & Cole, 2005).

Particular nutritional hazards await young adults who immigrate to the United States and decide to "eat American." They might avoid curry, hot peppers, or wasabi—each of which has been discovered to have health benefits—and indulge in more American fast food, which tends to be high in fat, sugar, and salt. Although older immigrants overall are healthier than native-born Americans, their young-adult offspring have significantly higher rates of obesity and diabetes than their parents did, particularly if their national origin is African or South Asian (Oza-Frank & Narayan, 2010).

No matter what their ancestry, today's emerging adults are fatter than past cohorts. One reason is that they earn less money, and healthy foods have become more expensive while unhealthy foods have become cheaper in the past 20 years (Duffey et al., 2010). (Adult obesity is discussed in Chapter 20.)

Supersize Large portions are a quick bargain. The real costs come later, often in lifelong compromised health and happiness.

Taking Risks

Now we look closely at something that brings both ecstasy and despair. A measure of caution, forethought, and planning can be considered a good health habit, but many emerging adults bravely, or foolishly, risk not only their health but life itself. Risk taking is age-related, as well as genetic and hormonal. Some people—more often males than females—are naturally more daring than others. Thus, those who are genetically impulsive *and* male *and* emerging adults are most likely to be brave or foolish.

Societies as well as individuals benefit precisely because emerging adults take chances. Enrolling in college, moving to a new state or nation, getting married, having a baby—all these endeavors are risky. So is starting a business, filming a documentary, entering an athletic contest, enlisting in the military, and joining the Peace Corps. Emerging adults take these risks, and the rest of society is grateful. Before lamenting risk taking, we need to recognize the attraction of **edgework**—that is, living on the edge by skillfully managing stress and fear in order to attain some goal (Lyng, 2005). The joy is in the intense concentration and mastery; edgework is more compelling if failure potentially entails disaster.

Dangers

Destructive risks are numerous, including having sex without a condom, driving without a seat belt, carrying a loaded gun, and abusing drugs. The addiction of an adrenaline rush is one reason people commit crimes or gamble (Cosgrave, 2010). In part because of risk taking, accidents, homicides, and suicides are the three leading causes of death among people aged 15 to 25—killing more of them than all diseases combined. This is true even in nations where infectious diseases and malnutrition are rampant. The only nation where this is not true is South Africa, where death from AIDS is more frequent than suicide, though AIDS is obviously connected to risk.

Although their bodies are strong, their organ reserve protective, and their reactions quick, emerging adults nonetheless have more accidents that land them in

>> **Response for Immigrants** (from page 478) Maintain your social supports. Ideally, emigrate with members of your close family, and join a religious or cultural community where you will find emotional understanding.

edgework Occupations or recreational activities that involve a degree of risk or danger. The prospect of "living on the edge" makes edgework compelling to some individuals.

>> **Response for Emerging Adults Seeking a New Place to Live** (from page 478) Since neighborhoods have a powerful impact on health, a person could ask to see the nearest park, to meet a neighbor who walks to work, or how to contact a neighborhood sports league.

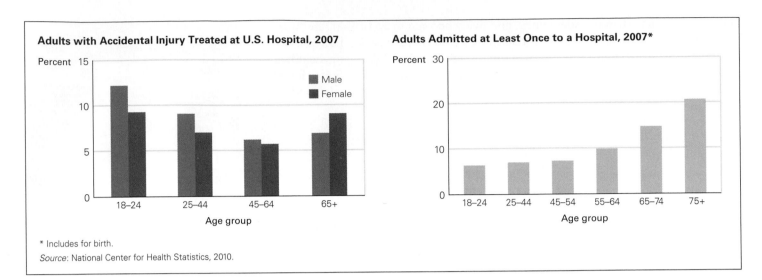

Adults with Accidental Injury Treated at U.S. Hospital, 2007

Percent

■ Male
■ Female

Age group

Adults Admitted at Least Once to a Hospital, 2007*

Percent

Age group

* Includes for birth.

Source: National Center for Health Statistics, 2010.

FIGURE 17.3

Send Them Home Accidents, homicides, and suicides occur more frequently during emerging adulthood than later, but emerging adults typically avoid hospitals unless they need emergency attention. They are usually stitched, bandaged, and injected and sent home.

emergency rooms than do people of other ages. The low rate of serious disease between ages 18 and 25 is counterbalanced by a high rate of serious injuries (see Figure 17.3, left). Fortunately, age is in their favor: The percent who are not only treated but also admitted to hospitals is lower than for adults of every age (see Figure 17.3, right).

Occupations

Many occupations include edgework, from firefighting to bond trading. One edgework occupation, bicycle messengering, has moments of timeless pleasure. As one social scientist explains, "Their entire lives are wrapped inside a distinct messenger lifestyle that cherishes thrills and threats of dodging cars as they speed through the city" (Kidder, 2006, p. 32).

Most companies pay messengers per delivery, which gives them incentive to run red lights and ride against traffic, but some exceptional firms pay per hour and provide health insurance. One skilled messenger quit his pay-per-delivery job and began to work for one of the exceptional companies because he was getting married and needed steady pay and health benefits. Soon he complained bitterly that the joy was gone (Kidder, 2006).

Edgework does not need to be physical. In the financial markets, some bankers or brokers gamble millions of corporate dollars on high-risk investments, operating outside established conventions and even beyond laws and ethics. These so-called rogue traders—usually young men—thrill in edgework, creating and then expanding investments that might fail (Wexler, 2010). The joy is in selling just at the right moment—the day before the market collapse.

Over the Edge Wearing no helmet, moving against traffic, and riding a racing bike among buses and trucks—these are a thrilling combination for bicycle messengers, almost all of whom are emerging-adult men.

extreme sports Forms of recreation that include apparent risk of injury or death and that are attractive and thrilling as a result. Motocross is one example.

Risky Sports

Many young adults cannot find work that satisfies their need for danger. Instead they seek the edge in recreation—climbing mountains, skydiving, and so on. Each of these activities has social guidelines that celebrate risk but not stupidity; novices are shunned until they are recognized as "members of the same tribe" (Laurendeau & Van Brunschot, 2006; Lyng, 2005, p. 4).

Other manifestations of the risk-taking impulse are competitive **extreme sports,** which were nonexistent until recently but became popular at about the same time that emerging adulthood was recognized as a distinct stage. For example, freestyle motocross was "practically invented" in the mid-1990s by Brian Deegan and Mike Metzger when they were about 20 years old (Higgins, 2006a). Motocross involves riding motorcycles over barriers and off ramps, including a 50-foot-high leap into "big air." As rider and cycle fall, points are gained by doing tricks, such as backward somersaults. As one reporter wrote:

> As a result of their longevity, Deegan and Metzger [now in their early thirties] are considered legends, graybeard veterans in a much younger man's game. . . . One has lost a kidney and broken a leg and both wrists; the other has broken arms and legs and lost a testicle. Watching them perform, many observers wonder whether they have lost their minds.
>
> *[Higgins, 2006a, p. D5]*

Observers who wonder about the sanity of these young men are usually themselves long past their daredevil days. However, many emerging adults prefer extreme sports. One, Travis Pastrana, won the 2006 X Games motocross competition at age 22 with a double backflip because, as he explained, "The two main things are that I've been healthy and able to train at my fullest, and a lot of guys have had major crashes this year" (quoted in Higgins, 2006b). Major crashes are part of every sport Pastrana enjoys. For example, he recently beat the record for the longest leap through big air in an automobile, as he drove over the ocean from a ramp on the shoreline in Long Beach California to a barge more than 250 feet out. He crashed into a barrier on the boat, but he emerged, seemingly ecstatic and unhurt, to the applause of thousands (Roberts, 2010).

Extreme sports attract thousands of adults, who travel long distances and spend large sums of money to jump off famous bridges (base jumping, with parachute), climb the sheer or icy sides of mountains, ride dangerous waves without a board (body surfing), and so on. Adventure has become a significant niche of tourism (Allman et al., 2009).

Drug Abuse

The same impulse that is admired in edgework can also lead to behaviors that are clearly destructive, not only for individuals but for the community as well. The most studied of these are drug abuse and addiction (Reith, 2005), which involve many substances—from the perfectly legal to the extremely illegal.

Drug abuse occurs whenever a person uses a drug that is harmful to physical, cognitive, or psychosocial well-being. Given what is known about health and tobacco, even occasional smoking can be abuse, and given the risk of arrest, even one use of an illegal drug can be abuse.

Drug abuse can lead to **drug addiction,** a condition of dependence in which the absence of a drug causes intense cravings for it in order to satisfy a need. The need may be either physical (e.g., to stop the shakes, settle one's stomach, or sleep) or psychological (e.g., to quiet anxiety or lift depression). Withdrawal symptoms are the telltale signs of addiction.

Although cigarettes and alcohol can be as addictive and destructive as the illegal drugs, from an emerging-adult perspective part of the lure of illegal drugs may be that they are illegal: There is a thrill in buying, carrying, and using, with the knowledge that one could be arrested and even imprisoned. Given the allure of edgework, it is not surprising that the use of illegal drugs peaks from ages 18 to 25 and declines more sharply than the use of cigarettes and alcohol (see Figure 17.4).

It may be surprising, however, that drug abuse is more common among college students than among their peers who are not in college. For instance, college students are most likely to engage in extreme binge drinking, with 25 percent of

drug abuse The ingestion of a drug to the extent that it impairs the user's biological or psychological well-being.

drug addiction A condition of drug dependence in which the absence of the given drug in the individual's system produces a drive—physiological, psychological, or both—to ingest more of the drug.

Especially for Substance Abuse Counselors Can you think of three possible explanations for the more precipitous drop in illegal drug use compared to legal ones? (see response, page 484)

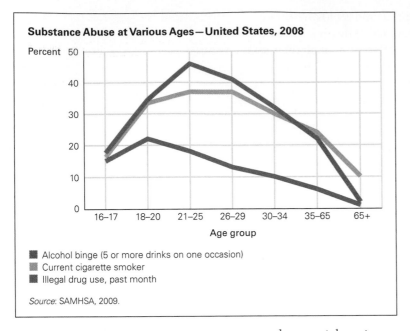

Substance Abuse at Various Ages—United States, 2008

Percent

- ■ Alcohol binge (5 or more drinks on one occasion)
- ■ Current cigarette smoker
- ■ Illegal drug use, past month

Source: SAMHSA, 2009.

FIGURE 17.4

Too Old for That As you can see, emerging adults are the biggest substance abusers, but illegal drug use drops much faster than cigarette use or binge drinking.

>> Response for Substance Abuse Counselors (from page 483) Legal drugs could be more addictive, or the thrill of illegality may diminish with age, or the fear of arrest may increase. In any case, treatment for young-adult substance abusers may need to differ from that for older ones.

young men and 5 percent of young women reporting that they consumed ten or more drinks in a row at least once in the previous two weeks (Johnston et al., 2009). Such extremes arise from the same drive as extreme sports or other risks—with the same possible consequence (death).

Being with peers, especially in college, seems to encourage drug abuse. In fact, the category of emerging adults least likely to abuse drugs is women who do not go to college, perhaps because many live with their families (Johnston et al., 2009). Patterns of use, abuse, and addiction are affected by historical trends as well as by age and culture; they vary from time to time and nation to nation. However, the overall trend is curvilinear, rising during emerging adulthood and then falling with maturity (see Figure 17.5).

Drugs illustrate a pattern of many kinds of risks for which the immediate benefits obscure the eventual costs. Most young adults use alcohol, for instance, to reduce social anxiety—a problem for many emerging adults as they enter college, start a new job, speak to strangers, or embark on a romance. It does not occur to them that they might become alcoholics.

Indeed, no matter what the drug, crossing the line between use and abuse does not ring alarms. This was apparent in a study of ketamine use among young adults in England, who justified its use—"a bargain"—even after signs of addiction were apparent (Moore & Measham, 2008). Although friends and family members are generally the first to know when a person is abusing drugs, this is much less likely during emerging adulthood. Family norms allow the most independence and privacy during this stage, and friends are often oblivious; disapproval of drug use is lower from age 18 to 25 than during any other age.

Yet longitudinal data show that early drug abuse impairs later life in many ways. Those who use drugs heavily in high school are less likely to go to college, and those who begin heavy drug use in college are less likely to earn a degree, find a

Higher Education College provides many benefits, but it also seems to encourage drug use. Everyone at this fraternity party appears to be using alcohol, and one young woman is drinking from a beer bong. Seeking admiration for drinking a lot in a short time is a sign that a person is at risk for alcoholism.

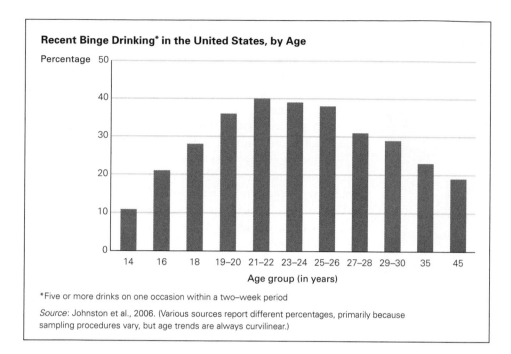

Recent Binge Drinking* in the United States, by Age

*Five or more drinks on one occasion within a two-week period

Source: Johnston et al., 2006. (Various sources report different percentages, primarily because sampling procedures vary, but age trends are always curvilinear.)

FIGURE 17.5

Laws and Choices Abusive drinking is common throughout adulthood. Laws seem to have some effect on those under the age of 21, and then experience and social setting affect adults as they mature.

good job, or sustain a romance (Johnston et al., 2009). Eventually, drug abusers lose friends, jobs, and relationships and are likely to get sick and die. Longitudinal research comes to this conclusion in every nation. For instance, a 21-year study in Scotland found that young-adult men who drank heavily doubled their risk of dying by middle age (Hart et al., 1999).

Social Norms

One discovery from the study of human development that might reduce risk taking and improve health habits among emerging adults is the power of *social norms*, which are customs for usual behavior within a particular society. Social norms exert a particularly strong influence on college students, since they are usually independent of their parents and do not yet have life partners or children. They want the approval of their peers; social norms matter.

Why Take Risks?

Social norms are one reason for the popularity of edgework. Not only are contemporary emerging adults immersed in social settings (colleges, parties, concerts, sports events) where risk takers are widely admired, they also tend to notice the risk takers—such as the classmate who brags that he waited until the last minute and wrote a term paper in one night or the star athlete who did something dangerous and unexpected. Noticing such individuals leads many emerging adults to overestimate the prevalence of risk takers and thus to be influenced by them. The stars of extreme sports seek adulation from others, as is evident in the Web sites of Deegan, Pastrana, and many others.

In one experiment, several small groups of college students were offered as much alcohol as they wanted while they socialized with one another. In some groups, one student was secretly recruited in advance to drink heavily; in others, one student was assigned to drink very little; in a third condition, there was no student confederate. In those groups with a heavy drinker, participants followed the norm set by the risk takers, not by the cautious ones (reported in W. R. Miller & Carroll, 2006).

Picture Yourself If you were taking the plunge in this photo, would you thrill at bungee-jumping with your partner or would you doubt your sanity? Your answer reflects your age, gender, culture, and parental status. Young, single, North American men might wish they were secured to that bungee cord; older mothers in developing nations would not dream of it.

DARRYL LENIUK / GETTY IMAGES

Risky Hero Johnathan Bopp, like many college students, is sometimes impulsive and brave—which is why reading about the Haiti earthquake led him to Port-Au-Prince despite the risk of possible aftershocks and disease. Here he comforts an orphaned child.

social norms approach A method of reducing risky behavior that uses emerging adults' desire to follow social norms by making them aware, through the use of surveys, of the prevalence of various behaviors within their peer group.

To be specific, the average alcohol consumption of the group with the light drinker and the group with no confederate were similar to each other but were significantly lower than the average for the group with the heavy drinker.

The power of social norms is evident in the popularity of extreme sports. For instance, a small group of young-adult British men formed the Dangerous Sports Club. They thought of trying bungee jumping on April Fools' Day in 1979. On that day, at first they all backed off, telling the press it was a foolish joke. But later, after drinking, one was filmed bungee jumping. Thousands of others saw the video, and before long, bungee jumping became a fad.

A similar story holds for other extreme sports—hang gliding, ice climbing, pond swooping, base jumping—that were never imagined until one daredevil young adult inspired thousands of others. Media coverage—especially video footage—increases participation (Bakir, 2010; Cockerham, 2006). Other risky sports, once attractive to hundred of thousands, have become safer, less edgy, and therefore less popular. Boxing, for example, was much more popular 50 years ago than today, now that rules make severe injury less likely.

A Way to Curb Alcohol Abuse in College

An understanding of the perceptions and needs of emerging adults, as well as the realization that college students abuse drugs even more than others their age, has led to a promising effort to reduce alcohol abuse on college campuses. This is the **social norms approach,** an attempt to reduce risk taking by conducting surveys of emerging adults and using the results to make them aware of the prevalence of various behaviors. About half the colleges in the United States have surveyed alcohol use on their campuses and reported the results. Almost always, students not only overestimate how much the average student drinks, but they also underestimate how their peers feel about the loud, late talking and other behaviors of drunk students (C. M. Lee et al., 2010).

In general, when survey results are reported and college students realize that most of their classmates study hard, avoid binge drinking, refuse drugs, and are sexually abstinent, faithful, or protected, they are more likely to follow these social norms. This is especially true if the survey is conducted and reported on the Web (not a paper questionnaire with written response) and if the students are not living with many heavy drinkers (Ward & Gryczynski, 2009). In the latter case, the social norm of their immediate residence may be more powerful than information about students overall. Of course, if social norms surveys suggest to lonely, temperate, conscientious students that they are odd, then the opposite may result: Those students might engage in more rather than less risky behavior (Schultz et al., 2007). But that is not the usual case.

Implications of Risks and Norms

Accurate knowledge about other people's thoughts and actions is useful, since people often misjudge what others are thinking. Even researchers are vulnerable: Those who immerse themselves in the groups where drug use and risk taking are normative tend to report the (often positive) perceptions of users, while those who study data on long-term effects in the population typically stress the risk of injury, impaired development, and death (Hunt et al., 2009).

Consider again the developmental problems raised by emerging adults' impulse to experiment and explore. We would all suffer if young adults were timid, traditional, and afraid of innovation. They need to befriend strangers, try new foods, explore ideas, travel abroad, and sometimes risk their lives. The tasks that await—graduating from college, finding a challenging job, getting married, becoming a parent—are all impossible for people who are overly cautious and unwilling to take chances.

But risks should be taken carefully. The independence of emerging adults may lead them to throw caution to the wind. Edgework may lead to permanent injury, life itself may be cut short. A college education correlates with better health—including more exercise, healthier eating, less drug use, and longer life (Adler & Snibbe, 2003). This is all the more reason to guard against the foolish risks that seem to accelerate during college.

One of my older students, John, told the class about his experience as an emerging adult. At first, he spoke with amused pride. But by the end of his narrative, he was troubled, partly because John was now the father of a little boy he adored, and he realized that his son might become an equally reckless young man.

John told us that, during a vacation break in his first year of college, he and two of his male friends were sitting, bored, on a beach. One friend proposed swimming to an island, barely visible on the horizon. They immediately set out. After swimming for a long time, John realized that he was only about one-third of the way there, that he was tired, that the island was merely an empty spit of sand, and that he would have to swim back. He turned around and swam to shore. The friend who made the proposal eventually reached the island. The third boy became exhausted and almost drowned (a passing boat rescued him).

What does this episode signify about the biosocial development of emerging adults? It is easy to understand why John started swimming. Male ego, camaraderie, boredom, and the overall context made this an attractive adventure. Young men like to be active, feeling their strong arms, legs, and lungs.

Like John, many adults fondly remember past risks. They forget the friends who caught STIs, who had abortions or unwanted births, who became addicts or alcoholics, or who died young; they ignore the fact that their younger siblings and children might do the same. Emerging adulthood is a strong and healthy age, but not without serious risks. Why swim to a distant island? More thinking (Chapter 18) is needed.

SUMMING UP

Good exercise and eating habits established in young adulthood contribute greatly to overall health in middle age and beyond, while sedentary individuals are more likely to develop diabetes and high blood pressure.

Risk taking is common during young adulthood. Some risks are beneficial; others are not. In general, males take more risks than females. Some choose edgework occupations—firefighting, for instance—that involve a degree of danger; others choose extreme sports because they are risky. Emerging adults—especially those in college—have high rates of drug and alcohol abuse. Social norms are powerful; knowledge about other's behavior and attitudes may help reduce alcohol abuse and other problems. ∎

SUMMARY

Growth and Strength

1. Emerging adulthood, from about age 18 to 25, is a new period of development characterized by later marriage and more education.

2. Most emerging adults are strong and healthy. All the body systems function optimally during these years; immunity is strong; death from disease is rare.

3. Homeostasis and organ reserve help ensure that emerging adults recover quickly from infections and injuries. The gradual slowdowns of senescence begin as soon as puberty is complete but are not yet noticed.

4. Emerging adults are usually physically and sexually attractive. This is also the peak time for sexual desire.

5. Reproduction is most successful during emerging adulthood because both male and female bodies are at their most fertile. However, most emerging adults do not yet want to become parents. Contraception helps to lower the risk of unwanted parenthood.

6. Sexual relationships before marriage are accepted by most young adults, although their sexual activity may have unanticipated consequences. Emotional connections often accompany sexual relationships, and disagreements about the purpose of sex—reproduction, relationship, or recreation—can cause stress.

7. Sexually transmitted infections are much more common now than in earlier generations because many young adults have several sexual relationships before marriage. Infertility and even death can result from untreated STIs.

Psychopathology

8. Generally, well-being increases during emerging adulthood, but so does the rate of psychological disorders. Although the roots of such problems can be traced to earlier ages, the stresses of this period push some people over the edge.

9. Mood and anxiety disorders are apparent at every period of life, but some of the social contexts that are more prevalent during emerging adulthood tend to worsen these problems. Therapy can help, but many young adults do not seek it.

10. Schizophrenia is an example of the diathesis–stress model. Genes underlie the vulnerability to schizophrenia, and good prenatal nutrition is protective, but the expression of this disorder occurs most often during emerging adulthood.

Good Health Habits

11. Many emerging adults engage in adequate exercise, protecting their long-term health by so doing. Ideally, they choose friends and neighborhoods that will keep them active.

12. Good nourishment is important lifelong. The body mass index (BMI) indicates whether an adult is of normal weight or is too heavy or too light. The BMIs of most emerging adults are normal (more so than at older ages), but some continue to display serious eating disorders such as anorexia and bulimia nervosa, and others are obese.

13. Risk taking increases during emerging adulthood, with the thrills of edgework being particularly attractive to young men. Many risks can have life-threatening consequences, including drug abuse and addiction, unprotected sex, and extreme sports.

14. Cultural as well as gender variations are evident in risk taking and violent death. Social norms are particularly powerful during these years. These two facts can reduce the hazards of risk taking, a lesson applied on many college campuses.

KEY TERMS

emerging adulthood (p. 465)
senescence (p. 468)
homeostasis (p. 468)
organ reserve (p. 468)

diathesis–stress model (p. 474)
hikikomori (p. 477)
set point (p. 480)

body mass index (BMI) (p. 480)
edgework (p. 481)
extreme sports (p. 482)

drug abuse (p. 483)
drug addiction (p. 483)
social norms approach (p. 486)

WHAT HAVE YOU LEARNED?

Growth and Strength

1. Why is maximum physical strength usually attained in emerging adulthood?

2. How is homeostasis apparent in the human need for nutrition?

3. How does organ reserve protect against heart attacks?

4. What advantages do emerging adults have in their physical appearance?

5. Why do most 20-year-olds not want to get married?

6. Biologically, what is the best age to have a baby?

Psychopathology

7. Why are STIs more common currently than 50 years ago?

8. What is the usual pattern of well-being during emerging adulthood?

9. Why do depressed people tend not to seek help?

10. What anxiety disorders are more likely in your culture?

11. What evidence suggests that schizophrenia is not totally genetic?

Good Health Habits

12. Why is the nutrition of emerging adults often better than that of other adults?

13. How does exercise in early adulthood affect health in late adulthood?

14. What are the social benefits of risk taking?

15. How do vocational choices change between early and later adulthood?

16. Why are some sports more attractive at some ages than others?

17. Why are serious accidents more common in emerging adulthood than later?

18. How can committing a crime be considered an example of edgework?

19. Why are college students more likely to abuse drugs than those not in college?

20. What is the difference between drug abuse and addiction?

21. Why are social norms particularly powerful in emerging adulthood?

APPLICATIONS

1. Describe an incident during your emerging adulthood when taking a risk could have led to disaster. What were your feelings at the time? What would you do if you knew that a child of yours was about to do the same thing?

2. Describe the daily patterns of someone you know who has unhealthy habits related to eating, exercise, drug abuse, risk taking, or some other aspect of lifestyle. What would it take for that person to change his or her habits? Consider the impact of time, experience, medical advice, and fear.

3. Use the library or Internet to investigate changes over the past 50 years in the lives of young adults in a particular nation or ethnic group. What caused those changes? Are they similar to the changes reported in the United States?

>>ONLINE CONNECTIONS

To accompany your textbook, you have access to a number of online resources, including quizzes for every chapter of the book, flashcards (in English and Spanish), critical thinking questions, and case studies. For access to any of these links, go to www.worthpublishers.com/bergerls8e. In addition to these free resources, you'll also find links to the podcasts, video clips, diagnostic quizzing with personalized study advice, and an ebook. Some of the videos and activities available online include:

- *Eating Disorders.* This activity covers the signs, symptoms, and impact of living with eating disorders. It also looks at cultural and gender differences.

- *The Effects of Psychological Stress.* What is stress, and how can it be managed? Activities let you measure your vulnerability to stress and determine your current stress level.

18

Emerging Adulthood: Cognitive Development

WHAT WILL YOU KNOW?

1. Do adults think about problems differently than adolescents do?

2. Are adults more moral than adolescents?

3. What nation has the highest proportion of young adults graduating from college?

4. How does college affect a person's thinking processes?

What did you learn today? When I asked my young children, I sometimes heard about things of no interest to me (like how a bunny eats a carrot); when I asked my adolescents, I sometimes got silence. A child might answer by reciting insignificant details; some adolescents might reply, "Nothing." What would you say if someone asked you now? Probably something that connects you with new ideas, something thoughtful. Beginning in early adulthood, cognition may change in quality, quantity, speed, efficiency, and depth, reflecting new values, interests, and skills. When and how this happens is explained in this book's three chapters on adulthood cognition.

Cognitive development has been studied using many approaches:

- The *stage approach* describes shifts in the nature of thought, as in a postformal stage that follows the formal stage discussed in Chapter 15.
- The *psychometric approach* analyzes intelligence via IQ tests and other measures.
- The *information-processing approach* studies encoding, storage, and retrieval of information.

All three approaches provide valuable insights into the complex patterns of adult cognition. Yet, as emphasized in Chapter 17, chronological age is an imperfect boundary in adulthood. It would be especially misleading to describe new forms of thinking beginning at age 18, 25, and 65—the ages at which emerging adulthood, adulthood, and late adulthood are said to begin. Therefore, each of the remaining chapters on cognitive development (this one, and Chapters 21 and 24) emphasizes only one of these three main research traditions.

This chapter focuses on postformal thought, Chapter 21 on psychometrics, and Chapter 24 on information processing. For all three, some examples extend beyond chronological age boundaries. Each cognitive chapter also includes age-related topics: college education here, expertise in Chapter 21, and wisdom and dementia in Chapter 24. For none of these are the boundaries exact. As you know, some college students are long past emerging adulthood, and some people become wise long before old age.

>> Postformal Thought

Thinking in adulthood differs from earlier thinking in three major ways: It is more practical, more flexible, and more dialectical. Each of these aspects of thinking will be discussed in turn. Taken together, they may constitute a fifth stage of cognitive development, combining a new "ordering of formal operations" with a "necessary subjectivity" (Sinnott, 1998, p. 24). This occurs gradually, not in any particular year or decade. However, it is normally in emerging adulthood that a person first develops the ability to think in this way.

The Practical and the Personal: A Fifth Stage?

postformal thought A proposed adult stage of cognitive development, following Piaget's four stages, that goes beyond adolescent thinking by being more practical, more flexible, and more dialectical (that is, more capable of combining contradictory elements into a comprehensive whole).

The term **postformal thought** originated because several developmentalists agreed that Piaget's fourth stage, formal operational thought, was inadequate to describe adult thinking. They proposed a fifth stage, characterized by "problem finding," not just "problem solving," wherein a person is more open to ideas and less concerned with absolute right and wrong (Yan & Arlin, 1995). As one group of scholars explained, in postformal thought, "one can conceive of multiple logics, choices, or perceptions . . . in order to better understand the complexities and inherent biases in 'truth'" (Griffin et al., 2009, p. 173).

Postformal thinkers do not wait for someone else to present a problem to solve. They take a more flexible and comprehensive approach instead, considering various aspects of a situation beforehand, noting difficulties and anticipating problems, dealing with them rather than denying, avoiding, or procrastinating. As a result, postformal thought is more practical as well as more creative and imaginative than is thought in previous stages (Wu & Chiou, 2008).

As you remember from Chapter 15, adolescents use two modes of thought (dual-processing), but combining them is difficult. They may use formal analysis to distill universal truths, develop arguments, and resolve the world's problems, or they may think spontaneously and emotionally, but they do not combine the two. For example, an adolescent may impulsively join a demonstration against genocide in Darfur but may forget to prepare for a chemistry exam. Both activities are important, but teenagers have difficulty setting priorities. They prefer quick responses. They *can* analyze, but they may not anticipate the consequences of their actions.

Time Management

One way to contrast postformal and formal thinking is to understand how adolescents and adults think in terms of time. In adulthood, intellectual skills are harnessed to real educational, occupational, and interpersonal concerns. Conclusions and consequences matter; setting priorities includes postponing some tasks in order to accomplish others.

Crammed Together Students flock to the Titan Student Union for All Night Study before final exams, making cramming a social experience. This is contrary to what scientific evidence has shown is the best way to learn—that is, through *distributed practice*, which means studying consistently throughout the semester, not bunching it all at the end. Is cramming simply the result of poor time management or is it a rational choice?

As an example familiar to most readers of this text, professors (in contrast to high school teachers) announce assignments and due dates for the entire semester and expect students "to decide for themselves when to do [the work] . . . invoking that dreaded phrase *time management*" (Howard, 2005, p. 15). Emerging adults struggle with this; time management is a challenge that adults gradually master as their cognition matures (Berg, 2008).

In the process of developing postformal thought, adults accept and adapt to the contradictions and inconsistencies of everyday experience, thereby becoming less playful and more practical. They consider most of life's answers to be provisional, not necessarily permanent; they take irrational and emotional factors into account. For example, planning when to begin writing a term paper that is due in a month may include personal emotions and traits (e.g., anxiety, perfectionism), other obligations (at home and at work), and practical considerations (fact checking, library reserves, computer availability, proper formatting). Ignoring all this until the last day is something teenagers might do; emerging adults usually know better.

No one always plans well for the future, however. A common logical error is **delay discounting,** the tendency to undervalue events in the future. If offered $100 now or $110 later, people will usually engage in delay discounting, which leads them to discount the delayed reward and choose the immediate one. Delay discounting occurs at every age; for example, lottery winners usually choose to take half of their winnings immediately, forfeiting the other half, rather than taking all in installments. Adolescents are particularly likely to underestimate delayed consequences, but gradually, over the years of early adulthood, as the prefrontal cortex matures, people become better able to plan ahead. Reflection is characteristic of adult postformal thought (Brookfield, 2009).

This tendency explains a paradox described in the previous chapter. As a result of school classes and media messages, almost all 18-year-olds know the life-threatening risks of drug abuse and unprotected sex. Nonetheless, many consume addictive drugs and have sex with partners whose history they do not know. Why? Delay discounting. Ironically, every psychoactive drug (especially alcohol and marijuana) distorts the sense of time and makes delay discounting more likely.

TSTB, Don't W8 The benefit of texting is its immediacy, the chance to respond TSTB (the sooner the better). Many texters think it rude to W8 (wait) until l8r (later) to reply, despite the potential risks of doing so while driving. Two weeks after this photo of Tina was taken, her state (New Hampshire) made it illegal to text while driving. Many emerging adults nevertheless disregard the future cost of arrest in order to respond to texts without delay.

delay discounting The tendency to undervalue, or downright ignore, future consequences and rewards in favor of more immediate gratification.

Really a Stage?

As you have read, some scholars doubt Piaget's stage theory of child cognition; many more question this fifth stage. Even Piaget never described a postformal stage for adults. Certainly, if *stage* means attaining a new set of intellectual abilities (such as the language explosion that distinguishes sensorimotor from preoperational thought), then adulthood has no stages.

However, as described in Chapter 15, the prefrontal cortex is not fully mature until one's early 20s, and new dendrites connect in adulthood. Moreover, the prefrontal cortex seems particularly connected to social understanding (Barbey et al., 2009). Several studies find that adults tend to think in ways that adolescents do not. For instance, one study of people aged 13 to 45 found that logical skills improved from adolescence to emerging adulthood and then stayed steady, as might be expected as formal operational thinking becomes well established. However, social understanding continued to advance (Demetriou & Bakracevic, 2009). (Social understanding includes knowing how best to interact with other people—making and keeping good friends, responding to social slights, helping others effectively, and so on.)

Of course, context and culture are crucial: A 30-year-old in one place and time may think quite differently from someone the same age in another place and at a different time (Baltes et al., 2006). But non-Western as well as Western cultures describe adult thought as qualitatively different from adolescent thought. In Hinduism, for instance, a period of social embeddedness (requiring social understanding) is thought to begin when people establish families of their own in early adulthood and to last through middle age. Then a new stage appears at which people are expected to be less engaged in immediate social concerns (Saraswathi, 2005).

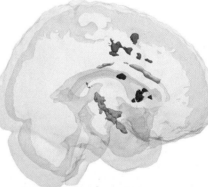

Thinking Away from Home Entering a residential college means experiencing new foods, new friends, and new neurons. A longitudinal study of 18-year-old students at the beginning and end of their first year in college (Dartmouth) found increases in the brain areas that integrate emotion and cognition—namely, the cingulate (blue and yellow), caudate (red), and insula (orange). Researchers also studied one-year changes in the brains of students over age 25 at the same college and found no dramatic growth.

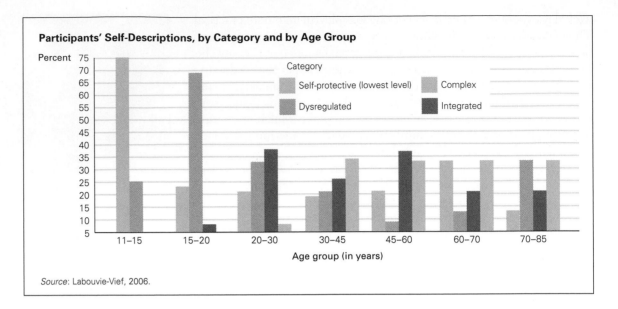

Participants' Self-Descriptions, by Category and by Age Group

Source: Labouvie-Vief, 2006.

FIGURE 18.1

Talk About Yourself People gradually became less self-centered and less confused as they described themselves over the years of adulthood. Many adults, but no children or adolescents, achieved a level of self-acceptance at which emotions and reason were integrated.

In one U.S. study, researchers who did not know the participants' ages categorized self-descriptions as *protective* (high in self-involvement, low in self-doubt), *dysregulated* (fragmented, overwhelmed by emotions or problems), *complex* (valuing openness and independence above all), or *integrated* (able to regulate emotions and logic). As life experiences accumulated, adults expressed themselves differently. No one under age 20 was at the advanced "integrated" stage, but some adults of every age were (see Figure 18.1). The largest shift occurred between adolescence and emerging adulthood (Labouvie-Vief, 2006). As the lead researcher wrote, adult thinking "can be ordered in terms of increasing levels of complexity and integration" (Labouvie-Vief et al., 2009, p. 182).

Thus, many scholars find that thinking changes both qualitatively and quantitatively during adulthood (Bosworth & Hertzog, 2009). The term *fifth stage* may be a misnomer, but adults can and often do reach a new cognitive level when their brains and life circumstances allow it.

Combining Subjective and Objective Thought

subjective thought Thinking that is strongly influenced by personal qualities of the individual thinker, such as past experiences, cultural assumptions, and goals for the future.

objective thought Thinking that is not influenced by the thinker's personal qualities but instead involves facts and numbers that are universally considered true and valid.

One of the practical skills of postformal thinking is the ability to combine subjective and objective thought. **Subjective thought** arises from personal experiences and perceptions; **objective thought** follows abstract, impersonal logic. Traditional models of formal operational thinking value impersonal logic (such as, on Piaget's balance scale, the mathematical relationship between weight and distance) and devalue subjective feelings, personal faith, and emotional experience.

Purely objective, logical thinking may be maladaptive when we are dealing with the complexities and commitments of daily life, especially for social understanding. Subjective feelings and individual experiences must be taken into account because objective reasoning alone is too limited, rigid, and impractical. Yet subjective thinking is also limited. Truly mature thought involves an interaction between abstract, objective forms of processing and expressive, subjective forms, the dual-processing described in Chapter 15. Adult thought does not abandon objectivity; instead, "postformal logic combines subjectivity and objectivity" (Sinnott, 1998, p. 55) to become personal and practical.

Solving the complex problem of combining affect (emotion) and cognition (logic) is the crucial intellectual accomplishment of adulthood. "Emerging adulthood truly does emerge as a somewhat crucial period of the life span . . . [because] complex, critical, and relativizing thinking emerges only in the 20s" (Labouvie-Vief, 2006, p. 78). Without this consolidation of intellect and emotion, behavioral extremes (such as binge eating, anorexia, obesity, addiction, and violence) or cognitive extremes (such as believing that one is the best or the worst person on Earth) are common. Those are typical of the egocentrism of adolescence—and of some emerging adults as well. By contrast, postformal thinkers are better able to balance personal experience with knowledge.

As an example of such balance, an emerging adult named Laura wrote:

> Unfortunately, alcoholism runs in my family. . . . I have seen it tear apart not only my uncle but my family also. . . . I have gotten sick from drinking, and it was the most horrifying night of my life. I know that I didn't have alcohol poisoning or anything, but I drank too quickly and was getting sick. All of these images flooded my head about how I didn't want to ever end up the way my uncle was. From that point on, whenever I have touched alcohol, it has been with extreme caution. . . . When I am old and gray, the last thing I want to be thinking about is where my next beer will come from or how I'll need a liver transplant.
>
> *[Laura, personal communication, 2004]*

Laura's thinking about alcohol is postformal in that it combines knowledge (e.g., of alcohol poisoning) with emotions (images flooding her head). Note that she is cautious, not abstinent: She does not need to go to the extreme of becoming an active alcoholic (as some college students do) and then to the other extreme of avoiding even one sip (as recovering alcoholics must).

This development of postformal thought regarding alcohol is seen in most U.S. adults over time. As explained in the previous chapter, those in their early 20s are more likely than people of any other age to abuse alcohol and other drugs, but with experience and cognitive maturity, most adults drink occasionally and moderately from then on (Schulenberg et al., 2005). Looking at all the research makes it apparent that teenagers tend to use either objective *or* subjective reasoning, but adults can combine the two.

Cognitive Flexibility

The ability to be practical—to predict, to plan, and to combine objective and subjective mental processes—is valuable; it is fortunate that adults can reach that postformal level. However, plans can go awry.

For example, corporate restructuring might require finding another job, a failure of birth control might mean an unwanted pregnancy, a parent's illness might require changing plans for higher education. Almost every adult experiences such events. Those with cognitive flexibility avoid retreating into either emotions or intellect. Research on practical problem solving instead finds that adults, given a complex problem with no pat solution (such as "what to do if your landlord will not pay for expensive repairs?"), reflect on their options, combining emotions and reason, taking time to select the best course of action (Berg, 2008).

Thus, a hallmark of postformal cognition is intellectual flexibility, a characteristic far more typical of emerging adults than of younger people. The "fundamental flux of emerging adulthood" (Tanner et al., 2009, p. 34) comes from the realization that each person's perspective is only one of many, that each problem has many potential solutions, and that knowledge is dynamic, not static. Emerging adults begin to realize that "there are multiple views of the same phenomenon" (Baltes et al., 1998, p. 1093). Listening to others, considering diverse opinions, is a sign of flexibility.

Especially for Someone Who Has to Make an Important Decision Which is better: to go with your gut feelings or to consider pros and cons as objectively as you can? (see response, page 496)

Working Together

Consider this problem:

> Every card in a pack has a letter on one side and a number on the other. Imagine that you are presented with the following four cards, each of which has something on the back. Turn over only those cards that will confirm or disconfirm this proposition: *If a card has a vowel on one side, then it always has an even number on the other side.*
>
> E 7 K 4
>
> Which cards must be turned over?

The difficulty of this puzzle is "notorious" (Moshman, 2005, p. 36). Almost everyone wants to turn over the E and the 4—and almost everyone is mistaken. In one experiment with college students working on their own, 91 percent got it wrong. However, when groups of college students who had guessed wrong on their own later discussed the problem together, 75 percent got it right: They avoided the 4 card (even if it has a consonant on the other side, the statement could still be true) and selected the E and the 7 cards (if the 7 has a vowel on the other side, the proposition is proved false). They were able to think things through, open to change after listening (Moshman & Geil, 1998). This is cognitive flexibility.

Alternate Solutions

Such data on behavioral change could be attributed to many factors other than cognitive flexibility. However, research specifically examining adult cognition finds that adults are more likely than children to imagine several solutions for every problem and then to take care in selecting the best one.

For example, young, middle-aged, and older adults in a particular study were asked to suggest solutions to various life problems (Artistico et al., 2010). Most participants found several possible solutions for each dilemma, as postformal thinkers (but not concrete or formal operational thinkers) usually do. The more familiar the problem, the more possibilities were suggested. For instance, the problem of losing motivation to finish a college degree evoked more solutions from younger adults, but wanting relatives to visit more frequently got more solutions from older adults.

Research on the problem-solving abilities of adults of various ages concludes that emerging adults are better problem solvers than both adolescents and the oldest adults. The reason is cognitive: They are better able to set aside their stereotypes and are not limited by familiar ideas (Klaczynski & Robinson, 2000; Thornton & Dumke, 2005). Openness to new ideas is one of the characteristics of emerging adults and of postformal thinkers (Cartwright et al., 2009; Tanner et al., 2009).

The ability to find multiple solutions to any practical problem is a hallmark of postformal thought (Sinnott, 1998). Of course, individuals differ in their cognitive flexibility, and experience helps. Evidence comes from another study, in which older adults were asked what a man should do if his lawn needs mowing but his doctor has told him to take it easy (Marsiske & Willis, 1995, 1998). Think of as many solutions as you can, and then look at Table 18.1.

If you see solutions that did not occur to you, remember that this problem is more familiar to older adults than to younger adults. After adolescence, when people encounter complex problems, maturity and experience help them become more strategic as well as more flexible: They seek advice and control their initial impulses (Berg, 2008).

>> **Response for Someone Who Has to Make an Important Decision** (from page 495) Both are necessary. Mature thinking requires a combination of emotions and logic. To make sure you use both, take your time (don't just act on your first impulse) and talk with people you trust. Ultimately, you will have to live with your decision, so do not ignore either intuitive or logical thought.

TABLE 18.1

Four Adults' Solutions to an Everyday Problem: Examples of Practical Creativity

Problem: Let's say that a 67-year-old man's doctor has told him to take it easy because of a heart condition. It's summertime and the man's yard needs to be mowed, but the man cannot afford to pay someone to mow the lawn. What should he do?

Subject A

- Do not mow the yard.
- Pray that someone will do it for me . . . Let my church know I have a need . . . Tell any help agency.
- If I have children . . . let them know of my need.

Subject B

- If the man has a yard, he must be living in a house. The best thing he could do would be to sell the house and move into an apartment with no yard or upkeep.
- He could trade services with a younger neighbor. The neighbor would mow his lawn in return for the man walking the neighbor's dog, watching his children, etc.
- He could call his city or county human services department . . . and ask if there are volunteers.
- He could ask a grandson to mow it without pay.

Subject C

- Immediately start planning to live in a situation that is suitable to his condition. Plan ahead.
- In the meanwhile, he should see whether a relative or friend could help him until he changes abode.
- Possibly he could exchange the mowing for some service he can do, like babysitting or tutoring.
- Be sure to get a second medical opinion.
- Talk to his church or organization people. Trade services.
- Check civic organizations.
- Possibly [borrowing] a riding mower might be suitable—until he changes abode.
- Get a part-time job, and earn enough to pay for help.

Subject D

- Move to quarters not having a yard to maintain.
- Cover lawn with black plastic sheeting . . . remove plastic in fall and sow rye grass.
- Rent a room to a man who will care for yard as part payment of room.
- Marry a young physical training teacher who loves yard work.
- Tether sheep in yard.
- Buy a reconditioned remote-controlled power mower, shrubbery, and flowers.
- Plant shade trees.
- Cover yard with river rock and/or concrete and apply weed killer when necessary.
- Plant a vegetable garden in yard.
- Plant a grain seed and sell harvest.

Sources: Marsiske & Willis, 1995, 1998. The problem is from Denney & Pearce, 1989.

Countering Stereotypes

Cognitive flexibility, particularly the ability to change one's childhood assumptions, is needed to counter stereotypes. Daily life for young adults shows many signs of such flexibility. The very fact that emerging adults marry and become parents later than did previous generations suggests that, couple by couple, their thinking processes are not determined by their own childhood family experiences or by traditional norms. Of course, early experiences are influential, but for the postformal thinker they are not determinative.

Stereotypes About Other People

Research on racial prejudice in adulthood merits closer study. Many American children and adults harbor some implicit bias against African Americans, detectable in their slower reaction time when mentally processing photos of African Americans as compared with photos of European Americans (Baron & Banaji, 2006).

By adulthood, however, most people in the United States believe that they are not racially prejudiced, and their behavior reveals no bias (at least in explicit tests in a research laboratory). Thus, many adults have both unconscious prejudice and rational nonprejudice—a combination that illustrates dual-processing. Cognitive flexibility allows adults to recognize their emotional biases and to change their behaviors—both difficult without openness and flexibility.

Stereotype Threat

stereotype threat The possibility that one's appearance or behavior will be misread to confirm another person's oversimplified, prejudiced attitudes.

People are often unaware of their own stereotypes, even when false beliefs harm them. One of the most pernicious is **stereotype threat,** the worry that other people assume that you yourself are stupid, lazy, oversexed, or worse because of your race, sex, age, or appearance. The mere *possibility* of being negatively stereotyped arouses emotions that can disrupt cognition as well as emotional regulation (Spencer et al., in press).

Stereotype threat is likely when circumstances remind a person of a possible threat "in the air," not an overt threat (Steele, 1997). One example begins with a statistic: African American men have lower grades in high school and earn only half as many college degrees as their genetic peers, African American women. This disparity has many possible causes; stereotype threat is one of them (Arnett & Brody, 2008). If African American males are made aware of the stereotype that they are poor scholars, they might become anxious. That anxiety would reduce their ability to focus on academics. Then, if they underachieve, they might disidentify with academic success in order to protect their pride. That would lead to disengagement from studying and ultimately to even lower achievement (Ogbu, 2008).

The Threat of Bias If students fear that others expect them to do poorly in school because of their ethnicity or gender, they might not identify with academic achievement and thus do worse on exams than they otherwise would have.

Observation Quiz Which of these three college students taking an exam is least vulnerable to stereotype threat? (see answer, page 501)

Indeed, exactly that downward pattern seems to occur, but African American men are not the only ones to experience it. Hundreds of studies show that almost all humans are harmed by stereotype threat: Women underperform in math, older people are more forgetful, bilingual students stumble with English, and every member of a stigmatized minority in every nation performs less well. Even those sometimes thought to be on top—White men—do less well in math if they think they will be negatively compared with Asian men, or they do less well in sports if they think they will be compared with African men (Schmader et al., 2008; Spencer et al., in press).

How do unconscious prejudices relate to postformal thought? Since everyone has some childhood stereotypes hidden in the brain, adults need flexible cognition to overcome them, abandoning the prejudices that were learned earlier. Many programs attempt to increase the achievement of individuals whose potential seems unrealized. Surprisingly successful in this regard are colleges that are predominantly for women or African Americans (Astin & Oseguera, 2004; Freeman & Thomas, 2002). Could one reason be that if every student has the same background, stereotype threat is diminished?

CORBIS

But what can reduce stereotype threat when students are a minority? One group of researchers developed a hypothesis: that stereotype threat will decrease and achievement will increase if people *internalize* (believe wholeheartedly, not just intellectually) the idea that intelligence is plastic rather than the inalterable product of one's genetic heritage. These scientists convinced African American college students that their ability depended on their personal efforts. That reduced stereotype threat and led to higher grades (Aronson et al., 2002). (See the Research Design.)

This study, and hundreds of others on stereotypes, provides hope. Instead of denying unconscious emotions about ourselves or others, postformal thinking allows people to overcome fears and anxieties. Is this wishful thinking, or can you recall prejudices you held about others, or about your own ability, that no longer impair your thoughts?

▶ **Research Design**

Scientists: Joshua Aronson, Carrie Fried, and Catherine Good.

Publication: *Journal of Experimental Social Psychology* (2002).

Participants: A total of 79 Stanford undergraduates of both sexes, 42 African American and 37 European American.

Design: Students were divided into three groups. Each group included the same proportions of African American and European American students. Group I had no intervention; Group II learned about multiple intelligences; and Group III learned that intelligence depends on effort, not innate ability. They twice answered questionnaires about attitudes toward college—once before and once after the experiment. IQ scores and college grades were also tallied. For Group I, no special intervention occurred. Students in Groups II and III read a letter supposedly written by a struggling junior high school student and were asked to write an encouraging response that included current research on intelligence. The difference between Groups II and III was in the particular research they learned about (via a video as well as written text), which they were asked to incorporate into their letters. Group II was told about multiple intelligences (see Chapter 11), and Group III was told how intellectual effort can cause new neurons to grow in the brain.

In the second session, for Groups I and II, the experimenter praised their letters and gave them a thank-you note, ostensibly from the younger student. They were then to encourage other young students by preparing a speech, which was videotaped as a first draft and later, at the third session, was taped again in a "final" version. All three sessions were designed to help them internalize a message about intelligence.

Major conclusion: The intervention succeeded. Compared with those in Groups I and II, participants in Group III changed their ideas about their own potential, and African Americans in particular became more favorable about academic achievement, reported more joy in learning, and increased their average grades (see Table 18.2).

TABLE 18.2						
Attitudes and Grades in Academic Term Following Stereotype-Threat Experiment						
	Group I (no intervention)		**Group II (IQ is multiple)**		**Group III (IQ is malleable)**	
	Blacks	Whites	Blacks	Whites	Blacks	Whites
Values placed on academics, from 1 (lowest) to 7 (highest)	3.5	5.7	3.9	5.7	4.8	5.6
Average grade	B	B+	B	B+	B+	A–

Source: Aronson et al., 2002.

Comment: This experiment intrigued thousands of researchers. They realized that this study required replication, since the participants were only 79 students at a highly selective university. Might other stereotyped groups respond differently? Soon thousands of other scientists replicated this study with many other groups. The results confirmed, again and again, that stereotype threat is pervasive and debilitating but that it can be alleviated.

dialectical thought The most advanced cognitive process, characterized by the ability to consider a thesis and its antithesis simultaneously and thus to arrive at a synthesis. Dialectical thought makes possible an ongoing awareness of pros and cons, advantages and disadvantages, possibilities and limitations.

thesis A proposition or statement of belief; the first stage of the process of dialectical thinking.

antithesis A proposition or statement of belief that opposes the thesis; the second stage of the process of dialectical thinking.

synthesis A new idea that integrates the thesis and its antithesis, thus representing a new and more comprehensive level of truth; the third stage of the process of dialectical thinking.

What Would It Take for You to March for a Cure? You know that breast cancer is a serious and all too common disease (affecting about one woman in eight) and that more research on it is needed. This thesis usually results in benign inaction, however; personal experience is often necessary to put antithesis into action. Actress and former model Gabrielle Union's antithesis occurred when her close friend was diagnosed with metastatic breast cancer at age 32. She moved dialectically, from indifference to despair and then to advocacy, first for her friend and then for an entire cause. Using personal tragedy to benefit others is the best kind of dialectical thinking.

Dialectical Thought

With all aspects of postformal thinking, advanced thinking at any point of adulthood is a "promise, not reality" (Labouvie-Vief, 2006). Postformal thought, at its best, becomes **dialectical thought,** said to be the most advanced cognitive process (Basseches, 1984, 1989; Riegel, 1975). The word *dialectic* refers to the philosophical concept, developed by the German philosopher Georg Hegel in the early nineteenth century, that every idea or truth bears within itself the opposite idea or truth.

To use the words of philosophers, each idea, or **thesis,** implies an opposing idea, or **antithesis.** Dialectical thought involves considering both these poles of an idea simultaneously and then forging them into a **synthesis**—that is, a new idea that integrates the original and its opposite. Note that the synthesis is not a compromise; it is a new concept that incorporates both original ones. For example, many young children idolize their parents (thesis), many adolescents are highly critical of their parents (antithesis), and many emerging adults appreciate their parents and forgive their shortcomings, which they attribute to background and age (synthesis).

Because ideas always initiate their opposites, change is continuous in dialectical thought. Each new synthesis deepens and refines the thesis and antithesis that initiated it, with "cognitive development as the dance of adaptive transformation" (Sinnott, 2009, p. 103). Thus, dialectical thinking involves the constant integration of beliefs and experiences with all the contradictions and inconsistencies of daily life.

Educators who agree with Vygotsky that learning is a social interaction within the zone of proximal development (with learners and mentors continually adjusting to each other) take a dialectical approach to education (Vianna & Stetsenko, 2006). Dialectical processes are readily observable by life-span researchers, who believe that "the occurrence and effective mastery of crises and conflicts represent not only risks, but also opportunities for new development" (Baltes et al., 1998, p. 1041). As Chapter 1 emphasized, life-span change is multidirectional, ongoing, and often surprising—a dynamic, dialectical process.

A "Broken" Marriage

Let's look at an example of dialectical thought familiar to many: the end of a love affair. A nondialectical thinker is likely to believe that each person has stable, independent traits. Faced with a troubled romance, then, a nondialectical thinker concludes that one partner (or the other) is at fault, or perhaps the relationship was a mistake from the beginning because the two were a bad match.

By contrast, dialectical thinkers see people and relationships as constantly evolving; partners are changed by time as well as by their interaction. Adjustment is necessary. Therefore, a romance becomes troubled not because the partners are fundamentally incompatible or because one or the other is at fault but because they both have changed without adapting. Marriages do not "break" or "fail"; they either continue to develop over time (dialectically) or they stagnate. Ideally, both members of a relationship develop dialectical processes, with each partner recognizing the needs of the other and moving forward with a new synthesis (McCarthy & McCarthy, 2004).

Does this happen in practice as well as in theory? Possibly. Certainly teenage marriages end in divorce more often than do adult marriages, perhaps because few adolescents think dialectically. People of all ages are upset when a romance fades, but neurological immaturity makes a young person overcome by jealousy or despair unable to find the synthesis (Fisher, 2006). Older couples think more dialectically and therefore move from thesis ("I love you because you are perfect") to antithesis ("I hate you—you can't do anything right") to synthesis ("Neither of us is perfect, but together we can grow").

New demands, roles, responsibilities, and even conflicts become learning opportunities for the dialectical thinker. A student might enroll in a course in an unfamiliar subject, an employee might apply for an unexpected promotion, a young adult might leave his parents' household and move to another town or nation. In such situations, when comfort collides with the desire for growth, dialectical thinkers find a new synthesis, gaining insight (Newirth, 2003).

Dialectical thinking is rare in adolescents, is more often found in middle-aged people, and is connected in complex and sometimes contradictory ways to ethnicity, intellect, and creativity (Paletz & Peng, 2009). Regression is possible. Degradation of complex thinking can be caused by any emotionally charged event. On the other hand, dialectical thinking may be more advanced than simple postformal thinking, at least according to current research in China (Yang et al., 2010), discussed next.

Culture and Dialectics

Several researchers have compared Asian and American adults' cognition, particularly in regard to dialectical thought. It may be that ancient Greek philosophy led Europeans and North Americans to use analytic, absolutist logic—to take sides in a battle between right and wrong, good and evil—whereas Confucianism and Taoism led the Chinese and other Asians to seek compromise, the "Middle Way." Asians tend to think holistically, about the whole rather than the parts, seeking the synthesis because "in place of logic, the Chinese developed a dialectic" (Nisbett et al., 2001, p. 305). One example is in art: Western art tends to focus on objects; Chinese art shows the entire context (Masuda et al., 2008).

A series of studies compared three groups of students: Koreans in Seoul, South Korea; Korean Americans who had lived most of their lives in the United States; and U.S.-born European Americans. Individuals in all three groups were told the following:

> Suppose you are the police officer in charge of a case involving a graduate student who murdered a professor. . . . As a police officer, you must establish motive.
>
> *[Choi et al., 2003]*

Participants were given a list of 97 items of information and were asked to identify the ones they would want to know as they looked for the killer's motive. Some of the 97 items were clearly relevant (e.g., whether the professor had publicly ridiculed the graduate student), and virtually everyone in all three groups chose them. Some were clearly irrelevant (e.g., the graduate student's favorite color), and almost everyone left them out. Other items were questionable (e.g., what the professor was doing that fateful night; how the professor was dressed). Compared with both groups of Americans, the students in Korea asked for 15 more items, on average. The researchers believe that their culture taught them to include the entire context in order to find a holistic, balanced synthesis (Choi et al., 2003).

Dialectical thought affects perspectives, priorities, and values (Masuda et al., 2008). Extensive cross-cultural research on well-being finds that Western adults are happiest when they achieve a personal triumph, but Chinese adults are happiest when they find a synthesis of several social roles (Lu, 2005). Other research

BRIAN SUMMERS / AGEFOTOSTOCK

What Do You See? At first glance, some might see people crossing a busy city street (in downtown Toronto) and perhaps a red light. Others who look longer see the larger context of multicolored buildings, cars as well as taxis and trucks, sun and shade, sky and street signs, and four red lights. If you saw the larger context, is there an Asian influence in your background?

>> Answer to Observation Quiz (from page 498) It depends on what is being tested and on the students' backgrounds. White males are generally least vulnerable, but if the test is about literature and if the male student believes that men are not as good as women at writing about poetry and fiction, his performance on the exam might be affected by that stereotype.

finds a positive correlation between the frequency of experiencing two seemingly opposite emotions—joy and distress—among Americans of Asian heritage as well as among Japanese in Japan. No such correlation was found among European and Hispanic Americans (Scollon et al., 2005). One interpretation is that dialectical thinkers seek a balance of happy and unhappy moments, reminding themselves of certain joys when they are sad and vice versa.

Researchers agree that notable differences between Eastern and Western thought are the result of nurture, not nature—that "cognitive differences have ecological, historical and sociological origins" (Choi et al., 2003, p. 47), not genetic ones. None insist that one way of thinking is always better than the other. In fact, the notion that there is one "best way" is not dialectical, although most developmentalists think that a flexible process of reflection and change is more advanced than simply sticking to one thesis.

SUMMING UP

A fifth stage of cognition, called postformal thought, may follow Piaget's fourth stage of formal operational thought. Postformal thinking entails practical, flexible, and dialectical thought. The real-life responsibilities that are typical in adulthood advance cognition, in part because neither logical analyses nor emotional reactions are adequate for the complex problems of adult life, especially problems involving social cognition. Cognitive advances and flexibility may allow adults to overcome their stereotypes and adapt their long-term relationships. Some adults think dialectically, with thesis leading to antithesis and then synthesis. This ever-changing, dynamic cognition of intellectually advanced adults may be more evident in some contexts and cultures than in others. ■

>> Morals and Religion

According to many researchers, adult responsibilities, experiences, and education affect moral reasoning and religious beliefs. The idea that maturation of values appears first in emerging adulthood and continues through middle age has been the mainstay of research over the past decades, not contradicted by more recent findings. As one expert said:

> Dramatic and extensive changes occur in young adulthood (the 20s and 30s) in
> the basic problem-solving strategies used to deal with ethical issues. . . . These
> changes are linked to fundamental reconceptualizations in how the person
> understands society and his or her stake in it.
>
> *[Rest, 1993, p. 201]*

This expert has found that college education is one stimulus for young adults' shifts in moral reasoning, especially if coursework includes extensive discussion of moral issues or if the student's future profession (such as law or medicine) requires ethical decisions. Even without college, another researcher finds that moral decisions are least likely in early adolescence and that their incidence rises as people mature and confront various issues (Nucci & Turiel, 2009).

Many emerging adults enter college expecting to deepen their values. In a U.S. survey of new college students, about 51 percent said they thought it was very important to develop a meaningful philosophy of life, and almost 70 percent thought it was very important to help other people who were in difficulty (*Chronicle of Higher Education*, 2009, 2010). In general, when students finish college, they report having experienced a "small, steady gain throughout college on developing their own values and ethical standards" (Komives & Nuss, 2005, p. 163).

Which Era? What Place?

As discussed in earlier chapters, moral values are powerfully affected by circumstances, including national background, culture, and era. Indeed, culture determines whether or not a particular issue is a moral one. For example, in the United States, abortion is considered a moral issue, with religious groups making pronouncements, often in absolute terms. This is not the case in Japan, where context (e.g., rape, incest, income) is more important regarding abortion than absolutes (Sahar & Karasawa, 2005).

The power of culture makes it difficult to assess whether adult morality changes with age because changing opinions can be judged as improvements or declines. For example, in the United States, older people tend to be less supportive of gay marriage and more troubled by divorce yet more supportive of public money for mass transit and health. Do these age trends suggest that people become more or less moral? Or is this a cohort difference because these are not really moral issues? Or are older people more stuck in their ways, using morality to justify their intransigence, instead of shifting when popular opinion and practice do? Even on answers to those questions, people disagree, with more older than younger people deciding these are moral issues (see Figure 18.2).

Despite such caveats, the research does indicate that the process (although not necessarily the outcome) of moral thinking improves with age. At least adult thinking may be more varied than adolescent thinking. As one scholar explains it, "The evolved human brain has provided humans with cognitive capacity that is so flexible and creative that every conceivable moral principle generates opposition and counter principles" (Kendler, 2002, p. 503).

Evidence for moral growth abounds in biographical and autobiographical literature. Most readers of this book probably know someone (or might even be that someone) who had a narrow, shallow outlook on the world at age 18 and then developed a broader, deeper perspective in adulthood. Few scientific studies of moral development have been published, but at least one longitudinal study found that individuals grew in understanding and empathy between adolescence and adulthood (Eisenberg et al., 2005). Many people would consider more open, dialectical, and flexible thinking (as in the postformal thinking just described) to also be more moral.

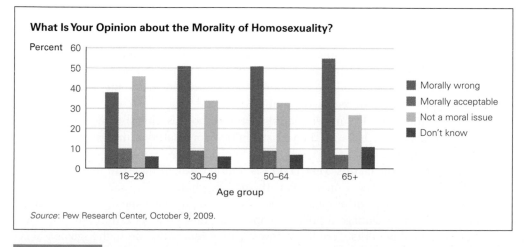

FIGURE 18.2

Don't Judge Me On many issues, not only this one, older adults are more likely to judge something right or wrong than are younger adults. Your own judgment may reflect your age and personal experience more than anything else.

Dilemmas for Emerging Adults

It is fortunate that adolescent egocentrism ebbs, because emerging adults often experience dilemmas that seem to raise moral issues. Most are no longer bound by their parents' rules or by their childhood culture, but they are not yet connected to a family of their own. As a result, they must decide for themselves what to do about sex, drugs, education, vocation, and many other matters.

Gender Differences

There is widespread disagreement about whether there are gender differences in morality. Carol Gilligan, a Harvard professor who challenged some of Kohlberg's work, believes that decisions about reproduction advance moral thinking, especially for women (Gilligan, 1981; Gilligan et al., 1990). According to Gilligan, the two sexes think differently about parenthood, abortion, and so on. Girls are raised to develop a **morality of care.** They give human needs and relationships the highest priority. In contrast, boys develop a **morality of justice;** they are taught to distinguish right from wrong.

Other research does not find gender differences in moral thinking. Factors such as education, specific dilemmas (some situations evoke care and some justice), and culture correlate more strongly than gender with whether a person's moral judgments emphasize relationships or absolutes (Juujärvi, 2005; Vikan et al., 2005; Walker, 1984). For example, a longitudinal study of high school students who were exceptionally talented in math found that as adults, the men were more likely to have advanced degrees in science and math and to be leaders in various fields of science, whereas many of the equally talented women had chosen to devote more time to their families (Ferriman et al., 2009). Is that a moral difference, a cultural pattern, or a gender one?

In any case, emerging adulthood is "a crucial time for the development of a world view" (Arnett, 2004, p. 166) about sex, relationships, career, and lifestyle. Finding a job and new friends, meeting coworkers and neighbors—all within a global economy and with advanced communications (Internet, satellite videos, international music)—means that contemporary emerging adults learn about ethical principles that differ radically from their own. Because these experiences cluster in early adulthood, young adults think deeply about moral issues.

Measuring Moral Growth

How can we assess whether a person uses postformal thinking regarding moral choices? In Lawrence Kohlberg's scheme (described in Chapter 13), people discuss standard moral dilemmas, responding however they choose to various probes. Over decades of longitudinal research, Kohlberg noted that some respondents in his sample seemed to regress at young adulthood, from postconventional to conventional thought. On further analysis of the responses, this shift was found to be a potential advance because the young adults incorporated human social concerns (Labouvie-Vief, 2006).

The **Defining Issues Test (DIT)** is another way to measure moral thinking. The DIT has a series of questions with specific choices. For example, in one DIT dilemma, a news reporter must decide whether to publish some old personal information that will damage a political candidate. Respondents rank their priorities, from personal benefits ("credit for investigative reporting") to higher goals ("serving society"). This ranking of items leads to a number score, which correlates with other aspects of adult cognition, experience, and life satisfaction (Schiller, 1998). In general, DIT scores rise with age because adults gradually become less doctrinaire and self-serving and more flexible and altruistic (Rest et al., 1999).

morality of care In Gilligan's view, moral principles that reflect the tendency of females to be reluctant to judge right and wrong in absolute terms because they are socialized to be nurturant, compassionate, and nonjudgmental.

morality of justice In Gilligan's view, moral principles that reflect the tendency of males to emphasize justice over compassion, judging right and wrong in absolute terms.

Defining Issues Test (DIT) A series of questions developed by James Rest and designed to assess respondents' level of moral development by having them rank possible solutions to moral dilemmas.

A study of adolescents and young adults in the Netherlands found intriguing results when they were given the DIT (Raaijmakers, 2005). Although there were many individual differences, some age trends were apparent: The responses of the participants shifted from justification for past behavior (adolescents) to guidance for future behavior (emerging adults). In adolescence, DIT scores gradually rose among those who rarely broke the law. However, for delinquents, DIT scores rose later but *preceded* a drop in delinquency. For emerging adults, then, moral thinking may produce moral behavior, not just vice versa.

Stages of Faith

A similar process may occur for the development of faith. Spiritual struggles, including "questioning one's religious/spiritual beliefs, feeling unsettled about religious or spiritual matters, struggling to understand evil, illness, and death, feeling angry at God" (Bryant & Astin, 2008, p. 3), are not unusual for emerging adults. Maturation may move them past the doctrinaire religion of childhood to a more flexible, dialectical, postformal faith. To describe this process, James Fowler (1981, 1986) developed a sequence of six stages of faith, building on the work of Piaget and Kohlberg:

- *Stage 1: Intuitive-projective faith.* Faith is magical, illogical, imaginative, and filled with fantasy, especially about the power of God and the mysteries of birth and death. It is typical of children ages 3 to 7.
- *Stage 2: Mythic-literal faith.* Individuals take the myths and stories of religion literally, believing simplistically in the power of symbols. God is seen as rewarding those who follow divine laws and punishing others. Stage 2 is typical from ages 7 to 11, but it also characterizes some adults. Fowler cites a woman who says extra prayers at every opportunity, to put them "in the bank."
- *Stage 3: Synthetic-conventional faith.* This is a conformist stage. Faith is conventional, reflecting concern about other people and favoring "what feels right" over what makes intellectual sense. Fowler quotes a man whose personal rules include "being truthful with my family. Not trying to cheat them out of anything. . . . I'm not saying that God or anybody else set my rules. I really don't know. It's what I feel is right."
- *Stage 4: Individual-reflective faith.* Faith is characterized by intellectual detachment from the values of the culture and from the approval of other people. College may be a springboard to stage 4, as the young person learns to question the authority of parents, teachers, and other powerful figures and to rely instead on his or her own understanding of the world. Faith becomes an active commitment.
- *Stage 5: Conjunctive faith.* Faith incorporates both powerful emotional ideas (such as the power of prayer and the love of God) and rational conscious values (such as the worth of life compared with that of property). People are willing to accept contradictions, obviously a postformal manner of thinking. Fowler says that this cosmic perspective is seldom achieved before middle age.
- *Stage 6: Universalizing faith.* People at this stage have a powerful vision of universal compassion, justice, and love that compels them to live their lives in a way that others may think is either saintly or foolish. A transforming experience

The Same Situation, Many Miles Apart: A Mature Faith In every religion, traditions and beliefs are passed down directly from the elders, as in the ordination of Roman Catholic priests in Paris *(top)* and the initiation of Buddhist monks in Thailand *(bottom)*. Does this indicate that moral thinking advances with experience?

is often the gateway to stage 6, as happened to Moses, Muhammad, the Buddha, and Saint Paul, as well as more recently to Mohandas Gandhi, Martin Luther King Jr., and Mother Teresa. Stage 6 is rarely achieved.

Although not everyone agrees with Fowler's particular stages, many people rely on faith to combat stress, overcome adversity, and analyze challenges. If Fowler is correct, faith, like other aspects of cognition, progresses from a simple, self-centered, one-sided perspective to a more complex, altruistic (unselfish), and many-sided view. Other evidence also suggests that faith develops over the years of adulthood, with emerging adults less likely than older or younger people to attend religious services and to pray (Wilhelm et al., 2007), even though most consider themselves at least as spiritual as they were when younger (Smith & Snell, 2009).

In any case, like almost all forms of thinking and analyzing, faith changes as life does. Cognition in adulthood is not stagnant. It is difficult, however, to imagine that one's own thinking, or morality, or faith is less advanced than it will be in another decade or two. My own experience is one example.

THINKING CRITICALLY

Faith and Tolerance

When I was in college, I spoke with a young woman whose religious beliefs seemed naive. She hadn't given her faith much thought. Wanting to deepen her thinking without being harsh, I asked, "How can you be so sure of what you believe?"

Instead of recognizing the immaturity of her thought, she startled me by replying, "I hope that someday you reach the certainty that I have."

In the years since that conversation, I have encountered many other people whose religious beliefs seem too pat, too unquestioning, too immature. Might they likewise think that my faith is less advanced than theirs? When people tell me that they are praying for my family and me, I now respond graciously, not judging their beliefs. Is this more flexible, dialectical? Has my own faith moved up the hierarchy that Fowler described?

Hunter Lewis (2000) observed that "people need to consider their own values, consider them seriously, consider them for themselves" (p. 248). I agree, and I think Fowler's description of six stages of faith aids such consideration. There is a problem, however. Do religious beliefs really advance? Few people are at the upper stages of Fowler's or Kohlberg's hierarchy, which implies that most of us are immature.

Judging someone else's faith, as Fowler seems to do, may be arrogant and self-satisfied—traits antithetical to my beliefs. Yet as a teacher, I assess my students' cognitive growth and delight when they question established beliefs. Is this one of the paradoxes that signifies postformal thinking, or am I justifying a particular set of values? It troubles me to describe stages of faith that are beyond most adults. I hope I am at stage 6, or at least 5. But at least I recognize that my own faith may be less advanced than I imagine.

SUMMING UP

Moral issues challenge cognitive processes as adults move beyond the acceptance of authority in childhood and beyond the reactive rebellion of adolescence. Cultural values, including gender norms, always affect beliefs, so it may not be valid to judge anyone else's morality. Some people become more open and reflective in their moral judgments and religious faith. As globalism advances, young adults encounter conflicting value systems and divergent religions; this exposure presents cognitive challenges. It is not obvious that some people are more advanced in morals and faith than others, although postformal thinking should advance moral judgment as well as other forms of thinking.

>> Cognitive Growth and Higher Education

Many readers of this textbook have a personal interest in the final topic of this chapter, the relationship between college education and cognition. All the evidence is positive: College graduates seem to be not only healthier and wealthier than other adults but also deeper and more flexible thinkers. These conclusions are so powerful that scientists view them with suspicion: Might selection effects or historical trends, rather than college education itself, lead to such encouraging correlations? Let us look at the data.

The Effects of College

Contemporary students attend college primarily to secure better jobs and to learn specific skills (especially in knowledge and service industries, such as information technology, global business, and health care). Their secondary goal is general education (Komives & Nuss, 2005). This is true not only in the United States (see Figure 18.3) but also in many other nations (Jongbloed et al., 1999).

One of my 18-year-old students acknowledged both goals:

> A higher education provides me with the ability to make adequate money so I can provide for my future. An education also provides me with the ability to be a mature thinker and to attain a better understanding of myself. . . . An education provides the means for a better job after college, which will support me and allow me to have a stable, comfortable retirement.

[E., personal communication]

Such worries about future costs and retirement may seem premature, but E. is not alone. More than half of all U.S. students take out loans to pay for college, 80 percent are employed while they are students, and many are concerned about these debts and their economic future. This is an example where delay discounting is not appropriate, since statistics confirm the economic value of college. For example, in the year 2007 in the United States, the average annual income of full-time workers with a BA degree was $73,000, compared with $36,000 for people with only a high school diploma (U.S. Bureau of the Census, 2009).

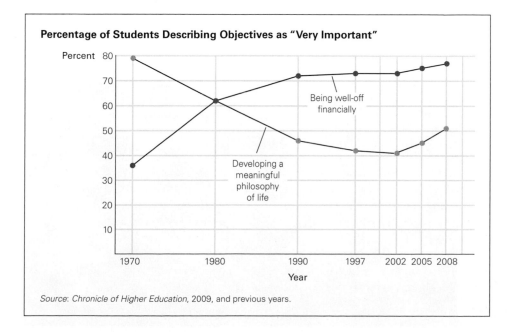

Percentage of Students Describing Objectives as "Very Important"

Being well-off financially

Developing a meaningful philosophy of life

Source: Chronicle of Higher Education, 2009, and previous years.

FIGURE 18.3

Wealth Versus Wisdom First-year college students have been surveyed every year. Cohort shifts are particularly significant regarding income.

Observation Quiz Does a generation gap exist between current professors and their students? (see answer, page 508)

>> Answer to Observation Quiz (from page 507) Maybe. If their professors are in their 60s and have not changed their values since their college days, a large gap is apparent. Other evidence presented in this chapter, however, suggests that neither of these conditions necessarily holds.

College also correlates with better health: College graduates everywhere smoke less, eat better, exercise more, and live longer. They are also more likely to be spouses, homeowners, and parents of healthy children. Does something gained in college—perhaps knowledge, self-control, confidence, better job prospects—affect health?

Looking specifically at cognitive development, does college make people more likely to combine the subjective and objective in a flexible, dialectical way? Probably. College improves verbal and quantitative abilities, adds knowledge of specific subject areas, teaches skills in various professions, fosters reasoning and reflection. According to one comprehensive review:

> Compared to freshmen, seniors have better oral and written communication skills, are better abstract reasoners or critical thinkers, are more skilled at using reason and evidence to address ill-structured problems for which there are no verifiably correct answers, have greater intellectual flexibility in that they are better able to understand more than one side of a complex issue, and can develop more sophisticated abstract frameworks to deal with complexity.
>
> *[Pascarella & Terenzini, 1991, p. 155]*

Note that many of these abilities characterize postformal thinking.

Some research finds that thinking becomes more reflective and expansive with *each year* of college (Clinchy, 1993; King & Kitchener, 1994; Perry, 1981). First-year students believe that clear and perfect truths exist; they are distressed if their professors do not explain these truths. Freshmen tend to gather knowledge as if facts were nuggets of gold, each one separate from other bits of knowledge and each one pure and true. One first-year student said he was like a squirrel, "gleaning little acorns of knowledge and burying them for later use" (quoted in Bozik, 2002, p. 145).

This initial phase is followed by a wholesale questioning of personal and social values, including doubts about the idea of truth itself. If a professor makes an assertion without extensive analysis and evidence, upper-level students are skeptical. No fact is taken at face value, much less stored intact for future use.

Finally, as graduation approaches, after considering many ideas, students become committed to certain values, even as they realize their opinions might change (Pascarella & Terenzini, 1991; Rest et al., 1999). Facts have become neither gold nor dross, but rather useful steps toward a greater understanding.

Thumbs Up! These graduates in Long Beach, California, are joyful that they have reached a benchmark. Ideally, their diplomas will earn them not only better jobs but also an intellectual perspective that will help them all their lives.

LOUISE GUBB / CORBIS

TABLE 18.3			
		Perry's Scheme of Cognitive and Ethical Development During College	
Freshmen	Position 1	Authorities know, and if we work hard, read every word, and learn Right Answers, all will be well.	
Dualism modified	Transition	But what about those Others I hear about? And different opinions? And Uncertainties? Some of our own Authorities disagree with each other or don't seem to know, and some give us problems instead of Answers	
	Position 2	True Authorities must be Right, the others are frauds. We remain Right. Others must be different and Wrong. Good Authorities give us problems so we can learn to find the Right Answer by our own independent thought	
	Transition	But even Good Authorities admit they don't know all the answers yet!	
	Position 3	Then some uncertainties and different opinions are real and legitimate temporarily, even for Authorities. They're working on them to get to the Truth.	
	Transition	But there are so many things they don't know the Answers to! And they won't for a long time	
Relativism discovered	Position 4a	Where Authorities don't know the Right Answers, everyone has a right to his own opinion; no one is wrong!	
	Transition	Then what right have They to grade us? About what?	
	Position 4b	In certain courses, Authorities are not asking for the Right Answer. They want us to think about things in a certain way, supporting opinion with data. That's what they grade us on.	
	Position 5	Then all thinking must be like this, even for Them. Everything is relative but not equally valid. You have to understand how each context works. Theories are not Truth but metaphors to interpret data with. You have to think about your thinking.	
	Transition	But if everything is relative, am I relative, too? How can I know I'm making the Right Choice?	
	Position 6	I see I'm going to have to make my own decisions in an uncertain world with no one to tell me I'm Right.	
	Transition	I'm lost if I don't. When I decide on my career (or marriage or values), everything will straighten out.	
Commitments in relativism developed	Position 7	Well, I've made my first Commitment!	
	Transition	Why didn't that settle everything?	
	Position 8	I've made several commitments. I've got to balance them—how many, how deep? How certain, how tentative?	
	Transition	Things are getting contradictory. I can't make logical sense out of life's dilemmas.	
Seniors	Position 9	This is how life will be. I must be wholehearted while tentative, fight for my values yet respect others, believe my deepest values right yet be ready to learn. I see that I shall be retracing this whole journey over and over—but, I hope, more wisely.	

Source: Perry, 1981, 1999.

According to one classic study (Perry, 1981, 1999), thinking progresses through nine levels of complexity over the four years that lead to a bachelor's degree, moving from a simplistic either/or dualism (right or wrong, success or failure) to a relativism that recognizes a multiplicity of perspectives (see Table 18.3). Perry found that the college experience itself causes this progression: Peers, professors, books, and class discussion all stimulate new questions and thoughts. In general, the more years of higher education and of life experience a person has, the deeper and more dialectical that person's reasoning becomes (Pascarella & Terenzini, 1991).

Which aspect of college is the primary catalyst for such growth? Is it the challenging academic work, professors' lectures, peer discussions, the new setting, living away from home? All are possible. Every scientist finds that social interaction and intellectual challenge advance thinking. College students expect classes and conversations to further their thinking—which is exactly what occurs (Kuh et al., 2005). This is not surprising, since development is a dialectical process between individuals and social structures, and college is an institution dedicated to fostering cognitive growth. Teachers and students alike can achieve postformal thought because of college, as the following suggests.

Especially for Those Considering Studying Abroad Given the effects of college, would it be better for a student to study abroad in the first year or last year of a college education? (see response, page 510)

College Advancing Thought

One of the leading thinkers in postformal thought is Jan Sinnott, a professor and now editor of the *Journal of Adult Development*. She describes the first course she taught:

> I did not think in a postformal way. . . . Teaching was good for passing information from the informed to the uninformed. . . . I decided to create a course in the psychology of aging . . . with a fellow graduate student. Being compulsive graduate students had paid off in our careers so far, so my colleague and I continued on that path. Articles and books and photocopies began to take over my house. And having found all this information, we seem to have unconsciously sworn to use all of it. . . .
>
> Each class day, my colleague and I would arrive with reams of notes and articles and lecture, lecture, lecture. Rapidly! . . . The discussion of death and dying came close to the end of the term (naturally). As I gave my usual jam-packed lecture, the sound of note taking was intense. But toward the end of the class . . . an extremely capable student burst into tears and said she had to drop the class. . . . Unknown to me, she had been the caretaker

of an older relative who had just died in the past few days. She had not said anything about this significant experience when we lectured on caretaking. . . . How could she? . . . We never stopped talking. "I wish I could tell people what it's really like," she said.

[*Sinnott, 2008, pp. 54–55*]

Sinnott changed her lesson plan. In the next class, the student told her story.

> In the end, the students agreed that this was a class when they . . . synthesized material and analyzed research and theory critically.

[*Sinnott, 2008, p. 56*]

Sinnott writes that she still lectures and gives multiple-choice exams, but she also realizes the impact of the personal story. She combines analysis and emotion; she includes the personal experiences of the students. Her teaching became postformal, dialectical, and responsive.

Changes in the College Context

You probably noticed that Perry's study was first published in 1981. He studied Harvard undergraduates. His decades-old conclusions may no longer apply, especially because both sides of the dialectic—students and faculty—have changed. Many recent books criticize colleges. Administrators and faculty still hope for intellectual growth, but the college context has changed. Has cognition suffered because of it?

Changes in the Students

College is no longer for the elite few. Far more emerging adults are in college today than ever before. For instance, in the first half of the twentieth century, fewer than one in every twenty young adults in western Europe, Japan, and North America earned a college degree—and only one in a thousand did so in the rest of the world. By contrast, in developed nations in 2010, almost one in two emerging adults earns a degree. In some nations, more than half of all 25- to 34-year-olds are college graduates (Canada, Korea, Russia, and Japan), with the United States ranking 12th, at about 41 percent (Montgomery & Williams, 2010; UNESCO, 2009). The percentages are far lower in Latin America, Africa, and Asia, but the rates of college graduation worldwide have multiplied in the past few decades. In 2010, China had more college graduates than the United States.

Not only have the numbers increased, but so have the demographics. The most obvious change is gender: In 1970, most college students were male; now in every developed nation (except Germany), most are female. In addition, ethnic, economic, religious, and cultural backgrounds are more varied. Compared to 1970, more students are parents, are older than age 24, attend part time, and live and

>> Response for Those Considering Studying Abroad (from page 509) Since one result of college is that students become more open to other perspectives while developing their commitment to their own values, foreign study might be most beneficial after several years of college. If they study abroad too early, some students might be either too narrowly patriotic (they are not yet open) or too quick to reject everything about their national heritage (they have not yet developed their own commitments).

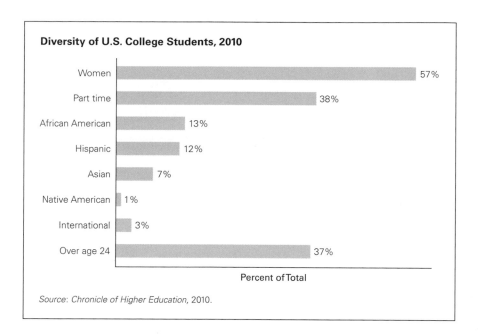

Diversity of U.S. College Students, 2010

Women	57%
Part time	38%
African American	13%
Hispanic	12%
Asian	7%
Native American	1%
International	3%
Over age 24	37%

Percent of Total

Source: *Chronicle of Higher Education*, 2010.

FIGURE 18.4

All Kinds of People If anything, this graph underestimates the diversity of the student body. For example, students who are full time for half the year and who work the other half are still considered full time. Another statistic summarizes the point: At one time, the typical college student was a full-time, single, European American emerging-adult male. Today, such individuals comprise only about 20 percent of the student body.

work off-campus—all true worldwide. Figure 18.4, which shows rates from the United States, makes the point.

Student experiences, histories, skills, and goals are changing as well. Most students are technologically savvy, having spent more hours using computers than watching television or reading. Personal blogs, chat rooms, and pages on Facebook and MySpace have exploded, often unbeknownst to college staff. College majors are changing. Fewer students concentrate in the liberal arts and more specialize in business and the professions (e.g., law and medicine). Students have different priorities today: Fewer seek general education and more seek financial security (see Figure 18.5).

The Same Situation, Many Miles Apart: Calculus Confusion College math has never been easy, be it at Grossmont College in California *(left)* or at the University of Chitre in Panama *(right)*. Nonetheless, many believe it fosters numeracy—the ability to understand numbers and statistics, an increasingly important ability for contemporary adults. Many aspects of human development, from risk analysis to research validity, depend on an understanding of math concepts.

Observation Quiz Although math has always been part of the college curriculum, two recent changes in college math classes are evident in both settings here. What are they? (see answer, page 512)

FIGURE 18.5

Personal Aspirations Note that raising a family and helping others are valued by today's 18-year-olds almost as much as wealth, and that close to one-fourth do not consider financial success very important. This may come as a surprise to many elders who, for example, regard the high rate of emerging adults' having premarital sex as immoral. Most developmentalists think contemporary 18-year-olds' priorities are just where they should be; later in life, their preferences might include more politics, poetry, and the arts.

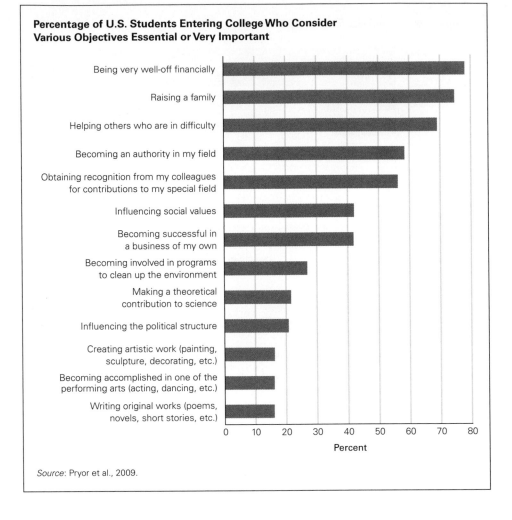

Percentage of U.S. Students Entering College Who Consider Various Objectives Essential or Very Important

Source: Pryor et al., 2009.

>> Answer to Observation Quiz (from page 511) Every student has a calculator (forbidden 50 years ago) and there are more women than men (women once shied away from college math).

Changes in the Institutions

As students are changing, so are colleges. Some nations, including China and Saudi Arabia, have recently built huge new universities. The United States has more than twice as many institutions of higher learning as it did 50 years ago. In 1955 in the United States, only 275 junior colleges existed; in 2010 there were almost 1,500 such colleges, now called community colleges. For-profit colleges were scarce until about 1980; now the United States has more than 1,300 of them. For 12 percent of four-year colleges, tuition (not room and board) costs more than $30,000 per year (*Chronicle of Higher Education*, 2010).

Other changes are evident. Compared with earlier decades, colleges today offer more career programs and hire more part-time faculty, more women, and more minorities. The proportion of tenured full professors who are European American males has decreased, although they still predominate; in 2008 in the United States, almost three-fourths of faculty at the top rank were men. The trend toward more non-White and part-time faculty is worldwide.

Enrollment in public colleges has expanded, with more than 25,000 undergraduates at *each* of 100 public universities in the United States. Private colleges still outnumber public ones by a ratio of about 3 to 2, but most U.S. college students (75 percent, about 14 million) attend publicly sponsored institutions. They are less expensive for students than private colleges, but no U.S. college is free.

Even students on full scholarships must pay for many items, including transportation, and every student earns less because they spend so much time in school.

Income, not ability, continues to be the most significant influence on whether a particular emerging adult will attend college and, once enrolled, will graduate (Bowen et al., 2009). In the United States, only 9 percent of the 24-year-olds in the lowest income bracket (family income below $38,340) have a bachelor's degree; the comparable statistic for those with family income above $107,000 is 54 percent (*Chronicle of Higher Education*, 2010). Noncompletion is particularly high among community college students. When they enroll, 80 percent say they are likely to earn a bachelor's degree; less than 20 percent do.

The chance of leaving college without a degree becomes greater as income falls, as the size of the college increases, and as other life obligations (such as employment and parenthood) accumulate (Bowen et al., 2009).

Distance Without Distance Online classes, in which students complete assignments and discuss issues via the Internet, were designed for those who live abroad or in distant rural areas. But they've become so popular that even some on-campus students use them to enhance their college experience. This senior at Black Hills University in South Dakota completes a distance-learning assignment while sitting in the college library.

Evaluating the Changes

This situation again raises the question of what today's students get out of attending college. The major changes just described might mean that college no longer produces the "greater intellectual flexibility" that earlier research found (Pascarella & Terenzini, 1991). Again, let's consider the data.

Diversity and Enrollment

All the evidence on cognition reviewed in this chapter suggests that interactions with people of different backgrounds and various views lead to intellectual challenges and deeper thought. Thus, the increased diversity of the student body is more likely to encourage learning than to discourage it. Colleges that make use of their diversity—via curriculum, class assignments, discussions, cooperative education, learning communities, and so on—help students stretch their understanding, not only of differences and similarities among people but also of themselves (Nagda et al., 2005). Young adults of all backgrounds are likely to benefit.

Of course, college education does not automatically produce a leap ahead in cognitive development. College tends to advance income, promote health, deepen thinking, and increase tolerance of differing political, social, and religious views, but not every student receives these benefits; nor is college the only path to cognitive growth.

Nonetheless, listening to students and professors from diverse backgrounds, thinking new thoughts, and reading scholarly books almost always broaden a person's perspective. College classes that are career-based, as well as courses in the liberal arts, raise ethical questions and promote moral thinking. Higher education still seems to be "a transforming element in human development" (Benjamin, 2003, p. 11).

A special benefit may come from students who are parents, are employed, attend school part time, and are older than 30. They enliven conversations and discussions with their fellow students. These students themselves make some crucial choices: Full-time study and part-time work are much more likely to foster learning than the opposite combination (Pascarella, 2005), which means that students of all backgrounds learn more if they involve themselves in the campus community. Some research suggests that those from the least wealthy backgrounds are most likely to benefit from a college degree. However, they are also the most likely to leave before graduation (Bowen et al., 2009).

Graduates and Dropouts

If postformal thinking—the ability to cope with the complexities of personal emotions and logical decision making—is the result of higher education, does a high dropout rate mean that many college students never reach that level of cognition? Do frustrating curricula, time-management complications, social challenges, and financial requirements prevent them from reaping the benefits of college? According to one research team, many young students lack the cultural knowledge or cognitive maturity to acquire the "social know-how" needed to navigate through college. Some "adapt to complexities better as they proceed through college," but that depends on their staying long enough to attain "basic skills or increased maturity" (Deil-Amen & Rosenbaum, 2003, p. 141).

Private, 4-year colleges offer advantages to young adults of all income levels and backgrounds, including less risk of dropping out (Bowen et al., 2009). By contrast, the expansion of public institutions and community colleges may make it harder for students to acquire the skills they need. However, "the extent of learning and cognitive growth that happens during the first year of college does not appear to be highly dependent on the characteristics of the institution one attends" (Pascarella, 2005, p. 130). Much more important are the student's openness to learning, engagement with education, and motivation.

A correlation between college education and later income is stronger currently than it was a few generations ago because fewer unskilled jobs are available and more knowledge-based jobs have been created. Though not perfect (1 percent of those in the top one-fifth income bracket are not high school graduates), the correlation is very high (77 percent in that top bracket have at least a bachelor's degree) (Swanson, 2007).

Skeptical readers might question linking college graduation to a wealthier and happier adulthood, since student characteristics before college affect their success

Among All Adults The percentage of U.S. residents with diplomas is increasing, as more of the oldest cohort (often without degrees) dies and the youngest cohorts aim for college. However, many people are insufficiently educated and less likely to find good jobs. It is not surprising that in the current recession, college enrollment is increasing. International data find that many European and East Asian nations have higher rates of degree holders.

Observation Quiz These data can be seen as encouraging or disappointing. What are both interpretations? (see answer, page 517)

TABLE 18.4			
Is High School Enough?			
Year	At Least a High School Diploma	An Associate Degree	At Least a Bachelor's Degree
Overall			
2000	81.4%	6.1%	24%
2008	85	7.5	28
European American			
2000	85.5	6.6	27
2008	91	7.9	30.7
African American			
2000	72.3	5.8	14.3
2008	80.7	7.4	17.5
Asian American			
2000	80.4	6.6	44.1
2008	85.1	6.6	49.7
Hispanic American			
2000	52.4	4.3	10.4
2008	60.8	5.3	12.9

Source: Robelen, 2010.

United States? Canada? Guess Again!
These students attend the University of Capetown in South Africa, where previous cohorts of Blacks and Whites would never have been allowed to socialize so freely. Such interactions foster learning, as long as stereotype threat does not interfere.

later on. Obviously, selection factors mean that students who are studious and financially secure are likely to apply to college, be admitted, and then graduate. However, when selection effects are taken into account, college still aids cognitive development. Even one year of college can make a difference. One expert explains:

> The growth in some content areas (e.g., English, mathematics, social sciences) and in critical thinking that occurs during the first year of college represents a substantial part of the total growth in those areas attributable to the undergraduate experience.
>
> *[Pascarella, 2005, p. 130]*

A valid comparison can be made with young adults who never attend college. When 18-year-old high school graduates of similar backgrounds and abilities are compared, those who begin jobs rather than college immediately after graduation eventually achieve less and are less satisfied by middle age than those who earned a college degree (Schulenberg et al., 2005). Even by age 24, those who attended college and postponed parenthood are more thoughtful, more secure, and seem to be better positioned for a successful adulthood (Osgood et al., 2005).

For many readers, none of this comes as a surprise. Tertiary education stimulates thought, no matter how old the student is. From first-year orientation to graduation, emerging adults do more than learn facts and skills pertaining to their majors: They think deeply and reflectively, as you and other postformal thinkers do.

SUMMING UP

Many life experiences advance thinking processes. College is one of them, as years of classroom discussion, guided reading, and conversations with fellow students from diverse backgrounds lead students to engage in more dynamic and dialectical reasoning. College enrollments have increased in many nations, particularly at publicly supported colleges and universities. A major problem is that many students drop out, but even a little higher education seems to advance cognition. Although the context differs from that of a few decades ago, college education still promotes cognitive development. ■

SUMMARY

Postformal Thought

1. Adult cognition can be studied in any of several ways: using a postformal approach, a psychometric approach, or an information-processing approach. This chapter focuses on postformal thinking.

2. Many researchers believe that, in adulthood, the complex and conflicting demands of daily life sometimes produce a new cognitive perspective, which can be called postformal thought. Postformal thinking is not the automatic result of maturation, so it is not a traditional "stage," but it is a higher level of thought.

3. Postformal thought is practical, flexible, and dialectical. Adults use their minds to solve the problems that they encounter, anticipating and deflecting difficulties.

4. One hallmark of adult thought is the ability to combine emotions and rational analysis. This ability is particularly useful in responding to social understanding and actions, because each relationship requires complex and flexible responses.

5. Stereotypes and stereotype threat interrupt thinking processes and thus can make people seem intellectually less capable. Ideally, adults find ways to overcome such liabilities.

6. Dialectical thinking synthesizes complexities and contradictions. Instead of seeking absolute, immutable truths, dialectical thought recognizes that people and situations are dynamic, ever-changing.

Morals and Religion

7. Thinking about questions of morality, faith, and ethics may also progress in adulthood. Specific moral opinions are strongly influenced by culture and context, but adults generally become less self-centered as they mature.

8. As people mature, life confronts them with ethical decisions, including many related to human relationships and the diversity of humankind. According to Fowler, religious faith also moves toward universal principles, past culture-bound concepts.

Cognitive Growth and Higher Education

9. Research over the past several decades indicates not only that college graduates are wealthier and healthier than other adults but also that they think at a more advanced level. Over the years of college, students gradually become less inclined to seek absolute truths from authorities and more inclined to make their own decisions.

10. Today's college students are unlike those of a few decades ago. In every nation, the sheer number of students has multiplied, and students' backgrounds are more diverse ethnically, economically, and in every other way.

11. Colleges as institutions have also changed, becoming larger, more focused on careers in business and health care, and less focused on knowledge for the sake of knowledge. In addition, enrollment in publicly funded institutions has increased. The cost of college has become a major consideration for many in the United States.

12. Not only students but also faculty are more often part time and of many backgrounds, although the older, established professors are still more often men of European heritage.

13. Students and institutions have changed, but college education still seems to benefit emerging adults, intellectually and financially. Some changes, particularly the increased diversity among students and faculty, are likely to foster deeper thinking.

KEY TERMS

postformal thought (p. 492)	stereotype threat (p. 498)	antithesis (p. 500)	morality of justice (p. 504)
delay discounting (p. 493)	dialectical thought (p. 500)	synthesis (p. 500)	Defining Issues Test (DIT)
subjective thought (p. 494)	thesis (p. 500)	morality of care (p. 504)	(p. 504)
objective thought (p. 494)			

WHAT HAVE YOU LEARNED?

Postformal Thought

1. Why did scholars choose the term *postformal* to describe the fifth stage of cognition?

2. How does postformal thinking differ from typical adolescent thought?

3. Why is time management a cognitive issue?

4. How does delay discounting relate to eating or exercising?

5. How does the maturation of the prefrontal cortex affect social understanding?

6. What is the relationship between subjective and objective thought?

7. How is listening to other opinions a measure of cognitive flexibility?

8. How could the threat of a stereotype affect cognition?

9. Which groups of people are vulnerable to stereotype threat and why?

10. Why does the phrase "broken home" indicate a lack of dialectical thought?

11. What differences are apparent in typical Asian and Western thinking?

Morals and Religion

12. Why do adults make more decisions involving morality than adolescents do?

13. Why do people disagree about whether or not something is a moral issue?

14. What is Gilligan's idea of the difference between male and female morality?

15. Why would decisions about reproduction be a catalyst for moral thought?

16. How are Fowler's stages similar to Piaget's and Kohlberg's stages?

17. Why might a devout person criticize Fowler's concept of the stages of faith?

Cognitive Growth and Higher Education

18. What do most students hope to gain from a college education?

19. According to Perry, how does students' thinking change during their college career?

20. How do current college enrollment patterns differ from those 50 years ago?

21. What are the differences between public and private colleges in the United States?

22. What evidence suggests that college fosters intellectual growth?

APPLICATIONS

1. Read a biography or autobiography that includes information about the person's thinking from age 18 to 60, paying particular attention to practical, flexible, or dialectical thought. How did personal experiences, education, and ideas affect the person's thinking?

2. Some ethical principles are thought to be universal, respected by people of every culture. Think of one such idea and analyze whether it is accepted by each of the world's major religions.

3. Statistics on changes in students and in colleges are fascinating, but only a few are reported here. Compare your nation, state, or province with another. Analyze the data and discuss causes and implications of differences.

4. One way to assess cognitive development during college is to study yourself or your classmates, comparing thoughts and decisions at the beginning and end of college. Since case studies are provocative but not definitive, identify some hypotheses that you might examine and explain how you would do so.

>> **Answer to Observation Quiz** (from page 514) The encouraging perspective is that rates are rising for everyone, with the only exception being associate degrees for Asian Americans, and the reason for that is itself encouraging—more of them are earning BAs. The discouraging perspective is that almost two-thirds of all adults and more than four-fifths of all Hispanics have no college degrees.

>>ONLINE CONNECTIONS

To accompany your textbook, you have access to a number of online resources, including quizzes for every chapter of the book, flashcards (in English and Spanish), critical thinking questions, and case studies. For access to any of these links, go to www.worthpublishers.com/bergerls8e. In addition to these free resources, you'll also find links to the podcasts, video clips, diagnostic quizzing with personalized study advice, and an ebook. Some of the videos and activities available online include:

- *Cheating.* Would you do it? Seventy-five percent of college students say they have cheated. This activity looks at the psychological and situational factors that make cheating more—or less—likely.

- *Interview with Kurt Fischer.* This noted developmentalist discusses the influence of experience on brain development.

Emerging Adulthood: Psychosocial Development

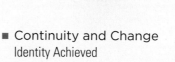

WHAT WILL YOU KNOW?

1. What happens to a shy child when he or she grows up?
2. Does cohabitation before marriage make a marriage happier?
3. In cases of spouse abuse, is it better for partners to be counseled or to separate?
4. Why do some emerging adults live with their parents?

In psychosocial development, even more than in physical or cognitive development, the hallmark of contemporary adult life is diversity. For emerging adults who are not restricted by family or culture, many choices of education, work, friends, and partners are possible. This is apparent worldwide for the current generation; in retrospect, developmentalists now see that young adults of earlier generations also began to forge paths quite different from those of their parents.

Looking back, I now see many signs of this new stage in the people I know. When I was 20, Phoebe and Peggy were my two closest friends. As expected by our parents and culture, we anticipated becoming happy brides, wives, and mothers, even describing our wedding dresses to each other and naming our children. Our anticipations were dashed by social change.

Over the years of our adulthood, the three of us had three husbands and five children—average for our culture and cohort. But Phoebe never married or had children. She started her own business and became a millionaire who now owns a house near the Pacific Ocean. Peggy married, divorced, remarried, and had one child at age 40. She earned a PhD and, after many academic jobs, finally found the work she loves, as a massage therapist. I married and had four children while working and learning, which was unusual for my generation. Another woman, a stranger I met at a party, on hearing about my four children, asked incredulously, "All from the same husband?" Yes, an odd path these days.

The culture shifted; none of us did what was expected when we were girls. About five years ago, I complained to Phoebe that my four grown daughters were not wives or mothers. She smiled, put her hand on mine, and said, "Please notice. I never married or had children. Yet I am happy." So is Peggy. So am I. Emerging adults do not always marry, secure lifelong careers, or become parents—but that does not necessarily mean they will be sad and lonely. Far from it.

>> Continuity and Change

A theme of human development is that continuity and change are evident throughout life. Thus, in emerging adulthood, the legacy of early development is apparent amidst new achievement, as Erikson recognized in his description of the fifth of his eight stages, identity versus role confusion. As you remember, the crisis of identity begins in adolescence, but it is not usually resolved until adulthood.

519

Identity Achieved

Erikson believed that the outcome of earlier crises provides the foundation of each new stage. The identity crisis is an example (see Table 19.1). Worldwide, emerging adults ponder all four arenas of identity—religious commitments, gender roles, political loyalties, and career options—trying to reconcile plans for the future with beliefs acquired in the past.

As explained in Chapter 16, the identity crisis sometimes causes confusion, diffusion, or foreclosure, but a more mature response occurs when emerging adults seek a moratorium, postponing identity achievement while they explore possibilities. Many examples of moratoria are apparent. For instance, earning a college degree is a socially acceptable way to avoid marriage and parenthood. College requirements discourage foreclosure: Usually students must take courses in many disciplines, exploring options rather than settling on a single identity.

TABLE 19.1

Erikson's Eight Stages of Development

Stage	Virtue/Pathology	Possible in Emerging Adulthood If Not Successfully Resolved
Trust vs. mistrust	Hope / withdrawal	Suspicious of others, making close relationships difficult
Autonomy vs. shame and doubt	Will / compulsion	Obsessively driven, single-minded, not socially responsive
Initiative vs. guilt	Purpose / inhibition	Fearful, regretful (e.g., very homesick in college)
Industry vs. inferiority	Competence / inertia	Self-critical of any endeavor, procrastinating, perfectionistic
Identity vs. role diffusion	Fidelity / repudiation	Uncertain and negative about values, lifestyle, friendships
Intimacy vs. isolation	Love / exclusivity	Anxious about close relationships, jealous, lonely
Generativity vs. stagnation	Care / rejection	[In the future] Fear of failure
Integrity vs. despair	Wisdom / disdain	[In the future] No "mindfulness," no life plan

Source: Erikson, 1982.

Past as Prologue In elaborating his eight stages of development, Erikson associated each stage with a particular virtue and a type of psychopathology, as shown here. He also thought that earlier crises could reemerge, taking a specific form at each stage. Listed are some possible problems (not directly from Erikson) that could occur in emerging adulthood if earlier crises were not resolved.

Societies offer many other moratoria: the military; religious mission work; apprenticeships; and various internships in government, academe, and industry. Any of these can reduce the pressure to achieve identity, offering a ready rejoinder to an older relative who urges settling down. Emerging adults in moratoria do what is required (as student, soldier, missionary, or whatever), which explains why a moratorium is considered more mature than diffusion. However, a moratorium is only temporary, a way to postpone identity achievement. This respite gives emerging adults some time to achieve in the two arenas of identity described by Erikson—political/ethnic identity and vocational identity—arenas that are particularly difficult in current times.

Ethnic Identity

In the United States and Canada, almost half of 18- to 25-year-olds are of African, Asian, Latino, or Native American heritage. Ethnicity is a significant aspect of their political identity (Phinney, 2006). During late adolescence and early adulthood, people are more likely to be proud, or at least accepting, of their ethnic background than younger adolescents are (Worrell, 2008). There is no doubt that "identity development . . . from the teenage years to the early 20s, if not through adulthood, . . . has been extended to explain the development of ethnic and racial identity" (Whitbourne et al., 2009, p. 1328).

Most emerging adults identify with very specific ethnic groups. For example, unlike adolescents, who might say that they are simply Asian American, emerging adults are more likely to specify that they are Vietnamese, Bangladeshi, or Korean

Americans (Dion, 2006). Similarly, people who are descendants of American slaves no longer call themselves colored or Negro, but African American or Caribbean American. Not surprisingly, the first age group to self-identify as African American was emerging adults; the years from 18 to 25 are the period in which people are particularly attuned to ethnic roots and future roles.

More than other age groups, emerging adults tend to have friends and acquaintances of many backgrounds. They become more aware of history, customs, and prejudices. As a longitudinal study of college students of every ethnic group found, a "strong sense of ethnic identity [was] related to both positive and negative experiences" (Syed & Azmitia, 2010, p. 218). As in this study, many European Americans, realizing the importance of ethnicity for their classmates, become more conscious of their own background. Another study found that Hispanic college students who resisted both assimilation and alienation fared best: They were able to maintain their ethnic identity, deflect stereotype threat, and become good students (Rivas-Drake & Mooney, 2009).

College classes (especially in history, ethnic studies, and sociology) attract many emerging adults who want to learn more about their own culture. In addition, various extracurricular groups help solidify identity as students encounter others of similar backgrounds who confront the same issues. Indeed, one study in a large multiethnic university found that students were most likely to find sexual partners (from hookups to marriage) within their own group (McClintock, 2010), even though most appreciated the ethnic diversity of their college. Intimacy was aided by cultural similarity.

When young adults' parents are from two ethnic groups, that heritage may push them toward being proudly biracial or toward self-identifying with whichever group experiences more prejudice (Chaudhari & Pizzolato, 2008; Herman, 2004). On a questionnaire, some emerging adults defiantly write "human" when asked "race," but in a multiethnic world, identity requires people to accept and reject parts of their background.

Young adults whose parents were immigrants experience added stresses because combining past and future means reconciling their heritage with their new social context. Conflicts arise, not only in choice of vocation or partner (as can happen with any emerging adult) but also in something more basic, that is, "the assumption that these choices should be made independently by the young adult daughter or son" (Dion, 2006, p. 303). Young immigrants are expected to be proud of their ethnic roots—and many are—but they are also expected by their peers to make independent choices. They encounter attitudes from the native-born that make them reexamine their identity (Rodriguez et al., 2010).

Ethnic identity is complex and pervasive, affecting language, manners, romance, employment, neighborhood, religion, clothing, and values. In addition (Trimble et al., 2003):

- It is reciprocal, both a personal choice and a response to others.
- It depends on context, so it changes with time and circumstances.
- It is multifaceted; emerging adults accept some aspects and reject others.

Consider Kevin Johnson, son of a European American father and a Mexican American mother. In high school, he thought of himself as Anglo, and in that social context, his Anglo identity was recognized. But as an emerging adult, he chose to identify with the Mexican half of his heritage, criticizing his mother

Proud Marchers Bicultural identity correlates with achievement and happiness in emerging adulthood. These students at Columbia University are also members of Ho Heup, dedicated to traditional Korean drumming.

Observation Quiz Where was this photo taken? (see answer, page 522)

A Woman Now Two young women (age 20) participate in the traditional coming-of-age ceremony in Japan. Their kimonos and hairstyles are elaborate and traditional, as is the sake (rice wine) they drink. This is part of the ceremony signifying passage from girlhood to womanhood.

>> Answer to Observation Quiz (from page 521) New York City. Most aspects of this scene could be seen in either Korea or the United States, but usually groups dedicated to a particular culture flourish when they are in the minority, as Koreans are in the United States. A further clue: The sign on the building has English letters.

For the Time Being Every company would like to hold on to its skilled employees. That is one reason the title of this young woman's job, at one of Starbucks' nearly 15,000 stores worldwide, is "barista," not "waitress." Nevertheless, most emerging adults consider their current jobs only temporary stops on the way toward lifelong careers.

TABLE 19.2

Top Six "Very Important" Objectives in Life*

Being well off financially	78%
Raising a family	75%
To make more money	71%
Helping others	69%
Becoming an authority in my field	59%
Obtaining recognition in my special field	56%

*Based on a national survey of students entering four-year colleges in the United States in the fall of 2010.
Source: Chronicle of Higher Education, 2010.

Look Again This research was already mentioned in Chapter 18, but now compare the cited objectives to the reality of the job market. Vocational identity is difficult for contemporary emerging adults. If projections prove accurate, many of them will not consider themselves "well off financially."

for not teaching him Spanish. He solidified his identity by marrying a Mexican American, giving his children Spanish names, and sending them to bilingual schools. Yet he decided to practice law in the United States and live in California (not Mexico). He writes in English about ethnic identity, his own and that of other Americans (K. R. Johnson, 1999, 2010; K. R. Johnson & Hing, 2007).

Like Johnson, adults choose how their ethnicity interacts with other aspects of their identity as well as how to express that interaction. In the globalization of the twenty-first century, combining past and future is complex yet crucial. Ethnic identity cannot be ignored, nor should it be foreclosed. As one young adult explained:

> Questioning their identity, as inevitable as that experience is, is not enough. To have passed through the ambiguities, contradictions, and frustration of cultural schizophrenia is to have passed only the first test in the process. . . . We need to embody our own history. *El pueblo que pierde su memoria pierde su destino:* The people who forgets its past, forfeits its future.
>
> [*Gaspar de Alba, 2003, pp. 211–212*]

Vocational Identity

Establishing a vocational identity is considered part of growing up not only by developmental psychologists influenced by Erikson but also by emerging adults themselves (Arnett, 2004). Many go to college, not only as a moratorium but also to prepare for a good job. Emerging adulthood is a "critical stage for the acquisition of resources"—including the education, skills, and experience needed for a lifelong family and career success (Tanner et al., 2009, p. 34) (see Table 19.2).

Part of the preparation for lifetime work often includes taking temporary jobs. Between ages 18 and 27, the average U.S. worker has held eight jobs, with the college-educated changing jobs even more than average (U.S. Bureau of the Census, 2009). This illustrates the exploration that is part of the identity search, and it is also a sign that achievement has not yet occurred: The worker is not yet climbing, rung by rung, a particular vocational ladder. For most emerging adults, "the process of identifying with society's work ethic, the core of this issue [identity achievement] in Erikson's scheme, continues to evolve throughout early adulthood" (Whitbourne et al., 2009, p. 1329).

Charles, a college graduate, is one example. He had worked for the same advertising agency for a year but still thought of himself as a "temp," likely to leave the company at any moment to pursue a career in music. He explained:

> I'm single. I don't have a car or a house or a mortgage or a significant other that's pulling me in another direction, or kids or anything. I'm highly portable, and I can basically do what I want as long as I can support myself.
>
> [*quoted in Arnett, 2004, p. 37*]

Many developmentalists wonder whether vocational identity is an illusion in the current global economy. Hiring and firing seem disconnected from the worker's training or need for a steady job, especially for young workers (Vaupel & Loichinger, 2006), who typically feel no loyalty to their particular employer. Perhaps adults of all ages should see their skills as "highly portable" (as Charles and many other young adults do), a way to earn money while they satisfy their creative, self-expressive impulses elsewhere. In many societies, pensions and schedules are structured as if every worker were steady and full time, but this may be an outdated social construction.

Some young adults assume that they will find a vocational niche that is perfect for their aspirations and talents. They have high expectations for work. They expect to find a job that will be an expression of their identity. . . . With such high expectations . . . some of them are likely to find that the actual job they end up in for the long term falls considerably short.

[Arnett, 2004, pp. 143, 163]

Ordinary Workers Most children and adolescents want to be sports heroes, entertainment stars, billionaires, or world leaders—yet fewer than one in 1 million succeed in doing so.

Personality in Emerging Adulthood

Continuity and change are evident in personality as well (McAdams & Olson, 2010). Of course, personality endures lifelong, which means that the self-doubt, anxiety, depression, and so on that are present in adolescence are often still evident years later. As you remember, the origins of personality are genetic, and then childhood experiences shape genetic impulses. Traits present at age 18 do not disappear by age 25.

Yet personality is not static. After adolescence, new personality dimensions may appear and negative traits may diminish. As the preceding two chapters have emphasized, emerging adults make choices that break with the past. Compared with previous generations, contemporary youth pursue education and avoid marriage and parenthood. This freedom from a settled lifestyle allows shifts in attitude and personality.

Rising Self-Esteem

Psychological research finds both continuity and improvement in attitudes. For example, one longitudinal study found that 17-year-olds who saw life in positive terms maintained their outlook as time went on, while those who were negative often shifted during emerging adulthood, becoming less worried, less anxious (Blonigen et al., 2008). Another team of researchers traced 3,912 U.S. high school seniors until age 23 or 24. Generally, transitions (entering college, starting a job, getting married) increased their well-being. Those in college who lived away from home showed the largest gains, and those who had become single parents or who still lived with their own parents showed the least. Even the latter, however, tended to be happier than they had been in high school (see Figure 19.1; Schulenberg et al., 2005). Similarly, 404 young adults in western Canada, repeatedly questioned from ages 18 to 25, reported increasing self-esteem (Galambos et al., 2006).

This positive trend of increasing happiness has become more evident over recent decades, perhaps because young adults are more likely to make their own life decisions (Twenge et al., 2008). Logically, the many stresses and transitions of emerging adulthood might reduce self-esteem, but that is not what the research finds. As you remember from Chapter 17, psychopathology may be increasing and some emerging adults develop serious disorders (Twenge et al., 2010), but most do not.

Worrisome Children Grow Up

Shifts toward positive development were also found in another longitudinal study, which began with 4-year-olds, particularly children at the extremes of one or the other of two traits known to have strong genetic roots: extreme shyness and marked aggression. These children tended to be shy or aggressive later in childhood as well. Surprisingly, they had changed in complex ways by emerging adulthood (Asendorpf et al., 2008).

Some developments were as expected. Those who had been very aggressive as children (compared to the average 4-year-old) had more conflicts with their

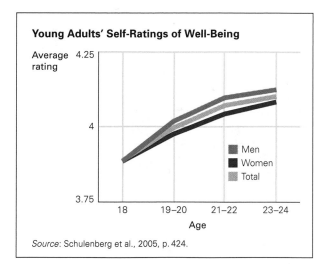

Young Adults' Self-Ratings of Well-Being

Source: Schulenberg et al., 2005, p. 424.

FIGURE 19.1

Worthy People This graph shows a steady increase in young adults' sense of well-being from age 18 to age 24, as measured by respondents' ratings of statements such as "I feel I am a person of worth." The ratings ranged from 1 (complete disagreement) to 5 (complete agreement). The average rating was already quite high at age 18, and it increased steadily over the years of emerging adulthood.

parents and friends when they became emerging adults. In addition, they were more likely to quit school and leave jobs before age 25; two-thirds had dropped out of high school before graduation, as had only one-third of their nonaggressive peers. By age 23, half had been arrested at least once, another sign of their unusually aggressive personalities.

Yet, unexpectedly, these aggressive young adults had as many friends as their average peers did. They wanted more education, and they rated themselves as quite conscientious. Their arrests were usually for minor offenses: Only one had been sent to prison, and only one other had been arrested several times. A closer examination of their school records found that their behavior in childhood led teachers to fail them; many had repeated the same grade while their classmates moved on, which meant that they were older than most of their fellow high school students. Many quit because of the school restrictions and people's assumptions, not because they hated learning. As emerging adults, most seemed to be developing well, controlling their aggression and putting their childhood problems behind them; some were employed and others had enrolled in college.

As for the emerging adults who had been inhibited as children, they were "cautious, reserved adults with few signs of internalizing problems" (Asendorpf et al., 2008, p. 1007). Perhaps because of their personalities, they were slower than average to secure a job, choose a career, or find a romance (at age 23, two-thirds had no current partner). However, they were no more anxious or depressed than others of their cohort, and their self-esteem was equally good. They had many friends, whom they saw often. Their delayed employment and later marriage were typical for the new cohort of emerging adults. In other words, the personality trait (shyness) that was considered to be a handicap in childhood may have become an asset.

Plasticity

In the research just discussed and in other research as well, plasticity is evident. Personality is not fixed by age 5, or 15, or 20, as it was once thought to be. Emerging adults are open to new experiences (a reflection of their adventuresome spirit), and this allows personality shifts as well as eagerness for more education (McAdams & Olson, 2010; Tanner et al., 2009). The trend is toward less depression and more joy, along with more insight into the self (Galambos et al., 2006; McAdams et al., 2006).

Going to college, leaving home, becoming independent, stopping drug abuse, moving to a new city, finding satisfying work and performing it well, making new friends, committing to a partner—each of these might alter a person's life course. Total change does not occur, since genes, childhood experiences, and family circumstances affect people lifelong. Nor do new experiences always result in desirable changes. But personality can shift in adulthood. Increased well-being may underlie another shift: Emerging adults become less self-centered and more caring of others (Eisenberg et al., 2005; Padilla-Walker et al., 2008). This can be seen as the foundation of the next psychosocial stage of development, which we now discuss.

Moving On Anna begins college with her father's help, but she will soon be on her own, with only her boxed items and comfy pillow to buffer her from the challenges of college life. When she returns home, her parents might be surprised by some of her newly shaped attitudes, ideas, and values.

SUMMING UP

The identity crisis continues in emerging adulthood, as young people seek to establish their own unique path toward adulthood. Ethnic identity is important but difficult, especially for those who realize they are a minority within their nation. Vocational identity is also an ongoing search. Most emerging adults hold many jobs between the ages of 18 and 25, but few feel they have established a career identity. Personality traits endure lifelong, partly because genes and early childhood are influential, but emerging adults modify some traits and develop others. Prediction of a person's future based only on his or her childhood personality and circumstances is often inaccurate. ■

>> Intimacy

In Erikson's theory, after achieving identity, people experience the crisis of **intimacy versus isolation.** This crisis arises from the powerful desire to share one's personal life with someone else. Without intimacy, adults suffer from loneliness and isolation. Erikson explains:

> The young adult, emerging from the search for and the insistence on identity, is eager and willing to fuse his identity with others. He is ready for intimacy, that is, the capacity to commit himself to concrete affiliations and partnerships and to develop the ethical strength to abide by such commitments, even though they call for significant sacrifices and compromises.
>
> *[Erikson, 1963, p. 263]*

As will be explained in Chapter 22, other theorists have different words for the same human need: *affiliation, affection, interdependence, communion, belonging, love.* All agree that adults seek to become friends, lovers, companions, and partners. The urge for social connection is a powerful human impulse, one reason our species has thrived.

All intimate relationships have much in common—not only in the psychic needs they satisfy but also in the behaviors they require (Reis & Collins, 2004). Intimacy progresses from attraction to close connection to ongoing commitment. Each relationship demands some personal sacrifice, including vulnerability that brings deeper self-understanding and shatters the isolation caused by too much self-protection. As Erikson explains, to establish intimacy, the young adult must

> face the fear of ego loss in situations which call for self-abandon: in the solidarity of close affiliations [and] sexual unions, in close friendship and in physical combat, in experiences of inspiration by teachers and of intuition from the recesses of the self. The avoidance of such experiences . . . may lead to a deep sense of isolation and consequent self-absorption.
>
> *[Erikson, 1963, pp. 163–164]*

According to a more recent theory, an important aspect of close human connections is "self-expansion," the idea that each of us enlarges our understanding, our experiences, and our resources through our intimate friends and lovers (Aron et al., 2005).

Friendship

Throughout life, friends defend against stress and provide joy. They are chosen for the very qualities that make them good companions, trustworthy confidants, and reliable sources of support (e.g., understanding, tolerance, loyalty, affection, humor). Unlike family members, friends are earned; they choose us. No wonder having close friends is positively correlated with happiness and self-esteem lifelong.

Friends in Emerging Adulthood

Friends, new and old, are particularly crucial during emerging adulthood, especially for those who do not have a steady romantic partner (Kalmijn, 2003). At this stage of life, family obligations are minimal because most emerging adults have no

intimacy versus isolation The sixth of Erikson's eight stages of development. Adults seek someone with whom to share their lives in an enduring and self-sacrificing commitment. Without such commitment, they risk profound aloneness and isolation.

spouse, children, or frail parents. Instead, they have friends, who provide companionship and critical support—they comfort each other when romance turns sour, take each other home if someone drank too much alcohol, advise each other on everything from what college to attend to what information should be shared with parents.

In college, work, and community, as well as in various chosen activities (from aerobics class to zoological society membership), young adults have acquaintances who provide advice, companionship, information, and sympathy (Radmacher & Azmitia, 2006). People tend to make more friends during these years than at any later period and rely on them more than people their age once did. They often use cell phone and computer connections not to distance themselves but to extend and deepen friendships that begin face to face (Subrahmanyam et al., 2008). Young adults who became friends when they lived near each other sometimes move away but maintain a strong friendship (A. J. Johnson et al., 2009).

Fears that increasing Internet use would diminish the number or quality of friendships have been proven to be false. If anything, heavy Internet users tend to have more face-to-face friends than do nonusers (Wang & Wellman, 2010). Thanks to technology, nonromantic friendships between men, between women, and between a man and a woman can last a lifetime, regardless of anyone's sexual orientation. In early adulthood, friends are more than a social nicety; they may be crucial for comfort and joy.

Gender and Friendship

It is a mistake to imagine that men and women have opposite friendship needs. All humans seek intimacy, lifelong. Claiming that men are from Mars and women are from Venus ignores reality: People are from Earth (Hyde, 2007).

Nevertheless, for cultural and biological reasons, some sex differences can be found (Monsour, 2002; Radmacher & Azmitia, 2006). Men tend to share activities and interests, and they talk about external matters—sports, work, politics,

Such Good Friends Friendship patterns vary from person to person, and gender stereotypes regarding these patterns are often wide of the mark. Nonetheless, friendships between women and friendships between men tend to take different directions. Women tend to spend more time in intimate conversation, with more emotion than activity, perhaps commiserating rather than calling attention to their accomplishments. Men, by contrast, typically do things together—with outdoor activities frequently preferred, especially if they lend themselves to showing off and friendly bragging.

cars. They are less likely to tell other men of their failures, emotional problems, and relationship dilemmas; if they do, they expect practical advice, not sympathy. Women's friendships are more intimate and emotional. They share secrets and engage in self-disclosing talk, including difficulties with their health, romances, and relatives. Women reveal their weaknesses and problems and receive an attentive and sympathetic ear, a shoulder to cry on, or a reassuring hug.

Lest this seem as if female friendships are better because they are closer, research finds that men are more tolerant; they demand less of their friends and thus have more friends. One specific detail from college dormitories: When strangers of the same sex are assigned as roommates (the practice for first-year students at most residential colleges), more women than men decide they are incompatible, requesting a change (Benenson et al., 2009).

Male tolerance does not extend to sexual orientation, however; more men than women are homophobic. For example, among U.S. college freshmen in 2009, 30 percent of the men but only 18 percent of the women agreed that laws should prohibit homosexual experiences (*Chronicle of Higher Education,* 2009). Probably for this reason, men avoid touching each other except in aggression, such as competitive athletics or military combat. The butt slapping or body slamming immediately after a sports victory, or the sobbing in a buddy's arms in the aftermath of a battlefield loss, rarely occurs among men in everyday life. By contrast, many women routinely hug friends in greeting or farewell.

Male–Female Friendships

As already noted, these gender differences may be cultural, not biological. They seem to be less salient among contemporary emerging adults. One sign of this is the frequency of male–female friendships, no longer rare (Lenton & Webber, 2006). To the extent that friendships expand the self, friendships across gender boundaries have much to commend them (Monsour, 2002).

These friendships are not usually preludes to romance, although sometimes romance does occur (Bleske-Rechek & Buss, 2001). Male–female friendships are less common for people at the extremes of gender identity (the very feminine girl or supermasculine boy); it is not known whether this is primarily nature or nurture (Lenton & Webber, 2006).

Problems may arise if outsiders assume that every male–female relationship is sexual. For this reason, when heterosexual couples are romantically committed to each other, they tend to have fewer cross-sex friendships, to avoid partner jealousy (S. Williams, 2005). Keeping a relationship "just friendly" may be difficult, and, if it becomes sexual, romance with a third person is almost impossible.

Humans apparently find it difficult to sustain more than one sexual/romantic relationship at a time. Indeed, even in nations where polygamy is accepted, 90 percent of husbands have only one wife (Georgas et al., 2006). A study of couples in Kenya found that actual or suspected sexual infidelity was the most common reason for breaking up (Clark et al., 2010), and a study in the United States found that emerging adults thought sexual fidelity was extremely important for a good, enduring relationship (Meier et al., 2009).

Especially for Young Men Why would you want at least one close friend who is a woman? (see response, page 529)

Romantic Partners

Love, romance, and lasting commitment are all of primary importance for emerging adults, although many specifics have changed. Most emerging adults are thought to be postponing, not abandoning, marriage. As one U.S. sociologist explains, "despite the culture of divorce, Americans remain optimistic about, and even eager to enter, marriages" (Hill, 2007, p. 295). This is good news to me, as the following explains.

A CASE TO STUDY

Changing Expectations About Marriage

In most nations of the world, marriage is not based on romantic love. Marriages connect families more than individuals. Increasingly, this traditional process is giving way to a new pattern that I personally welcome. Emerging adults seek partners who will be good lovers, confidants, companions, parents, and providers—as I think I had in my own marriage. Such multiple expectations may be the reason young adults marry later, if at all (Gibson-Davis et al., 2005; Glenn, 1998).

I take some comfort in that. I married late for my cohort (at age 25) and had children even later (two by age 30 and another two by age 40). Of my four children, only one is married, a wedding agreed on because she and her husband decided this was the only way for both of them to have health insurance. My other three daughters are older than I was when I married and are still single. I am proud of all four; they are admirable women working in professions that I respect. But I also wish they would find a life partner. I have hinted that their mate expectations may be too high; they glare angrily at that.

For those reasons, I pay attention to my students' thoughts about love and marriage. Emerging adult Kerri wrote:

> All young girls have their perfect guy in mind, their Prince Charming. For me he will be tall, dark, and handsome. He will be well-educated and have a career with a strong future . . . a great personality, and the same sense of humor as I do. I'm not sure I can do much to ensure that I meet my soul mate. I believe

that is what is implied by the term *soul mate*; you will meet them no matter what you do. Part of me is hoping this is true, but another part tells me the idea of soul mates is just a fable.

[Personal communication]

Kerri's classmate Chelsea, also an emerging adult, wrote:

> I dreamt of being married. The husband didn't matter specifically, as long as he was rich and famous and I had a long, off-the-shoulder wedding dress. Thankfully, my views since then have changed. . . . I have a fantastic boyfriend of almost two years who I could see myself marrying, as we are extremely compatible. Although we are different, we have mastered . . . communication and compromise. . . . I think I will be able to cope with the trials and tribulations life brings.

[Personal communication]

Neither of these students is naive. Kerri uses the words *Prince Charming* and *fable* to express her awareness that these ideas may be childish, and Chelsea seems to have let go of her "long, off-the-shoulder" wedding dress. I wish them both well, and I know my daughters are wise and wonderful. As a scientist, I read about divorce statistics and the pain of separation; I do not want that for my children. But as a mother, I wish they would all have loving husbands and live in houses with lawns and picket fences. That makes no sense. At least I know about cohorts and recognize that their ideas may be more suited to the twenty-first century than mine are. I hope so.

The relationship between love and marriage depends on era and culture, with three distinct patterns evident (Georgas et al., 2006). In about one-third of the world's families, love does not lead to marriage because parents arrange marriages that will join two families together.

In another third of families, adolescents meet only a select group (single-sex schools keep them from meeting unsuitable mates). Some then decide to marry, and young men ask the young women's fathers for "her hand in marriage." For these couples, parents supervise interactions, then young people choose their mates, then parental blessing is bestowed. (Historically, when young people could not secure parental approval, they separated with tears or eloped—neither of which occurs as often today).

Suggesting "a third" for each of these is a rough approximation. In former times, most all marriages were of the first type; young people almost never met and married people unknown to their parents (Apostolou, 2007). Currently, in developing nations, practice often blends these two types. For example, in modern India most brides believe they have a choice, but many meet their future husbands a few days before the wedding via parental arrangement. The young man or woman can then veto the match, but usually they do not (Desai & Andrist, 2010).

A third pattern is relatively new, although familiar to most readers of this book. Young people socialize with hundreds of others, are expected to fall in love but not marry until they are able, financially and emotionally, to be independent. Their choices tilt toward personal qualities observable at the moment—physical appearance, personal hygiene, personality, sexuality, a sense of humor—and not to qualities more important to parents, such as religion, ethnicity, or long-term stability. For instance, a person who has been married and divorced is seen much more negatively by parents than by unpartnered adults (Buunk et al., 2008).

For Western emerging adults, love is considered a prerequisite for marriage, according to 14,121 individuals of many ethnic groups and sexual orientations (Meier et al., 2009). They were asked to rate from 1 to 10 the importance of money, same racial background, long-term commitment, love, and faithfulness for a successful marriage or serious, committed relationship. Faithfulness was the most important of all (rated 10 by 89 percent) and love was almost as high (rated 10 by 86 percent). Virtually all the rest rated faithfulness and love as very important (rated 9). By contrast, most thought being the same race was not important (57 percent rated it 1, 2, or 3), and money, while important to many, was not nearly as crucial as faithfulness.

This survey was conducted in North America, but emerging adults worldwide share many of the same values. Halfway around the world, emerging adults in Kenya also reported that love was the primary reason for couples to connect and stay together; money was less important (Clark et al., 2010).

More than Yesterday, Less than Tomorrow
This is a sweet saying about love, but for Naveen and Supiya, it is literally true. They are typical young adults in many ways—married and in love, hoping someday to have children and grandchildren. But they differ from other Wisconsin couples in one respect: Their Indian parents arranged the marriage.

The Dimensions of Love

"Love" itself has many manifestations, which may differ from time to time. In a classic analysis, Robert Sternberg (1988) described three distinct aspects of love—passion, intimacy, and commitment. Sternberg believes that the relative presence or absence of these three components gives rise to seven different forms of love (see Table 19.3).

Early in a relationship, *passion* is evident in "falling in love," an intense physical, cognitive, and emotional onslaught characterized by excitement, ecstasy, and euphoria. The entire body and mind, hormones and neurons, are activated (Aron, 2010). Such moonstruck joy can become bittersweet once the two people involved get to know each other. As one observer explains, "Falling in love is absolutely no way of getting to know someone" (Sullivan, 1999, p. 225).

There is some evidence that passion fades with familiarity. Siblings who grow up together—even those who are not biological siblings (such as adopted children or children living together on a kibbutz)—typically are not attracted to each other sexually. In India, future brides who have lived in the groom's household since they were children have fewer offspring than do those who first met their future spouse after puberty (Lieberman, 2006).

Intimacy is knowing someone well, sharing secrets and nakedness as well as sex. This aspect of a romance is reciprocal, with each partner gradually revealing more of himself or herself as well as accepting more of the other's revelations. The research is not clear about the best schedule for passion and intimacy, whether they should progress slowly or quickly, for instance. According to some research,

TABLE 19.3			
Sternberg's Seven Forms of Love			
	Present in the Relationship?		
Form of Love	Passion	Intimacy	Commitment
Liking	No	Yes	No
Infatuation	Yes	No	No
Empty love	No	No	Yes
Romantic love	Yes	Yes	No
Fatuous love	Yes	No	Yes
Companionate love	No	Yes	Yes
Consummate love	Yes	Yes	Yes

Source: Sternberg, 1988.

>> **Response for Young Men** (from page 527) Not for sex! Women friends are particularly responsive to deep conversations about family relationships, personal weaknesses, emotional confusion. But women friends might be offended by sexual advances, bragging, or advice giving. Save these for a future romance.

they are not always connected, as lust and affection arise from different parts of the brain (L. M. Diamond, 2004).

Commitment takes time, at least for those who follow the current Western pattern of love and marriage. It grows gradually through decisions to be together, mutual caregiving, shared possessions, and forgiveness (Fincham et al., 2007). Maintaining a close romantic relationship over the years takes dedication and work (Dindia & Emmers-Sommer, 2006). Social forces strengthen commitment, which is why in-laws are often the topic of jokes and the cause of arguments. They have the power to strengthen or weaken a couple's long-term relationship.

Commitment is also affected by the culture. In fact, when cultures endorse arranged marriages, commitment occurs early on, before passion or intimacy (Georgas et al., 2006). Help from other people in sustaining a relationship may be needed in Western nations as well. For example, a study in Sweden found that couples living in detached houses (with yards between them) broke up more often than did couples in attached dwellings (such as apartments). Perhaps "single-family housing might have deleterious effects on couple stability due to the isolating lack of social support for couples staying together" (Lauster, 2008, p. 901). In other words, suburban couples may be too far from their neighbors to receive the help they might need when conflicts arise.

For both men and women, passion seems to fade, but commitment increases when children are born. This may be one reason why most sexually active young adults try to avoid pregnancy unless they believe their partner is a lifelong mate. (The relationship of parenthood to marital satisfaction is discussed in Chapter 22.)

The Ideal and the Real

In Europe in the Middle Ages, love, passion, and marriage were considered to be distinct phenomena, with "courtly love" disconnected from romance, which was also distinct from lifelong commitment (Singer, 2009). Currently, however, the Western ideal of consummate love includes all three components: passion, intimacy, and commitment. This ideal combines "the view of love promulgated in the movies . . . [and the] more prosaic conceptions of love rooted in daily and long-lived experience" (Gerstel, 2002, p. 555).

For developmental reasons, this ideal is difficult to achieve. Passion seems to be sparked by unfamiliarity, uncertainty, and risk, all diminished by the familiarity and security that contribute to intimacy and by the time needed for commitment.

In short, with time, passion may fade, intimacy may grow and stabilize, and commitment may develop. This pattern occurs for all types of couples—married, unmarried, and remarried; gay, lesbian, and straight; young, middle-aged, and old; in arranged, guided, and self-initiated relationships.

Romantic love moves from passion to intimacy to commitment. Sexual attraction is part of the process, but it is not enough to keep a couple together for decades. As one author explains, "Sex and love drift in and out of each other's territories and their foggy frontiers cannot be rigidly staked out. . . . Although lust does not contain love, love contains lust" (Sullivan, 1999, pp. 95–96).

Establishing an intimate nonsexual relationship and later moving toward a sexual one may be wiser than the converse—sex first and friendship later (Furman & Hand, 2006). Emerging adults refer to "friends with benefits," implying that sexual passion is less significant (an extra benefit, not the core attraction) than the friendship. However, if a friendship becomes sexual, complications arise (Bisson & Levine, 2009; Furman & Hand, 2006). Once the hormones of sexual intimacy are activated, people become more emotionally involved than they expected (H. E. Fisher, 2006).

Hookups Without Commitment

Sexual interactions can occur between people who are not friends. When this occurred in prior generations, it was either prostitution or illicit, as in a "fling" or a "dirty secret" of a married person. Now many emerging adults accept that their peers sometimes *hook up,* the term for a sexual encounter with neither intimacy nor commitment. **Hookups** are more common among first-year college students than among those about to graduate, perhaps because older students are looking for partners, and, as one put it, "if you hook up with someone it probably is just a hookup and nothing is going to come of it" (quoted in Bogle, 2008, p. 38).

The desire for physical intimacy without emotional commitment may be stronger in young men than in young women. If that is true, the reasons could be either hormonal (testosterone) or cultural (women want men to stay if children are born). Interestingly, emerging adults of both sexes say that if they want a serious relationship with someone, they are less likely to hook up with them, preferring to get to know them first (Bogle, 2008). This may vary with ethnicity as well as gender and age. At least in research on California undergraduates, African American men and Asian American women were more likely to hook up than were African American women and Asian American men (McClintock, 2010).

Given all these ethnic, gender, national, and historical differences, there is no formula that will necessarily lead to a good partnership. Emerging adults reject the patterns of the past: "Finding a love partner in your teens and continuing in that relationship with that person through your early twenties, culminating in marriage, is now viewed as unhealthy, a mistake, a path likely to lead to disaster" (Arnett, 2004, p. 73). However, emerging adults have not necessarily found a better way to connect.

Finding Each Other and Living Together

One major innovation of the current cohort of emerging adults is the use of **social networks.** Web sites such as MySpace and Facebook allow individuals to post their photos and personal information on the Internet, sharing the details of their daily lives to many others. Three-fourths of all 18- to 29-year-olds in the United States use social networking to keep in contact with hundreds, perhaps thousands, of others (Pew Research Center, 2010). Such sites often indicate whether an individual is, or is not, in a committed relationship.

In addition, many young adults seeking romance join one or more matchmaking Web sites that provide dozens of potential partners to meet and evaluate. A problem with such matches is that passion is hard to assess without meeting in person. As one journalist puts it, many people face "profound disappointment when the process ends in a face-to-face meeting with an actual, flawed human being who doesn't look like a JPEG or talk like an email message" (D. Jones, 2006, p. 13). Emerging adults overcome this by filtering their online connections, arranging a meeting with only those that seem promising, and then following through with only a few. Often physical attraction is the gateway to a relationship, but intimacy requires much more, and ongoing commitment even more.

Another problem with technology and matchmaking is more difficult to overcome. Social networking may produce too many potential partners, increasing **choice overload,** which occurs when too many options are available. Choice overload increases second thoughts after a choice is made and causes some people to refuse to make any selection (Iyengar & Lepper, 2000; Reutskaja & Hogarth, 2009). Choice overload has been demonstrated with many consumer goods— jams, chocolates, pens, restaurants—but it has not been proven for choosing a mate. Having many complex options that require weighing present and future

hookup A sexual encounter between two people who are not in a romantic relationship. Neither intimacy nor commitment are expected.

social network A Web site that allows users to publicly share details of their daily lives and connect with large numbers of friends, acquaintances, and potential romantic partners, among others.

choice overload Having so many possibilities that a thoughtful choice becomes difficult. This is particularly apparent when social networking and other technology make many potential romantic partners available.

Mail-Order Bride He was looking for a woman with green eyes and reddish hair but without strong religious convictions—his particular exclusion criteria, which he posted on the Web. That led to an e-mail courtship and eventually marriage to "the girl of my dreams."

FIGURE 19.2

More Together, Fewer Married As you see, the number of cohabiting male–female households in the United States has increased dramatically over the past decades. These numbers are an underestimate: Couples who do not tell the U.S. census takers that they are living together, or who cohabit within their parents' households, or who are same-sex couples (not tallied until 2000) are not included here. In addition, most emerging adults who are not now cohabiting may well be within a few years.

Observation Quiz Did the rate of cohabitation increase faster before or after the year 2000? (see answer, page 534)

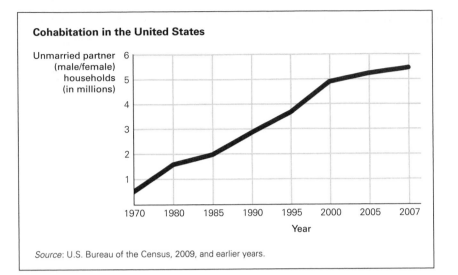

Cohabitation in the United States

Unmarried partner (male/female) households (in millions)

Source: U.S. Bureau of the Census, 2009, and earlier years.

cohabitation An arrangement in which a couple live together in a committed romantic relationship but are not formally married.

advantages and disadvantages (such trade-offs are inevitable in selecting a partner) makes choice overload more likely, although more research is needed (Scheibehenne et al., 2010).

A second major innovation among emerging adults is **cohabitation,** the term for living together in a romantic partnership without being married. Cohabitation was relatively unusual 40 years ago: In the United States, less than 1 percent of all households were comprised of a cohabiting man and woman (see Figure 19.2). Now more than 5 percent of all households are comprised of male–female cohabiting couples (with an additional 0.7 percent of same-sex couples not tallied as unmarried partners until 2000) (U.S. Bureau of the Census, 2009, and earlier years).

Most couples in the United States, Canada, northern Europe, England, and Australia cohabit during emerging adulthood, usually believing that cohabitation is a stage between dating and marriage. In other nations—including Japan, Ireland, and Italy—fewer people cohabit, although the rate is rising everywhere.

Variation is apparent in the purpose of cohabitation (Jose et al., 2010). About half of all cohabiting couples in the United States consider living together a prelude to marrying, which they expect to do when they are financially and emotionally ready. Longitudinal research (Casper & Bianchi, 2002) on a large group of male–female cohabiters who planned to marry found that, in five to seven years,

The Same Event, Many Miles Apart: Happy Young Women The British woman (*left*) and the Kenyan woman (*right*) are both developing just as their families had hoped they would. The major difference is that 23-year-old Kim is not yet married to Dave, while her contemporary already has a husband, son, and daughter.

about one-half had indeed married, one-sixth were still cohabiting, and only one-third had broken up. Some other couples live together but do not plan to marry each other; neither considers the relationship permanent. For them, longitudinal research finds that most separate in a few years, as described in the feature below.

The research just reported is from the United States. It is apparent that co-habitation differs not only by decade but also by nation. Most adults in Sweden, France, Jamaica, and Puerto Rico live together and do not plan to wed or separate. In most of the United States, committed same-sex couples are forced into this category, but not in Canada and many other nations. Many older heterosexual co-habiting couples in the United States—especially those who have been divorced—also expect to stay together but not to marry (King & Scott, 2005).

Especially for Social Scientists Suppose your 25-year-old Canadian friend, never married, says, "Look at the statistics. If I marry now, there is a 50/50 chance I will get divorced." What three statistical facts allow you to insist, "Your odds of divorce are much lower"? (see response, page 535)

THINKING CRITICALLY

Cohabitation

Although many emerging adults consider cohabitation to be a good prelude to marriage, a way for people to make sure they are compatible before tying the knot, research suggests they are mistaken. Cohabitants tend to be younger, poorer, and more likely to end their relationship than married couples—even when their relationship is quite satisfying (Bouchard, 2006; Brown et al., 2006). When they are angry with each other, they are more likely to fight. This seems true worldwide and was detailed with statistics from Latin America, where domestic violence is more common among cohabiting than among married couples (Flake & Forste, 2006).

Contrary to widespread belief, living together before marriage does not prevent problems that might arise after a wedding. The opposite is more likely. In a meta-analysis, a team of researchers examined the results of 26 scientific studies of the consequences of cohabitation for later marriage stability and quality and found that those who had lived together were more likely to divorce (Jose et al., 2010). Another study looked at the effects of dating, cohabitation, and marriage on happiness, as assessed by participants' answers to four questions (rated on a scale of 1 to 7) about how "ideal," "excellent," "satisfying," and "accomplished" their life was (Soons et al., 2009). At the start of

Bliss or Boredom If this moment is typical, the Swedish couple *(left)* find living together a joy and the U.S. couple *(right)* find their third year of cohabitation not much fun. However, almost every couple has moments of bliss—especially in the beginning of their relationship—as well as boredom—especially after several years together. The crucial question is what happens next, after the watermelon is cut and the photographers have gone.

a dating, cohabiting, or marriage relationship, happiness on all four indicators increased; at the end of any of these, happiness decreased. Both the increase and decrease were more affected by marriage than by cohabitation, implying that cohabitation is neither the ideal nor the marriage equivalent that many emerging adults believe.

Although the research suggests that cohabitation is not beneficial over the long term, most emerging adults do it. Developmentalists, like all good scientists, believe that published empirical data are more accurate than what the general population may assume, but developmentalists also consider historical trends. Since more and more individuals cohabit, might there be some advantages that are not measured by the published research?

One advantage, of course, is economic: People save money by living together. Beyond that, research in 30 nations finds that acceptance of cohabitation within the nation affects the happiness of those who cohabit. Demographic differences within those 30 nations (such as education, income, age, and religion among the married and cohabitants) affected the happiness gap as well (Soons & Kalmijn, 2009). Thus, earlier studies that simply evaluated those who did and did not cohabit may be unfair comparisons. Since emerging adults who have had several cohabiting relationships tend to be poorer and less religious than those who do not, that might affect their happiness, not the cohabitation itself.

This research suggests caution—that neither the popularity of cohabitation nor the immediate happiness of those who move in together proves that cohabitation is beneficial over the long term. On the other hand, in 2008 more than 12 million U.S. residents (6,209,000 couples, a number that includes same-sex couples) were in cohabiting relationships. They made a choice contrary to the one that seems wisest according to the published research. Critical thinking is needed.

What Makes Relationships Succeed

As already explained, friendships are similar to romances in many ways. They satisfy the human need for intimacy, and friends and mates are selected in similar ways. Furthermore, a good friendship or marriage helps an adult's self-esteem while providing practical support. However, research on maintaining friendships or even on long-term cohabitation is relatively scarce, so we focus here on marriage. As you read, think of applications to friendship as well.

Changes in Marriage Patterns

It is obvious that marriage is not what it once was—a legal and religious arrangement that couples sought as the exclusive avenue for sexual expression, the only legitimate prelude to childbearing, and a lifelong source of intimacy and support. As a sign of this change, the tie between marriage and childbearing is loosening in every nation. As many babies are born to unmarried as to married couples in some nations (including Denmark, France, and Sweden).

Further evidence is found in U.S. statistics (U.S. Bureau of the Census, 2009):

- Most adults aged 20 to 30 are not married. Indeed, of those aged 20 to 25, only 12 percent of the men and 20 percent of the women are married.
- Compared to any year in the past, fewer adults are married (57 percent) and more are divorced.
- The divorce rate is half the marriage rate (3.6 compared to 7.3 per 1,000)— not primarily because more people are divorcing but because fewer people are marrying.

From a developmental perspective, it is noteworthy that marriages evolve over time, sometimes getting better and sometimes worse (Waite & Luo, 2002). Among the factors that lead to improvement are good communication, financial security (more income or new employment), and the end of addiction or illness. Children are an added stress, with adolescents particularly trying for both parents (Cui & Donnellan, 2009). Another developmental factor is maturity. In general, the younger the partners, the more likely they are to separate, perhaps because, as Erikson recognized, intimacy is elusive before identity is achieved. An emerging

>> Answer to Observation Quiz (from page 532) Before! The *rate* of increase from 2000 to 2005 was about 4/49, or 8 percent, and the rate from 1985 to 1990 was about 9/20, a 45 percent increase.

adult who finally achieves identity might think, "I know who I am, and the person I am does not belong with the person you are."

Similarities and Differences

Similarity tends to solidify commitment, probably because similar people are likely to understand each other. Anthropologists distinguish between **homogamy,** or marriage within the same tribe or ethnic group, and **heterogamy,** marriage outside the group. Traditionally, homogamy meant marriage between people of the same cohort, religion, socioeconomic status, and ethnicity. For contemporary partners, homogamy and heterogamy also refer to similarity in interests, attitudes, and goals. Educational and economic similarity are becoming increasingly important (Clark et al., 2010; Hamplova, 2009; Schoen & Cheng, 2006).

One study of 168 young couples found that **social homogamy,** defined as similarity in preferred activities and roles, increased long-term commitment (Houts et al., 1996). When both partners enjoyed (or hated) picnicking, dancing, swimming, going to the movies, listening to music, eating out, or any of 44 other activities, they tended to be more "in love" and more committed. Similarly, if they agreed on roles such as who should cook, pay bills, and shop for groceries, ambivalence and conflict were reduced.

The authors of this study do not believe that "finding a mate compatible on many dimensions is an achievable goal." In reality, "individuals who are seeking a compatible mate must make many compromises if they are to marry at all" (Houts et al., 1996, p. 18). They found that, for any young adult, fewer than 1 in 100 potential mates share even three favorite leisure activities and three role preferences.

One thorny issue that arises among contemporary cohabiting couples as well as married ones is how domestic work is allocated. In earlier decades, if the husband had a good job and the wife kept the household running smoothly, each partner was content. No longer. Many twenty-first-century wives want their husbands to do much more housework than the men would prefer. On the other hand, many fathers want to be actively involved in decisions about child rearing, something women once assumed was their domain. If a couple cannot agree on division of household labor, cohabitants are likely to go their separate ways and married people are less satisfied (Brown et al., 2006; Hohmann-Marriott, 2006). Today, partners expect each other to be friends, lovers, and confidants as well as wage earners and caregivers, with both partners cooking, cleaning, and caring for children—a worldwide trend (Wong & Goodwin, 2009).

Happier relationships tend to be those in which both partners are adept at emotional perception and expression as well as hardworking. As women earn more money and men do more housework, overall marital satisfaction may have increased. Indeed, many aspects of romantic relationships have changed over the decades, some increasing happiness, some not—but couples overall seem as happy with their relationship as they ever were (Amato et al., 2003).

Conflict

Every intimate relationship has the potential to be destructive. The most extreme example comes from homicide statistics: If a civilian person is going to be killed, the perpetrator is usually a friend, acquaintance, or relative—especially a husband or wife (see Figure 19.3). Of course, that level of violence is rare, and usually friends who seriously disagree go their separate ways. Splitting is less acceptable, and more painful, for couples. We focus here on factors that make typical couples less happy than they might be, and then on intimate partner violence. Many of the conclusions apply to friendships as well.

homogamy Defined by developmentalists as marriage between individuals who tend to be similar with respect to such variables as attitudes, interests, goals, socioeconomic status, religion, ethnic background, and local origin.

heterogamy Defined by developmentalists as marriage between individuals who tend to be dissimilar with respect to such variables as attitudes, interests, goals, socioeconomic status, religion, ethnic background, and local origin.

social homogamy The similarity of a couple's leisure interests and role preferences.

>> **Response for Social Scientists**
(from page 533) First, no other nation has a divorce rate as high as the United States. Second, even the 50 percent divorce rate in the United States comes from dividing the number of divorces by the number of marriages. Because some people get married and divorced many times, that minority provides data that drive up the ratio and skew the average. (Actually, even in the United States, only one first marriage in three—not one in two—ends in divorce.) Finally, because you have read that teenage marriages are especially likely to end, you can deduce that older brides and grooms are less likely to divorce. The odds of your friend getting divorced are about one in five, as long as the couple has established a fair degree of social homogamy.

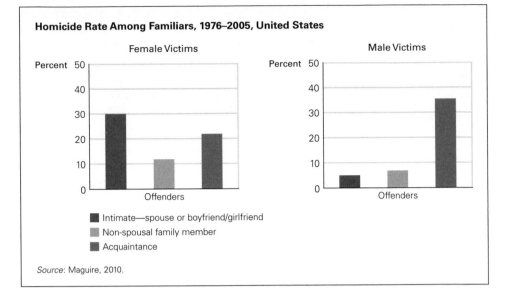

FIGURE 19.3

Fair Fight? Close relationships include passion and intimacy, which almost always leads to conflict at some point. Ideally, arguments should be dealt with using humor and love, yet if a woman is murdered, most likely her lover/husband is the killer. Does this mean that men are particularly hot-headed, or that women are particularly infuriating?

demand/withdraw interaction A situation in a romantic relationship wherein one partner wants to address an issue and the other refuses, resulting in opposite reactions—one insistent on talk while the other cuts short the conversation.

Learning to Listen

No relationship is always smooth, because each person has preferences and habits that differ from those of every other person. Early in my marriage, my husband organized the silverware drawer in our kitchen, thinking he was doing me a favor by separating salad and dinner forks, and so on. I was furious; I liked my way, resented his actions, and had half a dozen reasons why he was wrong and I was right. Fortunately, we figured out what was beneath my anger, and that fight became a joke in later decades.

According to John Gottman, who has videotaped and studied thousands of couples, conflict is less predictive of separation than disgust because disgust closes down intimacy. If a couple "fights fair," using humor and attending to each other's emotions as they disagree, conflict can contribute to commitment and intimacy (Gottman et al., 2002). Not every researcher agrees. Other studies of young couples (dating, cohabiting, and married) report that conflict may undermine a relationship (Kim et al., 2007). Much depends on how the conflict ends—with better understanding or with resentment.

One particularly destructive pattern is called **demand/withdraw interaction,** when one partner insists and the other retreats (e.g., "We need to talk about this" is met with "No—I'm too busy"). This is "consistently characteristic of ailing marriages," according to Gottman (Gottman et al., 2002, p. 22), and is probably evident among dating couples as well. An international study of young adults in romantic relationships (some dating, some cohabiting, some married) in Brazil, Italy, Taiwan, and the United States found that constructive communication was crucial for satisfaction (see the Research Design).

Women were more likely to be demanding and men, withdrawing, although the demand/withdraw interaction was also harmful if the sex roles were reversed. The authors explain:

> If couples cannot resolve their differences, then demand/withdraw interaction is likely not only to persist but also to become extreme. We believe that demand and withdraw may potentiate each other so that demanding leads to greater withdrawal and withdrawal leads to greater demanding. This repeated but frustrating and painful interaction can then damage relationship satisfaction.

[Christensen et al., 2006, p. 1040]

> **Research Design**

Scientists: Andrew Christensen, Kathleen Eldridge, Adriana Bokel Catta-Preta, Veronica R. Lim, and Rossella Santagata.

Publication: *Journal of Marriage and Family* (2006).

Participants: College students, aged 18 to 30, from Brazil, Italy, Taiwan, and the United States. Participants had to have been in their current relationship for less than 10 years (the average was 2½ years) and had to speak the native language fluently.

Design: Participants answered many written questions, focusing on communication patterns. Particular attention was given to the demand/withdraw pattern and to relationship satisfaction.

Major conclusion: Communication between both partners was impaired by demand/withdraw interaction. As this and many other studies have found, emerging adults in developing and developed nations need to talk and listen to each other, with neither partner demanding or withdrawing.

Comment: Such international research is needed and welcome, in part because some Westerners wonder whether Erikson's intimacy needs are merely a phenomenon of contemporary emerging adults in the United States. This study confirms universal patterns, albeit with some limitations pointed out by the authors: The participants were volunteers and the data were based on self-reports. This study is a good beginning. Needed is international longitudinal and behavioral research.

Intimate Partner Violence

Much worse than mere "damage to relationship satisfaction," sometimes an unmet demand leads to domestic abuse. In some abusive relationships, constructive communication may be impossible; in others, mediation can teach both partners how to improve their relationship. First, the background.

Surveys in the United States and Canada find that each year about 12 percent of all men say they have pushed, grabbed, shoved, or slapped their partner at least once. Between 1 and 3 percent have hit, kicked, beaten up, or threatened with a knife or a gun (Macmillan & Gartner, 1999; Straus & Gelles, 1995). Both of these studies had large samples and asked a variety of questions, so most experts consider them reliable.

You know, however, that survey accuracy depends on selection methods, honesty of participants, specifics of the questions, analysis, and cohort changes—all of which are particularly problematic in domestic violence. For these reasons, no one is certain of the rate of intimate partner violence (a better phrase than *spouse abuse*, which assumes marriage), which abusers are unlikely to recognize or admit. For example, some studies of intimate partner violence among Hispanics report higher rates than among European Americans; other studies report lower rates (Cunradi, 2009). Nonetheless, every expert and survey agree on three basic facts:

1. Emerging adults experience more intimate partner violence, both as victims and perpetrators, than those over age 25.
2. Alcohol and drugs make violence more likely and more severe.
3. Rates are high (10 percent is about the lowest) and would be higher if self-deception and dishonesty weren't factors but would be lower if various preventative measures were in place.

Surveys outside North America also report high rates. In China, 14 percent of women experienced "severe physical abuse" (hitting, kicking, beating, strangling, choking, burning, threatening to use or using a weapon) in their lifetime, with 6 percent reporting such abuse in the past year (almost always at the hands of their husbands) (Xu et al., 2005). In Iran, women reported widespread abuse by their husbands: 44 percent physical, 31 percent sexual, and 83 percent psychological (Vakili et al., 2010). When verbal abuse

Context Changes Shirley Hendricks signs documents sealing the deal on her new life. A former drug addict, victim, and perpetrator of couple violence, Shirley is now safe from abuse—much to the joy of her parole officer (in back). Now that she has her own apartment and a job, will she and her son, Ryan-James, finally be happy?

LEZLIE STERLING / THE SACRAMENTO BEE / ZUMA PRESS

(hostile or insulting comments such as "You're too fat" or "You're a lousy lover") was included, a New Zealand cohort of 25-year-olds reported that 70 percent of those in relationships (married or not) experienced abuse (Fergusson et al., 2005).

Traditionally, women, not men, were asked about domestic abuse because it was assumed that women were victims and men were abusers. It is true that more women are seriously injured or killed by their male lovers than vice versa, evident in every hospital emergency room or homicide summary. However, when the definition of abuse includes threats, insults, and slaps as well as physical battering, some studies find more abusive women than men (Archer, 2000; Fergusson et al., 2005; Swan et al., 2008).

The original, mistaken male-abuser/female-victim assumption occurred because abusive men are physically stronger, thus causing more injury, and because socialization makes men reluctant to admit that they are victims. Likewise, same-sex couples hesitate to publicly acknowledge that they have problems, although in domestic violence and most other aspects of relationships, they are very similar to heterosexual couples (Gelles, 1997; Kurdek, 2006; Langhinrichsen-Rohling, 2009).

Social scientists have identified numerous causes of domestic violence, including youth, poverty, personality (such as poor impulse control), mental illness (such as antisocial disorders), and drug and alcohol addiction. Developmentalists note that many children who are harshly punished, who are sexually abused, or who witness domestic assault grow up to become abusers or victims themselves. Neighborhood chaos is also a factor, as is the cultural acceptance of violence (Olsen et al., 2010). When women resist traditional roles, they are more likely to be abused—true in the United States as well as internationally. This is one reason why Hispanic women who were born in the United States are more likely to be abused than are those born in Latin America (Cunradi, 2009).

Knowing these causes points toward prevention. Halting child maltreatment, for instance, averts some later abuse. It is also useful to learn more about each abusive relationship. Researchers differentiate two forms of intimate partner abuse: **situational couple violence** and **intimate terrorism,** each of which has distinct causes, patterns, and means of prevention (M. P. Johnson, 2008; M. P. Johnson & Ferraro, 2000; Swan et al., 2008). *Situational couple violence* occurs when both partners fight—with words, slaps, and exclusion (leaving home, refusing sex, and so on)—and yet both partners are sometimes caring and affectionate. The situation brings out the anger, and then the partners abuse each other. This is the most common form, and women are at least as active in situational violence as men.

Situational couple violence can be reduced with maturation and counseling; both partners need to learn how to interact without violence. Often the roots are in the culture, not primarily in the individuals, which makes it possible for adults who love each other to learn how to overcome the culture of violence (Olsen et al., 2010).

Intimate terrorism is more violent and more demeaning. It is more likely to involve a male abuser and female victim and also more likely to lead to serious harm. It is dangerous to the victim and to anyone who tries to intervene, as well as more difficult to treat. The terrorist gets some satisfaction from abuse, and the victim usually cowers and apologizes. When the wife is terrorized, she is not only physically hurt but socially isolated, which makes her so beaten down that she does not resist—until the children are also hurt. With intimate terrorism, immediate separation from the abuser and relocation to a safe place are essential. The victim also needs help to restore her confidence and independence.

situational couple violence Fighting between romantic partners that is brought on more by the situation than by the deep personality problems of the individuals. Both partners are typically victims and abusers.

intimate terrorism A violent and demeaning form of abuse in a romantic relationship, where the victim (usually female) is frightened to fight back, seek help, or withdraw. In this case, the victim is in danger of physical as well as psychological harm.

Emerging Adults and Their Parents

It is hard to overestimate the importance of the family at any time of the life span. Families are "our most important individual support system" (Schaie, 2002, p. 318). Although made up of individuals, a family is much more than the persons who belong to it. In dynamic synergy, children grow, adults find support, and everyone is part of an ethos that gives meaning to, and provides models for, personal aspirations and decisions.

Linked Lives

Emerging adults are said to set out on their own, leaving their childhood home and parents behind. They strive for independence (Arnett, 2004). It might seem as if they no longer need parental support and guidance, but the data show that parents continue to be crucial—perhaps even more so than for previous generations. Fewer emerging adults have established their own families, secured high-paying jobs, or achieved a definitive understanding of their identity and their goals.

All members of each family have **linked lives,** meaning that the experiences and needs of family members at one stage of life are affected by those at other stages (Macmillan & Copher, 2005). We have seen this in earlier chapters: Children are affected by their parents' relationship, even if they are not directly involved in domestic disputes, financial stresses, parental alliances, and so on.

The same historical conditions that gave rise to the stage now called emerging adulthood may have an unanticipated benefit: stronger links between parents and their adult children. Because of demographic changes over the past few decades, most middle-aged parents have just one or two children, who were born within a few years of each other. As a result, the parents can attend to the needs of their emerging adults, since they have no babies or young children. Their concern is intensified by several factors: Their young adult children are usually not married, not parents, and almost never vocationally secure (long gone are the days when many of the young took over the family business or farm).

linked lives Lives in which the success, health, and well-being of each family member are connected to those of other members, including those of another generation, as in the relationship between parents and children.

Brilliant, Unemployed, and Laughing Not an unusual combination for contemporary college graduates. Melissa, in Missoula, Montana, graduated summa cum laude from George Washington University and is now one of many college graduates who live with their parents. The arrangement provides many financial and family benefits, but it is not known who cooked dinner and who will wash the dishes.

Many emerging adults still live at home, though this varies from nation to nation. Almost all unmarried young adults in Italy and Japan live with their parents, as do half of those in England (Manzi et al., 2006). Fewer do so in the United States, but many parents underwrite their young-adult children's independent living (Furstenberg, 2010).

Strong links between emerging adults and their parents may seem counterintuitive, as emerging adults are independent and cohort changes have occurred. Nonetheless, many studies have found congruence in attitudes between parents and their young-adult children. For instance, in North America as well as in the nations of northern Europe, adults of every age encourage young adults to become independent of their parents.

Furthermore, a detailed Dutch study found substantial agreement between parents and their adult children on issues that might, in theory, be contentious—such as cohabitation, same-sex partnerships, and divorce. Some generational differences appeared, but when parents were compared with their own children (not young adults in general), convergence of attitudes was apparent (Bucx et al., 2010). Adult children who still lived with their parents (about one-fourth of the sample) were more likely to agree with their parents than were adults who lived apart from them, but all groups showed "intergenerational convergence" (Bucx et al., 2010, p. 131).

In many nations, researchers find a connection among early attachment; adult perceptions of their current relationships with their parents; and adult relationships with friends, lovers, and children (Grossmann et al., 2005; Mikulincer & Goodman, 2006; Sroufe et al., 2005). Securely attached infants are more likely to become happily married adults; avoidant infants may hesitate to marry.

Financial Support

Parents of all income levels in the United States provide substantial help to their adult children, for many reasons. One is that they have more income than their children: Often both parents are employed and have some job seniority. In general, households with the highest average income are headed by someone aged 45 to 54 (U.S. Bureau of the Census, 2009). Furthermore, parents of emerging adults are not yet distracted by their own health or retirement concerns. In nations such as the United States, where neither college education nor young children's day care is free, parental financial help may be crucial (Furstenberg, 2010).

This is not to criticize earlier cohorts, because parents have always wanted to help their offspring. Now, however, more of them are able to give both money and time. Not surprisingly, then, one obvious connection between parents and adult children is financial. For example, very few young college students pay all their tuition and living expenses on their own. Parents provide support; loans, part-time employment, and partial scholarships also contribute.

About one-half of all emerging adults receive cash from their parents in addition to tuition, medical care, food, and other material support. Most are also given substantial gifts of time, such as help with laundry, moving, household repairs, and, if the young adult becomes a parent, free child care. This assistance makes possible the achievement of various goals (Schoeni & Ross, 2005). Getting a college degree is especially hard without family help.

Lack of family financial support is a problem for some emerging adults. College is costly; living expenses must be covered, and even with government subsidies many young adults from low-income families cannot afford higher education (see Figure 19.4). In every nation, college graduation rates decrease as family income falls (Organisation for Economic Co-operation and Development, 2008). A

Especially for Family Therapists More emerging-adult children today live with their parents than ever before, yet you have learned that families often function better when young adults live on their own. What would you advise? (see response, page 542)

"Don't give me too much, I'm not good with money."

How Old Is He? Appropriate financial planning is one of the skills of adulthood beyond the grasp of many emerging adults.

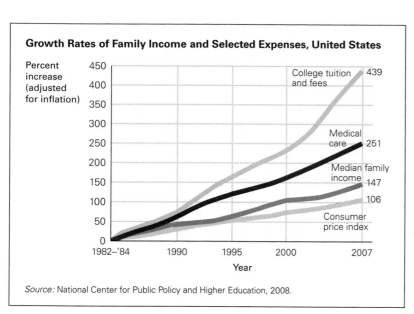

Growth Rates of Family Income and Selected Expenses, United States

Source: National Center for Public Policy and Higher Education, 2008.

FIGURE 19.4

Valuable, but Increasingly Unaffordable
In the past 25 years, U.S. family income (up 147 percent since 1982) has kept pace with rising prices except in two important sectors: health care (up 251 percent) and college tuition and fees (up 439 percent).

particular problem is evident for children who are in foster care: At age 18, they are considered adults, able to take their place in society. Given all that is now known about emerging adults, this is far too young (Avery & Freundlich, 2009).

A Global Perspective

Looking at many cultures, it is apparent that families can be destructive as well as helpful to emerging adults. For example, a study of enmeshment (e.g., parents always knowing what their emerging-adult children are doing and thinking) found that British emerging adults were less happy and less successful if their parents were too intrusive. However, emerging adults in Italy seem able to remain closely connected with their parents without hindering their own development (Manzi et al., 2006).

Some Westerners believe that family dependence is more evident in developing nations. There is some truth in this. For example, many African young adults marry someone approved by their parents and work to support their many relatives—siblings, parents, cousins, uncles, and so on. Individuals sacrifice personal goals for family concerns, and "collectivism often takes precedence and overrides individual needs and interests," which makes "the family a source of both collective identity and tension" (Wilson & Ngige, 2006, p. 248).

In cultures with arranged marriages, parents not only provide practical support (such as child care) and emotional encouragement, they may also protect their child. If the relationship is a disaster (for instance, the husband severely beats the wife, the wife refuses sex, the husband never works, or the wife never cooks), then the parents intervene. Again, each couple within each culture judges such intervention differently: What is expected in, say, Cambodia, would be unacceptable in, say, Colorado.

There are advantages to this family involvement. Each new baby is cared for by many people, so young adults are less burdened by child care. This may be one reason why parenthood begins much earlier in poor nations. By contrast, parenthood in the United States is a major impediment to higher education and career success (Osgood et al., 2005), which may be one reason why emerging adults postpone it (Furstenberg, 2010).

>> **Response for Family Therapists**
(from page 540) Remember that family function is more important than family structure. Sharing a home can work out well if contentious issues—like sexual privacy, money, and household chores—are clarified before resentments arise. You might offer a three-session preparation package, to explore assumptions and guidelines.

Cultural differences aside, in every nation young adults are encouraged to do well in school and to get good jobs, partly to make their families proud, partly so they will be able to care for their families when necessary, and partly for their own future. Immigrant young adults tend to be highly motivated to learn and work, and they reciprocate their parents' support. These values help them to become more successful than many native-born young adults (Mollenkopf et al., 2005).

When we look at actual lives, not the cultural image of independence or interdependence, emerging adults worldwide have much in common, including close family connections and a new freedom from parental limits (Georgas et al., 2006). Although specifics differ, it is a mistake to assume that emerging adults in Western nations abandon their parents. Indeed, some studies find that family relationships *improve* when young adults leave home (Graber & Brooks-Gunn, 1996; Smetana et al., 2004). Family members continue to feel obligated to one another. In fact, parents and adult children tend to expect more family obligation from their own generation than from the other generation (Bucx et al., 2010).

Sharing living quarters is not the best indicator of a supportive relationship. Emerging adults who live independently but who previously had close relationships with their parents are more likely to avoid serious risks to their health and safety than those who had been alienated from their parents. Interestingly, although most children are closer to their mothers than to their fathers, for emerging adults fathers are particularly influential, for good or ill (Schwartz et al., 2009).

As we think about the experiences of emerging adults overall, it is apparent that this stage of life has many pitfalls as well as benefits. These years may be crucial, as "decisions made during the transition to adulthood have a particularly long-lasting influence on the remainder of the life course because they set individuals on paths that are sometimes difficult to change" (Thornton et al., 2007, p. 13).

Fortunately, most emerging adults, like humans of all ages, have strengths as well as liabilities. Many survive risks, overcome substance abuse, combat loneliness, and deal with other problems through further education, friends and family, and maturation. If they postpone marriage, prevent parenthood, and avoid a set career until their identity is firmly established and their education complete, they may be ready for all the commitments and responsibilities of adulthood, described in the next chapters.

SUMMING UP

Intimacy needs are universal for all young adults, but the ways in which they are met vary by culture and cohort. In developed nations in the twenty-first century, most emerging adults have many friends, including some of the other sex, and a series of romantic relationships before marriage. Cohabitation is common, although it does not necessarily further the passion, intimacy, or commitment that emerging adults seek. In many other nations, arranged marriages are common. Parental support and linked lives are typical everywhere. In some families and nations, this support includes substantial financial assistance. ■

SUMMARY

Continuity and Change

1. Although Erikson thought that most people achieved identity by the end of adolescence, for today's youth the identity crisis continues into adulthood.

2. For emerging adults in multiethnic nations, ethnic identity becomes important but difficult to achieve. Combining local traditions and global concerns, accommodating both parental wishes and peer pressures, and accepting past heritage without past prejudices require complex psychosocial adjustment.

3. Vocational identity requires knowing what career one will have. Few young adults are certain about their career goals. Societies offer several moratoria on identity achievement (such as college) that allow postponement of vocational identity.

4. In today's job market, many adults of all ages switch jobs, with turnover particularly quick in emerging adulthood. Most short-term jobs are not connected to the young person's skills or ambitions. Vocational identity, as Erikson conceived it, is elusive.

5. Personality can change in emerging adulthood, but continuity is also apparent. Many emerging adults find an appropriate combination of education, friendship, and achievement that improves their self-esteem. Even unusually aggressive or shy children can become quite happy adults.

Intimacy

6. Close friendships typically include some other-sex as well as same-sex friends. Gender separation is less common than it once was, but women still exchange more confidences and physical affection than men do. Male friendships often center on shared activities.

7. Romantic love is complex, involving passion, intimacy, and commitment. In some nations, commitment is crucial and parents arrange marriages with that in mind. Among emerging adults in developed nations, passion is more important but does not necessarily lead to marriage.

8. Many emerging adults use social networking and matchmaking sites on the Internet to expand and deepen their friendship circles and mating options. This has advantages and disadvantages.

9. Cohabitation is increasingly common, with marked national variations. This arrangement does not necessarily improve marital happiness or stability.

10. Marriages work best if couples are able to communicate well and share responsibilities. Changes in relationships between spouses are evident over the past decades, but the impact of these changes seems both positive and negative.

11. Conflict is part of many intimate relationships. The pattern called demand/withdraw interaction harms a marriage. Intimate partner violence is common worldwide and may be an outgrowth of a culture of violence that can be mitigated, or of a deeply rooted psychosocial disorder that requires protection of the abused partner.

12. Family support is needed lifelong. Family members have linked lives, always affected by one another and often helping one another at every age.

13. In most nations, emerging adults and their parents are closely connected. Sometimes this means living in the same household, but even when it does not, complete separation of the two generations is unusual and impairs young adults' achievement.

14. Especially in nations with less public support for young adults, parents often pay college costs, provide free child care, and contribute in other ways to their young-adult children's welfare.

KEY TERMS

intimacy versus isolation (p. 525)
hookups (p. 531)
social networks (p. 531)

choice overload (p. 531)
cohabitation (p. 532)
homogamy (p. 535)
heterogamy (p. 535)

social homogamy (p. 535)
demand/withdraw interaction (p. 536)

situational couple violence (p. 538)
intimate terrorism (p. 538)
linked lives (p. 539)

WHAT HAVE YOU LEARNED?

Continuity and Change

1. How is attending college a moratorium?

2. How does ethnic pride change from early adolescence to adulthood?

3. Why are many emerging adults quite specific about their ethnic heritage?

4. How are romantic preferences related to ethnicity?

5. How does college help or hinder the development of vocational identity?

6. Why might vocational identity be an "outdated social construction"?

7. Which personality factors foster continuity and which encourage change?

8. What is the general trend of self-esteem during emerging adulthood?

Intimacy

9. How does the Internet affect friendship?

10. What gender differences in friendship are typical among men and among women?

11. What are the advantages and disadvantages of male–female friendships?

12. What do emerging adults seek in a romantic partner?

13. What are the three dimensions of love, according to Sternberg?

14. How has social networking changed the process of mate selection?

15. Why do many emerging adults cohabit instead of marrying?

16. What does most research conclude about the long-term effects of cohabitation?

17. What happens when couples choose partners who are unlike themselves?

18. Why is demand/withdraw interaction particularly destructive of a relationship?

19. When are counseling and mediation likely to succeed with intimate partner violence?

20. When is immediate protection and separation needed in intimate partner violence?

21. What are the gender differences in intimate partner violence?

22. Why do people assume that emerging adults are not influenced by their parents?

23. What kinds of support do parents provide their young-adult children?

24. How is family interaction affected when young adults live in their parents' homes?

APPLICATIONS

1. Talk to three people you would expect to have contrasting views on love and marriage (differences in age, gender, upbringing, experience, and religion might affect attitudes). Ask each the same questions and then compare their answers.

2. Analyze 50 marriage announcements (with photographs of the couples) in the newspaper. How much homogamy and heterogamy are evident?

3. Vocational identity is fluid in early adulthood. Talk with several people over age 30 about their work history. Are they doing what they expected they'd be doing when they were younger? Are they settled in their vocation and job? Pay attention to their age when they decided on their jobs. Was age 25 a turning point?

4. Observe couples walking together on your campus. Do your observation systematically, such as describing every third couple who walk past a particular spot. Can you tell the difference in body position or facial expression between men and women and between lovers, friends, and acquaintances? Once you have an answer, test your hypothesis by asking several of your observed couples what their relationship is.

>> ONLINE CONNECTIONS

To accompany your textbook, you have access to a number of online resources, including quizzes for every chapter of the book, flashcards (in English and Spanish), critical thinking questions, and case studies. For access to any of these links, go to www.worthpublishers.com/bergerls8e. In addition to these free resources, you'll also find links to the podcasts, video clips, diagnostic quizzing with personalized study advice, and an ebook. Some of the videos and activities available online include:

- *Transition to Parenthood.* Videos of couples in various stages of parenthood highlight the physical, emotional, social, household, and vocational changes that accompany this new responsibility.

- *Homosexuality: Genes versus Environment.* What makes someone gay? This video shows how the nature–nurture debate plays out when applied to this question.

Emerging Adulthood

BIOSOCIAL

Growth and Health Bodies are strong, healthy, and active. Homeostasis protects against too much stress in any one system, and sexual and reproductive potential are at their peak of the entire life span. Unlike in previous centuries, emerging adults no longer need to use all their physical strength and sexuality to work and bear children; thus, they must find other ways to express potential and avoid sexually transmitted diseases. Although most cope well with their new freedom, for some the stresses of this period make psychopathology more common, including major depression, anxiety, and schizophrenia.

Health Habits Good health habits include improving nutrition, increasing exercise, and avoiding dangerous risks and addictive drugs. Unfortunately, many emerging adults struggle to maintain good habits. Consequently, although death due to disease is rare, violent death and serious injury are far too common.

COGNITIVE

Postformal Thought Emerging adults may reach a fifth stage of cognition, called postformal thought. Whether this qualifies as a "stage" is controversial, but there is no doubt that adults learn to balance emotions and logic and that the experiences of adulthood move individuals toward deeper reflection and moral analysis. Religious faith may also become more mature.

College Tertiary education aims to advance critical thinking as well as to develop communication and practical skills. Usually, these goals are achieved. More and more emerging adults attend college, a trend particularly apparent among women (who traditionally achieved less education than men), members of minority groups, and in developing nations—especially in Asia and Africa. One result is that emerging adults everywhere are exposed to a wider range of ideas and values.

PSYCHOSOCIAL

Identity Achieved Emerging adults continue on the path toward identity achievement, finding vocational and ethnic identity particularly difficult as economic pressures and ethnic diversity increase. Personality patterns, inherited or developed in childhood, become more stable—although change is possible at every stage.

Intimacy Friendships become very important as a buffer against the stresses of emerging adulthood, as well as a way to find romantic partners. Many young adults cohabit with a partner, with the intent of getting married someday (but not just yet). Relationship problems, including domestic violence, are more common in early adulthood than later on.

Family Connections Families of origin continue to be supportive of their young-adult children, offering financial and emotional help and often providing a home as well. The impact of living with one's parents depends not only on the habits and personality of the emerging adult, but also on cultural norms.

P A R T

VII

CHAPTERS 20•21•22

adulthood

We now begin the seventh part of this text. These three chapters cover 40 years (ages 25 to 65), when bodies mature, minds master new material, and people work productively.

Adulthood covers four decades because no particular age connects to any one episode: Adults nurture marriages, raise children, and care for aging parents; they experience hiring and firing, poverty and wealth, births and deaths, weddings and divorces, disasters and wind-falls, illnesses and recovery—all as the moments of time bring them closer to late adulthood. Thus, adulthood is a long sweep, punctuated by many events, both joyful and sorrowful in turn, which may occur at any time during those 40 years.

Although not programmed by chronological age, events are not random: Adults build on their past development, creating their own ecological niche, with chosen people, activities, communities, and habits. For the most part, these are good years, when each person's goals become more attainable as people make decisions about the life they live.

Culture and context are always crucial. Indeed, the very concept that people choose their niche is assumed in North America but not in places where families, economics, and past history shape almost every aspect of life. Divorce, for instance, is a chosen sequel for almost half the marriages in the United States, but until recently divorce was not legal in three nations (Chile, Malta, and the Philippines). Some experiences thought to be part of adulthood—midlife crisis, sandwich generation, and empty nest among them—are unusual. These three chapters describe what is universal, what is usual, and what is not.

CHAPTER

Adulthood: Biosocial Development

WHAT WILL YOU KNOW?

1. When does a person's appearance start to show his or her age?

2. Which of the senses is most likely to decline before age 65?

3. Should couples bear children before age 30, 40, or 50?

4. How can you turn your stressors into challenges?

Jenny was in her early 30s, a star student in my human development class. She told the class that she was divorced, raising her son, daughter, and two orphaned nephews in public housing in the South Bronx. She spoke eloquently and enthusiastically about free activities for her children—public parks, museums, the zoo, Fresh Air camp. We were awed by her creativity and energy.

A year later, Jenny came to my office to speak privately. She told me she was four weeks pregnant. The father, Billy, was a married man who told her he would not leave his wife but would pay for an abortion. She thought she should terminate the pregnancy, but she wanted to talk to me first.

I learned more. She was not opposed to abortion on religious grounds; her son needed special education for a speech impediment; she thought she was too old to have another infant; she was a carrier for sickle-cell anemia, which had complicated her previous pregnancy; her crowded apartment was not "babyproof," since her youngest child was 7. She was about to graduate with honors and had found a job that would enable her to move out of her dangerous neighborhood. She was eager to get on with her adult life.

After a long talk, she thanked me profusely—although I had only asked questions, provided facts, and listened. Then came the surprise: "I'll have the baby," Jenny said. "Men come and go, but children are always with you." I had thought her narrative was leading her to a different conclusion, but her values shaped her life, not mine. We all make choices about our bodies and our futures.

Adulthood covers four decades, from ages 25 to 65. Despite feeling "too old" to have another baby, Jenny was a relatively young adult. Nonetheless, wondering about childbearing and child rearing is common among adults of all ages, as are worries about health and aging. This chapter explains the facts regarding the choices each adult makes about sex, reproduction, and aging.

This chapter also details the physiological changes of adulthood—changes in strength, appearance, and body functioning. Many people are concerned about some aspects of vision, hearing, and disease that occur long before they are senior citizens. Issues of habits, health, and medical care include many aspects of lifestyle and personal choices. You will read research and facts; as with Jenny, the conclusions are yours. At the end of this chapter, you will learn what happened to her after she left my office.

senescence A gradual physical decline related to aging. Senescence occurs in everyone and in every body part, but the rate of decline is highly variable within and between persons.

>> Senescence

Everyone ages. As soon as growth stops, **senescence,** a gradual physical decline over time, begins. Senescence affects every part of the body, visible and invisible.

The Experience of Aging

It is crucial to understand that, although senescence affects every part of the body, and although some parts of the body function less well because of it, senescence does not necessarily or directly cause illness or even impairment.

This may seem confusing, but it will become clear with an example. Two of the invisible aspects of aging are increases in blood pressure and in low-density lipoprotein (LDL) cholesterol. Both occur in everyone over time, and if either reaches high levels, that predicts heart disease. Thus, coronary heart disease correlates with certain blood measurements that correlate with senescence, but senescence does not directly *cause* heart disease. Indeed, most 25- to 65-year-olds' hearts beat strong, and, with good genes and good health habits, those hearts will be disease-free for many years after age 65.

Therefore, senescence is less disturbing than emerging adults might imagine. Fewer middle-aged adults are depressed than younger adults, and often happiness increases with age, as described in Chapter 25. Many middle-aged adults think they are years away from old age. One survey reported that emerging adults thought people became old at age 60, but the older an adult was, the later "old" was thought to begin: Those over age 64 thought old began at age 74. Furthermore, although half of the younger adults said they felt as old as they actually were (about one-fourth felt older and another fourth felt younger), that was not true of adults aged 30 to 65. Most of them felt 5 to 10 years younger than their chronological age (Pew Research Center, June 29, 2009). Other research confirms that most adults feel strong, capable, healthy, and "in their prime."

Some physiological aspects of the body protect adults. Chapter 17 explained two of them: organ reserve and homeostasis. Every organ has reserve power that allows normal functioning throughout the adult years: People rarely notice that their hearts, lungs, and so on are losing reserve capacity because hearts at rest function well until after age 70. Furthermore, homeostasis keeps every physical function in balance. For instance, vital capacity (the amount of air expelled after a deep breath) is reduced and oxygen dispersal into the bloodstream from the lungs drops about 4 percent per decade (faster for smokers), so breathing becomes quicker and more shallow as homeostasis keeps sufficient oxygen in the blood (P. S. Timiras & De Martinis, 2007). As a result, older adults may pause at the top of a long flight of stairs to "catch their breath," but that is a minor inconvenience, not a serious problem.

Physical stamina and power are influenced by many factors, not just age. Most adults make sure they can accomplish what they want. Suppose a 50-year-old wants to run a marathon. No problem—if he or she does practice runs, eats well, and gets enough rest for a year or more.

PATRICK FRASER / CORBIS OUTLINE

A Trick Question How old is he? His leg muscles and the angle of his stretch make him comparable to a fit 30-year-old. However, the placement of this photo should give you a clue about his real age—he is 61.

The Aging Brain

Like every other part of the body, the brain slows down with age. Neurons fire more slowly, and messages sent from the axon of one neuron are not picked up as quickly by the dendrite of another neuron, so reaction time lengthens. Brain size decreases, with fewer neurons and synapses in middle adulthood than earlier (Buckner et al., 2006). Multitasking becomes harder, processing takes longer, and complex working-memory tasks (e.g., repeating a series of eight numbers, then adding the first four, deleting the fifth one, subtracting the next two, and multiplying the new total by the last one—all in your head) may become impossible (Fabiani & Gratton, 2009).

A few individuals (less than 1 percent under age 65) experience significant brain loss with age, just as a few lose notable muscle strength. Those few "encounter a catastrophic rate of cognitive decline, passing through . . . the dementia threshold" (Dangour et al., 2007, p. 54). But for 99 percent of adults, neurological reserves and homeostasis within the brain make loss of neurons insignificant. Adults can perform the brain equivalent of a marathon—one reason that judges, bishops, and world leaders are usually at least 50 years old. If severe brain loss occurs in middle adulthood, the cause is not senescence but usually one of the following:

- *Drug abuse.* All psychoactive drugs can harm the brain, especially high consumption of alcohol over decades, which can cause Wernike-Korsakoff syndrome ("wet brain").
- *Poor circulation.* Everything that impairs blood flow—such as hypertension (high blood pressure) and heavy cigarette smoking—impairs cognition.
- *Viruses.* The blood–brain barrier keeps most viruses away, but a few—including HIV and the prion that causes mad cow disease—can destroy neurons.
- *Genes.* About one in a thousand persons inherits a dominant gene for Alzheimer disease, which destroys memory.

(These four factors are the common physiological reasons for brain slowdown in adulthood; cognitive function is described in the next chapter.)

Physical Appearance

Although a person's physical strength is no longer an important component of the ability to work, although most diseases are not yet lethal, and although brain function is more than adequate, one set of changes that senescence brings may be problematic in an age-conscious society. External changes—in skin, hair, agility, and body shape—show age. Few people want to look old. Yet even by age 30, they do, at least compared to themselves at 20.

Skin and Hair

The first visible changes are in the skin, which becomes dryer, rougher, and less regular in color. Collagen, the main component of the connective tissue of the body, decreases by about 1 percent per year, starting at age 20 (M. L. Timiras, 2007). By age 30, the skin is thinner and less flexible, the cells just beneath the surface are more variable, and wrinkles become visible, particularly around the eyes. Diet has an effect—fat slows down wrinkling—but aging is apparent in every layer of the skin (Nagata et al., 2010).

Wrinkles are not the only sign of skin senescence, of course. Especially on the face (the body part most exposed to sun, rain, heat, cold, and pollution), the skin loses "firmness and elasticity, leading to the formation of sagging areas such as the infamous double chin" (Whitbourne, 2008, p. 88). This is barely noticeable in young adulthood, but if you meet a typical pair of siblings, one 18 and the other 28, you can tell who is older by their skin. By age 60, all faces are wrinkled—some much more than others—and the smooth, taut, flexible young face has disappeared.

Hair usually turns gray and thins, first at the temples by age 40, and then over the rest of the scalp. This does not affect health, but since hair is a visible sign of aging, adults spend money and time on coloring, thickening, styling, and more.

Especially for Drivers A number of states have passed laws requiring that hands-free headphones be worn by people who use cell phones while driving. Do those measures cut down on accidents? (see response, page 552)

No Wrinkles An injection of Botox to plump the skin beneath her eyebrows is what this woman has decided she needs, although she is quite beautiful and shows no signs of aging.

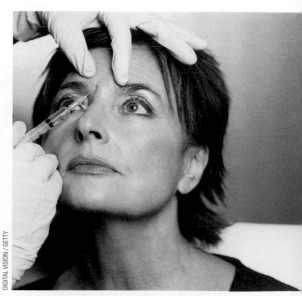

DIGITAL VISION / GETTY

>> Response for Drivers (from page 551)
No. Car accidents occur when the mind is distracted, not the hands.

Body hair (on the arms, legs, and pubic area) also becomes thinner and lighter. An occasional thick and unwanted hair may appear on the chin, inside the nose, or in some other place.

Shape and Agility

The body changes shape between ages 25 and 65. A "middle-age spread" increases waist circumference; all the muscles weaken; pockets of fat settle on the abdomen, the upper arms, the buttocks, and the chin; people stoop slightly when they stand (Whitbourne et al., 2008). By late middle age, even if they stretch to their tallest, adults are shorter than they were earlier in life. Back muscles, connective tissue, and bones lose density, making the vertebrae in the spine shrink. People lose about an inch of height (2 to 3 centimeters) by age 65. That loss occurs not in the leg bones but in the trunk, as the cushioning between spinal disks becomes compressed (Tilling et al., 2006)—another reason that waists widen.

Agility is also reduced, so rising from sitting on the floor, twisting in a dance, or even walking "with a spring in your step" is more difficult. The joints lose flexibility; stiffness is more evident; bending is harder, especially by middle age. Substantial variability is evident, not only from person to person but within each person. For instance, the fibers for Type II muscles (the fast ones needed for forceful actions in many sports) are said to be reduced 26 percent a decade beginning at age 30 (McCarter, 2006), but there is much less decline in Type I fibers, needed for slower, more routine muscle movements.

Compared with emerging adults, adults are less able to win a 100-meter dash than a marathon, less able to lift a heavy rock than to pick tomatoes all day. Loss of strength in the leg muscles may affect health, since walking helps blood circulation and digestion, both crucial for longevity. Thus, leg-strengthening and balance exercises are beneficial, not just for appearance but also for health.

The aging of the body is most evident in sports that require strength, agility, and speed: Gymnasts, boxers, and basketball players are among the athletes who benefit from youth but who experience slowdowns already by age 20. Of course, these are physiological slowdowns: The intellectual and emotional gains of adulthood may compensate for the physical changes, making some 30-year-olds better athletes than their younger teammates.

Sense Organs

All the senses become less acute with each decade. The effects on vision and hearing have been studied extensively, so we focus on them here.

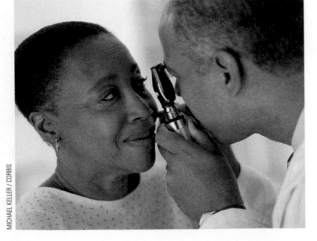

Healthy Eyes Annual examinations of the lens and retina are crucial for all middle-aged adults, especially those of African heritage.

MICHAEL KELLER / CORBIS

Vision

Not only does the rate of senescence vary from person to person and organ to organ, but each part of each organ is on its own timetable, as you already saw with muscles. Changes in the eyes are the most obvious example. Peripheral vision (at the sides) narrows faster than frontal vision; some aspects of color vision are reduced faster than others; near-sightedness and farsightedness follow different paths. To be specific, nearsightedness (difficulty seeing objects at a distance) increases gradually beginning in one's 20s (see Figure 20.1); by middle age, the process reverses as farsightedness (difficulty seeing objects that are close) increases—because the lens of the eye is less elastic and the cornea flattens (Schieber, 2006). This explains why, compared with 20-year-olds, 40-year-olds hold the newspaper much farther away (their near focus is blurry) and why many older adults need bifocals.

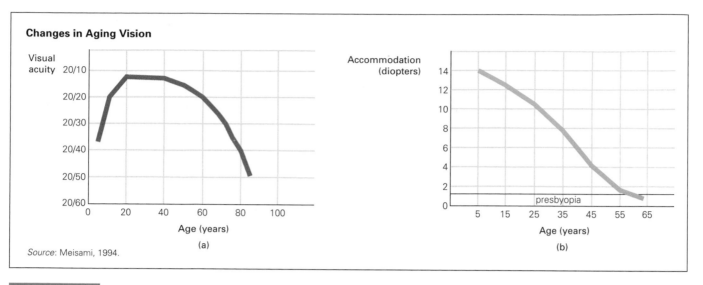

Changes in Aging Vision

(a)

Source: Meisami, 1994.

(b)

FIGURE 20.1

FIGURE 20.1

Age-Related Declines in Vision Every aspect of bodily functioning follows its own rate of senescence. Vision is a prime example. *(a)* Accurate vision overall increases in childhood and declines at about age 40, with faster decline after age 60. *(b)* By contrast, the ability to focus on a small point about 12 inches in front of the eyes declines from childhood on; at about age 60, the typical person becomes officially farsighted, thus needing reading glasses.

Other aspects of vision are also affected by age. It takes longer for the eyes to adjust to darkness (as when entering a movie theater after being in daylight) or to adjust to glare (as when headlights of an oncoming car temporarily blind the driver). In many other aspects as well, senescence may affect the vision needed for driving: Standard vision tests given for licenses do not measure whether vision is adequate for the rapid, wide scanning that helps to avoid accidents.

Hearing

Losses also occur in hearing, which is most acute at about age 10, again with specific intrapersonal variations—sounds at high frequencies (the voice of a small child) are lost earlier than sounds at low frequencies (the booming voice of a man). Although some middle-aged people hear much better than others, none hear perfectly. Actually, "perfect" hearing is impossible; hearing is always a matter of degree. (No one hears a conversation on the other side of town.) Deafness is rarely absolute, which is one reason the gradual hearing losses of age are not noticed until they begin to cause problems.

Typically, **presbycusis** (literally, "aging hearing") is not diagnosed until about age 60. One practical measure of presbycusis is the "whisper test." A person is asked to repeat something whispered by someone unseen who is 3 feet away (Pirozzo et al., 2003). Almost all emerging adults pass this test, as do two-thirds of people age 50, but only half of those over 65 do.

Although currently prebycusis is rarely problematic before age 60, an alarming study suggests that hearing problems may soon begin in middle age (Vogel et al., 2010). In this study, 30 percent of a large group of high school students (1,512 participants) reported that they already had symptoms of hearing loss (ringing, muffled sounds, temporary deafness) after they listened to music on MP3 players

Hard Rocking, Hard of Hearing Les Claypool is an example of the dangers posed by prolonged exposure to loud noise. Night after night of high-decibel rocking with his band, Primus, has damaged his hearing. When this photo was taken in 1999, Claypool was not only performing but also protecting his remaining hearing. He is active with HEAR—Hearing Education and Awareness for Rockers.

presbycusis A significant loss of hearing associated with senescence. Presbycusis usually is not apparent until after age 60.

or the like. Many had similar losses after attending concerts. Most listened to music with headphones for many hours each week, often at decibel levels known to damage the sensitive hairs of the inner ear (Vogel et al., 2010). Although many nations now mandate ear protection for workers to decrease damage from construction blasts and the like, no laws require similar protection from loud music and few individuals guard against it. (Technology to mitigate loss of hearing that has already occurred is described in Chapter 23.)

SUMMING UP

Senescence is the process of aging, evident in every body part from the moment that growth ends. The entire body slows down. However, changes in function are much less consequential today than in earlier centuries, when adults needed physical strength to complete their daily work; during most of adulthood, the brain continues to work well, which is crucial in the twenty-first century. Appearance reflects age: Skin becomes less smooth, hair is thinner and grayer, and bodies add fat. These changes have little impact on overall health, but many adults are concerned about them. All the senses become less acute over adulthood, with some aspects declining much faster than others. ▪

>> The Sexual-Reproductive System

As you just read, although senescence affects every body part, 60-year-olds can usually accomplish almost everything 30-year-olds can, albeit more slowly and selectively. There is no need to be appalled by thinner skin and weakened muscles, and many adults successfully mask superficial signs of aging, such as graying hair. However, one critical activity is virtually impossible for women and difficult for men as old age approaches—reproduction.

The aging of the sexual-reproductive system is universal, but what that means depends on historical context (especially medical advances) and local values. The most obvious example is birth control, which has transformed sexual relationships, as explained in Chapter 17. Specifics of contraception are powerfully influenced by local customs and national laws. For example, more than half the people who want to avoid conception in India rely on sterilization, more than half in Cuba use the intrauterine device (IUD), and more than half in Algeria (but very few in Japan) use the pill (T. M. Sullivan et al., 2006). Because medical contraception is unavailable to most couples in Bangladesh, they rely on early abortion (without calling it abortion) to control family size (Gipson & Hindin, 2008). Abortion itself, as you know, is illegal in some nations and readily available in others, with the United States somewhere between the extremes in practice but ideologically quite polarized.

The fact that there are a dozen or more effective ways to prevent unwanted births but that various groups practice some and avoid others is one example of a disconnect between the biology of the sexual-reproductive system and human psychology. This disconnect is also apparent in sexual arousal, orgasm, fertility, and menopause—all biological but strongly influenced by the mind. As one wag said: "The most important human sexual organ is between the . . . ears."

Sexual Responsiveness

Sexual arousal occurs more slowly with age, and orgasm takes longer. For some couples, these slowdowns are counterbalanced by reduced anxiety and better communication, as partners become more familiar with their own bodies and those of their mates. Distress at slower responsiveness seems less connected to age than to anxiety, troubled interpersonal relationships, and unrealistic fears and expectations (Duplassie & Daniluk, 2007; L. Siegel & Siegel, 2007).

According to a study of Chicago couples conducted in the early 1990s, most adults of all ages enjoy "very high levels of emotional satisfaction and physical pleasure from sex within their relationships" (Laumann & Michael, 2000, p. 250). That study found that both men and women were likely to report that they were "extremely satisfied" with sex if they were in a committed, monogamous relationship—a circumstance that was more likely during middle age (see Figure 20.2; Laumann & Michael, 2000).

A more recent U.S. study found that most people are sexually active throughout adulthood. On average, sexual intercourse (one expression of sexual activity) stopped at age 60 for women and 65 for men, with the gender difference attributed to availability of a partner. Many who considered themselves in good health were sexually active in their 70s and beyond (Lindau & Gavrilova, 2010).

Historical changes affect adult sexual experiences, which makes it hard to know what the biological changes signify. The current cohort of middle-aged adults had more contraceptive choices than did earlier cohorts, which has led to more sexual freedom. It may be that a combination of cohort and culture has made contemporary adults more comfortable with contraception and satisfied with one or two offspring; thus, they may be more sexually active because they worry less about pregnancy. They may welcome age-related slower climax because it allows longer lovemaking. Also related to better contraception, sex outside of marriage is becoming more common: This may have increased the average adult's sexual activity.

On the other hand, compared to a decade or two ago, more adults are divorced or never married: This may have reduced sexual activity. These opposite possibilities are both plausible, and each is true in some cases, but no one can be sure of the overall effect of these changes in society. One reason for this uncertainty is that research on sex raises thorny political and cultural issues; scientists avoid such research, and governments and foundations rarely fund it.

Fertility

Although sexual activity is understudied, there is considerable research on infertility (defined as being unable to conceive after trying for at least a year) (Hayden & Hallstein, 2010). For childless couples who want children, aging adds to their regret. For couples who prefer to remain childless, aging brings relief from unwanted questions. In cultures that expect adults to bear many offspring, Nigeria among them, a woman is not considered truly female until she bears a child: Obviously for such women, each year of infertility is a sad one (Hollos et al., 2009).

Infertility is most common in nations where medical care is scarce and sexually transmitted infections (STIs) are common, primarily very poor nations. In those places, fertility may be prized, partly because infertility and infant mortality are relatively common. Timing matters, too, with teenage pregnancy a cause for celebration in some developing nations but a cause for alarm in some developed ones. In the United States, about 15 percent of all adult couples are infertile, partly because many postpone childbearing long past adolescence. When North American

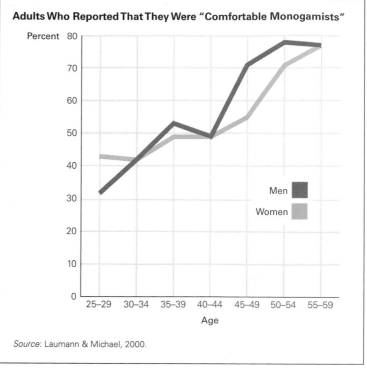

Adults Who Reported That They Were "Comfortable Monogamists"

Source: Laumann & Michael, 2000.

FIGURE 20.2

Sexually Satisfied with Monogamy In a cross section of more than 2,000 adults in the United States, most were "comfortable monogamists," a category for those who were happy with their one partner, with whom they usually had sex once or twice a week. Note that the percentages in this category were quite similar for men and women. The other categories differed by gender. For example, women could be "enthusiastic cohabiters," a category that included 25 percent of the women aged 25 to 39 and 10 percent of those aged 40 to 59. Men could be "enthusiastic polygamists," a category that included 10 percent of the 25- to 39-year-old men and 4 percent of those aged 40 to 59. Almost no women were polygamists, enthusiastic or not.

couples in their 40s try to conceive, about half are infertile and the other half risk various complications. Of course, risk is not reality: In 2007 in the United States, 113,000 babies were born to women age 40 and older (U.S. Bureau of the Census, 2009). Most such babies survive and thrive, becoming normal, healthy children.

As explained in Chapter 17, fertility peaks before age 25. From a biological (not psychosocial) perspective, women should try to conceive before age 30 and men before age 40. If they are unsuccessful, then medical interventions may help, especially if they are still relatively young (Bhasin, 2007). Although some older theories of biological health suggest that each birth reduces a woman's life span, recent analysis of the evidence does not support that finding (Mitteldorf, 2010). In fact, one large study found that having two or three children between ages 20 and 35 correlates with female longevity (Spence & Eberstein, 2009).

Causes of Infertility

When couples are infertile, about one-third of the time the problem can be traced to the man, about one-third of the time to the woman, and about one-third of the time the cause is a mystery. Remember that infertility is defined as no conception after a year of trying. Obviously, no couple conceives every time they have sex, and some infertile couples eventually do find themselves pregnant. Age is one factor, but not the determining one.

A common reason for male infertility is a low sperm count. Conception is most likely if a man ejaculates more than 20 million sperm per milliliter of semen, two-thirds of them mobile and viable, because each sperm's journey through the cervix and uterus is aided by millions of fellow travelers. In general, sperm count seems to have declined over the past century, but the count varies a great deal from place to place—higher in southern France than in Paris, in New York than in California, in Finland than in Sweden—for reasons that may be more connected to the specifics of the sample than to the health or age of the men (Merzenich et al., 2010).

Daily, about 100 million sperm reach maturity after a developmental process that lasts about 75 days. Anything that impairs body functioning over that 75-day period (e.g., fever, radiation, prescription drugs, time in a sauna, excessive stress, environmental toxins, drug abuse, alcoholism, cigarette smoking) can reduce sperm number, shape, and motility (activity), making conception less likely. Age also reduces sperm count, the probable explanation for an interesting statistic: Men take five times as many months to impregnate a woman when they are over 45 as when they are under 25 (Hassan & Killick, 2003). (This study controlled for frequency of sex and age of the woman.) Another problem is that bacteria sometimes attack sperm, although medicine can usually cure that. Overall, low sperm count is common but often easy to remedy.

As with men, women's fertility is affected by anything that impairs physical functioning—such as several diseases, smoking, extreme dieting, and obesity. Many infertile women do not even realize they have contracted one specific disease that could be the cause—*pelvic inflammatory disease (PID)*. PID creates scar tissue that blocks a woman's fallopian tubes, preventing the sperm from reaching an ovum. As with men, age itself also slows down every step of female reproduction—ovulation, implantation, fetal growth, labor, and birth.

Fertility Treatments

In the past 40 years, advances in medicine have solved about half of all fertility problems. Surgery repairs male or female reproductive systems, and *assisted reproductive technology* (ART) overcomes obstacles such as a low sperm count and blocked fallopian tubes. Some ART procedures, including in vitro fertiliza-

REUTERS / BOGDAN CRISTEL

A Happy 67-Year-Old Mother This Romanian woman gave birth after in vitro fertilization. Other nations would not allow IVF at her age, but every nation has new fathers who are that age or older.

Especially for Young Men A young man who impregnates a woman is often proud of his manhood. Is this reaction valid? (see response, page 558)

tion (IVF), were explained in Chapter 3. Donor sperm, donor ova, and donor wombs can help individuals whose partner is infertile or who have no partner of the other sex: All of these are biologically possible and have led to the births of tens of thousands of children, as well as raised moral questions in the minds of many people. For instance, since more than enough babies are born worldwide, ART may be unnecessary for the human species, but for many adults, ART is a welcome miracle.

Some uses of ART are acceptable to virtually everyone, especially when couples anticipate disease-related infertility. For example, many cancer patients freeze their sperm or ova before chemotherapy or radiation and thus can have children after they recover. In another example, only 20 years ago doctors recommended sterilization and predicted early death for those with HIV; now such individuals almost always use condoms for sex (to protect the uninfected partner), and couples can anticipate years together to raise their children. If the woman has the virus, medical help can almost always protect the fetus; if the man is HIV-positive, sperm can be collected and washed in the laboratory to rid them of the virus, and, via IVF, pregnancy can occur (Sauer et al., 2009).

Of the 15 percent of U.S. couples who are infertile, half are not helped by medical means, partly because ART is not always successful and partly because many avoid IVF because the process (in clinics, not bedrooms) is costly and arduous, without guarantees or privacy. The miscarriage rate (perhaps one in three embryos that have implanted) increases with both age and ART, causing added stress. All this is difficult for the adults, but not for ART children, who develop as well as other children (Wagenaar et al., 2008). Adoption is another option with its own joys and complications (discussed in Chapter 22).

Her Parents' Love Three-month-old Avery is blessed by having two adoring parents, Jared and Wendy Kennedy. It could even be said that she has a third parent—the woman who donated the ovum. That egg was fertilized through ART, to help this couple realize their dream of parenthood.

Menopause

During adulthood, the level of sex hormones circulating in the bloodstream declines—suddenly in women, gradually in men. As a result, sexual desire, frequency of intercourse, and odds of reproduction decrease. The specifics differ for women and men.

Women in Middle Age

For women, sometime between ages 42 and 58 (the average age is 51), ovulation and menstruation stop because of a marked drop in production of several hormones (Wise, 2006). This is **menopause.** If a woman has a *hysterectomy* (surgical removal of the uterus) that includes removal of her ovaries, then sudden, premature menopause occurs. In the United States, one in four women, usually between ages 35 and 55, undergoes this operation for any of various medical or personal reasons (M. K. Whiteman et al., 2008).

Removing the ovaries produces menopausal symptoms—most commonly disturbances of body temperature, including hot flashes (feeling hot), hot flushes (looking hot), and cold sweats (feeling chilled) (Gold et al., 2006). Natural menopause produces the same reactions, but not as suddenly and not in everyone. Symptoms vary by genes and ethnicity—with no marked disturbances for 40 percent of Asian Americans, 25 percent of European and Hispanic Americans, and 15 percent of African Americans.

The psychological consequences vary more than the physiological ones. Some menopausal women find new zest, while others become depressed (L. S. Cohen

menopause The time in middle age, usually around age 50, when a woman's menstrual periods cease and the production of estrogen, progesterone, and testosterone drops. Strictly speaking, menopause is dated one year after a woman's last menstrual period, although many months before and after that date are menopausal.

JENS LUCKING / STONE / GETTY IMAGES

Is She a Grandmother? Yes. Most middle-aged women are strong and competent, like this grandmother cutting wood in rural Italy.

hormone replacement therapy (HRT)
Taking hormones (in pills, patches, or injections) to compensate for hormone reduction. HRT is most common in women at menopause or after removal of the ovaries, but it is also used by men as their testosterone decreases. HRT has some medical uses but also carries health risks.

andropause A term coined to signify a drop in testosterone levels in older men, which normally results in reduced sexual desire, erections, and muscle mass. (Also called *male menopause*.)

>> **Response for Young Men** (from page 556) The answer depends on a person's definition of what a man is. No developmentalist would define a man as someone who has a high sperm count.

et al., 2006). The historical Western notion that menopausal women "temporarily lose their minds" (Neugarten & Neugarten, 1986) contrasts with the traditional view among Hindi women in India that menopause represents liberation (Menon, 2001).

Over the past 30 years, in **hormone replacement therapy (HRT),** millions of post-menopausal women took hormone supplements, usually estrogen combined with progesterone. Some did so to alleviate symptoms of menopause; others, to prevent osteoporosis (fragile bones), heart disease, strokes, or dementia. Correlational studies found that these diseases occurred less often among women who took hormones. Researchers now believe that the true cause of the correlation was not HRT but socioeconomic status (SES). In fact, in controlled longitudinal studies, the U.S. Women's Health Initiative found that taking estrogen for 10 years or more *increased* the risk of heart disease, stroke, and breast cancer and seems to have no effect on dementia (U.S. Preventive Services Task Force, 2002).

Estrogen replacement does reduce hot flashes and decrease osteoporosis, but women who want those benefits need to weigh the costs. Surprisingly, culture seems more influential than an objective cost-benefit analysis. Many U.S. women are now more anxious about hormone replacement than the research warrants (Powledge, 2007) and have thus stopped or outright rejected HRT.

By contrast, Australian research finds that additional estrogen is the most cost-effective way to prevent osteoporosis, and many Australian women take the hormone (Geelhoed et al., 2010). Similarly, many older women in Europe take estrogen; their doctors recommend it (Gompel & Plu-Bureau, 2007; Lip et al., 1995). Among the possible reasons are that the European form of estrogen differs from the one used in the Women's Health Initiative study and that diet and exercise make strokes less common than in the United States. Some research finds that estrogen may aid cognition after all (Erickson & Korol, 2009).

Men in Middle Age

Do men undergo anything like menopause? Some say yes, suggesting that the word **andropause** should be used to signify lower testosterone in older men, which reduces sexual desire, erections, and muscle mass. Even with erection-inducing drugs such as Viagra and Levitra, sexual desire and speed of orgasm decline with age, as do many other physiological and cognitive functions.

But most experts think that the term *andropause* (or *male menopause*) is misleading because it implies a sudden drop in reproductive ability or hormones. That does not occur in men, some of whom produce viable sperm throughout their lives. Sexual inactivity and anxiety reduce testosterone—a phenomenon similar to menopause but with a psychological, not physiological, cause. As one review explains, "Retirement, financial problems, unresolved anger, and dwindling social relationships can wreak havoc on some men's sense of masculinity and virility" (L. Siegel & Siegel, 2007, p. 239).

To combat the natural decline in testosterone, some men have turned to hormone replacement. Some women also take smaller amounts of testosterone to increase their sexual desire. But at least one longitudinal study with both sexes comparing testosterone supplements with a placebo found no benefits (sexual or otherwise) (Nair et al., 2006).

A few men have very low testosterone levels and therefore need supplemental hormones to reduce the risk of many disabilities (Morales, 2008). Age-related reductions in testosterone, however, are no more pathological than menopause is. One physician writes that men would be better off learning about "the health benefits of physical activity. . . . Tell them to take the $1,200 they'll spend on testosterone per year and join a health club; buy a Stairmaster—they'll have money left over for their new clothes" (Casey, 2008, p. 48).

Doctors are understandably cautious; supplemental doses of hormones may be harmful (Bhasin, 2007; Moffat, 2005; Sokol, 2009). For instance, overdoses of testosterone by athletes have led to sudden cardiac arrest. Yet low testosterone correlates with heart disease (Kaushik et al., 2010). Some people believe that new drugs, including hormones, should be approved more quickly, and some doctors—especially outside the United States—prescribe testosterone for older men. This debate is not settled, but all the evidence finds that adult health depends more on habits than on drugs. We discuss that next.

SUMMING UP

The efficiency of the sexual-reproductive system declines with age. This is evident in longer time to reach orgasm, declining frequency of sexual intercourse, and reduced fertility—although psychological aspects of sexual interaction may improve with age. About 15 percent of couples in the United States do not conceive after a year of trying; declining fertility with age is only one of many reasons. At about age 50, women experience menopause, a drop in estrogen that makes ovulation and menstruation cease. In men, hormone production also declines with age, although many men continue to produce viable sperm and thus could father a child. Hormone replacement therapy for either sex is controversial: Many U.S. physicians are concerned about possible side effects. ■

Naturally Happy Middle age seems to sit lightly on these married organic farmers in Virginia.

>> Health Habits and Age

Each person's routines and habits of daily life, not only currently but also since childhood, powerfully affect almost every disease and chronic condition. This is particularly true for problems associated with aging—from arthritis to varicose veins—that may first emerge after age 50 but actually begin decades before.

For instance, as already explained, every loud noise—traffic, music, construction—damages hearing to some extent. Many young adults (especially men, the sex more vulnerable to deafness) work with jackhammers without protection, enjoy the roar of their motorcycles, or listen to music at ear-splitting levels. The resulting damage accumulates, causing losses evident later on. As another example, you just read that sexual interest and fertility are affected by the relationship between partners, the treatment of STIs, and the availability of contraception. Age matters, too, but psychological and cultural factors seem more influential than biological ones.

Regarding fatal diseases, the rate of cancer increases with every decade of adulthood. However, 65 percent of all cancer deaths are attributable to lifestyle behaviors—specifically, smoking (30 percent), poor diet and obesity (30 percent), and lack of exercise (5 percent) (Willett & Trichopoulos, 1996). Let us look closely at the health habits of adults, with a particular goal: keeping adults healthy so that each one can develop well.

Drug Abuse

As described in Chapter 17, drug abuse, especially of illegal drugs, decreases markedly over adulthood—usually before age 25, almost always by age 40. Of the illegal drugs, marijuana use is slowest to decline; in the United States, about 8 percent of 25- to 34-year-olds still use it, impairing cognition and oral health. (More than one-fourth of people in their early 30s who regularly smoke marijuana have serious gum disease [Thomson et al., 2008].) However, abuse of legally prescribed drugs for physical pain or psychological distress increases in adulthood—partly because adults are slow to recognize addiction to prescribed drugs. We focus on the two drugs most commonly abused throughout adulthood: tobacco and alcohol.

Tobacco

Death rates for lung cancer (by far the leading cause of cancer deaths in North America) reflect smoking patterns of years earlier. Because North American men have been quitting for decades, lung cancer deaths for 55- to 64-year-old males are about half what they were in 1970 (see Appendix A, p. A-23). Relatively few women smoked at the beginning of the twentieth century, but their smoking increased over time and then decreased later than for men.

Consequently, in the United States, during the same 36 years that male lung cancer deaths declined, the rates for females increased (rates for 55- to 64-year-old women doubled from 1970 to 2005). Fifty years ago, more women died from the "female cancers" (breast, uterine, or ovarian) than from lung cancer; in 2008, about twice as many women died from lung cancer as from the combined total of those other three types (U.S. Bureau of the Census, 2009).

Fortunately, cigarette smoking over the past decade has been declining in North America (the United States, Canada, and Mexico) for every age and gender group. In 1970, half of U.S. adult men and one-third of women smoked, but by 2007 only 25 percent of men and 20 percent of women did. It is not yet time for celebration, however: Smoking is still costly (443,000 deaths and $193 billion in direct medical expenses per year in the United States) (MMWR, March 13, 2009).

North American projections are optimistic, as women are following the male pattern of quitting and as more and more offices, homes, and public places are becoming smoke-free (see Figure 20.3). Worldwide trends are less encouraging. Almost half the adults in Germany, Denmark, Poland, Holland, Switzerland, and Spain are smokers. In developing nations, rates of smoking are rising, especially among women. The World Health Organization calls tobacco "the single largest preventable cause of death and chronic disease in the world today" (Blas & Kurup, 2010, p. 199). Projections are almost a billion smoking-related deaths between 2010 and 2050 worldwide.

FIGURE 20.3

Quitters Win This figure shows the well-known historical declines in the number of people who start smoking and also shows that many adults quit. Half of all men aged 25 to 64 in 1970 smoked; 35 years later, almost all were over age 65 and almost all had quit. (Of course some had died, but most in that cohort were still alive and smoke-free.)

Observation Quiz Are the two sexes growing closer together or farther apart in rates of smoking in the United States? (see answer, page 562)

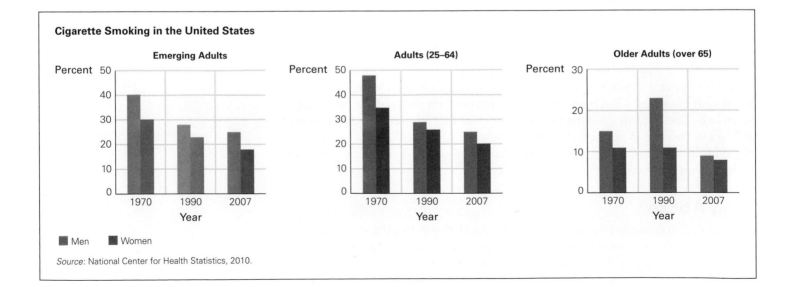

Cigarette Smoking in the United States

Source: National Center for Health Statistics, 2010.

Variations are dramatic from nation to nation. For instance, smoking is allowed in most Pakistani homes (92 percent) but in few Guatemalan ones (17 percent) (Bloch et al., 2008). The rate of lung cancer deaths in China, where 350 million adults now smoke, almost tripled from 1975 to 2005 (Xin, 2008). Although cigarettes are available everywhere, variations among nations, cohorts, and the sexes are evidence that smoking is powerfully influenced by social norms, laws, and advertising.

Alcohol Abuse

The harm from cigarettes is dose-related: Each puff, each day of smoking, each breath of secondhand smoke makes cancer, heart disease, strokes, and emphysema more likely. No such linear harm results from drinking alcohol. In fact, alcohol can be beneficial: People who drink wine, beer, or spirits *in moderation*—no more than two drinks a day—live longer than abstainers. The primary reason is that alcohol reduces coronary heart disease and strokes. It increases HDL (high-density lipoprotein), the "good" form of cholesterol, and reduces LDL (low-density lipoprotein), the "bad" cholesterol that causes clogged arteries and blood clots. It also lowers blood pressure and glucose (Klatsky, 2009).

However, moderation is impossible for some people. Alcoholics find it easier to abstain than to have one, and only one, drink a day. Furthermore, alcohol destroys brain cells; contributes to osteoporosis; decreases fertility; and accompanies many suicides, homicides, and accidents—while wreaking havoc in many families and harming children in the process. It is also implicated in 60 diseases, including not only liver damage but also cancer of the breast, stomach, and throat (Hampton, 2005). Even moderate consumption is unhealthy if it leads to smoking, overeating, or other destructive habits. In the United States, abstainers who are HIV-positive live, on average, three years longer than moderate drinkers and six years longer than heavy drinkers (Braithwaite et al., 2007).

There are stark international variations in alcohol abuse. It is rare in Muslim nations where alcohol is illegal, but it causes about half the deaths of Russian men under age 60 (Leon et al., 2007). About 20 percent of U.S. adults had five or more drinks on a single occasion in the past year; such *binge drinking* signals a problem (National Center for Health Statistics, 2007). In many nations, the risk of accidental death because of drinking is more common among younger adults, but the harm to families is more prevalent when the alcoholic is middle-aged (Blas & Kurup, 2010). The most devastating harm is experienced by men with little education, no matter what their culture, although alcoholism is a serious problem among adults of both sexes, every education level, and all religions.

The data suggest that "alcohol causes a disproportionate burden of harm in poorer countries" (Gonzalez, quoted in Grimm, 2008, p. 863) because prevention and treatment strategies have not been established and because enforcement of laws has not caught up with abuse. In general, low-income nations have more abstainers and more abusers, while more affluent nations have more moderate drinkers (Blas & Kurup, 2010). Alcohol in moderation may be healthy, but lack of moderation is often deadly.

Overeating

Although there are many ways to analyze the problems of overeating, a developmental view focuses on age. Metabolism decreases by one-third between ages 20 and 60. Thus, to stay the same weight, adults need to eat less and move more each year. Few adults do so; obesity increases with each decade of adulthood until old age, when the rates decrease. In the United States, longitudinal research

Guess His Age A man puffs on a bidi, a flavored cigarette, in Bangalore, India. He looks elderly but is actually middle-aged (about age 40). He is at risk of being among the 1 million Indians who die each year of smoking-related causes.

Especially for Doctors and Nurses If you had to choose between recommending various screening tests and recommending various lifestyle changes to a 35-year-old, which would you do? (see response, page 563)

TABLE 20.1

Obesity Worldwide: Percent Adults, Age 30 to 100, Whose BMI Is 30 or More

Country	Men	Women
Argentina	48	47
Australia	32	37
Brazil	16	32
Canada	30	32
China	5	5
France	13	11
Germany	31	31
India	3	3
Israel	26	37
Italy	14	14
Jamaica	10	53
Japan	3	2
Mexico	37	51
New Zealand	37	48
Nigeria	4	11
Peru	24	50
Poland	19	27
Russian Federation	14	35
South Africa	11	48
Spain	25	25
United Kingdom	32	34
United States	50	55

Source: World Health Organization Global InfoBase, 2010.

And Increasing This shows the rate of obesity (not just overweight) among adults age 30 and older in selected nations on each continent. In every case, the younger adults had much lower rates of obesity, which suggests that the cause is less genetic than overeating and underexercising over the decades of adulthood.

Observation Quiz In how many of the 22 nations shown are men more likely to be obese than women? (see answer, page 564)

>> **Answer to Observation Quiz** (from page 560) They are growing closer together. In fact, some data indicate that teenage girls are more likely to smoke than teenage boys are.

finds that adults gain one to two pounds a year on average, much more than their grandparents' generation did during adulthood. The basic problem is consumption of too many high-calorie foods combined with too little activity—a combination that leads to obesity for about half of all U.S. adults over age 30 and about one-fourth of adults worldwide (World Health Organization Global InfoBase, 2010) (see Table 20.1).

Consequences of Obesity

Excess weight increases the risk of every chronic disease; one example is diabetes, rapidly becoming more common, causing eye, heart, and foot problems as well as early death. The United States is the world leader in obesity and diabetes: Of all U.S. adults aged 18 and older, only 2 percent are underweight but 66 percent are overweight (with a body mass index, or BMI, above 25). Half of those overweight people are obese (with a BMI of 30 or more) and some of them (5 percent of the adult population) are morbidly obese (with a BMI of 40 or more) (National Center for Health Statistics, 2010). (BMI is defined in Chapter 11, and a BMI chart for adults is given in Table 17.2.) These numbers actually understate the problem from age 25 to 65 because emerging adults tend to be become heavier as they grow older, and the very old tend to lose weight.

If the BMI guidelines seem abstract, picture a person who is 5 feet, 8 inches tall. If that person weighs 150 pounds, BMI is about 24, a normal weight. If he or she weighs 200 pounds or more, BMI is 30 or higher and that person is obese. If he or she weighs more than 300 pounds, BMI is over 40 and that person is among the 5 percent who are morbidly obese. You may not realize how common this is because people who are that heavy are less likely to walk down your street, enroll in your college, or attend public events of any kind—a reflection of obesity's disabling consequences.

The consequences are psychological as well as physical, since prejudice against overweight people is pervasive and disabling. Adults who are overweight are targets of scorn and abuse, less likely to be chosen as marriage partners, as employees, and even as friends. The stigma endured by people who are overweight leads them to avoid medical checkups, eat more, and exercise less—with the result that their health is far more impaired than the mere fact of their weight would predict (Puhl & Heuer, 2010).

Perhaps the goal for people whose health is impaired by their weight should be to lose enough pounds to protect their health rather than to achieve a slender appearance. One result of stressing the ideal BMI may be unhealthy dieting and then weight gain (Shai & Stampfer, 2009). Many diets are tried and abandoned (see Table 20.2). Furthermore, there are some overweight adults who are not at risk of heart disease or diabetes, although many are. Genetic and ethnic factors vary, and a careful physician takes these into account (Young et al., 2007) (see the Research Design). The differences and the risks are among the reasons medical attention is especially needed for people who are overweight; social prejudice is one reason the obese are less likely than others to get the care they need (Puhl & Heuer, 2010).

Sustained counseling and encouragement are time-consuming for health practitioners but prove best in the long run. Past experience with weight-loss drugs urges caution (Li et al., 2005) since side effects can be severe, including addiction and morbidity. A major problem is that people drop out of drug studies because of side effects; positive results are reported when only those with few side effects complete the study (Fabricatore et al., 2009). Caution is also urged for gastric bypass surgery, which can produce dramatic weight loss but results in addi-

TABLE 20.2

Research on Weight-Loss Plans

Name of Diet	Description	Results
Mediterranean	Lots of vegetables, legumes, fruits, grains, fish, olive oil; low in meat, dairy, saturated fat	Longer life, less body fat
Atkins	Low in carbohydrates	Quick weight loss, then stable; improved cholesterol, lower blood pressure
Weight Watchers	Low in calories; group support	Weight loss over time; good on maintenance
Ornish	Low in fat	Quick loss; hard to sustain

Sources: Dansinger et al, 2005; Estruch et al., 2006; Gardner et al., 2007; Sacks et al., 2009; Shai et al., 2008.

A Dieter's Dream? Thousands of studies compare results over time. In general, eating fewer calories and less fat is more important for weight loss than are specifics. Nonetheless, here is a sampling of popular diets.

tional surgery for almost one-fourth of the patients and carries a high risk of death in the first month after the operation. Over time, however, those who are morbidly obese have higher death rates without the surgery: On balance, the surgery saves lives (Schauer et al., 2010), but it would be much better to stop the problem long before it gets to that point.

Causes of Weight Gain

Body weight is affected by genes, but as already explained, the *increase* in obesity cannot be blamed on genes because genes change little from one generation to the next. Something in the environment must be the cause.

What might that cause be? One likely possibility is diet. The typical U.S. family consumes more meat and fat, and less fiber, than people in other parts of the world or than Americans once did. For example, the Chinese traditionally eat several vegetables together with small bits of meat; some blame the recent Chinese weight increase on their new taste for American food. The Mediterranean diet (common in Italy and Greece) of lots of fiber, fish, and heart-healthy olive oil is becoming more common in North America—and adult obesity in the United States, although far too common, at least has not increased since 2000.

Details matter. Within cultures, specific food choices vary. For instance, is bread a good diet food? It depends on which bread. Among the Bedouins in the Middle East, bread is the mainstay of the diet. About half of the adults eat homemade whole wheat bread and the other half eat store-bought white bread. Among Bedouin adults, heart disease is 10 times higher among the white bread eaters (Abu-Saad et al., 2009).

Another possibility is the context of meals. For instance, the French gather at the table to talk as well as to eat, consuming smaller portions as they eat in a leisurely manner: Despite food sautéed in butter and desserts with heavy cream, their hearts are healthier than the heart of the average American (Rozin et al., 2003). By contrast, many Americans eat at fast-food restaurants several times a week. Indeed, in the United States simply living near fast-food establishments correlates with poorer nutrition and reduced health (Moore et al., 2009).

The final possibility is exercise, which merits an extensive discussion.

Research Design

Scientists: T. Kue Young, Peter Bjerregaard, Eric Dewailly, Patricia Risica, Marit E. Jorgensen, and Sven E. O. Ebbesson.

Publication: *American Journal of Public Health* (2007).

Participants: In four separate surveys conducted between 1990 and 2001, participants included 2,545 adults from Inuit groups in Alaska, Canada, and Greenland. Data were compared with findings from 2,200 people of European heritage living in Manitoba, northern Canada.

Design: Many biophysiological measures were taken for each individual, including weight, height, blood pressure, cholesterol level, and glucose level.

Major conclusion: Although increased weight correlated with various measures of risk for heart disease and diabetes, weight-related risk was lower for the Inuit than for the European Canadians. The authors point out that the Inuit have relatively high sitting height compared with leg length and that centuries of adaptation to the Arctic climate may have resulted in increased body fat without the same mortality risk as for other peoples.

Comment: This research reminds us that no one indicator (such as BMI) has the same effect on health for everyone. Although obesity is a health hazard no matter what a person's genetic background is, inherited body types differ, as do health risks with weight.

>> Response for Doctors and Nurses (from page 561) Obviously, much depends on the specific patient. Overall, however, far more people develop a disease or die because of years of poor health habits than because of various illnesses not spotted early. With some exceptions, age 35 is too early to detect incipient cancers or circulatory problems, but it's prime time for stopping cigarette smoking, curbing alcohol abuse, and improving exercise and diet.

"The fresh mountain air is starting to depress me."

Just Give Me the Usual Even bad habits can feel comfortable—that's what makes them habits.

TABLE 20.3

Percent of U.S. Residents Who Say They Exercise at Least Half an Hour a Day

Age	1998	2007
18–24	37	37
24–44	32	33
45–64	29	30

Source: U.S. Bureau of the Census, 2009.

>> **Answer to Observation Quiz** (from page 562) Only three nations: Japan, France, and Argentina. This raises a question not answered by the data: Why are women more often obese than men?

Inactivity

Regular physical activity at every stage of life protects against serious illness even if a person has other undesirable health habits such as smoking and overeating. Exercise reduces blood pressure; strengthens the heart and lungs; and makes depression, osteoporosis, heart disease, arthritis, and even some cancers less likely. Health benefits from exercise are substantial for men and women, old and young, former sports stars and those who never joined a team. If a person loses weight, the best predictor of maintaining that weight loss is an hour of exercise a day (Shai & Stampfer, 2009).

By contrast, sitting for long hours correlates with almost every unhealthy condition, especially heart disease and diabetes, both of which carry additional health hazards beyond the disease itself. Even a little movement—gardening, light housework, walking up the stairs or to the bus—helps.

As explained in Chapter 17, walking briskly for at least 30 minutes a day, five days a week, is a reasonable goal. More intense exercise (e.g., swimming, jogging, bicycling) is ideal. It is possible to exercise too much, but almost no adult aged 25 to 65 does. In fact, one study that used objective assessment of adult movement (electronic monitors) found that fewer than 5 percent of adults in the United States and England get even 30 minutes per day of exercise (Weiler et al., 2010). (Self-reports put the number at about 30 percent, not 5 percent; see Table 20.3.)

The close connection between exercise and health, both physical and mental, is well known, as is the influence of family, friends, and neighborhoods. Exercise-friendly communities have lower rates of obesity, hypertension, and depression (Lee et al., 2009). This is not merely a correlation but a cause: People who are more fit are likely to resist disease and to feel healthier as they age (Carnethon et al., 2003; Shirom et al., 2008).

Researchers are now trying to pin down specifics. Among the questions are whether the mode of exercise is crucial (fast walking, gardening, swimming, running?) and whether it is better to do half an hour each day or four hours on the weekend (Etnier, 2009). But no one doubts that adults need to move more. Many social scientists are seeking ways to encourage exercise and other good health habits among adults (Conner, 2008). Maintaining a healthy habit for life is the hardest part, as the following explains.

A VIEW FROM SCIENCE

A Habit Is Hard to Break

A paradox is apparent: People know that smoking cigarettes, abusing alcohol, overeating, and sedentary behavior are harmful, yet many have at least one destructive habit. Why don't we all just shape up and live right? Breaking New Year's resolutions; criticizing those whose bad habits are not our own; feeling guilty for consuming sweets, salt, fried foods, cigarettes, or alcohol; buying gym memberships that go unused or exercise equipment that becomes a coat rack or dust-gathering sculpture—these behaviors are common.

Social scientists have focused on this paradox (Conner, 2008; Shumaker et al., 2009). First, it helps to understand that the process of changing a habit is a long, multistepped one: Ignoring

that reality is one reason habits continue, because strategies that work at one stage fail at another. Different strategies are needed at each step. One list of these steps is: (1) denial, (2) awareness, (3) planning, (4) implementation, and (5) maintenance.

The first step, *denial,* occurs because all bad habits begin for a reason—they are also maintained for a reason. For example, with cigarettes, most smokers begin as teenagers in order to be socially accepted, to appear mature, and/or to control weight—all especially important during adolescence. When adults tell teenagers about lung cancer, that seems so far into the future as to be irrelevant. Then nicotine creates addiction; without the drug, smokers become anxious, confused, angry, and depressed—no wonder denial emerges. In fact, with many life-threatening addictions (including smoking), hearing how bad it is often leads to *more* smoking, drinking, and so on (Ben-Zur & Zeidner, 2009). Denial is one way to protect against stress, more drugs are another.

Awareness is attained by the person him- or herself. Others can help via *motivational interviewing,* encouraging the individual to describe the reasons why change is needed. Sometimes awareness comes after a particularly dramatic event—a doctor predicting death from continued smoking, a night in jail because of drinking, tipping the scale at 200 pounds (which seems much more than 199). Often people fluctuate between confused denial and dawning awareness; a good listener using motivated interviewing can tip the balance.

Planning is best when it is specific, with a date for quitting and strategies to overcome the many obstacles. A series of studies has found that humans tend to underestimate the power of their own impulses that make it difficult to break a habit (Nordgren et al., 2009). This seems true for smokers, dieters, and everyone else.

In one experiment, researchers gave students who were entering or leaving a college cafeteria a choice of packaged snacks and promised to give each of them about $10 (and the snack) if they did not eat it for a week. Those who were entering the cafeteria, presumably aware of the demands of hunger, planned to avoid temptation by choosing a less desirable snack. Most of them (61 percent) earned the money. However, those who had just eaten apparently underestimated their hunger. They chose a more desirable snack and often ate it before the week was up; only 39 percent earned the money (Nordgren et al., 2009).

Implementation is quitting the habit according to the plan. One crucial factor in achieving success is social support, such as (1) letting others know of the date and the plan, (2) finding a buddy, or (3) joining a group (Weight Watchers, Alcoholics Anonymous, or another 12-step program) or, better yet, all three. Private efforts often fail. Implementation is most successful when tackling one habit at a time: Quitting cigarettes on the same day as beginning an exercise routine is almost impossible; usually this double-barreled approach is short-lived.

Maintenance is the step that most people ignore. Although quitting any serious habit is difficult, even painful, many addicts have quit many times, only to relapse later on. Dieters go on and off diets so often that this phenomenon has a name—yo-yo dieting. The problem is that once implementation succeeds, people are overconfident. They forget the power of temptation. The recovered alcoholic might go out with friends who drink, confident that he will stick to juice instead of beer; the dieter will serve dessert to the rest of the family, certain she'll be able to resist a taste herself; the person who joined the gym will become overtired and skip a day, convinced he'll make up for it the following workout. Such actions are far more dangerous than people realize, at least according to the research.

Any stress is likely to undercut resolve and restart the habit. For example, in one study, dieters who were given a stressful task (remembering a nine-digit number) entered a room that had been set, seemingly at random, with either some tempting foods or with a scale and a diet book. They were asked to taste a milkshake and give their opinion; they were also told they could drink as much as they wanted. Those who saw eating clues drank more than those who saw dieting clues (Mann & Ward, 2007).

This phenomenon is called *attention myopia,* indicating that one's resolve (maintenance ability) fades when faced with stress. Many people who stop and start a habit explain that they did so under stress—a divorce, a new job, a rebellious teenager. Of course, sooner or later every adult is stressed; that is why maintenance strategies are crucial.

When the context encourages a slip, people mistakenly think that one cigarette, one drink, one slice of cake, one more swallow of milkshake, and so on is inconsequential—which it would be if the person stopped there. Unfortunately, the human mind is geared toward all or nothing, so one puff makes the next one more likely, one potato chip awakens the compulsion for another, and so on. With alcohol, the drink itself scrambles the mind; people are less aware of their cognitive lapses under the influence and thus likely to drink more when they have already had that first drink (Sayette et al., 2009).

Maintenance depends a great deal on the ecological context, which means that the attitudes and practices of other people and the circumstances of daily life are crucial. Once a person is aware of a destructive problem (step two), it is relatively easy to plan and implement a better habit (steps three and four), but sticking to it is difficult if the social context pushes in the opposite direction.

Accumulating Stressors

Every life is stressful, and some of those stresses become stressors. A **stressor** is an experience, circumstance, or condition that affects a person. Between ages 25 and 65, family members die, disasters destroy homes, jobs disappear, and even welcome events—a new marriage, birth, or job, for instance—cause stress. Daily life is also filled with minor stresses that accumulate—traffic jams, spilled food, noise at night, rude strangers, aches and pains, dirty pots, and much more. Together, daily hassles and major stresses can become stressors and destroy health.

stressor Any situation, event, experience, or other stimulus that causes a person to feel stressed. Many circumstances become stressors for some people but not for others.

Getting Somewhere To help employers reduce their health care costs and to encourage employees to keep fit, a noted manufacturer of office furniture offers a workstation that combines a treadmill and a computer.

problem-focused coping A strategy to deal with stress by tackling a stressful situation directly.

emotion-focused coping A strategy to deal with stress by changing feelings about the stressor rather than changing the stressor itself.

allostatic load The total, combined burden of physiological stresses (such as high blood pressure) that an individual lives with. A high allostatic load increases the risk of disease.

weathering The gradual accumulation of stressors over a long period of time, wearing down the resilience and resistance of a person.

If organ reserves are depleted, the physiological toll can lower immunity, increase blood pressure, speed up the heart, reduce sleep, and produce many other reactions that can lead to serious illness. A comprehensive review finds that "stress clearly affects the whole body" but also that the specific coping measures that work best vary for each illness and each person (Aldwin, 2007, p. 54).

Stressors increase all the bad habits just described—drug use, overeating, underexercising—sometimes ostensibly to relieve the stress but eventually making things worse. Stress does not merely correlate with illness—it *causes* illness. In an experiment, volunteers first indicated how stressed they felt and then agreed to have a cold virus squirted up their nostrils. A week later, some of them were stuffed, sneezing, and feverish. Others were fine. Stress was a crucial factor (S. Cohen et al., 1993).

Reactions to stress can cause more stress. For example, a longitudinal study of married couples in their 30s found that, if the husband's health deteriorated, the chance of divorce increased. This was apparent with all couples, but it was particularly evident for well-educated European Americans (Teachman, 2010).

Psychologists distinguish two major ways of coping with stress. In **problem-focused coping,** people try to solve their problems by attacking them in some way (for instance, confronting a difficult boss, moving out of a noisy neighborhood). In **emotion-focused coping,** people try to change their emotions (for instance, from anger to acceptance). In general, younger adults are more likely to attack a problem while older adults try to change their emotions (Aldwin, 2007).

Biologically, the two sexes respond differently to stress. Men are inclined to be problem-focused, reacting in a "fight-or-flight" manner. Their sympathetic nervous system (faster heart rate, increased adrenaline) prepares them for attack or escape. Their testosterone level rises when they attack a problem and decreases if they fail.

On the other hand, women are more emotion-focused, likely to "tend and befriend"—that is, to seek the company of other people when they are under pressure. Their bodies produce oxytocin, a hormone that leads them to seek confidential and caring interactions (S. E. Taylor, 2006; S. E. Taylor et al., 2000). This gender difference in coping explains why a woman might get upset if a man doesn't want to talk about his problems and why a man might get upset if a woman just wants to talk instead of taking action. Both problem- and emotion-focused coping can be effective in overcoming stresses; individuals need to learn from each other that every man and woman should sometimes fight and sometimes befriend.

As with this example, adults need both strategies, depending on the situation. Worse is no strategy at all—denying a problem until it escalates or until it takes a physical toll, such as causing high blood pressure. Medical researchers recognize **allostatic load,** an accumulation of various physiological reactions that typically increase with age and stressors, eventually causing illness.

The amount of stress a person has endured in childhood and adolescence may become evident in morbidity during the adult years. A U.S. study of 65,000 adults compared the indicators of poor health. The gradual accumulation of biochemical stressors, called **weathering,** was faster among African Americans than among European Americans such that, by age 60, they had aged, biologically, 10 years more. The authors believe this was the result of the "chronic stress" of living in a "race-conscious society" (Geronimus et al., 2006, p. 832).

Developmentalists urge people to consider the long term, including social contexts and childhood influences, as well as what might happen in future decades. Sometimes emotion-focused coping only seems best because "psychological defenses are extremely helpful in the short term but prove to be maladaptive over the long run" (Rahe, 2000, p. 543). Thus, if emotion-focused coping prevents problem solving, then repeated, ongoing stressors chip away at health. On the other hand, sometimes problem-focused coping makes a problem worse rather than letting it disappear on its own.

Consider an example. Suppose your teacher returns your term paper with red ink on every line, commenting that it is not worthy of a grade. You could:

1. Analyze your mistakes and try not to repeat them (problem-focused).
2. Complain to the teacher and the department chair (problem-focused).
3. Be grateful that the teacher read your paper carefully (emotion-focused).
4. Talk to fellow classmates, joking about the teacher (emotion-focused).
5. Tear up the paper, drop the class, and buy a bottle of rum (denial).

All but the last on this list might be the best choice, depending on specifics. Five general factors seem to help a person choose.

1. Social support. Talk to people who will listen carefully.
2. Stay well rested, nourished, and exercised, so you can think clearly.
3. Analyze alternatives—a cost-benefit analysis—but also listen to intuition. Wait until both analysis and intuition coalesce.
4. Take control. People with stressful jobs who delegate, pace themselves, and affect outcomes are much healthier than those who are passive.
5. Find meaning. Even in highly stressful situations—war, prison, natural disasters—some people believe there is something to be gained and ultimately find it.

Each of these strategies comes more easily to some people than to others, for reasons of personality, childhood mentoring, and culture. With age and experience, adults may learn to respond wisely. As reviewed in Chapter 25, over the years of adulthood, a more positive attitude toward life develops, which makes it easier to reinterpret stresses so that they do not fester (Charles & Carstensen, 2010). Often,

> Older individuals have had the opportunity to learn how to cope with stressful experiences and how to adjust their expectations. . . . On the basis of age and experience, older persons have developed more effective skills with which to manage stressful life events and to reduce emotional stress.

> *[Penninx & Deeg, 2000]*

Age brings another advantage. Emerging adulthood is "a time of heightened hassles" (Aldwin, 2007, p. 298). Once life settles down, some stresses (dating, job hunting, moving) are less frequent. Adults "are more adept at arranging their lives to minimize the occurrence of stressors" (Aldwin, 2007, p. 298).

Remember that attitude sometimes determines whether or not an event becomes a stressor. For instance, post-traumatic stress disorder (PTSD) is a common response to combat, especially if the person saw others seriously wounded or killed. But not everyone who has such combat experiences develops PTSD (Aldwin, 2007). Many psychologists are trying to figure out why, but it is clear that the external trauma is only one factor. Apparently, some adults learn to ignore some stresses and perceive other stresses as challenges, even if outsiders would consider them threats (Reich et al., 2010).

When challenges are successfully met, not only do people feel more effective and powerful but also the body's damaging responses to stress—increased heart and breathing rates, hormonal changes, and so on—are averted. Indeed, effective coping may strengthen the immune system and promote health (Bandura, 1997). Among adults, potential stressors can instead become positive turning points (Reich et al., 2010), as may have happened in the following case.

Staying on the Ball Professional athletes like New York Yankees pitcher Andy Pettitte know the value of regular exercise, especially as they get older—a lesson that many inactive adults need to learn.

A CASE TO STUDY

Coping with Katrina

There are limits to this stress/challenge/victory process. For instance, psychologists are following the psychological reactions of the hundreds of thousands of people in Louisiana and Mississippi who were uprooted by Hurricane Katrina. Many of them lost homes and jobs, went without food and water, knew people who died. Not surprisingly, their stressors increased. For instance, one study of survivors from New Orleans six months after the flood found that most had stress reactions: Almost all were irritable and had upsetting thoughts, and half had nightmares (see Figure 20.4).

The accumulation of stressors led to many physical and psychological problems. One in nine suffered serious mental health problems, twice as many as before the hurricane. Another 20 percent had mild to moderate mental illness, again double the earlier rate (Kessler et al., 2006). Given the trauma of the storm (a major stress) and the inept official response (ongoing hassles), this is not surprising.

However, there was one surprise. The same stresses also led to increased resilience, with three out of four reporting that they found a deeper sense of purpose after Katrina. Only one in 250 reported that they had made plans for suicide, which was one-tenth the reported rate before the storm. Adults aged 40 to 65 were particularly likely to cope well with the trauma (Kessler et al., 2006).

AP PHOTO / BILL HABER

Too Much to Ask Government paperwork is frustrating for everyone, but it became a major stressor for Karen Bazile, shown here applying for a federal loan six months after Hurricane Katrina damaged her home. Humans cope more easily with a major disaster, such as flooding, than with the ongoing stress of bureaucrats who are supposed to help but do not seem to care or understand.

A college student who traveled to Mississippi to help survivors provides a firsthand account. She was expecting to see people defeated by their losses. In her words:

> During spring break last March, I, along with more than 300 students from the University of Akron and Kent State University, came to Pass Christian, Miss., wanting to help alleviate the suffering that tugged at my conscience when I watched the news.
>
> What I didn't expect was how profoundly affected our group would be by the reality. More than six months after Katrina brought a vicious wall of sea water crashing down upon Pass Christian, it remained as if the hurricane had hit yesterday. Skeletons of homes littered the beachfront. Abandoned cars sat rusting in the street, clothing was strewn across tree branches and a crumbling doorstep signaled the spot where a home once stood. As I adjusted to the devastation, the last thing I expected to see was resilient optimism rising above the rubble.
>
> "You don't have time to sit down and cry. You've just got to get to work," said Ruby Blackwell, principal of the First Baptist Preschool. I met Blackwell as part of a group that assisted the school's teachers and helped sort through a mountain of donated books.
>
> I was awed when Blackwell told me that a month after the hurricane, teachers were already asking how soon the school could reopen, even as many were reeling from their own disasters. . . .
>
> From Blackwell and countless others, I learned a humbling truth. A local volunteer summarized the lesson in a simple, unforgettable phrase, "You make a living with what you earn; you make a life with what you give."

[Feerasta, 2006]

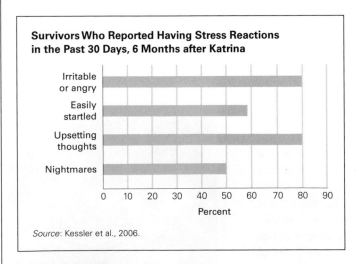

Survivors Who Reported Having Stress Reactions in the Past 30 Days, 6 Months after Katrina

Source: Kessler et al., 2006.

FIGURE 20.4

Lingering Effects of Hurricane Katrina Typically, most people involved in a natural disaster recover within weeks, but, as the chart shows, most Katrina victims were still feeling the psychological effects six months later. Two years after the hurricane, death rates from all causes in New Orleans were double what they had been.

Of course, this does not mean that trauma and stress are benevolent. Everyone who has tried to help the survivors of Katrina worries that ongoing stress may undermine even the most resilient survivors, and some other researchers question the conclusions of the Kessler study (Weisler et al., 2006).

However, similar to the organ reserve explained in Chapter 17 humans seem to have a recovery reserve that is activated under stress. According to a related set of studies, it seems that a reserve of effort and alertness is summoned when emergencies arise, even if the people are overtired and in a noisy environment. This reserve works well for the moments of the emergency, especially if people feel there is something they can do. No wonder the teachers wanted to get back to work. That initial activity may take a toll later on—when the emergency is over and the person must recover, unwind, sleep, relax, and so on (Hockey, 2005)—but at the moment, it helps.

This may explain a familiar reaction to final exams: Some students study intensely, perform well—and then collapse, maybe even getting sick after the last exam. Although more research is needed, it seems quite possible that over the years of adulthood, people can develop better coping skills to adapt to the stresses of life (Masten & Wright, 2010).

SUMMING UP

During adulthood, good health habits are crucial. If no adults smoked, drank too much, overate, underexercised, and accumulated stressors, almost everyone would reach age 65 in good health, ready for decades more of active life. Research on bad habits shows mixed results. Cigarette smoking is decreasing among adults in North America, but not in many other nations. By contrast, in Asia and Africa, people eat less and exercise more, but with affluence these good habits may be lost. Stressors accumulate, causing poor physical and mental health, but coping measures may improve with age. ■

>> Measuring Health

Most of the U.S. expenditure on health goes toward preventing death among people who are already sick rather than protecting health among people who are well. Increasingly, however, many doctors and scientists seek to improve **public health,** the health of everyone before anyone gets sick.

Primary and secondary prevention are the goals; education (such as information about handwashing and seat belts) and preparation (such as practice drills at hospitals so disaster does not mean chaos) are among their strategies. Public health researchers want to know how effective their work is and what else needs to be done. To do that, they need to measure health. There are at least four distinct measures: mortality, morbidity, disability, and vitality.

public health Measures that help prevent morbidity, mortality, and disability in the public at large, such as via immunization, monitoring the food and water supply, and increasing preventive health practices.

Mortality

Death is the ultimate loss of health. This basic indicator, **mortality,** is usually expressed as the annual number of deaths per thousand in the population. The figure for various age, gender, and racial groups in the United States ranged from about 0.1 (1 in 10,000 deaths per year for Asian American girls aged 5 to 14) to 143 (about 1 in 6 deaths per year for European American men over age 85) (U.S. Bureau of the Census, 2009). To compare health among nations, age-adjusted mortality rates are needed; otherwise, a nation with many people over age 80 will have an artificially high mortality rate. The age-adjusted mortality rate among people in the United States in 2005 was 7.8 per thousand, much better than 35 years earlier, when it was 12.3.

Mortality statistics are compiled from death certificates, which indicate age, sex, and immediate cause of death. This practice allows valid international and historical comparisons because deaths have been counted and recorded for

mortality Death. As a measure of health, mortality usually refers to the number of deaths each year per 1,000 members of a given population.

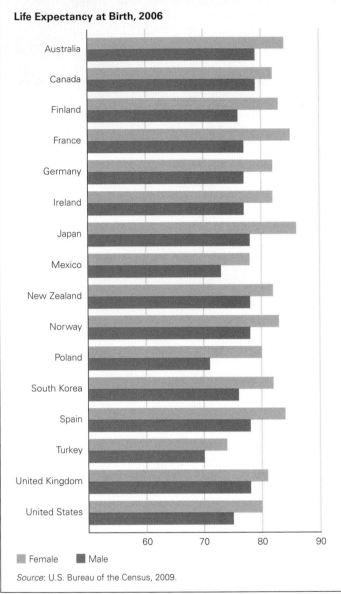

Life Expectancy at Birth, 2006

Australia
Canada
Finland
France
Germany
Ireland
Japan
Mexico
New Zealand
Norway
Poland
South Korea
Spain
Turkey
United Kingdom
United States

60   70   80   90

■ Female   ■ Male

Source: U.S. Bureau of the Census, 2009.

FIGURE 20.5

Not So Many Old Men International comparisons of life expectancy are useful for raising questions (why is the United States more similar to Mexico and Poland than to Australia and Canada?) and highlighting universals (females live longer, no matter what their culture or health care system).

morbidity Disease. As a measure of health, morbidity usually refers to the rate of diseases in a given population—physical and emotional, acute (sudden) and chronic (ongoing).

decades—sometimes for centuries. Japan has the world's lowest age-adjusted mortality rate (about 5 per 1,000) and Sierra Leone the highest (about 35 per 1,000); both of these rates are markedly lower than a few decades ago.

Mortality is lower for women (see Figure 20.5). Worldwide, women live 5 years longer than men. For example, men die an average of 12 years earlier than women in Russia (62 versus 74) but at the same age in Nigeria (both at 49). Worldwide, old women outnumber old men (by 2 to 1 in the United States for those over age 85), primarily because more young men and boys die. The sex ratio favors boys at birth, is about equal at age 20, and tilts toward women from then on.

This gender difference in mortality might be biological—the second X chromosome or extra estrogen could protect women from some illnesses. Or it might be cultural, since women tend to have more friends and take better care of themselves. One public health expert wrote:

> Men are socialized to project strength, individuality, autonomy, dominance, stoicism, and physical aggression, and to avoid demonstrations of emotion or vulnerability that could be construed as weakness. These [characteristics] . . . combine to increase health risks.
>
> [D. R. Williams, 2003, p. 726]

Mortality rates also vary by ethnicity, income, and place of residence, within nations as well as between them. For example, the overall risk of dying for a U.S. resident aged 35 to 65 is about 20 percent over those 30 years, but for some it is as high as 50 percent (e.g., Sioux men in South Dakota) or as low as 2 percent (e.g., Asian women in New Jersey). As one expert put it, "The way you age depends on where you live" (Cruikshank, 2003).

Morbidity

Another measure of health is **morbidity** (from the Latin word for "disease"), which refers to illnesses and impairments of all kinds—acute and chronic, physical and psychological. Morbidity statistics are derived from people's responses when asked if they have any diseases or impairments (e.g., deafness) and from doctors reporting on their patients.

Morbidity does not necessarily correlate with mortality. For example, in many African nations, a parasite causes "river blindness," destroying energy and eyesight in millions but not directly causing death (Basáñez et al., 2006). In the United States, almost half of older women have osteoarthritis; none die of it. As already noted, women live longer than men, but women have higher rates of morbidity for almost every chronic disease. Gender differences are particularly notable in most psychological illnesses: Women are severely depressed twice as often as men.

The relationship among mortality, morbidity, and medicine is not straightforward. The incidence of fatal heart attacks among middle-aged adults in North America and western Europe has been cut in half since 1960, primarily because of health habits (less smoking, better nutrition, and more exercise) but also because of drugs (to reduce hypertension and cholesterol), surgery (e.g., preemptive bypass), and immediate treatment (Unal et al., 2005). Mortality has decreased,

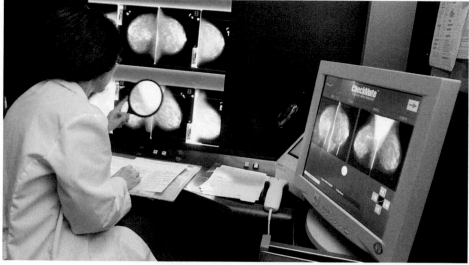

JOHN BERRY / THE IMAGE WORKS

Looking for Trouble A technician examines mammograms for breast abnormalities, such as tiny lumps that cannot be felt but may be malignant. At about age 50, the risks of developing breast cancer become greater than the risks of getting a false positive or having an unnecessary biopsy.

but morbidity has increased as more heart patients depend on medical advances (drugs, pacemakers) to keep them alive.

Similarly, death rates from many cancers are reduced, partly because of early detection and better treatment. However, screening measures themselves may increase morbidity without a marked reduction in mortality. For example, the common PSA blood test for prostate cancer may extend life by a few days on average, but overdiagnosis and negative biopsies result in increased morbidity (such as incontinence and impotence) (Barry, 2009). Likewise, mammograms for women under age 50 produce many false positives, which lead to needless biopsies (to ultimately determine no cancer) and heightened anxiety (while waiting for the results). Overall, depending on age and genetic or other risks, for many women, mammograms may be more harmful than helpful (Woloshin & Schwartz, 2010).

All Equally Sick? These photographs were used in a study that assessed physicians' biases in recommending treatment (Schulman et al., 1999). These supposed "heart patients" were described as identical in occupation, symptoms, and every other respect except age, race, and sex. However, the participating physicians who looked at the photos and the fictitious medical charts that accompanied them did not make identical recommendations. The appropriate treatment for the supposed symptoms would be catheterization; but for the younger, White, or male patients, catheterization was recommended 90, 91, and 91 percent of the time, respectively; for the older, female, or Black patients, 86, 85, and 85 percent of the time, respectively. Are you surprised that the bias differences were less than 10 percent? Or are you surprised that physician bias existed at all?

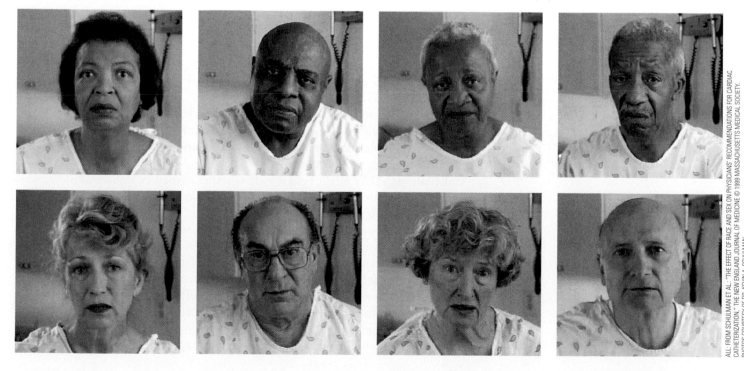

ALL: FROM SCHULMAN ET AL.: "THE EFFECT OF RACE AND SEX ON PHYSICIANS' RECOMMENDATIONS FOR CARDIAC CATHETERIZATION." THE NEW ENGLAND JOURNAL OF MEDICINE © 1999 MASSACHUSETTS MEDICAL SOCIETY. PHOTOS COURTESY OF DR. KEVIN A. SCHULMAN

Disability and Vitality

disability Difficulty in performing normal activities of daily life because of some physical, mental, or emotional condition.

Health is not only the absence of death and disease (mortality and morbidity) but also the ability to enjoy life. This is indicated by measures of disability and vitality.

Disability refers to difficulty in performing "activities of daily life" because of a "physical, mental, or emotional condition" (U.S. Bureau of the Census, 2009). Limitation in functioning (not severity of disease) is the hallmark of disability. Disability does not necessarily equal morbidity: In the United States, of the people who are disabled, 27 percent consider their health very good or excellent (MMWR, October 3, 2008).

Normal activities, and hence ability to perform them, vary by social context. For example, people who cannot walk 200 feet without resting could be said to have a disability if their job requires walking (a mail carrier) but not if they sit at work (a post office clerk). Disability hurts a society more than mortality or morbidity if disabled persons are less able to contribute to the general welfare.

DALYs (disability-adjusted life years) A measure of the reduced quality of life caused by disability.

Disability-adjusted life years, or **DALYs,** are one way to measure how impaired a person is because of a disability. The assumption is that a disabled person has somewhat less than a full life; thus, a person disabled from birth who lives to age 70 would be said to have 63 DALYs if the disability reduced his or her functioning by 10 percent. As you might imagine, the concept of DALYs is not welcomed by many people who are disabled; they do not consider their life any less full than that of a person with no disability—which again signifies that handicap depends on personality and context, not only the actual condition.

vitality A measure of health that refers to how healthy and energetic—physically, intellectually, and socially—an individual actually feels.

The fourth measure of health, **vitality,** refers to how healthy and energetic—physically, intellectually, and socially—an individual feels. Vitality is *joie de vivre,* the zest for living, the love of life (Gigante, 2007). A person can feel terrific despite having a serious disease or disability.

For example, in a Japanese study of people who had cancer and were in pain, some (not most) were high in vitality (Fujimori et al., 2006). Another study of older women in the United States with chronic diseases again found that many felt energetic and vital, at least some of the time (Crawford Shearer et al., 2009). Vitality is affected more by personality and social affirmation than by biology.

As you can see, mortality and morbidity are easy to measure, and disability is controversial—but in estimating one's own health, vitality is crucial. One way to measure vitality is by calculating **QALYs (quality-adjusted life years).** If people are fully vital, their quality of life is 100 percent, which means that a year of their life equals one QALY. A healthy, happy, energetic person who lives 70 years has 70 QALYs.

QALYs (quality-adjusted life years) A way of comparing mere survival without vitality to survival with good health. A full year of health is a full QALY; people with less than full health have a fraction of QALY each year. Thus, their total QALY is less than the total years they live.

A major reason for calculating DALYs or QALYs is to decide how to allocate public funds for health. No society spends enough to enable everyone to live life to the fullest. Without some measure of disability and vitality, the best health care goes to whoever has the most money.

Calculating QALYs might help decide whether taxpayers should subsidize kidney dialysis for young college students or intensive care for extremely low-birthweight newborns. If care of 500-gram babies costs $10 million per life saved yet those infants who survived were severely disabled, while dialysis cost $10,000 per life saved and the survivors led vital adult lives, then dialysis would be the priority. Would it matter, though, if those damaged kidneys were the result of drug abuse?

But that example is hypothetical; real choices are rarely that simple. Each person values his or her life, health, and appearance differently. As you read earlier in this chapter, for some people, visibly growing older reduces the quality of their life (they might avoid going out), so they temporarily lower their QALYs by undergoing the risk and pain of plastic surgery, hoping to regain their full QALYs. Others would never consider such surgery because their QALYs are unaffected by their aged appearance.

A similar dilemma was described earlier in this chapter, regarding in vitro fertilization for couples who cannot conceive a baby the usual way. From the overall society's perspective, IVF is unnecessary: If a society wants more babies, there are many less costly ways to accomplish that. But from the infertile couple's perspective, nothing could be more important. The province of Quebec in Canada recently became the first jurisdiction in North America to include IVF as part of subsidized health care; in the United States, virtually all IVF is financed privately. Each strategy can be justified: QALYs might help in weighing alternatives.

If we focus only on mortality and morbidity, prevention is likely to be tertiary (saving only the seriously ill from dying) or secondary (spotting early stages of ill health). If our goal is less disability and more vitality, then primary prevention (better diet, more exercise, and less smoking) becomes crucial. The World Health Organization and many health professionals are trying to reduce the global burden of disease by considering QALYs and DALYs, not just morbidity and mortality. The idea is to estimate the costs to society of polluting the air or water, parents' refusal to immunize their children, emerging adults' drug use, and even global warming and overuse of fossil fuels. If the cost is high, then laws might change.

That may seem idealistic, but QALYs can be quite practical. For example, two scientists calculated the cost to the health of American society of current smokers and overweight people; they found that smoking was more costly to society 10 years ago but that at current rates obesity is more costly (Jia & Lubetkin, 2010). Such analysis helps public officials know how to spend the limited public money they have.

Disabled but Vital Therapists find that the most serious consequence of losing a limb is losing the will to live. This young man not only learned to cope with crutches after losing a leg but also regained his spirit: He completed the 26.2-mile New York City marathon.

Correlating Income and Health

Money and education protect health in every nation. Well-educated, financially secure adults live longer and avoid morbidity and disability more than their fellow citizens. According to an economist who analyzed historical U.S. data, after age 35 the life span increases by 1.7 years for each year of education (Lleras-Muney, 2005). The reason may be that education teaches healthy habits. Obesity and cigarette smoking in the United States are almost twice as common among adults with the least education compared to those with postcollege degrees.

A related explanation is that education leads to higher income, which allows better medical care as well as a home distant from areas of high pollution and violence. Or education may merely be a marker for intelligence, and intelligence may be the key variable that predicts both income and health. This was one conclusion from a longitudinal study of an entire cohort in Scotland: Childhood IQ scores affected adult health more than any other factor (Deary et al., 2008). For whatever reason, differences can be dramatic. The 10 million Americans with the highest SES (and the best health care) outlive—by about 30 years—the 10 million with the lowest SES, who live in rundown areas (C. J. L. Murray et al., 2006).

SES is protective in comparisons between nations as well as within them: Rich nations have lower rates of disease, injury, and death than do poor nations. For example, a baby born in 2008 in East Asia can expect to live to age 75; in Southeast Asia, to 65; and in sub-Saharan Africa, to 53 (World Health Organization, 2010). Some rich nations do better than others. The United States has a lower life expectancy and a higher morbidity rate than several poorer nations (i.e., nations with a

Blue Skies Ahead Turkey is one of the nations where children still die at high rates but some adults live long, happy, and active lives. The social context, illustrated by this man riding a donkey, is the reason.

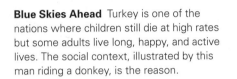
FIGURE 20.6

Immigrants Are Healthier Members of all these ethnic groups who were born in the United States are more likely to have arterial plaque than are their counterparts who were born elsewhere and emigrated to the United States. Plaque is a buildup of fatty substances (including cholesterol) that constricts blood flow inside an artery, increasing the risk of heart attack.

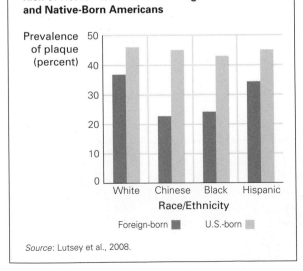

Risk of Heart Attack in U.S. Immigrants and Native-Born Americans

Source: Lutsey et al., 2008.

lower gross domestic product per capita)—among them, Spain, Portugal, Ireland, and Greece (Burd-Sharps et al., 2008).

Certain diseases, particularly lung and breast cancer, were once called *diseases of affluence* because they were more common among the rich than the poor (Krieger, 2002, 2003) and in wealthier ethnic groups even within one nation— Japanese Americans more than Filipino Americans, for instance. However, when smoking became cheaper (between 1920 and 1950), fast food more available, and cancer better diagnosed, the so-called diseases of affluence became more common among the poor.

Distinguishing the effects of income, education, cohort, and culture is difficult because, as you remember from Chapter 1, all these factors overlap. For instance, currently African American women are more likely to die of breast cancer than are women of other U.S. ethnic groups, but medical researchers are not sure why. The reason could be genetic, it could be quality of health care, it could be cultural eating habits, or it could be cultural fear of diagnosis and treatment.

Data on immigrants to the United States further complicate the relationship between economics and health because data that find greater health among the affluent are at odds with the data for immigrants. By almost every measure, immigrants are healthier yet poorer than the native-born. For example, see Figure 20.6, which shows the relationship between U.S. and foreign birth and one measure of heart attack risk (Lutsey et al., 2008).

The most extensive research on the health of immigrants has involved adults born in Mexico now living in the United States. The data are decisive: Although their income and education level are low, they are healthier and more vital than the average U.S. citizen, even the U.S.-born Mexican American. The same trends are apparent in all immigrant groups, and with each more acculturated generation, health worsens. Children and grandchildren of immigrants tend to surpass their elders in education, income, and English fluency—but as their SES rises, so does their drug use, obesity, inactivity, and incidence of virtually every illness, so that they reach the same level as their peers whose grandparents are native-born (Barger & Gallo, 2008; Bates et al., 2008).

One suggested explanation for this paradox is that healthy people of high SES are more likely to emigrate; then their good health protects them as they struggle in their new nation, even though they may be at the bottom of the social ladder in the United States. However, the data suggest that something beyond this "healthy migrant" theory is at work (Bates et al., 2008). Perhaps there are psychological or ethnic influences in other cultures that reduce drug use and increase nutrition and exercise.

One way to see whether this is true is to look at native-born African Americans, another group that, on average, has lower SES and shorter average life spans (by about 6 years) than do European Americans. However, if an African American man is screened for hypertension, glaucoma, and prostate cancer (all more common among middle-aged African American men than among other men), avoids cigarettes, eats healthily, and walks or runs an hour a day, he may live to age 100 or more, as 10,000 African Americans already are doing (U.S. Bureau of the Census, 2009).

That is hypothetical, but Jenny, whose story began this chapter, is a survivor. She is African American (did you guess that from the sickle-cell trait?), and at the beginning of this chapter you learned that she had decided to have another baby—with no prospects of marriage or building a family with the father, Billy, or even of leaving the South Bronx.

I hope you also noticed that she was smart, that others admired her, and that she herself reached out for social support, as evidenced by her seeking me out. She continued to find people to talk with, and she encouraged her children at school—establishing friendships with some of their teachers. After she had the baby, she continued her education and graduated with a BA as valedictorian, found a job that provided health benefits, and ultimately moved to a better neighborhood.

When Billy's wife found out about Jenny, she demanded a divorce. Soon afterward, Billy married Jenny, and they later moved to Florida. There, Jenny enjoyed biking, swimming, and gardening every day. She continues to do well, now working full time in education, having earned a master's degree. Her son with the learning disability eventually earned a PhD, and both her older daughter and the baby she decided to keep successfully graduated from college.

There are lessons here for everyone: As a society, we can do much to reduce disparities in health; as teachers and students, we can help one another develop better habits; as adults, we can make choices that enable us to have long and happy lives.

SUMMING UP

Health can be measured in at least four ways. Mortality, or death rate, is the easiest way to compare nations and cohorts: People are expected to live decades longer in the twenty-first century than they did in the twentieth, and decades longer in wealthy nations and neighborhoods than in poor ones. Morbidity measures chronic illness, which is more common in women than in men. Disability is indicated by difficulty performing daily tasks. It varies by social circumstances and demands, and it affects a society more than any other measure of health. Finally, vitality is the joy in life. It is sought by everyone, affected by culture and personal choices, and may be independent of mortality and morbidity. SES within nations and among nations has a dramatic impact on health. Yet individuals also can find ways to overcome the strikes against them.

Reach Higher Being able to work out at the local gym is rare for women in a low-income neighborhood, yet here they are in Dorchester, Massachusetts. In this case, the gym itself is unusual, too—it's a nonprofit establishment, partly supported by several for-profit Healthworks gyms in nearby Boston.

COURTESY HEALTHWORKS FOUNDATION

SUMMARY

Senescence

1. With each year of life, signs of senescence (a gradual physical decline associated with aging) become more apparent. All the body systems gradually become less efficient, though at varying rates, not only between different people but also between different organs within the same person.

2. The brain slows down and begins a gradual, usually imperceptible decline. Beyond measures to protect overall health, the brain is affected by psychoactive drugs, lack of sleep, and lack of exercise.

3. A person's appearance undergoes gradual but noticeable changes as middle age progresses, including more wrinkles, less hair, and more fat, particularly around the abdomen. With the exception of excessive weight gain, changes in appearance have little impact on health.

4. The rate of senescence is most apparent in the sense organs. Vision becomes less sharp with age, with both nearsightedness and farsightedness increasing gradually beginning in the 20s. Hearing also becomes less acute, with noticeable losses being more likely for pure tones (such as doorbells) and high-frequency sounds (such as a child's excited speech).

The Sexual-Reproductive System

5. Sexual responsiveness slows down with age, as does speed of recovery after orgasm. This is only a physical decline; many couples find that overall, sexual interaction improves with age.

6. Fertility problems become more common with increased age, for many reasons. The most common one for men is a reduced number of sperm, and for women, ovulation failure or blocked fallopian tubes. For both sexes, not only youth but also overall good health—especially sexual health—correlates with fertility.

7. A number of assisted reproductive technology (ART) procedures, including IVF (in vitro fertilization), offer potential answers to infertility. Donor sperm, donor ova, and/or donor wombs have helped thousands of infertile couples become parents.

8. At menopause, as a woman's menstrual cycle stops, ovulation ceases and levels of estrogen are markedly reduced. This hormonal change produces various symptoms, although most women find menopause much less troubling than they had expected.

9. Hormone production declines in men, too, though not as suddenly as in women. For both sexes, hormone replacement therapy (HRT) should be used cautiously, if at all.

Health Habits and Age

10. Adults in North America are smoking cigarettes much less than they once did, and rates of lung cancer and other diseases are falling, largely for that reason. Alcohol abuse remains a major health problem worldwide.

11. Good health habits include exercising regularly and not gaining weight. On both these counts, today's adults worldwide are faring worse than did previous generations. This is especially true in the United States. There is a worldwide "epidemic of obesity," as more people have access to abundant food and overeat as a result.

12. People experience many stresses over the 40 years of adulthood. They use various coping measures, both problem-focused and emotion-focused, depending on the particular issue as well as on the person's age. A combination of stressors increases allostatic load and reduces health.

Measuring Health

13. Variations in health can be measured in terms of mortality, morbidity, disability, and vitality. Although death and disease are easier to quantify, in terms of the health of a population, disability and vitality may be more significant. Quality-adjusted life years (QALYs) and disability-adjusted life years (DALYs) help doctors and public health advocates figure out how to allocate limited resources.

14. Aging and health status can be greatly affected by SES. In general, those who have more education and money are more likely to live longer and avoid illness than those who do not. However, low SES does not inevitably lead to poor health since genes and health habits are protective; avoiding drugs and obesity is possible at any income level.

KEY TERMS

senescence (p. 550)
presbycusis (p. 553)
menopause (p. 557)
hormone replacement therapy (HRT) (p. 558)
andropause (p. 558)
stressor (p. 565)
problem-focused coping (p. 566)
emotion-focused coping (p. 566)
allostatic load (p. 566)
weathering (p. 566)
public health (p. 569)
mortality (p. 569)
morbidity (p. 570)
disability (p. 572)
DALYs (disability-adjusted life years) (p. 572)
vitality (p. 572)
QALYs (quality-adjusted life years) (p. 572)

WHAT HAVE YOU LEARNED?

Senescence

1. What is the connection between senescence and serious disease?

2. How often and why do people lose significant brain function before age 65?

3. What are the visible changes in the skin between ages 25 and 65?

4. What are the visible changes in the hair between ages 25 and 65?

5. What are the visible changes in the body shape between ages 25 and 65?

6. How does aging affect nearsightedness and farsightedness?

7. Why are hearing losses expected to increase in the next generation?

The Sexual-Reproductive System

8. How are men and women affected by the changes in sexual responsiveness with age?

9. When a couple is infertile, which sex is usually responsible?

10. What are the reasons infertility is more problematic in Africa than in North America?

11. What are the advantages and disadvantages of HRT for women?

Health Habits and Age

12. What are the trends in cigarette smoking in North America?

13. How much alcohol should an adult drink and why?

14. What factors in the diet affect the rate of obesity?

15. What nonfood factors affect the rate of obesity?

16. What diseases and conditions are less likely in people who exercise every day?

17. When is problem-focused coping best?

18. When is emotion-focused coping best?

Measuring Health

19. What are the advantages and disadvantages of using mortality as a measure of health?

20. What are the advantages and disadvantages of using morbidity as a measure of health?

21. How do men and women compare in mortality and morbidity?

22. Why would a disabled person object to measuring DALYs?

23. What factors would increase a person's QALYs?

24. Are economic or educational factors more important in the correlation between SES and illness?

25. Why are there no more diseases of affluence?

APPLICATIONS

1. Guess the age of five people you know, and then ask them how old they are. Analyze the clues you used for your guesses and the people's reactions to your question.

2. Find a speaker willing to come to your class who is an expert on weight loss, adult health, smoking, or drinking. Write a one-page proposal explaining why you think this speaker would be good and what topics he or she should address. Give this proposal to your instructor, with contact information for your speaker. The instruc-

tor will call the potential speakers, thank them for their willingness, and decide whether or not to actually invite them to speak.

3. Attend a gathering for people who want to stop a bad habit or start a good one, such as an open meeting of Alcoholics Anonymous or another 12-step program, an introductory session of Weight Watchers or Smoke Enders, or a meeting of prospective gym members. Report on who attended, what you learned, and what your reactions were.

>>ONLINE CONNECTIONS

To accompany your textbook, you have access to a number of online resources, including quizzes for every chapter of the book, flashcards (in English and Spanish), critical thinking questions, and case studies. For access to any of these links, go to www.worthpublishers.com/bergerls8e. In addition to these free resources, you'll also find links to the podcasts, video clips, diagnostic quizzing with personalized study advice, and an ebook. Some of the videos and activities available online include:

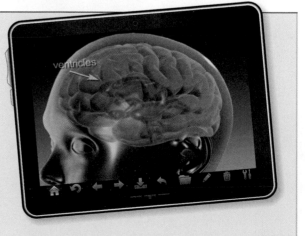

- *Brain Development: Middle Adulthood.* Animations show age-related loss of brain volume and compensatory increase in size of the ventricles and volume of cerebrospinal fluid

- *Signs of Aging.* Video, audio and illustrations demonstrate the physical and sensory changes that come with aging and older people's reactions to the process.

Adulthood: Cognitive Development

WHAT WILL YOU KNOW?

1. In what ways do adults get smarter as they grow older?

2. In what ways do adults get dumber as they grow older?

3. What kind of intelligence is most useful in adulthood?

4. How is your thinking about whatever you are an expert in different from ordinary thinking?

I asked my class if people get smarter or dumber as they grow older, the first two questions above. Opinions were divided until one student, himself over age 30, said: "Both."

Exactly. This chapter explains how we get smarter in some ways and dumber in others. Specifically, we describe adult cognitive development as measured by various tests. Scores from ages 18 to 88 are reported, although the focus is on adulthood, ages 25 to 65.

Remember that many research strategies are used to understand cognition throughout adulthood. Chapter 18 described postformal thinking as well as the impact of college. Chapter 24 will take an information-processing perspective and then highlight the aspects of processing that slow down cognition in old age. This chapter takes a psychometric approach (*metric* means "measure"; *psychometric* refers to measuring psychological characteristics) and considers various kinds of intelligence, including those that produce experts of one sort or another.

As you will see, psychometric conclusions about adult IQ keep changing. The reason is that each generation of scholars finds new answers to the crucial questions: What is intelligence and how should it be measured? Answers lead to different tests, subtests, and interpretations, and thus conclusions change. Intelligence was once thought to decline from age 20 on; now it is thought to rise throughout most of adulthood, declining at age 60, or 70, or 80. Which specific abilities and skills merit emphasis is also debatable; specifically, whether practical intelligence, used in daily life or on the job, is more important than the intelligence needed in school and college—which is helpful in understanding books such as this one!

>> What Is Intelligence?

For most of the twentieth century, everyone—scientists and the general public alike—assumed that there was such a thing as "intelligence"; that is, they assumed that some people are smarter than others because they have more intelligence than others. One leading theoretician who expressed this idea was Charles Spearman (1927), who proposed that there is a single entity, **general intelligence,** which he called **g.** Spearman contended that, although *g* cannot be measured directly, it

general intelligence (*g*) The idea of *g* assumes that intelligence is one basic trait, underlying all cognitive abilities. According to this concept, people have varying levels of this general ability.

can be inferred from various abilities, such as vocabulary, memory, and reasoning. By combining test scores on a diverse mix of items, a person could be assigned one overall IQ score, based on carefully standardized tests of intelligence. That score would indicate whether the person was a genius, average, or retarded.

The belief that there is a *g* continues to influence thinking on this subject. Many neuroscientists are searching for genetic underpinnings of the intellectual differences among adults, although efforts to find specific genes or abilities that comprise *g* have not succeeded (Deary et al., 2010; Haier et al., 2009). Many developmentalists seek one common factor that undergirds IQ—perhaps genetic inheritance, prenatal brain development, experiences in infancy, or physical health. Although many still believe "there are abilities and processes in intellectual functioning that are truly general" (Demetriou, 2002, p. 5), many others who study adulthood have abandoned this search.

Research on Age and Intelligence

Even though psychometricians throughout the twentieth century all believed that intelligence could be measured and quantified, and even though many tried to develop IQ tests to do so, they disagreed about interpreting the data—especially about whether general intelligence rises or falls after age 20 or so. Methodology was one reason for that disagreement.

NATIONAL ARCHIVES

Smart Enough for the Trenches? These young men were drafted to fight in World War I. Younger men (about age 17 or 18) did better on the military's intelligence tests than slightly older ones did.

Observation Quiz Beyond the test itself, what conditions of the testing favored the teenage men? (see answer, page 582)

Cross-Sectional Research

For the first half of the twentieth century, psychologists were convinced that intelligence increases in childhood, peaks in adolescence, and then gradually declines. This belief was based on the best evidence then available. For instance, the U.S. Army tested the aptitude of all literate draftees in World War I. When the scores of men of various ages were compared, it seemed apparent that intellectual ability reached its peak at about age 18, stayed at that level until the mid-20s, and then declined (Yerkes, 1923).

Similar results came from a classic study of 1,191 individuals, aged 10 to 60, from 19 carefully selected New England villages. Most of those studied had lived in the same village all their lives, as had all their relatives. This was ideal for the researchers, who wanted to measure the intelligence of people who differed in age but not in genes or life experience. The IQ scores of these New Englanders rose from ages 10 to 18, peaked between ages 18 and 21, and then gradually fell, with the average 55-year-old scoring the same as the average 14-year-old (Jones & Conrad, 1933).

Hundreds of other cross-sectional studies of IQ in many nations confirmed that younger adults outscored older adults. The case for an age-related decline in IQ was considered proven, and the two classic IQ tests, the Stanford-Binet and the WISC/WAIS (see pages 307–308), were normed to peak in late adolescence.

Longitudinal Research

Shortly after the middle of the twentieth century, Nancy Bayley and Melita Oden (1955) analyzed the adult intelligence of the people originally selected by Lewis Terman in 1921 for his study of child geniuses (a group studied by a succession of researchers over the past 80 years). Bayley was an expert in intelligence testing who knew that "the invariable findings had indicated that most intellectual functions decrease after about 21 years of age" (Bayley, 1966, p. 117). But she found, instead, that the IQ scores of these gifted individuals *increased* between ages 20 and 50.

Bayley wondered whether this group was atypical: Perhaps their high intelligence in childhood protected them against the usual age-related declines. To find out, she retested another group of adults who had been tested as children and who were then 36 years old. They had been selected in infancy as representative (not particularly smart) of the population of Berkeley, California. Bayley found that most of them, far from peaking at age 21, improved on tests of vocabulary, comprehension, and information (key subtests of adult intelligence scales). She concluded that the "intellectual potential for continued learning is unimpaired through 36 years" and probably beyond (Bayley, 1966, p. 136).

Why did these data contradict previous conclusions? Recall that Bayley's studies were longitudinal, whereas earlier studies were cross-sectional (see Chapter 1). As you remember, cross-sectional research can be misleading because each cohort has unique life experiences. Think of what those differences might be. Improvements in the quality and extent of adult education, greater variety of cultural opportunities (modes of travel, movies), and new sources of information from newspapers and radio (later, television and the Internet) resulted in intellectual growth after age 18.

When earlier research compared adults of various ages, such cross-sectional research did not take into account the fact that most of the sample of older adults had left school before eighth grade and were thus less likely to have developed their full academic intelligence, compared with younger cohorts. By contrast, adults who grew up later, when high school was normative, kept developing their intellect. For later cohorts, college became more common, which would mean that any cross-sectional comparison of cohorts would be comparing the effects of education as well as the effect of age. In cross-sectional comparisons of IQ, each younger generation would score higher than the previous one. But on longitudinal data, adults would have higher scores than they themselves had had earlier.

Powerful evidence that younger generations score higher because of education and health, not because of age, has come from research that compares test scores in many nations over time. In every country where data allow a valid comparison, more recent cohorts outscore older ones. As you remember from Chapter 11, this *Flynn effect* finds that younger people seem to gain in intelligence compared with older people (a trend evident in test scores) but not necessarily in basic abilities. That makes it unfair—and scientifically invalid—to compare IQ scores of a cross-section of adults of various ages. Older adults will score lower, but that does not mean that they have lost intellectual power.

Longitudinal research is more accurate than cross-sectional research when it comes to measuring development over the decades, but it is not perfect. One problem is that because the participants are tested repeatedly, they become practiced at taking the tests. Practice leads to learning. That means a longitudinal rise in IQ may reflect learning on specific test questions, or quicker test-taking strategies, rather than increased intelligence.

Another problem is that every longitudinal study loses some participants over time because some people move away and cannot be found, some people refuse to be retested, and—especially for studies that compare IQ scores on the same people throughout the entire life span—some people die. If the people who are not retested are similar in every other way to the people who stay in the study, the overall conclusions would not be affected. However, those who are not retested tend to be those whose IQ is declining. Indeed, one reason people refuse retesting

Especially for Older Brothers and Sisters If your younger siblings mock your ignorance of current TV shows and beat you at the latest video games, does that mean your intellect is fading? (see response, page 582)

>> Answer to Observation Quiz (from page 580) Sitting on the floor with no back support, with a test paper at a distance on your lap, and with someone standing over you holding a stopwatch—all are enough to rattle anyone, especially people over 18.

>> Response for Older Brothers and Sisters (from page 581) No. While it is true that each new cohort might be smarter than the previous one in some ways, cross-sequential research suggests that you are smarter than you used to be. Knowing that might help you respond wisely—smiling quietly rather than insisting that you are superior.

Seattle Longitudinal Study The first cross-sequential study of adult intelligence. This study began in 1956; the most recent testing was conducted in 2005.

is that they are not healthy and they believe their intellect is failing (Sliwinski et al., 2003). This would skew the results of longitudinal research because the people who return for retesting may not be typical but may be those who continue to improve. Their IQ scores might rise, but that does not mean everyone's intellect increases with age.

Even if careful efforts ensure that almost everyone in a longitudinal study is retested (and researchers now go to extraordinary lengths to ensure this), every longitudinal study is affected by another factor that cannot be avoided—history. Unusual events (e.g., a major war or a breakthrough in public health) affect each cohort, and more mundane changes—such as widespread use of the Internet and reductions in secondhand smoke—make the data on one cohort less relevant to later cohorts (Zelinski et al., 2009). Thus, longitudinal research on people born in 1930 may not predict the adult intelligence of people born decades later. The trend has been for each generation to be a little smarter than the previous one, but even that is not guaranteed; cohort effects might make a younger generation score lower, not higher, than their elders.

Cross-Sequential Research

The best method to understand the effects of age without the complications of historical change is to combine cross-sectional and longitudinal research. The story of how this method of study came about may be an inspiration to current students. As an undergraduate, K. Warner Schaie was already interested in adult intelligence, and he began to study it. In 1956, as a doctoral student, he tested a cross section of 500 adults, aged 20 to 50, on five standard primary mental abilities widely considered to be the foundation of intelligence: (1) verbal meaning (vocabulary), (2) spatial orientation, (3) inductive reasoning, (4) number ability, and (5) word fluency (rapid verbal associations).

Schaie's initial cross-sectional results showed a gradual decline in each ability with age, as others had found before him. He had read that longitudinal research reported an increase in IQ, so he planned to investigate this approach by retesting his population seven years later.

He then had a brilliant idea: He would not only retest his initial participants; he would also test a new group who were the same age that his earlier sample had been. He did so over his entire academic career, not just once but every seven years, adding a new group each time. By comparing the scores of the retested individuals with their own earlier scores (longitudinal) and with the scores of a new group (cross-sectional), he obtained a more accurate view of development than was possible from either kind of research alone.

Schaie's new design, called *cross-sequential research,* was illustrated in Chapter 1. Cross-age comparisons allow analysis of potential influences, including retesting, cohort differences, experience, and gender. The results of Schaie's ongoing project, known as the **Seattle Longitudinal Study,** confirmed and extended what others had found: People improve in most mental abilities during adulthood. As Figure 21.1 shows, each particular ability at each age and for each gender has a distinct pattern. Note the gradual rise and the eventual decline of all abilities, with men initially better at number skills and women at verbal skills—but then note the convergence of scores for men and women over time.

Other researchers from many nations have since found similar results (Alwin, 2009). For example, Paul Baltes (2003) tested hundreds of older Germans in Berlin and found that only at age 80 did the average of every cognitive ability show age-related declines. Adulthood is usually a time of increasing, or at least maintaining, IQ (Lee et al., 2008; Martin & Zimprich, 2005).

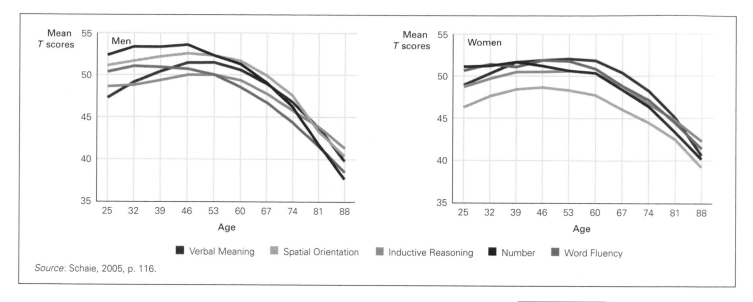

Source: Schaie, 2005, p. 116.

Schaie discovered substantial cohort effects, more detailed than the Flynn effect. Each successive cohort (born at seven-year intervals from 1889 to 1973) scored higher in adulthood than did the previous generations in verbal memory and inductive reasoning but scored lower in number ability. School curricula may explain these differences: By the mid-twentieth century, children were taught more reading, writing, and self-expression than math. In addition, another cohort effect was that the drop in scores with age occurred later, by about a decade, when those born after 1950 were compared with those born before 1900 (Schaie, 2005). It could be that those later-born children spent more years in school and then college, or it could be that they were less likely to have chronic illnesses such as hypertension and cigarette addiction, which are known to impair adult intelligence.

One correlate of higher ability is intellectual complexity at work and in personal life, which Schaie found tended to peak from ages 39 to 53. This has become more evident for more recent cohorts, particularly for women, who used to stay home or perform less challenging jobs. That may be the reason why adult women currently have higher IQ scores than adult women did 50 years ago. Other research also finds that a challenging job fosters high intelligence. One team found that those who retired from challenging work were more likely to lose intellectual power than were those who retired from less interesting jobs (Finkel et al., 2009). Much depends on what a person does after retirement: Intellectually demanding tasks, either paid or not, are likely to keep the mind working well (Schooler, 2009).

Many studies using sophisticated designs and statistics have now supplanted those early cross-sectional and longitudinal studies. It is apparent that people vary substantially in intellectual ability. Among the major reasons for the variation are inherited abilities and years of education, both of which are more influential than age during adulthood (Reynolds, 2008). Nonetheless, when it comes to a specific child, it is not easy to predict intelligence, even if that child's genes are known. For instance, a study of monozygotic and dizygotic twins in Sweden, aged 41 to 84, found that even among the monozygotic twins with equal education, verbal differences were apparent. However, that research also found that age

FIGURE 21.1

Age Differences in Intellectual Abilities
Cross-sectional data on intellectual abilities at various ages would show much steeper declines. Longitudinal research, in contrast, would show more notable rises. Because Schaie's research is cross-sequential, the trajectories it depicts are more revealing: None of the average scores for the five abilities at any age are above 55 or below 35. Because the methodology takes into account the cohort and historical effects, the age-related differences from ages 25 to 60 are very small.

Winners All St. Paul police chief Thomas Smith shows high school students how to read his thumbprint. Such mentoring obviously helps teenagers understand forensic science. Not as obvious are the advantages for Smith: Teaching others will help his 51-year-old mind stay sharp.

ELIZABETH FLORES / STAR TRIBUNE / ZUMA PRESS

matters, especially evident in the slowing down of memory and spatial ability (Finkel et al., 2009).

Considering all the research, it seems that over the many years of adulthood, intellectual abilities sometimes rise, fall, zigzag, or stay the same. Specific patterns are affected by each person's life. This illustrates the life-span perspective: Intelligence is multidirectional, multicultural, multicontextual, and plastic. Although several subtests show differences between the cognition of an average person at 25 and at 65, intellectual ability is usually maintained, and "decline prior to age 60 years of age is almost inevitably a symptom or precursor of pathological age changes" (Schaie 2005, p. 418). Can those pathological changes be avoided? Maybe, maybe not, as the following discusses.

THINKING CRITICALLY

How to Stay Smart

Adult intelligence may seem abstract when it is based on group averages, but individual cases reveal remarkable growth, decline, and stability (MacDonald et al., 2009). Using data from his Seattle Longitudinal Study, Schaie (1996) reported that "virtually every possible permutation of individual profiles has been observed in our study" (p. 351). For example, he reported changes in one of the five primary mental abilities, verbal meaning, for four people. See Figure 21.2.

The first two profiles represent two . . . women who throughout life functioned at very different levels. Subject 155510 is a high school graduate who has been a homemaker all of her adult life and whose husband is still alive and well-functioning. She started our testing program at a rather low level, but her performance has had a clear upward trend. The comparison participant subject (154503) had been professionally active as a teacher. Her performance remained fairly level and above the population average until her early sixties. Since that time she

has been divorced and retired from her teaching job; her performance in 1984 dropped to an extremely low level, which may reflect her experiential losses but could also be a function of increasing health problems.

The second pair of profiles shows the 28-year performance of two . . . men . . . Subject 153003, who started out somewhat below the population average, completed only grade school and worked as a purchasing agent prior to his retirement. He showed virtually stable performance until the late sixties; his performance actually increased after he retired, but he is beginning to experience health problems and has recently become a widower, and his latest assessment was below the earlier stable level. By contrast, subject 153013, a high school graduate who held mostly clerical types of jobs, showed gain until the early sixties and stability over the next assessment interval. By age 76, however, he showed substantial decrement that continued through the last assessment, which occurred less than a year prior to his death.

[Schaie, 1989, pp. 79–80]

FIGURE 21.2

Profiles of Verbal Memory These figures index changes in word-recognition scores for two pairs of comparable adults over time. Notice how distinctly different each profile is, although all four are from the same nation and cohort. These differences underscore the power of occupation, marriage, health, and other experiences that vary from one person to another.

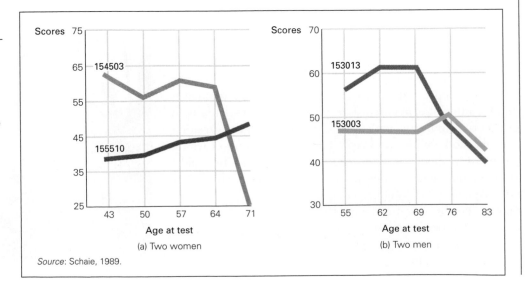

(a) Two women

(b) Two men

Source: Schaie, 1989.

Predictions about adult cognition are imprecise. No one could anticipate the middle-adulthood or late-life intellectual performance of these participants based on their early scores. Schaie found that education, occupation, marital status, and health—all of which vary from person to person—contribute to unique profiles. Other researchers agree: Eventually old age and poor health slow thinking, but this may not occur until late in life, and the decline may be gradual (Salthouse, 2006).

Some developmentalists downplay the factors within each person's control that Schaie stresses; they focus instead on genes, socioeconomic status (SES), ethnicity, or culture. What do you think is crucial for intelligence over the years of adulthood and beyond? More to the point, can you do anything to keep your intellect strong, even in your 80s? Personally, I like Schaie's interpretation and I have developed good health habits (as described in Chapter 20). I take comfort that I am thinner and more active than most adults of previous generations at my age, including my own parents, who nonetheless were still cogent when they died in their 90s. But my comfort may arise from wishful thinking. Critical thinking means applying the psychometric data to predict the future: If adults maintain their health, will they also maintain their intellect?

SUMMING UP

Psychometricians once believed that intelligence decreased beginning at about age 20 because that is what cross-sectional data revealed. Then longitudinal testing demonstrated that many people advance in intelligence with age. Cross-sequential research provided a more nuanced picture, finding that some abilities decrease and others increase throughout adulthood. Many factors—including challenging work, a stimulating marriage, and good health—protect intelligence and postpone any decline. ■

>> Components of Intelligence: Many and Varied

Responding to all these data, developmentalists are now looking closely at patterns of cognitive gains and losses over the adult years. Because virtually every pattern is possible, it is misleading to ask whether intelligence either increases or decreases; it does not move in lockstep. Instead, it often zigzags from one ability to another within the same person over time. There may be "vast domains of cognitive performance . . . that may not follow a common, age-linked trajectory of decline" (Dannefer & Patterson, 2009, p. 116).

Many psychologists envision several intellectual abilities, each of which independently rises and falls. They debate how many distinct abilities there are and how each might be affected by age. We now consider two proposals, one of which posits two such abilities and the other, three. (As you remember, Gardner's theory of multiple intelligences describes nine abilities, an idea with educational implications in childhood and therefore explained in Chapter 11.)

Two Clusters of Intelligence

In the 1960s, leading personality researcher Raymond Cattell teamed up with a promising graduate student, John Horn, to study intelligence tests. They concluded that adult intelligence is best understood if various measures are grouped into two categories, called fluid and crystallized.

Fluid Intelligence

As its name implies, **fluid intelligence** is like water, flowing to its own level no matter where it happens to be. Fluid intelligence is quick and flexible, enabling people to learn anything, even things that are unfamiliar and unconnected to what

fluid intelligence Those types of basic intelligence that make learning of all sorts quick and thorough. Abilities such as short-term memory, abstract thought, and speed of thinking are all usually considered part of fluid intelligence.

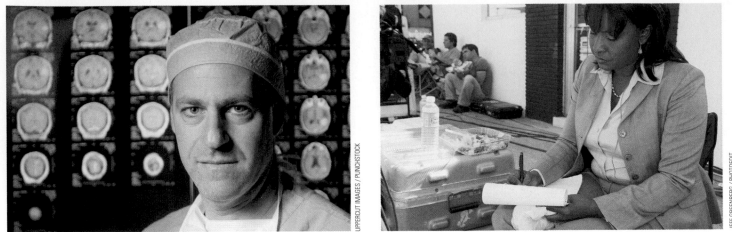

UPPERCUT IMAGES / PUNCHSTOCK

JEFF GREENBERG / PHOTOEDIT

Not Brain Surgery? Yes, it is! Both these adults need to combine fluid and crystallized intelligence, insight and intuition, logic and experience. One *(left)* is in fact a neurosurgeon, studying brain scans before picking up his scalpel. The other *(right)* is a court reporter for a TV station, jotting notes during a lunch recess before delivering her on-camera report on a trial.

they already know. Curiosity, learning for the joy of it and the thrill at discovering something new are marks of fluid intelligence (Silvia & Sanders, 2010).

People high in fluid abilities can draw inferences, understand relations between concepts, and readily process new ideas and facts. Someone high in fluid intelligence is quick and creative with words and numbers and enjoys intellectual puzzles. The kinds of questions that test fluid intelligence among Western adults might be:

What comes next in each of these two series?*
4 9 1 6 2 5 3
V X Z B D

Puzzles are often used to measure fluid intelligence, with speedy solutions given bonus points (as on many IQ tests). Immediate recall—of nonsense words, of numbers, of a sentence just read—is one indicator of fluid intelligence because working memory is considered crucial. Since fluid intelligence seems disconnected from past learning, it may seem impractical—not so. A study of adults aged 34 to 83 found that stresses and stressors did not vary by age but did vary by fluid intelligence. People high in fluid intelligence were more often exposed to stress but were less likely to suffer from it: They used their intellect to turn stressors into positive experiences (Stawski et al., 2010).

The ability to detoxify stress may be one reason that high fluid intelligence in emerging adulthood leads to longer life and higher IQ later in adulthood. Fluid intelligence is associated with openness to new experiences and overall brain health (Batterham et al., 2009; Silvia & Sanders, 2010).

Crystallized Intelligence

crystallized intelligence Those types of intellectual ability that reflect accumulated learning. Vocabulary and general information are examples. Some developmental psychologists think crystallized intelligence increases with age, while fluid intelligence declines.

The accumulation of facts, information, and knowledge as a result of education and experience is called **crystallized intelligence.** The size of a person's vocabulary, the knowledge of chemical formulas, and the long-term memory for dates in history all indicate crystallized intelligence. Tests designed to measure this intelligence might include questions like these:

What is the meaning of the word *misanthrope*?
Who would hold a harpoon?
Explain the formula for the area of a circle.
What was Sri Lanka called in 1950?

* The correct answers are 6 and F. These are fairly easy for people who know the alphabet and the times tables; some series are much more difficult to complete.

Although such questions seem to measure achievement more than aptitude, these two are connected, especially in adulthood. Intelligent adults read widely, think deeply, and remember what they learn so their achievement reflects their intellect. Vocabulary, for example, improves with reading and is a mainstay of most IQ tests, including the Wechsler tests, because a person's familiarity with words is a measure of intellect. Using the words *happiness, joy, ecstasy, bliss,* and *delight*—each appropriately, with a distinct meaning (quite apart from the drug, perfume, or yogurt that use these names)—is a sign of intelligence. Further, the more people know, the more they can learn, which explains why high crystallized intelligence in early adulthood predicts a high IQ later on, as well as why years of education is a rough indicator of adult IQ.

Both Together Now

To reflect the total picture of a person's intellectual aptitude, both fluid and crystallized intelligence must be measured. Age complicates the IQ calculation because scores on items measuring fluid intelligence decrease with age, whereas scores on items measuring crystallized intelligence increase. Subtests follow one or the other of these patterns, with verbal ability rising but speed falling (Horn & Masunaga, 2000). These two clusters, changing in opposite directions, make a person's IQ score (composed of diverse subtests) fairly steady from ages 30 to 70, even though particular abilities change.

The reason why age impairs fluid intelligence is that everything slows down with age, not only catching a speeding baseball but also putting together a puzzle. Fluid intelligence is age-sensitive. Although brain slowdown begins at age 20 or so, it is rarely apparent until massive declines in fluid intelligence begin to affect crystallized intelligence and overall IQ scores start to fall in late adulthood.

Horn and Cattell (1967) wrote that they had:

> shown intelligence to both increase and decrease with age—depending upon the definition of intelligence adopted, fluid or crystallized! Our results illustrate an essential fallacy implicit in the construction of omnibus measures of intelligence.
>
> [p. 124]

In other words, it is foolish to try to measure *g*, a single omnibus intelligence, because both components need to be measured separately. Otherwise, the real changes over time will be masked because changes in fluid and crystallized abilities cancel each other out.

Three Forms of Intelligence: Sternberg

Robert Sternberg (1988, 2003) agrees that a single intelligence score is misleading. As first mentioned in Chapter 11, Sternberg proposed three fundamental forms of intelligence: analytic, creative, and practical, each of which can be tested.

Analytic intelligence includes all the mental processes that foster academic proficiency by making efficient learning, remembering, and thinking possible. Thus, it draws on abstract planning, strategy selection, focused attention, and information processing, as well as on verbal and logical skills. Strengths in those areas are valuable in emerging adulthood, particularly in college, in graduate school, and in job training. Multiple-choice tests and brief essays that call forth remembered information, with one and only one right answer, indicate analytic intelligence.

Creative intelligence involves the capacity to be intellectually flexible and innovative. Creative thinking is divergent rather than convergent, valuing the unexpected, imaginative, and unusual, rather than standard and conventional answers. Sternberg developed tests of creative intelligence that include writing a short story

Quick and Smart Rotate the cubes until they match the picture: The faster you succeed at this task, the higher your IQ. Is this item on the WAIS (Wechsler Adult Intelligence Scale) equally valid for a midlife woman and an emerging-adult man? ["Wechsler Adult Intelligence Scale" and "WAIS" are trademarks, in the US and/or other countries, of Pearson Education, Inc. or its affiliate(s).]

analytic intelligence A form of intelligence that involves such mental processes as abstract planning, strategy selection, focused attention, and information processing, as well as verbal and logical skills.

creative intelligence A form of intelligence that involves the capacity to be intellectually flexible and innovative.

practical intelligence The intellectual skills used in everyday problem solving. (Sometimes called *tacit intelligence.*)

titled "The Octopus's Sneakers" or planning an advertising campaign for a new doorknob. High scores are earned by those with many unusual ideas.

Practical intelligence involves the capacity to adapt one's behavior to the demands of a given situation. This capacity includes an accurate grasp of the expectations and needs of the people involved and an awareness of the particular skills that are called for, along with the ability to use these insights effectively. Practical intelligence is sometimes called *tacit intelligence,* because it is not obvious on tests. Instead it comes from "the school of hard knocks" and is sometimes called "street smarts," not "book smarts."

Practical intelligence is useful for managing the conflicting personalities in a family or for convincing members of an organization (e.g., business, social group, school) to do something. Without practical intelligence, a solution found by analytic intelligence is doomed to fail because people resist academic brilliance as unrealistic and elite, as the term *ivory tower* implies. Similarly, a stunningly creative idea may be rejected as ridiculous and weird rather than seriously considered if it is not accompanied by practical intelligence.

For example, imagine a business manager, or a school principal, or a political leader without practical intelligence trying to change procedures. Unless the new policies are compatible with the organization and are understood by at least some of the people, the workers, teachers, or voters will misinterpret them, predict that they will fail, and balk at implementation. Both experience and flexibility are needed for practical intelligence (K. Sloan, 2009). As you remember from Chapter 18, these are the mental qualities that build during emerging adulthood. Ideally, they continue to be refined throughout adulthood because each new experience provides practice.

Listening Quietly This elementary school teacher appears to be explaining academic work to one of her students, a boy who seems attentive and quiet.

Observation Quiz If this situation is typical in this classroom, what kind of intelligence is valued? (see answer, page 591)

No abstract test can assess practical intelligence because context is crucial for practical problem solving. Preferably, adults would be observed as they cope with the challenges of their daily lives. For example, when hiring a new employee, one might test a candidate's practical intelligence by describing an actual situation and asking how the applicant would handle it. Such situational tests are now used by many companies to decide whether a prospective employee would be a good manager (Salter & Highhouse, 2009). Then the person is hired for a trial period, to see how he or she performs. Some excellent managers are not particularly brilliant or creative, but they are adept at overcoming the obstacles of daily life.

Sternberg believes that each of these three forms of intelligence is useful and that adults should deploy the strengths and guard against the limitations of each:

> People attain success, in part, by finding out how to exploit their own patterns of strengths and weaknesses. . . . Analytic ability involves critical thinking; it is the ability to analyze and evaluate ideas, solve problems, and make decisions. Creative ability involves going beyond what is given to generate novel and interesting ideas. Practical ability involves implementing ideas; it is the ability involved when intelligence is applied to real world contexts.

> [*Sternberg et al., 2000, p. 31*]

Age and Culture

Which kind of intelligence is most valued depends partly on age and partly on culture. Think about Steinberg's three types. Analytic intelligence is usually valued in high school and college, as students are expected to remember and analyze various ideas. Creative intelligence is prized if life circumstances change and new challenges arise; it is much more valued in some cultures and countries than others (Kaufman & Sternberg, 2006). In times of social upheaval, or in the arts, creativity is a better predictor of accomplishment than are traditional measures. Creativity allows people to find "a better match to one's skills, values, or desires" (Sternberg, 2002, p. 456). However, creativity can be so innovative and out of touch that creative people are scorned, ignored, or even killed. Many creative geniuses' contributions went unrecognized until years after their death.

The benefits of practical intelligence in adult life are obvious once we remember the tasks for which specific adults need, and do not need, to use their minds. Few adults need to define obscure words or deduce the next element in a number sequence (analytic intelligence); and few need to write a new type of music, restructure local government, or invent a new gadget (creative intelligence). Those few have already found a niche for themselves and have learned to rely on people with practical intelligence to develop their analytic or creative ideas.

However, almost every adult needs to solve real-world challenges: maintaining a home; advancing a career; managing family finances; analyzing information from media, mail, and the Internet; addressing the emotional needs of family members, neighbors, and colleagues (Blanchard-Fields, 2007). Schaie found that, more than scores on tests of the five primary abilities, scores on tests of practical intelligence were steady from age 20 to 70, with no notable decrement (Schaie, 2005).

Think about these three intelligences cross-culturally. Creative individuals would be critical of traditional authority and so would be tolerated only in some political environments (Sternberg, 2006). Analytic individuals might be seen as absentminded, head-in-the-clouds dreamers. Practical intelligence, although valued less within school settings, might be recognized as useful in every society.

Especially for Prospective Parents In terms of the intellectual challenge, what type of intelligence is most needed for effective parenthood? (see response, page 591)

An Example of Practical Intelligence in Kenya

Sternberg gives an example from rural Kenya, where a smart child is one who knows which herbal medicines cure which diseases, not one who excels in school. As Sternberg reported:

> Knowledge of these natural herbal medicines was negatively correlated both with school achievement in English and with scores on conventional tests of crystallized abilities. . . . [In rural Kenya,] children who spend a great deal of time on school-based learning may be viewed as rather foolish because they are taking away from the time they might be using to learn a trade and become economically self-sufficient. These results suggest that scores on ability or achievement tests always have to be understood in the cultural context.
>
> *[Sternberg et al., 2000, p. 19]*

This example highlights a problem: If a school curriculum is only analytic, and if analytic intelligence in some cultures is of little use in adulthood, then children with practical intelligence will not devote their time to study because they realize that, practically speaking, school success is irrelevant. Especially if a child is not especially talented in analytic intelligence, and especially if the family is poor and paying school fees is a hardship, children may leave school in order to start working at the tasks their culture values.

Note that this would not be true in most Western cultures, where school achievement is needed for adult success. A child who does well in school will also score well on college aptitude tests, be admitted to prestigious colleges and universities, and secure a high-paying job. In developed nations, all children benefit from high school and college—but children with practical intelligence might not realize that until adulthood.

FREDRICK ONYANGO

BLUE JEAN IMAGES / GETTY IMAGES

The Same Situation, Many Miles Apart: Men at Work The bean merchant in Nairobi, Kenya *(left),* and the construction supervisor in Beijing, China *(right),* have much in common: They are high in practical intelligence and they love their jobs. Context is also crucial since, if they changed places, each would be lost at first. However, practical intelligence could save the day—a few months of intensive instruction might enable each to master his new role.

At least, this is the usual sequence for academic learning and employment in societies such as twenty-first-century North America, where the information economy reigns. A century ago in the United States, an adult who never graduated from high school could be successful; no longer. The same shift may be occurring in Kenya and other cultures, but many rural families may not realize it. Meanwhile, many North American educators are broadening the curriculum to include creative and practical skills, sometimes specifically designed to measure the abilities that adults need, as the following illustrates.

A CASE TO STUDY

A Smart Mother

Tests of good infant care have been developed (e.g., McCall et al., 2010), one of which is the Knowledge of Infant Development Inventory (KIDI) (MacPhee, 1981). KIDI measures how much caregivers know about infant senses, motor skills, and communication. I would score high on such tests, but many mothers score low. For instance, one research team suggests that the inadequate knowledge of immigrant mothers (only 29 percent of immigrants know that 2-month-olds can tell some speech sounds apart, an item on the KIDI) might keep them from advancing their infants' language and social skills, handicapping their children later on (Bornstein & Cote, 2007).

None of the tests about infant development is designed as an intelligence test, but you can see that each culture makes assumptions about what a person should know and about what intelligence is. If an IQ test included only items on infant development, I would score close to genius; most U.S. mothers would do well enough, and immigrant mothers would be in the slow-learner range. My students believe I know a lot about babies:

I am not only a scholar and author—I also raised four children.

But many scholars suggest that tests of intelligence reflect a particular culture and cohort and may be less useful in practical ways. My daughters care for their children in ways different from my child-rearing practices. For example, I was distressed that Elissa did not give her newborn son a pacifier. She said the American Academy of Pediatrics recommended against it, an assertion I did not believe until she showed me the article online. Another example is that I proudly breast-fed all my children at birth, but at 2 months, I was also feeding them bananas and rice cereal; by 6 months, I was giving them store-bought baby food, mashed-up food from our dinner, and milk from the carton. If I did that with my grandchildren, my daughters would be horrified: They breast-fed exclusively (no other food, not even water or juice) for the first 6 months. Were my daughters to develop an updated test of ideal newborn care, I might fail.

Fortunately, my study of human development has taught me that infants thrive in wildly divergent cultures and that grandmothers should be supportive, not authoritarian. Many grandmothers have not yet learned this. I have one friend who infuriated her daughter when she answered her 8-year-old granddaughter's question about sex honestly. Another friend was about to help bathe her infant grandson when the baby's father ordered her to "Go sit in the living room now." An anthropologist repeatedly studied the Ache in Paraguay, who were always respectful and deferent year after year, until she and her husband

> arrived at their study site in the forest of Paraguay with their infant daughter in tow. The Ache greeted her in a whole new way. They took her aside and in friendly and intimate but no-nonsense terms told her all the things she was doing wrong as a mother. . . . "This older woman sat with me and told me I *must* sleep with my daughter. They were horrified that I brought a basket with me for her to sleep in." Here was a group of forest hunter-gatherers, people living in what Westerners would call basic conditions, giving instructions to a highly educated woman from a technologically sophisticated culture.
>
> [Small, 1998, p. 213]

Just as people differ in infant care, might each culture, each cohort, and maybe each individual have an understanding of intelligence that is adaptive in their community? Which of our measures are relevant to people in other cultures?

Keep Him Close Mothers everywhere keep their toddlers nearby, but it is particularly important in an environment where poisonous spiders and plants thrive. Thus, you can see why this Ache mother physically protects her son much more than would a typical North American mother—who might instead watch her son play in the house after removing small objects and covering the electric outlets.

Which Intelligence Is Valued?

Broad cultural and historical contexts emphasize one form of intelligence over the others (Park & Peterson, 2009). For example, as you read in Chapter 18, Chinese culture may be more dialectical and inclusive, seeking social compromises. As a result, the practical intelligence most needed by Chinese adults is social awareness and emotional regulation. A study of the use of anger in business negotiations found that an angry tone earned more concessions than a neutral tone from European American negotiators but was less successful than a neutral tone with an Asian negotiator (Adam et al., 2010). Thus, people high in practical intelligence would know when to express anger and when not to. Indeed, cultural display rules and conventions vary markedly, as found in a study of 33 nations (Matsumoto et al., 2009). If people simply use their logic or imagination (analytic or creative intelligence) to decide when to express anger, joy, or fear, they would be lost if the cultural context were not their own.

Similarly, understanding the historical context may be crucial for appreciating and displaying intelligence. Currently in North America, the arts are appreciated, but the Puritans in seventeenth-century colonial America considered dance and the visual arts the work of the devil. In that community, creative intelligence was not recognized or appreciated; thus, a child who was creative would learn not to express that creativity. Their contemporaries were Bach and Rembrandt, but if one of them had similar talent, no one would know.

Psychometric evaluation of intelligence was originally designed to indicate how children would learn in school, where the emphasis was on math and language. Since every test reflects cultural values and assumptions, as does every school, and since intelligence is now defined as the ability to adapt to life's demands,

>> **Answer to Observation Quiz** (from page 588) Solely academic learning. Neither practical nor creative intelligence is fostered by a student working quietly at her desk (the girl at right) or the boy coming up to the teacher for private instruction. Fortunately, there are signs that this moment is not typical: Notice the teacher's sweater, earrings, lipstick, and, especially, the apple on her desk.

>> **Response for Prospective Parents** (from page 589) Because parenthood demands flexibility and patience, Sternberg's practical intelligence is probably most needed. Anything that involves finding a single correct answer, such as analytic intelligence or number ability, would not be much help.

perhaps new tests are needed for adults. Paul Baltes (2003) believes that biology is significant during childhood (infants cannot talk, nor can schoolchildren reason abstractly because the requisite biological maturity of their brains has not occurred) but that culture becomes increasingly important with adulthood.

As more people live longer, Baltes suggests that intelligence should not be considered a matter of biological maturation and genetic gifts that allow school success; rather, it should measure the cultural qualities that allow adults to live their lives happily and successfully. That might also help us realize which cultural contexts impede adult development and which allow societies to change to foster adult intelligence—just as educators changed primary school to encourage all children to develop their talents.

A broader understanding of the power of education, both deliberate (as in college) and inadvertent (as in a marriage), is needed. Older adults can learn whatever their particular cultural setting encourages, including the skills tested on IQ tests, if that is what society requires. In the Seattle Longitudinal Study, a group of 60-year-olds who had declined markedly in spatial or reasoning skills were given five one-hour sessions of personalized training. Forty percent of them improved so much that they reached the level they had been at 14 years earlier, and their gains were still evident 7 years later (Schaie, 2005). For them, time didn't just stop—it moved backward.

Recent research finds intellectual spillover: Advances in one arena might aid other cognitive skills. For example, three diverse experiences—intellectual challenges, athletic practice, and video games—all improved people's abilities on psychometric tests (Green & Bavelier, 2008; Stine-Morrow et al., 2008).

It is apparent from the array of intellectual tests and abilities that cultural assumptions affect concepts of intelligence and the construction of IQ tests. How does this connect to developmental changes over adulthood? If a culture values youth and devalues age, this might explain why the very abilities that favor the young (e.g., quick reaction time, capacious short-term memory) are central to psychometric intelligence tests, whereas the strengths of older adults (e.g., emotional regulation and the upholding of traditional values) are not. Fluid intelligence is valued more in a youth-oriented culture than crystallized intelligence is. Curiously, a word often used to describe a highly intelligent person is *quick,* whereas a stupid person is considered *slow*—exactly what happens with age.

In Chapter 24, we will further explore the possibility that by late adulthood, senescence (perhaps in slower reaction time, reduced visual acuity, or decreased working memory) degrades specific abilities as well as overall IQ, no matter what an individual's context or habits (Lindenberger & Ghisletta, 2009; Salthouse, 2006). However, test results of adults in every culture find that most 25- to 65-year-olds are quite intelligent, especially when the contexts are considered. Stress, prejudice, and poor health undermine memory and other cognitive skills (Neupert et al., 2008), but, to return to the question that began this chapter, that does not mean that adults become dumber, not smarter, with age.

SUMMING UP

Intelligence may be not a single entity (*g*) but rather a combination of different abilities, sometimes categorized as fluid and crystallized or as analytic, creative, and practical. These abilities rise and fall partly because of events in each person's life, partly because of culture and cohort, and partly because of age. The overall picture of adult intelligence, as measured by various tests, is complex. One of the underlying issues of all the psychometric approaches to intelligence is the definition of intelligence: The specific intellectual abilities needed for success depend on context and culture.

>> Selective Gains and Losses

Aging neurons, cultural pressures, historical conditions, and past education all affect adult cognition. None of these are under direct individual control. However, many researchers believe that adults make deliberate choices about their intellectual development. For example, the fact that number skills declined more for recent cohorts than for earlier ones may be the result not of past math curricula (as was suggested) but of modern adults' tendency to use calculators instead of paper-and-pencil (or mental) calculations. If adults decided to trash their calculators, their math skills might improve. Of course, most adults would consider that strange: Spending more time on math might help number skills, but few modern adults want to do double-digit division in their heads.

Optimization with Compensation

Paul and Margret Baltes (1990) developed a theory, called **selective optimization with compensation,** to describe the "general process of systematic function" (P. B. Baltes, 2003, p. 25) as people maintain a balance in their lives as they grow older. The idea is that people seek to *optimize* their development, looking for the best ways to *compensate* for physical and cognitive losses and to become more proficient at activities they want to perform well. This helps explain the variations in intellectual abilities just reviewed. As other research has found, when older adults are motivated to do well, few age-related deficits are apparent; but, compared with younger adults, older adults are less motivated to put forth their best effort when the task at hand is not particularly engaging (Hess et al., 2009).

For example, suppose people who specialize in knowledge regarding one area of the world (perhaps East Timor or the Alaska coast) notice that aging affects their vision and memory and that they have difficulty reading fine print on a page or on their computer. They might buy reading glasses or increase the type size on their computers (compensation) or concentrate on articles that are relevant to their specialty, taking careful notes on current events in their particular area (selective) and skipping over most of the newspaper that they used to read. In that way, they build on their expertise (optimization). Similarly, although 55-year-old aircraft mechanics might move more slowly than younger workers, their ongoing practice might maintain their spatial and sequential abilities, thus allowing them to remain valuable employees.

An example that may be familiar to everyone is multitasking, which becomes more difficult with every passing decade (Reuter-Lorenz & Sylvester, 2005). This is obvious when people drive a car while talking on a cell phone—a particularly dangerous challenge for older drivers because their less flexible brain focuses on only the conversation, for example, making it difficult to perceive what the eyes see (Strayer & Drews, 2007). Some jurisdictions require drivers to use hands-free phones, as if the potential problem originates in the arms. These misguided laws have not reduced traffic accidents resulting from cell phone use because the multitasking brain is the problem, not the hands.

Some say that passenger conversation is as distracting as cell phone talk, but that is not true: Years of practice have taught adult passengers (though not young children) when to stop talking so the driver can focus on the road (S. G. Charlton, 2009)—and if passengers do not comply, older adult drivers tell them to be quiet because they know they have to concentrate.

selective optimization with compensation The theory, developed by Paul and Margaret Baltes, that people try to maintain a balance in their lives by looking for the best way to compensate for physical and cognitive losses and to become more proficient in activities they can already do well.

Brain Concentration Multitasking succeeds only when most of the tasks are automatic; deliberate reflection occurs one thought at a time. Thus, experienced drivers don't need to think about steering, much like experienced CEOs usually need to just listen. However, even if this phone call proposes an unexpected billion-dollar deal just when a truck swerves ahead, this man should instantly drop the phone and focus all his attention on the road.

"I can't do everything at once" is more often said by adults than by teenagers because adults have learned they must be selective, compensating for slower thinking by concentrating on one task at a time. Resources—of the brain as well as material resources—may be increasingly limited with age, but compensation allows optimal functioning (Freund, 2008).

One father tried to explain this concept to his son as follows:

> I told my son: triage
> Is the main art of aging.
> At midlife, everything
> Sings of it. In law
> Or healing, learning or play,
> Buying or selling—above all
> In remembering—the rule is
> Cut losses, let profits ring.
> Specifics rise and fall
> By selection.
>
> *[Hamill, 1991]*

Selective optimization with compensation applies to every aspect of life, from choosing friends to playing baseball. Each adult seeks to maximize gains and minimize losses, thus choosing to practice some abilities and ignore others. Such choices are critical, because every ability can be enhanced or diminished, depending on how, when, and why a person uses it. It is possible to "teach an old dog new tricks," but learning requires that adults choose and practice those "new tricks."

As Baltes and Baltes (1990) explain, selective optimization means that each person selects certain aspects of intelligence to optimize and neglects the rest. If those aspects that are ignored happen to be the ones measured by IQ tests, then intelligence scores will fall, even if a person's selection results in improvement (optimization) in other aspects of intellect. Many scholars believe that the brain is plastic over the entire life span, developing new dendrites and activation sequences, adjusting to those aspects of learning that are practiced and needed (Karmiloff-Smith, 2010; Macdonald et al., 2009).

Expert Cognition

Another way to express this idea is to say that everyone develops expertise. Each person becomes a **selective expert,** specializing in activities that are personally meaningful, whether they involve car repair, gourmet cooking, illness diagnosis, or fly fishing. As people develop expertise in some areas, they pay less attention to others. For example, each adult tunes out most channels on the TV, ignores some realms of human experience, and has no interest in attending particular events for which other people wait in line for hours to buy a ticket.

Culture and context guide all of us in selecting our areas of expertise. Many adults born 60 years ago are much better than more recent cohorts at writing letters with distinctive but legible handwriting. Because of their childhood culture, they selected and practiced penmanship, became expert in it, and maintained that expertise. Today's schools and children make other choices: Reading, for instance, is now crucial for every child, unlike a century ago when adult illiteracy was common.

Experts, as cognitive scientists define them, are not necessarily those with rare and outstanding proficiency. Although sometimes the term *expert* connotes an extraordinary genius, to researchers it means more—and less—than that (Charness & Krampe, 2008; Ericsson et al., 2006). To a developmentalist, an expert is nota-

Teacher and Student The novice on the left has two strikes against him—age and ethnicity. Older Hispanics are less likely to use computers than is any other group. However, the hands and facial expressions of these two suggest that this Latino student will be proficient soon. Personal motivation and a skilled instructor overcome any age-related barriers.

selective expert Someone who is notably more skilled and knowledgeable than the average person about whichever activities are personally meaningful.

bly more accomplished, proficient, and knowledgeable in a particular skill, topic, or task than the average person. Expertise is not innate, nor does it always correlate with basic abilities (such as the five abilities Schaie measured). Experts choose to be specialists (Masunaga & Horn, 2001); probably everyone is an expert at something.

An expert is not simply someone who knows more about something. At a certain point, accumulated knowledge, practice, and experience become transformative, putting the expert in a different league. The quality as well as the quantity of cognition is advanced. Expert thought is (1) intuitive, (2) automatic, (3) strategic, and (4) flexible, as we now describe.

Intuitive

Novices follow formal procedures and rules. Experts rely more on their past experiences and on immediate contexts. Their actions are therefore more intuitive and less stereotypic. The role of experience and intuition is evident, for example, during surgery. Outsiders might think medicine is straightforward, but experts understand the reality:

> Hospitals are filled with varieties of knives and poisons. Every time a medication is prescribed, there is potential for an unintended side effect. In surgery, collateral damage is inherent. External tissue must be cut to allow internal access so that a diseased organ may be removed, or some other manipulation may be performed to return the patient to better health.
>
> *[Dominguez, 2001, p. 287]*

In one study, many surgeons saw the same videotape of a gallbladder operation and were asked to talk about it. The experienced surgeons anticipated and described problems twice as often as did the residents (who had also removed gallbladders, just not as many) (Dominguez, 2001). Data on physicians indicate that the single most important question to ask a surgeon is, "How often have you performed this operation?" The novice, even with the best, most recent training, is less skilled than the expert.

Another example of expert intuition is *chicken-sexing,* the ability to tell whether a newborn chicken is male or female. As David Myers (2002) tells it:

> Poultry owners once had to wait five to six weeks before the appearance of adult feathers enabled them to separate cockerels (males) from pullets (hens). Egg producers wanted to buy and feed only pullets, so they were intrigued to hear that some Japanese had developed an uncanny ability to sex day-old chicks. . . . Hatcheries elsewhere then gave some of their workers apprenticeships under the Japanese. . . . After months of training and experience, the best Americans and Australians could almost match the Japanese, by sexing 800 to 1,000 chicks per hour with 99 percent accuracy. But don't ask them how they do it. The sex difference, as any chicken sexer can tell you, is too subtle to explain.
>
> *[p. 55]*

One of the intriguing recent discoveries in cognition is the role of intuition, thought to work unconsciously by sorting and weighing alternatives. In one experiment, participants were asked to choose the best of four apartments, each described with 12 characteristics. One was actually better (more of the 12 characteristics were positive) and people were more likely to select that one if they had time to think unconsciously (while another task prevented conscious thought) than if they had the same time to analyze the choice (Dijksterhuis, 2004). People making difficult decisions sometimes "sleep on it," so intuition can sort things out. This is not true for simple decisions—a person can pick well if only two variables are apparent—but works when the issues are complex and nuanced and many unequal factors need to be considered (Dijksterhuis & Nordgren, 2006).

One experiment that studied the relationship between expertise and intuition involved college students (fans, not players) who were asked to predict the winners of soccer games not yet played (see the Research Design). The students who were categorized as experts (they were avid fans) made better predictions when they had a few minutes of unconscious thought instead of when they had the same number of minutes to mull over their choice (see Figure 21.3). Those who didn't care much about soccer (the nonexperts) did worse overall, but they did especially poorly when they used unconscious intuition (Dijksterhuis et al., 2009).

▶ Research Design

Scientists: Ap Dijksterhuis, Maarten W. Bos, Andries van der Leij, and Rick B. van Baaren.

Publication: *Psychological Science* (2009).

Participants: A total of 468 undergraduates from the University of Amsterdam participated in one of two similar experiments. Since this study took place in the Netherlands among Dutch emerging adults, where the game of soccer (which they call *football*) is a national passion, about half the participants were categorized as experts, based on their knowlege of soccer teams.

Design: For 20 seconds, all participants were shown a computer screen with four soon-to-be-played soccer matches and were asked to predict the winners. One-third of the predictions were made immediately, one-third were made after two minutes of conscious thought, and one-third were made after two minutes when *only* unconscious thought could occur—because people randomly assigned to that group were required to calculate a series of mind-taxing math questions during those two minutes. In the first experiment, they predicted outcomes of matches between Dutch teams; in the second experiment, outcomes of World Cup matches.

Major conclusion: Nonexperts did no better than chance and did worse after thinking about their answer, especially when the thought was unconscious. Experts fared better than nonexperts (as would be expected), but the surprise was that their predictions were not much better than those of nonexperts when they guessed immediately, a little better when they had two minutes to think, and best of all after unconscious thought. Apparently, the experts' knowledge of soccer helped them most when they were consciously thinking of something else.

Comment: The idea that the unconscious is active is at least a century old, as evident in psychoanalytic theory (Chapter 2). However, this and other experiments have recently found that analysis may lead people astray and that unconscious thought may be best when multifactored decisions must be made. This experiment adds an important qualification: The unconscious works best if the person already has some expertise.

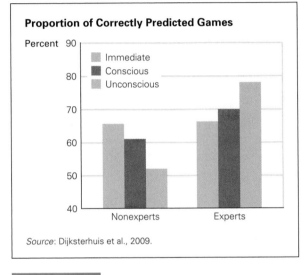

Proportion of Correctly Predicted Games

Source: Dijksterhuis et al., 2009.

FIGURE 21.3

If You Don't Know, Don't Think! Undergraduates at the University of Amsterdam were asked to predict winners of four World Cup soccer matches in one of three conditions: (1) immediate—as soon as they saw the names of the nations that were competing in each of the contests, (2) conscious—after thinking for two minutes about their answers, and (3) unconscious—after two minutes of solving distracting math tasks. As you can see, the experts were better at predicting winners after unconscious processing, but the nonexperts became less accurate when they thought about their answers, either consciously or unconsciously.

Automatic

Many elements of expert performance are automatic; that is, the complex action and thought required for such performance have become routine, making it appear that most aspects of the task are performed instinctively. Experts process incoming information more quickly and analyze it more efficiently than do nonexperts and then act in well-rehearsed ways that make their efforts appear unconscious. In fact, some automatic actions are no longer accessible to the conscious mind.

For example, adults are much better at tying their shoelaces than children are (adults can do it in the dark), but they are much worse at describing how they do it

(McLeod et al., 2005). When experts think, they engage in "automatic weighting" of various unverbalized factors. This automatic thinking can be disrupted by the words that nonexperts use, which distort rather than clarify the thinking process (Dijksterhuis et al., 2009, p. 1382).

This is apparent if you are an experienced driver and have attempted to teach someone else to drive. Excellent drivers who are inexperienced instructors find it hard to recognize or verbalize things that have become automatic—such as noticing pedestrians and cyclists on the far side of the road, or feeling the car shift gears as it heads up an incline, or hearing the tires lose traction on a bit of sand. Yet such factors differentiate the expert from the novice.

This may explain why, despite powerful motivation, quicker reactions, and better vision, teenagers have far more car accidents than middle-aged drivers do. Sometimes teenage drivers deliberately take risks (speeding, running a red light, and so on), but more often they simply misjudge and misperceive conditions that a more experienced driver would automatically notice. The same gap between knowledge and instruction occurs when a computer expert tries to teach a novice what to do: It is so much easier to click the mouse oneself than to teach what has become automatic.

Automatic processing is thought to be a crucial reason why expert chess and Go players are much better than novices. They see a configuration of game pieces and automatically encode it as a whole, rather than analyzing it bit by bit. A study of expert chess players (aged 17 to 81) found minor age-related declines, but expertise was much more important than age. This was particularly apparent for speedy recognition that the king was threatened: Older experts did it almost as quickly (in a fraction of a second) despite far steeper, age-related declines on standard tests of memory and speed (Jastrzembski et al., 2006).

automatic processing Thinking that occurs without deliberate, conscious thought. Experts process most tasks automatically, saving conscious thought for unfamiliar challenges.

Strategic

Experts have more and better strategies, especially when problems are unexpected (Ormerod, 2005). Indeed, strategy may be the most crucial difference between a skilled person and an unskilled one. Expert chess players not only have general strategies for winning, they also have even better specific strategies for the particular possibilities after a move that is their specialty (Bilalić et al., 2009).

Similarly, a strategy used by expert team leaders in the military as well as in civilian life is ongoing communication, especially during slow times, so that when stress builds, no team member misinterprets the previously rehearsed plans, commands, and requirements. You have witnessed the same phenomenon in expert professors: They have well-developed strategies to avoid problems later in the term.

Of course, strategies themselves need to be updated as situations change—and no chess game, or battle, or class is exactly like another. The monthly fire drill required by some schools, the standard lecture given by some professors, and the pat safety instructions read by airline attendants before takeoff become less effective than when they were first used. I recently heard a flight attendant precede his standard talk with, "For those of you who have not ridden in an automobile since 1960, this is how you buckle a seat belt." That was one of the few times I actually listened to the words.

The superior strategies of the expert permit selective optimization with compensation. Many developmentalists regard the capacity to accommodate to changes over time (compensation) as essential to successful aging (M. M. Baltes & Carstensen, 2003; Rowe & Kahn, 1998). People need to compensate for any slippage in their fluid abilities.

Such compensation was evident in a study of airplane pilots who were allowed to take notes on directions given by air traffic controllers in a flight simulation (Morrow et al., 2003). Experienced pilots took more accurate and complete notes and had developed their own shorthand to illustrate and emphasize ideas. For instance, they used more graphic symbols (such as arrows) than did pilots who were trained to understand air traffic instructions but who had little flight experience. In other words, even though nonexperts were trained and had the proper tools (paper, pencil, and a suggestion to take notes), they did not use them the way the experts did.

In actual flights, too, older pilots take more notes than younger ones do because they have mastered this strategy, perhaps to compensate for their slower working memory. Probably as a result, these researchers found no differences in the read-back proficiency among experienced pilots of three age groups: 22 to 40, 50 to 59, and 60 to 76 (Morrow et al., 2003). People who are not experts show age-related deficits in many studies (including this one, on other abilities), but experts of all ages often maintain their proficiency at their occupation for years past the time that other abilities decline.

Flexible

Finally, perhaps because they are intuitive, automatic, and strategic thinkers, experts are also more flexible in their thinking. The expert artist, musician, or scientist is creative and curious, deliberately experimenting and enjoying the challenge when things do not go according to plan (Csikszentmihalyi, 1996).

Consider the expert surgeon, who takes the most complex cases and prefers unusual patients over typical ones because operating on them might bring sudden, unexpected complications. Compared with the novice, the expert surgeon is not only more likely to notice telltale signs (an unexpected lesion, an oddly shaped organ, a rise or drop in a vital sign) that may signal a problem but is also more flexible and more willing to deviate from standard textbook procedures if those procedures are ineffective (Patel et al., 1999).

In the same way, experts in all walks of life adapt to individual cases and exceptions—like an expert chef who adjusts ingredients, temperature, technique, and timing as a dish develops, tasting to see if a little more ginger is needed, seldom following a recipe exactly. Standards are high: Some chefs throw food in the garbage rather than serve a dish that many people would happily eat. Expert chess players, auto mechanics, and violinists are similarly aware of nuances that might escape the novice.

In a study of forensic scientists. who must find clues from a mishmash of relevant and irrelevant things, the most expert were more methodical as well as more flexible, using more strategies to focus on the most relevant objects (Schraagen & Leijenhorst, 2001). A review of expertise finds that flexibility includes understanding which particular skills are necessary to become an expert in each profession—with repeated practice needed in typing, sports, and games; with collaboration skills needed for leadership; and with task management strategies needed for aviation (Morrow et al., 2009).

Expertise and Age

The relationship between expertise and age is not straightforward. One of the essential requirements for expertise is time. Not everyone becomes an expert as he or she grows older, but everyone needs months—or even years—of practice (depending on the task) to develop expertise (Ericsson et al., 2006). Some researchers think practice must be extensive, several hours a day for at least 10 years (Charness et al., 1996; Ericsson, 1996)—but that may be true in only some areas, not all. Circumstances, training, talent, ability, practice, and age all affect expertise, which means that experts in one specific field are often quite inexpert in other areas.

Expertise sometimes—but not always—overcomes the effects of age (Krampe & Charness, 2006). For example, in one study, participants aged 17 to 79 were asked to identify nine common tunes (such as "Happy Birthday" and "Old MacDonald Had a Farm") when notes from midsong were first played very slowly and then gradually faster until the listener identified the tune. The listeners were grouped according to their musical experience, from virtually none to 10 or more years of training and performing.

In this slow-to-fast phase of the experiment, responses correlated with expertise but not with age. Those individuals who had played more music themselves were quicker to recognize songs played very slowly (Andrews et al., 1998). In other words, no matter what their age, novices were similar to one another and were slower than the experts, who were equally proficient at all ages.

In another phase of this study, the songs were played very fast and then gradually slowed down. In this circumstance, the older adults took longer to recognize the tunes. Although all the experts of every age did better than the novices, the older expert adults were slower than the younger expert adults (Andrews et al., 1998). Note that pace made the difference here; speed is one part of fluid intelligence, which harkens back to the question raised earlier: What abilities should be tested on IQ tests? Perhaps "all measures of intelligence measure a form of developing expertise" (Sternberg, 2002, p. 452) and the specific tests used depend on which kind of expertise is valued. Speeded tests favor the young.

Make No Mistake Humans are not always expert at judging other humans. Juries have convicted some defendants who were later proved to be innocent and acquitted others who were actually guilty. If this lab technician is an expert at her work, and if the genetic evidence she is testing was carefully collected, DNA test results can provide objective proof of guilt or innocence.

Older Workers: Experts or Has-Beens?

Research on cognitive plasticity confirms that experienced adults often use selective optimization with compensation. This is particularly apparent in the everyday workplace. The best employees may be the older, more experienced ones—if they are motivated to do their best. Complicated work requires more cognitive practice and expertise than routine work; as a result, such work may have intellectual benefits for the workers themselves. In the Seattle Longitudinal Study, the cognitive complexity of the occupations of more than 500 workers was measured, including the complexities involved in the workers' interactions with other people, with things, and with data. In all three occupational challenges, older workers maintained their intellectual prowess (Schaie, 2005).

An intriguing study of age and job effectiveness comes from an occupation everyone is familiar with, driving a taxi. In major cities, taxi drivers must find the best route (factoring in traffic, construction, time of day, and many other details),

Voilà! This chemist is thinking intensely and watching carefully for a result that will merit an excited *"Voilà!"* ("There it is!") He is in France, so we can guess his linguistic expertise; but unless we are also experienced chemists, we would not recognize an important result if it happened. Expertise is astonishingly selective.

PHILIPPE GONTIER / THE IMAGE WORKS

all while knowing where new passengers are likely to be found and how to relate to customers, some of whom might want to talk, others not.

Research in England—where taxi drivers "have to learn the layout of 25,000 streets in London and the locations of thousands of places of interest, and pass stringent examinations" (Woollett et al., 2009, p. 1407)—found not only that the drivers became more expert with time, but also that their brains adjusted to the need for particular knowledge. In fact, some regions of their brains (areas thought to help with spatial representation) were more extensive and active than those of an average person (Woollett et al., 2009). On ordinary IQ tests, their scores were typical, but in navigating London, expertise was apparent. Other studies also show that people become more expert, and their brains adapt, as they practice various skills (Park & Reuter-Lorenz, 2009).

Family Skills

This discussion of expertise has focused on occupations—surgeons, pilots, taxi drivers—that once had far more male than female workers. In recent years, two important shifts have occurred that change this picture.

First, more women are working in occupations traditionally reserved for men. Remember from Chapter 4 that Virginia Apgar, when she earned her MD in 1933, was told she could not be a surgeon because only men were surgeons. Fortunately for the world, she became an anesthesiologist and developed a scale that has saved millions of newborns. Today that assumption has changed; almost half the new MDs in the United States are women (see Figure 21.4).

The second major shift is that **women's work** has gained new respect. In earlier generations, women said they were "just a housewife" or "a nonworking mom," but recently work at home has come to be considered important, and men as well as women do it. This relates to expertise, in that it has become increasingly clear that not all women are good mothers or wives and that some men become expert at the domestic emotional work that was once the domain of women. It is no longer assumed that a "maternal instinct" is innate to every mother and protective of every child; as you have read many times in previous chapters, many mothers experience postpartum depression, financial stress, or bursts of anger and are unable to provide the care that children need.

women's work A term formerly used to denigrate domestic and caregiving tasks that were once thought to be the responsibility of females.

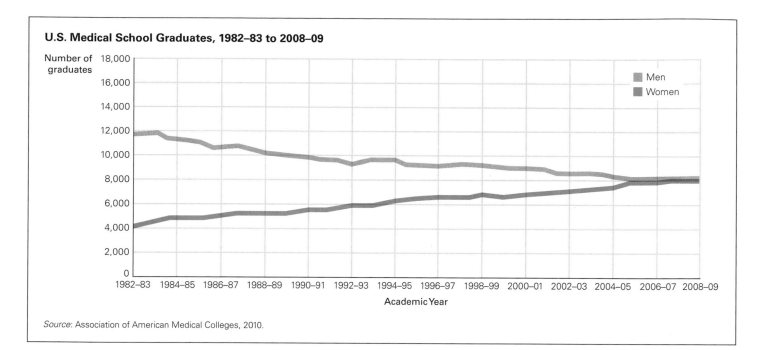

U.S. Medical School Graduates, 1982–83 to 2008–09

Source: Association of American Medical Colleges, 2010.

FIGURE 21.4

Expect a Woman Next time you hear "The doctor will see you now," the physician is as likely to be a woman as a man—unless the doctor is over age 40.

The skill, flexibility, and strategies needed to raise a family are a manifestation of expertise. This relates again to age as well as gender: You read in previous chapters that young women, in their late teens and early 20s, have the fewest complications of pregnancy. But you are also well aware that the biology of motherhood or fatherhood is only a start: In general, older parents are more patient and have lower rates of child abuse as well as more successful offspring.

Teenagers who feel they can talk with their own mother or father tend to stay away from drugs and other hazards, especially if the parent listens well and seems knowledgeable. Developmentalists have not yet pinned down all the components of an expert in the emotional work of raising a family, but at least there is no longer any doubt that such expertise exists and that all family members benefit from it.

SUMMING UP

People choose to become adept at some aspects of cognition, charting their course by using selective optimization with compensation. As a result, they can use their cognitive resources wisely, gaining intellectual power in areas that they choose. Choices and practice produce expertise, which is intuitive, automatic, strategic, and flexible. Expertise allows people to continue performing well throughout adulthood. ■

SUMMARY

What Is Intelligence?

1. It was traditionally assumed that there is one general entity called intelligence that individuals have in greater or lesser quantity and that it decreases over the years of adulthood. However, current evidence does not support this idea.

2. Longitudinal research has found that each person tends to increase in IQ, particularly in vocabulary and general knowledge, until age 60 or so. In addition, James Flynn found that average IQ scores increased over the twentieth century, perhaps because later cohorts had more education.

Components of Intelligence: Many and Varied

3. K. Warner Schaie found that some primary abilities decline with age while others (such as vocabulary) increase. Education, vocation, and family, as well as age, seem to affect these abilities.

4. Cattell and Horn concluded that while crystallized intelligence, which is based on accumulated knowledge, increases with time, one's fluid, flexible reasoning skills inevitably decline with age.

5. Sternberg proposed three fundamental forms of intelligence: analytic, creative, and practical. Most adults believe that while their analytic and creative abilities decline with age, their practical intelligence improves as they grow older. Research supports this belief.

6. Overall, cultural values and changing demands with age reward some cognitive abilities more than others. Each person and each culture responds to these demands, which may not be reflected in psychometric tests.

Selective Gains and Losses

7. As people grow older, they select certain aspects of their lives to focus on, optimizing development in those areas and compensating for declines in others, if need be. Applied to cognition, this means that people become selective experts in whatever intellectual skills they choose to develop. Meanwhile, abilities that are not exercised may fade.

8. In addition to being more experienced, experts are better thinkers than novices are because they are more intuitive; their cognitive processes are automatic, often seeming to require little conscious thought; they use more and better strategies to perform whatever task is required; and they are more flexible.

9. Expertise in adulthood is particularly apparent in the workplace. Experienced workers often surpass younger workers because of their ability to specialize and harness their efforts, compensating for any deficits that may appear.

10. Raising children and responding well to the emotional complexities and unanticipated challenges of family life are now recognized and valued as expert work. Experience and maturation increase the likelihood of family expertise.

KEY TERMS

general intelligence (*g*) (p. 579)
Seattle Longitudinal Study
  (p. 582)
fluid intelligence (p. 585)

crystallized intelligence (p. 586)
analytic intelligence (p. 587)
creative intelligence (p. 587)

practical intelligence (p. 588)
selective optimization with
  compensation (p. 593)

selective expert (p. 594)
automatic processing (p. 597)
women's work (p. 600)

WHAT HAVE YOU LEARNED?

What Is Intelligence?

1. How successful are geneticists at finding *g*?

2. What does cross-sectional research on IQ scores throughout adulthood usually find?

3. What does longitudinal research on IQ scores throughout adulthood usually find?

4. In what ways are younger generations more intelligent than older ones, according to cross-sequential research?

5. How do historical changes affect the results of longitudinal research?

6. How does cross-sequential research control for cohort effects?

7. What factors does Schaie think have significant impact on adult intelligence?

Components of Intelligence: Many and Varied

8. Why would a person want to be higher in crystallized intelligence than fluid intelligence?

9. Why would a person want to be higher in fluid intelligence than crystallized intelligence?

10. If you want to convince your professors that you are smart, what might you do and what intelligence does that involve?

11. If you want to convince your neighbors to compost their garbage, what might you do and what kind of intelligence does that involve?

12. What kinds of tests could measure creative intelligence?

Selective Gains and Losses

13. What might a person do to optimize ability in some area *not* discussed in the book, such as playing the flute, or growing tomatoes, or building a cabinet?

14. How might a person compensate for fading memory skills?

15. How does the saying "Can't see the forest for the trees" relate to what you have learned about adult cognition?

16. Think of an area of expertise that you have and most people do not. What mistakes do people make who are not experts in your area?

17. Two characteristics of experts—automatic and flexible— seem to work in opposite directions. Explain how an expert could avoid the problems of this polarity.

18. How specifically might intuition aid as well as diminish ability?

19. In what occupations would age be an asset, and why?

20. In what occupations would age be a liability, and why?

APPLICATIONS

1. The importance of context and culture is illustrated by the things that people think are basic knowledge. In pairs, both you and your partner write four questions that you think are hard but fair as measures of general intelligence. Then give your test to your partner, and answer the four questions that person has prepared for you. What did you learn from the results?

2. Skill at video games is sometimes thought to reflect intelligence. Interview three or four people who play such games. What abilities do they think video games require? What do you think these games reflect in terms of experience, age, and motivation?

3. Some people assume that almost any high school graduate can become a teacher, since most adults know the basic reading and math skills that elementary children need to learn. Describe aspects of expertise that experienced teachers need to master, with examples from your own experience.

C H A P T E R

Adulthood: Psychosocial Development

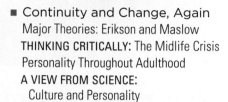

WHAT WILL YOU KNOW?

1. What happened to make the idea of the midlife crisis disappear?
2. What characterizes the interactions between parents and their adult children?
3. Why do people underestimate the pain of divorce?
4. Why do adults change jobs as often as they do?

I invited two long-married couples to our home for dinner. "George and I will be arriving separately," one of the wives told me. "No problem," I assured her. "I guess one of you will be coming directly from work."

"No, we are coming from our homes. We are divorced."

I was taken aback. I had had no idea that their marriage was in trouble. "I'm so sorry. Should I have invited only one of you?"

"Don't be sorry. We are happier and good friends."

I was stunned. I thought divorce meant a failed marriage, a broken home, and at least one bitter spouse. Not so. The dinner party was a success, with lots of laughter.

I am not the only one whose assumptions do not fit the current realities of adult development. As explained in this chapter, the *midlife crisis,* the *sandwich genera-tion,* and the *empty nest* are myths. Divorce, remarriage, and single adulthood are not always what people once assumed them to be. Some topics that could be cov-ered in this chapter (e.g., choosing friends, cohabitation) are discussed primarily in Chapter 19 and others are addressed in Chapter 25 (grandparenthood, retire-ment). This chapter focuses on personality, marriage, parenthood, caregiving, and employment—each sometimes joyous and sometimes not.

>> Continuity and Change, Again

Certain psychosocial needs and circumstances characterize the adult years, but variations are common, a theme already sounded in the "Continuity and Change" section in Chapter 19. The theme is repeated here, in more detail. The *social clock*—which once prescribed timetables for marriage, parenthood, and the like—no longer ticks as loud, if at all. Age-graded norms are said to be "obsolete" (Moen & Spencer, 2006).

There are now *multiple clocks,* some set by society and culture, some by cohort and generation, and some by family and the individual (Umberson et al., 2010). As described in earlier chapters, the social clock once said age 30 was too old to have a first child, but the current cohort, many relatives, and certainly individuals themselves no long accept even age 40 as "too old." Clocks still tick, in that people are still influenced by age norms, but there is no single timekeeper. This variation is recognized by many researchers and theorists, including the two psychosocial theorists first introduced in Chapter 2.

The Same Situation, Many Miles Apart: Beating the Clock The U.S. college graduate *(left)* is middle-aged, and the Israeli skydiver *(right)* is 80. Their activities are more typically done by emerging adults, not by older people.

Major Theories: Erikson and Maslow

Erikson originally envisioned eight stages of development, three of which follow adolescence. He deserves credit as "the one thinker who changed our minds about what it means to live as a person who has arrived at a chronologically mature position and yet continues to grow, to change, and to develop" (Hoare, 2002, p. 3).

Late in his life, Erikson stressed that stages and ages do not occur in lockstep. People of many ages can be in his fifth stage, *identity versus role confusion*, or in any of his three adult stages—called *intimacy versus isolation, generativity versus stagnation*, and *integrity versus despair* (McAdams, 2006) (see Table 22.1).

TABLE 22.1

Erikson's Stages of Adulthood

Unlike Freud or other early theorists who thought adults simply worked through the legacy of their childhood, Erikson described psychosocial needs after puberty in half of his eight stages. His most famous book, *Childhood and Society* (1963), devoted only two pages to each adult stage, but published and unpublished elaborations in later works led to a much richer depiction (Hoare, 2002).

Identity Versus Role Confusion
Although Erikson originally situated the identity crisis during adolescence, he realized that identity concerns could be lifelong. Identity combines values and traditions from childhood with the current social context. Since contexts keep evolving, many adults reassess all four types of identity (sexual/gender, vocational/work, religious/spiritual, and political/ethnic).

Intimacy Versus Isolation
Adults seek intimacy—a close, reciprocal connection with another human being. Intimacy is mutual, not self-absorbed, which means that adults need to devote time and energy to one another. This process begins in emerging adulthood and continues lifelong. Isolation is especially likely when divorce or death disrupts established intimate relationships.

Generativity Versus Stagnation
Adults need to care for the next generation, either by raising their own children or by mentoring, teaching, and helping younger people. Erikson's first description of this stage focused on parenthood, but later he included other ways to achieve generativity. Adults extend the legacy of their culture and their generation with ongoing care, creativity, and sacrifice.

Integrity Versus Despair
When Erikson himself was in his 70s, he decided that integrity, with the goal of combating prejudice and helping all humanity, was too important to be left to the elderly. He also thought that each person's entire life could be directed toward connecting a personal journey with the historical and cultural purpose of human society, the ultimate achievement of integrity.

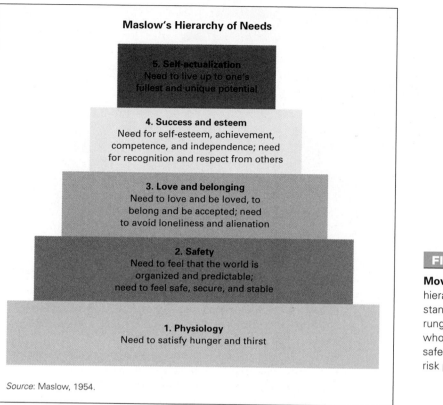

Maslow's Hierarchy of Needs

5. Self-actualization
Need to live up to one's
fullest and unique potential

4. Success and esteem
Need for self-esteem, achievement,
competence, and independence; need
for recognition and respect from others

3. Love and belonging
Need to love and be loved, to
belong and be accepted; need
to avoid loneliness and alienation

2. Safety
Need to feel that the world is
organized and predictable;
need to feel safe, secure, and stable

1. Physiology
Need to satisfy hunger and thirst

Source: Maslow, 1954.

FIGURE 22.1

Moving Up, Not Looking Back Maslow's hierarchy is like a ladder: Once a person stands firmly on a higher rung, the lower rungs are no longer needed. Thus, someone who has arrived at step 4 might devalue safety and security (step 2) and be willing to risk personal safety to gain success.

Abraham Maslow (1954) refused to link chronological age and adult development when he described a *hierarchy of needs* with five stages achieved in sequence (see Figure 22.1). Completion of each stage allows the person to move ahead. As an example, people who are in the third stage (*love and belonging,* similar to Erikson's *intimacy versus isolation*) seek to be loved and accepted by partners, family members, and friends. Without affection, people might stay stuck, needing love but never feeling satisfied. Those who experience abundant love move to the next level, *success and esteem.* They need at this stage to be respected and considered successful.

In his later years, Maslow, like Erikson, reassessed his final level, *self-actualization.* He suggested a sixth level, *self-transcendence* (Koltko-Rivera, 2006)—not usually attained until late in life. If the social timetable is so variable, why is the **midlife crisis** frequently referred to in the popular media? The answer is instructive as we consider cohort changes in the following.

Especially for People Under 20
Will future "decade" birthdays—30, 40, 50, and so on—be major turning points in your life? (see response, page 609)

midlife crisis A supposed period of unusual anxiety, radical self-reexamination, and sudden transformation that was once widely associated with middle age but that actually had more to do with developmental history than with chronological age.

THINKING CRITICALLY

The Midlife Crisis

The midlife crisis is, supposedly, a time of anxiety and radical change as age 40 approaches: Men, in particular, were said to leave their wives, buy red sports cars, and quit their jobs because midlife made them panic about their lives. This idea was popularized more than 30 years ago by Gail Sheehy (1976), who called it "the age 40 crucible," and Daniel Levinson (1978), who wrote that men in midlife experienced

tumultuous struggles within the self and with the external world. . . . Every aspect of their lives comes into question, and they are horrified by much that is revealed. They are full of recriminations against themselves and others.

[p. 199]

The midlife crisis continues to be referenced in popular movies, books, and songs. A 2010 Google search found more than

Midlife Purchase Steve Robinson (standing left) said his midlife crisis at age 49 included an urge to own an edgy sports car. Here he is, three years later, new owner of a company that manufactures cars with the external lines of classic late 1950s sport vehicles and the internal technology of the early twenty-first century.

8 million citations for "midlife crisis," including an article in the *Wall Street Journal* about successful middle-aged men experiencing this crisis (Clements, 2005) and a song title by the rock band Faith No More. However, no large study has found any normative midlife crisis (Austrian, 2008). How could earlier developmentalists have been so wrong?

Levinson studied just 40 men, all from one cohort, and the data were analyzed by men who were also middle-aged. That research design would no longer be considered good science. Sheehy was not a scientist; she supplemented Levinson's research with interviews of people she chose—the less objective way to use case studies. Neither used the replicated, multimethod, cross-sequential research designs that are the bedrock of developmental science today.

Of course, even imperfect and limited data, such as that of Levinson and Sheehy, might contain clues for new trends. With the midlife crisis, however, every attempt at replication has failed to confirm the existence of a midlife crisis for most adults.

In retrospect, cohort effects misled the researchers. Middle-class men who reached age 40 in about 1970 were affected by historic upheavals in their own families: Teenagers were rebellious (the 1960s generation coined the slogan "Don't trust anyone over 30") and wives were assertive (the first wave of modern feminism). Many of those men began marriages and careers in the 1950s, expecting grateful children, wives, employers, and coworkers. When they reached middle age, their world shifted and turned against them—no wonder some had a crisis. But that crisis was caused by personal and historical experiences, not chronological age.

This example highlights the need for critical thinking. Our personal experiences, and those of the people we know, may not represent a valid trend or universal experience of all humans as they age. Differences in cohort, ethnicity, nationality, sexuality, and culture abound in the psychosocial development of adults. As you read this chapter, be critical of some of the trends reported—and also be skeptical of your own critical thinking.

Personality Throughout Adulthood

Personality theories emphasize continuity based on temperament and early experiences. Genes, parental practices, culture, and adult circumstances all contribute to personality. Of these four, genes are probably the most influential, according to longitudinal studies of twins and other research (Pedersen et al., 2005). Since genes do not change over the life span, scientists confirm substantial coherence in personality. Longitudinal, cross-sectional, and multicultural research has identified five clusters of personality traits—called the **Big Five**—that generally remain quite stable throughout adult life:

Big Five The five basic clusters of personality traits that remain quite stable throughout adulthood: openness, conscientiousness, extroversion, agreeableness, and neuroticism.

- Openness: imaginative, curious, artistic, creative, open to new experiences
- Conscientiousness: organized, deliberate, conforming, self-disciplined
- Extroversion: outgoing, assertive, active
- Agreeableness: kind, helpful, easygoing, generous
- Neuroticism: anxious, moody, self-punishing, critical

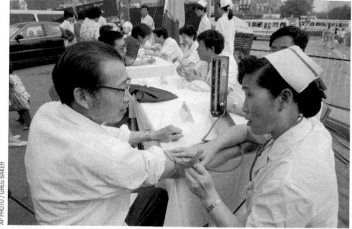

The Big Five correlate with every aspect of adulthood. That includes not only career choices and health habits but also education (conscientious people are more likely to graduate from college), marriage (extroverts are more likely to get married), divorce (which correlates with neuroticism), and intelligence (higher in people who are more open) (Duckworth et al., 2007; Pedersen et al., 2005; Silvia & Sanders, 2010).

Personality traits also affect lifestyle choices. In adulthood, people choose their particular social context, or **ecological niche.** Adults select vocations, mates, and neighborhoods. Even the decision to retire, and a person's reaction to retirement once it occurs, are related to the Big Five personality traits (Robinson et al., 2010). The idea of a chosen ecological niche may explain why, far from being a time of midlife crisis, ages 30 to 50 are marked by more stability of personality than are other periods of life (B. W. Roberts et al., 2006). Before age 30, many adults marry, divorce, quit jobs, move, and explore hidden aspects of their personality; after age 30, they make fewer changes.

Although genes push people toward one ecological niche or another, adult traits are not immutable. For example, marriage to a warm, supportive spouse affects the personality. Typically, those high in neuroticism do not find such a mate, but if they do, they become less neurotic (Rönkä et al., 2002). By contrast, neuroticism increases if a person experiences a hostile workplace, ill health, or poverty. If life circumstances are dramatically altered—perhaps by divorce or widowhood, recovery from addiction, forced emigration, treated depression, a sudden disabling disease—people may behave in new ways (Mroczek et al., 2006).

Often, however, new events bring out old personality patterns: A person might divorce and then remarry someone like the old partner, for instance, or people might find a job that reflects their personality rather than change their personality to fit their job. Those high in neuroticism, for example, tend to work in hazardous conditions—and complain about it (Sutin & Costa, 2010). Even happiness seems a matter of personality. Adults who experience things that temporarily make them overjoyed (e.g., winning a lottery) or depressed (e.g., losing a leg) often revert to the level of happiness they had before: Personality trumps experience (Gilbert, 2006).

None of this means personality is unchanging. The average person experiences slight personality shifts over the years. A massive study of midlife (called MIDUS) found that agreeableness and conscientiousness increased while openness, extroversion, and neuroticism decreased (Lachman & Bertrand, 2001)—a finding confirmed by other research (Allemand et al., 2008; Donnellan & Lucas, 2008).

The Same Situation, Many Miles Apart: Culture or Personality? Personality is more evident here than is culture, according to research on the ecological niche. The women in both of these photographs studied biology, but the more introverted one in Iceland *(left)* prefers to analyze samples of fish tissue on her own, while the more extroverted one in China *(right)* takes blood pressure readings in a city square.

ecological niche The particular lifestyle and social context that adults settle into because it is compatible with their individual personality needs and interests.

>> Response for People Under 20 (from page 607) Probably not. While many younger people associate certain ages with particular attitudes or accomplishments, few people find those ages significant when they actually live through them.

Young Stephen King

Especially for Immigrants and Children of Immigrants Poverty and persecution are the main reasons some people leave their home for another country, but personality is also influential. Which of the Big Five personality traits do you think is most characteristic of immigrants? (see response, page 612)

Culture has an impact. Many researchers who study personality find that people tend to adapt their traits to the culture in which they live, expressing them differently (Church, 2010). Traits that are considered pathological in one place (such as neuroticism in the United States) tend to be discouraged in children in that place and are therefore modified as people grow older (L. A. Clark, 2009). By contrast, traits that are valued (such as conscientiousness) endure. The following feature further examines how the culture of a particular place might affect personality.

A VIEW FROM SCIENCE

Culture and Personality

One hypothesis is that personality is powerfully shaped by culture, so that, say, a Mexican's personality would be quite different from a Canadian's. The opposite hypothesis is that personality is innate, fixed at birth and impervious to social pressures.

Evidence for the second hypothesis includes the fact that the same Big Five traits are found in many nations, with identical age-related trends. Other research, however, finds that culture does affect personality. For example, some social scientists believe that a sixth personality dimension, called *dependence on others,* should be added to the Big Five because it is significant for Asian cultures and is not captured by the standard five (Hofstede, 2007; Suh et al., 2008). To the consternation of Asian psychologists, Western psychiatrists may consider dependence on others a psychological disorder (Y. Chen et al., 2009).

Cultures differ in how they value openness, a trait prized in Western cultures as an indication of intelligence and willingness to learn. However, in some cultures, interpersonal collaboration is valued much more than individual initiative (Church, 2010). Attempts to measure openness in China have not found the same success as in the United States, leading one team to conclude: "Openness is not commonly used as a distinct dimension in the taxonomy of personality traits in Chinese culture" (Cheung et al., 2008, p. 103).

Consider a specific local example, comparing Big Five scores for people in each of the 50 U.S. states. According to an Internet survey of 619,397 Americans, New Yorkers are highest in openness, New Mexicans are highest in conscientiousness, North Dakotans are highest in both extroversion and agreeableness, and West Virginians are highest in neuroticism. Lowest in each of these five are, in order, residents of North Dakota, Alaska, Maryland, Alaska (again), and Utah (Rentfrow et al., 2008).

Do not draw too much from this study. People who respond to an Internet survey are not a random sample, nor does everyone in these states fit the local profile of personality traits: Unlike their neighbors, a particular North Dakota family may be quite disagreeable, for instance. Nevertheless, it is possible that local norms, institutions, history, and geography influence personality. Residents of Utah live among many Mormons (no drugs, large families, good health) and awesome mountains. Those sur-

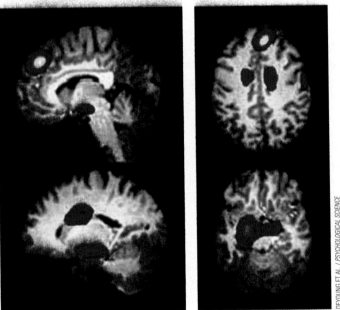

DEYOUNG ET AL. / *PSYCHOLOGICAL SCIENCE*

Active Brains, Active Personality The hypothesis that individual personality traits originate in the brain was tested by scientists who sought correlates between brain activity (red) and personality traits. People high in four of the Big Five (conscientiousness, extroversion, agreeableness, neuroticism—but not openness) activated brain regions known for comparable characteristics. Here are two side views *(left)* and a top and bottom view *(right)* of brains of people high in neuroticism. Regions sensitive to stress, depression, threat, and punishment (yellow bullseyes) were more active than in the low neurotic individuals (DeYoung et al., 2010).

roundings might make them less anxious, more serene, and thus low in neuroticism. Or it could be that people move to places where they feel at home. A North Dakotan who is high in openness might feel stifled and relocate to New York.

A decades-long study in Finland suggests that people do move partly because of their personality traits (Jokela et al., 2008; Silventoinen et al., 2008). Those Finns with an outgoing personality (high in extroversion, or sociability) were likely to relocate, especially from an isolated rural area to an urban one.

Consider again that sixth trait proposed, dependence on others. It could be cultural, in that children growing up in East Asia develop the trait because their parents, teachers, and community encourage it. Or it could be genetic if East Asians over the centuries who were innately strong in social dependence were more likely to survive and hence transmit their genes to the next generation. The relationship between culture and personality can be considered from many perspectives; a consensus is not yet apparent (Church, 2010).

Scientists confirm the niche-seeking aspect of personality: Adults select partners, neighbors, and jobs that allow them to express themselves. Whether or not culture nudges people to develop traits remains an open question.

SUMMING UP

Age boundaries in adulthood are fluid. Erikson and Maslow both described stages that occur in sequence (Erikson: identity, intimacy, generativity, and integrity; Maslow: physiological needs, safety, love and belonging, success and esteem, and self-actualization), but neither theorist set a schedule. Personality traits tend to be quite stable in adulthood, although some slight age-related trends are apparent: Conscientiousness peaks in middle age; openness and extroversion both decline slightly over the decades of adulthood. Personality traits are affected by genes, early experiences, life events, and perhaps geography and culture.

>> Intimacy

As you remember from Chapter 19, adults meet their need for intimacy through their relationships with other people. Specifics vary: Some adults are distant from their parents but close to partners and friends; others rely on family members but not on nonrelatives. The need for intimacy is universal yet dynamic: Each adult regulates closeness and reciprocity, with a combination of friends, acquaintances, and relatives (Lang et al., 2009).

Each person is part of a **social convoy,** a group of people who "provide a protective layer of social relations to guide, encourage, and socialize individuals as they go through life" (Antonucci et al., 2001, p. 572). The term *convoy* originally referred to a group of travelers in hostile territory, such as the pioneers in ox-drawn wagons headed for California or soldiers marching across unfamiliar terrain. Individuals were strengthened by the convoy, sharing the difficult conditions and defending one another when necessary.

As people move through life, their social convoy metaphorically functions as those earlier convoys did (Crosnoe & Elder, 2002; Lang et al., 2009). Current changes in the historical context, including greater globalization, longevity, and diversity, make many sources of intimacy increasingly important. We need our convoys (Antonucci et al., 2007).

social convoy Collectively, the family members, friends, acquaintances, and even strangers who move through life with an individual.

Friends and Acquaintances

Friends are crucial members of the social convoy, partly because they are chosen for the very traits that make them reliable fellow travelers. They are usually about the same age, with similar experiences and values. They often provide practical help and useful advice when serious problems—death of a family member, personal illness, loss of a job—arise; they also provide companionship, information, and laughter in daily life—helping to persuade a child to eat his carrots, to decide whether to remodel or replace the kitchen cabinets, to figure out when to ask for a raise, and, as time goes on, to determine how to deal with grandchildren, menopause, and retirement.

>> Response for Immigrants and Children of Immigrants (from page 610) Extroversion and neuroticism, according to some research. Perhaps because these traits decrease over adulthood, fewer older adults migrate.

consequential strangers People who are not in a person's closest friendship circle convoy but nonetheless have an impact.

A comprehensive research study (Fingerman et al., 2004) found that friendships tend to improve with age. During adolescence and emerging adulthood, people rate a significant minority of their friendships as ambivalent or problematic. By adulthood, almost all friendships are close, few are ambivalent, and almost none are problematic.

In addition to friends, hundreds of other acquaintances provide information, support, social integration, and new ideas (Fingerman, 2009). Neighbors, coworkers, store clerks, the local police officer, members of a religious or community group, and so on are **consequential strangers,** defined as people who are not in a person's closest convoy but who nonetheless have an impact. Among the consequential strangers in your life might be several dog owners if you walk a dog, your barber or beautician if you get your hair cut regularly, a street vendor from whom you buy a muffin every day. Sometimes a consequential stranger is literally a stranger: someone who sits next to you on an airplane, or directs you when you are lost, or gives you a seat on the bus.

Such acquaintances differ from most close friends and family members in that they include people of diverse religions, ethnic groups, ages, and political opinions—and that diversity is one reason they are consequential as well as particularly helpful in current times (Fingerman, 2009). The Internet has strengthened friendships and added more consequential strangers to many adult lives (Stern & Adams, 2010; Wang & Wellman, 2010).

The nature of all these networks varies by culture. In many African nations, almost anyone in the community might be a consequential stranger, who might stop by unannounced to visit. In both Germany and Hong Kong, adults have about an equal number of intimates, but the Germans tended to feel closer to their friends and the Chinese closer to their family members (Fung et al., 2008). Especially in regions where everyone has many siblings and cousins, close companions are also relatives, and almost all acquaintances are related somehow.

Family Bonds

A close friend is often referred to as being "like a sister" or "my brother." Such terms reflect the assumption that family connections are intimate.

Adult Children and Their Parents

Although most adults in modern societies leave their parents' homes to establish their own households, physical separation does not necessarily weaken family ties. In fact, relationships between parents and adult children are more likely to deteriorate if they live together (Ward & Spitze, 2007). (Intergenerational living may signify that either the parents or the children are unable to live independently.)

For that reason, living arrangements are a poor measure of family closeness. In rural Thailand, the greatest influence on whether a young married couple lives with the wife's parents (the traditional custom) or establishes their own household is income, not affection. Thai families establish separate households if they can afford to do so (Piotrowski, 2008). Noteworthy is that the main source of extra income for some of these Thai families is money voluntarily sent by adult children who work far from home. Thus, out of family loyalty, some adult children support independent households for their siblings, a practice that is probably a sign of closeness, not distance.

When adult children have serious financial, legal, or marital problems, their parents usually try to be supportive. In the economic recession that began around 2008, an increasing number of 25- to 34-year-old adults lived with their parents (Pew Social Trends Staff, 2010). In the Netherlands, about 5 percent of all 30- to

The Only One with Shorts Elizabeth Sheeran, age 29, is an oddity in this retirement community for adults over age 55, where she is living, temporarily, with her parents. Few such communities allow young adults to stay longer than a month.

RICK FRIEDMAN / THE NEW YORK TIMES / RDUX

Like Parent, Like Child Even when a child becomes bigger than a parent, as is evident with this Mexican son and California daughter, parents and adult children continue to admire each other.

40-year-olds live with their parents, and divorced men with children are particularly likely to move back with their parents (Smits et al., 2010).

The parent–child relationship is smoothest when both generations are independent and doing well but most troubled when an adult child has serious personal problems (such as drug addiction) and the middle-aged parent has no spouse to buffer his or her distress (E. A. Greenfield & Marks, 2006). Generally, parents are proud of their adult children and provide them more financial and emotional support than the children do for their parents. Yet parents have mixed emotions—especially if their children are not happily partnered and successful (Birditt et al., 2010).

Siblings and Other Relatives

Not only do parents and adult children often become mutually supportive, but siblings sometimes do as well. Although only about one-third of U.S. adolescents consider themselves close to their siblings, two-thirds of adults aged 25 to 65 and almost all the oldest adults count siblings as friends (Fingerman et al., 2004; see Figure 13.3).

Adult siblings help one another cope with children, marriage, and elderly relatives. For many adults, siblings provide practical support (especially between brothers) and emotional support (especially between sisters) (Voorpostel & van der Lippe, 2007). A middle-aged woman who lived thousands of miles from her four siblings said:

> I have a good relationship with my brothers. . . . Every time I come, they are very warm and loving, and I stayed with my brother for a week. . . . Sisters is another story. Sisters are best friends. Sisters is like forever. When I have a problem, I phone my sisters. When I'm feeling down, I phone my sisters. And they always pick me up.

[quoted in Connidis, 2007, p. 488]

In many families, adolescents usually criticize one another, emerging adults seek independence, and then older adults connect with the brother or sister they formerly avoided. Relationships with aunts, uncles, grandparents, nieces, nephews, and stepparents may also become closer, although not necessarily. Culture matters, as now discussed.

A Developmental View of Family Closeness

Over the years of adulthood, parents and adult children typically increase in closeness, forgiveness, and pride as both generations gain maturity. With age, adults become more likely to seek to maintain the family relationship rather than exit from it. To be specific, one study of 13- to 99-year-olds experiencing conflicts found that the youngest participants were likely to yell and walk away but that the oldest ones were likely to keep quiet and reconcile (Birditt & Fingerman, 2005).

Some family closeness is cultural. In North America, Europe, and Australia, older adults cherish their independence and dread burdening their children. Even frail parents seek to maintain independence, feeling that moving in with their children is a sign of failure. By contrast, in China and other nations where dependence on others is a desirable personality trait, intergenerational living does not necessarily reduce affection or signify a problem (Harvey & Yoshino, 2006).

Specifics of family bonds depend on many factors, including childhood attachments, cultural norms, and the financial and practical resources of each generation. One cultural norm is **familism,** the belief that family members should sacrifice personal freedom and success to care for one another. Familism (in Spanish, *familismo*) is particularly strong among Mexican Americans, for whom family solidarity cushions the strains of poverty, parenthood, and prejudice (Behnke et al., 2008).

In general, familism leads relatives to help one another, even if a family member is drug-addicted, abusive, or wanted by the police. For example, some families consider it betrayal for a family member to report a child-abusing relative; instead of calling the authorities, other family members are expected to take over child care.

A contrasting value is individuality. Some families expect all adults to be self-supporting and law-abiding. They would not subsidize a cousin who could not pay her bills or protect a nephew who broke the law. Two dramatic examples make the point: One of my students shot someone (he said it was justified) and then hid in his cousin's house. To his shock and anger, she called the police. Theodore Kaczynski (the "Unibomber") mailed letter bombs that killed 3 people and wounded 23 others. He escaped detection for 17 years until his suspicious younger brother alerted the police.

More mundane examples occur for everyone: Some people are expected to babysit for their siblings' children for free, drop out of college to help in a family emergency, or provide housing for distant relatives. Other people would consider such sacrifices unreasonable and foolish.

Family relationships sometimes are destructive, conflicted, or distant. A six-nation study found that close and affectionate relations between adults (average age 53) and their aging parents (average age 77) were most likely when the government provided many services (e.g., health care, residences) for the elderly (see the Research Design). England was highest in affection, the United States highest in conflict, and Germany highest in detachment. Israel, Spain, and Norway were closer to average on these dimensions (Silverstein et al., 2010).

Of course, each nation has many adults who differ from its trends, and in every nation, some adults wisely keep their distance from their blood relatives. They may instead become **fictive kin** in another family, that is, someone not related

familism The belief that family members should support one another, sacrificing individual freedom and success, if necessary, in order to preserve family unity.

fictive kin Someone who becomes accepted as part of a family to which he or she has no blood relation.

▶ Research Design

Scientists: Merril Silverstein, Daphna Gans, Ariel Lowenstein, Roseann Giarrusso, and Vern L. Bengtson.

Publication: *Journal of Marriage and Family* (2010).

Participants: Participants included more than 2,500 adults age 65 and older, with at least 400 from each of the following six nations: England, Germany, Israel, Norway, Spain, and the United States. They came from two longitudinal studies that collected data via surveys on dozens of characteristics. The older adults were asked many questions, including about their relationship with one of their adult children (randomly selected).

Design: Participants were asked about age, education, and mobility and were then asked questions about a single child. (If a person had several children, only the relationship with one child was selected.) Overall, answers were clustered so that the elders fit into one of four groups: *amicable* (close, got along well, high communication), *detached* (distant, low on communication), *disharmonious* (conflict, critical, arguing), and *ambivalent* (both close and critical, high on communication).

Major conclusions: Every nation had some elders in each of the four clusters, with amicable relationships the most common everywhere. Elders who were frail and dependent were more likely to experience friction, even though they often lived with their children. For all parent–child relationships, marriage and being a woman increased closeness; the most distant tended to be the divorced fathers and their unmarried sons.

National differences appeared in how common each cluster was, with England and Norway most amicable, Germany and Spain most detached, and Israel most ambivalent. No nations had many disharmonious relationships, but the United States had more (20 percent) than the other five nations.

Comment: This study has much to commend it, in that it has a large, longitudinal sample and compares many nations. Such research is difficult and expensive, but such empirical data on cultural differences and universal trends are crucial for understanding human development. There are two problems with this study, however. First, by randomly choosing one target child, the researchers may have gotten an incomplete picture—especially when there are several children, they may decide among themselves who is to be closest to the parents. Thus, the numbers of "detached" children may make it seem as if parents are more distant from their children than is the case. The second problem is that the U.S. sample all came from southern California. It may be that parent–child relationships there are unlike those in other parts of the country.

by blood who is accepted and treated like a family member. Fictive kin are usually introduced to a family by a friend who considers them to be like a brother or sister; gradually, they are accepted by the other family members. Especially if adults are rejected by their original family (perhaps because of their sexual orientation) or if they are far from home (perhaps immigrants), being adopted by a new family is a lifeline (Ebaugh & Curry, 2000; E. C. Kim, 2009; Muraco, 2006). Adults need kin, fictive or otherwise.

SUMMING UP

Intimacy is a universal need that is met in many ways—through friendship, family bonds, and romantic partnerships. Friends buffer against stress, and consequential strangers provide information and support. Throughout life, family financial assistance and emotional encouragement typically flow from older adults to younger ones. Some cultures encourage familism, including three-generational families living together, whereas other cultures expect independence from adults and therefore limit the sacrifices each adult is expected to make for relatives.

>> Committed Partners

As detailed earlier, people in every nation take longer than previous generations did to publicly commit to one long-term sexual partner. Nonetheless, although specifics differ (marriage at age 20 is late in some cultures and too young in others), adults everywhere seek committed partners to help meet their needs for intimacy as well as to raise children, share resources, and provide care when needed.

Although adults today marry later in life than earlier generations did, this change is more a shift in timing than a rejection of intimacy, as explained in Chapters 17 and 19. Recent data suggest that less than 10 percent of contemporary U.S. adults will *never* make a marriage-like commitment. In some other nations, marriage is even more common; less than 2 percent stay single lifelong. Both culture and cohort are influential. Of U.S. residents who were born before 1940, 96 percent married, usually before age 25 (U.S. Bureau of the Census, 2008).

Marriage and Happiness

From a developmental perspective, marriage is a useful institution. Adults thrive if another person is committed to their well-being; children benefit when they have two parents who are legally as well as emotionally dedicated to them; societies are stronger if individuals sort themselves into families.

From an individual perspective, the consequences are more mixed. Generally speaking, married people are a little happier, healthier, and richer than never-married ones—but not by much. A 16-nation survey 20 years ago found one nation (Portugal) where single people were happier than married ones, another (France) where both groups were equally content, and several where married adults were slightly more likely to be "very happy" than never-married adults. The largest differences were in the United States, where more married than single adults were "very happy" (37 versus 26 percent) (Inglehart, 1990). Overall, there is no doubt that a satisfying marriage improves health, wealth, and life happiness, but some marriages are not satisfying (Fincham & Beach, 2010).

One large longitudinal study of married adults found that

> there were as many people who ended up less happy than they started as there were people who ended up happier than they started (a fact that is particularly striking given that we restricted the sample to people who stayed married).

> [Lucas et al., 2003, p. 536]

Thus, most adults marry and expect ongoing happiness because of it, but some will be disappointed (Coontz, 2005). Those who never marry can be quite happy as well (DePaulo, 2006).

Not surprisingly, a meta-analysis of 93 studies found that personal well-being is affected by the quality of the marriage as well as vice versa, especially for people married eight years or longer (Proulx et al., 2007). The long-term quality of a marriage is affected by many factors, including the childhood experiences of both spouses (Overbeek et al., 2007), cohabitation before marriage (decreasing happiness), and the partners' personalities.

The sheer passage of time also makes a difference. For instance, the honeymoon period tends to be happy, but then frustration increases because conflicts arise. Domestic violence is more likely to appear early in a relationship than later

The Same Situation, Many Miles Apart: Happily Married Nebraska *(top)* and Siberia *(bottom)* are at opposite ends of the globe, but both places have much in common: sparse population, many farms, cold winters, and enduring marriages. In every nation, couples in rural areas are less likely to divorce.

on (H. K. Kim et al., 2008). Partnerships (including heterosexual marriages, committed cohabitations, same-sex couples) tend to be happiest in the beginning, then dip when the first child is an infant and dip again when children reach puberty (Umberson et al., 2010) (see At About This Time). Gradually, after a decade or two of declining satisfaction, partnerships improve as time goes on (Scarf, 2008).

These changes are relatively small; fluctuations are rarely dramatic. An abusive partnership may be better ended than endured until possible later improvement, and most marriages that are blissful in late adulthood were always pretty good. Part of the explanation for these trends, of course, is that many unhappy relationships end after a few years; this is particularly true for cohabitants.

Contrary to outdated impressions, the **empty nest** (the time when parents are alone again after their children have moved out and launched their own lives) often improves a relationship (Gorchoff et al., 2008). Simply spending time together, without the interruptions and stresses of child rearing and without the challenges of adolescents, reminds the couple why they chose each other in the first place. Another common problem, inadequate income, also tends to be less troublesome as marriages continue. The expense of child care or the lost income if the wife does not have a paid job is reduced as the last child enters school, and the later costs of college are more manageable when both middle-aged spouses are earning higher salaries than when they were first married.

Over time, some troubled marriages rebound, with spouses becoming happy again as they learn to understand and forgive each other (Fincham et al., 2007). In Chapter 19, you learned that shared backgrounds, values, and interests (homogamy) reduce conflict, while different backgrounds (heterogamy) raise issues that were not expected. Marriages among people of different ethnic groups, for instance, "soared more than 20-fold . . . from 1960 to 2000" (Lee & Bean, 2007, p. 562), but such marriages have a higher risk of divorce, probably because of racial tensions in the culture that the couple did not anticipate (Burton et al., 2010).

If they stay together, couples who initially were quite different may come closer together, especially if relatives accept them and if they develop some shared activities or traditions. One example is with religion: Simply belonging to the same faith does not improve the chance of a happy marriage, but having family religious rituals (such as praying at meals) does (Ellison et al., 2010).

Time does not fix every relationship, of course, and new stressors may occur. Economic stress causes marital friction no matter how many years a couple has been together (Conger et al., 2010), and contextual factors can undermine a couple's willingness to communicate and compromise (Karney & Bradbury, 2005). A long-standing relationship might crumble, especially under the weight of major crises—particularly financial (such as a foreclosed home, a stretch of unemployment) or relational (such as demanding in-laws or an extramarital affair) ones.

These generalities can obscure specifics. Some long-term marriages are blissful; others are horrible. Marriage has never been magical: It does not necessarily make adults happier or children successful (Acs, 2007; Foster & Kalil, 2007). As you remember from the discussion of family structure in Chapter 13, correlation is not causation, and there are happy adults and successful children in all kinds of families.

AT ABOUT THIS TIME

Marital Happiness over the Years

Interval After Wedding	Characterization
First 6 months	Honeymoon period—happiest of all
6 months to 5 years	Happiness dips; divorce is common; usual time for birth of first child
5 to 10 years	Happiness holds steady
10 to 20 years	Happiness dips as children reach puberty
20 to 30 years	Happiness rises when children leave the nest
30 to 50 years	Happiness is high and steady, barring serious health problems

empty nest The time in the lives of parents when their children have left the family home to pursue their own lives.

Especially for Young Couples Suppose you are one half of a turbulent relationship in which moments of intimacy alternate with episodes of abuse. Should you break up? (see response, page 619)

Gay and Lesbian Partners

Almost everything just described applies to gay and lesbian partners as well as to heterosexual ones (Biblarz & Savci, 2010; Herek, 2006). Some same-sex couples are faithful and supportive of each other; their emotional well-being benefits from their relationship. Others are conflicted, with problems of finances, communication, and domestic abuse resembling those of heterosexual marriages. A review of 15 years of same-sex marriages in Denmark, Sweden, and Norway finds that neither the greatest fears nor the greatest hopes are realized (Eskridge & Spedale, 2007).

Political and cultural contexts for same-sex couples are changing markedly. As of this writing, several nations, including Canada and Spain, and at least six U.S. states (Connecticut, Iowa, Maine, Massachusetts, New Hampshire, and Vermont) recognize same-sex marriage. Many other nations and U.S. states are ambivalent, and most countries, as well as about 30 states, explicitly outlaw same-sex marriage. Attitudes are changing as well, which might make earlier data no longer relevant.

However, up-to-date research with a large, randomly selected sample of gay and lesbian couples is not yet available, and many smaller studies are designed or cited to prove that gay marriage is, or is not, beneficial. About one-fourth of same-sex couples are raising children, either from a previous marriage or from using assisted reproductive technology (ART). Research on those families finds that they function at least as well as more conventional families do (Biblarz & Stacey, 2010).

It is not even known how many committed same-sex couples there are. According to the U.S. Bureau of the Census (2008), only 0.7 percent of U.S. households are headed by unmarried same-sex couples. All gay and lesbian groups, and most social scientists, consider this an underestimate because many such couples are reluctant to proclaim their status. Before 2000, the United States census defined an *unmarried couple* as a "cohabiting man and woman." Now *unmarried partners* are allowed to specify male–female, male–male, or female–female. The data (see Table 22.2) show a 31 percent increase in the number of gay couples between 2000 and 2006, probably because more same-sex couples are declaring themselves officially.

One study based on a 1978 survey of more than 1,000 each of four kinds of couples without children—gay, lesbian, cohabiting heterosexual, and married heterosexual—was only recently published (Kurdek, 2006). Then, as today, couples in romantic partnerships were all similar in most important ways. The greatest difference was not in the couples themselves but in their parents (Kurdek, 2006). Fathers were less likely to treat the mates of their gay and lesbian children "like family" than they did the mates of their married heterosexual children. Parental acceptance of cohabiting heterosexual partners was halfway between the two.

Newlyweds Well, not quite yet, but they are celebrating the marriage license they just acquired. Rocky Galloway and Reggie Stanley have been a couple for many years but were not allowed to marry until the day shown here—when same-sex marriages became legal in Washington, D.C.

TABLE 22.2				
Unmarried-Partner Households in the United States, 2000 and 2006*				
	Male–Female	Male–Male	Female–Female	Total Same-Sex
2000	4,881,377	301,026	293,365	594,391
2006	5,237,595	417,044	362,823	779,867
Increase from 2000 to 2006: Number and Percent				
	356,218 (7%)	116,018 (39%)	69,458 (24%)	185,476 (31%)

*Officially declared.
Source: *U.S. Bureau of the Census, 2002, 2008.*

Another interesting difference was that same-sex couples scored higher than the other couples on contact with friends. Apparently, they were more likely to meet their intimacy needs with their friends than with their relatives.

Divorce and Separation

Throughout this text, developmental events that seem isolated, personal, and transitory are shown to be interconnected, socially mediated, and subject to enduring consequences. Relationships never improve or end in a vacuum; they are influenced by the social and political context (Fine & Harvey, 2006). Divorce, separation, and the end of a cohabiting relationship are all affected by context, although most of the research has focused on divorce (see Table 22.3).

The Consequences of Divorce

Divorce occurs because at least one half of a couple believes that he or she would be happier not married. That conclusion is reached fairly often in the United States: Since 1980, almost half as many divorces or permanent separations have occurred as marriages. (About one-third of first marriages end in divorce; and with each subsequent marriage, the odds of divorce increase.)

Typically, people divorce because some aspects of the marriage have become difficult to endure; often they do not realize the impact on other aspects of their lives until months later. Divorce reduces income, severs friendships (many couples have only other couples as friends), and weakens family ties. Family problems arise not only with children (usually custodial parents become stricter and noncustodial parents feel excluded) but also with other relatives (C. Anderson, 2003; V. King, 2003). Self-esteem also falls: Many divorced people think they have failed, either as a spouse or in choosing a partner.

Although divorce may seem to be an event, from a developmental perspective it is a process that begins years before the official decree and that reverberates for decades after (Amato, 2010). Income, family welfare, and self-esteem are lower among the formerly married than among people of the same age who are still married or who have always been single. Children of divorce often develop academic or social problems, either immediately or later on, adding to their parents' stress (Amato & Cheadle, 2005). Although some research finds that women suffer from divorce more than men do (their income, particularly, is lower), aging divorced fathers are often lonely, alienated from their adult children and grandchildren (Lin, 2008a).

>> **Response for Young Couples** (from page 617) There is no simple answer, but you should bear in mind that, while abuse usually decreases with age, breakups become more difficult with every year, especially if children are involved.

TABLE 22.3
Factors That Make Divorce More Likely

Before Marriage
Divorced parents
Either partner under age 21
Family opposed
Cohabitation before marriage
Previous divorce of either partner
Large discrepancy in age, background, interests, values (heterogamy)

During Marriage
Divergent plans and practices regarding childbearing and child rearing
Financial stress, unemployment
Substance abuse
Communication difficulties
Lack of time together
Emotional or physical abuse
Relatives who do not support the relationship

In the Culture
High divorce rate in cohort
Weak religious values
Laws that make divorce easier
Approval of remarriage
Acceptance of single parenthood

Sources: Fine & Harvey, 2006; Gottman et al., 2002; R. A. Thompson & Wyatt, 1999; Wolfinger, 2005.

TOM CHENEY / THE NEW YORKER COLLECTION / CARTOONBANK.COM

"But you knew I was addicted to bad men when you married me."

Surprised? Many brides and grooms hope to rescue and reform their partners, but they should know better. Changing another person's habits, values, or addictions is very difficult.

This research on divorce is sobering. As with all of adult development, the shifting social context may have improved life for the formerly married, and some people escape the usual patterns. If divorce ends an abusive, destructive relationship (as it does about one-third of the time), it usually benefits at least one spouse and the children (Amato, 2010). Nonetheless, for adult development, divorce is never pain-free.

Repartnering

Divorce is most likely to occur within the first five years after a wedding, and cohabitation usually ends even sooner, with half of cohabiting relationships ending within two years (Kennedy & Bumpass, 2008). (These data are for the United States: Intimate relationships typically last longer in Canada and Europe.) Usually, both partners reestablish former friendships and resume dating. Often they marry again, especially if they are young men.

Women with children are less likely to remarry, but when they do, their new husbands often have children from a previous marriage also (Goldscheider & Sassler, 2006). About half of all U.S. marriages are remarriages for at least one partner, and many formerly married women as well as men begin new sexual partnerships, either cohabiting or having a steady mate whom they do not plan to marry.

Initially, remarriage brings intimacy, health, and financial security. For remarried fathers, bonds with their new stepchildren or with a new baby may replace strained relationships with their children from the earlier marriage (Hofferth & Anderson, 2003). Divorce usually increases depression and loneliness; remarriage brings relief. Most remarried adults are quite happy immediately after the wedding (Blekesaune, 2008).

However, such happiness may not endure. Remember that personality tends to change only slightly over the life span; people who were chronically unhappy in their first marriage may become unhappy in their second. Stepchildren add unexpected stresses (Sweeney, 2010). One theory is that because the culture has not yet codified the relationships and roles of stepfamilies, individuals may have clashing expectations of what they should and should not do.

Lewis Terman's 1921 research on gifted children has now produced longitudinal data on marriages that lasted 50 years. One finding is that adults who never married or who had only one marriage were notably healthier and more successful than were participants who married, divorced, and remarried (Tucker et al., 1996). Remember, however, the importance of cohort changes. As with same-sex partnerships and divorce, the social context of remarriage is changing. Remarriages are becoming more common. All this means that the data on people now in late adulthood may not predict what will occur for people now in their 20s who cohabit, marry, divorce, or remarry.

SUMMING UP

Marriage provides companionship, child-rearing help, and emotional support. Some adults (about 10 percent) never have a long-term romantic partnership but find other ways to meet their intimacy needs. Same-sex and different-sex couples seem to have similar needs and problems. The research on divorce finds that ties to relatives, financial security, and friendships are disrupted, and the consequences can last for decades. Remarriage resolves some loneliness and financial problems but also may create new complications, especially if children are involved. Many aspects of romantic commitments are changing: New studies of same-sex couples, divorce, and remarriage may not reach the same conclusions as those already published.

>> Generativity

According to Erikson, after the stage of *intimacy versus isolation* comes that of *generativity versus stagnation,* when adults seek to be productive in a caring way. Without generativity, adults experience "a pervading sense of stagnation and personal impoverishment" (Erikson, 1963, p. 267).

Adults satisfy their need to be generative in many ways; for instance, through creativity, caregiving, and employment. Of these three, the link between creativity and generativity has been least studied, although creative expression is recognized as an avenue for self-expression (as we will see in the next chapter). We now explore what has been learned about the two other generative activities: caregiving, particularly caring for children, and employment, particularly work that allows personal growth while producing goods or services that help others prosper. Balancing care and employment to achieve generativity is not easy, as we also discuss.

Caregiving

Erikson (1963) wrote that a mature adult "needs to be needed" (p. 266). Some caregiving involves meeting another person's physical needs—feeding, cleaning, and so on—but much of it has to do with fulfilling another person's psychological needs. As one study concludes:

> The time and energy required to provide emotional support to others must be reconceptualized as an important aspect of the *work* that takes place in families. . . . Care-giving, in whatever form, does not just emanate from within, but must be managed, focused, and directed so as to have the intended effect on the care recipient.
>
> [Erickson, 2005, p. 349]

Thus, caregiving includes responding to the emotions of people who need a confidant, a cheerleader, a counselor, a close friend. Parents and children care for one another, as do partners. Often neighbors, friends, and more distant relatives are caregivers as well. Most families include a **kinkeeper,** a caregiver who takes responsibility for maintaining communication among family members. The kinkeeper gathers everyone for holidays; spreads the word about anyone's illness, relocation, or accomplishments; buys gifts for special occasions; and reminds family members of one another's birthdays and anniversaries (Sinardet & Mortelmans, 2009). Guided by their kinkeeper, all the family members become generative.

Fifty years ago, kinkeepers were almost always women, usually the mother or grandmother of a large family. Now families are smaller and gender equity is more apparent, so some men and young women are kinkeepers—although most kinkeepers are still older women, typically the middle-aged or older mother who has several adult children. This role may seem burdensome, but caregiving provides both satisfaction and power (Mitchell, 2010). The best caregivers share the work; shared kinkeeping is generativity.

Caring for Biological Children

Although generativity can take many forms, its chief form is "establishing and guiding the next generation," usually through parenthood (Erikson, 1963, p. 267). Thus, many adults pass along their values as they decide how to respond to the hundreds of requests and unspoken needs of their children each day.

Parenting has been discussed many times in this text, primarily with a focus on its impact on children. Now we concentrate on the adult half of this interaction—

Four Generations of Caregiving These four women, from the great-grandmother to her 17-year-old great-granddaughter, all care for one another. Help flows to whoever needs it, not necessarily to the oldest or youngest.

kinkeeper A caregiver who takes responsibility for maintaining communication among family members.

The Same Situation, Many Miles Apart: Caregiving Dads Fathers are often caregivers for their young children, as shown here in Indonesia *(left)* and the United States *(right)*. Most developmentalists think that men have always nurtured their children, although in modern times employed mothers, plastic bottles, and sturdy baby carriers are among the specifics that have changed.

the impact of parenting on the parents themselves. Bearing and rearing children are labor-intensive expressions of generativity, "a transformative experience" with more costs than benefits when children are young (Umberson et al., 2010). Given adults' need to be generative, however, most adults choose to pay that price. As Erikson (1963) says, "The fashionable insistence on dramatizing the dependence of children on adults often blinds us to the dependence of the older generation on the younger one" (p. 266).

Every parent is tested by the dynamic experience of raising children. As experienced parents know, just when an adult thinks he or she has mastered the art of parenting, the child advances to the next stage and the parents must adjust all over again. Over the decades, new babies arrive and older children grow up, the financial burdens of child care change, family income almost never seems adequate, seldom is every child thriving. Illness or disability may suddenly require extra care.

If parents have only one child, they are often intensely focused on that child, and some aspect of development awakens concern. Problems and stresses increase as more children are born. As already mentioned, when children grow up, they usually bring more joy than distress to their parents, but if even one of several adult children is troubled, middle-aged and older parents are less happy (Birditt et al., 2010; Milkie et al., 2008). Most parents manage to cope with all these demands; resilience is evidence of their generativity.

Caring for Nonbiological Children

As described in Chapter 8, children can develop well in any family structure—nuclear or extended; heterosexual or same-sex; single-parent, two-parent, or grandparent. Can adults also thrive in any kind of parenting relationship?

Roughly one-third of all North American adults become stepparents, adoptive parents, or foster parents. These nonbiological parents face great challenges, but they also have abundant opportunities for generativity. One major challenge is the mistaken notion that the only "real" parents are the biological ones. This belief is a social construction that hinders a secure attachment between parents and their nonbiological children.

Although parent–child attachment does not depend on biology, many adopted or foster children remain attached to their birth parents, part of the normal human affection for familiar caregivers. However, if their birth parents were abusive, these children's early attachment can be problematic. Even worse, some children are not attached to anyone (as can happen when they spend years in an institution). They are mistrustful of all adults and fearful of loving anyone. Even in the best institutions, few 1-year-olds are securely attached (St. Petersburg–USA Orphanage Research Team, 2008). Secure attachment is hampered if both adult and child know that their connection can be severed for reasons unrelated to caregiving quality or relationship strength. Such separations often occur with foster children (Pew Commission on Children in Foster Care, 2004).

Foster parents face the dilemma of "whether to 'love' the children or maintain a cool, aloof posture with minimal sensitive or responsive interactions" (St. Petersburg–USA Orphanage Research Team, 2008, p. 15). A loving bond is better for both the foster parent and the child, and separation is harmful to both. Generative caring does not occur in the abstract; it involves a particular caregiver and care receiver, so everything needs to be done to foster attachment.

Most parents of stepchildren face special challenges. The average age of new stepchildren is 9 years old, which means that they may be strongly connected to their biological parents. This helps the child but hinders the stepparents. Stepmothers may hope to heal a broken family through love and understanding, whereas stepfathers may think their new children will welcome a benevolent disciplinarian. Neither expectation is realistic. Some stepparents go to the other extreme, remaining distant from the children. One reason they do so may be that they know their connection to their stepchildren depends on the strength of their relationship with their spouse, the biological parent.

Mother/Stepmother Remarriage gave Susan Heise *(far right)* a husband and stepchildren, joining her two biological progeny, both shown here. Erika, 16, converses with her at the table while Richard, 10, plays his trumpet, and Annie, 8, exercises in the doorway.

Observation Quiz Which one is the stepchild? (see answer, page 624)

Young stepchildren often get hurt, sick, lost, or disruptive; teenage stepchildren may get pregnant, drunk, or arrested. If adults overreact or are indifferent to such situations, the two generations become further alienated (Coleman et al., 2007). The temperament of the adults and the nature of the marriage affect whether a family will weather such storms (Ganong & Coleman, 2004). On the positive side, many men become "social fathers," providing fatherly care to children who are not their genetic progeny but who live with them. This can benefit both generations (Bzostek, 2008). Generativity, with patient, authoritative parenting, is needed. With time, most stepparents find satisfaction in their role (Ganong & Coleman, 2004).

Compared with stepparents, adoptive parents have several advantages: They are legally connected to their children for life, the biological parents are usually absent, and they desperately wanted the child. Strong bonds can develop, especially when the children are adopted as infants. Nevertheless, during adolescence, these bonds may stretch and loosen. Some adoptive children become intensely rebellious. As you remember, this can happen with a parent's biological teenagers as well, but it is more common among adoptees, who may reject family control as they seek to be reunited with their birth parents (J. K. Kohler et al., 2002).

Adoptive parents who undergo the complications of international adoption are usually intensely dedicated to their children, as are parents of domestic adoptees of a different background. From the parents' perspective, a child's ethnicity is not a barrier, although some parents become aware of community prejudice they did not recognize before. When the children grow up, they need to reconcile their appreciation of their adoptive parents with their pride in their ethnic identity (Trenka et al., 2006).

Despite all the stresses and complications associated with parenting, most parents cherish their experience. For instance, most adults who adopt seek a second child within a few years of the arrival of the first. At the same time, the birth rate in the United States decreased to the lowest rate ever in 2009. Obviously, adults want to provide a secure future for their children and are reluctant to have a baby in a depressed economy. As Erikson realized, adults want to raise their children well. Children offer their parents an opportunity to be generative every day.

Caring for Aging Parents

Because of their position in the generational hierarchy, many middle-aged adults are expected to help both the older and younger generations. They have been called the **sandwich generation,** a term that evokes an image of a layer of filling pressed between two slices of bread. This analogy suggests that the middle generation is squeezed between younger and older relatives. This sandwich metaphor is vivid, but it gives a false impression (Grundy & Henretta, 2006).

Caregiving is beneficial because people feel useful when they help one another. One study found that older adults, aged 50 to 75, were *less* likely to be depressed if they were providing support for their adult children than if they were not (Byers et al., 2008). Moreover, because of increased health and vitality in late adulthood, many adults do not need to provide extensive care for their elderly parents. If an elder needs care, typically the children and grandchildren are part of the caregiving team, but not the major providers, who usually are elders themselves (a spouse or a sibling). Since caregiving has benefits as well as costs, and since grown children are not usually full-time caregivers, few adults are sandwiched.

This is not to deny that, for a minority of adults—usually middle-aged women—providing care for an elderly relative impairs sibling relationships, marriages, or employment. For example, although siblings usually become closer in adulthood, a caregiving burden can disrupt that.

For instance, a caregiving sister described one of her two siblings as "real immature . . . a little slow" and the other as "very irresponsible," adding that "when it came right down to having to bathe and having to take care of physical tasks, neither of them would be able to handle it" (quoted in Ingersoll-Dayton et al., 2003, p. 209). A brother in another family resented his caregiving sister: "My sister reminds me all the time that she's taking care of [our parents]. They're actually pretty self-sufficient" (quoted in Ingersoll-Dayton et al., 2003, pp. 208–209).

Husbands and wives can become resentful, too, if care of one spouse's elderly relatives is not what the other spouse anticipated. Families and ethnic cultures differ in expectations, some believing that elderly parents should live with their children, others that elders should live alone as long as possible and then enter some care-providing residence (Parveen & Morrison, 2009; Ron, 2009). Cultures also differ as to how much care the children should provide, whether the husband's or the wife's parents should be helped more, and whether divorced, distant, or stepparents deserve care.

National policies vary as well, with some nations providing extensive care for the elderly and others (including the United States) assuming that most families care for their own (Funk & Kobayashi, 2009). The reality of linked lives (Chapter 19) means that everyone in the family—caregiver or not, sibling or parent—is strained when a family member becomes ill or disabled (Amirkhanyan & Wolf, 2006). Fortunately, however, most adults never need to deal with that strain because most elders never need full-time care from their adult children. Elder care is discussed again in Chapter 25.

sandwich generation The generation of middle-aged people who are supposedly "squeezed" by the needs of the younger and older members of their families. In reality, some adults do feel pressured by these obligations, but most are not burdened by them, either because they enjoy fulfilling them or because they choose to take on only some of them or none of them.

>> Answer to Observation Quiz (from page 623) Erika. There are two clues: The ages of the children make it more likely that the eldest is from the father's first marriage, and biological children often try to grab their mother's attention if she seems to focus on another child.

Employment

Besides family caregiving, the other major avenue for generativity is employment. Most of the research on employment has focused on productivity and career choice, important areas but not germane to this text. Social scientists need to put "thinking about working into the broader fabric of psychological theory and practice" (Blustein, 2006, p. xiv).

Developmental theory does not completely overlook employment. Erikson's *generativity versus stagnation* and Maslow's *success and esteem* stressed the importance of accomplishments in adulthood. Many other theorists also recognize employment when they study instrumental needs (as contrasted with emotional needs) and achievement-striving (as contrasted with affiliation). Adults want to accomplish something over the course of their lives, not simply to be loved and appreciated.

As is evident from the words *generativity, esteem, instrumental,* and *achievement,* adults have many psychosocial needs that employment can fulfill. The converse is also true: Unemployment is associated with higher rates of child abuse, alcoholism, depression, and many other social problems (Freisthler et al., 2006). Developmental researchers, influenced by the dynamic-systems perspective (explained in Chapter 1), see employment as part of a larger picture. Individuals seek to satisfy their needs through a combination of intimate relationships, caregiving, and employment: Because of "linked lives," each family member is affected by the others, with employment of one member affecting the family system, for good or ill.

Wages and Benefits

Salary is sometimes considered a mark of self-worth, or, if an individual is not salaried, being married to a high-wage earner is a sign of status. Beginning with Thorstein Veblen (1899/2007), sociologists have described *conspicuous consumption,* whereby people buy things—such as expensive cars, hip sunglasses, and MP3 players—primarily for the purpose of showing them off to others. Families seek to live in affluent neighborhoods not only for safety or community resources but also for status. A recent study found that people tend to buy more when they are depressed; money is a mood-changer, and people still display their wealth as a way of asserting their worth (Cryder et al., 2008).

Given this human characteristic, it is not surprising that raises and bonuses increase motivation and that salary cuts have emotional, not just financial, effects. Surprisingly, the absolute amount of income (whether a person earns $30,000 or $33,000 or $40,000 a year, for instance) is less significant to most people than how their income compares to that of others in their profession or neighborhood, or to their own salary a year or two ago. This might explain why even though average household income has doubled in the United States over the past 50 years, happiness has not increased. Worldwide, extreme poverty correlates with unhappiness, but most people of all incomes are mildly happy and some people at every income level are depressed (E. Diener & Biswas-Diener, 2008).

The sense of unfairness is innate and universal, encoded in the human brain (Hsu et al., 2008). Awareness of this helps explain some of the attitudes of adults about their work. British workers in one study were less happy and more likely to quit if they thought the salary ranking in their company was unfair, especially if the higher ranks were paid much more than the lower ones (G. D. A. Brown et al., 2008). In the United States, many are offended by the extremely high salaries of corporate executives. Women complain that men have higher average pay, minorities note that most millionaire executives

Lowered Expectations It was once realistic, a "secular trend," for adults to expect to be better off than their parents had been, but hard times have reduced the socioeconomic status of many adults.

are members of the majority, younger workers resent that older workers have seniority, and so on.

A sense of fairness is evident when benefits are compared. Consider health insurance. Globalization has made more Americans aware of the Canadian and European health care systems, which provide care for everyone; as a result, pressure for the United States to switch to a similarly all-inclusive system has been growing. Seniors who receive medical care paid by the government are fiercely protective of that benefit. In nations where family health care is provided primarily through employment, "health care coverage may be key to understanding who remains employed in the face of overwhelming caregiving demands" (Bianchi & Milkie, 2010. p. 719).

Working for More than Money

To understand human development, we must focus on the generative aspects of work—and there are many. Work provides a structure for daily life, a setting for human interaction, a source of social status and fulfillment (Wethington, 2002). In addition, work meets generativity needs by allowing people to do the following:

- Develop and use their personal skills
- Express their creative energy
- Aid and advise coworkers, as a mentor or friend
- Support the education and health of their families
- Contribute to the community by providing goods or services

The pleasure of "a job well done" is universal, as is the joy of having supportive supervisors and friendly coworkers. Job satisfaction correlates more strongly with challenge, creativity, productivity, and relationships among employees than with high pay or easy work (Pfeffer, 2007). Abusive supervisors and hostile coworkers reduce employee motivation and effectiveness. Workers quit their jobs more often because of unpleasant social interactions at the workplace than because of dissatisfaction with wages or benefits (LeBlanc & Barling, 2004). These facts highlight the distinction between the **extrinsic rewards of work**—which are the tangible benefits such as salary, health insurance, and pension—and the **intrinsic rewards of work**—which are the intangible gratifications of actually doing the job. Generativity is intrinsic.

A developmental view finds that extrinsic rewards tend to be more important at first, when young people enter the workforce and begin to establish their careers. Then, in a developmental shift, the "intrinsic rewards of work—satisfaction, relationships with coworkers, and a sense of participation in meaningful activity—become more important as an individual ages" (Sterns & Huyck, 2001, p. 452). The loss of jobs caused by the fiscal crisis that began in 2007 is chilling to developmentalists, who realize that even with unemployment benefits and savings, the intrinsic rewards of work are gone for many people—a fact that affects the psychological health of every affected worker and his or her family.

The power of intrinsic rewards explains why older employees display, on average, less absenteeism, less lateness, and more job commitment than do younger workers (Landy & Conte, 2007). A crucial factor may be that, in many jobs, older workers have more control

extrinsic rewards of work The tangible benefits, usually in the form of compensation (e.g., salary, health insurance, pension), that one receives for doing a job.

intrinsic rewards of work The intangible gratifications (e.g., job satisfaction, self-esteem, pride) that come from within oneself as a result of doing a job.

Stress or Stressor Facing a desk overflowing with income tax forms and checks is stressful, and this woman is new to the job—she began it less than a year ago. Will she quit? Perhaps not. She is mature enough to establish priorities and to cope with any unreasonable demands from her supervisor.

over what they do at work, as well as when and how they do it. This autonomy reduces strain and increases their dedication and vitality.

In a demonstration of this effect, one study began with 972 men who went back to work after having had a mild heart attack. Their work was categorized as (1) high strain (with many psychological demands but little personal control), (2) low strain (fewer demands but more control), or (3) mixed (moderate demands and some control). After controlling for age, high blood pressure, and 24 other factors that make heart attacks more likely, the researchers found that new heart problems (including death) were twice as common among those with high work strain (Aboa-Éboulé et al., 2007).

Another crucial factor is family support. When family members are appreciative and helpful regarding a worker's job requirements, that person's health benefits; conversely, when health impairs a husband's ability to work, divorce is more likely (Teachman, 2010).

Coping with Change

As discussed in Chapter 20, stresses in adulthood can become stressors, and every change has the potential to be a stressor. We focus here on changes at work, but the same potential problems exist for all the changes an adult might encounter. As you will see, flexibility and openness are needed.

Obviously, work is changing in many ways—some good for developing persons, some not. As a result of globalization, each nation exports what it does best (and cheapest) and imports what it needs. Specialization, interdependency, and international trade are increasing. Advanced nations are shifting from industry-based economies to information and service economies; poorer nations are shifting from subsistence agriculture to industry. Multinational corporations are replacing small, local businesses. Financial entrepreneurs seek to coordinate all this growth, investing to maximize profit.

These changes may affect human development by causing a clash between the best interests of workers and employers. For adults to attain intimacy and generativity, employees' psychological and physical health are more important than profit,

Especially for Entrepreneurs Suppose you are starting a business. In what ways would middle-aged adults be helpful to you? (see response, page 629)

T. S. SATYAN / DPA / THE IMAGE WORKS

JOHN B. BOYKIN / CORBIS

The Global Market These women sorting cashews *(left)* and the men working on an offshore oil rig *(right)* are participants in globalization—a phenomenon that has changed the economies of every nation and every family in the world. Radical changes coexist with traditional inequities. For instance, the women here are said to have easy, unskilled work, which is the reason they are paid less than 10 percent of the men's wages.

and family-friendly policies, such as paid child-care leave and flexible schedules, are needed. Yet owners, investors, and managers judge success on whether "the bottom line" shows a profit, not on whether the workplace fosters caregiving, creativity, comradeship, and esteem (Bianchi et al., 2005).

Diversity Within the Workplace

Developmentalists welcome employee diversity in background, gender, and ethnicity. Equal-opportunity policies make it more likely that all job seekers will find work that allows them to develop their potential. Discrimination is still evident, but employers increasingly hire the job applicants who are most likely to perform best, regardless of their background, and law requires that selection procedures be fair to people of all backgrounds (Outtz, 2010). In the United States, almost half the civilian labor force is female and almost one-fourth is of non-European ancestry—a marked change from even 20 years ago (see Figure 22.2).

Some occupations continue to be segregated by gender or ethnicity, but to a lesser extent than before. For example, in the United States, only 8 percent of nurses are men and only 15 percent of firefighters are women—but both these percentages are almost triple what they were 30 years ago (U.S. Bureau of the Census, 2009).

In a diverse workplace, functioning effectively and happily is a developmental need for everyone. Younger adults have an advantage here, since often they have studied and socialized with people of various backgrounds. Older people have their own advantage if their life experience has enabled them to shed their adolescent egocentrism. Much depends on the context: People who think their group is unfairly treated seek some other group to blame (Pettigrew et al., 2008).

Diversity in employees' backgrounds presents a challenge for employers as well as for workers. Not everyone has the same expectations, needs, and desires. Differences in these areas increase the need for **mentors,** people who can help new employees understand what is expected. Good mentoring is a difficult but gratifying form of generativity (Eby et al., 2006).

On the employer's part, working conditions must be adjusted to accommodate the diversity of the workforce. This involves much more than reconsidering the cafeteria menu and the holiday schedule. The social scientist's understanding of culture is helpful here, since culture includes very basic values, routines, and

mentor A skilled and knowledgeable person who advises or guides an inexperienced person.

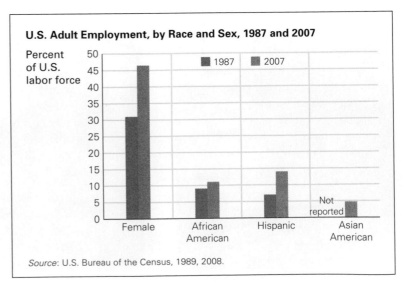

FIGURE 22.2

Closer to Equality In just 20 years, women and minorities achieved a significantly greater presence in the U.S. workforce. Today, each group's representation in the workforce is almost equal to its percentage of the population. Equality in pay and promotion remains elusive.

U.S. Adult Employment, by Race and Sex, 1987 and 2007

Source: U.S. Bureau of the Census, 1989, 2008.

assumptions, not just superficial differences. For example, one study found that U.S. employees are most stressed when they have little control over their work or when they have direct confrontations with their supervisors, whereas employees in China are most stressed by the possibility of negative job evaluations and indirect conflicts (C. Liu et al., 2007). Women may be discouraged by working conditions (such as sexual jokes or lack of child care) that men do not notice.

Well-intentioned people of one group do not necessarily know what words, policies, or mannerisms will impair the functioning of people from a marginalized group. Researchers have begun to explore *micro-aggressions*—small things unnoticed by the majority person that seem aggressive to the minority person (Sue, 2010).

For example, would you expect expressions of racism to impede the performance of African Americans? In one experiment, African and European Americans read transcripts of discussions among hiring teams who were supposedly analyzing job applicants (Salvatore & Shelton, 2007). Sometimes the discussants apparently judged applicants fairly, regardless of race; sometimes the judgments were clearly racist; sometimes a minority applicant was rejected with reasons that seemed plausible though not entirely convincing.

After reading the transcripts, the participants took a test that required mental concentration. The performance of the European Americans was impaired after they read the blatantly racist responses but not after they read the more subtle ones. The opposite was true for the African Americans—their intellectual sharpness was not affected by the clearly racist responses but was hindered by the ambiguous ones.

The experimenters believe that this result shows that the African Americans were not surprised by overt racism, so mentally processing the racist transcripts did not require much mental energy. However, more subtle prejudice did trouble them because considerable mental effort was required for them to decide whether racism was a factor.

Changing Jobs

One recent change in the labor market is the frequency of job changes; this increased incidence of hiring and firing impedes generativity. Between ages 25 and 42, the average worker in the United States has five different employers (U.S. Bureau of the Census, 2008). Some of these job changes are involuntary, resulting from companies' decisions to downsize, eliminate positions, relocate certain divisions, outsource work, cancel contracts, merge, and hire temporary employees. In other circumstances, frequent job changes are voluntary, stemming from workers' ambition or restlessness.

No matter what the origin, whenever social connections are broken, people suffer. The human costs of job change are confirmed by longitudinal research: People who frequently changed jobs by age 36 were three times more likely to have various health problems by age 42 (Kinnunen et al., 2005). This study controlled for cigarette smoking and excessive drinking. If it had not, the contrast would have been even greater, since poor health habits correlate with job instability.

Older workers find job changes particularly difficult, for at least three reasons:

1. Seniority brings higher salaries, more respect, and greater expertise; workers who leave lose their seniority and can no longer benefit from these advantages.
2. Many skills required for new jobs were not taught 20 years ago, so older workers who lose their jobs have more trouble finding another position.
3. Relocation is more difficult when a person has established a family and friends within a particular community.

>> **Response for Entrepreneurs** (from page 627) As employees, middle-aged workers are steady, with few absences and good "people skills," and they like to work. As customers, middle-aged adults will probably be able to afford your products or services because household income is likely to be higher at about age 50 than at any other time.

This last factor is crucial. Imagine that you are a middle-aged adult who loves living in Michigan, where unemployment is three times as high as in Idaho. Would you move 2,000 miles away from your family, church, and community to take a job in Boise, Idaho? If you were unemployed and in debt, and a new job was guaranteed, you might. But then, would it be fair to expect your spouse and children to leave their jobs, schools, and social networks and move with you?

Such difficulties are magnified for immigrants, who make up about 15 percent of the U.S. adult workforce and more than 20 percent of Canada's. Not only must they learn their new country's language, culture, and job skills, but they may also encounter hostility at work or in the community. Many immigrants seek housing help and social support from other immigrants, and most are strongly connected to their families, either in their new nation or their old one (Glick, 2010).

Variable Schedules

Another recent change in employment patterns is the proliferation of work schedules beyond the traditional 9-to-5, Monday-through-Friday one. In the United States, only about half of all employees work on the traditional schedule, with low-income workers and women far more likely to have nontraditional work hours (U.S. Bureau of the Census, 2009). In Europe, the proportion of employees on nonstandard work schedules varies from 25 percent in Sweden to 40 percent in Italy (see Figure 22.3; Presser et al., 2008).

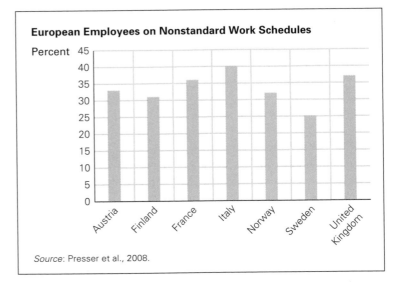

FIGURE 22.3

In Whose Favor? The traditional work schedule—Monday to Friday, 9:00 A.M. to 5:00 P.M.—is best for workers and their families. Employers and consumers, however, would prefer to have workers on the job on weekends and during evening and night shifts. European nations tilt toward the standard schedule. In the United States, about half of all workers have nonstandard schedules. In developing nations, most workers have nonstandard hours.

One crucial variable for job satisfaction is whether employees choose their own hours. Workers who can volunteer for overtime and who are paid at a higher rate for it are usually satisfied with their jobs; workers who are required to do overtime, even if they are paid for it, tend to be less satisfied (Beckers et al., 2008). **Flextime** is one response to the need for worker control of schedules and allows workers some leeway in deciding when to work. For instance, employees might be required to work from 10 A.M. to 3 P.M., Monday through Thursday, but can decide the other half of a 40-hour week. Thus, a worker can take a child to the doctor, attend a parent–teacher conference, or meet other personal obligations that occur on weekdays (Landy & Conte, 2007).

Another attempt in the same direction is **telecommuting,** whereby an employee can work from home and use videoconferencing, online communication, and faxing to keep in touch with the office. A telecommuter can interrupt work to

flextime An arrangement in which work schedules are flexible so that employees can balance personal and occupational responsibilities.

telecommuting Working at home and keeping in touch with the office via computer, telephone, and fax.

Ideal and Reality Perhaps Novi Vinod has found the perfect solution. Here she works at her home office, designing a program for computerized medical records while her 3-year-old daughter plays nearby. Or perhaps frequent interruptions and distractions will soon result in frustration, impatience, and exasperation.

answer the door, help a child with homework, or do a load of laundry. Employers like it because it requires less office space, and public officials like it because it reduces rush-hour traffic.

However, one study found that while telecommuters "experience the benefits of greater family enrichment," the demands of family life can increase the worker's stress by interfering with work efficiency (Golden et al., 2006, p. 1348). Furthermore, telecommuters who live alone miss many of the intrinsic rewards of work, such as the friendships and social interactions that occur when people work together. For some workers, telecommuting allows maintaining family life; for others, it means that the boundaries between home and work disappear, and the worker is more stressed by conflicting demands than before (Bianchi & Milkie, 2010).

A major problem is that flextime and telecommuting are less available to those in manufacturing, construction, or service jobs—even though a disproportionate number of young parents are employed in such jobs. Whether or not a worker has a nonstandard, flexible, or telecommuting schedule depends much more on the industry and status of the worker than on the worker's need to balance caregiving and employment (Presser et al., 2008).

In theory, part-time work and self-employment might allow adults to balance conflicting demands. But reality does not conform to the theory. In many nations (except the Netherlands, where half the workers are part time), part-time work is usually underpaid and offers no benefits. For these reasons, adults avoid it if possible. Instead, many adults prefer to work full time, with nonstandard schedules if they have young children, so one parent is always home. However, night work and other nonstandard work schedules correlate with personal, marital, and child-rearing difficulties (K. D. Davis et al., 2008; Joshi & Bogen, 2007; Perry-Jenkins et al., 2007).

Shift work creates a practical problem as well: Adult body rhythms do not allow a person to sleep deeply whenever they want to, day or night. Sleep-deprived adults are often cranky, impatient, and muddle-headed, especially with children. They are more often sick and in pain as well. For the optimal biosocial and psychosocial development of individuals and families, a regular schedule (even if it always includes odd hours) is better than an irregular one, and a steady job is better than one that involves intense overtime alternating with periods of no work (Presser, 2005). Obviously, developmentalists do not determine corporate policy.

Combining Intimacy and Generativity

To a great extent, job satisfaction depends on the particular job, the home situation, and the worker's ability to balance intimacy and generativity needs (Voydanoff, 2007). Chosen schedules (optional overtime, flexible hours) increase worker motivation, happiness, and health (Grzywacz et al., 2008; E. J. Hill et al., 2008). Although some employers consider the needs of developing persons as they schedule work, most do not (Breaugh & Frye, 2008). On their part, however, many families find ways to combine work and parenting.

When developmentalists look at the total picture of psychosocial development in adulthood, the scene is less discouraging than some specifics might imply. It is true that marriages are fewer, divorces more frequent, employment often stressful, and unemployment even worse. Diversity is increasingly apparent: In the United States, there are more couples who are not of the same ethnicity or religion, more same-sex couples, more cohabiting couples, more stepfamilies—and all of these entail additional stresses unknown to traditional couples of 50 years ago.

Parenthood is also more diverse, spread out over the years of the life span; about 40 percent of children are born to unmarried parents and about 15 percent have half-siblings because their parents also have children with other partners. Job changes are more frequent and coworkers more diverse; economic pressures mean some workers have too much work, others too little; most mothers as well as fathers are employed, forgoing leisure and wishing they had more time to spend with their children (Bianchi & Milkie, 2010; Cherlin, 2010).

Nonetheless, taking a broad view of psychosocial development of adults aged 25 to 65, it is hard to ignore encouraging evidence. Family members support one another across generations, with the older adults providing support for the younger adults, who, in turn, make the older adults proud. Flextime, telecommuting, non-standard schedules, and part-time work may not be the solutions to work–family tensions that some hoped they would be, but each of these allows some adults to balance their generativity needs in ways they could not do before. Partly because more mothers are employed, fathers spend far more time with their children than they did even a decade or two ago, and mothers do less housework, although their time spent with children has not diminished (Bianchi & Milkie, 2010).

Contrary to popular assumptions, the midlife crisis, the empty nest, and the sandwich generation are not common, and few unmarried mothers are alone: Half of them live with their children's father, and many of the others live with their own parents, who help them with child care (Smock & Greenland, 2010).

Overall, adults are confronted with many new challenges regarding intimacy and generativity, and some suffer because of it—but many cope quite well. We now turn to the final trio of chapters, on late adulthood: Again, the most pessimistic analysis of that stage of life is not in accord with the data.

SUMMING UP

Adults seek to be generative, which includes creativity, caregiving, and satisfying employment. Raising children is difficult but rewarding. Each stage of a child's development, and each type of biological and nonbiological parenthood, challenges adults to be generative. In addition to providing a livelihood, work has intrinsic rewards that are crucial from a developmental perspective. Work-related factors such as diversity of employees, frequent job changes, and nonstandard schedules are important influences on adult development.

SUMMARY

Continuity and Change, Again

1. The forty years of adulthood are characterized by many psychosocial challenges, with chronological age increasingly peripheral as a force of change. Adults become spouses, parents, employees, and even students primarily because of culture and circumstances, not age.

2. The midlife crisis is more myth than fact, more a cohort effect than a universal experience. Nonetheless, some individuals experience notable shifts, and many become more mature, as described by Erikson and Maslow.

3. The Big Five personality traits—openness, conscientiousness, extroversion, agreeableness, and neuroticism—are typically fairly stable in each individual over the decades of adulthood, as each person chooses a particular ecological niche. Culture and context affect everyone, with neuroticism most likely to be reduced with maturity.

4. Although chosen careers and partners typically reinforce existing personality traits, unexpected events (e.g., a major illness or financial windfall) can temporarily disrupt personality.

Intimacy

5. Intimacy is a universal human need, satisfied in diverse ways, with friends and family, romantic partners and consequential strangers. Each person has a social convoy of other people with whom he or she travels through life.

6. Friends are crucial for buffering stress, for sharing secrets, and for everyday companionship and guidance. This is true for both sexes.

7. Family members have linked lives, continuing to affect one another as they all grow older. They are less likely to live together than in earlier times and in other nations, but family members are often mutually supportive, emotionally and financially. Siblings typically become closer over the years of adulthood, and adult children and their parents continue to help one another in practical and emotional ways.

Committed Partners

8. Marriage typically occurs later than it did in early decades, but most adults still seek a partner (same sex or other sex) with whom to share life. Marital happiness often dips after the honeymoon period but improves over time, especially once children are grown.

9. Divorce is difficult for both partners as well as for their family members, not only immediately but also for years before and after the event. As divorce becomes more frequent, it may become less disruptive.

10. Remarriage is common, especially for men. This solves some of the problems (particularly financial and intimacy troubles) that are experienced by many divorced adults, but remarriage is complicated and may end in a second divorce.

Generativity

11. Adults seek to feel generative, achieving, successful, instrumental—all words used to describe a major psychosocial need. This need is met through creative work, caregiving, and employment.

12. Caring for partners, parents, children, and others is a major expression of generativity. Often one family member becomes the chief kinkeeper and caregiver, usually by choice.

13. Parenthood is a common expression of adult caregiving. Even wanted and planned biological children pose challenges to their parents; stepchildren, foster children, and adoptive children bring additional stresses. Adults usually consider this aspect of caregiving rewarding as well as challenging.

14. Many adults feel special concern for other adult members of their families. Caregiving is more likely to flow from the older generations to the younger ones, rather than vice versa. The "sandwich generation" metaphor is misleading.

15. Employment brings many rewards to adults, particularly intrinsic benefits such as pride and friendship. Changes in employment pattern—including job switches, shift work, and the diversity of fellow workers—can affect other aspects of adult development.

16. Combining work schedules, caregiving requirements, and intimacy needs is not easy, and consequences are mixed. Some adults benefit from the diversity of employment; others find that new patterns of work impair family well-being.

KEY TERMS

midlife crisis (p. 607)
Big Five (p. 608)
ecological niche (p. 609)
social convoy (p. 611)
consequential strangers (p. 612)

familism (p. 614)
fictive kin (p. 614)
empty nest (p. 617)
kinkeeper (p. 621)
sandwich generation (p. 624)

extrinsic rewards of work (p. 626)
intrinsic rewards of work (p. 626)

mentor (p. 628)
flextime (p. 630)
telecommuting (p. 630)

WHAT HAVE YOU LEARNED?

Continuity and Change, Again

1. What is the difference between the social clock and multiple clocks?

2. Why did people once believe that personality changed at midlife?

3. What personality changes occur in adulthood and why?

4. How does the ecological niche affect personality?

Intimacy

5. What are the differences between friends and consequential strangers?

6. How do people choose their friends?

7. What is the usual relationship between adult children and their parents?

8. What usually happens to sibling relationships over the course of adulthood?

9. What are the advantages and disadvantages of familism?

10. Why do people have fictive kin?

Committed Partners

11. How and why does marital happiness change from the wedding to old age?

12. What are the similarities and differences between same-sex and heterosexual partnerships?

13. What are the usual consequences of divorce?

14. What are the gender differences in remarriages and stepparenting?

Generativity

15. What are three different values regarding who should provide elder care for whom?

16. Why are work's extrinsic rewards more important for younger than older workers?

17. Why are developmentalists worried about the job losses in the economic downturn that began in 2007?

18. What innovations in work scheduling have helped families?

19. What innovations in work scheduling have hurt families?

20. What are the assets of older workers?

21. What are the advantages and disadvantages of greater ethnic diversity at work?

APPLICATIONS

1. Describe a relationship that you know of in which a middle-aged person and a younger adult learned from each other.

2. Did your parents' marital and employment status affect you? How would you have fared if they had chosen other marriage or work patterns?

3. Think about becoming a foster or adoptive parent yourself. What would you see as the personal benefits and costs?

4. Ask several people how their personalities have changed in the past decade. The research suggests that changes are usually minor. Is that what you found?

>>ONLINE CONNECTIONS

To accompany your textbook, you have access to a number of online resources, including quizzes for every chapter of the book, flashcards (in English and Spanish), critical thinking questions, and case studies. For access to any of these links, go to www.worthpublishers.com/bergerls8e. In addition to these free resources, you'll also find links to the podcasts, video clips, diagnostic quizzing with personalized study advice, and an ebook. Some of the videos and activities available online include:

- *Romantic Love and the Brain.* Explores neural and hormonal activity as the foundations of love and relationships and looks at the evolutionary benefit of pairing.

- *Caregivers Between Generations: What is the "Sandwich Generation"?* In this short video, two experts discuss the realities and stresses of caring for impaired elders.

Adulthood

BIOSOCIAL

Senescence As bodies age, internal as well as external organs show the effects of senescence. The brain slows down; skin becomes more wrinkled; the senses become less acute; lungs reduce capacity. Bodies change shape, with more fat in the middle and less strength in the muscles. There are many ways to measure health (mortality, morbidity, disability, vitality), but all depend on daily habits.

The Sexual-Reproductive System Sexual responsiveness and reproductive potential are reduced over the decades of adulthood. Women experience a dramatic drop in estrogen at menopause, which stops ovulation; men experience a more gradual decline in testosterone, which makes fatherhood less likely but not impossible in later adulthood. For both sexes, hormone replacement is an option, although most physicians are cautious about such use because of the side effects of adding hormones to the body.

COGNITIVE

What Is Intelligence? Researchers describe adult intelligence in many ways, noting that some intellectual abilities increase with age and others decline. Longitudinal research shows intelligence increasing over the years of adulthood, whereas cross-sectional research finds a decline. Over time, fluid intelligence declines and crystallized intelligence (especially vocabulary) improves. Practical intelligence, particularly social understanding, is increasingly needed through life's ups and downs.

Selective Gains and Losses Selective compensation with optimization is apparent in adulthood, as people become experts in areas of life that they choose to specialize in. This is apparent in many occupations, from surgeon to taxi driver. Brain connections as well as the knowledge base reflect a person's life experience. In general, people are more intuitive, automatic, strategic, and flexible when dealing with problems in their area of expertise than they are in other areas.

PSYCHOSOCIAL

Continuity and Change All the major theories of adult development note that people maintain personality traits yet show some change. For instance, people become more conscientious and less neurotic with age. The Big Five traits reflect culture and are strengthened by a person's chosen lifestyle and ecological niche.

Intimacy Adults depend on friends, family, and life partners. They usually find good friends and close partners (same sex or other sex), as well as have rewarding relationships with their adult children and their aging parents. Such rewarding social relationships do not always occur. Divorce and separation are common, although difficult for all concerned.

Generativity Caregiving is part of the joy as well as the obligation of adulthood. Many adults spend time and money on child rearing. Filial obligation is strong, with some adults caring for older family members. However, the sandwich generation concept is more myth than reality, and intergenerational support is usually mutual. Older generations usually provide financial and emotional support for younger generations. Employment is satisfying for many adults, although some trends, such as shift work and unemployment, harm optimal psychosocial development.

late adulthood

What emotions do you anticipate as you begin to read about late adulthood? Given the myths that abound, you might expect discomfort, depression, resignation, and sorrow. Expect another emotion: surprise. You will learn in Chapter 23 that thousands of centenarians are active, alert, and happy; in Chapter 24, that marked intellectual decline ("senility") is unusual; in Chapter 25, that relationships between older and younger generations are neither as close as some imagine nor as distant as others claim. Late adulthood continues earlier patterns rather than breaking from them. Instead of living in lonely isolation, most older adults remain social and independent.

This period of life, more than any other, is a magnet for misinformation and prejudice. Why? Think about that when the facts and research are unexpected.

CHAPTER

Late Adulthood: Biosocial Development

WHAT WILL YOU KNOW?

1. How could benevolent attitudes toward people of another group (the old, the young, people of another gender or ethnic group) be destructive of them?

2. Why is it a mistake for everyone to hope to "sleep like a baby"?

3. Does everyone who lives long enough get sick and feeble?

4. What is the quality of life for people who live to 100 or more?

I took Asa, my 1-year-old grandson, to the park yesterday. One mother warned me that the sandbox would soon be crowded because the day-care children were about to arrive. I asked for more information, and to my delight she told me details of curriculum, staffing, and tuition as if I were Asa's mother. Minutes later, I realized she probably was merely being polite because a girl, too young to be politely ageist, glanced at me and asked, "Is that your grandchild?"

I nodded.

"Where is the mother?" she asked.

Later that afternoon came the final blow. As I opened the gate for a middle-aged man, he said, "Thank you, young lady." That was benevolent ageism, and I realized that my pleasure at the first woman's words was a sign of my own prejudice.

Now we begin our study of the last phase of life, from age 65 or so until death. This chapter begins by exploring the prejudices that surround aging. Then we describe biosocial changes—in the senses, the vital organs, morbidity, and mortality. Underlying that is a crucial question: Why does aging occur? The answer might allow you to live to age 100 or beyond, joining the centenarians described at the end of the chapter.

First, a quiz to alert you to facts and prejudices. (Answers appear later in the chapter.)

1. In 2010, the proportion of the U.S. population over age 65 was about
   (a) 3 percent.   (d) 33 percent.
   (b) 13 percent.   (e) 50 percent.
   (c) 25 percent.

2. In 2010, the proportion of the world's population over age 65 was about
   (a) 2 percent.   (d) 20 percent.
   (b) 8 percent.   (e) 35 percent.
   (c) 12 percent.

3. Happiness in older people is
   (a) rare.
   (b) much less common than in younger adults.
   (c) at least as common as in younger adults.
   (d) apparent only among grandparents.
   (e) apparent only among those who have dementia.

Especially for People Who Guess on Quizzes On a multiple-choice quiz, it is better to guess than to leave an answer blank. People tend to choose *b* as a guess when they are not certain of the correct answer. Is this true for you? (see response, page 640)

639

4. Which senses become less acute in old age?
   (a) Sight and hearing
   (b) Taste and smell
   (c) Varied, as each sense improves in some people and declines in others
   (d) None if the person is healthy
   (e) All of them
5. The rate of automobile accidents per licensed driver over age 65 is
   (a) higher than for those under 65.
   (b) about the same as for those under age 65.
   (c) lower than for those under age 65.
   (d) unknown, because such statistics are not reported.
   (e) zero, because no one over age 65 drives.
6. What percent of U.S. residents over age 65 are in nursing homes or hospitals?
   (a) 4 percent   (d) 35 percent
   (b) 10 percent   (e) 50 percent
   (c) 25 percent
7. Compared with that of younger adults, the reaction time of older adults is
   (a) slower.   (d) slower for men, faster for women.
   (b) about the same.   (e) faster for men, slower for women.
   (c) faster.
8. After age 20, lung capacity (measured by how much air a person expels in one breath)
   (a) is reduced with age.
   (b) stays the same among nonsmokers.
   (c) increases among healthy adults.
   (d) is unrelated to age.
   (e) is unaffected by smoking.
9. Compared with those under age 65, an older adult's chance of being a victim of a violent crime is
   (a) lower.   (d) lower for men, higher for women.
   (b) about the same.   (e) higher for men, lower for women.
   (c) higher.
10. If a town passes a law that requires all teenage boys to be home by 10 P.M., that is
   (a) ageist, not sexist.   (d) a good way to stop crime.
   (b) sexist, not ageist.   (e) a good way to keep families together.
   (c) ageist and sexist.

[This quiz is adapted from a much larger one called *Facts on Aging* (Palmore, 1998).]

As you read this chapter, you will find the answers to these questions (on the following pages: 1, page 643; 2, page 643; 3, page 643; 4, page 646; 5, page 649; 6, page 645; 7, page 646; 8, page 647; 9, page 652; 10, page 641). Most people get at least half wrong, usually because prejudice—more negative than positive—clouds their judgment (Palmore et al., 2005).

>> Response for People Who Guess on Quizzes (from page 639) If you chose *b* as the answer to more than two of these quiz questions, you have made at least one wrong guess.

ageism A prejudice whereby people are categorized and judged solely on the basis of their chronological age.

>> Prejudice and Predictions

Prejudice about late adulthood is common among people of all ages, including children and older adults. It is called **ageism,** the idea that age determines who you are. Such stereotyping makes ageism "a social disease, much like racism and sexism . . . [causing] needless fear, waste, illness, and misery" (Palmore, 2005, p. 90).

Ageism can target people of any age. For example, curfew laws that require all teenagers to be off the streets by 10 P.M. are ageist. Ageism is not considered as harmful as racism or sexism—imagine the outcry if a curfew applied to all non-Whites or all teenage boys. The latter would be ageist and sexist (*Question 10*) and might disrupt families more than help them. But ageism may be equally destructive.

One reason why ageism is not recognized as harmful is that it sometimes seems benevolent ("young lady") (Bugental & Hehman, 2007). However, the effects of benevolent as well as hostile ageism are insidious, seeping into the older person's feelings of competence and undermining self-esteem. The resulting self-doubt allows anxiety, morbidity, and mortality to increase, and when it does, benevolent ageism might increase.

Believing the Stereotype

With racism or sexism, the targets of the prejudice learn to counter bias and alert others that a particular action is racist or sexist. However, when children believe an ageist idea, no one teaches them otherwise. When they become old, their lifetime prejudice is "extremely resistant to change," undercutting health and intellect (Golub & Langer, 2007, pp. 12–13). In one study, adults under age 50 were asked about the elderly. Thirty years later, 25 percent of the most ageist (e.g., those who believed that the old were absentminded) had had serious heart disease, as did only 13 percent of those with positive views of the elderly (Levy, 2009).

The Elderly's View of Ageism

Ageism becomes a self-fulfilling prophecy. Perhaps the worst part is that many older people themselves are ageist. Most people over age 70 think they are doing better than other people their age—who, they believe, have worse problems and are too self-absorbed (Cruikshank, 2009; Townsend et al., 2006). They refer to a "senior moment," not realizing the ageism inherent in that phrase, and when other people use ageist phrases (such as "dirty old man" or "second childhood") or offer patronizing compliments (such as "spry" or "having all her marbles"), they usually ignore the insult.

Stereotype threat (discussed in Chapter 18) can be as debilitating for the aged as for other groups (Chasteen et al., 2005). If the elderly fear they are losing their minds because they believe that old age inevitably brings dementia, that fear itself may undermine their cognitive competence (Hess et al., 2009).

One study measured perceived discrimination in older African and European Americans in Chicago (L. L. Barnes et al., 2008). The researchers were surprised: White Americans seemed more negatively affected if they felt ageist discrimination than Black Americans did. Perhaps people who had not experienced discrimination when they were younger had more trouble coping with it when they were old. In this study, the ultimate negative consequence was mortality: European Americans (but not African Americans) who reported more ageism were also more likely to die within the next five years.

This does not mean all is well with older African Americans: Another study found that their self-esteem fell more sharply with age than did that of European Americans (Shaw et al., 2010). One explanation that applies to both studies is that external prejudice may have less impact when ageism is already internalized.

The effect of internalized ageism was apparent in a second study, already a classic (Levy & Langer, 1994). This one did not include African Americans. Instead it involved two groups that might be less exposed to ageism: residents of China, where the old are traditionally venerated, and deaf people in North America, whose disability prevented them from hearing ageist talk. A third group was also included: North Americans with normal hearing, who presumably were exposed to whatever comments other people or the media had expressed.

In each of these three groups, half of the participants were young and half were old. Memory tests were administered to everyone, six clusters in total. In all three groups (Chinese, deaf, normal), the elders scored lower than their younger counterparts. This was expected, since older adults generally score lower on laboratory tests of memory than younger adults do.

The purpose of this study, however, was not to replicate earlier research on memory loss with age but to see if memory differences between younger and older adults would be affected by ageism. The answer was yes. The gap in scores between younger and older hearing North Americans (presumably those most exposed to ageism) was twice as wide as the gap between older and younger deaf North Americans, and it was five times wider than the gap among the Chinese. Apparently, ageism undercut the ability of the elders, a conclusion that has been found in numerous studies since then (Levy, 2009).

Ageism Leading to Illness

Ageism can also be harmful in everyday life. It may prevent depressed elderly people from seeking help. Could that be why elderly European American men have the highest suicide rate of any age, gender, or ethnic group? It may lead others to treat the elderly in ways that undermine their vitality. Health professionals are less aggressive in treating disease in older patients, researchers testing new prescription drugs enroll few older adults (who are the most likely ones to use those drugs), and caregivers diminish the independence of the aged by helping them too much (Cruikshank, 2009; Herrera et al., 2010).

The downward spiral caused by the interaction of aging and ageism is apparent in exercise. An ageist culture does not expect the elderly to move vigorously and often, which explains why team sports are organized for the young; why traditional dancing assumes a balanced sex ratio; and why many yoga, aerobic, and other classes are paced for younger adults. The elderly themselves exercise less, and their inaction increases stiffness; reduces range of motion; and slows down circulation, digestion, the brain, and so on. Balance is diminished, necessitating a slower gait and perhaps a walker or cane (Newell et al., 2006).

None of the normal physiological changes require older adults to end all exercise, although some of the specific activities may change (more walking, less sprinting). Health is protected by an hour of movement a day, but the combined ageism of the culture and the internalized ageism of the elderly result in inaction, then stagnation, and then poor health. Indeed, immobility is an ominous sign; the elder who does not move is at higher risk of virtually every illness, symptom, and sign of aging. That increasing frailty, of course, increases ageism in the person as well as in everyone else.

JUAN HERRERO / EPA / CORBIS

From the Neck Down If you could see only his body, would you guess that pole-vaulter Pierre Darrot is over age 80?

elderspeak A condescending way of speaking to older adults that resembles baby talk, with simple and short sentences, exaggerated emphasis, repetition, and a slower rate and a higher pitch than used in normal speech.

Elderspeak

One very specific aspect of ageism is common among many people who think they are compassionate toward the old. People tend to infantilize the elderly, acting as if they are children ("so cute," "second childhood"), not adults (Albert & Freedman, 2010). One example is **elderspeak.** Like baby talk, elderspeak uses simple and short sentences, exaggerated emphasis, slower speech, higher and louder pitch, and frequent repetition. Elderspeak is especially patronizing when people call an

older person "honey" or "dear" or use a nickname instead of a surname ("Billy" instead of "Mr. White").

Ironically, some features of elderspeak actually reduce comprehension (Kemper & Harden, 1999). For instance, elderspeak may use higher frequencies, as is common in baby talk, despite the reality that lower pitch is more audible for the elderly. Similarly, stretching out words makes comprehension worse, and shouting causes stress, reducing attention. Elderspeak is often used by service providers (such as social workers and nurses) who know only the person's age, not the person (Williams et al., 2009).

Especially for Young Adults Should you always speak louder and slower when talking to a senior citizen? (see response, page 644)

Gerontology and Geriatrics

Ageism is increasingly recognized as a prejudice, partly because of **gerontology,** the multidisciplinary study of old age. The people studied by gerontologists are typically community-dwelling adults (not in nursing homes or other institutions). Every study finds that most of those living in the community are healthy, active, and at least as happy and satisfied with their lives as younger adults (e.g., Jones & Peskin, 2010) (*Question 3*).

Gerontologists, benefiting from the life-span perspective as well as the data they collect, conclude that "aging is a process socially constructed to be a problem" (Cruikshank, 2009, p. 8). For example, older people walk more slowly than younger ones; this is a process that maintains balance and poses no problems—unless someone else is in a hurry or a red light is timed for faster-moving pedestrians.

Gerontology reaches conclusions quite different from those of **geriatrics,** the traditional medical specialty devoted to aging. Since geriatric physicians and nurses see hundreds of patients who are ill and infirm, they equate aging and illness; that is their experience. One geriatrician described "the patient seen in most geriatric practices, somewhat frail, with multiple medical conditions and taking multiple medications, possibly with some cognitive, functional, or mood impairment" (Leipzig, 2003, p. 4). There are millions of elderly patients like that, but there are ten times more elderly people who are not frail—and who see doctors occasionally for checkups, not frequently for impairments.

gerontology The multidisciplinary study of old age.

geriatrics The medical specialty devoted to aging.

demographic shift A shift in the proportions of the populations of various ages.

centenarian A person who has lived 100 years or more.

The Demographic Shift

Demography is the science that describes populations, including specific groups such as those of a particular age, gender, or region. Demographers describe a **demographic shift** in the proportions of the population of various ages. Once there were 20 times more children than older people. No longer.

The World's Aging Population

The United Nations estimates that nearly 8 percent of the world's population in 2010 was over age 65, compared with only 2 percent a century ago (*Question 2*)—and this number might double by the year 2050. Already 13 percent of the population in Canada, Australia, and the United States (*Question 1*) is age 65 or older, as is 16 percent in Great Britain, 19 percent in Italy, and 20 percent in Japan.

Every nation (except Japan) still has more people under age 16 than over age 64, and the world totals show four times as many children as elders. However, the fastest-growing age group is **centenarians,** people over age 100. Their numbers

Respect for the Aged You might show respect for an older woman by offering her a seat on the bus. By contrast, part of Respect for the Aged Day in Tokyo is an exercise class, as shown here. Japan has more elderly people than any other nation—do you think that's because of its cultural attitudes regarding elders and exercise or have the millions of elderly people worldwide changed age-old assumptions?

AP PHOTO / KOJI SASAHARA

>> **Response for Young Adults** (from page 643) No. Some seniors hear well, and they would resent it.

FIGURE 23.1

The Baby Boom Population Bulge Unlike earlier times, when each generation was slightly smaller than the one that followed, each cohort today has a unique position, determined by the reproductive patterns of the preceding generation and by the medical advances developed during their own lifetime. As a result, the baby boomers, born between 1947 and 1964, represent a huge bulge in the U.S. population. There are more people in their 50s than in their 40s.

are small, far less than 1 percent in any nation (0.03 percent in the United States in 2008, or 92,000 individuals). Given current survival rates, the United States may have twice that many centenarians by 2020, and the world may have 3.2 million by the year 2050—still far less than 1 percent.

Demographers often depict a given population as a series of stacked bars, one bar for each age cohort, with the bottom bar representing the youngest cohort and the top bar representing the oldest cohort (see Figure 23.1). Historically, the result is a shape called a *demographic pyramid*. Like a wedding cake, this diagram is widest at the base, and each higher level is narrower than the one beneath it for three reasons:

1. More children were born than the replacement rate of one per adult, so each new cohort was bigger than the previous one.
2. Before widespread sanitation and immunization, many babies died before age 5.
3. If people reached middle age and then had cancer or heart attacks, they rarely survived. Today, most people recover from those diseases if medical treatment catches them early. As a result of the fatality of these diseases in former years, each adult cohort was about 20 percent smaller than the following one.

Sometimes unusual world events caused a deviation from this wedding-cake pattern. For example, the Great Depression and World War II reduced births, and then postwar prosperity as well as the return of soldiers caused a baby boom between 1946 and 1964—just when the survival rate of young children increased. That increase in the birth rate led many demographers to fear that a worldwide population explosion would result in mass starvation and only a few feet of living space per person (Ehrlich, 1968).

That fear has been proven false. Birth rates have fallen worldwide and a "green revolution" has doubled the world's food supply. Some experts now warn of a new and very different population problem: not enough babies (Balter, 2006). The world

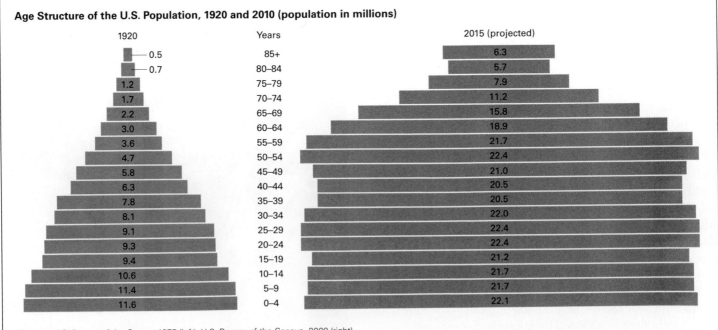

Age Structure of the U.S. Population, 1920 and 2010 (population in millions)

1920	Years	2015 (projected)
0.5	85+	6.3
0.7	80–84	5.7
1.2	75–79	7.9
1.7	70–74	11.2
2.2	65–69	15.8
3.0	60–64	18.9
3.6	55–59	21.7
4.7	50–54	22.4
5.8	45–49	21.0
6.3	40–44	20.5
7.8	35–39	20.5
8.1	30–34	22.0
9.1	25–29	22.4
9.3	20–24	22.4
9.4	15–19	21.2
10.6	10–14	21.7
11.4	5–9	21.7
11.6	0–4	22.1

Sources: U.S. Bureau of the Census, 1975 (left); U.S. Bureau of the Census, 2009 (right).

is experiencing a major demographic transition—fewer babies and more elders—that is affecting world health and politics (Albert & Freedman, 2010). As the birth rate declines and premature death becomes uncommon, countries' demographic stacks become a rectangle, not a pyramid, as is already the case in Germany, Italy, and Japan.

Unfortunately, the data are sometimes reported in racist or ageist ways designed to frighten people. If you got *Question 1* wrong, you can blame the press. For instance, if you read that people aged 90 and over are the fastest-growing age group and that their numbers in the United States in 2015 will be 120 percent of what they were in 2010, stop and think. You need to disentangle the statistics (the data are probably accurate, see the Research Design) to determine that the actual numbers are about 2.1 million in 2010 and 2.5 million in 2015. An increase of about 120 percent therefore means that the 90-and-older group's share of the total population is expected to rise from 0.7 percent to 0.8 percent—which means that in 2015, less than 1 percent of U.S. residents will be over age 90. That is certainly not overwhelming.

Those who worry about the demographic shift sometimes assume that everyone over age 65 must be supported by the young. Almost daily, news reports raise the specter of the aging baby boomers who will retire and create a crushing burden for the remaining able-bodied adults. That specter is based on false premises, for two reasons.

First, with technology, fewer workers are needed to provide food, shelter, and other goods that the rest of the population requires. In the United States two centuries ago, 90 percent of the people were farmers, harvesting barely enough to feed themselves, their large families, and the other 10 percent of the population. Societies needed everyone to work, and the infirm elderly were a burden. Now only about 1 percent of the U.S. labor force is in agriculture, yet the United States has more than enough food, shelter, and basic goods for everyone. In fact, the United States exports more food than it imports (U.S. Bureau of the Census, 2009), and unemployment is a more serious social problem than overwork.

Second, the assumption that people over age 65 need care is ageist. Most elders are fiercely independent, more likely to be caregivers than care receivers. Only 10 percent of those over age 65 are dependent on other people for basic care. In the United States, less than half of those (about 4 percent of the total number of elders, less than 1 percent of the total population) are in nursing homes or hospitals (*Question 6*). (Rates are even lower worldwide.)

Old, Older, and Oldest

One reason people overestimate the population in nursing homes is that they notice only the frail elderly, not the rest. Most people over age 65 function as well as they always did, living with their partner or alone, not with a younger family member or in an institution. As described in Chapter 22, financial and emotional support are more likely to flow down the generational ladder than up, at least until adults are age 85. Gerontologists distinguish among the *young-old*, the *old-old*, and the *oldest-old*. Only the oldest-old are dependent.

▶ Research Design

Scientists: Lars B. Johanson and hundreds of others.

Publication: *Statistical Abstract of the United States* (2010 and previous years).

Participants: Every 10 years, in the national census, the entire U.S. population is surveyed, and every year smaller samples are surveyed. The findings are analyzed, collated, and printed annually in the *Statistical Abstract of the United States*. Efforts are made to include the homeless, the hospitalized, and the undocumented.

Design: Interviewers are trained and are usually of the same culture and language background as the respondents. By law, answers are confidential and are safeguarded from inquiries by any government authority. Other national and international agencies also provide data.

Results: Social scientists study these statistics and comparable ones from other national and international groups, such as the United Nations. Most results are what researchers expect, but recent surprises in the United States include rising rates of low-birthweight infants, falling rates of teen pregnancy, more centenarians, and fewer serious crimes.

Major conclusions: Conclusions from the data in the *Statistical Abstract* are too many to list; they are presented throughout this text, in Appendix A, and in many other sources. Surprises are often found. For instance, which nation has most single parents? The United States has the highest rate (29 percent) of any developed nation, but many other nations are experiencing faster growth. In Ireland, single parenthood increased more than 300 percent in the past 25 years, while U.S. growth was only 50 percent.

Comment: The main problems are omissions: questions not asked, data not collected, statistics not included, and subgroups not described. Regarding the elderly, those age 65 to 75, 75 to 85, and 85 and over are not reported by income or ethnicity. Furthermore, ethnic backgrounds are not well distinguished: Jamaicans, Africans, and African Americans are all considered Black; those of European descent (including Finns, Turks, and Irish) are all considered White; Navajos and Eskimos are counted together; Pacific Islanders comprise a separate group, but all Asians are placed in one category, despite the many distinctions between, say, Pakistanis and Japanese.

Latinos (including those who speak no Spanish) are designated "Hispanic, may be of any race," and then another question requires them to specify a race (Latino is not an option; most choose White, some Black, and a few American Indian). Despite such problems, social scientists rely on these data because the *Statistical Abstract* is more comprehensive and accurate than many other sources.

An Old Lady? Tina Turner performed for thousands of adoring fans on her 50th Anniversary Tour across North America and western and eastern Europe. Here she is in Prague, at age 68.

The **young-old** make up the largest group of older adults. They are healthy, active, financially secure, and independent. Most of them expect that their future will be at least as good as the present, probably better (Fisher, 2010). The **old-old** suffer from some reductions in physical or mental ability or in social support, although they can still care for themselves and are proud of that. The **oldest-old** (about 10 percent of the aged) are infirm, at risk for illness and injury. In general, the young-old are age 60 to 75 and the oldest-old are over age 85, but age does not determine dependency; the middle group (the old-old) are not necessarily between ages 75 and 85—some are 100, others only 60.

Some gerontologists prefer terms that do not include the word *old*—namely, *optimal aging, usual aging,* and *impaired* or *pathological aging,* with about one-third of the population optimal, most people aging in the usual way, and only about 10 percent impaired (Depp & Jeste, 2009). (Specific definitions, and hence the proportions, vary, but every study agrees that the impaired are a minority.) The term *successful aging* is also used (Rowe & Kahn, 1998), signifying extensive social interaction and activity.

The Same Situation, Many Miles Apart: Keep Smiling Good humor seems to be a cause of longevity, and vice versa. This is true for both sexes, including the British men on Founders' Day *(left)*, and the German women on an ordinary sunny afternoon *(right)*.

young-old Healthy, vigorous, financially secure older adults (generally, those aged 60 to 75) who are well integrated into the lives of their families and communities.

old-old Older adults (generally, those over age 75) who suffer from physical, mental, or social deficits.

oldest-old Elderly adults (generally, those over age 85) who are dependent on others for almost everything, requiring supportive services such as nursing homes and hospital stays.

SUMMING UP

Ageism is a common but destructive prejudice. Ageism is evident in the patronizing tones of elderspeak as well as in the frightening predictions concerning the growing numbers of older people. Although the proportion of people who are over age 65 is increasing (from the current 13 percent in the United States and 8 percent worldwide), most elders are self-sufficient and independent. Most elderly people are young-old, likely to support younger generations. Only the oldest-old (perhaps 10 percent of those over age 65) are dependent on care by other people, whether by relatives or professionals. ■

>> Aging and Disease

As discussed in Chapters 17 and 20, reaction time slows with each passing decade after age 20 (*Question 7*); all the senses become less acute (*Question 4*); organ reserves are diminished; homeostasis takes longer; and skin, hair, and body shape show unmistakable signs of senescence. Underlying superficial signs are the invisible changes that take place in the internal organs. Many gerontologists believe that slowing the rate of senescence would decrease the incidence of many diseases; thus, they advocate less attention to wrinkle cream and hair thickening, less to specific diseases such as cancer or stroke, and more to the aging processes overall (Butler et al., 2008). If aging were slower, then the rate of every specific disease or debilitating condition would be reduced as well.

Primary and Secondary Aging

Gerontologists distinguish between **primary aging,** universal changes that occur with the passage of time, and **secondary aging,** the consequences of particular diseases, chosen health habits, and controllable environmental conditions. One explains:

> Primary aging is defined as the universal changes occurring with age that are not caused by diseases or environmental influences. Secondary aging is defined as changes involving interactions of primary aging processes with environmental influences and disease processes.
>
> [Masoro, 2006, p. 46]

primary aging The universal and irreversible physical changes that occur to all living creatures as they grow older.

secondary aging The specific physical illnesses or conditions that become more common with aging but are caused by health habits, genes, and other influences that vary from person to person.

High Blood Pressure and Cardiovascular Disease

As you might imagine, the distinction between primary and secondary aging is not clear-cut. For example, the leading cause of death for both men and women is **cardiovascular disease,** which is disease that involves the heart (*cardio*) and circulatory system (*vascular*). Cardiovascular disease is secondary aging because it is not universal and is more risk-related than age-related (Supiano, 2006).

cardiovascular disease Disease that involves the heart and the circulatory system.

For example, the Cardiovascular Health Study began with more than 5,000 people over age 65 in the United States who had healthy hearts. After six years, some had developed heart disease, but that onset did not correlate with age as much as with diabetes, smoking, abdominal fat, blood pressure, exercise, and cholesterol (Fried et al., 1998). Since most people in that study had healthy hearts after six years of aging, heart disease appears to be a manifestation of secondary aging. But that's too simple because high blood pressure (also called *hypertension*) is affected not only by lifestyle (diet, exercise, weight) but also by genes and age. Almost everyone develops hypertension if he or she lives long enough, and then it becomes more primary than secondary aging.

Thus, hypertension is age-related, and cardiovascular disease is hypertension-related, so it is misleading to conclude that hypertension is a risk factor for cardiovascular disease but that age is not. Indeed, primary aging makes every bodily system slower and less efficient and thus makes every disease more likely (Masoro, 2006). The heart pumps more slowly and the vascular network is less flexible, so blood pressure rises and increases the risk of stroke and heart attack. The lungs take in and expel less air with each breath (*Question 8*), reducing the level of oxygen in the blood and making chronic obstructive pulmonary disease more common. The digestive system slows, becoming less able to absorb nutrients and expel toxins. The kidneys become less efficient at regulating levels of water, potassium, and other substances, a situation that is particularly problematic if the older adult drinks less to reduce incontinence—which itself can be caused by an aging renal/urinary system.

Furthermore, recuperation is slower in the old, and reduced organ reserve makes the elderly more vulnerable if illness or an accident occurs (see Figure 23.2) (Arking, 2006). Young adults who contract pneumonia recover in a

FIGURE 23.2

Leading Causes of Death Among the Elderly This chart shows approximate ratios between the death rates for Americans over and under 65. Although older adults do not have more accidents or flu than younger adults, if an elderly person's organs have lost their reserve capacity, an accident may cause heart failure, and the flu may lead to pneumonia.

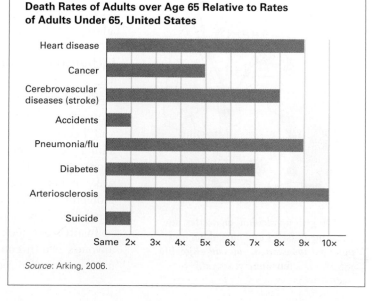

Death Rates of Adults over Age 65 Relative to Rates of Adults Under 65, United States

Source: Arking, 2006.

few weeks, but pneumonia can cause death if a person's organs are inefficient. One in every five older people hospitalized for pneumonia dies of it (O'Meara et al., 2005). In another example, because of senescence, surgery and drugs that help the young may create problems in the old (Herrera et al., 2010).

For instance, drug treatment is indicated when an adult's systolic blood pressure is above 140, but not when that person is older than 80. Mild hypertension may be protective in the oldest-old, since blood pressure that is too low is a risk factor for death; thus, a person whose blood pressure is slightly elevated could withstand a dip in pressure without disaster. However, when blood pressure is above 160, even 80-year-olds probably benefit from medication to reduce it (Beckett et al., 2008).

Diseases of the Elderly

The distinction between primary and secondary aging highlights an important fact: Most elderly people, even the oldest-old, do not have any particular disease. Less than half have cardiovascular disease, less than half have diabetes, less than half have dementia, and nobody dies merely because of old age. But almost every oldest-old person has at least one disease (which may be one of these serious ones) and many have several; age is a factor in all of them.

Some observers say that the rate of disease is increasing; others disagree (Albert & Freedman, 2010). There is no simple answer to this dispute because data vary, depending on several factors:

1. The medical cutoff (e.g., high systolic blood pressure was traditionally defined as having a reading above 160, but now it is above 140)
2. Detection (e.g., diabetes is spotted earlier)
3. The population (some groups are healthier)
4. Definitions

Regarding this last item, one study defined disease as any condition that required ongoing medical attention or interfered with daily life for at least a year. By that definition, 84 percent of U.S. residents over age 65 had at least one disease and 62 percent had two or more (Anderson & Horvath, 2004).

Selective Optimization with Compensation

Both primary and secondary aging undermine quality of life. However, if people respond with *selective optimization with compensation* (discussed in Chapter 21), they choose projects and activities (*selecting*) that they can do well (*optimizing*), thus adjusting (*compensation*) to disease, avoiding disability and maintaining vitality.

Individual Compensation: Sleep

The need for selective optimization with compensation is illustrated by sleep patterns. Older adults spend more time in bed, take longer to fall asleep, wake up more often (about 10 times per night), feel drowsy in the daytime more frequently, and, because of all this, are more distressed by their sleep patterns than younger adults are (Ayalon & Ancoli-Israel, 2009). The day–night circadian rhythm is less pronounced in the elderly than in the young, which means that many older people wake up before dawn and nap in the daytime. Some experts find that "sleep deficit problems are widespread in the elderly, adversely affect[ing] memory, performance capabilities, and general quality of life" (Dunlap et al., 2004, p. 363).

Insufficient deep sleep is particularly likely for smokers and for older men, but anyone's health could be affected, with depression and heart disease being the most common ailments that result from, or accompany, insomnia. One medical

"If you give up alcohol, cigarettes, sex, red meat, cakes and chocolate, and don't get too excited, you can enjoy life for a few more years yet."

CARTOONSTOCK.COM

response is to prescribe narcotics (Glass et al., 2005). However, the usual dose for a younger adult can overwhelm an older person, causing very heavy sleep and impaired wakefulness, with confusion, nausea, depression, and unsteadiness.

A self-administered drug chosen by some elderly insomniacs is alcohol—which also creates rebound symptoms. Many doctors advise people with insomnia to avoid all drugs, including caffeine. Others prescribe melatonin, a hormone naturally produced by the body that aids the circadian rhythm (Luthringer et al., 2009).

Optimization means making good use of sleep time. Evidence suggests that people with insomnia should restrict time in bed (not reading or watching television there), avoid naps, and reduce the amount of time they stay in bed after they wake up. These measures are all selective compensation, and they often induce bodies and brains to make good use of the limited sleep time.

Some sleep problems with age are connected to illness, and individualized medical help is needed. Often, however, the solution is cognitive, not medical. The elderly need to realize that sleep patterns change with age (McCurry et al., 2007; Sivertsen et al., 2006). (See Figure 23.3.) It is normal for an older person to awaken several times a night to urinate, to move the legs, to adjust the blankets. With age, the brain's electrical activity is reduced, which means less deep sleep, more half-awake time, and shorter dreams (Ayalon & Ancoli-Israel, 2009; Wise, 2006). If older adults realize all this, they may get up at dawn, untroubled by a short night. Not everyone should "sleep like a baby."

Social Compensation: Driving

Selective optimization with compensation is possible for families and societies, too. One example is driving. The elderly themselves compensate: They drive more slowly, many do not drive at night or when it is raining, and some licensed drivers have quit driving. As a result, elderly drivers have fewer accidents than do younger adults (see Figure 23.4) (*Question 5*), even though their sign-reading takes longer, head-turning is reduced, reaction time is slower, and night vision is worse. (When accidents are calculated per distance driven, not per licensed driver, then auto accidents are shown by a U-shaped curve: high among teenagers, low in middle age, then high again.)

But although many elderly drivers compensate, few societies do. If a crash occurs, people blame the driver but not the family, the context, or the laws (Satariano, 2006). The ageist stereotype is that either all older adults can drive or that none can. Most jurisdictions renew driver's licenses automatically, without retesting anyone (old or young). Retesting is especially needed to check peripheral vision because being able to see a wide range of movements aids in avoiding accidents (Johnson & Wilkinson, 2010; Wood, 2002). Even those places that

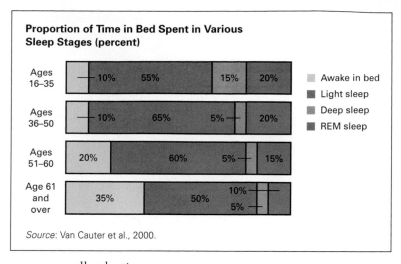

Proportion of Time in Bed Spent in Various Sleep Stages (percent)

Source: Van Cauter et al., 2000.

FIGURE 23.3

Don't Just Lie There One of the most common complaints of the elderly is that they spend too much time in bed but not sleeping. The solution is to get up and do something, not wait for sleep to come.

FIGURE 23.4

Too Slow? Teenage drivers are impatient with older drivers, yet the data suggest that driving more slowly also means driving more safely. In their defense, the accident rate of the youngest—five times that of the oldest—includes all accidents, even those caused by unlicensed drivers.

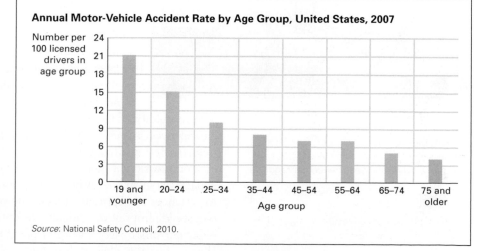

Annual Motor-Vehicle Accident Rate by Age Group, United States, 2007

Source: National Safety Council, 2010.

retest vision rarely test this important aspect, instead simply testing ability to read a sign straight ahead.

Beyond retesting, there is much else that societies can do. Larger-print signs with appropriate background before intersections, mirrors that replace the need to turn the neck 90 degrees, illuminated side streets and driveways, nonglaring headlights and hazard flashes, and warnings of ice or fog ahead would reduce accidents for everyone—especially the aged. Well-designed cars, roads, signs, lights, tests, laws, and law enforcement would allow selective optimization, with competent elderly drivers maintaining their independence and dangerous drivers (of all ages) staying off the road. Doctors, families, and the elderly themselves would not have to wait until an accident to know when someone else should take the wheel.

Compression of Morbidity

Unlike childhood diseases that can be prevented by vaccination, most adult diseases are impossible to prevent with a simple medical event. Indeed, if the goal is prevention, decades are needed. Many public health professionals believe that the first 50 years of life are crucial for the last 50 years and thus "the target of public health and aging efforts is not just the older adults of today but the children and adults who are the future elders" (Albert & Freedman, 2010, pp. 31–32).

Efforts in late adulthood may not stop illness completely but may postpone the onset of illness or limit its impact, reducing the duration of sickness, disability, and pain. This is **compression of morbidity,** a shortening of the time of illness before death.

compression of morbidity A shortening of the time a person spends ill or infirm, accomplished by postponing illness.

There is good news here: Morbidity and disability have both been compressed among the aged in recent years. Many of the old have been diagnosed with cancer, diabetes, or problems of the cardiovascular system, but most continue to be independent (Hamerman, 2007). Specific statistics reinforce this point: Between 1984 and 2004, the proportion of U.S. elderly who had difficulty doing housework or shopping declined from 16 to 12 percent, and the proportion who were more seriously disabled declined from 10 to 7 percent (Manton et al., 2006).

The gerontologist who first defined compression of morbidity provided the following example (see Figure 23.5). Imagine a pair of monozygotic twins who are exposed to the same pathogens, but one "smokes like a chimney, is fat, doesn't exercise, and has a poor diet," while the other has "fairly good health habits" (Fries, 1994, p. 314). Both get pneumonia at about age 25 (environmental exposure), and both recover quickly because their organ reserves and immune systems have barely begun to age. Both are genetically predisposed to the same illnesses—emphysema, heart attack, stroke, and lung cancer.

Beginning in middle age, one twin is sick with several serious illnesses and is often short of breath, but his brother is protected. The morbidity of the healthy twin is so delayed that his genetic vulnerability to cancer never appears. He has only a few compressed weeks of cardiovascular illness after a long, healthy life.

Reducing Risk The woman at left has some lifestyle factors, especially her excessive weight, that increase her risk of illness. On the plus side, however, she evidently has a cheerful attitude and sees her doctor regularly.

Compression of morbidity is a social and psychological blessing as well as a personal, biological one. A healthier person remains alert and active—in other words, experiences the optimal aging of the young-old person, not the impaired life of the oldest-old. Improved medical prevention, diagnosis, and treatment allow today's older persons to live with less pain, more mobility, better vision, stronger teeth, sharper hearing, clearer thinking, and enhanced vitality.

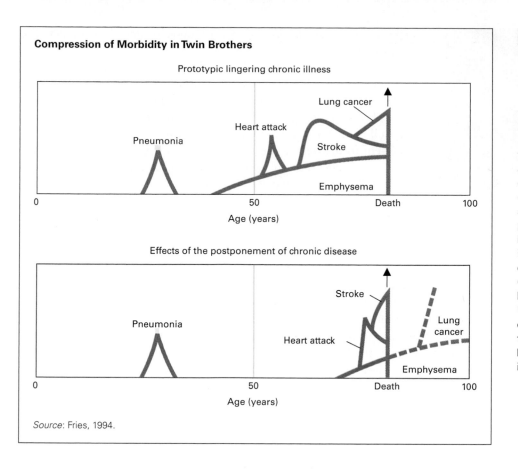

Compression of Morbidity in Twin Brothers

Prototypic lingering chronic illness

Pneumonia

Heart attack

Lung cancer

Stroke

Emphysema

0 50 Death 100

Age (years)

Effects of the postponement of chronic disease

Pneumonia

Stroke

Heart attack

Lung cancer

Emphysema

0 50 Death 100

Age (years)

Source: Fries, 1994.

FIGURE 23.5

Primary and Secondary Aging The interplay of primary and secondary aging is shown in this diagram of the illness and death of a hypothetical pair of monozygotic twins. Both are equally subject to certain illnesses—so both experience a bout of pneumonia at about age 25. Both also carry the same genetic clock, so they both die at age 80. However, genetic vulnerabilities to circulatory, heart, and lung problems affect each quite differently. The nonexercising smoker (*top*) suffers from an extended period of morbidity, as his various illnesses become manifest when his organ reserve is depleted, beginning at about age 45. By contrast, the healthy lifestyle of his twin (*bottom*) keeps disability and disease at bay until primary aging is well advanced. Indeed, he dies years before the emergence of lung cancer—which had been developing throughout late adulthood but was slowed by the strength of his organ reserve and immune system.

The Effects of Falling

With age, the bones become more porous, losing calcium and strength. This is a gradual process, more evident in women than in men. When this process is far advanced, it leads to a condition called *osteoporosis* (fragile bones); a person with osteoporosis can break a wrist or hip from a tumble that would have merely bruised a younger person.

A fall in late adulthood that causes a broken hip may also ultimately require hip replacement, hospitalization, and immobility—which may in turn cause infections, stresses, illnesses, and even death. Osteoporosis results from both primary and secondary aging because it is caused not only by aging but also by too much smoking and alcohol and too little calcium and weight-bearing exercise.

However, the most common liability elders experience from falling is fear. A prospective, longitudinal study of Dutch elders (Stel et al., 2004) found that one-third of those who fell became fearful and reduced their activity, thus causing all their organs to become less efficient. Ironically, only 6 percent of the falls resulted in serious injury, but the 94 percent with less serious injuries were as likely as the seriously injured 6 percent to reduce activity and thereby become sicker.

Exercise is another example of the need for selective compensation with optimization because those who become unsteady need to strengthen their muscles, aiding their cardiovascular, respiratory, and digestive bodily systems as well as their balance. Weight lifting is more likely to optimize the health of the old than the young because "strength training has the greatest impact on the most debilitated subjects" (Rice & Cunningham, 2002, p. 138). Walking may need to replace running, and care needs to be taken to make sure falling will not occur (some metal "walkers" are very stable), but exercise protects health at any age. Indeed,

Moving Along Her stiffening joints have made a walker necessary, but this elderly woman in Gujarat, India, is maintaining her mobility by walking every day.

AGE FOTOSTOCK / SUPERSTOCK

His Daily Bread An older man rides his bicycle home in Fecamp, France, after buying a loaf of fresh bread.

weight-bearing exercise slows down osteoporosis and thus protects the bones should a fall occur.

Overall, one of the best indicators of a person's physical and psychological health is mobility, so fear of falling should be confronted and eliminated, with special equipment, shoes, canes, and so on if needed. Those who move around are healthier and are more likely to maintain their well-being for years to come. Yet ageism, younger adults, and society seem to discourage the elderly from leaving home. For example, whenever an older person is robbed, raped, or assaulted, sensational news headlines make the elderly afraid and the young warn them not to venture outside.

In fact, however, the aged are far less likely to be victims of street crime than are younger adults (see Figure 23.6) (*Question 9*). Advertisements induce younger relatives to buy locks and medical-alert devices for their older relatives, feeling solicitous as they do so. It would be much better to go walking or biking with them.

Lest you think that bikes are only for children, an extensive study of five European nations (Germany, Italy, Finland, Hungary, the Netherlands) found that 15 percent of Europeans *over age* 75 ride their bicycles every day (Tacken & van Lamoen, 2005). In the United States, however, far fewer of the elderly ride bikes, perhaps because few bike paths are available and most bikes are designed for speed, not stability. Laws requiring bike helmets usually apply only to children—another example of ageism.

The Senses

For many of the elderly, the most troubling part of senescence is the loss of sensory ability. Much of social interaction depends on quick and accurate sensory responses, yet all the senses become slower and less sharp with each decade (Meisami et al., 2007) (*Question 4*). This is true for touch (particularly in the fingers), taste (particularly for sour and bitter), smell, and even pain, as well as for the more critical senses of sight and hearing. Only 10 percent of people of either sex over age 65 see well without glasses; by age 90, the average man is almost deaf, as are about half of the women (Aldwin & Gilmer, 2003). As with many of the other effects of senescence, an active effort to compress—not accept—and compensate is needed.

Corrective lenses, brighter lights, contrasting colors (black print on white paper, not blue on green), and sometimes magnifying glasses help most of the elderly read, recognize people, see where they are walking, and so on. For those with severe vision problems such as cataracts, glaucoma, and macular degeneration, early medical diagnosis and treatment can delay or even prevent blindness (see Table 23.1).

Medical care is less effective for presbycusis (age-related hearing loss) than for the specific diseases that cause poor vision: Currently, neither drugs nor surgery stops the progression of hearing loss or the ringing in the ears (tinnitus) that is more common with age. Fortunately, remediation is possible; unfortunately, ageism interferes. People wait a long time as their hearing worsens before visiting

---

FIGURE 23.6

Victims of Crime As people grow older, they are less likely to be crime victims. These figures come from personal interviews in which respondents were asked whether they had been the victim of a violent crime—assault, sexual assault, rape, or robbery—in the past several months. This approach yields more accurate results than official crime statistics because many crimes are never reported to the police.

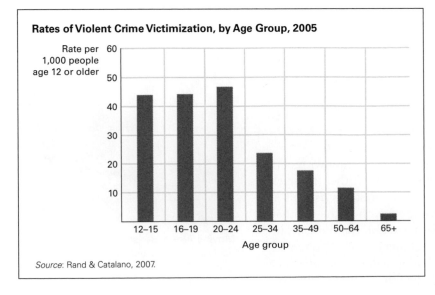

Rates of Violent Crime Victimization, by Age Group, 2005

Rate per 1,000 people age 12 or older

Source: Rand & Catalano, 2007.

TABLE 23.1

Common Vision Impairments Among the Elderly

- *Cataracts.* As early as age 50, about 10 percent of adults have cataracts, a thickening of the lens, causing vision to become cloudy, opaque, and distorted. By age 70, 30 percent do. Cataracts can be removed in outpatient surgery and replaced with an artificial lens.

- *Glaucoma.* About 1 percent of those in their 70s and 10 percent in their 90s have glaucoma, a buildup of fluid within the eye that damages the optic nerve. The early stages have no symptoms, but the later stages cause blindness, which can be prevented if an ophthalmologist or optometrist treats glaucoma before it becomes serious. African Americans and people with diabetes may develop glaucoma as early as age 40.

- *Macular degeneration.* About 4 percent of those in their 60s and about 12 percent over age 80 have a deterioration of the retina, called macular degeneration. An early warning occurs when vision is spotty (e.g., some letters missing when reading). Again, early treatment—in this case, medication—can restore some vision (Rosenfeld et al., 2006), but macular degeneration is progressive, causing blindness about five years after it starts.

Through Different Eyes These photographs depict the same scene as it would be perceived by a person with (*a*) normal vision, (*b*) cataracts, (*c*) glaucoma, or (*d*) macular degeneration. Thinking about how difficult it would be to find your own car if you had one of these disorders may help you remember to have your vision checked regularly.

an audiologist, and they often refuse even tiny, digital, personalized hearing aids because they associate a hearing aid with looking old (Meisami et al., 2007).

Ironically, individuals who mishear and misunderstand conversation strike others not only as old but also as mentally deficient. Even compared with the visually impaired, "hard-of-hearing individuals are often mistakenly thought to be retarded or mentally ill . . . [and] are more subject to depression, demoralization, and even at times psychotic symptomatology" (Butler et al., 1998, p. 181).

When people first notice the loss of some sensory abilities—when a newspaper page blurs or a dinner conversation is misunderstood—their usual reaction is denial. The problem may seem to disappear—eyes refocus, the brain completes the half-heard comments—so the elderly blame external circumstances, not their aging senses. However, senescence is ongoing. When people finally realize how much they do not perceive, they may shun social interactions or even avoid leaving home, sadly concluding that things will only get worse. Unless something is done, sensory loss does get worse, and isolation and depression follow.

Recognition and compensation, not denial or passive acceptance, are crucial (Meisami et al., 2007). This requires much more than a medical visit: Hearing aids need to be adjusted and personalized, which means several appointments with a professional for individualized training, readjustment, and calibration. Further compensation for sensory loss often involves technology that some elderly hesitate to use: attachments to televisions, radios, and telephones; canes that sense objects; infrared lenses that illuminate darkness; computers for the visually impaired that scan printed text and "speak" the words; or devices for the hearing-impaired that translate speech into print. For many sensory losses, service animals (not just dogs, but birds and monkeys, too) solve the problem, but the owner needs to get them, care for them, and use them.

Not only must individuals work to remedy their sensory losses, but societies also need to adjust. Virtually everything, from airplane seats to fashionable shoes, is designed for able-bodied, sensory-acute adults. Many disabilities would disappear with better design (Satariano, 2006). Look around at the built environment (the

Taking Her Ears for a Walk This profoundly deaf woman is greatly helped by Murphy, who is trained to get her attention whenever the telephone or doorbell rings or the smoke alarm goes off. Murphy's assistance enables her to remain in her home in Brainerd, Minnesota.

wear-and-tear theory A view of aging as a process by which the human body wears out because of the passage of time and exposure to environmental stressors.

layout and lighting of stores, streets, colleges, and homes), notice the print on medicine bottles, listen carefully to the public address systems in train stations. Even physical limitations are ignored: Ask yourself why most homes have entry stairs and most buses and cars require a big step to enter. Sensory loss does not signify brain loss, but without compensation, isolation and depression may lead to less intellectual stimulation. With blindness and deafness, morbidity can last for years.

SUMMING UP

Primary aging is inevitable and universal. Secondary aging involves diseases that occur as a result of poor health habits, disease, and environmental toxins combined with primary aging. Successful coping with senescence requires selective optimization with compensation by the community as well as by individuals. Some of the most troubling morbidities relate to the senses, particularly vision and hearing, because sensory impairment leads to depression and social isolation. The goal is compression of morbidity, so that aging is not accompanied by years of debilitating disease. ▪

>> Theories of Aging

Can aging be postponed, allowing the average person to live 100 healthy years or more? There are no definitive answers. Two decades ago, one expert categorized 300 theories of aging (Medvedev, 1990) and now there are more. Here we describe three clusters: wear and tear, genetic adaptation, and cellular aging.

Wear and Tear

The oldest, most general theory of aging is known as **wear and tear.** This theory contends that just as the parts of an automobile begin giving out as time and distance add up, the body wears out, part by part, after years of exposure to pollution, radiation, unhealthy foods, drugs, diseases, and other stresses. Organ reserve and repair processes are exhausted as the decades pass (Gavrilov & Gavrilova, 2006).

Is this true? For some body parts, yes. Athletes who put repeated stress on their shoulders or knees have chronically painful joints by middle adulthood; people who regularly work outdoors in strong sunlight damage their skin; industrial workers who inhale asbestos and smoke cigarettes destroy their lungs. By late adulthood, everyone's body has accumulated signs of wear. Scars leave their mark, bones reveal past fractures, the pupils of the eye narrow and the lenses cloud, the inner ear loses tiny hairs, fingernails become ridged, and so on.

At least three specific findings support the wear-and-tear theory. First, according to the "disposable soma" theory, each body (soma) has a certain amount of physical energy and strength, which gradually is spent (disposed of) over a lifetime (Finch & Kirkwood, 2000). For this reason, women who have never been pregnant live longer than others with the same health habits; perhaps pregnancy helps to wear out a person's body. Second, people who are overweight sicken and die at younger ages, perhaps because it takes more energy to maintain their bodies and thus less life force is available over time. Third, transplanted hearts and livers, artificial knees and hips, and implanted dentures can replace worn-out ones, adding years to life.

However, although wear and tear explains some aging, it is contradicted as well. Aerobic exercise improves heart and lung functioning; tai chi improves balance; weight training increases strength; breast-feeding reduces the risk of breast cancer; sexual activity stimulates the sexual-reproductive system; digestion is improved by

foods that require intestinal activity. In many ways, people are more likely to "rust out" from disuse than to wear out. Thus, although the wear-and-tear theory applies to senescence of some body parts, it is not a comprehensive explanation.

Genetic Adaptation

Humans may have a kind of **genetic clock,** a mechanism in the DNA of cells that regulates the aging process by triggering hormonal changes and controlling cellular reproduction and repair. Just as a genetic clock "switches off" growth genes (at about age 15), it might "switch on" aging genes.

Evidence for genetic aging comes from conditions that produce premature aging. People with Down syndrome (trisomy-21) are likely to develop heart disease, cancer, and Alzheimer disease in middle age. Children born with Hutchinson-Gilford syndrome (a genetic disease also called *progeria*) stop growing at about age 5 and begin to look old, with wrinkled skin and balding heads. These children die in their teens of heart diseases typically found in the elderly.

At the other end of the life span, people who live an extraordinarily long and healthy life usually have alleles that the average person does not (Halaschek-Wiener et al., 2009; Sierra et al., 2009). Probably hundreds of genes contribute to senescence, as do many epigenetic forces (Kim, 2008).

How Long Can Humans Live?

Genes seem to bestow on every species an inherent **maximum life span,** defined as the oldest possible age for members of that species (Wolf, 2010). Under ideal circumstances, the maximum that rats live seems to be 4 years; rabbits, 13; tigers, 26; house cats, 30; brown bats, 34; brown bears, 37; chimpanzees, 55; Indian elephants, 70; finback whales, 80; humans, 122; lake sturgeon, 150; giant tortoises, 180.

Maximum life span is quite different from **average life expectancy,** which is the average life span (calculated as median, not mean) of individuals in a particular group. In human groups, average life expectancy varies a great deal, depending on historical, cultural, and socioeconomic factors as well as genes (Sierra et al., 2009). Recent increases in life expectancy are attributed to reduction in deaths from adult diseases (heart attack, pneumonia, cancer, childbed fever). A dramatic change occurred over the past century, when women used to have a lower average life span than men because childbirth was a leading killer. Now women need never die in childbirth, and women live longer than men.

In the United States in 2010, average life expectancy at birth was about 76 years for men and 81 years for women. Those who are already 65 years old (no longer at risk of early death) are expected to live to 84; those who are already 80 die at age 89, on average. At about 90, the death rate seems to level off, which means that someone who is 95 is as likely to die within that year (about one chance in 6) as is someone who is 105.

Despite such variations, the genetic theory of aging contends that the *maximum* life span is as genetically fixed as it was a millennium or two ago. Thus, in ancient times, those few who survived past middle age died of the same aging-related causes that are evident in the twenty-first century. Just as people are genetically programmed to become capable of reproduction before age 20, humans may be genetically programmed to die, usually by age 90, with 122 the upper limit.

Some genes hasten aging. These could be genes that make a particular organ less efficient than normal. There are hundreds of such genes; every family has at least a few, such as a family weak stomach or a family tendency toward high blood pressure. Or there could be genes that switch on the aging process at a certain

genetic clock A purported mechanism in the DNA of cells that regulates the aging process by triggering hormonal changes and controlling cellular reproduction and repair.

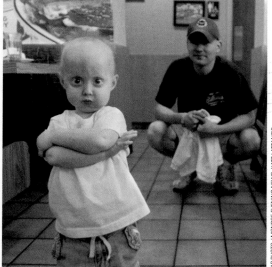

AP PHOTO / MONROE EVENING NEWS, KATI LATTANZIO

All Coats Barred In most ways, Lindsay is a typical 2-year-old, defiantly refusing to wear her coat when leaving the restaurant. Her father waits, more amused than annoyed. Lindsay acts her age, but her body does not. She has progeria and, before she reaches age 20, may die of a disease that more commonly affects the elderly.

maximum life span The oldest possible age that members of a species can live under ideal circumstances. For humans, that age is approximately 122 years.

average life expectancy The number of years the average newborn in a particular population group is likely to live.

Celebrating a Dozen Decades Only a few people live much beyond 100 years. Here, Jeanne Calment of France celebrates her 121st birthday; she died at 122 in 1997. Several other people are known to have lived to 122, and that age may be the upper limit for the human species. Even with the best medical care, most people die before age 80.

age. Some evidence for the latter is that some alleles—SIR2, ApoE4, def-2, among them—directly accelerate aging and death (Finch, 2010).

Much remains to be learned about the genetics of aging, but what has already been learned is intriguing. For instance, allele 2 of ApoE is protective, aiding survival. Of men in their 70s, 12 percent have ApoE2, but of men over age 85, 17 percent have it. That suggests that men with allele 2 are, for some reason, more likely to survive. Another common allele of the same gene, ApoE4, increases the risk of death by heart disease, stroke, dementia, and—if a person is HIV-positive—by AIDS (Kuhlmann et al., 2010).

Selective Adaptation

Evolutionary theory (discussed in Chapter 2) provides an explanation for the genetic diseases of late life (Hughes, 2010). At what point in the life span does a society need people to survive, and at what point is death not as harmful to the community? The answer is that young adults need to survive, but infants and old people are less needed. This requires some explanation: Since reproduction and child care are essential for species survival, and since young adults do almost all the birthing and infant care, that age group needs genetic protection. However, since infants and the very old need more care than they are able to give, their death from harmful genes did not impair survival of the species.

Genetic diseases, therefore, may be fatal to infants or to the old—as with Parkinson disease, Huntington disease, Alzheimer disease, type 2 diabetes, heart disease, and cancer—but rarely appear in young adulthood. Furthermore, those genetic diseases are passed on to the next generation because late-life genes have already been transmitted before they manifest themselves in the person. If there were a fatal gene that struck people down in emerging adulthood, those who had it would be more likely to die without passing it on.

An explanation for menopause at about age 50 is the "grandmother hypothesis"— that childbearing must cease so women can raise their children and help younger parents care for future generations (Lahdenperä et al., 2004). This hypothesis is appealing (especially to grandmothers), but it is not proven (van Bodegom et al., 2010).

Cellular Aging

Another cluster of theories holds that aging begins with molecules and cells, not whole body systems (Sedivy et al., 2008). Cells are damaged by the toxins of the environment over time, and minor errors in copying accumulate (remember, each cell contains the entire DNA of the person, and cells replace themselves thousands of times).

A damaged cell might be repaired or destroyed. Over time, in an "error catastrophe," imperfections proliferate, so the organism can no longer repair or overcome them all, resulting in senescence as well as in various cancers. This cellular damage is visible in skin cells: Cuts heal rapidly in children but more slowly in adults. In addition, benign growths, skin patches with changed color, or skin cancer appear in older adults (M. Timiras, 2007). In a similar way, invisibly, cellular imperfections accumulate in the entire body.

One specific hypothesis that explains the increase in cellular accidents is that *free radicals* (electrons that become detached [freed] from their nuclei) increase. Such electrons can wreak havoc on other molecules, splitting them or tearing them apart. Some free radicals are **oxygen free radicals,** in which the unpaired electron is highly reactive to any cell that includes some form of oxygen, as many cells do. Oxygen free radicals are especially destructive when they scramble DNA or mitochondria (Afanas'ev, 2009; Halliwell & Gutteridge, 2007). According to

oxygen free radicals Atoms of oxygen that, as a result of metabolic processes, have an unpaired electron. These atoms scramble DNA molecules or mitochondria, producing errors in cell maintenance and repair that, over time, may cause cancer, diabetes, and arteriosclerosis.

LIONEL CIRONNEAU / AP / WIDE WORLD PHOTOS

this theory, not only many diseases of aging but also the aging process itself occur because, over time, oxygen free radicals accumulate and cause damage to the normal cell-repair process.

In theory, **antioxidants,** which are chemical compounds that bind with electrons of oxygen free radicals, might reduce oxygen free radicals, slow cell aging, and extend life. However, although many older people take various antioxidant pills (e.g., vitamins A, C, and E and the mineral selenium), most research does not support this as a way to slow aging (Pocobelli et al., 2009). Indeed, the theory that oxygen free radicals cause aging is popular, but it is also widely criticized by scientists. One British team writes:

> The oxidative damage theory of aging once seemed almost proven. Yet recently the buzzards have been assembling in the blue skies above it. New challenges to the theory from work using nematode worms seem set to bring them down to peck at its bones.
>
> *[Gems & Doonan, 2009, p. 1681]*

This judgment is poetic but harsh. Nonetheless, it points to a problem with all of the research on aging: The experimental evidence comes primarily from fruit flies, worms, and mice—translation for humans is problematic.

The Immune System

A variant of the cellular theory of aging focuses on the immune system, which includes a complex array of cells that recognize foreign or abnormal substances, isolate them, and destroy them. **B cells** constitute one type of immune cells; they are so named because they are manufactured in the *bone* marrow. Once alerted to a specific infection via immunization or the actual disease, B cells produce antibodies that remain lifelong, protecting against a second bout of measles, mumps, and so on.

T cells (manufactured by the *thymus* gland) are multipurpose. They help the B cells produce more efficient antibodies and strengthen other aspects of the immune system. The immune system also includes NK (natural killer) cells, K (killer) cells, and white blood cells. Humans have developed an elaborate array of immune cells, necessary because humans are long-lived and thus encounter thousands of pathogens and parasites (Promislow et al., 2006). People with weaker immune systems (measured by analysis of T and B cells in the blood) die sooner than others, and people with many NK cells are healthy at age 85. The immune system weakens with age, so cancers grow and shingles emerge (the cause is latent herpes virus, which younger immune systems keep in check).

Drugs to stop cancer often involve killing all rapidly producing cells, which means temporarily shutting down the immune system. Shingles might be prevented with a new inoculation to bolster immunity, not completely effective because the aging immune system is difficult to activate (Oxman et al., 2005). Throughout life, immune systems are stronger in women than in men. That may be why women live longer and why men are more incapacitated by a virus (such as a cold). This female advantage has a downside, however; women develop more autoimmune diseases (such as lupus), caused by an immune system that goes awry.

Overall, there is ample evidence that the immune system becomes less effective with age, allowing many more pathogens to destroy the cells that sustain life (Wolf, 2010). It is also apparent that reactions to infection may cure the condition but also increase the rate of cell senescence overall (Evan & d'Adda di Fagagna, 2009). The hope is that, if the aging immune system can be repaired, then not only diseases but also cognitive losses can be halted, allowing an older person to function well for decades (Ron-Harel & Schwartz, 2009). The problem is that researchers do not know if decline in the immune system is the cause of aging or merely the result.

antioxidants Chemical compounds that nullify the effects of oxygen free radicals by forming a bond with their unattached oxygen electron.

SARAH LEEN / NATIONAL GEOGRAPHIC / GETTY IMAGES

A Sun Worshiper When this Australian man was a young lifeguard, he says, "We rubbed our bodies with coconut oil"—which did nothing to protect his skin from the sun's damaging rays. Deep tanning damaged his skin cells. Every dot of light represents a lesion that was removed to halt the spread of skin cancer.

B cells Immune cells manufactured in the bone marrow that create antibodies for isolating and destroying bacteria and viruses that invade the body.

T cells Immune cells manufactured in the thymus gland that produce substances that attack infected cells in the body.

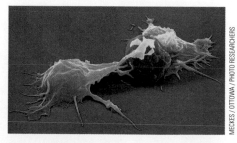

MECKES / OTTOWA / PHOTO RESEARCHERS

Natural Killers The immune system is always at war, attacking invading bacteria, viruses, and other destructive agents. Here two natural killer cells are overwhelming a leukemia cell. How healthy we are and how long we live are directly related to the strength and efficiency of our immune system.

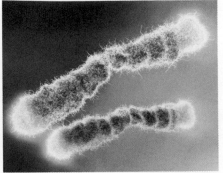

HYBRID MEDICAL / PHOTO RESEARCHERS, INC.

Old Caterpillars? No, these are young chromosomes, stained to show the glowing white telomeres at the ends.

Hayflick limit The number of times a human cell is capable of dividing into two new cells. The limit for most human cells is approximately 50 divisions, an indication that the life span is limited by our genetic program.

telomeres The ends of chromosomes in the cells; their length decreases with each cell duplication and seems to correlate with longevity.

telomerase An enzyme that increases the length of telomeres, which in turn may slow the advance of aging.

calorie restriction The practice of limiting dietary energy intake (while consuming sufficient quantities of vitamins, minerals, and other important nutrients) for the purpose of improving health and slowing down the aging process.

Especially for Biologists What are some immediate practical uses for research on the causes of aging? (see response, page 659)

Replication No More

Until about 50 years ago, scientists thought that all cells duplicate forever, as cancer cells do. Then, in a famous series of experiments, Leonard Hayflick allowed cells from humans of various ages to duplicate in ideal laboratory conditions, protected from anything that would produce errors or stop duplication. Instead of doubling indefinitely, the cells stopped after about 50 divisions if they came from an embryo, with less than 50 duplications if they came from a child, and fewer still if from an adult (Hayflick & Moorhead, 1961).

This research has been replicated hundreds of times with many species. Healthy cells stop replicating at a certain point, referred to as the **Hayflick limit,** found when the cells of people of various ages are allowed to duplicate. The Hayflick limit is also found when the cells from other animals are allowed to duplicate: The number of duplications seems related to the maximum life span of the particular species.

At the Hayflick limit, aged cells differ from young cells in many ways. One crucial difference is that the very ends of the chromosomes—called the **telomeres**—are much shorter in older cells. The length of telomeres signals longevity. Each cell duplication results in a shorter telomere and fewer remaining duplications. Eventually, the telomere is gone, duplication stops, and the creature dies (Shay & Wright, 2008).

The number of cell duplications and the length of telomeres are not identical for every person of a particular age. People who live to 100 have longer telomeres than others, and the length of their telomeres is related to their current health. Even among people who have already lived to 100 years or so, those with longer telomeres are often free of life-threatening disease (Terry et al., 2008).

Some experts believe "relengthening telomeres is the most efficient way to reset gene expression" (Fossel, 2004, p. 284), slowing the aging process. An enzyme, **telomerase,** increases the length of telomeres; adding telomerase to an organism may slow down aging (Shay & Wright, 2008). However, cancer cells make telomerase, and tumors grow rapidly when telomerase is abundant. To stop cancer, one proposal is to remove telomerase—with obvious dangers to the rest of the person (de Grey, 2007).

Hayflick himself believes that the Hayflick limit, and therefore aging, is caused by a natural loss of molecular fidelity—that is, by inevitable errors in transcription as each cell reproduces itself. He does not dispute the telomere research, but he calls *anti-aging* an oxymoron, a term that contradicts itself (Hayflick, 2004). He believes that aging is a natural process built into the very cells of our species.

Many other scientists in biology, psychology, neuroscience, and other fields call for a more dynamic, systems-based understanding of aging in humans (West & Bergman, 2009). It may be that humans can stave off morbidities and premature death; perhaps we can "add life to years" but not "add years to life." Or it may be that individuals or societies can add decades of healthy years for everyone, but few people really want that, as the following describes.

THINKING CRITICALLY

Calorie Restriction

One sure way to slow the aging process in most species is **calorie restriction,** drastically reducing daily calories while maintaining ample vitamins, minerals, fiber, and other important nutrients. Consuming fewer calories results in less frequent cell duplication, which in turn results in fewer free radicals, reduced duplication errors, and slower metabolism. It also

Two Long-Lived Monkeys Canto, left, and Owen, right, are about the same age, but Canto has been on a low-calorie diet most of his life whereas Owen has always eaten as much as he wants. As a result, Owen shows many more signs of aging, not only in his appearance but also in his metabolism, blood, and organ health.

enhances the mitochondria, which supports cell functioning (Finley & Haigis, 2009).

The benefits of calorie restriction have been demonstrated by careful research with dozens of nonhuman species, from fruit flies to mice to chimpanzees: Less aging and longer life (sometimes twice as long), as well as stronger hearts, less disease, and better cognition, result from keeping animals on a restricted diet after puberty (Bendlin et al., in press).

Controlled experiments with people would be unethical. Calorie restriction might be harmful for humans who are under age 21, or breast-feeding, or pregnant, and in everyone, calorie restriction reduces the sex drive, causes temporary infertility, and affects other body functions. Nonetheless, it seems plausible that throughout adulthood, a person could eat half as much and live decades longer.

Most scientists are skeptical, but many are curious. Rigorous experiments comparing hundreds of people—some required to eat as much as they wanted and some kept to a restricted diet—and testing them all every year or so are impossible. Fortunately, more than a thousand North Americans belong to the Calorie Restriction Society, voluntarily eating only 1,000 nutritious calories a day, none of them buttered or fried. One

leader of this group is Michael Rae, from Calgary, Canada. He explained to a reporter:

> Aging is a horror and it's got to stop right now. People are popping antioxidants, getting face lifts, and injecting Botox, but none of that is working. At the moment, C.R. [calorie restriction] is the only tool we have to stay younger longer.
>
> [quoted in Hochman, 2003, p. A9]

The reporter notes, "Mr. Rae is 6 feet tall, weighs just 115 pounds, and is often very hungry." The implication is that Rea is foolish. Scientists are trying to find some easier way—perhaps a drug or nutrient—that would achieve the same result (Barzilai & Bartke, 2009). Many people buy pills or eat strange foods, some endure surgery, and a few (perhaps 10, perhaps 1,000—no one knows for sure) have their bodies deep frozen (*cryogenic freezing*) at death, to be revived when technology has been developed to bring them back to life. Look at Owen and Canto. Would you give up junk food and sex to be more like Canto when you are 80? Why not?

112/63, 6 Feet, 135 Pounds These numbers are this man's blood pressure, height, and weight after six years on a calorie-restricted diet. So far, so good—he is now 36 years old.

SUMMING UP

There are hundreds of theories of aging. The wear-and-tear theory proposes that bodies wear out with age, but this theory does not explain the entire aging process. Genetic theories note the evolutionary limits on the maximum life span for various species. One genetic theory holds that selective adaptation for humans may have required, or at least allowed, humans to inherit genes for aging and death that did not become active until after they had produced and raised children to replace themselves. Cellular theories focus on damage from oxygen free radicals, on accumulated errors in cell duplication, on telomere shortening, and/or on the cells of the immune system. ■

>> **Response for Biologists** (from page 658) Although ageism and ambivalence limit the funding of research on the causes of aging, the applications include prevention of AIDS, cancer, senility, and physical damage from pollution—all urgent social priorities.

Centenarians Plus Every nation celebrates the very old, although some of these people may be younger than they are said to be. From left to right, counterclockwise: Juana Rodriquez, age 125, sits next to her 77-year-old son (Granma, Cuba); Walter Breuning, age 113, blows out his birthday candles (Montana, United States); Maria Capovilla, age 116, holds an old photo close to her heart (Guayaquil, Ecuador); Li Cain Rong, age 118, being a tourist (Foshan, China); Ali El Amri, age 130, sits on his bed (Tunisia); Hryhory Nestor, age 116, enjoys champagne (Lviv, Ukraine); Marie Hendrix and Gabrielle Vaudremer, age 100, are about to cut their cake (Belgium). The sisters are thought to be the oldest surviving twins; they share longevity but not mentality—Marie is notably more cogent than Gabrielle.

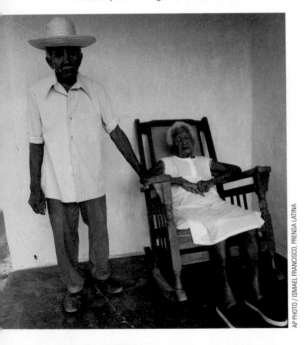

AP PHOTO / ISMAEL FRANCISCO, PRENSA LATINA

JOHN MOORE / GETTY IMAGES

>> The Centenarians

According to some scientists, most babies born today in developed countries will live to become centenarians (Kinsella, 2005). How might your life be at age 100?

Other Places, Other Stories

In the 1970s, three remote places—one in the former Soviet Union, one in Pakistan, and one in Ecuador—were in the news because many vigorous old people were found to live there, with several aged 100 or more. As one researcher wrote:

> Most of the aged work regularly. . . . Some even continue to chop wood and haul water. Close to 40 percent of the aged men and 30 percent of the aged women report good vision; that is, that they do not need glasses for any sort of work, including reading or threading a needle. Between 40 and 50 percent have reasonably good hearing. Most have their own teeth. Their posture is unusually erect, even into advanced age. Many take walks of more than two miles a day and swim in mountain streams.
>
> *[Benet, 1974, p. 9]*

A more comprehensive study (Pitskhelauri, 1982) found that the lifestyles in all three of these regions were similar in four ways:

- *Diet.* People ate mostly fresh vegetables and herbs, with little meat or fat. They thought it better to be a little bit hungry than too full.
- *Work.* Even the very old do farm work, household tasks, and child care.
- *Family and community.* The elderly are well integrated into families of several generations and interact frequently with friends and neighbors.
- *Exercise and relaxation.* Most take a walk every morning and evening (often up and down mountains), nap midday, and socialize in the evening.

Perhaps these factors—diet, activity, social respect, and exercise—lengthen life.

That the social context promotes longevity is buttressed by evidence from bumblebees. Genetically, worker bees and queen bees are the same, but worker bees survive for only about three months whereas queen bees, which are fed special food and treated with deference, live about five years. When a queen dies, a worker bee is chosen to become a queen, thereby living 20 times longer than it otherwise would.

The Truth About Life After 100

Surely your suspicions were raised by the preceding paragraphs. Humans have almost nothing in common with bumblebees—or fruit flies, for that matter—and the information about those long-lived people was published more than 30 years ago. Indeed, the three regions famous for long-lived humans have no verifiable birth or marriage records from 100 years ago. Beginning at about age 70, many people in these areas systematically exaggerate their age (Thorson, 1995). Everyone who claimed to be a centenarian was probably exaggerating, and every researcher who believed them was too eager to accept the idea that life would be long and wonderful if only the ills of modern civilization could be avoided.

The oldest well-documented life ended at age 122; Jeanne Calment died in France in 1997. No one has been proved to outlive Jeanne yet, despite the existence of documented birth dates for half a billion people who have died since 1997.

Do not give up too quickly, though. Several modern nations with good records report communities where many people live long, productive lives, including an island of Japan (Okinawa), an area of the United States (rural North Dakota),

and a religious group (Seventh Day Adventists). Those who study centenarians, wherever they live, find that many are quite happy (Jopp & Rott, 2006). Jeanne Calment was one: "I will die laughing," she said, and she enjoyed a glass of red wine and some olive oil each day.

Researchers in western Europe, East Asia, and North America find similarities between the centenarians they study and the aged in the former Soviet Union, Pakistan, and Ecuador (many of whom, while perhaps not reaching 100, were at least in their 80s): moderate diet, hard work, an optimistic attitude, intellectual curiosity, and social involvement.

Disease, disability, and dementia may eventually set in; studies disagree about how common these problems are at age 100. However, there is no doubt that many people celebrate a 100th birthday with energy, awareness, and optimism (Perls, 2008; Poon, 2008). Centenarians tend to have compressed morbidity and are upbeat about their life.

If this surprises you, you are not alone; many older people themselves would be surprised (Cruikshank, 2009). Ironically, the older people are, the more likely they are to believe that they are "exceptions to the usual pattern of aging, and that their health is superior to that of most of their age peers" (Hirsiaho & Ruopplia, 2005, p. 79). Ageism affects all of us, at every age. As explained in the beginning of this chapter, it can shorten your life. Don't let it. It is possible, as the next two chapters reiterate, to live a long life and enjoy it.

SUMMING UP

Research on centenarians finds no proof that anyone has lived longer than 122 years, but more and more people throughout the world are reaching 100. Many of them are quite happy and active. If people reach late adulthood in good health, their attitudes and activities may be crucial in determining the length and quality of their remaining years. The long-lived tend to eat a well-balanced diet and to exercise daily, both of which are even more important, but less common, in late adulthood than earlier.

SUMMARY

Prejudice and Predictions

1. Contrary to ageist stereotypes, most older adults are happy, quite healthy, and active. Although elderspeak persists, ageism is weakening because gerontologists provide a more optimistic picture of late adulthood than geriatricians do.

2. An increasing percentage of the population is over age 65, but these numbers are sometimes distorted in the media. Currently, about 13 percent of people in the U.S. population are elderly, and most of them are self-sufficient and productive.

3. Gerontologists sometimes distinguish among the young-old, the old-old, and the oldest-old, according to each age group's relative degree of dependency. Only 10 percent of the elderly are dependent (the old-old), and only 4 percent of the elderly are in nursing homes or hospitals.

Aging and Disease

4. The many apparent changes in skin, hair, and body shape that began earlier in adulthood continue in old age. The senses all become less acute, including vision. Almost all older people need glasses, and many have cataracts, glaucoma, or macular degeneration. Hearing also declines: Most older men are significantly hard-of-hearing, as are many women.

5. Selective optimization with compensation for sensory losses requires a combination of technology, specialist advice, and personal determination. These three have been underutilized in the past (exemplified by the underuse of hearing aids).

6. Primary aging happens to everyone, reducing organ reserve in body and brain. Although the particulars differ depending on the individual's past health habits and genes, eventually morbidity, disability, and risk of mortality increase. Compensation is possible and brings many benefits, including compression of morbidity.

Theories of Aging

7. Hundreds of theories address the causes of aging. Wear-and-tear theory suggests that living wears out the body; it applies to some parts of the body, but not to overall aging.

8. Another theory is that genes allow humans to survive through the reproductive years but then to become seriously ill and inevitably die. Each species seems to have a genetic timetable for decline and death.

9. Cellular theories of aging include the idea that the processes of DNA duplication and repair are affected by aging, making repair of errors more difficult. Oxidative stress, caused by oxygen free radicals, hinders cell maintenance and repair.

10. Age-related decline in the immune system may cause aging, as it contributes to elderly people's increasing vulnerability to disease.

11. Cells stop duplicating at a certain point, called the Hayflick limit. This stoppage seems to occur when the telomeres shorten and then disappear.

The Centenarians

12. It was once believed that many people in certain parts of the world lived long past 100 as a result of moderate diet, exercise, hard work, and respect for the aged. Such reports turned out to be exaggerated.

13. The number of centenarians is increasing, and many of them are quite healthy and happy. The personality and attitudes of the very old suggest that long-term survival may be welcomed more than feared.

KEY TERMS

ageism (p. 640)
elderspeak (p. 642)
gerontology (p. 643)
geriatrics (p. 643)
demographic shift (p. 643)
centenarian (p. 643)
young-old (p. 646)

old-old (p. 646)
oldest-old (p. 646)
primary aging (p. 647)
secondary aging (p. 647)
cardiovascular disease (p. 647)
compression of morbidity
  (p. 650)

wear-and-tear theory (p. 654)
genetic clock (p. 655)
maximum life span (p. 655)
average life expectancy (p. 655)
oxygen free radicals (p. 656)
antioxidants (p. 657)
B cells (p. 657)

T cells (p. 657)
Hayflick limit (p. 658)
telomeres (p. 658)
telomerase (p. 658)
calorie restriction (p. 658)

WHAT HAVE YOU LEARNED?

Prejudice and Predictions

1. What are the similarities among ageism, racism, and sexism?

2. What are the differences among ageism, racism, and sexism?

3. Is there any harm in being especially kind to people who are old?

4. Why don't the elderly exercise as much as the young?

5. How is elderspeak similar to baby talk?

6. What is the difference between gerontology and geriatrics?

7. Proportionally, why does Japan have 2½ times as many people over 65 as the world overall does?

8. What would need to happen for the demographic pyramid to become a square?

9. What are the differences among young-old, old-old, and oldest-old?

Aging and Disease

10. How does heart disease represent both primary and secondary aging?

11. How does diabetes both represent primary and secondary aging?

12. Why don't we know if diseases of the elderly are more common now than earlier?

13. What are the differences in the sleep patterns of the old and the young?

14. How should it be decided whether an elderly person should drive or not?

15. How is compression of morbidity related to mortality?

16. How is compression of morbidity good for society as well as the individual?

17. Why is falling a serious health problem in old age?

18. How can an older person compensate for declines in vision?

19. How can an older person compensate for declines in hearing?

20. How might declining touch, taste, and smell harm an older person?

Theories of Aging

21. Why is the wear-and-tear theory of aging no longer considered accurate?

22. According to the genetic theory of aging, what is the maximum human life span?

23. Why is the average life span so many decades lower than the maximum?

24. According to evolutionary theory, why are there more diseases of aging than of younger years?

25. What happens that damages cells as they age?

26. If the immune system breaks down, how can this be a cause of all aging?

The Centenarians

27. Why would people lie about their age by adding years to it?

28. What do studies of the very old suggest about the attitudes of other people?

29. What attitudes about life are more common in centenarians than younger people?

APPLICATIONS

1. Analyze Web sites that have information about aging for evidence of ageism, anti-aging measures, and exaggeration of longevity.

2. Compensating for sensory losses is difficult because it involves learning new habits. To better understand the experience, reduce your hearing or vision for a day by wearing earplugs or dark glasses that let in only bright lights. (Use caution and common sense:

Don't drive a car while wearing earplugs or cross streets while wearing dark glasses.) Report on your emotions, the responses of others, and your conclusions.

3. Ask five people of various ages if they want to live to age 100 and record their responses. Would they be willing to eat half as much, exercise much more, experience weekly dialysis, or undergo other procedures in order to extend life? Analyze the responses.

>>ONLINE CONNECTIONS

To accompany your textbook, you have access to a number of online resources, including quizzes for every chapter of the book, flashcards (in English and Spanish), critical thinking questions, and case studies. For access to any of these links, go to www.worthpublishers.com/bergerls8e. In addition to these free resources, you'll also find links to the podcasts, video clips, diagnostic quizzing with personalized study advice, and an ebook. Some of the videos and activities available online include:

- *Perceptions and Reality in Older Adulthood.* Discusses ageism, demographics, and the gains and losses associated with aging. In video clips, elders tell the real story of what it's like to age.

- *Brain Development: Late Adulthood.* Animated illustrations show normal age-related brain changes and changes associated with different types of dementia.

CHAPTER

Late Adulthood: Cognitive Development

WHAT WILL YOU KNOW?

1. Why is quicker thinking considered better thinking?
2. When older people tell memories of their childhood, should you believe them?
3. Is there any aspect of cognition that improves with age?
4. Does everyone who lives long enough become demented?
5. Are older people really wise?

Whenever I flew to Minnesota to visit my parents, who were in their 90s, friends would ask me, "How are their minds?"

"Good," I would answer.

"Isn't that wonderful!" they sometimes replied.

I wanted to shout "No! Not wonderful!" and then lecture about cognition in late adulthood. Instead I was quiet, thinking and remembering.

My parents were forgetful and repetitive; they could be stuck in the past, telling stories I had already heard. But my friends were asking if my parents had lost their minds, and they were glad this was not the case. My mother still had her wit, and my father still appreciated it. I asked Mom how it felt to be 90.

"Fine. But 89 felt better."

Dad chuckled. "She keeps coming up with these zingers. That's what I call them."

Like most of their peers, my parents were neither demented nor wonderful. Late-adulthood cognition is too complex to be captured in a brief conversation with a friend.

As you saw in the two earlier chapters on adult cognition (Chapters 18 and 21), during adulthood some abilities increase, others wane, and still others remain stable. By the end of adulthood, physical impairment, reduced perception, decreased energy, and slower reactions take an increasing toll. Yet even among the oldest-old, decline is not the entire story. The information-processing perspective, a focus of this chapter, highlights the complexity and variability of cognition in late adulthood.

The previous chapter explained that biosocial development in later adulthood may be "impaired," "usual," or "optimal." This chapter separates cognitive development into the same trio. Severe cognitive impairment (dementia) is discussed, as is optimal cognition (wisdom). Before describing the usual, the worst, and the best, we begin with the organ that supports cognition at every age, the brain.

>> The Aging Brain

New neurons form and dendrites grow in adulthood—a fact that once surprised many developmentalists who thought brain growth stopped in childhood (Yang et al., 2006). However, growth is slow. Just like the legs, the heart, and every other part of the body, the brain becomes less efficient as people grow older (Park & Reuter-Lorenz, 2009).

Brain Slowdown

Senescence reduces production of neurotransmitters—glutamate, acetylcholine, serotonin, and especially dopamine—that allow a nerve impulse to jump quickly across the synapse from one neuron to another. Neural fluid decreases, myelination thins, the corpus callosum is reduced, and cerebral blood circulates more slowly. The result is an overall brain slowdown, evident in reaction time, talking, and thinking.

Thinking is our focus here, and it is apparent that speed is crucial for many aspects of cognition. Older people need more time to perceive new sensations because their minds are still processing prior sensations. Their conclusions may be less comprehensive because slower thinking makes it difficult to hold in mind and analyze large quantities of information simultaneously.

At every age, working quickly slows down accuracy. Sometimes this trade-off is necessary—for instance, on a timed test at school or in a text message to a friend. However, in an experiment in which younger and older adults were asked to speed up answers and sacrifice a small bit of accuracy, the younger ones complied but the older ones did not, because "older participants are unwilling to make unnecessary errors to hasten their responding" (Starns & Ratcliff, 2010, p. 387).

Perhaps they were not merely *unwilling*; perhaps the slowness of their brain processing made them *unable* to speed up their answers. Does this make them less intelligent overall? Some experts believe that processing speed is the *g* mentioned in Chapter 11, the pivotal intellectual ability that is the foundation of all other aspects of intelligence. Evidence for this includes the fact that deterioration in cognitive ability correlates with slower walking as well as with almost every kind of physical disability (Kuo et al., 2007; Salthouse, 2010).

However, although all scientists agree that reduced speed is a component of late-life cognition, other factors may be more important, especially when declines in individuals are examined (Zimprich & Martin, 2009). For example, both past education and current intellectual challenge correlate with better neurological functioning in late adulthood. It may be that these factors create better connections and more dendrites, or it may be that past schooling slows down the slowdown, or it may merely be that decline is just as rapid but less noticeable if the person began late adulthood with higher ability (Salthouse, 2010).

Actually, the precise relationship among past education, current mental exercise, and intellectual functioning in late adulthood is controversial and complicated (Alley et al., 2007). Certainly good health correlates with education, and certainly health aids brain circulation, which correlates with faster thinking. Beyond that, experts disagree. It is agreed, however, that everyone's mind slows down markedly during late adulthood.

LARRY SMITH / THE NEW YORK TIMES / REDUX

Mind Over Matter Federal Judge Wesley Brown, age 103, compensates for diminished lung capacity by taking supplemental oxygen. He optimizes by no longer taking cases that might drag on, saying, "At my age, I no longer buy green bananas." Retired judges collect generous pensions, but Brown continues to work, hearing a full load of criminal cases—to the admiration of colleagues, lawyers, and defendants. Given what is known about cognitive variations in old age, he surely functions a bit more slowly than when President Kennedy first appointed him in 1962, but he may judge as well as ever.

Especially for People Who Are Proud of Their Intellect What can you do to keep your mind sharp all your life? (see response, page 668)

Evidence from Neuroscience

According to most neuroscientists, brain aging is measurable not only in speed but also in size: The brain gets smaller. Some areas shrink more than others, among them the hypothalamus (crucial for memory) and the prefrontal cortex (necessary for planning, inhibiting unwanted responses, and coordinating thoughts) (Kramer et al., 2006). Prefrontal shrinkage may explain inadequate inhibition, evident when some older people talk too much, with "off-target verbosity," to inattentive listeners (von Hippel, 2007).

In every part of the brain, on average, the volume of gray matter (crucial for processing new experiences) is reduced; as a consequence, many people must use their cognitive reserve to understand events (Park & Reuter-Lorenz, 2009). If the cognitive reserve is depleted (because it never was that big, or because life stresses reduced it, or because the person is among the oldest-old), then a person is less open to new experiences. As with all aspects of health and functioning in later adulthood, the amount of shrinkage—that is, the amount of gray matter lost—varies; those who have no cognitive decline have less shrinkage or perhaps none at all (Burgmans et al., 2009). Most scientists agree that some loss of gray matter is inevitable if a person lives long enough.

Using More of the Brain

Another finding from PET and fMRI scans is that, compared with younger adults, older adults use more parts of their brains, including both hemispheres, to solve problems. This was surprising at first, since it was assumed that older brains would be less active, not more so. What is the significance of this greater activity? There are at least three possibilities:

1. *Compensation.* Older adults may find that using only one brain region is inadequate for complex thinking, so they automatically use more parts. In this way, intellectual output may be unimpaired, even though the process of thinking has changed (Daselaar & Cabeza, 2005). Perhaps the plasticity explained in Chapter 1 includes "neuroplasticity as a compensatory response in the older brain" (Goh & Park, 2009, p. 391).
2. *Reduced brain reserves.* If brain reserves are reduced, cognitive abilities in several parts of the brain might combine to maintain cognition for relatively easy intellectual tasks, as in possibility #1 above. However, insufficient reserves might make more challenging tasks too hard (Cappell et al., 2010).
3. *Wandering minds.* Finally, if cognitive loss includes reduced control, the brain may "dedifferentiate," that is, stop using a focused region for each function, as younger brains do. Inhibition fails, attention wanders, and thinking becomes diffuse. Inadequate inhibition may allow daydreaming, intrusive memories, and irrelevant comments.

Multitasking

A study of multitasking, memory, and brain activation confirmed that older adults use more of their brains than younger ones do. However, these researchers reported a crucial difference: Older adults who were better at working memory and at multitasking used their prefrontal cortex; those who were worse did not (Goffaux et al., 2008). Thus, the general brain slowdown affects everyone, but some older adults are more adept at using the resources they have, perhaps because their prefrontal cortex still functions well.

Multitasking slows down people of every age, but older adults are more severely affected. When they are asked to do more tasks simultaneously, their performance

Atrophy Ranking

 Lowest

 25th Percentile

 Median

 75th Percentile

 Highest

IMAGE COURTESY J. M. WARDLAW

Not All Average A team of neuroscientists in Scotland (Farrell et al., 2009) published these images of the brains of healthy 65- to 70-year-olds. The images show normal brain loss (the white areas) from the lowest (5th percentile) *(top frame)* to the highest (95th percentile) *(bottom frame)*. Some atrophy is inevitable (even younger brains atrophy), but few elders are merely average.

Dynamic Duo Grandpa is methodical: He knows about scraping and priming and he bought waterproof paint. His grandson is quick, and he is eager to get their summer cabin painted in a day. As long as neither gets impatient with the other's contrasting style, this will be a very pleasant afternoon for both.

>> **Response for People Who Are Proud of Their Intellect** (from page 666) If you answered, "Use it or lose it" or "Do crossword puzzles," you need to read more carefully. No specific brain activity has been proved to prevent brain slowdown. Overall health is good for the brain as well as for the body, so exercise, a balanced diet, and well-controlled blood pressure are some smart answers.

becomes markedly worse (Voelcker-Rehage & Alberts, 2007). Particularly difficult is combining a motor task and a cognitive task—such as reading while walking, which requires both hemispheres (Albinet et al., 2006).

In daily life, suppose a grandfather, studying the newspaper, is interrupted by a grandchild's tugging at his leg, or suppose a grandmother, while getting dressed, is asked what bus she will take. Most likely the grandfather will put the newspaper down (or tell the child to go away) and the grandmother will first dress and then figure out transportation (avoiding mismatched shoes).

An older adult's difficulty with multitasking suggests that concentration on one task at a time is needed. Improved concentration may be the explanation for the results of a remarkable study (Fox & Charness, 2010). Older and younger adults took a test called Raven's Progressive Matrices, often used to indicate advanced reasoning processes. The researchers instructed half the participants to talk as they were being tested, that is, to say what was going on in their minds.

The talking did not help the younger adults (their scores were slightly lower), but the older adults gained 11 points compared with a matched age group who took the test silently. This gain represented almost 1 standard deviation, equivalent to the IQ difference between average intelligence and mental retardation. It may be that older brains benefit from activities that help them focus—screening out distractions, writing down reminders, or, in this case, talking to help them think.

SUMMING UP

The brain is an organ of the body, subject to the same forces of senescence that affect every other part. Cognition is slower in old age, probably because neurotransmitters are less abundant, myelination thins, and gray matter is reduced. As with the senses and other parts of the body, some brain functions are impaired while others remain strong. Older adults compensate for reductions in speed and attention, sometimes using more parts of their brain than younger people do to complete the same task. Implications are intriguing but inconclusive. ▪

>> The Usual: Information Processing After Age 65

As already implied in the discussion of ageism in Chapter 23, and as stated in the introduction to this chapter, most older people are neither demented nor wise. In between those extremes is the usual developmental course of cognition in late adulthood, not identical to that in earlier stages, but not radically different either. An information-processing approach, separating cognition into four steps—input (sensing), storage (memory), programming (control processes), and output (what the person says or does)—details the specifics.

Input

In order to process information, the senses must receive sensations to be transmitted to the brain. As you read in Chapter 23, no sense is as sharp at age 65 as at age 15. This reduced acuity impairs cognition because information must cross the *sensory threshold,* the divide between what is sensed and what is not, in order to be perceived.

Some information, such as the details of a road sign 300 feet away or the words of a conversation in a noisy place, never reaches older people's minds because

the senses do not detect the stimuli. Several researchers have wondered whether elderly people's underlying problem with sensory input is (1) directly due to their declining senses (the input never reaches the brain) or (2) rooted in the brain itself (the input is not registered correctly). The probable answer is both (Glass, 2007).

Awareness of the Loss

Sensory deficits are hard to notice at first; most older people believe they see and hear whatever is important. The brain automatically fills in missed sights and sounds, which means information may be distorted or lost without the person realizing it.

For example, in one study, more than 200 adults (half young, half old) were shown 10 video clips of men lying or telling the truth about whether they had stolen money. The older adults thought they could recognize the truth-tellers, but they were less accurate than the younger people (Stanley & Blanchard-Fields, 2008). The probable reason is that they missed the subtle indications—a pursing of the lips, a catch in the voice—that people use to detect a lie. A careful analysis by the researchers concluded that it was input, not processing, that led to the older adults' inaccuracy. This has an immediate practical application: Older people may be more likely to believe a con artist because they miss some cues.

Similar results were found in another study of older adults' ability to detect emotions based on body position and voice tone (not words). Adults aged 64 to 84 did not do as well on this as did adults aged 18 to 24 (Ruffman et al., 2009). A third study, which examined gaze-following (Slessor et al., 2008), found that older adults were less adept at knowing where someone was looking. Since understanding emotions is more likely if one knows when a conversation partner glances away and at what a person is gazing, older people are disadvantaged in social interactions. They may keep talking after their listener loses interest, or they may miss irony, humor, or sarcasm—all signaled with facial expressions as well as words. Finally, another study evaluated young, middle-aged, and older adults on how well they could read emotions by looking at the eyes. Deficits began at about age 50 (Pardini & Nichelli, 2009).

The upshot is that numerous clues as to meaning are deployed in communication, and fewer of these clues reach the aging brain. Older adults who think they hear and see as well as always are unaware that some subtle input is missed. They may be cognitively impaired without realizing it. Other people may notice, thinking the person's mind is failing, when actually the senses, not the brain, are at fault.

Interference

Reduced sensory input affects cognition in a second way, by increasing interference. Interference is a major impediment to effective and efficient cognition in the elderly (Park & Payer, 2006). Vital information may be lost because other, less important information captures attention, and it takes time to discard it.

For example, if reduced auditory input means that the word *interference* is heard as *in the ear ants,* then the brain uses resources to analyze the sounds and the context to figure out what was really said. Usually, people of all ages are successful at this, not even aware that they are processing the sounds. Studies of telephone talk, radio transmission, and public address systems reveal that some loss of fidelity (and saved expense) is acceptable because the human mind fills in the gaps.

Typically this is no problem, except when tiny audible differences are important, as when listening to music. However, dealing with gaps in a heard message

From Ten-Hut to Plant-Tending This man needed all his senses when he was on active duty as a colonel in the U.S. Marine Corps. Now, nearing age 90, he is partially deaf and has problems with balance. However, these sensory impairments don't keep him from enjoying the sights, smells, and textures of the plants he tends at a senior center's greenhouse in Louisiana.

AP PHOTO / THE NEWS-STAR, ARELY CASTILLO

tires the mind, depleting the mental energy needed to take the next step in information processing—that is, to judge whether the words should be remembered or not. Since older adults hear less well, they must spend more effort reducing interference. Mental energy is limited: Devoting attention to one task reduces attention for another.

Thus, for older people who constantly need to figure out what they have heard or seen, interference impedes thought, especially if many sensations occur quickly (Kramer et al., 2006). Indeed, a study examining "change blindness," the inability to see the difference between two similar sights, found that processing speed was the most important reason why older adults were significantly worse than younger adults at distinguishing the sights. Compared with 18- to 28-year-olds, more of the 60- to 84-year-olds were slower to see differences. That made them less adept at detecting change (Costello et al., 2010).

Memory

The second step of information processing is memory, a particularly sensitive topic since memory loss is the first symptom of the dreaded Alzheimer disease. Remember stereotype threat: If older people fear their memories are fading, or suspect that other people believe their memories are fading, anxiety itself impairs memory—a phenomenon especially apparent among those with more education (Hess et al., 2009). The probable explanation is that people who have earned college degrees have been proud of their intellectual achievements all their lives, which makes them particularly upset when they feel their intellect is slowing.

To confront this anxiety, it is critical to realize that only some aspects of memory fade, while others do not. Just because an older person cannot remember the name of, say, the mayor of the town, does not mean that all aspects of memory are disappearing. Recalling names is a type of memory likely to decline with age, while memory for vocabulary (semantic memory) is likely to increase.

Remember from Chapter 20 that each area of sensory decline is quite specific. That is true cognitively as well. Detailed research on semantic memory finds specific variations, depending on how vocabulary is assessed (Salthouse, 2010). For instance, an older person's vocabulary is as good as, or better than, that of an average younger adult if the purpose of the test is to indicate a particular object among a set of pictures—such as being asked to point to the spatula among a group of household utensils. But an elder's vocabulary is not as good when he or she is asked to name objects depicted—such as a drawing of a spatula, a garlic press, a corkscrew, and so on. Unfortunately, people are more likely to notice losses more than gains: When older people cannot quickly name someone, the tendency is to conclude that their memory is diminished, but when older people use vocabulary that younger people rarely employ, few conclude that memory improves with age.

Working Memory

You learned in earlier chapters that there are many kinds of memory, each with its own developmental pattern. One broad distinction is between *working memory* (short-term memory) and *long-term memory*. Working memory is the information that the brain holds at a given moment, allowing processing of new ideas. Most research on working memory finds deficiencies with age (Bopp & Verhaeghen, 2005). This is no small matter: Evaluating, calculating, inferring, and so on—all helpful in deciding whether recent information is to be accepted or discarded—depend on working memory. When brain slowdown requires more time to perceive and process sensations, working memory is reduced and forgotten information undercuts every aspect of cognition.

This might explain why vocabulary recognition is the final ability to show decline: Speed is not a factor in deciding whether *chartreuse* is a color, a tool, or an emotion. However, speed is crucial in repeating a list of six digits backwards (a common test of working memory) because a slow-thinking person may already have lost the memory of the first digits when it is time to repeat them.

Some research finds that when older people can take their time and concentrate and the task is not overwhelming, working memory seems as good as ever. For example, a study of reading ability found that older people were more likely to reread a phrase than younger people were, but they were equally accurate in understanding what they read (Stine-Morrow et al., 2010). Older college students tend to spend more time studying than younger students do, which allows them to achieve as well as people one-third their age.

Long-Term Memory

One cognitive task required of older adults is to remember the past: They may have the institutional memory, or the family history, or the experienced perspective that younger adults need. However, it is difficult to obtain an accurate assessment of long-term memory. Many older adults recount details of their childhood, which suggests intact long-term memories. But people of all ages misremember, even when they are convinced that their memories are true (Loftus et al., 2007). When listening to Grandpa describe his boyhood, how does a grandchild assess accuracy?

Some researchers test long-term memory via verifiable public events, such as presidential elections and space flights, finding "replicable findings of age-related decline, stability and even in some cases increase" (Zacks & Hasher, 2006, p. 162). One question often used in the United States to assess memory is, "Who is the current president . . . and who was the president before that . . . and before that?" Many older adults name more presidents than younger adults do. However, political awareness may increase more over the years than long-term memory decreases, and personal experience with past presidents may trump learned history. If so, this test is unfair to the young.

A recent study seems more valid. Beginning on September 12, 2001, 64 younger adults (average age 33) and 67 older adults (average age 71) were asked how they heard about the attack on the World Trade Center (called a *flashbulb memory* because the entirety of the circumstances is typically encoded in a flash) (Kvavilashvili et al., 2010). After they freely recalled what they could, they were asked five specific questions (when they heard the news, from whom, where they were, what they were doing, who was with them). They were also screened to make sure they were healthy and mentally capable (signified by several measures, including memory for 10 words).

Two years later, all were asked the same five questions. Both groups remembered the specifics very well (see Figure 24.1). Almost no inconsistencies were found between immediate and later memories. The researchers thus concluded that "older adults' autobiographical memories (whether flashbulb or ordinary) appear to be much better retained and more consistent than one would predict from numerous laboratory studies" (Kvavilashvili et al., 2010, p. 401).

The practical implication is that emotional memories encoded at one point in life tend to endure, without marked loss or distortion (Kensinger, 2009). Short-term memory

Recognition At every age, recognition memory is much better than recall. Chances are that few of my high school classmates could describe how I looked back then, but all of them could point out my picture among the hundreds of photos in our yearbook.

FIGURE 24.1

Some Memories Stick As you can see, older adults score lower than younger adults on short-term memory, but their memory for emotional events is almost as good as that of younger adults. This study also reported a somewhat larger standard deviation among the old: Perhaps a few of them were in the early, undetectable stages of dementia. If they were eliminated from this data (impossible to do until years later, when dementia would be diagnosed), long-term memory might be revealed to be even better for the older adults.

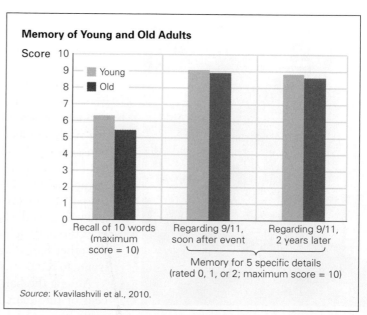

Memory of Young and Old Adults

Source: Kvavilashvili et al., 2010.

Especially for Students If you want to remember something you learn in class for the rest of your life, what should you do? (see response, page 674)

control processes The part of the information-processing system that regulates the analysis and flow of information. Memory and retrieval strategies, selective attention, and rules or strategies for problem solving are all useful control processes.

Don't Forget As a retrieval strategy, this Maryland shop owner posts dozens of reminders for herself on the wall.

AP PHOTO / SALISBURY DAILY TIMES, BRICE STUMP

usually declines, but long-term memory stays strong. When Grandpa talks about his childhood, usually his memories are as accurate as they ever were. If he exaggerates, it is not because he does not remember.

Control Processes

If late-life cognitive impairment involved only senses and short-term memory, then eyeglasses, hearing aids, PDAs, and written lists would correct it. But many older adults have impaired **control processes.** As first explained in Chapter 12, control processes are the various methods used to regulate the analysis and flow of information, including memory and retrieval strategies, selective attention, and rules or strategies for problem solving. Control processes usually depend on the prefrontal cortex, which may shrink with age (Raz, 2005).

The elderly tend to rely on prior knowledge, general principles, familiarity, and rules of thumb in their decision making (Jacoby & Rhodes, 2006). This is called a *top-down strategy,* which involves deductive rather than inductive reasoning—or, to use the terms of Chapter 15, intuitive rather than analytic thought. As you remember, such reasoning is not necessarily wrong, but it is limited.

For decision making, for instance, intuitive thinking is quicker and older adults' decisions usually are good enough (Mata & Nunes, 2010). Nonetheless, for complex decisions, analytic thinking may be best for the elderly (Queen & Hess, 2010). This is at odds with expert findings presented in Chapter 21, probably because the unconscious processes are, in late adulthood, also diminished. Relying on them instead of on analysis might lead one astray.

Retrieval, Not Storage

Two aspects of memory are storage, which refers to memories stored in the brain, and retrieval, which is the ability to produce a stored memory on demand. Retrieval is a crucial control process that is typically reduced in late adulthood. Many elders have stored knowledge that they fail to access. An older person who says, "I know it, I just can't remember it," may be quite accurate.

That something is amiss with retrieval is one explanation for many deficits found in cognitive tests of older adults: They have extensive vocabularies (measured by written tests) but limited fluency (when they write or talk), they are much better at recognition than recall, they are particularly likely to have tip-of-the-tongue forgetfulness, their spelling is far poorer than their speech. In the study just mentioned about long-term memories, the participants were first asked to freely recall their circumstances when hearing about September 11th and were then asked the five questions. You saw that answers to specific questions were as good for the old as for the young. Not shown is another finding: Free recall was worse for the old. This indicates again that retrieval, not storage, is reduced.

Some evidence suggests that the elderly need better strategies. For example, in one study, adults of varying ages were given props for 30 odd and memorable actions, such as kissing an artificial frog or stepping into a large plastic bag (Thomas & Bulevich, 2006). They were instructed to perform 15 of these actions (and did so) and told to *imagine* themselves performing the other 15. Two weeks later, all the participants read a list of 45 actions (15 performed, 15 imagined, and 15 new) and were asked which ones had been performed, had been imagined, or were new. Half the participants read the list and simply answered performed/imagined/new; the other half were guided in particular memory strategies that might help (e.g., trying to remember sensations, such as the feel of the frog while kissing it).

Among the half who merely read the list, the younger adults assigned 78 percent of the items to the correct categories, compared with only 52 percent for the older adults. As for the half who were taught memory strategies, the younger adults still got 78 percent correct, but the older ones got 66 percent right (Thomas & Bulevich, 2006). Thus, strategies were more helpful to the old than to the young.

In general, many gerontologists think elders would benefit from using strategies to strengthen control of their cognition. Unfortunately, though, many older adults resist the idea because they believe that declines are "inevitable or irreversible [although] a high sense of control is associated with being happy, healthy, and wise" (Lachman et al., 2009, p. 144).

Reminding People of What They Know

Another control strategy is **priming,** when a person is given a clue before being asked to remember something or when some technique is used to jog the person's memory. For example, hearing a word before being asked to remember it primes the brain to recall the word later. When your professor begins class with a review of last week's class, that primes you to connect what you already know to what you are about to learn. When elders are primed with words like *smart* and *wise,* they perform better on cognitive tests than when they are primed with words like *senile* and *fading* (Bennett & Gaines, 2010). Some people use priming on their own, such as recalling a person's name by remembering the first letter. Priming benefits older people, although they are less likely than younger adults to use it spontaneously (Fleischman, 2007).

Memory is especially shaky in elderly people who lack adequate control processes, and priming would make a marked difference. For example, if older adults are asked to describe the face of their best friend in third grade, they might find that impossible and become anxious that they had forgotten. Instead of anxiety, they might use priming, asking themselves if the friend had brown, black, or blond hair, and so on. With proper control processes, cognition in late adulthood is quite good.

Priming is a simple example of a control process that could advance cognition in the elderly. There are many others. Many developmentalists wonder why the elderly do not use strategies to control their cognition as much as they could. It is known that anxiety, fear, and depression reduce control processes (Banich et al., 2009), and it is also known that internalized ageism and aroused stereotype threat can trigger those emotions in the elderly. Thus, a major impediment to elderly cognition and learning is what they, and others, think about their intellectual potential (Bennett & Gaines, 2010).

Output

The final step in information processing is output. In the Seattle Longitudinal Study (described in Chapter 21), the measured output of all the five primary mental abilities (verbal meaning, spatial orientation, inductive reasoning, number ability, and word fluency) began to decline at about age 60. This was particularly notable in the subtests affected by spatial perception and processing speed (Schaie, 2005).

Similar results are found in many tests of cognition: Thus, the usual path of cognition in late adulthood is gradual decline, at least in output (Salthouse, 2010). Gradual decline of output over the years of late adulthood is present in every study worldwide. For instance, a Japanese study of nondemented elderly, including 68 people over age 100, found that cognition on a standard test declined gradually every decade from age 60 on (Inagaki et al., 2009). In every nation, however, two important factors modify this decline: health and training.

priming Words or ideas presented in advance that make it easier to remember something. It is also possible for priming to impair cognition, as with stereotype threat.

Does She Need Her Shopping List? A shopping list may help when memory fails. If this shopper wrote a list and then misplaced it, however, she could use control processes, such as scanning the store shelves and imagining her kitchen cupboards. She probably would recall almost every item she needs.

Observation Quiz What are two signs that this woman is over 60? (see answer, page 675)

>> **Response for Students** (from page 672): Learn it very well now, and you will probably remember it in 50 years, with a little review.

terminal decline An overall slowdown of cognitive abilities in the weeks and months before death. (Also called *terminal drop*.)

Health and Well-Being

Remember that health is measured not only by mortality and morbidity but also by disability and vitality. These measures of health predict late-life cognition better than age does. Indeed, sometimes cognition in late life goes counter to the trend; people improve rather than decline. The most likely reason is that they gained a sense of control over their health and feel better because of it (Lachman et al., 2009).

Another indicator that health may be pivotal is found in studies of adults who are tested repeatedly as long as they are alive. In such studies, some participants happen to die relatively soon (at age 70 or so) while others keep returning for retesting past age 100. The data show that years past birth are much less important for cognition than are years until death. Most elders think quite well until the end nears, and then many experience **terminal decline** (also called *terminal drop*), an overall slowdown of cognitive abilities (Rabbitt et al., 2008; Thorvaldsson et al., 2009). By contrast, no matter how old they are, those who will live many more years experience much less cognitive decline.

This is closely connected to the emotional impact of the control processes just mentioned. Longitudinal research on more than 10,000 people who died found that an overall sense of well-being was quite steady, declining only slightly over time, until a relatively steep decline that began about four years before death—no matter at what age death occurred (Gerstorf et al., 2010). Another, smaller study found that the two strongest predictors of whether new residents (171 of them) in a nursing home would die in the next year (29 percent did) were intellectual decline and depression—not morbidity (Kane et al., 2010).

Of course, this nursing home study does not mean that physical health is unimportant: Virtually every resident of a nursing home has a serious medical condition that could cause death. Furthermore, some medical conditions such as hypertension, diabetes, arteriosclerosis, emphysema, and many other chronic conditions slow down cognition; their effects are evident even in middle age. Thus, the link between cognition and mortality in the nursing home could be indirectly connected to disease. But it is noteworthy that once a person is in a nursing home, cognition and mood are more predictive of mortality than is disease. The converse is also true: Maintaining good health habits, particularly exercise and nutrition, may be as important for the mind as for the body.

New Tricks With a grandchild as a patient tutor, this woman, like other older people, is delighted to learn how to use a laptop computer.

Training

The second important modifier of cognitive decline in late adulthood is training (Lustig et al., 2009). In the Seattle Longitudinal Study, some 60-year-olds were given five one-hour sessions of personalized training and practice. Those five hours had an impact: The trainees regained the spatial understanding they had had 14 years earlier (Schaie, 2005). Similar results have been found in many other training programs targeted at specific skills. One conclusion now accepted by almost all researchers is that it is quite possible to improve virtually any specific cognitive ability in the young-old if the educational process is carefully targeted to the individual's needs and abilities.

This success has led to two new questions: (1) Can the old-old benefit from training? (2) Can training in one particular task transfer to other tasks? The answer to both questions is a *qualified* yes (C. S. Green & Bavelier, 2008). Apparently, the old adage "You can't teach an old dog new tricks" is ageist, at least when

used to refer to people (and probably dogs, too). But note that that yes is qualified; it does not apply to every older person or to every type of training.

For example, one study began with healthy 80-year-olds divided into two groups who performed equally well on cognitive tests (Buschkuehl et al., 2008). Then half completed various tasks designed to improve visual memory, about 20 hours in all over three months. For instance, a sequence of animals (dog, cat, iguana, rabbit, mouse, toad, butterfly, and bee) appeared and then disappeared on a computer screen; the same animals were then presented in different sequence. The 80-year-olds were asked to click on the animal that was previously second in the series. Meanwhile, the other participants were taught to ride an exercise bicycle (set at a low speed to avoid the cognitive benefit of aerobic exercise), which they did for the same 20 hours.

The results led to that qualified yes. The bicycle group stayed at the same cognitive level, while the experimental group improved in tests of visual working memory (related to the training, but not the same as the training). However, they did not improve in other tests of working memory, such as repeating a long string of digits. Furthermore, a year later, they had lost some of what they had gained: They did no better or worse than the retested bicycle group (Buschkuehl et al., 2008).

Another group of researchers (Basak et al., 2008) targeted the aspect of cognition that is most reduced with age: executive control processes that enable an adult to be flexible despite distractions, changing tasks, and new goals. Volunteers, averaging age 69, were again divided into an experimental and a control group. The experimental group spent about 24 hours over five weeks playing a video game that required making quick decisions, task-switching, and monitoring several parts of the screen at once. The members of the control group were tested at the beginning (when their scores equaled those of the experimental group), in the middle, and then at the end. Final results showed that training worked: Participation in the video game led to significant improvements in executive control (see the Research Design).

Some of this research has led to the notion that older people should exercise their minds in order to keep intellectually fit. Most developmentalists are suspicious of this "use it or lose it" hypothesis, especially when it produces intellectual puzzles for the elderly that are supposed to stave off dementia or touts a particular video game that will supposedly make every older person smarter.

Gerontologist Timothy Salthouse (2006) analyzed evidence that mental exercise reduces mental aging and concluded that "although my professional opinion is that . . . the mental-exercise hypothesis is more of an optimistic hope than an empirical reality, my personal recommendation is that people should behave as if it is true" (p. 84). In other words, we all should keep our minds active, as well as our

>> **Answer to Observation Quiz** (from page 673) Her gray hair and poor vision. She is holding the paper about 24 inches away from her face, a sign of aging eyes. Younger people see best if an object is about 10 inches away.

▶ Research Design

Scientists: Chandramallika Basak, Walter R. Boot, Michelle W. Voss, and Arthur Kramer.

Publication: *Psychology and Aging* (2008).

Participants: Forty older adults, living near Urbana-Champaign, Illinois. All of them were right-handed, had good vision (sometimes corrected with glasses), and showed no signs of dementia. They were volunteers, recruited via flyers and word of mouth. None of them were video game players.

Design: Before, during, and after the five-week training, all the participants took a battery of cognitive tests that presumably evaluated executive function. The experimental group were taught to play a video game called "Quick Battle" that was set to begin at the easiest level. No collaboration was allowed. After each game, they were told their score, as well as how that compared to their previous score. Then another game began. This continued for five sessions, each of which included several episodes of this new game.

Results: The experimental group improved on most of the tests when compared to the control group, with the most powerful improvement on a task called *n-back*, in which the person is asked to quickly judge whether a newly appearing letter is the same as one that appeared previously, either one back ($n = 1$), two back ($n = 2$), and so on.

Major conclusion: Training can produce transfer of cognitive skill, even for control processes. The researchers emphasized that not every video game provides the same result; this game was carefully chosen to allow practice of particular skills.

Comment: In other research as well, video games improve the performance of elders on a variety of cognitive tasks. One problem with this study, however, is that the participants were not retested a year or more later. But other similar research has reported that some transferred skills endure. Another problem is that the control group had no alternate task, which allows the possibility that being in the training program, rather than practicing the particular video game, produced the results. The practical question, which these scientists posed, is whether such control-processes training leads to transfer in daily life. For instance, were these elders better drivers because of their video game experiences? Such questions are the focus of ongoing research.

Talking 'bout My Generation Measuring brain age is the goal of a Nintendo DS game. Shown here front and center is Alf Carreta giving the game a "test drive" at a trade show in London. He's the lead singer for the Zimmers, a British rock band of 40 pensioners who recorded a best-selling cover of "My Generation," earlier popularized by The Who. At age 90, Alf's brain age was 59.

bodies healthy and our spirits up, but no one should assume cognitive decline with age is thereby banished.

Ecological Validity

There is one more aspect of output that needs to be explained. Since output can be improved via training, to design the training we must first decide what cognition is needed in late adulthood. Surely older adults do not *need* to score high on IQ tests, or to finish a crossword puzzle in record time, or to name past presidents.

ecological validity The idea that cognition should be measured in settings that are as realistic as possible and that the abilities measured should be those needed in real life.

Ecological validity is the idea that cognition should be measured in everyday tasks and circumstances, not as laboratory tests assess it, and that the abilities measured should be those that people need. Ecological validity is important at every age but particularly for the elderly, who are handicapped in many ways by traditional practices (Marsiske & Margrett, 2006). For example, older adults are at their best in the morning, just when adolescents are half asleep. It would be inaccurate to compare the two groups in late afternoon, as some researchers have done.

Similarly, it is unfair to use a timed test to measure accuracy because, as already explained, older adults are unable or unwilling to speed up their responses (Costello et al., 2010). Almost invariably, the more realistic the testing circumstances (as when people are quizzed at home instead of in a university laboratory), the better an older person performs.

Ecological validity is a concern of many gerontologists (Berg, 2008). The problem is that "there is no objective way to evaluate the degree of ecological validity at the current time because ecological validity is a subjective concept" (Salthouse, 2010, p. 77). It is impossible to be totally objective in assessing cognition because people have different opinions about the ecological value of various parts of thinking. Nonetheless, awareness of the need for ecological validity is crucial to evaluate the research.

Traditional tests of memory, knowledge, intellect, and speed measure cognitive abilities that are valued by the young, especially in schools; however, problem solving and emotional regulation may be the cognitive abilities needed for the old. Both of these are likely to improve with age, but neither is usually measured (Hall, 2010).

When scientists study the relationship of cognition to the challenges of daily life, they find that older adults develop or ignore various cognitive skills. This is evident from research on vocational complexity (Finkel et al., 2009). Before retirement, older adults whose jobs require complex interpersonal understanding (mentoring, supervising, collaborating, and so on) gain in verbal and spatial skills while those in simpler, less challenging jobs do not. After retirement, apparently the former have less opportunity to use their skills whereas the latter have more opportunity, because those who left mindless jobs gained compared to those who had complex work (see Figure 24.2).

When real-life situations are assessed, sometimes the old outperform the young. For example, one kind of memory is called *prospective memory,* which is remembering to do something in the future. One might imagine that prospective memory would be particularly poor in the elderly, since more of their life has passed than remains in the future. That is what laboratory research finds—reduced prospective memory with age. However, in real life, prospective memory is better among the old than the young (Henry et al., 2004; McDaniel et al., 2008).

In daily life, older adults use routines, pacing, strategies, and cues to "help ameliorate, and sometimes eliminate, age-related memory impairment" (Moscovitch et al., 2001). Compared with college students, older adults score lower on fill-in-the-blanks tests of newly learned material (as might be given in a college class) and in recalling nonsense syllables (a traditional memory test), but they are better at remembering to send birthday cards, to take their vitamins, and even to brush their teeth. Awareness of the need for ecological validity has helped scientists restructure research on working memory, finding fewer deficits than originally thought.

Certainly ecological validity is an important qualifier whenever an older person's cognitive ability is found wanting. Does loss of cognition affect the older person's daily life? The answer is "Not usually." Sometimes, however, the answer is "Yes, drastically." We now turn to the group for whom cognitive impairment destroys daily life.

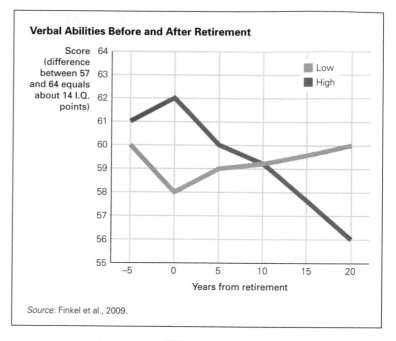

FIGURE 24.2

Thoughtful Work At least in one study, the verbal abilities of workers with cognitively demanding jobs increased as they approached retirement (designated here by zero) and then decreased when life became less challenging. The opposite was true for those with mindless work. No wonder some people look forward to retirement and others dread it.

SUMMING UP

Usually cognition in late adulthood shows some fading, particularly in sensory input, short-term memory, and control strategies. However, other aspects remain strong, including vocabulary and long-term memory. Health and exercise protect mental abilities, and a positive attitude may be crucial in maintenance of the mind. The number of years to death, not years since birth, affects cognitive decline. Training can improve specific intellectual abilities. The awareness of ecological validity has led scientists to realize that some laboratory tests of cognition may be unfair to the old and that, in their daily lives, some of the old think as well as, or even better than, the young. ■

>> The Impaired: Diseases That Affect the Brain

The patterns of normal aging challenge another assumption—that senility is typical. Actually, *senile* simply means "old," and in that sense, senility happens to everyone. However, senility is commonly used to signify severe mental impairment, implying that old age brings intellectual failure—an ageist and false idea.

Dementia and Age

dementia Irreversible loss of intellectual functioning caused by organic brain damage or disease. Dementia becomes more common with age, but it is abnormal and pathological even in the very old.

delirium A temporary loss of memory, often accompanied by hallucinations, terror, grandiosity, and irrational behavior.

Dementia is a better term than *senility* for irreversible, pathological loss of brain functioning caused by organic brain damage or disease. The word *dementia* literally means "out of mind," referring to severely impaired judgment, memory, or problem-solving ability. It is diagnosed when a person has chronic "multiple cognitive deficits . . . sufficiently severe to cause impairment in occupational or social functioning" (American Psychiatric Association, 2000, p. 148). More than 70 diseases can cause dementia, each different in onset, sequence, severity, and particulars—although all are characterized by mental confusion and forgetfulness. Dementia is chronic, which means it is long-lasting, unlike **delirium,** which is acute, with severe memory loss and confusion that disappears in hours or days (Inouye, 2006).

Traditionally, dementia occurring before age 60 was called *presenile dementia;* that occurring after age 60 was called *senile dementia* or *senile psychosis.* However, age 60 is a meaningless divide, because those few people who become demented before age 60 have the same symptoms and causes as those who develop it later.

Estimates about prevalence are often exaggerated, a manifestation of the age-ism described in Chapter 23. To obtain accurate data, researchers examined a representative sample of people over age 70 from every part of the United States, checked medical records and test results, and asked detailed questions of someone who knew the older person well. They found that 14 percent had some form of dementia (see Table 24.1; Plassman et al., 2007). The fact that only 1 percent of people in their 60s, and even fewer younger than 60, have dementia suggests that about 4 million U.S. residents now have dementia of one type or another. As you see from the table, incidence rises with age. As adults live longer, the number who have dementia will increase.

Not Everyone Gets It Most elderly people never experience dementia. Among people in their 70s, only 1 person in 20 does, and most of those who reach 90 or 100 are not demented. Presented another way, the prevalence data sound more dire: Almost 4 million people in the United States have dementia.

TABLE 24.1

Prevalence of Dementia Among the Elderly, by Age, United States

Age	All Dementia (%)	Alzheimer Disease (%)	Vascular Dementia (%)
70–79	5	2.3	1
80–89	24.2	18.2	4.1
90+	37.4	29.7	6.2
Overall (70+)	13.9	9.7	2.4

Source: Plassman et al., 2007.

Internationally, rates of dementia vary by nation, from about 2 percent to 25 percent of those over age 65 (Kalaria et al., 2008). Valid cross-cultural studies are not yet available, although in the poorest nations only the very healthy live past 75, which makes the incidence of dementia lower (Kalaria et al., 2008). Genetics, culture, health, and nutrition may also reduce the rates in some nations, but that is not yet known (Bondi et al., 2009).

Alzheimer Disease

Alzheimer disease (AD) The most common cause of dementia, characterized by gradual deterioration of memory and personality and marked by the formation of plaques of beta-amyloid protein and tangles of tau in the brain. (Sometimes called *senile dementia of the Alzheimer type.*)

The most feared and the most frequent type of dementia in North America and western Europe is **Alzheimer disease (AD),** sometimes called *senile dementia of the Alzheimer type* (SDAT) (Weiner & Lipton, 2009). Alzheimer disease is characterized by the proliferation of *plaques* and *tangles* in the cerebral cortex. These abnormalities destroy the ability of neurons to communicate with one another, eventually halting cortex function.

Plaques are clumps of a protein called **beta-amyloid,** found in the tissues surrounding the neurons; tangles are twisted masses of threads made of a protein called **tau** that is found within the neurons. A normal brain contains some beta-amyloid and tau, but in AD these plaques and tangles proliferate, especially in the hippocampus (the brain structure that is crucial for memory). Forgetfulness is usually the dominant symptom, with short-term memory the first to disappear. Although finding many plaques and tangles at autopsy is definitive for Alzheimer disease, some autopsies reveal plaques and tangles in people who did not appear demented when they were alive. Perhaps they compensated by using other parts of their brains.

Genes and Alzheimer Disease

Alzheimer disease is partly genetic. When it appears before age 60, either trisomy-21 (Down syndrome) or one of three dominant genes—APP (amyloid precursor protein), presenilin 1, or presenilin 2—is the reason. With those genetic causes, the disease progresses quickly, reaching the last phase within three to five years.

Usually AD appears much later, at age 75 or so, although many researchers believe it actually begins 10 or even 20 years before diagnosis. The most frequent forms are polygenetic, with SORL1 and ApoE4 among the genes that increase the risk. People who live to age 80 and who inherit one copy of ApoE4 (as about one-fifth of all U.S. residents do) have about a 50/50 chance of developing AD. Those who inherit two copies of the gene almost always develop the disease if they live long enough, although many die before dementia is diagnosed because ApoE4 increases the likelihood of many other serious ailments (Plassman et al., 2007).

The frequency of the ApoE4 allele varies from place to place: high in Finland, low in Greece, high among South Africans, low among South Asians (Kalaria et al., 2008). Genetic tests are rarely used to predict AD because they might evoke false fear or deceptive reassurance. Many people with no known genetic risk develop AD, and some people with the ApoE4 gene never do (Salthouse, 2010).

Stages: From Confusion to Death

Alzheimer disease usually runs through a progressive course of five identifiable stages, beginning with forgetfulness and ending in death. Even before the first stage, many people have **mild cognitive impairment,** which is forgetfulness and loss of verbal fluency that is worse than the usual brain slowdown and reduced short-term memory described previously. About half of those with mild cognitive impairment remain mildly impaired for decades or even improve, while the other half develop Alzheimer disease.

Thousands of scientists seek biomarkers or test questions that will definitively distinguish those people who will remain mildly impaired from those who will develop AD (Miller, 2009). No success yet. Once symptoms of Alzheimer disease begin, they increase gradually, in five stages.

Stage 1. People in the first stage forget recent events or newly acquired information, particularly the names of people and places. For example, they might be unable to remember where they just put something. This first stage is not much worse than mild cognitive impairment, with some but not all people aware that something is wrong. In a study of 1,883 people over age 65 (average age 75), 5 percent complained about memory

beta-amyloid A protein that makes up the plaques that are found in the tissues surrounding neurons.

tau A protein that makes up the tangles found within neurons.

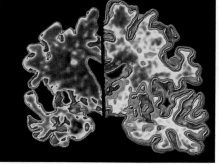

The Alzheimer Brain This computer graphic shows a vertical slice through a brain ravaged by Alzheimer disease *(left)* compared with a similar slice of a normal brain *(right).* The diseased brain is shrunken as a result of the degeneration of neurons.

Especially for Genetic Counselors Would you perform a test for ApoE4 if someone asked for it? (see response, page 681)

mild cognitive impairment Forgetfulness and loss of verbal fluency that often comes before the first stage of Alzheimer disease.

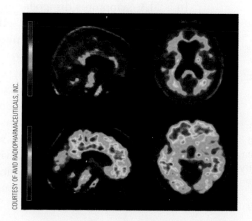

Visible Too Late Magnetic resonance imaging (MRI) shows normal *(top)* and Alzheimer *(bottom)* brains at work; the red areas represent amyloid plaques that block communication between neurons. Every brain has some amyloid, but most people naturally rid themselves of it. Although some scientists are testing drugs to reduce amyloid, plaque builds up years before the first symptoms of dementia are evident. People would need to begin treatment before they even know they have the disease.

I Love You, Dad This man, who is in the last stage of Alzheimer disease, no longer remembers his daughter, but she obviously has fond memories of his fatherly affection.

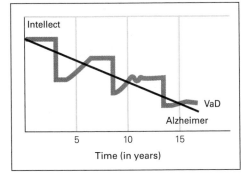

ALAN ODDIE / PHOTOEDIT, INC.

FIGURE 24.3

The Progression of Vascular Dementia and Alzheimer Disease Cognitive decline is apparent in both Alzheimer disease and multi-infarct dementia. However, the pattern of decline for each disease is different. Victims of AD show steady, gradual decline, while those who suffer from VaD get suddenly much worse, improve somewhat, and then experience another serious loss.

vascular dementia (VaD) A form of dementia characterized by sporadic, and progressive, loss of intellectual functioning caused by repeated infarcts, or temporary obstructions of blood vessels, which prevent sufficient blood from reaching the brain. (Also called *multi-infarct dementia*.)

problems. Three years later, 15 percent of those who complained initially, and 6 percent of those who had not, had developed dementia (Wang et al., 2004). Even experts cannot always distinguish early Alzheimer disease from other conditions. For example, in retrospect, President Ronald Reagan had early AD symptoms while in office, but no one diagnosed it.

Stage 2. Generalized confusion develops, with deficits in concentration and short-term memory. Speech becomes aimless and repetitive, vocabulary is limited, words get mixed up. People at stage 2 may read a newspaper article and forget it completely the next moment. Personality traits become exaggerated as rational thought disappears: Those who are suspicious by nature may decide that others have stolen the things that they have mislaid; a tidy person may become compulsively neat; someone with a quick temper may display explosive rages; an asocial person may become more withdrawn. One writer worked obsessively to chronicle his losses, relying on spell-check because his spelling had deteriorated; he quit trying in stage 2 because he spent five minutes struggling to spell *hour* (DeBaggio, 2002).

Stage 3. Eventually, memory loss becomes dangerous. A person might forget to turn off a lit stove or a hot iron, causing a fire; might forget to eat; or might fail to dress properly, leaving home barefoot in winter or walking naked about the neighborhood, crossing streets against the light and forgetting the way home. For some, the part of the brain that recognizes objects becomes tangled, so the person does not know whether something is a fork, a hat, or a beloved family member.

Stage 4. At the fourth stage, full-time care is needed. Sufferers cannot care for themselves, communicate clearly, or even recognize their closest loved ones, not because they have forgotten them but because the part of the brain that recognizes people has further deteriorated. Their speech is short and simple; ultimately, talking stops. Reading is impossible; they stare blankly at the TV or into space.

Stage 5. Finally, people with AD become unresponsive. Identity and personality are gone; they recognize no one. When former president Ronald Reagan was at this stage, a longtime friend who visited him was asked, "Did he recognize you?" The friend answered, "Worse than that—I didn't recognize him." Death comes 10 to 15 years after the first signs appear.

Vascular Dementia

The second common cause of dementia is a stroke (a temporary obstruction of a blood vessel in the brain) or a series of strokes, called *TIAs* (transient ischemic attacks, or ministrokes). The interruption in blood flow reduces oxygen in the affected area of the brain, which destroys brain tissue. As part of the brain dies, immediate symptoms (blurred vision, weak or paralyzed limbs, slurred speech, and mental confusion) appear.

In a TIA, symptoms disappear quickly—in hours or even minutes—and may be so slight that no one (even the victim) notices. However, repeated TIAs produce more damage, and **vascular dementia (VaD),** also called *multi-infarct dementia,* occurs. Vascular dementia is also common when the elderly have surgery under general anesthesia, especially if hypertension or diabetes has already weakened the brain. A momentary stroke may occur during or after the surgery, and some people's brains cannot recover (Gorelick & Bowler, 2010). Either way, the progression of VaD differs from that of Alzheimer disease, but the result is similar (see Figure 24.3).

In North America and Europe, VaD is the primary diagnosis in about 15 to 20 percent of people with dementia, with AD the primary diagnosis for about 50 percent. (Comorbidity is common: Many people have the other as a secondary diagnosis.) By contrast, in Japan and China, VaD is more common than Alzheimer disease (De la Torre et al., 2002).

Other Dementias

About 30 years ago, people used the words *dementia* and *Alzheimer disease* interchangeably. No longer. There are many other kinds of dementia.

Frontal lobe dementia, or *frontotemporal lobar degeneration* (Pick disease is the most common form), may cause 15 percent of all dementias in the United States. Parts of the brain that regulate emotions and social behavior (the amygdala and the frontal lobes) deteriorate, making the person disinhibited, impulsive, and emotionally indifferent (Mathias & Morphett, 2010). As a result, personality changes—not memory loss—are the main symptom. A loving mother might reject her children or a businessman might invest in a scheme he would have avoided earlier. Frontal lobe dementia may be worse than Alzheimer or vascular dementia in that compassion, self-awareness, and judgment fade in a person who otherwise seems normal. Frontal lobe dementia usually begins before age 60 and progresses rapidly, leading to death in about five years.

Many other dementias begin with impaired motor control (shaking when picking up a coffee cup, falling or shuffling when trying to walk), not with impaired thinking. The most common of these is **Parkinson disease,** which does not always lead to dementia but is the cause of about 3 percent of all cases of dementia (Aarsland et al., 2005). Parkinson disease starts with rigidity or tremor of the muscles, as neurons that produce dopamine degenerate, affecting movement long before cognition is notably impaired. Younger adults with Parkinson disease have sufficient cognitive reserve to avoid dementia for years; older people develop dementia sooner (Pfeiffer et al., 2011). Depression and anxiety are common with Parkinson, partly caused by brain damage.

Another 3 to 5 percent of all dementias in the United States are **Lewy body dementia,** named after round deposits of protein (Lewy bodies) in the neurons (Zaccai et al., 2005). Lewy bodies are also present in Parkinson disease, but in Lewy body dementia they are more numerous and dispersed throughout the brain. Motor movements and cognition are both impacted, although the effects are less severe than the motor deficits of Parkinson disease or the memory loss of Alzheimer disease (Bondi et al., 2009). People with this disorder may have vivid visual hallucinations, momentary loss of attention, and loss of inhibition. As a result of this brain abnormality, they may fall, faint, take risks, gamble, or express inappropriate sexual urges.

Our focus in this chapter is on late adulthood, but we should briefly mention some other causes of dementia that usually begin before age 65. Among these are Huntington disease; multiple sclerosis; severe head injury; and the last stages of syphilis, AIDS, and bovine spongiform encephalitis (BSE, or mad cow disease). Timing and symptoms vary; comorbid conditions produce quicker and more severe dementia.

With some dementias, blood tests and brain scans (MRIs) reveal the cause; with others, psychological tests show a pattern that indicates one form or another. However, for many late-life dementias, the definitive diagnosis comes after death, when a pathologist sees plaques and tangles, dead brain areas, a shrunken prefrontal cortex, or unusual neurons that signify AD, vascular, frontal lobe, or Lewy body dementia.

Prevention and Treatment

Slowing down senescence postpones dementia, as does improving blood circulation and preventing hypertension and diabetes. In addition, "some brain-cellular changes seen in normal aging can be slowed or reversed with exercise" (Woodlee &

frontal lobe dementia Deterioration of the amygdala and frontal lobes that may be the cause of 15 percent of all dementias. (Also called *frontotemporal lobar degeneration*.)

Parkinson disease A chronic, progressive disease that is characterized by muscle tremor and rigidity, and sometimes dementia; caused by a reduction of dopamine production in the brain.

Lewy body dementia A form of dementia characterized by an increase in Lewy body cells in the brain. Symptoms include visual hallucinations, momentary loss of attention, falling, and fainting.

>> Response for Genetic Counselors (from page 679) A general guideline for genetic counselors is to provide clients with whatever information they seek; but because of both the uncertainty of diagnosis from such a test and the devastation of Alzheimer disease, the ApoE4 test is not available at present. This may change (as was the case with the test for HIV) if early methods of prevention and treatment become more effective.

KAREN KASMAUSKI / CORBIS

Waiting for a Bath This woman is in a Tokyo facility that provides baths for physically or cognitively impaired elderly people—not just as a hygienic necessity, but also as a soothing, sensual experience.

Observation Quiz Should someone take that doll away? (see answer, page 684)

Schallert, 2006, p. 203). Because brain plasticity continues throughout life, exercise may build brain capacity, not merely prevent loss (Kramer & Erickson, 2007). Medication may help, too. A study in Finland began with all the older people who did not have dementia. Half of them were given drugs to reduce lipids (primarily cholesterol) in their blood. Years later, fewer of this group had developed any type of dementia (Solomon et al., 2010).

For some dementias, people can avoid specific pathogens: Beef can be tested for mad cow disease, condoms can protect against AIDS, syphilis can be cured with antibiotics before it reaches the brain. For most dementias, prevention is not yet certain. There is no evidence that doing puzzles or that avoiding toxins that were once hypothesized to cause AD—lead, aluminum, copper, and pesticides among them—makes any difference. The same discouraging results come from controlled studies testing many possible treatments—including hormones, aspirin, coffee, antioxidants, and statins (Zandi et al., 2005).

The good news is that thousands of scientists are working to discover ways to halt the production of beta-amyloid or tau or to diagnose Alzheimer disease 10 or 15 years before the first outward signs. In a massive cooperative effort between the U.S. federal government and the major pharmaceutical companies, some early markers for dementia—in brain scans or cerebrospinal fluid—have been identified experimentally. Once early diagnosis is possible, drugs can be tested to see if they halt the disease. Some anti-Alzheimer drugs seem successful in mice, but studies with human participants thus far are disappointing (Miller, 2009).

Cure is not yet possible, and even halting the progression is difficult. The first step is to improve overall health: High blood pressure, diabetes, arteriosclerosis, and emphysema all disrupt the flow of oxygen to the brain and worsen the symptoms of dementia (Caplan & Schooler, 2003; Elias et al., 2004). Sadly, that first step sometimes occurs years after symptoms appear. Diagnosis is often missed or delayed (Bradford et al., 2009) partly because symptoms are ignored and few primary care physicians are trained to combine clinical judgment with tests of behavior, cognition, blood, spinal fluid, and brain—all of which are expensive, time-consuming, and stressful (Aluise et al., 2008; Besga et al., 2010; Mattsson et al., 2009).

All experts believe that early treatment can make a difference. Rehabilitation can overcome much initial brain damage from VaD, and diet, drugs, and exercise can prevent another TIA. Several drugs, especially cholinesterase inhibitors (e.g., donepezil) and memantine, allow years of close-to-normal functioning for those with Alzheimer disease (Kaduszkiewicz et al., 2005; Kavirajan & Schneider, 2007). Other drugs are helpful for Parkinson disease, and surgery and perhaps stem cells can restore lost movement control, although care is needed because treatment may increase impulsive behavior (Frank et al., 2007). Drugs can also help Lewy body dementia—but the drugs for Alzheimer disease may make this form of dementia worse.

This leads to a pressing need: more professionals who are willing and able to provide early diagnosis and then individualized medical and psychological care. Patients and caregivers are more often relieved than depressed to be told why someone is confused and forgetful; having a plan of action undercuts distress (Carpenter, 2009).

Reversible Impairment

Accurate diagnosis is even more crucial when a person is mistakenly thought to have dementia. True dementias destroy parts of the brain and thus cannot be cured, but many older people are thought to be losing their minds when in fact a reversible problem is at fault.

Mental Illness

The most common reversible cause of dementia symptoms is depression. An older person who repeatedly complains about losing his or her mind, or despairs at every memory lapse, probably has a treatable mental illness. Normally, older people are quite content with their lives; constant sadness or anxiety is a sign that something is wrong.

Ironically, people with untreated anxiety or depression exaggerate minor memory losses or refuse to talk. Quite the opposite reaction occurs with Alzheimer disease, when victims are surprised that they cannot answer questions, or with Lewy body or frontal lobe dementia, when people talk without thinking. Specifics of memory also provide clues. People with dementia might forget what they just said, heard, or did but might well be able to describe in detail something that happened long ago. The opposite is often true for emotional disorders: People are impaired or delusional in episodic memory (months or years ago) but not in short-term memory.

Other Causes

Malnutrition, dehydration, brain tumors, physical illness, and overmedication can all cause symptoms that seem to be dementia (Milosevic et al., 2007). With age, bodies become less efficient at digesting food and using its nutrients. A varied and healthful diet, emphasizing fresh fruits and vegetables, is even more essential in late adulthood than earlier. Deficits of B vitamins, particularly B_{12} and folic acid, correlate with cognitive decline (Stanger et al., 2009).

Scientists urge caution here. Almost monthly, someone finds certain vitamins, minerals, or foods that might protect against dementia. For instance, a Scandinavian study found that consumption of tea, chocolate, and wine correlated with better cognition (Nurk et al., 2009)—welcome news for people who already enjoy these items, but regarded with suspicion by others. Similarly, selenium, blueberries, olive oil, red grapes, garlic, giant knotweed, and turmeric have all been mentioned as fighting disease or dementia, but according to the triage theory of nutrition, too much of any one substance might put the body out of balance (McCann & Ames, 2009).

That caution is especially needed when people take several medications, a circumstance called **polypharmacy.** At home as well as in the hospital, most elderly people take numerous drugs. For instance, even in Canada, where the government takes a more active role in health care and prescription medication, a detailed study found that the cost of prescription drugs for people over age 65 almost doubled from 2002 to 2008 (Canadian Institute for Health Information, 2010). Some increase was due to inflation, some was due to increases in population, but most was due to the fact that doctors were writing more prescriptions and elders were taking more drugs. The per capita cost of drugs for Canadians over age 65 was about $1,400 a year (see Figure 24.4).

The disturbing data on prescription drugs actually underestimate polypharmacy because almost every older person also takes over-the-counter drugs and

And the Print Is Too Small Patients, physicians, and pharmacists have reason to be confused about the eight or more drugs that the average elderly person takes. Very few patients take their medicines exactly as prescribed. Moreover, in addition to prescription drugs, most elderly people also take over-the-counter medications, vitamins, and herbal remedies as well as consume caffeinated or alcoholic drinks. It is no wonder that drug interactions cause drowsiness, unsteadiness, and confusion in about half of all elderly persons.

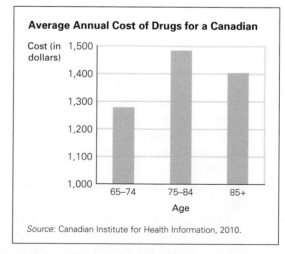

Average Annual Cost of Drugs for a Canadian

Cost (in dollars) — y-axis: 1,000 to 1,500
Age — x-axis: 65–74, 75–84, 85+

Source: Canadian Institute for Health Information, 2010.

FIGURE 24.4

And in Canada Drugs Are Cheaper In every developed nation, older people take far more drugs than do younger adults. The Canadian health system allows accurate estimates of the cost per person, and you can see that even in a nation where the government keeps the cost down, medication is very common for the elderly.

polypharmacy Refers to a situation in which elderly people are prescribed several medications. The various side effects and interactions of those medications can result in dementia symptoms.

TONY FREEMAN / PHOTOEDIT, INC.

many use herbal remedies (Hajjar et al., 2007). Added to that, most older adults have been drinking alcohol all their lives, unaware that in late adulthood alcohol combined with medicine can make even one drink too much. Moreover, few professionals or family members recognize polypharmacy. Audrey, a widow who was addicted to Valium, Placidyl, and alcohol, was a classic case.

A CASE TO STUDY

Drug Addiction in a Grandmother

Polypharmacy and drug abuse are not rare among the elderly, although ageism often leads family members to believe that an elderly relative's mood swings, rage, and confusion are simply normal signs of aging. As at every age, addicts hide their addiction, lie about their drug use, and become angry at those who confront them. Fortunately, again at any age, recovery is possible. Consider Audrey.

> A 70-year-old widow named Audrey . . . was covered with large black bruises and burns from her kitchen stove. Audrey no longer had an appetite, so she ate little and was emaciated. One night she passed out in her driveway and scraped her face. The next morning, her neighbor found her face down on the pavement in her nightgown.
>
> Audrey couldn't be trusted with the grandchildren anymore, so family visits were fewer and farther between. She rarely showered and spent most days sitting in a chair alternating between drinking, sleeping, and watching television. She stopped calling friends, and social invitations had long since ceased.
>
> Audrey obtained prescriptions for Valium, a tranquilizer, and Placidyl, a sleep inducer. Both medications, which are addictive

and have more adverse effects in patients over age 60, should only be used for short periods of time. Audrey had taken both medications for years at three to four times the prescribed dosage. She mixed them with large quantities of alcohol. She was a full-fledged addict . . . close to death.

> Her children knew she had a problem, but they . . . couldn't agree among themselves on the best way to help her. Over time, they became desensitized to the seriousness of her problem—until it progressed to a dangerously advanced stage. Luckily for Audrey, she was referred to a new doctor who recognized her addiction. . . . Once Audrey was in treatment and weaned off the alcohol and drugs, she bloomed. Audrey's memory improved; her appetite returned; she regained her energy; and she started walking, swimming and exercising every day. Now, a decade later, Audrey plays an important role in her grandchildren's lives, gardens, and she lives creatively and with meaning.

[Colleran & Jay, 2003, p. 11]

Audrey is a stunning example of the danger of ageist assumptions. Her children did not realize that she could and should have an intellectually and socially productive life.

>> Answer to Observation Quiz (from page 682) No. Note that the woman is holding the doll close, with both hands and her chin. The photograph makes a valid point about the universal need for comfort.

One reason doctors overmedicate is that recommended doses are determined primarily by clinical trials with younger adults (Herrera et al., 2010). The metabolism and digestive systems of young adults rid their bodies of excess drugs sooner than do those of the elderly, which may alter the proper dose—but research does not say how. Logically, less medication might be needed to avoid overdosing, or, alternatively, more medication might be needed because absorption is impaired.

An added problem is that people of every age forget when they are supposed to take which drugs (before, during, or after meals? after dinner, before breakfast, at bedtime?). Although prospective memory is better in the old than in the young, anyone can misunderstand exactly how medication is to be taken, a problem multiplied as more drugs are prescribed (Bosworth & Ayotte, 2009).

Even when medications are taken as written, drug interactions can produce confusion and psychotic behavior. Cognitive side effects (such as confusion and depression) can occur with almost any drug, and many doctors prescribe drugs for depression, anxiety, or insomnia that have cognitive changes as the main effect. In addition, anesthesia in a hospital often triggers hallucinations, and pain medication can produce delirium. If a drugged and confused patient is discharged from a hospital to a nursing home, the initial intake interview may lead to more medication, unnecessarily.

The solution to polypharmacy seems simple: Eliminate drugs. But doing so requires careful analysis of harm, benefits, and interactions. For instance, Coumadin is life saving for people with abnormal heart rhythms, but it destroys vitamin K, which is needed for overall health (McCann & Ames, 2009). Most of the oldest-old are treated by multiple physicians, but not every one of those doctors may be aware of the drugs being prescribed by the others—and no one knows the side effects of them all.

Many drugs interact with the person's genetic characteristics, which makes it even harder for a professional to know which drug and dose to prescribe. Added to that, the elderly themselves may find some drugs too expensive and make harmful substitutions, or they might try various supplements, compounds, and herbal preparations that contain mind-altering toxins. Just as it is folly to assume that all adults become demented, it is folly to think that every medication does what it is supposed to do, and only that.

Regarding medication or nutrition or any other issue in late adulthood, it is crucial to remember the difference between science—which requires replication, controlled studies, large numbers of participants, and multicultural research—and wishful thinking. Especially regarding aging and dementia, cross-sequential studies over several years are needed. When good scientific methods are used, no miracle food or smart pill is found (Moats & Rimm, 2007; Pocobelli et al., 2009, 2010).

SUMMING UP

Dementia, characterized by memory loss and confusion, is neither usual nor rare. The main causes of dementia are Alzheimer disease, small strokes (TIAs) resulting in vascular dementia, frontal lobe dementia, Parkinson disease, and Lewy body dementia—although there are many other reasons a person's brain might be impaired. Each condition follows a somewhat different pattern. Researchers are working to detect dementia years before the behavioral symptoms appear; to discover causes; and to test drugs, surgery, or stem cells that might stop its insidious progression.

No cure is yet known, although exercise and good health can delay the onset or slow the progression. Not everyone who is mentally confused or who notices memory lapses has dementia. Some may have mild cognitive impairment and continue in that condition for years; others have reversible problems, including depression, anxiety disorders, malnutrition, and polypharmacy.

>> The Optimal: New Cognitive Development

You have learned that most older adults maintain adequate intellectual power. Some losses—in rapid responses, for instance—are quite manageable in daily life, and only a minority become demented. But one principle of the life-span perspective is that at every period, there are gains as well as losses. Are there cognitive gains in late adulthood? Sometimes. New depth, enhanced creativity, and even wisdom are possible.

Erikson and Maslow

Both Erik Erikson and Abraham Maslow were particularly interested in the perspective of the elderly, interviewing older people in depth to understand their views. Erikson's final book, *Vital Involvement in Old Age* (Erikson et al., 1986), written when he was in his 90s, was based on responses from other 90-year-olds—the individuals who had been studied since they were babies in Berkeley, California.

self-actualization The final stage in Maslow's hierarchy of needs, characterized by aesthetic, creative, philosophical, and spiritual understanding.

That older cohort gained interest in the arts, in children, and in human experience as a whole. Erikson called them "social witnesses," aware of the interdependence of the generations as well as of all of human experience. In his eighth stage, *integrity versus despair* (discussed in Chapter 25), life comes together in a "re-synthesis of all the resilience and strengths already developed" (Erikson et al., 1986, p. 40).

Maslow maintained that older adults are more likely than younger people to reach the highest level of development, **self-actualization.** Remember that Maslow rejected a rigid age-based sequence of life stages, refusing to confine self-actualization to the old. Some youth might already be self-actualizers and some elders might still be at earlier steps of his hierarchy, seeking love or success, for instance. However, Maslow also believed that life experience helps people move forward, so more of the old reach the final stage.

Self-actualization is characterized by aesthetic, creative, philosophical, and spiritual understanding (Maslow, 1970). Many older people are more likely to engage in various religious practices—reading scriptures, attending services, praying. A self-actualized person might have a deeper spirituality than ever; or might be especially appreciative of nature; or might find life amusing, laughing often at him- or herself. Studies of centenarians also find that they frequently have such traits, including a deep spiritual grounding and a surprising sense of humor—surprising, that is, if one mistakenly assumes that people with limited sight, poor hearing, and recurrent pain have nothing to laugh about (Perls, 2008; Poon, 2008).

Aesthetic Sense and Creativity

For many, "old age can be a time of emotional sensory awareness and enjoyment" (R. N. Butler et al., 1998, p. 65). For that reason, some of the elderly take up gardening, bird-watching, sculpting, painting, or making music, even if they have never done so before.

A great example of late creative development is Anna Moses, who was a farm wife in upstate New York. For most of her life, she expressed her artistic impulses by stitching quilts and embroidering in winter, when farm work was slow. At age 75, arthritis made needlework impossible, so she took to "dabbling in oil."

Four years later, three of her paintings, displayed in a local drugstore, caught the eye of a New York City art dealer. He bought them, drove to her house, and bought 15 more. The following year, at age 80, "Grandma Moses" had a one-woman show in Manhattan, receiving international recognition for her unique "primitive" style. She continued to paint, her work having "developed and changed considerably over the course of her twenty-year career" (Cardinal, 2001). Anna Moses died at age 101.

Other people were well-known artists all their lives, and for them old age became a time of renewed inspiration (Lindauer, 2003). Famous examples abound: Michelangelo painted the awe-inspiring frescoes in the Sistine Chapel at age 75; Verdi composed the opera *Falstaff* when he was 80; Frank Lloyd Wright completed the design of New York City's Guggenheim Museum, an innovative architectural masterpiece, when he was 91.

In a study of extraordinarily creative people, almost none of them felt that their ability, their goals, or the quality of their work had been much impaired with age. The researcher observed, "In their seventies, eighties, and nineties, they may lack the fiery ambition of earlier years, but they are just as focused, efficient, and committed as before . . . perhaps more so" (Csikszentmihalyi, 1996, p. 503).

What about older people who were never particularly attuned to art or music? One theory is that the logical, methodical parts of the brain (often located in the

Hard to Replace Playing the sitar and drawing kanji were widely admired talents when these men were boys. Now, decades later, Ravi Shankar, performing at age 79 in India *(left)*, and Karamata-sensei, drawing a poster at an off-track betting theater in Japan *(right)*, are masters. Few young adults are.

Observation Quiz What two signs of compensation are visible for Shankar? (see answer, page 688)

left hemisphere) become weaker in late adulthood (remember that more areas in both hemispheres are activated among the old). This allows the more creative parts of the brain (often located in the right hemisphere) to come to the fore. Thus, formerly suppressed parts of the brain allow expression and appreciation of music in the elderly (Sacks, 2007).

The creative impulse is one that family members and everyone else should encourage in the elderly, according to many professionals. Expressing one's creativity and aesthetic sense is said to aid in social skills, resilience, and even brain health (McFadden & Basting, 2010).

The Life Review

Erikson recognized that many older people become more reflective and philosophical, thinking about their own history, putting their lives in perspective, assessing their accomplishments and failures (Birren & Schroots, 2006). One outcome of such reflection may be a **life review,** an elderly person's examination of the part he or she has played in human history, connecting the past with the future by writing or telling his or her story. A person's relationship to prior generations, to humanity, to God, and to life is reconsidered; memories are revived, reinterpreted, and finally reintegrated (Kotre, 1995).

The life review is more social than solitary (Webster & Gould, 2007). Elderly people want to tell their stories to others, and often their tales are not solely about themselves but also about their family, cohort, or ethnic group. Such stories tend to be richer in interesting details than those told by younger adults. Robert Butler, the psychiatrist and gerontologist who coined the word *ageism,* says that:

> We have been taught that this nostalgia represents living in the past and a preoccupation with self and that it is generally boring, meaningless, and time-consuming. Yet as a natural healing process it represents one of the underlying

life review An examination of one's own role in the history of human life, engaged in by many elderly people.

>> Answer to Observation Quiz (from page 687) He has a back-up sitar player (his daughter) and he wears a hearing aid.

human capacities on which all psychotherapy depends. The life review should be recognized as a necessary and healthy process in daily life as well as a useful tool in the mental health care of older people.

[R. N. Butler et al., 1998, p. 91]

The importance of connecting past to present is illustrated by Butler's life. His parents left him at 11 months to the care of his grandparents. He adored them, but his grandfather died when he was 7 and his grandmother lost everything, even having her house burn down. However, she never lost her enthusiasm for life and her devotion to her grandson. Butler said, "What I remember even more than the hardships of those years was my grandmother's triumphant spirit and determination. Experiencing at first hand an older person's struggle to survive, I was myself helped to survive as well." (quoted in Martin, 2010, p. A13).

As an adult, Butler's memories of the older adults in his youth helped him recognize how society underestimates the contributions of the old. He wrote a Pulitzer Prize–winning book (*Why Survive? Being Old in America*, 1975); founded and then led several gerontological organizations; lectured, wrote, researched; and "just days before his death [at age 83], he was still putting in a 60-hour work week as CEO of the International Longevity Center" (Tapper, 2010).

Wisdom

The idea that older people are wise is a "hoped-for antidote to views that have cast the process of aging in terms of intellectual deficit and regression" (Labouvie-Vief, 1990, p. 52). The belief that old age brings wisdom, like the opposite idea that aging always means dementia, may be a false generality (Brugman, 2006).

When scientists try to define and measure wisdom, they are not convinced that the old are wise. However, a survey of 3,435 college students in 26 nations on every continent, most of whom had frequent contact with older people, found that people in every nation agreed that wisdom was a characteristic of the elderly (Löckenhoff et al., 2009). Such massive international agreement is impossible to dismiss, even though specifics are not proven.

In the Beginning Creation myths echo through millennia in the tales that elders tell. This woman in northern Australia is recounting to these teenagers the legendary origin of the bluff behind them.

To decide whether the elderly are indeed wise, we need an operational definition of wisdom. One summary describes wisdom as an "expert knowledge system dealing with the conduct and understanding of life" (P. B. Baltes & Smith, 2008, p. 58). Several factors just mentioned—including the life review (perspective on living), the ability to put aside one's personal needs (as in self-actualization), and a self-reflective honesty (as in integrity)—are part of wisdom. Hence, the elderly may be likely to have some of the attributes of wisdom.

Whether a person is *perceived* as wise depends on who is judging the person's thoughts or actions. Wisdom is a social virtue that involves recognizing and responding to enduring cultural values and current social conditions (Staudinger & Werner, 2003). In certain social conflicts, or in making decisions about health treatments (e.g., cancer), elders seem wiser than younger people because a lifetime of experience has taught them to resist fads and irrational emotions and instead consider strategies and options that younger people have not considered (Hall, 2010; Hess et al., 2005).

Philosophers, psychologists, and the general public connect this social virtue (wisdom) with old age. Although there is no widely accepted, empirical test of wisdom that is accepted by the scientific community, two psychologists who have studied wisdom explain:

> Wisdom is one domain in which some older individuals excel. . . . [They have] a combination of psychosocial characteristics and life history factors, including openness to experience, generativity, cognitive style, contact with excellent mentors, and some exposure to structured and critical life experiences.
>
> *[P. B. Baltes & Smith, 2008, p. 60]*

These researchers posed life dilemmas to adults of various ages and asked others to judge whether the responses were wise or not. The results were that wisdom is rare at any age and that even some young adults are wise, but, unlike physical strength and cognitive quickness, wisdom was not less common in the old.

Similarly, the author of a detailed longitudinal study of 814 people concluded that wisdom is not reserved for the old—although humor, perspective, and altruism increase over the decades, making wisdom more possible. He then wrote:

> To be wise about wisdom we need to accept that wisdom does—and wisdom does not—increase with age. Age facilitates a widening social radius and more balanced ways of coping with adversity, but thus far no one can prove that wisdom is great in old age. Perhaps we are wisest when we keep our discussion of wisdom simple and when we confine ourselves to words of one and two syllables. Winston Churchill, that master of wise simplicity and simple wisdom, reminds us, "We are all happier in many ways when we are old than when we are young. The young sow wild oats. The old grow sage."
>
> *[Vaillant, 2002, p. 256]*

SUMMING UP

On balance, mental processes in late adulthood can be adaptive and creative, as people seek integrity and self-actualization. These qualities are particularly apparent in the work of artists, who seem as creative and passionate about their work in later adulthood as they were earlier. Others, who were not particularly gifted, develop a strong aesthetic sense and appreciation of music in old age. Many elders seek to tell their life story to other people, and such life reviews may be inspirational to the teller and to the listener. Wisdom is not the sole domain of the old, nor are all older people wise. Nonetheless, many are insightful, creative, and reflective, using their life experience wisely. ∎

Atrophy Ranking

Lowest

25th Percentile

Median

75th Percentile

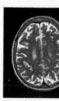

Highest

IMAGE COURTESY J. M. WARDLAW

What Is Lost? These five brain scans of healthy 75- to 80-year-olds show cognitive loss (the white areas), especially in the cortex (at the perimeter). Note that there is substantial variation from the 5th percentile *(top)* to the 95th percentile *(bottom)*. What effect do those losses have? Is there anything you perceive that would better be forgotten? One scientist suggests that the very old are likely to see the forest, not the trees.

SUMMARY

The Aging Brain

1. Brain scans and measurements show that the speed of processing slows down, parts of the brain shrink, and more areas of the brain are activated in older people.

2. Often the elderly activate more parts of their brain when thinking than younger adults do. Although thinking processes become slower and less sharp once a person reaches adulthood, there is much variation.

The Usual: Information Processing After Age 65

3. As the senses become dulled, some stimuli never reach the sensory memory. Interference with the sensory signals can usually be overcome, but this takes mental effort and thus can reduce cognition.

4. Working memory shows notable declines with age because slower processing means that some things are lost. Long-term memory is difficult to measure. However, especially for memories with strong emotional impact, long-term memory may remain strong.

5. Control processes are less effective with age, as retrieval strategies become less efficient. Anxiety may prevent older people from using the strategies they need.

6. In daily life, most of the elderly are not seriously handicapped by cognitive difficulties. The need for ecologically valid, real-life measures of cognition is increasingly apparent to developmental scientists.

The Impaired: Diseases That Affect the Brain

7. Dementia, whether it occurs in late adulthood or earlier, is characterized by cognitive loss—at first minor lapses, then more serious impairment, and finally such extreme losses that recognition of even the closest family members may fade.

8. The most common cause of dementia in the United States is Alzheimer disease, an incurable ailment that becomes more prevalent with age and worsens over time. Genetic factors (especially the ApoE4 gene) contribute to the onset of Alzheimer disease.

9. Vascular dementia (also called multi-infarct dementia) results from a series of ministrokes (transient ischemic attacks, or TIAs) that occur when impairment of blood circulation destroys portions of brain tissue.

10. Other dementias, including frontal lobe dementia and Lewy body dementia, also become more common with age. The primary impact of Parkinson disease is to reduce muscle control, but it can also cause dementia, particularly in the old.

11. Dementia is sometimes mistakenly diagnosed when the individual is actually suffering from a reversible problem. Malnutrition, anxiety, depression, and polypharmacy can cause dementia symptoms.

The Optimal: New Cognitive Development

12. Many people become more interested and adept in creative endeavors, as well as more philosophical, as they grow older. The life review is a personal reflection that many older people undertake, remembering earlier experiences, putting their entire lives into perspective, and achieving integrity or self-actualization.

13. Wisdom does not necessarily increase as a result of age, but some elderly people are unusually wise or insightful.

KEY TERMS

control processes (p. 672)	delirium (p. 678)	mild cognitive impairment (p. 679)	Parkinson disease (p. 681)
priming (p. 673)	Alzheimer disease (AD) (p. 678)	vascular dementia (VaD) (p. 680)	Lewy body dementia (p. 681)
terminal decline (p. 674)	beta-amyloid (p. 679)	frontal lobe dementia (p. 681)	polypharmacy (p. 683)
ecological validity (p. 676)	tau (p. 679)		self-actualization (p. 686)
dementia (p. 678)			life review (p. 687)

WHAT HAVE YOU LEARNED?

The Aging Brain

1. What aspects of the brain slow down with age?

2. Why does slower thinking reduce scores on IQ tests?

3. Why do the elderly use more parts of their brains at once to think?

4. Why is multitasking particularly difficult in late adulthood?

The Usual: Information Processing After Age 65

5. How does sensory loss affect cognition?

6. Why does interference affect thinking, even if the person eventually reaches an accurate conclusion?

7. Which kinds of things are harder to remember with age?

8. Which kinds of memories seem well preserved or even improved with age?

9. What is the difference between short-term and long-term memory in the elderly?

10. How are short-term and long-term memory measured?

11. Why are the elderly likely to benefit from learning control strategies?

12. How does priming help people remember?

13. Why is ecological validity especially important for prospective memory?

14. Why is the number of years until death a better measure of late-life cognition than years since birth?

15. What diseases or conditions correlate with loss of cognition?

16. In what specific ways does exercise affect the brain?

17. How and why does training in cognitive skills help the elderly?

The Impaired: Diseases That Affect the Brain

18. Why is calling a demented person senile an example of ageism?

19. What proof is there that Alzheimer disease is partly genetic?

20. How might a person in stage 2 of Alzheimer disease function in daily life?

21. Why are most people unaware of the early stages of vascular dementia?

22. In what ways is frontal lobe dementia worse than Alzheimer disease?

23. If a person has Parkinson disease, what effect does that person's age have?

24. Why is Lewy body dementia sometimes mistaken for Parkinson disease?

25. How successful are scientists at preventing dementia?

The Optimal: New Cognitive Development

26. What is the purpose of the life review?

27. Why might older people become more creative, musical, and spiritual than before?

28. Why do scientists hesitate to say that wisdom comes with age?

APPLICATIONS

1. At all ages, memory is selective. People forget much more than they remember. Choose someone—a sibling, a former classmate, or a current friend—who went through some public event with you. Sit down together, write separate lists of all the details each of you remembers about the event, and then compare your accounts. What insight does this exercise give you into the kinds of things adults remember and forget?

2. Many factors affect intellectual sharpness. Think of an occasion when you felt stupid and an occasion when you felt smart.

How did the contexts of the two experiences differ? How might those differences affect the performance of elderly and young adults who go to a university laboratory for testing?

3. Visit someone in a hospital. Note all the elements in the environment—such as noise, lights, schedules, and personnel—that might cause an elderly patient to seem demented.

>> ONLINE CONNECTIONS

To accompany your textbook, you have access to a number of online resources, including quizzes for every chapter of the book, flashcards (in English and Spanish), critical thinking questions, and case studies. For access to any of these links, go to www.worthpublishers.com/bergerls8e. In addition to these free resources, you'll also find links to the podcasts, video clips, diagnostic quizzing with personalized study advice, and an ebook. Some of the videos and activities available online include:

- *Old Age and Multitasking.* Can you walk and think at the same time? This video demonstrates how physical movement requires more of people's cognitive resources as they grow older.

- *Alzheimer Disease.* Outlines the progressive course of Alzheimer disease, as well as the types and limits of treatments. Includes video about the effects of chronic stress on two caregivers.

CHAPTER

Late Adulthood: Psychosocial Development

WHAT WILL YOU KNOW?

1. How is an older person's health affected by retirement?
2. Why don't older people all move into their grown children's homes?
3. Does marriage get better or worse in late adulthood?
4. Why would anyone abuse an older person?

Gilbert and Sadie are centenarians, more than 100 years old. They have been married for 80 years and retired for 40. They live together in their own home, with no outside helpers. They often talk about their offspring, who are already old themselves. Gilbert is proud of Sadie's agility:

> "She gets out of bed—I timed her this morning, just for fun. I got up first, but while I was in the bathroom, she gets up, she comes out here first and puts the coffee on. Got back and washed up and got dressed and just twelve minutes after she got out of bed—just twelve minutes this morning—I had her right on the watch."
>
> Sadie chuckles. "I don't have any secrets anymore."
> "So then you have breakfast together?" I ask.
> "Oh, yes!"
> "And then read the paper?"
> "After we get the dishes washed, we sit down and read the paper for a couple of hours."

[N. Ellis, 2002, pp. 107–108]

Few of the oldest-old live as well as Gilbert and Sadie: Many are widowed; most no longer live independently. But Gilbert and Sadie are not unusual in taking comfort in their families, pleasure in their daily routines, and interest in current events. Like them, many other elderly people are socially embedded, physically active, and mentally alert. It is ageist to assume otherwise.

In this chapter, we describe the variability and complexity of development in later life. Activities of daily life often include working and socializing as well as self-care. In long-lasting marriages, both partners help each other stay active. We also examine the conditions for the minority of elderly people who are frail and unable to care for themselves. Most of them are well cared for, but frail elders are vulnerable to abuse from family members and others.

>> Theories of Late Adulthood

It is probably true that development is more diverse in late adulthood than at any other age: Some elderly people run marathons and lead nations, while others no longer walk or talk. Moreover, each person varies in almost every measure of performance from day to day, with some days much better than others (Newell et al., 2009). Many social scientists have tried to understand the significance and origin of these variations as well as the general course of old age.

Some theories of late adulthood have been called *self theories* because they focus on individuals' perceptions of themselves and their ability to meet challenges to their identity. Other theories are called *stratification theories* because they describe the ways in which societies place people on a particular life path.

Self Theories

It can be said that people become more truly themselves as they grow old. The essential self is protected and fulfilled, despite all the changes that may occur. Thus, self theories emphasize "the ways people negotiate challenges to the self" (Sneed & Whitbourne, 2005, p. 380). Such negotiation is particularly crucial when older adults are confronted with multiple challenges like illness, retirement, and the death of loved ones.

A central idea of **self theories** is that each person ultimately depends on himself or herself. As one woman explained:

> I actually think I value my sense of self more importantly than my family or relationships or health or wealth or wisdom. I do see myself as on my own, ultimately. . . . Statistics certainly show that older women are likely to end up being alone, so I really do value my own self when it comes right down to things in the end.
>
> *[quoted in J. Kroger, 2007, p. 203]*

self theories Theories of late adulthood that emphasize the core self, or the search to maintain one's integrity and identity.

Integrity

The most comprehensive self theory came from Erik Erikson. His eighth and final stage of development is called **integrity versus despair,** a period in which older adults seek to integrate their unique experiences with their vision of community (Erikson et al., 1986). The word *integrity* is often used to mean honesty, but it also means a feeling of being whole, not scattered, comfortable with oneself. (*Integrity* comes from the same root word as *integer,* a math term meaning a whole number, not a fraction.)

As an example of how integrity is achieved, many older people develop pride and contentment regarding their personal history: They are proud of their past, even when they skipped school, took drugs, escaped arrest, or were beaten by their parents. Psychologists sometimes call this the *"sucker or saint" phenomenon*—that is, people interpret their experiences as signs of their nobility (saintly endurance or rebellion), not their foolishness (Jordan & Monin, 2008). As Erikson (1963) explains it, such distortion is far better than losing hope, "feeling that the time is now short, too short for the attempt to start another life" (p. 269).

As with every crisis described by Erikson, tension occurs between the two opposing aspects of development at this stage. Past crises, particularly *identity versus role confusion,* reappear when the usual pillars of the self-concept (such as employment or good looks) crumble. One 70-year-old said, "I know who I've been, but who am I now?" (quoted in J. Kroger, 2007, p. 201).

This tension helps advance the person toward a more complete understanding. In this last stage,

> life brings many, quite realistic reasons for experiencing despair: aspects of the present that cause unremitting pain; aspects of a future that are uncertain and frightening. And, of course, there remains inescapable death, that one aspect of the future which is both wholly certain and wholly unknowable. Thus, some despair must be acknowledged and integrated as a component of old age.
>
> *[Erikson et al., 1986, p. 72]*

integrity versus despair The final stage of Erik Erikson's developmental sequence, in which older adults seek to integrate their unique experiences with their vision of community.

Still Helping Virginia Ryder, here helping Betty Baldwin put on her coat, is a lifelong helper. She cared for younger children when she was a child, and she has been a senior companion for the past 19 years, again often for younger people. She is 89.

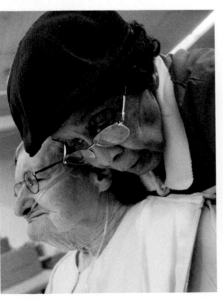

AP PHOTO / COLUMBUS DAILY DISPATCH, ERIC ALBRECHT

Holding On to One's Self

Most older people consider their personalities and attitudes to have remained quite stable over their life span, even as they recognize the physical changes of their bodies (Fischer et al., 2008). One 103-year-old woman observed, "My core has stayed the same. Everything else has changed" (quoted in Troll & Skaff, 1997, p. 166). This is not always easy. Older persons who are the victim of a crime feel that their sense of self-efficacy is threatened, especially if they are African American (DeLisi et al., 2010). As both their bodies and their social relationships change, adults may need to revise their self-theory about their own identity.

The importance of maintaining the self explains some of the behaviors that younger people may think are foolish. For example, many elders hate to give up driving a car because "the loss felt, for men in particular, is deeper than that of simply not being able to get from A to B; it is a loss of a sense of self, of the meaning of manhood" (Davidson, 2008, p. 46). When older adults are asked to select a "cherished object," most pick ordinary and inexpensive things that have great personal meaning (Sherman & Dacher, 2005). Objects and places become more precious in late adulthood than they were earlier, as people seek a way to hold on to identity (J. Kroger, 2007; Whitmore, 2001).

The tendency to cling to familiar places and possessions may be problematic if it leads to **compulsive hoarding.** This urge to accumulate old papers, pieces of furniture, and mementos becomes stronger with age, and family members often complain that an elderly person foolishly saves things that take up space and become a fire hazard (Thobaben, 2006). In fact, however, compulsive hoarding can be seen as a sign of self theory: Most elderly hoarders compulsively saved things when they were much younger. With time, the problem becomes worse, partly because there are more things to save, but the hoarding impulse is a lifelong expression of self (Ayers et al., 2010).

Similarly, many older people resist moving from a drafty and dangerous dwelling into a smaller, safer place, not because they are oblivious to the benefits of the move but because they fear that abandoning familiar places will mean abandoning themselves. They may avoid surgery for the same reason. Preserving the self is crucial, even if it shortens life.

The need to protect oneself explains why many of the old strive to maintain the cultural and religious values of their youth. For instance, grandparents may painstakingly teach a grandchild a language that is rarely used in their current community or encourage the child to repeat rituals and prayers they themselves learned almost a century ago. In cultures that emphasize youth and novelty, the elderly worry that their old values may be lost and thus that they themselves will disappear.

This is apparent among U.S. immigrants who were raised never to question their elders, unlike U.S. children. Older people from India, living with their offspring in New Jersey, reported to researchers that their grandchildren were disrespectful and that "Indian culture is ignored, compartmentalized, and debased in America" (Kalavar & van Willigen, 2005, p. 228).

The Positivity Effect

As you remember from Chapter 23, some people cope successfully with the changes of late adulthood through *selective optimization with compensation*. This concept is central to self theories. Individuals set their personal goals, assess their own abilities, and figure out how to accomplish what they want to achieve despite limitations and declines. For some people, simply maintaining their identity correlates with well-being (Ebner et al., 2006).

compulsive hoarding The urge to accumulate and hold on to familiar objects and possessions, sometimes to the point of their becoming health and/or safety hazards. This impulse tends to increase with age.

Fiercely Independent In the first half of his life, Nelson Mandela led the fight against apartheid in his native South Africa—until he was convicted of sabotage and sentenced to life in prison. Remarkably, he stayed true to his beliefs; released 27 years later to lead once again, he was elected president and served from 1994 to 1999. Still his true self, he next formed The Elders, pledged to be "a fiercely independent force for good." At age 92, he sits with two other Elders, Desmond Tutu (72) and Jimmy Carter (79).

AP PHOTO / JEFF MOORE, POOL

positivity effect The tendency for elderly people to perceive, prefer, and remember positive images and experiences more than negative ones.

One example of selective optimization is known as the **positivity effect.** Elderly people are more likely to perceive, prefer, and remember positive images and experiences than negative ones (Carstensen et al., 2006). The compensation occurs via selective memory: Unpleasant experiences are reinterpreted as inconsequential.

Research has found that the positivity effect has both cognitive and social aspects. For example, in one study people of various ages were shown photographs of faces—some happy, some angry, some neutral. Later they were shown photographs again, including new ones and those they had seen before, and asked whether they had already seen each person or not. Compared with the younger adults, the elderly were more likely to recognize those who had had happy expressions (Werheid et al., 2010) (see the Research Design).

The positivity effect is found not only in hundreds of laboratory experiments; it is also apparent in daily life. For example, adults in one study were asked about recent instances of personal confrontation (Sorkin & Rook, 2006). More than one-third (39 percent) of those over age 65 could not think of any negative social exchanges. Of those who remembered unpleasant encounters, 60 percent said that their primary goal after the event was to maintain goodwill. Only a few sought to change the other person's behavior (see Figure 25.1). The

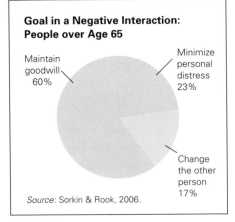

Goal in a Negative Interaction: People over Age 65

Maintain goodwill 60%

Minimize personal distress 23%

Change the other person 17%

Source: Sorkin & Rook, 2006.

FIGURE 25.1

Keep the Peace When someone does something mean or unpleasant, what is your goal in your interaction with that person? If your goal is to maintain goodwill, as was the case for a majority of older adults studied, you are likely to be quicker to forgive and forget.

A. RAMEY / PHOTOEDIT, INC.

Not Completely Identical These 90-year-old monozygotic twins have the same genes, but, judging from their faces, life has not treated them the same way. Continuity of self in late adulthood reflects earlier experiences, not just genes.

> ### ► Research Design
>
> **Scientists:** Katja Werheid, Maria Gruno, Norbert Kathmann, Håkan Fischer, Ove Almkvist, and Bengt Winblad—all in Germany or Sweden.
>
> **Publication:** *Psychology and Aging* (2010).
>
> **Participants:** In four experiments, a total of 132 European individuals, 60 young (average age 25) and 72 old (average age 66), 12 of whom had been diagnosed with mild cognitive impairment. All participants were screened for good physical and mental health—that is, no history of substance abuse, head injury, or psychological disorders.
>
> **Design:** Participants looked at photographs of happy, neutral, or angry faces; they were then shown the same faces and an equal number of new faces either one day (experiments 1, 2, and 3) or two weeks (experiment 4) later, when they were asked which faces had been seen previously and which were new. The main result of interest was whether memory of happy faces would differ among the groups by age or cognitive ability.
>
> **Major conclusion:** In all four experiments, the positivity effect was present, even for those who were mildly cognitively impaired. For instance, in the first experiment, the older adults were slightly better than the younger ones at recognizing happy faces (74 to 70 percent), slightly worse at recognizing angry faces (81 to 84 percent) or neutral faces (65 to 69 percent). They were also significantly more likely to believe that new happy faces had been seen before (false positives of 22 to 7 percent). As expected, the older adults were less proficient overall at accurate memory.
>
> **Comment:** The positivity effect is not found in every experimental design, which makes it noteworthy that it was apparent here, especially among European groups. (Most of the earlier research had occurred in the United States.) Note that the effect was not huge, with the false positives showing the biggest difference. This means that older adults usually remember quite well, but when they misremember, their most likely mistake is to imagine positive things that did not actually happen.

goal of achieving harmony led to strategies such as compromise, not assertion, a strategy that led to a happier outcome:

> Participants whose primary coping goal was to preserve goodwill reported the highest levels of perceived success and the least intense and shortest duration of distress. In contrast, participants whose . . . goal was to change the other person reported the lowest levels of perceived success and the most intense and longest lasting distress.
>
> *[Sorkin & Rook, 2006, p. 723]*

Preserving the self normally leads to happiness rather than despair. Most people realize they could have chosen other paths through life, especially if they lived in other cultures, but they also appreciate their particular self. As Erikson (1963) put it, the older person

> knows that an individual life is the accidental coincidence of but one life cycle with but one segment of history and that for him all human integrity stands or falls with the one style of integrity of which he partakes. . . . In such a final consolation, death loses its sting.
>
> *[p. 268]*

With age, there is less distance between what people hope for themselves (the ideal self) and how they perceive themselves (the real self) (George, 2006). As self theory contends, self-acceptance leads to happiness.

Stratification Theories

A second set of theories emphasize that "stratification remains at the heart of life course studies" (O'Rand, 2006, p. 158). **Stratification theories** focus on the relationship between social forces and the individual, particularly the consequences of social forces that place each older person in a category or role. According to stratification theories, categorization limits people throughout life. The effects accumulate to make one older person's life unlike another's and every older person distinct from younger people (O'Rand, 2006).

Stratification by Age

Industrialized nations segregate elderly people, gradually shutting them out of the mainstream of society as they grow older (Achenbaum, 2005). According to stratification theory, segregation by age harms everyone because it "creates socialization deficits for members of all age groups" (Hagestad & Dannefer, 2001, p. 13). A "socialization deficit" is a lack of needed social experiences: Younger as well as older people have a narrow perspective on life if they interact only with people their own age.

The most controversial version of age-stratification theory is **disengagement theory** (Cumming & Henry, 1961). According to this theory, as people age, traditional roles become unavailable or unimportant, the social circle shrinks, coworkers stop asking for help, and adult children turn away to focus on their own children. This process is mutual, according to disengagement theory. Children want to be with other children, adults with other adults, and older adults with one another or by themselves. Thus, younger people disengage from the old, who themselves voluntarily disengage from younger

stratification theories Theories that emphasize that social forces, particularly those related to a person's social stratum or social category, limit individual choices and affect a person's ability to function in late adulthood because past stratification continues to limit life in various ways.

disengagement theory The view that aging makes a person's social sphere increasingly narrow, resulting in role relinquishment, withdrawal, and passivity.

Silver on Display In the foreground is Layla Eneboldsen, enjoying the company of three other elderly people who live with her. Since more than 90 percent of the elderly in the United States are White (and mostly female), like this group of friends, and since the furniture, lights, and artwork date from about 60 years ago, this might seem to be a scene from the 1940s in the United States. In fact, this is twenty-first-century Denmark.

STEPHANIE MAZE / CORBIS

adults. They relinquish past roles, withdrawing from life's action. If they can afford it, they move to senior residences where no young people are allowed.

Disengagement theory provoked a storm of protest because people feared it justified ageism. Many gerontologists insisted that older people need new involvements. Some developed an opposite theory, called **activity theory,** which holds that the elderly seek to remain actively involved with relatives, friends, and community groups. If the elderly disengage and withdraw, activity theorists contend, they do so unwillingly (J. R. Kelly, 1993; Rosow, 1985).

Research supports both theories. Many of the elderly disengage, but most studies find that happier and healthier elders are quite active, filling various roles (worker, wife, husband, mother, father, neighbor) (Lampinen et al., 2006; Rowe & Kahn, 1998). Indeed, literally being active—bustling around the house, climbing stairs, walking to work—lengthens life and increases satisfaction (Manini et al., 2006).

Since the elderly are diverse in needs, personality, and background as well as age, neither disengagement nor activity theories fit everyone. A leading gerontologist wrote:

> Staff members working with old people . . . reported having very mixed feelings when trying to "activate" certain old people. They maintained that activity is good, but they nevertheless confessed feeling that they were doing something wrong when they try to drag certain older people to various forms of arranged social activity or activity therapy.
>
> *[Tornstam, 2005, p. 34]*

A similar cautionary note comes from research in China. Among the young-old, activity correlated with health, particularly if the activities involved social interactions. But among the oldest-old, activity did not correlate with longevity: For some of them, disengagement was more closely associated with health (R. Sun & Liu, 2008). When all the research is considered, there is evidence that many of the elderly disengage from some social roles and activities, but overall, healthy older adults who see decades of life after retirement compensate for such losses by finding new roles and activities (Freund et al., 2009).

Stratification by Gender

Feminist theory draws attention to stratification on the basis of gender. From the newborn's pink or blue blanket to the flowers or stripes on the bedspread in a nursing home, gender is signaled lifelong. Society guides and pressures males and females into divergent paths.

The ongoing implications of gender differences were revealed by a study of retirement and caregiving among older married couples. Both men and women provided care if their spouse needed it, but they did so in opposite ways: Women quit their jobs, whereas men worked longer. To be specific, employed women whose husbands needed care were five times more likely to retire than were other older women who were not caregivers. By contrast, when employed husbands had a sick wife, they retired only half as often as other men did (Dentinger & Clarkberg, 2002).

The responses of both husbands and wives make sense in terms of caregiving: The men who kept working could afford household help, and the women who quit working had time to provide care. Both responses result from past stratification: Men are more likely to have had jobs with better pay and benefits, while women are socialized to be caregivers. However, the female strategy is more likely than the male one to lead to poverty and social isolation.

Irrational, gender-based fear may also limit women's independence. For example, citing safety, adult children persuade their elderly mothers more than their

activity theory The view that elderly people want and need to remain active in a variety of social spheres—with relatives, friends, and community groups—and become withdrawn only unwillingly, as a result of ageism.

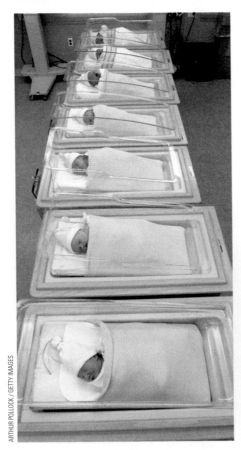
Boys in Pink Not really, but why does it matter?

fathers to stop traveling or living alone (as increasing numbers of older women do). However, the data show that men living alone are more likely than women to have a sudden health crisis, and only 2 percent of violent crime victims are women over age 65 (it's about 5 percent for older men) (P. Klaus, 2005). Indeed, if avoiding travel protects against crime, then emerging adults (who are much more likely to be victims) should stay home—but that would be a sign of pathology in the young.

Many of the oldest-old women married men older than they were and outlived them. Especially if they lived in rural areas (as most Americans did until about 1950), they relied on their husbands to drive, to manage money, and to keep up with politics. Such accumulated lifelong stratification may lead to poverty, frailty, and dependence when old age and widowhood co-occur.

Gender-stratification theory has recently recognized that men, too, are pushed into certain roles because of their sex, roles that may ultimately harm them in late adulthood. For instance, men have connected masculinity with stoicism, and they are less likely to be open about their emotions or to seek medical care than women are. That may be why older men endure pain silently and die at higher rates than do older women (Mansfield et al., 2008).

Stratification by Ethnicity

Like age and gender, ethnic background affects every aspect of development, including education, health, place of residence, and employment. Stratification theory suggests that these factors accumulate, creating large discrepancies in income by old age (see Figure 25.2).

One example is home ownership, which provides financial security for many seniors. However, racial stratification prevented many older African Americans from buying homes when they were young, making poverty more likely in old age. If they did have homes, their mortgages were higher, as were rates of foreclosure on them.

Health disparities also accumulate, a phenomenon called *weathering*—that is, various past stresses and medical disabilities creating a high *allostatic load,* an accumulation of problems (such as hypertension and obesity) that make a person vulnerable to serious disease. This may be the reason life expectancy for 65-year-olds (no longer vulnerable to infant or adolescent mortality) is three years shorter for African Americans (81 years) than for European Americans (84 years) (see Figure 25.3). It also may explain changes in self-esteem over the years: In general,

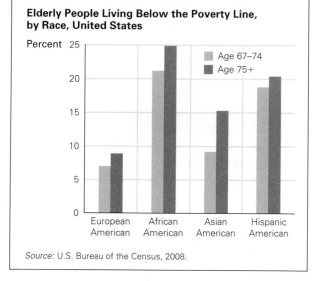

Elderly People Living Below the Poverty Line, by Race, United States

Source: U.S. Bureau of the Census, 2008.

FIGURE 25.2

Ethnic Gaps in Poverty Other data show that, overall, those under age 25 are more likely to be poor than elders are but that ethnic discrepancies in income are much greater among the old. This is what theories of cumulative stratification would predict.

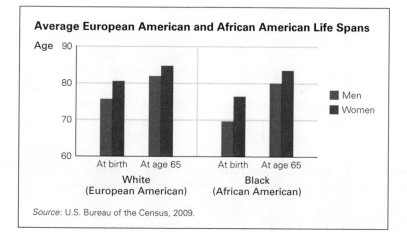

Source: U.S. Bureau of the Census, 2009.

FIGURE 25.3

Age as the Equalizer? As you see, once a person survives the hazards of childhood and adolescence, he or she is likely to live until age 80 or more. (The terms *Black* and *White* are used here because that is how the data are reported. White includes most Hispanics, and Black includes most Africans; the ethnic differences would be greater if the data compared European and African Americans.)

Observation Quiz Do the data suggest that gender or ethnicity is the more powerful stratification? (see answer, page 700)

Dig Deeper A glance at this woman at her outdoor pump might evoke sympathy. Her home's lack of plumbing suggests that she is experiencing late adulthood in poverty, in a rural community that probably offers few social services. Her race and gender put her at additional risk of problems as she ages. However, a deeper understanding might reveal many strengths: religious faith, strong family ties, and gritty survival skills.

older people have lower self-esteem than they did earlier, but this drop is steeper and starts earlier (age 65, not 85) for African Americans (Shaw et al., 2010).

A particular form of ethnic stratification affects elders born in another nation, a number that increased in the United States from 2.7 million in 1990 to 4.4 million in 2008 (Leach, 2008–2009). Some grew up in one country and then came to the United States, where age and ethnic norms are often different from those in their original nations. As one example, elders often expect to live with their children, as is traditional in most African, eastern European, and Asian nations. However, the U.S. age norms expect the elderly to be independent as long as possible, and that expectation is reflected in housing designs, employment patterns, and pensions (which many immigrants do not receive).

An immigrant elder may expect to become a revered family leader, but his or her children may expect the elder to become household help, and the grandchildren may notice that their grandparent has neither income nor English. Many older immigrants are lonely and sad (Treas, 2008–2009). In this case, stratification comes not only from the assumptions of outsiders but also from the acculturation of the younger generations.

Consider the fate of an elderly man born in Russia. He was placed by his U.S.-born son in an assisted-living center for senior citizens. The man hated the place and left. He rented a room from an 85-year-old Russian widow, to whom he became attached. But when the landlady became frail and the elderly man began taking care of her, his son moved him out. Once again, the father was on his own and unhappy. He said:

> Would I like to live with my kids? Of course. But I know that's impossible. They don't want me. . . . not that they don't love me. I understand that. In the old days, a hundred years ago, old people stayed at home.
>
> *[quoted in Koch, 2000, p. 53]*

As a result of this cultural divide, the man's life was described as one of "lonely independence . . . a quintessentially American tragedy" (Koch, 2000, p. 55).

Finally, the crucial stratification variable in the well-being of the elderly may be income, which correlates with gender and ethnicity but is not directly caused by them (Achenbaum, 2006–2007). Sexist and racist practices are always harmful, of course, but income disparities in childhood lead to less education, less control over work, and worse health—all of which build stress and increase disability (Bowen & González, 2010). What may seem to be a burden of gender or ethnicity may result from lifelong stratification based on socioeconomic status (SES) (O'Rand, 2006).

SUMMING UP

Many theories attempt to organize and explain development in late adulthood. Self theories emphasize that each person becomes more himself or herself in old age. Erikson's final stage of development, integrity versus despair, can be the culmination of self-affirmation. An older person's wish to stay in the same home, to hold on to familiar possessions, and to maintain traditional values may be an attempt to protect the self. Stratification theories emphasize the power of social groupings, in which one category of person is treated differently from another. Disengagement theory and activity theory reach opposite conclusions, but both focus on age stratification. Gender and ethnic stratification may lead to substantial burdens in late adulthood, particularly if they also reflect economic stratification. Low SES in childhood harms late-life development. ■

>> Answer to Observation Quiz (from page 699) Both have an impact, but by late adulthood, the gender gap is greater than the ethnic gap, at least in the way that the U.S. Census defines it.

The Same Situation, Many Miles Apart: Sustained by Mother Nature These elderly men are similar in that they both benefit from the growth of plants.

Observation Quiz What are two important differences between these men? (see answer, page 702)

>> Activities in Late Adulthood

Activities in late adulthood are intense and varied. This might come as a surprise to younger adults, who see few elders at sports events, political rallies, job sites, or midnight concerts. In fact, most college students consider the elderly relatively passive and inactive (Wurtele, 2009). However, the elderly are engaged with life in many ways.

Work

Developmentalists are aware of "a growing body of research that points to the positive physical and psychological impacts, for women as well as men, of employment" (Moen & Spencer, 2006, p. 135). Work provides social support and status, boosting self-esteem. For many people, employment allows generativity and is evidence of "productivity, effectiveness, and independence," all cherished Western values (Tornstam, 2005, p. 23).

This is not to ignore the fact that some elders keep working because they need the money, increasingly apparent as pensions and investments shrink. In the current economic crisis, those who have job security tend to keep working—more true for men than women and for professionals than low-wage workers (see Figure 25.4). Besides needing the money, some employees over age 65 stay on the job because they appreciate the social recognition and self-fulfillment that work brings. Elder participation in the labor force is higher among nonunionized low-wage workers (who probably need the income) and professionals (who may enjoy the recognition) than among those in between. Many older adults prefer to keep working part time, but phased retirement and part-time work is not valued, or even possible, in many U.S. workplaces (Sheaks, 2007).

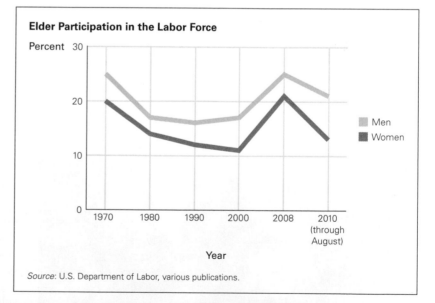

Elder Participation in the Labor Force

Source: U.S. Department of Labor, various publications.

FIGURE 25.4

Along with Everyone Else Although younger adults might imagine that older people stop work as soon as they can, this is clearly not the case for everyone.

>> Answer to Observation Quiz (from page 701) Dozens of differences are apparent, but the two most influential are nationality (United States and India) and income (one can afford to grow plants as a hobby; the other sells coconuts to earn a living). Both of these involuntary differences point to the fact that social stratification persists into old age.

Retirement

Many people once believed that older adults were healthier and happier when they were employed. They warned about "the presumed traumatic aspects of retirement" (Tornstam, 2005, p. 19). Accordingly, in the 1980s, U.S. legislators outlawed mandatory retirement (except in special occupations, such as that of jet pilot).

The paradox is that since 1980, when older workers were no longer required to quit their jobs at age 65, the average age of retirement has *decreased*. Rather than preferring to work until they die, many older adults retire as soon as they can (Hardy, 2006). Only when retirement is precipitated by poor health or fading competence does it correlate with illness (A. Shapiro & Yarborough-Hayes, 2008). On the other hand, some people choose not to retire. As with other aspects of life, at least for North Americans, having some control over change reduces stress.

In more than a dozen European nations where adequate pensions are offered to employees in their 50s, half the workers retire before age 60 and many of those who remain in the labor force after age 60 work part time (Hardy, 2006). In the United States, Social Security payments increase if people wait until age 70 to stop working; nonetheless, most stop working years before that. If income is adequate, the data suggest that retirement is likely to make older adults healthy and happy, not sick and sad.

Of course, just as employment does not always bring joy, retirees are not always happy. Planning is often inadequate, and married couples may disagree as to who should retire, when retirement should begin, and how their lives should be restructured (Moen et al., 2005). Many retirees live longer than they expected to, not realizing that inflation reduces buying power, that some pensions stop, and that Medicare does not cover all health care expenses. Furthermore, after retirees' initial months of completing long-postponed projects (anything from traveling to China to painting the porch), their former goals need "expanding, reducing, concentrating and diffusing" (Nimrod, 2007, p. 91).

Volunteer Work

Volunteering offers some of the advantages of paid employment (generativity, social connections). The benefits are many—for the individual (better health, less depression) as well as for society (help in providing health, education, and other social services)—and "gerontologists have been strongly attracted to the idea that active engagement [volunteering and political activity] in society is related to well-being in later life" (Morrow-Howell & Freedman, 2006–2007, p. 6).

Mutual Help Senior citizens are steady volunteers at this Tokyo day-care center. Small children benefit from personal attention as they learn new skills. The elders benefit from social interaction with the children.

KAREN KASMAUSKI / CORBIS

Is the connection between well-being and volunteering merely an "idea"? No; empirical data reveal that it is much more. Cross-sectional research finds a strong link between good health and volunteering. As with any correlation, it is not obvious which comes first: Healthy elders are more likely to be volunteers, as well as vice versa. However, many signs indicate that volunteering itself aids well-being. Advantages are strongest when volunteering occurs in moderation—for 2 hours a week, not 20; for one organization, not several—and when volunteers feel useful and socially involved (M. A. Musick et al., 1999; Windsor et al., 2008).

As self theory would predict, volunteer work attracts older people who have been strongly committed to their community. Many have volunteered earlier in adulthood and now are "mentors, guides, and repositories of experience" for younger people (Settersten, 2002, p. 65). The rate of volunteering varies by culture; the elderly in Nordic nations (e.g., Sweden and Norway) volunteer far more often than those in Mediterranean nations (e.g., Italy and Greece), differences that persist when illness is taken into account (Erlinghagen & Hank, 2006).

The data reveal two areas of concern. First, contrary to what most people imagine, older, retired people are less likely to volunteer than are middle-aged, employed people. Three-fourths of people over 65 do no volunteer work (see Figure 25.5). Second, less than half of all adults of any age volunteer. This may be a sign of social isolation and disconnection from the community (Bellah et al., 2007; Putnam, 2000).

Some gerontologists wonder if the push for more volunteering is a way for public institutions to avoid hiring paid workers (Minkler & Holstein, 2008). However, most wish that volunteering were more common among the elderly and have offered four possible explanations as to why more elders do not volunteer:

1. *Social culture.* Ageism may discourage meaningful volunteering. Many volunteer opportunities are geared toward the young, who are attracted to intense, short-term experiences. A few weeks of building a house during spring break or a few years of working in an undeveloped nation with the Peace Corps are not designed for older volunteers (Morrow-Howell & Freedman, 2006–2007).
2. *Organizations.* Institutions lack recruitment, training, and implementation strategies for attracting older volunteers. For instance, although most primary school students would benefit from a personal mentor, schools have barriers (e.g., health exams, background checks, long flights of stairs) that discourage elders, and few schools provide space, time, and training for tutors.
3. *The elderly themselves.* Perhaps older adults are too self-absorbed, more concerned with their own needs than with the needs of strangers. This is suggested by other statistics: About half of the elderly who volunteer do so within their own religious organizations, and only one in six work with youth, compared with about one in three younger adult volunteers (U.S. Bureau of Labor Statistics, 2008).
4. *The researchers.* The problem may lie not with the people but with the science. Surveys of volunteer work ignore daily caregiving and informal helping. Babysitting, caring for an ill spouse, shopping for an infirm neighbor—perhaps if such activities were included, the data would reveal higher rates.

Home Sweet Home

One of the favorite activities of many retirees is caring for their own homes. Typically, both men and women do more housework after retirement (Kleiber, 1999; Szinovacz, 2000). They also do yard work, redecorate, build shelves, rearrange furniture. Gardening is popular: More than half the elderly in the United States cultivate a garden each year (see Figure 25.6). Challenging hobbies and home-repair activities correlate with lower rates of dementia (E. Kröger et al., 2008).

In keeping up with household tasks and maintaining their property, many older people demonstrate that they prefer

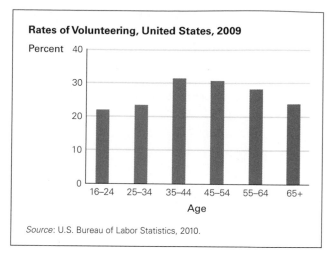

Rates of Volunteering, United States, 2009

Source: U.S. Bureau of Labor Statistics, 2010.

FIGURE 25.5

Official Volunteers As you can see, older adults volunteer less often than middle-aged adults, according to official statistics. However, this counts people who volunteer for organizations—schools, churches, social service groups, and so on. Not counted is all the volunteer help that people give to friends, family members, neighbors, and even strangers. If that were counted, would everyone of every age be a volunteer?

Beautiful When It Snows George and Margaret bought a retirement condo (in University Commons) near their alma mater in Michigan. Their preference for staying near home is typical of most seniors.

AP PHOTO / PAUL SANCYA

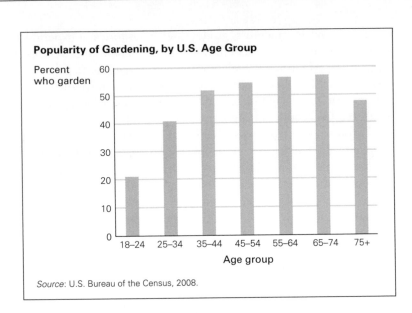

FIGURE 25.6

Dirty Fingernails Almost three times as many 60-year-olds as 20-year-olds are gardeners. What is it about dirt, growth, and time that makes gardening an increasingly popular hobby as people age?

Popularity of Gardening, by U.S. Age Group

Source: U.S. Bureau of the Census, 2008.

aging in place Remaining in the same home and community in later life, adjusting but not leaving when health fades.

naturally occurring retirement community (NORC) A neighborhood or apartment complex whose population is mostly retired people who moved to the location as younger adults and never left.

aging in place, not moving to another residence. If they must move, they prefer to stay near their old neighborhood, perhaps in a smaller apartment in a building with an elevator, but not in a different city or state.

The preference for aging in place is evident in state statistics. Of the 50 states, Florida has the highest proportion of people over age 65, but the next three states —Maine, West Virginia, and Pennsylvania—are not places most older people would move to but places where they have always lived. Obviously, many people stay where they grew up rather than move to the Sunbelt.

Sometimes a neighborhood or an apartment complex becomes a **naturally occurring retirement community (NORC)** when young adults who moved in decades earlier never leave. Many elderly people in NORCs are content to live alone. They stay on after their children move away and their partners die, in part because they are familiar with their community and they have friends there (C. C. Cook et al., 2007). One reason the elderly enjoy home repair, housework, and gardening is that neighbors notice and appreciate the new curtains, the polished door, the blooming rosebush.

To age in place successfully, elderly people need many community services (K. Black, 2008). If a person is living alone in dilapidated housing, especially in a rural or high-crime urban community, simply pointing out the danger is not enough. Someone needs to help them move out or remodel. Aging in place does not mean that seniors need to be left alone; it means that care should come to them (Golant, 2008). NORCs can replace after-school programs with senior centers if that is what the community needs.

Religious Involvement

Especially for Religious Leaders Why might the elderly have strong faith but poor church attendance? (see response, page 706)

Religious practices of all kinds correlate with physical and emotional health (Idler, 2006). Social scientists have found several reasons for this: (1) Faith encourages health (less drug use, for instance); (2) social relationships are increased; (3) faith gives meaning to life, age, and death, thus reducing stress (Atchley, 2009). Older adults attend fewer religious services than the middle-aged, but faith and praying increase with age.

Religious identity and religious institutions are especially important for older members of minority groups, many of whom feel a stronger commitment to their religious heritage than to their national or cultural background. For example, although Westerners may note only the national origin of Nigerians or Iraqis or Turks, elderly people in those groups may focus on their Muslim, or Christian, or Jewish faith (Gelfand, 2003). They may identify more closely with a particular branch of their religion than with their nation—as is evident in Iraq, with its sharp distinctions between the Shiite and Sunni branches of Islam.

Religious institutions fulfill many needs, and a nearby house of worship is one reason why American elders prefer to age in place. Particularly for older African Americans, their churches may be a cherished spiritual home, providing practical activities (choir, study, meals) as well as close, supportive friends. Many churches also have social service programs (e.g., feeding the homeless, counseling drug abusers, sponsoring after-school activities). Such programs give members a convenient way to "do the Lord's work" while obtaining the benefits of volunteering mentioned earlier (Carlton-LaNey, 2006–2007).

Religious faith may explain an oddity of mortality statistics. In the United States, suicide after age 65 is more common among elderly European American men than among African American women, by a ratio of about 50-to-1. So few elderly African American women kill themselves that their suicide rate is almost zero (R. L. Walker & Hunter, 2008). A possible explanation is that African American women's religious faith is often very strong, making them less depressed about their daily lives (Colbert et al., 2009).

For all elderly people, no matter what their particular faith or ethnicity, psychological health depends on feeling that they are part of traditions that were handed down by their ancestors and will be carried on by their descendants. At least one gerontologist believes that an "increasing feeling of cosmic communion" comes with age, that older people are better able to see beyond their own immediate needs and to care about other people, ask enduring questions, and emphasize spiritual needs (Tornstam, 2005, p. 41). Every religion helps elders deal with these concerns (Idler, 2006).

Political Activism

Younger adults might be forgiven if they think that elderly people are not politically active. Fewer older people turn out for massive rallies, and only about 2 percent volunteer in political campaigns. Nor do they vote as a bloc. In Europe as well as in the United States, the elderly do not seem to be actively involved in politics (U.S. Bureau of the Census, 2008; A. Walker, 2006).

By other measures, however, the elderly are more politically active than people of any other age. More of them write letters to their elected representatives, vote, and identify with a political party.

Over the past 20 years in off-year (nonpresidential) U.S. elections, an average of 60 percent of those over age 65 voted, compared with 15 percent of those aged 18 to 20 (U.S. Bureau of the Census, 2008). This difference seems more a result of age than of cohort: As Table 25.1 shows, the number of people of a given age who are registered to vote in nonpresidential elections remains quite steady over time.

Like Sadie and Gilbert at the beginning of this chapter, the elderly are more likely than younger adults to keep up with the news. For example, the Pew Research Center for the People and the Press periodically asks U.S. residents questions on current events. In 2008, elders (age 65 and over) beat the youngest (age 18–30) by a ratio of about 3-to-2 in knowing who was the Speaker of the U.S.

TABLE 25.1			
Voter Registration in Nonpresidential Election Years, by Age Group			
Age Group	**Voters Registered in Election Year (%)**		
	1974	1990	2006
18–20	36	35	37
21–24	45	43	45
25–34	55	56	50
35–44	67	66	59
45–64	74	71	70
65+	71	77	75

Source: U.S. Bureau of the Census, 2008.

House of Representatives (Nancy Pelosi) or what nation Nicolas Sarkozy led (France) (Pew Research Center, 2008).

AARP (originally the American Association of Retired Persons), the largest organized interest group in the world, advocates for the elderly. In 2008, AARP had nearly 40 million members, many of whom were baby boomers (members must be over 50 but need not be retired). About 8 percent of AARP's budget goes to research and action regarding politics (Binstock, 2006–2007).

AARP's political influence is thought to be one reason that the U.S. Social Security program is called "the third rail" of domestic politics, named for the high-voltage electrical rail that delivers power to trains and could electrocute a person who touches it. The idea is that advocating changes in Social Security may be fatal to a politician's career—even though most experts believe that reform is needed. Similar concerns are raised in any nation that attempts to reduce benefits for older citizens. For instance, in 2010 a massive, one-day strike in France was triggered by an attempt to move the pension age from 60 to 62 (smaller protests and strikes continued for months thereafter).

Many government policies affect the elderly, especially those regarding housing, pensions, prescription drugs, and medical costs. However, members of this age group do not necessarily vote their own economic interests. Some are swayed by opposite perspectives on various issues, including global warming, military conflicts, and public education. For example, the elderly tend to support public spending for schools and often vote to commit their own tax dollars to educate children who are not theirs.

AARP A U.S. organization of people aged 50 and older that advocates for the elderly. It was originally called the American Association of Retired Persons, but now only the initials AARP are used, since members need not be retired.

There is one exception to this generous outlook: Elders who have moved from one part of the country to another, such as new arrivals in Arizona or Florida, are less likely to approve bonds for public education (Berkman & Plutzer, 2004). It seems that elders who age in place are likely to support their neighborhood children but elders who come to a new place are less giving to children from families they do not know.

Generally, the political opinions of the elderly reflect national trends and their own personal history more than their chronological age (A. Walker, 2006). The idea that their political or economic concerns clash with those of the young is not confirmed by the data: Many older people are passionate about the well-being of future generations who are not their direct descendants. A particular concern is the legacy of the natural environment, whether the "golden pond will be polluted and fresh water will be running out" (Moody, 2009–2010, p. 70).

In fact, the idea of "gray power" may be a myth, designed to reduce support among younger people for programs that support health care for the old (A. Walker, 2006, p. 349). Given that ageism fluctuates from hostile to benign—and is often based on beliefs that are far from reality—it is not surprising that political perceptions of the elderly zigzag from compassion to fury, as "older persons [are] attacked as too powerful and, at the same time, as a burdensome responsibility" (Schulz & Binstock, 2008, p. 8). As you know, neither of these accusations is true.

DAVID YOUNG-WOLFF / PHOTOEDIT, INC.

Still Politically Active The man with the microphone is Floyd Red Crow Westerman, a Lakota Sioux who is an actor (in *Dances with Wolves,* among many other films) and a director. Many members of his cohort fought in Vietnam. Disapproval of the war in Iraq was greater among his generation than among both older and younger cohorts.

SUMMING UP

Older adults who keep working, whether as paid employees or as unpaid volunteers, tend to feel productive and socially connected. Most who retire enjoy their newfound leisure time, especially working at home. If having a job is an economic necessity, if retirement is mandated, or if volunteering is overwhelming or underappreciated, older adults do not benefit from being retired. Elders prefer to grow older in the same com-

>> Response for Religious Leaders (from page 704) There are many possible answers, including the specifics of getting to church (transportation, stairs), physical comfort in church (acoustics, temperature), and content (unfamiliar hymns and language).

munities in which they spent the earlier years of adulthood. Often their religious involvement within their local community is one reason for this preference. Many elders are connected to politics, in that they vote more and are better informed about current events than are younger adults.

■

>> Friends and Relatives

Humans are social animals, dependent on one another for survival and drawn to one another for joy. This is as true in late life as in infancy and every stage in between.

Remember from Chapter 22 that every person travels the life course in the company of other people, who make up the social convoy (Antonucci et al., 2007). Bonds formed over a lifetime allow people to share triumphs and tragedies with others who understand their past victories and defeats. Siblings, old friends, and spouses are ideal convoy members.

Long-Term Partnerships

Spouses buffer each other against the problems of old age, thus extending life. This was one conclusion from a meta-analysis of dozens of studies with a combined total of 250,000 participants (Manzoli et al., 2007). Married older adults are healthier, wealthier, and happier than unmarried people their age.

Elderly divorced people are lower in health and happiness than are those who are still married, although some argue that income and personality are the reasons, not marital status (Manzoli et al., 2007). Obviously, not every marriage is good for every older person: About one in every six long-term marriages is not satisfying to the couple, and in that case, neither health nor happiness is increased by the relationship (Waldinger & Schultz, 2010). Divorce is rare in later adulthood, but the rate is increasing (Wu & Schimmele, 2007).

Personal happiness increases with the length as well as the quality of an intimate relationship—an association that is more apparent in longitudinal than in cross-sectional research (Proulx et al., 2007; Scarf, 2008). A lifetime of shared experiences—living together, raising children, and dealing with financial and emotional crises—brings partners closer in memories and values. Often couples develop "an exceedingly positive portrayal" (O'Rourke & Cappeliez, 2005) of their mate, seeing their personality as better than their own.

In general, older couples have learned how to disagree and actually consider their conflicts to be discussions, not fights. I know a politically active couple in their 60s who seem happily married, are the proud parents of two young adults, yet vote for opposing candidates. That puzzled me until the wife explained: "We sit together on the fence, seeing both perspectives, and then, when it is time to get off the fence and vote, Bob and I fall on opposite sides." I always knew who would fall on which side, but to this couple, both the discussion and the final choice were productive. Their

The Same Situation, Many Miles Apart: Partners Whether in the living room of their home in the United States (*left*) or at a senior center in the Philippines (*right*), elderly people are more likely to smile when they are with one another than when they are alone.

Observation Quiz What does the clothing of the people in these photographs indicate about their economic status? (see answer, page 709)

JEAN MICHEL FOUJOLS / ZEFA / CORBIS

SEAN SPRAGUE / THE IMAGE WORKS

Bride and Groom The Robinsons walked down the aisle 75 years ago and were pronounced "man and wife." Now they are *husband* and wife, and walking is more difficult, but they still enjoy holding hands.

long-term affection kept disagreements from becoming fights. Most other long-married couples deal with their disputes in the same way.

Partners become interdependent over time, as we saw with Sadie and Gilbert at the opening of this chapter. In one U.S. study of long-lasting marriages, 86 percent of the partners surveyed thought their relationship was about equal in give-and-take (Gurung et al., 2003). Similar results were found in a comparison of similar couples in various European nations. Objectively, wives were less equal in some nations (e.g., Portugal) than others (e.g., France), but subjectively they felt fairly treated (M. Braun et al., 2008).

Outsiders might judge many long-term marriages as unequal, since one or the other spouse usually provides most of the money, or needs most of the care, or does most of the housework. Yet such disparities do not seem to bother the partners. Generally, older spouses accept each other's frailties and dependencies, assisting with the partner's physical and psychological needs, remembering times (perhaps decades ago) when the situation was reversed. Elders who are disabled (have difficulty walking, bathing, and performing other activities of daily life) are less depressed and anxious if they are in a close marital relationship (Mancini & Bonanno, 2006). A couple can achieve selective optimization with compensation: The one who is bedbound but alert can keep track of what the mobile but confused one is supposed to do, for instance.

Besides caregiving, sexual intimacy is another major aspect of long-lasting marriages. Younger adults, and many researchers, tend to measure sexual activity by frequency of orgasm; by that measure, sexual activity decreases with each decade. Many older couples' sexual behavior changes, but sex remains important (M. Johnson, 2007). One couple had this to say about their sex life:

Husband: We have sex less frequently now, but it's satisfying to me. Now that we are both home, we could spend all our time in bed. But it's still more amorous when we go away. When we travel, it's like a second honeymoon.

Wife: Sex has been important in our marriage, but not the most important. The most important thing has been our personal relationship, our fondness, respect, and friendship.

[quoted in Wallerstein & Blakeslee, 1995, p. 318]

Relationships with Younger Generations

In past centuries, most adults died before their grandchildren were born (Uhlenberg, 1996). Today, some families span five generations, consisting of elders and their children, grandchildren, great-grandchildren, and great-great-grandchildren. The result is "longer years of 'shared lives' across generations" (Bengtson, 2001, p. 6).

Since the average couple now has fewer children, the *beanpole family*, with multiple generations but only a few members in each one, is becoming more common (see Figure 25.7). Some members of the youngest generation have no cousins, brothers, or sisters but a dozen or more elderly relatives. Intergenerational relationships are becoming more important as many grandparents have only one or two grandchildren (Bengtson, 2001; Silverstein, 2006).

Although elderly people's relationships with members of younger generations are usually positive, they can also include tension and conflict. Few older adults stop parenting simply because their children are grown. As one 82-year-old woman put it: "No matter how old a mother is, she watches her middle-aged children for signs of improvement" (Scott-Maxwell, 1968). Adult children also imagine parental disapproval, even if it is not outwardly expressed.

Family members throughout life tend to support one another. As you remember, *familism* prompts siblings, cousins, and even more distant relatives to seek out one another as adulthood unfolds. **Filial responsibility** is the obligation of adult children to care for their aging parents. Members of the younger generations in every culture feel responsible for their parents, and older generations want to help the younger ones. As explained in Chapter 22, this can impact the younger generation negatively as well as positively. This is already found in Europe, where beanpole families have been common for several decades (Saraceno, 2010).

filial responsibility The obligation of adult children to care for their aging parents.

When parents need material goods, their adult children often sacrifice to provide them, but emotional support is more crucial and more complex, sometimes increasing when financial help is not needed (Silverstein, 2006). Some elders resent exactly the same supportive behaviors that other elders expect from their children, such as visiting frequently, giving presents, cleaning the refrigerator, calling the doctor, or even paying the telephone bill.

A longitudinal study of attitudes found no evidence that recent changes in family structure (including divorce) reduce the sense of filial responsibility (Gans & Silverstein, 2006). In fact, younger cohorts (born in the 1950s and 1960s) endorsed *more* responsibility toward older generations, "regardless of the sacrifices involved," than did earlier cohorts (born in the 1930s and 1940s).

Amazingly, belief in filial responsibility was weaker among the elderly, who were most likely to need care. After midlife and especially after the death of their own parents, members of the older generation were *less* likely to express the view that children should provide substantial care for their parents and more likely to strive to be helpful to their children. The authors of this study conclude that, as adults become more likely to receive than to give intergenerational care, "reappraisals are likely the result of altruism (growing relevance as a potential receiver) or role loss (growing irrelevance as a provider)" (Gans & Silverstein, 2006, p. 974). This observation echoes an idea introduced in Chapter 22: Adults of all ages like to be needed, not needy.

Culture is crucial in determining what specific support people expect. Most in the United States want to be self-sufficient or to rely on a spouse, not a child. Adult children may be more willing to offer support than their parents are to receive it. This is not true in most Asian nations, where parents depend on sons, not daughters, for support in their old age. Often the first-born son encourages his elderly parents to move in with him. Indeed, a study in rural China found depression more common among the elderly people whose daughters took care of them instead of their daughters-in-law (Cong & Silverstein, 2008).

Tensions Between Older and Younger Adults

As noted in Chapter 22, a good relationship with successful grown children enhances a parent's well-being, especially when both generations do whatever the other generation expects. By contrast, a poor relationship makes life worse for everyone. Ironically, conflict is more likely in emotionally close relationships than in distant ones (Silverstein et al., 2010), especially when either generation becomes dependent on the other (Birditt et al., 2009).

Extensive research has found that relationships between parents and adult children are affected by many factors:

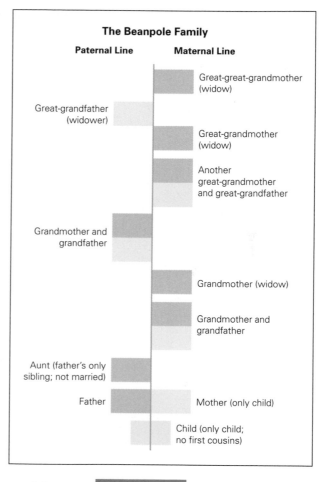

FIGURE 25.7

Many Households, Few Members The traditional nuclear family consists of two parents and their children living together. Today, as couples have fewer children, the beanpole family is becoming more common. This kind of family has many generations, each typically living in its own household, with only a few members in each generation.

>> **Answer to Observation Quiz** (from page 707) The U.S. couple is relatively rich (their nightclothes look new, and pajamas are mostly the preference of well-to-do men); the Filipina women are relatively poor (they are wearing identical dresses, a gift from the agency that runs this senior center).

- Assistance arises from need and from the ability to provide.
- Frequency of contact is related to geographical proximity, not affection.
- Love is influenced by the interaction remembered from childhood.
- Sons feel stronger obligation; daughters feel stronger affection.

Although all family members are supportive across the generations, members of each generation tend to overestimate how much they contribute (Lin, 2008b; Mandemakers & Dykstra, 2008). Contrary to popular perceptions, financial assistance and emotional support typically flow more from the older generation down instead of from the younger generation up, although much depends on who needs what (Silverstein, 2006). Only when an elder becomes frail is he or she more likely to receive family assistance than to give it. (Caring for the frail elderly is discussed later.)

Grandchildren

Most (85 percent) U.S. elders over age 65 are grandparents. (The rate was lower in some previous cohorts, because the birth rate fell during the 1930s, and is expected to be lower again.) Personality, background, and past family interactions all influence the nature of the grandparent–grandchild relationship, as do the child's age and personality. As with parents and children, the relationship between grandparents and grandchildren depends partly on the age of the grandchildren. One of my college students realized this when she wrote:

> Brian and Brianna are twins and are turning 13 years old this coming June. Over the spring break my family celebrated my grandmother's 80th birthday and I overheard the twins' talking about how important it was for them to still have grandma around because she was the only one who would give them money if they really wanted something their mom wasn't able to give them. . . . I lashed out . . . how lucky we were to have her around and that they were two selfish little brats. . . . Now that I am older, I learned to appreciate her for what she really is. She's the rock of the family and "the bank" is the least important of her attributes now.
>
> *[Giovanna, personal communication, 2010]*

Although a century ago grandparents almost always lived with the family of at least one of their grandchildren, now most do not. As in this case, the grandparent–grandchild connection can be very strong without co-residence, which is now more voluntary and varied (Thiele & Whelan, 2008). The existence of a good relationship between elderly parents and their grown children makes a good relationship more likely between grandparents and grandchildren. Fathers are particularly influential in the grandfathers' relationships with grandchildren; mothers affect the grandmothers' relationships (Monserud, 2008).

In the United States, contemporary grandparents follow one of four approaches to dealing with their grandchildren (Szinovacz, 1998):

1. *Remote grandparents* (sometimes called *distant grandparents*) are emotionally distant from their grandchildren. They are esteemed elders who are honored, respected, and obeyed, expecting to get help whenever they need it.

2. *Companionate grandparents* (sometimes called *"fun-loving" grandparents*) entertain and "spoil" their grandchildren—especially in ways, or for reasons, that the parents would not.

3. *Involved grandparents* are active in the day-to-day lives of their grandchildren. They live near them and see them daily.

4. *Surrogate parents* raise their grandchildren, usually because the parents are unable or unwilling to do so.

"They grow up too fast."

Ignorant? Each generation has much to teach as well as much to learn.

MIKE BALDWIN / CARTOONSTOCK.COM

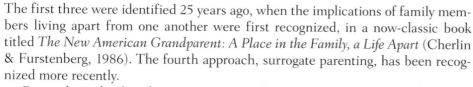

The first three were identified 25 years ago, when the implications of family members living apart from one another were first recognized, in a now-classic book titled *The New American Grandparent: A Place in the Family, a Life Apart* (Cherlin & Furstenberg, 1986). The fourth approach, surrogate parenting, has been recognized more recently.

Currently, in developed nations, most grandparents are companionate, partly because all three generations expect them to be beloved older companions rather than authority figures (Hayslip & Patrick, 2003). Grandparents themselves enjoy their independence from the demands of child rearing. If grandparents become too involved and intrusive, parents tend to be forgiving but not appreciative (Pratt et al., 2008).

Most are proud of their grandchildren and care about their well-being but keep their distance if possible. They provide babysitting and financial help but not advice or discipline. Their involvement leads to generativity and joy (Thiele & Whelan, 2008).

Such generative distance is not possible for grandparents who become surrogates when the biological parents are incapable. Difficult grandchildren (such as drug-affected infants and rebellious school-age boys) are more likely to live with grandparents. Social workers often seek grandparents for kinship foster care (see Chapter 8). The most vulnerable grandparents (disproportionately non-White and low-income) are pushed into surrogate parenting (Dunifon & Kowaleski-Jones, 2007).

Grandparents who are responsible full time for grandchildren have more illness, depression, and marital problems than other elders do. This is true in Europe as well as in North America, although the frequency of this family form depends on local and national culture (Hank & Buber, 2009; S. J. Kelley & Whitley, 2003; Solomon & Marx, 2000). Not surprisingly, few surrogate parents welcome their role. As one explains:

> I don't know if God thought I did a poor job and wanted to give me a second chance, or thought I did well enough to be given the task one more time. My daughter tells me she cannot handle the children anymore, but maybe I won't be able to manage them either.
>
> *[quoted in Strom & Strom, 2000, p. 291]*

When a married couple takes over care of their grandchildren, employed grandfathers postpone retirement and grandmothers are likely to quit work (Y. Wang & Marcotte, 2007). Single grandfathers who become surrogate parents usually stop working. None of these outcomes increase the elders' satisfaction, as the following explains.

MARKO HAGERTY / THE IMAGE BANK / GETTY IMAGES

Alone, But Not Lonely Ten million women in the United States are widows. Most, like this woman, are over age 60 and live alone. Many, though not all, are financially secure and well adjusted to their newly independent way of life.

A VIEW FROM SCIENCE

Not Always Grand

It is a myth that grandparents always enjoy their grandchildren and vice versa. Another assumption is that the more time grandparents spend with grandchildren, the better. Those are among the reasons that social workers prefer grandparents for kinship care (as just noted) and judges protect the visitation rights of grandparents, even when parents are adequate and do not want the grandparents around (T. J. Stein, 2007).

The data suggest a more varied outcome: Sometimes all three generations benefit from grandparenting, sometimes not—responses vary depending on which generation is asked about which aspect of their relationship (Thiele & Whelan, 2008). One common assumption is that as more families take on the beanpole structure, and as more single parents and dual-earner couples raise children, grandparents become more important. This is sometimes true (Griggs et al., 2010) but not always.

For example, researchers compared groups of 5- to 15-year olds to test their hypothesis that the children who lived with their grandparents would have higher academic achievement than those who did not because the grandparents would provide stability, homework help, and encouragement (Dunifon & Kowaleski-Jones, 2007). The researchers considered ethnic backgrounds and family structure. They found that European American children did better, on average, when living with both older generations, but the math scores of African American children were highest when they lived with single mothers and no other adult. This suggests that, in some families, three generations living together signifies poverty and stress (Dunifon & Kowaleski-Jones, 2007).

Another study examined depression and self-esteem in emerging adults who had single parents. Some of them had a good relationship with their grandparents and some did not (Ruiz & Silverstein, 2007). The researchers again expected the grandparent relationship to be crucial, but surprisingly, the child–parent relationship was the pivotal one. A close relationship with a grandparent meant less depression only when the emerging adult had a good relationship with his or her mother.

This finding was confirmed by another aspect of this study. In second marriages, the mothers often became less supportive of their children (they were more involved with their new spouse), and unfortunately the grandparents became more distant as well. Then the young adults became depressed, withdrawing from both older generations (see Figure 25.8; Ruiz & Silverstein, 2007).

It is apparent from these studies and from other research that grandparents can provide security and joy for their grandchildren, but not all of them do so. As the discussion of family structure and family function in Chapter 13 explained, the crucial variable is what actually occurs in their interaction, not simply the amount of contact or the formal structure.

The fact that grandparenting is not always wonderful should not obscure the more typical situation: Most grandparents enjoy their role, gain generativity from it, and are appreciated by younger family members (C. L. Kemp, 2005; Thiele & Whelan, 2008). International college students, despite being thousands of miles away from their grandparents, often express warmth, respect, and affection for at least one of them (usually their maternal grandmother) back home (A. C. Taylor et al., 2005). In most conditions, grandparenting benefits all three generations.

The animal kingdom may help us see the bigger picture. Wild elephants normally live in multigenerational herds. In one region of Africa, elephant poachers killed most of the oldest generation (until strict laws put an end to killing mature elephants for their tusks). In those herds, when the younger elephants became adults, many were infertile and most had higher levels of stress than elephants normally do (Gobush et al., 2008). Like humans, elephants benefit from having grandparents around.

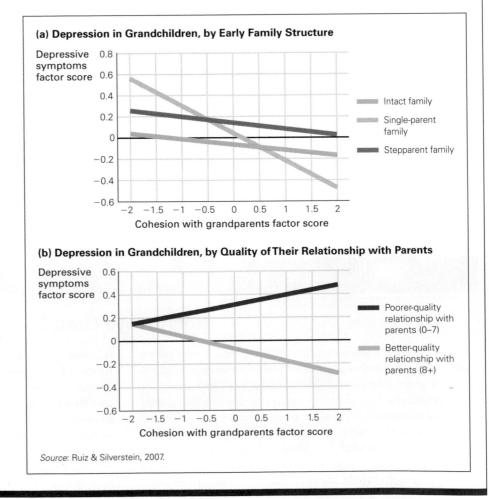

(a) Depression in Grandchildren, by Early Family Structure

(b) Depression in Grandchildren, by Quality of Their Relationship with Parents

Source: Ruiz & Silverstein, 2007.

FIGURE 25.8

One Puzzling Curve In these graphs, the vertical axis represents depressive symptoms, so lines that slope downward indicate that closeness to grandparents reduces depression in grandchildren. However, as part (b) shows, when the relationship with parents is poor, the relationship with grandparents also suffers, and depression is more likely.

Good to See You Again Older men, like younger ones, appreciate one another's friendship but seldom get together just to talk. These Delaware farmers met again at a melon auction and took the opportunity to get caught up on their families, their aches and pains, and the price of watermelon.

Together by Choice Elderly women outnumber elderly men in China by a wide margin, but that does not stop their social impulses. These six women in a public park in Guangzhou seek out one another for daily conversation, often bringing their own chairs.

Friendship

Of people currently over age 65 in the United States, only 4 percent (1.4 million) have never married, making this oldest generation the most-married cohort in history (U.S. Bureau of the Census, 2008). The next cohort will include far fewer married people. Many middle-aged adults, married and unmarried, have no children. Will they be lonely and lack social support?

Probably not. Members of the current oldest generation who never married are usually quite content, and not usually lonely. Some of them are in gay or lesbian partnerships and some have heterosexual romances, either sharing a residence or "living apart together"; all seem just as happy as traditionally married people (Brown & Kawamura, 2010). In future generations, as the number of unmarried elderly adults increases, the size of their social networks is likely to increase as well.

Recent widowhood or divorce is almost always difficult, but elderly people who never married usually have friendships, activities, and social connections that keep them busy and happy (DePaulo, 2006). This is true internationally. A Dutch study of 85 currently single elders (divorced, widowed, and never married) found that their level of well-being was similar to that of people in long-term equitable marriages. They were happier than either recent widows or the married adults in unequal marriages (Hagedoorn et al., 2006).

All the research finds that older adults need at least one close companion. For many (especially husbands), this intimate friend is also a spouse; for many others, the friend is another member of the social convoy. Sometimes an older person is not aware of the importance of a confidant until the relationship is severed. For example, one man was unexpectedly depressed when he retired voluntarily. He anticipated being happy on leaving his job, but something was wrong. "For over forty years, he had car-pooled with another man who worked in the same office. They traveled to and from work; an hour's drive each way. They had spent ten hours each week together, for over forty years, sharing their lives, hopes, dreams, and demons" (Rosowsky, 2007, p. 39).

He had not realized how important that relationship was to him until he quit work. There is a lesson here: Many people do not realize the importance of social relationships until they are gone. Quality (not quantity) of friendship is crucial, especially among the oldest-old (Krause, 2006). A study of widows found that those who fared best increased their contact with close friends after the death of their spouse (Zettel & Rook, 2004). Successful aging requires that people not be socially isolated, as explained in the following.

THINKING CRITICALLY

Social Networking

Older people text, tweet, and stream less than younger ones. Compared with emerging adults, older adults own fewer computers, are less connected to the Internet, and avoid social networking (Charness & Boot, 2009). One statistic makes the point: In the United States in 2010, 80 percent of all 18- to 29-year-olds had broadband connections *at home,* but only 31 percent of those over age 65 did (Smith, 2010).

Older adults may not realize what they are missing: "Seniors are significantly less likely than other age groups to view a lack of broadband access as a major disadvantage across a range of topics—from finding out about job or career opportunities to using government services," with only one elder in nine considering lack of Internet connection "a major disadvantage" (Smith, 2010, p.16). Meanwhile, adolescents and emerging adults are often distraught if their online connections are disrupted. Indeed, their technology use has led to prohibitions not contemplated a few years ago: Some school guards confiscate

cell phones, some professors forbid laptops in class, and some partners tell their mates never to take BlackBerries to bed.

The digital age gap is particularly apparent for social networking. Facebook, Twitter, MySpace, LinkedIn, online dating, and so on are populated by millions of 15- to 25-year-olds, with fewer participants at every older age. A contrary trend is emerging, however. Many seniors who acquire Internet access join social-networking sites soon after they cross that digital divide. In one recent year, the rates of social networking among those aged 65 and older increased 100 percent, while rates for 18- to 29-year-olds rose only 15 percent (see Figure 25.9). As one newspaper reported:

Richard Bosak joined Facebook on Thursday, after his buddy Ray Urbans recommended the ubiquitous social networking site a few days earlier. Bosack is 89. Urbans is 96. . . . The hottest growth segment in online social networking sites is guys like

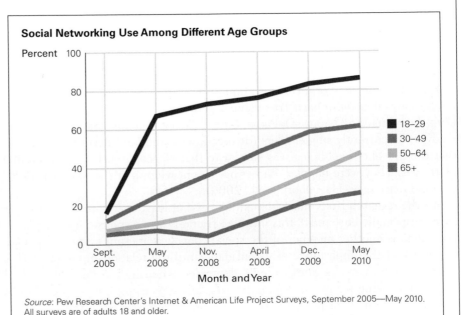

Social Networking Use Among Different Age Groups

Legend:
- 18–29
- 30–49
- 50–64
- 65+

Source: Pew Research Center's Internet & American Life Project Surveys, September 2005—May 2010. All surveys are of adults 18 and older.

FIGURE 25.9

Clear Data Social networking is already widespread among emerging adults and is increasing rapidly among older ones. Still murky is what this means—new connections, new problems, or the same human behaviors and emotions in a new format?

Richard and Ray and their lady friends. That's right. Grampy and Grammy are down with "the Face."

[Gregory, 2010]

From a developmental perspective, this is good news. As the text explains, elders who have strong social networks, close friends, and cognitively stimulating activities tend to live long and healthy lives—but this would not be the case if their activities were routine and passive (Akbaraly et al., 2009). Involved, interacting elders are more cogent and happier than their relatively lonely and isolated peers. Internet use and social networking correlate with more frequent contact with friends, family, and community organizations (Hogeboom et al., 2010).

Pause to appreciate the scope of this historical change. A few decades ago, social networks were maintained through direct contact. Neighbors were *neighborly*, a word that means "friendly and helpful." Everyone shopped, worshipped, studied, and played at the same places, and they saw one another often. People always answered their phone and doorbell and complained if their friends did not "stay in touch."

Many of the elderly grew up that way—in one study, only those over age 80 said they would not mind if a friend dropped by unannounced (Felmlee & Muraco, 2009). Such direct and informal contact is no longer the norm, and even older adults who want frequent, informal contact are less able to have it: Aging makes them less likely to go to work, take part in political rallies, enjoy late-night parties, volunteer, or even attend church. Technology may remedy this. For people of all ages, Internet use correlates with more offline friends, partly because friendships seem strengthened through online contact (Wang & Wellman, 2010).

Then why is this a topic for critical thinking instead of celebration? Two reasons: Social networking may increase prejudice and decrease community activism.

First, with wider access, people become more exclusive and selective about their contacts, lists, and news sources—screening out those who disagree. Humans take comfort in reading opinions that reinforce their own point of view. Yet

GREGORY

"I used to call people, then I got into e-mailing, then texting, and now I just ignore everyone."

on blogs, in chat rooms, and on YouTube, much more so than in newspapers and magazines, rumors and prejudices become viral, infecting thousands before anyone discovers a hoax, lie, or distortion. This makes reflection and analysis more necessary than ever, yet the prefrontal cortex that enables such thinking shrinks with age.

People of all ages tend to seek information to confirm their stereotypes, and the elderly may be particularly vulnerable. They are less tolerant of gays, immigrants, the poor, and so on (e.g., 53 percent of those age 18 to 29 but only 29 percent of those over age 65 favor gay marriage [Pew Research Center for the People and the Press, 2010]). Might social networking increase narrow thinking?

Second, although social networking increases the frequency of contact with friends, it may also decrease true intimacy and commitment. As Malcolm Gladwell (2010) explains:

> The platforms of social media are built around weak ties. . . . Facebook is a tool for effectively managing your acquaintances, for keeping up with the people you would not otherwise be able to stay in touch with.

[p. 44]

Weak ties, Gladwell contends, do not spur people to action; instead, they encourage comfort, lip service, and passivity—thus maintaining the status quo.

Two eminent scholars, Thomas Sander and Robert Putnam (2010), also fear this possibility. They hope that "technological innovators may yet master the elusive social alchemy that will enable online behavior to produce real and enduring civic effects," but they do not see it thus so far (p. 15).

A non-Internet study of the relationship between taking action after telling or not telling good intentions to another person found that public expression actually reduced intended behavior (Gollwitzer et al., 2009). Admittedly, this study focused on college students' plans to study and thus might not be relevant to social networking. However, Gladwell (2010) reported that the thousands of people who declared their support on Facebook for a group dedicated to ending the violence in Darfur gave an average of only 9 cents each to that cause. Might declaring support online make people less likely to donate, rally, write letters, or anything else?

Any answer is premature. Sander and Putnam (2010) note that "posts on Twitter (known as 'tweets') convey people's meal and sock choices, instant movie reactions, rush-hour rants, and occasionally even their profound reflections," and they "remain agnostic . . . about whether [these] replace traditional social ties" (p. 15). Two other social scientists conclude: "Changing social connectivity is, after all, neither a dystopian loss nor a utopian gain but an intricate, multifaceted, fundamental social transformation" (Wang & Wellman, 2010, p. 1164). Apparently all of us—old and young alike—are in the thralls of this transformation. Critical thinking may help us prevent the harm and reap the benefits of social networking.

SUMMING UP

SUMMING UP

In late adulthood, the social convoy continues to provide emotional and psychological support as well as practical help. People in long-term partnerships typically live longer, healthier, and happier lives because of their mutual dependence. Relationships with adult children and with grandchildren are usually mutually supportive, although the older generation is more likely to help the younger ones than vice versa. Friends are needed and wanted in late adulthood, particularly by elderly people who do not have a living spouse or children.

■

>> The Frail Elderly

Remember that aging can be *usual, impaired,* or *optimal.* Thus far, we have focused on the usual and optimal—on those elderly people who are active and enjoy the support of friends and family. Now we look at the **frail elderly,** those who are infirm, very ill, or cognitively impaired. Usually the frail elderly are the oldest-old, not only over age 85 but also severely disabled.

Activities of Daily Life

The crucial indicator of frailty is the inability to perform the tasks of self-care needed to maintain independence. Gerontologists often refer to these tasks in terms of five physical **activities of daily life (ADLs)**—namely, eating, bathing, toileting, dressing, and moving (transferring) from a bed to a chair.

Equally important may be the **instrumental activities of daily life (IADLs),** which require intellectual competence and forethought (Stone, 2006). It is more difficult to measure IADLs because they vary from culture to culture. In developed nations, IADLs include shopping for groceries, paying bills, driving a car, taking medications as prescribed, and keeping appointments (see Table 25.2). In rural areas of other nations, feeding the chickens, cultivating the garden, mending clothes, getting water from the well, and making dinner might be considered IADLs.

frail elderly People over age 65, and often over age 85, who are physically infirm, very ill, or cognitively disabled.

activities of daily life (ADLs) Typically identified as five tasks of self-care that are important to independent living: eating, bathing, toileting, dressing, and transferring from a bed to a chair. The inability to perform any of these tasks is a sign of frailty.

instrumental activities of daily life (IADLs) Actions (for example, paying bills and driving a car) that are important to independent living and that require some intellectual competence and forethought. The ability to perform these tasks may be even more critical to self-sufficiency than ADL ability.

TABLE 25.2	
Instrumental Activities of Daily Life	
Domain	Exemplar Task
Managing medications	Determining how many doses of cough medicine can be taken in a 24-hour period Completing a patient medical-history form
Shopping for necessities	Ordering merchandise from an online catalog Comparing brands of a product
Managing one's finances	Comparing Medigap insurance plans Completing income tax returns
Using transportation	Computing taxi rates versus bus rates Interpreting driver's right-of-way laws
Using the telephone	Determining amount to pay from a phone bill Determining emergency phone information
Maintaining one's household	Following instructions for operating a household appliance Comprehending an appliance warranty
Preparing meals and understanding nutrition	Evaluating nutritional information on food labels Following recipe directions

Source: Adapted from Willis, 1996.

Cultural Shift This list of IADLs in the United States is less than two decades old, yet you can already see that culture and cohort are crucial. For today's elderly, understanding Medicare part D, obtaining a free flu vaccination, evaluating cell phone carriers, and interpreting the salt content of packaged foods might replace some items listed here.

Everywhere, the inability to perform IADLs makes people frail, even if they can perform all five ADLs (Stone, 2006). Ideally, compression of morbidity and good medical care will reduce the amount of time during which the average elderly person needs help with either ADLs or IADLs (Willis et al., 2006).

There are marked cultural differences in care for the frail elderly, as already mentioned. Many Asian and African cultures emphasize family responsibility and respect for the aged. India passed a law in 2007 making it a crime to neglect one's elderly parents. However, gerontologists have criticized government policies that place too much reliance on family obligation, noting that some families are overburdened while others have no frail elders (Aboderin, 2004; Ogawa, 2004; Phillipson, 2006).

Governments, families, and aging individuals sometimes blame one another for frailty. The responsibility actually rests with all three. To take a simple example, a person whose leg muscles are weakening might make choices that lead toward, or away from, frailty. This person might avoid stairs altogether and stay in bed, while an oversolicitous caregiver brings meals and a remote for a new large-screen TV in the bedroom. Alternatively, he or she might start strength training and purchase a walker that allows long, daily excursions.

Family members as well as friendly volunteers could walk with the elderly person on pathways that the local government has built to be safe and pleasant. Someone could help that elderly person buy that sturdy walker, and public funds could underwrite the purchase. Thus, all three—the elder, the family, and the community—could prevent or at least postpone frailty or could make it worse. Consider another example, this one not theoretical.

An Odd Couple This tiny short-haired chihuahua and big, mustached Hispanic man may seem an odd pair, but what you see here is admirable self-protection. The cognitive demands of a mobile wheelchair and the physical demands of a dog are likely to prevent frailty for years to come.

JEFF GREENBERG / PHOTO EDIT

A CASE TO STUDY

When Protection Doesn't Help

A 70-year-old Hispanic man came to his family doctor following a visit to his family in Colombia, where he had appeared to be disoriented (he said he believed he was in the United States, and he did not recognize places that were known to be familiar to him) and he was very agitated, especially at night. An interview with the patient and a family member revealed a history that had progressed over the past six years, at least, of gradual worsening cognitive deficit which that family had interpreted as part of normal aging. Recently his symptoms had included difficulty operating simple appliances, misplacement of items, and difficulty finding words, with the latter attributed to his having learned English in his late 20s. . . . [His] family had been very protective and increasingly had compensated for his cognitive problems.

. . . He had a lapse of more than five years without proper control of his medical problems [hypertension and diabetes] because of difficulty gaining access to medical care. . . .

Based on the medical history, a cognitive exam . . . and a magnetic resonance imaging of the brain . . . the diagnosis of moderate Alzheimer's disease was made. Treatment with ChEI

[cholinesterase inhibiters] was started. . . . His family noted that his apathy improved and that he was feeling more connected with the environment.

[Griffith & Lopez, 2009]

In this example, you can see that the community (those five years without treatment for hypertension and diabetes, both known to impair cognition) and the family (making excuses, protecting him) allowed him to reach a stage of dementia that should have been delayed, if not prevented. Improvement came once treatment began. One hopes that his family also learned how to help, not just protect. If he himself had known more about his condition, he would have realized that taking a trip to Colombia was the worst thing he could do; disorientation of place is one of the first signs of dementia, and traveling to another country is disorienting for anyone. Thus, even with dementia, as well as with all other kinds of physical and mental impairment, delay, moderation, and sometimes prevention is possible.

Caring for the Frail Elderly

The caregiver of a frail elderly person is usually the spouse, who is also elderly. If an impaired person has no living partner, often a sibling or an adult daughter provides care. Nursing homes are usually considered as a last resort.

Family caregivers experience substantial stress. Their health may suffer, and their risk of depression increases, especially if the care receiver has dementia (Pinquart & Sörensen, 2003; Roth et al., 2008). After listing the problems and frustrations of caring for someone who is mentally incapacitated but physically strong, the authors of one overview note:

> The effects of these stresses on family caregivers can be catastrophic. . . . They may include increased levels of depression and anxiety as well as higher use of psychotropic medicine such as tranquilizers, poorer self-reported health, compromised immune function, and increased mortality.
>
> *[Gitlin et al., 2003, p. 362]*

However, not all caregivers feel overwhelmed. Indeed, some feel fulfilled because they are returning past caregiving and everyone, including the care receiver, expresses appreciation. In fact, when caregivers feel increasingly supported by family, they experience less emotional stress as time goes on, even though the frail person's needs increase (Roth et al., 2005).

The designated caregiver of a frail elderly person is chosen less for practical reasons (e.g., the relative with the most patience, time, and skill) than for cultural ones. In the United States, the spouse is the usual caregiver, perhaps helped by the eldest daughter. In some European nations, most of the care is provided through a social safety net of senior day-care centers, seniors' homes, and skilled nurses. In some cultures, an older person who is dying is taken to a hospital to extend life; in other cultures, such intervention is seen as interference with the natural order.

Traditionally in Asian nations, a son and his wife provide elder care. In a 1990s study in South Korea, for instance, 80 percent of those with dementia were cared for by daughters-in-law and only 7 percent by spouses. In contrast, among Ameri-

Morning, Afternoon, Evening, Bedtime Less than half of all adults follow doctors' orders about medication. For seniors, this negligence can lead to dementia or even death. Family caregiving usually begins with IADLs, as with this daughter, who is sorting her mother's 16 medications into a tray that is marked to help the older woman remember when to take them.

Observation Quiz Do this mother and daughter live together? (see answer, page 720)

DENNIS MACDONALD / PHOTO EDIT

cans of Korean descent with dementia, 19 percent were cared for by daughters-in-law and 40 percent by spouses, with some of the rest in nursing homes (which almost never happened in Korea) (Youn et al., 1999).

In every culture, emotional and physical needs, as well as expectations, vary. Some older people would rather accept help from a paid stranger than from a son or a daughter; others insist on the opposite. Some cultures admire caregivers; others isolate them. That may explain why at least one study found that caregiving African Americans are less depressed than caregivers of other ethnicities (Roth et al., 2008), although generalities by ethnicity obscure many individual variations.

Even in ideal circumstances with cultural and community support, family caregiving can present problems:

- If one adult child is the primary caregiver, other siblings feel both relief and jealousy. The caregiver wants siblings to do more; they resent being told what to do.

- Care receivers and caregivers often disagree about schedules, menus, doctor visits, and so on. Resentments on both sides disrupt mutual affection and appreciation.

- Public agencies rarely provide services unless a crisis arises.

This last item is of particular concern to developmentalists, who are trained to see "changes over time." From a life-span perspective, frailty should be anticipated and postponed. Caregiver exhaustion and elder abuse are potential problems that can be prevented. In many nations, public policy and cultural values result in "a system that places inappropriate burdens of elder care upon the family" (Seki, 2001, p. 101).

One cause of this burden is the widespread horror of nursing homes, even though many of them provide excellent care (as will soon be discussed). Some elderly people regard going into a nursing home as a fate worse than death; some families feel shame if they place an elderly relative into a nursing home.

Developmentalists, concerned about the well-being of people of all ages, advocate more help for families caring for frail elders (see Fortinsky et al., 2007; Stone, 2006). The most important need is for some relief from full responsibility, including more free time (via professional providers of respite care or family members who take over on a regular basis), and better medical attention (usually with visiting nurses who provide medical and psychological care for both caregiver and care receiver). Such measures can make home care tolerable, even fulfilling, for caregivers.

Sweet But Sad Family support is evident here, as an older sister (Lillian, age 75) escorts the younger (Julia, age 71) to the doctor. Unseen is how family support wrecked their lives: The sisters lost their life savings and their childhood home because their nephew was addicted to crack.

NICOLE BENGIVENO / THE NEW YORK TIMES

Elder Abuse

When caregiving results in resentment and social isolation, the risk of depression, poor health, and abuse (of either the frail person or the caregiver) escalates. Abuse is likely if the caregiver suffers from emotional problems or substance abuse, if the care receiver is frail, and if care occurs in an isolated place where visitors are few. Ironically, although relatives are less prepared to cope with difficult patients than professionals are, they often provide round-the-clock care with little outside help or supervision and may believe that overmedication, locked doors, and physical restraints are their only options.

>> Answer to Observation Quiz (from page 718) Probably not. Clues include the small (not family-size) refrigerator, the mother's medical-alert pendant, and the fact that the daughter is organizing medications for an entire week (as indicated by the large number of compartments in the tray), not just a single day.

Professionals consider all these measures abusive. Extensive public and personal safety nets for the frail elderly are needed to prevent maltreatment (Mellor & Brownell, 2006).

Sometimes the caregiver becomes the victim, cursed or even attacked by the confused elderly person. As with other forms of abuse, the dependency of the victim makes prosecution difficult (Mellor & Brownell, 2006). This problem gets worse when a family's pride, secrecy, and suspicion keep outsiders away.

Researchers find that about 5 percent of elders say they are abused and that up to one-fourth of all elders are vulnerable but do not report abuse (Cooper et al., 2008). Because elders who are mistreated by family members are ashamed to admit it, the actual rate is probably close to that one-fourth. Accurate measurement is complicated by lack of consensus regarding standards of care: Some elders feel abused, but caregivers disagree.

Long-Term Care

Many elders and their relatives, horrified by headlines and photographs of abuse in nursing homes, are convinced that those institutions should be avoided no matter what. And some institutions are dehumanizing. One 61-year-old woman with cerebral palsy, who spent time in a nursing home, said:

> I would rather die than have to exist in such a place where residents are neglected, ignored, patronized, infantilized, demeaned; where the environment is chaotic, noisy, cold, clinical, even psychotic.
>
> *[quoted in W. H. Thomas, 2007, p. 159]*

Fortunately, outright abuse is now rare in nursing homes. Laws forbid the use of physical restraints except temporarily in specific, extraordinary circumstances. Some nursing homes provide individualized, humane care, allowing residents to decide what to eat, where to walk, whether or not to have a pet (W. H. Thomas, 2007).

In North America and particularly in western Europe, good nursing-home care is available for those who can afford it and know what to look for. Among the signs of a humane setting are provisions for independence, individual choice, and privacy. As with day care for young children, continuity of care is crucial: An institution with a high rate of staff turnover is to be avoided.

Especially for Those Uncertain About Future Careers Would you like to work in a nursing home? (see response, page 722)

Training and workload of the staff, especially of the aides who provide the most frequent and most personal care, are also crucial: Such simple tasks as helping a frail person out of bed can be done clumsily, painfully, or skillfully. The difference depends on proficiency, experience, and patience—all possible with a sufficient number of well-trained and well-paid staff. Currently, however, most front-line workers have little training, low pay, and many patients (Stone, 2006).

Quality care is labor-intensive and expensive; the average nursing home cost in the United States in 2005 was $75,000 a year; some facilities charged more than $200,000. In an AARP survey, only 8 percent of middle-aged adults guessed within 20 percent of the actual cost of nursing-home care in their community (L. L. Barrett, 2006). Most thought that Medicare or Medicaid covered such care—another misconception (Feng et al., 2008).

In the United States, the trend over the past 20 years has been toward fewer nursing-home residents (currently about 1.5 million people nationwide), and those few are very frail and confused, needing assistance with both ADLs and IADLs (Stone, 2006). Although 90 percent of elders are independent and community dwelling at any given moment, half of them will need nursing-home care at some point, usually for less than a month as they recuperate from hospitalization. It is

KAREN KASMAUSKI / CORBIS

Help with an ADL A frail elderly man who can no longer bathe himself (one of the basic activities of daily living) is assisted by trained attendants in a model home for the aged in Tokyo.

projected that one in eight will need such care for over a year, and a few will need it for 10 years or more (Stone, 2006). These statistics mean that everyone needs to be concerned about the quality of nursing-home care, because everyone will ultimately need it for themselves or for a close family member.

Alternative Care

Most elder-care arrangements—home care, aging in place, and NORCs—are less costly and more individualized than nursing homes. One common form in the United States is called **assisted living,** an arrangement that combines some of the privacy and independence of home life with some of the medical supervision of a nursing home (Imamoglu, 2007).

An assisted-living residence might provide a private room for each person, allowing pets and furnishings just as in a traditional home. Services might include one communal meal per day, special bus trips and activities, and optional arrangements for household cleaning and minor repairs. Usually, medical assistance is readily available—from daily supervision of pill taking to emergency help, with a doctor and ambulance provided when necessary.

Assisted-living facilities range from group homes for three or four elderly people to large apartment or townhouse developments for hundreds of residents (Stone, 2006). Each state in the United States has its own standards for assisted-living facilities, but many such places are unlicensed. International variation is also wide: Some regions of the world (northern Europe) have many residential options for older residents, and others (sub-Saharan Africa) have almost none.

We close with an example of family care and nursing-home care at their best. A young adult named Rob related that his 98-year-old great-grandmother "began to fail. We had no idea why and thought, well, maybe she is growing old" (quoted in L. P. Adler, 1995, p. 242). All three younger generations of the family conferred and reluctantly decided that it was time to move the matriarch from her suburban home, where she had lived for decades, into a nearby nursing home. She, reluctantly, agreed.

assisted living A living arrangement for elderly people that combines privacy and independence with medical supervision.

>> **Response for Those Uncertain About Future Careers** (from page 720) Why not? The demand for good workers will obviously increase as the population ages, and the working conditions are likely to improve. An important problem is that the quality of nursing homes varies, so you need to make sure you work in one whose policies incorporate the view that the elderly can be quite capable, social, and independent.

Fortunately, this nursing home encouraged independence and did not assume that decline is always a sign of "final failing." The doctors there discovered that the woman's heart pacemaker was not working properly. Rob tells what happened next:

> We were very concerned to have her undergo surgery at her age, but we finally agreed. . . . Soon she was back to being herself, a strong, spirited, energetic, independent woman. It was the pacemaker that was wearing out, not Great-grandmother.

[quoted in L. P. Adler, 1995, p. 242]

This story contains a lesson repeated throughout this book. When a toddler does not talk, or a preschooler grabs a toy, or a teenager gets drunk, or an emerging adult takes dangerous risks, or an older person seems to be failing, one might conclude that such problems are normal for that particular age. There is truth in that: Each of these is more common at those stages.

But each of those behaviors should also alert caregivers, who can encourage talking, sharing, moderation, caution, or self-care. The life-span perspective holds that, at every age, people can be "strong, spirited, and energetic" if all of us do our part.

SUMMING UP

Some elderly people become frail, unable to perform the activities of daily life (such as bathing and dressing) or the instrumental activities of daily life (such as taking medication and paying bills). If an elderly person needs full-time care, usually the spouse or another family member provides it. Full-time caregiving of a frail elder, performed by an isolated and untrained family member, is stressful and sometimes leads to ill health in the caregiver and to abuse of either the care receiver or the caregiver. Alternate provisions for elder care, including assisted-living settings and nursing homes, are sometimes preferable to family care.

SUMMARY

Theories of Late Adulthood

1. Several self theories hold that adults make personal choices in ways that allow them to become fully themselves. Erikson believed that individuals seek integrity that connects them to the human community; research finds substantial continuity in personality traits as well as the existence of the positivity effect and appreciation of self and others.

2. Stratification theories maintain that social forces—such as ageism, racism, and sexism—limit personal choices throughout the life span. One such theory blames stratification for the disengagement of older adults, but that view is opposed by activity theory, which holds that older people wish to be active.

Activities in Late Adulthood

3. At every age, employment can provide social and personal satisfaction as well as needed income. However, retirement may be welcomed by the elderly.

4. Some elderly people perform volunteer work, and many are active politically—writing letters, voting, staying informed. These activities enhance the health and well-being of the elderly and benefit the larger society.

5. More common among retirees are an increase in religious activity (but not church attendance) and a wish to "age in place." Many of the elderly engage in home improvement or redecoration, preferring to stay in their own homes.

Friends and Relatives

6. A spouse is the most important member of a person's social convoy. Older adults in long-standing marriages tend to be satis-

fied with their relationships and to safeguard each other's health. As a result, married elders tend to live longer, happier, and healthier lives than unmarried ones.

7. The death of a spouse is always difficult. Wives are more likely to experience this loss, and, partly because many of their women friends have the same experiences, women are more likely than men to adjust to the death of a partner.

8. Relationships with adult children and grandchildren are usually mutually supportive. Most of the elderly prefer to maintain their independence, living alone, but some become surrogate parents, raising their grandchildren. This surrogate parenting benefits many family members and society as a whole, but it adds to the stress of the older generation.

The Frail Elderly

9. Most elderly people are self-sufficient, but some eventually become frail. They need help with their activities of daily life, either with physical tasks (such as eating and bathing) or with instrumental ones (such as paying bills and arranging transportation).

10. Care of the frail elderly is usually undertaken by adult children or spouses, who are often elderly themselves. Most families have a strong sense of filial responsibility, although elder abuse may occur when the stress of care is great and social support is lacking.

11. Nursing homes, assisted living, and professional home care are of varying quality and availability. Each of these arrangements can provide necessary and beneficial care, but good care for the frail elderly cannot be taken for granted.

KEY TERMS

self theories (p. 694)
integrity versus despair (p. 694)
compulsive hoarding (p. 695)
positivity effect (p. 696)
stratification theories (p. 697)

disengagement theory (p. 697)
activity theory (p. 698)
aging in place (p. 704)
naturally occurring retirement
　community (NORC) (p. 704)

AARP (p. 706)
filial responsibility (p. 709)
frail elderly (p. 716)
activities of daily life (ADLs)
　(p. 716)

instrumental activities of daily
　life (IADLs) (p. 716)
assisted living (p. 721)

WHAT HAVE YOU LEARNED?

Theories of Late Adulthood

1. How does Erikson's use of the word *integrity* differ from its usual meaning?

2. How is self theory reflected in older adults' wish to age in place?

3. How does hoarding relate to self theory?

4. What are the advantages of the positivity effect?

5. What are the disadvantages of the positivity effect?

6. How can disengagement be a mutual process?

7. If activity theory is correct, what does that suggest older adults should do?

8. What are the problems with being female, according to stratification theory?

9. What are the problems with being male, according to stratification theory?

10. In terms of independence, how is old age difficult for members of minority groups, according to stratification theory?

Activities in Late Adulthood

11. How does retirement affect the health of people who have worked all their lives?

12. Why would a person choose not to retire?

13. What are the age differences in how likely someone is to choose to volunteer?

14. Of the four possible reasons listed for lack of volunteering among the elderly, which do you think is most valid and why?

15. What are the benefits and liabilities for elders who want to age in place?

16. How does religion affect the well-being of the aged?

17. How does the political activism of older and younger adults differ?

Friends and Relatives

18. What is the usual relationship between older adults who have been partners for decades?

19. Who benefits most from relationships between older adults and their grown children?

20. Which type of grandparenting seems to benefit both generations the most?

The Frail Elderly

21. Inability to perform which of the ADLs do you think is most indicative of frailty and why?

22. Why are IADLs considered even more important than ADLs in assessing frailty in an elderly person?

23. What three factors increase the likelihood of elder abuse?

24. What are the advantages and disadvantages of assisted living for the elderly?

25. When is a nursing home a good solution for the problems of the frail elderly?

APPLICATIONS

1. Attitudes about disabilities are influential. Visit the disability office on your campus, asking both staff and students what they see as the effects of attitude on the performance of all students. How do your findings relate to the elderly?

2. People of different ages, cultures, and experiences vary in their values regarding family caregiving, including the need for safety, privacy, independence, and professional help. Find four people whose backgrounds (age, ethnicity, SES) differ. Ask their opinions, and analyze the results.

3. Visit a nursing home or assisted-living residence in your community. Record details about the physical setting, the social interactions of the residents, and the activities of the staff. Would you like to work or live in this place? Why or why not?

>>ONLINE CONNECTIONS

To accompany your textbook, you have access to a number of online resources, including quizzes for every chapter of the book, flashcards (in English and Spanish), critical thinking questions, and case studies. For access to any of these links, go to www.worthpublishers.com/bergerls8e. In addition to these free resources, you'll also find links to the podcasts, video clips, diagnostic quizzing with personalized study advice, and an ebook. Some of the videos and activities available online include:

■ *Making the Most of Life During Adulthood.* Explains the keys to successful aging and discusses Erikson's final three stages of development. Video clips show how culture affects the experience of aging.

■ *Grandparents as Parents.* In text and video, find out how elders cope with this growing phenomenon and how it affects grandparents and grandchildren.

Late Adulthood

BIOSOCIAL

Predictions, Aging, and Disease Ageism is prevalent and insidious, as prejudice about the old limits the elderly population's health and happiness. Both primary and secondary aging increase morbidity; ageism accelerates the process. Although all the senses eventually decline and every disease becomes more common, much can be done to slow down senescence and "add life to years" if not years to life.

Theories of Aging Many scientists are working to understand the aging process. While it is true that some parts of the body wear down with use, the opposite seems more the case, with exercise particularly important for reducing the effects of age. Each species seems to have a maximum life span because of aging cells, which themselves may be affected by genetic forces and by an aging immune system.

Centenarian More people are living past 100 years, although their prevalence in the society is far less than 1 percent. Although most experience serious disease in late adulthood and often show the neurological effects of aging brains, a sizable proportion of those who live to be very old are surprisingly healthy, happy, and independent.

COGNITIVE

The Usual Most people are able to think and plan relatively well in late adulthood. Problems are apparent in short-term memory, but long-term memory seems good. For some, emotional restraint—a main function of the prefrontal cortex—decreases with age, such that feelings, reactions, and memories may be more vivid for the elderly than for younger people.

The Impaired Dementia is not the usual consequence of old age, but it is devastating when it occurs. The worst common form is Alzheimer disease, which destroys memory. Vascular dementia is also widespread, although efforts to reduce high blood pressure and obesity help reduce the ministrokes that characterize vascular dementia.

The Optimal Interest and ability in the arts may increase with age, as does the wish to become more spiritual. The life review helps elders understand their role in human experience, and they recount past history and enduring values. Wisdom is not necessarily the consequence of old age, but some elders are exceptionally wise.

PSYCHOSOCIAL

Activities of Later Adulthood Generally, older adults are quite active. Activity theory seems more accurate than disengagement theory. Some older adults are employed, some volunteer, some are politically active.

Friends and Family Long-term marriages tend to be supportive, long-time friends are usually loyal, and relationships with grown children and grandchildren are satisfying. None of this is inevitable, of course; grandparents who take over child care from their sick or absent children, for example, find surrogate parenting difficult.

The Frail Elderly Some elderly are frail, unable to perform the physical activities of daily life (ADLs) or the instrumental ones (IADLs). They depend on others for their care (often a spouse or a sibling who is also elderly), assisted living, or nursing home care. Elder abuse is common and, like child abuse, is the result of a dangerous interaction of care receiver, caregiver, and social context.

Death and Dying

> **WHAT WILL YOU KNOW?**
>
> 1. Should children be told that someone has died?
> 2. Why do people disagree about when a person is dead?
> 3. How does a hospice death differ from a typical death?
> 4. Is it important, psychologically, for people to sob at a funeral?

On September 11, 2001, I left lower Manhattan at 7:00 A.M. to teach in the Bronx. Two hours later, my students told me about the attack on the World Trade Center. I thought first about my family. I knew three of my daughters were far away from the site; I phoned the fourth one—she assured me that she was safe. My husband, Martin, worked near the towers, but when I left home that morning he was on his way to an appointment uptown.

When I finally got home that night, Martin told me he had walked toward his office after his appointment, undaunted by crowds running the other way. Finally, the police stopped him. Apparently, his first impulse was to maintain normal life—irrational, but not unlike my impulse to check on my family.

Martin died 16 months later. The immediate cause was an infection, which was exacerbated by steroids, which he took because they helped him breathe, which he needed because he had lung cancer, which occurred because his lungs were compromised by the smoke from the burning towers, added to 50 years of smoking cigarettes. For that, I blame myself; I never got him to quit smoking. I blame the U.S. Army, too, because they gave him free cigarettes when he was a 17-year-old volunteer. And I blame the culture because boys smoked to act like men. I even blame Hitler, already dead when Martin enlisted, but Martin had grown up wanting to fight him.

My search for causes—steroids, September 11th, pollution, addiction, me, the military, machismo, Hitler—arises from emotions of anger, guilt, and sorrow, not from acceptance of death as a natural and inevitable part of the life span. As you will read, people react to death in many ways; I am not the only irrational mourner.

This chapter discusses that and much more. Dying is a process that begins with personal choices (such as smoking cigarettes) and social contexts (such as the toxic smoke from the destroyed buildings), involving loved ones and strangers. Sometimes blame is irrational, bereavement takes many forms, dying is difficult to recognize, and death is hard to accept.

Thanatology is the study of all this. Perhaps surprisingly, thanatology is neither morbid nor gloomy. Rather, it reveals the *hope* in death, *acceptance* of dying, and *reaffirmation* of life. This chapter describes some insights that thanatologists have gained. As a social science, thanatology is a stellar example of the many developmental, cultural, and contextual variations in a universal human experience. We all die, but we do it in our own way. Begin with hope.

thanatology The study of death and dying, especially of the social and emotional aspects.

>> Death and Hope

You may not realize that hope is the human response to death. Yet death is often considered a beginning, not an end; a community event, not a personal one; welcomed, not dreaded. A life-span perspective allows us to see that death is viewed through many cultural prisms. A culture's attitude toward death is affected by historical changes (see Table EP.1) as well as by age, both of the person who dies and the one who mourns.

Understanding Death Throughout the Life Span

In order to understand what death means to people, we begin with developmental differences. The meaning assigned to death—either a person's own death or the death of another—depends partly on cognitive maturation and personal experience. As humans age, death becomes more likely, understanding deepens, and hope becomes stronger.

Death in Childhood

Some adults think children are oblivious to death; others believe children are aware of death and should therefore participate in funerals and other rituals, just as adults do. You know from your study of childhood cognition that neither view is completely correct.

Children as young as 2 have some understanding of death, but their perspective differs from that of older people. If a child encounters death, parents should listen with full attention, neither ignoring the child's concerns nor expecting mourning (Kenyon, 2001). Children are more impulsive than deliberate (remember that the brain matures very gradually) and may seem happy one day and morbidly sad the next. Children neither forget the death of a loved one nor do they dwell on it.

Children who themselves are fatally ill typically fear that death means being abandoned by beloved and familiar people (Wolchik et al., 2008). Consequently, parents are advised to stay with a dying child day and night, holding, reading, singing, and sleeping, always ensuring that the child is not alone. Frequent and caring contact is more important than logic.

A child who loses a friend, a relative, or a pet typically demonstrates sadness, loneliness, anger, and other signs of mourning, but adults cannot be certain how a particular child might react. Thus, one 7-year-old boy who lost three grandparents and an uncle within two years was especially upset when his dog, Twick, died. His parents, each grieving for a dead mother, were taken aback by the depth of the boy's emotions. They regretted that they had not taken their son to the veterinarian's office to say goodbye to the dog. The boy refused to go back to school, saying, "I wanted to see him one more time. . . . You don't understand. . . . I play with Twick every day" (quoted in K. R. Kaufman & Kaufman, 2006, pp. 65–66).

TABLE EP.1

How Death Has Changed in the Past 100 Years

Death occurs later. A century ago, the average life span worldwide was less than 40 years (47 in the rapidly industrializing United States). Half of the world's babies died before age 5. Now newborns are expected to live to age 78; in many nations, elderly people age 85 and over are the fastest-growing age group.

Dying takes longer. In the early 1900s, death was usually fast and unstoppable; once the brain, the heart, or other vital organs failed, the rest of the body quickly followed. Now death can often be postponed through medical intervention: Hearts can beat for years after the brain stops functioning, respirators can replace lungs, and dialysis can do the work of failing kidneys. As a result, dying is often a lengthy process.

Death often occurs in hospitals. A hundred years ago, death almost always occurred at home, with the dying person surrounded by familiar faces. Now many deaths occur in hospitals, surrounded by medical personnel and technology.

The main causes of death have changed. People of all ages once died of infectious diseases (tuberculosis, typhoid, smallpox), and many women and infants died in childbirth. Now disease deaths before age 50 are rare, and almost all newborns (99 percent) and their mothers (99.99 percent) live, unless the infant is very frail or medical care of the mother is grossly inadequate.

And after death . . . People once knew about life after death. Some believed in heaven and hell; others, in reincarnation; others, in the spirit world. Many prayers were repeated—some on behalf of the souls of the deceased, some for remembrance, some to the dead asking for protection. Believers were certain that their prayers were heard. Today's young adults are aware of cultural and religious diversity, which makes them question what earlier generations believed, raising doubts that never occurred to their ancestors.

Source: Adapted from Kastenbaum, 2006; data from U.S. Bureau of the Census, 2007 and earlier editions.

Because the loss of a particular companion is a young child's prime concern, it is not helpful to say that a dog can be replaced, that Grandma is sleeping, that God wanted his or her sister in heaven, or that Grandpa went on a trip. The child may take such explanations literally, thinking that someone should wake up Grandma, complain to God, or tell Grandpa to come home. Even a 2-year-old knows that a new puppy is not the same dog and might be angry or confused that an adult would think so. If adults are afraid to say that death has occurred, a child might conclude that death is so horrible that adults cannot talk about it—a terrifying conclusion.

As children become older and more concrete operational thinkers, they seek specific facts, such as exactly how a person died and where he or she is now. But their understanding is still childlike. In a study of 4- to 8-year-olds, those who knew more about the specifics of a loved one's death were less anxious about death and dying (Slaughter & Griffiths, 2007).

When 3- to 12-year-olds in a different U.S. study saw a puppet skit about a sick mouse that was eaten by an alligator, nearly all of them said that the mouse was dead and would never be alive again. However, most of the younger children did not really understand what it meant to be dead. Many thought the dead mouse still felt sick, lonely, scared, and so on (Bering & Bjorklund, 2004) (see Figure EP.1).

When this study was replicated in Spain (Bering et al., 2005), children from Spanish public and religious schools also thought the dead mouse still felt sick, lonely, and so on, with those in Catholic schools more likely to believe that the dead mouse could still hear voices and taste food. Rather than dismissing such children's notions, the lead researcher thinks an innate belief in an afterlife is evidence that "we are a species characterized—defined perhaps—by altruism, self-sacrifice, and charity" (Johnson & Bering, 2009, p. 27).

Double Sorrow Responses to death vary by age, culture, and significance. Jean and Don Masten arranged a memorial service for a dead newborn whose parents abandoned it; they then put a rose on the snowy grave of their own stillborn daughter, who died 21 years ago.

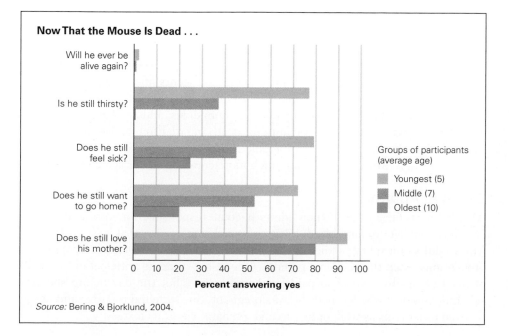

Source: Bering & Bjorklund, 2004.

FIGURE EP.1

Love Endures Even the youngest children knew that the mouse was dead, but most of them believed that it still had feelings, needs, and wishes. For children, death does not stop life. These researchers also surveyed 20 college students, 13 of whom (65 percent) thought that love for one's mother continues after one's death. (In this series of studies, not every age group was asked every question, which explains why only two sets of responses are shown for two of the questions here.)

Death in Adolescence and Emerging Adulthood

"Live fast, die young, and leave a good-looking corpse." This widely repeated saying was the title of a biography of actor James Dean, who died in a car crash at age 24. At what age would a person be most likely to agree with this advice? Age 25 and under, of course.

Worldwide, teenagers and emerging adults seem to have little fear of death, which may be their way of controlling anxiety rather than evidence that they do not care. They take risks, place a high value on appearance, and seek thrills, predicting they will die long before they are old (de Bruin et al., 2007).

One way to keep death anxiety at bay is to take death-defying risks and emerge unscathed. Social scientists have developed **terror management theory (TMT)** to explain some illogical responses people have about death, including why young people take risks (Mosher & Danoff-Burg, 2007). Many studies have found, as already noted in our discussion of emerging adulthood, that "a health promotion message that equates smoking with death may ironically have the exact opposite effect" (Goldenberg & Arndt, 2008, p. 1049); it may increase smoking in those who want to protect their pride and self-esteem. Likewise, college students who heard about the death risks of binge drinking were more willing to binge, not less so (Jessop & Wade, 2008).

Other research in many nations finds that when adolescents and emerging adults think about death, they sometimes "strive to maintain self-esteem and faith in their cultural worldviews, at least in part to protect themselves from death-related anxiety" (Maxfield et al., 2007, p. 342). This makes people more likely to accept stereotypes and to be intolerant of people of other ethnicities because they want to convince themselves that members of their own group (and thus they) are more worthy of life. Some even blame people who died because of severe injuries through no fault of their own (Hirschberger, 2006; Renkema et al., 2008), and some distance themselves from people with cancer but take more risks themselves to avoid anxiety about their own death (Hart et al., 2010).

How might the developmental tendency among older adolescents and emerging adults to take risks (see Figure EP.2) be connected to death anxiety? One reason why adolescents and emerging adults die in suicides, homicides, and accidents (especially when drunk) may be that they romanticize death in order to manage the fear of it. That combination makes them vulnerable to cluster suicides, foolish dares, fatal gang fights, and drunk driving—all much more common under age 25 than over.

Death in Adulthood

A shift in attitudes occurs when adults become responsible for work and family. Death is no longer romanticized; it is to be avoided instead—or at least postponed. Many adults quit taking addictive drugs, start wearing seat belts, and adopt other precautions when they become parents. One of my students anticipated the thrill of her first skydive. She had paid for it in advance, but the day before she was scheduled to dive, she learned she was pregnant. She forfeited the dive and chose to avoid other risks as well, opting to take prenatal vitamins instead.

terror management theory (TMT) The idea that people adopt cultural values and moral principles in order to cope with their fear of death. This system of beliefs protects individuals from anxiety about their mortality and bolsters their self-esteem, so they react harshly when other people go against any of the moral principles involved.

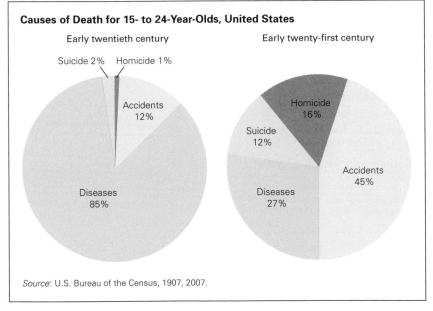

Causes of Death for 15- to 24-Year-Olds, United States

Early twentieth century

Suicide 2%   Homicide 1%

Accidents 12%

Diseases 85%

Early twenty-first century

Homicide 16%

Suicide 12%

Accidents 45%

Diseases 27%

Source: U.S. Bureau of the Census, 1907, 2007.

FIGURE EP.2

Typhoid Versus Driving into a Tree In 1905, most young adults in the United States who died were victims of diseases, usually infectious ones like tuberculosis and typhoid. In 2005, 25 times more died in the most common type of accident (motor vehicle) than died of the most common lethal disease (leukemia).

To defend themselves against the fear of aging and untimely death, adults do not readily accept the death of others—even when those others are ready to die. Thus, when Dylan Thomas was about age 30, he wrote his most famous poem, addressed to his dying father: "Do not go gentle into that good night. / Rage, rage against the dying of the light" (D. Thomas, 1957). Nor do they readily accept their own death. A woman diagnosed at age 42 with a rare and almost always fatal cancer (a sarcoma) wrote:

> I hate stories about people dying of cancer, no matter how graceful, noble, or beautiful. . . . I refuse to accept that I am dying; I prefer denial, anger, even desperation. . . . I resist the lure of dignity; I refuse to be graceful, beautiful, beloved."
>
> *[Robson, in Bauer-Maglin & Perry, 2010, pp. 19, 27, 28]*

When adults hear about another's death, their reaction is closely connected to the person's age. Death in the prime of life is much harder to accept (especially for people who are that age themselves) than is death in late adulthood. As an example of the power of age, consider the public reaction to the deaths of two U.S. presidents, Ronald Reagan and John Fitzgerald Kennedy. Reagan was probably the more popular of the two; he was president for eight years (Kennedy held office for only three) and was elected twice by a far wider margin. Yet Kennedy's violent death at age 46 continues to evoke far more public sorrow than did Reagan's death from Alzheimer disease at age 93.

Likewise, reactions to one's own terminal illness differ depending on developmental stage. From ages 25 to 60, terminally ill adults worry about leaving something undone or leaving family members—especially children—alone. One such adult was Randy Pausch, a 47-year-old professor and the father of three young children. Ten months before he died of cancer in 2008, he delivered a famous "last lecture," detailing his childhood dreams and saluting those who would continue his work. After advising his students to follow their own dreams, he concluded, "This talk is not for you, it's for my kids" (Pausch, 2008).

Adults' attitudes about death are often irrational. Rationally, people should work to change social factors that increase the risk of mortality—such as air pollution, junk foods, and unsafe transportation. Instead, many people react more strongly to events that only rarely cause death, such as anthrax outbreaks and avalanches, or to the deaths of people they know.

Often, when adults hear about someone's death, they want to donate to an organization that works to fight against that cause of death, as well as learn details in order to convince themselves that their situation is different. This is easy if the deceased was much older; if not, the impulse is to distinguish oneself from that person—who had genes, or had bad habits, or engaged in foolish behavior (unlike oneself).

The most feared deaths are the seemingly random ones, such as a freak accident or a mysterious poison. For this reason, many more people are afraid of flying than of driving; although the latter is much more likely to be fatal, adults in cars believe they are in control. Ironically, the crashing of four airplanes in the September 11th attacks led people to drive instead of fly; as an indirect result, 2,300 people died in car crashes that would not have occurred if fear were logical (Blalock et al., 2009).

In general, adults ignore their own life-shortening behavior, such as smoking cigarettes, eating a poor diet, and having unsafe sex. In

"For My Kids" Randy Pausch was a brilliant, innovative scientist who specialized in virtual-reality research at Pittsburgh's Carnegie Mellon University. When he was diagnosed with terminal pancreatic cancer, he gave a talk that became famous worldwide as "The Last Lecture," titled "Really Achieving Your Childhood Dreams." He devoted the final 10 months of his life to his family—his wife Jai and their children Chlöe, Dylan, and Logan.

reading this book, you probably have a reaction similar to mine as I write it: Those risky behaviors I myself engage in get less attention than the behaviors I avoid. For example, I blamed cigarettes for my husband's death and earlier linked smoking to heart attacks, dementia, and many cancers. Those links are proven, but would I have stressed them less if I were a smoker?

As a general example, statistics reveal that more people die *each day* of heart disease in the United States than died in the attacks of September 11th, but that statistic has little impact on public policy or private behavior. Intensified airport security measures seem protective, yet people eat food that clogs their arteries and drive everywhere instead of taking an occasional walk. Not logical, but very human.

That people do not follow their moral principles when thinking about death is one explanation for a classic puzzle called the *trolley car dilemma* (Thomson, 1986). When adults are asked whether they would pull a switch that would kill one innocent person but save five others, almost everyone would save the five, saying that is the ethical choice. But if asked whether they would push someone off a footbridge to stop a trolley car that otherwise would kill five, most adults say they would not. Brain activation (seen in fMRIs) in response to the trolley car and other dilemmas confirms that life-or-death choices activate the emotional parts of the brain, not necessarily the logical ones (J. D. Greene et al., 2001).

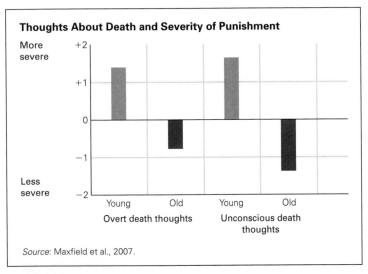

Thoughts About Death and Severity of Punishment

Source: Maxfield et al., 2007.

FIGURE EP.3

A Toothache Worse Than Death? Young (average age 21) and old (average age 74) adults were divided into three groups. One group wrote about death (so that they had overt thoughts about it), another did a puzzle with some words about death (so that their thoughts about death were unconscious), and the third wrote about dental pain (so that they served as the control group). Then they all judged how harshly people should be punished for various moral transgressions, using a scale of severity from 1 to 15. The groups who wrote about dental pain are represented by the zero point on this graph, meaning that they were not influenced by thoughts of death in making their ratings. Compared with those groups, the older groups who thought about death were less punitive, but the younger adults were more so. The difference in the ratings of the young and old groups was more pronounced if their thoughts about death were unconscious than if they were overt.

Death in Late Adulthood

In late adulthood, attitudes about death shift once more. Anxiety decreases and hope rises. Life-threatening illnesses reduce satisfaction with life more among the middle-aged than the elderly (Wurm et al., 2008). Some older people are quite happy even when they know their remaining time is short. The irrational and seemingly immoral reactions that help people manage terror are less evident at this stage (see Figure EP.3; Maxfield et al., 2007).

This shift in attitude is beneficial. Indeed, many developmentalists believe that one sign of mental health among older adults is acceptance of mortality (e.g., M. M. Baltes & Carstensen, 2003; Erikson et al., 1986; Schindler et al., 2006), which leads to altruistic concern about those who will live on after them.

As evidence of the change in attitude, older people write their wills, designate health care proxies, read scriptures, reconcile with estranged family members, and, in general, tie up all the loose ends that most young adults avoid (Kastenbaum, 2006). Sometimes adults are troubled when their elderly parents take specific actions, such as allocating heirlooms, choosing funeral music, or buying a burial plot, but all those might well be developmentally appropriate toward the end of life.

This acceptance of death does not mean that the elderly give up on living. On the contrary, most try to maintain their health and independence. However, they adjust their priorities. In an intriguing series of studies, people were presented with the following scenario, often used to demonstrate socioemotional selectivity, described in Chapter 25:

> Imagine that in carrying out the activities of everyday life, you find that you have half an hour of free time, with no pressing commitments. You have decided that you'd like to spend this time with another person. Assuming that the following three persons are available to you, who would you want to spend that time with?

A member of your immediate family
The author of a book you have just read
An acquaintance with whom you seem to have much in common

Older adults, more than younger ones, choose the family member. The researchers' explanation is that such conversations become more important when death seems imminent. This is supported by a study in which the same question was asked of middle-aged gay men before the discovery of protease inhibitors (used to treat HIV/AIDS). One group already had AIDS and expected to die within a few years, a second group was HIV-positive but had no symptoms, and a third group was HIV-negative. Compared with the latter two groups, the men with AIDS more often chose time with family (Carstensen & Fredrickson, 1998).

A similar study involved 329 people of various ages who had recently been diagnosed with cancer and another group of 170 people (of the same ages) who had no serious illness (Pinquart & Silbereisen, 2006). The most marked difference in how the participants would prefer to spend their time was between those with or without cancer, regardless of age (see Figure EP.4). This awareness of life-threatening illness, more common in late adulthood but not directly caused by age, seems to change a person's attitude toward life, people, and death.

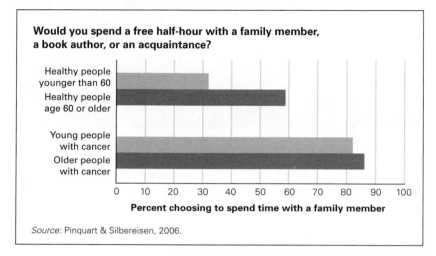

Would you spend a free half-hour with a family member, a book author, or an acquaintance?

Source: Pinquart & Silbereisen, 2006.

FIGURE EP.4

Turning to Family as Death Approaches
Both young and old people diagnosed with cancer (one-fourth of whom died within five years) were found to be more likely to prefer to spend a free half-hour having a conversation with a family member rather than with an interesting person whom they did not know well. A larger difference was found between older and younger adults who did not have a serious disease: The healthy younger people were less likely to say they'd prefer to spend the time with a family member rather than with an interesting acquaintance.

Religions and Hope

People who think they might die soon are also more likely than others to believe in life after death (Vail et al., 2010). This is one reason why the aged in the United States tend to be more religious than the young, praying more—although not necessarily attending church, temple, or mosque more frequently (Pyne, 2010). It may also explain why people in nations with higher death rates tend to be more devout.

An interesting connection exists among prayer, attendance at religious services, and readiness to die for one's faith (either as a martyr or a warrior). A study of six nations and three religions (Islam, Christianity, Judaism) found a strong positive correlation between attendance at services and belief in martyrdom but found no correlation overall between prayer and belief in martyrdom (Ginges et al., 2009). Apparently, the community of believers, more than connection to God, encourages dedication (or is it fanaticism?) to the faith.

Every religion provides rites and customs to honor the dead and comfort the living, a method of terror management that is much healthier than the risk taking common among the young (Vail et al., 2010). Specifics vary: "Rituals in the world's religions, especially those for the major tragic and significant events of bereavement and death, have a bewildering diversity" (Idler, 2006, p. 285).

Some details illustrate this diversity. According to many branches of Hinduism, for example, a person should die on the floor, surrounded by family, who neither eat nor wash until the funeral pyre is extinguished. By contrast, among some (not all) Christian denominations, funerals include food, drink, music, and dancing. Cremation is expected in many Asian cultures, whereas an open casket and then burial is standard practice in many Christian ones. Caskets themselves can be luxurious, silk-lined and enclosed in strong metal—or families can opt for "a plain pine box," as some religions prescribe (Sanders, 2010).

The Same Situation, Many Miles Apart: Gateway to Heaven or Final Rest
Many differences are obvious between a Roman Catholic burial in Mbongolwane, South Africa *(left),* and a Buddhist funeral procession before cremation in Bali, Indonesia *(right).* In both places, however, friends and neighbors gather to honor the dead person and to comfort his or her family members.

In some religions, the community insists that mourners eat; in others, mourners are supposed to fast; and in still others, specific foods are prepared for the dead—not to be eaten by the living. As another contrast, in many Muslim cultures, the dead person is bathed by the next of kin; among some Native Americans (e.g., the Navajo), no one touches the dead person.

That being said, however, not everyone in these religions necessarily observes the customs just mentioned; every faith has marked regional and individual variations that are evident in many aspects of death and dying. For example, each of the world's major religions includes opinions for *and* against organ donation after death (Bresnahan et al., 2010). Obviously, medical professionals must show extraordinary sensitivity to family and cultural traditions, which might include values that are quite different from their own (Schim et al., 2006).

Despite such diversity, some universals are apparent. In all religions and cultures, death is considered a passage, not an endpoint; it is a reason for people to come together, diminishing rather than magnifying their differences. In every tradition, throughout history and currently, religion provides hope (C. Kemp & Bhungalia, 2002; Shushan, 2009). Such hope takes many forms. For example, the ancient Greeks developed myths about those who died; the ancient Egyptians wrote the Book of the Dead, constructed magnificent pyramids as royal tombs, and preserved mummies for eternal life. Similarly, the ancient Mayans held elaborate funerals for dead rulers.

Many elderly people seek to return to their religious roots through devotion to traditional rituals, deeper spirituality, or an actual journey. Many dying adults ask that their bodies or ashes be returned to their birthplace, sometimes thousands of miles away. When adults were asked what they would want for their last meal if they knew they were to die soon, many chose foods that bespoke their cultural origins, although those foods were not what they ate in daily life (Friese & Hofmann, 2008).

ED KASHI / IPN / AURORA PHOTOS

The Same Faith in Another Country An open coffin, pictures of saints, and burning candles are traditional features of many Christian funerals worldwide, including this Ukrainian Orthodox ceremony.

Even coming close to death is often an occasion for religious affirmation. This is most obvious in what is called a *near-death experience,* in which a person almost dies but survives and reports having left his or her body and moved toward a bright white light while feeling peacefulness and joy. The following classic report is typical:

> I was in a coma for approximately a week. . . . I felt as though I were lifted right up, just as though I didn't have a physical body at all. A brilliant white light appeared. . . . The most wonderful feelings came over me—feelings of peace, tranquility, a vanishing of all worries.
>
> *[quoted in R. A. Moody, 1975, p. 56]*

Near-death experiences often include religious elements (angels have been seen, celestial music heard), and survivors often adopt a more spiritual, less materialistic view of life as a result (Vaillant, 2008). To some, near-death experiences prove that there is a heaven (Piper & Murphey, 2004). Scientists are more skeptical, claiming that

> there is no evidence that what happens when a person really dies and "stays dead" has any relationship to the experience reported by those who have recovered from a life-threatening episode. In fact, it is difficult to imagine how there could ever be such evidence.
>
> *[Kastenbaum, 2006, p. 448]*

Hope, of course, is not based on evidence.

SUMMING UP

For those who are dying or mourning, age influences emotions. Children's reactions are neither absent nor identical to those of their elders. Terror management theory notes that many adolescents and emerging adults take risks and use drugs to cope with death anxiety. Adults seek reasons to believe that the circumstances of a particular death that they hear about do not apply to them. Adults who are dying worry about things undone. Older adults tend to be more accepting, sometimes even planning their own funerals. Religions have diverse rituals and beliefs, but all foster hope, affirming that each life and death has meaning.

>> Dying and Acceptance

People everywhere hope for a good death (Abramovitch, 2005), one that is:

- At the end of a long life
- Peaceful
- Quick
- In familiar surroundings
- With family and friends present
- Without pain, confusion, or discomfort

A *bad death* (lacking these six characteristics) is dreaded, particularly by the elderly. Many of them have known people who died in hospitals, semiconscious and alone.

Attending to the Needs of the Dying

In some ways, modern medicine has made a good death more likely. The first item on the list has become the norm: Death usually occurs at the end of a long life. Young people still get sick, but surgery, drugs, radiation, and rehabilitation usually mean that, in developed countries, the ill go to the hospital, are treated, and then return home.

Among the young, the death rate from violent causes is far higher than the death rate from disease, although death from either cause is less common than it was even 50 years ago. Even violent deaths are usually quick and thus avoid the lengthy lingering that characterizes a bad death.

In other ways, however, contemporary advances have made a bad death more likely. When a cure is impossible, lack of acceptance may make physical and emotional care deteriorate. Instead of acceptance, which would allow people to die peacefully at home with close friends, dying in a hospital often means surgery and drugs that professionals do not expect to restore health. Instead of loved ones being together, families are separated from the dying person, who may become delirious or unconscious and thus unable to reach a psychological peace.

Doctors spend less time with their dying patients than with patients who are likely to survive, pain medication is often inadequate, physical comfort is not prioritized, visitors are kept away, and nurses respond more slowly:

> Nurses were surprised and upset when told of this differential response pattern . . . and resolved to . . . respond promptly to terminally ill patients. After a few weeks, however, the original pattern reinstated itself.
>
> *[Kastenbaum, 2006, p. 113]*

Fortunately, three practices that make a good death more likely have increased: honest talk, the hospice, and palliative care.

Honest Conversation

In about 1960, researcher Elisabeth Kübler-Ross (1969, 1975) asked the administrator of a large Chicago hospital for permission to speak with dying patients. He informed her that no one in the hospital was dying! Eventually, she found a few terminally ill patients who, to everyone's surprise, wanted very much to talk.

From ongoing interviews, Kübler-Ross identified emotions experienced by dying people, which she divided into a sequence of five stages:

1. Denial ("I am not really dying.")
2. Anger ("I blame my doctors, or my family, or God for my death.")
3. Bargaining ("I will be good from now on if I can live.")

4. Depression ("I don't care about anything; nothing matters anymore.")
5. Acceptance ("I accept my death as part of life.")

Another set of stages of dying is based on Abraham Maslow's hierarchy of needs, discussed in Chapters 2 and 22 (Zalenski & Raspa, 2006).

1. Physiological needs (freedom from pain)
2. Safety (no abandonment)
3. Love and acceptance (from close family and friends)
4. Respect (from caregivers)
5. Self-actualization (appreciating one's unique past and present)

Maslow later suggested a possible sixth stage, *self-transcendence* (Koltko-Rivera, 2006), which emphasizes the acceptance of death.

Other researchers have *not* found sequential stages in dying people's approach to death. The adult, cited on page Ep-5, who was dying of a sarcoma said that she would never accept death and that Kübler-Ross should have included desperation as a stage. Many thanatologists find that Kübler-Ross's stages of denial, anger, and depression disappear and reappear; that bargaining is brief because it is fruitless; and that acceptance may never occur. Regarding Maslow, comfort, safety, love, respect, and self-expression are important throughout the dying process, and transcendence does not require completion of the first five stages.

Nevertheless, both lists remind caregivers that each dying person has emotions and needs that may be unlike those of another dying person—or even unlike that same person's emotions and needs a few days or weeks earlier. Most important, the emotions of the dying may not be what family, medical personnel, and others might expect.

As Kübler-Ross and others have discovered, most dying people want to spend time with loved ones and to talk honestly with medical and religious professionals. Human relationships are crucial: People continue to need each other (Planalp & Trost, 2008). Dying patients do not want to be cut off from daily life; they want to know what their relatives and friends are doing and how they are feeling. One consequence of Kübler-Ross's research is that the patient's right to be told the truth is now widely accepted in Western hospitals. It is considered unethical to withhold information if the patient asks for it.

Kübler-Ross also stressed that each person responds to death in his or her own way; this means that some people do *not* want the whole truth. In some cultures, telling people they are dying is thought to destroy hope. Indeed, even maintaining human relationships via long, intimate conversations may be counter to some religious beliefs (Baugher, 2008). Hospital personnel need to respond carefully and honestly to each individual, not always as someone who must be informed that death is near. Among some Japanese, dying people want the family to know the facts and to decide what treatment is warranted, but they do not want to be informed themselves (Kogan et al., 2000).

The Hospice

In 1950s London, Cecily Saunders opened the first modern **hospice,** where terminally ill people could spend their last days in comfort (Saunders, 1978). Thousands of other such places have since opened throughout the world. Some dying people receive hospice care at home, dying in familiar surroundings with friends and family nearby.

Hospice caregivers provide skilled treatment to relieve pain and discomfort, including massage, bathing, and so on. They avoid measures that merely delay death; their aim is to make dying easier. There are two principles for hospice care:

hospice An institution or program in which terminally ill patients receive palliative care to reduce suffering; family and friends of the dying are helped as well.

- Each patient's autonomy and decisions are respected. For example, pain medication is readily available as needed, not on a strict schedule or at a strict dosage.
- Family members and friends are counseled before the death, taught to provide care, and guided in mourning.

When a hospice patient remains at home (as occurs about half the time), family members are the main caregivers. When a person is in a hospice facility, a relative or a close friend is encouraged (and sometimes required) to stay with the patient. Hospice staff believe that the needs of the caregivers, both before and after the death, are as important as the needs of the patient. In fact, thanks partly to hospice work, it is now recognized that long-time caregivers may require professional help as they mourn and restart their lives (Orzeck & Silverman, 2008).

Unfortunately, many dying people never begin hospice care or enter it only in the last days before death. The reasons for this delay are detailed in Table EP.2. One report says that half of all hospice patients receive less than three weeks of specialized care before they die—not enough time for the personal, medical, and emotional needs of a dying person and their loved ones to be assessed and satisfied (J. E. Brody, 2007).

Another expert describes many impediments to good hospice care; for example, U.S. Medicare pays for hospice only if a doctor attests that the person has less than six months to live, and doctors can be sued for fraud if a patient lives longer (Kiernan, 2010). He writes that "while seven-eighths of the population want to die at home, without needless suffering, less than one-fifth actually do so" (p. 177). A British report found that only 10 percent of patients die in a hospice and that many of the rest receive inadequate medical attention (Charlton, 2007).

Hospice care is far from universally available (Kiernan, 2010). People who are dying of heart disease are only half as likely to be in hospice as are people dying of cancer, even though heart failure is the most common cause of death (Setoguchi et al., 2009). Hospice care correlates

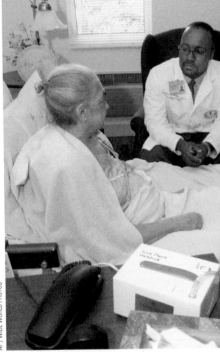

AP / WIDE WORLD PHOTOS

To Meet a Need The idea of hospice care has traveled far from its birthplace in London. Dr. Theodore Turnquest, shown here speaking with a patient in Lifepath Hospice House in Florida, plans to open the first hospice in his native country, the Bahamas.

Especially for Relatives of a Person Who Is Dying Why would a healthy person want the attention of hospice caregivers? (see response, page Ep-15)

TABLE EP.2
Barriers to Entering Hospice Care
■ Hospice patients must be terminally ill, with death anticipated within six months, but such predictions are difficult to make. For example, in one study of noncancer patients, physician predictions were 90 percent accurate for those who died within a week but only 13 percent accurate when death was predicted in three to six weeks (usually the patients died sooner) (Brandt et al., 2006).
■ Patients and caregivers must accept death. Traditionally, entering a hospice meant the end of curative treatment (chemotherapy, dialysis, and so on). This is no longer true (Abelson, 2007; Sulmasy, 2006). About 12 percent of patients live longer than expected, and about 2 to 3 percent are discharged (J. W. Finn, 2005). Nonetheless, many people avoid hospice because they want to keep hope alive.
■ Hospice care is expensive, especially if curative therapy continues. Many skilled workers—doctors, nurses, psychologists, social workers, clergy, music therapists, and so on—provide individualized care day and night.
■ Availability varies. Hospice care is more common in England than in mainland Europe and is a luxury in poor nations. In the United States, western states have more hospices than southern states do. Even in one region (northern California) and among clients of one insurance company (Kaiser), the likelihood that people with terminal cancer will enter hospice depends on exactly where they live (N. L. Keating et al., 2006).

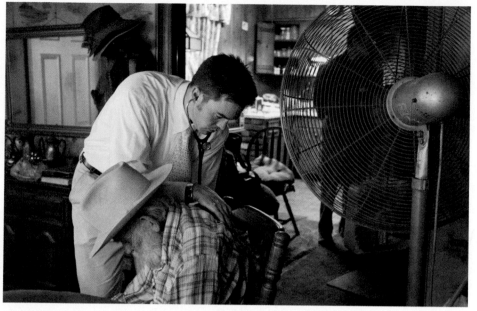

ZUMA PRESS / NEWSCOM

Hospice at Home Lester Albury is dying from COPD (chronic obstructive pulmonary disease), as do many elderly men who smoked for decades. But Lester is fortunate: He will die in his home with hospice care from Derek Robben, who checks lung function and provides medicine to ease the final breaths.

with ethnicity: European American heart patients are twice as likely as Latinos or African Americans to have hospice care (Givens et al., 2010).

One reason for differential rates is that cancer is seen as more deadly, and people equate hospice with terminal disease and hospitals with survival. Geography matters, too: A dying person is more likely to receive hospice care in California than in Mississippi, in England than in Italy—even though death does not change at borders.

Palliative Medicine

The same "bad death" conditions that inspired the hospice movement have led to a medical specialty called **palliative care,** designed to relieve pain and suffering, which some people fear more than any other aspect of dying. Powerful painkillers were once prescribed sparingly. Now physicians realize that no harm results if a dying person becomes drug addicted.

Morphine and other opiates have a **double effect:** They relieve pain (a positive effect), but they also slow down respiration (a negative effect). A painkiller that reduces both pain and breathing is considered acceptable in law, ethics, and medical practice. In England, for instance, it is illegal to cause the death of a terminally ill patient (even one who asks to die); the double effect, however, is not only legal, it is common, associated with one-third of English deaths (Seale, 2006).

Choices and Controversies

Because listening to the wishes of the dying and providing hospice and palliative care are now widely accepted as good practice by doctors and nurses, a good death is more likely today than it was 50 years ago. But new controversies have emerged in the wake of dramatic medical advances: Breathing can continue with respirators, a heart that has stopped can be restarted, and nutrition can be provided to a comatose person via a stomach tube.

Choices regarding such measures are made in almost every life-threatening condition in hospitals. Treatments are avoided, started, or stopped, with either life-prolonging or death-hastening effects (B. Rosenfeld, 2004). Vehement disagreements about appropriate care arise, not only between national governments (as evidenced

palliative care Care designed not to treat an illness but to provide physical and emotional comfort to the patient and support and guidance to his or her family.

double effect A situation in which an action (such as administering opiates) has both a positive effect (relieving a terminally ill person's pain) and a negative effect (hastening death by suppressing respiration).

by radically different laws) but also within nations, among family members, religious advisers, and doctors (Engelhardt, 2005; Prado, 2008; R. Young, 2007).

Even experts hesitate to declare someone brain-dead, although when a person cannot breathe, see, or respond to anything, brain death can be declared (Wijdicks et al., 2010). (See the Research Design on the next page.) Culture, beliefs, and past experiences all influence every choice made in end-of-life care. Even determining when death occurs is not straightforward; as you'll see in the following feature, it requires critical thought.

THINKING CRITICALLY

When Is a Person Dead?

Historically, death was determined by listening to a person's heart: No heartbeat meant death. To make sure, a feather was put to the person's nose as an indicator of respiration—a person who did not exhale was pronounced dead. Modern medicine has changed that, with hearts that can be restarted artificially and respirators that can pump air into the lungs of people who do not breathe on their own.

One way people currently choose to die is to refuse all food, but such a choice needs to be made consciously and communicated clearly; otherwise, a feeding tube is inserted into the stomach and nutrition continues. In these and many other ways, people who otherwise would have died are kept alive. Now that such life-support measures are widely available, how do people know when death has occurred? Answers change as medicine does.

In the late 1970s, a group of Harvard physicians decided that the determining factor was brain function. They concluded that when brain waves ceased, brain death occurred and thus the person was dead. This definition was accepted by a U.S. presidential commission in 1981 and is now used worldwide (Wijdicks et al., 2010). However, in recent years, many people have suggested that death might occur even if primitive brain waves continue (Kellehear, 2008; Truog, 2007).

This newer definition of death is controversial (see Table EP.3 for descriptions of various physical states). Some researchers have attempted to distinguish between people who are in a permanent vegetative state (and thus will never regain the ability to think) and those who are in a coma but could recover. Many scientists seek to define death more precisely than was

possible 30 years ago. One crucial factor is whether the person could ever again breathe without a respirator, but that is hard to guarantee if "ever again" includes the distant future. Understandably, experts still find "severe limitations in the current evidence base" (Wijdicks et al., 2010, p. 1914).

The question becomes a philosophical and religious as well as a biological and medical one: What does it mean to say that a person is alive or dead?

TABLE EP.3
Dead or Not? Yes, No, and Maybe
Brain death: Prolonged cessation of all brain activity with complete absence of voluntary movements; no spontaneous breathing; no response to pain, noise, and other stimuli. Brain waves have ceased; the EEG is flat; *the person is dead.*
Locked-in syndrome: The person cannot move, except for the eyes, but brain waves are still apparent; *the person is not dead.*
Coma: A state of deep unconsciousness from which the person cannot be aroused. Some people awaken spontaneously from a coma; others enter a vegetative state; *the person is not dead.*
Vegetative state: A state of deep unconsciousness in which all cognitive functions are absent, although eyes may open, sounds may be emitted, and breathing may continue; *the person is not yet dead.* This state can be *transient*, with recovery possible, *persistent*, or *permanent.* No one has ever recovered after two years; most who recover (about 15 percent) improve within three weeks (Preston & Kelly, 2006). After time has elapsed, the person may, effectively, be dead.

Hastening or Postponing Death

Powerful emotions are connected to dying. Many elderly people fear being kept alive too long when death is near, and many younger people fear dying too soon. Since death can now be postponed with drugs, surgery, respirators to facilitate breathing, shocks to restart the heart, stomach tubes to provide nutrition, and antibiotics to halt infections, the average person lives twice as long as the average

▶ Research Design

Scientists: Eelco F. M. Wijdicks, Panayiotis N. Varelas, Gary S. Gronseth, and David M. Greer.

Publication: *Neurology* (2010).

Participants: This research was a meta-analysis, which involves gathering all the studies on a particular topic and compiling the results. Meta-analyses are especially useful for controversial subjects when published results of individual studies are not definitive or reach contradictory conclusions. This particular meta-analysis was requested by a subcommittee of the American Academy of Neurology. In 1995, neurologists had established criteria for brain death, and the hope was that most recent research would update those criteria. The authors searched the Internet for all published reports on "brain death" that were empirical, in English, and about adults. They found 38 such articles.

Design: Each article was read by at least two experts who used preset measures to answer five questions regarding brain death—specifically, timing, signs, tests, apnea, and misleading movements.

Results: For many of the relevant issues, there was insufficient evidence. For instance, it was not proven how many hours or days must elapse between an initial lack of responsiveness and irreversible brain death. More research is needed to spare people from weeks or months of misleading hope. It was confirmed that eye responses and spontaneous breathing are absent when a person is brain-dead, as well as that mechanical ventilators and so on occasionally give misleading indications of brain activity when none exists. No one who was declared brain-dead based on earlier (1995) criteria has ever recovered.

Major conclusion: More research is needed to refine indicators of brain death, but the standard 1995 indicators remain valid.

Comment: A meta-analysis, especially one called for by a society of experts, is a useful way to sift through controversial and emotional research. As this article points out, it would benefit the dying and those who love them to find a surefire way to determine quickly that a person is brain-dead, but there is not yet a definitive, instant test.

>> **Response for Relatives of a Person Who Is Dying** (from page Ep-12) Death affects the entire family, including children and grandchildren. I learned this myself when my mother was dying. A hospice nurse not only gave her pain medication (which made it easier for me to be with her) but also counseled me. At the nurse's suggestion, I asked for forgiveness. My mother indicated that there was nothing to forgive. We both felt a peace that would have eluded us without hospice care.

person did a century ago. These measures have saved many lives but also raise new ethical questions—especially regarding suicide and euthanasia.

In **passive euthanasia,** a person is allowed to die. The chart of a patient may include a **DNR (do not resuscitate)** order, which instructs the medical staff not to restore breathing or restart the heart if breathing or pulsating stops. A DNR usually reflects the expressed wishes of the patient or health care proxy (discussed below).

Passive euthanasia is legal everywhere and is relatively frequent (Löfmark et al., 2008), although a distinction is sometimes made between removing life-support equipment and not beginning medical intervention in the first place. Both have the same result, but many emergency personnel start artificial respiration and stimulate hearts without ascertaining whether a DNR has been chosen. If a dying patient is revived, the issue of passive euthanasia then becomes more complex because some consider removing life support to be active euthanasia.

Active euthanasia involves directly causing a person's death, as by giving the person a lethal drug. Some physicians perform active euthanasia when confronted with suffering they cannot relieve, an illness they cannot cure, and a patient who wants to die. It is legal under some circumstances in the Netherlands, Belgium, Luxembourg, and Switzerland, but it is illegal (yet rarely prosecuted) in most other nations.

Many see a major moral distinction between active and passive euthanasia, although the final result is the same (McLachlan, 2008; Prado, 2008). A survey of physicians in the United States found that while a majority (69 percent) objected to active euthanasia, few (18 percent) objected to sedation that had a double effect. Even fewer (5 percent) objected to withdrawing life support when a patient

passive euthanasia A situation in which a seriously ill person is allowed to die naturally, through the cessation of medical intervention.

DNR (do not resuscitate) A written order from a physician (sometimes initiated by a patient's advance directive or by a health care proxy's request) that no attempt should be made to revive a patient if he or she suffers cardiac or respiratory arrest.

active euthanasia A situation in which someone takes action to bring about another person's death, with the intention of ending that person's suffering.

was brain-dead (Curlin et al., 2008), in part because no brain-dead person has ever been revived (Wijdicks et al., 2010). A similar survey in seven other nations found wide variations within and among them, with some physicians saying they would never perform active euthanasia and others reporting they had done so (Löfmark et al., 2008).

Between passive and active euthanasia there is another action: Someone may provide the means for a patient to end his or her own life. According to a survey conducted in 33 nations, opposite and adamant opinions about this action can be found among physicians, politicians, and laypeople.

Some people advocate **physician-assisted suicide,** whereby a doctor provides lethal medication that a patient can then swallow in order to die. The state of Oregon legalized this practice in 1994, explicitly asserting that such deaths should be called "death with dignity," not suicide. No matter what the name, acceptance varies markedly by culture (Prado, 2008). Reasons have less to do with experience with dying than with religion, education, and local values (Verbakel & Jaspers, 2010).

For example, in some Asian nations, suicides can be seen as noble, as when Buddhist monks publicly burned themselves to death to protest the war in Vietnam or when people choose to die for the honor of their nation or themselves. However, in the United States, physicians of Asian heritage are *less* likely to condone physician-assisted suicide than are non-Asian physicians (Curlin et al., 2008). The debate about assisted suicide is especially heated in England as a result of several lawsuits brought by terminally ill citizens who were determined to die. The question became: Do individuals have a legal "right to die" or not (Finlay, 2009)?

physician-assisted suicide A form of active euthanasia in which a doctor provides the means for someone to end his or her own life.

Watching Her Die Diane Pretty suffered from motor neuron disease, a degenerative condition that destroyed her ability to move but did not affect her mind. She wanted her husband, Michael, to be legally allowed to help her die, but her petitions to the British courts and then to the European Court of Human Rights were denied. She died 13 days after this photograph of the couple was taken.

© REUTERS / CORBIS

When Physician-Assisted Suicide Is Legal

The Netherlands has permitted active euthanasia and physician-assisted suicide since 1980, refining the law in 2002. The emphasis is on halting "unbearable suffering," and the patient must be clear and aware in making the request (Buiting et al., 2009). Only half the patients who ask for help in dying receive it (one-fourth die before receiving medical approval and one-fourth are denied or dissuaded) (Jansen-van der Weide et al., 2005). When Dutch patients ask for help in dying, physicians first explain alternatives, often increasing pain medication (Buiting et al., 2009). At that point, some patients withdraw their request for death, but often they refuse the alternatives.

Two other nations near Holland—Belgium and Luxembourg—now have similar laws, in part because it is clear that those people who decide to die and want medical help are a tiny minority, perhaps 2 percent (van Alphen et al., 2010; van der Heide et al., 2007).

Oregon voters approved physician-assisted "death with dignity" (but not other forms of active euthanasia) in 1994 and again in 1997. The first such legal deaths occurred in 1998. The law requires the following:

- The dying person must be an adult and an Oregon resident.
- The dying person must request the lethal drugs twice orally and once in writing.
- Fifteen days must elapse between the first request and prescription of the lethal drugs.
- Two physicians must confirm that the person is terminally ill, has less than six months to live, and is competent (i.e., not mentally impaired or depressed).

The law also requires record-keeping and annual reporting. About one-third of the requests are granted, and about one-third of those who are approved never take the drugs. Instead, they have the deadly drugs as reassurance, but they prefer to die naturally.

Between 1998 and 2009, over 100,000 people in Oregon died. Only 461 of them (less than half of 1 percent of the total deaths) obtained prescriptions for lethal drugs and used them to die. Note that a diagnosis of terminal illness is required for physician-assisted suicide in Oregon, but, unlike in the Netherlands, intense pain is not considered sufficient reason (perhaps because palliative care has become much more prevalent since 1980).

As Table EP.4 shows, Oregon residents requested the drugs primarily for psychological, not biological, reasons—they were more concerned about their autonomy than their pain (Ganzini et al., 2009). In 2009, 95 Oregonians obtained lethal prescriptions, 53 used them, 30 died naturally, and 12 were still alive at year's end (according to data from previous years, about 6 of those 12 are likely to use the drugs in the future) (Oregon Department of Health, 2010).

Many people fear that legalizing euthanasia or physician-assisted suicide will create a **slippery slope,** that hastening death at the request of the terminally ill will cause a society to slide into killing people who are *not* ready to die—especially the old and the poor. The evidence from the Netherlands and Oregon suggests that no such slippery slope occurs. Indeed, people in Oregon who obtain a lethal prescription tend to be advantaged, not disadvantaged. Almost all were European American (98 percent) and had health insurance; most were well-educated (67 percent had attended college). At age 71, the average person was old but not among the oldest-old, with almost none over age 90. Almost all died at home, with close friends or family nearby.

Worldwide, most voters and lawmakers are not convinced by the data from Oregon or the Netherlands. Proposals to legalize physician-assisted suicide have been defeated in five U.S. states and in several nations (e.g., by Great Britain's House of Lords in 2006). However, in the state of Washington, just north of Oregon, 58 percent of the voters approved a Death with Dignity law in November 2008; in 2009, Luxembourg joined the Netherlands and Belgium in allowing active euthanasia.

Advance Directives

Many places have attempted to increase personal choice about death, although, as just detailed, in most places they stop short of legalizing medical assistance. For example, a massive effort in Hawaii to inform people about end-of-life issues resulted in *less* support for physician-assisted suicide but *more* support for advance directives—an individual's instructions regarding end-of-life medical care, written before such care is needed (K. L. Braun et al., 2005).

Even this is controversial. An original part of the U.S. health care bill passed in 2010 allowed doctors to be paid for informing the dying of their treatment options—a measure that had the support of many physicians (e.g., Kettl, 2010, in the *Journal of the American Medical Association*). That measure, after it began to be called "death panels" by some opponents of the bill, almost torpedoed the entire package of benefits and so was dropped.

Generally, in the United States, once people understand the processes and complications of dying, they seek to control many aspects of their deaths. That control is often exerted through creating a living will and assigning a health care proxy.

A **living will** indicates what sort of medical intervention a person wants or does not want in the event that he or she becomes unable to express those preferences.

TABLE EP.4	
Reasons Oregon Residents Gave for Requesting Physician Assistance in Dying, 1998–2005	
Reason	Patients Giving Reason (%)
Loss of autonomy	86
Less able to enjoy life	85
Loss of dignity	83
Loss of control over body	57
Burden on others	37
Pain	22

Source: Oregon Department of Human Services, 2006.

slippery slope The argument that a given action will start a chain of events that will culminate in an undesirable outcome.

living will A document that indicates what medical intervention an individual prefers if he or she is not conscious when a decision is to be expressed. For example, some do not want mechanical breathing.

(If the person is conscious, hospital personnel often ask about each specific procedure. Then patients who are conscious and lucid can choose to override any written instructions they had earlier written in their living will.) Living wills include phrases such as "incurable," "reasonable chance of recovery," and "extraordinary measures" because a patient may not anticipate exactly what that means. In fact, doctors and family members disagree about what such phrases mean.

Accordingly, people may designate a **health care proxy,** someone who can make medical decisions if the person becomes incapable of doing so. Only about 25 percent of all North Americans (mostly older adults) have arranged to have both a living will and a health care proxy, although both are recommended for everyone (Preston & Kelly, 2006).

However, neither a living will nor a health care proxy guarantees that medical care will be exactly what a person would choose if able. For one thing, designated proxies often find it difficult to choose death over even the slimmest chance of recovery for a loved one, nor do they know what the person would want in every instance, nor do doctors want to say that there is no hope. The risks, benefits, and alternatives to every medical procedure have rarely been contemplated in advance by anyone. Even people who have been married for years do not necessarily know their partner's wishes; husbands are more likely to believe they know but are less likely to be accurate (Zettel-Watson et al., 2008).

Furthermore, doctors and nurses may object to the specifics of a living will. For example, as already mentioned, if breathing suddenly fails, many emergency personnel automatically begin artificial respiration—learning only later that the patient did not want that. Conversely, many medical people think the stomach tube is overused; it prolongs life but does not cure illness. Many laypeople, however, consider artificial feeding normal, not an extraordinary measure (Orentlicher & Callahan, 2004).

health care proxy A person chosen by another person to make medical decisions if the second person becomes unable to do so.

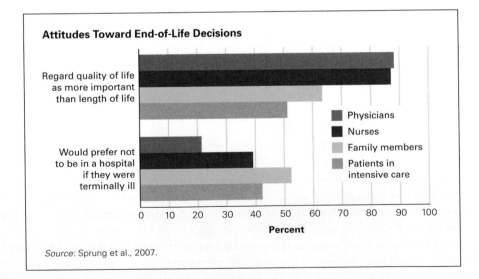

Attitudes Toward End-of-Life Decisions

FIGURE EP.5

Interesting Discrepancies Responding to a survey taken in six European nations' intensive-care units (ICUs), higher percentages of ICU doctors and nurses than of ICU patients and their families said they considered quality of life more important than a long life.

Source: Sprung et al., 2007.

The discrepancy among the views of doctors, patients, and families was evident in a survey conducted in six European nations. Doctors more than family members chose quality of life over length of life (see Figure EP.5; Sprung et al., 2007). In recent years, options have expanded and variations have become more evident. Documents help, but most people do not have them; thus, it is crucial for people to talk to others about dying, so that friends, family, and physicians know their wishes, as explained in the following. This is increasingly recognized in law and practice (Sabatino, 2010).

Especially for People Without Advance Directives Why do very few young adults have living wills? (see response, page Ep-20)

A CASE TO STUDY

Terri Schiavo

Theresa Marie Schiavo was 26 years old in 1990 when her heart suddenly stopped and anoxia destroyed some brain cells. Emergency personnel restarted her heart, but she fell into a deep coma. Like most people her age, Terri had no advance directive, so a court designated Michael, her husband of six years, as her health care proxy.

Eleven years after Terri's collapse, following numerous attempts to bring back his wife, Michael accepted her doctors' diagnosis: Terri was in a persistent vegetative state. He petitioned to have her feeding tube removed. The court agreed, noting witnesses who said that Terri had told them that she never wanted life support. Terri's parents appealed but lost.

The Florida legislature then passed "Terri's Law," requiring that the tube be reinserted. It was, but Florida courts soon ruled that Terri's Law was unconstitutional. After three more years of legal wrangling, the U.S. Supreme Court ruled that the lower courts were correct. By this point, every North American newspaper and TV station was following the case. Congress passed a law requiring that artificial feeding be continued, but that law, too, was overturned. The stomach tube was removed, and Terri died on March 31, 2005—although some maintained that she had really died 15 years earlier.

Partly because of the conflicts among family members, and between appointed judges and elected politicians, Terri's case caught media attention, inspiring vigils and protests. Lost in that blitz are the thousands of other mother and fathers, husbands and wives, sons and daughters, judges and legislators, doctors and nurses, who struggle with similar issues. Advance directives are intended to help people avoid such anguish, but even with signed and notarized documents, honest conversation is needed long before a crisis occurs (Sabatino, 2010).

Is She Thinking? This photo of Terri Schiavo with her mother was released by those who believed Terri could recover. Other photos (not released) and other signs told the opposite story. Although autopsy showed that Terri's brain had shrunk markedly, remember that hope is part of being human. It is easy to understand why some people were passionately opposed to removal of Terri's stomach tube.

SUMMING UP

Modern medical care has postponed death but does not necessarily make for a good death, one that occurs peacefully, at home, with family nearby. Hospice workers ease discomfort and help patients as well as caregivers cope emotionally with death. Pain management has become more widespread. Controversies include how death should be defined and what actions may be taken to hasten or postpone death. Everyone should have a living will and a health care proxy because the range of medical measures is vast and people disagree vehemently about medical intervention for the dying. In addition, death and dying should be discussed by everyone in order to avoid the anguish that seems inevitable when explicit directions are not known.

>> Bereavement

In her book entitled *The Year of Magical Thinking,* Joan Didion (2005), a highly respected author known for her honesty and logic, confessed that after her husband died suddenly of a heart attack, she decided not to give away his shoes. She reasoned that he would need them if he came back. With similar illogic, when someone dies, the bereaved often wonder how the world can continue functioning just as it did before.

>> **Response for People Without Advance Directives** (from page Ep-18)
Young adults tend to avoid thinking realistically about their own deaths. This attitude is emotional, not rational. The actual task of preparing the documents is easy (the forms can be downloaded; no lawyer is needed). Young adults have no trouble doing other future-oriented things, such as getting a tetanus shot or enrolling in a pension plan.

bereavement The complicated and multifaceted feelings of loss following a death.

grief The deep sorrow that people feel at the death of another. Grief is personal and unpredictable.

mourning The ceremonies and behaviors that a religion or culture prescribes for people to employ in expressing their bereavement after a death.

Normal Grief

The death of a loved one arouses powerful emotions in surviving relatives and friends, including anger and shock, sadness and depression (Qualls & Kasl-Godley, 2010). Denial—as in Didion's thought that her husband might return—alternates with deep sadness and feelings of loss. Humans may be bewildered when they find themselves more overwhelmed by one death than by the deaths of thousands. As one woman said:

> Although I'm 62, I still miss my mother. . . . Since 9/11 it has been even harder. People make me feel ashamed. After all, they're right when they say to me, "Look at all the youngsters who were killed; their lives were just beginning. Your mother lived a full life, what more do you want?"
>
> *[quoted in Schachter, 2003, p. 20]*

Grief, Mourning, and Bereavement

As we consider how people react to a death, some distinctions are in order. **Bereavement** is the sense of loss following a death. Grief and mourning are both aspects of bereavement, but they are quite different from each other.

Grief is the powerful sorrow that an individual feels at the death of another. It is a highly personal emotion, an anguish that overtakes daily life. It is manifest in uncontrollable crying, sleeplessness, and irrational and delusional thoughts—the "magical thinking" of Didion's title:

> Grief has no distance. Grief comes in waves, paroxysms, sudden apprehensions that weaken the knees and blind the eyes and obliterate the dailiness of life. . . . I see now that my insistence on spending that first night alone was more complicated than it seemed, a primitive instinct. . . . There was a level on which I believed that what had happened remained reversible. That is why I needed to be alone. . . . I needed to be alone so that he could come back. This was the beginning of my year of magical thinking.
>
> *[Didion, 2005, pp. 27, 32, 33]*

The Flowers of Youth In many cultural traditions, mourners bring a token of their presence to funeral rites. Such items as pebbles, stuffed animals, notes, candles, and flowers are left at gravesites throughout the world. These young women are placing flowers on the coffin of a friend who was killed in a drive-by shooting.

A. RAMEY / PHOTOEDIT, INC.

Mourning is the public and ritualistic expression of bereavement, the ceremonies and behaviors that a religion or culture prescribes to honor the dead. These may include special clothing, food, prayers, and informal shrines at the place where someone died, as well as the gestures of friends, who may send cards, bring food, and stay near the bereaved family.

Mourning is needed because the grief-stricken are vulnerable not only to irrational thoughts but also to self-destructive acts. Physical as well as mental health dips in the recently bereaved, and the rate of suicide increases (Ajdacic-Gross et al., 2008; Elwert & Christakis, 2008).

After natural or human-caused disasters, including hurricanes and wars, many people die of causes not directly attributable to the disaster. They are victims of the indifference of others or of their own diminished self-care. Grief splinters people into jumbled pieces, making them vulnerable. Mourning reassembles them, making them whole again and able to rejoin the larger community.

Mourning customs are designed to move grief from loss toward reaffirmation (Harlow, 2005). For this reason, eulogies emphasize the dead person's good qualities; people who did not personally know the deceased person attend wakes, funerals, or memorial services to help comfort the survivors. If the dead person was a public figure, mourners could include thousands, even millions. They express their sorrow to one another, weep as they watch memorials on television, and promise themselves to affirm the best of that person as they ignore whatever criticisms they might have had.

Mourning is often time-limited by cultural custom or religious tradition. Examples include the Jewish custom of sitting shiva at home for a week, or the three days of active sorrow among some Muslim groups. Memories often return on the anniversary of a death, so mourning includes annual rituals such as visiting a grave or lighting a candle. Having a specific time, prayer, and place for remembering the dead (such as a home altar in China or a gravesite in places where burial is customary) helps bereaved people express their grief without being overwhelmed by it.

Placing Blame and Seeking Meaning

A common impulse after death is for the survivors to assess blame—for medical measures not taken, laws not enforced, unhealthy habits not changed. The bereaved sometimes blame the dead person, sometimes themselves, and sometimes distant others. For public tragedies, nations may blame one another. Blame is not necessarily rational; for instance, outrage at the assassination of Archduke Francis Ferdinand of Austria by a Serbian terrorist in 1914 provoked a conflict between the governments of Austria and Serbia that led to the four years and 16 million deaths of World War I.

As you remember, denial and anger appear first on Kübler-Ross's list of reactions to death; ideally, people move on to acceptance of a deeper meaning to death. The need to find meaning may be crucial to the reaffirmation that follows grief. In some cases, this search starts with preserving memories: Displaying photographs and personal effects and telling anecdotes about the dead person are central to many memorial services.

Mourners may also be helped by strangers who have experienced a similar loss, especially when friends are unlikely to understand. This explains why groups have been organized for parents of murdered children, mothers whose adolescents were killed by drunk drivers, widows of firefighters who died at the World Trade Center, relatives of passengers who died in the same plane crash, and so on.

Mourners sometimes want strangers to know about a death. Pages of paid obituaries are found in every major newspaper, and spontaneous memorials (graffiti, murals, stuffed animals, flowers) appear in public spaces, such as at the spot on a roadside where a fatal crash occurred. This practice was once rare and discouraged in the United States but now is common; such memorials are taken down by authorities only when complaints are lodged after a period of time (Dickinson & Hoffmann, 2010).

Sometimes "meaning becomes grounded in action" to honor the dead (Armour, 2003, p. 538). Organizations devoted to causes such as fighting cancer and banning handguns find their most dedicated supporters among people who have lost a loved one to that particular circumstance. Often when someone dies, the close family designates a charity that is somehow connected to the deceased, inviting other mourners to make contributions.

Wins and Losses The most poignant deaths are the young, unexpected ones, such as when Dylan Bradshaw collapsed after a high school football practice. Adults blame coaches, helmets, and doctors, but mourning teammates pledge to play hard and win the next game for their special number 1.

No Peace Without Justice Jasmine Hightower sobs at a makeshift memorial in the Newark, New Jersey, schoolyard where her older sister, Iofemi, and two other college students were fatally shot during a random robbery that ended in murder in 2007. (A fourth victim was seriously wounded but survived.) Tears and the comfort of relatives and friends can help people cope with such sudden and senseless deaths. It may also be helpful to locate the blame and seek justice: Six young men with gang associations were soon arrested for these murders.

An action that allayed one mother's grief was carrying around a bag containing the personal effects of her murdered son. She showed them, item by item, to young gang members, telling them:

> "This is all I had left of my son. A pair of tennis shoes and a pair of underwear that had no blood on them. He loved this little chain he had on. And you see it's broken up, with a shot?". . . These groups of young kids are sitting there . . . . Driving home from that group, I just get warm, like affirmation.
>
> *[quoted in Armour, 2003, p. 532]*

Thus, the normal grief reaction is intense and irrational at first but gradually eases, as time, social support, and traditions help first with the initial outpouring of emotion and then with the search for meaning and reaffirmation. The individual may engage in *grief work,* experiencing and expressing strong emotions and then moving toward wholeness, which includes recognizing the larger story of human life and death.

Complicated Grief

In recent times, mourning has become more private, less emotional, and less religious. As a result, new complications in the grieving process have emerged. Emblematic of this change are funeral trends in the United States: Whereas older generations prefer burial after a traditional funeral, younger generations are likely to prefer small memorial services after cremation. This may, in the abstract, seem a simpler, more rational way to deal with death, but that is not always the case.

Decisions about what to do with the ashes after cremation may be fraught with denial and controversy and thus complicate grief (Cranwell, 2010). About 10 percent of all mourners experience what is known as **complicated grief,** a type of grief that impedes the person's future life (Neimeyer & Currier, 2009).

complicated grief A type of grief that impedes a person's future life, usually because the person clings to sorrow or is buffeted by contradictory emotions.

Grief Without Mourning

As mourning rituals diminish, many bereavement counselors have noted specific problems that may become pathological (Qualls & Kasl-Godley, 2010; van der Houwen et al., 2010). One is **absent grief,** in which a bereaved person does not seem to mourn at all. This may be a first reaction, as some people cannot face the reality of the death, but if it continues, absent grief can trigger physical or psychological symptoms—for instance, trouble breathing or walking, sudden panic attacks, or depression. If such disabilities seem to appear for no reason, the underlying cause might be a death that was never mourned.

absent grief A situation in which mourners do not grieve, either because other people do not allow grief to be expressed or because the mourners do not allow themselves to feel sadness.

Absent grief may be more common in modern society than it was earlier. People who live and work where no one knows their personal lives have no community or recognized customs to help them grieve. Indeed, for workers at large corporations or students in universities, grief becomes "an unwelcome intrusion (or violent intercession) into the normal efficient running of everyday life" (M. Anderson, 2001, p. 141). This leads to silence and isolation—exactly the opposite of what bereaved people need.

Modern life also increases the incidence of **disenfranchised grief,** wherein people who feel grief are not allowed to mourn publicly because of cultural customs or social restrictions. Unmarried lovers (of the same or other sex), divorced wives or husbands, young children, and close friends at work may be excluded (perhaps by the relatives, either deliberately or through ignorance) from saying goodbye to the dying person, viewing the corpse, or participating in the aftermath of death. Parents may grieve the loss of a fetus or newborn, but others may wonder why.

disenfranchised grief A situation in which certain people, although they are bereaved, are prevented from mourning publicly by cultural customs or social restrictions.

Typically, only a current spouse or close blood relative decides on funeral arrangements, disposal of the body, and other matters. This made sense when all adults were closely connected to their relatives, but it may result in "gagged grief and beleaguered bereavement" when, for instance, a long-time but unmarried partner is excluded (L. Green & Grant, 2008, p. 275).

Mourning That Does Not Heal

Another possible problem is **incomplete grief.** Murders and suicides often trigger police investigations and press reports, which interfere with the grief process. An autopsy complicates grieving for those who believe that the body will rise again or that the soul does not leave the body immediately. The inability to recover a body, as happens for soldiers who are missing in action or some victims of a major flood or fire, impedes mourning and hence halts a bereaved person's progress toward reaffirmation.

incomplete grief A situation in which circumstances, such as a police investigation or an autopsy, interfere with the process of grieving.

Sometimes events interrupt the responses of the community. The bereaved need attention to their particular loss, and the grief process may be incomplete if mourning is cut short or if other people are distracted from their role in recovery. When death occurs on a major holiday, immediately after another death or disaster, or during wartime, it is harder for the survivors to grieve.

One widow whose husband died of cancer on September 10, 2001, complained, "People who attended the funeral talked only about the terrorist attack of September 11, and my husband wasn't given the respect he deserved" (quoted in Schachter, 2003, p. 20). Although she expressed concern for her husband, it is apparent that she herself needed sympathy.

Empty Boots The body of a young army corporal killed near Baghdad has been shipped home to his family in Mississippi for a funeral and burial, but his fellow soldiers in Iraq also need to express their grief. The custom is to hold an informal memorial service, placing the dead soldier's boots, helmet, and rifle in the middle of a circle of mourners, who weep, pray, and reminisce.

Diversity of Reactions

Bereaved people depend on the customs and attitudes of their community, as well as on their social network, to guide them through their irrational thoughts and grief. Particulars depend on the specific culture. For example, mourners who keep the dead person's possessions, talk to the deceased, and frequently review memories are notably *less* well adjusted 18 months after the death if they live in the United States but are *better* adjusted if they live in China (Lalande & Bonanno, 2006).

Legacy of Earlier Loss

Childhood experiences also affect bereavement. Adults whose parents died when they were children are more distraught by death. Attachment history may be important (Hansson & Stroebe, 2007). Older adults who were securely attached may be more likely to experience normal grief. Those whose attachment was insecure-avoidant may have absent grief. Those who were insecure-resistant may become stuck, unable to find meaning in the living and dying of someone they love and thus perhaps unable to reaffirm their own lives.

Reaffirmation does not mean forgetting the dead person; many *continuing bonds* are evident years after death. Although a mourner hallucinating visions of the dead person (seeing ghosts, hearing voices) is a sign of complicated grief, some continuing bonds such as recalling fond memories and seeing the dead person as a role model are "linked to greater personal growth" (Field & Filanosky, 2010, p. 20).

Bereavement theory once held that everyone should immediately do grief work and then move on, realizing that the dead person is gone forever. It was thought that if this did not happen, pathological grief could result in the person either not grieving enough (absent grief) or grieving too long (incomplete grief). Current research finds a much wider variety of reactions.

Research Findings

It is easy to see why some earlier studies overestimated the frequency of pathological grief. For obvious reasons, scientists often began their research on mourning with mourners—that is, with people who had recently experienced the death of a loved one. Furthermore, they often studied people who needed psychological help. Some experienced absent grief; others felt disenfranchised grief; some were overcome by unremitting sadness many months after the loss; others could not find meaning in a violent, sudden, unexpected death.

Such mourners are *not* typical. Almost everyone experiences several deaths over a lifetime—of parents and grandparents, of a spouse or close friend. Most feel sadness at first but then resume their customary activities, functioning as well a few months later as they did before. And only a small subset, about 10 to 15 percent, exhibit extreme or complicated grief (Bonanno & Lilienfeld, 2008).

The variety of grief reactions was evident in a longitudinal study that began by interviewing and assessing married older adults who lived in greater Detroit. Over several years, 319 became widows or widowers. Most were reinterviewed at 6 and 18 months after the death of their spouse, and about one-third were seen again years later (Boerner et al., 2004, 2005).

General trends were evident. Almost all the widows and widowers idealized their past marriages, a normal phenomenon that other research finds may be connected to psychological health, not pathology (O'Rourke & Cappeliez, 2005). In this study, recollections after death were rosier than the descriptions they had given of their relationships when their spouse was still alive. Another trend was that many thought of their spouse several times each day immediately after the death; with time, such thoughts became less frequent.

Reactions to the spouse's death were clustered into five categories (see Figure EP.6; Boerner et al., 2004, 2005):

1. Fifty percent were resilient. They were sad at first, but by 6 months later they were about as happy and productive as they had been before the death.
2. Eleven percent experienced normal grief, with increased depression for 6 months after the death but recovery by 18 months.
3. Eighteen percent were *less* depressed after the death than before, perhaps because they had been caregivers for their seriously ill partners.
4. Eleven percent were slow to recover, functioning poorly even at 18 months. By four years after the death, however, they functioned almost as well as they had before the death. This slow and incomplete recovery suggests that some of them had complicated grief.
5. Ten percent were depressed at every assessment, before as well as after the death. If this research had begun only after the death, it might seem that the loss caused depression. However, the pre-loss assessment suggests that these people were chronically depressed, not stuck in grief.

Practical Applications

This research might help someone who is grieving or who knows someone in mourning. The first step is simply to be aware that powerful, complicated, and

Reactions to Spouse's Death

Source: Boerner et al., 2005.

FIGURE EP.6

As Time Goes By . . . Grief varies, in duration and depth. A few mourners may never recover after a spouse dies, but that is a small minority. In one study, 18 months after such a death, one in nine survivors was still grieving. Most (68 percent) widows and widowers were no longer depressed after 6 months; indeed, some (18 percent) were happier after the death than before. Another group (10 percent) were chronically depressed, even before the death, and some (11 percent) took 18 months to regain their equilibrium. Specifics from other studies vary, but all the research finds that time heals most sadness; grief that lasts more than a year is unusual.

unexpected emotions are likely: A friend should listen and sympathize, never implying that the person is too grief-stricken or not grief-stricken enough.

The bereaved person *might or might not* want to visit the grave, light a candle, cherish a memento, pray, or sob. Those who have been taught to bear grief stoically may be doubly distressed if a friend advises them to cry but they cannot. Conversely, those whose cultures expect loud wailing may resent it if they are urged to hush.

Even absent grief—in which the bereaved refuses to do any of these things— might be appropriate. So might the opposite reaction, when people want to talk about their loss, gathering sympathy, ascribing blame, and finding meaning. If emotions can be expressed in action—joining a bereavement group; protesting some government policy; planting a garden; walking, running, or biking to raise money for some cause—that may help. Remember the 7-year-old boy whose grandparents, uncle, and dog (Twick) died? The boy wrote a memorial poem for the dog, which his parents framed and hung in the living room. This helped the boy (K. R. Kaufman & Kaufman, 2006).

No matter what rituals are followed or what pattern is evident in human reactions to death, the result may give the living a deeper appreciation of themselves as well as of the value of human relationships. In fact, a theme frequently sounded by those who work with the dying and the bereaved is that the lessons of death may lead to a greater appreciation of life, especially of the value of intimate, caring relationships.

George Vaillant is a psychiatrist who has studied the lives of a group of men from the time they were Harvard students through old age. He writes about funerals: "With tears of remembrance running down our cheeks, we are reunited with our remembrance of past love. . . . Remembered love lives triumphantly today" (Vaillant, 2008, p. 133).

It is fitting to end this Epilogue, and this book, with a reminder of the creative work of living. As first described in Chapter 1, the study of human development is a science, with topics to be researched, understood, and explained. But the process of living is an art as well as a science, with strands of love and sorrow woven into each person's unique tapestry. Dying, when it is accepted; death, when it leads to hope; grief, when it is allowed expression; and mourning, when it fosters reaffirmation—all give added meaning to birth, growth, development, and human relationships.

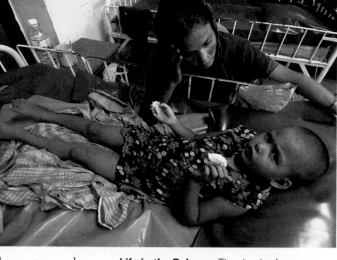

Life in the Balance The death of a young child is especially devastating to families. This girl is in a hospital in Bangladesh; she is suffering from cholera, which kills more than 2,000 children a year worldwide, most of them in areas with unsafe water supplies.

Especially for Educators How might a teacher help a young child cope with death? (see response, page Ep-27)

SUMMING UP

Rituals help the living come to terms with both mourning (the public process) and grief (the private emotion). Grief is neither rational nor predictable; grief and mourning vary a great deal from person to person, death to death, and culture to culture. One problem in modern societies is that some of the bereaved may not be granted the time and social support they need for mourning. Since reactions to death vary, other people need to be especially responsive to whatever needs a grieving person may have. Most bereaved people recover within a year, although sometimes grief is complicated and explicit help from professionals is beneficial.

SUMMARY

Death and Hope

1. Death has various meanings, depending partly on the age of the person involved and whether that person is dying or mourning. For example, young children are more concerned about being separated from those they see every day; adults are concerned about their own life plans; older adults are more accepting of death.

2. Religious and cultural customs vary a great deal, but all attempt to help people find meaning in life and hope after death.

Dying and Acceptance

3. People who are dying need to be treated with honesty and respect. Their emotions may change over time. Some may move from denial to acceptance, although stages of dying vary much more than originally proposed. Honest conversation helps many, but not all, dying persons.

4. Hospice nurses and other workers meet the biological and psychological needs of fatally ill people and their families. This can occur at home or at a specific place.

5. Palliative care relieves pain and other uncomfortable aspects of dying, in modern hospitals as well as in hospices. Such care makes a good death much more possible, although other aspects of modern medicine seem more likely to have the opposite effect.

6. Drugs that reduce pain as well as hasten dying, producing a double effect, are acceptable by many. However, both passive and active euthanasia and physician-assisted suicide are controversial. A few nations and U.S. states allow some forms of these, but many others do not.

7. Since 1980, death has been defined as occurring when brain waves stop; however, many modern measures can prolong life when no conscious thinking occurs. The need for a more precise, updated definition is apparent, but professionals and the public do not agree on what that new definition should be.

8. A living will and a health care proxy are recommended for everyone, although it is impossible to anticipate the possible interventions in dying that may occur. Family members often disagree about specifics.

Bereavement

9. Variations in grief and mourning are wide. Mourning rituals are cultural or religious expressions that aid survivors and the entire community.

10. Grief may be irrational and complicated, absent or disenfranchised. Most people find meaning in death that eventually helps them live a fuller life; a feeling of having an ongoing bond with the deceased is no longer thought to be pathological.

KEY TERMS

thanatology (p. Ep-1)
terror management theory (TMT) (p. Ep-4)
hospice (p. Ep-11)
palliative care (p. Ep-13)
double effect (p. Ep-13)

passive euthanasia (p. Ep-15)
DNR (do not resuscitate) (p. Ep-15)
active euthanasia (p. Ep-15)
physician-assisted suicide (p. Ep-16)

slippery slope (p. Ep-17)
living will (p. Ep-17)
health care proxy (p. Ep-18)
bereavement (p. Ep-20)
grief (p. Ep-20)
mourning (p. Ep-20)

complicated grief (p. Ep-22)
absent grief (p. Ep-22)
disenfranchised grief (p. Ep-22)
incomplete grief (p. Ep-23)

WHAT HAVE YOU LEARNED?

Death and Hope

1. What do fatally ill children fear most?

2. What do children believe about death, according to the study with the puppet mouse?

3. How does terror management theory explain young people's risk taking?

4. What is the difference in attitudes about death between younger and older adults?

5. How does parenthood affect people's thoughts about their own death?

6. How is the trolley car dilemma an example of the illogic of people when they think about death?

7. What is the effect of religious faith on thoughts of death?

8. What is one example of contrasting rituals about death?

9. Why are near-death experiences controversial?

Dying and Acceptance

10. What is a good death?

11. What is a bad death?

12. Why doesn't everyone agree with Kübler-Ross's stages of death?

13. What are the guiding principles of hospice care?

14. Why is the double effect legal everywhere, even though it speeds death?

15. Why is the definition of death controversial?

16. What is the difference between a DNR order and euthanasia?

17. Why does Oregon use the phrase *death with dignity* instead of *physician-assisted suicide*?

18. Why do some people want to speed up their own dying process?

19. Why would a person who has a living will also need a health care proxy?

Bereavement

20. What is the difference between grief and mourning?

21. How do bereavement customs help people who are grieving?

22. How can a grieving person find meaning in death?

23. When are people not allowed to express their grief?

24. Who is expected to decide on the details of funerals, burial, cremation, and so on?

25. If a person still feels a loss six months after a death, is that pathological?

APPLICATIONS

1. Death is sometimes said to be hidden, even taboo. Ask 10 people if they have ever been with someone who was dying. Note not only the yes and no answers but also the details and reactions. For instance, how many of the deaths occurred in hospitals?

2. Find quotes about death in *Bartlett's Familiar Quotations* or a similar collection. Do you see any historical or cultural patterns of acceptance, denial, or fear?

3. Every aspect of dying is controversial in modern society. Do an Internet search for a key term such as *euthanasia* or *grief*. Analyze the information and the underlying assumptions. What is your opinion, and why?

4. People of varying ages have different attitudes toward death. Ask people of different ages (ideally, at least one young person under 20, one adult under 60, and one older person) what thoughts they have about their own death. What differences do you find?

>> Response for Educators (from page Ep-25) Death has varied meanings, so a teacher needs to take care not to contradict the child's cultural background. In general, however, specific expressions of mourning are useful, and acting as if the death did not happen is destructive.

>>ONLINE CONNECTIONS

To accompany your textbook, you have access to a number of online resources, including quizzes for every chapter of the book, flashcards (in English and Spanish), critical thinking questions, and case studies. For access to any of these links, go to www.worthpublishers.com/bergerls8e. In addition to these free resources, you'll also find links to the podcasts, video clips, diagnostic quizzing with personalized study advice, and an ebook. Some of the videos and activities available online include:

- *Bereavement.* This in-depth activity covers the four stages of the grieving process and bereavement at different points in the life span. People share their personal experiences of loss.

- *Preparing to Die.* Experts discuss the process of dying, and dying people tell their stories. Covers death at different ages, palliative and hospice care, and more.

Appendix A

>> Supplemental Charts, Graphs, and Tables

Often, examining specific data is useful, even fascinating, to developmental researchers. The particular numbers reveal trends and nuances not apparent from a more general view. Each chart, graph, or table in this appendix contains information not generally known.

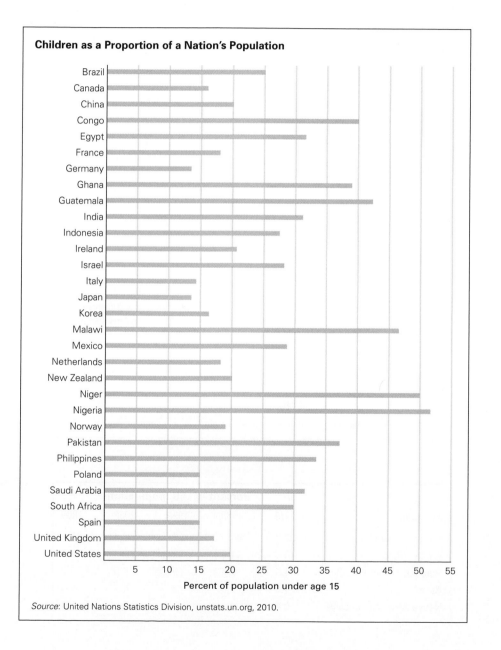

Children as a Proportion of a Nation's Population

Percent of population under age 15

Source: United Nations Statistics Division, unstats.un.org, 2010.

More Children, Worse Schools? (Chapter 1)

Nations that have high birth rates also have high death rates, short life spans, and more illiteracy. A systems approach suggests that these variables are connected: For example, the Montessori and Reggio Emilia early-childhood education programs, said to be the best in the world, originated in Italy, and Italy has one of the lowest proportions of children under 15.

Ethnic Composition of the U.S. Population (Chapter 2)

Thinking about the ethnic makeup of the U.S. population helps explain the rising importance of sociocultural theory. If you look only at the table, you will not see dramatic differences over the past 40 years: Whites are still the majority, Native Americans (Indians) are still a tiny minority, and African Americans are still about 12 percent of the population. However, if you look at the chart, you can see why every group feels that much has changed. Because the proportions of Hispanic Americans and Asian Americans have increased dramatically, European Americans see the current non-White population at almost one-third of the total, and African Americans see that Hispanics now outnumber them. There are also interesting regional differences within the United States; for example, the Los Angeles metropolitan area has the largest number of Native Americans (125,000) and the largest number of Asians (1.8 million). Remember that racial categories (e.g., White, Black) are often rejected by social scientists but used in the U.S. Census and other data sources. Also note that the terms for each group vary; some people prefer one term, some another.

Observation Quiz Which ethnic group is growing most rapidly since 1980 in rate of increase (not in numbers added)? (see answer, page A-4)

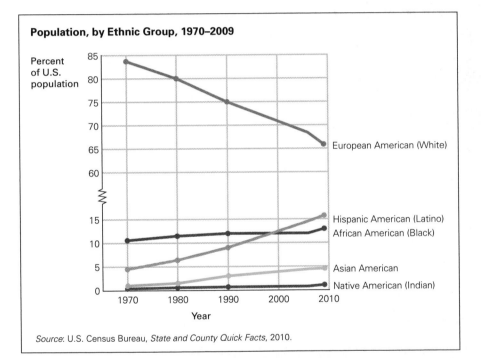

Population, by Ethnic Group, 1970–2009

Source: U.S. Census Bureau, *State and County Quick Facts*, 2010.

Ancestry	Percent of U.S. population				
	1970	1980	1990	2006	2009
European (White)	83.7	80	75	68.4	65.1
African (Black)	10.6	11.5	12	12	12.9
Hispanic (Latino)	4.5	6.4	9	14.5	15.8
Asian	1.0	1.5	3	4.3	4.6
Native American (Indian)	0.4	0.6	0.7	0.82	1.0

The Genetics of Blood Types (Chapter 3)

Blood types A and B are dominant traits, and type O is recessive. The percentages given in the first column of this chart represent the odds that a child born to the parents with the various combinations of genotypes will have the genotype given in the second column.

Genotypes of Parents*	Genotype of Offspring	Phenotype	Can Donate Blood to (Phenotype)	Can Receive Blood from (Phenotype)
AA + AA (100%) AA + AB (50%) AA + AO (50%) AB + AB (25%) AB + AO (25%) AO + AO (25%)	AA (inherits one A from each parent)	A	A or AB	A or O
AA + OO (100%) AB + OO (50%) AO + AO (50%) AO + OO (50%) AB + AO (25%) AB + BO (25%)	AO	A	A or AB	A or O
BB + BB (100%) AB + BB (50%) BB + BO (50%) AB + AB (25%) AB + BO (25%) BO + BO (25%)	BB	B	B or AB	B or O
BB + OO (100%) AB + OO (50%) BO + BO (50%) BO + OO (50%) AB + AO (25%) AB + BO (25%)	BO	B	B or AB	B or O
AA + BB (100%) AA + AB (50%) AA + BO (50%) AB + AB (50%) AB + BB (50%) AO + BB (50%) AB + BO (25%) AO + BO (25%)	AB	AB	AB only	A, B, AB, O ("universal recipient")
OO + OO (100%) AO + OO (50%) BO + OO (50%) AO + AO (25%) AO + BO (25%) BO + BO (25%)	OO	O	A, B, AB, O ("universal donor")	O only

*Blood type is not sex-linked because blood type comes equally from each parent.
Source: Adapted from Hartl & Jones, 1999.

Saving Young Lives: Childhood and Adolescent Immunizations (Chapter 5)

Recommended Childhood and Adolescent Immunization Schedule, United States, 2006

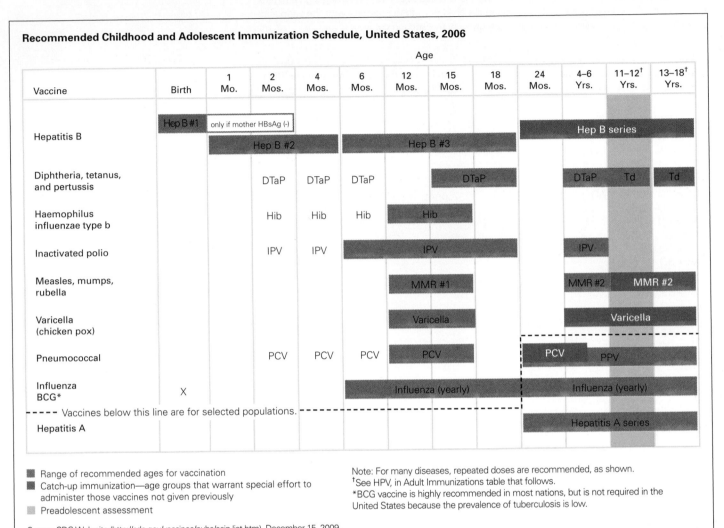

Vaccine	Birth	1 Mo.	2 Mos.	4 Mos.	6 Mos.	12 Mos.	15 Mos.	18 Mos.	24 Mos.	4–6 Yrs.	11–12[†] Yrs.	13–18[†] Yrs.
Hepatitis B	Hep B #1	only if mother HBsAg (-)	Hep B #2			Hep B #3			Hep B series			
Diphtheria, tetanus, and pertussis			DTaP	DTaP	DTaP		DTaP			DTaP	Td	Td
Haemophilus influenzae type b			Hib	Hib	Hib	Hib						
Inactivated polio			IPV	IPV	IPV					IPV		
Measles, mumps, rubella						MMR #1				MMR #2	MMR #2	
Varicella (chicken pox)						Varicella				Varicella		
Pneumococcal			PCV	PCV	PCV	PCV			PCV	PPV		
Influenza BCG*	X				Influenza (yearly)				Influenza (yearly)			
Hepatitis A									Hepatitis A series			

‑ ‑ ‑ ‑ Vaccines below this line are for selected populations. ‑ ‑ ‑ ‑

■ Range of recommended ages for vaccination
■ Catch-up immunization—age groups that warrant special effort to administer those vaccines not given previously
■ Preadolescent assessment

Note: For many diseases, repeated doses are recommended, as shown.
[†]See HPV, in Adult Immunizations table that follows.
*BCG vaccine is highly recommended in most nations, but is not required in the United States because the prevalence of tuberculosis is low.

Source: CDC Web site (http://cdc.gov/vaccines/pubs/acip-list.htm), December 15, 2009.

Adult Immunizations (Chapter 5)

Vaccine	Recommended Immunization Schedule
Tetanus, diphtheria, pertussis	Dtap: Before age 65—Dtap every 10 years. Adults older than 65—1 dose Td booster every 10 years.
Human papillomavirus (HPV)	Females age 9–26 (before any sexual activity).
Influenza	Adults—every year.
Pneumococcal	Before age 65—recommended if some other risk factor is present. Adults older than 65—every year.
Meningococcal	Recommended if other risk factor is present.

First Sounds and First Words: Similarities Among Many Languages (Chapter 6)

	Baby's word for:	
Language	**Mother**	**Father**
English	mama, mommy	dada, daddy
Spanish	mama	papa
French	maman, mama	papa
Italian	mamma	babbo, papa
Latvian	mama	te-te
Syrian Arabic	mama	baba
Bantu	ba-mama	taata
Swahili	mama	baba
Sanskrit	nana	tata
Hebrew	ema	abba
Korean	oma	apa

>> Answer to Observation Quiz (from page A-2)
Asian Americans, whose share of the U.S. population has quadrupled in the past 30 years. Latinos are increasing most rapidly in numbers, but not in proportion.

Breast-feeding in the United States (Chapter 7)

Differentiating excellent from destructive mothering is not easy, once the child's basic needs for food and protection are met. However, psychosocial development depends on responsive parent–infant relationships. Breast-feeding is one sign of intimacy between mother and infant.

Regions of the world differ dramatically in rates of breast-feeding, with the highest rate in Southeast Asia, where half of all 2-year-olds are still breast-fed. In the United States, factors that affect the likelihood of breast-feeding are ethnicity, maternal age, and education.

Breast-feeding in the United States					
Socio-demographic factors	Ever breast-feeding	Breast-feeding at 6 months	Breast-feeding at 12 months	Exclusive breast-feeding* at 3 months	Exclusive breast-feeding* at 6 months
U.S. National	75.0%	43.0%	22.4%	33.0%	13.3%
Sex of baby					
Male	75.4	42.6	22.0	33.1	12.9
Female	74.6	43.5	22.8	32.9	13.7
Birth order					
First born	74.5	44.1	23.7	33.4	13.8
Not first born	75.6	41.8	20.8	32.6	12.6
Ethnicity					
Native American (Indian)	73.8	42.4	20.7	27.6	13.2
Asian or Pacific Islander	83.0	56.4	32.8	34.1	14.5
Hispanic or Latino	80.6	46.0	24.7	32.4	13.2
African American (non-Hispanic)	59.7	27.9	12.9	22.7	8.2
European (non-Hispanic)	77.7	45.1	23.6	35.3	14.4
Mother's age					
Less than 20	59.7	22.2	10.7	18.1	7.9
20–29	69.7	33.4	16.1	28.8	10.2
More than 30	79.3	50.5	27.1	36.6	15.5
Mother's education					
Less than high school	67.0	37.0	21.9	33.7	9.2
High school	66.1	31.4	15.1	25.8	8.9
Some college	76.5	41.0	20.5	34.1	14.4
College graduate	88.3	59.9	31.1	45.9	19.6
Mother's marital status					
Married	81.7	51.6	27.5	39.0	16.7
Unmarried[†]	61.3	25.5	11.9	20.9	6.4
Residence					
Central city	75.5	43.9	24.4	32.8	13.3
Urban	77.9	45.3	22.3	34.9	13.9
Suburban and rural	66.4	35.0	17.4	28.8	11.8

*Exclusive breast-feeding is defined as only breast milk—no solids, no water, and no other liquids.
†Unmarried includes never married, widowed, separated, and divorced.
Source: National Immunization Survey, Centers for Disease Control and Prevention, Department of Health and Human Services, 2010.

Height Gains from Birth to Age 18 (Chapters 5, 8, 11)

The range of height (on this page) and weight (see page A-7) of children in the United States. The columns labeled "50th" (the fiftieth percentile) show the average; the columns labeled "90th" (the ninetieth percentile) show the size of children taller and heavier than 90 percent of their contemporaries; and the columns labeled "10th" (the tenth percentile) show the size of children who are taller than only 10 percent of their peers. Note that girls are slightly shorter, on average, than boys.

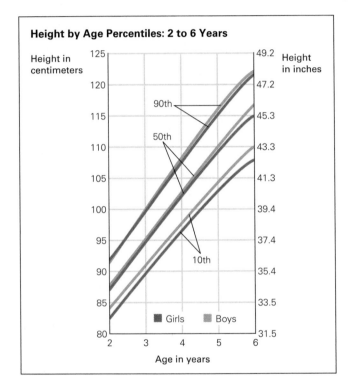

Height by Age Percentiles: 2 to 6 Years

Same Data, Different Form

The columns of numbers in the table at the right provide detailed and precise information about height ranges for every year of childhood. The illustration above shows the same information in graphic form for ages 2–6. The same is done for weight ranges on page A-7. Ages 2–6 are singled out because that is the period during which a child's eating habits are set. Which form of data presentation do you think is easier to understand?

	Length in Centimeters (and Inches)					
	Boys: percentiles			**Girls: percentiles**		
AGE	**10th**	**50th**	**90th**	**10th**	**50th**	**90th**
Birth	47.5 (18¾)	50.5 (20)	53.5 (21)	46.5 (18¼)	49.9 (19¾)	52.0 (20½)
1 month	51.3 (20¼)	54.6 (21½)	57.7 (22¾)	50.2 (19¾)	53.5 (21)	56.1 (22)
3 months	57.7 (22¾)	61.1 (24)	64.5 (25½)	56.2 (22¼)	59.5 (23½)	62.7 (24¾)
6 months	64.4 (25¼)	67.8 (26¾)	71.3 (28)	62.6 (24¾)	65.9 (26)	69.4 (27¼)
9 months	69.1 (27¼)	72.3 (28½)	75.9 (30)	67.0 (26½)	70.4 (27¾)	74.0 (29¼)
12 months	72.8 (28¾)	76.1 (30)	79.8 (31½)	70.8 (27¾)	74.3 (29¼)	78.0 (30¾)
18 months	78.7 (31)	82.4 (32½)	86.6 (34)	77.2 (30½)	80.9 (31¾)	85.0 (33½)
24 months	83.5 (32¾)	87.6 (34½)	92.2 (36¼)	82.5 (32½)	86.5 (34)	90.8 (35¾)
3 years	90.3 (35½)	94.9 (37¼)	100.1 (39½)	89.3 (35¼)	94.1 (37)	99.0 (39)
4 years	97.3 (38¼)	102.9 (40½)	108.2 (42½)	96.4 (38)	101.6 (40)	106.6 (42)
5 years	103.7 (40¾)	109.9 (43¼)	115.4 (45½)	102.7 (40½)	108.4 (42¾)	113.8 (44¾)
6 years	109.6 (43¼)	116.1 (45¾)	121.9 (48)	108.4 (42¾)	114.6 (45)	120.8 (47½)
7 years	115.0 (45¼)	121.7 (48)	127.9 (50¼)	113.6 (44¾)	120.6 (47½)	127.6 (50¼)
8 years	120.2 (47¼)	127.0 (50)	133.6 (52½)	118.7 (46¾)	126.4 (49¾)	134.2 (52¾)
9 years	125.2 (49¼)	132.2 (52)	139.4 (55)	123.9 (48¾)	132.2 (52)	140.7 (55½)
10 years	130.1 (51¼)	137.5 (54¼)	145.5 (57¼)	129.5 (51)	138.3 (54½)	147.2 (58)
11 years	135.1 (53¼)	143.33 (56½)	152.1 (60)	135.6 (53½)	144.8 (57)	153.7 (60½)
12 years	140.3 (55¼)	149.7 (59)	159.4 (62¾)	142.3 (56)	151.5 (59¾)	160.0 (63)
13 years	145.8 (57½)	156.5 (61½)	167.0 (65¾)	148.0 (58¼)	157.1 (61¾)	165.3 (65)
14 years	151.8 (59¾)	63.1 (64¼)	173.8 (68½)	151.5 (59¾)	160.4 (63¼)	168.7 (66½)
15 years	158.2 (62¼)	169.0 (66½)	178.9 (70½)	153.2 (60¼)	161.8 (63¾)	170.5 (67¼)
16 years	163.9 (64½)	173.5 (68¼)	182.4 (71¾)	154.1 (60¾)	162.4 (64)	171.1 (67¼)
17 years	167.7 (66)	176.2 (69¼)	184.4 (72½)	155.1 (61)	163.1 (64¼)	171.2 (67½)
18 years	168.7 (66½)	176.8 (69½)	185.3 (73)	156.0 (61½)	163.7 (64½)	171.0 (67¼)

Source: These data are those of the National Center for Health Statistics (NCHS), Health Resources Administration, DHHS. They were based on studies of The Fels Research Institute, Yellow Springs, Ohio. These data were first made available with the help of William M. Moore, M.D., of Ross Laboratories, who supplied the conversion from metric measurements to approximate inches and pounds. This help is gratefully acknowledged.

Weight Gains from Birth to Age 18 (Chapters 5, 8, 11)

These height and weight charts present rough guidelines; a child might differ from these norms and be quite healthy and normal. However, if a particular child shows a discrepancy between height and weight (for instance, at the 90th percentile in height but only the 20th percentile in weight) or is much larger or smaller than most children the same age, a pediatrician should see if disease, malnutrition, or genetic abnormality is part of the reason.

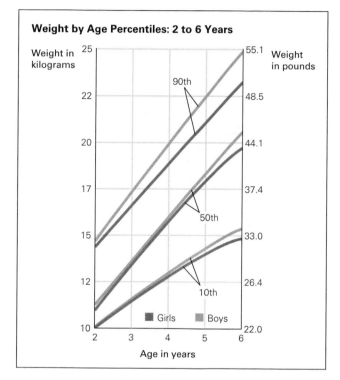

Weight by Age Percentiles: 2 to 6 Years

Weight in kilograms

Weight in pounds

90th

50th

10th

■ Girls   ■ Boys

Age in years

Comparisons

Notice that the height trajectories for boys and girls on page A-6 are much closer together than the weight trajectories shown above. By age 18, the height range amounts to only about 6 inches, but there is a difference of about 65 pounds between the 10th and the 90th percentiles.

Critical Thinking Question How can this gender discrepancy between height and weight ranges be explained? (see answer, page A-8)

	Weight in Kilograms (and Pounds)					
	Boys: percentiles			Girls: percentiles		
AGE	10th	50th	90th	10th	50th	90th
Birth	2.78 (6¼)	3.27 (7¼)	3.82 (8½)	2.58 (5¾)	3.23 (7)	3.64 (8)
1 month	3.43 (7½)	4.29 (9½)	5.14 (11¼)	3.22 (7)	3.98 (8¾)	4.65 (10¼)
3 months	4.78 (10½)	5.98 (13¼)	7.14 (15¾)	4.47 (9¾)	5.40 (12)	6.39 (14)
6 months	6.61 (14½)	7.85 (17¼)	9.10 (20)	6.12 (13½)	7.21 (16)	8.38 (18½)
9 months	7.95 (17½)	9.18 (20¼)	10.49 (23¼)	7.34 (16¼)	8.56 (18¾)	9.83 (21¾)
12 months	8.84 (19½)	10.15 (22½)	11.54 (25½)	8.19 (18)	9.53 (21)	10.87 (24)
18 months	9.92 (21¾)	11.47 (25¼)	13.05 (28¾)	9.30 (20½)	10.82 (23¾)	12.30 (27)
24 months	10.85 (24)	12.59 (27¾)	14.29 (31½)	10.26 (22½)	11.90 (26¼)	13.57 (30)
3 years	12.58 (27¾)	14.62 (32¼)	16.95 (37¼)	12.26 (27)	14.10 (31)	16.54 (36½)
4 years	14.24 (31½)	16.69 (36¾)	19.32 (42½)	13.84 (30½)	15.96 (35¼)	18.93 (41¾)
5 years	15.96 (35¼)	18.67 (41¼)	21.70 (47¾)	15.26 (33¾)	17.66 (39)	21.23 (46¾)
6 years	17.72 (39)	20.69 (45½)	24.31 (53½)	16.72 (36¾)	19.52 (43)	23.89 (52¾)
7 years	19.53 (43)	22.85 (50¼)	27.36 (60¼)	18.39 (40½)	21.84 (48¼)	27.39 (60½)
8 years	21.39 (47¼)	25.30 (55¾)	31.06 (68½)	20.45 (45)	24.84 (54¾)	32.04 (70¾)
9 years	23.33 (51½)	28.13 (62)	35.57 (78½)	22.92 (50½)	28.46 (62¾)	37.60 (83)
10 years	25.52 (56¼)	31.44 (69¼)	40.80 (90)	25.76 (56¾)	32.55 (71¾)	43.70 (96¼)
11 years	28.17 (62)	35.30 (77¾)	46.57 (102¾)	28.97 (63¾)	36.95 (81½)	49.96 (110¼)
12 years	31.46 (69¼)	39.78 (87¾)	52.73 (116¼)	32.53 (71¼)	41.53 (91½)	55.99 (123½)
13 years	35.60 (78½)	44.95 (99)	59.12 (130¼)	36.35 (80¼)	46.10 (101¾)	61.45 (135½)
14 years	40.64 (89½)	50.77 (112)	65.57 (144½)	40.11 (88½)	50.28 (110¾)	66.04 (145½)
15 years	46.06 (101½)	56.71 (125)	71.91 (158½)	43.38 (95¾)	53.68 (118¼)	69.64 (153¼)
16 years	51.16 (112¾)	62.10 (137)	77.97 (172)	45.78 (101)	55.89 (123¼)	71.68 (158)
17 years	55.28 (121¾)	66.31 (146¼)	83.58 (184¼)	47.04 (103¾)	56.69 (125)	72.38 (159½)
18 years	57.89 (127½)	68.88 (151¾)	88.41 (195)	47.47 (104¾)	56.62 (124¾)	72.25 (159¼)

Source: Data are those of the National Center for Health Statistics, Health Resources Administration, DHHS, collected in its Health Examination Surveys.

Children Are the Poorest Americans (Chapters 10, 11)

It probably comes as no surprise that the rate of poverty is twice as high in some states as in others. What is surprising is how much the rates vary between age groups within the same state.

Observation Quiz In which nine states is the proportion of poor children more than twice as high as the proportion of poor people over age 65? (see answer, page A-9)

>> Answer to Critical Thinking Question (from page A-7) Nutrition is generally adequate in the United States and that is why height differences are small. But as a result of the strong influence that family and culture have on eating habits, almost half of all North Americans are overweight or obese.

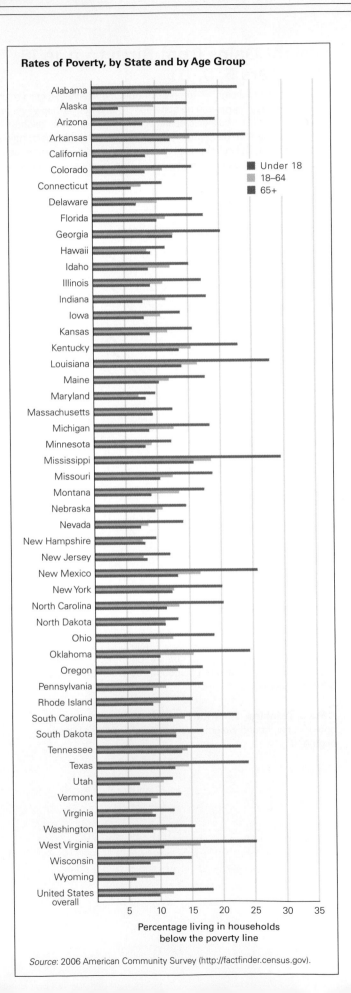

Rates of Poverty, by State and by Age Group

Percentage living in households below the poverty line

Legend: ■ Under 18   ■ 18–64   ■ 65+

Source: 2006 American Community Survey (http://factfinder.census.gov).

DSM-IV-TR Criteria for Attention-Deficit/ Hyperactivity Disorder (ADHD), Conduct Disorder (CD), Oppositional Defiant Disorder (ODD), Autistic Disorder, and Asperger Disorder (Chapter 11)

The specific symptoms for these various disorders overlap. Many other childhood disorders also have some of the same symptoms. Differentiating one problem from another is the main purpose of DSM-IV-TR. That is no easy task, which is one reason the book is now in its fourth major revision and is more than 900 pages long. Those pages include not only the type of diagnostic criteria shown here but also discussions of prevalence, age and gender statistics, cultural aspects, and prognosis for about 400 disorders or subtypes, 40 of which appear primarily in childhood. Thus, the diagnostic criteria reprinted here for five disorders represent less than 1 percent of the contents of DSM-IV-TR. Note that publication of the DSM-5 is expected in 2013, and some criteria will change.

>> Answer to Observation Quiz (from page A-8): Alaska, Arizona, California, Delaware, Indiana, Michigan, Oklahoma, West Virginia, and Wisconsin.

>> Diagnostic Criteria for Attention-Deficit/Hyperactivity Disorder

A.   Either (1) or (2):

(1) Six (or more) of the following symptoms of **inattention** have persisted for at least 6 months to a degree that is maladaptive and inconsistent with developmental level:

INATTENTION

(a) often fails to give close attention to details or makes careless mistakes in schoolwork, work, or other activities
(b) often has difficulty sustaining attention in tasks or play activities
(c) often does not seem to listen when spoken to directly
(d) often does not follow through on instructions and fails to finish schoolwork, chores, or duties in the workplace (not due to oppositional behavior or failure to understand instructions)
(e) often has difficulty organizing tasks and activities
(f) often avoids, dislikes, or is reluctant to engage in tasks that require sustained mental effort (such as schoolwork or homework)
(g) often loses things necessary for tasks or activities (e.g., toys, school assignments, pencils, books, or tools)
(h) is often easily distracted by extraneous stimuli
(i) is often forgetful in daily activities

(2) Six (or more) of the following symptoms of **hyperactivity-impulsivity** have persisted for at least 6 months to a degree that is maladaptive and inconsistent with developmental level:

HYPERACTIVITY

(a) often fidgets with hands or feet or squirms in seat
(b) often leaves seat in classroom or in other situations in which remaining seated is expected
(c) often runs about or climbs excessively in situations in which it is inappropriate (in adolescents or adults, may be limited to subjective feelings of restlessness)
(d) often has difficulty playing or engaging in leisure activities quietly
(e) is often "on the go" or often acts as if "driven by a motor"
(f) often talks excessively

IMPULSIVITY

(g) often blurts out answers before questions have been completed

(h) often has difficulty awaiting turn

(i) often interrupts or intrudes on others (e.g., butts into conversations or games)

B.   Some hyperactive-impulsive or inattentive symptoms that caused impairment were present before age 7 years.

C.   Some impairment from the symptoms is present in two or more settings (e.g., at school [or work] and at home).

D.   There must be clear evidence of clinically significant impairment in social, academic, or occupational functioning.

>> Diagnostic Criteria for Conduct Disorder

A.   A repetitive and persistent pattern of behavior in which the basic rights of others or major age-appropriate societal norms or rules are violated, as manifested by the presence of three (or more) of the following criteria in the past 12 months, with at least one criterion present in the past 6 months:

AGGRESSION TO PEOPLE AND ANIMALS

(1) often bullies, threatens, or intimidates others

(2) often initiates physical fights

(3) has used a weapon that can cause serious physical harm to others (e.g., a bat, brick, broken bottle, knife, gun)

(4) has been physically cruel to people

(5) has been physically cruel to animals

(6) has stolen while confronting a victim (e.g., mugging, purse snatching, extortion, armed robbery)

(7) has forced someone into sexual activity

DESTRUCTION OF PROPERTY

(8) has deliberately engaged in fire setting with the intention of causing serious damage

(9) has deliberately destroyed others' property (other than by fire setting)

DECEITFULNESS OR THEFT

(10) has broken into someone else's house, building, or car

(11) often lies to obtain goods or favors or to avoid obligations (i.e., "cons" others)

(12) has stolen items of nontrivial value without confronting a victim (e.g., shoplifting, but without breaking and entering; forgery)

SERIOUS VIOLATIONS OF RULES

(13) often stays out at night despite parental prohibitions, beginning before age 13 years

(14) has run away from home overnight at least twice while living in parental or parental surrogate home (or once without returning for a lengthy period)

(15) is often truant from school, beginning before age 13 years

B. The disturbance in behavior causes clinically significant impairment in social, academic, or occupational functioning.

>> Diagnostic Criteria for Oppositional Defiant Disorder

A. A pattern of negativistic, hostile, and defiant behavior lasting at least 6 months, during which four (or more) of the following are present:

(1) often loses temper

(2) often argues with adults

(3) often actively defies or refuses to comply with adults' requests or rules

(4) often deliberately annoys people

(5) often blames others for his or her mistakes or misbehavior

(6) is often touchy or easily annoyed by others

(7) is often angry and resentful

(8) is often spiteful or vindictive

Note: Consider a criterion met only if the behavior occurs more frequently than is typically observed in individuals of comparable age and developmental level.

B. The disturbance in behavior causes clinically significant impairment in social, academic, or occupational functioning.

>> Diagnostic Criteria for Autistic Disorder

A. A total of six (or more) items from (1), (2), and (3), with at least two from (1) and one each from (2) and (3):

(1) qualitative impairment in social interaction, as manifested by at least two of the following:

    (a) marked impairment in the use of multiple nonverbal behaviors such as eye-to-eye gaze, facial expression, body postures, and gestures to regulate social interaction

    (b) failure to develop peer relationships appropriate to developmental level

    (c) a lack of spontaneous seeking to share enjoyment, interests, or achievements with other people (e.g., by a lack of showing, bringing, or pointing out objects of interest)

    (d) lack of social or emotional reciprocity

(2) qualitative impairments in communication as manifested by at least one of the following:

    (a) delay in, or total lack of, the development of spoken language (not accompanied by an attempt to compensate through alternative modes of communication such as gesture or mime)

    (b) in individuals with adequate speech, marked impairment in the ability to initiate or sustain a conversation with others

    (c) stereotyped and repetitive use of language or idiosyncratic language

    (d) lack of varied, spontaneous make-believe play or social imitative play appropriate to developmental level

  (3) restricted repetitive and stereotyped patterns of behavior, interests, and activities, as manifested by at least one of the following:

    (a) encompassing preoccupation with one or more stereotyped and restricted patterns of interest that is abnormal either in intensity or focus

    (b) apparently inflexible adherence to specific, nonfunctional routines or rituals

    (c) stereotyped and repetitive motor mannerisms (e.g., hand or finger flapping or twisting, or complex whole-body movements)

    (d) persistent preoccupation with parts of objects

B. Delays or abnormal functioning in at least one of the following areas, with onset prior to age 3 years:

  (1) social interaction

  (2) language as used in social communication

  (3) symbolic or imaginative play

C. The disturbance is not better accounted for by Rett's Disorder or Childhood Disintegrative Disorder.

▶▶ Diagnostic Criteria for Asperger Disorder

A. Qualitative impairment in social interaction, as manifested by at least two of the following:

  (1) marked impairment in the use of multiple nonverbal behaviors such as eye-to-eye gaze, facial expression, body postures, and gestures to regulate social interaction

  (2) failure to develop peer relationships appropriate to developmental level

  (3) a lack of spontaneous seeking to share enjoyment, interests, or achievements with other people (e.g., by a lack of showing, bringing, or pointing out objects of interest to other people)

  (4) lack of social or emotional reciprocity

B. Restricted repetitive and stereotyped patterns of behavior, interests, and activities, as manifested by at least one of the following:

  (1) encompassing preoccupation with one or more stereotyped and restricted patterns of interest that is abnormal either in intensity or focus

  (2) apparently inflexible adherence to specific, nonfunctional routines or rituals

  (3) stereotyped and repetitive motor mannerisms (e.g., hand or finger flapping or twisting, or complex whole-body movements)

  (4) persistent preoccupation with parts of objects

C. The disturbance causes clinically significant impairment in social, occupational, or other important areas of functioning.

D. There is no clinically significant general delay in language (e.g., single words used by age 2 years, communicative phrases used by age 3 years).

E. There is no clinically significant delay in cognitive development or in the development of age-appropriate self-help skills, adaptive behavior (other than in social interaction), and curiosity about the environment in childhood.

F. Criteria are not met for another specific Pervasive Developmental Disorder or Schizophrenia.

Motivation or Achievement? (Chapters 12, 15)

The PISA (Programme for International Student Assessment) is an international test of students' abilities to apply their knowledge. One explanation for the high scores of China and low scores of the United States is motivation of the students: Chinese young people are said to want to show national pride. Most experts believe that students in the United States are not as strongly motivated to learn in school—so they don't.

Science		Reading		Math	
Country	PISA Score	Country	PISA Score	Country	PISA Score
Shanghai	575	Shanghai	556	Shanghai	600
Finland	554	Korea	539	Singapore	562
Hong Kong	549	Finland	536	Hong Kong	555
Singapore	542	Hong Kong	533	Korea	546
Japan	539	Singapore	526	Taiwan	543
Korea	538	Canada	524	Finland	541
New Zealand	532	New Zealand	521	Liechtenstein	536
Canada	529	Japan	520	Switzerland	534
Estonia	528	Australia	515	Japan	529
Australia	527	Netherlands	508	Canada	527
Netherlands	522	Belgium	506	Netherlands	526
Taiwan	520	Norway	503	New Zealand	519
Germany	520	Estonia	501	Belgium	515
Liechtenstein	520	Switzerland	501	Australia	514
Switzerland	517	Poland	500	Germany	513
Britain	514	Iceland	500	Estonia	512
Slovenia	512	**United States**	**500**	Iceland	507
Poland	508	Liechtenstein	499	Denmark	503
Ireland	508	Sweden	497	Slovenia	501
Belgium	507	Germany	497	Norway	498
Hungary	503	Ireland	496	France	497
United States	**502**	France	496	Slovakia	497
AVERAGE SCORE	501	Taiwan	495	AVERAGE SCORE	497
Czech Republic	500	Denmark	495	Austria	496
Norway	500	Britain	494	Poland	495
Denmark	499	Hungary	494	Sweden	494
France	498	AVERAGE SCORE	494	Czech Republic	493
Iceland	496	Portugal	489	Britain	492
Sweden	495	Italy	486	Hungary	490
Austria	494	Latvia	484	Luxembourg	489
Latvia	494	Slovenia	483	**United States**	**487**
Portugal	493	Greece	483	Ireland	487

Changes in the Average Weekly Amount of Time Spent by 6- to 11-Year-Olds in Various Activities (Chapter 12)

Facts are the bedrock of science, but facts can be presented in many ways, with many interpretations. Your opinions about these facts reflect your values, which may be quite different from those of the parents and teachers of these children.

Average Amount of Time Spent in Activity, per Week, United States				
Activity	In 1981	In 1997	In 2004	Change in Time Spent Since 1981
School	25 hrs, 17 min.	33 hrs, 52 min.	33 hrs, 33 min.	+8 hrs, 16 min.
Organized sports	3 hrs, 5 min.	4 hrs, 56 min.	2 hrs, 28 min.	–32 min.
Studying	1 hr, 46 min.	2 hrs, 50 min.	3 hrs, 25 min.	+1 hr, 21 min.
Reading	57 min.	1 hr, 15 min.	1 hr, 28 min.	+31 min.
Being outdoors	1 hr, 17 min.	39 min.	56 min.	–21 min.
Playing	12 hrs, 52 min.	10 hrs, 5 min.	10 hrs, 25 min.	–2 hrs, 27 min.
Watching TV	15 hrs, 34 min.	13 hrs, 7 min.	14 hrs, 19 min.	–1 hr, 15 min.

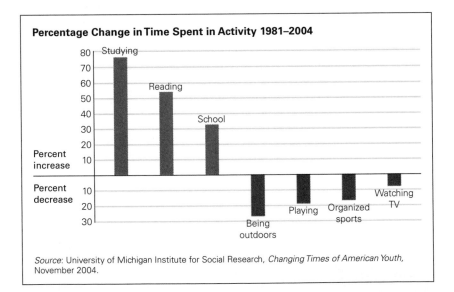

Percentage Change in Time Spent in Activity 1981–2004

Source: University of Michigan Institute for Social Research, *Changing Times of American Youth*, November 2004.

Who Is Raising the Children? (Chapter 13)

Most children still live in households with a male/female couple, who may be the children's married or unmarried biological parents, grandparents, stepparents, foster parents, or adoptive parents. However, the proportion of households headed by single parents has risen—by 350 percent for single fathers and by almost 200 percent for single mothers. (In 2008, 66 percent of U.S. households had *no* children under age 18.)

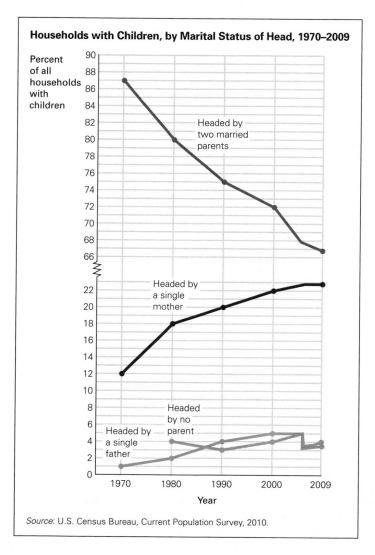

Households with Children, by Marital Status of Head, 1970–2009

Source: U.S. Census Bureau, Current Population Survey, 2010.

Major Sexually Transmitted Infections: Some Basics (Chapter 14)

These and other STIs, if left untreated, may lead to serious reproductive and other health problems or even, as with HIV/AIDS and syphilis, to death. STIs can be avoided by consistently using condoms, having sex only in a relationship with an uninfected partner, or abstaining from sex.

Sexually Transmitted Infection (and Cause)	Symptoms	Treatment
Chlamydia (bacterium)	The most frequently reported bacterial STI in the United States. In women, abnormal vaginal discharge or burning sensation when urinating; may be followed by pain in low abdomen or low back, nausea, fever, pain during intercourse, or bleeding between menstrual periods. In men, discharge from penis or burning sensation when urinating.	Antibiotics
Genital HPV infection (virus)	One of the most common STIs in the world. Causes no symptoms or health problems in most people, but certain types may cause genital warts and others can cause cervical cancer in women and other cancers of the genitals in both sexes.	A vaccine is now available and is recommended for 11- and 12-year-old girls who are not yet sexually active.
Genital herpes (virus)	Blisters on or around the genitals or rectum that break and leave sores, which may take 2 to 4 weeks to heal; some people may experience fever, swollen glands, and other flu-like symptoms. Later outbreaks are usually less severe and shorter. Many people never have sores and may take years to realize they are infected. May lead to potentially fatal infections in babies and makes infected person more susceptible to HIV infection.	There is no vaccine or cure, but antiviral medications can shorten and prevent outbreaks.
Gonorrhea (bacterium)	Some men and most women have no symptoms. In men, a burning sensation when urinating; a white, yellow, or green discharge from the penis; painful or swollen testicles. In women, symptoms—pain or burning during urination, increased vaginal discharge, vaginal bleeding between periods—may be so mild or nonspecific that they are mistaken for a bladder or vaginal infection. May cause pelvic inflammatory disease (PID) in women and infertility in both sexes. Infected person can more easily contract HIV.	Antibiotics
Pelvic inflammatory disease (PID) (various bacteria)	A common and serious complication in women who have certain other STIs, especially chlamydia and gonorrhea. Pain in lower abdomen, fever, unusual vaginal discharge that may have a foul odor, painful intercourse, painful urination, irregular menstrual bleeding, and (rarely) pain in the right upper abdomen. May lead to blocked fallopian tubes, causing infertility.	Administration of at least two antibiotics that are effective against a wide range of infectious agents. In severe cases, surgery.
HIV/AIDS (virus)	Infection with the human immunodeficiency virus (HIV) eventually leads to acquired immune deficiency syndrome (AIDS). Infection with other STIs increases a person's likelihood of both acquiring and transmitting HIV. Soon after exposure, some people have flu-like symptoms: fever, headache, tiredness, swollen lymph glands. Months or years later, when the virus has weakened the immune system, the person may experience lack of energy, weight loss, frequent fevers and sweats, yeast infections, skin rashes, short-term memory loss. Symptoms of full-blown AIDS include certain cancers (Kaposi's sarcoma and lymphomas), seizures, vision loss, and coma. A leading cause of death among young adults in many nations.	There is no vaccine or cure, but antiretroviral drugs can slow the growth of the virus; antibiotics can cure some secondary infections, and various treatments are available to relieve painful or unpleasant symptoms.
Syphilis (bacterium)	Symptoms may not appear for years. Primary stage: One or more sores (chancres) a few days or weeks after exposure. Secondary stage: Skin rash, lesions of mucous membranes, fever, swollen lymph glands, sore throat, patchy hair loss, headaches, weight loss, muscle aches, fatigue. Latent stage: Primary and secondary symptoms disappear, but infection remains in the body. Late stage (10 to 20 years after first infection): Damage to brain, nerves, eyes, heart, blood vessels, liver, bones, and joints, progressing to difficulty coordinating muscle movements, paralysis, numbness, blindness, dementia.	Penicillin injections will kill the syphilis bacterium and prevent further damage but cannot repair damage already done.
Trichomoniasis (Trichomonas *vaginalis*, *a single-celled* protozoan parasite)	Most men have no symptoms, but some may temporarily have an irritation inside the penis, mild discharge, or slight burning after urination or ejaculation. Women may have a frothy, yellow-green, strong-smelling vaginal discharge and may experience discomfort during intercourse and urination; irritation and itching of the genital area; and, rarely, lower abdominal pain.	A single oral dose of metronidazole or tinidazole

Source: Centers for Disease Control and Prevention, 2009, July 14.

Sexual Behaviors of U.S. High School Students, 2009 (Chapters 14, 15)

These percentages, as high as they may seem, are actually lower than they were in the early 1990s. (States not listed did not participate fully in the survey.) The data in this table reflect responses from students in the 9th to 12th grades. When only high school seniors are surveyed, the percentages are higher: Nationwide, 62 percent of seniors have had sexual intercourse, and 21 percent have had four or more partners.

State	Ever had sexual intercourse (%)			Had first sexual intercourse before age 13 (%)			Has had four or more sex partners during lifetime (%)			Is currently sexually active (%)		
	Female	Male	Total	Female	Male	Total	Female	Male	Total	Female	Male	Total
Alabama	51.4	61.8	**56.6**	4.1	16.2	**10.1**	14.4	25.7	**19.9**	42.0	40.9	**41.5**
Arizona	44.8	52.1	**48.6**	2.9	7.8	**5.5**	10.4	17.4	**14.1**	34.4	34.2	**34.5**
Arkansas	51.4	55.9	**53.6**	6.7	14.3	**10.3**	15.5	20.8	**18.0**	39.9	37.6	**38.9**
Colorado	36.2	43.7	**40.0**	2.7	6.4	**4.6**	11.0	16.5	**13.8**	25.6	29.1	**27.4**
Delaware	57.1	57.9	**57.5**	5.8	13.4	**9.7**	18.0	23.9	**21.1**	44.2	41.5	**42.9**
Florida	47.7	53.4	**50.6**	4.3	12.0	**8.3**	11.4	21.4	**16.6**	37.0	36.8	**37.0**
Hawaii	45.8	42.7	**44.3**	4.1	7.8	**6.0**	11.3	10.9	**11.1**	33.9	27.2	**30.5**
Idaho	39.2	38.8	**39.0**	3.4	4.9	**4.2**	—	—	—	—	—	—
Kansas	46.2	47.0	**46.6**	1.7	7.2	**4.5**	11.8	16.4	**14.2**	35.2	33.3	**34.2**
Kentucky	47.8	49.0	**48.3**	4.0	9.3	**6.7**	10.7	14.7	**12.7**	36.1	31.2	**33.6**
Maine	45.9	45.9	**46.0**	2.8	7.3	**5.0**	10.7	13.1	**11.9**	37.1	33.3	**35.3**
Massachusetts	44.6	48.0	**46.4**	3.0	8.0	**5.4**	10.6	15.2	**12.9**	36.0	33.1	**34.6**
Michigan	44.3	46.9	**45.6**	3.0	7.2	**5.1**	11.5	15.7	**13.6**	35.6	32.6	**34.1**
Missouri	47.3	50.2	**48.7**	3.4	7.9	**5.7**	13.6	18.3	**16.0**	36.3	34.9	**35.5**
Montana	47.0	48.1	**47.6**	3.7	7.7	**5.7**	14.7	17.3	**16.0**	33.6	30.8	**32.2**
Nevada	45.3	52.6	**49.0**	3.4	10.0	**6.7**	10.9	20.3	**15.7**	32.8	32.5	**32.7**
New York	38.4	45.6	**42.0**	3.3	8.8	**6.1**	8.4	18.4	**13.4**	29.7	33.2	**31.5**
North Carolina	48.2	54.2	**51.1**	5.1	10.1	**7.5**	12.2	19.2	**15.7**	35.7	37.5	**36.6**
North Dakota	46.7	42.3	**44.6**	2.1	4.8	**3.5**	11.6	11.7	**11.7**	37.2	29.3	**33.3**
Oklahoma	50.7	51.2	**44.6**	3.4	6.0	**4.7**	15.2	20.1	**17.6**	40.3	39.5	**39.8**
Rhode Island	42.8	45.6	**44.2**	2.4	8.0	**5.2**	8.6	13.7	**11.2**	32.6	32.0	**32.3**
South Carolina	50.7	56.3	**53.4**	6.3	12.2	**9.2**	14.8	24.9	**19.7**	37.0	40.4	**38.6**
South Dakota	46.9	47.1	**47.0**	3.7	7.6	**5.7**	14.4	16.0	**15.2**	38.9	33.7	**36.3**
Tennessee	51.2	55.6	**53.4**	3.3	11.5	**7.5**	13.3	19.8	**16.6**	38.4	39.1	**38.8**
Texas	49.3	53.9	**51.6**	3.1	9.1	**6.1**	12.7	20.3	**16.5**	38.5	36.9	**37.7**
West Virginia	54.7	53.6	**54.1**	4.6	7.5	**6.0**	14.6	16.4	**15.5**	42.4	38.2	**40.3**
Wisconsin	41.1	40.7	**40.9**	2.5	4.4	**3.4**	8.7	11.0	**9.9**	31.7	26.9	**29.3**
Wyoming	51.6	49.6	**50.6**	3.0	8.8	**5.0**	16.8	19.0	**17.9**	40.4	35.0	**37.8**
U.S. median	**46.8**	**48.5**	**48.2**	**3.3**	**7.8**	**5.7**	**11.6**	**17.3**	**14.5**	**36.2**	**33.4**	**35.4**

Source: National Center for Chronic Disease Prevention and Health Promotion, Youth Risk Behavior Surveillance System, *MMWR*, June 4, 2010.

Smoking Behavior Among U.S. High School Students, 1991–2009 (Chapters 14, 16)

The data in these two tables reveal many trends. For example, do you see that African American adolescents are much less likely to smoke than Hispanics or European Americans, but that this racial advantage is decreasing? Are you surprised to see that White females smoke more than White males?

Percentage of High School Students Who Reported Smoking Cigarettes							
Smoking Behavior	1991	1995	1999	2003	2005	2007	2009
Lifetime (ever smoked)	70.1	71.3	70.4	58.4	54.3	50.3	46.3
Current (smoked at least once in past 30 days)	27.5	34.8	34.8	21.9	23.0	20.0	19.5
Current frequent (smoked 20 or more times in past 30 days)	12.7	16.1	16.8	9.7	9.4	8.1	7.3

Percentage of High School Students Who Reported Current Smoking, by Sex, Ethnicity, and Grade							
Characteristic	1991	1995	1999	2003	2005	2007	2009
Sex							
Female	27.3	34.3	34.9	21.9	23.0	18.7	19.1
Male	27.6	35.4	34.7	21.8	22.9	21.3	19.8
Ethnicity							
White, non-Hispanic	30.9	38.3	38.6	24.9	25.9	23.2	22.5
Female	*31.7*	*39.8*	*39.1*	*26.6*	*27.0*	*22.5*	*22.8*
Male	*30.2*	*37.0*	*38.2*	*23.3*	*24.9*	*23.8*	*22.3*
Black, non-Hispanic	12.6	19.2	19.7	15.1	12.9	11.6	9.5
Female	*11.3*	*12.2*	*17.7*	*10.8*	*11.9*	*8.4*	*8.4*
Male	*14.1*	*27.8*	*21.8*	*19.3*	*14.0*	*14.9*	*10.7*
Hispanic	25.3	34.0	32.7	18.4	22.0	16.7	18.0
Female	*22.9*	*32.9*	*31.5*	*17.7*	*19.2*	*14.6*	*16.7*
Male	*27.9*	*34.9*	*34.0*	*19.1*	*24.8*	*18.7*	*19.4*
Grade							
9th	23.2	31.2	27.6	17.4	19.7	14.3	13.5
10th	25.2	33.1	34.7	21.8	21.4	19.6	18.3
11th	31.6	35.9	36.0	23.6	24.3	21.6	22.3
12th	30.1	38.2	42.8	26.2	27.6	26.5	25.2

Source: MMWR (2010, July 9).

United States Homicide Victim and Offender Rates, by Race and Gender, Ages 13–16 (Chapters 16, 17)

Teenage boys are more often violent offenders than victims. The ratio of victimization to offense has varied for teenage girls over the years. The good news is that rates have decreased dramatically over the past 10 years for every category of adolescents—male and female, Black and White. (Similar declines are apparent for Asian and Hispanic Americans.) The bad news is that rates are far higher in the United States than in any other developed nation.

Number of Homicide Victims, Ages 13–16

Year	Total	Male	Female	White	Black
2001	390	291	99	190	182
2004	411	325	86	177	218
2005	467	426	41	176	272
2006	485	395	90	217	259
2007	487	380	107	206	265
2008	496	447	48	197	272
2009	400	319	81	190	199

Source: U.S. Department of Justice—Federal Bureau of Investigation, 2010.

Number of Homicide Offenders, Ages 13–16

Year	Total	Male	Female	White	Black
2001	454	388	63	196	234
2004	480	440	39	210	256
2005	467	426	41	176	272
2006	610	560	47	213	377
2007	542	493	47	187	344
2008	496	447	48	197	272
2009	465	422	43	186	264

Source: U.S. Department of Justice—Federal Bureau of Investigation, 2010.

The charts, graphs, and tables in this Appendix offer readers the opportunity to analyze raw data and draw their own conclusions. The same information may be presented in a variety of ways. On this page, you can create your own bar graph or line graph, depicting some noteworthy aspect of the data presented in the three tables. First, consider all the possibilities the tables offer by answering these five questions:

1. Are male or female teenagers more likely to be victims of homicide?
2. These are annual rates. How many African Americans in 1,000 were likely to commit homicide in 2006?
3. Which age group is *most* likely to commit homicide?
4. Which age group is *least* likely to be victims of homicide?
5. Of the four groups of adolescents, which has shown the greatest decline in rates of both victimization and perpetration of homicide over the past decade? Which has shown the least decline?

Answers: 1. Boys—at least 4 times as often. 2. Less than one. 3. 17–24. 4. 0–12. 5. Black males had the greatest decline, and White females had the least (but these two groups have always been highest and lowest, respectively, in every year).
Now—use the grid provided at right to make your own graph.

Overall Number of Homicides by Age, 2009, United States (Chapters 16, 17)

Late adolescence and early adulthood are the peak times for murders—both for victims and offenders. The question for developmentalists is whether something changes before age 18 to decrease the rates in young adulthood.

Age group	Victims	Killers
0–12	634	11
13–16	400	465
17–24	3672	4447
25–34	3475	2917
35–49	3137	1964
50–64	1468	762

Demographic Changes (Chapter 17)

These numbers show dramatic shifts in family planning, with teenage births continuing to fall and births after age 30 rising again. These data come from the United States, but the same trends are apparent in almost every nation (see top of page A-21). Can you tell when contraception became widely available?

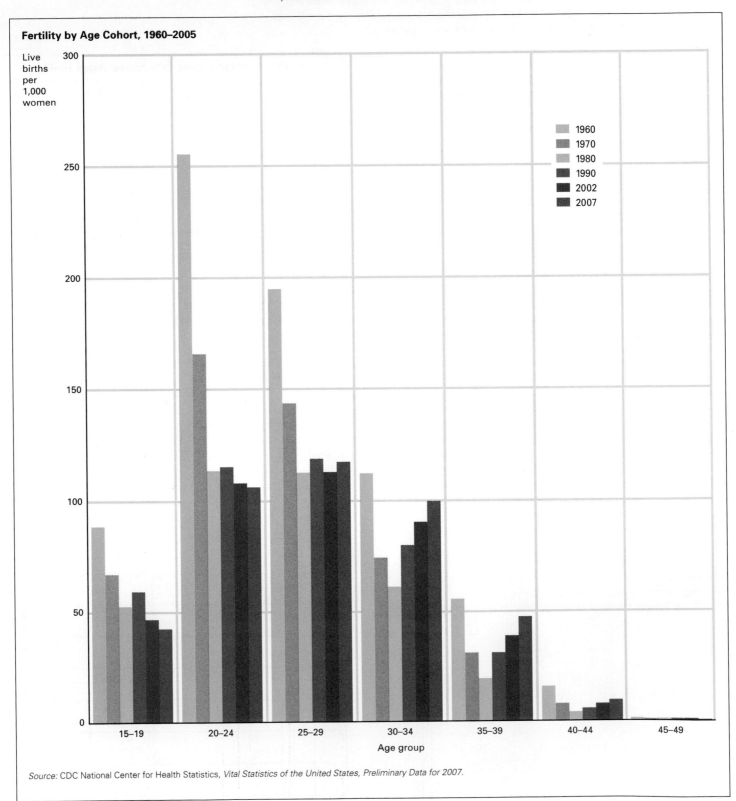

Fertility by Age Cohort, 1960–2005

Source: CDC National Center for Health Statistics, *Vital Statistics of the United States, Preliminary Data for 2007.*

A New Norm (Chapter 17)

As you can see, birth without marriage has become normal in many nations. These rates are for all births—first births are more often before marriage, later births more often follow marriage. Typically, the parents live together: They are ready for a baby but not for a wedding.

Births to Unmarried Woman by Country: 1980 to 2007					
Country	1980	1990	2000	2006	2007
United States	18.4	28.0	33.2	38.5	39.7
Canada	12.8	24.4	28.3	27.1	(NA)
Japan	0.8	1.1	1.6	2.1	(NA)
Denmark	33.2	46.4	44.6	46.4	46.1
France	11.4	30.1	43.6	50.5	51.7
Germany	(NA)	15.1	23.4	30.0	30.8
Ireland	5.9	14.6	31.5	33.2	(NA)
Italy	4.3	6.5	9.7	16.2	(NA)
Netherlands	4.1	11.4	24.9	37.1	39.5
Spain	3.9	9.6	17.7	28.4	(NA)
Sweden	39.7	47.0	55.3	55.5	54.8
United Kingdom	11.5	27.9	39.5	43.7	(NA)

NA: Not available
Source: U.S. Bureau of the Census, 2009.

Suicide Rates in the United States (Chapters 17, 25)

These are the rates per 100,000. When there is no bar for a given age group, that means there are too few suicides in that age group to calculate an accurate rate. Overall, the highest rates are among older European American men.

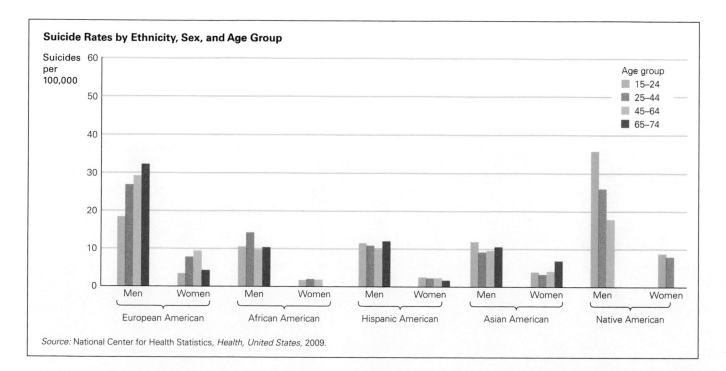

Suicide Rates by Ethnicity, Sex, and Age Group

Source: National Center for Health Statistics, *Health, United States*, 2009.

Education Affects Income (Chapter 18)

Although there is some debate about the cognitive benefits of college education, there is no doubt about the financial benefits. No matter what a person's ethnicity or gender is, an associate's degree more than doubles his or her income compared to that of someone who has not completed high school. These data are for the United States; similar trends, often with steeper increases, are found in other nations.

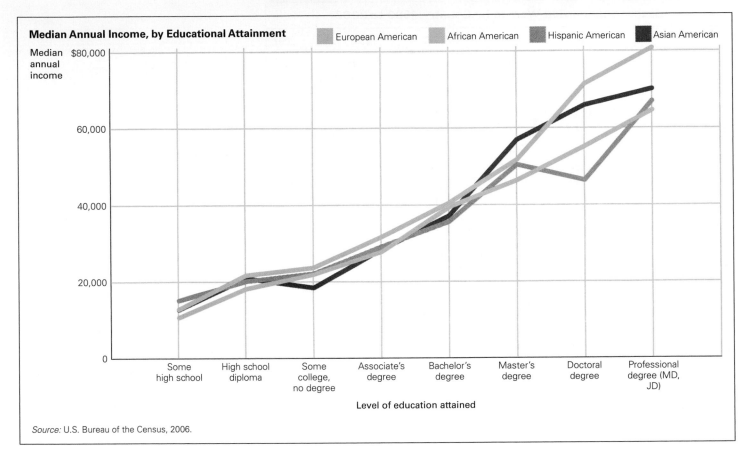

Median Annual Income, by Educational Attainment ▪ European American ▪ African American ▪ Hispanic American ▪ Asian American

Source: U.S. Bureau of the Census, 2006.

Obesity in the United States, 1976 to 2006 (Chapter 20)

About a third of all adults in the United States have a BMI of 30 or higher, which is not just overweight but seriously too heavy. Other data show that another third are overweight (not yet obese), again with increases over the past decades.

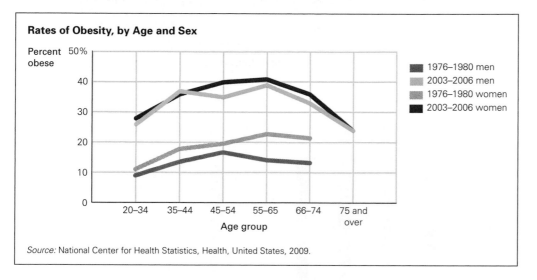

Rates of Obesity, by Age and Sex

Legend:
- 1976–1980 men
- 2003–2006 men
- 1976–1980 women
- 2003–2006 women

Source: National Center for Health Statistics, Health, United States, 2009.

Dying of Lung Cancer: It's Not Just Genes and Gender (Chapter 20)

For lung cancer as well as most other diseases, the male death rate is markedly higher than the female death rate in the United States. Moreover, the death rate for African Americans is almost twice the average, and for Asian Americans it is almost half the average. Genes and gender do not explain these discrepancies, however. As you can see, European American women are at greater risk than Hispanic or Native American men, and the rate for African American men went down as the rate for some other groups rose. (These are "age-adjusted" rates, which means that they reflect the fact that more Asians reach old age and fewer Native Americans do. In other words, the sex and ethnic differences shown here are real—not artifacts of the age distribution.)

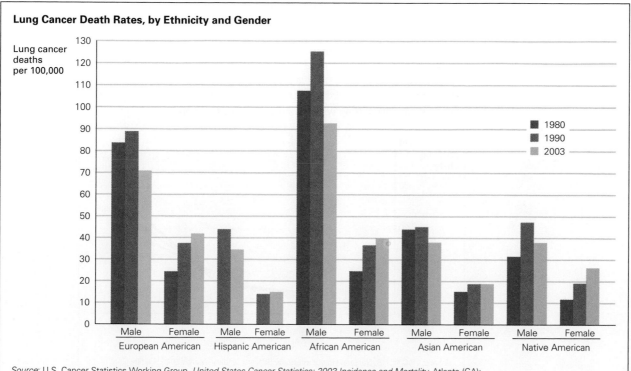

Lung Cancer Death Rates, by Ethnicity and Gender

Legend:
- 1980
- 1990
- 2003

Source: U.S. Cancer Statistics Working Group. *United States Cancer Statistics: 2003 Incidence and Mortality.* Atlanta (GA): Department of Health and Human Services, Centers for Disease Control and Prevention, and National Cancer Institute; 2007.

Grandparents Parenting Grandchildren (Chapters 22, 25)

In 2009, 3.8% of U.S. households included grandparents living with grandchildren. In 40 percent of those households, 2.69 million grandparents were directly responsible for the care of their grandchildren.

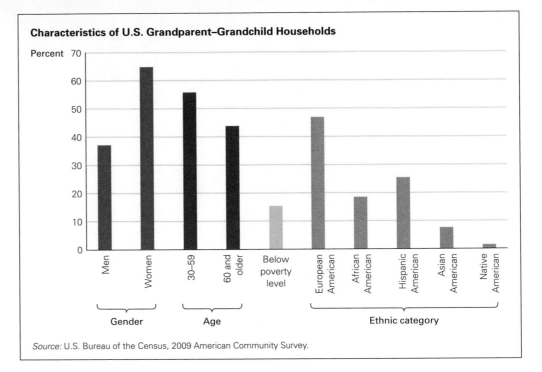

Characteristics of U.S. Grandparent–Grandchild Households

Source: U.S. Bureau of the Census, 2009 American Community Survey.

Trouble with Personal Care (Chapters 23, 25)

As you see, with age people are more likely to need help with daily activities, such as taking a shower, getting dressed, and even getting out of bed. What is not shown is who provides that help. Usually it is a husband or wife, sometimes a grown child (who often is elderly), and, only for the oldest and least capable, the aides in a nursing home.

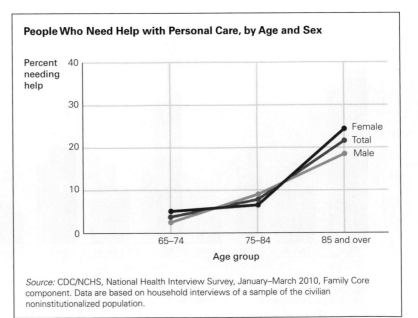

People Who Need Help with Personal Care, by Age and Sex

Source: CDC/NCHS, National Health Interview Survey, January–March 2010, Family Core component. Data are based on household interviews of a sample of the civilian noninstitutionalized population.

Dementia Around the World (Chapter 24)

More than 24 million of the 6 billion people worldwide have been diagnosed with Alzheimer's disease. This number is expected to double by 2020, since one of the major risk factors is advanced age. That also is the main reason rates are lower in nations with poor medical care—most people with health problems die and fewer are diagnosed. At the moment, 60 percent of people with Alzheimer's disease live in developing countries, making it a "disease of affluence."

Region	Percentage of population over 60 with dementia, 2001
Africa	1.6
India and South Asia	1.9
Indonesia, Sri Lanka, and Thailand	2.7
Middle East and North Africa	3.6
Developing western Pacific countries (including China, Korea, Vietnam)	4.0
Developed countries in the western Pacific (including Japan, Australia, New Zealand)	4.3
Europe	4.36
Latin America	4.6
North America	6.4

Source: C. P. Ferri et al. (2005). Global prevalence of dementia: A Delphi consensus study. *The Lancet, 366:* 2112–2117. Adapted from Table 2.

The Human Brain

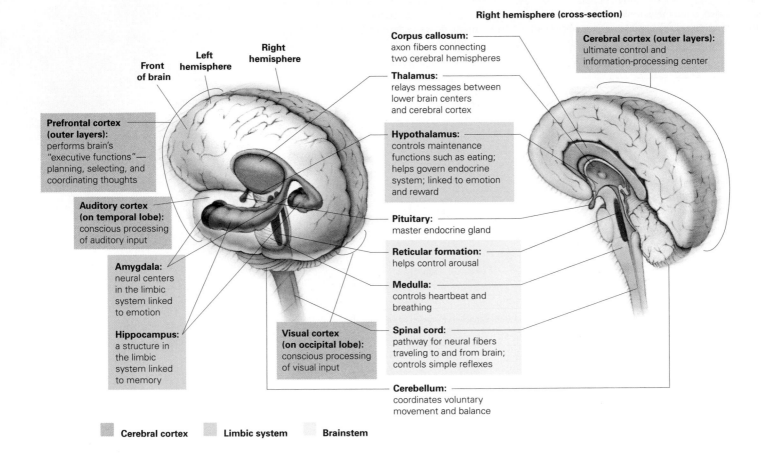

Right hemisphere (cross-section)

Left hemisphere

Right hemisphere

Front of brain

Corpus callosum: axon fibers connecting two cerebral hemispheres

Thalamus: relays messages between lower brain centers and cerebral cortex

Cerebral cortex (outer layers): ultimate control and information-processing center

Prefrontal cortex (outer layers): performs brain's "executive functions"—planning, selecting, and coordinating thoughts

Auditory cortex (on temporal lobe): conscious processing of auditory input

Amygdala: neural centers in the limbic system linked to emotion

Hippocampus: a structure in the limbic system linked to memory

Hypothalamus: controls maintenance functions such as eating; helps govern endocrine system; linked to emotion and reward

Pituitary: master endocrine gland

Reticular formation: helps control arousal

Medulla: controls heartbeat and breathing

Visual cortex (on occipital lobe): conscious processing of visual input

Spinal cord: pathway for neural fibers traveling to and from brain; controls simple reflexes

Cerebellum: coordinates voluntary movement and balance

Cerebral cortex   Limbic system   Brainstem

Appendix B
More About
Research Methods

This appendix explains how to learn about any topic. It is crucial that you distinguish valid conclusions from wishful thinking. Such learning begins with your personal experience.

>> Make It Personal

Think about your life, observe your behavior, and watch the people around you. Pay careful attention to details of expression, emotion, and behavior. The more you see, the more fascinated, curious, and reflective you will become. Ask questions and listen carefully and respectfully to what other people say regarding development.

Whenever you ask specific questions as part of an assignment, **remember that observing ethical standards (see Chapter 1) comes first.** *Before* you interview anyone, inform the person of your purpose and assure him or her of confidentiality. Promise not to identify the person in your report (use a pseudonym) and do not repeat any personal details that emerge in the interview to anyone (friends or strangers). Your instructor will provide further ethical guidance. If you might publish what you've learned, get in touch with your college's Institutional Research Board (IRB).

>> Read the Research

No matter how deeply you think about your own experiences, and no matter how intently you listen to others whose background is unlike yours, you also need to read scholarly published work in order to fully understand any topic that interests you. Be skeptical about magazine or newspaper reports; some are bound to be simplified, exaggerated, or biased.

Professional Journals and Books

Part of the process of science is that conclusions are not considered solid until they are corroborated in many studies, which means that you should consult several sources on any topic. Four **journals in human development** are:

- *Developmental Psychology* (published by the American Psychological Association)
- *Child Development* (Society for Research in Child Development)
- *Developmental Review* (Elsevier)
- *Human Development* (Karger)

These journals differ in the types of articles and studies they publish, but all are well respected and *peer-reviewed,* which means that other scholars review each article submitted and recommend that it be accepted, rejected, or revised. Every article includes references to other recent work.

Beyond these four are literally thousands of other professional journals, each with a particular perspective or topic. To judge them, look for journals that are peer-reviewed. Also consider the following details: the background of the author (research funded by corporations tends to favor their products); the nature of the publisher (professional organizations, as in the first two journals above, protect their reputations); how long the journal has been published (the volume number tells you that). Some interesting work does not meet these criteria, but these are guides to quality.

Many **books** cover some aspect of development. Single-author books are likely to present only one viewpoint. That view may be insightful, but it is limited. You might consult a *handbook,* which is a book that includes many authors and many topics. Two good handbooks in development, both now in their sixth editions (a sign that past scholars have found them useful) are:

- *Handbook of Child Psychology* (2006, Damon & Lerner, eds.), four volumes, published by Wiley
- *Handbook of Aging* (2011), three volumes (biology, psychology, and social sciences), published by Academic Press

Again, dozens of good handbooks are available, many of which focus on a particular age or topic.

The Internet

The **Internet** is a mixed blessing, useful to every novice and experienced researcher but dangerous as well. Every library worldwide and most homes in North America, western Europe, and East Asia have computers that provide access to journals and other information. Ask for help from the librarians; many are highly skilled. In addition, other students, friends, and even strangers can be helpful.

Virtually everything is on the Internet, not only massive national and international statistics but also very personal accounts. Photos, charts, quizzes, ongoing experiments, newspapers from around the world, videos, and much more are available at the click of a mouse. Every journal has a Web site, with tables of contents, abstracts, and sometimes full texts (an abstract gives the key findings; for the full text, you may need to consult the library's copy of the print version).

Unfortunately, you can spend many frustrating hours sifting through information that is useless, trash, or tangential. *Directories* (which list general topics or areas and then move you step by step in the direction you choose) and *search engines* (which give you all the sites that use a particular word or words) can help you select appropriate information. Each directory or search engine provides somewhat different lists; none provides only the most comprehensive and accurate sites. With experience and help, you will find the best sites for you, but you will also encounter some junk no matter how experienced you are.

Anybody can put anything on the Web, regardless of its truth or fairness, so evaluate with a very critical eye everything you find. Make sure you have several divergent sources for every "fact" you find; consider who provided the information and why. Every controversial issue has sites that forcefully advocate opposite viewpoints, sometimes with biased statistics and narrow perspectives.

Here are seven Internet sites that are quite reliable:

- *www.worthpublishers.com/berger* Includes links to Web sites, quizzes, PowerPoint slides, and activities keyed to every chapter of the textbook.
- *embryo.soad.umich.edu* The Multidimensional Human Embryo. Presents MRI images of a human embryo at various stages of development, accompanied by brief explanations.

- *www.cdipage.com* Child Development Institute. A useful site, with links and articles on child development and information on common childhood psychological disorders.
- *ericeece.org* ERIC Clearinghouse. Provides links to many education-related sites and includes brief descriptions of each.
- *site.educ.indiana.edu/cafs* Adolescence Directory online (ADOL) is an electronic guide to information on adolescent issues. It is a service of the Center for Adolescent and Family Studies at Indiana University.
- *www.nih.gov.nia/* National Institute on Aging. Includes information about current research on aging.
- *www.cdc.gov/nchs/hus.htm* The National Center for Health Statistics issues an annual report on health trends, called *Health, United States.*

Every source—you, your interviewees, journals, books, and the Internet—is helpful. Do not depend on any particular one. Especially if you use the Web, also check print resources. Avoid plagiarism and prejudice by citing every source and noting objectivity, validity, and credibility. Your own analysis, opinions, words, and conclusions are crucial.

>> Additional Terms and Concepts

As emphasized throughout this text, the study of development is a science. Social scientists spend years in graduate school, studying methods and statistics. Chapter 1 touches on some of these matters (observation and experiments; correlation and statistical significance; independent and dependent variables; experimental and control groups; cross-sectional, longitudinal, and cross-sequential research), but there is much more. A few additional aspects of research are presented here, to help you evaluate research wherever you find it.

Who Participates?

The entire group of people about whom a scientist wants to learn is called the **population.** Generally, a research population is quite large—not usually the world's entire population of almost 8 billion, but perhaps all the 4 million babies born in the United States last year, or all the 25 million Japanese currently over age 65.

The particular individuals who are studied in a specific research project are called the **participants.** They are used as a **sample** of the larger group. Ideally, a large number of people are used as a **representative sample,** that is, a sample who reflect the entire population. Every peer-reviewed published study reports details on the sample.

Selection of the sample is crucial. Volunteers, or people with telephones, or people treated with some particular condition, are not a *random sample,* in which everyone in that population is equally likely to be selected. To avoid *selection bias,* some studies are *prospective,* beginning with an entire cluster (for instance, every baby born on a particular day) and then tracing the development of some particular characteristic.

For example, prospective studies find the antecedents of heart disease, or child abuse, or high school dropout rates—all of which are much harder to find if the study is *retrospective,* beginning with those who had heart attacks, experienced abuse, or left school. Thus, although retrospective research finds that most high school dropouts say they disliked school, prospective research finds that some who like school still decide to drop out and then later say they hated school, while others dislike school but stay to graduate. Prospective research discovers how many students are in these last two categories; retrospective research on people who have already dropped out does not.

population The entire group of individuals who are of particular concern in a scientific study, such as all the children of the world or all newborns who weigh less than 3 pounds.

participants The people who are studied in a research project.

sample A group of individuals drawn from a specified population. A sample might be the low-birthweight babies born in four particular hospitals that are representative of all hospitals.

representative sample A group of research participants who reflect the relevant characteristics of the larger population whose attributes are under study.

Research Design

Every researcher begins not only by formulating a hypothesis but also by learning what other scientists have discovered about the topic in question and what methods might be useful and ethical in designing research. Often they include measures to guard against inadvertently finding only the results they expect. For example, the people who actually gather the data may not know the purpose of the research. Scientists say that these data gatherers are **blind** to the hypothesized outcome. Participants are sometimes "blind" as well, because otherwise they might, for instance, respond the way they think they should.

Another crucial aspect of research design is to define exactly what is to be studied. Researchers establish an **operational definition** of whatever phenomenon they will be examining, defining each variable by describing specific, observable behavior. This is essential in quantitative research (see Chapter 1), but it is also useful in qualitative research. For example, if a researcher wants to know when babies begin to walk, does *walking* include steps taken while holding on? Is one unsteady step enough? Some parents say yes, but the usual operational definition of walking is "takes at least three steps without holding on." This operational definition allows comparisons worldwide, making it possible to discover, for example, that well-fed African babies tend to walk earlier than well-fed European babies.

Operational definitions are difficult but essential when personality traits are studied. How should *aggression* or *sharing* or *shyness* be defined? Lack of an operational definition leads to contradictory results. For instance, some say that infant day care makes children more aggressive, but others say it makes them less passive. Similarly, as explained in the Epilogue, the operational definition of death is the subject of heated disputes. For any scientist, operational definitions are crucial.

Reporting Results

You already know that results should be reported in sufficient detail so that another scientist can analyze the conclusions and replicate the research. Various methods, populations, and research designs may produce divergent conclusions. For that reason, handbooks, some journals, and some articles are called *reviews*: They summarize past research. Often, when studies are similar in operational definitions and methods, the review is a **meta-analysis,** combining the findings of many studies to present an overall conclusion.

Table 1.3 describes some statistical measures. One of them is *statistical significance,* which indicates whether or not a particular result could have occurred by chance.

Another statistic that is often crucial is **effect size,** a way of measuring how much impact one variable has on another. Effect size ranges from 0 (no effect) to 1 (total transformation, never found in actual studies). Effect size may be particularly important when the sample size is large, because a large sample often leads to highly "significant" results (unlikely to have occurred by chance) that have only a tiny effect on the variable of interest.

Hundreds of statistical measures are used by developmentalists. Often the same data can be presented in many ways: Some scientists examine statistical analysis intently before they accept conclusions as valid. A specific example involved methods to improve students' writing ability between grades 4 and 12. A meta-analysis found that many methods of writing instruction have a significant impact, but effect size is much larger for some methods (teaching strategies and summarizing) than for others (prewriting exercises and studying models). For teachers, this statistic is crucial, for they want to know what has a big effect, not merely what is better than chance (significant).

---

blind The condition of data gatherers (and sometimes participants as well) who are deliberately kept ignorant of the purpose of the research so that they cannot unintentionally bias the results.

operational definition A description of the specific, observable behavior that will constitute the variable that is to be studied, so that any reader will know whether that behavior occurred or not. Operational definitions may be arbitrary (e.g., an IQ score at or above 130 is operationally defined as "gifted"), but they must be precise.

meta-analysis A technique of combining results of many studies to come to an overall conclusion. Meta-analysis is powerful, in that small samples can be added together to lead to significant conclusions, although variations from study to study sometimes make combining them impossible.

effect size A way to indicate, statistically, how much of an impact the independent variable had on the dependent variable.

Numerous articles published in the past decade are meta-analyses that combine similar studies to search for general trends. Often effect sizes are also reported, which is especially helpful for meta-analysis since standard calculations almost always find some significance if the number of participants is in the thousands. Here are three recent examples, to help you grasp the use and implications of meta-analyses and effect size.

- **Twenge, Jean M., Gentile, Brittany, DeWall, C. Nathan, Ma, Debbie, Lacefield, Katharine, & Schurtz, David R.** (2010). Birth cohort increases in psychopathology among young Americans, 1938–2007: A cross-temporal meta-analysis of the MMPI. *Clinical Psychology Review, 30,* 145–154. [Using responses to the Minnesota Multiphasic Personality Inventory (the MMPI, an old chestnut, originally developed to spot psychopathology), this meta-analysis finds increasing prevalence of psychological disorders among adolescents and emerging adults in the United States. The reported effect size is large, 1.05. The authors hypothesize that contemporary culture is too materialistic and selfish, leading youth to ignore the deeper meaning of life. Note, however, that impressive statistics, as shown here, do not prove or disprove a causal explanation.]

- **Grote, Nancy K., Bridge, Jeffrey A., Gavin, Amelia R., Melville, Jennifer L., Iyengar, Satish, & Katon, Wayne J.** (2010). A meta-analysis of depression during pregnancy and the risk of preterm birth, low birthweight, and intrauterine growth restriction. *Archives of General Psychiatry, 67,* 1012–1024. [This meta-analysis confirms that pregnant women who are depressed are more likely to have low-birthweight newborns. The article also shows one of the benefits of meta analysis—the possibility of comparing people in different contexts on the same variables. In this case, depressed women in less developed nations were more at risk, and, within the United States, maternal depression has a more marked effect on low-income women. This meta-analysis makes a very convincing case that maternal mood and fetal growth are connected. Of course, additional variables may cause both the depression and the prenatal complications.]

- **Webb, Thomas L., Joseph, Judith, Yardley, Lucy, & Michie, Susan.** (2010). Using the internet to promote health behavior change: A systematic review and meta-analysis of the impact of theoretical basis, use of behavior change techniques, and mode of delivery on efficacy. *Journal of Medical Internet Research, 12,* e4. [The conclusion this article makes is not surprising: Messages sent via the Internet and texting can effectively promote health. Again, however, the advantages of meta-analyses are notable. In this study, the effect size of electronic messages on health was very small (d = 0.16). Such small effects might be ignored in studies with fewer participants, but a meta-analytic study can find them, with useful implications. For instance, if texting health messages annually saves only one life in 100,000, and if cost-benefit analysis finds no negative effects, then universal health texting in the United States would save 3,000 lives per year.]

Glossary

23rd pair The chromosome pair that, in humans, determines sex. The other 22 pairs are autosomes; inherited equally by males and females.

A

AARP A U.S. organization of people aged 50 and older that advocates for the elderly. It was originally called the American Association of Retired Persons, but now only the initials AARP are used, since members need not be retired.

absent grief A situation in which mourners do not grieve, either because other people do not allow grief to be expressed or because the mourners do not allow themselves to feel sadness.

accommodation The restructuring of old ideas to include new experiences.

achievement test A measure of mastery or proficiency in reading, mathematics, writing, science, or some other subject.

active euthanasia A situation in which someone takes action to bring about another person's death, with the intention of ending that person's suffering.

activities of daily life (ADLs) Typically identified as five tasks of self-care that are important to independent living: eating, bathing, toileting, dressing, and transferring from a bed to a chair. The inability to perform any of these tasks is a sign of frailty.

activity theory The view that elderly people want and need to remain active in a variety of social spheres—with relatives, friends, and community groups—and become withdrawn only unwillingly, as a result of ageism.

adolescence-limited offender A person whose criminal activity stops by age 21.

adolescent egocentrism A characteristic of adolescent thinking that leads young people (ages 10 to 13) to focus on themselves to the exclusion of others.

adoption A legal proceeding in which an adult or couple unrelated to a child is granted the joys and obligations of being that child's parent(s).

adrenal glands Two glands, located above the kidneys, that produce hormones (including the "stress hormones" epinephrine [adrenaline] and norepinephrine).

affordance An opportunity for perception and interaction that is offered by a person, place, or object in the environment.

age of viability The age (about 22 weeks after conception) at which a fetus may survive outside the mother's uterus if specialized medical care is available.

ageism A prejudice whereby people are categorized and judged solely on the basis of their chronological age.

aggressive-rejected Rejected by peers because of antagonistic, confrontational behavior.

aging in place Remaining in the same home and community in later life, adjusting but not leaving when health fades.

allele A variation that makes a gene different in some way from other genes for the same characteristics. Many genes never vary; others have several possible alleles.

allostatic load The total, combined burden of physiological stresses (such as high blood pressure) that an individual lives with. A high allostatic load increases the risk of disease.

Alzheimer disease (AD) The most common cause of dementia, characterized by gradual deterioration of memory and personality and marked by the formation of plaques of beta-amyloid protein and tangles of tau in the brain. (Sometimes called *senile dementia of the Alzheimer type.*)

amygdala A tiny brain structure that registers emotions, particularly fear and anxiety.

analytic intelligence A form of intelligence that involves such mental processes as abstract planning, strategy selection, focused attention, and information processing, as well as verbal and logical skills.

analytic thought Thought that results from analysis, such as a systematic ranking of pros and cons, risks and consequences, possibilities and facts. Analytic thought depends on logic and rationality.

andropause A term coined to signify a drop in testosterone levels in older men, which normally results in reduced sexual desire, erections, and muscle mass. (Also called *male menopause.*)

animism The belief that natural objects and phenomena are alive.

anorexia nervosa An eating disorder characterized by self-starvation. Affected individuals voluntarily undereat and often overexercise, depriving their vital organs of nutrition. Anorexia can be fatal.

anoxia A lack of oxygen that, if prolonged, can cause brain damage or death.

antioxidants Chemical compounds that nullify the effects of oxygen free radicals by forming a bond with their unattached oxygen electron.

antipathy Feelings of dislike or even hatred for another person.

antisocial behavior Feelings and actions that are deliberately hurtful or destructive to another person.

antithesis A proposition or statement of belief that opposes the thesis; the second stage of the process of dialectical thinking.

Apgar scale A quick assessment of a newborn's health. The baby's color, heart rate, reflexes, muscle tone, and respiratory effort are given a score of 0, 1, or 2 twice—at one minute and five minutes after birth—and each time the total of all five scores is compared with the maximum score of 10 (rarely attained).

apprenticeship in thinking Vygotsky's term for how cognition is stimulated and developed in people by older and more skilled members of society.

aptitude The potential to master a specific skill or to learn a certain body of knowledge.

assimilation The reinterpretation of new experiences to fit into old ideas.

assisted living A living arrangement for elderly people that combines privacy and independence with medical supervision.

assisted reproductive technology (ART) A general term for the techniques designed to help infertile couples conceive and then sustain a pregnancy.

asthma A chronic disease of the respiratory system in which inflammation narrows the airways from the nose and mouth to the lungs, causing difficulty in breathing. Signs and symptoms include wheezing, shortness of breath, chest tightness, and coughing.

attachment According to Ainsworth, an affectional tie that an infant forms with a caregiver—a tie that binds them together in space and endures over time.

attention-deficit/hyperactivity disorder (ADHD) A condition in which a person not only has great difficulty concentrating for more than a few moments but also is inattentive, impulsive, and overactive.

authoritarian parenting An approach to child rearing that is characterized by high behavioral standards, strict punishment of misconduct, and little communication.

authoritative parenting An approach to child rearing in which the parents set limits but listen to the child and are flexible.

autism A developmental disorder marked by an inability to relate to other people normally, extreme self-absorption, and an inability to acquire normal speech.

autistic spectrum disorder Any of several disorders characterized by inadequate social skills, impaired communication, and unusual play.

automatic processing Thinking that occurs without deliberate, conscious thought. Experts process most tasks automatically, saving conscious thought for unfamiliar challenges.

automatization A process in which repetition of a sequence of thoughts and actions makes the sequence routine, so that it no longer requires conscious thought.

autonomy versus shame and doubt Erikson's second crisis of psychosocial development. Toddlers either succeed or fail in gaining a sense of self-rule over their own actions and bodies.

average life expectancy The number of years the average newborn in a particular population group is likely to live.

axon A fiber that extends from a neuron and transmits electrochemical impulses from that neuron to the dendrites of other neurons.

B

B cells Immune cells manufactured in the bone marrow that create antibodies for isolating and destroying bacteria and viruses that invade the body.

babbling The extended repetition of certain syllables, such as *ba-ba-ba*, that begins when babies are between 6 and 9 months old.

balanced bilingual A person who is fluent in two languages, not favoring one over the other.

base rate neglect A common fallacy in which a person ignores the overall frequency of some behavior or characteristic (called the *base rate*) in making a decision. For example, a person might bet on a "lucky" lottery number without considering the odds that that number will be selected.

behavioral teratogens Agents and conditions that can harm the prenatal brain, impairing the future child's intellectual and emotional functioning.

behaviorism A grand theory of human development that studies observable behavior. Behaviorism is also called *learning theory* because it describes the laws and processes by which behavior is learned.

bereavement The complicated and multifaceted feelings of loss following a death.

beta-amyloid A protein that makes up the plaques that are found in the tissues surrounding neurons.

bickering Petty, peevish arguing, usually repeated and ongoing.

Big Five The five basic clusters of personality traits that remain quite stable throughout adulthood: openness, conscientiousness, extroversion, agreeableness, and neuroticism.

bilingual schooling A strategy in which school subjects are taught in both the learner's original language and the second (majority) language.

binocular vision The ability to focus the two eyes in a coordinated manner in order to see one image. This ability is absent at birth.

bipolar disorder A condition characterized by extreme mood swings, from euphoria to deep depression, not caused by outside experiences.

BMI (body mass index) A person's weight in kilograms divided by the square of height in meters.

body image A person's idea of how his or her body looks.

body mass index (BMI) The ratio of a person's weight in kilograms divided by his or her height in meters squared.

Brazelton Neonatal Behavioral Assessment Scale (NBAS) A test often administered to newborns that measures responsiveness and records 46 behaviors, including 20 reflexes.

bulimia nervosa An eating disorder characterized by binge eating and subsequent purging, usually by induced vomiting and/or use of laxatives.

bully-victim Someone who attacks others and who is attacked as well. (Also called *provocative victims* because they do things that elicit bullying, such as stealing a bully's pencil.)

bullying Repeated, systematic efforts to inflict harm through physical, verbal, or social attack on a weaker person.

bullying aggression Unprovoked, repeated physical or verbal attack, especially on victims who are unlikely to defend themselves.

C

calorie restriction The practice of limiting dietary energy intake (while consuming sufficient quantities of vitamins, minerals, and other important nutrients) for the purpose of improving health and slowing down the aging process.

cardiovascular disease Disease that involves the heart and the circulatory system.

carrier A person whose genotype includes a gene that is not expressed in the phenotype. Such an unexpressed gene occurs in half of the carrier's gametes and thus is passed on to half of the carrier's children, who will most likely be carriers, too. Generally, only when such a gene is inherited from both parents does the characteristic appear in the phenotype.

centenarian A person who has lived 100 years or more.

center day care Child care that occurs in a place especially designed for the purpose, where several paid adults care for many children. Usually, the children are grouped by age, the day-care center is licensed, and providers are trained and certified in child development.

centration A characteristic of preoperational thought in which a young child focuses (centers) on one idea, excluding all others.

cerebral palsy A disorder that results from damage to the brain's motor centers. People with cerebral palsy have difficulty with muscle control, so their speech and/or body movements are impaired.

cesarean section (c-section) A surgical birth, in which incisions through the mother's abdomen and uterus allow the fetus to be removed quickly, instead of being delivered through the vagina. (Also called simply *section*.)

charter school A public school with its own set of standards that is funded and licensed by the state or local district in which it is located.

child abuse Deliberate action that is harmful to a child's physical, emotional, or sexual well-being.

child maltreatment Intentional harm to or avoidable endangerment of anyone under 18 years of age.

child neglect Failure to meet a child's basic physical, educational, or emotional needs.

child sexual abuse Any erotic activity that arouses an adult and excites, shames, or confuses a child, whether or not the victim protests and whether or not genital contact is involved.

child-directed speech The high-pitched, simplified, and repetitive way adults speak to infants. (Also called *baby talk* or *motherese*.)

choice overload Having so many possibilities that a thoughtful choice becomes difficult. This is particularly apparent when social networking and other technology make many potential romantic partners available.

chromosome One of the 46 molecules of DNA (in 23 pairs) that virtually each cell of the human body contains and that, together, contain all the genes. Other species have more or fewer chromosomes.

classical conditioning The learning process in which a meaningful stimulus (such as the smell of food to a hungry animal) is connected with a neutral stimulus (such as the sound of a tone) that had no special meaning before conditioning. (Also called *respondent conditioning*.)

classification The logical principle that things can be organized into groups (or categories or classes) according to some characteristic they have in common.

clinical depression Feelings of hopelessness, lethargy, and worthlessness that last two weeks or more.

clique A group of adolescents made up of close friends who are loyal to one another while excluding outsiders.

cluster suicides Several suicides committed by members of a group within a brief period of time.

co-sleeping A custom in which parents and their children (usually infants) sleep together in the same room.

code of ethics A set of moral principles that members of a profession or group are expected to follow.

cognitive equilibrium In cognitive theory, a state of mental balance in which people are not confused because they can use their existing thought processes to understand current experiences and ideas.

cognitive theory A grand theory of human development that focuses on changes in how people think over time. According to this theory, our thoughts shape our attitudes, beliefs, and behaviors.

cohabitation An arrangement in which a couple live together in a committed romantic relationship but are not formally married.

cohort A group defined by the shared age of its members. Each cohort was born at about the same time and moves through life together, experiencing the same historical events and cultural shifts.

comorbid Refers to the presence of two or more unrelated disease conditions at the same time in the same person.

complicated grief A type of grief that impedes a person's future life, usually because the person clings to sorrow or is buffeted by contradictory emotions.

compression of morbidity A shortening of the time a person spends ill or infirm, accomplished by postponing illness.

compulsive hoarding The urge to accumulate and hold on to familiar objects and possessions, sometimes to the point of their becoming health and/or safety hazards. This impulse tends to increase with age.

concrete operational thought Piaget's term for the ability to reason logically about direct experiences and perceptions.

conditioning According to behaviorism, the processes by which responses become linked to particular stimuli and learning takes place. The word *conditioning* is used to emphasize the importance of repeated practice, as when an athlete conditions his or her body to perform well by training for a long time.

consequential strangers People who are not in a person's closest friendship circle convoy but nonetheless have an impact.

conservation The principle that the amount of a substance remains the same (i.e., is conserved) even when its appearance changes.

control processes The part of the information-processing system that regulates the analysis and flow of information. Memory and retrieval strategies, selective attention, and rules or strategies for problem solving are all useful control processes. Also called *executive processes*.)

conventional moral reasoning Kohlberg's second level of moral reasoning, emphasizing social rules.

corpus callosum A long, thick band of nerve fibers that connects the left and right hemispheres of the brain and allows communication between them.

correlation A number between +1.0 and −1.0 that indicates the degree of relationship between two variables, expressed in terms of the likelihood that one variable will (or will not) occur when the other variable does (or does not). A correlation indicates only that two variables are related, not that one variable causes the other to occur.

cortex The outer layers of the brain in humans and other mammals. Most thinking, feeling, and sensing involve the cortex. (Sometimes called the *neocortex*.)

couvade Symptoms of pregnancy and birth experienced by fathers.

creative intelligence A form of intelligence that involves the capacity to be intellectually flexible and innovative.

critical period A time when a particular type of developmental growth (in body or behavior) must happen if it is ever going to happen.

cross-sectional research A research design that compares groups of people who differ in age but are similar in other important characteristics.

cross-sequential research A hybrid research design in which researchers first study several groups of people of different ages (a cross-sectional approach) and then follow those groups over the years (a longitudinal approach). (Also called *cohort-sequential research* or *time-sequential research*.)

crowd A larger group of adolescents who have something in common but who are not necessarily friends.

crystallized intelligence Those types of intellectual ability that reflect accumulated learning. Vocabulary and general information are examples. Some developmental psychologists think crystallized intelligence increases with age, while fluid intelligence declines.

culture of children The particular habits, styles, and values that reflect the set of rules and rituals that characterize children as distinct from adult society.

cutting An addictive form of self-mutilation that is most prevalent among adolescent girls and that correlates with depression and drug abuse.

cyberbullying Bullying that occurs when one person spreads insults or rumors about another by means of e-mails, text messages, or cell phone videos.

D

DALYs (disability-adjusted life years) A measure of the reduced quality of life caused by disability.

deductive reasoning Reasoning from a general statement, premise, or principle, through logical steps, to figure out (deduce) specifics. (Also called *top-down reasoning*.)

deferred imitation A sequence in which an infant first perceives something that someone else does and then performs the same action a few hours or even days later.

Defining Issues Test (DIT) A series of questions developed by James Rest and designed to assess respondents' level of moral development by having them rank possible solutions to moral dilemmas.

delay discounting The tendency to undervalue, or downright ignore, future consequences and rewards in favor of more immediate gratification.

delirium A temporary loss of memory, often accompanied by hallucinations, terror, grandiosity, and irrational behavior.

demand/withdraw interaction A situation in a romantic relationship wherein one partner wants to address an issue and the other refuses, resulting in opposite reactions—one insistent on talk while the other cuts short the conversation.

dementia Irreversible loss of intellectual functioning caused by organic brain damage or disease. Dementia becomes more common with age, but it is abnormal and pathological even in the very old.

demographic shift A shift in the proportions of the populations of various ages.

dendrite A fiber that extends from a neuron and receives electrochemical impulses transmitted from other neurons via their axons.

deoxyribonucleic acid (DNA) The chemical composition of the molecules that contain the genes, which are the chemical instructions for cells to manufacture various proteins.

dependent variable In an experiment, the variable that may change as a result of whatever new condition or situation the experimenter adds. In other words, the dependent variable depends on the independent variable.

developmental psychopathology The field that uses insights into typical development to understand and remediate developmental disorders, and vice versa.

developmental theory A group of ideas, assumptions, and generalizations that interpret and illuminate the thousands of observations that have been made about human growth. A developmental theory provides a framework for explaining the patterns and problems of development.

deviancy training Destructive peer support in which one person shows another how to rebel against authority or social norms.

dialectical thought The most advanced cognitive process, characterized by the ability to consider a thesis and its antithesis simultaneously and thus to arrive at a synthesis. Dialectical thought makes possible an ongoing awareness of pros and cons, advantages and disadvantages, possibilities and limitations.

diathesis–stress model The view that psychological disorders, such as schizophrenia, are produced by the interaction of a genetic vulnerability (the diathesis) and stressful environmental factors and life events.

disability Difficulty in performing normal activities of daily life because of some physical, mental, or emotional condition.

disenfranchised grief A situation in which certain people, although they are bereaved, are prevented from mourning publicly by cultural customs or social restrictions.

disengagement theory The view that aging makes a person's social sphere increasingly narrow, resulting in role relinquishment, withdrawal, and passivity.

disorganized attachment (type D) A type of attachment that is marked by an infant's inconsistent reactions to the caregiver's departure and return.

distal parenting Caregiving practices that involve remaining distant from a baby, providing toys, food, and face-to-face communication with minimal holding and touching.

dizygotic (DZ) twins Twins who are formed when two separate ova are fertilized by two separate sperm at roughly the same time. (Also called *fraternal twins*.)

DNR (do not resuscitate) A written order from a physician (sometimes initiated by a patient's advance directive or by a health care proxy's request) that no attempt should be made to revive a patient if he or she suffers cardiac or respiratory arrest.

dominant–recessive pattern The interaction of a heterozygous pair of alleles in such a way that the phenotype reveals the influence of one allele (the dominant gene) more than that of the other (the recessive gene).

double effect A situation in which an action (such as administering opiates) has both a positive effect (relieving a terminally ill person's pain) and a negative effect (hastening death by suppressing respiration).

doula A woman who helps with the birth process. Traditionally in Latin America, a doula was the only professional who attended childbirth. Now doulas are likely to arrive at the woman's home during early labor and later work alongside a hospital's staff.

Down syndrome A condition in which a person has 47 chromosomes instead of the usual 46, with 3 rather than 2 chromosomes at the 21st site. People with Down syndrome typically have distinctive characteristics, including unusual facial features, heart abnormalities, and language difficulties. (Also called *trisomy-21*.)

drug abuse The ingestion of a drug to the extent that it impairs the user's biological or psychological well-being.

drug addiction A condition of drug dependence in which the absence of the given drug in the individual's system produces a drive—physiological, psychological, or both—to ingest more of the drug.

dual-process model The notion that two networks exist within the human brain, one for emotional and one for analytical processing of stimuli.

dynamic perception Perception that is primed to focus on movement and change.

dynamic-systems theory A view of human development as an ongoing, ever-changing interaction between the physical and emotional being and between the person and every aspect of his or her environment, including the family and society.

dyslexia Unusual difficulty with reading; thought to be the result of some neurological underdevelopment.

E

eclectic perspective The approach taken by most developmentalists, in which they apply aspects of each of the various theories of development rather than adhering exclusively to one theory.

ecological niche The particular lifestyle and social context that adults settle into because it is compatible with their individual personality needs and interests.

ecological validity The idea that cognition should be measured in settings that are as realistic as possible and that the abilities measured should be those needed in real life.

ecological-systems approach The view that in the study of human development, the person should be considered in all the contexts and interactions that constitute a life. (Later renamed *bioecological theory.*)

edgework Occupations or recreational activities that involve a degree of risk or danger. The prospect of "living on the edge" makes edgework compelling to some individuals.

effortful control The ability to regulate one's emotions and actions through effort, not simply through natural inclination.

egocentrism Piaget's term for children's tendency to think about the world entirely from their own personal perspective.

elderspeak A condescending way of speaking to older adults that resembles baby talk, with simple and short sentences, exaggerated emphasis, repetition, and a slower rate and a higher pitch than used in normal speech.

Electra complex The unconscious desire of girls to replace their mother and win their father's romantic love.

embryo The name for a developing human organism from about the third through the eighth week after conception.

embryonic period The stage of prenatal development from approximately the third through the eighth week after conception, during which the basic forms of all body structures, including internal organs, develop.

emerging adulthood The period of life between the ages of 18 and 25. Emerging adulthood is now widely thought of as a separate developmental stage.

emotion-focused coping A strategy to deal with stress by changing feelings about the stressor rather than changing the stressor itself.

emotional regulation The ability to control when and how emotions are expressed.

empathy The ability to understand the emotions and concerns of another person, especially when they differ from one's own.

empirical Based on observations, repeated experiences, verifiable experiments; not theoretical.

empty nest The time in the lives of parents when their children have left the family home to pursue their own lives.

epigenetic Referring to environmental factors that affect genes and genetic expression; enhancing, halting, shaping, or altering the expression of genes, resulting in a phenotype that may differ markedly from the genotype.

ESL (English as a second language) An approach to teaching English in which all children who do not speak English are placed together in an intensive course to learn basic English so that they can be educated in the same classroom as native English speakers.

estradiol A sex hormone, considered the chief estrogen. Females produce much more estradiol than males do.

ethnic group People whose ancestors were born in the same region and who often share a language, culture, and religion.

ethnotheory A theory that underlies the values and practices of a culture but is not usually apparent to the people within the culture.

experience-dependent brain functions Brain functions that depend on particular, variable experiences and that therefore may or may not develop in a particular infant.

experience-expectant brain functions Brain functions that require certain basic common experiences (which an infant can be expected to have) in order to develop normally.

experiment A research method in which the researcher tries to determine the cause-and-effect relationship between two variables by manipulating one (called the *independent variable*) and then observing and recording the ensuing changes in the other (called the *dependent variable*).

explicit memory Memory that is easy to retrieve on demand (as in a specific test), usually with words. Most explicit memory involves consciously learned words, data and concepts.

extended family A family of three or more generations living in one household.

externalizing problems Difficulty with emotional regulation that involves expressing powerful feelings through uncontrolled physical or verbal outbursts, as by lashing out at other people or breaking things.

extreme sports Forms of recreation that include apparent risk of injury or death and that are attractive and thrilling as a result. Motocross is one example.

extremely low birthweight (ELBW) A body weight at birth of less than 2 pounds, 3 ounces (1,000 grams).

extrinsic motivation A drive, or reason to pursue a goal, that arises from the need to have one's achievements rewarded from outside, perhaps by receiving material possessions or another person's esteem.

extrinsic rewards of work The tangible benefits, usually in the form of compensation (e.g., salary, health insurance, pension), that one receives for doing a job.

F

familism The belief that family members should support one another, sacrificing individual freedom and success, if necessary, in order to preserve family unity.

family day care Child care that occurs in the home of someone to whom the child is not related and who usually cares for several children of various ages.

family function The way a family works to meet the needs of its members. Children need families to provide basic material necessities, to encourage learning, to help them develop self-respect, to nurture friendships, and to foster harmony and stability.

family structure The legal and genetic relationships among relatives living in the same home; includes nuclear family, extended family, stepfamily, and so on.

fast-mapping The speedy and sometimes imprecise way in which children learn new words by tentatively placing them in mental categories according to their perceived meaning.

fetal alcohol syndrome (FAS) A cluster of birth defects, including abnormal facial characteristics, slow physical growth, and retarded mental development, that may occur in the child of a woman who drinks alcohol while pregnant.

fetal period The stage of prenatal development from the ninth week after conception until birth, during which the fetus gains about 7 pounds (more than 3,000 grams) and organs become more mature, gradually able to function on their own.

fetus The name for a developing human organism from the start of the ninth week after conception until birth.

fictive kin Someone who becomes accepted as part of a family to which he or she has no blood relation.

filial responsibility The obligation of adult children to care for their aging parents.

fine motor skills Physical abilities involving small body movements, especially of the hands and fingers, such as drawing and picking up a coin. (The word *fine* here means "small.")

flextime An arrangement in which work schedules are flexible so that employees can balance personal and occupational responsibilities.

fluid intelligence Those types of basic intelligence that make learning of all sorts quick and thorough. Abilities such as short-term memory, abstract thought, and speed of thinking are all usually considered part of fluid intelligence.

Flynn effect The rise in average IQ scores that has occurred over the decades in many nations.

fMRI Functional magnetic resonance imaging, a measuring technique in which the brain's electrical excitement indicates activation anywhere in the brain; fMRI helps researchers locate neurological responses to stimuli.

focus on appearance A characteristic of preoperational thought in which a young child ignores all attributes that are not apparent.

foreclosure Erikson's term for premature identity formation, which occurs when an adolescent adopts parents' or society's roles and values wholesale, without questioning or analysis.

formal operational thought In Piaget's theory, the fourth and final stage of cognitive development, characterized by more systematic logical thinking and by the ability to understand and systematically manipulate abstract concepts.

foster care A legal, publicly supported system in which a maltreated child is removed from the parents' custody and entrusted to another adult or family, which is reimbursed for expenses incurred in meeting the child's needs.

fragile X syndrome A genetic disorder in which part of the X chromosome seems to be attached to the rest of it by a very thin string of molecules. The cause is a single gene that has more than 200 repetitions of one triplet.

frail elderly People over age 65, and often over age 85, who are physically infirm, very ill, or cognitively disabled.

frontal lobe dementia Deterioration of the amygdala and frontal lobes that may be the cause of 15 percent of all dementias. (Also called *frontotemporal lobar degeneration*.)

G

gamete A reproductive cell; that is, a sperm or ovum that can produce a new individual if it combines with a gamete from the other sex to make a zygote.

gender differences Differences in the roles and behavior of males and females that are prescribed by the culture.

gender identity A person's acceptance of the roles and behaviors that society associates with the biological categories of male and female.

gender schema A cognitive concept or general belief based on one's experiences—in this case, a child's understanding of sex differences.

gene A small section of a chromosome; the basic unit for the transmission of heredity. A gene consists of a string of chemicals that provide instructions for the cell to manufacture certain proteins.

general intelligence (g) The idea of g assumes that intelligence is one basic trait, underlying all cognitive abilities. According to this concept, people have varying levels of this general ability.

generational forgetting The idea that each new generation forgets what the previous generation learned. As used here, the term refers to knowledge about the harm drugs can do.

genetic clock A purported mechanism in the DNA of cells that regulates the aging process by triggering hormonal changes and controlling cellular reproduction and repair.

genetic counseling Consultation and testing by trained experts that enable individuals to learn about their genetic heritage, including harmful conditions that they might pass along to any children they may conceive.

genome The full set of genes that are the instructions to make an individual member of a certain species.

genotype An organism's entire genetic inheritance, or genetic potential.

geriatrics The medical specialty devoted to aging.

germinal period The first two weeks of prenatal development after conception, characterized by rapid cell division and the beginning of cell differentiation.

gerontology The multidisciplinary study of old age.

gonads The paired sex glands (ovaries in females, testicles in males). The gonads produce hormones and gametes.

goodness of fit A similarity of temperament and values that produces a smooth interaction between an individual and his or her social context, including family, school, and community.

grammar All the methods—word order, verb forms, and so on—that languages use to communicate meaning, apart from the words themselves.

grief The deep sorrow that people feel at the death of another. Grief is personal and unpredictable.

gross motor skills Physical abilities involving large body movements, such as walking and jumping. (The word *gross* here means "big.")

growth spurt The relatively sudden and rapid physical growth that occurs during puberty. Each body part increases in size on a schedule: Weight usually precedes height, and growth of the limbs precedes growth of the torso.

guided participation The process by which people learn from others who guide their experiences and explorations.

H

habituation The process of getting used to an object or event through repeated exposure to it.

Hayflick limit The number of times a human cell is capable of dividing into two new cells. The limit for most human cells is approximately 50 divisions, an indication that the life span is limited by our genetic program.

head-sparing A biological mechanism that protects the brain when malnutrition affects body growth. The brain is the last part of the body to be damaged by malnutrition.

health care proxy A person chosen by another person to make medical decisions if the second person becomes unable to do so.

heritability A statistic that indicates what percentage of the variation in a particular trait within a particular population, in a particular context and era, can be traced to genes.

heterogamy Defined by developmentalists as marriage between individuals who tend to be dissimilar with respect to such variables as attitudes, interests, goals, socioeconomic status, religion, ethnic background, and local origin.

heterozygous Referring to two genes of one pair that differ in some way. Typically one allele has only a few base pairs that differ from the other member of the pair.

hikikomori A Japanese word literally meaning "pull away," it is the name of an anxiety disorder common among young adults in Japan. Sufferers isolate themselves from the outside world by staying inside their homes for months or even years at a time.

hidden curriculum The unofficial, unstated, or implicit rules and priorities that influence the academic curriculum and every other aspect of learning in a school.

high-stakes test An evaluation that is critical in determining success or failure. If a single test determines whether a student will graduate or be promoted, it is a high-stakes test.

hippocampus A brain structure that is a central processor of memory, especially memory for locations.

holophrase A single word that is used to express a complete, meaningful thought.

homeostasis The adjustment of all the body's systems to keep physiological functions in a state of equilibrium. As the body ages, it takes longer for these homeostatic adjustments to occur, so it becomes harder for older bodies to adapt to stress.

homogamy Defined by developmentalists as marriage between individuals who tend to be similar with respect to such variables as attitudes, interests, goals, socioeconomic status, religion, ethnic background, and local origin.

homozygous Referring to two genes of one pair that are exactly the same in every letter of their code. Most gene pairs are homozygous.

hookup A sexual encounter between two people who are not in a romantic relationship. Neither intimacy nor commitment are expected.

hormone An organic chemical substance that is produced by one body tissue and conveyed via the bloodstream to another to affect some physiological function.

hormone replacement therapy (HRT) Taking hormones (in pills, patches, or injections) to compensate for hormone reduction. HRT is most common in women at menopause or after removal of the ovaries, but it is also used by men as their testosterone decreases. HRT has some medical uses but also carries health risks.

hospice An institution or program in which terminally ill patients receive palliative care to reduce suffering; family and friends of the dying are helped as well.

HPA (hypothalamus–pituitary–adrenal) axis A sequence of hormone production originating in the hypothalamus and moving to the pituitary and then to the adrenal glands.

HPG (hypothalamus–pituitary–gonad) axis A sequence of hormone production originating in the hypothalamus and moving to the pituitary and then to the gonads.

Human Genome Project An international effort to map the complete human genetic code. This effort was essentially completed in 2001, though analysis is ongoing.

humanism A theory that stresses the potential of all humans for good and the belief that all people have the same basic needs, regardless of culture, gender, or background.

hypothalamus A brain area that responds to the amygdala and the hippocampus to produce hormones that activate other parts of the brain and body.

hypothetical thought Reasoning that includes propositions and possibilities that may not reflect reality.

I

identification An attempt to defend one's self-concept by taking on the behaviors and attitudes of someone else.

identity achievement Erikson's term for the attainment of identity, or the point at which a person understands who he or she is as a unique individual, in accord with past experiences and future plans.

identity versus role confusion Erikson's term for the fifth stage of development, in which the person tries to figure out "Who am I?" but is confused as to which of many possible roles to adopt.

imaginary audience The other people who, in an adolescent's egocentric belief, are watching and taking note of his or her appearance, ideas, and behavior. This belief makes many teenagers very self-conscious.

immersion A strategy in which instruction in all school subjects occurs in the second (usually the majority) language that a child is learning.

implantation The process, beginning about 10 days after conception, in which the developing organism burrows into the placenta that lines the uterus, where it can be nourished and protected as it continues to develop.

implicit memory Unconscious or automatic memory that is usually stored via habits, emotional responses, routine procedures, and various sensations.

in vitro fertilization (IVF) Fertilization that takes place outside a woman's body (as in a glass laboratory dish). The procedure involves mixing sperm with ova that have been surgically removed from the woman's ovary. If a zygote is produced, it is inserted into the woman's uterus, where it may implant and develop into a baby.

incomplete grief A situation in which circumstances, such as a police investigation or an autopsy, interfere with the process of grieving.

independent variable In an experiment, the variable that is introduced to see what effect it has on the dependent variable. (Also called *experimental variable.*)

individual education plan (IEP) A document that specifies educational goals and plans for a child with special needs.

inductive reasoning Reasoning from one or more specific experiences or facts to reach (induce) a general conclusion. (Also called *bottom-up reasoning.*)

industry versus inferiority The fourth of Erikson's eight psychosocial crises, during which children attempt to master many skills, developing a sense of themselves as either industrious or inferior, competent or incompetent.

information-processing theory A perspective that compares human thinking processes, by analogy, to computer analysis of data, including sensory input, connections, stored memories, and output.

initiative versus guilt Erikson's third psychosocial crisis, in which children undertake new skills and activities and feel guilty when they do not succeed at them.

injury control/harm reduction Practices that are aimed at anticipating, controlling, and preventing dangerous activities; these practices reflect the beliefs that accidents are not random and that injuries can be made less harmful if proper controls are in place.

insecure-avoidant attachment (type A) A pattern of attachment in which an infant avoids connection with the caregiver, as when the infant seems not to care about the caregiver's presence, departure, or return.

insecure-resistant/ambivalent attachment (type C) A pattern of attachment in which anxiety and uncertainty are evident, as when an infant becomes very upset at separation from the caregiver and both resists and seeks contact on reunion.

Institutional Review Board (IRB) A group that exists within most educational and medical institutions whose purpose is to ensure that research follows established guidelines and remains ethical.

instrumental activities of daily life (IADLs) Actions (for example, paying bills and driving a car) that are important to independent living and that require some intellectual competence and forethought. The ability to perform these tasks may be even more critical to self-sufficiency than ADL ability.

instrumental aggression Behavior that hurts someone else because the aggressor wants to get or keep a possession or a privilege.

integrity versus despair The final stage of Erik Erikson's developmental sequence, in which older adults seek to integrate their unique experiences with their vision of community.

internalizing problems Difficulty with emotional regulation that involves turning one's emotional distress inward, as by feeling excessively guilty, ashamed, or worthless.

intimacy versus isolation The sixth of Erikson's eight stages of development. Adults seek someone with whom to share their lives in an enduring and self-sacrificing commitment. Without such commitment, they risk profound aloneness and isolation.

intimate terrorism A violent and demeaning form of abuse in a romantic relationship, where the victim (usually female) is frightened to fight back, seek help, or withdraw. In this case, the victim is in danger of physical as well as psychological harm.

intrinsic motivation A drive, or reason to pursue a goal, that comes from inside a person, such as the need to feel smart or competent.

intrinsic rewards of work The intangible gratifications (e.g., job satisfaction, self-esteem, pride) that come from within oneself as a result of doing a job.

intuitive thought Thought that arises from an emotion or a hunch, beyond rational explanation, and is influenced by past experiences and cultural assumptions.

invincibility fable An adolescent's egocentric conviction that he or she cannot be overcome or even harmed by anything that might defeat a normal mortal, such as unprotected sex, drug abuse, or high-speed driving.

IQ test A test designed to measure intellectual aptitude, or ability to learn in school. Originally, intelligence was defined as mental age divided by chronological age, times 100—hence the term intelligence quotient, or IQ.

irreversibility A characteristic of preoperational thought in which a young child thinks that nothing can be undone. A thing cannot be restored to the way it was before a change occurred.

K

kangaroo care A form of newborn care in which mothers (and sometimes fathers) rest the baby between their breasts, like a kangaroo that carries her immature newborn in a pouch on her abdomen.

kinkeeper A caregiver who takes responsibility for maintaining communication among family members.

kinship care A form of foster care in which a relative of a maltreated child, usually a grandparent, becomes the approved caregiver.

knowledge base A body of knowledge in a particular area that makes it easier to master new information in that area.

kwashiorkor A disease of chronic malnutrition during childhood, in which a protein deficiency makes the child more vulnerable to other diseases, such as measles, diarrhea, and influenza.

L

language acquisition device (LAD) Chomsky's term for a hypothesized mental structure that enables humans to learn language, including the basic aspects of grammar, vocabulary, and intonation.

latency Freud's term for middle childhood, during which children's emotional drives and psychosexual needs are quiet (latent). Freud thought that sexual conflicts from earlier stages are only temporarily submerged, bursting forth again at puberty.

lateralization Literally, sidedness, referring to the specialization in certain functions by each side of the brain, with one side dominant for each activity. The left side of the brain controls the right side of the body, and vice versa.

learning disability A marked delay in a particular area of learning that is not caused by an apparent physical disability, by mental retardation, or by an unusually stressful home environment.

least restrictive environment (LRE) A legal requirement that children with special needs be assigned to the most general educational context in which they can be expected to learn.

leptin A hormone that affects appetite and is believed to affect the onset of puberty. Leptin levels increase during childhood and peak at around age 12.

Lewy body dementia A form of dementia characterized by an increase in Lewy body cells in the brain. Symptoms include visual hallucinations, momentary loss of attention, falling, and fainting.

life review An examination of one's own role in the history of human life, engaged in by many elderly people.

life-course-persistent offender A person whose criminal activity typically begins in early adolescence and continues throughout life; a career criminal.

life-span perspective An approach to the study of human development that takes into account all phases of life, not just childhood or adulthood.

linked lives Lives in which the success, health, and well-being of each family member are connected to those of other members, including those of another generation, as in the relationship between parents and children.

"little scientist" The stage-five toddler (age 12 to 18 months) who experiments without anticipating the results, using trial and error in active and creative exploration.

living will A document that indicates what medical intervention an individual prefers if he or she is not conscious when a decision is to be expressed. For example, some do not want mechanical breathing.

long-term memory The component of the information-processing system in which virtually limitless amounts of information can be stored indefinitely.

longitudinal research A research design in which the same individuals are followed over time and their development is repeatedly assessed.

low birthweight (LBW) A body weight at birth of less than 5½ pounds (2,500 grams).

M

marasmus A disease of severe protein-calorie malnutrition during early infancy, in which growth stops, body tissues waste away, and the infant eventually dies.

maximum life span The oldest possible age that members of a species can live under ideal circumstances. For humans, that age is approximately 122 years.

menarche A girl's first menstrual period, signaling that she has begun ovulation. Pregnancy is biologically possible, but ovulation and menstruation are often irregular for years after menarche.

menopause The time in middle age, usually around age 50, when a woman's menstrual periods cease and the production of estrogen, progesterone, and testosterone drops. Strictly speaking, menopause is dated one year after a woman's last menstrual period, although many months before and after that date are menopausal.

mentor A skilled and knowledgeable person who advises or guides an inexperienced person.

metacognition "Thinking about thinking," or the ability to evaluate a cognitive task in order to determine how best to accomplish it, and then to monitor and adjust one's performance on that task.

middle childhood The period between early childhood and early adolescence, approximately from ages 6 to 11.

middle school A school for children in the grades between elementary and high school. Middle school usually begins with grade 6 and ends with grade 8.

midlife crisis A supposed period of unusual anxiety, radical self-reexamination, and sudden transformation that was once widely associated with middle age but that actually had more to do with developmental history than with chronological age.

mild cognitive impairment Forgetfulness and loss of verbal fluency that often comes before the first stage of Alzheimer disease.

mirror neurons Cells in an observer's brain that respond to an action performed by someone else in the same way they would if the observer had actually performed that action.

modeling The central process of social learning, by which a person observes the actions of others and then copies them. (Also called *observational learning.*)

monozygotic (MZ) twins Twins who originate from one zygote that splits apart very early in development. (Also called *identical twins.*) Other monozygotic multiple births (such as triplets and quadruplets) can occur as well.

Montessori schools Schools that offer early-childhood education based on the philosophy of Maria Montessori, which emphasizes careful work and tasks that each young child can do.

morality of care In Gilligan's view, moral principles that reflect the tendency of females to be reluctant to judge right and wrong in absolute terms because they are socialized to be nurturant, compassionate, and nonjudgmental.

morality of justice In Gilligan's view, moral principles that reflect the tendency of males to emphasize justice over compassion, judging right and wrong in absolute terms.

moratorium An adolescent's choice of a socially acceptable way to postpone making identity-achievement decisions. Going to college is a common example.

morbidity Disease. As a measure of health, morbidity usually refers to the rate of diseases in a given population—physical and emotional, acute (sudden) and chronic (ongoing).

mortality Death. As a measure of health, mortality usually refers to the number of deaths each year per 1,000 members of a given population.

motor skills The learned abilities to move some part of the body, in actions ranging from a large leap to a flicker of the eyelid. (The word *motor* here refers to movement of muscles.)

mourning The ceremonies and behaviors that a religion or culture prescribes for people to employ in expressing their bereavement after a death.

multifactorial Referring to a trait that is affected by many factors, both genetic and environmental expression; enhancing, halting, shaping, or altering the expression of genes, resulting in a phenotype that may differ markedly from the genotype.

multiple intelligences The idea that human intelligence is comprised of a varied set of abilities rather than a single, all-encompassing one.

myelination The process by which axons become coated with myelin, a fatty substance that speeds the transmission of nerve impulses from neuron to neuron.

N

naming explosion A sudden increase in an infant's vocabulary, especially in the number of nouns, that begins at about 18 months of age.

National Assessment of Educational Progress (NAEP) An ongoing and nationally representative measure of U.S. children's achievement in reading, mathematics, and other subjects over time; nicknamed "the Nation's Report Card."

naturally occurring retirement community (NORC) A neighborhood or apartment complex whose population is mostly retired people who moved to the location as younger adults and never left.

nature A general term for the traits, capacities, and limitations that each individual inherits genetically from his or her parents at the moment of conception.

neglectful/uninvolved parenting An approach to child rearing in which the parents are indifferent toward their children and unaware of what is going on in their children's lives.

neurons The billions of nerve cells in the central nervous system, especially the brain.

No Child Left Behind Act A U.S. law enacted in 2001 that was intended to increase accountability in education by requiring states to qualify for federal educational funding by administering standardized tests to measure school achievement.

nuclear family A family that consists of a father, a mother, and their biological children under age 18.

nurture A general term for all the environmental influences that affect development after an individual is conceived.

O

obesity In a child, having a BMI above the 95th percentile, according to the U.S. Centers for Disease Control's 1980 standards for children of a given age.

object permanence The realization that objects (including people) still exist when they can no longer be seen, touched, or heard.

objective thought Thinking that is not influenced by the thinker's personal qualities but instead involves facts and numbers that are universally considered true and valid.

Oedipus complex The unconscious desire of young boys to replace their father and win their mother's romantic love.

old-old Older adults (generally, those over age 75) who suffer from physical, mental, or social deficits.

oldest-old Elderly adults (generally, those over age 85) who are dependent on others for almost everything, requiring supportive services such as nursing homes and hospital stays.

operant conditioning The learning process by which a particular action is followed by something desired (which makes the person or animal more likely to repeat the action) or by something unwanted (which makes the action less likely to be repeated). (Also called *instrumental conditioning*.)

organ reserve The capacity of organs to allow the body to cope with stress, via extra, unused functioning ability.

overregularization The application of rules of grammar even when exceptions occur, making the language seem more "regular" than it actually is.

overweight In a child, having a BMI above the 85th percentile, according to the U.S. Centers for Disease Control's 1980 standards for children of a given age.

oxygen free radicals Atoms of oxygen that, as a result of metabolic processes, have an unpaired electron. These atoms scramble DNA molecules or mitochondria, producing errors in cell maintenance and repair that, over time, may cause cancer, diabetes, and arteriosclerosis.

P

palliative care Care designed not to treat an illness but to provide physical and emotional comfort to the patient and support and guidance to his or her family.

parasuicide Any potentially lethal action against the self that does not result in death.

parent–infant bond The strong, loving connection that forms as parents hold, examine, and feed their newborn.

parental alliance Cooperation between a mother and a father based on their mutual commitment to their children. In a parental alliance, the parents support each other in their shared parental roles.

parental monitoring Parents' ongoing awareness of what their children are doing, where, and with whom.

Parkinson disease A chronic, progressive disease that is characterized by muscle tremor and rigidity, and sometimes dementia; caused by a reduction of dopamine production in the brain.

passive euthanasia A situation in which a seriously ill person is allowed to die naturally, through the cessation of medical intervention.

peer pressure Encouragement to conform to one's friends or contemporaries in behavior, dress, and attitude; usually considered a negative force, as when adolescent peers encourage one another to defy adult authority.

people preference A universal principle of infant perception, consisting of an innate attraction to other humans, which is evident in visual, auditory, tactile, and other preferences.

percentile A point on a ranking scale of 0 to 100. The 50th percentile is the midpoint; half the people in the population being studied rank higher and half rank lower.

perception The mental processing of sensory information when the brain interprets a sensation. Perception occurs in the cortex.

permanency planning An effort by child-welfare authorities to find a long-term living situation that will provide stability and support for a maltreated child. A goal is to avoid repeated changes of caregiver or school, which can be particularly harmful to the child.

permissive parenting An approach to child rearing that is characterized by high nurturance and communication but little discipline, guidance, or control.

perseveration The tendency to persevere in, or stick to, one thought or action for a long time.

personal fable An aspect of adolescent egocentrism characterized by an adolescent's belief that his or her thoughts, feelings, and experiences are unique, more wonderful or awful than anyone else's.

phallic stage Freud's third stage of development, when the penis becomes the focus of concern and pleasure.

phenotype The observable characteristics of a person, including appearance, personality, intelligence, and all other traits.

phenylketonuria (PKU) A genetic disorder in which a child's body is unable to metabolize an amino acid called phenylalanine. Unless the infant immediately begins a special diet, the resulting buildup of phenylalanine in body fluids causes brain damage, progressive mental retardation, and other symptoms.

phonics approach Teaching reading by first teaching the sounds of each letter and of various letter combinations.

physician-assisted suicide A form of active euthanasia in which a doctor provides the means for someone to end his or her own life.

PISA (Programme for International Student Assessment) An international test taken by 15-year-olds in 50 nations that is designed to measure problem solving and cognition in daily life.

pituitary A gland in the brain that responds to a signal from the hypothalamus by producing many hormones, including those that regulate growth and control other glands, among them the adrenal and sex glands.

polygamous family A family consisting of one man, several wives, and the biological children of the man and his wives.

polygenic Referring to a trait that is influenced by many genes.

polypharmacy Refers to a situation in which elderly people are prescribed several medications. The various side effects and interactions of those medications can result in dementia symptoms.

positivity effect The tendency for elderly people to perceive, prefer, and remember positive images and experiences more than negative ones.

post-traumatic stress disorder (PTSD) An anxiety disorder that develops as a delayed reaction to having experienced or witnessed a profoundly shocking or frightening event, such as rape, severe beating, war, or natural disaster. Its symptoms may include flashbacks to the event, hyperactivity and hypervigilance, displaced anger, sleeplessness, nightmares, sudden terror or anxiety, and confusion between fantasy and reality.

postconventional moral reasoning Kohlberg's third level of moral reasoning, emphasizing moral principles.

postformal thought A proposed adult stage of cognitive development, following Piaget's four stages, that goes beyond adolescent thinking by being more practical, more flexible, and more dialectical (that is, more capable of combining contradictory elements into a comprehensive whole).

postpartum depression A new mother's feelings of inadequacy and sadness in the days and weeks after giving birth.

practical intelligence The intellectual skills used in everyday problem solving. (Sometimes called *tacit intelligence*.)

pragmatics The practical use of language that includes the ability to adjust language communication according to audience and context.

preconventional moral reasoning Kohlberg's first level of moral reasoning, emphasizing rewards and punishments.

prefrontal cortex The area of cortex at the front of the brain that specializes in anticipation, planning, and impulse control.

preoperational intelligence Piaget's term for cognitive development between the ages of about 2 and 6; it includes language and imagination (which involve symbolic thought), but logical, operational thinking is not yet possible.

presbycusis A significant loss of hearing associated with senescence. Presbycusis usually is not apparent until after age 60.

preterm A birth that occurs 3 or more weeks before the full 38 weeks of the typical pregnancy—that is, at 35 or fewer weeks after conception.

primary aging The universal and irreversible physical changes that occur to all living creatures as they grow older.

primary circular reactions The first of three types of feedback loops in sensorimotor intelligence, this one involving the infant's own body. The infant senses motion, sucking, noise, and other stimuli, and tries to understand them.

primary prevention Actions that change overall background conditions to prevent some unwanted event or circumstance, such as injury, disease, or abuse.

primary sex characteristics The parts of the body that are directly involved in reproduction, including the vagina, uterus, ovaries, testicles, and penis.

priming Words or ideas presented in advance that make it easier to remember something. It is also possible for priming to impair cognition, as with stereotype threat.

private speech The internal dialogue that occurs when people talk to themselves (either silently or out loud).

problem-focused coping A strategy to deal with stress by tackling a stressful situation directly.

Progress in International Reading Literacy Study (PIRLS) Inaugurated in 2001, a planned five-year cycle of international trend studies in the reading ability of fourth-graders.

prosocial behavior Feelings and actions that are helpful and kind but are of no obvious benefit to oneself.

protein-calorie malnutrition A condition in which a person does not consume sufficient food of any kind. This deprivation can result in several illnesses, severe weight loss, and even death.

proximal parenting Caregiving practices that involve being physically close to a baby, with frequent holding and touching.

psychoanalytic theory A grand theory of human development that holds that irrational, unconscious drives and motives, often originating in childhood, underlie human behavior.

psychological control A disciplinary technique that involves threatening to withdraw love and support and that relies on a child's feelings of guilt and gratitude to the parents.

psychopathology An illness or disorder of the mind.

puberty The time between the first onrush of hormones and full adult physical development. Puberty usually lasts three to five years. Many more years are required to achieve psychosocial maturity.

public health Measures that help prevent morbidity, mortality, and disability in the public at large, such as via immunization, monitoring the food and water supply, and increasing preventive health practices.

Q

QALYs (quality-adjusted life years) A way of comparing mere survival without vitality to survival with good health. A full year of health is a full QALY; people with less than full health have a fraction of QALY each year. Thus, their total QALY is less than the total years they live.

qualitative research Research that considers qualities instead of quantities. Descriptions of particular conditions and participants' expressed ideas are often part of qualitative studies.

quantitative research Research that provides data that can be expressed with numbers, such as ranks or scales.

R

race A group of people who are regarded by themselves or by others as distinct from other groups on the basis of physical appearance. Social scientists think race is a misleading concept.

reaction time The time it takes to respond to a stimulus, either physically (with a reflexive movement such as an eyeblink) or cognitively (with a thought).

reactive aggression An impulsive retaliation for another person's intentional or accidental action, verbal or physical.

reflex An unlearned, involuntary action or movement that responds to a stimulus. A reflex occurs without conscious thought.

Reggio Emilia A famous program of early-childhood education that originated in the town of Reggio Emilia, Italy, and that encourages each child's creativity in a carefully designed setting.

reinforcement A technique for conditioning behavior in which that behavior is followed by something desired, such as food for a hungry animal or a welcoming smile for a lonely person.

relational aggression Nonphysical acts, such as insults or social rejection, aimed at harming the social connection between the victim and other people.

REM sleep Rapid eye movement sleep, a stage of sleep characterized by flickering eyes behind closed lids, dreaming, and rapid brain waves.

reminder session A perceptual experience that is intended to help a person recollect an idea, a thing, or an experience, without testing whether the person remembers it at the moment.

replication The repetition of a study, using different participants.

reported maltreatment Harm or endangerment about which someone has notified the authorities.

resilience The capacity to adapt well to significant adversity and to overcome serious stress.

response to intervention An educational strategy intended to help children in early grades who demonstrate below-average achievement by means of special intervention.

role confusion A situation in which an adolescent does not seem to know or care what his or her identity is. (Sometimes called *identity diffusion*.)

rough-and-tumble play Play that mimics aggression through wrestling, chasing, or hitting, but in which there is no intent to harm.

rumination Repeatedly thinking and talking about past experiences; can contribute to depression.

S

sandwich generation The generation of middle-aged people who are supposedly "squeezed" by the needs of the younger and older members of their families. In reality, some adults do feel pressured by these obligations, but most are not burdened by them, either because they enjoy fulfilling them or because they choose to take on only some of them or none of them.

scaffolding Temporary support that is tailored to a learner's needs and abilities and aimed at helping the learner master the next task in a given learning process.

science of human development The science that seeks to understand how and why people of all ages and circumstances change or remain the same over time.

scientific method A way to answer questions using empirical research and data-based conclusions.

scientific observation A method of testing a hypothesis by unobtrusively watching and recording participants' behavior in a systematic and objective manner—in a natural setting, in a laboratory, or in searches of archival data.

Seattle Longitudinal Study The first cross-sequential study of adult intelligence. This study began in 1956; the most recent testing was conducted in 2005.

secondary aging The specific physical illnesses or conditions that become more common with aging but are caused by health habits, genes, and other influences that vary from person to person.

secondary circular reactions The second of three types of feedback loops in sensorimotor intelligence, this one involving people and objects. Infants respond to other people, to toys, and to any other object they can touch or move.

secondary education Literally, the period after primary education (elementary or grade school) and before tertiary education (college). It usually occurs from about age 12 to 18, although there is some variation by school and by nation.

secondary prevention Actions that avert harm in a high-risk situation, such as stopping a car before it hits a pedestrian.

secondary sex characteristics Physical traits that are not directly involved in reproduction but that indicate sexual maturity, such as a man's beard and a woman's breasts.

secular trend The long-term upward or downward direction of a certain set of statistical measurements, as opposed to a smaller, shorter cyclical variation. As an example, over the last two centuries, because of improved nutrition and medical care, children have tended to reach their adult height earlier and their adult height has increased.

secure attachment (type B) A relationship in which an infant obtains both comfort and confidence from the presence of his or her caregiver.

selective adaptation The process by which living creatures (including people) adjust to their environment. Genes that enhance survival and reproductive ability are selected, over generations, to become more frequent.

selective attention The ability to concentrate on some stimuli while ignoring others.

selective expert Someone who is notably more skilled and knowledgeable than the average person about whichever activities are personally meaningful.

selective optimization with compensation The theory, developed by Paul and Margret Baltes, that people try to maintain a balance in their lives by looking for the best way to compensate for physical and cognitive losses and to become more proficient in activities they can already do well.

self theories Theories of late adulthood that emphasize the core self, or the search to maintain one's integrity and identity.

self-actualization The final stage in Maslow's hierarchy of needs, characterized by aesthetic, creative, philosophical, and spiritual understanding.

self-awareness One's realization that he or she is a distinct individual, whose body, mind, and actions are separate from those of other people.

self-concept A person's understanding of who he or she is, in relation to self-esteem, appearance, personality, and various traits.

self-efficacy In social learning theory, the belief of some people that they are able to change themselves and effectively alter the social context.

self-righting The inborn drive to remedy a developmental deficit; literally, to return to sitting or standing upright, after being tipped over. People of all ages have self-righting impulses, for emotional as well as physical imbalance.

senescence The process of aging, whereby the body becomes less strong and efficient.

sensation The response of a sensory system (eyes, ears, skin, tongue, nose) when it detects a stimulus.

sensitive period A time when a certain type of development is most likely, although it may still happen later. For example, early childhood is considered a sensitive period for language learning.

sensorimotor intelligence Piaget's term for the way infants think—by using their senses and motor skills—during the first period of cognitive development.

sensory memory The component of the information-processing system in which incoming stimulus information is stored for a split second to allow it to be processed. (Also called the *sensory register.*)

separation anxiety An infant's distress when a familiar caregiver leaves, most obvious between 9 and 14 months.

set point A particular body weight that an individual's homeostatic processes strive to maintain.

sex differences Biological differences between males and females, in organs, hormones, and body type.

sexual orientation A term that refers to whether a person is sexually and romantically attracted to others of the same sex, the opposite sex, or both sexes.

sexually transmitted infection (STI) A disease spread by sexual contact, including syphilis, gonorrhea, genital herpes, chlamydia, and HIV.

shaken baby syndrome A life-threatening injury that occurs when an infant is forcefully shaken back and forth, a motion that ruptures blood vessels in the brain and breaks neural connections.

single-parent family A family that consists of only one parent and his or her biological children under age 18.

situational couple violence Fighting between romantic partners that is brought on more by the situation than by the deep personality problems of the individuals. Both partners are typically victims and abusers.

slippery slope The argument that a given action will start a chain of events that will culminate in an undesirable outcome.

small for gestational age (SGA) A term for a baby whose birthweight is significantly lower than expected, given the time since conception. For example, a 5-pound (2,265-gram) newborn is considered SGA if born on time but not SGA if born two months early. (Also called *small-for-dates.*)

social cognition The ability to understand social interactions, including the causes and consequences of human behavior.

social comparison The tendency to assess one's abilities, achievements, social status, and other attributes by measuring them against those of other people, especially one's peers.

social convoy Collectively, the family members, friends, acquaintances, and even strangers who move through life with an individual.

social homogamy The similarity of a couple's leisure interests and role preferences.

social learning Learning that is accomplished by observing others—both what they do and how other people react to that behavior.

social learning theory An extension of behaviorism that emphasizes the influence that other people have over a person's behavior. Even without specific reinforcement, every individual learns many things through observation and imitation of other people.

social mediation Human interaction that expands and advances understanding, often through words that one person uses to explain something to another.

social network A Web site that allows users to publicly share details of their daily lives and connect with large numbers of friends, acquaintances, and potential romantic partners, among others.

social norms approach A method of reducing risky behavior that uses emerging adults' desire to follow social norms by making them aware, through the use of surveys, of the prevalence of various behaviors within their peer group.

social referencing Seeking information about how to react to an unfamiliar or ambiguous object or event by observing someone else's expressions and reactions. That other person becomes a social reference.

social smile A smile evoked by a human face, normally evident in infants about 6 weeks after birth.

sociocultural theory An emergent theory that holds that development results from the dynamic interaction of each person with the surrounding social and cultural forces.

sociodramatic play Pretend play in which children act out various roles and themes in stories that they create.

socioeconomic status (SES) A person's position in society as determined by income, wealth, occupation, education, and place of residence. (Sometimes called *social class*.)

spermarche A boy's first ejaculation of sperm. Erections can occur as early as infancy, but ejaculation signals sperm production. Spermarche may occur during sleep (in a "wet dream") or via direct stimulation.

static reasoning A characteristic of preoperational thought in which a young child thinks that nothing changes. Whatever is now has always been and always will be.

stem cells Cells from which any other specialized type of cell can form.

stereotype threat The possibility that one's appearance or behavior will be misread to confirm another person's oversimplified, prejudiced attitudes.

still-face technique An experimental practice in which an adult keeps his or her face umoving and expressionless in face-to-face interaction with an infant.

Strange Situation A laboratory procedure for measuring attachment by evoking infants' reactions to stress in eight episodes, lasting three minutes each.

stranger wariness An infant's expression of concern—a quiet stare, clinging to a familiar person, or sadness—when a stranger appears.

stratification theories Theories that emphasize that social forces, particularly those related to a person's social stratum or social category, limit individual choices and affect a person's ability to function in late adulthood because past stratification continues to limit life in various ways.

stressor Any situation, event, experience, or other stimulus that causes a person to feel stressed. Many circumstances become stressors for some people but not for others.

stunting The failure of children to grow to a normal height for their age due to severe and chronic malnutrition.

subjective thought Thinking that is strongly influenced by personal qualities of the individual thinker, such as past experiences, cultural assumptions, and goals for the future.

substantiated maltreatment Harm or endangerment that has been reported, investigated, and verified.

suicidal ideation Thinking about suicide, usually with some serious emotional and intellectual or cognitive overtones.

sunk cost fallacy The mistaken belief that if money, time, or effort that cannot be recovered (a "sunk cost," in economic terms) has already been invested in some endeavor, then more should be invested in an effort to reach the goal. Because of this fallacy, people spend money trying to fix a "lemon" of a car or send more troops to fight a losing battle.

superego In psychoanalytic theory, the judgmental part of the personality that internalizes the moral standards of the parents.

survey A research method in which information is collected from a large number of people by interviews, written questionnaires, or some other means.

synapse The intersection between the axon of one neuron and the dendrites of other neurons.

synchrony A coordinated, rapid, and smooth exchange of responses between a caregiver and an infant.

synthesis A new idea that integrates the thesis and its antithesis, thus representing a new and more comprehensive level of truth; the third stage of the process of dialectical thinking.

T

T cells Immune cells manufactured in the thymus gland that produce substances that attack infected cells in the body.

tau A protein that makes up the tangles found within neurons.

telecommuting Working at home and keeping in touch with the office via computer, telephone, and fax.

telomerase An enzyme that increases the length of telomeres, which in turn may slow the advance of aging.

telomeres The ends of chromosomes in the cells; their length decreases with each cell duplication and seems to correlate with longevity.

temperament Inborn differences between one person and another in emotions, activity, and self-regulation. Temperament originates in genes and prenatal development and is affected by early experiences.

teratogens Agents and conditions, including viruses, drugs, and chemicals, that can impair prenatal development and result in birth defects or even death.

terminal decline An overall slowdown of cognitive abilities in the weeks and months before death. (Also called *terminal drop*.)

terror management theory (TMT) The idea that people adopt cultural values and moral principles in order to cope with their fear of death. This system of beliefs protects individuals from anxiety about their mortality and bolsters their self-esteem, so they react harshly when other people go against any of the moral principles involved.

tertiary circular reactions The third of three types of feedback loops in sensorimotor intelligence, this one involving active exploration and experimentation. Infants explore a range of new activities, varying their responses as a way of learning about the world.

tertiary prevention Actions, such as immediate and effective medical treatment, that are taken after an adverse event (such as illness or injury) occurs and that are aimed at reducing the harm or preventing disability.

testosterone A sex hormone, the best known of the androgens (male hormones); secreted in far greater amounts by males than by females.

thanatology The study of death and dying, especially of the social and emotional aspects.

theory of mind A person's theory of what other people might be thinking. In order to have a theory of mind, children must realize that other people are not necessarily thinking the same thoughts that they themselves are. That realization is seldom possible before age 4.

theory-theory The idea that children attempt to explain everything they see and hear by constructing theories.

thesis A proposition or statement of belief; the first stage of the process of dialectical thinking.

threshold effect A situation in which a certain teratogen is relatively harmless in small doses but becomes harmful once exposure reaches a certain level (the threshold).

time-out A disciplinary technique in which a child is separated from other people for a specified time.

transient exuberance The great but temporary increase in the number of dendrites that occurs in an infant's brain during the first two years of life.

transitive inference The ability to figure out the unspoken link between one fact and another.

Trends in Math and Science Study (TIMSS) An international assessment of the math and science skills of fourth- and eighth-graders. Although the TIMSS is very useful, different countries' scores are not always comparable because sample selection, test administration, and content validity are hard to keep uniform.

trust versus mistrust Erikson's first psychosocial crisis. Infants learn basic trust if their basic needs (for food, comfort, attention, and so on) are met.

U

ultrasound An image of a fetus (or an internal organ) produced by using high-frequency sound waves. (Also called *sonogram.*)

V

vascular dementia (VaD) A form of dementia characterized by sporadic, and progressive, loss of intellectual functioning caused by repeated infarcts, or temporary obstructions of blood vessels, which prevent sufficient blood from reaching the brain. (Also called *multi-infarct dementia.*)

very low birthweight (VLBW) A body weight at birth of less than 3 pounds, 5 ounces (1,500 grams).

visual cliff An experimental apparatus that gives an illusion of a sudden drop-off between one horizontal surface and another.

vitality A measure of health that refers to how healthy and energetic—physically, intellectually, and socially—an individual actually feels.

voucher Permission for a parent to choose the school for the child, with some or all of the cost of that's child's education borne by the local government. Parents who have vouchers for their children often can choose a public or private school, although the specifics vary a great deal from one jurisdiction to another.

W

wasting The tendency for children to be severely underweight for their age as a result of malnutrition.

wear-and-tear theory A view of aging as a process by which the human body wears out because of the passage of time and exposure to environmental stressors.

weathering The gradual accumulation of stressors over a long period of time, wearing down the resilience and resistance of a person.

whole-language approach Teaching reading by encouraging early use of all language skills—talking and listening, reading and writing.

withdrawn-rejected Rejected by peers because of timid, withdrawn, and anxious behavior.

women's work A term formerly used to denigrate domestic and caregiving tasks that were once thought to be the responsibility of females.

working memory The component of the information-processing system in which current conscious mental activity occurs. (Formerly called *short-term memory.*)

working model In cognitive theory, a set of assumptions that the individual uses to organize perceptions and experiences. For example, a person might assume that other people are trustworthy and be surprised by evidence that this working model of human behavior is erroneous.

X

X-linked Referring to a gene carried on the X chromosome. If a male inherits an X-linked recessive trait from his mother, he expresses that trait because the Y from his father has no counteracting gene. Females are more likely to be carriers of X-linked traits but are less likely to express them.

XX A 23rd chromosome pair that consists of two X-shaped chromosomes, one each from the mother and the father. XX zygotes become females.

XY A 23rd chromosome pair that consists of an X-shaped chromosome from the mother and a Y-shaped chromosome from the father. XY zygotes become males.

Y

young-old Healthy, vigorous, financially secure older adults (generally, those aged 60 to 75) who are well integrated into the lives of their families and communities.

Z

zone of proximal development (ZPD) In sociocultural theory, a metaphorical area, or "zone," surrounding a learner that includes all the skills, knowledge, and concepts that the person is close ("proximal") to acquiring but cannot yet master without help.

zygote The single cell formed from the union of two gametes, a sperm and an ovum.

References

Aarnoudse-Moens, Cornelieke S. H., Smidts, Diana P., Oosterlaan, Jaap, Duivenvoorden, Hugo J., & Weisglas-Kuperus, Nynke. (2009). Executive function in very preterm children at early school age. *Journal of Abnormal Child Psychology, 37,* 981–993.

Aarsland, Dag, Zaccai, Julia, & Brayne, Carol. (2005). A systematic review of prevalence studies of dementia in Parkinson's disease. *Movement Disorders, 20,* 1255–1263.

Abdool Karim, Quarraisha, Abdool Karim, Salim S., Frohlich, Janet A., Grobler, Anneke C., Baxter, Cheryl, Mansoor, Leila E., et al. (2010). Effectiveness and safety of tenofovir gel, an antiretroviral microbicide, for the prevention of HIV infection in women. *Science, 329,* 1168–1174.

Abelson, Reed. (2007, February 10). A chance to pick hospice, and still hope to live. *New York Times,* pp. A1, C4.

Aboa-Éboulé, Corine, Brisson, Chantal, Maunsell, Elizabeth, Mâsse, Benoît, Bourbonnais, Renée, Vézina, Michel, et al. (2007). Job strain and risk of acute recurrent coronary heart disease events. *Journal of the American Medical Association, 298,* 1652–1660.

Aboderin, Isabella. (2004). Intergenerational family support and old age economic security in sub-Saharan Africa: The importance of understanding shifts, processes and expectations. An example from Ghana. In Peter Lloyd-Sherlock (Ed.), *Living longer: Ageing, development and social protection* (pp. 210–229). London: Zed Books.

Aboud, Frances E., & Amato, Maria. (2001). Developmental and socialization influences on intergroup bias. In Rupert Brown & Samuel L. Gaertner (Eds.), *Blackwell handbook of social psychology: Intergroup processes* (pp. 65–85). Malden, MA: Blackwell.

Aboud, Frances E., & Mendelson, Morton J. (1998). Determinants of friendship selection and quality: Developmental perspectives. In William M. Bukowski, Andrew F. Newcomb, & Willard W. Hartup (Eds.), *The company they keep: Friendship in childhood and adolescence* (pp. 87–112). New York: Cambridge University Press.

Abramovitch, Henry. (2005). Where are the dead? Bad death, the missing, and the inability to mourn. In Samuel Heilman (Ed.), *Death, bereavement, and mourning* (pp. 53–67). New Brunswick, NJ: Transaction.

Abrams, Dominic, Rutland, Adam, Ferrell, Jennifer M., & Pelletier, Joseph. (2008). Children's judgments of disloyal and immoral peer behavior: Subjective group dynamics in minimal intergroup contexts. *Child Development, 79,* 444–461.

Abreu, Guida de. (2008). From mathematics learning out-of-school to multicultural classrooms: A cultural psychology perspective. In Lyn D. English, Maria Bartolini Bussi, Graham A. Jones, Richard A. Lesh, & Bharath Sriraman (Eds.), *Handbook of international research in mathematics education* (2nd ed., pp. 323–353). New York: Routledge.

Abrevaya, Jason. (2009). Are there missing girls in the United States? Evidence from birth data. *American Economic Journal: Applied Economics, 1,* 1–34.

Abu-Saad, Kathleen, Shai, Iris, Kaufman-Shriqui, Vered, German, Larissa, Vardi, Hillel, & Fraser, Drora. (2009). Bread type intake is associated with lifestyle and diet quality transition among Bedouin Arab adults. *British Journal of Nutrition, 102,* 1513–1522.

Accardo, Pasquale. (2006). Who's training whom? *The Journal of Pediatrics, 149,* 151–152.

Achenbaum, W. Andrew. (2005). *Older Americans, vital communities: A bold vision for societal aging.* Baltimore: Johns Hopkins University Press.

Achenbaum, W. Andrew. (2006–2007). A history of civic engagement of older people. *Generations, 30,* 18–23.

Ackerman, Joshua M., & Kenrick, Douglas T. (2009). Cooperative courtship: Helping friends raise and raze relationship barriers. *Personality and Social Psychology Bulletin, 35,* 1285–1300.

Acs, Gregory. (2007). Can we promote child well-being by promoting marriage? *Journal of Marriage and Family, 69,* 1326–1344.

Adam, Emma K., Klimes-Dougan, Bonnie, & Gunnar, Megan R. (2007). Social regulation of the adrenocortical response to stress in infants, children, and adolescents: Implications for psychopathology and education. In Donna Coch, Geraldine Dawson, & Kurt W. Fischer (Eds.), *Human behavior, learning, and the developing brain: Atypical development* (pp. 264–304). New York: Guilford Press.

Adam, Hajo, Shirako, Aiwa, & Maddux, William W. (2010). Cultural variance in the interpersonal effects of anger in negotiations. *Psychological Science, 21,* 882–889.

Adamson, Lauren B., & Bakeman, Roger. (2006). Development of displaced speech in early mother-child conversations. *Child Development, 77,* 186–200.

Adler, Lynn Peters. (1995). *Centenarians: The bonus years.* Santa Fe, NM: Health Press.

Adler, Nancy E., & Snibbe, Alana Conner. (2003). The role of psychosocial processes in explaining the gradient between socioeconomic status and health. *Current Directions in Psychological Science, 12,* 119–123.

Adolph, Karen E., & Berger, Sarah E. (2005). Physical and motor development. In Marc H. Bornstein & Michael E. Lamb (Eds.), *Developmental science: An advanced textbook* (5th ed., pp. 223–281). Mahwah, NJ: Erlbaum.

Adolph, Karen E., Vereijken, Beatrix, & Shrout, Patrick E. (2003). What changes in infant walking and why. *Child Development, 74,* 475–497.

Afanas'ev, Igor B. (2009). *Signaling mechanisms of oxygen and nitrogen free radicals.* Boca Raton, FL: Taylor & Francis.

Afifi, Tracie O., Enns, Murray W., Cox, Brian J., Asmundson, Gordon J. G., Stein, Murray B., & Sareen, Jitender. (2008). Population attributable fractions of psychiatric disorders and suicide ideation and attempts associated with adverse childhood experiences. *American Journal of Public Health, 98,* 946–952.

Ahmed, Parvez, & Jaakkola, Jouni J. K. (2007). Maternal occupation and adverse pregnancy outcomes: A Finnish population-based study. *Occupational Medicine, 57,* 417–423.

Ainsworth, Mary D. Salter. (1973). The development of infant-mother attachment. In Bettye M. Caldwell & Henry N. Ricciuti (Eds.), *Review of child development research* (Vol. 3, pp. 1–94). Chicago: University of Chicago Press.

Ajdacic-Gross, Vladeta, Ring, Mariann, Gadola, Erika, Lauber, Christoph, Bopp, Matthias, Gutzwiller, Felix, et al. (2008). Suicide after bereavement: An overlooked problem. *Psychological Medicine, 38,* 673–676.

Akbaraly, Tasmine N., Portet, Florence, Fustinoni, Sarah, Dartigues, Jean-François, Artero, Sylvaine, Rouaud, Olivier, et al. (2009). Leisure activities and the risk of dementia in the elderly: Results from the Three-City Study. *Neurology, 73,* 854–861.

Akiba, Daisuke, & García Coll, Cynthia. (2004). Effective interventions with children of color and their families: A contextual developmental approach. In Timothy B. Smith (Ed.), *Practicing multiculturalism: Affirming diversity in counseling and psychology* (pp. 123–144). Boston: Pearson/Allyn and Bacon.

Akinbami, Lara J., Lynch, Courtney D., Parker, Jennifer D., & Woodruff, Tracey J. (2010). The association between childhood asthma prevalence and monitored air pollutants in metropolitan areas, United States, 2001–2004. *Environmental Research, 110,* 294–301.

Albert, Steven M., & Freedman, Vicki A. (2010). *Public health and aging: Maximizing function and well-being* (2nd ed.). New York: Springer.

Alberts, Amy, Elkind, David, & Ginsberg, Stephen. (2007). The personal fable and risk-taking in early adolescence. *Journal of Youth and Adolescence, 36,* 71–76.

Albinet, Cédric, Temporowski, Phillip, & Beasman, Kathryn. (2006). Aging and concurrent task performance: Cognitive demand and motor control. *Educational Gerontology, 32,* 689–706.

Aldwin, Carolyn M. (2007). *Stress, coping, and development: An integrative perspective* (2nd ed.). New York: Guilford Press.

Aldwin, Carolyn M., & Gilmer, Diane F. (2003). *Health, illness, and optimal aging: Biological and psychosocial perspectives.* Thousand Oaks, CA: Sage.

Alexander, Robin. (2000). *Culture and pedagogy: International comparisons in primary education.* Malden, MA: Blackwell.

Allemand, Mathias, Zimprich, Daniel, & Martin, Mike. (2008). Long-term correlated change in personality traits in old age. *Psychology and Aging, 23,* 545–557.

Allen, Elizabeth, Bonell, Chris, Strange, Vicki, Copas, Andrew, Stephenson, Judith, Johnson, Anne, et al. (2007). Does the UK government's teenage pregnancy strategy deal with the correct risk factors? Findings from a secondary analysis of data from a randomised trial of sex education and their implications for policy. *Journal of Epidemiology & Community Health, 61,* 20–27.

Allen, Joseph P., Porter, Maryfrances R., McFarland, F. Christy, Marsh, Penny, & McElhaney, Kathleen Boykin. (2005). The two faces of adolescents' success with peers: Adolescent popularity, social adaptation, and deviant behavior. *Child Development, 76,* 747–760.

Allen, Shanley. (2007). The future of Inuktitut in the face of majority languages: Bilingualism or language shift? *Applied Psycholinguistics, 28,* 515–536.

Alley, Dawn, Suthers, Kristen, & Crimmins, Eileen. (2007). Education and cognitive decline in older Americans: Results from the AHEAD sample. *Research on Aging, 29,* 73–94.

Allis, C. David, Jenuwein, Thomas, & Reinberg, Danny (Eds.). (2007). *Epigenetics.* Cold Spring Harbor, NY: Cold Spring Harbor Laboratory Press.

Allman, Tara L., Mittelstaedt, Robin D., Martin, Bruce, & Goldenberg, Marni. (2009). Exploring the motivations of BASE jumpers: Extreme sport enthusiasts. *Journal of Sport & Tourism, 14,* 229–247.

Alloy, Lauren B., & Abramson, Lyn Y. (2007). The adolescent surge in depression and emergence of gender differences: A biocognitive vulnerability-stress model in developmental context. In Daniel Romer & Elaine F. Walker (Eds.), *Adolescent psychopathology and the developing brain: Integrating brain and prevention science* (pp. 284–312). New York: Oxford University Press.

Alm, Bernt. (2007). To co-sleep or not to sleep. *Acta Pædiatrica, 96,* 1385–1386.

Alsaker, Françoise D., & Flammer, August (2006). Pubertal development. In Sandy Jackson & Luc Goossens (Eds.), *Handbook of adolescent development* (pp. 30–50). Hove, East Sussex, UK: Psychology Press.

Aluise, Christopher D., Sowell, Rena A., & Butterfield, D. Allan. (2008). Peptides and proteins in plasma and cerebrospinal fluid as biomarkers for the prediction, diagnosis, and monitoring of therapeutic efficacy of Alzheimer's disease. *Biochimica et Biophysica Acta (BBA)/Molecular Basis of Disease, 1782,* 549–558.

Alwin, Duane F. (2009). History, cohorts, and patterns of cognitive aging, *Aging and cognition: Research methodologies and empirical advances* (pp. 9–38). Washington, DC: American Psychological Association.

Amato, Paul R. (2010). Research on divorce: Continuing trends and new developments. *Journal of Marriage and Family, 72,* 650–666.

Amato, Paul R., & Cheadle, Jacob. (2005). The long reach of divorce: Divorce and child well-being across three generations. *Journal of Marriage and Family, 67,* 191–206.

Amato, Paul R., Johnson, David R., Booth, Alan, & Rogers, Stacy J. (2003). Continuity and change in marital quality between 1980 and 2000. *Journal of Marriage & Family, 65,* 1–22.

Ambady, Nalini, & Bharucha, Jamshed. (2009). Culture and the brain. *Current Directions in Psychological Science, 18,* 342–345.

American Psychiatric Association (APA). (2000). *Diagnostic and statistical manual of mental disorders: DSM-IV-TR* (4th ed.). Washington, DC: Author.

American Psychological Association. (2010). *Ethical principles of psychologists and code of conduct 2002: 2010 amendments.* Retrieved September 11, 2010, from the World Wide Web: http://www.apa.org/ethics/code/index.aspx

Amirkhanyan, Anna A., & Wolf, Douglas A. (2006). Parent care and the stress process: Findings from panel data. *Journals of Gerontology: Series B: Psychological Sciences and Social Sciences, 61,* S248–S255.

Anderson, Carol. (2003). The diversity, strength, and challenges of single-parent households. In Froma Walsh (Ed.), *Normal family processes: Growing diversity and complexity* (3rd ed., pp. 121–152). New York: Guilford Press.

Anderson, Craig A., Gentile, Douglas A., & Buckley, Katherine E. (2007). *Violent video game effects on children and adolescents: Theory, research, and public policy.* New York: Oxford University Press.

Anderson, Craig A., Sakamoto, Akira, Gentile, Douglas A., Ihori, Nobuko, Shibuya, Akiko, Yukawa, Shintaro, et al. (2008). Longitudinal effects of violent video games on aggression in Japan and the United States. *Pediatrics, 122,* e1067–1072.

Anderson, Gerard, & Horvath, Jane. (2004). The growing burden of chronic disease in America. *Public Health Reports, 119,* 263–270.

Anderson, Michael. (2001). 'You have to get inside the person' or making grief private: Image and metaphor in the therapeutic reconstruction of bereavement. In Jenny Hockey, Jeanne Katz & Neil Small (Eds.) *Grief, mourning, and death ritual* (pp.135–143). Hull University, UK: Open University Press.

Andrade, Susan E., Gurwitz, Jerry H., Davis, Robert L., Chan, K. Arnold, Finkelstein, Jonathan A., Fortman, Kris, et al. (2004). Prescription drug use in pregnancy. *American Journal of Obstetrics and Gynecology, 191,* 398–407.

Andreassen, Carol, & West, Jerry. (2007). Measuring socioemotional functioning in a national birth cohort study. *Infant Mental Health Journal, 28,* 627–646.

Andrews, Melinda W., Dowling, W. Jay, Bartlett, James C., & Halpern, Andrea R. (1998). Identification of speeded and slowed familiar melodies by younger, middle-aged, and older musicians and nonmusicians. *Psychology & Aging, 13,* 462–471.

Anis, Tarek. (2007). Hormones involved in male sexual function. In Annette Fuglsang Owens & Mitchell S. Tepper (Eds.), *Sexual health: Vol. 2. Physical foundations* (pp. 79–113). Westport, CT: Praeger/Greenwood.

Anjum, Afshan, Gait, Priyanka, Cullen, Kathryn R., & White, Tonya. (2010). Schizophrenia in adolescents and young adults. In Jon E. Grant & Marc N. Potenza (Eds.), *Young adult mental health* (pp. 362–378). New York: Oxford University Press.

Ansary, Nadia S., & Luthar, Suniya S. (2009). Distress and academic achievement among adolescents of affluence: A study of externalizing and internalizing problem behaviors and school performance. *Development and Psychopathology, 21,* 319–341.

Antonucci, Toni C., Akiyama, Hiroko, & Merline, Alicia. (2001). Dynamics of social relationships in midlife. In Margie E. Lachman (Ed.), *Handbook of midlife development* (pp. 571–598). New York: Wiley.

Antonucci, Toni C., Jackson, James S., & Biggs, Simon. (2007). Intergenerational relations: Theory, research, and policy. *Journal of Social Issues, 63,* 679–693.

Apgar, Virginia. (1953). A proposal for a new method of evaluation of the newborn infant. *Current Researches in Anesthesia and Analgesia, 32,* 260–267.

Apostolou, Menelaos. (2007). Sexual selection under parental choice: The role of parents in the evolution of human mating. *Evolution and Human Behavior, 28,* 403–409.

Applegate, Anthony J., Applegate, Mary DeKonty, McGeehan, Catherine M., Pinto, Catherine M., & Kong, Ailing. (2009). The assessment of thoughtful literacy in NAEP: Why the states aren't measuring up. *Reading Teacher, 62,* 372–381.

Appoh, Lily Yaa. (2004). Consequences of early malnutrition for subsequent social and emotional behaviour of children in Ghana. *Journal of Psychology in Africa, 14,* 87–94.

Appoh, Lily Yaa, & Krekling, Sturla. (2004). Effects of early childhood malnutrition on cognitive performance of Ghanaian children. *Journal of Psychology in Africa: South of the Sahara, the Caribbean, and Afro-Latin America, 14,* 1–7.

Archambault, Isabelle, Janosz, Michel, Fallu, Jean-Sebastien, & Pagani, Linda S. (2009). Student engagement and its relationship with early high school dropout. *Journal of Adolescence, 32,* 651–670.

Archer, John. (2000). Sex differences in aggression between heterosexual partners: A meta-analytic review. *Psychological Bulletin, 126,* 651–680.

Arita, Isao, Nakane, Miyuki, & Fenner, Frank. (2006, May 12). Is polio eradication realistic? *Science, 312,* 852–854.

Arking, Robert. (2006). *The biology of aging: Observations and principles* (3rd ed.). New York: Oxford University Press.

Armour, Marilyn. (2003). Meaning making in the aftermath of homicide. *Death Studies, 27,* 519–540.

Armson, B. Anthony. (2007). Is planned cesarean childbirth a safe alternative? *Canadian Medical Association Journal, 176,* 475–476.

Armstrong, Lyle, Tilgner, Katarzyna, Saretzki, Gabriele, Atkinson, Stuart P., Stojkovic, Miodrag, Moreno, Ruben, et al. (2010). Human induced pluripotent stem cell lines show stress defense mechanisms and mitochondrial regulation similar to those of human embryonic stem cells. *Stem Cells, 28,* 661–673.

Arnett, Jeffrey Jensen. (2002). The psychology of globalization. *American Psychologist, 57,* 774–783.

Arnett, Jeffrey Jensen. (2004). *Emerging adulthood: The winding road from the late teens through the twenties.* New York: Oxford University Press.

Arnett, Jeffrey Jensen. (2010). Oh, grow up! *Perspectives on Psychological Science, 5,* 89–92.

Arnett, Jeffrey Jensen, & Brody, Gene H. (2008). A fraught passage: The identity challenges of African American emerging adults. *Human Development, 51,* 291–293.

Arnold, L. Eugene, Farmer, Cristan, Kraemer, Helena Chmura, Davies, Mark, Witwer, Andrea, Chuang, Shirley, et al. (2010). Moderators, mediators, and other predictors of risperidone response in children with autistic disorder and irritability. *Journal of Child and Adolescent Psychopharmacology, 20,* 83–93.

Aron, Arthur. (2010). Behavior, the brain, and the social psychology of close relationships. In Christopher R. Agnew, Donald E. Carlston, William G. Graziano, & Janice R. Kelly (Eds.), *Then a miracle occurs: Focusing on behavior in social psychological theory and research* (pp. 283–298). New York: Oxford University Press.

Aron, Arthur, McLaughlin-Volpe, Tracy, Mashek, Debra, Lewandowski, Gary, Wright, Stephen C., & Aron, Elaine N. (2005). Including others in the self. *European Review of Social Psychology, 15,* 101–132.

Aronson, Joshua, Fried, Carrie B., & Good, Catherine. (2002). Reducing the effects of stereotype threat on African American college students by shaping theories of intelligence. *Journal of Experimental Social Psychology, 38,* 113–125.

Artistico, Daniele, Orom, Heather, Cervone, Daniel, Krauss, Stephen, & Houston, Eric. (2010). Everyday challenges in context: The influence of contextual factors on everyday problem solving among young, middle-aged, and older adults. *Experimental Aging Research, 36,* 230–247.

Aseltine, Robert H., Jr., & DeMartino, Robert. (2004). An outcome evaluation of the SOS suicide prevention program. *American Journal of Public Health, 94,* 446–451.

Asendorpf, Jens B., Denissen, Jaap J. A., & van Aken, Marcel A. G. (2008). Inhibited and aggressive preschool children at 23 years of age: Personality and social transitions into adulthood. *Developmental Psychology, 44,* 997–1011.

Ash, Caroline, Jasny, Barbara R., Roberts, Leslie, Stone, Richard, & Sugden, Andrew M. (2008, February 8). Reimagining cities. *Science, 319,* 739.

Ash, Katie. (2009, October 21). Maine 1-to-1 effort moves forward: Student laptop program expands into high schools. *Education Week's Digital Directions, 3,* 14–15.

Aspinall, Richard J. (2003). *Aging of organs and systems.* Boston: Kluwer Academic.

Asscheman, Henk. (2009). Gender identity disorder in adolescents. *Sexologies, 18,* 105–108.

Association of American Medical Colleges. (2010). *AAMC data book: Medical schools and teaching hospitals by the numbers 2010.* Washington, DC: Author.

Astin, Alexander W., & Oseguera, Leticia. (2004). The declining "equity" of American higher education. *Review of Higher Education, 27,* 321–341.

Atchley, Robert C. (2009). *Spirituality and aging.* Baltimore: Johns Hopkins University Press.

Atkinson, Janette, & Braddick, Oliver. (2003). Neurobiological models of normal and abnormal visual development. In Michelle De Haan & Mark H. Johnson (Eds.), *The cognitive neuroscience of development* (pp. 43–71). New York: Psychology Press.

Attar-Schwartz, Shalhevet, Tan, Jo-Pei, Buchanan, Ann, Flouri, Eirini, & Griggs, Julia. (2009). Grandparenting and adolescent adjustment in two-parent biological, lone-parent, and step-families. *Journal of Family Psychology, 23,* 67–75.

Audrey, Suzanne, Holliday, Jo, & Campbell, Rona. (2006). It's good to talk: Adolescent perspectives of an informal, peer-led intervention to reduce smoking. *Social Science & Medicine, 63,* 320–334.

Aunola, Kaisa, & Nurmi, Jari-Erik. (2004). Maternal affection moderates the impact of psychological control on a child's mathematical performance. *Developmental Psychology, 40,* 965–978.

Austrian, Sonia G. (2008). *Developmental theories through the life cycle* (2nd ed.). New York: Columbia University Press.

Avery, Rosemary J., & Freundlich, Madelyn. (2009). You're all grown up now: Termination of foster care support at age 18. *Journal of Adolescence, 32,* 247–257.

Ayalon, Liat, & Ancoli-Israel, Sonia. (2009). Normal sleep in aging. In Teofilo L. Lee-Chiong (Ed.), *Sleep medicine essentials* (pp. 173–176). Hoboken, NJ: Wiley-Blackwell.

Ayduk, Özlem, & Kross, Ethan. (2008). Enhancing the pace of recovery. *Psychological Science, 19,* 229–231.

Ayers, Catherine R., Saxena, Sanjaya, Golshan, Shahrokh, & Wetherell, Julie Loebach. (2010). Age at onset and clinical features of late life compulsive hoarding. *International Journal of Geriatric Psychiatry, 25,* 142–149.

Azrin, Nathan H., & Foxx, Richard M. (1974). *Toilet training in less than a day.* New York: Simon and Schuster.

Badaloo, Asha V., Forrester, Terrence, Reid, Marvin, & Jahoor, Farook. (2006). Lipid kinetic differences between children with kwashiorkor and those with marasmus. *American Journal of Clinical Nutrition, 83,* 1283–1288.

Baddeley, Alan D. (2007). *Working memory, thought, and action.* New York: Oxford University Press.

Bagner, Daniel M., Pettit, Jeremy W., Lewinsohn, Peter M., & Seeley, John R. (2010). Effect of maternal depression on child behavior: A sensitive period? *Journal of the American Academy of Child and Adolescent Psychiatry, 49,* 699–707.

Bailey, Kira, West, Robert, & Anderson, Craig A. (2010). A negative association between video game experience and proactive cognitive control. *Psychophysiology, 47,* 34–42.

Baillargeon, Renée. (1994). How do infants learn about the physical world? *Current Directions in Psychological Science, 3,* 133–140.

Baillargeon, Renée. (2000). How do infants learn about the physical world? In Darwin Muir & Alan Slater (Eds.), *Infant development: The essential readings* (pp. 195–212). Malden, MA: Blackwell.

Baillargeon, Renée, & DeVos, Julie. (1991). Object permanence in young infants: Further evidence. *Child Development, 62,* 1227–1246.

Baker, Jason K., Fenning, Rachel M., Crnic, Keith A., Baker, Bruce L., & Blacher, Jan. (2007). Prediction of social skills in 6-year-old children with and without developmental delays: Contributions of early regulation and maternal scaffolding. *American Journal on Mental Retardation, 112,* 375–391.

Baker, Jeffrey P. (2000). Immunization and the American way: 4 childhood vaccines. *American Journal of Public Health, 90,* 199–207.

Baker, Susan P. (2000). Where have we been and where are we going with injury control? In Dinesh Mohan & Geetam Tiwari (Eds.), *Injury prevention and control* (pp. 19–26). London: Taylor & Francis.

Bakir, Vian. (2010). Media and risk: Old and new research directions. *Journal of Risk Research, 13,* 5–18.

Baldwin, Dare A. (1993). Infants' ability to consult the speaker for clues to word reference. *Journal of Child Language, 20,* 395–418.

Balter, Michael. (2006, June 30). The baby deficit. *Science, 312,* 1894–1897.

Baltes, Margret M., & Carstensen, Laura L. (2003). The process of successful aging: Selection, optimization and compensation. In Ursula M. Staudinger & Ulman Lindenberger (Eds.),

Understanding human development: Dialogues with lifespan psychology (pp. 81–104). Dordrecht, The Netherlands: Kluwer.

Baltes, Paul B. (2003). On the incomplete architechture of human ontogeny: Selection, optimization and compensation as foundation of developmental theory. In Ursula M. Staudinger & Ulman Lindenberger (Eds.), *Understanding human development: Dialogues with lifespan psychology* (pp. 17–43). Dordrecht, The Netherlands: Kluwer.

Baltes, Paul B., & Baltes, Margret M. (1990). Psychological perspectives on successful aging: The model of selective optimization with compensation. In Paul B. Baltes & Margret M. Baltes (Eds.), *Successful aging: Perspectives from the behavioral sciences* (pp. 1–34). New York: Cambridge University Press.

Baltes, Paul B., Lindenberger, Ulman, & Staudinger, Ursula M. (1998). Life-span theory in developmental psychology. In William Damon (Series Ed.) & Richard M. Lerner (Vol. Ed.), *Handbook of child psychology: Vol. 1. Theoretical models of human development* (5th ed., pp. 1029–1144). New York: Wiley.

Baltes, Paul B., Lindenberger, Ulman, & Staudinger, Ursula M. (2006). Life span theory in developmental psychology. In William Damon & Richard M. Lerner (Series Eds.) & Richard M. Lerner (Vol. Ed.), *Handbook of child psychology: Vol. 1. Theoretical models of human development* (6th ed., pp. 569–664). Hoboken, NJ: Wiley

Baltes, Paul B., & Smith, Jacqui. (2008). The fascination of wisdom: Its nature, ontogeny, and function. *Perspectives on Psychological Science, 3,* 56–64.

Bamford, Christi, & Lagattuta, Kristin Hansen. (2010). A new look at children's understanding of mind and emotion: The case of prayer. *Developmental Psychology, 46,* 78–92.

Bandura, Albert. (1977). *Social learning theory.* Englewood Cliffs, NJ: Prentice Hall.

Bandura, Albert. (1986). *Social foundations of thought and action: A social cognitive theory.* Englewood Cliffs, NJ: Prentice Hall.

Bandura, Albert. (1997). The anatomy of stages of change. *American Journal of Health Promotion, 12,* 8–10.

Bandura, Albert. (2006). Toward a psychology of human agency. *Perspectives on Psychological Science, 1,* 164–180.

Bandura, Albert, Barbaranelli, Claudio, Caprara, Gian Vittorio, & Pastorelli, Concetta. (2001). Self-efficacy beliefs as shapers of children's aspirations and career trajectories. *Child Development, 72,* 187–206.

Bandura, Albert, & Bussey, Kay. (2004). On broadening the cognitive, motivational, and sociostructural scope of theorizing about gender development and functioning: Comment on Martin, Ruble, and Szkrybalo (2002). *Psychological Bulletin, 130,* 691–701.

Banerjee, Robin, & Lintern, Vicki. (2000). Boys will be boys: The effect of social evaluation concerns on gender-typing. *Social Development, 9,* 397–408.

Banich, Marie T., Mackiewicz, Kristen L., Depue, Brendan E., Whitmer, Anson J., Miller, Gregory A., & Heller, Wendy. (2009). Cognitive control mechanisms, emotion and memory: A neural perspective with implications for psychopathology. *Neuroscience & Biobehavioral Reviews, 33,* 613–630.

Bansal, Vishal, Fortlage, Dale, Lee, Jeanne, Costantini, Todd, Potenza, Bruce, & Coimbra, Raul. (2009). Hemorrhage is more prevalent than brain injury in early trauma deaths: The golden six hours. *European Journal of Trauma and Emergency Surgery, 35,* 26–30.

Barber, Brian K. (Ed.). (2002). *Intrusive parenting: How psychological control affects children and adolescents.* Washington, DC: American Psychological Association.

Barbey, Aron K., Krueger, Frank, & Grafman, Jordan. (2009). An evolutionarily adaptive neural architecture for social reasoning. *Trends in Neurosciences, 32,* 603–610.

Barbey, Aron K., & Sloman, Steven A. (2007). Base-rate respect: From ecological rationality to dual processes. *Behavioral and Brain Sciences, 30,* 241–254.

Barger, Steven D., & Gallo, Linda C. (2008). Ability of ethnic self-identification to partition modifiable health risk among US residents of Mexican ancestry. *American Journal of Public Health, 98,* 1971–1978.

Barinaga, Marcia. (2003, January 3). Newborn neurons search for meaning. *Science, 299,* 32–34.

Barkin, Shari, Scheindlin, Benjamin, Ip, Edward H., Richardson, Irma, & Finch, Stacia. (2007). Determinants of parental discipline practices: A national sample from primary care practices. *Clinical Pediatrics, 46,* 64–69.

Barkley, Russell A. (2006). *Attention-deficit hyperactivity disorder: A handbook for diagnosis and treatment* (3rd ed.). New York: Guilford Press.

Barnes, Grace M., Hoffman, Joseph H., Welte, John W., Farrell, Michael P., & Dintcheff, Barbara A. (2006). Effects of parental monitoring and peer deviance on substance use and delinquency. *Journal of Marriage and Family, 68,* 1084–1104.

Barnes, Lisa L., de Leon, Carlos F. Mendes, Lewis, Tené T., Bienias, Julia L., Wilson, Robert S., & Evans, Denis A. (2008). Perceived discrimination and mortality in a population-based study of older adults. *American Journal of Public Health, 98,* 1241–1247.

Barnett, Kylie J., Finucane, Ciara, Asher, Julian E., Bargary, Gary, Corvin, Aiden P., Newell, Fiona N., et al. (2008). Familial patterns and the origins of individual differences in synaesthesia. *Cognition, 106,* 871–893.

Barnett, Mark, Watson, Ruth, & Kind, Peter. (2006). Pathways to barrel development. In Reha Erzurumlu, William Guido, & Zoltán Molnár (Eds.), *Development and plasticity in sensory thalamus and cortex* (pp. 138–157). New York: Springer.

Barnett, W. Steven. (2007). Benefits and costs of quality early childhood education. *Children's Legal Rights Journal, 27,* 7–23.

Barnett, W. Steven, Epstein, Dale J., Friedman, Allison H., Boyd, Judi Stevenson, & Hustedt, Jason T. (2008). *The state of preschool 2008.* New Brunswick, NJ: The National Institute for Early Education Research.

Baron, Andrew Scott, & Banaji, Mahzarin R. (2006). The development of implicit attitudes: Evidence of race evaluations from ages 6 and 10 and adulthood. *Psychological Science, 17,* 53–58.

Barrett, Justin L. (2008). Why Santa Claus is not a god. *Journal of Cognition and Culture, 8,* 149–161.

Barrett, Karen Caplovitz. (2005). The origins of social emotions and self-regulation in toddlerhood: New evidence. *Cognition & Emotion, 19,* 953–979.

Barrett, Linda L. (2006). *The costs of long-term care: Public perceptions versus reality in 2006.* Washington, DC: AARP.

Barry, Michael J. (2009). Screening for prostate cancer—The controversy that refuses to die. *New England Journal of Medicine, 360,* 1351–1354.

Barry, Patrick. (2007, September 8). Genome 2.0: Mountains of new data are challenging old views. *Science News, 172,* 154.

Barzilai, Nir, & Bartke, Andrzej. (2009). Biological approaches to mechanistically understand the healthy life span extension achieved by calorie restriction and modulation of hormones. *Journals of Gerontology Series A: Biological Sciences and Medical Sciences, 64A,* 187–191.

Basak, Chandramallika, Boot, Walter R., Voss, Michelle W., & Kramer, Arthur F. (2008). Can training in a real-time strategy video game attenuate cognitive decline in older adults? *Psychology and Aging, 23,* 765–777.

Basáñez, María-Gloria, Pion, Sébastien D. S., Churcher, Thomas S., Breitling, Lutz P., Little, Mark P., & Boussinesq, Michel. (2006). River blindness: A success story under threat? *PLoS Medicine, 3,* e371.

Basseches, Michael. (1984). *Dialectical thinking and adult development.* Norwood, NJ: Ablex.

Basseches, Michael. (1989). Dialectical thinking as an organized whole: Comments on Irwin and Kramer. In Michael L. Commons, Jan D. Sinnott, Francis A. Richards, & Cheryl Armon (Eds.), *Adult development: Vol. 1. Comparisons and applications of developmental models* (pp. 161–178). New York: Praeger.

Bates, Gillian, Harper, Peter S., & Jones, Lesley (Eds.). (2002). *Huntington's disease* (3rd ed.). Oxford, UK: Oxford University Press.

Bates, Lisa M., Acevedo-Garcia, Dolores, Alegria, Margarita, & Krieger, Nancy. (2008). Immigration and generational trends in body mass index and obesity in the United States: Results of the National Latino and Asian American Survey, 2002–2003. *American Journal of Public Health, 98,* 70–77.

Bateson, Patrick. (2005, February 4). Desirable scientific conduct. *Science, 307,* 645.

Batterham, Philip J., Christensen, Helen, & Mackinnon, Andrew J. (2009). Fluid intelligence is independently associated with all-cause mortality over 17 years in an elderly community sample: An investigation of potential mechanisms. *Intelligence, 37,* 551–560.

Bauer, Patricia J. (2006). Event memory. In William Damon & Richard M. Lerner (Series Eds.) & Deanna Kuhn & Robert S. Siegler (Vol. Eds.), *Handbook of child psychology: Vol. 2. Cognition, perception, and language* (6th ed., pp. 373–425). Hoboken, NJ: Wiley.

Bauer, Patricia J., San Souci, Priscilla, & Pathman, Thanujeni. (2010). Infant memory. *Wiley Interdisciplinary Reviews: Cognitive Science, 1,* 267–277.

Baugher, John Eric. (2008). Facing death: Buddhist and western hospice approaches. *Symbolic Interaction, 31,* 259–284.

Baum, Katrina. (2005). *Juvenile victimization and offending, 1993–2003* (NCJ 209468). Washington, DC: U.S. Department of Justice, Office of Justice Programs.

Baum, Steven K. (2008). *The psychology of genocide: Perpetrators, bystanders, and rescuers.* New York: Cambridge University Press.

Baumeister, Roy F., & Blackhart, Ginnette C. (2007). Three perspectives on gender differences in adolescent sexual development. In Rutger C. M. E. Engels, Margaret Kerr, & Håkan Stattin (Eds.), *Friends, lovers, and groups: Key relationships in adolescence* (pp. 93–104). Hoboken, NJ: Wiley.

Baumeister, Roy F., Campbell, Jennifer D., Krueger, Joachim I., & Vohs, Kathleen D. (2003). Does high self-esteem cause better performance, interpersonal success, happiness, or healthier lifestyles? *Psychological Science in the Public Interest, 4,* 1–44.

Baumrind, Diana. (1967). Child care practices anteceding three patterns of preschool behavior. *Genetic Psychology Monographs, 75,* 43–88.

Baumrind, Diana. (1971). Current patterns of parental authority. *Developmental Psychology, 4*(1:2), 1–103.

Baumrind, Diana. (2005). Patterns of parental authority and adolescent autonomy. *New Directions for Child and Adolescent Development, 2005,* 61–69.

Bayer, Carey Roth. (2007). Understanding family planning, birth control, and contraception. In Annette Fuglsang Owens & Mitchell S. Tepper (Eds.), *Sexual health: Vol. 4. State-of-the-art treatments and research* (pp. 211–233). Westport, CT: Praeger/Greenwood.

Bayer, Jordana K., Hiscock, Harriet, Hampton, Anne, & Wake, Melissa. (2007). Sleep problems in young infants and maternal mental and physical health. *Journal of Paediatrics and Child Health, 43,* 66–73.

Bayley, Nancy. (1966). Learning in adulthood: The role of intelligence. In Herbert J. Klausmeier & Chester William Harris (Eds.), *Analyses of concept learning* (pp. 117–138). New York: Academic Press.

Bayley, Nancy, & Oden, Melita H. (1955). The maintenance of intellectual ability in gifted adults. *Journal of Gerontology Series B, 10,* 91–107.

Beal, Susan. (1988). Sleeping position and sudden infant death syndrome. *The Medical Journal of Australia, 149,* 562.

Beaudoin, Kathleen M., & Schonert-Reichl, Kimberly A. (2006). Epistemic reasoning and adolescent egocentrism: Relations to internalizing and externalizing symptoms in problem youth. *Journal of Youth and Adolescence, 35,* 999–1014.

Beck, Melinda. (2009, May 26). How's your baby? Recalling the Apgar score's namesake. *Wall Street Journal,* pp. D1.

Beck, Martha Nibley. (1999). *Expecting Adam: A true story of birth, rebirth, and everyday magic.* New York: Times Books.

Beckers, Debby G. J., van der Linden, Dimitri, Smulders, Peter G. W., Kompier, Michiel A. J., Taris, Toon W., & Geurts, Sabine A. E. (2008). Voluntary or involuntary? Control over overtime and rewards for overtime in relation to fatigue and work satisfaction. *Work & Stress, 22,* 33–50.

Beckett, Nigel S., Peters, Ruth, Fletcher, Astrid E., Staessen, Jan A., Liu, Lisheng, Dumitrascu, Dan, et al. (2008). Treatment of hypertension in patients 80 years of age or older. *New England Journal of Medicine, 358,* 1887–1898.

Begos, Kevin. (2010, Winter). A wounded hero. *CR, 5,* 30–35, 62–63.

Behne, Tanya, Carpenter, Malinda, Call, Josep, & Tomasello, Michael. (2005). Unwilling versus unable: Infants' understanding of intentional action. *Developmental Psychology, 41,* 328–337.

Behnke, Andrew O., MacDermid, Shelley M., Coltrane, Scott L., Parke, Ross D., Duffy, Sharon, & Widaman, Keith F. (2008). Family cohesion in the lives of Mexican American and European American parents. *Journal of Marriage and Family, 70,* 1045–1059.

Beilin, Lawrence, & Huang, Rae-Chi. (2008). Childhood obesity, hypertension, the metabolic syndrome and adult cardiovascular disease. *Clinical and Experimental Pharmacology and Physiology, 35,* 409–411.

Belamarich, Peter, & Ayoob, Keith-Thomas. (2001). Keeping teenage vegetarians healthy and in the know. *Contemporary Pediatrics, 10,* 89–108.

Belfield, Clive R., Nores, Milagros, Barnett, Steve, & Schweinhart, Lawrence. (2006). The High/Scope Perry Preschool Program: Cost benefit analysis using data from the age-40 followup. *Journal of Human Resources, 41,* 162–190.

Belizán, José M., Althabe, Fernando, Barros, Fernando C., & Alexander, Sophie. (1999). Rates and implications of caesarean sections in Latin America: Ecological study. *British Medical Journal, 319,* 1397–1402.

Belka, David. (2004). Substituting skill learning for traditional games in early childhood. *Teaching Elementary Physical Education, 15,* 25–27.

Bell, Joanna H., & Bromnick, Rachel D. (2003). The social reality of the imaginary audience: A ground theory approach. *Adolescence, 38,* 205–219.

Bell, Richard Q., & Harper, Lawrence V. (1977). *Child effects on adults.* Hillsdale, NJ: Erlbaum.

Bell, Ruth. (1998). *Changing bodies, changing lives: A book for teens on sex and relationships* (Expanded 3rd ed.). New York: Times Books.

Bellah, Robert Neelly, Madsen, Richard, Sullivan, William M., Swidler, Ann, & Tipton, Steven M. (2007). *Habits of the heart: Individualism and commitment in American life* (3rd ed.). Berkeley, CA: University of California Press.

Belsky, Jay, Bakermans-Kranenburg, Marian J., & Van IJzendoorn, Marinus H. (2007). For better and for worse: Differential susceptibility to environmental influences. *Current Directions in Psychological Science, 16,* 300–304.

Belsky, Jay, & Pluess, Michael. (2009). The nature (and nurture?) of plasticity in early human development. *Perspectives on Psychological Science, 4,* 345–351.

Belsky, Jay, Steinberg, Laurence, Houts, Renate M., Halpern-Felsher, Bonnie L., & The NICHD Early Child Care Research Network. (2010). The development of reproductive strategy in females: Early maternal harshness → earlier menarche → increased sexual risk taking. *Developmental Psychology, 46,* 120–128.

Ben-Zur, Hasida, & Zeidner, Moshe. (2009). Threat to life and risk-taking behaviors: A review of empirical findings and explanatory models. *Personality and Social Psychology Review, 13,* 109–128.

Benacerraf, Beryl R. (2007). *Ultrasound of fetal syndromes* (2nd ed.). Philadelphia: Churchill Livingstone/Elsevier.

Bendlin, Barbara B., Canu, Elisa, Willette, Auriel A., Kastman, Erik K., McLaren, Donald G., Kosmatka, Kris J., et al. (in press). Effects of aging and calorie restriction on white matter in rhesus macaques. *Neurobiology of Aging.*

Benenson, Joyce F., Markovits, Henry, Fitzgerald, Caitlin, Geoffroy, Diana, Flemming, Julianne, Kahlenberg, Sonya M., et al. (2009). Males' greater tolerance of same-sex peers. *Psychological Science, 20,* 184–190.

Benet, Sula. (1974). *Abkhasians: The long-living people of the Caucasus.* New York: Holt, Rinehart & Winston.

Bengtson, Vern L. (2001). Beyond the nuclear family: The increasing importance of multigenerational bonds (The Burgess Award Lecture). *Journal of Marriage & the Family, 63,* 1–16.

Benjamin, Georges C. (2004). The solution is injury prevention. *American Journal of Public Health, 94,* 521.

Benjamin, Roger. (2003). *The coming transformation of the American university.* New York: Council for Aid to Education/An Independent Subsidiary of RAND.

Benner, Aprile D., & Graham, Sandra. (2007). Navigating the transition to multi-ethnic urban high schools: Changing ethnic congruence and adolescents' school-related affect. *Journal of Research on Adolescence, 17,* 207–220.

Bennett, Teri, & Gaines, Jean. (2010). Believing what you hear: The impact of aging stereotypes upon the old. *Educational Gerontology, 36,* 435–445.

Bentley, Gillian R., & Mascie-Taylor, C. G. Nicholas. (2000). Introduction. In Gillian R. Bentley & C. G. Nicholas Mascie-Taylor (Eds.), *Infertility in the modern world: Present and future prospects* (pp. 1–13). Cambridge, England: Cambridge University Press.

Berenbaum, Sheri A., Martin, Carol Lynn, Hanish, Laura D., Briggs, Phillip T., & Fabes, Richard A. (2008). Sex differences in children's play. In Jill B. Becker, Karen J. Berkley, Nori Geary, Elizabeth Hampson, James P. Herman, & Elizabeth Young (Eds.), *Sex differences in the brain: From genes to behavior* (pp. 275–290). New York: Oxford University Press.

Berg, Cynthia A. (2008). Everyday problem solving in context. In Scott M. Hofer & Duane F. Alwin (Eds.), *Handbook of cognitive aging: Interdisciplinary perspectives* (pp. 207–223). Thousand Oaks, CA: Sage.

Berg, Sandra J., & Wynne-Edwards, Katherine E. (2002). Salivary hormone concentrations in mothers and fathers becoming parents are not correlated. *Hormones & Behavior, 42,* 424–436.

Berger, Kathleen Stassen. (2007). Update on bullying at school: Science forgotten? *Developmental Review, 27,* 90–126.

Berger, Lawrence M., Paxson, Christina, & Waldfogel, Jane. (2009). Income and child development. *Children and Youth Services Review, 31,* 978–989.

Bering, Jesse M., & Bjorklund, David F. (2004). The natural emergence of reasoning about the afterlife as a developmental regularity. *Developmental Psychology, 40,* 217–233.

Bering, Jesse M., Blasi, Carlos Hernández, & Bjorklund, David F. (2005). The development of 'afterlife' beliefs in religiously and secularly schooled children. *British Journal of Developmental Psychology, 23,* 587–607.

Berkey, Catherine S., Gardner, Jane D., Frazier, A. Lindsay, & Colditz, Graham A. (2000). Relation of childhood diet and body size to menarche and adolescent growth in girls. *American Journal of Epidemiology, 152,* 446–452.

Berkman, Michael B., & Plutzer, Eric. (2004). Gray peril or loyal support? The effects of the elderly on educational expenditures. *Social Science Quarterly, 85,* 1178–1192.

Berman, Alan L., Jobes, David A., & Silverman, Morton M. (2006). *Adolescent suicide: Assessment and intervention* (2nd ed.). Washington, DC: American Psychological Association.

Berndt, Thomas J., & Murphy, Lonna M. (2002). Influences of friends and friendships: Myths, truths, and research recommendations. In Robert V. Kail (Ed.), *Advances in child development and behavior* (Vol. 30, pp. 275–310). San Diego, CA: Academic Press.

Bernstein, Mary. (2005). Identity politics. *Annual Review of Sociology, 31,* 47–74.

Besga, Ariadna, Ortiz, Laura, Fernández, Alberto, Maestu, Fernando, Arrazola, Juan, Gil-Gregorio, Pedro, et al. (2010). Structural and functional patterns in healthy aging, mild cognitive impairment, and Alzheimer disease. *Alzheimer Disease and Associated Disorders, 24,* 1–10.

Bhasin, Shalender. (2007). Approach to the infertile man. *Journal of Clinical Endocrinology & Metabolism, 92,* 1995–2004.

Bhattacharjee, Yudhijit. (2008, February 8). Choking on fumes, Kolkata faces a noxious future. *Science, 319,* 749.

Bhutta, Zulfiqar A., Ali, Samana, Cousens, Simon, Ali, Talaha M., Haider, Batool Azra, Rizvi, Arjumand, et al. (2008). Interventions to address maternal, newborn, and child survival: What difference can integrated primary health care strategies make? *Lancet, 372,* 972–989.

Bialystok, Ellen, & Viswanathan, Mythili. (2009). Components of executive control with advantages for bilingual children in two cultures. *Cognition, 112,* 494–500.

Bianchi, Suzanne M., Casper, Lynne M., & King, Rosalind Berkowitz (Eds.). (2005). *Work, family, health, and well-being.* Mahwah, NJ: Erlbaum.

Bianchi, Suzanne M., & Milkie, Melissa A. (2010). Work and family research in the first decade of the 21st century. *Journal of Marriage and Family, 72,* 705–725.

Biblarz, Timothy J., & Savci, Evren. (2010). Lesbian, gay, bisexual, and transgender families. *Journal of Marriage and Family, 72,* 480–497.

Biblarz, Timothy J., & Stacey, Judith. (2010). How does the gender of parents matter? *Journal of Marriage and Family, 72,* 3–22.

Biederman, Joseph, Spencer, Thomas J., Monuteaux, Michael C., & Faraone, Stephen V. (2010). A naturalistic 10-year prospective study of height and weight in children with attention-deficit hyperactivity disorder grown up: Sex and treatment effects. *The Journal of Pediatrics, 157,* 635–640. e631.

Biehl, Michael C., Natsuaki, Misaki N., & Ge, Xiaojia. (2007). The influence of pubertal timing on alcohol use and heavy drinking trajectories. *Journal of Youth and Adolescence, 36,* 153–167.

Bienvenu, Thierry. (2005). Rett syndrome. In Merlin Gene Butler & F. John Meaney (Eds.), *Genetics of developmental disabilities* (pp. 477–519). Boca Raton, FL: Taylor & Francis.

Bijou, Sidney W., & Baer, Donald M. (1978). *Behavior analysis of child development.* Englewood Cliffs, NJ: Prentice-Hall.

Bilalić, Merim, McLeod, Peter, & Gobet, Fernand. (2009). Specialization effect and its influence on memory and problem solving in expert chess players. *Cognitive Science, 33,* 1117–1143.

Binstock, Robert. (2006–2007). Older people and political engagement: From avid voters to 'cooled-out marks'. *Generations, 30,* 24–30.

Birch, Susan A. J., & Bloom, Paul. (2003). Children are cursed: An asymmetric bias in mental-state attribution. *Psychological Science, 14,* 283–286.

Birditt, Kira S., & Fingerman, Karen L. (2005). Do we get better at picking our battles? Age group differences in descriptions of behavioral reactions to interpersonal tensions. *The Journals of Gerontology Series B: Psychological Sciences and Social Sciences, 60,* P121–P128.

Birditt, Kira S., Fingerman, Karen L., & Zarit, Steven H. (2010). Adult children's problems and successes: Implications for intergenerational ambivalence. *The Journals of Gerontology Series B: Psychological Sciences and Social Sciences, 65B,* 145–153.

Birditt, Kira S., Miller, Laura M., Fingerman, Karen L., & Lefkowitz, Eva S. (2009). Tensions in the parent and adult child relationship: Links to solidarity and ambivalence. *Psychology and Aging, 24,* 287–295.

Birdsong, David. (2006). Age and second language acquisition and processing: A selective overview. *Language Learning, 56*(Suppl. 1), 9–49.

Birney, Damian P., Citron-Pousty, Jill H., Lutz, Donna J., & Sternberg, Robert J. (2005). The development of cognitive and intellectual abilities. In Marc H. Bornstein & Michael E. Lamb (Eds.), *Developmental science: An advanced textbook* (5th ed., pp. 327–358). Mahwah, NJ: Erlbaum.

Biro, Frank M., McMahon, Robert P., Striegel-Moore, Ruth, Crawford, Patricia B., Obarzanek, Eva, Morrison, John A., et al. (2001). Impact of timing of pubertal maturation on growth in black and white female adolescents: The National Heart, Lung, and Blood Institute Growth and Health Study. *Journal of Pediatrics, 138,* 636–643.

Biro, Frank M., Striegel-Moore, Ruth H., Franko, Debra L., Padgett, Justina, & Bean, Judy A. (2006). Self-esteem in adolescent females. *Journal of Adolescent Health, 39,* 501–507.

Birren, James E., & Schroots, Johannes J. F. (2006). Autobiographical memory and the narrative self over the life span. In James E. Birren & K. Warner Schaie (Eds.), *Handbook of the psychology of aging* (6th ed., pp. 477–498). Amsterdam: Elsevier.

Bisiacchi, Patrizia Silvia, Mento, Giovanni, & Suppiej, Agnese. (2009). Cortical auditory processing in preterm newborns: An ERP study. *Biological Psychology, 82,* 176–185.

Bisson, Melissa, & Levine, Timothy. (2009). Negotiating a friends with benefits relationship. *Archives of Sexual Behavior, 38,* 66–73.

Bitensky, Susan H. (2006). *Corporal punishment of children: A human rights violation.* Boston: Brill.

Bjorklund, David F., Dukes, Charles, & Brown, Rhonda Douglas. (2009). The development of memory strategies. In Mary L. Courage & Nelson Cowan (Eds.), *The development of memory in infancy and childhood* (2nd ed., pp. 145–175). New York: Psychology Press.

Black, Corri, Kaye, James A., & Jick, Hershel. (2005). Cesarean delivery in the United Kingdom: Time trends in the General Practice Research Database. *Obstetrics & Gynecology, 106,* 151–155.

Black, Kathy. (2008). Health and aging-in-place: Implications for community practice. *Journal of Community Practice, 16,* 79–95.

Blair, Peter S., & Ball, Helen L. (2004). The prevalence and characteristics associated with parent-infant bed-sharing in England. *Archives of Disease in Childhood, 89,* 1106–1110.

Blakemore, Sarah-Jayne. (2008). Development of the social brain during adolescence. *The Quarterly Journal of Experimental Psychology, 61,* 40–49.

Blalock, Garrick, Kadiyali, Vrinda, & Simon, Daniel H. (2009). Driving fatalities after 9/11: A hidden cost of terrorism. *Applied Economics, 41,* 1717–1729.

Blanchard-Fields, Fredda. (2007). Everyday problem solving and emotion: An adult developmental perspective. *Current Directions in Psychological Science, 16,* 26–31.

Blas, Erik, & Kurup, Anand Sivasankara (Eds.). (2010). *Equity, social determinants, and public health programmes.* Geneva, Switzerland: World Health Organization.

Blekesaune, Morten. (2008). Partnership transitions and mental distress: Investigating temporal order. *Journal of Marriage and Family, 70,* 879–890.

Bleske-Rechek, April L., & Buss, David M. (2001). Opposite-sex friendship: Sex differences and similarities in initiation, selection, and dissolution. *Personality and Social Psychology Bulletin, 27,* 1310–1323.

Bloch, Michele, Althabe, Fernando, Onyamboko, Marie, Kaseba-Sata, Christine, Castilla, Eduardo E., Freire, Salvio, et al. (2008). Tobacco use and secondhand smoke exposure during pregnancy: An investigative survey of women in 9 developing nations. *American Journal of Public Health, 98,* 1833–1840.

Blonigen, Daniel M., Carlson, Marie D., Hicks, Brian M., Krueger, Robert F., & Iacono, William G. (2008). Stability and change in personality traits from late adolescence to early adulthood: A longitudinal twin study. *Journal of Personality, 76,* 229–266.

Bloom, Barbara, Cohen, Robin A., & Freeman, Gulnur. (2009). Summary health statistics for U.S. children: National Health Interview Survey, 2008. *Vital and Health Statistics, 10*(244).

Bloom, Lois. (1993). *The transition from infancy to language: Acquiring the power of expression.* New York: Cambridge University Press.

Bloom, Lois. (1998). Language acquisition in its developmental context. In William Damon (Series Ed.) & Deanna Kuhn & Robert S. Siegler (Vol. Eds.), *Handbook of child psychology: Vol. 2. Cognition, perception, and language* (5th ed., pp. 309–370). New York: Wiley.

Blum, Deborah. (2002). *Love at Goon Park: Harry Harlow and the science of affection.* Cambridge, MA: Perseus.

Blum, Nathan J., Taubman, Bruce, & Nemeth, Nicole. (2003). Relationship between age at initiation of toilet training and duration of training: A prospective study. *Pediatrics, 111*(4, Pt. 1), 810–814.

Blum, Robert W., Beuhring, Trisha, Shew, Marcia L., Bearinger, Linda H., Sieving, Renee E., & Resnick, Michael D. (2000). The effects of race/ethnicity, income, and family structure on adolescent risk behaviors. *American Journal of Public Health, 90,* 1879–1884.

Blum, Robert Wm., & Nelson-Mmari, Kristin. (2004). Adolescent health from an international perspective. In Richard M. Lerner & Laurence D. Steinberg (Eds.), *Handbook of adolescent psychology* (2nd ed., pp. 553–586). Hoboken, NJ: Wiley.

Blurton-Jones, Nicholas G. (1976). Rough-and-tumble play among nursery school children. In Jerome S. Bruner, Alison Jolly, & Kathy Sylva (Eds.), *Play: Its role in development and evolution* (pp. 352–363). New York: Basic Books.

Blustein, David Larry. (2006). *The psychology of working: A new perspective for career development, counseling, and public policy.* Mahwah, NJ: Erlbaum.

Bodrova, Elena, & Leong, Deborah J. (2005). High quality preschool programs: What would Vygotsky say? *Early Education and Development, 16,* 435–444.

Boehnke, Klaus. (2008). Peer pressure: A cause of scholastic underachievement? A cross-cultural study of mathematical achievement among German, Canadian, and Israeli middle school students. *Social Psychology of Education, 11,* 149–160.

Boerner, Kathrin, Schulz, Richard, & Horowitz, Amy. (2004). Positive aspects of caregiving and adaptation to bereavement. *Psychology and Aging, 19,* 668–675.

Boerner, Kathrin, Wortman, Camille B., & Bonanno, George A. (2005). Resilient or at risk? A 4-year study of older adults who initially showed high or low distress following conjugal loss. *Journals of Gerontology: Series B: Psychological Sciences and Social Sciences, 60,* P67–P73.

Bogle, Kathleen A. (2008). *Hooking up: Sex, dating, and relationships on campus.* New York: New York University Press.

Boles, David B., Barth, Joan M., & Merrill, Edward C. (2008). Asymmetry and performance: Toward a neurodevelopmental theory. *Brain and Cognition, 66,* 124–139.

Bonanno, George A., & Lilienfeld, Scott O. (2008). Let's be realistic: When grief counseling is effective and when it's not. *Professional Psychology: Research and Practice, 39,* 377–378.

Bondi, Mark W., Salmon, David P., & Kaszniak, Alfred W. (2009). The neuropsychology of dementia. In Igor Grant & Kenneth M. Adams (Eds.), *Neuropsychological assessment of neuropsychiatric and neuromedical disorders* (3rd ed., pp. 159–198). New York: Oxford University Press.

Booth, James R. (2007). Brain bases of learning and development of language and reading. In Donna Coch, Kurt W. Fischer, & Geraldine Dawson (Eds.), *Human behavior, learning, and the developing brain: Typical development* (pp. 279–300). New York: Guilford.

Bopp, Kara L., & Verhaeghen, Paul. (2005). Aging and verbal memory span: A meta-analysis. *The Journals of Gerontology Series B: Psychological Sciences and Social Sciences, 60,* P223–P233.

Borke, Jörn, Lamm, Bettina, Eickhorst, Andreas, & Keller, Heidi. (2007). Father-infant interaction, paternal ideas about early child care, and their consequences for the development of children's self-recognition. *Journal of Genetic Psychology, 168,* 365–379.

Borkowski, John G., Farris, Jaelyn Renee, Whitman, Thomas L., Carothers, Shannon S., Weed, Keri, & Keogh, Deborah A. (2007). *Risk and resilience: Adolescent mothers and their children grow up.* Mahwah, NJ: Erlbaum.

Bornstein, Marc H. (2002). Parenting infants. In Marc H. Bornstein (Ed.), *Handbook of parenting: Vol. 1. Children and parenting* (2nd ed., pp. 3–43). Mahwah, NJ: Erlbaum.

Bornstein, Marc H. (2006). Parenting science and practice. In William Damon & Richard M. Lerner (Series Eds.) & K. Ann Renninger & Irving E. Sigel (Vol. Eds.), *Handbook of child psychology: Vol. 4. Child psychology in practice* (6th ed., pp. 893–949). Hoboken, NJ: Wiley.

Bornstein, Marc H., Arterberry, Martha E., & Mash, Clay. (2005). Perceptual development. In Marc H. Bornstein & Michael E. Lamb (Eds.), *Developmental science: An advanced textbook* (5th ed., pp. 283–325). Mahwah, NJ: Erlbaum.

Bornstein, Marc H., & Cote, Linda R. (2007). Knowledge of child development and family interactions among immigrants to America: Perspectives from developmental science. In Jennifer E. Lansford, Kirby Deater-Deckard, & Marc H. Bornstein (Eds.), *Immigrant families in contemporary society* (pp. 121–136). New York: Guilford Press.

Bornstein, Marc H., & Lamb, Michael E. (2005). *Developmental science: An advanced textbook* (5th ed.). Mahwah, NJ: Erlbaum

Borrelli, Belinda, McQuaid, Elizabeth L., Novak, Scott P., Hammond, S. Katharine, & Becker, Bruce. (2010). Motivating Latino caregivers of children with asthma to quit smoking: A randomized trial. *Journal of Consulting and Clinical Psychology, 78,* 34–43.

Bors, Philip, Dessauer, Mark, Bell, Rich, Wilkerson, Risa, Lee, Joanne, & Strunk, Sarah L. (2009). The active living by design national program: Community initiatives and lessons learned. *American Journal of Preventive Medicine, 37*(Suppl. 2), S313–S321.

Bortz, Walter M. (2005). Biological basis of determinants of health. *American Journal of Public Health, 95,* 389–392.

Bos, Henny M. W., Sandfort, Theo G. M., de Bruyn, Eddy H., & Hakvoort, Esther M. (2008). Same-sex attraction, social relationships, psychosocial functioning, and school performance in early adolescence. *Developmental Psychology, 44,* 59–68.

Bossé, Yohan, & Hudson, Thomas J. (2007). Toward a comprehensive set of asthma susceptibility genes. *Annual Review of Medicine, 58,* 171–184.

Bosworth, Hayden B., & Ayotte, Brian J. (2009). The role of cognitive and social function in an applied setting: Medication adherence as an example. In Hayden B. Bosworth & Christopher Hertzog (Eds.), *Aging and cognition: Research methodologies and empirical advances* (pp. 219–239). Washington, DC: American Psychological Association.

Bosworth, Hayden B., & Hertzog, Christopher. (2009). *Aging and cognition: Research methodologies and empirical advances.* Washington, DC: American Psychological Association.

Bouchard, Geneviève. (2006). Cohabitation versus marriage: The role of dyadic adjustment in relationship dissolution. *Journal of Divorce & Remarriage, 46,* 107–117.

Bowen, Mary Elizabeth, & González, Hector M. (2010). Childhood socioeconomic position and disability in later life: results of the health and retirement study. *American Journal of Public Health, 100*(Suppl. 1), S197–S203.

Bowen, William G., Chingos, Matthew M., McPherson, Michael S., & Tobin, Eugene M. (2009). *Crossing the finish line: Completing college at America's public universities.* Princeton, NJ: Princeton University Press.

Bower, Bruce. (2007, February 17). Net heads. *Science News, 171,* 104–106.

Bowers, Jeffrey S., Mattys, Sven L., & Gage, Suzanne H. (2009). Preserved implicit knowledge of a forgotten childhood language. *Psychological Science, 20,* 1064–1069.

Bowlby, John. (1969). *Attachment and loss: Vol. 1. Attachment.* New York: Basic Books.

Bowlby, John. (1973). *Attachment and loss: Vol. 2. Separation: Anxiety and anger.* New York: Basic Books.

Bowlby, John. (1988). *A secure base: Clinical applications of attachment theory.* London: Routledge.

Boyce, W. Thomas, Essex, Marilyn J., Alkon, Abbey, Goldsmith, H. Hill, Kraemer, Helena C., & Kupfer, David J. (2006). Early father involvement moderates biobehavioral susceptibility to mental health problems in middle childhood. *Journal of the American Academy of Child and Adolescent Psychiatry, 45,* 1510–1520.

Boyd, William L. (2007). The politics of privatization in American education. *Educational Policy, 21,* 7–14.

Bozik, Mary. (2002). The college student as learner: Insight gained through metaphor analysis. *College Student Journal, 36,* 142–151.

Bradford, Andrea, Kunik, Mark E., Schulz, Paul, Williams, Susan P., & Singh, Hardeep. (2009). Missed and delayed diagnosis of dementia in primary care: Prevalence and contributing factors. *Alzheimer Disease and Associated Disorders, 23,* 306–314.

Bradley, Robert H., & Corwyn, Robert F. (2005). Productive activity and the prevention of behavior problems. *Developmental Psychology, 41,* 89–98.

Braithwaite, R. Scott, Conigliaro, Joseph, Roberts, Mark S., Shechter, Steven, Schaefer, Andrew, McGinnis, Kathleen, et al. (2007). Estimating the impact of alcohol consumption on survival for HIV+ individuals. *AIDS Care, 19,* 459–466.

Branca, Francesco, Nikogosian, Haik, & Lobstein, Tim (Eds.). (2007). *The challenge of obesity in the WHO European Region and the strategies for response.* Copenhagen, Denmark: WHO Regional Office for Europe.

Brandone, Amanda C., & Wellman, Henry M. (2009). You can't always get what you want. *Psychological Science, 20,* 85–91.

Brandt, Hella E., Ooms, Marcel E., Ribbe, Miel W., Wal, Gerrit van der, & Deliens, Luc. (2006). Predicted survival vs. actual survival in terminally ill noncancer patients in Dutch nursing homes. *Journal of Pain and Symptom Management, 32,* 560–566.

Braun, Kathryn L., Zir, Ana, Crocker, Joanna, & Seely, Marilyn R. (2005). Kokua Mau: A statewide effort to improve end-of-life care. *Journal of Palliative Medicine, 8,* 313–323.

Braun, Michael, Lewin-Epstein, Noah, Stier, Haya, & Baumgärtner, Miriam K. (2008). Perceived equity in the gendered division of household labor. *Journal of Marriage and Family, 70,* 1145–1156.

Brazelton, T. Berry, & Sparrow, Joshua D. (2006). *Touchpoints: Birth to 3: Your child's emotional and behavioral development* (2nd ed.). Cambridge, MA: Da Capo Press.

Breaugh, James, & Frye, N. Kathleen. (2008). Work-family conflict: The importance of family-friendly employment practices and family-supportive supervisors. *Journal of Business and Psychology, 22,* 345–353.

Brendgen, Mara, Lamarche, Véronique, Wanner, Brigitte, & Vitaro, Frank. (2010). Links between friendship relations and early adolescents' trajectories of depressed mood. *Developmental Psychology, 46,* 491–501.

Brennan, Arthur, Ayers, Susan, Ahmed, Hafez, & Marshall-Lucette, Sylvie. (2007). A critical review of the Couvade syndrome: the pregnant male. *Journal of Reproductive and Infant Psychology, 25,* 173–189.

Bresnahan, Mary Jiang, & Mahler, Kevin. (2010). Ethical debate over organ donation in the context of brain death. *Bioethics, 24,* 54–60.

Bretherton, Inge. (2010). Fathers in attachment theory and research: A review. *Early Child Development and Care, 180,* 9–23.

Brickhouse, Tegwyn H., Rozier, R. Gary, & Slade, Gary D. (2008). Effects of enrollment in Medicaid versus the State Children's Health Insurance Program on kindergarten children's untreated dental caries. *American Journal of Public Health, 98,* 876–881.

Bridge, Jeffrey A., Iyengar, Satish, Salary, Cheryl B., Barbe, Remy P., Birmaher, Boris, Pincus, Harold Alan, et al. (2007). Clinical response and risk for reported suicidal ideation and suicide attempts in pediatric antidepressant treatment: A meta-analysis of randomized controlled trials. *Journal of the American Medical Association, 297,* 1683–1696.

Briggs, Gerald G., Freeman, Roger K., & Yaffe, Sumner J. (2008). *Drugs in pregnancy and lactation: A reference guide to fetal and neonatal risk* (8th ed.). Philadelphia: Lippincott Williams & Wilkins.

Briley, Mike, & Sulser, Fridolin (Eds.). (2001). *Molecular genetics of mental disorders: The place of molecular genetics in basic mechanisms and clinical applications in mental disorders.* London: Martin Dunitz.

Brody, Gene H., Beach, Steven R. H., Philibert, Robert A., Chen, Yi-fu, & Murry, Velma McBride. (2009). Prevention effects moderate the association of 5–HTTLPR and youth risk behavior initiation: Gene x environment hypotheses tested via a randomized prevention design. *Child Development, 80,* 645–661.

Brody, Jane E. (2007, January 23). A humorist illuminates the blessings of hospice. *New York Times,* pp. F7.

Brokaw, Tom. (1998). *The greatest generation.* New York: Random House.

Bronfenbrenner, Urie. (1974). Developmental research, public policy, and the ecology of childhood. *Child Development, 45,* 1–5.

Bronfenbrenner, Urie. (1977). Toward an experimental ecology of human development. *American Psychologist, 32,* 513–531.

Bronfenbrenner, Urie, & Morris, Pamela A. (2006). The bioecological model of human development. In William Damon & Richard M. Lerner (Eds.), *Handbook of child psychology: Vol. 1. Theoretical models of human development* (6th ed., pp. 793–828). Hoboken, NJ: Wiley.

Bronte-Tinkew, Jacinta, Moore, Kristin A., Matthews, Gregory, & Carrano, Jennifer. (2007). Symptoms of major depression in a sample of fathers of infants: Sociodemographic correlates and links to father involvement. *Journal of Family Issues, 28,* 61–99.

Brooker, Robert J. (2009). *Genetics: Analysis & principles* (3rd ed.). New York: McGraw-Hill.

Brookfield, Stephen. (2010). Critical reflection as an adult learning process. In Nona Lyons (Ed.), *Handbook of Reflection and Reflective Inquiry* (pp. 215–236). New York: Springer.

Brotman, Melissa A., Guyer, Amanda E., Lawson, Evin S., Horsey, Sarah E., Rich, Brendan A., Dickstein, Daniel P., et al. (2008). Facial emotion labeling deficits in children and adolescents at risk for bipolar disorder. *American Journal of Psychiatry, 165,* 385–389.

Brotman, Melissa A., Rich, Brendan A., Guyer, Amanda E., Lunsford, Jessica R., Horsey, Sarah E., Reising, Michelle M., et al. (2010). Amygdala activation during emotion processing of neutral faces in children with severe mood dysregulation versus ADHD or bipolar disorder. *American Journal of Psychiatry, 167,* 61–69.

Brown, Angela M., & Lindsey, Delwin T. (2009). Contrast insensitivity: The critical immaturity in infant visual performance. *Optometry and Vision Science, 86,* 572–576.

Brown, B. Bradford. (2004). Adolescents' relationships with peers. In Richard M. Lerner & Laurence D. Steinberg (Eds.), *Handbook of adolescent psychology* (2nd ed., pp. 363–394). Hoboken, NJ: Wiley.

Brown, B. Bradford. (2006). A few "course corrections" to Collins & van Dulmen's "The course of true love." In Ann C. Crouter & Alan Booth (Eds.), *Romance and sex in adolescence and emerging adulthood: Risks and opportunities* (pp. 113–123). Mahwah, NJ: Erlbaum.

Brown, B. Bradford, & Larson, James. (2009). Peer relationships in adolescence, *Handbook of adolescent psychology: Vol. 2. Contextual influences on adolescent development* (3rd ed., pp. 74–103). Hoboken, NJ: John Wiley & Sons.

Brown, Gordon D. A., Gardner, Jonathan, Oswald, Andrew J., & Qian, Jing. (2008). Does wage rank affect employees well-being? *Industrial Relations, 47,* 355–389.

Brown, Susan L. (2004). Family structure and child well-being: The significance of parental cohabitation. *Journal of Marriage and Family, 66,* 351–367.

Brown, Susan L., & Kawamura, Sayaka. (2010). Relationship quality among cohabitors and marrieds in older adulthood. *Social Science Research, 39,* 777–786.

Brown, Susan L., Sanchez, Laura Ann, Nock, Steven L., & Wright, James D. (2006). Links between premarital cohabitation and subsequent marital quality, stability, and divorce: A comparison of covenant versus standard marriages. *Social Science Research, 35,* 454–470.

Brown, Tony N., Tanner-Smith, Emily E., Lesane-Brown, Chase L., & Ezell, Michael E. (2007). Child, parent, and situational correlates of familial ethnic/race socialization. *Journal of Marriage and Family, 69,* 14–25.

Bruce, Susan, & Muhammad, Zayyad. (2009). The development of object permanence in children with intellectual disability, physical disability, autism, and blindness. *International Journal of Disability, Development and Education, 56,* 229–246.

Bruck, Maggie, Ceci, Stephen J., & Principe, Gabrielle F. (2006). The child and the law. In William Damon & Richard M. Lerner (Series Eds.) & K. Ann Renninger & Irving E. Sigel (Vol. Eds.), *Handbook of child psychology: Vol. 4. Child psychology in practice* (6th ed., pp. 776–816). Hoboken, NJ: Wiley.

Brugman, Gerard M. (2006). Wisdom and aging. In James E. Birren & K. Warner Schaie (Eds.), *Handbook of the psychology of aging* (6th ed., pp. 445–475). Amsterdam: Elsevier.

Bryant, Alyssa N., & Astin, Helen S. (2008). The correlates of spiritual struggle during the college years. *Journal of Higher Education, 79,* 1–27.

Bryant, Brenda K., & Donnellan, M. Brent. (2007). The relation between socio-economic status concerns and angry peer conflict resolution is moderated by pet provisions of support. *Anthrozoös, 20,* 213–223.

Bryant, Gregory A., & Barrett, H. Clark. (2007). Recognizing intentions in infant-directed speech: Evidence for universals. *Psychological Science, 18,* 746–751.

Buccino, Giovanni, & Amore, Mario. (2008). Mirror neurons and the understanding of behav-ioural symptoms in psychiatric disorders. *Current Opinion in Psychiatry, 21,* 281–285.

Buccino, Giovanni, Binkofski, Ferdinand, & Riggio, Lucia. (2004). The mirror neuron system and action recognition. *Brain and Language, 89,* 370–376.

Buckhalt, Joseph A., El-Sheikh, Mona, & Keller, Peggy. (2007). Children's sleep and cognitive functioning: Race and socioeconomic status as moderators of effects. *Child Development, 78,* 213–231.

Buckley, Maureen, & Saarni, Carolyn. (2009). Emotion regulation: Implications for positive youth development. In Rich Gilman, E. Scott Huebner, & Michael J. Furlong (Eds.), *Handbook of positive psychology in schools* (pp. 107–118). New York: Routledge/Taylor & Francis.

Buckner, Randy, Head, Denise, & Lustig, Cindy. (2006). Brain changes in aging: A lifespan perspective. In Ellen Bialystok & Fergus I. M. Craik (Eds.), *Lifespan cognition: Mechanisms of change* (pp. 27–42). Oxford, UK: Oxford University Press.

Bucx, Freek, Raaijmakers, Quinten, & van Wel, Frits. (2010). Life course stage in young adulthood and intergenerational congruence in family attitudes. *Journal of Marriage and Family, 72,* 117–134.

Bugental, Daphne Blunt, & Grusec, Joan E. (2006). Socialization theory. In William Damon & Richard M. Lerner (Series Eds.) & Nancy Eisenberg (Vol. Ed.), *Handbook of child psychology: Vol. 3. Social, emotional, and personality development* (6th ed., pp. 366–428). Hoboken, NJ: Wiley.

Bugental, Daphne Blunt, & Happaney, Keith. (2004). Predicting infant maltreatment in low-income families: The interactive effects of maternal attributions and child status at birth. *Developmental Psychology, 40,* 234–243.

Bugental, Daphne Blunt, & Hehman, Jessica A. (2007). Ageism: A review of research and policy implications. *Social Issues and Policy Review, 1,* 173–216.

Bugental, Daphne Blunt, & Schwartz, Alex. (2009). A cognitive approach to child mistreatment prevention among medically at-risk infants. *Developmental Psychology, 45,* 284–288.

Buiting, Hilde, van Delden, Johannes, Onwuteaka-Philpsen, Bregje, Rietjens, Judith, Rurup, Mette, van Tol, Donald, et al. (2009). Reporting of euthanasia and physician-assisted suicide in the Netherlands: Descriptive study. *BMC Medical Ethics, 10,* 18.

Bulbulia, Joseph A. (2007). Evolution of religion. In R. I. M. Dunbar & Louise Barrett (Eds.), *Oxford handbook of evolutionary psychology* (pp. 621–636). New York: Oxford University Press.

Bulik, Cynthia M., Thornton, Laura, Pinheiro, Andréa Poyastro, Plotnicov, Katherine, Klump, Kelly L., Brandt, Harry, et al. (2008). Suicide attempts in anorexia nervosa. *Psychosomatic Medicine, 70,* 378–383.

Burd-Sharps, Sarah, Lewis, Kristen, & Martins, Eduardo Borges. (2008). *The measure of America: American human development report, 2008–2009.* New York: Columbia University Press.

Burgmans, Saartje, van Boxtel, Martin P. J., Vuurman, Eric F. P. M., Smeets, Floortje, Gronenschild, Ed H. B. M., Uylings, Harry B. M., et al. (2009). The prevalence of cortical gray matter atrophy may be overestimated in the healthy aging brain. *Neuropsychology, 23,* 541–550.

Burkitt, Esther. (2004). Drawing conclusions from children's art. *The Psychologist, 17,* 566–568.

Burt, S. Alexandra. (2009). Rethinking environmental contributions to child and adolescent psychopathology: A meta-analysis of shared environmental influences. *Psychological Bulletin, 135,* 608–637.

Burt, S. Alexandra, McGue, Matt, & Iacono, William G. (2009). Nonshared environmental mediation of the association between deviant peer affiliation and adolescent externalizing behaviors over time: Results from a cross-lagged monozygotic twin differences design. *Developmental Psychology, 45,* 1752–1760.

Burton, Linda M., Bonilla-Silva, Eduardo, Ray, Victor, Buckelew, Rose, & Hordge Freeman, Elizabeth. (2010). Critical race theories, colorism, and the decade's research on families of color. *Journal of Marriage and Family, 72,* 440–459.

Buschkuehl, Martin, Jaeggi, Susanne M., Hutchison, Sara, Perrig-Chiello, Pasqualina, Dapp, Christoph, Muller, Matthias, et al. (2008). Impact of working memory training on memory performance in old-old adults. *Psychology and Aging, 23,* 743–753.

Buss, David M. (2003). *The evolution of desire: Strategies of human mating* (Revised ed.). New York: Basic Books.

Buss, David M. (2007). *Evolutionary psychology: The new science of the mind* (3rd ed.). Boston: Pearson/Allyn and Bacon.

Buss, David M., Haselton, Martie G., Shackelford, Todd K., Bleske, April L., & Wakefield, Jerome C. (1998). Adaptations, exaptations, and spandrels. *American Psychologist, 53,* 533–548.

Busse, William W., & Lemanske, Robert F. (Eds.). (2005). *Lung biology in health and disease: Vol. 195. Asthma prevention.* Boca Raton, FL: Taylor & Francis.

Bussey, Kay, & Bandura, Albert. (1999). Social cognitive theory of gender development and differentiation. *Psychological Review, 106,* 676–713.

Butler, Merlin Gene, & Meaney, F. John. (2005). *Genetics of developmental disabilities.* Boca Raton, FL: Taylor & Francis.

Butler, Robert N. (1975). *Why survive? Being old in America* (1st ed.). New York: Harper & Row.

Butler, Robert N., Lewis, Myrna I., & Sunderland, Trey. (1998). *Aging and mental health: Positive psychosocial and biomedical approaches* (5th ed.). Boston: Allyn & Bacon.

Butler, Robert N., Miller, Richard A., Perry, Daniel, Carnes, Bruce A., Williams, T Franklin, Cassel, Christine, et al. (2008). New model of health promotion and disease prevention for the 21st century. *British Medical Journal, 337,* 149–150.

Buunk, Abraham P., Park, Justin H., & Dubbs, Shelli L. (2008). Parent-offspring conflict in mate preferences. *Review of General Psychology, 12,* 47–62.

Byers, Amy L., Levy, Becca R., Allore, Heather G., Bruce, Martha L., & Kasl, Stanislav V. (2008). When parents matter to their adult children: Filial reliance associated with parents' depressive symptoms. *The Journals of Gerontology Series B: Psychological Sciences and Social Sciences, 63,* P33–40.

Byers-Heinlein, Krista, Burns, Tracey C., & Werker, Janet F. (2010). The roots of bilingualism in newborns. *Psychological Science, 21,* 343–348.

Byng-Hall, John. (2008). The significance of children fulfilling parental roles: Implications for family therapy. *Journal of Family Therapy, 30,* 147–162.

Byram, Michael S., & Feng, Anwei. (2005). Teaching and researching intercultural competence. In Eli Hinkel (Ed.), *Handbook of research in second language teaching and learning* (pp. 911–930). Mahwah, NJ: Erlbaum.

Bzostek, Sharon H. (2008). Social fathers and child well-being. *Journal of Marriage and Family, 70,* 950–961.

Cabrera, Natasha J., Shannon, Jacqueline D., West, Jerry, & Brooks-Gunn, Jeanne. (2006). Parental interactions with Latino infants: Variation by country of origin and English proficiency. *Child Development, 77,* 1190–1207.

Cain, Daphne S., & Combs-Orme, Terri. (2005). Family structure effects on parenting stress and practices in the African American family. *Journal of Sociology & Social Welfare, 32,* 19–40.

Calkins, Susan D., & Keane, Susan P. (2009). Developmental origins of early antisocial behavior. *Development and Psychopathology, 21,* 1095–1109.

Callaghan, Tara, Rochat, Philippe, Lillard, Angeline, Claux, Mary Louise, Odden, Hal, Itakura, Shoji, et al. (2005). Synchrony in the onset of mental-state reasoning: Evidence from five cultures. *Psychological Science, 16,* 378–384.

Calvert, Karin. (2003). Patterns of childrearing in America. In Willem Koops & Michael Zuckerman (Eds.), *Beyond the century of the child: Cultural history and developmental psychology* (pp. 62–81). Baltimore: University of Pennsylvania Press.

Camarata, Stephen, & Woodcock, Richard. (2006). Sex differences in processing speed: Developmental effects in males and females. *Intelligence, 34,* 231–252.

Cameron, Judy, & Pierce, W. David. (2002). *Rewards and intrinsic motivation: Resolving the controversy.* Westport, CT: Bergin & Garvey.

Cameron, James D., Bulpitt, Christopher J., Pinto, Elisabete S., & Rajkumar, Chakravarthi. (2003). The aging of elastic and muscular arteries. *Diabetes Care, 26,* 2133–2138.

Cameron, Judy L. (2004). Interrelationships between hormones, behavior, and affect during adolescence: Understanding hormonal, physical, and brain changes occurring in association with pubertal activation of the reproductive axis. Introduction to Part III. In Ronald E. Dahl & Linda Patia Spear (Eds.), *Adolescent brain development: Vulnerabilities and opportunities* (Vol. 1021, pp. 110–123). New York: New York Academy of Sciences.

Cameron, Nicole M., Fish, Eric W., & Meaney, Michael J. (2008). Maternal influences on the sexual behavior and reproductive success of the female rat. *Hormones and Behavior, 54,* 178–184.

Camilli, Gregory, Vargas, Sadako, Ryan, Sharon, & Barnett, W. Steven. (2010). Meta-analysis of the effects of early education interventions on cognitive and social development. *Teachers College Record, 112,* 579–620.

Campbell, Frances A., Pungello, Elizabeth P., Miller-Johnson, Shari, Burchinal, Margaret, & Ramey, Craig T. (2001). The development of cognitive and academic abilities: Growth curves from an early childhood educational experiment. *Developmental Psychology, 37,* 231–242.

Camras, Linda A., & Shutter, Jennifer M. (2010). Emotional facial expressions in infancy. *Emotion Review, 2,* 120–129.

Canadian Institute for Health Information. (2010). *Drug use among seniors on public drug programs in Canada, 2002 to 2008.* Ottawa, ON, Canada: Author.

Canadian Psychological Association. (2000). *Canadian code of ethics for psychologists* (3rd ed.). Ottawa, Ontario, Canada: Author.

Cantor-Graae, Elizabeth, & Selten, Jean-Paul. (2005). Schizophrenia and migration: A meta-analysis and review. *American Journal of Psychiatry, 162,* 12–24.

Caplan, Leslie J., & Schooler, Carmi. (2003). The roles of fatalism, self-confidence, and intellectual resources in the disablement process in older adults. *Psychology & Aging, 18,* 551–561.

Cappell, Katherine A., Gmeindl, Leon, & Reuter-Lorenz, Patricia A. (2010). Age differences in prefontal recruitment during verbal working memory maintenance depend on memory load. *Cortex, 46,* 462–473.

Caravita, Simona C. S., Di Blasio, Paola, & Salmivalli, Christina. (2010). Early adolescents' participation in bullying: Is ToM involved? *The Journal of Early Adolescence, 30,* 138–170.

Cardinal, Roger. (2001). The sense of time and place. In Jane Kallir (Ed.), *Grandma Moses in the 21st century* (pp. 79–102). Alexandria, VA: Art Services International.

Carlson, Susan A., Fulton, Janet E., Lee, Sarah M., Maynard, L. Michele, Brown, David R., Kohl, Harold W., III, et al. (2008). Physical education and academic achievement in elementary school: Data from the early childhood longitudinal study. *American Journal of Public Health, 98,* 721–727.

Carlson, Stephanie M. (2003). Executive function in context: Development, measurement, theory and experience. *Monographs of the Society for Research in Child Development, 68*(3, Serial No. 274), 138–151.

Carlton-LaNey, Iris. (2006–2007). 'Doing the lord's work': African American elders' civic engagement. *Generations, 30,* 47–50.

Carnethon, Mercedes R., Gidding, Samuel S., Nehgme, Rodrigo, Sidney, Stephen, Jacobs, David R., Jr., & Liu, Kiang. (2003). Cardiorespiratory fitness in young adulthood and the development of cardiovascular disease risk factors. *Journal of the American Medical Association, 290,* 3092–3100.

Carpendale, Jeremy I. M., & Lewis, Charlie. (2004). Constructing an understanding of mind: The development of children's social understanding within social interaction. *Behavioral and Brain Sciences, 27,* 79–96.

Carpenter, Brian. (2009). 'You have Alzheimer's disease.' How to reveal a diagnosis and how to deal with the reactions. *Generations, 33*(1), 82–85.

Carstensen, Laura L., & Fredrickson, Barbara L. (1998). Influence of HIV status and age on cognitive representations of others. *Health Psychology, 17,* 494–503.

Carstensen, Laura L., Mikels, Joseph A., & Mather, Mara. (2006). Aging and the intersection of cognition, motivation, and emotion. In James E. Birren & K. Warner Schaie (Eds.), *Handbook of the psychology of aging* (6th ed., pp. 343–362). Amsterdam: Elsevier.

Cartwright, Kelly, Galupo, M., Tyree, Seth, & Jennings, Jennifer. (2009). Reliability and validity of the complex postformal thought questionnaire: Assessing adults' cognitive development. *Journal of Adult Development, 16,* 183–189.

Case-Smith, Jane, & Kuhaneck, Heather Miller. (2008). Play preferences of typically developing children and children with developmental delays between ages 3 and 7 years. *OTJR: Occupation, Participation and Health, 28,* 19–29.

Casey, Richard. (2008). The use of hormonal therapy in "andropause": The con side. *Canadian Urological Association Journal, 2,* 47–48.

Casper, Lynne M., & Bianchi, Suzanne M. (2002). *Continuity & change in the American family.* Thousand Oaks, CA: Sage.

Caspi, Avshalom, McClay, Joseph, Moffitt, Terrie, Mill, Jonathan, Martin, Judy, Craig, Ian W., et al. (2002, August 2). Role of genotype in the cycle of violence in maltreated children. *Science, 297,* 851–854.

Caspi, Avshalom, Moffitt, Terrie E., Morgan, Julia, Rutter, Michael, Taylor, Alan, Arseneault, Louise, et al. (2004). Maternal expressed emotion predicts children's antisocial behavior problems: Using monozygotic-twin differences to identify environmental effects on behavioral development. *Developmental Psychology, 40,* 149–161.

Caspi, Avshalom, & Shiner, Rebecca L. (2006). Personality development. In William Damon & Richard M. Lerner (Series Eds.) & Nancy Eisenberg (Vol. Ed.), *Handbook of child psychology: Vol. 3. Social, emotional, and personality development* (Vol. 6, pp. 300–365). Hoboken, NJ: Wiley.

Cassia, Viola Macchi, Kuefner, Dana, Picozzi, Marta, & Vescovo, Elena. (2009).

Early experience predicts later plasticity for face processing: Evidence for the reactivation of dormant effects. *Psychological Science, 20,* 853–859.

Castle, David J., & Morgan, Vera. (2008). Epidemiology. In Kim T. Mueser & Dilip V. Jeste (Eds.), *Clinical handbook of schizophrenia* (pp. 14–24). New York: Guilford Press.

Catani, Claudia, Gewirtz, Abigail H., Wieling, Elizabeth, Schauer, Elizabeth, Elbert, Thomas, & Neuner, Frank. (2010). Tsunami, war, and cumulative risk in the lives of Sri Lankan schoolchildren. *Child Development, 81,* 1176–1191.

Cavanagh, Sean. (2005). Poor math scores on world stage trouble U.S. *Education Week, 24,* 1–18.

Cavanagh, Sean. (2007). Top-achieving nations beat U.S. states in math and science. *Education Week, 27.*

Cavanagh, Sean. (2007, December 13). Poverty's effect on U.S. scores greater than for other nations. *Education Week, 27,* 1, 13.

CBS News. (2005, Feb 8). *World's smallest baby goes home: Cellphone-sized baby is discharged from hospital.* Retrieved September 27, 2010, from the World Wide Web: http://www.cbsnews.com/stories/2005/02/08/health/main672488.shtml

Center for Sexual Health Promotion. (2010). *National Survey of Sexual Health and Behavior (NSSHB).* Retrieved November 13, 2010, from the World Wide Web: http://nationalsexstudy.indiana.edu/

Centers for Disease Control and Prevention. (n.d.). *Pneumococcal vaccination.* Retrieved August 3, 2010, from the World Wide Web: http://www.cdc.gov/vaccines/vpd-vac/pneumo/default.htm

Centers for Disease Control and Prevention (CDC) (Ed.). (2007). *Epidemiology and prevention of vaccine-preventable diseases* (10th ed.). Washington, DC: Public Health Foundation.

Centre for Community Child Health and Telethon Institute for Child Health Research. (2009). *A snapshot of early childhood development in Australia: Australian Early Development Index (AEDI) national report 2009.* Australian Government Department of Education. Retrieved October 24, 2010, from the World Wide Web: http://www.rch.org.au/aedi/media/Snapshot_of_Early_Childhood_DevelopmentinAustralia_AEDI_National_Report.pdf

Cesario, Sandra K., & Hughes, Lisa A. (2007). Precocious puberty: A comprehensive review of literature. *Journal of Obstetric, Gynecologic, & Neonatal Nursing, 36,* 263–274.

Chaddock, Laura , Erickson, Kirk I., Prakash, Ruchika Shaurya, VanPatter, Matt, Voss, Michelle W., Pontifex, Matthew B., et al. (2010). Basal ganglia volume is associated with aerobic fitness in preadolescent children. *Developmental Neuroscience, 32,* 249–256.

Chambers, Bette, Cheung, Alan C., Slavin, Robert E., Smith, Dewi, & Laurenzano, Mary. (2010). *Effective early childhood education programs: A systematic review.* Baltimore, MD: Johns Hopkins University, Center for Research and Reform in Education.

Chan, Cheri C. Y., Brandone, Amanda C., & Tardif, Twila. (2009). Culture, context, or behavioral control? English- and Mandarin-speaking mothers' use of nouns and verbs in joint book reading. *Journal of Cross-Cultural Psychology, 40,* 584–602.

Chan, Siu Mui, Bowes, Jennifer, & Wyver, Shirley. (2009). Parenting style as a context for emotion socialization. *Early Education & Development, 20,* 631–656.

Chan, Tak Wing, & Koo, Anita. (2010). *Parenting style and youth outcomes in the UK.* Retrieved December 21, 2010, from the World Wide Web: http://esr.oxfordjournals.org/content/early/2010/03/05/esr.jcq013.abstract

Chao, Ruth K. (2001). Extending research on the consequences of parenting style for Chinese Americans and European Americans. *Child Development, 72,* 1832–1843.

Chao, Y. May, Pisetsky, Emily M., Dierker, Lisa C., Dohm, Faith-Anne, Rosselli, Francine, May, Alexis M., et al. (2008). Ethnic differences in weight control practices among U.S. adolescents from 1995 to 2005. *International Journal of Eating Disorders, 41,* 124–133.

Chaplin, Lan Nguyen, & John, Deborah Roedder. (2007). Growing up in a material world: Age differences in materialism in children and adolescents. *Journal of Consumer Research, 34,* 480–493.

Charles, Eric P., & Rivera, Susan M. (2009). Object permanence and method of disappearance: Looking measures further contradict reaching measures. *Developmental Science, 12,* 991–1006.

Charles, Susan T., & Carstensen, Laura L. (2010). Social and emotional aging. *Annual Review of Psychology, 61,* 383–409.

Charlton, Rodger. (2007). The demise of palliative care. *The British Journal of General Practice, 57,* 247.

Charlton, Samuel G. (2009). Driving while conversing: Cell phones that distract and passengers who react. *Accident Analysis and Prevention, 41,* 160–173.

Charness, Neil, & Boot, Walter R. (2009). Aging and information technology use: Potential and barriers. *Current Directions in Psychological Science, 18,* 253–258.

Charness, Neil, & Krampe, Ralf T. (2008). Expertise and knowledge. In Scott M. Hofer & Duane F. Alwin (Eds.), *Handbook of cognitive aging: Interdisciplinary perspectives.* (pp. 244–258). Thousand Oaks, CA: Sage.

Charness, Neil, Krampe, Ralf, & Mayr, Ulrich. (1996). The role of practice and coaching in entrepreneurial skill domains: An international comparison of life-span chess skill acquisition. In Karl Anders Ericsson (Ed.), *The road to excellence: The acquisition of expert performance in the arts and sciences, sports, and games* (pp. 51–80). Hillsdale, NJ: Erlbaum.

Chassin, Laurie, Hussong, Andrea, Barrera, Manuel, Jr., Molina, Brooke S. G., Trim, Ryan, & Ritter, Jennifer. (2004). Adolescent substance use. In Richard M. Lerner & Laurence D. Steinberg (Eds.), *Handbook of adolescent psychology* (2nd ed., pp. 665–696). Hoboken, NJ: Wiley.

Chassin, Laurie, Hussong, Andrea, & Beltran, Iris. (2009). Adolescent substance use. In Richard M. Lerner & Laurence Steinberg (Eds.), *Handbook of adolescent psychology: Individual bases of adolescent development* (3rd ed., pp. 723–763). Hoboken, NJ: John Wiley & Sons.

Chasteen, Alison L., Bhattacharyya, Sudipa, Horhota, Michelle, Tam, Raymond, & Hasher, Lynn. (2005). How feelings of stereotype threat influence older adults' memory performance. *Experimental Aging Research, 31,* 235–260.

Chattopadhyay, Amit. (2008). Oral health disparities in the United States. *Dental Clinics of North America, 52,* 297–318.

Chaudhari, Prema, & Pizzolato, Jane E. (2008). Understanding the epistemology of ethnic identity development in multiethnic college students. *Journal of College Student Development, 49,* 443–458.

Chawarska, Katarzyna, Klin, Ami, Paul, Rhea, & Volkmar, Fred. (2007). Autism spectrum disorder in the second year: Stability and change in syndrome expression. *Journal of Child Psychology and Psychiatry, 48,* 128–138.

Chein, Isidor. (2008). *The science of behavior and the image of man.* New Brunswick, NJ: Transaction Publishers. (Original work published 1972)

Chen, Edith, Cohen, Sheldon, & Miller, Gregory E. (2010). How low socioeconomic status affects 2-year hormonal trajectories in children. *Psychological Science, 21,* 31–37.

Chen, Hong, & Jackson, Todd. (2009). Predictors of changes in weight esteem among mainland Chinese adolescents: A longitudinal analysis. *Developmental Psychology, 45,* 1618–1629.

Chen, Xinyin, Cen, Guozhen, Li, Dan, & He, Yunfeng. (2005). Social functioning and adjustment in Chinese children: The imprint of historical time. *Child Development, 76,* 182–195.

Chen, Xinyin, Rubin, Kenneth H., & Sun, Yuerong. (1992). Social reputation and peer relationships in Chinese and Canadian children: A cross-cultural study. *Child Development, 63,* 1336–1343.

Chen, Xinyin, Wang, Li, & Wang, Zhengyan. (2009). Shyness-sensitivity and social, school, and psychological adjustment in rural migrant and urban children in China. *Child Development, 80,* 1499–1513.

Chen, Yuju, Nettles, Margaret E., & Chen, Shun-Wen. (2009). Rethinking dependent personality disorder: Comparing different human relatedness in cultural contexts. *The Journal of Nervous and Mental Disease, 197,* 793–800

Cherbuin, Nicolas, & Brinkman, Cobie. (2006). Hemispheric interactions are different in left-handed individuals. *Neuropsychology, 20,* 700–707.

Cherlin, Andrew J. (2010). Demographic trends in the united states: A review of research in the 2000s. *Journal of Marriage and Family, 72,* 403–419.

Cherlin, Andrew J., & Furstenberg, Frank F. (1986). *The new American grandparent: A place in the family, a life apart.* New York: Basic Books.

Cheung, Fanny M., Shu Fai Cheung, Jianxin Zhang, Leung, Kwok, Leong, Frederick, & Kuang Huiyeh. (2008). Relevance of openness as a personality dimension in Chinese culture. *Journal of Cross-Cultural Psychology, 39,* 81–108.

Cheurprakobkit, Sutham, & Bartsch, Robert A. (2005). Security measures on school crime in Texas middle and high schools. *Educational Research, 47,* 235–250.

Children's Bureau. (2010). *Child maltreatment 2008.* Washington, DC: U.S. Department of Health and Human Services, Administration for Children and Families, Administration on Children, Youth and Families, .

Chin, Vivien S., Skike, Candice E. Van, & Matthews, Douglas B. (2010). Effects of ethanol on hippocampal function during adolescence: a look at the past and thoughts on the future. *Alcohol, 44,* 3–14.

Choi, Incheol, Dalal, Reeshad, Kim-Prieto, Chu, & Park, Hyekyung. (2003). Culture and judgment of causal relevance. *Journal of Personality & Social Psychology, 84,* 46–59.

Chomsky, Noam. (1968). *Language and mind.* New York: Harcourt Brace & World.

Chomsky, Noam. (1980). *Rules and representations.* New York: Columbia University Press.

Chouinard, Michelle M. (2007). Children's questions: A mechanism for cognitive development. *Monographs of the Society for Research in Child Development, 72*(1, Serial No. 286), vii–112.

Christensen, Andrew, Eldridge, Kathleen, Catta-Preta, Adriana Bokel, Lim, Veronica R., & Santagata, Rossella. (2006). Cross-cultural consistency of the demand/withdraw interaction pattern in couples. *Journal of Marriage and Family, 68,* 1029–1044.

Christenson, Sandra L., & Thurlow, Martha L. (2004). School dropouts: Prevention considerations, interventions, and challenges. *Current Directions in Psychological Science, 13,* 36–39.

Christian, Cindy W., Block, Robert, & the Committee on Child Abuse and Neglect. (2009). Abusive head trauma in infants and children. *Pediatrics, 123,* 1409–1411.

Chronicle of Higher Education. (2009). *Almanac of higher education 2009–10.* Washington, DC: Author.

Chronicle of Higher Education. (2010). *Almanac of higher education 2010–2011.* Washington, DC: Author.

Church, A. Timothy (2010). Current perspectives in the study of personality across cultures. *Perspectives on Psychological Science, 5,* 441–449.

Cicchetti, Dante, Rogosch, Fred A., & Sturge-Apple, Melissa L. (2007). Interactions of child maltreatment and serotonin transporter and monoamine oxidase A polymorphisms: Depressive symptomatology among adolescents from low socioeconomic status backgrounds. *Development and Psychopathology, 19,* 1161–1180.

Cicchetti, Dante, & Toth, Sheree L. (2009). The past achievements and future promises of developmental psychopathology: the coming of age of a discipline. *Journal of Child Psychology and Psychiatry, 50,* 16–25.

Cillessen, Antonius H. N., & Mayeux, Lara. (2004). From censure to reinforcement: Developmental changes in the association between aggression and social status. *Child Development, 75,* 147–163.

Clancy, Susan A. (2010). *The trauma myth: The truth about the sexual abuse of children—and its aftermath.* New York: Basic Books.

Clark, Lee Anna. (2009). Stability and change in personality disorder. *Current Directions in Psychological Science, 18,* 27–31.

Clark, Shelley, Kabiru, Caroline, & Mathur, Rohini. (2010). Relationship transitions among youth in urban Kenya. *Journal of Marriage and Family, 72,* 73–88.

Clark, Sharon E., & Symons, Douglas K. (2009). Representations of attachment relationships, the self, and significant others in middle childhood. *Journal of the Canadian Academy of Child and Adolescent Psychiatry, 18,* 316–321.

Clarke, Ann M., & Clarke, Alan D. B. (2003). *Human resilience: A fifty year quest.* London: Jessica Kingsley.

Clements, Jonathan. (2005, October 5). *Rich, successful—and miserable: New research probes mid-life angst.* Retrieved December 5, 2010, from the World Wide Web: http://online.wsj.com/public/article/SB112846380547659946.html

Cleveland, Michael J., Gibbons, Frederick X., Gerrard, Meg, Pomery, Elizabeth A., & Brody, Gene H. (2005). The impact of parenting on risk cognitions and risk behavior: A study of mediation and moderation in a panel of African American adolescents. *Child Development, 76,* 900–916.

Clinchy, Blythe McVicker. (1993). Ways of knowing and ways of being: Epistemological and moral development in undergraduate women. In Andrew Garrod (Ed.), *Approaches to moral development: New research and emerging themes* (pp. 180–200). New York: Teachers College Press.

Cockerham, William C. (2006). *Society of risk-takers: Living life on the edge.* New York: Worth.

Coghlan, Misia, Bergeron, Caroline, White, Karen, Sharp, Caroline, Morris, Marian, & Rutt, Simon. (2009). *Narrowing the gap in outcomes for young children through effective practices in the early years.* London: Centre for Excellence and Outcomes in Children and Young People's Services.

Cohen, David. (2006). *The development of play* (3rd ed.). New York: Routledge.

Cohen, Daniel, & Soto, Marcelo. (2007). Growth and human capital: Good data, good results. *Journal of Economic Growth, 12,* 51–76.

Cohen, Joel E., & Malin, Martin B. (Eds.). (2010). *International perspectives on the goals of universal basic and secondary education.* New York: Routledge.

Cohen, Jon. (2004, June 4). HIV/AIDS in China: Poised for takeoff? *Science, 304,* 1430–1432.

Cohen, Jon. (2007, September 7). DNA duplications and deletions help determine health. *Science, 317,* 1315–1317.

Cohen, Jon. (2007, March 9). Hope on new AIDS drugs, but breast-feeding strategy backfires. *Science, 315,* 1357.

Cohen, Larry, Chávez, Vivian, & Chehimi, Sana. (2007). *Prevention is primary: Strategies for community well-being.* San Francisco: Jossey-Bass.

Cohen, Lee S., Soares, Claudio N., Vitonis, Allison F., Otto, Michael W., & Harlow, Bernard L. (2006). Risk for new onset of depression during the menopausal transition. *Archives of General Psychiatry, 63,* 385–390.

Cohen, Leslie B., & Cashon, Cara H. (2006). Infant cognition. In William Damon & Richard M. Lerner (Series Eds.) & Deanna Kuhn & Robert S. Siegler (Vol. Eds.), *Handbook of child psychology: Vol. 2. Cognition, perception, and language* (6th ed., pp. 214–251). Hoboken, NJ: Wiley.

Cohen, Sheldon, Tyrrell, David A., & Smith, Andrew P. (1993). Negative life events, perceived stress, negative affect, and susceptibility to the common cold. *Journal of Personality and Social Psychology, 64,* 131–140.

Cohen, William I. (2005). Medical care of the child with Down syndrome. In Merlin Gene Butler & F. John Meaney (Eds.), *Genetics of developmental disabilities* (pp. 223–245). Boca Raton, FL: Taylor & Francis.

Colbert, Linda K., Jefferson, Joseph L., Gallo, Ralph, & Davis, Ronnie. (2009). A study of religiosity and psychological well-being among African Americans: Implications for counseling and psychotherapeutic processes. *Journal of Religion and Health, 48,* 278–289.

Cole, Claire, & Winsler, Adam. (2010). Protecting children from exposure to lead: Old problem, new data, and new policy needs. *Social Policy Report, 24,* 3–29.

Coleman, Marilyn, Ganong, Lawrence H., & Warzinik, Kelly. (2007). *Family life in 20th-century America.* Westport, CT: Greenwood Press.

Coles, Robert. (1997). *The moral intelligence of children: How to raise a moral child.* New York: Random House.

Colleran, Carol, & Jay, Debra. (2003). Surviving addiction: Audrey's story. *Aging Today, 24,* 11.

Collins, Juliet, Johnson, Susan L., & Krebs, Nancy F. (2004). Screen for and treat overweight in 2- to 5-year-olds? Yes! *Contemporary Pediatrics, 21,* 60–74.

Collins, Michael F. (with Kay, Tess). (2003). *Sport and social exclusion.* London: Routledge.

Collins, W. Andrew, & Laursen, Brett. (2004). Parent-adolescent relationships and influences. In Richard M. Lerner & Laurence D. Steinberg (Eds.), *Handbook of adolescent psychology* (2nd ed., pp. 331–361). Hoboken, NJ: Wiley.

Compas, Bruce E. (2004). Processes of risk and resilience during adolescence: Linking contexts and individuals. In Richard M. Lerner & Laurence D. Steinberg (Eds.), *Handbook of adolescent psychology* (2nd ed., pp. 263–296). Hoboken, NJ: Wiley.

Compian, Laura J., Gowen, L. Kris, & Hayward, Chris. (2009). The interactive effects of puberty and peer victimization on weight concerns and depression symptoms among early adolescent girls. *The Journal of Early Adolescence, 29,* 357–375.

Conboy, Barbara T., & Thal, Donna J. (2006). Ties between the lexicon and grammar: Cross-sectional and longitudinal studies of bilingual toddlers. *Child Development, 77,* 712–735.

Cong, Zhen, & Silverstein, Merril. (2008). Intergenerational support and depression among elders in rural China: Do daughters-in-law matter? *Journal of Marriage and Family, 70,* 599–612.

Conger, Rand D., Conger, Katherine J., & Martin, Monica J. (2010). Socioeconomic status, family processes, and individual development. *Journal of Marriage and Family, 72,* 685–704.

Conger, Rand D., Wallace, Lora Ebert, Sun, Yumei, Simons, Ronald L., McLoyd, Vonnie C., & Brody, Gene H. (2002). Economic pressure in African American families: A replication and extension of the family stress model. *Developmental Psychology, 38,* 179–193.

Conley, Colleen S., & Rudolph, Karen D. (2009). The emerging sex difference in adolescent depression: Interacting contributions of puberty and peer stress. *Development and Psychopathology, 21,* 593–620.

Conner, Mark (2008). Initiation and maintenance of health behaviors. *Applied Psychology, 57,* 42–50.

Connidis, Ingrid Arnet. (2007). Negotiating inequality among adult siblings: Two case studies. *Journal of Marriage and Family, 69,* 482–499.

Cook, Christine C., Martin, Peter, Yearns, Mary, & Damhorst, Mary Lynn. (2007). Attachment to "place" and coping with losses in changed communities: A paradox for aging adults. *Family & Consumer Sciences Research Journal, 35,* 201–214.

Cooke, Bill, Mills, Albert J., & Kelley, Elizabeth S. (2005). Situating Maslow in cold war America: A recontextualization of management theory. *Group & Organization Management,* 129–152.

Coontz, Stephanie. (2005). *Marriage, a history: From obedience to intimacy or how love conquered marriage.* New York: Viking.

Cooper, Claudia, Selwood, Amber, & Livingston, Gill. (2008). The prevalence of elder abuse and neglect: A systematic review. *Age and Ageing, 37,* 151–160.

Cooper, Carey E., McLanahan, Sara S., Meadows, Sarah O., & Brooks-Gunn, Jeanne. (2009). Family structure transitions and maternal parenting stress. *Journal of Marriage and Family, 71,* 558–574.

Coovadia, Hoosen M., & Wittenberg, Dankwart F. (Eds.). (2004). *Paediatrics and child health: A manual for health professionals in developing countries* (5th ed.). New York: Oxford University Press.

Coplan, Robert J., & Weeks, Murray. (2009). Shy and soft-spoken: Shyness, pragmatic language, and socio-emotional adjustment in early childhood. *Infant and Child Development, 18,* 238–254.

Corballis, Michael C. (2010). Mirror neurons and the evolution of language. *Brain and Language, 112,* 25–35.

Correa-Chavez, Maricela, Rogoff, Barbara, & Arauz, Rebeca Mejia. (2005). Cultural patterns in attending to two events at once. *Child Development, 76,* 664–678.

Cosgrave, James F. (2010). Embedded addiction: The social production of gambling knowledge and the development of gambling markets. *Canadian Journal of Sociology, 35,* 113–134.

Costello, Matthew C., Madden, David J., Mitroff, Stephen R., & Whiting, Wythe L. (2010). Age-related decline of visual processing components in change detection. *Psychology and Aging, 25,* 356–368.

Côté, James E. (2006). Emerging adulthood as an institutionalized moratorium: Risks and benefits to identity formation. In Jeffrey Jensen Arnett & Jennifer Lynn Tanner (Eds.), *Emerging adults in America: Coming of age in the 21st century* (pp. 85–116). Washington, DC: American Psychological Association.

Côté, James E. (2009). Identity formation and self-development in adolescence. In Richard M. Lerner & Laurence Steinberg (Eds.), *Handbook of adolescent psychology: Vol. 1. Individual bases of adolescent development* (3rd ed., pp. 266–304). Hoboken, NJ: John Wiley & Sons.

Côté, Sylvana M., Borge, Anne I., Geoffroy, Marie-Claude, Rutter, Michael, & Tremblay, Richard E. (2008). Nonmaternal care in infancy and emotional/behavioral difficulties at 4 years old: Moderation by family risk characteristics. *Developmental Psychology, 44,* 155–168.

Courage, Mary L., Reynolds, Greg D., & Richards, John E. (2006). Infants' attention to patterned stimuli: Developmental change from 3 to 12 months of age. *Child Development, 77,* 680–695.

Covington, Martin V., & Dray, Elizabeth. (2002). The developmental course of achievement motivation: A need-based approach. In Allan Wigfield & Jacquelynne S. Eccles (Eds.), *Development of achievement motivation* (pp. 33–56). San Diego, CA: Academic Press.

Cowan, Nelson (Ed.). (1997). *The development of memory in childhood.* Hove, East Sussex, UK: Psychology Press.

Cowan, Nelson. (2010). The magical mystery four. *Current Directions in Psychological Science, 19,* 51–57.

Cowan, Nelson, & Alloway, Tracy. (2009). Development of working memory in childhood. In Mary L. Courage & Nelson Cowan (Eds.), *The development of memory in infancy and childhood* (2nd ed., pp. 303–342). New York: Psychology Press.

Coward, Fiona. (2008, March 14). Standing on the shoulders of giants. *Science, 319,* 1493–1495.

Crain, William C. (2005). *Theories of development: Concepts and applications* (5th ed.). Upper Saddle River, NJ: Prentice Hall.

Cramer, Robert, Lipinski, Ryan, Bowman, Ashley, & Carollo, Tanner. (2009). Subjective distress to violations of trust in Mexican American close relationships conforms to evolutionary principles. *Current Psychology, 28,* 1–11.

Cranwell, Brian. (2010). Care and control: What motivates people's decisions about the disposal of ashes. *Bereavement Care, 29,* 10–12.

Crawford, Emily, Wright, Margaret O'Dougherty, & Masten, Ann S. (2006). Resilience and spirituality in youth. In Eugene C. Roehlkepartain, Pamela Ebstyne King, Linda Wagener, & Peter L. Benson (Eds.), *The handbook of spiritual development in childhood and adolescence* (pp. 355–370). Thousand Oaks, CA: Sage Publications.

Crawford Shearer, Nelma B., Fleury, Julie D., & Reed, Pamela G. (2009). The rhythm of health in older women with chronic illness. *Research and Theory for Nursing Practice, 23,* 148–160.

Crews, Douglas E. (2003). *Human senescence: Evolutionary and biocultural perspectives.* New York: Cambridge University Press.

Crinion, Jenny, Turner, R., Grogan, Alice, Hanakawa, Takashi, Noppeney, Uta, Devlin, Joseph T., et al. (2006, June 9). Language control in the bilingual brain. *Science, 312,* 1537–1540.

Cronce, Jessica M., & Corbin, William R. (2010). College and career. In Jon E. Grant & Marc N. Potenza (Eds.), *Young adult mental health* (pp. 80–95). New York, NY: Oxford University Press.

Crone, Eveline A., & Westenberg, P. Michiel. (2009). A brain-based account of developmental changes in social decision making. In Michelle de Haan & Megan R. Gunnar (Eds.), *Handbook of developmental social neuroscience* (pp. 378–396). New York: Guilford.

Crosnoe, Robert, & Elder, Glen H., Jr. (2002). Successful adaptation in the later years: A life course approach to aging. *Social Psychology Quarterly, 65,* 309–328.

Crosnoe, Robert, Johnson, Monica Kirkpatrick, & Elder, Glen H., Jr. (2004). Intergenerational bonding in school: The behavioral and contextual correlates of student-teacher relationships. *Sociology of Education, 77,* 60–81.

Crosnoe, Robert, Leventhal, Tama, Wirth, Robert John, Pierce, Kim M., Pianta, Robert C., & Network, NICHD Early Child Care Research. (2010). Family socioeconomic status and consistent environmental stimulation in early childhood. *Child Development, 81,* 972–987.

Crosnoe, Robert, & Needham, Belinda. (2004). Holism, contextual variability, and the study of friendships in adolescent development. *Child Development, 75,* 264–279.

Cruikshank, Margaret. (2003). *Learning to be old: Gender, culture, and aging.* Lanham, MD: Rowman & Littlefield.

Cruikshank, Margaret. (2009). *Learning to be old: Gender, culture, and aging* (2nd ed.). Lanham, MD: Rowman & Littlefield.

Cruz, Alvaro A., Bateman, Eric D., & Bousquet, Jean. (2010). The social determinants of asthma. *European Respiratory Journal, 35,* 239–242.

Cryder, Cynthia E., Lerner, Jennifer S., Gross, James J., & Dahl, Ronald E. (2008). Misery is not miserly: Sad and self-focused individuals spend more. *Psychological Science, 19,* 525–530.

Csikszentmihalyi, Mihaly. (1996). *Creativity: Flow and the psychology of discovery and invention.* New York: HarperCollins.

Cui, Ming, & Donnellan, M. Brent. (2009). Trajectories of conflict over raising adolescent children and marital satisfaction. *Journal of Marriage and Family, 71,* 478–494.

Cuijpers, Pim, Brännmark, Jessica G., & van Straten, Annemieke. (2008). Psychological treatment of postpartum depression: a meta-analysis. *Journal of Clinical Psychology, 64,* 103–118.

Cullen, Karen Weber, & Zakeri, Issa. (2004). Fruits, vegetables, milk, and sweetened beverages consumption and access to a la carte/snack bar meals at school. *American Journal of Public Health, 94,* 463–467.

Cumming, Elaine, & Henry, William Earl. (1961). *Growing old: The process of disengagement.* New York: Basic Books.

Cumsille, Patricio, Darling, Nancy, & Martínez, M. Loreto. (2010). Shading the truth: The patterning of adolescents' decisions to avoid issues, disclose, or lie to parents. *Journal of Adolescence, 33,* 285–296.

Cunningham, Solveig Argeseanu, Ruben, Julia D., & Narayan, K. M. Venkat. (2008). Health of foreign-born people in the United States: A review. *Health & Place, 14,* 623–635.

Cunradi, Carol B. (2009). Intimate partner violence among Hispanic men and women: The role of drinking, neighborhood disorder, and acculturation-related factors. *Violence and Victims, 24,* 83–97.

Curlin, Farr A., Nwodim, Chinyere, Vance, Jennifer L., Chin, Marshall H., & Lantos, John D. (2008). To die, to sleep: US physicians' religious and other objections to physician-assisted suicide, terminal sedation, and withdrawal of life support. *American Journal of Hospice and Palliative Medicine, 25,* 112–120.

Currie, Janet, & Widom, Cathy Spatz. (2010). Long-term consequences of child abuse and neglect on adult economic well-being. *Child Maltreatment, 15,* 111–120.

Curtis, W. John, & Cicchetti, Dante. (2003). Moving research on resilience into the 21st century: Theoretical and methodological considerations in examining the biological contributors to resilience. *Development & Psychopathology, 15,* 773–810.

D'Angelo, Denise, Williams, Letitia, Morrow, Brian, Cox, Shanna, Harris, Norma,

Harrison, Leslie, et al. (2007). Preconception and interconception health status of women who recently gave birth to a live-born infant—Pregnancy Risk Assessment Monitoring System (PRAMS), United States, 26 reporting areas, 2004. *MMWR Surveillance Summaries, 56*(SS10), 1–35.

Daddis, Christopher. (2010). Adolescent peer crowds and patterns of belief in the boundaries of personal authority. *Journal of Adolescence, 33,* 699–708.

Dahl, Ronald E. (2004). Adolescent brain development: A period of vulnerabilities and opportunities. Keynote address. In Ronald E. Dahl & Linda Patia Spear (Eds.), *Adolescent brain development: Vulnerabilities and opportunities* (Vol. 1021, pp. 1–22). New York: New York Academy of Sciences.

Dahl, Ronald E., & Gunnar, Megan R. (2009). Heightened stress responsiveness and emotional reactivity during pubertal maturation: Implications for psychopathology. *Development and Psychopathology, 21,* 1–6.

Daley, Dave, Jones, Karen, Hutchings, Judy, & Thompson, Margaret. (2009). Attention deficit hyperactivity disorder in pre-school children: Current findings, recommended interventions and future directions. *Child: Care, Health and Development, 35,* 754–766.

Dalman, Christina, Allebeck, Peter, Gunnell, David, Harrison, Glyn, Kristensson, Krister, Lewis, Glyn, et al. (2008). Infections in the CNS during childhood and the risk of subsequent psychotic illness: A cohort study of more than one million Swedish subjects. *American Journal of Psychiatry, 165,* 59–65.

Damasio, Antonio R. (2003). *Looking for Spinoza: Joy, sorrow, and the feeling brain.* Orlando, FL: Harcourt.

Damon, William, & Lerner, Richard M. (Eds.). (2006). *Handbook of child psychology* (6th ed., Vol. 1–4). Hoboken, NJ: Wiley.

Danel, Isabella, Berg, Cynthia, Johnson, Christopher H., & Atrash, Hani. (2003). Magnitude of maternal morbidity during labor and delivery: United States, 1993–1997. *American Journal of Public Health, 93,* 631–634.

Dangour, Alan D., Fletcher, Astrid E., & Grundy, Emily M. D. (2007). *Ageing well: Nutrition, health, and social interventions.* Boca Raton, FL: CRC Press/Taylor & Francis.

Dannefer, Dale, & Patterson, Robin Shura. (2008). The missing person: Some limitations in the contemporary study of cognitive aging. In Scott M. Hofer & Duane F. Alwin (Eds.), *Handbook of cognitive aging: Interdisciplinary perspectives* (pp. 105–119). Thousand Oaks, CA: Sage.

Dansinger, Michael L., Gleason, Joi Augustin, Griffith, John L., Selker, Harry P., & Schaefer, Ernst J. (2005). Comparison of the Atkins, Ornish, Weight Watchers, and Zone diets for weight loss and heart disease risk reduction: A randomized trial. *Journal of the American Medical Association, 293,* 43–53.

Darling, Nancy, Cumsille, Patricio, & Martinez, M. Loreto. (2008). Individual dif-

ferences in adolescents' beliefs about the legitimacy of parental authority and their own obligation to obey: A longitudinal investigation. *Child Development, 79,* 1103–1118.

Daro, Deborah. (2002). Public perception of child sexual abuse: Who is to blame? *Child Abuse & Neglect, 26,* 1131–1133.

Darwin, Charles. (1859). *On the origin of species by means of natural selection.* London: J. Murray.

Daselaar, Sander, & Cabeza, Roberto. (2005). Age-related changes in hemispheric organization. In Roberto Cabeza, Lars Nyberg, & Denise Park (Eds.), *Cognitive neuroscience of aging: Linking cognitive and cerebral aging* (pp. 325–353). New York: Oxford University Press.

Dasen, Pierre R. (2003). Theoretical frameworks in cross-cultural developmental psychology: An attempt at integration. In T. S. Saraswati (Ed.), *Cross-cultural perspectives in human development: Theory, research, and applications* (pp. 128–165). New Delhi, India: Sage.

Datan, Nancy. (1986). Oedipal conflict, platonic love: Centrifugal forces in intergenerational relations. In Nancy Datan, Anita L. Greene, & Hayne W. Reese (Eds.), *Life-span developmental psychology: Intergenerational relations* (pp. 29–50). Hillsdale, NJ: Erlbaum.

David, Barbara, Grace, Diane, & Ryan, Michelle K. (2004). The gender wars: A self-categorization perspective on the development of gender identity. In Mark Bennett & Fabio Sani (Eds.), *The development of the social self* (pp. 135–157). Hove, East Sussex, England: Psychology Press.

Davidson, Julia O'Connell. (2005). *Children in the global sex trade.* Malden, MA: Polity.

Davidson, Kate. (2008). Declining health and competence: Men facing choices about driving cessation. *Generations, 32,* 44–47.

Davila, Joanne. (2008). Depressive symptoms and adolescent romance: Theory, research, and implications. *Child Development Perspectives,* 26–31.

Davis, Elysia Poggi, Parker, Susan Whitmore, Tottenham, Nim, & Gunnar, Megan R. (2003). Emotion, cognition, and the hypothalamic-pituitary-adrenocortical axis: A developmental perspective. In Michelle de Haan & Mark H. Johnson (Eds.), *The cognitive neuroscience of development* (pp. 181–206). New York: Psychology Press.

Davis, Kelly D., Goodman, W. Benjamin, Pirretti, Amy E., & Almeida, David M. (2008). Nonstandard work schedules, perceived family well-being, and daily stressors. *Journal of Marriage and Family, 70,* 991–1003.

Davis, Mark, & Squire, Corinne (Eds.). (2010). *HIV treatment and prevention technologies in international perspective.* New York: Palgrave Macmillan.

Davis-Kean, Pamela E., Jager, Jager, & Collins, W. Andrew (2009). The self in action: An emerging link between self-beliefs and behaviors in middle childhood. *Child Development Perspectives, 3,* 184–188.

Davison, Kirsten Krahnstoever, Werder, Jessica L., Trost, Stewart G., Baker, Birgitta L., & Birch, Leann L. (2007). Why are early maturing girls less active? Links between pubertal development, psychological well-being, and physical activity among girls at ages 11 and 13. *Social Science & Medicine, 64,* 2391–2404.

Dawson, Geraldine. (2010). Recent advances in research on early detection, causes, biology, and treatment of autism spectrum disorders. *Current Opinion in Neurology, 23,* 95–96.

Dawson, Lorne L. (2010). The study of new religious movements and the radicalization of homegrown terrorists: Opening a dialogue. *Terrorism and Political Violence, 22,* 1–21.

Dawson, Michelle, Soulières, Isabelle, Gernsbacher, Morton Ann, & Mottron, Laurent. (2007). The level and nature of autistic intelligence. *Psychological Science, 18,* 657–662.

de Bruin, Wändi Bruine, Parker, Andrew M., & Fischhoff, Baruch. (2007). Can adolescents predict significant life events? *The Journal of Adolescent Health, 41,* 208–210.

De Dreu, Carsten K. W., Nijstad, Bernard A., & van Knippenberg, Daan. (2008). Motivated information processing in group judgment and decision making. *Personality and Social Psychology Review,* 22–49.

de Grey, Aubrey D. N. J. (with Rae, Michael). (2007). *Ending aging: The rejuvenation breakthroughs that could reverse human aging in our lifetime.* New York: St. Martin's Press.

de Haan, Amaranta D., Prinzie, Peter, & Dekovic, Maja. (2009). Mothers' and fathers' personality and parenting: The mediating role of sense of competence. *Developmental Psychology, 45,* 1695–1707.

de Haan, Michelle, & Johnson, Mark H. (2003). Mechanisms and theories of brain development. In Michelle De Haan & Mark H. Johnson (Eds.), *The cognitive neuroscience of development* (pp. 1–18). Hove, East Sussex, England: Psychology Press.

De la Torre, Jack C., Kalaria, Raj, Nakajima, Kenji, & Nagata, Ken (Eds.). (2002). *Annals of the New York Academy of Sciences: Vol. 977. Alzheimer's disease: Vascular etiology and pathology.* New York: New York Academy of Sciences.

De Lee, Joseph Bolivar. (1938). *The principles and practice of obstetrics* (7th ed.). Philadelphia: Saunders.

De Neys, Wim. (2006). Dual processing in reasoning: Two systems but one reasoner. *Psychological Science, 17,* 428–433.

De Neys, Wim, & Van Gelder, Elke. (2009). Logic and belief across the lifespan: The rise and fall of belief inhibition during syllogistic reasoning. *Developmental Science, 12,* 123–130.

de Schipper, Elles J., Riksen-Walraven, J. Marianne, & Geurts, Sabine A. E. (2006). Effects of child-caregiver ratio on the interactions between caregivers and children in child-care centers: An experimental study. *Child Development, 77,* 861–874.

Dean, Angela J, Walters, Julie, & Hall, Anthony. (2010). A systematic review of interventions to enhance medication adherence in children and adolescents with chronic illness. *Archives of Disease in Childhood, 95,* 717–723.

Dearing, Eric, Wimer, Christopher, Simpkins, Sandra D., Lund, Terese, Bouffard, Suzanne M., Caronongan, Pia, et al. (2009). Do neighborhood and home contexts help explain why low-income children miss opportunities to participate in activities outside of school? *Developmental Psychology, 45,* 1545–1562.

Deary, Ian J., Batty, G. David, Pattie, Alison, & Gale, Catharine R. (2008). More intelligent, more dependable children live longer: A 55-year longitudinal study of a representative sample of the Scottish nation. *Psychological Science, 19,* 874–880.

Deary, Ian J., Penke, Lars, & Johnson, Wendy. (2010). The neuroscience of human intelligence differences. *Nature Reviews Neuroscience, 11,* 201–211.

DeBaggio, Thomas. (2002). *Losing my mind: An intimate look at life with Alzheimer's.* New York: Free Press.

Decety, Jean, & Meyer, Meghan. (2008). From emotion resonance to empathic understanding: A social developmental neuroscience account. *Development and Psychopathology, 20,* 1053–1080.

Deci, Edward L., Koestner, Richard, & Ryan, Richard M. (1999). A meta-analytic review of experiments examining the effects of extrinsic rewards on intrinsic motivation. *Psychological Bulletin, 125,* 627–668.

Dehue, Francine, Bolman, Catherine, & Völlink, Trijntje. (2008). Cyberbullying: Youngsters' experiences and parental perception. *CyberPsychology & Behavior, 11,* 217–223.

Deil-Amen, Regina, & Rosenbaum, James E. (2003). The social prerequisites of success: Can college structure reduce the need for social know-how? In Kathleen M. Shaw & Jerry A. Jacobs (Eds.), *Community colleges: New environments, new directions* (Vol. 586, pp. 120–143). Thousand Oaks, CA: Sage.

DeLisi, Matt, Jones-Johnson, Gloria, Johnson, W. Roy, & Hochstetler, Andy. (2010). *The aftermath of criminal victimization: Race, self-esteem, and self-efficacy.* Retrieved December 15, 2010, from the World Wide Web: http://cad.sagepub.com/content/early/2010/01/22/0011128709354036.abstract

Demetriou, Andreas, & Bakracevic, Karin. (2009). Reasoning and self-awareness from adolescence to middle age: Organization and development as a function of education. *Learning and Individual Differences, 19,* 181–194.

Demetriou, Andreas, Christou, Constantinos, Spanoudis, George, & Platsidou, Maria. (2002). The development of mental processing: Efficiency, working memory, and thinking. *Monographs of the Society for Research in Child Development, 67.*

Denham, Susanne A., Blair, Kimberly A., DeMulder, Elizabeth, Levitas, Jennifer, Sawyer, Katherine, Auerbach-Major, Sharon, et al. (2003). Preschool emotional competence: Pathway to social competence. *Child Development, 74,* 238–256.

Denney, Nancy W., & Pearce, Kathy A. (1989). A developmental study of practical problem solving in adults. *Psychology & Aging, 4,* 438–442.

Denny, Dallas, & Pittman, Cathy. (2007). Gender identity: From dualism to diversity. In Mitchell S. Tepper & Annette Fuglsang Owens (Eds.), *Sexual health: Vol. 1. Psychological foundations* (pp. 205–229). Westport, CT: Praeger/Greenwood.

Dentinger, Emma, & Clarkberg, Marin. (2002). Informal caregiving and retirement timing among men and women: Gender and caregiving relationships in late midlife. *Journal of Family Issues, 23,* 857–879.

Denton, Melinda Lundquist, Pearce, Lisa D., & Smith, Christian. (2008). *Religion and spirituality on the path through adolescence* (Research Report Number 8). Chapel Hill, NC: National Study of Youth and Religion, University of North Carolina at Chapel Hill.

DePaulo, Bella M. (2006). *Singled out: How singles are stereotyped, stigmatized, and ignored and still live happily ever after.* New York: St. Martin's Press.

Depp, Colin A., & Jeste, Dilip V. (2009). Definitions and predictors of successful aging: A comprehensive review of larger quantitative studies. *Focus, 7,* 137–150.

Derman, Orhan, Kanbur, Nuray Öksöz, & Kutluk, Tezer. (2003). Tamoxifen treatment for pubertal gynecomastia. *International Journal of Adolescent Medicine and Health, 15,* 359–363.

Derryberry, Douglas, Reed, Marjorie A., & Pilkenton-Taylor, Carolyn. (2003). Temperament and coping: Advantages of an individual differences perspective. *Development & Psychopathology, 15,* 1049–1066.

Desai, Sonalde, & Andrist, Lester. (2010). Gender scripts and age at marriage in India. *Demography, 47,* 667–687.

DesJardin, Jean L., Ambrose, Sophie E., & Eisenberg, Laurie S. (2009). Literacy skills in children with cochlear implants: The importance of early oral language and joint storybook reading. *Journal of Deaf Studies and Deaf Education, 14,* 22–43.

Desoete, Annemie, Stock, Pieter, Schepens, Annemie, Baeyens, Dieter, & Roeyers, Herbert. (2009). Classification, seriation, and counting in grades 1, 2, and 3 as two-year longitudinal predictors for low achieving in numerical facility and arithmetical achievement? *Journal of Psychoeducational Assessment, 27,* 252–264.

Devi, Sharmila. (2008). Progress on childhood obesity patchy in the USA. *Lancet, 371,* 105–106.

DeVito, Loren M., Kanter, Benjamin R., & Eichenbaum, Howard. (2010). The hippocampus contributes to memory expression during transitive inference in mice. *Hippocampus, 20,* 208–217.

DeYoung, Colin G., Hirsh, Jacob B., Shane, Matthew S., Papademetris, Xenophon, Rajeevan, Nallakkandi, & Gray, Jeremy R. (2010). Testing predictions from personality neuroscience. *Psychological Science, 21,* 820–828.

Di Martino, Adriana, Ross, Kathryn, Uddin, Lucina Q., Sklar, Andrew B., Castellanos, F. Xavier, & Milham, Michael P. (2009). Functional brain correlates of social and nonsocial processes in autism spectrum disorders: An activation likelihood estimation meta-analysis. *Biological Psychiatry, 65,* 63–74.

Diamanti-Kandarakis, Evanthia, Bourguignon, Jean-Pierre, Giudice, Linda C., Hauser, Russ, Prins, Gail S., Soto, Ana M., et al. (2009). Endocrine-disrupting chemicals: An endocrine society scientific statement. *Endocrine Society, 30,* 293–342.

Diamond, Adele, & Amso, Dima. (2008). Contributions of neuroscience to our understanding of cognitive development. *Current Directions in Psychological Science, 17,* 136–141.

Diamond, Adele, Barnett, W. Steven, Thomas, Jessica, & Munro, Sarah. (2007, November 30). Preschool program improves cognitive control. *Science, 318,* 1387–1388.

Diamond, Adele, & Kirkham, Natasha. (2005). Not quite as grown-up as we like to think: Parallels between cognition in childhood and adulthood. *Psychological Science, 16,* 291–297.

Diamond, David M., Dunwiddie, Thomas V., & Rose, Gregory M. (1988). Characteristics of hippocampal primed burst potentiation in vitro and in the awake rat. *Journal of Neuroscience, 8,* 4079–4088.

Diamond, Lisa M. (2004). Emerging perspectives on distinctions between romantic love and sexual desire. *Current Directions in Psychological Science, 13,* 116–119.

Diamond, Lisa M., & Fagundes, Christopher P. (2010). Psychobiological research on attachment. *Journal of Social and Personal Relationships, 27*(2), 218–225.

Diamond, Lisa M., & Savin-Williams, Ritch C. (2003). The intimate relationships of sexual-minority youths. In Gerald R. Adams & Michael D. Berzonsky (Eds.), *Blackwell handbook of adolescence* (pp. 393–412). Malden, MA: Blackwell.

Diamond, Marion C. (1988). *Enriching heredity.* New York: The Free Press.

Diamond, Mathew E. (2007). Neuronal basis of perceptual intelligence. In Flavia Santoianni & Claudia Sabatano (Eds.), *Brain development in learning environments: Embodied and perceptual advancements* (pp. 98–108). Newcastle, UK: Cambridge Scholars.

Dickinson, George E., & Hoffmann, Heath C. (2010). Roadside memorial policies in the United States. *Mortality, 15,* 154–167.

Didion, Joan. (2005). *The year of magical thinking.* New York: Knopf.

Diener, Ed, & Biswas-Diener, Robert. (2008). *Happiness: Unlocking the mysteries of psychological wealth.* Malden, MA: Blackwell.

Diener, Marissa. (2000). Gift from the gods: A Balinese guide to early child rearing. In Judy S. DeLoache & Alma Gottlieb (Eds.), *A world of babies: Imagined childcare guides for seven societies* (pp. 96–116). New York: Cambridge University Press.

Dietrich, Anne. (2008). *When the hurting continues: Revictimization and perpetration in the lives of childhood maltreatment survivors.* Saarbrücken, Germany: VDM Verlag.

Dietz, William H., & Robinson, Thomas N. (2005). Overweight children and adolescents. *New England Journal of Medicine, 352,* 2100–2109.

DiGirolamo, Ann, Thompson, Nancy, Martorell, Reynaldo, Fein, Sara, & Grummer-Strawn, Laurence. (2005). Intention or experience? Predictors of continued breastfeeding. *Health Education & Behavior, 32,* 208–226.

Dijksterhuis, Ap. (2004). Think different: The merits of unconscious thought in preference development and decision making. *Journal of Personality and Social Psychology, 87,* 586–598.

Dijksterhuis, Ap, & Aarts, Henk. (2010). Goals, attention, and (un)consciousness. *Annual Review of Psychology, 61,* 467–490.

Dijksterhuis, Ap, Bos, Maarten W., van der Leij, Andries, & van Baaren, Rick B. (2009). Predicting soccer matches after unconscious and conscious thought as a function of expertise. *Psychological Science, 20,* 1381–1387.

Dijksterhuis, Ap, & Nordgren, Loran F. (2006). A theory of unconscious thought. *Perspectives on Psychological Science, 1,* 95–109.

Dilworth-Bart, Janean E., & Moore, Colleen F. (2006). Mercy mercy me: Social injustice and the prevention of environmental pollutant exposures among ethnic minority and poor children. *Child Development, 77,* 247–265.

Dindia, Kathryn, & Emmers-Sommer, Tara M. (2006). What partners do to maintain their close relationships. In Patricia Noller & Judith A. Feeney (Eds.), *Close relationships: Functions, forms and processes* (pp. 305–324). Hove, England: Psychology Press/Taylor & Francis.

Dion, Karen Kisiel. (2006). On the development of identity: Perspectives from immigrant families. In Ramaswami Mahalingam (Ed.), *Cultural psychology of immigrants* (pp. 299–314). Mahwah, NJ: Erlbaum

DiPietro, Janet A., Hilton, Sterling C., Hawkins, Melissa, Costigan, Kathleen A., & Pressman, Eva K. (2002). Maternal stress and affect influence fetal neurobehavioral development. *Developmental Psychology, 38,* 659–668.

Dirix, Chantal E. H., Nijhuis, Jan G., Jongsma, Henk W., & Hornstra, Gerard. (2009). Aspects of fetal learning and memory. *Child Development, 80,* 1251–1258.

Dishion, Thomas J., & Bullock, Bernadette Marie. (2002). Parenting and adolescent problem behavior: An ecological analysis of the nurturance hypothesis. In John G. Borkowski, Sharon Landesman Ramey, & Marie Bristol-Power (Eds.), *Parenting and the child's world: Influences on academic, intellectual, and social-emotional development* (pp. 231–249). Mahwah, NJ: Erlbaum.

Dishion, Thomas J., Poulin, François, & Burraston, Bert. (2001). Peer group dynamics associated with iatrogenic effects in group interventions with high-risk young adolescents. In William Damon (Series Ed.) & Douglas W. Nangle & Cynthia A. Erdley (Vol. Eds.), *New directions for child and adolescent development: No. 91. The role of friendship in psychological adjustment* (pp. 79–92). San Francisco: Jossey-Bass.

Dishion, Thomas J., Véronneau, Marie-Hélène, & Myers, Michael W. (2010). Cascading peer dynamics underlying the progression from problem behavior to violence in early to late adolescence. *Development and Psychopathology, 22,* 603–619.

Dixon, Roger A., & Lerner, Richard M. (1999). History and systems in developmental psychology. In Marc H. Bornstein & Michael E. Lamb (Eds.), *Developmental psychology: An advanced textbook* (4th ed., pp. 3–45). Mahwah, NJ: Erlbaum.

Dodge, Kenneth A. (2009). Mechanisms of gene-environment interaction effects in the development of conduct disorder. *Perspectives on Psychological Science, 4,* 408–414.

Dodge, Kenneth A., Coie, John D., & Lynam, Donald R. (2006). Aggression and antisocial behavior in youth. In William Damon & Richard M. Lerner (Series Eds.) & Nancy Eisenberg (Vol. Ed.), *Handbook of child psychology: Vol. 3. Social, emotional, and personality development* (6th ed., pp. 719–788). New York: Wiley.

Doidge, Norman. (2007). *The brain that changes itself: Stories of personal triumph from the frontiers of brain science.* New York: Viking.

Dominguez, Cynthia O. (2001). Expertise in laparoscopic surgery: Anticipation and affordances. In Eduardo Salas & Gary Klein (Eds.), *Linking expertise and naturalistic decision making* (pp. 287–301). Mahwah, NJ: Erlbaum.

Donaldson, Margaret C. (2003). *A study of children's thinking.* New York: Routledge. (Original work published 1963)

Donnellan, M. Brent, & Lucas, Richard E. (2008). Age differences in the Big Five across the life span: Evidence from two national samples. *Psychology and Aging, 23,* 558–566.

dosReis, Susan, Mychailyszyn, Matthew P., Evans-Lacko, Sara E., Beltran, Alicia, Riley, Anne W., & Myers, Mary Anne. (2009). The meaning of attention-deficit/hyperactivity disorder medication and parents' initiation and continuity of treatment for their child. *Journal of Child and Adolescent Psychopharmacology, 19,* 377–383.

dosReis, Susan, & Myers, Mary Anne. (2008). Parental attitudes and involvement in psychopharmacological treatment for ADHD: A conceptual model. *International Review of Psychiatry, 20,* 135–141.

Doumbo, Ogobara K. (2005, February 4). It takes a village: Medical research and ethics in Mali. *Science, 307,* 679–681.

Dowling, John E. (2004). *The great brain debate: Nature or nurture?* Washington, DC: Joseph Henry Press.

Drover, James, Hoffman, Dennis R., Castañeda, Yolanda S., Morale, Sarah E., & Birch, Eileen E. (2009). Three randomized controlled trials of early long-chain polyunsaturated fatty acid supplementation on means-end problem solving in 9-month-olds. *Child Development, 80,* 1376–1384.

Duckworth, Angela L., Peterson, Christopher, Matthews, Michael D., & Kelly, Dennis R. (2007). Grit: Perseverance and passion for long-term goals. *Journal of Personality and Social Psychology, 92,* 1087–1101.

Duffey, Kiyah J., Gordon-Larsen, Penny, Shikany, James M., Guilkey, David, Jacobs, David R., Jr, & Popkin, Barry M. (2010). Food price and diet and health outcomes: 20 years of the CARDIA study. *Archives of Internal Medicine, 170,* 420–426.

Dugger, Celia W. (2006, April 30). Mothers of Nepal vanquish a killer of children. *New York Times,* pp. A1, A16.

Dukes, Richard L., Stein, Judith A., & Zane, Jazmin I. (2009). Effect of relational bullying on attitudes, behavior and injury among adolescent bullies, victims and bully-victims. *Social Science Journal, 46,* 671–688.

Duncan, Greg J., Ziol-Guest, Kathleen M., & Kalil, Ariel. (2010). Early-childhood poverty and adult attainment, behavior, and health. *Child Development, 81,* 306–325.

Dunifon, Rachel, & Kowaleski-Jones, Lori. (2007). The influence of grandparents in single-mother families. *Journal of Marriage and Family, 69,* 465–481.

Dunlap, Jay C., Loros, Jennifer J., & DeCoursey, Patricia J. (2004). *Chronobiology: Biological timekeeping.* Sunderland, MA: Sinauer Associates.

Dunn, Judy, & Hughes, Claire. (2001). "I got some swords and you're dead!": Violent fantasy, antisocial behavior, friendship, and moral sensibility in young children. *Child Development, 72,* 491–505.

Dunphy, Dexter C. (1963). The social structure of urban adolescent peer groups. *Sociometry, 26,* 230–246.

Duplassie, Danielle, & Daniluk, Judith C. (2007). Sexuality: Young and middle adulthood. In Mitchell S. Tepper & Annette Fuglsang Owens (Eds.), *Sexual health: Vol. 1. Psychological foundations* (pp. 263–289). Westport, CT: Praeger/Greenwood.

Durvasula, Srinivas, Lysonski, Steven, & Watson, John. (2001). Does vanity describe other cultures? A cross-cultural examination of the vanity scale. *Journal of Consumer Affairs, 35,* 180–199.

Dweck, Carol S. (2007). Is math a gift? Beliefs that put females at risk. In Stephen J. Ceci & Wendy M. Williams (Eds.), *Why aren't more women in science: Top researchers debate the evidence* (pp. 47–55). Washington, DC: American Psychological Association.

Dye, Jane Lawler. (2005). *Fertility of American women: June 2004* (Current Population Reports P20–55). Washington, DC: U.S. Census Bureau.

Dye, Kelly, Mills, Albert J., & Weatherbee, Terrance. (2005). Maslow: Man interrupted: Reading management theory in context. *Management Decision, 43,* 1375–1395.

Ebaugh, Helen Rose, & Curry, Mary. (2000). Fictive kin as social capital in new immigrant communities. *Sociological Perspectives, 43,* 189–209.

Ebner, Natalie C., Freund, Alexandra M., & Baltes, Paul B. (2006). Developmental changes in personal goal orientation from young to late adulthood: From striving for gains to maintenance and prevention of losses. *Psychology and Aging, 21,* 664–678.

Eby, Lillian T., Durley, Jaime R., Evans, Sarah C., & Ragins, Belle Rose. (2006). The relationship between short-term mentoring benefits and long-term mentor outcomes. *Journal of Vocational Behavior, 69,* 424–444.

Eccles, Jacquelynne S. (2004). Schools, academic motivation, and stage-environment fit. In Richard M. Lerner & Laurence D. Steinberg (Eds.), *Handbook of adolescent psychology* (2nd ed., pp. 125–153). Hoboken, NJ: Wiley.

Eckstein, Daniel G., Rasmussen, Paul R., & Wittschen, Lori. (1999). Understanding and dealing with adolescents. *Journal of Individual Psychology, 55,* 31–50.

Edenberg, Howard J., Koller, Daniel L., Xuei, Xiaoling, Wetherill, Leah, McClintick, Jeanette N., Almasy, Laura, et al. (2010). Genome-wide association study of alcohol dependence implicates a region on chromosome 11. *Alcoholism Clinical and Experimental Research, 34,* 840–852.

Education Sector. (2009). *Growing pains: Scaling up the nation's best charter schools.* Washington, DC: Author.

Education Week. (2010, January 14). *Chance for success.* Retrieved August 25, 2010, from the World Wide Web: http://www.edweek.org/media/ew/qc/2010/17sos.h29.chance.pdf

Edwards, Judge Leonard. (2010). Relative placement in child protection cases: A judicial perspective. *Juvenile and Family Court Journal, 61,* 1–44.

Edwards, Judge Leonard P. (2007). Achieving timely permanency in child protection courts: The importance of frontloading the court process. *Juvenile and Family Court Journal, 58,* 1–37.

Egan, Kieran, & Ling, Michael. (2002). We began as poets: Conceptual tools and the arts in early childhood. In Liora Bresler & Christine Marme Thompson (Eds.), *The arts in children's lives: Context, culture, and curriculum* (pp. 93–100). Dordrecht, The Netherlands: Kluwer.

Ehrlich, Paul R. (1968). *The population bomb.* New York: Ballantine Books.

Eisenberg, Nancy, Cumberland, Amanda, Guthrie, Ivanna K., Murphy, Bridget C., & Shepard, Stephanie A. (2005). Age changes in prosocial responding and moral reasoning in adolescence and early adulthood. *Journal of Research on Adolescence, 15,* 235–260.

Eisenberg, Nancy, Fabes, Richard A., & Spinrad, Tracy L. (2006). Prosocial development. In William Damon & Richard M. Lerner (Series Eds.) & Nancy Eisenberg (Vol. Ed.), *Handbook of child psychology: Vol. 3. Social, emotional, and personality development* (6th ed., pp. 646–718). Hoboken, NJ: Wiley.

Eisenberg, Nancy, Hofer, Claire, Spinrad, Tracy L., Gershoff, Elizabeth T., Valiente, Carlos, Losoya, Sandra, et al. (2008). Understanding mother-adolescent conflict discussions: Concurrent and across-time prediction from youths' dispositions and parenting. *Monographs of the Society for Research in Child Development, 73* (2, Serial No. 290), vii–viii, 1–160.

Eisenberg, Nancy, Spinrad, Tracy L., Fabes, Richard A., Reiser, Mark, Cumberland, Amanda, Shepard, Stephanie A., et al. (2004). The relations of effortful control and impulsivity to children's resiliency and adjustment. *Child Development, 75,* 25–46.

Eklund, Jenny M., Kerr, Margaret, & Stattin, Håkan. (2010). Romantic relationships and delinquent behaviour in adolescence: The moderating role of delinquency propensity. *Journal of Adolescence, 33,* 377–386.

El-Chaar, Darine, Yang, Qiuying, Gao, Jun, Jim, Bottomley, Leader, Arthur, Wen, Shi Wu, et al. (2009). Risk of birth defects increased in pregnancies conceived by assisted human reproduction. *Fertility and Sterility, 92,* 1557–1561.

El-Sheikh, Mona, & Harger, JoAnn. (2001). Appraisals of marital conflict and children's adjustment, health, and physiological reactivity. *Developmental Psychology, 37,* 875–885.

Elder, Glen H., Jr,, & Shanahan, Michael J. (2006). The life course and human development. In William Damon & Richard M. Lerner (Series Eds.) & Richard M. Lerner (Vol. Ed.), *Handbook of child psychology: Vol. 1. Theoretical models of human development* (6th ed., pp. 665–715). Hoboken, NJ: Wiley.

Elia, Josephine, & Vetter, Victoria L. (2010). Cardiovascular effects of medications for the treatment of attention-deficit hyperactivity disorder: What is known and how should it influence prescribing in children? *Pediatric Drugs, 12,* 165–175.

Elias, Merrill F., Robbins, Michael A., Budge, Marc M., Elias, Penelope K., Hermann, Barbara A., & Dore, Gregory A. (2004). Studies of aging, hypertension and cognitive functioning: With contributions from the Maine-Syracuse Study. In Paul T. Costa & Ilene C. Siegler (Eds.), *Recent advances in psychology and aging* (Vol. 15, pp. 89–132). Amsterdam: Elsevier.

Elkind, David. (1967). Egocentrism in adolescence. *Child Development, 38,* 1025–1034.

Elkind, David. (2007). *The power of play: How spontaneous, imaginative activities lead to happier, healthier children.* Cambridge, MA: Da Capo Press.

Elliott, Leslie, Arbes, Samuel J., Jr., Harvey, Eric S., Lee, Robert C., Salo, Päivi M., Cohn, Richard D., et al. (2007). Dust weight and asthma prevalence in the National Survey of Lead and Allergens in Housing (NSLAH). *Environmental Health Perspectives, 115,* 215–220.

Ellis, Bruce J. (2004). Timing of pubertal maturation in girls: An integrated life history approach. *Psychological Bulletin, 130,* 920–958.

Ellis, Bruce J., & Boyce, W. Thomas. (2008). Biological sensitivity to context. *Current Directions in Psychological Science, 17,* 183–187.

Ellis, Neenah. (2002). *If I live to be 100: Lessons from the centenarians.* New York: Crown.

Ellison, Christopher G., Burdette, Amy M., & Wilcox, W. Bradford. (2010). The couple that prays together: Race and ethnicity, religion, and relationship quality among working-age adults. *Journal of Marriage and Family, 72,* 963–975.

Else-Quest, Nicole M., Hyde, Janet Shibley, Goldsmith, H. Hill, & Van Hulle, Carol A. (2006). Gender differences in temperament: A meta-analysis. *Psychological Bulletin, 132,* 33–72.

Elwert, Felix, & Christakis, Nicholas A. (2008). The effect of widowhood on mortality by the causes of death of both spouses. *American Journal of Public Health, 98,* 2092–2098.

Engelberts, Adèle C., & de Jonge, Guustaaf Adolf. (1990). Choice of sleeping position for infants: Possible association with cot death. *Archives of Disease in Childhood, 65,* 462–467.

Engelhardt, H. Tristram. (2005). What is Christian about Christian bioethics? metaphysical, epistemological, and moral differences. *Christian Bioethics, 11,* 241–253.

Engels, Rutger C. M. E., Scholte, Ron H. J., van Lieshout, Cornelis F. M., de Kemp, Raymond, & Overbeek, Geertjan. (2006). Peer group reputation and smoking and alcohol consumption in early adolescence. *Addictive Behaviors, 31,* 440–449.

Englander, Elizabeth, Mills, Elizabeth, & McCoy, Meghan. (2009). Cyberbullying and information exposure: User-generated content in post-secondary education. *International Journal of Contemporary Sociology, 46,* 213–230.

Epstein, Jeffery N., Langberg, Joshua M., Lichtenstein, Philip K., Altaye, Mekibib, Brinkman, William B., House, Katherine, et al. (2010). Attention-deficit/hyperactivity disorder outcomes for children treated in community-based pediatric settings. *Archives of Pediatrics & Adolescent Medicine, 164,* 160–165.

Epstein, Leonard H., Handley, Elizabeth A., Dearing, Kelly K., Cho, David D., Roemmich, James N., Paluch, Rocco A., et al. (2006). Purchases of food in youth: Influence of price and income. *Psychological Science, 17,* 82–89.

Erath, Stephen A., Keiley, Margaret K., Pettit, Gregory S., Lansford, Jennifer E., Dodge, Kenneth A., & Bates, John E. (2009). Behavioral predictors of mental health service utilization in childhood through adolescence. *Journal of Developmental & Behavioral Pediatrics, 30,* 481–488.

Erickson, Kirk I., & Korol, Donna L. (2009). Effects of hormone replacement therapy on the brains of postmenopausal women: A review of human neuroimaging studies. In Wojtek Chodzko-Zajko, Arthur F. Kramer, & Leonard W. Poon (Eds.), *Enhancing cognitive functioning and brain plasticity* (pp. 133–158). Champaign, IL: Human Kinetics.

Erickson, Rebecca J. (2005). Why emotion work matters: Sex, gender, and the division of household labor. *Journal of Marriage and Family, 67,* 337–351.

Ericsson, K. Anders. (1996). The acquisition of expert performance: An introduction to some of the issues. In Karl Anders Ericsson (Ed.), *The road to excellence: The acquisition of expert perfor-*

mance in the arts and sciences, sports, and games (pp. 1–50). Hillsdale, NJ: Erlbaum.

Ericsson, K. Anders, Charness, Neil, Feltovich, Paul J., & Hoffman, Robert R. (Eds.). (2006). *The Cambridge handbook of expertise and expert performance.* New York: Cambridge University Press.

Eriks-Brophy, Alice, & Crago, Martha. (2003). Variation in instructional discourse features: Cultural or linguistic? Evidence from Inuit and non-Inuit teachers of Nunavik. *Anthropology & Education Quarterly, 34,* 396–419.

Erikson, Erik H. (1963). *Childhood and society* (2nd ed.). New York: Norton.

Erikson, Erik H. (1968). *Identity: Youth and crisis.* New York: Norton.

Erikson, Erik H. (1969). *Gandhi's truth: On the origins of militant nonviolence.* New York: Norton.

Erikson, Erik H. (1982). *The life cycle completed: A review.* New York: Norton.

Erikson, Erik H., Erikson, Joan M., & Kivnick, Helen Q. (1986). *Vital involvement in old age.* New York: Norton.

Erlandsson, Kerstin, Dsilna, Ann, Fagerberg, Ingegerd, & Christensson, Kyllike. (2007). Skin-to-skin care with the father after cesarean birth and its effect on newborn crying and prefeeding behavior. *Birth: Issues in Perinatal Care, 34,* 105–114.

Erlinghagen, Marcel, & Hank, Karsten. (2006). The participation of older Europeans in volunteer work. *Ageing & Society, 26,* 567–584.

Ertmer, David J., Young, Nancy M., & Nathani, Suneeti. (2007). Profiles of vocal development in young cochlear implant recipients. *Journal of Speech, Language, and Hearing Research, 50,* 393–407.

Eskridge, William N., & Spedale, Darren R. (2006). *Gay marriage: For better or for worse? What we've learned from the evidence.* New York: Oxford University Press.

Estruch, Ramon, Martinez-Gonzalez, Miguel Angel, Corella, Dolores, Salas-Salvado, Jordi, Ruiz-Gutierrez, Valentina, Covas, Maria Isabel, et al. (2006). Effects of a Mediterranean-style diet on cardiovascular risk factors: A randomized trial. *Annals of Internal Medicine, 145,* 1–11.

Etchu, Koji. (2007). Social context and preschoolers' judgments about aggressive behavior: Social domain theory. *Japanese Journal of Educational Psychology, 55,* 219–230.

Etnier, Jennifer L. (2009). Physical activity programming to promote cognitive function: Are we ready for prescription? In Wojtek Chodzko-Zajko, Arthur F. Kramer, & Leonard W. Poon (Eds.), *Enhancing cognitive functioning and brain plasticity.* (pp. 159–175). Champaign, IL: Human Kinetics.

Evan, Gerard I., & d'Adda di Fagagna, Fabrizio. (2009). Cellular senescence: Hot or what? *Current Opinion in Genetics & Development, 19,* 25–31.

Evans, David W., & Leckman, James F. (2006). Origins of obsessive-compulsive disorder:

Developmental and evolutionary perspectives. In Dante Cicchetti & Donald J. Cohen (Eds.), *Developmental psychopathology: Vol. 3. Risk, disorder, and adaptation* (2nd ed., pp. 404–435). Hoboken, NJ: Wiley

Evans, David W., Leckman, James F., Carter, Alice, Reznick, J. Steven, Henshaw, Desiree, King, Robert A., et al. (1997). Ritual, habit, and perfectionism: The prevalence and development of compulsive-like behavior in normal young children. *Child Development, 68,* 58–68.

Evans, Jonathan St. B. T. (2008). Dual-processing accounts of reasoning, judgment, and social cognition. *Annual Review of Psychology, 59,* 255–278.

Eyer, Diane E. (1992). *Mother-infant bonding: A scientific fiction.* New Haven, CT: Yale University Press.

Fabiani, Monica, & Gratton, Gabriele. (2009). Brain imaging probes into the cognitive and physiological effects of aging. In Wojtek Chodzko-Zajko, Arthur F. Kramer, & Leonard W. Poon (Eds.), *Enhancing cognitive functioning and brain plasticity* (pp. 1–13). Champaign, IL: Human Kinetics.

Fabricatore, Anthony N., Wadden, Thomas A., Moore, Reneé H., Butryn, Meghan L., Gravallese, Elizabeth A., Erondu, Ngozi E., et al. (2009). Attrition from randomized controlled trials of pharmacological weight loss agents: A systematic review and analysis. *Obesity Reviews, 10,* 333–341.

Fagard, Jacqueline, & Lockman, Jeffrey J. (2010). Change in imitation for object manipulation between 10 and 12 months of age. *Developmental Psychobiology, 52,* 90–99.

Falk, Dean. (2004). Prelinguistic evolution in early hominins: Whence motherese? *Behavioral and Brain Sciences, 27,* 491–503, discussion 503–483.

Farahani, Mansour, Subramanian, S. V., & Canning, David. (2009). The effect of changes in health sector resources on infant mortality in the short-run and the long-run: A longitudinal econometric analysis. *Social Science & Medicine, 68,* 1918–1925.

Faraone, Stephen V., Sergeant, Joseph, Gillberg, Christopher, & Biederman, Joseph. (2003). The worldwide prevalence of ADHD: Is it an American condition? *World Psychiatry, 2,* 104–113.

Faraone, Stephen V., & Wilens, Timothy. (2003). Does stimulant treatment lead to substance use disorders? *Journal of Clinical Psychiatry, 64,* 9–13.

Farrar, Ruth D., & Al-Qatawneh, Khalil S. (2010). Interdisciplinary theoretical foundations for literacy teaching and learning. *European Journal of Social Sciences, 13,* 56–66.

Farrell, C., Chappell, F., Armitage, Paul A., Keston, P., Maclullich, Alasdair, Shenkin, Susan, et al. (2009). Development and initial testing of normal reference MR images for the brain at ages 65–70 and 75–80 years. *European Radiology, 19,* 177–183.

Farrelly, Matthew C., Davis, Kevin C., Haviland, M. Lyndon, Messeri, Peter, &

Healton, Cheryl G. (2005). Evidence of a dose-response relationship between "truth" antismoking ads and youth smoking prevalence. *American Journal of Public Health, 95,* 425–431.

Fechter-Leggett, Molly O., & O'Brien, Kirk. (2010). The effects of kinship care on adult mental health outcomes of alumni of foster care. *Children and Youth Services Review, 32,* 206–213.

Feerasta, Aniqa. (2006, February 11). Voices of Katrina: 'A humbling truth'. *USA Today,* pp. A12.

Feldman, Ruth. (2007). Parent-infant synchrony and the construction of shared timing; Physiological precursors, developmental outcomes, and risk conditions. *Journal of Child Psychology and Psychiatry, 48,* 329–354.

Feldman, Ruth, & Eidelman, Arthur I. (2004). Parent-infant synchrony and the social-emotional development of triplets. *Developmental Psychology, 40,* 1133–1147.

Feldman, Ruth, Weller, Aron, Sirota, Lea, & Eidelman, Arthur I. (2002). Skin-to-skin contact (kangaroo care) promotes self-regulation in premature infants: Sleep-wake cyclicity, arousal modulation, and sustained exploration. *Developmental Psychology, 38,* 194–207.

Felmlee, Diane, & Muraco, Anna. (2009). Gender and friendship norms among older adults. *Research on Aging, 31,* 318–344.

Feng, Zhanlian, Grabowski, David C., Intrator, Orna, Zinn, Jacqueline, & Mor, Vincent. (2008). Medicaid payment rates, case-mix reimbursement, and nursing home staffing—1996–2004. *Medical Care, 46,* 33–40.

Fenson, Larry, Bates, Elizabeth, Dale, Philip, Goodman, Judith, Reznick, J. Steven, & Thal, Donna. (2000). Measuring variability in early child language: Don't shoot the messenger. *Child Development, 71,* 323–328.

Ferber, Sari Goldstein, & Makhoul, Imad R. (2004). The effect of skin-to-skin contact (kangaroo care) shortly after birth on the neurobehavioral responses of the term newborn: a randomized, controlled trial. *Pediatrics, 113,* 858–865.

Ferguson Publishing. (2007). *Encyclopedia of careers and vocational guidance* (14th ed.). New York: Ferguson.

Fergusson, David M., Horwood, L. John, & Ridder, Elizabeth M. (2005). Partner violence and mental health outcomes in a New Zealand birth cohort. *Journal of Marriage and Family, 67,* 1103–1119.

Fergusson, Emma, Maughan, Barbara, & Golding, Jean. (2008). Which children receive grandparental care and what effect does it have? *Journal of Child Psychology and Psychiatry, 49,* 161–169.

Fernyhough, Charles. (2010). Vygotsky, Luria, and the social brain. In Bryan W. Sokol, Ulrich Müller, Jeremy I. M. Carpendale, Arlene R. Young, & Grace Iarocci (Eds.), *Self and social regulation: Social interaction and the development of social understanding and executive functions* (pp. 56–79). New York: Oxford University Press.

Ferri, Cleusa, P., Prince, Martin, Brayne, Carol, Brodaty, Henry, Fratiglioni, Laura,

Ganguli, Mary, et al. (2005). Global prevalence of dementia: A Delphi consensus study. *The Lancet, 366:* 2112–2117.

Ferriman, Kimberley, Lubinski, David, & Benbow, Camilla P. (2009). Work preferences, life values, and personal views of top math/science graduate students and the profoundly gifted: Developmental changes and gender differences during emerging adulthood and parenthood. *Journal of Personality and Social Psychology, 97,* 517–532.

Field, Nigel P., & Filanosky, Charles. (2010). Continuing bonds, risk factors for complicated grief, and adjustment to bereavement. *Death Studies, 34,* 1–29.

Finch, Caleb E. (2010). Evolution of the human lifespan and diseases of aging: Roles of infection, inflammation, and nutrition. *Proceedings of the National Academy of Sciences, 107*(Suppl. 1), 1718–1724.

Finch, Caleb E., & Kirkwood, Thomas B. L. (2000). *Chance, development, and aging.* New York: Oxford University Press.

Fincham, Frank D., & Beach, Steven R. H. (2010). Of memes and marriage: Toward a positive relationship science. *Journal of Family Theory & Review, 2,* 4–24.

Fincham, Frank D., Stanley, Scott M., & Beach, Steven R. H. (2007). Transformative processes in marriage: An analysis of emerging trends. *Journal of Marriage and Family, 69,* 275–292.

Fine, Mark A., & Harvey, John H. (2006). *Handbook of divorce and relationship dissolution.* Mahwah, NJ: Erlbaum.

Fingerman, Karen L. (2009). Consequential strangers and peripheral ties: The importance of unimportant relationships. *Journal of Family Theory & Review, 1,* 69–86.

Fingerman, Karen L., Hay, Elizabeth L., & Birditt, Kira S. (2004). The best of ties, the worst of ties: Close, problematic, and ambivalent social relationships. *Journal of Marriage and Family, 66,* 792–808.

Finkel, Deborah, Andel, Ross, Gatz, Margaret, & Pedersen, Nancy L. (2009). The role of occupational complexity in trajectories of cognitive aging before and after retirement. *Psychology and Aging, 24,* 563–573.

Finkelhor, David, & Jones, Lisa M. (2004). *Explanations for the decline in child sexual abuse cases.* Office of Juvenile Justice and Delinquency Prevention. Retrieved July 19, 2009, from the World Wide Web: http://www.ncjrs.gov/html/ojjdp/199298/contents.html

Finlay, Ilora. (2009). Dying and choosing. *Lancet, 373,* 1840–1841.

Finley, Lydia W. S., & Haigis, Marcia C. (2009). The coordination of nuclear and mitochondrial communication during aging and calorie restriction. *Ageing Research Reviews, 8,* 173–188.

Finn, John W. (2005). Stories of Pearl: Surviving end-of-life care. In Donald E. Gelfand, Richard Raspa, Sherylyn H. Briller, & Stephanie Myers Schim (Eds.), *End-of-life stories: Crossing disciplinary boundaries* (pp. 134–147). New York: Springer.

Fischer, Regina Santamäki, Norberg, Astrid, & Lundman, Berit. (2008). Embracing opposites: Meanings of growing old as narrated by people aged 85. *International Journal of Aging and Human Development, 67,* 259–271.

Fisher, Helen E. (2006). Broken hearts: The nature and risks of romantic rejection. In Ann C. Crouter & Alan Booth (Eds.), *Romance and sex in adolescence and emerging adulthood: Risks and opportunities* (pp. 3–28). Mahwah, NJ: Erlbaum.

Fisher, Linda L. (2010). *Sex, romance, and relationships: AARP survey of midlife and older adults* (Publication D19234). Washington, DC: AARP.

Flake, Dallan F., & Forste, Renata. (2006). Fighting families: Family characteristics associated with domestic violence in five Latin American countries. *Journal of Family Violence, 21,* 19–29.

Fleischman, Debra A. (2007). Repetition priming in aging and Alzheimer's disease: An integrative review and future directions. *Cortex, 43,* 889–897.

Fletcher, Anne C., Steinberg, Laurence, & Williams-Wheeler, Meeshay. (2004). Parental influences on adolescent problem behavior: Revisiting Stattin and Kerr. *Child Development, 75,* 781–796.

Fletcher, Jack M., & Vaughn, Sharon. (2009). Response to intervention: Preventing and remediating academic difficulties. *Child Development Perspectives, 3,* 30–37.

Fletcher, Jason M. (2009). Beauty vs. brains: Early labor market outcomes of high school graduates. *Economics Letters, 105,* 321–325.

Flory, Richard W., & Miller, Donald E. (2000). *GenX religion.* New York: Routledge.

Flynn, James R. (1999). Searching for justice: The discovery of IQ gains over time. *American Psychologist, 54,* 5–20.

Flynn, James R. (2007). *What is intelligence? Beyond the Flynn effect.* New York: Cambridge University Press.

Forget-Dubois, Nadine, Dionne, Ginette, Lemelin, Jean-Pascal, Pérusse, Daniel, Tremblay, Richard E., & Boivin, Michel. (2009). Early child language mediates the relation between home environment and school readiness. *Child Development, 80,* 736–749.

Fortinsky, Richard H., Tennen, Howard, Frank, Natalie, & Affleck, Glenn. (2007). Health and psychological consequences of caregiving. In Carolyn M. Aldwin, Crystal L. Park, & Avron Spiro III (Eds.), *Handbook of health psychology and aging* (pp. 227–249). New York: Guilford Press.

Fortuna, Keren, & Roisman, Glenn I. (2008). Insecurity, stress, and symptoms of psychopathology: Contrasting results from self-reports versus interviews of adult attachment. *Attachment & Human Development, 10,* 11–28.

Fossel, Michael. (2004). *Cells, aging, and human disease.* New York: Oxford University Press.

Foster, Eugene A., Jobling, Mark A., Taylor, P. G., Donnelly, Peter, de Knijff, Peter, Mieremet, Rene, et al. (1998, November 5). Jefferson fathered slave's last child. *Nature, 396,* 27–28.

Foster, E. Michael, & Kalil, Ariel. (2007). Living arrangements and children's development in low-income White, Black, and Latino families. *Child Development, 78,* 1657–1674.

Fowler, James H., & Schreiber, Darren. (2008, November 7). Biology, politics, and the emerging science of human nature. *Science, 322,* 912–914.

Fowler, James W. (1981). *Stages of faith: The psychology of human development and the quest for meaning.* San Francisco: Harper & Row.

Fowler, James W. (1986). Faith and the structuring of meaning. In Craig Dykstra & Sharon Parks (Eds.), *Faith development and Fowler* (pp. 15–42). Birmingham, AL: Religious Education Press.

Fox, Emily, & Riconscente, Michelle. (2008). Metacognition and self-regulation in James, Piaget, and Vygotsky. *Educational Psychology Review, 20*(4), 373–389.

Fox, Mark C., & Charness, Neil. (2010). How to gain eleven IQ points in ten minutes: Thinking aloud improves Raven's Matrices performance in older adults. *Aging, Neuropsychology, and Cognition, 17,* 191–204.

Fox, Nathan A., Henderson, Heather A., Rubin, Kenneth H., Calkins, Susan D., & Schmidt, Louis A. (2001). Continuity and discontinuity of behavioral inhibition and exuberance: Psychophysiological and behavioral influences across the first four years of life. *Child Development, 72,* 1–21.

Foxman, Betsy, Newman, Mark, Percha, Bethany, Holmes, King K., & Aral, Sevgi O. (2006). Measures of sexual partnerships: Lengths, gaps, overlaps, and sexually transmitted infection. *Sexually Transmitted Diseases, 33,* 209–214.

Frank, Michael J., Samanta, Johan, Moustafa, Ahmed A., & Sherman, Scott J. (2007, November 23). Hold your horses: Impulsivity, deep brain stimulation, and medication in parkinsonism. *Science, 318,* 1309–1312.

Frankenburg, William K., Dodds, Josiah, Archer, Philip, Shapiro, Howard, & Bresnick, Beverly. (1992). The Denver II: A major revision and restandardization of the Denver Developmental Screening Test. *Pediatrics, 89,* 91–97.

Franklin, Anna, Pitchford, Nicola, Hart, Lynsey, Davies, Ian R. L., Clausse, Samantha, & Jennings, Siobhan. (2008). Salience of primary and secondary colours in infancy. *British Journal of Developmental Psychology, 26,* 471–483.

Franko, Debra L., Thompson, Douglas, Affenito, Sandra G., Barton, Bruce A., & Striegel-Moore, Ruth H. (2008). What mediates the relationship between family meals and adolescent health issues. *Health Psychology, 27*(Suppl. 2), S109–S117.

Frayling, Timothy M., Timpson, Nicholas J., Weedon, Michael N., Zeggini, Eleftheria, Freathy, Rachel M., Lindgren, Cecilia M., et al. (2007, May 11). A common variant in the FTO gene is associated with body mass index and predisposes to childhood and adult obesity. *Science, 316,* 889–894.

Frazier, Thomas W., & Hardan, Antonio Y. (2009). A meta-analysis of the corpus callosum in autism. *Biological psychiatry, 66,* 935–941.

Fredricks, Jennifer A., Blumenfeld, Phyllis C., & Paris, Alison H. (2004). School engagement: Potential of the concept, state of the evidence. *Review of Educational Research, 74,* 59–109.

Fredricks, Jennifer A., & Eccles, Jacquelynne S. (2002). Children's competence and value beliefs from childhood through adolescence: Growth trajectories in two male-sex-typed domains. *Developmental Psychology, 38,* 519–533.

Fredricks, Jennifer A., & Eccles, Jacquelynne S. (2006). Is extracurricular participation associated with beneficial outcomes? Concurrent and longitudinal relations. *Developmental Psychology, 42,* 698–713.

Freeman, Kassie, & Thomas, Gail E. (2002). Black colleges and college choice: Characteristics of students who choose HBCUs. *Review of Higher Education, 25,* 349–358.

Freisthler, Bridget, Merritt, Darcey H., & LaScala, Elizabeth A. (2006). Understanding the ecology of child maltreatment: A review of the literature and directions for future research. *Child Maltreatment, 11,* 263–280.

Freud, Anna. (2000). Adolescence. In James B. McCarthy (Ed.), *Adolescent development and psychopathology* (Vol. 13, pp. 29–52). Lanham, MD: University Press of America. (Reprinted from *Psychoanalytic Study of the Child,* pp. 255–278, 1958, New Haven, CT: Yale University Press)

Freud, Sigmund. (1935). *A general introduction to psychoanalysis* (Joan Riviere, Trans.). New York: Liveright.

Freud, Sigmund. (1938). *The basic writings of Sigmund Freud* (A. A. Brill, Trans.). New York: Modern Library.

Freud, Sigmund. (1964). An outline of psychoanalysis. In James Strachey (Ed. and Trans.) (Ed.), *The standard edition of the complete psychological works of Sigmund Freud* (Vol. 23, pp. 144–207). London: Hogarth Press. (Original work published 1940)

Freund, Alexandra M. (2008). Successful aging as management of resources: The role of selection, optimization, and compensation. *Research in Human Development, 5,* 94–106.

Freund, Alexandra M., Nikitin, Jana, & Ritter, Johannes O. (2009). Psychological consequences of longevity: The increasing importance of self-regulation in old age. *Human Development, 52,* 1–37.

Fried, Linda P., Kronmal, Richard A., Newman, Anne B., Bild, Diane E., Mittelmark, Maurice B., Polak, Joseph F., et al. (1998). Risk factors for 5-year mortality in older adults: The Cardiovascular Health Study. *Journal of the American Medical Association, 279,* 585–592.

Fries, Alison B. Wismer, & Pollak, Seth D. (2007). Emotion processing and the developing brain. In Donna Coch, Kurt W. Fischer, & Geraldine Dawson (Eds.), *Human behavior, learning, and the developing brain. Typical development* (pp. 329–361). New York: Guilford Press.

Fries, James F. (1994). *Living well: Taking care of your health in the middle and later years.* Reading, MA: Addison-Wesley.

Friese, Malte, & Hofmann, Wilhelm (2008). What would you have as a last supper? Thoughts about death influence evaluation and consumption of food products. *Journal of Experimental Social Psychology, 44,* 1388–1394.

Frost, Joe L. (2009). *A history of children's play and play environments: Toward a contemporary child-saving movement.* New York: Routledge.

Fujimori, Maiko, Kobayakawa, Makoto, Nakaya, Naoki, Nagai, Kanji, Nishiwaki, Yutaka, Inagaki, Masatoshi, et al. (2006). Psychometric properties of the Japanese version of the quality of life-Cancer Survivors Instrument. *Quality of Life Research, 15,* 1633–1638.

Fuligni, Andrew J., & Hardway, Christina. (2006). Daily variation in adolescents' sleep, activities, and psychological well-being. *Journal of Research on Adolescence, 16,* 353–378.

Fuligni, Andrew J., Hughes, Diane L., & Way, Niobe. (2009). Ethnicity and immigration. In Richard M. Lerner & Laurence Steinberg (Eds.), *Handbook of adolescent psychology: Vol. 2. Contextual influences on adolescent development* (3rd ed., pp. 527–569). Hoboken, NJ: John Wiley & Sons.

Fung, Helene H., Stoeber, Franziska S., Yeung, Dannii Yuen-lan, & Lang, Frieder R. (2008). Cultural specificity of socioemotional selectivity: Age differences in social network composition among Germans and Hong Kong Chinese. *Journals of Gerontology Series B: Psychological Sciences and Social Sciences, 63,* 156–164.

Fung, Joey J., & Lau, Anna S. (2009). Punitive discipline and child behavior problems in Chinese-American immigrant families: The moderating effects of indigenous child-rearing ideologies. *International Journal of Behavioral Development, 33,* 520–530.

Funk, Laura M., & Kobayashi, Karen M. (2009). "Choice" in filial care work: Moving beyond a dichotomy. *Canadian Review of Sociology/Revue canadienne de sociologie, 46,* 235–252.

Furman, Wyndol, & Hand, Laura Shaffer. (2006). The slippery nature of romantic relationships: Issues in definition and differentiation. In Ann C. Crouter & Alan Booth (Eds.), *Romance and sex in adolescence and emerging adulthood: Risks and opportunities* (pp. 171–178). Mahwah, NJ: Erlbaum.

Furstenberg, Frank F., Jr. (2010). On a new schedule: Transitions to adulthood and family change. *Future of Children, 20,* 67–87.

Gabrieli, John D. E. (2009, July 17). Dyslexia: A new synergy between education and cognitive neuroscience. *Science, 325,* 280–283.

Gaertner, Bridget M., Spinrad, Tracy L., Eisenberg, Nancy, & Greving, Karissa A. (2007). Parental childrearing attitudes as correlates of father involvement during infancy. *Journal of Marriage and Family, 69,* 962–976.

Gagnon, John H., Giami, Alain, Michaels, Stuart, & de Colomby, Patrick. (2001). A comparative study of the couple in the social organization of sexuality in France and the United States. *Journal of Sex Research, 38,* 24–34.

Galambos, Nancy L., Barker, Erin T., & Krahn, Harvey J. (2006). Depression, self-esteem, and anger in emerging adulthood: Seven-year trajectories. *Developmental Psychology, 42,* 350–365.

Gall, Stanley (Ed.). (1996). *Multiple pregnancy and delivery.* St. Louis, MO: Mosby.

Gallese, Vittorio, Fadiga, Luciano, Fogassi, Leonardo, & Rizzolatti, Giacomo. (1996). Action recognition in the premotor cortex. *Brain, 119,* 593–609.

Gallup, Gordon G., Anderson, James R., & Shillito, Daniel J. (2002). The mirror test. In Marc Bekoff, Colin Allen, & Gordon M. Burghardt (Eds.), *The cognitive animal: Empirical and theoretical perspectives on animal cognition* (pp. 325–333). Cambridge, MA: MIT Press.

Galotti, Kathleen M. (2002). *Making decisions that matter: How people face important life choices.* Mahwah, NJ: Erlbaum.

Gandara, Patricia, & Rumberger, Russell W. (2009). Immigration, language, and education: How does language policy structure opportunity? *Teachers College Record, 111,* 750–782.

Gandini, Leila, Hill, Lynn, Cadwell, Louise, & Schwall, Charles (Eds.). (2005). *In the spirit of the studio: Learning from the atelier of Reggio Emilia.* New York: Teachers College Press.

Gangestad, Steven W., & Simpson, Jeffry A. (2007). *The evolution of mind: Fundamental questions and controversies.* New York: Guilford Press.

Ganiban, Jody M., Saudino, Kimberly J., Ulbricht, Jennifer, Neiderhiser, Jenae M., & Reiss, David. (2008). Stability and change in temperament during adolescence. *Journal of Personality and Social Psychology, 95,* 222–236.

Ganong, Lawrence H., & Coleman, Marilyn. (2004). *Stepfamily relationships: Development, dynamics, and interventions.* New York: Kluwer Academic/Plenum.

Gans, Daphna, & Silverstein, Merril. (2006). Norms of filial responsibility for aging parents across time and generations. *Journal of Marriage and Family, 68,* 961–976.

Ganzini, Linda, Goy, Elizabeth R., & Dobscha, Steven K. (2009). Oregonians' reasons for requesting physician aid in dying. *Archives of Internal Medicine, 169,* 489–492.

García, Fernando, & Gracia, Enrique. (2009). Is always authoritative the optimum parenting style? Evidence from Spanish families. *Adolescence, 44,* 101–131.

Garcia-Segura, Luis Miguel. (2009). *Hormones and brain plasticity.* New York: Oxford University Press.

Gardner, Christopher D., Kiazand, Alexandre, Alhassan, Sofiya, Kim, Soowon, Stafford, Randall S., Balise, Raymond R., et al. (2007). Comparison of the Atkins, Zone, Ornish, and LEARN diets for change in weight and related risk factors among overweight premenopausal women: The A TO Z Weight Loss Study: a randomized trial. *Journal of the American Medical Association, 297,* 969–977.

Gardner, Howard. (1983). *Frames of mind: The theory of multiple intelligences.* New York: Basic Books.

Gardner, Howard. (1999). Are there additional intelligences? The case for naturalist, spiritual, and existential intelligences. In Jeffrey Kane (Ed.), *Education, information, and transformation: Essays on learning and thinking* (pp. 111–131). Upper Saddle River, NJ: Merrill.

Gardner, Howard. (2006). *Multiple intelligences: New horizons in theory and practice* (Completely rev. and updated ed.). New York: Basic Books.

Gardner, Howard, & Moran, Seana. (2006). The science of multiple intelligences theory: A response to Lynn Waterhouse. *Educational Psychologist, 41,* 227–232.

Gardner, Margo, & Steinberg, Laurence. (2005). Peer influence on risk taking, risk preference, and risky decision making in adolescence and adulthood: An experimental study. *Developmental Psychology, 41,* 625–635.

Garofalo, Robert, Wolf, R. Cameron, Wissow, Lawrence S., Woods, Elizabeth R., & Goodman, Elizabeth. (1999). Sexual orientation and risk of suicide attempts among a representative sample of youth. *Archives of Pediatrics & Adolescent Medicine, 153,* 487–493.

Gaspar de Alba, Alicia. (2003). Rights of passage: From cultural schizophrenia to border consciousness in Cheech Marin's Born in East L.A. In Alicia Gaspar de Alba (Ed.), *Velvet barrios: Popular culture & Chicana/o sexualities* (pp. 199–214). Basingstoke, England: Palgrave Macmillan.

Gathercole, Susan E., Pickering, Susan J., Ambridge, Benjamin, & Wearing, Hannah. (2004). The structure of working memory from 4 to 15 years of age. *Developmental Psychology, 40,* 177–190.

Gathwala, Geeta, Singh, Bir, & Balhara, Bharti. (2008). KMC facilitates mother baby attachment in low birth weight infants. *The Indian Journal of Pediatrics, 75,* 43–47.

Gauvain, Mary. (2005). Scaffolding in socialization. *New Ideas in Psychology, 23,* 129–139.

Gavrilov, Leonid A., & Gavrilova, Natalia S. (2006). Reliability theory of aging and longevity. In Edward J. Masoro & Steven N. Austad (Eds.), *Handbook of the biology of aging* (6th ed., pp. 3–42). Amsterdam: Elsevier Academic Press.

Gdalevich, Michael, Mimouni, Daniel, & Mimouni, Marc. (2001). Breast-feeding and the risk of bronchial asthma in childhood: A systematic review with meta-analysis of prospective studies. *Journal of Pediatrics, 139,* 261–266.

Ge, Xiaojia, Natsuaki, Misaki N., Neiderhiser, Jenae M., & Reiss, David. (2007). Genetic and environmental influences on pubertal timing: Results from two national sibling studies. *Journal of Research on Adolescence, 17,* 767–788.

Geary, Nori, & Lovejoy, Jennifer. (2008). Sex differences in energy metabolism, obesity, and eating behavior. In Jill B. Becker, Karen J. Berkley, Nori Geary, Elizabeth Hampson, James P. Herman, & Elizabeth Young (Eds.), *Sex differences in the brain: From genes to behavior* (pp. 253–274). New York: Oxford University Press.

Geelhoed, Elizabeth, Harris, Anthony, & Prince, Richard. (1994). Cost-effectiveness analysis of hormone replacement therapy and lifestyle intervention for hip fracture. *Australian Journal of Public Health, 18,* 153–160.

Geitz, Henry, Heideking, Jürgen, & Herbst, Jurgen. (2006). *German influences on education in the United States to 1917* (1st paperback ed.). Washington, DC: German Historical Institute.

Gelfand, Donald E. (2003). *Aging and ethnicity: Knowledge and services* (2nd ed.). New York: Springer.

Geller, Barbara, Tillman, Rebecca, Bolhofner, Kristine, & Zimerman, Betsy. (2008). Child bipolar I disorder: Prospective continuity with adult bipolar I disorder; Characteristics of second and third episodes; Predictors of 8-year outcome. *Archives of General Psychiatry, 65,* 1125–1133.

Gelles, Richard J. (1997). *Intimate violence in families* (3rd ed.). Thousand Oaks, CA: Sage.

Gelman, Susan A., & Kalish, Charles W. (2006). Conceptual development. In Deanna Kuhn & Robert S. Siegler (Series Eds.) & William Damon & Richard M. Lerner (Vol. Eds.), *Handbook of child psychology: Vol. 2. Cognition, perception, and language* (6th ed., pp. 687–733). Hoboken, NJ: Wiley.

Gems, David, & Doonan, Ryan. (2009). Antioxidant defense and aging in C. elegans: Is the oxidative damage theory of aging wrong? *Cell Cycle, 8,* 1681–1687.

Genesee, Fred. (2008). Early dual language learning. *Zero to Three, 29,* 17–23.

Genesee, Fred, & Nicoladis, Elena. (2007). Bilingual first language acquisition. In Erika Hoff & Marilyn Shatz (Eds.), *Blackwell handbook of language development* (pp. 324–342). Malden, MA: Blackwell.

Gentile, Douglas A. (2009). Pathological video-game use among youth ages 8 to 18: A National Study. *Psychological Science, 20,* 594–602.

Gentile, Douglas A., Saleem, Muniba, & Anderson, Craig A. (2007). Public policy and the effects of media violence on children. *Social Issues and Policy Review, 1,* 15–61.

Gentner, Dedre, & Boroditsky, Lera. (2001). Individuation, relativity, and early word learning. In Melissa Bowerman & Stephen C. Levinson (Eds.), *Language acquisition and conceptual development* (pp. 215–256). Cambridge, UK: Cambridge University Press.

Georgas, James, Berry, John W., van de Vijver, Fons J. R., Kagitçibasi, Çigdem, & Poortinga, Ype H. (2006). *Families across cultures: A 30-nation psychological study.* Cambridge, UK: Cambridge University Press.

George, Linda K. (2006). Perceived quality of life. In Robert H. Binstock & Linda K. George (Eds.), *Handbook of aging and the social sciences* (6th ed., pp. 320–336). Amsterdam: Elsevier.

Georgieff, Michael K., & Rao, Raghavendra. (2001). The role of nutrition in cognitive development. In Charles A. Nelson & Monica Luciana (Eds.), *Handbook of developmental cognitive neuroscience* (pp. 149–158). Cambridge, MA: MIT Press.

Geronimus, Arline T., Hicken, Margaret, Keene, Danya, & Bound, John. (2006).

"Weathering" and age patterns of allostatic load scores among Blacks and Whites in the United States. *American Journal of Public Health, 96,* 826–833.

Gerrard, Meg, Gibbons, Frederick X., Houlihan, Amy E., Stock, Michelle L., & Pomery, Elizabeth A. (2008). A dual-process approach to health risk decision making: The prototype willingness model. *Developmental Review, 28,* 29–61.

Gershkoff-Stowe, Lisa, & Hahn, Erin R. (2007). Fast mapping skills in the developing lexicon. *Journal of Speech, Language, and Hearing Research, 50,* 682–696.

Gershoff, Elizabeth Thompson. (2002). Corporal punishment by parents and associated child behaviors and experiences: A meta-analytic and theoretical review. *Psychological Bulletin, 128,* 539–579.

Gerstel, Naomi Ruth. (2002). Book reviews [Review of the book *Talk of love: How culture matters*]. *Journal of Marriage and the Family, 64,* 549–556.

Gerstorf, Denis, Ram, Nilam, Mayraz, Guy, Hidajat, Mira, Lindenberger, Ulman, Wagner, Gert G., et al. (2010). Late-life decline in well-being across adulthood in Germany, the United Kingdom, and the United States: Something is seriously wrong at the end of life. *Psychology and Aging, 25,* 477–485.

Giardino, Angelo P., & Alexander, Randell. (2011). *Child maltreatment* (4th ed.). St. Louis: G.W. Medical.

Gibson, Eleanor J. (1969). *Principles of perceptual learning and development.* New York: Appleton-Century-Crofts.

Gibson, Eleanor J. (1988). Exploratory behavior in the development of perceiving, acting, and the acquiring of knowledge. *Annual Review of Psychology, 39,* 1–42.

Gibson, Eleanor J. (1997). An ecological psychologist's prolegomena for perceptual development: A functional approach. In Cathy Dent-Read & Patricia Zukow-Goldring (Eds.), *Evolving explanations of development: Ecological approaches to organism-environment systems* (pp. 23–54). Washington, DC: American Psychological Association.

Gibson, Eleanor J., & Walk, Richard D. (1960). The "visual cliff." *Scientific American, 202,* 64–71.

Gibson, James Jerome. (1979). *The ecological approach to visual perception.* Boston: Houghton Mifflin.

Gibson-Davis, Christina M., & Brooks-Gunn, Jeanne. (2006). Couples' immigration status and ethnicity as determinants of breastfeeding. *American Journal of Public Health, 96,* 641–646.

Gibson-Davis, Christina M., Edin, Kathryn, & McLanahan, Sara. (2005). High hopes but even higher expectations: The retreat from marriage among low-income couples. *Journal of Marriage and Family, 67,* 1301–1312.

Gifford-Smith, Mary E., & Rabiner, David L. (2004). Social information processing and children's social adjustment. In Janis B. Kupersmidt & Kenneth A. Dodge (Eds.), *Children's peer relations: From development to intervention* (pp. 61–79). Washington, DC: American Psychological Association.

Gigante, Denise. (2007). Zeitgeist. *European Romantic Review, 18,* 265–272.

Gigerenzer, Gerd. (2008). Why heuristics work. *Perspectives on Psychological Science, 3,* 20–29.

Gilbert, Daniel. (2006). *Stumbling on happiness.* New York: Knopf.

Gilchrist, Heidi, & Sullivan, Gerard. (2006). The role of gender and sexual relations for young people in identity construction and youth suicide. *Culture, Health & Sexuality, 8,* 195–209.

Giles-Sims, Jean, & Lockhart, Charles. (2005). Culturally shaped patterns of disciplining children. *Journal of Family Issues, 26,* 196–218.

Gillespie, Michael Allen. (2010). Players and spectators: Sports and ethical training in the American university. In Elizabeth Kiss & J. Peter Euben (Eds.), *Debating moral education: Rethinking the role of the modern university* (pp. 293–316). Durham: Duke University Press.

Gilligan, Carol. (1981). Moral development in the college years. In A. Chickering (Ed.), *The modern American college: Responding to the new realities of diverse students and a changing society* (pp. 139–156). San Francisco: Jossey-Bass.

Gilligan, Carol. (1982). *In a different voice: Psychological theory and women's development.* Cambridge, MA: Harvard University Press.

Gilligan, Carol, Murphy, John Michael, & Tappan, Mark B. (1990). Moral development beyond adolescence. In Charles N. Alexander & Ellen J. Langer (Eds.), *Higher stages of human development: Perspectives on adult growth* (pp. 208–225). London: Oxford University Press.

Gilliland, Frank D. (2009). Outdoor air pollution, genetic susceptibility, and asthma management: Opportunities for intervention to reduce the burden of asthma. *Pediatrics, 123*(Suppl. 3), S168–173.

Gillis, John R. (2008). The islanding of children: Reshaping the mythical landscapes of childhood. In Marta Gutman & Ning De Coninck-Smith (Eds.), *Designing modern childhoods: History, space, and the material culture of children* (pp. 316–329). New Brunswick, NJ: Rutgers University Press.

Gimelbrant, Alexander, Hutchinson, John N., Thompson, Benjamin R., & Chess, Andrew. (2007, November 16). Widespread monoallelic expression on human autosomes. *Science, 318,* 1136–1140.

Ginges, Jeremy, Hansen, Ian, & Norenzayan, Ara. (2009). Religion and support for suicide attacks. *Psychological Science, 20,* 224–230.

Gintis, Herb, Bowles, Samuel, Boyd, Robert, & Fehr, Ernst. (2007). Explaining altruistic behaviour in humans. In R. I. M. Dunbar & Louise Barrett (Eds.), *Oxford handbook of evolutionary psychology* (pp. 605–620). New York: Oxford University Press.

Gipson, Jessica D., & Hindin, Michelle J. (2008). "Having another child would be a life or death situation for her": Understanding pregnancy termination among couples in rural Bangladesh. *American Journal of Public Health, 98,* 1827–1832.

Gitlin, Laura N., Belle, Steven H., Burgio, Louis D., Czaja, Sara J., Mahoney, Diane, Gallagher-Thompson, Dolores, et al. (2003). Effect of multicomponent interventions on caregiver burden and depression: The REACH multisite initiative at 6-month follow-up. *Psychology & Aging, 18,* 361–374.

Givens, Jane L., Tjia, Jennifer, Zhou, Chao, Emanuel, Ezekiel, & Ash, Arlene S. (2010). Racial and ethnic differences in hospice use among patients with heart failure. *Archives of Internal Medicine, 170,* 427–432.

Gladwell, Malcolm. (2010, October 4). Small change. *New Yorker, 86,* 41–49.

Glanville, Jennifer L., Sikkink, David, & Hernández, Edwin I. (2008). Religious involvement and educational outcomes: The role of social capital and extracurricular participation. *Sociological Quarterly, 49,* 105–137.

Glass, Jennifer, Lanctôt, Krista L., Herrmann, Nathan, Sproule, Beth A., & Busto, Usoa E. (2005). Sedative hypnotics in older people with insomnia: Meta-analysis of risks and benefits. *British Medical Journal, 331,* 1–7.

Glass, Jennifer M. (2007). Visual function and cognitive aging: Differential role of contrast sensitivity in verbal versus spatial tasks. *Psychology and Aging, 22,* 233–238.

Glass, Roger I., & Parashar, Umesh D. (2006). The promise of new rotavirus vaccines. *New England Journal of Medicine, 354,* 75–77.

Glenn, Norval D. (1998). The course of marital success and failure in five American 10-year marriage cohorts. *Journal of Marriage & the Family, 60,* 569–576.

Glick, Jennifer E. (2010). Connecting complex processes: A decade of research on immigrant families. *Journal of Marriage and Family, 72,* 498–515.

Glover, Evam Kofi, Bannerman, Angela, Pence, Brian Wells, Jones, Heidi, Miller, Robert, Weiss, Eugene, et al. (2003). Sexual health experiences of adolescents in three Ghanaian towns. *International Family Planning Perspectives, 29,* 32–40.

Gluckman, Peter D., & Hanson, Mark A. (2006). *Developmental origins of health and disease.* Cambridge, England: Cambridge University Press.

Gobush, Kathleen S., Mutayoba, Benezeth M., & Wasser, Samuel K. (2008). Long-term impacts of poaching on relatedness, stress physiology, and reproductive output of adult female African elephants. *Conservation Biology, 22,* 1590–1599.

Goffaux, Philippe, Phillips, Natalie A., Sinai, Marco, & Pushkar, Dolores. (2008). Neurophysiological measures of task-set switching: Effects of working memory and aging. *Journals of Gerontology Series B: Psychological Sciences and Social Sciences, 63,* 57–66.

Goh, Joshua O., & Park, Denise C. (2009). Neuroplasticity and cognitive aging: The scaffolding theory of aging and cognition. *Restorative Neurology and Neuroscience, 27,* 391–403.

Golant, Stephen M. (2008). Commentary: Irrational exuberance for the aging in place of vulnerable low-income older homeowners. *Journal of Aging & Social Policy, 20,* 379–397.

Gold, Ellen B., Colvin, Alicia, Avis, Nancy, Bromberger, Joyce, Greendale, Gail A., Powell, Lynda, et al. (2006). Longitudinal analysis of the association between vasomotor symptoms and race/ethnicity across the menopausal transition: Study of women's health across the nation. *American Journal of Public Health, 96,* 1226–1235.

Goldberg, Wendy A., Prause, JoAnn, Lucas-Thompson, Rachel, & Himsel, Amy. (2008). Maternal employment and children's achievement in context: A meta-analysis of four decades of research. *Psychological Bulletin, 134,* 77–108.

Golden, Timothy D., Veiga, John F., & Simsek, Zeki. (2006). Telecommuting's differential impact on work-family conflict: Is there no place like home? *Journal of Applied Psychology, 91,* 1340–1350.

Goldenberg, Jamie L., & Arndt, Jamie. (2008). The implications of death for health: A terror management health model for behavioral health promotion. *Psychological Review, 115,* 1032–1053.

Goldin-Meadow, Susan. (2006). Nonverbal communication: The hand's role in talking and thinking. In William Damon & Richard M. Lerner (Series Eds.) & Deanna Kuhn & Robert S. Siegler (Vol. Eds.), *Handbook of child psychology: Vol. 2. Cognition, perception, and language* (6th ed., pp. 336–369). Hoboken, NJ: Wiley.

Goldin-Meadow, Susan. (2009). How gesture promotes learning throughout childhood. *Child Development Perspectives, 3,* 106–111.

Goldscheider, Frances, & Sassler, Sharon. (2006). Creating stepfamilies: Integrating children into the study of union formation. *Journal of Marriage and Family, 68,* 275–291.

Goldstein, Michael H., Schwade, Jennifer A., & Bornstein, Marc H. (2009). The value of vocalizing: Five-month-old infants associate their own noncry vocalizations with responses from caregivers. *Child Development, 80,* 636–644.

Goldston, David B., Molock, Sherry Davis, Whitbeck, Leslie B., Murakami, Jessica L., Zayas, Luis H., & Hall, Gordon C. Nagayama. (2008). Cultural considerations in adolescent suicide prevention and psychosocial treatment. *American Psychologist, 63,* 14–31.

Gollwitzer, Peter M., Sheeran, Paschal, Michalski, Verena, & Seifert, Andrea E. (2009). When intentions go public: Does social reality widen the intention-behavior gap? *Psychological Science, 20,* 612–618.

Golub, Sarit A., & Langer, Ellen J. (2007). Challenging assumptions about adult development: implications for the health of older adults. In Carolyn M. Aldwin, Crystal L. Park, & Avron Spiro, III (Eds.), *Handbook of health psychology and aging* (pp. 9–29). New York: Guilford Press.

Gompel, Anne, & Plu-Bureau, Geneviève. (2007). Hormone replacement therapy and breast cancer. The European view. *European Clinics in Obstetrics and Gynaecology, 3,* 7–15.

Gonzales, Nancy A., Dumka, Larry E., Deardorff, Julianna, Carter, Sara Jacobs, & McCray, Adam. (2004). Preventing poor mental health and school dropout of Mexican American adolescents following the transition to junior high school. *Journal of Adolescent Research, 19,* 113–131.

Goodman, Sherryl H., & Gotlib, Ian H. (2002). *Children of depressed parents: Mechanisms of risk and implications for treatment.* Washington, DC: American Psychological Association.

Goodwin, Geoffrey P., & Johnson-Laird, Philip. N. (2008). Transitive and pseudo-transitive inferences. *Cognition, 108,* 320–352.

Gopnik, Alison. (2001). Theories, language, and culture: Whorf without wincing. In Melissa Bowerman & Stephen C. Levinson (Eds.), *Language acquisition and conceptual development* (pp. 45–69). Cambridge, UK: Cambridge University Press.

Gopnik, Alison, & Schulz, Laura. (2007). *Causal learning: Psychology, philosophy, and computation.* New York: Oxford University Press.

Gorchoff, Sara M., John, Oliver P., & Helson, Ravenna. (2008). Contextualizing change in marital satisfaction during middle age: An 18-year longitudinal study. *Psychological Science, 19,* 1194–1200.

Gordis, Elana B., Granger, Douglas A., Susman, Elizabeth J., & Trickett, Penelope K. (2008). Salivary alpha amylase-cortisol asymmetry in maltreated youth. *Hormones and Behavior, 53,* 96–103.

Gordon, Peter. (2004, August 19). Numerical cognition without words: Evidence from Amazonia. *Science, 306,* 496–499.

Gorelick, Philip B., & Bowler, John V. (2010). Advances in vascular cognitive impairment. *Stroke, 41,* 93–98.

Gormley, William T., Jr., Phillips, Deborah, & Gayer, Ted. (2008, June 27). Preschool programs can boost school readiness. *Science, 320,* 1723–1724.

Goss, David A. (2002). More evidence that near work contributes to myopia development. *Indiana Journal of Optometry, 5,* 11–13.

Gottesman, Irving I., Laursen, Thomas Munk, Bertelsen, Aksel, & Mortensen, Preben Bo. (2010). Severe mental disorders in offspring with 2 psychiatrically ill parents. *Archives of General Psychiatry, 67,* 252–257.

Gottfried, Adele Eskeles, Marcoulides, George A., Gottfried, Allen W., & Oliver, Pamella H. (2009). A latent curve model of parental motivational practices and developmental decline in math and science academic intrinsic motivation. *Journal of Educational Psychology, 101,* 729–739.

Gottlieb, Alma. (2000). Luring your child into this life: A Beng path for infant care. In Judy S.

DeLoache & Alma Gottlieb (Eds.), *A world of babies: Imagined childcare guides for seven societies* (pp. 55–90). New York: Cambridge University Press.

Gottlieb, Gilbert. (1992). *Individual development and evolution: The genesis of novel behavior.* New York: Oxford University Press.

Gottlieb, Gilbert. (2002). *Individual development and evolution: The genesis of novel behavior.* Mahwah, NJ: Erlbaum. (Original work published 1992)

Gottlieb, Gilbert. (2007). Probabilistic epigenesis. *Developmental Science, 10,* 1–11.

Gottman, John Mordechai, Murray, James D., Swanson, Catherine, Tyson, Rebecca, & Swanson, Kristin R. (2002). *The mathematics of marriage: Dynamic nonlinear models.* Cambridge, MA: MIT Press.

Gould, Madelyn. (2003). Suicide risk among adolescents. In Daniel Romer (Ed.), *Reducing adolescent risk: Toward an integrated approach* (pp. 303–320). Thousand Oaks, CA: Sage.

Goymer, Patrick. (2007). Genes know their left from their right. *Nature Reviews Genetics, 8,* 652.

Graber, Julia A. (2004). Internalizing problems during adolescence. In Richard M. Lerner & Laurence D. Steinberg (Eds.), *Handbook of adolescent psychology* (2nd ed., pp. 587–626). Hoboken, NJ: Wiley.

Graber, Julia A., & Brooks-Gunn, Jeanne. (1996). Expectations for and precursors to leaving home in young women. In Julia A. Graber & Judith Semon Dubas (Eds.), *Leaving home: Understanding the transition to adulthood* (pp. 21–38). San Francisco: Jossey-Bass.

Graber, Julia A., Nichols, Tracy R., & Brooks-Gunn, Jeanne. (2010). Putting pubertal timing in developmental context: implications for prevention. *Developmental psychobiology, 52,* 254–262.

Graham-Bermann, Sandra A., Gruber, Gabrielle, Howell, Kathryn H., & Girz, Laura. (2009). Factors discriminating among profiles of resilience and psychopathology in children exposed to intimate partner violence (IPV). *Child Abuse & Neglect: The International Journal, 33,* 648–660.

Grandin, Temple, & Johnson, Catherine. (2009). *Animals make us human: Creating the best life for animals.* Boston: Houghton Mifflin Harcourt.

Granic, Isabela, & Patterson, Gerald R. (2006). Toward a comprehensive model of antisocial development: A dynamic systems approach. *Psychological Review, 113,* 101–131.

Granpeesheh, Doreen, Tarbox, Jonathan, & Dixon, Dennis R. (2009). Applied behavior analytic interventions for children with autism: A description and review of treatment research. *Annals of Clinical Psychiatry, 21,* 162–173.

Granpeesheh, Doreen, Tarbox, Jonathan, Dixon, Dennis R., Wilke, Arthur E., Allen, Michael S., & Bradstreet, James Jeffrey. (2010). Randomized trial of hyperbaric oxygen therapy for children with autism. *Research in Autism Spectrum Disorders, 4,* 268–275.

Grant, Jon E., & Potenza, Marc N. (Eds.). (2010). *Young adult mental health.* New York: Oxford University Press.

Green, C. Shawn, & Bavelier, Daphne. (2008). Exercising your brain: A review of human brain plasticity and training-induced learning. *Psychology and Aging, 23,* 692–701.

Green, Lorraine, & Grant, Victoria. (2008). "Gagged grief and beleaguered bereavements?" An analysis of multidisciplinary theory and research relating to same sex partnership bereavement. *Sexualities, 11,* 275–300.

Greene, Joshua D., Sommerville, R. Brian, Nystrom, Leigh E., Darley, John M., & Cohen, Jonathan D. (2001). An fMRI investigation of emotional engagement in moral judgment. *Science, 293,* 2105–2108.

Greene, Melissa L., & Way, Niobe. (2005). Self-esteem trajectories among ethnic minority adolescents: A growth curve analysis of the patterns and predictors of change. *Journal of Research on Adolescence, 15,* 151–178.

Greene, Melissa L., Way, Niobe, & Pahl, Kerstin. (2006). Trajectories of perceived adult and peer discrimination among Black, Latino, and Asian American adolescents: Patterns and psychological correlates. *Developmental Psychology, 42,* 218–238.

Greenfield, Emily A., & Marks, Nadine F. (2006). Linked lives: Adult children's problems and their parents' psychological and relational well-being. *Journal of Marriage and Family, 68,* 442–454.

Greenfield, Patricia M. (2009, January 2). Technology and informal education: What is taught, what is learned. *Science, 323,* 69–71.

Greenhalgh, Susan. (2008). *Just one child: Science and policy in Deng's China.* Berkeley, CA: University of California Press.

Greenough, William T., Black, James E., & Wallace, Christopher S. (1987). Experience and brain development. *Child Development, 58,* 539–559.

Greenough, William T., & Volkmar, Fred R. (1973). Pattern of dendritic branching in occipital cortex of rats reared in complex environments. *Experimental Neurology, 40,* 491–504.

Gregory, Ted (2010, August 28). Grampy down with 'the Face'. *Chicago Tribune.*

Griebel, Wilfried, & Niesel, Renate. (2002). Co-constructing transition into kindergarten and school by children, parents, and teachers. In Hilary Fabian & Aline-Wendy Dunlop (Eds.), *Transitions in the early years: Debating continuity and progression for young children in early education* (pp. 64–75). New York: RoutledgeFalmer.

Griffin, James, Gooding, Sarah, Semesky, Michael, Farmer, Brittany, Mannchen, Garrett, & Sinnott, Jan. (2009). Four brief studies of relations between postformal thought and non-cognitive factors: Personality, concepts of god, political opinions, and social attitudes. *Journal of Adult Development, 16,* 173–182.

Griffith, Patrick, & Lopez, Oscar. (2009). Disparities in the diagnosis and treatment of Alzheimer's disease in African American and Hispanic patients: A call to action. *Generations, 33*(1), 37–46.

Griggs, Julia, Tan, Jo-Pei, Buchanan, Ann, Attar-Schwartz, Shalhevet, & Flouri, Eirini. (2010). 'They've always been there for me':

Grandparental involvement and child well-being. *Children & Society, 24,* 200–214.

Grimm, David. (2008, May 16). Staggering toward a global strategy on alcohol abuse. *Science, 320,* 862–863.

Grobman, Kevin H. (2008). *Learning & teaching developmental psychology: Attachment theory, infancy, & infant memory development.* Retrieved October 30, 2010, from the World Wide Web: http://www.devpsy.org/questions/attachment_theory_memory.html

Grollmann, Philipp, & Rauner, Felix. (2007). Exploring innovative apprenticeship: Quality and costs. *Education & Training, 49,* 431–446.

Grolnick, Wendy S., McMenamy, Jannette M., & Kurowski, Carolyn O. (2006). Emotional self-regulation in infancy and toddlerhood. In Lawrence Balter & Catherine S. Tamis-LeMonda (Eds.), *Child psychology: A handbook of contemporary issues* (2nd ed., pp. 3–25). New York: Psychology Press.

Gros-Louis, Julie, West, Meredith J., Goldstein, Michael H., & King, Andrew P. (2006). Mothers provide differential feedback to infants' prelinguistic sounds. *International Journal of Behavioral Development, 30,* 509–516.

Grossmann, Klaus E., Grossmann, Karin, & Waters, Everett (Eds.). (2005). *Attachment from infancy to adulthood: The major longitudinal studies.* New York: Guilford Press.

Grosvenor, Theodore. (2003). Why is there an epidemic of myopia? *Clinical and Experimental Optometry, 86,* 273–275.

Grubeck-Loebenstein, Beatrix. (2010). Fading immune protection in old age: Vaccination in the elderly. *Journal of Comparative Pathology, 142*(Suppl. 1), S116–S119.

Grundy, Emily, & Henretta, John C. (2006). Between elderly parents and adult children: A new look at the intergenerational care provided by the 'sandwich generation'. *Ageing & Society, 26,* 707–722.

Grzywacz, Joseph, Carlson, Dawn, & Shulkin, Sandee. (2008). Schedule flexibility and stress: Linking formal flexible arrangements and perceived flexibility to employee health. *Community, Work & Family, 11,* 199–214.

Guerra, Nancy G., & Williams, Kirk R. (2010). Implementing bullying prevention in diverse settings: Geographic, economic, and cultural influences. In Eric M. Vernberg & Bridget K. Biggs (Eds.), *Preventing and treating bullying and victimization* (pp. 319–336). New York: Oxford University Press.

Guerri, Consuelo, & Pascual, María. (2010). Mechanisms involved in the neurotoxic, cognitive, and neurobehavioral effects of alcohol consumption during adolescence. *Alcohol, 44,* 15–26.

Guillaume, Michele, & Lissau, Inge. (2002). Epidemiology. In Walter Burniat, Tim J. Cole, Inge Lissau, & Elizabeth M. E. Poskitt (Eds.), *Child and adolescent obesity: Causes and consequences, prevention and management* (pp. 28–49). New York: Cambridge University Press.

Gummerum, Michaela, Keller, Monika, Takezawa, Masanori, & Mata, Jutta. (2008).

To give or not to give: Children's and adolescents' sharing and moral negotiations in economic decision situations. *Child Development, 79,* 562–576.

Guo, Sufang, Padmadas, Sabu S., Zhao, Fengmin, Brown, James J., & Stones, R. William. (2007). Delivery settings and caesarean section rates in China. *Bulletin of the World Health Organization, 85,* 755–762.

Gurung, Regan A. R., Taylor, Shelley E., & Seeman, Teresa E. (2003). Accounting for changes in social support among married older adults: Insights from the MacArthur Studies of Successful Aging. *Psychology & Aging, 18,* 487–496.

Guyer, Ruth Levy. (2006). *Baby at risk: The uncertain legacies of medical miracles for babies, families, and society.* Sterling, VA: Capital Books.

Guzell, Jacqueline R., & Vernon-Feagans, Lynne. (2004). Parental perceived control over caregiving and its relationship to parent-infant interaction. *Child Development, 75,* 134–146.

Hackman, Daniel A., & Farah, Martha J. (2009). Socioeconomic status and the developing brain. *Trends in Cognitive Sciences, 13,* 65–73.

Hagedoorn, Mariët, Van Yperen, Nico W., Coyne, James C., van Jaarsveld, Cornelia H. M., Ranchor, Adelita V., van Sonderen, Eric, et al. (2006). Does marriage protect older people from distress? The role of equity and recency of bereavement. *Psychology and Aging, 21,* 611–620.

Hagestad, Gunhild O., & Dannefer, Dale. (2001). Concepts and theories of aging: Beyond microfication in social science approaches. In Robert H. Binstock (Ed.), *Handbook of aging and the social sciences* (5th ed., pp. 3–21). San Diego, CA: Academic Press.

Hahn, Robert, Fuqua-Whitley, Dawna, Wethington, Holly, Lowy, Jessica, Crosby, Alex, Fullilove, Mindy, et al. (2007). Effectiveness of universal school-based programs to prevent violent and aggressive behavior: A systematic review. *American Journal of Preventive Medicine, 33,* S114–S129.

Haier, Richard J., Colom, Roberto, Schroeder, David H., Condon, Christopher A., Tang, Cheuk, Eaves, Emily, et al. (2009). Gray matter and intelligence factors: Is there a neuro-g? *Intelligence, 37,* 136–144.

Hajjar, Emily R., Cafiero, Angela C., & Hanlon, Joseph T. (2007). Polypharmacy in elderly patients. *American Journal of Geriatric Pharmacotherapy, 5,* 345–351.

Halaschek-Wiener, Julius, Amirabbasi-Beik, Mahsa, Monfared, Nasim, Pieczyk, Markus, Sailer, Christian, Kollar, Anita, et al. (2009). *Genetic variation in healthy oldest-old.* Retrieved December 11, 2010, from the World Wide Web: http://www.plosone.org/article/info:doi/10.1371/journal.pone.0006641

Halford, Graeme S., & Andrews, Glenda. (2006). Reasoning and problem solving. *Handbook of child psychology: Vol. 2. Cognition, perception, and language.* 557–608.

Hall, Lynn K. (2008). *Counseling military families: What mental health professionals need to know.* New York: Taylor and Francis.

Hall, Stephen S. (2010). *Wisdom: From philosophy to neuroscience.* New York: Alfred A. Knopf.

Hall-Lande, Jennifer A., Eisenberg, Marla E., Christenson, Sandra L., & Neumark-Sztainer, Dianne. (2007). Social isolation, psychological health, and protective factors in adolescence. *Adolescence, 42,* 265–286.

Halliwell, Barry, & Gutteridge, John M. C. (2007). *Free radicals in biology and medicine* (4th ed.). New York: Oxford University Press.

Halpern, Carolyn Tucker, King, Rosalind Berkowitz, Oslak, Selene G., & Udry, J. Richard. (2005). Body mass index, dieting, romance, and sexual activity in adolescent girls: Relationships over time. *Journal of Research on Adolescence, 15,* 535–559.

Hamerman, David. (2007). *Geriatric bioscience: The link between aging and disease.* Baltimore: Johns Hopkins University Press.

Hamerton, John L., & Evans, Jane A. (2005). Sex chromosome anomalies. In Merlin Gene Butler & F. John Meaney (Eds.), *Genetics of developmental disabilities* (pp. 585–650). Boca Raton, FL: Taylor & Francis.

Hamill, Paul J. (1991). Triage: An essay. *The Georgia Review, 45,* 463–469.

Hamilton, Brady E., Martin, Joyce A., & Sutton, Paul P. (2004, November 23). Births: Preliminary data for 2003. *National Vital Statistics Reports, 53*(9), 1–17.

Hamm, Jill V., & Faircloth, Beverly S. (2005). The role of friendship in adolescents' sense of school belonging. *New Directions for Child and Adolescent Development, 107,* 61–78.

Hammond, Christopher J., Andrew, Toby, Mak, Ying Tat, & Spector, Tim D. (2004). A susceptibility locus for myopia in the normal population is linked to the PAX6 gene region on chromosome 11: A genomewide scan of dizygotic twins. *American Journal of Human Genetics, 75,* 294–304.

Hamplova, Dana. (2009). Educational homogamy among married and unmarried couples in Europe: Does context matter? *Journal of Family Issues, 30,* 28–52.

Hampton, Tracy. (2005). Alcohol and cancer. *Journal of the American Medical Association, 294,* 1481.

Hane, Amie Ashley, & Fox, Nathan A. (2006). Ordinary variations in maternal caregiving influence human infants' stress reactivity. *Psychological Science, 17,* 550–556.

Hank, Karsten, & Buber, Isabella. (2009). Grandparents caring for their grandchildren: Findings from the 2004 Survey of Health, Ageing, and Retirement in Europe. *Journal of Family Issues, 30,* 53–73.

Hannan, Claire, Buchanan, Anna DeBlois, & Monroe, Judy. (2009). Maintaining the vaccine safety net. *Pediatrics, 124*(Suppl. 5), S571–572.

Hanoch, Yaniv, Miron-Shatz, Talya, & Himmelstein, Mary. (2010). Genetic testing and risk interpretation: How do women understand lifetime risk results? *Judgment and Decision Making, 5,* 116–123.

Hansson, Robert O., & Stroebe, Margaret S. (2007). *Bereavement in late life: Coping, adaptation, and developmental influences.* Washington, DC: American Psychological Association.

Hanushek, Eric A. (2009). Building on No Child Left Behind. *Science, 326,* 802–803.

Hanushek, Eric A., & Woessmann, Ludger. (2009). *Do better schools lead to more growth? Cognitive skills, economic outcomes, and causation* (IZA Discussion Paper 4575). Bonn, Germany: Institute for the Study of Labor.

Hanushek, Eric A., & Woessmann, Ludger. (2010). *The high cost of low educational performance: The long-run economic impact of improving pisa outcomes.* Paris: Organisation for Economic Co-operation and Development.

Hardisty, David J., Johnson, Eric J., & Weber, Elke U. (2010). A dirty word or a dirty world? Attribute framing, political affiliation, and query theory. *Psychological Science, 21,* 86–92.

Hardy, Melissa. (2006). Older workers. In Robert H. Binstock & Linda K. George (Eds.), *Handbook of aging and the social sciences* (6th ed., pp. 201–218). Amsterdam: Elsevier.

Harjes, Carlos E., Rocheford, Torbert R., Bai, Ling, Brutnell, Thomas P., Kandianis, Catherine Bermudez, Sowinski, Stephen G., et al. (2008, January 18). Natural genetic variation in lycopene epsilon cyclase tapped for maize biofortification. *Science, 319,* 330–333.

Harlor, Allen D. Buz, Jr., & Bower, Charles. (2009). Hearing assessment in infants and children: Recommendations beyond neonatal screening. *Pediatrics, 124,* 1252–1263.

Harlow, Harry F. (1958). The nature of love. *American Psychologist, 13,* 673–685.

Harlow, Harry Frederick. (1986). *From learning to love: The selected papers of H. F. Harlow* (Clara Mears Harlow, Trans.). New York: Praeger.

Harlow, Ilana. (2005). Shaping sorrow: Creative aspects of public and private mourning. In Samuel Heilman (Ed.), *Death, bereavement, and mourning* (pp. 33–52). New Brunswick, NJ: Transaction.

Harmon, Amy. (2004, June 20). In new tests for fetal defects, agonizing choices for parents. *New York Times,* pp. A1, A19.

Harris, Christine. (2004, January-February). The evolution of jealousy, 92, 62.

Harris, Judith Rich. (1998). *The nurture assumption: Why children turn out the way they do.* New York: Free Press.

Harris, Judith Rich. (2002). Beyond the nurture assumption: Testing hypotheses about the child's environment. In John G. Borkowski, Sharon Landesman Ramey, & Marie Bristol-Power (Eds.), *Parenting and the child's world: Influences on academic, intellectual, and social-emotional development* (pp. 3–20). Mahwah, NJ: Erlbaum.

Hart, Betty, & Risley, Todd R. (1995). *Meaningful differences in the everyday experience of young American children.* Baltimore: Brookes.

Hart, Carole L., Smith, George Davey, Hole, David J., & Hawthorne, Victor M. (1999). Alcohol consumption and mortality from all causes, coronary heart disease, and stroke: Results from a prospective cohort study of Scottish men with 21 years of follow up. *British Medical Journal, 318,* 1725–1729.

Hart, Daniel, Atkins, Robert, & Fegley, Suzanne. (2003). Personality and development in childhood: A person-centered approach. *Monographs of the Society for Research in Child Development, 68*(Serial No. 272), vii–109.

Hart, Joshua, Schwabach, James A., & Solomon, Sheldon. (2010). Going for broke: Mortality salience increases risky decision making on the Iowa gambling task. *British Journal of Social Psychology, 49,* 425–432.

Harter, Susan. (1999). *The construction of the self: A developmental perspective.* New York: Guilford Press.

Harter, Susan. (2006). The self. In William Damon & Richard M. Lerner (Series Eds.) & Nancy Eisenberg (Vol. Ed.), *Handbook of child psychology: Vol. 3. Social, emotional, and personality development* (6th ed., pp. 505–570). Hoboken, NJ: Wiley.

Hartl, Daniel L., & Jones, Elizabeth W. (1999). *Essential genetics* (2nd ed.). Sudbury, MA: Jones and Bartlett.

Hartmann, Donald P., & Pelzel, Kelly E. (2005). Design, measurement, and analysis in developmental research. In Marc H. Bornstein & Michael E. Lamb (Eds.), *Developmental science: An advanced textbook* (5th ed., pp. 103–184). Mahwah, NJ: Erlbaum.

Harvey, Carol D. H., & Yoshino, Satomi. (2006). Social policy for family caregivers of elderly: A Canadian, Japanese, and Australian comparison. *Marriage & Family Review, 39,* 143–158.

Hasebe, Yuki, Nucci, Larry, & Nucci, Maria S. (2004). Parental control of the personal domain and adolescent symptoms of psychopathology: A cross-national study in the United States and Japan. *Child Development, 75,* 815–828.

Hassan, Mohamed A. M., & Killick, Stephen R. (2003). Effect of male age on fertility: Evidence for the decline in male fertility with increasing age. *Fertility and Sterility, 79,* 1520–1527.

Hassett, Janice M., Siebert, Erin R., & Wallen, Kim. (2008). Sex differences in rhesus monkey toy preferences parallel those of children. *Hormones and Behavior, 54,* 359–364.

Hastie, Peter A. (2004). Problem-solving in teaching sports. In Jan Wright, Lisette Burrows, & Doune MacDonald (Eds.), *Critical inquiry and problem-solving in physical education* (pp. 62–73). London: Routledge.

Hauser-Cram, Penny, Warfield, Marji Erickson, Stadler, Jennifer, & Sirin, Selcuk R. (2006). School environments and the diverging pathways of students living in poverty. In Aletha C. Huston & Marika N. Ripke (Eds.), *Developmental contexts in middle childhood: Bridges to adolescence and adulthood* (pp. 198–216). New York: Cambridge University Press.

Hawkley, Louise C., Thisted, Ronald A., Masi, Christopher M., & Cacioppo, John T. (2010). Loneliness predicts increased blood pressure: 5-year cross-lagged analyses in middle-aged and older adults. *Psychology and Aging, 25,* 132–141.

Hawthorne, Joanna. (2009). Promoting development of the early parent-infant relationship using the Neonatal Behavioural Assessment Scale. In Jane Barlow & P. O. Svanberg (Eds.), *Keeping the baby in mind: Infant mental health in practice* (pp. 39–51). New York: Routledge/Taylor & Francis Group.

Hay, Dale F., Pawlby, Susan, Waters, Cerith S., Perra, Oliver, & Sharp, Deborah. (2010). Mothers' antenatal depression and their children's antisocial outcomes. *Child Development, 81,* 149–165.

Hayatbakhsh, Mohammad R., Kingsbury, Ann M., Flenady, Vicki, Gilshenan, Kristen S., Hutchinson, Delyse M., & Najman, Jake M. (2010). *Illicit drug use before and during pregnancy at a tertiary maternity hospital 2000–2006.* Retrieved November 10, 2010, from the World Wide Web: http://dx.doi.org/10.1111/j.1465-3362.2010.00214.x

Hayden, Sara, & Hallstein, D. Lynn O. (Eds.). (2010). *Contemplating maternity in an era of choice: Explorations into discourses of reproduction.* Lanham, MD: Lexington Books.

Haydon, Jo. (2007). *Genetics in practice: A clinical approach for healthcare practitioners.* Hoboken, NJ: Wiley.

Hayes, Rachel A., & Slater, Alan. (2008). Three-month-olds' detection of alliteration in syllables. *Infant Behavior & Development 31,* 153–156.

Hayflick, Leonard. (2004). "Anti-aging" is an oxymoron. *Journals of Gerontology: Series A: Biological Sciences and Medical Sciences, 59A,* 573–578.

Hayflick, Leonard, & Moorhead, Paul S. (1961). The serial cultivation of human diploid cell strains. *Experimental Cell Research, 25,* 585–621.

Hayne, Harlene, & Simcock, Gabrielle. (2009). Memory development in toddlers. In Mary L. Courage & Nelson Cowan (Eds.), *The development of memory in infancy and childhood* (2nd ed., pp. 43–68). New York: Psychology Press.

Hayslip, Bert, & Patrick, Julie Hicks. (2003). Custodial grandparenting viewed from within a life-span perpective. In Bert Hayslip, Jr. & Julie Hicks Patrick (Eds.), *Working with custodial grandparents* (pp. 3–11). New York: Springer.

Hayward, Diane W., Gale, Catherine M., & Eikeseth, Svein. (2009). Intensive behavioural intervention for young children with autism: A research-based service model. *Research in Autism Spectrum Disorders, 3,* 571–580.

Heine, Steven J. (2007). Culture and motivation: What motivates people to act in the ways that they do? In Shinobu Kitayama & Dov Cohen (Eds.), *Handbook of cultural psychology* (pp. 714–733). New York: Guilford Press.

Hemminki, Kari, Sundquist, Jan, & Lorenzo Bermejo, Justo. (2008). Familial risks for cancer as the basis for evidence-based clinical referral and counseling. *The Oncologist, 13,* 239–247.

Henderson, Heather A., Marshall, Peter J., Fox, Nathan A., & Rubin, Kenneth H. (2004). Psychophysiological and behavioral evidence for varying forms and functions of nonsocial behavior in preschoolers. *Child Development, 75,* 251–263.

Henig, Robin Marantz. (2004, November 30). Sorry. Your eating disorder doesn't meet our criteria. *New York Times Magazine,* pp. 32–37.

Henry, Julie D., MacLeod, Mairi S., Phillips, Louise H., & Crawford, John R. (2004). A meta-analytic review of prospective memory and aging. *Psychology and Aging, 19,* 27–39.

Herek, Gregory M. (2006). Legal recognition of same-sex relationships in the United States: A social science perspective. *American Psychologist, 61,* 607–621.

Herman, Melissa. (2004). Forced to choose: Some determinants of racial identification in multiracial adolescents. *Child Development, 75,* 730–748.

Herman-Giddens, Marcia E., Wang, Lily, & Koch, Gary. (2001). Secondary sexual characteristics in boys: Estimates from the National Health and Nutrition Examination Survey III, 1988–1994. *Archives of Pediatrics & Adolescent Medicine, 155,* 1022–1028.

Herrera, Angelica P., Snipes, Shedra Amy, King, Denae W., Torres-Vigil, Isabel, Goldberg, Daniel S., & Weinberg, Armin D. (2010). Disparate inclusion of older adults in clinical trials: Priorities and opportunities for policy and practice change. *American Journal of Public Health, 100,* S105–S112.

Herring, Ann, & Swedlund, Alan C. (Eds.). (2010). *Plagues and epidemics: Infected spaces past and present.* New York: Berg.

Herrmann, Esther, Call, Josep, Hernàndez-Lloreda, María Victoria, Hare, Brian, & Tomasello, Michael. (2007, September 7). Humans have evolved specialized skills of social cognition: The cultural intelligence hypothesis. *Science, 317,* 1360–1366.

Herschensohn, Julia Rogers. (2007). *Language development and age.* New York: Cambridge University Press.

Hertenstein, Matthew J., & Campos, Joseph J. (2001). Emotion regulation via maternal touch. *Infancy, 2,* 549–566.

Heslop, Richard (2006). "Doing a Maslow": Humanistic education and diversity in police training *The Police Journal, 79,* 331–342.

Hess, Thomas, Hinson, Joey, & Hodges, Elizabeth. (2009). Moderators of and mechanisms underlying stereotype threat effects on older adults' memory performance. *Experimental Aging Research, 35,* 153–177.

Hess, Thomas M., Germain, Cassandra M., Rosenberg, Daniel C., Leclerc, Christina M., & Hodges, Elizabeth A. (2005). Aging-related selectivity and susceptibility to irrelevant affective information in the construction of attitudes. *Aging, Neuropsychology, and Cognition, 12,* 149–174.

Hess, Thomas M., Leclerc, Christina M., Swaim, Elizabeth, & Weatherbee, Sarah R. (2009). Aging and everyday judgments: the impact of motivational and processing resource factors. *Psychology and Aging, 24,* 735–740.

Higgins, Matt. (2006a, August 5). Risk of injury is simply an element of motocross. *New York Times,* pp. D5.

Higgins, Matt. (2006b, August 7). A series of flips creates some serious buzz. *New York Times,* pp. D7.

Higuchi, Susumu, Matsushita, Sachio, Muramatsu, Taro, Murayama, Masanobu, & Hayashida, Motoi. (1996). Alcohol and aldehyde dehydrogenase genotypes and drinking behavior in Japanese. *Alcoholism: Clinical and Experimental Research, 20,* 493–497.

Hill, E. Jeffrey, Jacob, Jenet, Shannon, Laurie, Brennan, Robert, Blanchard, Victoria, & Martinengo, Giuseppe. (2008). Exploring the relationship of workplace flexibility, gender, and life stage to family-to-work conflict, and stress and burnout. *Community, Work & Family, 11,* 165–181.

Hill, Nancy E., Bush, Kevin R., & Roosa, Mark W. (2003). Parenting and family socialization strategies and children's mental health: Low-income, Mexican-American and Euro-American mothers and children. *Child Development, 74,* 189–204.

Hill, Nancy E., & Tyson, Diana F. (2009). Parental involvement in middle school: A meta-analytic assessment of the strategies that promote achievement. *Developmental Psychology, 45,* 740–763.

Hill, Shirley A. (2007). Transformative processes: Some sociological questions. *Journal of Marriage and Family, 69,* 293–298.

Hillier, Dawn. (2003). *Childbirth in the global village: Implications for midwifery education and practice.* New York: Routledge.

Hillman, Richard. (2005). Expanded newborn screening and phenylketonuria (PKU). In Merlin Gene Butler & F. John Meaney (Eds.), *Genetics of developmental disabilities* (pp. 651–664). Boca Raton, FL: Taylor & Francis.

Hilton, Irene V., Stephen, Samantha, Barker, Judith C., & Weintraub, Jane A. (2007). Cultural factors and children's oral health care: A qualitative study of carers of young children. *Community Dentistry and Oral Epidemiology, 35,* 429–438.

Hindman, Annemarie H., Skibbe, Lori E., Miller, Alison, & Zimmerman, Marc. (2010). Ecological contexts and early learning: Contributions of child, family, and classroom factors during Head Start, to literacy and mathematics growth through first grade. *Early Childhood Research Quarterly, 25,* 235–250.

Hines, Melissa. (2004). *Brain gender.* Oxford, England: Oxford University Press.

Hipwell, Alison E., Keenan, Kate, Loeber, Rolf, & Battista, Deena. (2010). Early predictors of sexually intimate behaviors in an urban sample of young girls. *Developmental Psychology, 46,* 366–378.

Hirsch, Eric Donald, Jr. (2008). Plugging the hole in state standards. *American Educator, 32,* 8–12.

Hirschberger, Gilad. (2006). Terror management and attributions of blame to innocent victims: Reconciling compassionate and defensive responses. *Journal of Personality and Social Psychology, 91,* 832–844.

Hirsiaho, Nina, & Ruoppila, Isto. (2005). Physical health and mobility. In Heidrun

Mollenkopf, Fiorella Marcellini, Isto Ruoppila, Zsuzsa Széman, & Mart Tacken (Eds.), *Enhancing mobility in later life: Personal coping, environmental resources and technical support. The out-of-home mobility of older adults in urban and rural regions of five European countries* (pp. 77–104). Amsterdam: IOS Press.

Ho, Caroline, Bluestein, Deborah N., & Jenkins, Jennifer M. (2008). Cultural differences in the relationship between parenting and children's behavior. *Developmental Psychology, 44,* 507–522.

Hoare, Carol Hren. (2002). *Erikson on development in adulthood: New insights from the unpublished papers.* New York: Oxford University Press.

Hobbes, Thomas. (1997). *Leviathan: Authoritative text, backgrounds, interpretations* (Richard E. Flathman & David Johnston, Trans.). New York: Norton. (Original work published 1651)

Hochman, David. (2003, November 23). Food for holiday thought: Eat less, live to 140? *The New York Times,* pp. A9.

Hockey, Robert J. (2005). Operator functional state: The prediction of breakdown in human performance. In John Duncan, Peter McLeod, & Louise H. Phillips (Eds.), *Measuring the mind: Speed, control, and age* (pp. 373–394). New York: Oxford University Press.

Hofer, Scott M., & Piccinin, Andrea M. (2010). Toward an integrative science of life-span development and aging. *The Journals of Gerontology: Series B: Psychological Sciences and Social Sciences, 65B,* 269–278.

Hoff, David J. (2007). Not all agree on meaning of NCLB proficiency. *Education Week, 26*(33), 1, 23.

Hoff, Erika. (2003). The specificity of environmental influence: Socioeconomic status affects early vocabulary development via maternal speech. *Child Development, 74,* 1368–1378.

Hofferth, Sandra L., & Anderson, Kermyt G. (2003). Are all dads equal? Biology versus marriage as a basis for paternal investment. *Journal of Marriage & Family, 65,* 213–232.

Hoffman, Edward. (2009). Rollo May on Maslow and Rogers: "No theory of evil." *Journal of Humanistic Psychology,* 484–485.

Hofstede, Geert. (2007). A European in Asia. *Asian Journal of Social Psychology, 10,* 16–21.

Hogeboom, David L., McDermott, Robert J., Perrin, Karen M., Osman, Hana, & Bell-Ellison, Bethany A. (2010). Internet use and social networking among middle aged and older adults. *Educational Gerontology, 36,* 93–111.

Hohmann-Marriott, Bryndl E. (2006). Shared beliefs and the union stability of married and cohabiting couples. *Journal of Marriage and Family, 68,* 1015–1028.

Holden, Constance. (2006, June 30). An evolutionary squeeze on brain size. *Science, 312,* 1867b.

Holden, Constance. (2009, October 16). Fetal cells again? *Science, 326,* 358–359.

Holland, James D., & Klaczynski, Paul A. (2009). Intuitive risk taking during adolescence. *Prevention Researcher, 16,* 8–11.

Hollich, George J., Hirsh-Pasek, Kathy, Golinkoff, Roberta Michnick, Brand, Rebecca J., Brown, Ellie, Chung, He Len, et al. (2000). Breaking the language barrier: An emergentist coalition model for the origins of word learning. *Monographs of the Society for Research in Child Development, 65*(3, Serial No. 262), v–123.

Holliday, Robin. (1995). *Understanding ageing.* Cambridge, England: Cambridge University Press.

Hollos, Marida, Larsen, Ulla, Obono, Oka, & Whitehouse, Bruce. (2009). The problem of infertility in high fertility populations: Meanings, consequences and coping mechanisms in two Nigerian communities. *Social Science & Medicine, 68,* 2061–2068.

Holm, Stephanie M., Forbes, Erika E., Ryan, Neal D., Phillips, Mary L., Tarr, Jill A., & Dahl, Ronald E. (2009). Reward-related brain function and sleep in pre/early pubertal and mid/late pubertal adolescents. *The Journal of Adolescent Health, 45,* 326–334.

Holtzman, Jennifer. (2009). Simple, effective—and inexpensive—strategies to reduce tooth decay in children. *ICAN: Infant, Child, & Adolescent Nutrition, 1,* 225–231.

Hong, Ying-yi, Morris, Michael W., Chiu, Chi-yue, & Benet-Martinez, Veronica. (2000). Multicultural minds: A dynamic constructivist approach to culture and cognition. *American Psychologist, 55,* 709–720.

Hooley, Jill M. (2004). Do psychiatric patients do better clinically if they live with certain kinds of families? *Current Directions in Psychological Science, 13,* 202–205.

Hormann, Elizabeth. (2007). Sleeping with your baby: A parent's guide to co-sleeping. *Birth, 34,* 355–356.

Horn, Ivor B., Brenner, Ruth, Rao, Malla, & Cheng, Tina L. (2006). Beliefs about the appropriate age for initiating toilet training: Are there racial and socioeconomic differences? *The Journal of Pediatrics, 149,* 165–168.

Horn, John L., & Cattell, Raymond B. (1967). Age differences in fluid and crystallized intelligence. *Acta Psychologica, 26,* 107–129.

Horn, John L., & Masunaga, Hiromi. (2000). New directions for research into aging and intelligence: The development of expertise. In Timothy J. Perfect & Elizabeth A. Maylor (Eds.), *Models of cognitive aging* (pp. 125–159). London: Oxford University Press.

Hougaard, Karin S., & Hansen, Åse M. (2007). Enhancement of developmental toxicity effects of chemicals by gestational stress. A review. *Neurotoxicology and Teratology, 29,* 425–445.

Houts, Renate M., Robins, Elliot, & Huston, Ted L. (1996). Compatibility and the development of premarital relationships. *Journal of Marriage & the Family, 58,* 7–20.

Howard, Andrea L., Galambos, Nancy L., & Krahn, Harvey J. (2010). Paths to success in young adulthood from mental health and life transitions in emerging adulthood. *International Journal of Behavioral Development, 34,* 538–546.

Howard, Jeffrey A. (2005). Why should we care about student expectations? In Thomas E. Miller, Barbara E. Bender, John H. Schuh, & Associates (Eds.), *Promoting reasonable expectations: Aligning student and institutional views of the college experience* (pp. 10–33). San Francisco: Jossey-Bass.

Howe, Mark L. (2004). The role of conceptual recoding in reducing children's retroactive interference. *Developmental Psychology, 40,* 131–139.

Howlin, Patricia, Magiati, Iliana, Charman, Tony, & MacLean, William E., Jr. (2009). Systematic review of early intensive behavioral interventions for children with autism. *American Journal on Intellectual and Developmental Disabilities, 114,* 23–41.

Hrabosky, Joshua I., & Thomas, Jennifer J. (2008). Elucidating the relationship between obesity and depression: Recommendations for future research. *Clinical Psychology: Science and Practice, 15,* 28–34.

Hsia, Yingfen, & Maclennan, Karyn. (2009). Rise in psychotropic drug prescribing in children and adolescents during 1992–2001: A population-based study in the UK. *European Journal of Epidemiology, 24,* 211–216.

Hsu, Ming, Anen, Cedric, & Quartz, Steven R. (2008, May 23). The right and the good: Distributive justice and neural encoding of equity and efficiency. *Science, 320,* 1092–1095.

Hu, Frank B., Li, Tricia Y., Colditz, Graham A., Willett, Walter C., & Manson, JoAnn E. (2003). Television watching and other sedentary behaviors in relation to risk of obesity and type 2 diabetes mellitus in women. *Journal of the American Medical Association, 289,* 1785–1791.

Huang, Chien-Chung. (2009). Mothers' reports of nonresident fathers' involvement with their children: Revisiting the relationship between child support payment and visitation. *Family Relations, 58,* 54–64.

Huang, Jannet. (2007). Hormones and female sexuality. In Annette Fuglsang Owens & Mitchell S. Tepper (Eds.), *Sexual health: Vol. 2. Physical foundations* (pp. 43–78). Westport, CT: Praeger/Greenwood.

Huesmann, L. Rowell, Dubow, Eric F., & Boxer, Paul. (2009). Continuity of aggression from childhood to early adulthood as a predictor of life outcomes: Implications for the adolescent-limited and life-course-persistent models. *Aggressive Behavior, 35,* 136–149.

Hughes, Kimberly A. (2010). Mutation and the evolution of ageing: From biometrics to system genetics. *Philosophical Transactions of the Royal Society B: Biological Sciences, 365,* 1273–1279.

Hughes, Sonya M., & Gore, Andrea C. (2007). How the brain controls puberty, and implications for sex and ethnic differences. *Family & Community Health, 30*(Suppl. 1), S112–S114.

Huijbregts, Sanne K., Tavecchio, Louis, Leseman, Paul, & Hoffenaar, Peter. (2009). Child rearing in a group setting: Beliefs of Dutch, Caribbean Dutch, and Mediterranean Dutch caregivers in center-based child care. *Journal of Cross-Cultural Psychology, 40,* 797–815.

Hulbert, Ann. (2007, April 1). Re-education. *New York Times Magazine*, pp. 34ff.

Hunt, Geoffrey, Moloney, Molly, & Evans, Kristin. (2009). Epidemiology meets cultural studies: Studying and understanding youth cultures, clubs and drugs. *Addiction Research & Theory, 17,* 601–621.

Hunt, Ruskin H., & Thomas, Kathleen M. (2008). Magnetic resonance imaging methods in developmental science: A primer. *Development and Psychopathology, 20,* 1029–1051.

Hussey, Jon M., Chang, Jen Jen, & Kotch, Jonathan B. (2006). Child maltreatment in the United States: Prevalence, risk factors, and adolescent health consequences. *Pediatrics, 118,* 933–942.

Hust, Stacey J. T., Brown, Jane D., & L'Engle, Kelly Ladin. (2008). Boys will be boys and girls better be prepared: An analysis of the rare sexual health messages in young adolescents' media. *Mass Communication and Society, 11,* 3–23.

Huston, Aletha C., & Aronson, Stacey Rosenkrantz. (2005). Mothers' time with infant and time in employment as predictors of mother-child relationships and children's early development. *Child Development, 76,* 467–482.

Huston, Aletha C., & Ripke, Marika N. (2006). Middle childhood: Contexts of development. In Aletha C. Huston & Marika N. Ripke (Eds.), *Developmental contexts in middle childhood: Bridges to adolescence and adulthood* (pp. 1–22). New York: Cambridge University Press.

Huver, Rose M. E., Otten, Roy, de Vries, Hein, & Engels, Rutger C. M. E. (2010). Personality and parenting style in parents of adolescents. *Journal of Adolescence, 33,* 395–402.

Hyde, Janet Shibley. (2007). New directions in the study of gender similarities and differences. *Current Directions in Psychological Science, 16,* 259–263.

Hyde, Janet S., Lindberg, Sara M., Linn, Marcia C., Ellis, Amy B., & Williams, Caroline C. (2008, July 25). Gender similarities characterize math performance. *Science, 321,* 494–495.

Hyson, Marilou, Copple, Carol, & Jones, Jacqueline. (2006). Early childhood development and education. In William Damon & Richard M. Lerner (Series Eds.) & K. Ann Renninger & Irving E. Sigel (Vol. Eds.), *Handbook of child psychology: Vol. 4. Child psychology in practice* (6th ed., pp. 3–47). Hoboken, NJ: Wiley.

Iacoboni, Marco. (2009). Imitation, empathy, and mirror neurons. *An ● al Review of Psychology, 60,* 653–670.

Idler, Ellen. (2006). Religion and aging. In Robert H. Binstock & Linda K. George (Eds.), *Handbook of aging and the social sciences* (6th ed., pp. 277–300). Amsterdam: Elsevier.

Imamoglu, Çagri. (2007). Assisted living as a new place schema: A comparison with homes and nursing homes. *Environment and Behavior, 39,* 246–268.

Inagaki, Hiroki, Gondo, Yasuyuki, Hirose, Nobuyoshi, Masui, Yukie, Kitagawa, Koji, **Arai, Yasumichi, et al.** (2009). Cognitive function in Japanese centenarians according to the mini-mental state examination. *Dementia and Geriatric Cognitive Disorders, 28,* 6–12.

Ingersoll-Dayton, Berit, Neal, Margaret B., Ha, Jung-Hwa, & Hammer, Leslie B. (2003). Redressing inequity in parent care among siblings. *Journal of Marriage & Family, 65,* 201–212.

Inglehart, Ronald. (1990). *Culture shift in advanced industrial society.* Princeton, NJ: Princeton University Press.

Inhelder, Bärbel, & Piaget, Jean. (1958). *The growth of logical thinking from childhood to adolescence: An essay on the construction of formal operational structures.* New York: Basic Books.

Inhelder, Bärbel, & Piaget, Jean. (1964). *The early growth of logic in the child.* New York: Harper & Row.

Inouye, Sharon K. (2006). Delirium in older persons. *New England Journal of Medicine, 354,* 1157–1165.

Insel, Beverly J., & Gould, Madelyn S. (2008). Impact of modeling on adolescent suicidal behavior. *Psychiatric Clinics of North America, 31,* 293–316.

Institute of Medicine, Committee on Food Marketing and the Diets of Children and Youth. (2006). *Food marketing to children and youth: Threat or opportunity?* Washington, DC: National Academies Press.

Irwin, Scott, Galvez, Roberto, Weiler, Ivan Jeanne, Beckel-Mitchener, Andrea, & Greenough, William. (2002). Brain structure and the functions of FMR1 protein. In Randi Jenssen Hagerman & Paul J. Hagerman (Eds.), *Fragile X syndrome: Diagnosis, treatment, and research* (3rd ed., pp. 191–205). Baltimore: Johns Hopkins University Press.

Ispa, Jean M., Fine, Mark A., Halgunseth, Linda C., Harper, Scott, Robinson, JoAnn, Boyce, Lisa, et al. (2004). Maternal intrusiveness, maternal warmth, and mother-toddler relationship outcomes: Variations across low-income ethnic and acculturation groups. *Child Development, 75,* 1613–1631.

Iverson, Jana M., & Fagan, Mary K. (2004). Infant vocal-motor coordination: Precursor to the gesture-speech system? *Child Development, 75,* 1053–1066.

Iyengar, Sheena S., & Lepper, Mark R. (2000). When choice is demotivating: Can one desire too much of a good thing? *Journal of personality and social psychology, 79,* 995–1006.

Izard, Carroll E. (2009). Emotion theory and research: Highlights, unanswered questions, and emerging issues. *Annual Review of Psychology, 60,* 1–25.

Izard, Carroll E., Fine, Sarah, Mostow, Allison, Trentacosta, Christopher, & Campbell, Jan. (2002). Emotion processes in normal and abnormal development and preventive intervention. *Development & Psychopathology, 14,* 761–787.

Jackson, Debra J., Lang, Janet M., Swartz, William H., Ganiats, Theodore G., Fullerton, **Judith, Ecker, Jeffrey, et al.** (2003). Outcomes, safety, and resource utilization in a collaborative care birth center program compared with traditional physician-based perinatal care. *American Journal of Public Health, 93,* 999–1006.

Jackson, Richard J. J., & Tester, June. (2008). Environment shapes health, including children's mental health. *Journal of the American Academy of Child & Adolescent Psychiatry, 47,* 129–131.

Jacob, Jenet I. (2009). The socio-emotional effects of non-maternal childcare on children in the USA: A critical review of recent studies. *Early Child Development and Care, 179,* 559–570.

Jacoby, Larry L., & Rhodes, Matthew G. (2006). False remembering in the aged. *Current Directions in Psychological Science, 15,* 49–53.

Jaffe, Eric. (2004). Mickey Mantle's greatest error: Yankee star's false belief may have cost him years. *Observer, 17*(9), 37.

Jaffee, Sara R., Caspi, Avshalom, Moffitt, Terrie E., Polo-Tomás, Monica, & Taylor, Alan. (2007). Individual, family, and neighborhood factors distinguish resilient from nonresilient maltreated children: A cumulative stressors model. *Child Abuse & Neglect, 31,* 231–253.

James, Raven. (2007). Sexually transmitted infections. In Annette Fuglsang Owens & Mitchell S. Tepper (Eds.), *Sexual health: Vol. 4. State-of-the-art treatments and research* (pp. 235–267). Westport, CT: Praeger/Greenwood.

Jansen-van der Weide, Marijke C., Onwuteaka-Philipsen, Bregje D., & van der Wal, Gerrit. (2005). Granted, undecided, withdrawn, and refused requests for euthanasia and physician-assisted suicide. *Archives of Internal Medicine, 165,* 1698–1704.

Jansson, Ulla-Britt, Hanson, M., Sillen, Ulla, & Hellstrom, Anna-Lena. (2005). Voiding pattern and acquisition of bladder control from birth to age 6 years—A longitudinal study. *Journal of Urology, 174,* 289–293.

Jastrzembski, Tiffany S., Charness, Neil, & Vasyukova, Catherine. (2006). Expertise and age effects on knowledge activation in chess. *Psychology and Aging, 21,* 401–405.

Jenson, Jeffrey M., & Fraser, Mark W. (2006). *Social policy for children & families: A risk and resilience perspective.* Thousand Oaks, CA: Sage.

Jessop, Donna C., & Wade, Jennifer. (2008). Fear appeals and binge drinking: A terror management theory perspective. *British Journal of Health Psychology, 13,* 773–788.

Jia, Haomiao, & Lubetkin, Erica I. (2010). Trends in quality-adjusted life-years lost contributed by smoking and obesity. *American Journal of Preventive Medicine, 38,* 138–144.

Johnson, Amy Janan, Becker, Jennifer A. H., Craig, Elizabeth A., Gilchrist, Eileen S., & Haigh, Michel M. (2009). Changes in friendship commitment: Comparing geographically close and long-distance young-adult friendships. *Communication Quarterly, 57,* 395–415.

Johnson, Chris A., & Wilkinson, Mark E. (2010). Vision and driving: The United States. *Journal of Neuro-Ophthalmology, 30,* 170–176.

Johnson, Dominic, & Bering, Jesse. (2009). Hand of God, mind of man: Punishment and cognition in the evolution of cooperation. In Jeffrey Schloss & Michael J. Murray (Eds.), *The believing primate: Scientific, philosophical, and theological reflections on the origin of religion* (pp. 26–43). New York: Oxford University Press.

Johnson, Dana E. (2000). Medical and developmental sequelae of early childhood institutionalization in Eastern European adoptees. In Charles A. Nelson (Ed.), *The Minnesota symposia on child psychology: Vol. 31. The effects of early adversity on neurobehavioral development* (pp. 113–162). Mahwah, NJ: Erlbaum.

Johnson, Kevin R. (1999). *How did you get to be Mexican? A white/brown man's search for identity.* Philadelphia: Temple University Press.

Johnson, Kevin R. (2010). How racial profiling in America became the 'law of the land': United States v. Brignoni-Ponce and Whren v. United States and the need for rebellious lawyering. *Georgetown Law Journal, 98,* 1005–1077.

Johnson, Kevin R., & Hing, Bill O. (2007). The immigrant rights marches of 2006 and the prospects for a new civil rights movement. *Harvard Civil Rights-Civil Liberties Law Review, 42,* 99–138.

Johnson, Mark H. (2005). Developmental neuroscience, psychophysiology and genetics. In Marc H. Bornstein & Michael E. Lamb (Eds.), *Developmental science: An advanced textbook* (5th ed., pp. 187–222). Mahwah, NJ: Erlbaum.

Johnson, Mark H. (2007). The social brain in infancy: A developmental cognitive neuroscience approach. In Donna Coch, Kurt W. Fischer, & Geraldine Dawson (Eds.), *Human behavior, learning, and the developing brain. Typical development* (pp. 115–137). New York: Guilford Press.

Johnson, Mark H., Grossmann, Tobias, & Kadosh, Kathrin Cohen. (2009). Mapping functional brain development: Building a social brain through interactive specialization. *Developmental Psychology, 45,* 151–159.

Johnson, Mary. (2007). Our guest editors talk about couples in later life. *Generations, 31,* 4–5.

Johnson, Michael P. (2008). *A typology of domestic violence: Intimate terrorism, violent resistance, and situational couple violence.* Hanover, NH: Northeastern University Press.

Johnson, Michael P., & Ferraro, Kathleen J. (2000). Research on domestic violence in the 1990s: Making distinctions. *Journal of Marriage and Family, 62,* 948–963.

Johnson, Scott P., & Shuwairi, Sarah M. (2009). Learning and memory facilitate predictive tracking in 4-month-olds. *Journal of Experimental Child Psychology, 102,* 122–130.

Johnson, Wendy. (2010). Understanding the genetics of intelligence: Can height help? Can corn oil? *Current Directions in Psychological Science, 19,* 177–182.

Johnston, Lloyd D., O'Malley, Patrick M., Bachman, Jerald G., & Schulenberg, John E. (2006). *Monitoring the Future national survey results on drug use, 1975–2006: Volume II. College students and adults ages 19–45* (NIH Publication No. 06–5884). Bethesda, MD: National Institute on Drug Abuse.

Johnston, Lloyd D., O'Malley, Patrick M., Bachman, Jerald G., & Schulenberg, John E. (2008). *Monitoring the Future national results on adolescent drug use: Overview of key findings, 2007* (NIH Publication No. 08–6418). Bethesda, MD: National Institute on Drug Abuse.

Johnston, Lloyd D., O'Malley, Patrick M., Bachman, Jerald G., & John E. Schulenberg. (2010). *Monitoring the Future national results on adolescent drug use: Overview of key findings, 2009* (NIH Publication No. 10–7583). Bethesda, MD: National Institute on Drug Abuse.

Johnston, Lloyd D., O'Malley, Patrick M., Bachman, Jerald G., & Schulenberg, John E. (2009). *Monitoring the Future national survey results on drug use, 1975–2008: Vol. II. College students and adults ages 19–50* (NIH Publication No. 09–7403). Bethesda, MD: National Institute on Drug Abuse.

Jokela, Markus, Elovainio, Marko, Kivimäki, Mika, & Keltikangas-Järvinen, Liisa. (2008). Temperament and migration patterns in Finland. *Psychological Science, 19,* 831–837.

Jones, Constance, & Peskin, Harvey. (2010). Psychological health from the teens to the 80s: Multiple developmental trajectories. *Journal of Adult Development, 17,* 20–32.

Jones, Daniel. (2006, February 12). You're not sick, you're just in love. *New York Times,* pp. 1, 13.

Jones, Diane, & Crawford, Joy. (2005). Adolescent boys and body image: Weight and muscularity concerns as dual pathways to body dissatisfaction. *Journal of Youth and Adolescence, 34,* 629–636.

Jones, Edward P. (2003). *The known world.* New York: Amistad.

Jones, Edward P. (2003). *Lost in the city: Stories.* New York: Amistad. (Original work published 1992)

Jones, Harold Ellis, & Conrad, Herbert S. (1933). The growth and decline of intelligence: A study of a homogeneous group between the ages of ten and sixty. *Genetic Psychology Monographs, 13,* 223–298.

Jones, Maggie. (2006, January 15). Shutting themselves in. *New York Times Magazine,* pp. 46–51.

Jones, Mary Cover. (1965). Psychological correlates of somatic development. *Child Development, 36,* 899–911.

Jones, Steve. (2006, December 22). Prosperous people, penurious genes. *Science, 314,* 1879.

Jong, Jyh-Tsorng, Kao, Tsair, Lee, Liang-Yi, Huang, Hung-Hsuan, Lo, Po-Tsung, & Wang, Hui-Chung. (2010). Can temperament be understood at birth? The relationship between neonatal pain cry and their temperament: A preliminary study. *Infant Behavior and Development, 33,* 266–272.

Jongbloed, Ben W. A., Maassen, Peter A. M., & Neave, Guy R. (Eds.). (1999). *From the eye of the storm: Higher education's changing institution.* Dordrecht, The Netherlands: Kluwer Academic Publishers.

Jopp, Daniela, & Rott, Christoph. (2006). Adaptation in very old age: Exploring the role of resources, beliefs, and attitudes for centenarians' happiness. *Psychology and Aging, 21,* 266–280.

Jordan, Alexander H., & Monin, Benoît. (2008). From sucker to saint: Moralization in response to self-threat. *Psychological Science, 19,* 809–815.

Jose, Anita, Daniel O'Leary, K., & Moyer, Anne. (2010). Does premarital cohabitation predict subsequent marital stability and marital quality? a meta-analysis. *Journal of Marriage and Family, 72,* 105–116.

Joshi, Pamela, & Bogen, Karen. (2007). Nonstandard schedules and young children's behavioral outcomes among working low-income families. *Journal of Marriage and Family, 69,* 139–156.

Juujärvi, Soile. (2005). Care and justice in real-life moral reasoning. *Journal of Adult Development, 12,* 199–210.

Juvonen, Jaana, Nishina, Adrienne, & Graham, Sandra. (2006). Ethnic diversity and perceptions of safety in urban middle schools. *Psychological Science, 17,* 393–400.

Kaduszkiewicz, Hanna, Zimmermann, Thomas, Beck-Bornholdt, Hans-Peter, & van den Bussche, Hendrik. (2005). Cholinesterase inhibitors for patients with Alzheimer's disease: Systematic review of randomised clinical trials. *British Medical Journal, 331,* 321–327.

Kagan, Jerome. (2007). A trio of concerns. *Perspectives on Psychological Science, 2,* 361–376.

Kagan, Jerome. (2008). In defense of qualitative changes in development. *Child Development, 79,* 1606–1624.

Kagan, Jerome, & Herschkowitz, Elinore Chapman. (2005). *Young mind in a growing brain.* Mahwah, NJ: Erlbaum.

Kagan, Jerome, & Norbert Herschkowitz (with Herschkowitz, Elinore Chapman). (2005). *A young mind in a growing brain.* Mahwah, NJ: Erlbaum.

Kagan, Jerome, Snidman, Nancy, Kahn, Vali, & Towsley, Sara. (2007). The preservation of two infant temperaments into adolescence. *Monographs of the Society for Research in Child Development, 72*(Serial No. 287), 1–95.

Kagitcibasi, Cigdem. (2003). Human development across cultures: A contextual-functional analysis and implications for interventions. In T. S. Saraswati (Ed.), *Cross-cultural perspectives in human development: Theory, research, and applications* (pp. 166–191). New Delhi, India: Sage.

Kahana-Kalman, Ronit, & Walker-Andrews, Arlene S. (2001). The role of person familiarity in young infants' perception of emotional expressions. *Child Development, 72,* 352–369.

Kaiser, Jocelyn. (2008, January 25). A plan to capture human diversity in 1000 genomes. *Science, 319,* 395.

Kakihara, Fumiko, & Tilton-Weaver, Lauree. (2009). Adolescents' interpretations of parental control: Differentiated by domain and types of control. *Child Development, 80,* 1722–1738.

Kalambouka, Afroditi, Farrell, Peter, Dyson, Alan, & Kaplan, Ian. (2007). The impact of placing pupils with special educational needs in mainstream schools on the achievement of their peers. *Educational Research, 49,* 365–382.

Kalaria, Raj N., Maestre, Gladys E., Arizaga, Raul, Friedland, Robert P., Galasko, Doug, Hall, Kathleen, et al. (2008). Alzheimer's disease and vascular dementia in developing countries: prevalence, management, and risk factors. *The Lancet Neurology, 7,* 812–826.

Kalavar, Jyotsna, & van Willigen, John. (2005). Older Asian Indians resettled in America: Narratives about households, culture and generation. *Journal of Cross-Cultural Gerontology, 20,* 213–230.

Kalliala, Marjatta. (2006). *Play culture in a changing world.* Maidenhead, England: Open University Press.

Kalmijn, Matthijs. (2003). Shared friendship networks and the life course: An analysis of survey data on married and cohabiting couples. *Social Networks, 25,* 231–249.

Kane, Katherine D., Yochim, Brian P., & Lichtenberg, Peter A. (2010). Depressive symptoms and cognitive impairment predict all-cause mortality in long-term care residents. *Psychology and Aging, 25,* 446–452.

Kanner, Leo. (1943). Autistic disturbances of affective contact. *Nervous Child, 2,* 217–250.

Karabinus, David S. (2009). Flow cytometric sorting of human sperm: MicroSort® clinical trial update. *Theriogenology, 71,* 74–79.

Karama, Sherif, Ad-Dab'bagh, Yasser, Haier, Richard J., Deary, Ian J., Lyttelton, Oliver C., Lepage, Claude, et al. (2009). Positive association between cognitive ability and cortical thickness in a representative US sample of healthy 6 to 18-year-olds. *Intelligence, 37,* 145–155.

Karmiloff-Smith, Annette. (2010). A developmental perspective on modularity. In Britt Glatzeder, Vinod Goel, & Albrecht Müller (Eds.), *Towards a theory of thinking* (pp. 179–187). Heidelberg, Germany: Springer.

Karney, Benjamin R., & Bradbury, Thomas N. (2005). Contextual influences on marriage: Implications for policy and intervention. *Current Directions in Psychological Science, 14,* 171–174.

Kasinitz, Philip, Mollenkopf, John H., Waters, Mary C., & Holdaway, Jennifer. (2008). *Inheriting the city: The children of immigrants come of age.* New York: Russell Sage Foundation.

Kast, Kelly R., Berg, Rob, Deas, Ann, Lezotte, Dennis, & Crane, Lori A. (2008). Colorado dental practitioners' attitudes and practices regarding tobacco-use prevention activities for 8- through 12-year-old patients. *Journal of the American Dental Association, 139,* 467–475.

Kastenbaum, Robert. (2006). *Death, society, and human experience* (9th ed.). Boston: Allyn and Bacon.

Kaufman, James C., & Sternberg, Robert J. (2006). *The international handbook of creativity.* New York: Cambridge University Press.

Kaufman, Kenneth R., & Kaufman, Nathaniel D. (2006). And then the dog died. *Death Studies, 30,* 61–76.

Kaushik, Manu, Sontineni, Siva P., & Hunter, Claire. (2010). Cardiovascular disease and androgens: A review. *International Journal of Cardiology, 142,* 8–14.

Kavirajan, Harish, & Schneider, Lon S. (2007). Efficacy and adverse effects of cholinesterase inhibitors and memantine in vascular dementia: A meta-analysis of randomised controlled trials. *Lancet Neurology, 6,* 782–792.

Keating, Daniel P. (2004). Cognitive and brain development. In Richard M. Lerner & Laurence D. Steinberg (Eds.), *Handbook of adolescent psychology* (2nd ed., pp. 45–84). Hoboken, NJ: Wiley.

Keating, Nancy L., Herrinton, Lisa J., Zaslavsky, Alan M., Liu, Liyan, & Ayanian, John Z. (2006). Variations in hospice use among cancer patients. *Journal of the National Cancer Institute, 98,* 1053–1059.

Kedar, Yarden, Casasola, Marianella, & Lust, Barbara. (2006). Getting there faster: 18- and 24-month-old infants' use of function words to determine reference. *Child Development, 77,* 325–338.

Keel, Pamela K., & Brown, Tiffany A. (2010). Update on course and outcome in eating disorders. *International Journal of Eating Disorders, 43,* 195–204.

Kelemen, Deborah, Callanan, Maureen A., Casler, Krista, & Perez-Granados, Deanne R. (2005). Why things happen: Teleological explanation in parent-child conversation. *Developmental Psychology, 41,* 251–264.

Kellehear, Allan. (2008). Dying as a social relationship: A sociological review of debates on the determination of death. *Social Science & Medicine, 66,* 1533–1544.

Keller, Heidi, Lamm, Bettina, Abels, Monika, Yovsi, Relindis, Borke, Jörn, Jensen, Henning, et al. (2006). Cultural models, socialization goals, and parenting ethnotheories: A multicultural analysis. *Journal of Cross-Cultural Psychology, 37,* 155–172.

Keller, Heidi, Yovsi, Relindis, Borke, Joern, Kärtner, Joscha, Jensen, Henning, & Papaligoura, Zaira. (2004). Developmental consequences of early parenting experiences: Self-recognition and self-regulation in three cultural communities. *Child Development, 75,* 1745–1760.

Keller, Meret A., & Goldberg, Wendy A. (2004). Co-sleeping: Help or hindrance for young children's independence? *Infant and Child Development, 13,* 369–388.

Kelley, Susan J., & Whitley, Deborah M. (2003). Psychological distress and physical health problems in grandparents raising grandchildren: Development of an empirically-based intervention model. In Bert Hayslip, Jr. & Julie Hicks Patrick (Eds.), *Working with custodial grandparents* (pp. 127–144). New York: Springer.

Kellman, Philip J., & Arterberry, Martha E. (2006). Infant visual perception. In William Damon & Richard M. Lerner (Series Eds.) &

Deanna Kuhn & Robert S. Siegler (Vol. Eds.), *Handbook of child psychology: Vol. 2. Cognition, perception, and language* (6th ed., pp. 109–160). Hoboken, NJ: Wiley.

Kelly, John R. (1993). *Activity and aging: Staying involved in later life.* Newbury Park, CA: Sage.

Kemp, Charles, & Bhungalia, Sonal. (2002). Culture and the end of life: A review of major world religions. *Journal of Hospice & Palliative Nursing, 4,* 235–242.

Kemp, Candace L. (2005). Dimensions of grandparent-adult grandchild relationships: From family ties to intergenerational friendships. *Canadian Journal on Aging, 24,* 161–177.

Kempe, Ruth S., & Kempe, C. Henry. (1978). *Child abuse.* Cambridge, MA: Harvard University Press.

Kemper, Susan, & Harden, Tamara. (1999). Experimentally disentangling what's beneficial about elderspeak from what's not. *Psychology & Aging, 14,* 656–670.

Kempner, Joanna, Perlis, Clifford S., & Merz, Jon F. (2005, February 11). Forbidden knowledge. *Science, 307,* 854.

Kendler, Howard H. (2002). Unified knowledge: Fantasy or reality? [Review of the book *Unity of knowledge: The convergence of natural and human science*]. *Contemporary Psychology: APA Review of Books, 47,* 501–503.

Kennedy, Colin R., McCann, Donna C., Campbell, Michael J., Law, Catherine M., Mullee, Mark, Petrou, Stavros, et al. (2006). Language ability after early detection of permanent childhood hearing impairment. *New England Journal of Medicine, 354,* 2131–2141.

Kennedy, Sheela, & Bumpass, Larry. (2008). Cohabitation and children's living arrangements: New estimates from the United States. *Demographic Research, 19,* 1663–1692.

Kensinger, Elizabeth A. (2009). *Emotional memory across the adult lifespan.* New York: Psychology Press.

Kenyon, Brenda L. (2001). Current research in children's conceptions of death: A critical review. *Omega: Journal of Death and Dying, 43,* 63–91.

Keogh, Barbara K. (2004). The importance of longitudinal research for early intervention practices. In Peggy D. McCardle & Vinita Chhabra (Eds.), *The voice of evidence in reading research* (pp. 81–102). Baltimore: Brookes.

Keri, Szabolcs. (2009). Genes for psychosis and creativity: A promoter polymorphism of the neuregulin 1 gene is related to creativity in people with high intellectual achievement. *Psychological Science, 20,* 1070–1073.

Kessler, Ronald C., Aguilar-Gaxiola, Sergio, Alonso, Jordi, Chatterji, Somnath, Lee, Sing, Ormel, Johan, et al. (2009). The global burden of mental disorders: An update from the WHO World Mental Health (WMH) Surveys. *Epidemiologia e Psichiatria Sociale, 18,* 23–33.

Kessler, Ronald C., Galea, Sandro, Jones, Russell T., & Parker, Holly A. (2006). Mental illness and suicidality after Hurricane Katrina. *Bulletin of the World Health Organization, 84,* 930–939.

Kettl, Paul. (2010). One vote for death panels. *Journal of the American Medical Association, 303,* 1234–1235.

Keysers, Christian, & Gazzola, Valeria. (2010). Social neuroscience: Mirror neurons recorded in humans. *Current Biology, 20,* R353–R354.

Khaleque, Abdul, & Rohner, Ronald P. (2002). Perceived parental acceptance-rejection and psychological adjustment: A meta-analysis of cross-cultural and intracultural studies. *Journal of Marriage & the Family, 64,* 54–64.

Khan, Laura Kettel, Sobush, Kathleen, Keener, Dana, Goodman, Kenneth, Lowry, Amy, Kakietek, Jakub, et al. (2009, July 24). Recommended community strategies and measurements to prevent obesity in the United States. *Morbidity and Mortality Weekly Report Recommendations and Reports, 58*(RR07), 1–26.

Khanna, Sunil K. (2010). *Fetal/fatal knowledge: New reproductive technologies and family-building strategies in India.* Belmont, CA: Wadsworth/Cengage Learning.

Khawaja, Marwan, Jurdi, Rozzet, & Kabakian-Khasholian, Tamar. (2004). Rising trends in cesarean section rates in Egypt. *Birth: Issues in Perinatal Care, 31,* 12–16.

Khoury-Kassabri, Mona. (2009). The relationship between staff maltreatment of students and bully-victim group membership. *Child Abuse & Neglect: The International Journal, 33,* 914–923.

Kiang, Lisa, & Harter, Susan. (2008). Do pieces of the self-puzzle fit? Integrated/fragmented selves in biculturally-identified Chinese Americans. *Journal of Research in Personality, 42,* 1657–1662.

Kiang, Lisa, Witkow, Melissa, Baldelomar, Oscar, & Fuligni, Andrew. (2010). Change in ethnic identity across the high school years among adolescents with Latin American, Asian, and European backgrounds. *Journal of Youth and Adolescence, 39,* 683–693.

Kidder, Jeffrey L. (2006). "It's the job that I love": Bike messengers and edgework. *Sociological Forum, 21,* 31–54.

Kiernan, Stephen P. (2010). The transformation of death in America. In Nan Bauer-Maglin & Donna Perry (Eds.), *Final acts: Death, dying and the choices we make* (pp. 163–182). New Brunswick, NJ: Rutgers.

Killen, Melanie. (2007). Children's social and moral reasoning about exclusion. *Current Directions in Psychological Science, 16,* 32–36.

Killen, Melanie, Lee-Kim, Jennie, McGlothlin, Heidi, & Stangor, Charles. (2002). How children and adolescents evaluate gender and racial exclusion. *Monographs of the Society for Research in Child Development, 67*(4, Serial No. 271).

Killen, Melanie, Margie, Nancy Geyelin, & Sinno, Stefanie. (2006). Morality in the context of intergroup relationships. In Melanie Killen & Judith G. Smetana (Eds.), *Handbook of moral development* (pp. 155–183). Mahwah, NJ: Erlbaum.

Killen, Melanie, & Smetana, Judith. (2007). The biology of morality: Human development and moral neuroscience. *Human Development, 50,* 241–243.

Killgore, William D. S., Vo, Alexander H., Castro, Carl A., & Hoge, Charles W. (2006). Assessing risk propensity in American soldiers: Preliminary reliability and validity of the Evaluation of Risks (EVAR) scale-English version. *Military Medicine, 171,* 233–239.

Kilmer, Ryan P., & Gil-Rivas, Virginia. (2010). Exploring posttraumatic growth in children impacted by Hurricane Katrina: Correlates of the phenomenon and developmental considerations. *Child Development, 81,* 1211–1227.

Kim, Dong-Sik, & Kim, Hyun-Sun. (2009). Body-image dissatisfaction as a predictor of suicidal ideation among Korean boys and girls in different stages of adolescence: A two-year longitudinal study. *The Journal of Adolescent Health, 45,* 47–54.

Kim, Esther Chihye. (2009). "Mama's family": Fictive kinship and undocumented immigrant restaurant workers. *Ethnography, 10,* 497–513.

Kim, Geunyoung, Walden, Tedra A., & Knieps, Linda J. (2010). Impact and characteristics of positive and fearful emotional messages during infant social referencing. *Infant Behavior and Development, 33,* 189–195.

Kim, Hyoun K., Capaldi, Deborah M., & Crosby, Lynn. (2007). Generalizability of Gottman and colleagues' affective process models of couples' relationship outcomes. *Journal of Marriage and Family, 69,* 55–72.

Kim, Hyoun K., Laurent, Heidemarie K., Capaldi, Deborah M., & Feingold, Alan. (2008). Men's aggression toward women: A 10-year panel study. *Journal of Marriage and Family, 70,* 1169–1187.

Kim, Stuart K. (2008). Genome-wide views of aging gene networks. In Leonard Guarente, Linda Partridge, & Douglas C. Wallace (Eds.), *Molecular biology of aging* (pp. 215–235). Cold Spring Harbor, NY: Cold Spring Harbor Laboratory Press.

Kim-Cohen, Julia, Moffitt, Terrie E., Caspi, Avshalom, & Taylor, Alan. (2004). Genetic and environmental processes in young children's resilience and vulnerability to socioeconomic deprivation. *Child Development, 75,* 651–668.

King, Alan R., & Terrance, Cheryl. (2006). Relationships between personality disorder attributes and friendship qualities among college students. *Journal of Social and Personal Relationships, 23,* 5–20.

King, Pamela Ebstyne, & Furrow, James L. (2004). Religion as a resource for positive youth development: Religion, social capital, and moral outcomes. *Developmental Psychology, 40,* 703–713.

King, Pamela Ebstyne, & Roeser, Robert W. (2009). Religion and spirituality in adolescent development. In Richard M. Lerner & Laurence Steinberg (Eds.), *Handbook of adolescent psychology: Vol. 1. Individual bases of adolescent development* (3rd ed., pp. 435–478). Hoboken, NJ: John Wiley & Sons.

King, Patricia M., & Kitchener, Karen S. (1994). *Developing reflective judgment: Understanding and promoting intellectual growth and critical thinking in adolescents and adults.* San Francisco: Jossey-Bass.

King, Sara, Waschbusch, Daniel A., Pelham, William E., Frankland, Bradley W., Corkum, Penny V., & Jacques, Sophie. (2009). Subtypes of aggression in children with attention deficit hyperactivity disorder: Medication effects and comparison with typical children. *Journal of Clinical Child and Adolescent Psychology, 38,* 619–629.

King, Valarie. (2003). The legacy of a grandparent's divorce: Consequences for ties between grandparents and grandchildren. *Journal of Marriage and Family, 65,* 170–183.

King, Valarie, & Scott, Mindy E. (2005). A comparison of cohabiting relationships among older and younger adults. *Journal of Marriage and Family, 67,* 271–285.

Kinney, Hannah C., & Thach, Bradley T. (2009). The sudden infant death syndrome. *New England Journal of Medicine, 361,* 795–805.

Kinnunen, Marja-Liisa, Kaprio, Jaakko, & Pulkkinen, Lea. (2005). Allostatic load of men and women in early middle age. *Journal of Individual Differences, 26,* 20–28.

Kinsella, Kevin G. (2005). Future longevity-demographic concerns and consequences. *Journal of the American Geriatrics Society, 53,* S299–S303.

Kirby, Douglas, & Laris, B. A. (2009). Effective curriculum-based sex and STD/HIV education programs for adolescents. *Child Development Perspectives, 3,* 21–29.

Kirkbride, James B., Fearon, Paul, Morgan, Craig, Dazzan, Paola, Morgan, Kevin, Tarrant, Jane, et al. (2006). Heterogeneity in incidence rates of schizophrenia and other psychotic syndromes: Findings from the 3-center AESOP study. *Archives of General Psychiatry, 63,* 250–258.

Kirkorian, Heather L., Pempek, Tiffany A., Murphy, Lauren A., Schmidt, Marie E., & Anderson, Daniel R. (2009). The impact of background television on parent-child interaction. *Child Development, 80,* 1350–1359.

Kitzinger, Sheila. (2001). *Rediscovering birth.* New York: Simon & Schuster.

Klaczynski, Paul, Daniel, David B., & Keller, Peggy S. (2009). Appearance idealization, body esteem, causal attributions, and ethnic variations in the development of obesity stereotypes. *Journal of Applied Developmental Psychology, 30,* 537–551.

Klaczynski, Paul A. (2001). Analytic and heuristic processing influences on adolescent reasoning and decision-making. *Child Development, 72,* 844–861.

Klaczynski, Paul A. (2005). Metacognition and cognitive variability: A dual-process model of decision making and its development. In Janis E. Jacobs & Paul A. Klaczynski (Eds.), *The development of judgment and decision making in children and adolescents* (pp. 39–76). Mahwah, NJ: Erlbaum.

Klaczynski, Paul A., & Robinson, Billi. (2000). Personal theories, intellectual ability, and epistemological beliefs: Adult age differences in everyday reasoning biases. *Psychology and Aging*, 15, 400–416.

Klahr, David, & Nigam, Milena. (2004). The equivalence of learning paths in early science instruction: Effects of direct instruction and discovery learning. *Psychological Science*, 15, 661–667.

Klassen, Terry P., Kiddoo, Darcie, Lang, Mia E., Friesen., Carol, Russell, Kelly, Spooner, Carol, et al. (2006). *The effectiveness of different methods of toilet training for bowel and bladder control* (AHRQ Publication No. 07-E003). Rockville, MD: Agency for Healthcare Research and Quality.

Klatsky, Arthur L. (2009). Alcohol and cardiovascular diseases. *Expert Review of Cardiovascular Therapy*, 7, 499–506.

Klaus, Marshall H., & Kennell, John H. (1976). *Maternal-infant bonding: The impact of early separation or loss on family development*. St. Louis, MO: Mosby.

Klaus, Patsy. (2005). *Crimes against persons age 65 or older, 1993–2002* (NCJ 206154). Washington, DC: Bureau of Justice Statistics.

Kleiber, Douglas A. (1999). *Leisure experience and human development: A dialectical interpretation*. New York: Basic Books.

Klimke, Martin A., & Scharloth, Joachim. (2008). *1968 in Europe: A history of protest and activism, 1956–1977*. New York: Palgrave Macmillan.

Kline, Kathleen Kovner. (2008). *Authoritative communities: The scientific case for nurturing the whole child*. New York: Springer.

Klöppel, Stefan, Vongerichten, Anna, Eimeren, Thilo van, Frackowiak, Richard S. J., & Siebner, Hartwig R. (2007). Can left-handedness be switched? Insights from an early switch of handwriting. *Journal of Neuroscience*, 27, 7847–7853.

Klug, William, Cummings, Michael, Spencer, Charlotte, & Palladino, Michael. (2008). *Concepts of genetics* (9th ed.). San Francisco: Pearson/Benjamin Cummings.

Koch, Tom. (2000). *Age speaks for itself: Silent voices of the elderly*. Westport, CT: Praeger.

Kochanska, Grazyna, Aksan, Nazan, Prisco, Theresa R., & Adams, Erin E. (2008). Mother-child and father-child mutually responsive orientation in the first 2 years and children's outcomes at preschool age: Mechanisms of influence. *Child Development*, 79, 30–44.

Kochanska, Grazyna, Gross, Jami N., Lin, Mei-Hua, & Nichols, Kate E. (2002). Guilt in young children: Development, determinants, and relations with a broader system of standards. *Child Development*, 73, 461–482.

Kogan, Michael D., Blumberg, Stephen J., Schieve, Laura A., Boyle, Coleen A., Perrin, James M., Ghandour, Reem M., et al. (2009, October 5). *Prevalence of parent-reported diagnosis of autism spectrum disorder among children in the US, 2007*. Retrieved December 21, 2010, from the World Wide Web: http://pediatrics.aappublications.org/cgi/content/abstract/peds.2009-1522v1

Kogan, Shari L., Blanchette, Patricia L., & Masaki, Kamal. (2000). Talking to patients about death and dying: Improving communication across cultures. In Kathryn Braun, James H. Pietsch, & Patricia L. Blanchette (Eds.), *Cultural issues in end-of-life decision making* (pp. 305–325). Thousand Oaks, CA: Sage.

Kohl, Patricia L., Jonson-Reid, Melissa, & Drake, Brett. (2009). Time to leave substantiation behind. *Child Maltreatment*, 14, 17–26.

Kohlberg, Lawrence. (1963). The development of children's orientations toward a moral order: I. Sequence in the development of moral thought. *Vita Humana*, 6, 11–33.

Kohlberg, Lawrence, Levine, Charles, & Hewer, Alexandra. (1983). *Moral stages: A current formulation and a response to critics*. New York: Karger.

Kohler, Julie K., Grotevant, Harold D., & McRoy, Ruth G. (2002). Adopted adolescents' preoccupation with adoption: The impact on adoptive family relationships. *Journal of Marriage & Family*, 64, 93–104.

Koivisto, Maila. (2004). A follow-up survey of anti-bullying interventions in the comprehensive schools of Kempele in 1990–98. In Peter K. Smith, Debra Pepler, & Ken Rigby (Eds.), *Bullying in schools: How successful can interventions be?* (pp. 235–249). New York: Cambridge University Press.

Kolb, Bryan, & Whishaw, Ian Q. (2008). *Fundamentals of human neuropsychology* (6th ed.). New York: Worth.

Kolling, Thorsten, Goertz, Claudia, Frahsek, Stefanie, & Knopf, Monika. (2009). Stability of deferred imitation in 12- to 18-month-old infants: A closer look into developmental dynamics. *European Journal of Developmental Psychology*, 6, 615–640.

Koltko-Rivera, Mark E. (2006). Rediscovering the later version of Maslow's hierarchy of needs: Self-transcendence and opportunities for theory, research, and unification. *Review of General Psychology*, 10, 302–317.

Komives, Susan R., & Nuss, Elizabeth M. (2005). Life after college. In Thomas E. Miller, Barbara E. Bender, & John H. Schuh (Eds.), *Promoting reasonable expectations: Aligning student and institutional views of the college experience* (pp. 140–174). San Francisco: Jossey-Bass.

Konner, Melvin. (2007). Evolutionary foundations of cultural psychology. In Shinobu Kitayama & Dov Cohen (Eds.), *Handbook of cultural psychology* (pp. 77–105). New York: Guilford Press.

Koops, Willem. (2003). Imaging childhood. In Willem Koops & Michael Zuckerman (Eds.), *Beyond the century of the child: Cultural history and developmental psychology* (pp. 1–18). Philadelphia: University of Pennsylvania Press.

Koretz, Daniel. (2009). Moving past No Child Left Behind. *Science*, 326, 803–804.

Kornblum, Janet. (2008, July 15). Cyberbullying grows bigger and meaner with photos, video. *USA Today*.

Kotre, John N. (1995). *White gloves: How we create ourselves through memory*. New York: Free Press.

Kovacs, Maria, Joormann, Jutta, & Gotlib, Ian H. (2008). Emotion (dys)regulation and links to depressive disorders. *Child Development Perspectives*, 2, 149–155.

Kovas, Yulia, Hayiou-Thomas, Marianna E., Oliver, Bonamy, Dale, Philip S., Bishop, Dorothy V. M., & Plomin, Robert. (2005). Genetic influences in different aspects of language development: The etiology of language skills in 4.5-year-old twins. *Child Development*, 76, 632–651.

Kramer, Arthur F., & Erickson, Kirk I. (2007). Capitalizing on cortical plasticity: Influence of physical activity on cognition and brain function. *Trends in Cognitive Sciences*, 11, 342–348.

Kramer, Arthur F., Fabiani, Monica, & Colcombe, Stanley J. (2006). Contributions of cognitive neuroscience to the understanding of behavior and aging. In James E. Birren & K. Warner Schaie (Eds.), *Handbook of the psychology of aging* (6th ed., pp. 57–83). Amsterdam: Elsevier.

Krampe, Ralf Th., & Charness, Neil. (2006). Aging and expertise. In K. Anders Ericsson, Neil Charness, Paul J. Feltovich, & Robert R. Hoffman (Eds.), *The Cambridge handbook of expertise and expert performance* (pp. 723–742). New York: Cambridge University Press.

Krause, Neal. (2006). Social relationships in late life. In Robert H. Binstock & Linda K. George (Eds.), *Handbook of aging and the social sciences* (6th ed., pp. 181–200). Amsterdam: Elsevier.

Krebs, Dennis L. (2008). Morality: An evolutionary account. *Perspectives on Psychological Science*, 3, 149–172.

Krebs, John R. (2009). The gourmet ape: Evolution and human food preferences. *American Journal of Clinical Nutrition*, 90, 707S-711S.

Krentz, Ursula C., & Corina, David P. (2008). Preference for language in early infancy: The human language bias is not speech specific. *Developmental Science*, 11, 1–9.

Krieger, Nancy. (2002). Is breast cancer a disease of affluence, poverty, or both? The case of African American women. *American Journal of Public Health*, 92, 611–613.

Krieger, Nancy. (2003). Does racism harm health? Did child abuse exist before 1962? On explicit questions, critical science, and current controversies: An ecosocial perspective. *American Journal of Public Health*, 93, 194–199.

Kröger, Edeltraut, Andel, Ross, Lindsay, Joan, Benounissa, Zohra, Verreault, René, & Laurin, Danielle. (2008). Is complexity of work associated with risk of dementia? The Canadian Study of Health and Aging. *American Journal of Epidemiology*, 167, 820–830.

Kroger, Jane. (2007). *Identity development: Adolescence through adulthood* (2nd ed.). Thousand Oaks, CA: Sage.

Kroger, Jane, Martinussen, Monica, & Marcia, James E. (2010). Identity status change during adolescence and young adulthood: A meta-analysis. *Journal of Adolescence*, 33, 683–698.

Kronenberg, Mindy E., Hansell, Tonya Cross, Brennan, Adrianne M., Osofsky, Howard J., Osofsky, Joy D., & Lawrason,

Beverly. (2010). Children of Katrina: Lessons learned about postdisaster symptoms and recovery patterns. *Child Development, 81,* 1241–1259.

Kruk, Margaret E., Prescott, Marta R., & Galea, Sandro. (2008). Equity of skilled birth attendant utilization in developing countries: Financing and policy determinants. *American Journal of Public Health, 98,* 142–147.

Kryzer, Erin M., Kovan, Nikki, Phillips, Deborah A., Domagall, Lindsey A., & Gunnar, Megan R. (2007). Toddlers' and preschoolers' experience in family day care: Age differences and behavioral correlates. *Early Childhood Research Quarterly, 22,* 451–466.

Kübler-Ross, Elisabeth. (1969). *On death and dying.* New York: Macmillan.

Kübler-Ross, Elisabeth. (1975). Death: The final stage of growth. xxii, 175.

Kuh, George D., Gonyea, Robert M., & Williams, Julie M. (2005). What students expect from college and what they get. In Thomas E. Miller, Barbara E. Bender, John H. Schuh, & Associates (Eds.), *Promoting reasonable expectations: Aligning student and institutional views of the college experience* (pp. 34–64). San Francisco: Jossey-Bass.

Kuhlmann, Inga, Minihane, Anne, Huebbe, Patricia, Nebel, Almut, & Rimbach, Gerald. (2010). Apolipoprotein E genotype and hepatitis C, HIV and herpes simplex disease risk: A literature review. *Lipids in Health and Disease, 9,* 8.

Kuhn, Deanna. (2009). The importance of learning about knowing: Creating a foundation for development of intellectual values. *Child Development Perspectives, 3,* 112–117.

Kuhn, Deanna, & Franklin, Sam. (2006). The second decade: What develops (and how). In William Damon & Richard M. Lerner (Series Eds.) & Deanna Kuhn & Robert Siegler (Vol. Eds.), *Handbook of child psychology: Vol. 2. Cognition, perception, and language* (6th ed., pp. 953–993). Hoboken, NJ: Wiley.

Kuhn, Louise, Reitz, Cordula, & Abrams, Elaine J. (2009). Breastfeeding and AIDS in the developing world. *Current Opinion in Pediatrics, 21,* 83–93.

Kulkofsky, Sarah, & Klemfuss, J. Zoe. (2008). What the stories children tell can tell about their memory: Narrative skill and young children's suggestibility. *Developmental Psychology, 44,* 1442–1456.

Kun, Jürgen F. J., May, Jürgen, & Noedl, Harald. (2010). Surveillance of malaria drug resistance: Improvement needed? *Future Medicine, 7,* 3–6.

Kuo, Hsu-Ko, Leveille, Suzanne G., Yu, Yau-Hua, & Milber, William P. (2007). Cognitive function, habitual gait speed, and late-life disability in the National Health and Nutrition Examination Survey (NHANES) 1999–2002. *Gerontology, 53,* 102–110.

Kupersmidt, Janis B., Coie, John D., & Howell, James C. (2004). Resilience in children exposed to negative peer influences. In Kenneth I. Maton, Cynthia J. Schellenbach, Bonnie J. Leadbeater, & Andrea L. Solarz (Eds.), *Investing in children, youth, families, and communities: Strengths-based research and policy* (pp. 251–268). Washington, DC: American Psychological Association.

Kuppens, Sofie, Grietens, Hans, Onghena, Patrick, & Michiels, Daisy. (2009). Associations between parental control and children's overt and relational aggression. *British Journal of Developmental Psychology, 27,* 607–623.

Kurdek, Lawrence A. (2006). Differences between partners from heterosexual, gay, and lesbian cohabiting couples. *Journal of Marriage and Family, 68,* 509–528.

Kutob, Randa M., Senf, Janet H., Crago, Marjorie, & Shisslak, Catherine M. (2010). Concurrent and longitudinal predictors of self-esteem in elementary and middle school girls. *Journal of School Health, 80,* 240–248.

Kvavilashvili, Lia, Mirani, Jennifer, Schlagman, Simone, Erskine, James A. K., & Kornbrot, Diana E. (2010). Effects of age on phenomenology and consistency of flashbulb memories of September 11 and a staged control event. *Psychology and Aging, 25,* 391–404.

Kwok, Sylvia Y. C. Lai, & Shek, Daniel T. L. (2010). Hopelessness, parent-adolescent communication, and suicidal ideation among Chinese adolescents in Hong Kong. *Suicide and Life-Threatening Behavior, 40,* 224–233.

LaBar, Kevin S. (2007). Beyond fear: Emotional memory mechanisms in the human brain. *Current Directions in Psychological Science, 16,* 173–177.

Labouvie-Vief, Gisela. (1990). Wisdom as integrated thought: Historical and developmental perspectives. In Robert J. Sternberg (Ed.), *Wisdom: Its nature, origins, and development* (pp. 52–83). Cambridge, England: Cambridge University Press.

Labouvie-Vief, Gisela. (2006). Emerging structures of adult thought. In Jeffrey Jensen Arnett & Jennifer Lynn Tanner (Eds.), *Emerging adults in America: Coming of age in the 21st century* (pp. 59–84). Washington, DC: American Psychological Association.

Labouvie-Vief, Gisela, Grühn, Daniel, & Mouras, Harold. (2009). Dynamic emotion-cognition interactions in adult development: Arousal, stress, and the processing of affect. In Hayden B. Bosworth & Christopher Hertzog (Eds.), *Aging and cognition: Research methodologies and empirical advances* (pp. 181–196). Washington, DC: American Psychological Association.

Lachman, Margie E., & Bertrand, Rosanna M. (2001). Personality and the self in midlife. In Margie E. Lachman (Ed.), *Handbook of midlife development* (pp. 279–309). New York: Wiley.

Lachman, Margie E., Rosnick, Christopher B., & Röcke, Christina. (2009). The rise and fall of control beliefs and life satisfaction in adulthood: Trajectories of stability and change over ten years. In Hayden B. Bosworth & Christopher Hertzog (Eds.), *Aging and cognition: Research methodologies and empirical advances* (pp. 143–160). Washington, DC: American Psychological Association.

Ladd, Gary W. (2005). *Children's peer relations and social competence: A century of progress.* New Haven, CT: Yale University Press.

Lahdenperä, Mirkka, Lummaa, Virpi, Helle, Samuli, Tremblay, Marc, & Russell, Andrew F. (2004). Fitness benefits of prolonged post-reproductive lifespan in women. *Nature, 428,* 178–181.

Laible, Deborah, Panfile, Tia, & Makariev, Drika. (2008). The quality and frequency of mother-toddler conflict: Links with attachment and temperament. *Child Development, 79,* 426–443.

Lalande, Kathleen M., & Bonanno, George A. (2006). Culture and continuing bonds: A prospective comparison of bereavement in the United States and the People's Republic of China. *Death Studies, 30,* 303–324.

Lamb, Michael E. (1982). Maternal employment and child development: A review. In Michael E. Lamb (Ed.), *Nontraditional families: Parenting and child development* (pp. 45–69). Hillsdale, NJ: Erlbaum.

Lamb, Michael E. (Ed.). (2010). *The role of the father in child development* (5th ed.). Hoboken, NJ: Wiley.

Lamb, Michael E., & Lewis, Charlie (2005). The role of parent-child relationships in child development. In Marc H. Bornstein & Michael E. Lamb (Eds.), *Developmental science: An advanced textbook* (5th ed., pp. 429–468). Mahwah, NJ: Erlbaum.

Lambert, Nathaniel M., Fincham, Frank D., Stillman, Tyler F., Graham, Steven M., & Beach, Steven R.H. (2010). Motivating change in relationships. *Psychological Science, 21,* 126–132.

Lamm, Bettina, Keller, Heidi, Yovsi, Relindis D., & Chaudhary, Nandita. (2008). Grandmaternal and maternal ethnotheories about early child care. *Journal of Family Psychology, 22,* 80–88.

Lampinen, Päivi, Heikkinen, Riitta-Liisa, Kauppinen, Markku, & Heikkinen, Eino. (2006). Activity as a predictor of mental well-being among older adults. *Aging & Mental Health, 10,* 454–466.

Landry, David J., Darroch, Jacqueline E., Singh, Susheela, & Higgins, Jenny. (2003). Factors associated with the content of sex education in U.S. public secondary schools. *Perspectives on Sexual and Reproductive Health, 35,* 261–269.

Landy, Frank J., & Conte, Jeffrey M. (2007). *Work in the 21st century: An introduction to industrial and organizational psychology* (2nd ed.). Malden, MA: Blackwell.

Lane, Scott D., Cherek, Don R., Pietras, Cynthia J., & Steinberg, Joel L. (2005). Performance of heavy marijuana-smoking adolescents on a laboratory measure of motivation. *Addictive Behaviors, 30,* 815–828.

Lang, Frieder R., Wagner, Jenny, & Neyer, Franz J. (2009). Interpersonal functioning across the lifespan: Two principles of relationship regulation. *Advances in Life Course Research, 14,* 40–51.

Langhinrichsen-Rohling, Jennifer. (2010). Controversies involving gender and intimate partner violence: Response to commentators. *Sex Roles, 62,* 221–225.

Långström, Niklas, Rahman, Qazi, Carlström, Eva, & Lichtenstein, Paul. (2010).

Genetic and environmental effects on same-sex sexual behavior: A population study of twins in Sweden. *Archives of Sexual Behavior, 39,* 75–80.

Lapsley, Daniel K. (1993). Toward an integrated theory of adolescent ego development: The "new look" at adolescent egocentrism. *American Journal of Orthopsychiatry, 63,* 562–571.

Lara, Marielena, Akinbami, Lara, Flores, Glenn, & Morgenstern, Hal. (2006). Heterogeneity of childhood asthma among Hispanic children: Puerto Rican children bear a disproportionate burden. *Pediatrics, 117,* 43–53.

Laraway, Kelly A., Birch, Leann L., Shaffer, Michele L., & Paul, Ian M. (2010). Parent perception of healthy infant and toddler growth. *Clinical Pediatrics, 49,* 343–349.

Larson, Nicole I., Neumark-Sztainer, Dianne, Hannan, Peter J., & Story, Mary. (2007). Trends in adolescent fruit and vegetable consumption, 1999–2004: Project EAT. *American Journal of Preventive Medicine, 32,* 147–150.

Larson, Reed, & Wilson, Suzanne. (2004). Adolescence across place and time: Globalization and the changing pathways to adulthood. In Richard M. Lerner & Laurence D. Steinberg (Eds.), *Handbook of adolescent psychology* (2nd ed., pp. 299–330). Hoboken, NJ: Wiley.

Larzelere, Robert E., & Kuhn, Brett R. (2005). Comparing child outcomes of physical punishment and alternative disciplinary tactics: A meta-analysis. *Clinical Child and Family Psychology Review, 8,* 1–37.

Laska, Melissa Nelson, Larson, Nicole I., Neumark-Sztainer, Dianne, & Story, Mary. (2010). Dietary patterns and home food availability during emerging adulthood: Do they differ by living situation? *Public Health Nutrition, 13,* 222–228.

Laumann, Edward O., Gagnon, John H., Michael, Robert T., & Michaels, Stuart. (1994). *The social organization of sexuality: Sexual practices in the United States.* Chicago: University of Chicago Press.

Laumann, Edward O., & Michael, Robert T. (2000). *Sex, love, and health in America: Private choices and public policies.* Chicago: University of Chicago Press.

Laumann, Edward O., & Michael, Robert T. (2001). Setting the scene. In Edward O. Laumann & Robert T. Michael (Eds.), *Sex, love, and health in America: Private choices and public policies* (pp. 1–38). Chicago: University of Chicago Press.

Laurendeau, Jason, & Van Brunschot, Erin E. Gibbs (2006). Policing the edge: Risk and social control in skydiving. *Deviant Behavior, 27,* 173–201.

Laursen, Brett, Bukowski, William M., Nurmi, Jari-Eri, Marion, Donna, Salmela-Aro, Katariina, & Kiuru, Noona. (2010). Opposites detract: Middle school peer group antipathies. *Journal of Experimental Child Psychology, 106,* 240–256.

Laursen, Brett, & Collins, W. Andrew. (2009). Parent-child relationships during adolescence. In Richard M. Lerner & Laurence Steinberg (Eds.), *Handbook of adolescent psychology: Vol. 2. Contextual influences on adolescent development* (3rd ed., pp. 3–42). Hoboken, NJ: John Wiley & Sons.

Laursen, Brett, & Mooney, Karen S. (2007). Individual differences in adolescent dating and adjustment. In Rutger C. M. E. Engels, Margaret Kerr, & Håkan Stattin (Eds.), *Friends, lovers, and groups: Key relationships in adolescence* (pp. 81–92). Hoboken, NJ: Wiley.

Lauster, Nathanael T. (2008). Better homes and families: Housing markets and young couple stability in Sweden. *Journal of Marriage and Family, 70,* 891–903.

Lavelli, Manuela, & Fogel, Alan. (2005). Developmental changes in the relationship between the infant's attention and emotion during early face-to-face communication: The 2-month transition. *Developmental Psychology, 41,* 265–280.

Layden, Tim. (2004, November 15). Get out and play! *Sports Illustrated, 101,* 80–93.

Leach, Mark. (2008–2009). America's older immigrants: A profile. *Generations, 32*(4), 34–39.

Leach, Penelope. (1997). *Your baby & child: From birth to age five* (3rd ed.). New York: Knopf.

Leach, Penelope. (2009). *Child care today: Getting it right for everyone.* New York: Knopf.

Leadbeater, Bonnie J., & Hoglund, Wendy L. G. (2009). The effects of peer victimization and physical aggression on changes in internalizing from first to third grade. *Child Development, 80,* 843–859.

Leather, Nicola C. (2009). Risk-taking behaviour in adolescence: A literature review. *Journal of Child Health Care, 13,* 295–304.

LeBlanc, Manon Mireille, & Barling, Julian. (2004). Workplace aggression. *Current Directions in Psychological Science, 13,* 9–12.

Lee, Christine M., Geisner, Irene M., Patrick, Megan E., & Neighbors, Clayton. (2010). The social norms of alcohol-related negative consequences. *Psychology of Addictive Behaviors, 24,* 342–348.

Lee, Hoyee Flora, Gorsuch, Richard L., Saklofske, Donald H., & Patterson, Colleen A. (2008). Cognitive differences for ages 16 to 89 years (Canadian WAIS-III): Curvilinear with Flynn and Processing Speed corrections. *Journal of Psychoeducational Assessment, 26,* 382–394.

Lee, I-Min, Ewing, Reid, & Sesso, Howard D. (2009). The built environment and physical activity levels: The Harvard Alumni Health Study. *American Journal of Preventive Medicine, 37,* 293–298.

Lee, Jennifer, & Bean, Frank D. (2007). Reinventing the color line: Immigration and America's new racial/ethnic divide. *Social Forces, 86,* 561–586.

Lee, Joyce M., Kaciroti, Niko, Appugliese, Danielle, Corwyn, Robert F., Bradley, Robert H., & Lumeng, Julie C. (2010). Body mass index and timing of pubertal initiation in boys. *Archives of Pediatric and Adolescent Medicine, 164,* 139–144.

Leerkes, Esther M., Blankson, A. Nayena, & O'Brien, Marion. (2009). Differential effects of maternal sensitivity to infant distress and nondistress on social-emotional functioning. *Child Development, 80,* 762–775.

Lefkowitz, Eva S., & Gillen, Meghan M. (2006). "Sex is just a normal part of life": Sexuality in emerging adulthood. In Jeffrey Jensen Arnett & Jennifer Lynn Tanner (Eds.), *Emerging adults in America: Coming of age in the 21st century* (pp. 235–255). Washington, DC: American Psychological Association.

Lehmann, Martin, & Hasselhorn, Marcus. (2010). The dynamics of free recall and their relation to rehearsal between 8 and 10 years of age. *Child Development, 81,* 1006–1020.

Lehmann, Wolfgang. (2004). "For some reason, I get a little scared": Structure, agency, and risk in school-work transitions. *Journal of Youth Studies, 7,* 379–396.

Lei, Joy L. (2003). (Un)necessary toughness?: Those "loud black girls" and those "quiet Asian boys." *Anthropology & Education Quarterly, 34,* 158–181.

Leipzig, Rosanne M. (2003). Evidence-based medicine and geriatrics. In Christine K. Cassel, Rosanne Leipzig, Harvey Jay Cohen, Eric B. Larson, & Diane E. Meier (Eds.), *Geriatric medicine: An evidence-based approach* (4th ed., pp. 3–14). New York: Springer.

Leman, Patrick J., & Björnberg, Marina. (2010). Conversation, development, and gender: A study of changes in children's concepts of punishment. *Child Development, 81,* 958–971.

Lenneberg, Eric H. (1967). *Biological foundations of language.* New York: Wiley.

Lenroot, Rhoshel K., & Giedd, Jay N. (2008). The changing impact of genes and environment on brain development during childhood and adolescence: Initial findings from a neuroimaging study of pediatric twins. *Development and Psychopathology, 20,* 1161–1175.

Lenton, Alison, & Webber, Laura. (2006). Cross-sex friendships: Who has more? *Sex Roles, 54,* 809–820.

Leon, David A., Saburova, Ludmila, Tomkins, Susannah, Andreev, Evgueni M., Kiryanov, Nikolay, McKee, Martin, et al. (2007, June 16). Hazardous alcohol drinking and premature mortality in Russia: A population based case-control study. *Lancet, 369,* 2001–2009.

Leonard, Christiana M. (2003). Neural substrate of speech and language development. In Michelle De Haan & Mark H. Johnson (Eds.), *The cognitive neuroscience of development* (pp. 127–156). New York: Psychology Press.

Lepper, Mark R., Greene, David, & Nisbett, Richard E. (1973). Undermining children's intrinsic interest with extrinsic reward: A test of the "overjustification" hypothesis. *Journal of Personality & Social Psychology, 28,* 129–137.

Lerner, Claire, & Dombro, Amy Laura. (2004). Finding your fit: Some temperament tips for parents. *Zero to Three, 24,* 42–45.

Lerner, Richard M., & Steinberg, Laurence D. (2009). *Handbook of adolescent psychology* (3rd ed.). Hoboken, NJ: John Wiley & Sons.

Leung, Angel Nga-Man, Wong, Stephanie Siu-fong, Wong, Iris Wai-yin, & McBride-Chang, Catherine. (2010). Filial piety and psychosocial adjustment in Hong Kong Chinese early adolescents. *The Journal of Early Adolescence, 30,* 651–667.

Levinson, Daniel J. (1978). *The seasons of a man's life.* New York: Knopf.

Levy, Becca. (2009). Stereotype embodiment: A psychosocial approach to aging. *Current Directions in Psychological Science, 18,* 332–336.

Levy, Becca, & Langer, Ellen. (1994). Aging free from negative stereotypes: Successful memory in China among the American deaf. *Journal of Personality & Social Psychology, 66,* 989–997.

Lewin, Kurt. (1943). Psychology and the process of group living. *Journal of Social Psychology, 17,* 113–131.

Lewin-Benham, Ann. (2008). *Powerful children: Understanding how to teach and learn using the Reggio approach.* New York: Teachers College Press.

Lewis, Hunter. (2000). *A question of values: Six ways we make personal choices that shape our lives* (Rev. and updated ed.). Crozet, VA: Axios Press.

Lewis, Lawrence B., Antone, Carol, & Johnson, Jacqueline S. (1999). Effects of prosodic stress and serial position on syllable omission in first words. *Developmental Psychology, 35,* 45–59.

Lewis, Michael, & Brooks, Jeanne. (1978). Self-knowledge and emotional development. In Michael Lewis & L. A. Rosenblum (Eds.), *Genesis of behavior: Vol. 1. The development of affect* (pp. 205–226). New York: Plenum Press.

Lewis, Michael, & Ramsay, Douglas. (2005). Infant emotional and cortisol responses to goal blockage. *Child Development, 76,* 518–530.

Lewkowicz, David J. (2010). Infant perception of audio-visual speech synchrony. *Developmental Psychology, 46,* 66–77.

Li, Zhaoping, Maglione, Margaret, Tu, Wenli, Mojica, Walter, Arterburn, David, Shugarman, Lisa R., et al. (2005). Meta-analysis: Pharmacologic treatment of obesity. *Annals of Internal Medicine, 142,* 532–546.

Libertus, Melissa E., & Brannon, Elizabeth M. (2009). Behavioral and neural basis of number sense in infancy. *Current Directions in Psychological Science, 18,* 346–351.

Lieberman, Debra. (2006). Mate selection: Adaptive problems and evolved cognitive programs. In Patricia Noller & Judith A. Feeney (Eds.), *Close relationships: Functions, forms and processes* (pp. 245–266). Hove, England: Psychology Press/ Taylor & Francis.

Lieu, Tracy A., Ray, G. Thomas, Black, Steven B., Butler, Jay C., Klein, Jerome O., Breiman, Robert F., et al. (2000). Projected cost-effectiveness of pneumococcal conjugate vaccination of healthy infants and young children. *Journal of the American Medical Association, 283,* 1460–1468.

Lillard, Angeline, & Else-Quest, Nicole. (2006, September 29). Evaluating Montessori education. *Science, 313,* 1893–1894.

Lillard, Angeline Stoll. (2005). *Montessori: The science behind the genius.* New York: Oxford University Press.

Lim, Boo Yeun. (2004). The magic of the brush and the power of color: Integrating theory into practice of painting in early childhood settings. *Early Childhood Education Journal, 32,* 113–119.

Lin, I-Fen. (2008a). Consequences of parental divorce for adult children's support of their frail parents. *Journal of Marriage and Family, 70,* 113–128.

Lin, I-Fen. (2008b). Mother and daughter reports about upward transfers. *Journal of Marriage and Family, 70,* 815–827.

Lincove, Jane A., & Painter, Gary (2006). Does the age that children start kindergarten matter? Evidence of long-term educational and social outcomes. *Educational Evaluation And Policy Analysis, 28,* 153–179

Lindau, Stacy Tessler, & Gavrilova, Natalia. (2010). Sex, health, and years of sexually active life gained due to good health: Evidence from two US population based cross sectional surveys of ageing. *British Medical Journal, 340,* c810.

Lindauer, Martin S. (2003). *Aging, creativity, and art: A positive perspective on late-life development.* New York: Plenum.

Lindenberger, Ulman, & Ghisletta, Paolo. (2009). Cognitive and sensory declines in old age: Gauging the evidence for a common cause. *Psychology and Aging, 24,* 1–16.

Lindfors, Kaj, Elovainio, Marko, Wickman, Sanna, Vuorinen, Risto, Sinkkonen, Jari, Dunkel, Leo, et al. (2007). Brief report: The role of ego development in psychosocial adjustment among boys with delayed puberty. *Journal of Research on Adolescence, 17,* 601–612.

Linn, Susan, & Novosat, Courtney L. (2008). Calories for sale: Food marketing to children in the twenty-first century. *Annals of the American Academy of Political and Social Science, 615,* 133–155.

Lip, Gregory Y. H., Beevers, Gareth, & Zarifis, John. (1995). Hormone replacement therapy and cardiovascular risk: The cardiovascular physicians' viewpoint. *Journal of Internal Medicine, 238,* 389–399.

Lipkin, Nicole A., & Perrymore, April J. (2009). *Y in the workplace: Managing the "Me First" generation.* Franklin Lakes, NJ: The Career Press.

Lipton, Jennifer S., & Spelke, Elizabeth S. (2003). Origins of number sense: Large-number discrimination in human infants. *Psychological Science, 14,* 396–401.

Liszkowski, Ulf, Schäfer, Marie, Carpenter, Malinda, & Tomasello, Michael. (2009). Prelinguistic infants, but not chimpanzees, communicate about absent entities. *Psychological Science, 20*(5), 654–660.

Little, Peter (Ed.). (2002). *Genetic destinies.* Oxford, England: Oxford University Press.

Liu, Cong, Spector, Paul E., & Shi, Lin. (2007). Cross-national job stress: A quantitative and qualitative study. *Journal of Organizational Behavior, 28,* 209–239.

Liu, David, Sabbagh, Mark A., Gehring, William J., & Wellman, Henry M. (2009). Neural correlates of childrens theory of mind development. *Child Development, 80,* 318–326.

Liu, David, Wellman, Henry M., Tardif, Twila, & Sabbagh, Mark A. (2008). Theory of mind development in Chinese children: A meta-analysis of false-belief understanding across cultures and languages. *Developmental Psychology, 44,* 523–531.

Livas-Dlott, Alejandra, Fuller, Bruce, Stein, Gabriela L., Bridges, Margaret, Mangual Figueroa, Ariana, & Mireles, Laurie. (2010). Commands, competence, and *cariño*: Maternal socialization practices in Mexican American families. *Developmental Psychology, 46,* 566–578.

Lleras-Muney, Adriana. (2005). The relationship between education and adult mortality in the United States. *Review of Economic Studies, 72,* 189–221.

Lloyd-Fox, Sarah, Blasi, Anna, Volein, Agnes, Everdell, Nick, Elwell, Claire E., & Johnson, Mark H. (2009). Social perception in infancy: A near infrared spectroscopy study. *Child Development, 80,* 986–999.

Lobstein, Tim, & Dibb, Sue. (2005). Evidence of a possible link between obesogenic food advertising and child overweight. *Obesity Reviews, 6,* 203–208.

Löckenhoff, Corinna E., De Fruyt, Filip, Terracciano, Antonio, McCrae, Robert R., De Bolle, Marleen, Costa, Paul T., Jr., et al. (2009). Perceptions of aging across 26 cultures and their culture-level associates. *Psychology and Aging, 24,* 941–954.

Lockhart, Kristi L., Chang, Bernard, & Story, Tyler. (2002). Young children's beliefs about the stability of traits: Protective optimism? *Child Development, 73,* 1408–1430.

Loe, Irene M., & Feldman, Heidi M. (2007). Academic and educational outcomes of children with ADHD. *Journal of Pediatric Psychology, 32,* 643–654.

Loeb, Susanna, Bridges, Margaret, Bassok, Daphna, Fuller, Bruce, & Rumberger, Russell. (2005). *How much is too much? The influence of preschool centers on children's social and cognitive development.* Retrieved December 23, 2010 from the World Wide Web: http://ideas.repec.org/p/nbr/nberwo/11812.html.

Löfmark, Rurik, Nilstun, Tore, Cartwright, Colleen, Fischer, Susanne, van der Heide, Agnes, Mortier, Freddy, et al. (2008, February 12). *Physicians' experiences with end-of-life decision-making: Survey in 6 European countries and*

Australia. Retrieved December 18, 2010, from the World Wide Web: http://www.biomedcentral.com/1741–7015/6/4

Loftus, Elizabeth F., Doyle, James M., & Dysart, Jennifer E. (2007). *Eyewitness testimony: Civil and criminal* (4th ed.). Charlottesville, VA: LexisNexis.

Loland, Sigmund. (2002). *Fair play in sport: A moral norm system*. London: Routledge.

Longmore, Monica, Eng, Abbey, Giordano, Peggy , & Manning, Wendy. (2009). Parenting and adolescents' sexual initiation. *Journal of Marriage and Family, 71,* 969–982.

Losin, Elizabeth A. Reynolds, Dapretto, Mirella, & Iacoboni, Marco. (2009). Culture in the mind's mirror: How anthropology and neuroscience can inform a model of the neural substrate for cultural imitative learning. *Progress in Brain Research, 178,* 175–190.

Lovecky, Deirdre V. (2009). Moral sensitivity in young gifted children. In Tracy Cross & Don Ambrose (Eds.), *Morality, ethics, and gifted minds* (pp. 1–16). New York: Springer.

Lu, Luo. (2005). In pursuit of happiness: The cultural psychological study of SWB. *Chinese Journal of Psychology, 47,* 99–112.

Lucas, Richard E., Clark, Andrew E., Georgellis, Yannis, & Diener, Ed. (2003). Reexamining adaptation and the set point model of happiness: Reactions to changes in marital status. *Journal of Personality and Social Psychology, 84,* 527–539.

Lucast, Erica K. (2007). Informed consent and the misattributed paternity problem in genetic counseling. *Bioethics, 21,* 41–50.

Luna, Beatriz, Padmanabhan, Aarthi, & O'Hearn, Kirsten. (2010). What has fMRI told us about the development of cognitive control through adolescence? *Brain and Cognition, 72,* 101–113.

Lustig, Cindy, Shah, Priti, Seidler, Rachael, & Reuter-Lorenz, Patricia A. (2009). Aging, training, and the brain: A review and future directions. *Neuropsychology Review, 19,* 504–522.

Luthar, Suniya S., Cicchetti, Dante, & Becker, Bronwyn. (2000). The construct of resilience: A critical evaluation and guidelines for future work. *Child Development, 71,* 543–562.

Luthar, Suniya S., D'Avanzo, Karen, & Hites, Sarah. (2003). Maternal drug abuse versus other psychological disturbances: Risks and resilience among children. In Suniya S. Luthar (Ed.), *Resilience and vulnerability: Adaptation in the context of childhood adversities* (pp. 104–129). New York: Cambridge University Press.

Luthringer, Remy, Muzet, Muriel, Zisapel, Nava, & Staner, Luc. (2009). The effect of prolonged-release melatonin on sleep measures and psychomotor performance in elderly patients with insomnia. *International Clinical Psychopharmacology, 24,* 239–249.

Lutsey, Pamela L., Diez Roux, Ana V., Jacobs, David R., Jr., Burke, Gregory L., Harman, Jane, Shea, Steven, et al. (2008). Associations of acculturation and socioeconomic status with subclinical cardiovascular disease in the Multi-Ethnic Study of Atherosclerosis. *American Journal of Public Health, 98,* 1963–1970.

Lyng, Stephen (Ed.). (2005). *Edgework: The sociology of risk taking*. New York: Routledge.

Lynn, Richard, & Mikk, Jaan. (2007). National differences in intelligence and educational attainment. *Intelligence, 35,* 115–121.

Lynne, Sarah D., Graber, Julia A., Nichols, Tracy R., Brooks-Gunn, Jeanne, & Botvin, Gilbert J. (2007). Links between pubertal timing, peer influences, and externalizing behaviors among urban students followed through middle school. *Journal of Adolescent Health, 40,* 181. e187–181.e113.

Lyons-Ruth, Karlen, Bronfman, Elisa, & Parsons, Elizabeth. (1999). IV. Maternal frightened, frightening, or atypical behavior and disorganized infant attachment patterns. *Monographs of the Society for Research in Child Development, 64*(3, Serial No. 258), 67–96.

Ma, Lang, Phelps, Erin, Lerner, Jacqueline V., & Lerner, Richard M. (2009). Academic competence for adolescents who bully and who are bullied: Findings from the 4-H Study of Positive Youth Development. *The Journal of Early Adolescence, 29,* 862–897.

Maas, Carl, Herrenkohl, Todd I., & Sousa, Cynthia. (2008). Review of research on child maltreatment and violence in youth. *Trauma, Violence & Abuse, 9,* 56–67.

Maccoby, Eleanor E. (2000). Parenting and its effects on children: On reading and misreading behavior genetics. *Annual Review of Psychology, 51,* 1–27.

MacDorman, Marian F., & Mathews, T. J. (2008). *Recent trends in infant mortality in the United States* (NCHS Data Brief No. 9). Hyattsville, MD: National Center for Health Statistics.

Macgregor, Stuart, Lind, Penelope A., Bucholz, Kathleen K., Hansell, Narelle K., Madden, Pamela A. F., Richter, Melinda M., et al. (2009). Associations of ADH and ALDH2 gene variation with self report alcohol reactions, consumption and dependence: An integrated analysis. *Human Molecular Genetics, 18,* 580–593.

MacMillan, Harriet L., Wathen, C. Nadine, Barlow, Jane, Fergusson, David M., Leventhal, John M., & Taussig, Heather N. (2009). Interventions to prevent child maltreatment and associated impairment. *The Lancet, 373*(9659), 250–266.

Macmillan, Ross, & Copher, Ronda. (2005). Families in the life course: Interdependency of roles, role configurations, and pathways. *Journal of Marriage and Family, 67,* 858–879.

Macmillan, Ross, & Gartner, Rosemary. (1999). When she brings home the bacon: Labor-force participation and the risk of spousal violence against women. *Journal of Marriage and the Family, 61,* 947–958.

MacPhee, David. (1981). *Knowledge of Infant Development Inventory (KIDI)*. (Unpublished manuscript). Ewing, NJ: Educational Testing Service.

Madden, Mary, & Lenhart, Amanda. (2009). *Teens and distracted driving: Texting, talking and other uses of the cell phone behind the wheel*. Washington, DC: Pew Internet & American Life Project.

Magen, Zipora. (1998). *Exploring adolescent happiness: Commitment, purpose, and fulfillment*. Thousand Oaks, CA: Sage.

Maguire, Kathleen. (2010). *Sourcebook of criminal justice statistics*. Washington, DC: U.S. Department of Justice.

Mah, Timothy, & Halperin, Daniel. (2010). Concurrent sexual partnerships and the HIV epidemics in Africa: Evidence to move forward. *AIDS and Behavior, 14,* 11–16.

Mahler, Margaret S., Pine, Fred, & Bergman, Anni. (1975). *The psychological birth of the human infant: Symbiosis and individuation*. New York: Basic Books.

Mahmoud, Adel. (2004, July 9). The global vaccination gap. *Science, 305,* 147.

Majercsik, Eszter. (2005). Hierachy of needs of geriatric patients. *Gerontology, 51,* 170–173.

Malina, Robert M., Bouchard, Claude, & Bar-Or, Oded. (2004). *Growth, maturation, and physical activity* (2nd ed.). Champaign, IL: Human Kinetics.

Malloy, Michael H. (2009). Impact of cesarean section on intermediate and late preterm births: United States, 2000–2003. *Birth: Issues in Perinatal Care, 36,* 26–33.

Mancini, Anthony D., & Bonanno, George A. (2006). Marital closeness, functional disability, and adjustment in late life. *Psychology and Aging, 21,* 600–610.

Mandemakers, Jornt J., & Dykstra, Pearl A. (2008). Discrepancies in parent's and adult child's reports of support and contact. *Journal of Marriage and Family, 70,* 495–506.

Mandler, Jean Matter. (2004). *The foundations of mind: Origins of conceptual thought*. Oxford, England: Oxford University Press.

Mandler, Jean M. (2007). On the origins of the conceptual system. *American Psychologist, 62,* 741–751.

Manfra, Louis, & Winsler, Adam. (2006). Preschool children's awareness of private speech. *International Journal of Behavioral Development, 30,* 537–549.

Mange, Elaine Johansen, & Mange, Arthur P. (1999). *Basic human genetics* (2nd ed.). Sunderland, MA: Sinauer Associates.

Manini, Todd M., Everhart, James E., Patel, Kushang V., Schoeller, Dale A., Colbert, Lisa H., Visser, Marjolein, et al. (2006). Daily activity energy expenditure and mortality among older adults. *Journal of the American Medical Association, 296,* 171–179.

Mann, Joshua R., McDermott, Suzanne, Bao, Haikun, & Bersabe, Adrian. (2009). Maternal genitourinary infection and risk of cerebral palsy.

Developmental Medicine & Child Neurology, 51, 282–288.

Mann, Ronald D., & Andrews, Elizabeth B. (Eds.). (2007). *Pharmacovigilance* (2nd ed.). Hoboken, NJ: Wiley.

Mann, Traci, & Ward, Andrew. (2007). Attention, self-control, and health behaviors. *Current Directions in Psychological Science, 16,* 280–283.

Mansfield, Abigail, Syzdek, Matthew, Green, Jonathan, & Addis, Michael. (2008). Understanding and increasing help-seeking in older men. *Generations, 32*(1), 15–20.

Manton, Kenneth G., Gu, XiLiang, & Lamb, Vicki L. (2006). Change in chronic disability from 1982 to 2004/2005 as measured by long-term changes in function and health in the U.S. elderly population. *Proceedings of the National Academy of Sciences, 103,* 18374–18379.

Manzi, Claudia, Vignoles, Vivian L., Regalia, Camillo, & Scabini, Eugenia. (2006). Cohesion and enmeshment revisited: Differentiation, identity, and well-being in two European cultures. *Journal of Marriage and Family, 68,* 673–689.

Manzoli, Lamberto, Villari, Paolo, Pironec, Giovanni M., & Boccia, Antonio. (2007). Marital status and mortality in the elderly: A systematic review and meta-analysis. *Social Science & Medicine, 64,* 77–94.

Mao, Amy, Burnham, Melissa M., Goodlin-Jones, Beth L., Gaylor, Erika E., & Anders, Thomas F. (2004). A comparison of the sleep-wake patterns of cosleeping and solitary-sleeping infants. *Child Psychiatry and Human Development, 35,* 95–105.

March, John S., Franklin, Martin E., Leonard, Henrietta L., & Foa, Edna B. (2004). Obsessive-compulsive disorder. In Tracy L. Morris & John S. March (Eds.), *Anxiety disorders in children and adolescents* (2nd ed., pp. 212–240). New York: Guilford Press.

Marcia, James E. (1966). Development and validation of ego-identity status. *Journal of Personality & Social Psychology, 3,* 551–558.

Marcia, James E., Waterman, Alan S., Matteson, David R., Archer, Sally L., & Orlofsky, Jacob L. (1993). *Ego identity: A handbook for psychosocial research.* New York: Springer-Verlag.

Margueron, Raphaël, & Reinberg, Danny. (2010). Chromatin structure and the inheritance of epigenetic information. *Nature Reviews Genetics, 11,* 285–296.

Marlow-Ferguson, Rebecca (Ed.). (2002). *World education encyclopedia: A survey of educational systems worldwide* (2nd ed.). Detroit, MI: Gale Group.

Marsh, Louise, McGee, Rob, Nada-Raja, Shyamala, & Williams, Sheila. (2010). Text bullying and traditional bullying among New Zealand secondary school students. *Journal of Adolescence, 33,* 237–240.

Marshall, Peter J. (2009). Relating psychology and neuroscience: Taking up the challenges. *Perspectives on Psychological Science, 4,* 113–125.

Marsiske, Michael, & Margrett, Jennifer A. (2006). Everyday problem solving and decision making. In James E. Birren & K. Warren Schaie (Eds.), *Handbook of the psychology of aging* (6th ed.). Burlington, MA: Elsevier Academic Press.

Marsiske, Michael, & Willis, Sherry L. (1995). Dimensionality of everyday problem solving in older adults. *Psychology & Aging, 10,* 269–283.

Marsiske, Michael, & Willis, Sherry L. (1998). Practical creativity in older adults' everyday problem solving: Life span perspectives. In Carolyn E. Adams-Price (Ed.), *Creativity and successful aging: Theoretical and empirical approaches* (pp. 73–113). New York: Springer.

Martel, Jane G. (1974). *Smashed potatoes: A kid's-eye view of the kitchen.* Boston: Houghton Mifflin.

Martin, Andrew J. (2009). Motivation and engagement across the academic life span: A developmental construct validity study of elementary school, high school, and university/college students. *Educational and Psychological Measurement, 69,* 794–824.

Martin, Carol Lynn, Ruble, Diane N., & Szkrybalo, Joel. (2002). Cognitive theories of early gender development. *Psychological Bulletin, 128,* 903–933.

Martin, Douglas. (2010, July 7). Robert Butler, aging expert, is dead at 83. *New York Times,* pp. A13.

Martin, Joyce A., Hamilton, Brady E., Sutton, Paul D., Ventura, Stephanie J., Menacker, Fay, Kirmeyer, Sharon, et al. (2009). Births: Final data for 2006. *National Vital Statistics Reports, 57*(7).

Martin, Mike, & Zimprich, Daniel (2005). Cognitive development in midlife. In Sherry L. Willis & Mike Martin (Eds.), *Middle adulthood: A lifespan perspective* (pp. 179–206). Thousand Oaks, CA: Sage.

Martorell, Reynaldo, Melgar, Paul, Maluccio, John A., Stein, Aryeh D., & Rivera, Juan A. (2010). The nutrition intervention improved adult human capital and economic productivity. *The Journal of Nutrition, 140,* 411–414.

Masche, J. Gowert. (2010). Explanation of normative declines in parents' knowledge about their adolescent children. *Journal of Adolescence, 33,* 271–284.

Mascolo, Michael F., Fischer, Kurt W., & Li, Jin. (2003). Dynamic development of component systems of emotions: Pride, shame, and guilt in China and the United States. In Richard J. Davidson, Klaus R. Scherer, & H. Hill Goldsmith (Eds.), *Handbook of affective sciences* (pp. 375–408). Oxford, England: Oxford University Press.

Mashburn, Andrew J., Justice, Laura M., Downer, Jason T., & Pianta, Robert C. (2009). Peer effects on children's language achievement during pre-kindergarten. *Child Development, 80,* 686–702.

Maslow, Abraham H. (1954). *Motivation and personality.* New York: Harper.

Maslow, Abraham H. (1970). *Motivation and personality* (2nd ed.). New York: Harper & Row.

Maslow, Abraham H. (1971). *The farther reaches of human nature.* New York: Viking Press.

Maslow, Abraham H. (1999). *Toward a psychology of being* (3rd ed.). New York: J. Wiley & Sons. (Original work published 1962)

Masoro, Edward J. (2006). Are age-associated diseases an integral part of aging? In Edward J. Masoro & Steven N. Austad (Eds.), *Handbook of the biology of aging* (6th ed., pp. 43–62). Amsterdam: Elsevier Academic Press.

Masten, Ann S. (2004). Regulatory processes, risk, and resilience in adolescent development. In Ronald E. Dahl & Linda Patia Spear (Eds.), *Adolescent brain development: Vulnerabilities and opportunities* (Vol. 1021, pp. 310–319). New York: New York Academy of Sciences.

Masten, Ann S., & Wright, Margaret O'Dougherty. (2010). Resilience over the life-span: Developmental perspectives on resistance, recovery, and transformation. In John W. Reich, Alex J. Zautra, & John Stuart Hall (Eds.), *Handbook of adult resilience* (pp. 213–237). New York: Guilford Press.

Masten, Carrie L., Guyer, Amanda E., Hodgdon, Hilary B., McClure, Erin B., Charney, Dennis S., Ernst, Monique, et al. (2008). Recognition of facial emotions among maltreated children with high rates of posttraumatic stress disorder. *Child Abuse & Neglect, 32,* 139–153.

Masuda, Takahiko, Gonzalez, Richard, Kwan, Letty, & Nisbett, Richard E. (2008). Culture and aesthetic preference: Comparing the attention to context of East Asians and Americans. *Personality and Social Psychology Bulletin,* 1260–1275.

Masunaga, Hiromi, & Horn, John. (2001). Expertise and age-related changes in components of intelligence. *Psychology & Aging, 16,* 293–311.

Mata, Rui, & Nunes, Ludmila. (2010). When less is enough: Cognitive aging, information search, and decision quality in consumer choice. *Psychology and Aging, 25,* 289–298.

Mathias, Jane L., & Morphett, Kylie. (2010). Neurobehavioral differences between Alzheimer's disease and frontotemporal dementia: A meta-analysis. *Journal of Clinical and Experimental Neuropsychology, 32,* 682–698.

Matsumoto, David. (2004). Reflections on culture and competence. In Robert J. Sternberg & Elena L. Grigorenko (Eds.), *Culture and competence: Contexts of life success* (pp. 273–282). Washington, DC: American Psychological Association.

Matsumoto, David. (2009). Teaching about culture. In Regan A. R. Gurung & Loreto R. Prieto (Eds.), *Getting culture: Incorporating diversity across the curriculum* (pp. 3–10). Sterling, VA: Stylus.

Matsumoto, David, Yoo, Seung Hee, & Fontaine, Johnny. (2009). Hypocrisy or maturity? Culture and context differentiation. *European Journal of Personality, 23,* 251–264.

Mattsson, Niklas, Zetterberg, Henrik, Hansson, Oskar, Andreasen, Niels, Parnetti, Lucilla, Jonsson, Michael, et al. (2009). CSF biomarkers and incipient Alzheimer disease in patients with mild cognitive impairment. *Journal of the American Medical Association, 302,* 385–393.

Maxfield, Molly, Pyszczynski, Tom, Kluck, Benjamin, Cox, Cathy R., Greenberg, Jeff, Solomon, Sheldon, et al. (2007). Age-related differences in responses to thoughts of one's own death: Mortality salience and judgments of moral transgressions. *Psychology and Aging, 22,* 341–353.

Mayes, Rick, Bagwell, Catherine, & Erkulwater, Jennifer L. (2009). *Medicating children: ADHD and pediatric mental health.* Cambridge, Mass.: Harvard University Press.

Mayeux, Lara, & Cillessen, Antonius H. N. (2007). Peer influence and the development of antisocial behavior. In Rutger C. M. E. Engels, Margaret Kerr, & Håkan Stattin (Eds.), *Friends, lovers, and groups: Key relationships in adolescence* (pp. 33–46). Hoboken, NJ: Wiley.

Maynard, Ashley E. (2002). Cultural teaching: The development of teaching skills in Maya sibling interactions. *Child Development, 73,* 969–982.

Mazin, Alexander L. (2009). Suicidal function of DNA methylation in age-related genome disintegration. *Ageing Research Reviews, 8,* 314–327.

Mazzocco, Michèle M. M., & Ross, Judith L. (2007). *Neurogenetic developmental disorders: Variation of manifestation in childhood.* Cambridge, MA: MIT Press.

McAdams, Dan P. (2006). The redemptive self: Generativity and the stories Americans live by. *Research in Human Development, 3,* 81–100.

McAdams, Dan P., Bauer, Jack J., Sakaeda, April R., Anyidoho, Nana Akua, Machado, Mary Anne, Magrino-Failla, Katie, et al. (2006). Continuity and change in the life story: A longitudinal study of autobiographical memories in emerging adulthood. *Journal of Personality, 74,* 1371–1400.

McAdams, Dan P., & Olson, Bradley D. (2010). Personality development: Continuity and change over the life course. *Annual Review of Psychology, 61,* 517–542.

McAdams, Dan P., & Pals, Jennifer L. (2006). A new big five: Fundamental principles for an integrative science of personality. *American Psychologist, 61,* 204–217.

McCall, Robert B., Groark, Christina J., & Fish, Larry. (2010). A caregiver–child socioemotional and relationship rating scale. *Infant Mental Health Journal, 31,* 201–219.

McCann, Joyce C., & Ames, Bruce N. (2009). Vitamin K, an example of triage theory: Is micronutrient inadequacy linked to diseases of aging? *The American Journal of Clinical Nutrition, 90,* 889–907.

McCarter, Roger J. M. (2006). Differential aging among skeletal muscles. In Edward J. Masoro & Steven N. Austad (Eds.), *Handbook of the biology of aging* (6th ed., pp. 470–497). Amsterdam: Elsevier Academic Press.

McCarthy, Barry W., & McCarthy, Emily J. (2004). *Getting it right the first time: Creating a healthy marriage.* New York: Brunner-Routledge.

McCarthy-Keith, Desireé M., Schisterman, Enrique F., Robinson, Randal D., O'Leary, Kathleen, Lucidi, Richard S., & Armstrong, Alicia Y. (in press). Will decreasing assisted reproduction technology costs improve utilization and outcomes among minority women? *Fertility and Sterility.*

McCartney, Kathleen, Burchinal, Margaret, Clarke-Stewart, Alison, Bub, Kristen L., Owen, Margaret T., Belsky, Jay, et al. (2010). Testing a series of causal propositions relating time in child care to children's externalizing behavior. *Developmental Psychology, 46,* 1–17, 17a.

McClain, Paula D., Johnson Carew, Jessica D., Walton, Eugene, Jr., & Watts, Candis S. (2009). Group membership, group identity, and group consciousness: Measures of racial identity in American politics? *Annual Review of Political Science, 12,* 471–485.

McClintock, Elizabeth Aura. (2010). When does race matter? Race, sex, and dating at an elite university. *Journal of Marriage and Family, 72,* 45–72.

McConkie-Rosell, Allyn, & O'Daniel, Julianne. (2007). Beyond the diagnosis: The process of genetic counseling. In Michèle M. M. Mazzocco & Judith L. Ross (Eds.), *Neurogenetic developmental disorders: Variation of manifestation in childhood* (pp. 367–389). Cambridge, MA: MIT Press.

McCormick, Cheryl M., Mathews, Iva Z., Thomas, Catherine, & Waters, Patti. (2010). Investigations of HPA function and the enduring consequences of stressors in adolescence in animal models. *Brain and Cognition, 72,* 73–85.

McCowan, Lesley M. E., Dekker, Gustaaf A., Chan, Eliza, Stewart, Alistair, Chappell, Lucy C., Hunter, Misty, et al. (2009). Spontaneous preterm birth and small for gestational age infants in women who stop smoking early in pregnancy: Prospective cohort study. *BMJ, 338,* b1081.

McCrae, Robert R., & Costa, Paul T. (2003). *Personality in adulthood: A five-factor theory perspective* (2nd ed.). New York: Guilford Press.

McCurry, Susan M., Logsdon, Rebecca G., Teri, Linda, & Vitiello, Michael V. (2007). Evidence-based psychological treatments for insomnia in older adults. *Psychology and Aging, 22,* 18–27.

McDaniel, Mark A., Howard, Daniel C., & Butler, Karin M. (2008). Implementation intentions facilitate prospective memory under high attention demands. *Memory & Cognition, 36,* 716–724.

McFadden, Susan H., & Basting, Anne D. (2010). Healthy aging persons and their brains: Promoting resilience through creative engagement. *Clinics in Geriatric Medicine, 26,* 149–161.

McGrath, Susan K., & Kennell, John H. (2008). A randomized controlled trial of continuous labor support for middle-class couples: Effect on cesarean delivery rates. *Birth, 35,* 92–97.

McGuigan, Leigh. (2008). Systems thinking and culture change in urban school districts. In Wayne K. Hoy & Michael F. DiPaola (Eds.), *Improving schools: Studies in leadership and culture* (pp. 99–116). Charlotte, NC: Information Age.

McIntyre, Donald A. (2002). *Colour blindness: Causes and effects.* Chester, UK: Dalton.

McKinley, Jesse. (2010, June 24). Whooping cough kills 5 in California; State declares an epidemic. *New York Times,* pp. A15.

McKown, Clark, & Strambler, Michael J. (2009). Developmental antecedents and social and academic consequences of stereotype-consciousness in middle childhood. *Child Development, 80,* 1643–1659.

McKusick, Victor A. (2007). Mendelian Inheritance in Man and its online version, OMIM. *American Journal of Human Genetics, 80,* 588–604.

McLachlan, Hugh V. (2008). The ethics of killing and letting die: Active and passive euthanasia. *Journal of Medical Ethics, 34,* 636–638.

McLanahan, Sara. (2009). Fragile families and the reproduction of poverty. *The ANNALS of the American Academy of Political and Social Science, 621,* 111–131.

McLeod, Bryce D., Wood, Jeffrey J., & Weisz, John R. (2007). Examining the association between parenting and childhood anxiety: A meta-analysis. *Clinical Psychology Review, 27,* 155–172.

McLeod, Jane D., Pescosolido, Bernice A., Takeuchi, David T., & Falkenberg White, Terry (2004). Public attitudes toward the use of psychiatric medications for children. *Journal of Health and Social Behavior, 45,* 53–67.

McLeod, Peter, Sommerville, Peter, & Reed, Nick. (2005). Are automated actions beyond conscious access? In John Duncan, Peter McLeod, & Louise H. Phillips (Eds.), *Measuring the mind: Speed, control, and age* (pp. 359–372). New York: Oxford University Press.

McLoyd, Vonnie C. (2006). The legacy of Child Development's 1990 special issue on minority children: An editorial retrospective. *Child Development, 77,* 1142–1148.

McLoyd, Vonnie C., Aikens, Nikki L., & Burton, Linda M. (2006). Childhood poverty, policy, and practice. In William Damon & Richard M. Lerner (Series Eds.) & K. Ann Renninger & Irving E. Sigel (Vol. Eds.), *Handbook of child psychology: Vol. 4. Child psychology in practice* (6th ed., pp. 700–775). Hoboken, NJ: Wiley.

McLoyd, Vonnie C., Kaplan, Rachel, Hardaway, Cecily R., & Wood, Dana. (2007). Does endorsement of physical discipline matter? Assessing moderating influences on the maternal and child psychological correlates of physical discipline in African American families. *Journal of Family Psychology, 21,* 165–175.

McNally, Richard J., & Geraerts, Elke. (2009). A new solution to the recovered memory debate. *Perspectives on Psychological Science, 4,* 126–134.

McNeil, Nicole M., & Uttal, David H. (2009). Rethinking the use of concrete materials in learning: Perspectives from development and education. *Child Development Perspectives, 3,* 137–139.

McNeil, Nicole M., Uttal, David H., Jarvin, Linda, & Sternberg, Robert J. (2009). Should you show me the money? Concrete objects both hurt and help performance on mathematics problems. *Learning and Instruction, 19,* 171–184.

McShane, Kelly E., & Hastings, Paul D. (2009). The New Friends Vignettes: Measuring parental psychological control that confers risk for anxious adjustment in preschoolers. *International Journal of Behavioral Development, 33,* 481–495.

Meadows, Sara. (2006). *The child as thinker: The development and acquisition of cognition in childhood* (2nd ed.). New York: Routledge.

Meaney, Michael J. (2010). Epigenetics and the biological definition of gene–environment interactions. *Child Development, 81,* 41–79.

Medscape Psychiatry & Mental Health. (2005). *Autism first-hand: An expert interview with Temple Grandin, PhD.* Retrieved July 6, 2009, from the World Wide Web: http://cme.medscape.com/viewarticle/498153

Medvedev, Zhores A. (1990). An attempt at a rational classification of theories of ageing. *Biological Reviews, 65,* 375–398.

Mehta, Clare M., & Strough, JoNell. (2009). Sex segregation in friendships and normative contexts across the life span. *Developmental Review, 29,* 201–220.

Meier, Ann, Hull, Kathleen E., & Ortyl, Timothy A. (2009). Young adult relationship values at the intersection of gender and sexuality. *Journal of Marriage and Family, 71,* 510–525.

Meisami, Esmail. (1994). Aging of the sensory systems. In Paola S. Timiras (Ed.), *Physiological basis of aging and geriatrics* (2nd ed., pp. 115–132). Boca Raton, FL: CRC Press.

Meisami, Esmail, Brown, Chester M., & Emerle, Henry F. (2007). Sensory systems: Normal aging, disorders, and treatments of vision and hearing in humans. In Paola S. Timiras (Ed.), *Physiological basis of aging and geriatrics* (4th ed., pp. 109–136). New York: Informa Healthcare.

Meissner, Christian A., & Brigham, John C. (2001). Thirty years of investigating the own-race bias in memory for faces: A meta-analytic review. *Psychology, Public Policy, and Law, 7,* 3–35.

Melhuish, Edward, & Petrogiannis, Konstantinos. (2006). An international overview of early childhood care and education. In Edward Melhuish & Konstantinos Petrogiannis (Eds.), *Early childhood care and education: International perspectives* (pp. 167–178). London: Routledge.

Melhuish, Edward C., Phan, Mai B., Sylva, Kathy, Sammons, Pam, Siraj-Blatchford, Iram, & Taggart, Brenda. (2008). Effects of the home learning environment and preschool center experience upon literacy and numeracy development in early primary school. *Journal of Social Issues, 64,* 95–114.

Mell, Loren K., Ogren, David S., Davis, Robert L., Mullooly, John P., Black, Steven B., Shinefield, Henry R., et al. (2005). Compliance with national immunization guidelines for children younger than 2 years, 1996–1999. *Pediatrics, 115,* 461–467.

Mellor, M. Joanna, & Brownell, Patricia J. (Eds.). (2006). *Elder abuse and mistreatment: Policy, practice, and research.* New York: Haworth Press.

Meltzoff, Andrew N. (2007). 'Like me': A foundation for social cognition. *Developmental Science, 10,* 126–134.

Meltzoff, Andrew N., & Moore, M. Keith. (1999). A new foundation for cognitive development in infancy: The birth of the representational infant. In Ellin Kofsky Scholnick, Katherine Nelson, Susan A. Gelman, & Patricia H. Miller (Eds.), *Conceptual development: Piaget's legacy* (pp. 53–78). Mahwah, NJ: Erlbaum.

Mendle, Jane, Harden, K. Paige, Turkheimer, Eric, Van Hulle, Carol A., D'Onofrio, Brian M., Brooks-Gunn, Jeanne, et al. (2009). Associations between father absence and age of first sexual intercourse. *Child Development, 80,* 1463–1480.

Menon, Usha. (2001). Middle adulthood in cultural perspectives: The imagined and the experienced in three cultures. *Handbook of midlife development,* 40–74.

Merikangas, Kathleen R., & Pato, Michael. (2009). Recent developments in the epidemiology of bipolar disorder in adults and children: Magnitude, correlates, and future directions. *Clinical Psychology: Science and Practice, 16,* 121–133.

Meririnne, Esa, Kiviruusu, Olli, Karlsson, Linnea, Pelkonen, Mirjami, Ruuttu, Titta, Tuisku, Virpi, et al. (2010). Brief report: Excessive alcohol use negatively affects the course of adolescent depression—One year naturalistic follow-up study. *Journal of Adolescence, 33,* 221–226.

Merriman, William E. (1999). Competition, attention, and young children's lexical processing. In Brian MacWhinney (Ed.), *The emergence of language* (pp. 331–358). Mahwah, NJ: Erlbaum.

Mervis, Jeffrey. (2008, March 21). Expert panel lays out the path to algebra—And why it matters. *Science, 319,* 1605.

Merz, Emily C., & McCall, Robert B. (2010). Behavior problems in children adopted from psychosocially depriving institutions. *Journal of Abnormal Child Psychology, 38,* 459–470

Merzenich, Hiltrud, Zeeb, Hajo, & Blettner, Maria. (2010). Decreasing sperm quality: A global problem? *BMC Public Health, 10,* 24.

Meshcheryakov, Boris G. (2005). Psychometric approach to child animism. *Cultural-Historical Psychology, 1,* 70–86.

Mesquita, Batja, & Leu, Janxin. (2007). The cultural psychology of emotion. In Shinobu Kitayama & Dov Cohen (Eds.), *Handbook of cultural psychology* (pp. 734–759). New York: Guilford Press.

Messer, Karen, Trinidad, Dennis R., Al-Delaimy, Wael K., & Pierce, John P. (2008). Smoking cessation rates in the United States: A comparison of young adult and older smokers. *American Journal of Public Health, 98,* 317–322.

Messing, Jacqueline. (2007). Multiple ideologies and competing discourses: Language shift in Tlaxcala, Mexico. *Language in Society, 36,* 555–577.

Messinger, Daniel S., Mahoor, Mohammad H., Chow, Sy-Miin, & Cohn, Jeffrey F. (2009). Automated measurement of facial expression in infant-mother interaction: A pilot study. *Infancy, 14,* 285–305.

Mikami, Amori Yee, Szwedo, David E., Allen, Joseph P., Evans, Meredyth A., & Hare, Amanda L. (2010). Adolescent peer relationships and behavior problems predict young adults' communication on social networking websites. *Developmental Psychology, 46,* 46–56.

Miklowitz, David Jay, & Cicchetti, Dante (Eds.). (2010). *Understanding bipolar disorder: A developmental psychopathology perspective.* New York: Guilford.

Mikulincer, Mario, & Goodman, Gail S. (2006). *Dynamics of romantic love: Attachment, caregiving, and sex.* New York: Guilford Press.

Miles, Lynden K. (2009). Who is approachable? *Journal of Experimental Social Psychology, 45,* 262–266.

Milkie, Melissa A., Bierman, Alex, & Schieman, Scott. (2008). How adult children influence older parents' mental health: Integrating stress-process and life-course perspectives. *Social Psychology Quarterly, 71,* 86–105.

Milkman, Katherine L., Chugh, Dolly, & Bazerman, Max H. (2009). How can decision making be improved? *Perspectives on Psychological Science, 4,* 379–383.

Miller, Greg. (2006, March 31). The thick and thin of brainpower: Developmental timing linked to IQ. *Science, 311,* 1851.

Miller, Greg. (2006, January 27). The unseen: Mental illness's global toll. *Science, 311,* 458–461.

Miller, Greg. (2008, June 13). Growing pains for fMRI. *Science, 320,* 1412–1414.

Miller, Greg. (2009, October 16). Alzheimer's biomarker initiative hits its stride. *Science, 326,* 386–389.

Miller, Joan G. (2004). The cultural deep structure of psychological theories of social development. In Robert J. Sternberg & Elena L. Grigorenko (Eds.), *Culture and competence: Contexts of life success* (pp. 111–138). Washington, DC: American Psychological Association.

Miller, Orlando J., & Therman, Eeva. (2001). *Human chromosomes* (4th ed.). New York: Springer.

Miller, Patrick, & Plant, Martin. (2010). Parental guidance about drinking: Relationship with teenage psychoactive substance use. *Journal of Adolescence, 33,* 55–68.

Miller, Patricia H. (2011). *Theories of developmental psychology* (5th ed.). New York: Worth.

Miller, Patricia Y., & Simon, William. (1980). The development of sexuality in adolescence. In Joseph Adelson (Ed.), *Handbook of adolescent psychology* (pp. 383–407). New York: Wiley.

Miller, Torri W., Nigg, Joel T., & Miller, Robin L. (2009). Attention deficit hyperactivity disorder in African American children: What can be concluded from the past ten years? *Clinical Psychology Review, 29,* 77–86.

Miller, William R., & Carroll, Kathleen. (2006). *Rethinking substance abuse: What the science shows, and what we should do about it.* New York: Guilford Press.

Mills, Britain, Reyna, Valerie F., & Estrada, Steven. (2008). Explaining contradictory relations between risk perception and risk taking. *Psychological Science, 19,* 429–433.

Mills, Jon (Ed.). (2004). *Psychoanalysis at the limit: Epistemology, mind, and the question of science.* Albany, NY: State University of New York Press.

Mills, James L., McPartlin, Joseph M., Kirke, Peadar N., Lee, Young J., Conley, Mary R., Weir, Donald G., et al. (1995). Homocysteine metabolism in pregnancies complicated by neural-tube defects. *Lancet, 345,* 149–151.

Milosevic, Dragoslav P., Kostic, Svetlana, Potic, Bojana, Kalašić, Aleksandra, Svorcan, Petar, Bojic, Daniela, et al. (2007). Is there such thing as "reversible dementia" (RD)? *Archives of Gerontology and Geriatrics, 44,* 271–277.

Min, Pyong Gap. (2000). Korean Americans' language use. In Sandra Lee McKay & Sau-ling Cynthia Wong (Eds.), *New immigrants in the United States: Readings for second language educators* (pp. 306–332). Cambridge, UK: Cambridge University Press.

Mindell, Jodi A., & Owens, Judith A. (2010). *A clinical guide to pediatric sleep: Diagnosis and management of sleep problems* (2nd ed.). Philadelphia: Lippincott Williams & Wilkins.

Minkler, Meredith, & Holstein, Martha B. (2008). From civil rights to . . . civic engagement? Concerns of two older critical gerontologists about a "new social movement" and what it portends. *Journal of Aging Studies, 22,* 196–204.

Mintz, Toben H. (2005). Linguistic and conceptual influences on adjective acquisition in 24- and 36-month-olds. *Developmental Psychology, 41,* 17–29.

Mitchell, Barbara A. (2010). Happiness in midlife parental roles: A contextual mixed methods analysis. *Family Relations, 59,* 326–339.

Mitchell, Edwin A. (2009). SIDS: Past, present and future. *Acta Pædiatrica, 98,* 1712–1719.

Mitchell, Philip B., Meiser, Bettina, Wilde, Alex, Fullerton, Janice, Donald, Jennifer, Wilhelm, Kay, et al. (2010). Predictive and diagnostic genetic testing in psychiatry. *Psychiatric Clinics of North America, 33,* 225–243.

Mitteldorf, Joshua. (2010). Female fertility and longevity. *AGE, 32,* 79–84.

Mize, Krystal D., Shackelford, Todd K., & Shackelford, Viviana A. (2009). Hands-on killing of intimate partners as a function of sex and relationship status/state. *Journal of Family Violence, 24,* 463–470.

MMWR. (1998, August 14). Youth risk behavior surveillance—United States, 1997. *MMWR Surveillance Summaries, 47*(SS-3).

MMWR. (2002, September 13). Folic acid and prevention of spina bifida and anencephaly: 10 years after the U.S. public health service recommendation. *MMWR Recommendations and Reports, 51*(RR13), 1–3.

MMWR. (2005, August 26). Surveillance for dental caries, dental sealants, tooth retention, edentulism, and enamel fluorosis—United States, 1988–1994 and 1999–2002. *54*(3), 1–44.

MMWR. (2005, January 14). Reducing childhood asthma through community-based service delivery—New York City, 2001–2004. *Morbidity and Mortality Weekly Report, 54,* 11–14.

MMWR. (2005, May 27). Blood lead levels—United States, 1999–2002. *Morbidity and Mortality Weekly Report, 54,* 513–516.

MMWR. (2007, February 9). Prevalence of autism spectrum disorders—Autism and Developmental Disabilities Monitoring Network, six sites, United States, 2000. *MMWR Surveillance Summaries, 56*(SS01), 1–11.

MMWR. (2008, January 18). School-associated student homicides—United States, 1992–2006. *Morbidity and Mortality Weekly Report, 57*(2), 33–36.

MMWR. (2008, July 11). Disparities in second-hand smoke exposure—United States, 1988–1994 and 1999–2004. *Morbidity and Mortality Weekly Report, 57,* 744–747.

MMWR. (2008, June 6). Youth risk behavior surveillance—United States, 2007. *MMWR Surveillance Summaries, 57*(SS04), 1–131.

MMWR. (2008, October 3). Racial/ethnic disparities in self-rated health status among adults with and without disabilities—United States, 2004–2006. *Morbidity and Mortality Weekly Report, 57,* 1069–1073.

MMWR. (2009, July 24). QuickStats. *Morbidity and Mortality Weekly Report, 58,* 782–794.

MMWR. (2009, June 12). Assisted reproductive technology surveillance—United States, 2006. *MMWR Surveillance Summaries, 58*(SS-5), 1–25.

MMWR. (2009, March 13). State-specific prevalence and trends in adult cigarette smoking—United States, 1998–2007. *Morbidity and Mortality Weekly Report, 58,* 221–226.

MMWR. (2009, October 9). Availability of less nutritious snack foods and beverages in secondary schools—Selected states, 2002–2008. *MMWR Surveillance Summaries, 58*(39), 1102–1104.

MMWR. (2009, October 23). Reduction in rotavirus after vaccine introduction—United States, 2000–2009. *Morbidity and Mortality Weekly Report, 58,* 1146–1149.

MMWR. (2010, June 4). Youth risk behavior surveillance—United States, 2009. *MMWR Surveillance Summaries, 59*(SS05), 1–142.

Moats, Caroline, & Rimm, Eric B. (2007). Vitamin intake and risk of coronary disease: Observation versus intervention. *Current Atherosclerosis Reports, 9,* 508–514.

Mocan, Naci H., & Tekin, Erdal. (2006). *Ugly criminals* (IZA Discussion Paper No. 2048). Bonn, Germany: Institute for the Study of Labor (IZA).

Moen, Phyllis, & Spencer, Donna. (2006). Converging divergences in age, gender, health, and well-being: Strategic selection in the third age. In Robert H. Binstock & Linda K. George (Eds.), *Handbook of aging and the social sciences* (6th ed., pp. 127–144). Amsterdam: Elsevier.

Moen, Phyllis, Sweet, Stephen, & Swisher, Raymond. (2005). Embedded career clocks: The case of retirement planning. In Ross Macmillan (Ed.), *The structure of the life course: Standardized? Individualized? Differentiated?* (pp. 237–265). Greenwich, CT: Elsevier/JAI Press.

Moffat, Scott D. (2005). Effects of testosterone on cognitive and brain aging in elderly men. In Richard G. Cutler, S. Mitchell Harman, Chris Heward, & Mike Gibbons (Eds.), *Longevity health sciences: The Phoenix conference* (Vol. 1055, pp. 80–92). New York: New York Academy of Sciences.

Moffitt, Terrie E. (2003). Life-course-persistent and adolescence-limited antisocial behavior: A 10-year research review and a research agenda. In Benjamin B. Lahey, Terrie E. Moffitt, & Avshalom Caspi (Eds.), *Causes of conduct disorder and juvenile delinquency* (pp. 49–75). New York: Guilford Press.

Moffitt, Terrie E., Caspi, Avshalom, & Rutter, Michael. (2006). Measured gene-environment interactions in psychopathology: Concepts, research strategies, and implications for research, intervention, and public understanding of genetics. *Perspectives on Psychological Science, 1,* 5–27.

Moffitt, Terrie E., Caspi, Avshalom, Rutter, Michael, & Silva, Phil A. (2001). *Sex differences in antisocial behaviour: Conduct disorder, delinquency, and violence in the Dunedin Longitudinal Study.* New York: Cambridge University Press.

Mofidi, Mahyar, Zeldin, Leslie P., & Rozier, R. Gary. (2009). Oral health of Early Head Start children: A qualitative study of staff, parents, and pregnant women. *American Journal of Public Health, 99,* 245–251.

Molina, Brooke S. G., Hinshaw, Stephen P., Swanson, James W., Arnold, L. Eugene, Vitiello, Benedetto, Jensen, Peter S., et al. (2009). The MTA at 8 years: Prospective follow-up of children treated for combined-type ADHD in a multisite study. *Journal of the American Academy of Child & Adolescent Psychiatry, 48,* 484.

Mollenkopf, John, Waters, Mary C., Holdaway, Jennifer, & Kasinitz, Philip. (2005). The ever-winding path: Ethnic and racial diversity in the transition to adulthood. In Richard A. Settersten, Jr., Frank F. Furstenberg, Jr., & Rubén G. Rumbaut (Eds.), *On the frontier of adulthood: Theory, research, and public policy* (pp. 454–497). Chicago: University of Chicago Press.

Monahan, Kathryn C., Steinberg, Laurence, & Cauffman, Elizabeth. (2009). Affiliation with antisocial peers, susceptibility to peer influence, and antisocial behavior during the transition to adulthood. *Developmental Psychology, 45,* 1520–1530.

Monastersky, Richard. (2007, January 12). Who's minding the teenage brain? *Chronicle of Higher Education, 53,* A14–A18.

Monroe, Kristen Renwick, Hankin, James, & Vechten, Renée Bukovchik Van. (2000). The psychological foundations of identity politics. *Annual Review of Political Science, 3,* 419–447.

Monserud, Maria A. (2008). Intergenerational relationships and affectual solidarity between grandparents and young adults. *Journal of Marriage and Family, 70,* 182–195.

Monsour, Michael. (2002). *Women and men as friends: Relationships across the life span in the 21st century.* Mahwah, NJ: Erlbaum.

Monteiro, Carlos A., Conde, Wolney L., & Popkin, Barry M. (2004). The burden of disease from undernutrition and overnutrition in countries undergoing rapid nutrition transition: A view from Brazil. *American Journal of Public Health, 94,* 433–434.

Monteiro, Carlos A., Conde, Wolney L., & Popkin, Barry M. (2007). Income-specific trends in obesity in Brazil: 1975–2003. *American Journal of Public Health, 97,* 1808–1812.

Montgomery, Leigh, & Williams, Stacie. (2010). *Countries with the highest college graduation rates.* Retrieved November 21, 2010, from the World Wide Web: http://www.csmonitor.com/USA/Education/2010/0809/Countries-with-the-highest-college-graduation-rates/Ireland-43.9-percent

Moody, Harry R. (2009–2010). Eco-elders: Legacy and environmental advocacy. *Generations, 33*(4), 70–74.

Moody, Raymond A. (1975). *Life after life: The investigation of a phenomenon—Survival of bodily death.* Atlanta, GA: Mockingbird Books.

Moore, Ginger A., & Calkins, Susan D. (2004). Infants' vagal regulation in the still-face paradigm is related to dyadic coordination of mother-infant interaction. *Developmental Psychology, 40,* 1068–1080.

Moore, Karenza, & Measham, Fiona. (2008). "It's the most fun you can have for twenty quid": Motivations, consequences and meanings of British ketamine use. *Addiction Research & Theory, 16,* 231–244.

Moore, Keith L., & Persaud, Trivedi V. N. (2003). *The developing human: Clinically oriented embryology* (7th ed.). Philadelphia: Saunders.

Moore, Keith L., & Persaud, Trivedi V. N. (2007). *The developing human: Clinically oriented embryology* (8th ed.). Philadelphia: Saunders/Elsevier.

Moore, Latetia V., Diez Roux, Ana V., Nettleton, Jennifer A., Jacobs, David R., & Franco, Manuel. (2009). Fast-food consumption, diet quality, and neighborhood exposure to fast food: The multi-ethnic study of atherosclerosis. *American Journal of Epidemiology, 170,* 29–36.

Moore, Susan, & Rosenthal, Doreen. (2006). *Sexuality in adolescence: Current trends* (2nd ed.). New York: Routledge.

Morales, Alvaro. (2008). The use of hormonal therapy in "andropause": The pro side. *Canadian Urological Association Journal, 2,* 43–46.

Morasch, Katherine C., & Bell, Martha Ann. (2009). Patterns of brain-electrical activity during declarative memory performance in 10-month-old infants. *Brain and Cognition, 71,* 215–222.

Morelli, Gilda A., & Rothbaum, Fred. (2007). Situating the child in context: Attachment relationships and self-regulation in different cultures. In Shinobu Kitayama & Dov Cohen (Eds.), *Handbook of cultural psychology* (pp. 500–527). New York: Guilford Press.

Moreno, Carmen, Laje, Gonzalo, Blanco, Carlos, Jiang, Huiping, Schmidt, Andrew B., & Olfson, Mark. (2007). National trends in the outpatient diagnosis and treatment of bipolar disorder in youth. *Archives of General Psychiatry, 64,* 1032–1039.

Morgan, Craig, Kirkbride, James, Leff, Julian, Craig, Tom, Hutchinson, Gerard, McKenzie, Kwame, et al. (2007). Parental separation, loss and psychosis in different ethnic groups: A case-control study. *Psychological Medicine, 37,* 495–503.

Morgan, Ian G. (2003). The biological basis of myopic refractive error. *Clinical and Experimental Optometry, 86,* 276–288.

Morris, Amanda Sheffield, Silk, Jennifer S., Steinberg, Laurence, Myers, Sonya S., & Robinson, Lara Rachel. (2007). The role of the family context in the development of emotion regulation. *Social Development, 16,* 361–388.

Morris, John A., Jordan, Cynthia L., & Breedlove, S. Marc. (2004). Sexual differentiation of the vertebrate nervous system. *Nature Neuroscience, 7,* 1034–1039.

Morris, Pamela, & Kalil, Ariel. (2006). Out-of-school time use during middle childhood in a low-income sample: Do combinations of activities affect achievement and behavior? In Aletha C. Huston & Marika N. Ripke (Eds.), *Developmental contexts in middle childhood: Bridges to adolescence and adulthood* (pp. 237–259). New York: Cambridge University Press.

Morrison, Frederick J., Ponitz, Claire Cameron, & McClelland, Megan M. (2010). Self-regulation and academic achievement in the transition to school. In Susan D. Calkins & Martha Ann Bell (Eds.), *Child development at the intersection of emotion and cognition* (pp. 203–224). Washington, DC: American Psychological Association.

Morrissey, Taryn. (2009). Multiple child-care arrangements and young children's behavioral outcomes. *Child Development, 80,* 59–76.

Morrow, Daniel G., Miller, Lisa M. Soederberg, Ridolfo, Heather E., Magnor, Clifford, Fischer, Ute M., Kokayeff, Nina K., et al. (2009). Expertise and age differences in pilot decision making. *Aging, Neuropsychology, and Cognition, 16,* 33–55.

Morrow, Daniel G., Ridolfo, Heather E., Menard, William E., Sanborn, Adam, Stine-Morrow, Elizabeth A. L., Magnor, Cliff, et al. (2003). Environmental support promotes expertise-based mitigation of age differences on pilot communication tasks. *Psychology & Aging, 18,* 268–284.

Morrow-Howell, Nancy, & Freedman, Marc. (2006). Introduction: Bringing civic engagement into sharper focus. *Generations, 30*(4), 6–9.

Moscovitch, Morris, Fernandes, Myra, & Troyer, Angela. (2001). Working-with-memory and cognitive resources: A component-process account of divided attention and memory. In Moshe Naveh-Benjamin, Morris Moscovitch, & Henry L. Roediger (Eds.), *Perspectives on human memory and cognitive aging: Essays in honour of Fergus Craik* (pp. 171–192). New York: Psychology Press.

Mosher, Catherine E., & Danoff-Burg, Sharon. (2007). Death anxiety and cancer-related stigma: A terror management analysis. *Death Studies, 31,* 885–907.

Moshman, David. (2005). *Adolescent psychological development: Rationality, morality, and identity* (2nd ed.). Mahwah, NJ: Erlbaum.

Moshman, David, & Geil, Molly. (1998). Collaborative reasoning: Evidence for collective rationality. *Thinking & Reasoning, 4,* 231–248.

Mosholder, Andrew D., Gelperin, Kate, Hammad, Tarek A., Phelan, Kathleen, & Johann-Liang, Rosemary. (2009). Hallucinations and other psychotic symptoms associated with the use of attention-deficit/hyperactivity disorder drugs in children. *Pediatrics, 123,* 611–616.

Moster, Dag, Lie, Rolv T., Irgens, Lorentz M., Bjerkedal, Tor, & Markestad, Trond. (2001). The association of Apgar score with subsequent death and cerebral palsy: A population-based study in term infants. *Journal of Pediatrics, 138,* 798–803.

Moulson, Margaret C., Westerlund, Alissa, Fox, Nathan A., Zeanah, Charles H., & Nelson, Charles A. (2009). The effects of early experience on face recognition: An event-related potential study of institutionalized children in Romania. *Child Development, 80,* 1039–1056.

Mowbray, Carol T., Megivern, Deborah, Mandiberg, James M., Strauss, Shari, Stein, Catherine H., Collins, Kim, et al. (2006). Campus mental health services: Recommendations for change. *American Journal of Orthopsychiatry, 76,* 226–237.

Mroczek, Daniel K., Spiro, Avion, III, & Griffin, Paul W. (2006). Personality and aging. In James E. Birren & K. Warner Schaie (Eds.), *Handbook of the psychology of aging* (6th ed., pp. 363–377). Amsterdam: Elsevier.

Mrozek-Budzyn, Dorota, Kieltyka, Agnieszka, & Majewska, Renata. (2010). Lack of association between measles-mumps-rubella vaccination and autism in children: A case-control study. *The Pediatric Infectious Disease Journal, 29,* 397–400

Müller, Ulrich, Dick, Anthony Steven, Gela, Katherine, Overton, Willis F., & Zelazo, Philip David. (2006). The role of negative priming in preschoolers' flexible rule use on the dimensional change card sort task. *Child Development, 77,* 395–412.

Mullis, Ina V. S., Martin, Michael O., & Foy, Pierre. (2008). *TIMSS 2007 international mathematics report: Findings from IEA's Trends in International Mathematics and Science Study at the fourth and eighth grades.* Chestnut Hill, MA: TIMSS & PIRLS International Study Center, Boston College.

Mullis, Ina V. S., Martin, Michael O., Gonzalez, Eugenio J., & Chrostowski, Steven J.

(2004). *TIMSS 2003 international mathematics report: Findings from IEA's Trends in International Mathematics and Science Study at the eighth and fourth grades*. Chestnut Hill, MA: TIMSS & PIRLS International Study Center, Lynch School of Education, Boston College.

Munroe, Robert L., & Romney, A. Kimbal. (2006). Gender and age differences in same-sex aggregation and social behavior: A four-culture study. *Journal of Cross-Cultural Psychology, 37*, 3–19.

Muraco, Anna. (2006). Intentional families: Fictive kin ties between cross-gender, different sexual orientation friends. *Journal of Marriage and Family, 68*, 1313–1325.

Murphy, Kevin, & Delanty, Norman. (2007). Sleep deprivation: A clinical perspective. *Sleep and Biological Rhythms, 5*, 2–14.

Murphy, Laura M. Bennett, Laurie-Rose, Cynthia, Brinkman, Tara M., & McNamara, Kelly A. (2007). Sustained attention and social competence in typically developing preschool-aged children. *Early Child Development and Care, 177*, 133–149.

Murray, Christopher J. L., Kulkarni, Sandeep C., Michaud, Catherine, Tomijima, Niels, Bulzacchelli, Maria T., Iandiorio, Terrell J., et al. (2006). Eight Americas: Investigating mortality disparities across races, counties, and race-counties in the United States. *PLoS Medicine, 3*, e260.

Murray, Erin K., Ricketts, Sue, & Dellaport, Jennifer. (2007). Hospital practices that increase breastfeeding duration: Results from a population-based study. *Birth, 34*, 202–211.

Musick, Marc A., Herzog, A. Regula, & House, James S. (1999). Volunteering and mortality among older adults: Findings from a national sample. *Journals of Gerontology: Series B: Psychological Sciences & Social Sciences, 54B*, S173–S180.

Mutti, Donald O., & Zadnik, Karla. (2009). Has near work's star fallen? *Optometry & Vision Science, 86*, 76–78.

Myers, David G. (2002). *Intuition: Its powers and perils*. New Haven, CT: Yale University Press.

Nagata, Chisato, Nakamura, Kozue, Wada, Keiko, Oba, Shino, Hayashi, Makoto, Takeda, Noriyuki, et al. (2010). Association of dietary fat, vegetables and antioxidant micronutrients with skin ageing in Japanese women. *British Journal of Nutrition, 103*, 1493–1498.

Nagda, Biren A., Gurin, Patricia, & Johnson, Shawnti M. (2005). Living, doing and thinking diversity: How does pre-college diversity experience affect first-year students' engagement with college diversity? In Robert S. Feldman (Ed.), *Improving the first year of college: Research and practice* (pp. 73–108). Mahwah, NJ: Erlbaum.

Nair, K. Sreekumaran, Rizza, Robert A., O'Brien, Peter, Dhatariya, Ketan, Short, Kevin R., Nehra, Ajay, et al. (2006). DHEA in elderly women and DHEA or testosterone in elderly men. *New England Journal of Medicine, 355*, 1647–1659.

Narvaez, Darcia, & Lapsley, Daniel K. (2009). Moral identity, moral functioning, and the development of moral character. In H. Ross Brian (Ed.), *Psychology of Learning and Motivation* (Vol. 50, pp. 237–274): Academic Press.

National Academy of Sciences & Institute of Medicine. (2008). *Science, evolution, and creationism*. Washington, DC: National Academies Press.

National Center for Education Statistics, Institute of Education Sciences. (2009). *The condition of education 2009* (NCES 2009-081). Washington, DC: U.S. Department of Education

National Center for Education Statistics, Institute of Education Sciences. (2010). *The condition of education 2010* (NCES 2010–028). Washington, DC: U.S. Department of Education

National Center for Health Statistics. (2007). *Health, United States, 2007, with chartbook on trends in the health of Americans* (DHSS Publication No. 2007–1232). Hyattsville, MD: Author.

National Center for Health Statistics. (2008). *Deaths: Final data for 2005*. U.S. Department Of Health And Human Services. Retrieved October 21, 2010, from the World Wide Web: http://www.cdc.gov/nchs/data/nvsr/nvsr56/nvsr56_10.pdf

National Center for Health Statistics. (2010). *Health, United States, 2009: With special feature on medical technology*. Author: Government Printing Office.

National Center for Public Policy and Higher Education. (2008). *Measuring up 2008*. Retrieved August 25, 2009, from http://measuringup2008.highereducation.org/

National Governors Association Center for Best Practices (NGA Center) and the Council of Chief State School Officers (CCSSO). (2010). *Common Core State Standards Initiative*. National Governors Association. Retrieved October 25, 2010, from the World Wide Web: http://corestandards.org/

National Heart, Lung, and Blood Institute. (n.d.). *Body mass index table*. Retrieved November 20, 2010, from the World Wide Web: http://www.nhlbi.nih.gov/guidelines/obesity/bmi_tbl.htm

National Research Council. (2009). *Science and decisions: Advancing risk assessment*. Washington, DC: National Academies Press.

National Safety Council. (2010). *Injury facts*. Itasca, IL: Author.

National Sleep Foundation. (2006). *Summary findings of the 2006 Sleep in America poll*. Retrieved July 17, 2008, from the World Wide Web: http://www.sleepfoundation.org/atf/cf/%7BF6BF2668-A1B4-4FE8-8D1A-A5D39340D9CB%7D/2006_summary_of_findings.pdf

Naudé, H., Marx, J., Pretorius, E., & Hislop-Esterhuyzen, N. (2007). Evidence of early childhood defects due to prenatal over-exposure to vitamin A: A case study. *Early Child Development and Care, 177*, 235–253.

Neal, David T., Wood, Wendy, & Quinn, Jeffrey M. (2006). Habits—A repeat performance. *Current Directions in Psychological Science, 15*, 198–202.

Neave, Nick. (2008). *Hormones and behaviour: A psychological approach*. New York: Cambridge University Press.

Neigh, Gretchen N., Gillespie, Charles F., & Nemeroff, Charles B. (2009). The neurobiological toll of child abuse and neglect. *Trauma, Violence, & Abuse, 10*, 389–410.

Neimeyer, Robert A., & Currier, Joseph M. (2009). Grief therapy: Evidence of efficacy and emerging directions. *Current Directions in Psychological Science, 18*, 352–356.

Nelson, Charles A., de Haan, Michelle, & Thomas, Kathleen M. (2006). *Neuroscience of cognitive development: The role of experience and the developing brain*. Hoboken, NJ: Wiley.

Nelson, Charles A., III, Thomas, Kathleen M., & de Haan, Michelle. (2006). Neural bases of cognitive development. In William Damon & Richard M. Lerner (Series Eds.) & Deanna Kuhn & Robert S. Siegler (Vol. Eds.), *Handbook of child psychology: Vol. 2. Cognition, perception, and language* (6th ed., pp. 3–57). Hoboken, NJ: Wiley.

Nelson, Charles A., III, Zeanah, Charles H., Fox, Nathan A., Marshall, Peter J., Smyke, Anna T., & Guthrie, Donald. (2007, December 21). Cognitive recovery in socially deprived young children: The Bucharest Early Intervention Project. *Science, 318*, 1937–1940.

Nelson, Jennifer A., Chiasson, Mary Ann, & Ford, Viola. (2004). Childhood overweight in a New York City WIC population. *American Journal of Public Health, 94*, 458–462.

Nelson, Larry J., Hart, Craig H., & Evans, Cortney A. (2008). Solitary-functional play and solitary-pretend play: Another look at the construct of solitary-active behavior using playground observations. *Social Development, 17*, 812–831.

Nelson, R. Michael, & DeBacker, Teresa K. (2008). Achievement motivation in adolescents: The role of peer climate and best friends. *Journal of Experimental Education, 76*, 170–189.

Nesselroade, John R., & Molenaar, Peter C. M. (2003). Quantitative models for developmental processes. In Jaan Valsiner & Kevin J. Connolly (Eds.), *Handbook of developmental psychology* (pp. 622–639). Thousand Oaks, CA: Sage.

Netting, Nancy S., & Burnett, Matthew L. (2004). Twenty years of student sexual behavior: Subcultural adaptations to a changing health environment. *Adolescence, 39*, 19–38.

Neugarten, Bernice L., & Neugarten, Dail A. (1986). Changing meanings of age in the aging society. In Alan J. Pifer & Lydia Bronte (Eds.), *Our aging society: Paradox and promise* (pp. 33–52). New York: Norton.

Neupert, Shevaun D., Mroczek, Daniel K., & Spiro, Avron, III. (2008). Neuroticism moderates the daily relation between stressors and memory failures. *Psychology and Aging, 23*, 287–296.

Newell, Karl M., Mayer-Kress, Gottfried, & Liu, Yeou-Teh. (2009). Aging, time scales, and sensorimotor variability. *Psychology and Aging, 24*, 809–818.

Newell, Karl M., Vaillancourt, David E., & Sosnoff, Jacob J. (2006). Aging, complexity, and motor performance. In James E. Birren & K. Warner Schaie (Eds.), *Handbook of the psychology of aging* (6th ed., pp. 163–182). Amsterdam: Elsevier.

Newirth, Joseph. (2003). *Between emotion and cognition: The generative unconscious.* New York: Other Press.

Newnham, Carol A., Milgrom, Jeannette, & Skouteris, Helen. (2009). Effectiveness of a modified mother-infant transaction program on outcomes for preterm infants from 3 to 24 months of age. *Infant Behavior and Development, 32,* 17–26.

Ng, Nawi, Weinehall, Lars, & Öhman, Ann. (2007). 'If I don't smoke, I'm not a real man'—Indonesian teenage boys' views about smoking. *Health Education Research, 22,* 794–804.

Ngui, Emmanuel, Cortright, Alicia, & Blair, Kathleen. (2009). An investigation of paternity status and other factors associated with racial and ethnic disparities in birth outcomes in Milwaukee, Wisconsin. *Maternal and Child Health Journal, 13,* 467–478.

Nguyen, Simone P., & Murphy, Gregory L. (2003). An apple is more than just a fruit: Cross-classification in children's concepts. *Child Development, 74,* 1783–1806.

Nic Gabhainn, Saoirse, Baban, Adriana, Boyce, William, & Godeau, Emmanuelle. (2009). How well protected are sexually active 15-year olds? Cross-national patterns in condom and contraceptive pill use 2002–2006. *International Journal of Public Health, 54,* 209–215.

Niccols, Alison. (2007). Fetal alcohol syndrome and the developing socio-emotional brain. *Brain and Cognition, 65,* 135–142.

NICHD Early Child Care Research Network (Ed.). (2005). *Child care and child development: Results from the NICHD Study of Early Child Care and Youth Development.* New York: Guilford Press.

NICHD Early Child Care Research Network. (2007). Age of entry to kindergarten and children's academic achievement and socioemotional development. *Early Education and Development, 18,* 337–368.

Nichols, Sharon L., & Berliner, David C. (2007). *Collateral damage: How high-stakes testing corrupts America's schools.* Cambridge, MA: Harvard Education Press.

Nichols, Tracy R., Graber, Julia A., Brooks-Gunn, Jeanne, & Botvin, Gilbert J. (2006). Sex differences in overt aggression and delinquency among urban minority middle school students. *Journal of Applied Developmental Psychology, 27,* 78–91.

Nielsen, Mark. (2006). Copying actions and copying outcomes: Social learning through the second year. *Developmental Psychology, 42,* 555–565.

Nielsen, Mark, Suddendorf, Thomas, & Slaughter, Virginia. (2006). Mirror self-recognition beyond the face. *Child Development, 77,* 176–185.

Nielsen, Mark, & Tomaselli, Keyan. (2010). Overimitation in Kalahari Bushman children and the origins of human cultural cognition. *Psychological Science, 21,* 729–736.

Nieto, Sonia. (2000). *Affirming diversity: The sociopolitical context of multicultural education* (3rd ed.). New York: Longman.

Nihtilä, Elina, & Martikainen, Pekka. (2008). Institutionalization of older adults after the death of a spouse. *American Journal of Public Health, 98,* 1228–1234.

Nimrod, Galit. (2007). Expanding, reducing, concentrating and diffusing: Post retirement leisure behavior and life satisfaction. *Leisure Sciences, 29,* 91–111.

Nisbett, Richard E., Peng, Kaiping, Choi, Incheol, & Norenzayan, Ara. (2001). Culture and systems of thought: Holistic versus analytic cognition. *Psychological Review, 108,* 291–310.

Nishida, Tracy K., & Lillard, Angeline S. (2007). The informative value of emotional expressions: 'Social referencing' in mother-child pretense. *Developmental Science, 10,* 205–212.

Nishina, Adrienne, & Juvonen, Jaana. (2005). Daily reports of witnessing and experiencing peer harassment in middle school. *Child Development, 76,* 435–450.

Nord, Mark, Andrews, Margaret, & Carlson, Steven. (2009). *Household food security in the United States, 2008.* (Economic Research Report No. 83). Washington, DC: U.S. Dept. of Agriculture.

Nordgren, Loran F., Harreveld, Frenk van, & Pligt, Joop van der. (2009). The restraint bias: How the illusion of self-restraint promotes impulsive behavior. *Psychological Science, 20,* 1523–1528.

Normile, Dennis. (2007, April 13). Japan picks up the 'innovation' mantra. *Science, 316,* 186.

Norris, Pippa. (2001). *Digital divide: Civic engagement, information poverty, and the internet worldwide.* New York: Cambridge University Press.

Nsamenang, A. Bame. (2004). *Cultures of human development and education: Challenge to growing up African.* New York: Nova Science Publishers.

Nucci, Larry, & Turiel, Elliot. (2009). Capturing the complexity of moral development and education. *Mind, Brain, and Education, 3,* 151–159.

Nurk, Eha, Refsum, Helga, Drevon, Christian A., Tell, Grethe S., Nygaard, Harald A., Engedal, Knut, et al. (2009). Intake of flavonoid-rich wine, tea, and chocolate by elderly men and women is associated with better cognitive test performance. *The Journal of Nutrition, 139,* 120–127.

Nurmi, Jari-Erik. (2004). Socialization and self-development: Channeling, selection, adjustment, and reflection. In Richard M. Lerner & Laurence D. Steinberg (Eds.), *Handbook of adolescent psychology* (2nd ed., pp. 85–124). Hoboken, NJ: Wiley.

O'Doherty, Kieran. (2006). Risk communication in genetic counselling: A discursive approach to probability. *Theory & Psychology, 16,* 225–256.

O'Donnell, Lydia, Stueve, Ann, Duran, Richard, Myint-U, Athi, Agronick, Gail, Doval, Alexi San, et al. (2008). Parenting practices, parents' underestimation of daughters' risks, and alcohol and sexual behaviors of urban girls. *Journal of Adolescent Health, 42,* 496–502.

O'Meara, Ellen S., White, Mark, Siscovick, David S., Lyles, Mary F., & Kuller, Lewis H. (2005). Hospitalization for pneumonia in the cardiovascular health study: Incidence, mortality, and influence on longer-term survival. *Journal of the American Geriatrics Society, 53,* 1108–1116.

O'Rahilly, Ronan R., & Müller, Fabiola. (2001). *Human embryology & teratology* (3rd ed.). New York: Wiley-Liss.

O'Rand, Angela M. (2006). Stratification and the life course: Life course capital, life course risks, and social inequality. In Robert H. Binstock & Linda K. George (Eds.), *Handbook of aging and the social sciences* (6th ed., pp. 145–162). Amsterdam: Elsevier.

O'Rourke, Norm, & Cappeliez, Philippe. (2005). Marital satisfaction and self-deception: Reconstruction of relationship histories among older adults. *Social Behavior and Personality, 33,* 273–282.

O'Rourke, Norm, Neufeld, Eva, Claxton, Amy, & Smith, JuliAnna Z. (2010). Knowing me-Knowing you: Reported personality and trait discrepancies as predictors of marital idealization between long-wed spouses. *Psychology and Aging, 25,* 412–421.

Oakes, J. Michael. (2009). The effect of media on children. *American Behavioral Scientist, 52,* 1136–1151.

Oddy, Wendy H. (2004). A review of the effects of breastfeeding on respiratory infections, atopy, and childhood asthma. *Journal of Asthma, 41,* 605–621.

Odlaug, Brian L., Mahmud, Waqar, Goddard, Andrew, & Grant, Jon E. (2010). Anxiety disorders. In Jon E. Grant & Marc N. Potenza (Eds.), *Young adult mental health* (pp. 231–254). New York: Oxford University Press.

Offit, Paul A. (2008). *Autism's false prophets: Bad science, risky medicine, and the search for a cure.* New York: Columbia University Press.

Ogawa, Tetsuo. (2004). Ageing in Japan: An issue of social contract in welfare transfer or generational conflict? In Peter Lloyd-Sherlock (Ed.), *Living longer: Ageing, development and social protection* (pp. 141–159). London: Zed Books.

Ogbu, John U. (2008). *Minority status, oppositional culture, and schooling.* New York: Routledge.

Ogden, Cynthia L., Carroll, Margaret D., & Flegal, Katherine M. (2008). High body mass index for age among US children and adolescents, 2003–2006. *Journal of the American Medical Association, 299,* 2401–2405.

Oh, Seungmi, & Lewis, Charlie. (2008). Korean preschoolers' advanced inhibitory control and its relation to other executive skills and mental state understanding. *Child Development, 79,* 80–99.

Oken, Emily, & Bellinger, David C. (2008). Fish consumption, methylmercury and child neurodevelopment. *Current Opinion in Pediatrics, 20,* 178–183.

Oldershaw, Lynn. (2002). *A national survey of parents of young children.* Toronto, ON, Canada: Invest in Kids.

Olfson, Mark, Crystal, Stephen, Huang, Cecilia, & Gerhard, Tobias. (2010). Trends in antipsychotic drug use by very young, privately insured children. *Journal of the American Academy of Child and Adolescent Psychiatry, 49,* 13–23.

Olsen, James P., Parra, Gilbert R., & Bennett, Shira A. (2010). Predicting violence in romantic relationships during adolescence and emerging adulthood: A critical review of the mechanisms by which familial and peer influences operate. *Clinical Psychology Review, 30,* 411–422.

Olson, Kristina R., & Dweck, Carol S. (2008). A blueprint for social cognitive development. *Perspectives on Psychological Science, 3,* 193–202.

Olweus, Dan. (1993). Victimization by peers: Antecedents and long-term outcomes. In Kenneth H. Rubin & Jens B. Asendorpf (Eds.), *Social withdrawal, inhibition, and shyness in childhood* (pp. 315–341). Hillsdale, NJ: Erlbaum.

Olweus, Dan, Limber, Sue, & Mahalic, Sharon F. (1999). *Bullying prevention program.* Boulder, CO: Center for the Study and Prevention of Violence, Institute of Behavioral Science, University of Colorado at Boulder.

Omariba, D. Walter Rasugu, & Boyle, Michael H. (2007). Family structure and child mortality in sub-Saharan Africa: Cross-national effects of polygyny. *Journal of Marriage and Family, 69,* 528–543.

Ontai, Lenna L., & Thompson, Ross A. (2008). Attachment, parent-child discourse and theory-of-mind development. *Social Development, 17,* 47–60.

Oosterman, Mirjam, Schuengel, Carlo, Slot, N. Wim, Bullens, Ruud A. R., & Doreleijers, Theo A. H. (2007). Disruptions in foster care: A review and meta-analysis. *Children and Youth Services Review, 29,* 53–76.

Oregon Department of Health (2010). 2009 summary of Oregon's Death with Dignity Act. Retrieved September 2010 from http://oregon.gov/DHS/ph/pas/ar-index.shtml.

Oregon Department of Human Services. (2006). *State of Oregon: Death with dignity act.* Retrieved December 18, 2010, from the World Wide Web: http://oregon.gov/DHS/ph/pas/index.shtml

Oregon Department of Human Services. (2010). *2009 Summary of Oregon's Death with Dignity Act.* Salem, OR: Author.

Orentlicher, David, & Callahan, Christopher M. (2004). Feeding tubes, slippery slopes, and physician-assisted suicide. *Journal of Legal Medicine, 25,* 389–409.

Organisation for Economic Co-operation and Development (OECD). (2008). *Education at a glance 2008: OECD indicators.* Paris: OECD Publications.

Orlich, Donald C., Harder, Robert J., Callahan, Richard C., Trevisan, Michael S., & Brown, Abbie H. (2009). *Teaching strategies: A guide to effective instruction* (9th ed.). Boston: Cengage Learning.

Ormerod, Thomas C. (2005). Planning and ill-defined problems. In Robin Morris & Geoff Ward (Eds.), *The cognitive psychology of planning* (pp. 53–70). New York: Psychology Press.

Orzeck, Pam, & Silverman, Marjorie. (2008). Recognizing post-caregiving as part of the caregiving career: Implications for practice. *Journal of Social Work Practice, 22,* 211–220.

Osgood, D. Wayne, Ruth, Gretchen, Eccles, Jacquelynne S., Jacobs, Janis E., & Barber, Bonnie L. (2005). Six paths to adulthood: Fast starters, parents without careers, educated partners, educated singles, working singles, and slow starters. In Richard A. Settersten, Jr., Frank F. Furstenberg, Jr., & Rubén G. Rumbaut (Eds.), *On the frontier of adulthood: Theory, research, and public policy* (pp. 320–355). Chicago: University of Chicago Press.

Osher, David, Bear, George G., Sprague, Jeffrey R., & Doyle, Walter. (2010). How can we improve school discipline? *Educational Researcher, 39,* 48–58.

Outtz, James. (2010). *Adverse impact: Implications for organizational staffing and high stakes selection.* New York: Psychology Press.

Over, Harriet, & Gattis, Merideth. (2010). Verbal imitation is based on intention understanding. *Cognitive Development, 25,* 46–55.

Overbeek, Geertjan, Stattin, Håkan, Vermulst, Ad, Ha, Thao, & Engels, Rutger C. M. E. (2007). Parent-child relationships, partner relationships, and emotional adjustment: A birth-to-maturity prospective study. *Developmental Psychology, 43,* 429–437.

Oxman, Michael N., Levin, Myron J., Johnson, Gary R., Schmader, Kenneth E., Straus, Stephen E., Arbeit, Robert D., et al. (2005). A vaccine to prevent herpes zoster and postherpetic neuralgia in older adults. *New England Journal of Medicine, 352,* 2271–2284.

Oyekale, Abayomi Samuel, & Oyekale, Tolulope Olayemi. (2009). Do mothers' educational levels matter in child malnutrition and health outcomes in Gambia and Niger? *The Social Sciences, 4,* 118–127.

Oza-Frank, Reena, & Narayan, K. M. Venkat. (2010). Overweight and diabetes prevalence among U.S. immigrants. *American Journal of Public Health, 100,* 661–668.

Ozer, Emily J., & Weiss, Daniel S. (2004). Who develops posttraumatic stress disorder? *Current Directions in Psychological Science, 13,* 169–172.

Padilla-Walker, Laura M., Barry, Carolyn McNamara, Carroll, Jason S., Madsen, Stephanie D., & Nelson, Larry J. (2008). Looking on the bright side: The role of identity status and gender on positive orientations during emerging adulthood. *Journal of Adolescence, 31,* 451–467.

Pagani, Linda S., Japel, Christa, Girard, Alain, Farhat, Abdeljelil, Cote, Sylvana, & Tremblay, Richard E. (2006). Middle childhood life course trajectories: Links between family dysfunction and children's behavioral development. In Aletha C. Huston & Marika N. Ripke (Eds.), *Developmental contexts in middle childhood: Bridges to adolescence and adulthood* (pp. 130–149). New York: Cambridge University Press.

Paletz, Susannah B. F., & Peng, Kaiping. (2009). Problem finding and contradiction: Examining the relationship between naive dialectical thinking, ethnicity, and creativity. *Creativity Research Journal, 21,* 139–151.

Palmer, Raymond F., Blanchard, Stephen, Jean, Carlos R., & Mandell, David S. (2005). School district resources and identification of children with autistic disorder. *American Journal of Public Health, 95,* 125–130.

Palmore, Erdman. (1998). *The facts on aging quiz* (2nd ed.). New York: Springer.

Palmore, Erdman. (2005). Three decades of research on ageism. *Generations, 29*(1), 87–90.

Palmore, Erdman, Branch, Laurence G., & Harris, Diana K. (2005). *Encyclopedia of ageism.* Binghamton, NY: Haworth.

Pardini, Matteo, & Nichelli, Paolo F. (2009). Age-related decline in mentalizing skills across adult life span. *Experimental Aging Research, 35,* 98–106.

Park, Denise C., & Payer, Doris. (2006). Working memory across the adult lifespan. In Ellen Bialystok & Fergus I. M. Craik (Eds.), *Lifespan cognition: Mechanisms of change* (pp. 128–142). New York: Oxford University Press.

Park, Denise C., & Reuter-Lorenz, Patricia. (2009). The adaptive brain: Aging and neurocognitive scaffolding. *Annual Review of Psychology, 60,* 173–196.

Park, D. J. J., & Congdon, Nathan G. (2004). Evidence for an "epidemic" of myopia. *Annals, Academy of Medicine, Singapore, 33,* 21–26.

Park, Nansook, & Peterson, Christopher. (2009). Achieving and sustaining a good life. *Perspectives on Psychological Science, 4,* 422–428.

Parke, Ross D., & Buriel, Raymond. (2006). Socialization in the family: Ethnic and ecological perspectives. In William Damon & Richard M. Lerner (Series Eds.) & Nancy Eisenberg (Vol. Ed.), *Handbook of child psychology: Vol. 3. Social, emotional, and personality development* (6th ed., pp. 429–504). Hoboken, NJ: Wiley.

Parke, Ross D., Coltrane, Scott, Duffy, Sharon, Buriel, Raymond, Dennis, Jessica, Powers, Justina, et al. (2004). Economic stress, parenting, and child adjustment in Mexican American and European American families. *Child Development, 75,* 1632–1656.

Parker, Susan W., & Nelson, Charles A. (2005). The impact of early institutional rearing on the ability to discriminate facial expressions of emotion: An event-related potential study. *Child Development, 76,* 54–72.

Parten, Mildred B. (1932). Social participation among pre-school children. *The Journal of Abnormal and Social Psychology, 27,* 243–269.

Parveen, Sahdia, & Morrison, Val. (2009). Predictors of familism in the caregiver role: A pilot study. *Journal of Health Psychology, 14,* 1135–1143.

Pascarella, Ernest T. (2005). Cognitive impacts of the first year of college. In Robert S. Feldman (Ed.), *Improving the first year of college: Research and practice* (pp. 111–140). Mahwah, NJ: Erlbaum.

Pascarella, Ernest T., & Terenzini, Patrick T. (1991). *How college affects students: Findings and insights from twenty years of research.* San Francisco: Jossey-Bass Publishers.

Pashler, Harold, McDaniel, Mark, Rohrer, Doug, & Bjork, Robert. (2008). Learning styles: Concepts and evidence. *Psychological Science in the Public Interest, 9,* 105–119.

Pastore, Ann L., & Maguire, Kathleen. (2005). *Sourcebook of criminal justice statistics,*

2003 (NCJ 208756). Rockville, MD: Justice Statistics Clearinghouse/NCJRS.

Patel, Vimla L., Arocha, José F., & Kaufman, David R. (1999). Expertise and tacit knowledge in medicine. In Robert J. Sternberg & Joseph A. Horvath (Eds.), *Tacit knowledge in professional practice: Researcher and practitioner perspectives* (pp. 75–99). Mahwah, NJ: Erlbaum.

Patrick, Kevin, Norman, Gregory J., Calfas, Karen J., Sallis, James F., Zabinski, Marion F., Rupp, Joan, et al. (2004). Diet, physical activity, and sedentary behaviors as risk factors for overweight in adolescence. *Archives of Pediatrics & Adolescent Medicine, 158,* 385–390.

Patton, George C., Hemphill, Sheryl A., Beyers, Jennifer M., Bond, Lyndal, Toumbourou, John W., McMorris, Barbara J., et al. (2007). Pubertal stage and deliberate self-harm in adolescents. *Journal of the American Academy of Child & Adolescent Psychiatry, 46,* 508–514.

Pauli-Pott, Ursula, Mertesacker, Bettina, & Beckmann, Dieter. (2004). Predicting the development of infant emotionality from maternal characteristics. *Development & Psychopathology, 16,* 19–42.

Pausch, Randy (with Jeffrey Zaslow). (2007). *The last lecture.* New York: Hyperion.

Pedersen, Nancy L., Spotts, Erica, & Kato, Kenji. (2005). Genetic influences on midlife functioning. In Sherry L. Willis & Mike Martin (Eds.), *Middle adulthood: A lifespan perspective* (pp. 65–98). Thousand Oaks, CA: Sage.

Pelham, William E., Jr., & Fabiano, Gregory A. (2008). Evidence-based psychosocial treatments for attention-deficit/hyperactivity disorder. *Journal of Clinical Child and Adolescent Psychology, 37,* 184–214.

Pellegrini, Anthony D. (2009). Research and policy on children's play. *Child Development Perspectives, 3,* 131–136.

Pellegrini, Anthony D., Dupuis, Danielle, & Smith, Peter K. (2007). Play in evolution and development. *Developmental Review, 27,* 261–276.

Pellegrini, Anthony D., & Smith, Peter K. (Eds.). (2005). *The nature of play: Great apes and humans.* New York: Guilford Press.

Peng, Duan, & Robins, Philip K. (2010). Who should care for our kids? The effects of infant child care on early child development. *Journal of Children and Poverty, 16,* 1–45.

Penninx, Brenda W. J. H., & van den Brink, S. (2000). Aging and psychological stress. In George Fink (Ed.), *Encyclopedia of stress* (pp. 104–110). San Diego: Academic Press.

Pennisi, Elizabeth. (2009, November 6). No genome left behind. *Science, 326,* 794–795.

Pepler, Debra, Craig, Wendy, Yuile, Amy, & Connolly, Jennifer. (2004). Girls who bully: A developmental and relational perspective. In Martha Putallaz & Karen L. Bierman (Eds.), *Aggression, antisocial behavior, and violence among girls: A developmental perspective* (pp. 90–109). New York: Guilford Press.

Perels, Franziska, Merget-Kullmann, Miriam, Wende, Milena, Schmitz, Bernhard, & Buchbinder, Carla. (2009). Improving self-regulated learning of preschool children: Evaluation of training for kindergarten teachers. *British Journal of Educational Psychology, 79,* 311–327.

Perfetti, Jennifer, Clark, Roseanne, & Fillmore, Capri-Mara. (2004). Postpartum depression: Identification, screening, and treatment. *Wisconsin Medical Journal, 103,* 56–63.

Perie, Marianne, Grigg, Wendy S., & Dion, Gloria S. (2005). *The nation's report card: Mathematics 2005* (NCES 2006–453). Washington, DC: U.S. Department of Education, National Center for Education Statistics.

Perls, Thomas T. (2008). Centenarians and genetics. In Catherine Y. Read, Robert C. Green, & Michael A. Smyer (Eds.), *Aging, biotechnology, and the future* (pp. 89–99). Baltimore: Johns Hopkins University.

Perner, Josef. (2000). About + belief + counterfactual. In Peter Mitchell & Kevin John Riggs (Eds.), *Children's reasoning and the mind* (pp. 367–401). Hove, England: Psychology Press.

Perry, William G., Jr. (1981). Cognitive and ethical growth: The making of meaning. In A. Chickering (Ed.), *The modern American college: Responding to the new realities of diverse students and a changing society* (pp. 76–116). San Francisco: Jossey-Bass.

Perry, William G. (1999). *Forms of intellectual and ethical development in the college years: A scheme.* San Francisco: Jossey-Bass.

Perry-Jenkins, Maureen, Goldberg, Abbie E., Pierce, Courtney P., & Sayer, Aline G. (2007). Shift work, role overload, and the transition to parenthood. *Journal of Marriage and Family, 69,* 123–138.

Persaud, Trivedi V. N., Chudley, Albert E., & Skalko, Richard G. (1985). *Basic concepts in teratology.* New York: Liss.

Peterson, Jordan B., & Flanders, Joseph L. (2005). Play and the regulation of aggression. In Richard Ernest Tremblay, Willard W. Hartup, & John Archer (Eds.), *Developmental origins of aggression* (pp. 133–157). New York: Guilford Press.

Pettigrew, Thomas F., Christ, Oliver, Wagner, Ulrich, Meertens, Roel W., van Dick, Rolf, & Zick, Andreas. (2008). Relative deprivation and intergroup prejudice. *Journal of Social Issues, 64,* 385–401.

Pew Commission on Children in Foster Care. (2004). *Safety, permanence and well-being for children in foster care.* Retrieved June 23, 2007, from the World Wide Web: http://pewfostercare.org/research/docs/FinalReport.pdf

Pew Commission on Children in Foster Care. (2004). *Fostering the future: Safety, permanence and well-being for children in foster care.* Retrieved June 25, 2009, from the World Wide Web: http://pewfostercare.org/research/docs/FinalReport.pdf

Pew Research Center. (2007). *A portrait of "Generation Next": How young people view their lives, futures and politics.* Pew Research Center. Retrieved November 19, 2009, from the World Wide Web: http://people-press.org/reports/pdf/300.pdf

Pew Research Center. (2008, December 15). *Hillary's new job better known than Dow Jones Average.* Retrieved December 15, 2010, from the World Wide Web: http://pewresearch.org/pubs/1055/hillarys-new-job-better-known-than-dow-jones-average

Pew Research Center. (2009). *Growing old in america: Expectations vs. reality.* Washington, DC: Pew Research Center.

Pew Research Center. (2010). *Teen and young adult internet use.* Retrieved November 15, 2010, from the World Wide Web: http://www.pewinternet.org/Infographics/2010/Internet-acess-by-age-group-over-time-Update.aspx

Pew Research Center. (2010). *Millennials: A portrait of "Generation Next." Confident. Connected. Open to change.* Retrieved November 24, 2010, from the World Wide Web: http://pewsocialtrends.org/files/2010/10/millennials-confident-connected-open-to-change.pdf

Pew Research Center. (2010, November 18). *The decline of marriage and rise of new families: VI. New family types.* Washington, DC: Pew Research Center: Social and Demographic Trends.

Pew Research Center for the People & the Press. (2009). *Independents take center stage in Obama era.* Washington, DC: Author.

Pew Research Center for the People & the Press. (2009, October 9). *Most still oppose gay marriage, but support for civil unions continues to rise.* Retrieved November 20, 2010, from the World Wide Web: http://pewresearch.org/pubs/1375/gay-marriage-civil-unions-opinion

Pew Research Center for the People & the Press. (2010). *Support for same-sex marriage edges upward.* Washington, DC: Author.

Pew Social Trends Staff. (2010, March 18). *The return of the multi-generational family household.* Washington, DC: Pew Research Center: Social & Demographic Trends.

Pfeffer, Jeffrey. (2007). Human resources from an organizational behavior perspective: Some paradoxes explained. *Journal of Economic Perspectives, 21,* 115–134.

Pfeiffer, Ronald F., Wszolek, Zbigniew K., & Ebadi, Manuchair (Eds.). (2011). *Parkinson's disease* (2nd ed.). Boca Raton, FL: CRC Press.

Philips, Sharon, & Tolmie, Andrew. (2007). Children's performance on and understanding of the Balance Scale problem: The effects of parental support. *Infant and Child Development, 16,* 95–117.

Philipsen, Nina, & Brooks-Gunn, Jeanne. (2008). Overweight and obesity in childhood. In Thomas P. Gullotta & Gary M. Blau (Eds.), *Handbook of childhood behavioral issues: Evidence-based approaches to prevention and treatment* (pp. 125–146). New York: Routledge/Taylor & Francis.

Phillips, Deborah A., Gormley, William T., Jr., & Lowenstein, Amy E. (2009). Inside the pre-kindergarten door: Classroom climate and instructional time allocation in Tulsa's pre-K programs. *Early Childhood Research Quarterly, 24,* 213–228.

Phillips, Mary L. (2010). Coming of age? Neuroimaging biomarkers in youth. *American Journal of Psychiatry, 167,* 4–7.

Phillips, Tommy M., & Pittman, Joe F. (2007). Adolescent psychological well-being by identity style. *Journal of Adolescence, 30,* 1021–1034.

Phillipson, Chris. (2006). Ageing and globalization. In John A. Vincent, Chris R. Phillipson, & Murna Downs (Eds.), *The futures of old age* (pp. 201–207). Thousand Oaks, CA: Sage.

Phillipson, Sivanes, & Phillipson, Shane N. (2007). Academic expectations, belief of ability, and involvement by parents as predictors of child achievement: A cross-cultural comparison. *Educational Psychology, 27,* 329–348.

Phinney, Jean S. (2006). Ethnic identity exploration in emerging adulthood. In Jeffrey Jensen Arnett & Jennifer Lynn Tanner (Eds.), *Emerging adults in America: Coming of age in the 21st century* (pp. 117–134). Washington, DC: American Psychological Association.

Piaget, Jean. (1929). *The child's conception of the world* (Joan Tomlinson & Andrew Tomlinson, Trans.). New York: Harcourt, Brace and Company.

Piaget, Jean. (1952). *The origins of intelligence in children* (M. Cook, Trans.). Oxford, England: International Universities Press.

Piaget, Jean. (1954). *The construction of reality in the child* (Margaret Cook, Trans.). New York: Basic Books.

Piaget, Jean. (1962). *Play, dreams and imitation in childhood* (C. Gattegno & F. M. Hodgson, Trans.). New York: Norton. (Original work published 1945)

Piaget, Jean. (1972). *The psychology of intelligence.* Totowa, NJ: Littlefield. (Original work published 1950)

Piaget, Jean. (1997). *The moral judgment of the child* (Marjorie Gabain, Trans.). New York: Simon and Schuster. (Original work published 1932)

Piaget, Jean, & Inhelder, Bärbel. (1969). *The psychology of the child.* New York: Basic Books.

Piaget, Jean, Voelin-Liambey, Daphne, & Berthoud-Papandropoulou, Ioanna. (2001). *Problems of class inclusion and logical implication* (Robert L. Campbell, Trans.). Hove, E. Sussex, England: Psychology Press. (Original work published 1977)

Piazza, Manuela, Facoetti, Andrea, Trussardi, Anna Noemi, Berteletti, Ilaria, Conte, Stefano, Lucangeli, Daniela, et al. (2010). Developmental trajectory of number acuity reveals a severe impairment in developmental dyscalculia. *Cognition, 116,* 33–41.

Pin, Tamis, Eldridge, Beverley, & Galea, Mary P. (2007). A review of the effects of sleep position, play position, and equipment use on motor development in infants. *Developmental Medicine & Child Neurology, 49,* 858–867.

Pinborg, Anja, Loft, Anne, & Nyboe Andersen, Anders. (2004). Neonatal outcome in a Danish national cohort of 8602 children born after in vitro fertilization or intracytoplasmic sperm injection: The role of twin pregnancy. *Acta Obstetricia et Gynecologica Scandinavica, 83,* 1071–1078.

Pinheiro, Andréa Poyastro (Ed.). (2006). *World report on violence against children.* Geneva, Switzerland: United Nations.

Pinker, Steven. (2007). *The stuff of thought: Language as a window into human nature.* New York: Viking.

Pinquart, Martin, & Silbereisen, Rainer K. (2006). Socioemotional selectivity in cancer patients. *Psychology and Aging, 21,* 419–423.

Pinquart, Martin, & Sörensen, Silvia. (2003). Associations of stressors and uplifts of caregiving with caregiver burden and depressive mood: A meta-analysis. *Journals of Gerontology: Series B: Psychological Sciences & Social Sciences, 58B,* P112–P128.

Piontelli, Alessandra. (2002). *Twins: From fetus to child.* London: Routledge.

Piotrowski, Martin. (2008). Migrant remittances and household division: The case of Nang Rong, Thailand. *Journal of Marriage and Family, 70,* 1074–1087.

Piper, Don (with Cecil B. Murphey). (2004). *90 minutes in heaven: A true story of death & life.* Grand Rapids, MI: Revell.

Pirozzo, Sandi, Papinczak, Tracey, & Glasziou, Paul. (2003). Whispered voice test for screening for hearing impairment in adults and children: Systematic review. *British Medical Journal, 327,* 967–960.

PISA. (2009). *Learning mathematics for life: A perspective from PISA* Paris: OECD.

Pitskhelauri, G. Z. (1982). *The longliving of Soviet Georgia* (Gari Lesnoff-Caravaglia, Trans.). New York: Human Sciences Press.

Pizer, Ginger, Walters, Keith, & Meier, Richard P. (2007). Bringing up baby with baby signs: Language ideologies and socialization in hearing families. *Sign Language Studies, 7,* 387–430.

Planalp, Sally, & Trost, Melanie R. (2008). Communication issues at the end of life: Reports from hospice volunteers. *Health Communication, 23,* 222–233.

Plank, Stephen B., & MacIver, Douglas J. (2003). Educational achievement. In Marc H. Bornstein, Lucy Davidson, Corey L. M. Keyes, & Kristin Moore (Eds.), *Well-being: Positive development across the life course* (pp. 341–354). Mahwah, NJ: Erlbaum.

Plassman, Brenda L., Langa, Kenneth M., Fisher, Gwenith G., Heeringa, Steven G., Weir, David R., Ofstedal, Mary Beth, et al. (2007). Prevalence of dementia in the United States: The aging, demographics, and memory study. *Neuroepidemiology, 29,* 125–132.

Plomin, Robert, DeFries, John C., Craig, Ian W., & McGuffin, Peter. (2003). *Behavioral genetics in the postgenomic era.* Washington, DC: American Psychological Association.

Plomin, Robert, Defries, John C., McClearn, Gerald E., & McGuffin, Peter. (2008). *Behavioral genetics* (5th ed.). New York: Worth.

Pluess, Michael, & Belsky, Jay. (2009). Differential susceptibility to rearing experience: The case of childcare. *Journal of Child Psychology and Psychiatry and Allied Disciplines, 50,* 396–404.

Plutchik, Robert. (2003). *Emotions and life: Perspectives from psychology, biology, and evolution.* Washington, DC: American Psychological Association.

Pocobelli, Gaia, Kristal, Alan R., Patterson, Ruth E., Potter, John D., Lampe, Johanna W., Kolar, Ann, et al. (2010). Total mortality risk in relation to use of less-common dietary supplements. *The American Journal of Clinical Nutrition, 91,* 1791–1800.

Pocobelli, Gaia, Peters, Ulrike, Kristal, Alan R., & White, Emily. (2009). Use of supplements of multivitamins, vitamin C, and vitamin E in relation to mortality. *American Journal of Epidemiology, 170,* 472–483.

Pollak, Seth D., Cicchetti, Dante, Hornung, Katherine, & Reed, Alex. (2000). Recognizing emotion in faces: Developmental effects of child abuse and neglect. *Developmental Psychology, 36,* 679–688.

Poon, Leonard W. (2008). What can we learn from centenarians?, *Aging, biotechnology and the future* (pp. 100–110). Baltimore, MD: Johns Hopkins University.

Porche, Michelle V., Ross, Stephanie J., & Snow, Catherine E. (2004). From preschool to middle school: The role of masculinity in low-income urban adolescent boys' literacy skills and academic achievement. In Niobe Way & Judy Y. Chu (Eds.), *Adolescent boys: Exploring diverse cultures of boyhood* (pp. 338–360). New York: New York University Press.

Posner, Michael I., Rothbart, Mary K., Sheese, Brad E., & Tang, Yiyuan. (2007). The anterior cingulate gyrus and the mechanism of self-regulation. *Cognitive, Affective & Behavioral Neuroscience, 7,* 391–395.

Poulin-Dubois, Diane, & Chow, Virginia. (2009). The effect of a looker's past reliability on infants' reasoning about beliefs. *Developmental Psychology, 45,* 1576–1582.

Poulsen, Pernille, Esteller, Manel, Vaag, Allan, & Fraga, Mario F. (2007). The epigenetic basis of twin discordance in age-related diseases. *Pediatric Research, 61*(5, Pt. 2), 38R–42R.

Powell, Douglas R. (2006). Families and early childhood interventions. In William Damon & Richard M. Lerner (Series Eds.) & K. Ann Renninger & Irving E. Sigel (Vol. Eds.), *Handbook of child psychology: Vol. 4. Child psychology in practice* (6th ed., pp. 548–591). Hoboken: Wiley.

Powell, Kendall. (2006). Neurodevelopment: How does the teenage brain work? *Nature, 442,* 865–867.

Powledge, Tabitha M. (2007, October). Easing hormone anxiety. *Scientific American, 297,* 32, 34.

Powlishta, Kimberly. (2004). Gender as a social category: Intergroup processes and gender-role development. In Mark Bennett & Fabio Sani (Eds.), *The development of the social self* (pp. 103–133). Hove, East Sussex, England: Psychology Press.

Prado, Carlos G. (2008). *Choosing to die: Elective death and multiculturalism.* New York: Cambridge University Press.

Pratt, Michael W., Norris, Joan E., Cressman, Kate, Lawford, Heather, & Hebblethwaite, Shannon. (2008). Parents' stories of grandparenting concerns in the three-generational family: Generativity, optimism, and forgiveness. *Journal of Personality, 76,* 581–604.

Pratt, Michael W., Norris, Joan E., Lawford, Heather, & Arnold, Mary Louise. (2010). What he said to me stuck: Adolescents' narratives of grandparents and their identity development in emerging adulthood. In Kate C. McLean & Monisha Pasupathi (Eds.), *Narrative development in adolescence: Creating the storied self* (pp. 93–112). New York: Springer Science + Business Media.

Presser, Harriet B. (2005). *Working in a 24/7 economy: Challenges for American families* (Paperback ed.). New York: Russell Sage.

Presser, Harriet B., Gornick, Janet C., & Parashar, Sangeeta. (2008). Gender and nonstandard work hours in 12 European countries. *Monthly Labor Review, 131,* 83–103.

Pressley, Michael, & Hilden, Katherine. (2006). Cognitive strategies: Production deficiencies and successful strategy instruction everywhere. In William Damon & Richard M. Lerner (Series Eds.) & Deanna Kuhn & Robert S. Siegler (Vol. Eds.), *Handbook of child psychology: Vol. 2. Cognition, perception, and language* (6th ed., pp. 511–556). Hoboken, NJ: Wiley.

Preston, Tom, & Kelly, Michael. (2006). A medical ethics assessment of the case of Terri Schiavo. *Death Studies, 30,* 121–133.

Priess, Heather A., Lindberg, Sara M., & Hyde, Janet Shibley. (2009). Adolescent gender-role identity and mental health: Gender intensification revisited. *Child Development, 80,* 1531–1544.

Print, Murray, Ugarte, Carolina, Naval, Concepción, & Mihr, Anja. (2008). Moral and human rights education: The contribution of the United Nations. *Journal of Moral Education, 37,* 115–132.

Promislow, Daniel, Fedorka, Ken, & Burger, Joep. (2006). Evolutionary biology of aging: Future directions. In Edward J. Masoro & Steven N. Austad (Eds.), *Handbook of the biology of aging* (6th ed., pp. 217–242). Amsterdam: Elsevier Academic Press.

Proulx, Christine M., Helms, Heather M., & Buehler, Cheryl. (2007). Marital quality and personal well-being: A meta-analysis. *Journal of Marriage and Family, 69,* 576–593.

Pruden, Shannon M., Hirsh-Pasek, Kathy, Golinkoff, Roberta Michnick, & Hennon, Elizabeth A. (2006). The birth of words: Ten-month-olds learn words through perceptual salience. *Child Development, 77,* 266–280.

Pryor, John H., Hurtado, Sylvia, DeAngelo, Linda, Palucki Blake, Laura, & Tran, Serge. (2009). *The American freshman: National norms fall 2009.* Los Angeles: Higher Education Research Institute, UCLA.

Puhl, Rebecca M., & Heuer, Chelsea A. (2010). Obesity stigma: Important considerations for public health. *American Journal Of Public Health, 100,* 1019–1028.

Pullmann, Helle, & Allik, Jüri. (2008). Relations of academic and general self-esteem to school achievement. *Personality and Individual Differences, 45,* 559–564.

Puri, Sunita, & Nachtigall, Robert D. (2010). The ethics of sex selection: a comparison of the attitudes and experiences of primary care physicians and physician providers of clinical sex selection services. *Fertility and Sterility, 93,* 2107–2114.

Purves, Dale, Augustine, George J., Fitzpatrick, David, Hall, William C., LaMantia, Anthony-Samuel, McNamara, James O., et al. (Eds.). (2004). *Neuroscience* (3rd ed.). Sunderland, MA: Sinauer Associates.

Putnam, Robert D. (2000). *Bowling alone: The collapse and revival of American community.* New York: Simon & Schuster.

Pyne, Derek Arnold. (2010). A model of religion and death. *Journal of Socio-Economics, 39,* 46–54.

Qin, Lili, Pomerantz, Eva M., & Wang, Qian. (2009). Are gains in decision-making autonomy during early adolescence beneficial for emotional functioning? The case of the United States and China. *Child Development, 80,* 1705–1721.

Qualls, Sarah Honn, & Kasl-Godley, Julia E. (2010). *End-of-life issues, grief, and bereavement: What clinicians need to know.* Hoboken, NJ: Wiley.

Quas, Jodi A., Bauer, Amy, & Boyce, W. Thomas. (2004). Physiological reactivity, social support, and memory in early childhood. *Child Development, 75,* 797–814.

Queen, Tara L., & Hess, Thomas M. (2010). Age differences in the effects of conscious and unconscious thought in decision making. *Psychology and Aging, 25,* 251–261.

Quinn, Alexander E., Georges, Arthur, Sarre, Stephen D., Guarino, Fiorenzo, Ezaz, Tariq, & Graves, Jennifer A. Marshall. (2007, April 20). Temperature sex reversal implies sex gene dosage in a reptile. *Science, 316,* 411.

Quinn, Paul C. (2004). Development of subordinate-level categorization in 3- to 7-month-old infants. *Child Development, 75,* 886–899.

Raaijmakers, Quinten A. W., Engels, Rutger C. M. E., & Van Hoof, Anne. (2005). Delinquency and moral reasoning in adolescence and young adulthood. *International Journal of Behavioral Development, 29,* 247–258.

Rabbitt, Patrick, Lunn, Mary, & Wong, Danny. (2008). Death, dropout, and longitudinal measurements of cognitive change in old age. *Journals of Gerontology Series B: Psychological Sciences and Social Sciences, 63,* 271–278.

Race, Ethnicity, and Genetics Working Group of the National Human Genome Research Institute. (2005). The use of racial, ethnic, and ancestral categories in human genetics research. *American Journal of Human Genetics, 77,* 519–532.

Radmacher, Kimberley, & Azmitia, Margarita. (2006). Are there gendered pathways to intimacy in early adolescents' and emerging adults' friendships? *Journal of Adolescent Research, 21,* 415–448.

Rahe, Richard H. (2000). Coping, stress and. In George Fink (Ed.), *Encyclopedia of stress* (pp. 541–546). San Diego: Academic Press.

Rajaratnam, Julie Knoll, Marcus, Jake R., Flaxman, Abraham D., Wang, Haidong, Levin-Rector, Alison, Dwyer, Laura, et al. (2010). Neonatal, postneonatal, childhood, and under-5 mortality for 187 countries, 1970–2010: A systematic analysis of progress towards Millennium Development Goal 4. *Lancet, 375,* 1988–2008.

Ramón, Rosa, Ballester, Ferran, Aguinagalde, Xabier, Amurrio, Ascensión, Vioque, Jesús, Lacasaña, Marina, et al. (2009). Fish consumption during pregnancy, prenatal mercury exposure, and anthropometric measures at birth in a prospective mother-infant cohort study in Spain. *American Journal of Clinical Nutrition, 90,* 1047–1055.

Rand, Michael R., & Catalano, Shannan M. (2007). *Criminal victimization, 2006* (NCJ 219413). Washington, DC: U.S. Department of Justice.

Rankin, Jane L., Lane, David J., Gibbons, Frederick X., & Gerrard, Meg. (2004). Adolescent self-consciousness: Longitudinal age changes and gender differences in two cohorts. *Journal of Research on Adolescence, 14,* 1–21.

Ravizza, Kenneth. (2007). Peak experiences in sport. In Daniel Smith & Michael Bar-Eli (Eds.), *Essential readings in sport and exercise psychology* (pp. 122–125). Champaign, IL: Human Kinetics.

Raz, Naftali. (2005). The aging brain observed in vivo: Differential changes and their modifiers. In Roberto Cabeza, Lars Nyberg, & Denise Park (Eds.), *Cognitive neuroscience of aging: Linking cognitive and cerebral aging* (pp. 19–57). New York: Oxford University Press.

Ream, Geoffrey L., & Savin-Williams, Ritch C. (2003). Religious development in adolescence. In Gerald R. Adams & Michael D. Berzonsky (Eds.), *Blackwell handbook of adolescence* (pp. 51–59). Malden, MA: Blackwell.

Recchia, Holly E., & Howe, Nina. (2009). Associations between social understanding, sibling relationship quality, and siblings' conflict strategies and outcomes. *Child Development, 80,* 1564–1578.

Reece, E. Albert, & Hobbins, John C. (Eds.). (2007). *Handbook of clinical obstetrics: The fetus & mother handbook* (2nd ed.). Malden, MA: Blackwell.

Reese, Elaine, Bird, Amy, & Tripp, Gail. (2007). Children's self-esteem and moral self: Links to parent-child conversations regarding emotion. *Social Development, 16,* 460–478.

Reich, John W., Zautra, Alex J., & Hall, John Stuart (Eds.). (2010). *Handbook of adult resilience.* New York: Guilford Press.

Reilly, Sheena, Eadie, Patricia, Bavin, Edith L., Wake, Melissa, Prior, Margot, Williams, Joanne, et al. (2006). Growth of infant communication between 8 and 12 months: A population study. *Journal of Paediatrics and Child Health, 42,* 764–770.

Reis, Harry T., & Collins, W. Andrew. (2004). Relationships, human behavior, and psychological science. *Current Directions in Psychological Science, 13*, 233–237.

Reith, Gerda. (2005). On the edge: Drugs and the consumption of risk in late modernity. In Stephen Lyng (Ed.), *Edgework: The sociology of risk taking* (pp. 227–246). New York: Routledge.

Renk, Kimberly, Donnelly, Reesa, McKinney, Cliff, & Agliata, Allison Kanter. (2006). The development of gender identity: Timetables and influences. In Kam-Shing Yip (Ed.), *Psychology of gender identity: An international perspective* (pp. 49–68). Hauppauge, NY: Nova Science.

Renkema, Lennart J., Stapel, Diederik A., Maringer, Marcus, & van Yperen, Nico W. (2008). Terror management and stereotyping: Why do people stereotype when mortality is salient? *Personality and Social Psychology Bulletin, 34*, 553–564.

Rentfrow, Peter J., Gosling, Samuel D., & Potter, Jeff. (2008). A theory of the emergence, persistence, and expression of geographic variation in psychological characteristics. *Perspectives on Psychological Science, 3*, 339–369.

Rentner, Diane Stark, Scott, Caitlin, Kober, Nancy, Chudowsky, Naomi, Chudowsky, Victor, Joftus, Scott, et al. (2006). *From the capital to the classroom: Year 4 of the No Child Left Behind Act.* Washington, DC: Center on Education Policy.

Rest, James. (1993). Research on moral judgment in college students. In Andrew Garrod (Ed.), *Approaches to moral development: New research and emerging themes* (pp. 201–211). New York: Teachers College Press.

Rest, James, Narvaez, Darcia, Bebeau, Muriel J., & Thoma, Stephen J. (1999). *Postconventional moral thinking: A neo-Kohlbergian approach.* Mahwah, NJ: Erlbaum.

Rettig, Michael. (2005). Using the multiple intelligences to enhance instruction for young children and young children with disabilities. *Early Childhood Education Journal, 32*, 255–259.

Retting, Richard A., Ferguson, Susan A., & McCartt, Anne T. (2003). A review of evidence-based traffic engineering measures designed to reduce pedestrian-motor vehicle crashes. *American Journal of Public Health, 93*, 1456–1463.

Reuter-Lorenz, Patricia A., & Sylvester, Ching-Yune C. (2005). The cognitive neuroscience of working memory and aging. In Roberto Cabeza, Lars Nyberg, & Denise C. Park (Eds.), *Cognitive neuroscience of aging: Linking cognitive and cerebral aging* (pp. 186–217). New York: Oxford University Press.

Reutskaja, Elena, & Hogarth, Robin M. (2009). Satisfaction in choice as a function of the number of alternatives: When "goods satiate." *Psychology and Marketing, 26*, 197–203.

Reynolds, Arthur J. (2000). *Success in early intervention: The Chicago Child-Parent Centers.* Lincoln, NE: University of Nebraska Press.

Reynolds, Arthur J., & Temple, Judy A. (2008). Cost-effective early childhood development programs from preschool to third grade. *Annual Review of Clinical Psychology, 4*, 109–139.

Reynolds, Arthur J., Temple, Judy A., Ou, Suh-Ruu, Robertson, Dylan L., Mersky, Joshua P., Topitzes, James W., et al. (2007). Effects of a school-based, early childhood intervention on adult health and well-being: A 19-year follow-up of low-income families. *Archives of Pediatrics & Adolescent Medicine, 161*, 730–739.

Reynolds, Chandra A. (2008). Genetic and environmental influences on cognitive change. In Scott M. Hofer & Duane F. Alwin (Eds.), *Handbook of cognitive aging: Interdisciplinary perspectives* (pp. 557–574). Thousand Oaks, CA: Sage.

Rhee, Kyung. (2008). Childhood overweight and the relationship between parent behaviors, parenting style, and family functioning. *Annals of the American Academy of Political and Social Science, 615*, 12–37.

Riccio, Cynthia A., & Rodriguez, Olga L. (2007). Integration of psychological assessment approaches in school psychology. *Psychology in the Schools, 44*, 243–255.

Riccio, Cynthia A., Sullivan, Jeremy R., & Cohen, Morris J. (2010). *Neuropsychological assessment and intervention for childhood and adolescent disorders.* Hoboken, NJ: John Wiley.

Rice, Charles L., & Cunningham, David A. (2002). Aging of the neuromuscular system: Influences of gender and physical activity. In Roy J. Shephard (Ed.), *Gender, physical activity, and aging* (pp. 121–150). Boca Raton, FL: CRC Press.

Richardson, Rick, & Hayne, Harlene. (2007). You can't take it with you: The translation of memory across development. *Current Directions in Psychological Science, 16*, 223–227.

Riegel, Klaus F. (1975). Toward a dialectical theory of development. *Human Development, 18*, 50–64.

Riordan, Jan (Ed.). (2005). *Breastfeeding and human lactation* (3rd ed.). Sudbury, MA: Jones and Bartlett.

Riordan, Jan, & Wambach, Karen (Eds.). (2009). *Breastfeeding and human lactation* (4th ed.). Sudbury, MA: Jones and Bartlett Publishers.

Ripke, Marika N., Huston, Aletha C., & Casey, David M. (2006). Low-income children's activity participation as a predictor of psychosocial and academic outcomes in middle childhood and adolescence. In Aletha C. Huston & Marika N. Ripke (Eds.), *Developmental contexts in middle childhood: Bridges to adolescence and adulthood* (pp. 260–282). New York: Cambridge University Press.

Rivas-Drake, Deborah, & Mooney, Margarita. (2009). Neither colorblind nor oppositional: Perceived minority status and trajectories of academic adjustment among Latinos in elite higher education. *Developmental Psychology, 45*, 642–651.

Rivers, Ian, Poteat, V. Paul, Noret, Nathalie, & Ashurst, Nigel. (2009). Observing bullying at school: The mental health implications of witness status. *School Psychology Quarterly, 24*, 211–223.

Rizzolatti, Giacomo, & Sinigaglia, Corrado. (2008). *Mirrors in the brain: How our minds share actions and emotions* (Frances Anderson, Trans.). New York: Oxford University Press.

Robelen, Erik W. (2010). Panel moves toward "next generation" science standards. *Education Digest, 76*, 32–33.

Roberts, Brent W., Kuncel, Nathan R., Shiner, Rebecca, Caspi, Avshalom, & Goldberg, Lewis R. (2007). The power of personality: The comparative validity of personality traits, socioeconomic status, and cognitive ability for predicting important life outcomes. *Perspectives on Psychological Science, 2*, 313–345.

Roberts, Brent W., Walton, Kate E., & Viechtbauer, Wolfgang. (2006). Patterns of mean-level change in personality traits across the life course: A meta-analysis of longitudinal studies. *Psychological Bulletin, 132*, 1–25.

Roberts, Donald F., & Foehr, Ulla G. (2004). *Kids and media in America: Patterns of use at the millennium.* New York: Cambridge University Press.

Roberts, Leslie. (2007, October 26). Battling over bed nets. *Science, 318*, 556–559.

Roberts, Soraya. (2010, January 1). Travis Pastrana breaks world record for longest rally car jump on New Year's Eve. *New York Daily News.*

Robertson, Bruce C., Elliott, Graeme P., Eason, Daryl K., Clout, Mick N., & Gemmell, Neil J. (2006). Sex allocation theory aids species conservation. *Biology Letters, 2*, 229–231.

Robinson, Oliver C., Demetre, James D., & Corney, Roslyn. (2010). Personality and retirement: Exploring the links between the Big Five personality traits, reasons for retirement and the experience of being retired. *Personality and Individual Differences, 48*, 792–797.

Robson, Ruthann. (2010). Notes on my dying. In Nan Bauer-Maglin & Donna Marie Perry (Eds.), *Final acts: Death, dying, and the choices we make* (pp. 19–28). New Brunswick, NJ: Rutgers University Press.

Rochat, Philippe. (2001). *The infant's world.* Cambridge, MA: Harvard University Press.

Roche, Alex F., & Sun, Shumei S. (2003). *Human growth: Assessment and interpretation.* Cambridge, UK: Cambridge University Press.

Rodgers, Joseph. (2003). EMOSA sexuality models, memes, and the tipping point: Policy & program implications. In Daniel Romer (Ed.), *Reducing adolescent risk: Toward an integrated approach* (pp. 185–192). Thousand Oaks, CA: Sage.

Rodkin, Philip C., & Roisman, Glenn I. (2010). Antecedents and correlates of the popular-aggressive phenomenon in elementary school. *Child Development, 81*, 837–850.

Rodriguez, Liliana, Schwartz, Seth J., & Whitbourne, Susan Krauss. (2010). American identity revisited: The relation between national, ethnic, and personal identity in a multiethnic sample of emerging adults. *Journal of Adolescent Research, 25*, 324–349.

Roebers, Claudia M., Schmid, Corinne, & Roderer, Thomas. (2009). Metacognitive monitoring and control processes involved in primary school children's test performance. *British Journal of Educational Psychology, 79,* 749–767.

Rogaev, Evgeny I., Grigorenko, Anastasia P., Faskhutdinova, Gulnaz, Kittler, Ellen L. W., & Moliaka, Yuri K. (2009, November 6). Genotype analysis identifies the cause of the "royal disease." *Science, 326,* 817.

Rogers, Carl R. (2004). *On becoming a person: A therapist's view of psychotherapy.* London: Constable. (Original work published 1961)

Rogers, Lesley J., & Andrew, Richard John (Eds.). (2008). *Comparative vertebrate lateralization* (Paperback ed.). New York: Cambridge University Press.

Rogoff, Barbara. (2003). *The cultural nature of human development.* New York: Oxford University Press.

Rogoff, Barbara, Correa-Chávez, Maricela, & Cotuc, Marta Navichoc. (2005). A cultural/historical view of schooling in human development. In David B. Pillemer & Sheldon H. White (Eds.), *Developmental psychology and social change: Research, history and policy* (pp. 225–263). New York: Cambridge University Press.

Ron, Pnina. (2009). Daughters as caregivers of aging parents: The shattering myth. *Journal of Gerontological Social Work, 52,* 135–153.

Ron-Harel, Noga, & Schwartz, Michal. (2009). Immune senescence and brain aging: Can rejuvenation of immunity reverse memory loss? *Trends in Neurosciences, 32,* 367–375.

Rönkä, Anna, Oravala, Sanna, & Pulkkinen, Lea. (2002). "I met this wife of mine and things got onto a better track": Turning points in risk development. *Journal of Adolescence, 25,* 47–63.

Roopnarine, Jaipaul L., Johnson, James E., & Hooper, Frank H. (Eds.). (1994). *Children's play in diverse cultures.* Albany, NY: State University of New York Press.

Rose, Amanda J., & Asher, Steven R. (2004). Children's strategies and goals in response to help-giving and help-seeking tasks within a friendship. *Child Development, 75,* 749–763.

Rose, Steven. (2008, January 31). Drugging unruly children is a method of social control [Correspondence]. *Nature, 451,* 521.

Rose, Susan A., Feldman, Judith F., & Jankowski, Jeffery J. (2009). A cognitive approach to the development of early language. *Child Development, 80,* 134–150.

Rose, Susan A., Feldman, Judith F., Jankowski, Jeffery J., & Van Rossem, Ronan. (2008). A cognitive cascade in infancy: Pathways from prematurity to later mental development. *Intelligence, 36,* 367–378.

Roseberry, Sarah, Hirsh-Pasek, Kathy, Parish-Morris, Julia, & Golinkoff, Roberta M. (2009). Live action: Can young children learn verbs from video? *Child Development, 80,* 1360–1375.

Rosenberg, Rebecca, Mandell, David, Farmer, Janet, Law, J., Marvin, Alison, & Law, Paul. (2010). Psychotropic medication use among children with autism spectrum disor-

ders enrolled in a national registry, 2007–2008. *Journal of Autism and Developmental Disorders, 40,* 342–351.

Rosenfeld, Barry. (2004). *Assisted suicide and the right to die: The interface of social science, public policy, and medical ethics.* Washington, DC: American Psychological Association.

Rosenfeld, Philip J., Brown, David M., Heier, Jeffrey S., Boyer, David S., Kaiser, Peter K., Chung, Carol Y., et al. (2006). Ranibizumab for neovascular age-related macular degeneration. *New England Journal of Medicine, 355,* 1419–1431.

Rosenfield, Robert L., Lipton, Rebecca B., & Drum, Melinda L. (2009). Thelarche, pubarche, and menarche attainment in children with normal and elevated body mass index. *Pediatrics, 123,* 84–88.

Rosenthal, Miriam K. (1991). The relation of peer interaction among infants and toddlers in family day care to characteristics of the child care environment. *Journal of Reproductive and Infant Psychology, 9,* 151–167.

Rosow, Irving. (1985). Status and role change through the life cycle. In Robert H. Binstock & Ethel Shanas (Eds.), *Handbook of aging and the social sciences* (2nd ed., pp. 62–93). New York: Van Nostrand Reinhold.

Rosowsky, Erlene. (2007). Loss of the 'supplementary spouse' in marriages in later life. *Generations, 31*(3), 38–40.

Ross, Colin A. (2009). Ethics of gender identity disorder. *Ethical Human Psychology and Psychiatry, 11,* 165–170.

Rossignol, Daniel, Rossignol, Lanier, Smith, Scott, Schneider, Cindy, Logerquist, Sally, Usman, Anju, et al. (2009). Hyperbaric treatment for children with autism: A multicenter, randomized, double-blind, controlled trial. *BMC Pediatrics, 9,* 21.

Roth, David L., Ackerman, Michelle L., Okonkwo, Ozioma C., & Burgio, Louis D. (2008). The four-factor model of depressive symptoms in dementia caregivers: A structural equation model of ethnic differences. *Psychology and Aging, 23,* 567–576.

Roth, David L., Mittelman, Mary S., Clay, Olivio J., Madan, Alok, & Haley, William E. (2005). Changes in social support as mediators of the impact of a psychosocial intervention for spouse caregivers of persons with Alzheimer's disease. *Psychology and Aging, 20,* 634–644.

Rothbart, Mary K., & Bates, John E. (2006). Temperament. In William Damon & Richard M. Lerner (Series Eds.) & Nancy Eisenberg (Vol. Ed.), *Handbook of child psychology: Vol. 3. Social, emotional, and personality development* (6th ed., pp. 99–166). Hoboken, NJ: Wiley.

Rothbaum, Fred, Pott, Martha, Azuma, Hiroshi, Miyake, Kazuo, & Weisz, John. (2000). The development of close relationships in Japan and the United States: Paths of symbiotic harmony and generative tension. *Child Development, 71,* 1121–1142.

Rothenberg, Richard. (2007). The relevance of social epidemiology in HIV/AIDS and drug abuse

research. *American Journal of Preventive Medicine, 32*(Suppl. 6), S147–S153.

Rothrauff, Tanja C., Cooney, Teresa M., & An, Jeong Shin. (2009). Remembered parenting styles and adjustment in middle and late adulthood. *The Journals of Gerontology Series B: Psychological Sciences and Social Sciences, 64B,* 137–146.

Rouchka, Eric C., & Cha, I. Elizabeth. (2009). Current trends in pseudogene detection and characterization. *Current Bioinformatics, 4,* 112–119.

Rovee-Collier, Carolyn. (1987). Learning and memory in infancy. In Joy Doniger Osofsky (Ed.), *Handbook of infant development* (2nd ed., pp. 98–148). New York: Wiley.

Rovee-Collier, Carolyn. (1990). The "memory system" of prelinguistic infants. In Adele Diamond (Ed.), *The development and neural bases of higher cognitive functions* (Vol. 608, pp. 517–542). New York: New York Academy of Sciences.

Rovee-Collier, Carolyn. (2001). Information pick-up by infants: What is it, and how can we tell? *Journal of Experimental Child Psychology, 78,* 35–49.

Rovee-Collier, Carolyn, & Cuevas, Kimberly. (2009a). The development of infant memory. In Mary L. Courage & Nelson Cowan (Eds.), *The development of memory in infancy and childhood* (2nd ed.). ed., pp. 11–41). New York: Psychology Press.

Rovee-Collier, Carolyn, & Cuevas, Kimberly. (2009b). Multiple memory systems are unnecessary to account for infant memory development: An ecological model. *Developmental Psychology, 45,* 160–174.

Rovee-Collier, Carolyn, & Hayne, Harlene. (1987). Reactivation of infant memory: Implications for cognitive development. In Hayne W. Reese (Ed.), *Advances in child development and behavior* (Vol. 20, pp. 185–238). San Diego, CA: Academic Press.

Rovi, Sue, Chen, Ping-Hsin, & Johnson, Mark S. (2004). The economic burden of hospitalizations associated with child abuse and neglect. *American Journal of Public Health, 94,* 586–590.

Rowe, John W., & Kahn, Robert Louis. (1998). *Successful aging.* New York: Pantheon.

Rozin, Paul. (2007). Food and eating. In Shinobu Kitayama & Dov Cohen (Eds.), *Handbook of cultural psychology* (pp. 391–416). New York: Guilford Press.

Rozin, Paul, Kabnick, Kimberly, Pete, Erin, Fischler, Claude, & Shields, Christy. (2003). The ecology of eating: Smaller portion sizes in France than in the United States help explain the French paradox. *Psychological Science, 14,* 450–454.

Rubie-Davies, Christine M. (2007). Classroom interactions: Exploring the practices of high- and low-expectation teachers. *British Journal of Educational Psychology, 77,* 289–306.

Rubin, Kenneth H., Coplan, Robert J., & Bowker, Julie C. (2009). Social withdrawal in childhood. *Annual Review of Psychology, 60,* 141–171.

Ruble, Diane N., Martin, Carol Lynn, & Berenbaum, Sheri. (2006). Gender development. In William Damon & Richard M. Lerner (Series Eds.) & Nancy Eisenberg (Vol. Ed.), *Handbook of child psychology: Vol. 3. Social, emotional, and personality development* (6th ed., pp. 858–932). Hoboken, NJ: Wiley.

Ruder, Debra Bradley. (2008, September-October). The teen brain. *Harvard Magazine, 111,* 8–10.

Rueda, M. Rosario, Rothbart, Mary K., Saccomanno, Lisa, & Posner, Michael I. (2007). Modifying brain networks underlying self regulation. In Daniel Romer & Elaine F. Walker (Eds.), *Adolescent psychopathology and the developing brain: Integrating brain and prevention science* (pp. 401–419). Oxford, UK: Oxford University Press.

Rueter, Martha A., & Kwon, Hee-Kyung. (2005). Developmental trends in adolescent suicidal ideation. *Journal of Research on Adolescence, 15,* 205–222.

Ruffman, Ted, Sullivan, Susan, & Dittrich, Winand. (2009). Older adults' recognition of bodily and auditory expressions of emotion. *Psychology and Aging, 24,* 614–622.

Ruiz, Sarah A., & Silverstein, Merril. (2007). Relationships with grandparents and the emotional well-being of late adolescent and young adult grandchildren. *Journal of Social Issues, 63,* 793–808.

Rutter, Michael. (2006). The psychological effects of early institutional rearing. In Peter J. Marshall & Nathan A. Fox (Eds.), *The development of social engagement: Neurobiological perspectives* (pp. 355–391). New York: Oxford University Press.

Rutter, Michael, Colvert, Emma, Kreppner, Jana, Beckett, Celia, Castle, Jenny, Groothues, Christine, et al. (2007). Early adolescent outcomes for institutionally-deprived and non-deprived adoptees. I: Disinhibited attachment. *Journal of Child Psychology and Psychiatry, 48,* 17–30.

Rutters, Femke, Nieuwenhuizen, Arie G., Vogels, Neeltje, Bouwman, Freek, Mariman, Edwin, & Westerterp-Plantenga, Margriet S. (2008). Leptin-adiposity relationship changes, plus behavioral and parental factors, are involved in the development of body weight in a Dutch children cohort. *Physiology & Behavior, 93,* 967–974.

Ruys, Jan H., de Jonge, Guus A., Brand, Ronald, Engelberts, Adèle, C., & Semmekrot, Ben A. (2007). Bed-sharing in the first four months of life: A risk factor for sudden infant death. *Acta Pædiatrica, 96,* 1399–1403.

Ryalls, Brigette Oliver. (2000). Dimensional adjectives: Factors affecting children's ability to compare objects using novel words. *Journal of Experimental Child Psychology, 76,* 26–49.

Ryan, Michael J. (2005, June 8). Punching out in Little League. *Boston Herald.*

Ryan, Suzanne, Franzetta, Kerry, Manlove, Jennifer, & Holcombe, Emily. (2007). Adolescents' discussions about contraception or STDs with partners before first sex. *Perspectives on Sexual and Reproductive Health, 39,* 149–157.

Ryan, Suzanne, Franzetta, Kerry, Manlove, Jennifer S., & Schelar, Erin. (2008). Older sexual partners during adolescence: Links to reproductive health outcomes in young adulthood. *Perspectives on Sexual and Reproductive Health, 40,* 17–26.

Rymer, Russ. (1994). *Genie: A scientific tragedy.* New York: Harper Perennial. (Original work published 1945)

Saarni, Carolyn, Campos, Joseph J., Camras, Linda A., & Witherington, David. (2006). Emotional development: Action, communication, and understanding. In William Damon & Richard M. Lerner (Series Eds.) & Nancy Eisenberg (Vol. Ed.), *Handbook of child psychology: Vol. 3. Social, emotional, and personality development* (6th ed., pp. 226–299). Hoboken, NJ: Wiley.

Sabatino, Charles P. (2010). The evolution of health care advance planning law and policy. *Milbank Quarterly, 88,* 211–239.

Sacks, Frank M., Bray, George A., Carey, Vincent J., Smith, Steven R., Ryan, Donna H., Anton, Stephen D., et al. (2009). Comparison of weight-loss diets with different compositions of fat, protein, and carbohydrates. *New England Journal Of Medicine, 360,* 859–873.

Sacks, Oliver W. (1995). *An anthropologist on Mars: Seven paradoxical tales.* New York: Knopf.

Sacks, Oliver W. (2007). *Musicophilia: Tales of music and the brain.* New York: Knopf.

Sadeh, Avi, Mindell, Jodi A., Luedtke, Kathryn, & Wiegand, Benjamin. (2009). Sleep and sleep ecology in the first 3 years: A web-based study. *Journal of Sleep Research, 18,* 60–73.

Sadeh, Avi, Tikotzky, Liat, & Scher, Anat. (2010). Parenting and infant sleep. *Sleep medicine reviews, 14,* 89–96.

Sadler, Philip M., Sonnert, Gerhard, Tai, Robert H., & Klopfenstein, Kristin (Eds.). (2010). *AP: A critical examination of the advanced placement program.* Cambridge, MA: Harvard Education Press.

Saey, Tina Hesman. (2008, May 24). Epic genetics: Genes' chemical clothes may underlie the biology behind mental illness. *Science News, 173,* 14–19.

Safe Kids USA. (2008). *Report to the nation: Trends in unintentional childhood injury mortality and parental views on child safety.* Washington, DC: Safe Kids Worldwide.

Saffran, Jenny R., Werker, Janet F., & Werner, Lynne A. (2006). The infant's auditory world: Hearing, speech, and the beginnings of language. In William Damon & Richard M. Lerner (Series Eds.) & Deanna Kuhn & Robert S. Siegler (Vol. Eds.), *Handbook of child psychology: Vol. 2. Cognition, perception, and language* (pp. 58–108). Hoboken, NJ: Wiley.

Sahar, Gail, & Karasawa, Kaori. (2005). Is the personal always political? A cross-cultural analysis of abortion attitudes. *Basic and Applied Social Psychology, 27,* 285–296.

Salkind, Neil J. (2004). *An introduction to theories of human development.* Thousand Oaks, CA: Sage.

Salmivalli, Christina. (2010). Bullying and the peer group: A review. *Aggression and Violent Behavior, 15,* 112–120.

Salter, Nicholas P., & Highhouse, Scott. (2009). Assessing managers' common sense using situational judgment tests. *Management Decision, 47,* 392–398.

Salthouse, Timothy A. (2006). Mental exercise and mental aging: Evaluating the validity of the "use it or lose it" hypothesis. *Perspectives on Psychological Science, 1,* 68–87.

Salthouse, Timothy A. (2010). *Major issues in cognitive aging.* New York: Oxford University Press.

Salvatore, Jessica, & Shelton, J. Nicole. (2007). Cognitive costs of exposure to racial prejudice. *Psychological Science, 18,* 810–815.

SAMHSA (Substance Abuse and Mental Health Services Administration). (2009). *Results from the 2008 National Survey on Drug Use and Health: National findings* (Office of Applied Studies, NSDUH Series H-36, HHS Publication No. SMA 09-4434). Rockville, MD: U.S. Department of Health and Human Services.

Sander, Thomas H., & Putnam, Robert D. (2010). Still bowling alone? The post-9/11 split. *Journal of Democracy, 21,* 9–16.

Sanders, George. (2010). The dismal trade as culture industry. *Poetics, 38,* 47–68.

Sandstrom, Marlene J., & Zakriski, Audrey L. (2004). Understanding the experience of peer rejection. In Janis B. Kupersmidt & Kenneth A. Dodge (Eds.), *Children's peer relations: From development to intervention* (pp. 101–118). Washington, DC: American Psychological Association.

Sangrigoli, Sandy, Pallier, Christophe, Argenti, Anne-Marie, Ventureyra, Valérie A. G., & de Schonen, Scania. (2005). Reversibility of the other-race effect in face recognition during childhood. *Psychological Science, 16,* 440–444.

Santelli, John S., & Melnikas, Andrea J. (2010). Teen fertility in transition: Recent and historic trends in the United States. *Annual Review of Public Health, 31,* 371–383.

Santosh, Paramala J., & Canagaratnam, Myooran. (2008). Paediatric bipolar disorder—an update. *Psychiatry, 7,* 349–352.

Saraceno, Chiara. (2010). Social inequalities in facing old-age dependency: A bi-generational perspective. *Journal of European Social Policy, 20,* 32–44.

Saraswathi, T. S. (2005). Hindu worldview in the development of selfways: The "Atman" as the real self. In Lene Arnett Jensen & Reed W. Larson (Eds.), *New Horizons in Developmental Theory and Research* (pp. 43–50). San Francisco: Jossey-Bass.

Satariano, William. (2006). *Epidemiology of aging: An ecological approach.* Sudbury, MA: Jones and Bartlett.

Sauer, Mark V., Wang, Jeff G., Douglas, Nataki C., Nakhuda, Gary S., Vardhana, Pratibhashri, Jovanovic, Vuk, et al. (2009). Providing fertility care to men seropositive for human immunodeficiency virus: Reviewing 10 years of experience and 420 consecutive cycles of in vitro fertilization and intracytoplasmic sperm injection. *Fertility and Sterility, 91,* 2455–2460.

Saunders, Cicely M. (1978). *The management of terminal disease.* London: Arnold.

Savin-Williams, Ritch C. (2005). *The new gay teenager.* Cambridge, MA: Harvard University Press.

Saw, Seang-Mei, Cheng, Angela, Fong, Allan, Gazzard, Gus, Tan, Donald T. H., & Morgan, Ian. (2007). School grades and myopia. *Ophthalmic and Physiological Optics, 27,* 126–129.

Sawires, Sharif R., Dworkin, Shari L., Fiamma, Agnès, Peacock, Dean, Szekeres, Greg, & Coates, Thomas J. (2007). Male circumcision and HIV/AIDS: challenges and opportunities. *The Lancet, 369,* 708–713.

Saxe, Geoffrey B. (1999). Sources of concepts: A cultural-developmental perspective. In Ellin Kofsky Scholnick, Katherine Nelson, Susan A. Gelman, & Patricia H. Miller (Eds.), *Conceptual development: Piaget's legacy* (pp. 253–267). Mahwah, NJ: Erlbaum.

Saxe, Geoffrey B. (2004). Practices of quantification from a socio-cultural perspective. In Andreas Demetriou & Athanassios Raftopoulos (Eds.), *Cognitive developmental change: Theories, models and measurement* (pp. 241–263). New York: Cambridge University.

Sayette, Michael A., Reichle, Erik D., & Schooler, Jonathan W. (2009). Lost in the sauce: The effects of alcohol on mind wandering. *Psychological Science, 20,* 747–752.

Saylor, Megan M., & Sabbagh, Mark A. (2004). Different kinds of information affect word learning in the preschool years: The case of part-term learning. *Child Development, 75,* 395–408.

Scales, Peter C., Benson, Peter L., & Mannes, Marc. (2006). The contribution to adolescent well-being made by nonfamily adults: An examination of developmental assets as contexts and processes. *Journal of Community Psychology, 34,* 401–413.

Scambler, Douglas J., Hepburn, Susan L., Rutherford, Mel, Wehner, Elizabeth A., & Rogers, Sally J. (2007). Emotional responsivity in children with autism, children with other developmental disabilities, and children with typical development. *Journal of Autism and Developmental Disorders, 37,* 553–563.

Scannapieco, Maria, & Connell-Carrick, Kelli. (2005). *Understanding child maltreatment: An ecological and developmental perspective.* New York: Oxford University Press.

Scarf, Maggie. (2008). *September songs: The good news about marriage in the later years.* New York: Riverhead Books.

Schachter, Sherry R. (2003). 9/11: A grief therapist's journal. In Marcia Lattanzi-Licht & Kenneth J. Doka (Eds.), *Living with grief: Coping with public tragedy* (pp. 15–25). New York: Brunner-Routledge.

Schafer, Graham. (2005). Infants can learn decontextualized words before their first birthday. *Child Development, 76,* 87–96.

Schaffer, H. Rudolph. (2000). The early experience assumption: Past, present, and future. *International Journal of Behavioral Development, 24,* 5–14.

Schaie, K. Warner. (1989). Individual differences in rate of cognitive change in adulthood. In Vern L. Bengtson & K. Warner Schaie (Eds.), *The course of later life: Research and reflections* (pp. 65–85). New York: Springer.

Schaie, K. Warner. (1996). *Intellectual development in adulthood: The Seattle Longitudinal Study.* New York: Cambridge University Press.

Schaie, K. Warner. (2002). The impact of longitudinal studies on understanding development from young adulthood to old age. In Willard W. Hartup & Rainer K. Silbereisen (Eds.), *Growing points in developmental science: An introduction* (pp. 307–328). New York: Psychology Press.

Schaie, K. Warner. (2005). *Developmental influences on adult intelligence: The Seattle longitudinal study* (Rev. ed.). New York: Oxford University Press.

Schardein, James L. (1976). *Drugs as teratogens.* Cleveland, OH: CRC Press.

Schauer, Daniel P., Arterburn, David E., Livingston, Edward H., Fischer, David, & Eckman, Mark H. (2010). Decision modeling to estimate the impact of gastric bypass surgery on life expectancy for the treatment of morbid obesity. *Archives of Surgery, 145,* 57–62.

Scheffler, Richard M., Brown, Timothy T., Fulton, Brent D., Hinshaw, Stephen P., Levine, Peter, & Stone, Susan. (2009). Positive association between attention-deficit/hyperactivity disorder medication use and academic achievement during elementary school. *Pediatrics, 123,* 1273–1279.

Scheibehenne, Benjamin, Greifeneder, Rainer, & Todd, Peter M. (2010). Can there ever be too many options? a meta-analytic review of choice overload. *Journal of Consumer Research, 37,* 409–425.

Schick, Adina, & Melzi, Gigliana. (2010). The development of children's oral narratives across contexts. *Early Education & Development, 21,* 293–317.

Schieber, Frank. (2006). Vision and aging. In James E. Birren & K. Warner Schaie (Eds.), *Handbook of the psychology of aging* (6th ed., pp. 129–161). Amsterdam: Elsevier.

Schiller, Ruth A. (1998). The relationship of developmental tasks to life satisfaction, moral reasoning, and occupational attainment at age 28. *Journal of Adult Development, 5,* 239–254.

Schim, Stephanie Myers, Doorenbos, Ardith Zwyghuizen, & Borse, Nagesh N. (2006). Enhancing cultural competence among hospice staff. *American Journal of Hospice and Palliative Medicine, 23,* 404–411.

Schindler, Ines, Staudinger, Ursula M., & Nesselroade, John R. (2006). Development and structural dynamics of personal life investment in old age. *Psychology and Aging, 21,* 737–753.

Schmader, Toni, Johns, Michael, & Forbes, Chad. (2008). An integrated process model of stereotype threat effects on performance. *Psychological Review, 115,* 336–356.

Schmeer, Kammi. (2009). Father absence due to migration and child illness in rural Mexico. *Social Science & Medicine, 69,* 1281–1286.

Schmidt, Marie Evans, Pempek, Tiffany A., Kirkorian, Heather L., Lund, Anne Frankenfield, & Anderson, Daniel R. (2008). The effects of background television on the toy play behavior of very young children. *Child Development, 79,* 1137–1151.

Schneider, Wolfgang, & Lockl, Kathrin. (2008). Procedural metacognition in children: Evidence for developmental trends. In John Dunlosky & Robert A. Bjork (Eds.), *Handbook of metamemory and memory* (pp. 391–409). New York: Psychology Press.

Schoen, Robert, & Cheng, Yen-Hsin Alice. (2006). Partner choice and the differential retreat from marriage. *Journal of Marriage and Family, 68,* 1–10.

Schoeni, Robert F., & Ross, Karen E. (2005). Material assistance from families during the transition to adulthood. In Richard A. Settersten, Jr., Frank F. Furstenberg, Jr., & Rubén G. Rumbaut (Eds.), *On the frontier of adulthood: Theory, research, and public policy* (pp. 396–416). Chicago: University of Chicago Press.

Schön, Daniele, Boyer, Maud, Moreno, Sylvain, Besson, Mireille, Peretz, Isabelle, & Kolinsky, Régine. (2008). Songs as an aid for language acquisition. *Cognition, 106,* 975–983.

Schooler, Carmi. (2009). The effects of the cognitive complexity of occupational conditions and leisure-time activities on the intellectual functioning of older adults. In Wojtek Chodzko-Zajko, Arthur F. Kramer, & Leonard W. Poon (Eds.), *Enhancing cognitive functioning and brain plasticity.* (pp. 15–34). Champaign, IL: Human Kinetics.

Schraagen, Jan Maarten, & Leijenhorst, Henk. (2001). Searching for evidence: Knowledge and search strategies used by forensic scientists. In Eduardo Salas & Gary A. Klein (Eds.), *Linking expertise and naturalistic decision making* (pp. 263–274). Mahwah, NJ: Erlbaum.

Schreck, Christopher J., Burek, Melissa W., Stewart, Eric A., & Miller, J. Mitchell. (2007). Distress and violent victimization among young adolescents: Early puberty and the social interactionist explanation. *Journal of Research in Crime and Delinquency, 44,* 381–405.

Schroedel, Jean Reith, & Fiber, Pamela. (2001). Punitive versus public health oriented responses to drug use by pregnant women. *Yale Journal of Health Policy, Law, and Ethics, 1,* 217–235.

Schulenberg, John, O'Malley, Patrick M., Bachman, Jerald G., & Johnston, Lloyd D. (2005). Early adult transitions and their relation to well-being and substance use. In Richard A. Settersten, Jr., Frank F. Furstenberg, Jr., & Rubén G. Rumbaut (Eds.), *On the frontier of adulthood: Theory, research, and public policy* (pp. 417–453). Chicago: University of Chicago Press.

Schulenberg, John, & Zarrett, Nicole R. (2006). Mental health during emerging adulthood:

Continuity and discontinuity in courses, causes, and functions. In Jeffrey Jensen Arnett & Jennifer Lynn Tanner (Eds.), *Emerging adults in America: Coming of age in the 21st century* (pp. 135–172). Washington, DC: American Psychological Association.

Schulman, Kevin A., Berlin, Jesse A., Harless, William, Kerner, Jon F., Sistrunk, Shyrl, Gersh, Bernard J., et al. (1999). The effect of race and sex on physicians' recommendations for cardiac catheterization. *New England Journal of Medicine, 340,* 618–626.

Schultz, P. Wesley, Nolan, Jessica M., Cialdini, Robert B., Goldstein, Noah J., & Griskevicius, Vladas. (2007). The constructive, destructive, and reconstructive power of social norms. *Psychological Science, 18,* 429–434.

Schulz, James H., & Binstock, Robert H. (2008). *Aging nation: The economics and politics of growing older in America* (Paperback ed.). Baltimore: Johns Hopkins University Press.

Schumann, Cynthia Mills, Hamstra, Julia, Goodlin-Jones, Beth L., Lotspeich, Linda J., Kwon, Hower, Buonocore, Michael H., et al. (2004). The amygdala is enlarged in children but not adolescents with autism; the hippocampus is enlarged at all ages. *Journal of Neuroscience, 24,* 6392–6401.

Schwartz, Carl E., Kunwar, Pratap S., Greve, Douglas N., Moran, Lyndsey R., Viner, Jane C., Covino, Jennifer M., et al. (2010). Structural differences in adult orbital and ventromedial prefrontal cortex predicted by infant temperament at 4 months of age. *Archives of General Psychiatry, 67,* 78–84.

Schwartz, David, & Collins, Francis. (2007, May 4). Environmental biology and human disease. *Science, 316,* 695–696.

Schwartz, Jeffrey, & Begley, Sharon. (2002). *The mind and the brain: Neuroplasticity and the power of mental force.* New York: Regan Books.

Schwartz, Paul D., Maynard, Amanda M., & Uzelac, Sarah M. (2008). Adolescent egocentrism: A contemporary view. *Adolescence, 43,* 441–448.

Schwartz, Pepper. (2006). What elicits romance, passion, and attachment, and how do they affect our lives throughout the life cycle? In Ann C. Crouter & Alan Booth (Eds.), *Romance and sex in adolescence and emerging adulthood: Risks and opportunities* (pp. 49–60). Mahwah, NJ: Erlbaum.

Schwartz, Seth J., Zamboanga, Byron L., Ravert, Russell D., Kim, Su Yeong, Weisskirch, Robert S., Williams, Michelle K., et al. (2009). Perceived parental relationships and health-risk behaviors in college-attending emerging adults. *Journal of Marriage and Family, 71,* 727–740.

Schweinhart, Lawrence J., Montie, Jeanne, Xiang, Zongping, Barnett, W. Steven, Belfield, Clive R., & Nores, Milagros. (2005). *Lifetime effects: The High/Scope Perry Preschool Study through age 40.* Ypsilanti, MI: High/Scope Press.

Schweinhart, Lawrence J., & Weikart, David P. (1997). *Lasting differences: The High/Scope Preschool Curriculum Comparison Study through age 23.* Ypsilanti, MI: High/Scope Educational Research Foundation.

Schwekendiek, Daniel. (2009). Height and weight differences between North and South Korea. *Journal of Biosocial Science, 41,* 51–55.

Scollon, Christie Napa, Diener, Ed, Oishi, Shigehiro, & Biswas-Diener, Robert. (2005). An experience sampling and cross-cultural investigation of the relation between pleasant and unpleasant affect. *Cognition & Emotion, 19,* 27–52.

Scott, Kate M., Wells, J. Elisabeth, Angermeyer, Matthias C., Brugha, Traolach S., Bromet, Evelyn, Demyttenaere, Koen, et al. (2010). Gender and the relationship between marital status and first onset of mood, anxiety and substance use disorders. *Psychological Medicine, 40,* 1495–1505.

Scott, Lisa S., & Monesson, Alexandra. (2009). The origin of biases in face perception. *Psychological Science, 20,* 676–680.

Scott, Lisa S., Pascalis, Olivier, & Nelson, Charles A. (2007). A domain-general theory of the development of perceptual discrimination. *Current Directions in Psychological Science, 16,* 197–201.

Scott-Maxwell, Florida. (1968). *The measure of my days.* New York: Knopf.

Seale, Clive. (2006). Characteristics of end-of-life decisions: Survey of UK medical practitioners. *Palliative Medicine, 20,* 653–659.

Sears, Malcolm R., Greene, Justina M., Willan, Andrew R., Wiecek, Elizabeth M., Taylor, D. Robin, Flannery, Erin M., et al. (2003). A longitudinal, population-based, cohort study of childhood asthma followed to adulthood. *New England Journal of Medicine, 349,* 1414–1422.

Sebastian, Catherine, Burnett, Stephanie, & Blakemore, Sarah-Jayne. (2008). Development of the self-concept during adolescence. *Trends in Cognitive Sciences, 12,* 441–446.

Sebastián-Gallés, Núria. (2007). Biased to learn language. *Developmental Science, 10,* 713–718.

Sedivy, John M., Munoz-Najar, Ursula M., Jeyapalan, Jessie C., & Campisi, Judith. (2008). Cellular senescence: A link between tumor suppression and organismal aging? In Leonard Guarente, Linda Partridge, & Douglas C. Wallace (Eds.), *Molecular biology of aging* (pp. 185–214). Cold Spring Harbor, NY: Cold Spring Harbor Laboratory Press.

Seedat, Soraya, Scott, Kate Margaret, Angermeyer, Matthias C., Berglund, Patricia, Bromet, Evelyn J., Brugha, Traolach S., et al. (2009). Cross-national associations between gender and mental disorders in the world health organization world mental health surveys. *Archives of General Psychiatry, 66,* 785–795.

Seifer, Ronald, LaGasse, Linda L., Lester, Barry, Bauer, Charles R., Shankaran, Seetha, Bada, Henrietta S., et al. (2004). Attachment status in children prenatally exposed to cocaine and other substances. *Child Development, 75,* 850–868.

Seki, Fusako. (2001). The role of the government and the family in taking care of the frail elderly: A comparison of the United States and Japan. In David N. Weisstub, David C. Thomasma, Serge Gauthier, & George F. Tomossy (Eds.), *Aging: Caring for our elders* (pp. 83–105). Dordrecht, The Netherlands: Kluwer.

Senju, Atsushi, Southgate, Victoria, Miura, Yui, Matsui, Tomoko, Hasegawa, Toshikazu, Tojo, Yoshikuni, et al. (2010). Absence of spontaneous action anticipation by false belief attribution in children with autism spectrum disorder. *Development and Psychopathology, 22,* 353–360.

Setlik, Jennifer, Bond, G. Randall, & Ho, Mona. (2009). Adolescent prescription ADHD medication abuse is rising along with prescriptions for these medications. *Pediatrics, 124,* 875–880.

Setoguchi, Soko, Glynn, Robert J., May, Christopher W., Schaefer, Kristen G., Levin, Raisa, Lewis, Eldrin F., et al. (2009). Abstract 3143: Hospice enrollment and duration for patients with heart failure versus cancer. *Circulation, 120*(Suppl. 2), S748.

Settersten, Richard A. (2002). Social sources of meaning in later life. In Robert S. Weiss & Scott A. Bass (Eds.), *Challenges of the third age: Meaning and purpose in later life* (pp. 55–79). London: Oxford University Press.

Shahin, Hashem, Walsh, Tom, Sobe, Tama, Lynch, Eric, King, Mary-Claire, Avraham, Karen, et al. (2002). Genetics of congenital deafness in the Palestinian population: Multiple connexin 26 alleles with shared origins in the Middle East. *Human Genetics, 110,* 284–289.

Shai, Iris, Schwarzfuchs, Dan, Henkin, Yaakov, Shahar, Danit R., Witkow, Shula, Greenberg, Ilana, et al. (2008). Weight loss with a low-carbohydrate, Mediterranean, or low-fat diet. *New England Journal of Medicine, 359,* 229–241.

Shai, Iris, & Stampfer, Meir J. (2008). Weight-loss diets—Can you keep it off? *American Journal of Clinical Nutrition, 88,* 1185–1186.

Shanahan, Lilly, McHale, Susan M., Osgood, Wayne, & Crouter, Ann C. (2007). Conflict frequency with mothers and fathers from middle childhood to late adolescence: Within- and between-families comparisons. *Developmental Psychology, 43,* 539–550.

Shannon, Joyce Brennfleck (Ed.). (2007). *Eating disorders sourcebook: Basic consumer health information about anorexia nervosa, bulimia nervosa, binge eating, compulsive exercise, female athlete triad, and other eating disorders* (2nd ed.). Detroit, MI: Omnigraphics.

Shapiro, Adam, & Yarborough-Hayes, Raijah. (2008). Retirement and older men's health. *Generations, 32,* 49–53.

Shapiro, James A. (2009). Revisiting the central dogma in the 21st century. In Günther Witzany (Ed.), *Annals of the New York Academy of Sciences: Vol. 1178. Natural genetic engineering and natural genome editing* (pp. 6–28). New York: New York Academy of Sciences.

Sharma, Monica. (2008). Twenty-first century pink or blue: How sex selection technology facilitates gendercide and what we can do about it. *Family Court Review, 46,* 198–215.

Shattuck, Paul T. (2006). The contribution of diagnostic substitution to the growing administrative prevalence of autism in US special education. *Pediatrics, 117,* 1028–1037.

Shaw, Benjamin A., Liang, Jersey, & Krause, Neal. (2010). Age and race differences in the trajectories of self-esteem. *Psychology and Aging, 25,* 84–94.

Shay, Jerry W., & Wright, Woodring E. (2008). Telomeres and telomerase in aging and cancer. In Leonard Guarente, Linda Partridge, & Douglas C. Wallace (Eds.), *Molecular biology of aging* (pp. 575–597). Cold Spring Harbor, NY: Cold Spring Harbor Laboratory Press.

Sheaks, Chantel. (2007). The state of phased retirement: Facts, figures, and policies. *Generations, 31*(1), 57–62.

Sheehy, Gail. (1976). *Passages: Predictable crises of adult life.* New York: Dutton.

Shepard, Thomas H., & Lemire, Ronald J. (2004). *Catalog of teratogenic agents* (11th ed.). Baltimore: Johns Hopkins University Press.

Sherblom, Stephen. (2008). The legacy of the "Care challenge": Re-envisioning the outcome of the justice-care debate. *Journal of Moral Education, 37,* 81–98.

Sherman, Edmund, & Dacher, Joan. (2005). Cherished objects and the home: Their meaning and roles in late life. In Graham D. Rowles & Habib Chaudhury (Eds.), *Home and identity in late life international perspectives* (pp. 63–79). New York: Springer.

Sherman, Stephanie. (2002). Epidemiology. In Randi Jenssen Hagerman & Paul J. Hagerman (Eds.), *Fragile X syndrome: Diagnosis, treatment, and research* (3rd ed., pp. 136–168). Baltimore: Johns Hopkins University Press.

Shirom, Arie, Toker, Sharon, Berliner, Shlomo, Shapira, Itzhak, & Melamed, Samuel. (2008). The effects of physical fitness and feeling vigorous on self-rated health. *Health Psychology, 27,* 567–575.

Shirtcliff, Elizabeth A., Dahl, Ronald E., & Pollak, Seth D. (2009). Pubertal development: Correspondence between hormonal and physical development. *Child Development, 80,* 327–337.

Shonkoff, Jack P., Boyce, W. Thomas, & McEwen, Bruce S. (2009). Neuroscience, molecular biology, and the childhood roots of health disparities: Building a new framework for health promotion and disease prevention. *Journal of the American Medical Association, 301,* 2252–2259.

Shuler, Carly. (2009). *Pockets of potential: Using mobile technologies to promote children's learning.* New York: The Joan Ganz Cooney Center at Sesame Workshop.

Shumaker, Sally A., Ockene, Judith K., & Riekert, Kristin A. (Eds.). (2009). *The handbook of health behavior change* (3rd ed.). New York: Springer.

Shushan, Gregory. (2009). *Conceptions of the afterlife in early civilizations: Universalism, constructivism, and near-death experience.* London: Continuum.

Shweder, Richard A. (1994). Are moral intuitions self-evident truths? *Criminal Justice Ethics, 13,* 24–32.

Siebenbruner, Jessica, Zimmer-Gembeck, Melanie J., & Egeland, Byron. (2007). Sexual partners and contraceptive use: A 16-year prospective study predicting abstinence and risk behavior. *Journal of Research on Adolescence, 17,* 179–206.

Siegel, Lawrence A., & Siegel, Richard M. (2007). Sexual changes in the aging male. In Annette Fuglsang Owens & Mitchell S. Tepper (Eds.), *Sexual health: Vol. 2. Physical foundations* (pp. 223–255). Westport, CT: Praeger/Greenwood.

Siegler, Robert S. (2009). Improving the numerical understanding of children from low-income families. *Child Development Perspectives, 3,* 118–124.

Sierra, Felipe, Hadley, Evan, Suzman, Richard, & Hodes, Richard. (2009). Prospects for life span extension. *Annual Review of Medicine, 60,* 457–469.

Silva, Katie G., Correa-Chávez, Maricela, & Rogoff, Barbara. (2010). Mexican-heritage children's attention and learning from interactions directed to others. *Child Development, 81,* 898–912.

Silventoinen, Karri, Hammar, Niklas, Hedlund, Ebba, Koskenvuo, Markku, Ronnemaa, Tapani, & Kaprio, Jaakko. (2008). Selective international migration by social position, health behaviour and personality. *European Journal of Public Health, 18,* 150–155.

Silverman, Wendy K., & Dick-Niederhauser, Andreas. (2004). Separation anxiety disorder. In Tracy L. Morris & John S. March (Eds.), *Anxiety disorders in children and adolescents* (2nd ed., pp. 164–188). New York: Guilford Press.

Silverstein, Merril. (2006). Intergenerational family transfers in social context. In Robert H. Binstock & Linda K. George (Eds.), *Handbook of aging and the social sciences* (6th ed., pp. 165–180). Amsterdam: Elsevier.

Silverstein, Merril, Gans, Daphna, Lowenstein, Ariela, Giarrusso, Roseann, & Bengtson, Vern L. (2010). Older parent–child relationships in six developed nations: Comparisons at the intersection of affection and conflict. *Journal of Marriage and Family, 72,* 1006–1021.

Silvia, Paul J., & Sanders, Camilla E. (2010). Why are smart people curious? Fluid intelligence, openness to experience, and interest. *Learning and Individual Differences, 20,* 242–245.

Simpkins, Sandra D., Fredricks, Jennifer A., Davis-Kean, Pamela E., & Eccles, Jacquelynne S. (2006). Healthy mind, healthy habits: The influence of activity involvement in middle childhood. In Aletha C. Huston & Marika N. Ripke (Eds.), *Developmental contexts in middle childhood: Bridges to adolescence and adulthood* (pp. 283–302). New York: Cambridge University Press.

Simpson, Jeffry A., & Rholes, W. Steven. Attachment and relationships: Milestones and future directions. *Journal of Social and Personal Relationships, 27,* 173–180.

Sinardet, Dave, & Mortelmans, Dimitri. (2009). The feminine side to Santa Claus. Women's work of kinship in contemporary gift-giving relations. *The Social Science Journal, 46,* 124–142.

Singer, Irving. (2009). *The nature of love.* Cambridge, MA: MIT Press.

Singh, Leher. (2008). Influences of High and Low Variability on Infant Word Recognition. *Cognition, 106*(2), 833–870.

Sinnott, Jan D. (1998). *The development of logic in adulthood: Postformal thought and its applications.* New York: Plenum Press.

Sinnott, Jan D. (2008). Cognitive and representational development in adults. In Kelly B. Cartwright (Ed.), *Literacy processes: Cognitive flexibility in learning and teaching* (pp. 42–68). New York: Guilford.

Sinnott, Jan D. (2009). Cognitive development as the dance of adaptive transformation: Neo-Piagetian perspectives on adult cognitive development, *Handbook of research on adult learning and development* (pp. 103–134). New York: Routledge/Taylor & Francis Group.

Siu, Angela F. Y. (2007). Using friends to combat internalizing problems among primary school children in Hong Kong. *Journal of Cognitive and Behavioral Psychotherapies, 7,* 11–26.

Sivertsen, Børge, Omvik, Siri, Pallesen, Ståle, Bjorvatn, Bjørn, Havik, Odd E., Kvale, Gerd, et al. (2006). Cognitive behavioral therapy vs zopiclone for treatment of chronic primary insomnia in older adults. *Journal of the American Medical Association, 295,* 2851–2858.

Skinner, B. F. (1953). *Science and human behavior.* New York: Macmillan.

Skinner, B. F. (1957). *Verbal behavior.* New York: Appleton-Century-Crofts.

Slaughter, Virginia, & Griffiths, Maya. (2007). Death understanding and fear of death in young children. *Clinical Child Psychology and Psychiatry, 12,* 525–535.

Slavin, Robert E., Lake, Cynthia, & Groff, Cynthia. (2009). Effective programs in middle and high school mathematics: A best-evidence synthesis. *Review of Educational Research, 79,* 839–911.

Slessor, Gillian, Phillips, Louise H., & Bull, Rebecca. (2008). Age-related declines in basic social perception: Evidence from tasks assessing eye-gaze processing. *Psychology and Aging, 23,* 812–822.

Sliwinski, Martin J., Hofer, Scott M., Hall, Charles, Buschke, Herman, & Lipton, Richard B. (2003). Modeling memory decline in older adults: The importance of preclinical dementia, attrition, and chronological age. *Psychology & Aging, 18,* 658–671.

Sloan, Ken. (2009). The role of personality in a manager's learning effectiveness. *European Journal of Social Sciences, 12,* 31–42.

Sloan, Mark. (2009). *Birth day: A pediatrician explores the science, the history, and the wonder of childbirth.* New York: Ballantine Books.

Slobin, Dan I. (2001). Form-function relations: How do children find out what they are? In Melissa Bowerman & Stephen C. Levinson (Eds.), *Language acquisition and conceptual development* (pp. 406–449). Cambridge, UK: Cambridge University Press.

Small, Meredith F. (1998). *Our babies, ourselves: How biology and culture shape the way we parent.* New York: Anchor Books.

Smedley, Audrey, & Smedley, Brian D. (2005). Race as biology is fiction, racism as a social problem is real: Anthropological and historical perspectives on the social construction of race. *American Psychologist, 60,* 16–26.

Smetana, Judith G. (2008). "It's 10 o'clock: Do you know where your children are?" Recent advances in understanding parental monitoring and adolescents' information management. *Child Development Perspectives, 2,* 19–25.

Smetana, Judith G., Metzger, Aaron, & Campione-Barr, Nicole. (2004). African American late adolescents' relationships with parents: Developmental transitions and longitudinal patterns. *Child Development, 75,* 932–947.

Smith, Aaron. (2010). *Home broadband 2010.* Washington, DC: Pew Research Center's Internet & American Life Project.

Smith, Christian, & Snell, Patricia. (2009). *Souls in transition: The religious and spiritual lives of emerging adults.* New York: Oxford University Press.

Smith, Christian (with Denton, Melinda Lundquist). (2005). *Soul searching: The religious and spiritual lives of American teenagers.* Oxford, UK: Oxford University Press.

Smith, Margaret G., & Fong, Rowena. (2004). *The children of neglect: When no one cares.* New York: Brunner-Routledge.

Smith, Peter K., Mahdavi, Jess, Carvalho, Manuel, Fisher, Sonja, Russell, Shanette, & Tippett, Neil. (2008). Cyberbullying: Its nature and impact in secondary school pupils. *Journal of Child Psychology and Psychiatry, 49,* 376–385.

Smith, Peter K., Pepler, Debra J., & Rigby, Ken. (2004). *Bullying in schools: How successful can interventions be?* New York: Cambridge University Press.

Smith, Tom W. (2005). Generation gaps in attitudes and values from the 1970s to the 1990s. In Richard A. Settersten, Jr., Frank F. Furstenberg, Jr., & Rubén G. Rumbaut (Eds.), *On the frontier of adulthood: Theory, research, and public policy* (pp. 177–221). Chicago: University of Chicago Press.

Smits, Annika, Van Gaalen, Ruben I., & Mulder, Clara H. (2010). Parent–child coresidence: Who moves in with whom and for whose needs? *Journal of Marriage and Family, 72,* 1022–1033.

Smock, Pamela J., & Greenland, Fiona Rose. (2010). Diversity in pathways to parenthood: Patterns, implications, and emerging research directions. *Journal of Marriage and Family, 72,* 576–593.

Smokowski, Paul Richard, Rose, Roderick, & Bacallao, Martica. (2010). Influence of risk factors and cultural assets on latino adolescents' trajectories of self-esteem and internalizing symptoms. *Child Psychiatry & Human Development, 41,* 133–155.

Smyth, Joshua M. (2007). Beyond self-selection in video game play: An experimental examination of the consequences of massively multiplayer online role-playing game play. *CyberPsychology & Behavior, 10,* 717–727.

Sneed, Joel R., & Whitbourne, Susan Krauss. (2005). Models of the aging self. *Journal of Social Issues, 61,* 375–388.

Snow, Catherine E., & Kang, Jennifer Yusun. (2006). Becoming bilingual, biliterate, and bicultural. In William Damon & Richard M. Lerner (Series Eds.) & K. Ann Renninger & Irving E. Sigel (Vol. Eds.), *Handbook of child psychology: Vol. 4. Child psychology in practice* (6th ed., pp. 75–102). Hoboken, NJ: Wiley.

Snow, Catherine E., Porche, Michelle V., Tabors, Patton O., & Harris, Stephanie Ross. (2007). *Is literacy enough? Pathways to academic success for adolescents.* Baltimore: Brookes.

Snow, David. (2006). Regression and reorganization of intonation between 6 and 23 months. *Child Development, 77,* 281–296.

Snyder, James, Schrepferman, Lynn, Oeser, Jessica, Patterson, Gerald, Stoolmiller, Mike, Johnson, Kassy, et al. (2005). Deviancy training and association with deviant peers in young children: Occurrence and contribution to early-onset conduct problems. *Development & Psychopathology, 17,* 397–413.

Snyder, Thomas D., & Dillow, Sally A. (2010). *Digest of education statistics, 2009.* Washington, DC: National Center for Education Statistics.

Snyder, Thomas D., Tan, Alexandra G., & Hoffman, Charlene M. (2006). *Digest of education statistics, 2005* (NCES 2006–030). Washington, DC: National Center for Education Statistics.

Social Security Administration. (2009, May 8). *Popular baby names.* Retrieved June 1, 2009, from the World Wide Web: http://www.ssa.gov/OACT/babynames/

Soekadar, Surjo R., Haagen, Klaus, & Birbaumer, Niels. (2008). Brain-computer interfaces (BCI): Restoration of movement and thought from neuroelectric and metabolic brain activity. In Armin Fuchs & Viktor K. K. Jirsa (Eds.), *Coordination: Neural, behavioral and social dynamics* (pp. 229–252). New York: Springer.

Soenens, Bart, & Vansteenkiste, Maarten. (2010). A theoretical upgrade of the concept of parental psychological control: Proposing new insights on the basis of self-determination theory. *Developmental Review, 30,* 74–99.

Sokol, Rebecca Z. (2009). Is androgen therapy indicated for aging men? *Sexuality, Reproduction & Menopause, 7,* 27–30.

Soley, Gaye, & Hannon, Erin E. (2010). Infants prefer the musical meter of their own culture: A cross-cultural comparison. *Developmental Psychology, 46,* 286–292.

Solomon, Alina, Sippola, Risto, Soininen, Hilkka, Wolozin, Benjamin, Tuomilehto, Jaakko, Laatikainen, Tiina, et al. (2010). Lipid-lowering treatment is related to decreased risk of dementia: A population-based study (FINRISK). *Neurodegenerative Diseases, 7,* 180–182.

Solomon, Jennifer Crew, & Marx, Jonathan. (2000). The physical, mental, and social health of custodial grandparents. In Bert Hayslip, Jr. & Robin Goldberg-Glen (Eds.), *Grandparents raising grandchildren: Theoretical, empirical, and clinical perspectives* (pp. 183–205). New York: Springer.

Soons, Judith P. M., & Kalmijn, Matthijs. (2009). Is marriage more than cohabitation? Well-being differences in 30 European countries. *Journal of Marriage and Family, 71,* 1141–1157.

Soons, Judith P. M., Liefbroer, Aart C., & Kalmijn, Matthijs. (2009). The long-term consequences of relationship formation for subjective well-being. *Journal of Marriage and Family, 71,* 1254–1270.

Sorkin, Dara H., & Rook, Karen S. (2006). Dealing with negative social exchanges in later life: Coping responses, goals, and effectiveness. *Psychology and Aging, 21,* 715–725.

Sowell, Elizabeth R., Thompson, Paul M., & Toga, Arthur W. (2007). Mapping adolescent brain maturation using structural magnetic resonance imaging. In Daniel Romer & Elaine F. Walker (Eds.), *Adolescent psychopathology and the developing brain: Integrating brain and prevention science* (pp. 55–84). Oxford, UK: Oxford University Press.

Spandorfer, Philip R., Alessandrini, Evaline A., Joffe, Mark D., Localio, Russell, & Shaw, Kathy N. (2005). Oral versus intravenous rehydration of moderately dehydrated children: A randomized, controlled trial. *Pediatrics, 115,* 295–301.

Spearman, Charles Edward. (1927). *The abilities of man, their nature and measurement.* New York: Macmillan.

Spelke, Elizabeth S. (1993). Object perception. In Alvin I. Goldman (Ed.), *Readings in philosophy and cognitive science* (pp. 447–460). Cambridge, MA: MIT Press.

Spence, Naomi J., & Eberstein, Isaac W. (2009). Age at first birth, parity, and postreproductive mortality among white and black women in the US, 1982–2002. *Social Science & Medicine, 68,* 1625–1632.

Spencer, John P., Blumberg, Mark S., McMurray, Bob, Robinson, Scott R., Samuelson, Larissa K., & Tomblin, J. Bruce. (2009). Short arms and talking eggs: Why we should no longer abide the nativist–empiricist debate. *Child Development Perspectives, 3,* 79–87.

Spencer, Steven, Logel, Christine, & Davies, Paul G. (in press). Stereotype threat. *Annual Review of Psychology, 62.*

Spinillo, Arsenio, Montanari, Laura, Gardella, Barbara, Roccio, Marianna, Stronati, Mauro, & Fazzi, Elisa. (2009). Infant sex, obstetric risk factors, and 2-year neurodevelopmental outcome among preterm infants. *Developmental Medicine & Child Neurology, 51,* 518–525.

Spittle, Alicia J., Treyvaud, Karli, Doyle, Lex W., Roberts, Gehan, Lee, Katherine J., Inder, Terrie E., et al. (2009). Early emergence of behavior and social-emotional problems in very preterm infants. *Journal of the American Academy of Child and Adolescent Psychiatry, 48,* 909–918.

Sprung, Charles L., Carmel, Sara, Sjokvist, Peter, Baras, Mario, Cohen, Simon L., Maia, Paulo, et al. (2007). Attitudes of European physicians, nurses, patients, and families regarding end-of-life decisions: The ETHICATT study. *Intensive Care Medicine, 33,* 104–110.

Sroufe, L. Alan, Egeland, Byron, Carlson, Elizabeth A., & Collins, W. Andrew. (2005). *The development of the person: The Minnesota study of risk and adaptation from birth to adulthood.* New York: Guilford Press.

St Clair, David, Xu, Mingqing, Wang, Peng, Yu, Yaqin, Fang, Yourong, Zhang, Feng, et al. (2005). Rates of adult schizophrenia following prenatal exposure to the Chinese famine of 1959–1961. *JAMA, 294,* 557–562.

St. Petersburg-USA Orphanage Research Team. (2008). The effects of early social-emotional and relationship experience on the development of young orphanage children. *Monographs of the Society for Research in Child Development, 73*(3), 1–262.

Staiger, Annegret Daniela. (2006). *Learning difference: Race and schooling in the multiracial metropolis.* Stanford, CA: Stanford University Press.

Stanger, Olaf, Fowler, Brian, Piertzik, Klaus, Huemer, Martina, Haschke-Becher, Elisabeth, Semmler, Alexander, et al. (2009). Homocysteine, folate and vitamin B12 in neuropsychiatric diseases: Review and treatment recommendations. *Expert Review of Neurotherapeutics, 9,* 1393–1412.

Stanley, Jennifer Tehan, & Blanchard-Fields, Fredda. (2008). Challenges older adults face in detecting deceit: The role of emotion recognition. *Psychology and Aging, 23,* 24–32.

Stanton, Cynthia K., & Holtz, Sara A. (2006). Levels and trends in cesarean birth in the developing world. *Studies in Family Planning, 37,* 41–48.

Starns, Jeffrey J., & Ratcliff, Roger. (2010). The effects of aging on the speed-accuracy compromise: Boundary optimality in the diffusion model. 25, 377–390.

Stattin, Håkan, & Kerr, Margaret. (2000). Parental monitoring: A reinterpretation. *Child Development, 71,* 1072–1085.

Staudinger, Ursula M., & Lindenberger, Ulman. (2003). Why read another book on human development? Understanding human development takes a metatheory and multiple disciplines. In Ursula M. Staudinger & Ulman E. R. Lindenberger (Eds.), *Understanding human development: Dialogues with lifespan psychology* (pp. 1–13). Boston: Kluwer.

Staudinger, Ursula M., & Werner, Ines. (2003). Wisdom: Its social nature and lifespan development. In Jaan Valsiner & Kevin J. Connolly (Eds.), *Handbook of developmental psychology* (pp. 584–602). Thousand Oaks, CA: Sage.

Stawski, Robert S., Almeida, David M., Lachman, Margie E., Tun, Patricia A., & Rosnick, Christopher B. (2010). Fluid cognitive ability is associated with greater exposure and smaller reactions to daily stressors. *Psychology and Aging, 25,* 330–342.

Stearns, Elizabeth, & Glennie, Elizabeth J. (2010). Opportunities to participate: Extracurricular activities' distribution across and academic correlates in high schools. *Social Science Research, 39,* 296–309.

Steele, Claude M. (1997). A threat in the air: How stereotypes shape intellectual identity and performance. *American Psychologist, 52,* 613–629.

Steemers, Jeanette. (2010). *Creating preschool television: A story of commerce, creativity and curriculum.* New York: Palgrave Macmillan.

Stein, Arlene. (2006). *Shameless: Sexual dissidence in American culture.* New York: New York University Press.

Stein, Theodore J. (2007). Court-ordered grandparent visitation: Welcome event or unwarranted intrusion into family life? *Social Service Review, 81,* 229–243.

Steinberg, Laurence. (2001). We know some things: Parent-adolescent relationships in retrospect and prospect. *Journal of Research on Adolescence, 11,* 1–19.

Steinberg, Laurence. (2004). Risk taking in adolescence: What changes, and why? In Ronald E. Dahl & Linda Patia Spear (Eds.), *Adolescent brain development: Vulnerabilities and opportunities* (Vol. 1021, pp. 51–58). New York: New York Academy of Sciences

Steinberg, Laurence. (2007). Risk taking in adolescence: New perspectives from brain and behavioral science. *Current Directions in Psychological Science, 16,* 55–59.

Steinberg, Laurence. (2008). A social neuroscience perspective on adolescent risk-taking. *Developmental Review, 28,* 78–106.

Steinberg, Laurence, Lamborn, Susie D., Darling, Nancy, Mounts, Nina S., & Dornbusch, Sanford M. (1994). Over-time changes in adjustment and competence among adolescents from authoritative, authoritarian, indulgent, and neglectful families. *Child Development, 65,* 754–770.

Steiner, Meir, & Young, Elizabeth A. (2008). Hormones and mood. In Jill B. Becker, Karen J. Berkley, Nori Geary, Elizabeth Hampson, James P. Herman, & Elizabeth Young (Eds.), *Sex differences in the brain: From genes to behavior* (pp. 405–426). New York: Oxford University Press.

Stel, Vianda S., Smit, Johannes H., Pluijm, Saskia M. F., & Lips, Paul. (2004). Consequences of falling in older men and women and risk factors for health service use and functional decline. *Age and Ageing, 33,* 58–65.

Sterck, Elisabeth H. M., & Begeer, Sander. (2010). Theory of Mind: Specialized capacity or emergent property? *European Journal of Developmental Psychology, 7,* 1–16.

Stern, Michael J., & Adams, Alison E. (2010). Do rural residents really use the internet to build social capital? An empirical investigation. *American Behavioral Scientist, 53,* 1389–1422.

Sternberg, Robert J. (1988). Triangulating love. In Robert J. Sternberg & Michael L. Barnes (Eds.), *The psychology of love* (pp. 119–138). New Haven, CT: Yale University Press.

Sternberg, Robert J. (1988). *The triarchic mind: A new theory of human intelligence.* New York: Viking.

Sternberg, Robert J. (1996). *Successful intelligence: How practical and creative intelligence determine success in life.* New York: Simon & Schuster.

Sternberg, Robert J. (2002). Beyond g: The theory of successful intelligence. In Robert J. Sternberg & Elena L. Grigorenko (Eds.), *The general factor of intelligence: How general is it?* (pp. 447–479). Mahwah, NJ: Erlbaum.

Sternberg, Robert J. (2003). *Wisdom, intelligence, and creativity synthesized.* New York: Cambridge University Press.

Sternberg, Robert J. (2006). Introduction. In James C. Kaufman & Robert J. Sternberg (Eds.), *The international handbook of creativity* (pp. 1–9). New York: Cambridge University Press.

Sternberg, Robert J., Forsythe, George B., Hedlund, Jennifer, Horvath, Joseph A., Wagner, Richard K., Williams, Wendy M., et al. (2000). *Practical intelligence in everyday life.* New York: Cambridge University Press.

Sterns, Harvey L., & Huyck, Margaret Hellie. (2001). The role of work in midlife. In Margie E. Lachman (Ed.), *Handbook of midlife development* (pp. 447–486). New York: Wiley.

Stevenson, Olive. (2007). *Neglected children and their families* (2nd ed.). Malden, MA: Blackwell.

Stevenson, Richard J., Oaten, Megan J., Case, Trevor I., Repacholi, Betty M., & Wagland, Paul. (2010). Children's response to adult disgust elicitors: Development and acquisition. *Developmental Psychology, 46,* 165–177.

Stewart, Endya B. (2008). School structural characteristics, student effort, peer associations, and parental involvement: The influence of school- and individual-level factors on academic achievement. *Education and Urban Society, 40,* 179–204.

Stigler, James W., & Hiebert, James. (2009). *The teaching gap: Best ideas from the world's teachers for improving education in the classroom* (1st Free Press trade paperback ed.). New York: Free Press. (Original work published 1999)

Stiles, Joan. (2008). *The fundamentals of brain development: Integrating nature and nurture.* Cambridge, MA: Harvard University Press.

Stillman, Robert J., Richter, Kevin S., Banks, Nicole K., & Graham, James R. (2009). Elective single embryo transfer: A 6-year progressive implementation of 784 single blastocyst transfers and the influence of payment method on patient choice. *Fertility and Sterility, 92,* 1895–1906.

Stine-Morrow, Elizabeth A. L., Parisi, Jeanine M., Morrow, Daniel G., & Park, Denise C. (2008). The effects of an engaged lifestyle on cognitive vitality: A field experiment. *Psychology and Aging, 23,* 778–786.

Stine-Morrow, Elizabeth A. L., Shake, Matthew C., Miles, Joseph R., Lee, Kenton, Gao, Xuefei, & McConkie, George. (2010). Pay now or pay later: Aging and the role of boundary salience in self-regulation of conceptual integration in sentence processing. *Psychology and Aging, 25,* 168–176.

Stokstad, Erik. (2003, December 12). The vitamin D deficit. *Science, 302,* 1886–1888.

Stone, Robyn I. (2006). Emerging issues in long-term care. In Robert H. Binstock & Linda K. George (Eds.), *Handbook of aging and the social sciences* (6th ed., pp. 397–418). Amsterdam: Elsevier

Strasburger, Victor C., Wilson, Barbara J., & Jordan, Amy B. (2009). *Children, adolescents, and the media* (2nd ed.). Los Angeles: Sage.

Straus, Murray A., & Gelles, Richard J. (with Smith, Christine) (Eds.). (1995). *Physical violence in American families: Risk factors and adaptations to violence in 8,145 families* (Paperback ed.). New Brunswick, NJ: Transaction.

Straus, Murray A., & Paschall, Mallie J. (2009). Corporal punishment by mothers and development of children's cognitive ability: A longitudinal study of two nationally representative age cohorts. *Journal of Aggression, Maltreatment & Trauma, 18,* 459–483.

Strayer, David L., & Drews, Frank A. (2007). Cell-phone-induced driver distraction. *Current Directions in Psychological Science, 16,* 128–131.

Streissguth, Ann P., & Connor, Paul D. (2001). Fetal alcohol syndrome and other effects of prenatal alcohol: Developmental cognitive neuroscience implications. In Charles A. Nelson & Monica Luciana (Eds.), *Handbook of developmental cognitive neuroscience* (pp. 505–518). Cambridge, MA: MIT Press.

Stright, Anne Dopkins, Gallagher, Kathleen Cranley, & Kelley, Ken. (2008). Infant temperament moderates relations between maternal parenting in early childhood and children's adjustment in first grade. *Child Development, 79,* 186–200.

Strom, Robert D., & Strom, Shirley K. (2000). Goals for grandparents and support groups. In Bert Hayslip, Jr. & Robin Goldberg-Glen (Eds.), *Grandparents raising grandchildren: Theoretical, empirical, and clinical perspectives* (pp. 289–303). New York: Springer.

Strouse, Darcy L. (1999). Adolescent crowd orientations: A social and temporal analysis. In Jeffrey A. McLellan & Mary Jo V. Pugh (Eds.), *The role of peer groups in adolescent social identity: Exploring the importance of stability and change* (pp. 37–54). San Francisco, CA: Jossey-Bass.

Stubben, Jerry D. (2001). Working with and conducting research among American Indian families. *American Behavioral Scientist, 44,* 1466–1481.

Štulhofer, Aleksandar, Graham, Cynthia, Božićević, Ivana, Kufrin, Krešimir, & Ajduković, Dean. (2009). An assessment of HIV/STI vulnerability and related sexual risk-taking in a nationally representative sample of young Croatian adults. *Archives of Sexual Behavior, 38,* 209–225.

Subrahmanyam, Kaveri, Reich, Stephanie M., Waechter, Natalia, & Espinoza, Guadalupe. (2008). Online and offline social networks: Use of social networking sites by emerging adults. *Journal of Applied Developmental Psychology, 29,* 420–433.

Sue, Derald Wing. (2010). *Microaggressions and marginality: Manifestation, dynamics, and impact.* Hoboken, NJ: Wiley.

Suh, Eunkook M., Diener, Ed, & Updegraff, John A. (2008). From culture to priming conditions: Self-construal influences on life satisfaction judgments. *Journal of Cross-Cultural Psychology, 39,* 3–15.

Sullivan, Sheila. (1999). *Falling in love: A history of torment and enchantment.* London: Macmillan.

Sullivan, Tara M., Bertrand, Jane T., Rice, Janet, & Shelton, James D. (2006). Skewed contraceptive method mix: Why it happens, why it matters. *Journal of Biosocial Science, 38,* 501–521.

Sulmasy, Daniel P. (2006). Spiritual issues in the care of dying patients: ". . . It's okay between me and god." *Journal of the American Medical Association, 296,* 1385–1392.

Sun, Min, & Rugolotto, Simone. (2004). Assisted infant toilet training in a Western family setting. *Journal of Developmental & Behavioral Pediatrics, 25,* 99–101.

Sun, Rongjun, & Liu, Yuzhi. (2008). The more engagement, the better? A study of mortality of the oldest old in China. In Zeng Yi, Dudley L. Poston, Jr., Denese Ashbaugh Vlosky, & Danan Gu (Eds.), *Healthy longevity in China* (pp. 177–192). Dordrecht, The Netherlands: Springer.

Sunstein, Cass R. (2008). Adolescent risk-taking and social meaning: A commentary. *Developmental Review, 28,* 145–152.

Suomi, Stephen, van der Horst, Frank, & van der Veer, René. (2008). Rigorous experiments on monkey love: An account of Harry F. Harlow's role in the history of attachment theory. *Integrative Psychological and Behavioral Science, 42,* 354–369.

Suomi, Steven J. (2002). Parents, peers, and the process of socialization in primates. In John G. Borkowski, Sharon Landesman Ramey, & Marie Bristol-Power (Eds.), *Parenting and the child's world: Influences on academic, intellectual, and social-emotional development* (pp. 265–279). Mahwah, NJ: Erlbaum.

Supiano, Mark A. (2006). Hypertension in later life. *Generations, 30*(3), 11–16.

Surgeoner, Brae V., Chapman, Benjamin J., & Powell, Douglas A. (2009). University students' hand hygiene practice during a gastrointestinal outbreak in residence: What they say they do and what they actually do. *Journal of Environmental Health, 72,* 24–28.

Suris, Joan-Carles, Michaud, Pierre-André, Akre, Christina, & Sawyer, Susan M. (2008). Health risk behaviors in adolescents with chronic conditions. *Pediatrics, 122,* e1113–e1118.

Susman, Elizabeth J., Dockray, Samantha, Schiefelbein, Virginia L., Herwehe, Suellen, Heaton, Jodi A., & Dorn, Lorah D. (2007). Morningness/eveningness, morning-to-afternoon cortisol ratio, and antisocial behavior problems during puberty. *Developmental Psychology, 43,* 811–822.

Susman, Elizabeth J., Houts, Renate M., Steinberg, Laurence, Belsky, Jay, Cauffman, Elizabeth, DeHart, Ganie, et al. (2010). Longitudinal development of secondary sexual characteristics in girls and boys between ages 9-1/2 and 15-1/2 years. *Archives of Pediatrics & Adolescent Medicine, 164,* 166–173.

Sutin, Angelina R., & Costa, Paul T., Jr. (2010). Reciprocal influences of personality and job characteristics across middle adulthood. *Journal of Personality, 78,* 257–288.

Sutton-Smith, Brian. (1997). *The ambiguity of play.* Cambridge, MA: Harvard University Press.

Swan, Suzanne C., Gambone, Laura J., Caldwell, Jennifer E., Sullivan, Tami P., & Snow, David L. (2008). A review of research on women's use of violence with male intimate partners. *Violence and Victims, 23,* 301–314.

Swanson, Richard A. (2007). *Analysis for improving performance: Tools for diagnosing organizations and documenting workplace expertise* (2nd ed.). San Francisco: Berrett-Koehler Publishers.

Sweeney, Megan M. (2010). Remarriage and stepfamilies: Strategic sites for family scholarship in the 21st century. *Journal of Marriage and Family, 72,* 667–684.

Syed, Moin, & Azmitia, Margarita. (2010). Narrative and ethnic identity exploration: A longitudinal account of emerging adults' ethnicity-related experiences. *Developmental Psychology, 46,* 208–219.

Szinovacz, Maximiliane. (1998). Grandparent research: Past, present and future. In Maximiliane Szinovacz (Ed.), *Handbook on grandparenthood* (pp. 1–20). Westport, CT: Greenwood Press.

Szinovacz, Maximiliane E. (2000). Changes in housework after retirement: A panel analysis. *Journal of Marriage & the Family, 62,* 78–92.

Tacken, Mart, & van Lamoen, Ellemieke (2005). Transport behaviour and realised journeys and trips. In Heidrun Mollenkopf, Fiorella Marcellini, Isto Ruoppila, Zsuzsa Széman, & Mart Tacken (Eds.), *Enhancing mobility in later life: Personal coping, environmental resources and technical support. The out-of-home mobility of older adults in urban and rural regions of five European countries* (pp. 105–139). Amsterdam: IOS Press.

Taga, Keiko A., Markey, Charlotte N., & Friedman, Howard S. (2006). A longitudinal investigation of associations between boys' pubertal timing and adult behavioral health and well-being. *Journal of Youth and Adolescence, 35,* 401–411.

Takahashi, Hidehiko, Kato, Motoichiro, Matsuura, Masato, Mobbs, Dean, Suhara, Tetsuya, & Okubo, Yoshiro. (2009, February 13). When your gain is my pain and your pain is my gain: Neural correlates of envy and schadenfreude. *Science, 323,* 937–939.

Takata, Yutaka, Ansai, Toshihiro, Soh, Inho, Kimura, Yasuo, Yoshitake, Yutaka, Sonoki, Kazuo, et al. (2008). Physical fitness and cognitive function in an 85-year-old community-dwelling population. *Gerontology, 54,* 354–360.

Talge, Nicole M., Neal, Charles, & Glover, Vivette. (2007). Antenatal maternal stress and long-term effects on child neurodevelopment: How and why? *Journal of Child Psychology and Psychiatry, 48,* 245–261.

Tamay, Zeynep, Akcay, Ahmet, Ones, Ulker, Guler, Nermin, Kilic, Gurkan, & Zencir, Mehmet. (2007). Prevalence and risk factors for allergic rhinitis in primary school children. *International Journal of Pediatric Otorhinolaryngology, 71,* 463–471.

Tamis-LeMonda, Catherine, Kahana-Kalman, Ronit, & Yoshikawa, Hirokazu. (2009). Father involvement in immigrant and ethnically diverse families from the prenatal period to the second year: Prediction and mediating mechanisms. *Sex Roles, 60,* 496–509.

Tamis-LeMonda, Catherine S., Bornstein, Marc H., & Baumwell, Lisa. (2001). Maternal responsiveness and children's achievement of language milestones. *Child Development, 72,* 748–767.

Tamis-LeMonda, Catherine S., Way, Niobe, Hughes, Diane, Yoshikawa, Hirokazu, Kalman, Ronit Kahana, & Niwa, Erika Y. (2008). Parents' goals for children: The dynamic coexistence of individualism and collectivism in cultures and individuals. *Social Development, 17,* 183–209.

Tanaka, Yuko, & Nakazawa, Jun. (2005). Job-related temporary father absence (Tanshinfunin) and child development. In David W. Shwalb, Jun Nakazawa, & Barbara J. Shwalb (Eds.), *Applied developmental psychology: Theory, practice, and research from Japan* (pp. 241–260). Greenwich, CT: Information Age.

Tang, Chao-Hsiun, Wang, Han-I, Hsu, Chun-Sen, Su, Hung-Wen, Chen, Mei-Ju, & Lin, Herng-Ching. (2006). *Risk-adjusted cesarean section rates for the assessment of physician performance in Taiwan: A population-based study.* BioMed Central. Retrieved April 27, 2007, from the World Wide Web: http://www.biomedcentral.com/1471-2458/6/246

Tangney, June Price, Stuewig, Jeff, & Mashek, Debra J. (2007). Moral emotions and moral behavior. *Annual Review of Psychology, 58,* 345–372.

Tanner, Jennifer L., Arnett, Jeffrey J., & Leis, Julie A. (2009). Emerging adulthood: Learning and development during the first stage of adulthood. In M. Cecil Smith (Ed.), *Handbook of research on adult learning and development* (pp. 34–67). New York: Routledge/Taylor & Francis Group.

Tapper, Joshua. (2010, July 7). *A last conversation with Dr. Robert Butler.* Retrieved December 13, 2010, from the World Wide Web: http://newoldage.blogs.nytimes.com/2010/07/07/a-last-conversation-with-dr-robert-butler/

Tarullo, Amanda R., & Gunnar, Megan R. (2006). Child maltreatment and the developing HPA axis. *Hormones and Behavior, 50,* 632–639.

Tay, Marc Tze-Hsin, Au Eong, Kah Guan, Ng, C. Y., & Lim, M. K. (1992). Myopia and educational attainment in 421,116 young Singaporean males. *Annals, Academy of Medicine, Singapore, 21,* 785–791.

Taylor, Alan C., Robila, Mihaela, & Lee, Hae Seung. (2005). Distance, contact, and intergenerational relationships: Grandparents and adult grandchildren from an international perspective. *Journal of Adult Development, 12,* 33–41.

Taylor, Donald H., Jr., Cook-Deegan, Robert M., Hiraki, Susan, Roberts, J. Scott, Blazer, Dan G., & Green, Robert C. (2010). Genetic testing for Alzheimer's and long-term care insurance. *Health Affairs, 29,* 102–108.

Taylor, James A., Geyer, Leah J., & Feldman, Kenneth W. (2010). Use of supplemental vitamin D among infants breastfed for prolonged periods. *Pediatrics, 125,* 105–111.

Taylor, Marjorie, Carlson, Stephanie M., Maring, Bayta L., Gerow, Lynn, & Charley, Carolyn M. (2004). The characteristics and correlates of fantasy in school-age children: Imaginary companions, impersonation, and social understanding. *Developmental Psychology, 40,* 1173–1187.

Taylor, Ronald D., Seaton, Eleanor, & Dominguez, Antonio. (2008). Kinship support, family relations, and psychological adjustment among low-income African American mothers and adolescents. *Journal of Research on Adolescence, 18,* 1–22.

Taylor, Rachael W., Murdoch, Linda, Carter, Philippa, Gerrard, David F., Williams, Sheila M., & Taylor, Barry J. (2009). Longitudinal study of physical activity and inactivity in preschoolers: The FLAME study. *Medicine & Science in Sports & Exercise, 41,* 96–102.

Taylor, Shelley E. (2006). Tend and befriend: Biobehavioral bases of affiliation under stress. *Current Directions in Psychological Science, 15,* 273–277.

Taylor, Shelley E., Klein, Laura Cousino, Lewis, Brian P., Gruenewald, Tara L., Gurung, Regan A. R., & Updegraff, John A. (2000). Biobehavioral responses to stress in females: Tend-and-befriend, not fight-or-flight. *Psychological Review, 107,* 411–429.

Teachman, Jay. (2008). Complex life course patterns and the risk of divorce in second marriages. *Journal of Marriage and Family, 70,* 294–305.

Teachman, Jay. (2010). Work-related health limitations, education, and the risk of marital disruption. *Journal of Marriage and Family, 72,* 919–932.

Tedeschi, Alberto, & Airaghi, Lorena. (2006). Is affluence a risk factor for bronchial asthma and type 1 diabetes? *Pediatric Allergy and Immunology, 17,* 533–537.

Teitler, Julien O. (2002). Trends in youth sexual initiation and fertility in developed countries: 1960–1995. *Annals of the American Academy of Political & Social Science, 580,* 134–152.

Teo, Alan R. (2010). A new form of social withdrawal in Japan: A review of hikikomori. *International Journal of Social Psychiatry, 56,* 178–185.

ter Bogt, Tom, Schmid, Holger, Gabhainn, Saoirse Nic, Fotiou, Anastasios, & Vollebergh, Wilma. (2006). Economic and cultural correlates of cannabis use among mid-adolescents in 31 countries. *Addiction, 101,* 241–251.

Tercyak, Kenneth P. (2008). Editorial: Prevention in child health psychology and the Journal of Pediatric Psychology. *Journal of Pediatric Psychology, 33,* 31–34.

Terracciano, Antonio. (2010). Secular trends and personality. *Perspectives on Psychological Science, 5,* 93–96.

Terry, Dellara F., Nolan, Vikki G., Andersen, Stacy L., Perls, Thomas T., & Cawthon, Richard. (2008). Association of longer telomeres with better health in centenarians. *Journals Of Gerontology Series A: Biological Sciences And Medical Sciences, 63,* 809–812.

Tester, June M., Rutherford, George W., Wald, Zachary, & Rutherford, Mary W. (2004). A matched case-control study evaluating the effectiveness of speed humps in reducing child pedestrian injuries. *American Journal of Public Health, 94,* 646–650.

Thaler, Richard H., & Sunstein, Cass R. (2008). *Nudge: Improving decisions about health, wealth, and happiness.* New Haven, CT: Yale University Press.

The EXPRESS Group. (2009). One-year survival of extremely preterm infants after active perinatal care in Sweden. *Journal of the American Medical Association, 301*(21), 2225–2233.

Thelen, Esther, & Corbetta, Daniela. (2002). Microdevelopment and dynamic systems: Applications to infant motor development. In Nira Granott & Jim Parziale (Eds.), *Microdevelopment: Transition processes in development and learning* (pp. 59–79). New York: Cambridge University Press.

Thelen, Esther, & Smith, Linda B. (2006). Dynamic systems theories. In William Damon & Richard M. Lerner (Series Eds.) & Richard M. Lerner (Vol. Ed.), *Handbook of child psychology: Vol. 1. Theoretical models of human development* (6th ed., pp. 258–312). Hoboken, NJ: Wiley.

Theriot, Matthew T., & Dupper, David R. (2010). Student discipline problems and the transition from elementary to middle school. *Education and Urban Society, 42,* 205–222.

Thiele, Dianne M., & Whelan, Thomas A. (2008). The relationship between grandparent satisfaction, meaning, and generativity. *International Journal of Aging and Human Development, 66,* 21–48.

Thobaben, Marshelle. (2006). Understanding compulsive hoarding. *Home Health Care Management Practice, 18,* 152–154.

Thomaes, Sander, Reijntjes, Albert, Orobio de Castro, Bram, Bushman, Brad J., Poorthuis, Astrid, & Telch, Michael J. (2010). I like me if you like me: On the interpersonal modulation and regulation of preadolescents' state self-esteem. *Child Development, 81,* 811–825.

Thomas, Alexander, & Chess, Stella. (1977). *Temperament and development:* Oxford, England: Brunner/Mazel.

Thomas, Ayanna K., & Bulevich, John B. (2006). Effective cue utilization reduces memory errors in older adults. *Psychology and Aging, 21,* 379–389.

Thomas, Dylan. (1957). *The collected poems of Dylan Thomas* (6th ed.). New York: New Directions.

Thomas, Lori M. (2008). The changing role of parents in neonatal care: A historical review. *Neonatal Network, 27,* 91–100.

Thomas, Michael S. C., & Johnson, Mark H. (2008). New advances in understanding sensitive periods in brain development. *Current Directions in Psychological Science, 17,* 1–5.

Thomas, Michael S. C., Van Duuren, Mike, Purser, Harry R. M., Mareschal, Denis, Ansari, Daniel, & Karmiloff-Smith, Annette. (2010). The development of metaphorical language comprehension in typical development and in Williams syndrome. *Journal of Experimental Child Psychology, 106,* 99–114.

Thomas, William H. (2007). *What are old people for? How elders will save the world* (Paperback ed.). Acton, MA: VanderWyk & Burnham.

Thompson, Elisabeth Morgan, & Morgan, Elizabeth M. (2008). "Mostly straight" young women: Variations in sexual behavior and identity development. *Developmental Psychology, 44,* 15–21.

Thompson, Ross A. (2006). The development of the person: Social understanding, relationships, conscience, self. In William Damon & Richard M. Lerner (Series Eds.) & Nancy Eisenberg (Vol. Ed.), *Handbook of child psychology: Vol. 3. Social, emotional, and personality development* (6th ed., pp. 24–98). Hoboken, NJ: Wiley.

Thompson, Ross A., & Nelson, Charles A. (2001). Developmental science and the media: Early brain development. *American Psychologist, 56,* 5–15.

Thompson, Ross A., & Raikes, H. Abigail. (2003). Toward the next quarter-century: Conceptual and methodological challenges for attachment theory. *Development & Psychopathology, 15,* 691–718.

Thompson, Ross A., & Wyatt, Jennifer M. (1999). Values, policy, and research on divorce: Seeking fairness for children. In Ross A. Thompson & Paul R. Amato (Eds.), *The postdivorce family: Children, parenting, and society* (pp. 191–232). Thousand Oaks, CA: Sage.

Thomson, Judith Jarvis. (1986). *Rights, restitution, and risk: Essays in moral theory* (William Parent, Trans.). Cambridge, MA: Harvard University Press.

Thomson, W. Murray, Poulton, Richie, Broadbent, Jonathan M., Moffitt, Terrie E., Caspi, Avshalom, Beck, James D., et al. (2008). Cannabis smoking and periodontal disease among young adults. *Journal of the American Medical Association, 299,* 525–531.

Thornton, Arland, Axinn, William G., & Xie, Yu. (2007). *Marriage and cohabitation.* Chicago: University of Chicago Press.

Thornton, Wendy J. L., & Dumke, Heike A. (2005). Age differences in everyday problem-solving and decision-making effectiveness: A meta-analytic review. *Psychology and Aging, 20,* 85–99.

Thorson, James A. (1995). *Aging in a changing society.* Belmont, CA: Wadsworth.

Thorvaldsson, Valgeir, Hofer, Scott M., Hassing, Linda B., & Johansson, Boo. (2008). Cognitive change as conditional on age heterogeneity in onset of mortality-related processes and repeated testing effects. In Scott M. Hofer & Duane F. Alwin (Eds.), *Handbook of cognitive aging: Interdisciplinary perspectives* (pp. 284–297). Thousand Oaks, CA: Sage Publications.

Thurber, James. (1999). The secret life of James Thurber. In James Thurber (Ed.), *The Thurber carnival* (pp. 35–41). New York: Harper Perennial.

Tilling, Kate, Lawlor, Debbie A., Davey Smith, George, Chambless, Lloyd, & Szklo, Moyses. (2006). The relation between components of adult height and intimal-medial thickness in middle age: The Atherosclerosis Risk in Communities Study. *American Journal of Epidemiology, 164,* 136–142.

Tilton-Weaver, Lauree, Kerr, Margaret, Pakalniskeine, Vilmante, Tokic, Ana, Salihovic, Selma, & Stattin, HÂkan. (2010). Open up or close down: How do parental reactions affect youth information management? *Journal of Adolescence, 33,* 333–346.

Timiras, Mary L. (2007). The skin. In Paola S. Timiras (Ed.), *Physiological basis of aging and geriatrics* (4th ed., pp. 345–352). New York: Informa Healthcare.

Timiras, Paola S., & De Martinis, Massimo. (2007). The pulmonary respiration, hematopoiesis, and erythrocytes. In Paola S. Timiras (Ed.), *Physiological basis of aging and geriatrics* (4th ed., pp. 277–296). New York: Informa Healthcare.

Tishkoff, Sarah A, & Kidd, Kenneth K. (2004). Implications of biogeography of human populations for 'race' and medicine. *Nature Genetics, 36,* S21–S27.

Titus, Dale N. (2007). Strategies and resources for enhancing the achievement of mobile students. *NASSP Bulletin, 91,* 81–97.

Tluczek, Audrey, Koscik, Rebecca L., Modaff, Peggy, Pfeil, Darci, Rock, Michael J., Farrell, Philip M., et al. (2006). Newborn screening for cystic fibrosis: Parents' preferences regarding counseling at the time of infants' sweat test. *Journal of Genetic Counseling, 15,* 277–291.

Tokunaga, Robert S. (2010). Following you home from school: A critical review and synthesis of research on cyberbullying victimization. *Computers in Human Behavior, 26*(3), 277–287.

Tomalski, Przemyslaw, & Johnson, Mark H. (2010). The effects of early adversity on the adult and developing brain. *Current Opinion in Psychiatry, 23,* 233–238.

Tomasello, Michael. (2001). Perceiving intentions and learning words in the second year of life. In Melissa Bowerman & Stephen C. Levinson (Eds.), *Language acquisition and conceptual development* (pp. 132–158). Cambridge, UK: Cambridge University Press.

Tomasello, Michael. (2006). Acquiring linguistic constructions. In William Damon & Richard M. Lerner (Series Eds.) & Deanna Kuhn & Robert S. Siegler (Vol. Eds.), *Handbook of child psychology: Vol. 2. Cognition, perception, and language* (6th ed., pp. 255–298). Hoboken, NJ: Wiley.

Tomasello, Michael. (2009). Cultural transmission: A view from chimpanzees and human infants. In Ute Schönpflug (Ed.), *Cultural transmission: Psychological, developmental, social, and methodological aspects* (pp. 33–47). New York: Cambridge University Press.

Tomasello, Michael, Carpenter, Malinda, & Liszkowski, Ulf. (2007). A new look at infant pointing. *Child Development, 78,* 705–722.

Tonn, Jessica L. (2006). Later high school start times: A reaction to research. *Education Week, 25,* 5, 17.

Tornstam, Lars. (2005). *Gerotranscendence: A developmental theory of positive aging.* New York: Springer.

Towner, Elizabeth, & Mytton, Julie. (2009). Prevention of unintentional injuries in children. *Paediatrics and Child Health, 19,* 517–521.

Townsend, Jean, Godfrey, Mary, & Denby, Tracy. (2006). Heroines, villains and victims: Older people's perceptions of others. *Ageing & Society, 26,* 883–900.

Toyama, Miki. (2001). Developmental changes in social comparison in preschool and elementary school children: Perceptions, feelings, and behavior. *Japanese Journal of Educational Psychology, 49,* 500–507.

Tracy, Erin E. (2009, August). Does home birth empower women, or imperil them and their babies? *OBG Management, 21,* 45–52.

Trautmann-Villalba, Patricia, Gschwendt, Miriam, Schmidt, Martin H., & Laucht, Manfred. (2006). Father-infant interaction patterns as precursors of children's later externalizing behavior problems: A longitudinal study over 11 years. *European Archives of Psychiatry and Clinical Neuroscience, 256,* 344–349.

Treas, Judith. (2008–2009). Four myths about older adults in America's immigrant families. *Generations, 32*(4), 40–45.

Trenholm, Christopher, Devaney, Barbara, Fortson, Ken, Quay, Lisa, Wheeler, Justin, & Clark, Melissa. (2007). *Impacts of four Title V, Section 510 abstinence education programs final report.* U.S. Department of Health and Human Services. Retrieved August 22, 2007, from the World Wide Web: http://www.mathematica-mpr.com/abstinencereport.asp

Trenka, Jane Jeong, Oparah, Julia Chinyere, & Shin, Sun Yung (Eds.). (2006). *Outsiders within: Writing on transracial adoption.* Cambridge, MA: South End Press.

Trimble, Joseph, Root, Maria P. P., & Helms, Janet E. (2003). Psychological perspectives on ethnic and racial psychology. *Racial and*

ethnic minority psychology series: Vol. 4. Handbook of racial & ethnic minority psychology, 239–275.

Troll, Lillian E., & Skaff, Marilyn McKean. (1997). Perceived continuity of self in very old age. *Psychology & Aging, 12,* 162–169.

Tronick, Edward Z. (1989). Emotions and emotional communication in infants. *American Psychologist, 44,* 112–119.

Tronick, Edward Z., & Weinberg, M. Katherine. (1997). Depressed mothers and infants: Failure to form dyadic states of consciousness. In Lynne Murray & Peter J. Cooper (Eds.), *Postpartum depression and child development* (pp. 54–81). New York: Guilford Press.

Truog, Robert D. (2007). Brain death—Too flawed to endure, too ingrained to abandon. *The Journal of Law, Medicine & Ethics, 35,* 273–281.

Trzesniewski, Kali H., & Donnellan, M. Brent. (2010). Rethinking "Generation Me." *Perspectives on Psychological Science, 5,* 58–75.

Trzesniewski, Kali H., Donnellan, M. Brent, Moffitt, Terrie E., Robins, Richard W., Poulton, Richie, & Caspi, Avshalom. (2006). Low self-esteem during adolescence predicts poor health, criminal behavior, and limited economic prospects during adulthood. *Developmental Psychology, 42,* 381–390.

Tsao, Feng-Ming, Liu, Huei-Mei, & Kuhl, Patricia K. (2004). Speech perception in infancy predicts language development in the second year of life: A longitudinal study. *Child Development, 75,* 1067–1084.

Tu, Wanzhu, Batteiger, Byron E., Wiehe, Sarah, Ofner, Susan, Van Der Pol, Barbara, Katz, Barry P., et al. (2009). Time from first intercourse to first sexually transmitted infection diagnosis among adolescent women. *Archives of Pediatrics & Adolescent Medicine, 163,* 1106–1111.

Tucker, Joan S., Friedman, Howard S., Wingard, Deborah L., & Schwartz, Joseph E. (1996). Marital history at midlife as a predictor of longevity: Alternative explanations to the protective effect of marriage. *Health Psychology, 15,* 94–101.

Tudge, Jonathan. (2008). *The everyday lives of young children: Culture, class, and child rearing in diverse societies.* New York: Cambridge University Press.

Tudge, Jonathan R. H., Doucet, Fabienne, Odero, Dolphine, Sperb, Tania M., Piccinini, Cesar A., & Lopes, Rita S. (2006). A window into different cultural worlds: Young children's everyday activities in the United States, Brazil, and Kenya. *Child Development, 77,* 1446–1469.

Tulgan, Bruce. (2009). *Not everyone gets a trophy: How to manage Generation Y.* San Francisco, CA: Jossey-Bass.

Turiel, Elliot. (2006). The development of morality. In William Damon & Richard M. Lerner (Series Eds.) & Nancy Eisenberg (Vol. Ed.), *Handbook of child psychology: Vol. 3. Social, emotional, and personality development* (6th ed., pp. 789–857). Hoboken, NJ: Wiley.

Turiel, Elliot. (2008). Thought about actions in social domains: Morality, social conventions, and social interactions. *Cognitive Development, 23,* 136–154.

Turner, Val D., & Berkowitz, Marvin W. (2005). Scaffolding morality: Positioning a socio-cultural construct. *New Ideas in Psychology, 23,* 174–184.

Twenge, Jean M. (2006). *Generation Me: Why today's young Americans are more confident assertive, entitled—and more miserable than ever before.* New York: Free Press.

Twenge, Jean M., & Campbell, W. Keith. (2009). *The narcissism epidemic.* New York: Free Press.

Twenge, Jean M., & Campbell, W. Keith. (2010). Birth cohort difference in the Monitoring the Future dataset and elsewhere: Further evidence for Generation Me—Commentary on Trzesniewski & Donnellan. *Perspectives on Psychological Science, 5,* 81–88.

Twenge, Jean M., Gentile, Brittany, DeWall, C. Nathan, Ma, Debbie, Lacefield, Katharine, & Schurtz, David R. (2010). Birth cohort increases in psychopathology among young Americans, 1938–2007: A cross-temporal meta-analysis of the MMPI. *Clinical Psychology Review, 30,* 145–154.

Twenge, Jean M., Konrath, Sara, Foster, Joshua D., Campbell, W. Keith, & Bushma, Brad J. (2008). Egos inflating over time: A cross-temporal meta-analysis of the narcissistic personality inventory. *Journal of Personality, 76,* 875–902.

Tyzio, Roman, Cossart, Rosa, Khalilov, Ilgam, Minlebaev, Marat, Hubner, Christian A., Represa, Alfonso, et al. (2006, December 15). Maternal oxytocin triggers a transient inhibitory switch in GABA signaling in the fetal brain during delivery. *Science, 314,* 1788–1792.

Tzeng, Shih-Jay. (2007). Learning disabilities in Taiwan: A case of cultural constraints on the education of students with disabilities. *Learning Disabilities Research & Practice, 22,* 170–175.

U.S. Bureau of Labor Statistics. (2008, January 23). *Volunteering in the United States, 2007* (Press release USDL 08-0090). Washington, DC: Author.

U.S. Bureau of Labor Statistics. (2010, January 26). *Volunteering in the United States, 2009* (Press release USDL-10-0097). Washington, DC: Author.

U.S. Bureau of the Census. (1907). *Statistical abstract of the United States: 1907* (30th ed.). Washington, DC: U.S. Government Printing Office.

U.S. Bureau of the Census. (1975). *Statistical abstract of the United States: 1975* (96th ed.). Washington, DC: U.S. Government Printing Office.

U.S. Bureau of the Census. (1989). *Statistical abstract of the United States: 1989* (109th ed.). Washington, DC: U.S. Government Printing Office.

U.S. Bureau of the Census. (2002). *Statistical abstract of the United States, 2001: The national data book* (121st ed.). Washington, DC: U.S. Department of Commerce.

U.S. Bureau of the Census. (2007). *Statistical abstract of the United States: 2008* (127th ed.). Washington, DC: U.S. Department of Commerce.

U.S. Bureau of the Census. (2008). *Statistical abstract of the United States: 2009* (128th ed.). Washington, DC: U.S. Department of Commerce.

U.S. Bureau of the Census. (2009). *Statistical abstract of the United States: 2010* (129th ed.). Washington, DC: U.S. Government Printing Office.

U.S. Bureau of the Census. (2010). *America's families and living arrangements: 2009.* Retrieved November 4, 2010, from the World Wide Web: http://www.census.gov/population/www/socdemo/hh-fam/cps2009.html

U.S. Census Bureau. (2008, August 26). *American Community Survey.* Retrieved September 11, 2010, from the World Wide Web: http://factfinder.census.gov/servlet/DatasetMainPageServlet?_program=ACS&_submenuId=&_lang=en&_ds_name=ACS_2008_3YR_G00_&ts=

U.S. Census Bureau. (2009). *Statistical abstract of the United States: 2010* (129th ed.). Washington, DC: U.S. Government Printing Office.

U.S. Department of Health and Human Services. (2010). *Head Start impact study: Final report.* Washington, DC: Author.

U.S. Preventive Services Task Force. (2002). Postmenopausal hormone replacement therapy for primary prevention of chronic conditions: Recommendations and rationale. *Annals of Internal Medicine, 137,* 834–839.

Uekermann, Jennifer, Kraemer, Markus, Abdel-Hamid, Mona, Schimmelmann, Benno G., Hebebrand, Johannes, Daum, Irene, et al. (2010). Social cognition in attention-deficit hyperactivity disorder (ADHD). *Neuroscience & Biobehavioral Reviews, 34,* 734–743.

Uhlenberg, Peter. (1996). The burden of aging: A theoretical framework for understanding the shifting balance of caregiving and care receiving as cohorts age. *Gerontologist, 36,* 761–767.

Umana-Taylor, Adriana J., & Guimond, Amy B. (2010). A longitudinal examination of parenting behaviors and perceived discrimination predicting Latino adolescents' ethnic identity. *Developmental Psychology, 46,* 636–650.

Umberson, Debra, Pudrovska, Tetyana, & Reczek, Corinne. (2010). Parenthood, childlessness, and well-being: A life course perspective. *Journal of Marriage and Family, 72,* 612–629.

Unal, Belgin, Critchley, Julia Alison, & Capewell, Simon. (2005). Modelling the decline in coronary heart disease deaths in England and Wales, 1981–2000: Comparing contributions from primary prevention and secondary prevention. *British Medical Journal, 331,* 614–617.

UNESCO. (2005). *Education for all: Global monitoring report 2006: Literacy for life.* Paris: United Nations Educational, Scientific and Cultural Organization.

UNESCO. (2008). *Global education digest: Comparing education statistics across the world.* Montreal, Quebec, Canada: UNESCO Institute for Statistics.

UNESCO. (2009). *Global education digest 2009: Comparing education statistics across the world.* Montreal, Quebec, Canada: UNESCO Institute for Statistics.

UNICEF. (2007). *Progress for children: A world fit for children statistical review.* New York: UNICEF.

UNICEF. (2009). *The state of the world's children special edition: Celebrating 20 years of the Convention on the Rights of the Child.* New York: Author.

UNICEF (United Nations Children's Fund). (2008). *The state of the world's children 2009: Maternal and newborn health.* New York: Author.

United Nations. (2007). *World population prospects: The 2006 revision, highlights* (Working Paper No. ESA/P/WP.202). New York: United Nations, Department of Economic and Social Affairs, Population Division.

United States Department of Transportation. (2009). *Traffic safety facts: 2008 data* (DOT HS 811 162). Washington, DC: National Center for Statistics and Analysis.

Unnever, James D. (2005). Bullies, aggressive victims, and victims: Are they distinct groups? *Aggressive Behavior, 31,* 153–171.

Vail, Kenneth E., Rothschild, Zachary K., Weise, Dave R., Solomon, Sheldon, Pyszczynski, Tom, & Greenberg, Jeff. (2010). A terror management analysis of the psychological functions of religion. *Personality and Social Psychology Review, 14,* 84–94.

Vaillant, George E. (2002). *Aging well: Surprising guideposts to a happier life from the landmark Harvard Study of Adult Development.* Boston: Little Brown.

Vaillant, George E. (2008). *Spiritual evolution: A scientific defense of faith.* New York: Broadway Books.

Vakili, Mahmood, Nadrian, Haidar, Fathipoor, Mohammad, Boniadi, Fatemeh, & Morowatisharifabad, Mohammad Ali. (2010). Prevalence and determinants of intimate partner violence against women in Kazeroon, Islamic Republic of Iran. *Violence and Victims, 25,* 116–127.

Valentino, Kristin, Cicchetti, Dante, Rogosch, Fred A., & Toth, Sheree L. (2008). True and false recall and dissociation among maltreated children: The role of self-schema. *Development and Psychopathology, 20,* 213–232.

Valentino, Kristin, Cicchetti, Dante, Toth, Sheree L., & Rogosch, Fred A. (2006). Mother-child play and emerging social behaviors among infants from maltreating families. *Developmental Psychology, 42,* 474–485.

Valkenburg, Patti M., & Peter, Jochen. (2009). Social consequences of the internet for adolescents. *Current Directions in Psychological Science, 18,* 1–5.

Valsiner, Jaan. (2006). Developmental epistemology and implications for methodology. In William Damon & Richard M. Lerner (Series Eds.) & Richard M. Lerner (Vol. Ed.), *Handbook of child psychology: Vol. 1. Theoretical models of human development* (6th ed., pp. 166–209). Hoboken, NJ: Wiley.

van Alphen, Jojanneke E., Donker, Gé A., & Marquet, Richard L. (2010). Requests for euthanasia in general practice before and after implementation of the Dutch Euthanasia Act. *British Journal of General Practice, 60,* 263–267.

van Bodegom, David, Rozing, Maarten, May, Linda, Kuningas, Maris, Thomese, Fleur, Meij, Hans, et al. (2010). When grandmothers matter. *Gerontology, 56,* 214–216.

Van Cauter, Eve, Leproult, Rachel, & Plat, Laurence. (2000). Age-related changes in slow wave sleep and REM sleep and relationship with growth hormone and cortisol levels in healthy men. *Journal of the American Medical Association, 284,* 861–868.

van den Ban, Els, Souverein, Patrick, Swaab, Hanna, van Engeland, Herman, Heerdink, Rob, & Egberts, Toine. (2010). Trends in incidence and characteristics of children, adolescents, and adults initiating immediate- or extended-release methylphenidate or atomoxetine in the Netherlands during 2001–2006. *Journal of Child and Adolescent Psychopharmacology, 20,* 55–61.

van den Berg, Stéphanie M., & Boomsma, Dorret I. (2007). The familial clustering of age at menarche in extended twin families. *Behavior Genetics, 37,* 661–667.

van den Brink, Carolien L., Tijhuis, Marja, van den Bos, Geertrudis A. M., Giampaoli, Simona, Kivinen, Paula, Nissinen, Aulikki, et al. (2004). Effect of widowhood on disability onset in elderly men from three European countries. *Journal of the American Geriatrics Society, 52,* 353–358.

van der Heide, Agnes, Onwuteaka-Philipsen, Bregje D., Rurup, Mette L., Buiting, Hilde M., van Delden, Johannes J.M., Hanssen-de Wolf, Johanna E., et al. (2007). End-of-life practices in the Netherlands under the euthanasia act. *New England Journal of Medicine, 356,* 1957–1965.

van der Houwen, Karolijne, Stroebe, Margaret, Schut, Henk, Stroebe, Wolfgang, & van den Bout, Jan. (2010). Mediating processes in bereavement: The role of rumination, threatening grief interpretations, and deliberate grief avoidance. *Social Science & Medicine, 71,* 1669–1676.

van Dijk, Jan A. G. M. (2005). *The deepening divide: Inequality in the information society.* Thousand Oaks, CA: Sage.

van Hof, Paulion, van der Kamp, John, & Savelsbergh, Geert J. P. (2008). The relation between infants' perception of catchableness and the control of catching. *Developmental Psychology, 44,* 182–194.

van IJzendoorn, Marinus H., & Bakermans-Kranenburg, Marian J. (2010). Invariance of adult attachment across gender, age, culture, and socioeconomic status? *Journal of Social and Personal Relationships, 27,* 200–208.

van IJzendoorn, Marinus H., Bakermans-Kranenburg, Marian J., Pannebakker, Fieke, & Out, Dorothée. (2010). In defence of situational morality: Genetic, dispositional and situational determinants of children's donating to charity. *Journal of Moral Education, 39,* 1–20.

Van IJzendoorn, Marinus H., Bakermans-Kranenburg, Marian J., & Sagi-Schwartz,

Abraham. (2006). Attachment across diverse sociocultural contexts: The limits of universality. In Kenneth H. Rubin & Ock Boon Chung (Eds.), *Parenting beliefs, behaviors, and parent-child relations: A cross-cultural perspective* (pp. 107–142). New York: Psychology Press.

Van Leijenhorst, Linda, Zanolie, Kiki, Van Meel, Catharina S., Westenberg, P. Michiel, Rombouts, Serge A.R.B., & Crone, Eveline A. (2010). What motivates the adolescent? brain regions mediating reward sensitivity across adolescence. *Cerebral Cortex, 20,* 61–69.

van Schijndel, Tessa J. P., Singer, Elly, van der Maas, Han L. J., & Raijmakers, Maartje E. J. (2010). A sciencing programme and young children's exploratory play in the sandpit. *European Journal of Developmental Psychology, 7,* 603–617.

Van Zundert, Rinka M. P., Van Der Vorst, Haske, Vermulst, Ad A., & Engels, Rutger C. M. E. (2006). Pathways to alcohol use among Dutch students in regular education and education for adolescents with behavioral problems: The role of parental alcohol use, general parenting practices, and alcohol-specific parenting practices. *Journal of Family Psychology, 20,* 456–467.

Vartanian, Lesa Rae. (2001). Adolescents' reactions to hypothetical peer group conversations: Evidence for an imaginary audience? *Adolescence, 36,* 347–380.

Vaupel, James W., & Loichinger, Elke. (2006, June 30). Redistributing work in aging Europe. *Science, 312,* 1911–1913.

Veblen, Thorstein. (2007). *The theory of the leisure class.* New York: Oxford University Press. (Original work published 1899)

Verbakel, Ellen, & Jaspers, Eva. (2010). A comparative study on permissiveness toward euthanasia. *Public Opinion Quarterly, 74,* 109–139.

Vered, Karen Orr. (2008). *Children and media outside the home: Playing and learning in after-school care.* Houndmills, Basingstoke, Hampshire, England: Palgrave Macmillan.

Verona, Sergiu. (2003). Romanian policy regarding adoptions. In Victor Littel (Ed.), *Adoption update* (pp. 5–10). New York: Nova Science.

Verté, Sylvie, Geurts, Hilde M., Roeyers, Herbert, Oosterlaan, Jaap, & Sergeant, Joseph A. (2005). Executive functioning in children with autism and Tourette syndrome. *Development & Psychopathology, 17,* 415–445.

Viadero, Debra. (2007, April 5). Long after Katrina, children show symptoms of psychological distress. *Education Week, 26*(32), 7.

Vianna, Eduardo, & Stetsenko, Anna. (2006). Embracing history through transforming it: Contrasting Piagetian versus Vygotskian (activity) theories of learning and development to expand constructivism within a dialectical view of history. *Theory & Psychology, 16,* 81–108.

Victora, Cesar G., Adair, Linda, Fall, Caroline, Hallal, Pedro C., Martorell, Reynaldo, Richter, Linda, et al. (2008). Maternal and child undernutrition: consequences for adult health and human capital. *The Lancet, 371,* 340–357.

Vieno, Alessio, Nation, Maury, Pastore, Massimiliano, & Santinello, Massimo. (2009). Parenting and antisocial behavior: A model of the relationship between adolescent self-disclosure, parental closeness, parental control, and adolescent antisocial behavior. *Developmental Psychology, 45,* 1509–1519.

Vikan, Arne, Camino, Cleonice, & Biaggio, Angela. (2005). Note on a cross-cultural test of Gilligan's ethic of care. *Journal of Moral Education, 34,* 107–111.

Viner, Russell M., & Cole, Tim J. (2005). Adult socioeconomic, educational, social, and psychological outcomes of childhood obesity: A national birth cohort study. *British Medical Journal, 330,* 1354–1357.

Vitale, Susan, Sperduto, Robert D., & Ferris, Frederick L., III. (2009). Increased prevalence of myopia in the United States between 1971–1972 and 1999–2004. *Archives of Ophthalmology, 127,* 1632–1639.

Vitiello, Benedetto, Zuvekas, Samuel H., & Norquist, Grayson S. (2006). National estimates of antidepressant medication use among U.S. children, 1997–2002. *Journal of the American Academy of Child & Adolescent Psychiatry, 45,* 271–279.

Voelcker-Rehage, Claudia, & Alberts, Jay L. (2007). Effect of motor practice on dual-task performance in older adults. *The Journals of Gerontology Series B: Psychological Sciences and Social Sciences, 62B,* 141–148.

Vogel, Ineke, Verschuure, Hans, van der Ploeg, Catharina P. B., Brug, Johannes, & Raat, Hein. (2010). Estimating adolescent risk for hearing loss based on data from a large school-based survey. *American Journal of Public Health, 100,* 1095–1100.

von Hippel, William. (2007). Aging, executive functioning, and social control. *Current Directions in Psychological Science, 16,* 240–244.

Voorpostel, Marieke, & van der Lippe, Tanja. (2007). Support between siblings and between friends: Two worlds apart? *Journal of Marriage and Family, 69,* 1271–1282.

Vouloumanos, Athena, & Werker, Janet F. (2007). Listening to language at birth: Evidence for a bias for speech in neonates. *Developmental Science, 10,* 159–164.

Voydanoff, Patricia. (2007). *Work, family, and community: Exploring interconnections.* Mahwah, NJ: Erlbaum.

Vygotsky, Lev S. (1986). *Thought and language* (Eugenia Hanfmann & Gertrude Vakar, Trans. Revised ed.). Cambridge, MA: MIT Press. (Original work published 1934)

Vygotsky, Lev S. (1987). *Thinking and speech* (Norris Minick, Trans. Vol. 1). New York: Plenum Press. (Original work published 1934)

Vygotsky, Lev S. (1994). Principles of social education for deaf and dumb children in Russia (Theresa Prout, Trans.). In Rene van der Veer & Jaan Valsiner (Eds.), *The Vygotsky reader* (pp. 19–26). Cambridge, MA: Blackwell. (Original work published 1925)

Vygotsky, Lev S. (1994). The development of academic concepts in school aged children (Theresa Prout, Trans.). In Rene van der Veer & Jaan Valsiner (Eds.), *The Vygotsky reader* (pp. 355–370). Cambridge, MA: Blackwell. (Original work published 1934)

Waber, Deborah P. (2010). *Rethinking learning disabilities: Understanding children who struggle in school.* New York: Guilford Press.

Wagenaar, Karin, Huisman, Jaap, Cohen-Kettenis, Peggy T., & Adelemarre-van De Waal, Henriette. (2008). An overview of studies on early development, cognition, and psychosocial well-being in children born after in vitro fertilization. *Journal of Developmental & Behavioral Pediatrics, 29,* 219–230.

Wagner, Carol L., Greer, Frank R., & and the Section on Breastfeeding and Committee on Nutrition of the American Academy of Pediatrics. (2008). Prevention of rickets and vitamin D deficiency in infants, children, and adolescents. *Pediatrics, 122,* 1142–1152.

Wahlstrom, Dustin, Collins, Paul, White, Tonya, & Luciana, Monica. (2010). Developmental changes in dopamine neurotransmission in adolescence: Behavioral implications and issues in assessment. *Brain and Cognition, 72,* 146–159.

Wahlstrom, Kyla L. (2002). Accommodating the sleep patterns of adolescents within current educational structures: An uncharted path. In Mary A. Carskadon (Ed.), *Adolescent sleep patterns: Biological, social, and psychological influences* (pp. 172–197). New York: Cambridge University Press.

Waite, Linda J., & Luo, Ye. (2002, August). *Marital quality and marital stability: Consequences for psychological well-being.* Paper presented at the Annual Meetings of the American Sociological Association, Chicago.

Wakefield, Melanie, Flay, Brian, Nichter, Mark, & Giovino, Gary. (2003). Effects of anti-smoking advertising on youth smoking: A review. *Journal of Health Communication, 8,* 229–247.

Waldfogel, Jane. (2006). What do children need? *Public Policy Research, 13,* 26–34.

Waldinger, Robert J., & Schulz, Marc S. (2010). What's love got to do with it? Social functioning, perceived health, and daily happiness in married octogenarians. *Psychology and Aging, 25,* 422–431.

Walker, Alan. (2006). Aging and politics: An international perspective. In Robert H. Binstock & Linda K. George (Eds.), *Handbook of aging and the social sciences* (6th ed., pp. 339–359). Amsterdam: Elsevier.

Walker, Lawrence J. (1984). Sex differences in the development of moral reasoning: A critical review. *Child Development, 55,* 677–691.

Walker, Peter, Bremner, J. Gavin, Mason, Uschi, Spring, Jo, Mattock, Karen, Slater, Alan, et al. (2010). Preverbal infants' sensitivity to synaesthetic cross-modality correspondences. *Psychological Science, 21,* 21–25.

Walker, Rob. (2009, November 1). Consumed: Hummer love. *New York Times,* pp. MM22.

Walker, Rheeda L., & Hunter, Lora Rose. (2008). From anxiety and depression to suicide and self-harm. In Helen A. Neville, Brendesha M. Tynes, & Shawn O. Utsey (Eds.), *Handbook of African American psychology* (pp. 401–416). Thousand Oaks, CA: Sage.

Waller, Erika M., & Rose, Amanda J. (2010). Adjustment trade-offs of co-rumination in mother-adolescent relationships. *Journal of Adolescence, 33,* 487–497.

Wallerstein, Judith S., & Blakeslee, Sandra. (1995). *The good marriage: How and why love lasts.* Boston: Houghton Mifflin.

Walsh, Bridget A., & Petty, Karen. (2007). Frequency of six early childhood education approaches: A 10-year content analysis of early childhood education journal. *Early Childhood Education Journal, 34,* 301–305.

Wang, A. Ting, Lee, Susan S., Sigman, Marian, & Dapretto, Mirella. (2006). Developmental changes in the neural basis of interpreting communicative intent. *Social Cognitive and Affective Neuroscience, 1,* 107–121.

Wang, Hua, & Wellman, Barry. (2010). Social connectivity in America: Changes in adult friendship network size from 2002 to 2007. *American Behavioral Scientist, 53,* 1148–1169.

Wang, Li, van Belle, Gerald, Crane, Paul K., Kukull, Walter A., Bowen, James D., McCormick, Wayne C., et al. (2004). Subjective memory deterioration and future dementia in people aged 65 and older. *Journal of the American Geriatrics Society, 52,* 2045–2051.

Wang, Qi, Shao, Yi, & Li, Yexin Jessica. (2010). "My way or mom's way?" The bilingual and bicultural self in Hong Kong Chinese children and adolescents. *Child Development, 81,* 555–567.

Wang, Richard Y., Needham, Larry L., & Barr, Dana B. (2005). Effects of environmental agents on the attainment of puberty: Considerations when assessing exposure to environmental chemicals in the National Children's Study. *Environmental Health Perspectives, 113,* 1100–1107.

Wang, Ying, & Marcotte, Dave E. (2007). Golden years? The labor market effects of caring for grandchildren. *Journal of Marriage and Family, 69,* 1283–1296.

Ward, Brian W., & Gryczynski, Jan. (2009). Social learning theory and the effects of living arrangement on heavy alcohol use: Results from a national study of college students. *Journal of Studies on Alcohol and Drugs, 70,* 364–372.

Ward, Russell A., & Spitze, Glenna D. (2007). Nestleaving and coresidence by young adult children: The role of family relations. *Research on Aging, 29,* 257–277.

Warneken, Felix, & Tomasello, Michael. (2009). The roots of human altruism. *British Journal of Psychology, 100,* 455–471.

Warren, Charles W., Jones, Nathan R., Eriksen, Michael P., & Asma, Samira. (2006). Patterns of global tobacco use in young people and implications for future chronic disease burden in adults. *Lancet, 367,* 749–753.

Warshofsky, Fred. (1999). *Stealing time: The new science of aging.* New York: TV Books.

Washington, Harriet A. (2006). *Medical apartheid: The dark history of medical experimentation on Black Americans from colonial times to the present.* New York: Doubleday.

Watson, John B. (1928). *Psychological care of infant and child.* New York: Norton.

Watson, John B. (1998). *Behaviorism.* New Brunswick, NJ: Transaction. (Original work published 1924)

Waxman, Sandra R., & Lidz, Jeffrey L. (2006). Early word learning. In William Damon & Richard M. Lerner (Series Eds.) & Deanna Kuhn & Robert S. Siegler (Vol. Eds.), *Handbook of child psychology: Vol. 2. Cognition, perception, and language* (6th ed., pp. 299–335). Hoboken, NJ: Wiley.

Way, Niobe, Gingold, Rachel, Rotenberg, Mariana, & Kuriakose, Geena. (2005). Close friendships among urban, ethnic-minority adolescents. In Niobe Way & Jill V. Hamm (Eds.), *The experience of close friendships in adolescence* (Vol. 107, pp. 41–59). San Francisco: Jossey-Bass.

Webster, Jeffrey Dean, & Gould, Odette. (2007). Reminiscence and vivid personal memories across adulthood. *International Journal of Aging & Human Development, 64,* 149–170.

Weichold, Karina, Silbereisen, Rainer K., & Schmitt-Rodermund, Eva. (2003). Short-term and long-term consequences of early versus late physical maturation in adolescents. In Chris Hayward (Ed.), *Gender differences at puberty* (pp. 241–276). New York: Cambridge University Press.

Weikart, David P. (Ed.). (1999). *What should young children learn? Teacher and parent views in 15 countries.* Ypsilanti, MI: High/Scope Press.

Weikum, Whitney M., Vouloumanos, Athena, Navarra, Jordi, Soto-Faraco, Salvador, Sebastian-Galles, Nuria, & Werker, Janet F. (2007, May 25). Visual language discrimination in infancy. *Science, 316,* 1159.

Weil, Andrew. (2007, May & June). The truth about the fountain of youth. *AARP The Magazine,* 40–41.

Weiler, Richard, Stamatakis, Emmanuel, & Blair, Steven. (2010). Should health policy focus on physical activity rather than obesity? Yes. *British Medical Journal, 340,* c2603.

Weiner, Myron F., & Lipton, Anne M. (Eds.). (2009). *The American Psychiatric Publishing textbook of Alzheimer disease and other dementias.* Washington, DC: American Psychiatric Publishing.

Weis, Robert, & Cerankosky, Brittany C. (2010). Effects of video-game ownership on young boys' academic and behavioral functioning. *Psychological Science, 21,* 463–470.

Weisgram, Erica S., Bigler, Rebecca S., & Liben, Lynn S. (2010). Gender, values, and occupational interests among children, adolescents, and adults. *Child Development, 81,* 778–796.

Weisler, Richard H., Barbee, James G. I. V., & Townsend, Mark H. (2006). Mental health and recovery in the Gulf Coast after hurricanes Katrina and Rita. *Journal of the American Medical Association, 296,* 585–588.

Wellman, Henry M., Cross, David, & Watson, Julanne. (2001). Meta-analysis of theory-of-mind development: The truth about false belief. *Child Development, 72,* 655–684.

Wenner, Melinda. (2009, February). The serious need for play. *Scientific American Mind,* 23–29.

Werheid, Katja, Gruno, Maria, Kathmann, Norbert, Fischer, Håkan, Almkvist, Ove, & Winblad, Bengt. (2010). Biased recognition of positive faces in aging and amnestic mild cognitive impairment. *Psychology and Aging, 25,* 1–15.

Werner, Emmy E. (1979). *Cross-cultural child development: A view from the planet Earth.* Monterey, CA: Brooks/Cole.

Werner, Emmy E., & Smith, Ruth S. (1992). *Overcoming the odds: High risk children from birth to adulthood.* Ithaca, NY: Cornell University Press.

Werner, Emmy E., & Smith, Ruth S. (2001). *Journeys from childhood to midlife: Risk, resilience, and recovery.* Ithaca, NY: Cornell University Press.

Werner, Nicole E., & Hill, Laura G. (2010). Individual and peer group normative beliefs about relational aggression. *Child Development, 81,* 826–836.

West, Geoffrey B., & Bergman, Aviv. (2009). Toward a systems biology framework for understanding aging and health span. *The Journals of Gerontology Series A: Biological Sciences and Medical Sciences, 64A,* 205–208.

Wethington, Elaine. (2002). The relationship of turning points at work to perceptions of psychological growth and change. In Richard A. Settersten & Timothy J. Owens (Eds.), *Advances in life course research: Vol. 7. New frontiers in socialization* (pp. 93–110). Amsterdam: JAI.

Wexler, Mark N. (2010). Financial edgework and the persistence of rogue traders. *Business and Society Review, 115,* 1–25.

Wheatley, Thalia, Milleville, Shawn C., & Martin, Alex. (2007). Understanding animate agents: Distinct roles for the social network and mirror system. *Psychological Science, 18,* 469–474.

Whelchel, Lisa. (2000). *Creative correction: Extraordinary ideas for everyday discipline.* Wheaton, IL: Tyndale House.

Whitbourne, Susan Krauss. (2008). *Adult development & aging: Biopsychosocial perspectives* (3rd ed.). Hoboken, NJ: John Wiley & Sons.

Whitbourne, Susan Krauss, Sneed, Joel R., & Sayer, Aline. (2009). Psychosocial development from college through midlife: A 34-year sequential study. *Developmental Psychology, 45,* 1328–1340.

Whitehead, Kevin A., Ainsworth, Andrew T., Wittig, Michele A., & Gadino, Brandy. (2009). Implications of ethnic identity exploration and ethnic identity affirmation and belonging for intergroup attitudes among adolescents. *Journal of Research on Adolescence, 19,* 123–135.

Whiteman, Maura K., Hillis, Susan D., Jamieson, Denise J., Morrow, Brian, Podgornik, Michelle N., Brett, Kate M., et al. (2008). Inpatient hysterectomy surveillance in the United States, 2000–2004. *American Journal of Obstetrics and Gynecology, 198,* 34.e31–34.e34, e37.

Whiteside-Mansell, Leanne, Bradley, Robert H., Casey, Patrick H., Fussell, Jill J., & Conners-Burrow, Nicola A. (2009). Triple risk: Do difficult temperament and family conflict increase the likelihood of behavioral maladjustment in children born low birth weight and preterm? *Journal of Pediatric Psychology, 34,* 396–405.

Whitfield, Keith E., & McClearn, Gerald. (2005). Genes, environment, and race: Quantitative genetic approaches. *American Psychologist, 60,* 104–114.

Whitlock, Janis L., Powers, Jane L., & Eckenrode, John. (2006). The virtual cutting edge: The internet and adolescent self-injury. *Developmental Psychology, 42,* 407–417.

Whitmore, Heather. (2001). Value that marketing cannot manufacture: Cherished possessions as links to identity and wisdom. *Generations, 25,* 57–63.

Wicherts, Jelte M., Dolan, Conor V., & van der Maas, Han L. J. (2010). The dangers of unsystematic selection methods and the representativeness of 46 samples of African test-takers. *Intelligence, 38,* 30–37.

Wigfield, Allan, Eccles, Jacquelynne S., Yoon, Kwang Suk, Harold, Rena D., Arbreton, Amy J. A., Freedman-Doan, Carol, et al. (1997). Change in children's competence beliefs and subjective task values across the elementary school years: A 3-year study. *Journal of Educational Psychology, 89,* 451–469.

Wijdicks, Eelco F.M., Varelas, Panayiotis N., Gronseth, Gary S., & Greer, David M. (2010). Evidence-based guideline update: Determining brain death in adults. *Neurology, 74,* 1911–1918.

Wilhelm, Mark O., Rooney, Patrick M., & Tempel, Eugene R. (2007). Changes in religious giving reflect changes in involvement: Age and cohort effects in religious giving, secular giving, and attendance. *Journal for the Scientific Study of Religion, 46,* 217–232.

Willatts, Peter. (1999). Development of means-end behavior in young infants: Pulling a support to retrieve a distant object. *Developmental Psychology, 35,* 651–667.

Willett, Walter C., & Trichopoulos, Dimitrios. (1996). Nutrition and cancer: A summary of the evidence. *Cancer Causes Control, 7,* 178–180.

Williams, David R. (2003). The health of men: Structured inequalities and opportunities. *American Journal of Public Health, 93,* 724–731.

Williams, Justin H. G., Waiter, Gordon D., Gilchrist, Anne, Perrett, David I., Murray, Alison D., & Whiten, Andrew. (2006). Neural mechanisms of imitation and 'mirror neuron' functioning in autistic spectrum disorder. *Neuropsychologia, 44,* 610–621.

Williams, Kristine N., Herman, Ruth, Gajewski, Byron, & Wilson, Kristel. (2009). Elderspeak communication: Impact on dementia care. *American Journal of Alzheimer's Disease and Other Dementias, 24,* 11–20.

Williams, Preston. (2009, March 5). Teens might need to sleep more, but schools have to work efficiently. *The Washington Post.*

Williams, Shirlan A. (2005). Jealousy in the cross-sex friendship. *Journal of Loss and Trauma, 10,* 471–485.

Williams, Wendy M., & Ceci, Stephen J. (2007). Introduction: Striving for perspective in the debate on women in science. In Stephen J. Ceci & Wendy M. Williams (Eds.), *Why aren't more women in science: Top researchers debate the evidence* (pp. 3–23). Washington, DC: American Psychological Association.

Williamson, Rebecca A., Meltzoff, Andrew N., & Markman, Ellen M. (2008). Prior experiences and perceived efficacy influence 3-year-olds' imitation. *Developmental Psychology, 44,* 275–285.

Willis, Sherry L., Tennstedt, Sharon L., Marsiske, Michael, Ball, Karlene, Elias, Jeffrey, Koepke, Kathy Mann, et al. (2006). Long-term effects of cognitive training on everyday functional outcomes in older adults. *Journal of the American Medical Association, 296,* 2805–2814.

Wilson, Stephan M., & Ngige, Lucy W. (2006). Families in sub-Saharan Africa. In Bron B. Ingoldsby & Suzanna D. Smith (Eds.), *Families in global and multicultural perspective* (2nd ed., pp. 247–273). Thousand Oaks, CA: Sage.

Windsor, Timothy D., Anstey, Kaarin J., & Rodgers, Bryan. (2008). Volunteering and psychological well-being among young-old adults: How much is too much? *Gerontologist, 48,* 59–70.

Winsler, Adam, Manfra, Louis, & Díaz, Rafael M. (2007). "Should I let them talk?": Private speech and task performance among preschool children with and without behavior problems. *Early Childhood Research Quarterly, 22,* 215–231.

Wise, Phyllis. (2006). Aging of the female reproductive system. In Edward J. Masoro & Steven N. Austad (Eds.), *Handbook of the biology of aging* (6th ed., pp. 570–590). Amsterdam: Elsevier Academic Press.

Witherington, David C., Campos, Joseph J., & Hertenstein, Matthew J. (2004). Principles of emotion and its development in infancy. In Gavin Bremner & Alan Fogel (Eds.), *Blackwell handbook of infant development* (Paperback ed., pp. 427–464). Malden, MA: Blackwell.

Witt, Ellen D. (2007). Puberty, hormones, and sex differences in alcohol abuse and dependence. *Neurotoxicology and Teratology, 29,* 81–95.

Wittrock, Merlin C. (2010). Learning as a generative process. *Educational Psychologist, 45,* 40–45

Wolak, Janis, Finkelhor, David, Mitchell, Kimberly J., & Ybarra, Michele L. (2008). Online "predators" and their victims: Myths, realities, and implications for prevention and treatment. *American Psychologist, 63,* 111–128.

Wolchik, Sharlene A., Ma, Yue, Tein, Jenn-Yun, Sandler, Irwin N., & Ayers, Tim S. (2008). Parentally bereaved children's grief: Self-system beliefs as mediators of the relations between grief and stressors and caregiver-child relationship quality. *Death Studies, 32,* 597–620.

Wolf, Norman S. (Ed.). (2010). *Comparative biology of aging.* New York: Springer.

Wolfinger, Nicholas H. (2005). *Understanding the divorce cycle: The children of divorce in their own marriages.* New York: Cambridge University Press.

Woloshin, Steven, & Schwartz, Lisa M. (2010). The benefits and harms of mammography screening: Understanding the trade-offs. *Journal of the American Medical Association, 303,* 164–165.

Wong, Sowan, & Goodwin, Robin. (2009). Experiencing marital satisfaction across three cultures: A qualitative study. *Journal of Social and Personal Relationships, 26,* 1011–1028.

Wood, Joanne M. (2002). Aging, driving and vision. *Clinical and Experimental Optometry, 85,* 214–220.

Woodlee, Martin T., & Schallert, Timothy. (2006). The impact of motor activity and inactivity on the brain: Implications for the prevention and treatment of nervous-system disorders. *Current Directions in Psychological Science, 15,* 203–206.

Woodward, Amanda L., & Markman, Ellen M. (1998). Early word learning. In William Damon (Series Ed.) & Deanna Kuhn & Robert S. Siegler (Vol. Eds.), *Handbook of child psychology: Vol. 2. Cognition, perception and language* (5th ed., pp. 371–420). New York: Wiley.

Woollett, Katherine, Spiers, Hugo J., & Maguire, Eleanor A. (2009). Talent in the taxi: A model system for exploring expertise. *Philosophical Transactions of the Royal Society of London, 364,* 1407–1416.

World Food Programme. (2008). *WFP Strategic Plan 2008–2011.* Rome: Author.

World Health Organization. (2005). *Sexually transmitted infections among adolescents: Issues in adolescent health and development.* Geneva, Switzerland: World Health Organization.

World Health Organization. (2010). *Chronic diseases and health promotion.* Geneva, Switzerland: World Health Organization.

World Health Organization (WHO). (2010). *World health statistics 2010.* Geneva, Switzerland: WHO Press.

World Health Organization. (2010, October 5). *WHO global infobase: NCD indicators.*

Worrell, Frank C. (2008). Nigrescence attitudes in adolescence, emerging adulthood, and adulthood. *Journal of Black Psychology, 34,* 156–178.

Worthman, Carol M. (2010). *Formative experiences: The interaction of caregiving, culture, and developmental psychobiology.* New York: Cambridge University Press.

Worthman, Carol M., Plotsky, Paul M., Schechter, Daniel S., & Cummings, Constance A. (Eds.). (2010). *Formative experiences: The interaction of caregiving, culture, and developmental psychobiology.* New York: Cambridge University Press.

Wosje, Karen S., Khoury, Philip R., Claytor, Randal P., Copeland, Kristen A., Hornung, Richard W., Daniels, Stephen R., et al. (2010). Dietary patterns associated with fat and bone mass in young children. *American Journal of Clinical Nutrition, 92,* 294–303.

Wu, Pai-Lu, & Chiou, Wen-Bin. (2008). Postformal thinking and creativity among late adolescents: a post-Piagetian approach. *Adolescence, 43,* 237–251.

Wu, Zheng, & Schimmele, Christoph. (2007). Uncoupling in late life. *Generations, 31*(3), 41–46.

Wurm, Susanne, Tomasik, Martin, & Tesch-Römer, Clemens. (2008). Serious health events and their impact on changes in subjective health and life satisfaction: The role of age and a positive view on ageing. *European Journal of Ageing, 5,* 117–127.

Wurtele, Sandy K. (2009). "Activities of older adults" survey: Tapping into student views of the elderly. *Educational Gerontology, 35,* 1026–1031.

Xin, Hao. (2008, August 29). Mortality survey offers mixed message. *Science, 321,* 1155.

Xu, Xiao, Zhu, Fengchuan, O'Campo, Patricia, Koenig, Michael A., Mock, Victoria, & Campbell, Jacquelyn. (2005). Prevalence of and risk factors for intimate partner violence in China. *American Journal of Public Health, 95,* 78–85.

Yajnik, Chittaranjan S. (2004). Early life origins of insulin resistance and type 2 diabetes in India and other Asian countries. *Journal of Nutrition, 134,* 205–210.

Yamaguchi, Susumu, Greenwald, Anthony G., Banaji, Mahzarin R., Murakami, Fumio, Chen, Daniel, Shiomura, Kimihiro, et al. (2007). Apparent universality of positive implicit self-esteem. *Psychological Science, 18,* 498–500.

Yan, Bernice, & Arlin, Patricia. (1995). Nonabsolute/relativistic thinking: A common factor underlying models of postformal reasoning? *Journal of Adult Development, 2,* 223–240.

Yang, Chao-Chin, Wan, Chin-Shen, & Chiou, Wen-Bin. (2010). Dialectical thinking and creativity among young adults: A postformal operations perspective. *Psychological Reports, 106,* 79–92.

Yang, Lixia, Krampe, Ralf T., & Baltes, Paul B. (2006). Basic forms of cognitive plasticity extended into the oldest-old: Retest learning, age, and cognitive functioning. *Psychology and Aging, 21,* 372–378.

Yarber, William L., Milhausen, Robin R., Crosby, Richard A., & Torabi, Mohammad R. (2005). Public opinion about condoms for HIV and STD prevention: A midwestern state telephone survey. *Perspectives on Sexual and Reproductive Health, 37,* 148–154.

Yehuda, Rachel (Ed.). (2006). *Annals of the New York Academy of Sciences: Vol. 1071. Psychobiology of posttraumatic stress disorder: A decade of progress.* Boston: Blackwell.

Yen, Ju-Yu, Ko, Chih-Hung, Yen, Cheng-Fang, Chen, Sue-Huei, Chung, Wei-Lun, & Chen, Cheng-Chung. (2008). Psychiatric symptoms in adolescents with internet addiction: Comparison with substance use. *Psychiatry and Clinical Neurosciences, 62,* 9–16.

Yerkes, Robert Mearns. (1923). Testing the human mind. *Atlantic Monthly, 131,* 358–370.

Yerys, Benjamin E., & Munakata, Yuko. (2006). When labels hurt but novelty helps: Children's perseveration and flexibility in a card-sorting task. *Child Development, 77,* 1589–1607.

Yeung, Melinda Y. (2006). Postnatal growth, neurodevelopment and altered adiposity after preterm birth—From a clinical nutrition perspective. *Acta Paediatrica, 95,* 909–917.

Yeung, W. Jean, & Conley, Dalton. (2008). Black-White achievement gap and family wealth. *Child Development, 79,* 303–324.

Yli-Kuha, Anna-Niina, Gissler, Mika, Luoto, Riitta, & Hemminki, Elina. (2009). Success of infertility treatments in Finland in the period 1992–2005. *European Journal of Obstetrics, Gynecology, and Reproductive Biology, 144,* 54–58.

Youn, Gahyun, Knight, Bob G., Jeong, Hyun-Suk, & Benton, Donna. (1999). Differences in familism values and caregiving outcomes among Korean, Korean American, and White American dementia caregivers. *Psychology & Aging, 14,* 355–364.

Young, Elizabeth A., Korszun, Ania, Figueiredo, Helmer F., Banks-Solomon, Matia, & Herman, James P. (2008). Sex differences in HPA axis regulation. In Jill B. Becker, Karen J. Berkley, Nori Geary, Elizabeth Hampson, James P. Herman, & Elizabeth Young (Eds.), *Sex differences in the brain: From genes to behavior* (pp. 95–105). New York: Oxford University Press.

Young, John K. (2010). Anorexia nervosa and estrogen: Current status of the hypothesis. *Neuroscience & Biobehavioral Reviews, 34,* 1195–1200.

Young, Robert. (2007). *Medically assisted death.* Cambridge, UK: Cambridge University Press.

Young, T. Kue, Bjerregaard, Peter, Dewailly, Eric, Risica, Patricia M., Jorgensen, Marit E., & Ebbesson, Sven E. O. (2007). Prevalence of obesity and its metabolic correlates among the circumpolar Inuit in 3 countries. *American Journal of Public Health, 97,* 691–695.

Zaccai, Julia, McCracken, Cherie, & Brayne, Carol. (2005). A systematic review of prevalence and incidence studies of dementia with Lewy bodies. *Age and Ageing, 34,* 561–566.

Zacks, Rose T., & Hasher, Lynn. (2006). Aging and long-term memory: Deficits are not inevitable. In Ellen Bialystok & Fergus I. M. Craik

(Eds.), *Lifespan cognition: Mechanisms of change* (pp. 162–177). New York: Oxford University Press.

Zahn-Waxler, Carolyn, Park, Jong-Hyo, Usher, Barbara, Belouad, Francesca, Cole, Pamela, & Gruber, Reut. (2008). Young children's representations of conflict and distress: A longitudinal study of boys and girls with disruptive behavior problems. *Development and Psychopathology, 20,* 99–119.

Zalenski, Robert J., & Raspa, Richard. (2006). Maslow's hierarchy of needs: A framework for achieving human potential in hospice. *Journal of Palliative Medicine, 9,* 1120–1127.

Zalesak, Martin, & Heckers, Stephan. (2009). The role of the hippocampus in transitive inference. *Psychiatry Research: Neuroimaging, 172,* 24–30.

Zandi, Peter P., Sparks, D. Larry, Khachaturian, Ara S., Tschanz, JoAnn, Norton, Maria, Steinberg, Martin, et al. (2005). Do statins reduce risk of incident dementia and Alzheimer disease? The Cache County Study. *Archives of General Psychiatry, 62,* 217–224.

Zani, Bruna, & Cicognani, Elvira. (2006). Sexuality and intimate relationships in adolescence. In Sandy Jackson & Luc Goossens (Eds.), *Handbook of adolescent development* (pp. 200–222). Hove, East Sussex, UK: Psychology Press.

Zarate, Carlos A., Jr. (2010). Psychiatric disorders in young adults: Depression assessment and treatment. *Young adult mental health.* (pp. 206–230): New York: Oxford University Press.

Zelazo, Philip David, Müller, Ulrich, Frye, Douglas, & Marcovitch, Stuart. (2003). The development of executive function in early childhood. *Monographs of the Society for Research in Child Development, 68*(3, Serial No. 274), 11–27.

Zelinski, Elizabeth M., Kennison, Robert F., Watts, Amber, & Lewis, Kayan L. (2009). Convergence between cross-sectional and longitudinal studies: Cohort matters. In Hayden B. Bosworth & Christopher Hertzog (Eds.), *Aging and cognition: Research methodologies and empirical advances* (pp. 101–118). Washington, DC: American Psychological Association.

Zentner, Marcel, & Bates, John E. (2008). Child temperament: An integrative review of concepts, research programs, and measures. *European Journal of Developmental Science, 2,* 7–37.

Zettel, Laura A., & Rook, Karen S. (2004). Substitution and compensation in the social networks of older widowed women. *Psychology and Aging, 19,* 433–443.

Zettel-Watson, Laura, Ditto, Peter H., Danks, Joseph H., & Smucker, William D. (2008). Actual and perceived gender differences in the accuracy of surrogate decisions about life-sustaining medical treatment among older spouses. *Death Studies, 32,* 273–290.

Zhang, Ying. (2009). *State high school exit exams: Trends in test programs, alternate pathways, and pass rates.* Washington, DC: Center on Education Policy.

Zhu, Qi, Song, Yiying, Hu, Siyuan, Li, Xiaobai, Tian, Moqian, Zhen, Zonglei, et al. (2010). Heritability of the specific cognitive ability of face perception. *Current Biology, 20,* 137–142.

Zhu, Ying, Zhang, Li, Fan, Jin, & Han, Shihui. (2007). Neural basis of cultural influence on self-representation. *NeuroImage, 34,* 1310–1316.

Zigler, Edward, & Styfco, Sally J. (Eds.). (2004). *The Head Start debates.* Baltimore: Brookes.

Zimmer-Gembeck, Melanie J., & Collins, W. Andrew. (2003). Autonomy development during adolescence. In Gerald R. Adams & Michael D. Berzonsky (Eds.), *Blackwell handbook of adolescence* (pp. 175–204). Malden, MA: Blackwell.

Zimmerman, Frederick J., & Bell, Janice F. (2010). Associations of television content type and obesity in children. *American Journal of Public Health, 100,* 334–340.

Zimprich, Daniel, & Martin, Mike. (2009). A multilevel factor analysis perspective on intellectual development in old age. *Aging and cognition: Research methodologies and empirical advances,* 53–76.

Zuvekas, Samuel H., Vitiello, Benedetto, & Norquist, Grayson S. (2006). Recent trends in stimulant medication use among U.S. children. *American Journal of Psychiatry, 163,* 579–585.

Name Index

Subject Index